S0-CEW-484

INTERNATIONAL *Antiques* PRICE GUIDE

THERE ARE MANY ANTIQUE SHIPPERS IN BRITAIN BUT...

... few, if any, who are as quality conscious as Norman Lefton, Chairman and Managing Director of British Antique Exporters Ltd. of Burgess Hill, Nr. Brighton, Sussex.

Thirty years' experience of shipping goods to all parts of the globe have confirmed his original belief that the way to build clients' confidence in his services is to supply them only with goods which are in first class saleable condition. To this end, he employs a cottage industry staff of over 50, from highly skilled antique restorers, polishers and packers to representative buyers and executives.

Through their knowledgeable hands passes each piece of furniture before it leaves the B.A.E. warehouses, ensuring that the overseas buyer will only receive the best and most saleable merchandise for their particular market. This attention to detail is obvious on a visit to the Burgess Hill showrooms where potential customers can view what must be the most varied assortment of Georgian, Victorian, Edwardian and 1930s furniture in the UK. One cannot fail to be impressed by, not only the varied range of merchandise, but also the fact that each piece is in showroom condition awaiting shipment.

As one would expect, packing is considered somewhat of an art at B.A.E. and the manager in charge of the works ensures that each piece will reach its final destination in the condition a customer would wish. B.A.E. set a very high standard and, as a further means of improving each container load, their customer/container liaison dept, invites each customer to return detailed information on the saleability of each piece in the container, thereby ensuring successful future shipments.

This feedback of information is the all important factor which guarantees the profitability of future containers. "By this method" Mr. Lefton explains, "we have established that an average £12,500 container will immediately it is unpacked at its final destination realise in the region of £20,000 to £27,000 for our clients selling

the goods on a quick wholesale turnover basis."

In an average 20-foot container B.A.E. put approximately 75 to 100 pieces carefully selected to suit the particular destination. There are always at least 10 outstanding or unusual items in each shipment, but every piece included looks as though it has something special about it.

Burgess Hill is 15 minutes away from Gatwick Airport, 7 miles from Brighton and 39 miles from London on a direct rail link, (only 40 minutes journey), the Company is ideally situated to ship containers to all parts of the world. The showrooms, restoration and packing departments are open to overseas buyers and no visit to purchase antiques for re-sale in other countries is complete without a visit to their Burgess Hill premises where a welcome is always found.

BRITISH ANTIQUE EXPORTERS LTD,
SCHOOL CLOSE, QUEEN ELIZABETH AVENUE,
BURGESS HILL, WEST SUSSEX RH15 9RX, ENGLAND.
Telephone BURGESS HILL (04 44) 245577.
Fax (04 44) 232014.
Tel from USA 011 44 444 245577

MEMBER
LAPADA MEMBER

MEMBER

INTERNATIONAL
Antiques
PRICE GUIDE

Consultants
Judith and Martin Miller

General Editor
Josephine Davis

1994

MILLER'S INTERNATIONAL ANTIQUES PRICE GUIDE 1994

Created and designed by
Millers
The Cellars, High Street,
Tenterden, Kent, TN30 6BN
Tel: 0580 766411

Consultants: Judith & Martin Miller

First published in Great Britain in 1993
by Millers, an imprint of
Reed Consumer Books Limited,
Michelin House, 81 Fulham Road,
London SW3 6RB
and Auckland, Melbourne, Singapore and Toronto

This edition distributed in the US
by
Antique Collectors' Club Ltd
Market Street Industrial Park
Wappingers Falls
New York
12590

ISBN 1-85732-241-X

Bromide output by Final Word, Tonbridge, Kent
Illustrations by G.H. Graphics, St. Leonards-on-Sea
Colour origination by Scantrans, Singapore
Printed and bound in England by William Clowes Ltd,
Beccles and London

KEY TO ILLUSTRATIONS

Please find below a listing of Auctioneers (denoted by *) and Dealers (•) who submitted pictures in this year's Guide. Advertisers in this year's Directory are denoted by †.

†* Academy Auctioneers & Valuers, Northcote House, Northcote Avenue, Ealing, London W5. Tel: 081 579 7466
* Abbotts Auction Rooms, Campsea Ashe, Woodbridge, Suffolk. Tel: 0728 746323
• A. & F. Gordon, c/o B.A.D.A. Tel: 071 589 4128
* Anderson & Garland, Marlborough House, Marlborough Crescent, Newcastle-upon-Tyne. Tel: 091 232 6278
†* Andrew Hartley, Victoria Hall, Little Lane, Ilkley, West Yorkshire. Tel: 0943 816363
• Adrian Hornsey Ltd, Three Bridge Mill, Twyford, Buckingham, Bucks. Tel: 0296 738373
• A. J. Partners, Stand J28, Gray's In the Mews, 1-7 Davies Mews, London W1. Tel: 071 629 1649
†• Ann Lingard, Ropewalk Antiques, Ropewalk, Rye, Sussex. Tel: 0797 223486
†* Allen & Harris, Bristol Auction Rooms, St John's Place, Apsley Road, Clifton, Bristol, Avon. Tel: 0272 737201
†• Allan Smith Antiques, Amity Cottage, 162 Beechcroft Road, Upper Stratton, Swindon, Wilts. Tel: 0793 822977
†* Andrew Pickford, The Hertford Saleroom, Castle Hall, Hertford. Tel: 0992 501421
†• Apollo Antiques Ltd, The Saltisford, Birmingham Road, Warwick. Tel: 0926 494746 and 07695 3342
†• Arenski, Stand 107, Gray's Antique Market, 58 Davies Street, London W1. Tel: 071 499 6824
†• AS Antiques, 26 Broad Street, Pendleton, Salford 6, Lancashire. Tel: 061 737 5938
* Boardman, Station Road Corner, Haverhill, Suffolk. Tel: 0440 703784
• British Collectables, 1st Floor, 9 Georgian Village, Camden Passage, Islington, London N1. Tel: 071 359 4560
* Bearnes, Rainbow, Avenue Road, Torquay, Devon. Tel: 0803 296277
†• Janice Paull, Beehive House, 125 Warwick Road, Kenilworth, Warwicks. Tel: 0926 52253
†• Bell Antiques, 68 Harold Street, Grimsby, South Humberside. Tel: 0472 695110
• Douglas Berryman, Bartlett Street Antique Centre, Bath, Avon. Tel: 0225 446841
†* Bonhams, Montpelier Galleries, Montpelier Street, London SW7. Tel: 071 584 9161
†* Brown & Merry, Brook Street, Tring, Herts. Tel: 0442 826446
* Bracketts, 27-29 High Street, Tunbridge Wells, Kent. Tel: 0892 533733
†• Breck Antiques, 762 Mansfield Road, Nottingham. Tel: 0602 605263
†• Bow-Well Antiques, 103 West Bow, Edinburgh, Scotland. Tel: 031 225 3335
* Biddle & Webb, Ladywood Middleway, Birmingham. Tel: 021 455 8042
* Christie, Manson & Woods Ltd, 8 King Street, St James's, London SW1. Tel: 071 839 9060
†* Canterbury Auction Galleries, 40 Station Road West, Canterbury, Kent. Tel: 0227 763337
• Cain Antiques, Littleton House, Littleton, Nr Somerton, Somerset. Tel: 0458 72341
• The China Doll, 31 Walcot Street, Bath, Avon. Tel: 0225 465849
†* Charles Edwards & Co Ltd, 4/8 Lynwood Road, Blackburn, Lancs. Tel: 0254 691748
* Christie's (International) SA, 8 Place de la Taconnerie, 1204 Geneva, Switzerland. Tel: 010 4122 311 17 66
• Chelsea Lion, Steve Clark, Chenil Galleries, 181/183 Kings's Road, London SW3. Tel: 071 351 9338
• Country Interiors, 10 Great Western Antiques Centre, Bartlett Street, Bath. Tel: 0225 310388/421505
†• The Clock Clinic Ltd, 85 Lower Richmond Road, Putney, London SW15. Tel: 081 788 1407
* Christie's (Monaco), S.A.M., Park Palace, 98000, Monte Carlo. Tel: 010 339 325 1933
†* Christie, Manson & Woods International Inc., 502 Park Avenue, New York, NY 10022, USA. Tel: (212) 546 1000 (including Christie's East)
†* Cooper Hirst, The Granary Saleroom, Victoria Road, Chelmsford, Essex. Tel: 0245 260535
†• Country Pine Antiques, The Barn, Upper Bush Farm, Upper Bush, Kent. Tel: 0634 717982
• Chris Partington, 41 Berwick Road, Shrewsbury, Shropshire. Tel: 0743 369373
†* Christie's Scotland Ltd, 164-166 Bath Street, Glasgow. Tel: 041 332 8134
†• Christopher Sykes Antiques, The Old Parsonage, Woburn, Bucks. Tel: 0525 290259
* Christie's South Kensington Ltd, 85 Old Brompton Road, London SW7. Tel: 071 581 7611
†* Dee, Atkinson & Harrison, The Exchange Saleroom, Driffield, East Yorks. Tel: 0377 43151
* David Dockree, 224 Moss Lane, Bramhall, Stockport, Cheshire. Tel: 061 485 1258
• Andrew Dando, 4 Wood St, Queen Square, Bath, Avon. Tel: 0225 422702
* Dickinson, Davy & Markham, Wrawby Street, Brigg, South Humberside. Tel: 0652 53666
• Ann Delores, Bartlett Street Antique Centre, Bath, Avon. Tel: 0225 310457
* Dreweatt Neate, Donnington Priory, Donnington, Newbury, Berkshire. Tel: 0635 31234
• Drummonds of Bramley, Birtley Farm, Horsham Road, Bramley, Guildford, Surrey. Tel: 0483 898766
* Ewbank Fine Art, Welbeck House, High St, Guildford, Surrey. Tel: 0483 232134
†* Francis Fine Art Auctioneers, The Tristar Business Centre, Star Industrial Estate, Partridge Green, Horsham, Sussex. Tel: 0403 710567
†• Fenwick Billiards, Tonedale Mills, Wellington, Somerset. Tel: 0643 706165.
• Frank Dux Antiques, 33 Belvedere, Bath, Avon. Tel: 0225 312367
• Forget Me Not Antiques (Heather Sharp), By George Antique Centre, 23 George Street, St Albans, Herts. Tel: 0727 53032/ 0923 261172
†* G.A. Key, Aylsham Saleroom, off Palmers Lane, Aylsham, Norfolk. Tel: 0263 733195
†• Gerard Campbell, Maple House, Market Place, Lechlade-on-Thames, Glos. Tel: 0367 252267

- * Giles Haywood, The Auction House, St. John's Road, Stourbridge, West Midlands. Tel: 0384 370891
- • David Gibson, 4 Wood Street, Queen Square, Bath, Avon. Tel: 0225 446646
- • Grange Farm Ltd, Grange Farm, Tongham, Surrey. Tel: 0258 2993/2804
- †• Gordon Reece Gallery, Finkle Street, Knaresborough, N. Yorks. Tel: 0423 866219
- * Graves, Son & Pilcher, 71 Church Road, Hove, East Sussex. Tel: 0273 735266
- * Hamptons, 6 Artlington Street, St James's, London SW1. Tel: 071 493 8222
- * Hobbs & Chambers, 'At The Sign of the Bell', Market Place, Cirencester, Glos. Tel: 0285 4736
- †* HY Duke & Son, 40 South Street, Dorchester, Dorset. Tel: 0305 265080
- • Heritage Antiques, Unit 14, Georgian Village, 30 Islington Greet, Camden Passage, London N1. Tel: 071 226 9822 Wed & Sat only
- †* Holloways, 49 Parsons Street, Banbury, Oxon. Tel: 0295 253197
- * Henry Spencer & Sons, 20 The Square, Retford, Notts. Tel: 0777 708633
- †* Ibbett Mosely, 125 High Street, Sevenoaks, Kent. Tel: 0732 452246
- * Jacobs & Hunt, Lavant Street, Petersfield, Hants. Tel: 0730 62744
- †• Jonathan Horne (Antiques) Ltd, 66B & C, Kensington Church Street, London, W8. Tel: 071 221 5658
- • Joy Luke, The Gallery, 300E Grove Street, Bloomington, IL 61701, USA. Tel: (309) 828 5533
- • J & M Collectables (Maurice & Judith Coombs). Tel: 0580 891657
- †• Jamie Maxtone Graham, Lyne Haugh, Lyne Station, Peebles, Scotland. Tel: 07214 304
- †* John Nicholson, 1 Crossways Court, Fernhurst, Haslemere, Surrey. Tel: 0428 653727
- • Key Antiques, 11 Horsefair, Chipping Norton, Oxon. Tel: 0608 643777
- †* George Kidner, The Old School, Pennington, Lymington, Hants. Tel: 0590 670070
- * Lawrences of Crewkerne, South Street, Crewkerne, Somerset. Tel: 0460 73041
- * Langlois, Westaway Chambers, Don Street, St Helier, Jersey. Tel: 0534 22441
- • Lawrence Black Antiques of Scotland, 45 Cumberland Street, Edinburgh. Tel: 031 557 4545
- * Locke & England, Black Horse Agencies, 18 Guy Street, Leamington Spa, Warwicks. Tel: 0926 889100
- †* Lambert & Foster, 102 High Street, Tenterden, Kent. Tel: 0580 763233
- * Lots Road Chelsea Auction Galleries, 71 Lots Road, London SW10. Tel: 071 351 7771
- †* Louis Taylor Fine Art Auctioneers & Valuers, Britannia House, 10 Town Road, Hanley, Stoke-on-Trent. Tel: 0782 214111
- †* Lawrences Auctioneers, Norfolk House, High Street, Bletchingley, Surrey. Tel: 0883 743323
- * Morphets of Harrogate, 4-6 Albert Street, Harrogate, North Yorks. Tel: 0423 502282
- * Christopher Matthews, 23 Mount Street, Harrogate, Yorks. Tel: 0423 871756
- * Mervyn Carey, Twysden Cottage, Benenden, Cranbrook, Kent. Tel: 0580 240283
- †* McCartney's Portcullis Salerooms, Ludlow, Shropshire. Tel: 0584 872636
- • Merrifield Studios, 110/112 Heath Street, Hampstead, London NW3. Tel: 071 794 0343
- †* Mitchells, Fairfield House, Station Road, Cockermouth, Cumbria. Tel: 0900 822016

- †* Michael J. Bowman, 6 Haccombe House, Netherton, Newton Abbot, Devon. Tel: 0626 872890
- • Mark J West, Cobb Antiques Ltd, 39a High Street, Wimbledon Village, London SW19. Tel: 081 946 2811
- †• Millers of Chelsea Antiques Ltd, Netherbrook House, 86 Christchurch Road, Ringwood, Hants. Tel: 0425 472062
- • Mark Rees Tools, Barrow Mead Cottage, Rush Hill, Bath. Tel: 0225 837031
- †* Michael Stainer Ltd, St Andrew's Hill, Boscombe, Bournemouth. Tel: 0202 309999
- †* Marilyn Swain Auctions, The Old Barracks, Sandon Road, Grantham. Tel: 0476 68861
- • Nicolaus Boston, Kensington Church Street Antique Centre, London W8. Tel: 071 376 0425/0722 326906
- • New Century Antiques, 69 Kensington Church Street, W8. Tel: 071 376 2810
- †* D. M. Nesbit & Co., Southsea Salerooms, 7 Clarendon Road, Southsea, Hants. Tel: 0705 864321
- †• The Old Cinema, 160 Chiswick High Road, London W4. Tel: 081-995 4166
- * Onslows, Metrostore, Townmead Road, London SW6. Tel: 071 793 0240
- †• Pieter Oosthuizen, The Georgian Village, 30 Islington Green, Camden Passage, London N1. Wed & Sat. Tel: 071 376 3852
- †* Phillips, Blenstock House, 101 New Bond Street, London W1. Tel: 071 629 6602
- †• P A Oxley, The Old Rectory, Cherhill, Nr Calne, Wiltshire. Tel: 0249 816227
- • Park House Antiques, Park Street, Stow-on-the-Wold, Nr Cheltenham, Glos.
- †* Peter Cheney, Western Road Auction Rooms, Western Road, Littlehampton, West Sussex. Tel: 0903 722264/713418
- †• Paul Hopwell Antiques, 30 High Street, West Haddon, Northants. Tel: 0788 510636
- †• Peter Jackson Antiques, 3 Market Place, Brackley, Northants. Tel: 0993 882415/0280 703259
- * Phillips, Hepper House, 17a East Parade, Leeds. Tel: 0532 448011
- • Mrs I Morton-Smith, The Plough, Maysleith, Milland, Nr Liphook, Hants. Tel: 0428 76323
- †• Sylvia Powell Decorative Arts, 28 The Mall, Camden Passage, London N1. Tel: 071 354 2977/081 458 4543
- * Phillips, 49 London Road, Sevenoaks, Kent. Tel: 0732 740310
- * Phillips Scotland, 65 George Street, Edinburgh. Tel: 031 225 2266. Also 207 Bath Street, Glasgow. Tel: 041 221 8377
- • Patrick & Susan Gould, Stand L17, Gray's Antique Market, Davies Street, London W1. Tel: 071 408 0129
- †• Pieces of Time, Grays Mews, 1-7 Davies Street, London W1. Tel: 071 629 2422
- * Rye Auction Galleries, Rock Channel, Rye, East Sussex. Tel: 0797 222124
- †* Russell, Baldwin & Bright, Fine Art Salerooms, Ryelands Road, Leominster, Hereford. Tel: 0568 611166
- †• Rogers de Rin, 76 Royal Hospital Road, Paradise Walk, London SW3. Tel: 071 352 9007
- • Relic Antiques at Brillscote Farm, Lea, Malmesbury, Wilts. Tel: 0666 822332
- * R. H. Ellis & Sons, 44-46 High Street, Worthing, Sussex. Tel: 0903 238999
- †* Riddetts of Bournemouth, 26 Richmond Hill, Bournemouth, Hants. Tel: 0202 555686
- • Richard Kimbell, Riverside, Market Harborough, Leics. Tel: 0858 433444
- †* Rosebery's, The Old Railway Booking Hall, Crystal Palace Station Road, London SE19. Tel: 081 778 4024
- †* Raymond P. Inman, The Auction Galleries, 35 & 40 Temple Street, Brighton, Sussex. Tel: 0273 774777
- †• Rumours Decorative Arts, 10 The Mall, Upper Street, Camden Passage, Islington, London N1. Tel: 0582 873561
- †• Roy W. Bunn Antiques, 34-36 Church Street, Barnoldswick, Colne, Lancashire. Tel: 0282 813703
- * Sotheby's, 34-35 New Bond Street, London W1. Tel: 071 493 8080
- †• Somerville Antiques & Country Furniture Ltd, Killanley, Ballina, Co Mayo, Ireland. Tel: 096 36275
- * Stride & Son, Southdown House, St John's Street, Chichester. Tel: 0243 782626
- • Serendipity, 168 High Street, Deal, Kent. Tel: 0304 369165/366536
- * Sotheby's, 13 Quai du Mont Blanc, CH-1201 Geneva. Tel: 41 (22) 732 8585
- †* Auction Centres, Highgate, Hawkhurst, Kent. Tel: 0580 753463
- †* Simmons & Sons, 32 Bell Street, Henley-on-Thames, Oxfordshire. Tel: 0491 591111
- * Sotheby's, 1334 York Avenue, New York, NY 10021, USA. Tel: (212) 606 7000
- †• Somervale Antiques, 6 Radstock Road, Midsomer Norton, Bath. Tel: 0761 412686
- • Station Pine Antiques, 103 Carrington Street, Nottingham. Tel: 0602 582710
- * Sotheby's, Summers Place, Billingshurst, West Sussex. Tel: 0403 783933
- * Suffolk Sales, Half Moon House, High Street, Clare, Suffolk. Tel: 0787 277993
- †* Sworders, G. E. Sworder & Sons, 15 Northgate End, Bishops Stortford, Herts. Tel: 0279 651388
- * Taviners Ltd, Prewett Street, Redcliffe, Bristol. Tel: 0272 265996
- †• Teddy Bears of Witney, 99 High Street, Witney, Oxon. Tel: 0993 702616
- * Thos. Mawer & Son, The Lincoln Saleroom, 63 Monks Road, Lincoln. Tel: 0522 524984
- †• The Pine Cellars, 39 Jewry Street, Winchester, Hants. Tel: 0962 67014
- • The Trumpet, West End, Minchinhampton, Glos. Tel: 0453 883027
- • The Talking Machine, 30 Watford Way, London NW4. Tel: 081 202 3473
- • Teme Valley Antiques, 1 The Bull Ring, Ludlow, Shropshire. Tel: 0584 874686
- • Utopia Pine & Country Furniture, Holme Mills, Burton-in-Kendal, Carnforth, Lancs. Tel: 0524 781739
- • Valerie Howard, 131e Kensington Church Street, London W8. Tel: 071 792 9702
- †* T. Vennett-Smith, 11 Nottingham Road, Gotham, Nottingham. Tel: 0602 830541
- †* Walter's, No. 1 Mint Lane, Lincoln. Tel: 0522 525454
- • Windmill Antiques, 4 Montpelier Mews, Harrogate, Yorks. Tel: 0423 530502/0845 401330
- †* Wallis & Wallis, West Street Auction Galleries, Lewes, Sussex. Tel: 0273 480208
- • Welsh Bridge Salerooms, Welsh Bridge, Shrewsbury, Shropshire. Tel: 0743 231212
- • W.G.T. Burne, 11 Elystan Street, London SW3. Tel: 071 589 6074
- * Peter Wilson, Victoria Gallery, Market Street, Nantwich, Cheshire. Tel: 0270 623878
- * Wintertons Ltd, Lichfield Auction Centre, Wood End Lane, Fradley, Lichfield, Staffs. Tel: 0543 263256
- • Whytock & Reid, Sunbury House, Belford Mews, Edinburgh. Tel: 031 226 4911.
- * Woolley & Wallis, The Castle Auction Mart, Castle Street, Salisbury. Tel: 0722 212711
- • Walker & Walker, Halfway Manor, Halfway, Nr Newbury, Berkshire. Tel: 0488 58693/0831 147480
- • Zeitgeist, 58 Kensington Church Street, London W8. Tel: 071 938 4817

The Old Mint House

HIGH STREET, PEVENSEY
NEAR EASTBOURNE, EAST SUSSEX BN24 5LF

The Largest Antique Business in the South of England

ALL ENQUIRIES To Head Office (0323) 762337
(0323) 641142 (After Hours)
(0323) 762337 (Fax)

Couriers Welcome

All trains met by appointment

Business hours:
Monday thru to Saturday 9.00 hrs to 17.30 hrs
(or by appointment)

The Old Mint House Antiques, established since 1901, with 33 showrooms containing a large and varied stock of Georgian, Victorian, Edwardian, inlaid and marquetry furniture, also we carry a large stock of porcelain, clocks and metalware. We can cater for a client wishing to purchase one item or an entire container.

A rapidly changing stock, but always 20,000 items available, with new consignments arriving daily.

LOCATION MAP

1 hr from Gatwick, 1½hrs from London ½hr from Brighton

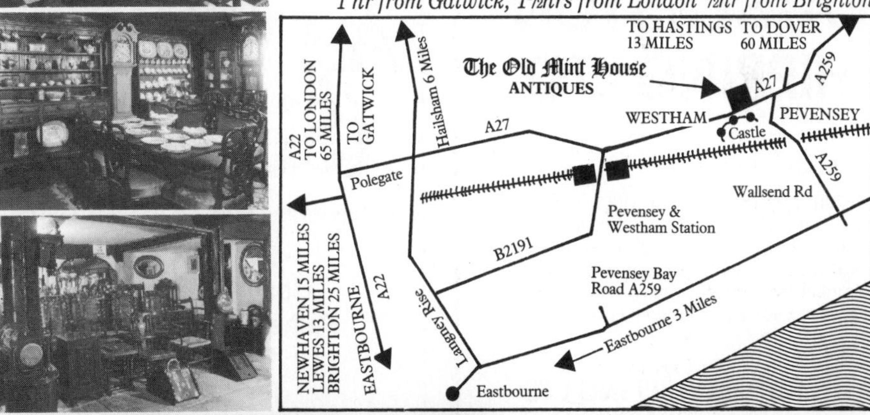

Also our shipping and export division situated at

45 TURKEY ROAD, BEXHILL, E. SUSSEX. Tel: (0424) 216056

which specialises in Victorian and Pre-War oak, mahogany and inlaid shipping furniture for the large trade buyer, who wishes to find most of his requirements at one location.

This 20,000 sq. ft. purpose built warehouse contains on two levels a huge selection of goods at the absolute lowest open trade prices

Video (all systems) available for the larger buyer

ACKNOWLEDGEMENTS

The publishers would like to acknowledge the great assistance given by our consultants:

POTTERY & PORCELAIN:	**Christopher Spencer,** *Greystones, 29 Mostyn Road, Merton Park, London SW19 3LL*
OAK & COUNTRY FURNITURE:	**Paul Hopwell,** *30 High Street, West Haddon, Northants NN6 7AP*
CLOCKS:	**James Lowe,** *27 Victoria Road, Mortlake, London SW14 8EX*
	Brian Loomes, *Calf Haugh, Pateley Bridge, N. Yorks*
GLASS:	**Wing Cdr R. G. Thomas,** *Somervale Antiques, 6 Radstock Road, Midsomer Norton, Bath, Avon.*
DOLLS:	**Olivia Bristol,** *Christie's South Kensington, 85 Old Brompton Road, London SW7*
DECORATIVE ARTS:	**Fiona Baker,** *Phillips, Blenstock House, 101 New Bond Street, London W1*
SCOTCH WHISKY:	**Martin Green,** *Christie's Scotland Ltd, 164-166 Bath Street, Glasgow G2 4TG*
SILVER:	**Stephen Clarke,** *Christie's Manson & Woods, 8 King Street, St. James's, London SW1*

An Austin J40 Roadster pedal car, c1950.
$900-1,050

CONTENTS

A flying scale model of a Sopwith 'Taperwing Camel', the fabric covered wooden air frame with working elevator control surfaces, with single cylinder glow-plug engine, wingspan 42in (106.5cm)
$900-1,050

INTRODUCTION

'An American edition of a British price guide?' you may be thinking. True, Miller's Antiques Price Guide long has been a must-have book in England. Wait. Look again. It's *Miller's International Antiques Price Guide*. As anyone familiar with today's antiques market will attest, antiques of every description, and from every source, are being collected in every corner of the world.

We shop wherever we may be - along winding village streets in Southern Italy, at antiques fairs in London, in antiques malls in Ohio, and any place we see the sign 'Antique Auction'. That's the fun of being a collector. Yet, as an appraiser, I've long been fascinated by varying degrees of success achieved by my clients in their antiques purchases.

Why is it that some collectors come away with sound, even remarkable buys, whether American or Oriental, silver or furniture - pieces of quality purchased at good, fair prices - while others come up short and spend too much money on the not-good-enough piece? Knowledge, of course, is the answer. When there are so many enticing and wonderful objects to choose from, knowledge, both of the object itself and the current marketplace, is the essential ingredient to making wise purchases.

That's what distinguishes this volume from many other price guides, which are generally less concrete in their identification of specific pieces, and which are compiled from a much smaller market scope. Within these pages there is a wealth of information that you need to know about the antiques being bought and sold, not just in the United States, but around the world. In fact, you won't be the only one who finds this price guide to be an invaluable tool.

Appraisers, antiques dealers, and others in the trade already find this single volume indispensable in their daily research. Its pages bring to your fingertips facts and figures that would require thousands of hours and endless travel to compile first-hand.

First, each object is clearly pictured. Then, beneath each picture of the actual object, in addition to the price that it sold for and where it was sold, is the all-important caption that cites specific features of that piece. These captions hold the clues the savvy collector looks for.

By carefully studying them and making comparative judgements among the pictured pieces, you will soon better understand why, for example, one piece is priced in the lower, $3,000-5,000 range and another slips up into the $7,000-9,000 category. This is invaluable information when you're ready to begin making your own purchase.

Yes, the antiques market in America is strong - the published prices that the pieces actually sold for attest to that. There are, of course, the expected regional differences, seasonal fluctuations, and even slumps in entire segments of the market which are not as popular (and therefore expensively priced) as they were only a few years ago. But ask any dealer, decorator, or auctioneer and you'll hear that fine quality objects, in good condition, and sensibly priced, are moving as strongly as ever. In fact the 1990s are bringing new buying opportunities to American collectors as a large volume of objects, long privately held, is making a return to the market.

Many choice antiques - silver, ceramics, furniture, decorative accessories - bought in the 1920s, '30s and '40s, when serious antique collecting first became an American obsession, are now leaving private homes and returning to the shops and auction blocks. Yet these pieces have had an additional 50-70 years' worth of wear and tear. When does condition make a notable price difference? What influence do decorating trends have on pricing? What unexpected markets are there? The editorial introductions to each general category and in-depth treatment of each area of decorative objects - textiles, dolls and toys, silver, even arms and armour - are invaluable in unravelling many of the puzzles in the antiques pricing world.

So when you begin your search through these pages, remember that it is arranged to make the guide as easy to use as possible by breaking the larger sections down into smaller sub-sections. When looking for a particular item, first consult the contents on page 21 to find the main heading, for example, Furniture. Then turn to the section and look at the sub-headings, which appear in alphabetical order, to find your particular area of interest, such as Desks. If you are looking for a particular designer or craftsman or even factory, consult the index which starts on page 801.

Also remember Miller's pricing policy: this is a price GUIDE, not a price LIST. Price ranges, worked out by a team of dealers and auction house experts, and based on actual prices realized, reflect variables such as condition, location, desirability, alterations. and so on. Don't forget that if you are selling, it is possible that you will be offered less than the price range.

Lastly, we are always keen to improve the Guide. If you feel that we have left something important out, if you disagree with our panel of experts, or have any other comments about the book, we'd like to hear from you. Write and let us know. We value feedback from the people who use this Guide to tell us how to make it even better for next year.

Emyl Jenkins

Dates	British Monarch	British Period	French Period
1558-1603	Elizabeth I	Elizabethan	Renaissance
1603-1625	James I	Jocobean	
1625-1649	Charles I	Carolean	Louis XIII (1610-1643)
1649-1660	Commonwealth	Cromwellian	Louis XIV (1643-1715)
1660-1685	Charles II	Restoration	
1685-1689	James II	Restoration	
1689-1694	William & Mary	William & Mary	
1694-1702	William III	William III	
1702-1714	Anne	Queen Anne	
1714-1727	George I	Early Georgian	Régence (1715-1723)
1727-1760	George II	Early Georgian	Louis XV (1723-1774)
1760-1811	George III	Late Georgian	Louis XVI (1774-1793) Directoire (1793-1799) Empire (1799-1815)
1812-1820	George III	Regency	Restauration (1815-1830)
1820-1830	George IV	Regency	
1830-1837	William IV	William IV	Louis Philippe (1830-1848) 2nd Empire (1848-1870) 3rd Republic (1871-1940)
1837-1901	Victoria	Victorian	
1901-1910	Edward VII	Edwardian	

<table>
<tr><th>German Period</th><th>U.S. Period</th><th>Style</th><th>Woods</th></tr>
<tr><td rowspan="2">Renaissance</td><td rowspan="3">Early Colonial</td><td>Gothic</td><td rowspan="12">Oak Period (to c1670)

Walnut period (c1670-1735)

Early mahogany period (c1735-1770)

Late mahogany period (c1770-1810)</td></tr>
<tr><td rowspan="3">Baroque (c1620-1700)</td></tr>
<tr><td rowspan="3">Renaissance/ Baroque (c1650-1700)</td></tr>
<tr><td>William & Mary</td></tr>
<tr><td>Dutch Colonial</td><td rowspan="3">Rococo (c 1695-1760)</td></tr>
<tr><td>Baroque (c1700-1730)</td><td>Queen Anne</td></tr>
<tr><td>Rococo (c1730-1760)</td><td>Chippendale (from 1750)</td></tr>
<tr><td>Neo-classicism (c1760-1800)

Empire (c1800-1815</td><td>Early Federal (1790-1810)

American Directoire (1798-1804)

American Empire (1804-1815)</td><td>Neo-classical (c1755-1805)

Empire (c1799-1815)</td></tr>
<tr><td>Biedermeier (c1815-1848</td><td rowspan="2">Late Federal (1810-1830)</td><td>Regency (c1812-1830)</td></tr>
<tr><td rowspan="3">Revivale (c1830-1880)

Jugendstil (c1880-1920)</td><td rowspan="2">Eclectic (c1830-1880)

Arts & Crafts (c1880-1900)</td></tr>
<tr><td>Victorian</td></tr>
<tr><td>Art Nouveau (c1900-1920)</td><td>Art Nouveau (c1900-1920)</td></tr>
</table>

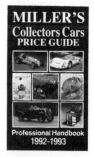

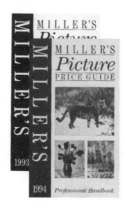

OAK & COUNTRY FURNITURE

It certainly cannot be long before the lower end, price wise, of the oak furniture market starts to improve. At the moment, 18th and 19th Century furniture of a plain but original condition is extremely inexpensive and represents excellent value for money.

Unusual and rare pieces of 17th Century oak are becoming excellent value for money considering the cost of the equivalent mahogany items.

Why should anybody want to buy the reproduction equivalent at the same price or more, with no - or very little - second-hand value?

When buying 17th and 18th Century oak and country furniture remember two things. First, the colour and patina represent fifty per cent of the value of the item - oak will not stand cleaning and French polishing like mahogany. Secondly, buy from people who specialise solely in the early oak furniture - there is no other reliable oak outlet.

Choose the best that you can afford, this will pay off in the long run. If I may quote William Shakespeare: 'The bitterness of poor quality long outlasts the sweetness of low price' *The Merchant of Venice*. Remember also that Continental oak only makes half the price of English oak in this country.

At the moment it is a buyer's market, so my advice to you is to go out and buy. Prices are at an all-time low, and they can only go up!

18th & 19thC Furniture - plain but of original condition

Hanging oak corner cupboards
$550-1,200
Georgian oak 6-8 seater oblong dining tables
$550-1,200
Pairs of country oak, ash and elm chairs
$300-750
Sets of 6 country chairs
$750-1,800
Dressers
$3,750-6,750
Chests of drawers (oak, ash and elm)
$750-1,800
Panelled coffers
$750-1,500
Livery cupboards/wardrobes
$1,200-2,250
Delft racks
$750-1,800
Oak longcase clocks
$1,200-5,250

17thC Oak - unusual and rare pieces

Side tables
$3,000-9,000
Court cupboards
$6,000-18,000
Single chairs
$750-2,100
Carved coffers
$975-6,000
Joined stools
$1,500-6,000
Dresser bases
$7,500-22,500
Four poster beds
$6,000-15,000 (restored)
$18,000-45,000 (good condition)

Paul Hopwell
Paul Hopwell Antiques

Beds

An oak bedstead, the panelled headboard and footrest carved with linenfold and with tablets of scrolling foliage, fruit and mythical beasts, with turned baluster short posts carved with roundels and foliage, the back legs applied with atlantes and caryatids, with box spring and mattress, 62in (157cm) wide.
$4,500-6,000

Bureaux

A George III oak bureau with fitted interior, bracket feet, 33in (84cm) wide.
$1,500-2,250

A William and Mary oak bureau-on-stand, with shaped stretcher, original bun feet, c1695.
$7,500-9,000

An early Georgian oak slope front bureau, with stepped interior including a well, 36in (91.5cm) wide.
$1,500-2,250

An early George III oak bureau, with fall front enclosing fitted interior, on bracket feet with pierced C-scroll spandrels, damaged, 41in (104cm).
$1,200-1,500

A Queen Anne oak bureau, the fall front revealing a well and stationery compartments, with two short and two long drawers above bracket feet, 33in (84cm).
$2,250-3,000

A George II oak bureau, with walnut crossbanding, c1740.
$5,250-7,500

A George III oak bureau, the fall front enclosing drawers and pigeonholes above 4 graduated drawers, on plinth base.
$750-1,200

An oak bureau, the sloping flap enclosing a cupboard, drawers and pigeonholes, with 4 graduated drawers below, on shaped bracket feet, mid-18thC, 38in (96.5cm).
$1,050-1,350

A George III oak bureau, with hinged fall front enclosing a fitted interior, on bracket feet, 35in (89cm).
$1,500-2,250

A George III oak bureau, with mahogany crossbanded decoration, the fall front opening to reveal a fitted interior.
$1,200-1,500

An oak bureau bookcase, early 18thC, 36in (91.5cm).
$5,250-6,000

Cabinets

A Dutch oak display cabinet, the glazed upper section with a pair of astragal doors and canted sides, above a pair of cupboard doors, damaged, c1750, 62in (158cm).
$4,500-6,000

A George III yew wood Windsor armchair, c1790.
$1,800-2,700

A George IV yew wood, ash and beechwood Windsor armchair, with crinoline stretcher, c1825.
$750-1,200

Chairs

A matched pair of elm and yew wood Windsor armchairs, attributed to Robert Prior of Uxbridge, each with arched spindle-filled back and pierced vase shaped splat, one carved with a wheel, the other carved with a roundel, with dished seats on turned legs, on double Y-shaped stretchers, one with fruitwood legs, the other with damage to toprail.
$1,500-2,250

The roundel centred pierced vase shaped splat and overall shape of these chairs reflect closely the stamped work of Robert Prior of Uxbridge, the second generation of a dynasty started in the second half of the 18thC by his father John Prior. Stamped variants exist with both the wheel and the roundel splats.

A yew and fruitwood high hoop back Windsor armchair, 19thC, 46in (116.5cm) high.
$375-450

Windsor Chairs

- Windsor chairs are the most popular and recognisable type of English provincial chair.
- Predominantly made between 1800 and 1840.
- The backs are usually composed of 'sticks', sometimes with a central decorative splat and, more rarely, with alternate plain straight and decorative sticks.
- A central splat adds to the value.
- Hoop-shaped top is typically English, and the comb back Windsor chair from c1765 has a characteristically American form.
- The great many reproductions made in the 1920s and 30s are of insignificant value.
- Replacements will seriously reduce value.

A George III yew wood and elm Windsor comb back armchair, with waved top rail and spindle filled back, the dished seat on cabriole legs joined by H-shaped stretchers on pad feet, Thames Valley, restoration, with repair to one front foot.
$1,500-2,250

The comb back, waved top rail and cabriole legs are characteristic of Thames Valley Windsor armchairs in the period 1775-1800. The cabriole legs are more often found on hoop backed chairs.

A set of 7 Windsor scroll back small chairs, including one with arms, in beech, fruitwood and elm, each with triple baluster spindles beneath an arcaded top rail, dished panel seat and turned underframe, repaired, stamped RW on rear edge of seat, 19thC.
$1,500-2,250

This style of chair was made by many of the High Wycombe chair manufacturers.

A yew wood and elm Windsor armchair, with splat back and crinoline stretcher, early 19thC.
$900-1,500

A yew, ash and elm Windsor armchair, with splat back and crinoline stretcher, early 19thC.
$600-750

A George III ash Windsor armchair, with a fruitwood cresting rail and sycamore seat, on turned legs.
$1,050-1,350

An English carved oak side chair, c1690.
$900-1,500

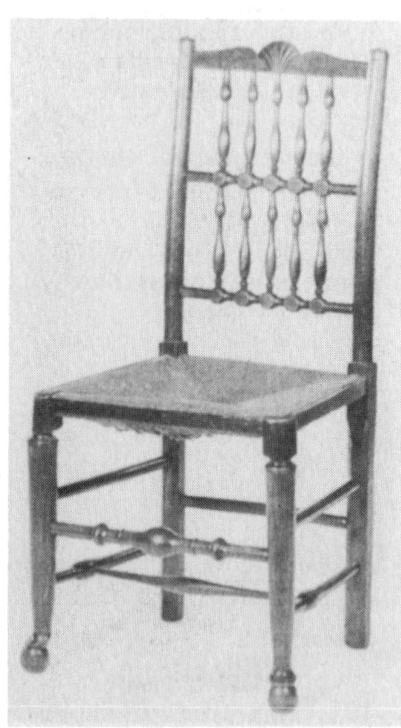

A set of 6 ash spindle back chairs, probably Cheshire, each with a shell-carved top rail and rush seat, on turned legs with pad feet joined by stretchers, stamped C. Leicester, mid-19thC.
$1,800-2,700

Charles Leicester is recorded as a chair maker working in Macclesfield, Cheshire, with premises situated at 120-121 Chestergate. He shared these premises with his son Charles until they both moved to Derby Street c1855.

A set of 3 Hereford style kitchen chairs, late 19thC.
$180-225

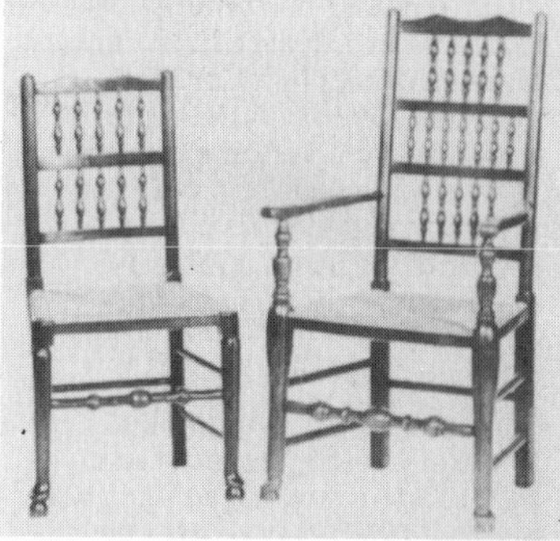

A matched set of 8 ash and birch spindle back chairs, including a pair of armchairs, with rush seats and turned tapering legs, on pad and bun feet joined by stretchers, seats re-rushed, Lancashire/ Cheshire, c1900.
$3,000-4,500

A set of 6 George III fruitwood ladder back dining chairs, with rush seats, on turned baluster legs with pad feet joined by turned stretchers, probably Lancashire, c1900.
$3,000-3,750

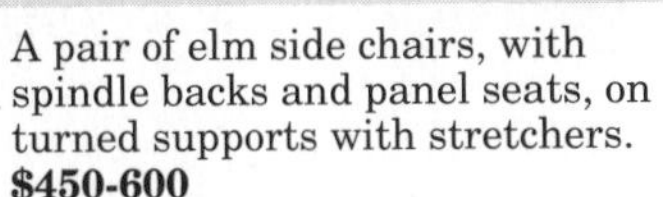

A pair of elm side chairs, with spindle backs and panel seats, on turned supports with stretchers.
$450-600

A George II laburnham ladder back armchair, c1730.
$1,800-2,700

Two similar oak panel back chairs, on square and ring turned legs joined by stretchers, Lancashire, late 17thC.
$1,800-2,700

An oak rush seat chair, early 19thC, 41in (104cm) high.
$225-255

A panel back lambing armchair, with shaped toprail, fielded panel back, outset wings with flat arms and enclosed sides, the sprung seat with panelled base, c1740.
$3,000-4,500

A George III oak lambing chair, the arched canopy with geometric pierced frieze, the detachable solid seat revealing a well, on turned feet with rocking supports.
$1,500-2,250

A Queen Anne oak armchair, early 18thC.
$1,200-1,800

A pair of Charles II walnut side chairs, c1680.
$5,250-6,000

A William IV oak and alder rocking lambing chair, c1830.
$2,700-3,300

A Charles II oak side chair, c1680.
$1,800-2,700

A William and Mary caned oak child's high chair, late 17thC.
$3,000-3,750

A William and Mary carved panel back side chair, North Lancashire, c1690.
$1,800-2,700

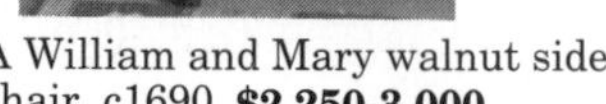

A William and Mary walnut side chair, c1690. **$2,250-3,000**

An oak Turner's chair with bobbin and baluster turnings and squab seat, legs re-toed, c1700.
$750-900

A carved oak open arm elbow wainscot chair, the back decorated with rosettes, flowers and leaves, with upholstered seat, on inverted baluster supports with stretchers, 17thC.
$1,200-1,500

A Dutch oak triangular chair, with arched toprail and bobbin turned arms, the triangular seat on turned legs joined by turned stretchers, c1630.
$1,500-2,250

This chair was originally purchased from Thornton Smith, Soho Square, London, together with a similar chair, for £10.

An oak wainscot elbow chair, with curved arms on baluster shape supports, panel seat and turned front supports joined by stretchers, damaged and repaired, 17thC.
$12,000-15,000

A George III country-made ash and fruit wood corner library chair, the back with 2 solid shaped splats and turned supports, wood seat and straight legs with stretchers.
$600-750

A pair of oak chairs, with embossed leather back and seat, 34½in (87.5cm) high.
$600-750

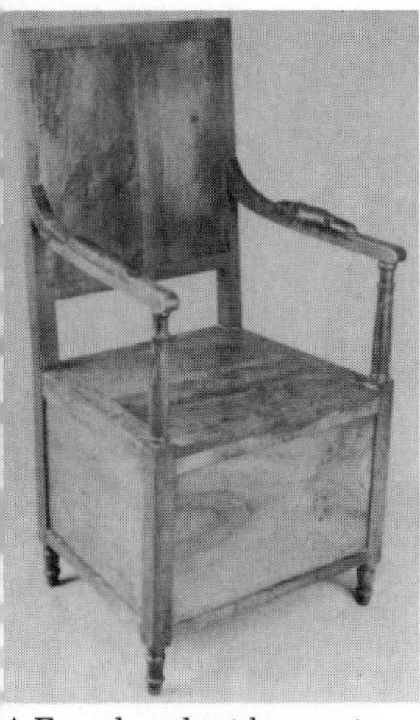

A French walnut box seat armchair, with padded arms and side door, 18thC.
$375-525

A pair of oak open armchairs, the panelled backs carved with stylised flowerheads, Romanesque arches, initials 'CF', with solid seats, fluted seat rails, ring turned legs and moulded stretchers, with crushed dark red foliate cut velvet squab cushions, dated 1652.
$7,500-9,000

An elm and beech child's chair, English, c1840.
$1,200-1,500

An oak settle, the triple panel back above a hinged seat, on a box base, some alterations, 18thC, 55in (141cm).
$1,800-2,700

An oak settle, the carved ribbon surmount above a continuous carved frieze with grape and foliate motif, above panels carved with initials 'I.I.S. 1728', with panelled back, shaped arms, boxseat with a rising lid and central drawer, 18thC, 72in (182.5cm).
$3,000-4,500

An oak settle, 18thC.
$1,500-2,250

A carved oak settle, the fielded panel back above an enclosed base with a hinged seat, on stile feet, 72½in (184cm).
$1,050-1,350

A Charles II oak settee, the upholstered wing back and seat raised on turned supports joined by stretchers, re-railed, late 17thC, 42½in (108cm), together with a loose needlework cushion.
$3,000-4,500

An oak box settle, with a 4 panel back, hinged seat, on stile feet, early 18thC, 53in (135cm).
$2,250-3,000

A carved dark oak hall settle, with lift-up seat and serpent's head arms, earlier back panel, with Apostle and jardinière panels, 19thC, 44in (111.5cm).
$600-750

A panelled oak box settle, the back with slanting stiles and 3 recessed panels, shaped arms with turned front supports above the lift up box seat, 3 panelled front and panelled sides, on stump feet, 18thC.
$2,700-3,300

An oak settle, with a panelled back and baluster turned legs joined by stretchers, restored, late 18thC.
$1,050-1,350

A late George III West Country oak settle, the panelled back centred by a pair of doors above a solid seat, with flat scroll arms on turned supports, the panelled base centred by a pair of doors, the reverse with storage label of W. Stevens, Ridgeway, Plymouth inscribed in ink Montague Eliot Esq./Port Eliot/St. Germans/Cornwall, 74in (188cm).
$1,500-2,250

The curved movable settle, with grocery storage cupboard below the seat and high bacon cupboard above, were a common feature of Devon and West Country vernacular interiors well into this century. The curve was intended to trap the heat of the fire rather than to reflect any architectural feature.

An oak church bench, the back with pierced Gothic panels and chevron banding, scroll arms, plank seat, the frieze fitted a drawer, on panel legs, 18thC, 72in (182.5cm).
$1,200-1,500

Chests

A Charles II oak and snake wood 3 part enclosed chest.
$4,500-6,000

A Charles II oak chest, with moulded top above 4 drawers with geometric moulded fronts, on bun feet, c1665, 38in (97cm).
$3,000-4,500

Purchased by Mr Mountain at the sale of contents of Groombridge Place, 23 and 24 September 1919, lot 78.

Miller's is a price GUIDE not a price LIST

An oak chest of drawers, veneered with snake wood, c1660.
$9,000-12,000

A Charles II oak and cedar wood veneered chest, with hinged top now enclosing a camphor lined interior, the geometrically panelled front including mother-of-pearl and bone stylised flora inlay, with dummy apron drawer above later bun feet, altered, 51in (129cm).
$1,800-2,700

A Charles II oak chest, with 4 geometrically panelled drawers, on stile feet, late 17thC, 34in (87cm).
$2,700-3,300

A George III oak mule chest.
$750-1,200

A Charles II oak chest, with applied geometric moulding, on bun feet, c1670, 41in (104cm).
$3,000-3,750

A George I oak chest-on-stand in 2 sections, with brass drop handles and elaborate pierced back plates, with shaped skirt below, early 18thC, 24in (61cm).
$2,700-3,300

An oak chest of drawers in 2 parts, the top half with a 4 plank top with an oak banded edge and moulded lip above a dentil work frieze, the lower section fitted with 2 long drawers, brass drop handles, on stile feet, late 17thC, 45in (114cm).
$1,200-1,800

An oak bachelor's chest, with folding top above 3 short and 3 long graduated drawers, on bracket feet, mid-18thC, 23½in (60cm).
$5,250-7,500

An oak chest of drawers, with brushing slide, early 19thC, 30in (76cm).
$2,250-3,000

An oak joined chest with hinged top, the interior with a lidded compartment, a walnut frieze carved with foliate scrolls and 'GG 1623', above 3 carved panels and a border of flowers, some later carving , 17thC, 51in (130cm).
$750-900

An oak coffer, with solid panelled hinged lid, iron ring handles and double lock hasp, the front later carved with scenes of gallantry, early 16thC, 71in (180cm).
$5,250-6,000
Reputed to have come from Wyckhamford, near Evesham, Worcestershire, and to have been a parish chest.

Coffers

A James I oak coffer, with moulded edge to the top, the frieze carved with a compressed guilloche design above 3 arcaded panels, inlaid uprights and on stile feet, 65½in (166cm).
$1,800-2,700

An oak coffer, with moulded top above a band of guilloche and 3 panels inlaid with marquetry geometric patterns divided by fluted and stop-fluted pilasters, early 17thC, 56in (142cm).
$3,000-4,500

An Elizabethan oak coffer, with inlaid parquetry, and a parquetry frieze, 54in (137cm).
$3,000-4,500

An oak carved panelled coffer, English, c1670.
$2,250-3,000

A Charles I oak coffer, with moulded top above triple carved arched panels, fluted pilasters, on stile feet, mid-17thC, 52in (132cm).
$2,250-3,000

An oak carved 6 plank coffer, English, c1690.
$1,050-1,350

An oak 3 panelled coffer, with carved top rail and ebony and holly chevron inlay, raised on high stiles, 17thC, 42in (106.5cm).
$900-1,500

A Charles II oak carved panelled coffer, c1680.
$2,250-3,000

An oak coffer, with moulded top above foliate carved triple panel front outlined with ebonised bands, on stile feet, late 17thC, 46½in (118cm).
$1,200-1,800

A Charles II oak coffer, with fluted frieze and multi-fielded panel front, c1680, 52in (132cm).
$1,200-1,800

A carved oak coffer, with triple panelled rectangular lid above arched frieze and 3 panels with diamond foliate motifs, on stem feet, 18thC.
$450-600

A carved oak coffer, with candle box to interior, replacement hinges, c1700, 52in (132cm).
$600-750

A Flemish oak and fruit wood coffer, with triple arched front panels inlaid with vases of flowers, geometric decoration and barber's pole band, panelled sides and carrying handles, with later quadruple panelled top, mid-17thC, 55in (104cm).
$3,000-4,500

A miniature oak coffer, with hinged top and 3 ogee arched panels above 2 drawers, English, mid-18thC, 24in (62cm).
$1,800-2,700

A George III Welsh oak coffer bach, c1760.
$7,500-9,000

A Welsh coffer bach, c1780.
$2,700-3,300

Cupboards

An early 16thC style oak aumbry, the top above a cornice moulding with a pair of plain doors, shaped iron hinges flanked by 2 pairs of small linenfold panels, with plain panelled sides, late 19thC, 35½in (90cm) high.
$3,000-4,500

An oak aumbry, with a pair of linenfold doors with iron butterfly hinges divided by a linenfold panel, above 2 short drawers, the sides with pierced sections, raised on moulded legs, constructed from earlier fragments, 51in (129cm).
$4,500-6,000

Aumbry

An aumbry is a medieval cupboard, sometimes raised on a stand, used for storing weapons or food. It is also called a hutch.

A Georgian oak hanging corner cupboard, the door inlaid in the centre with an ebony and light oak star, 21in (52cm).
$750-1,200

A German medieval style aumbry, with moulded top above 2 doors carved with beasts, armorials and foliage with scroll strap hinges, flanked by rectangular moulded leaf carved panels above 2 moulded and leaf carved drawers, the sides with linenfold carving, on chamfered legs joined by a rectangular platform, late 19thC, 50in (127cm).
$3,000-4,500

A George III oak and mahogany crossbanded standing corner cupboard, 43in ((109cm).
$2,700-3,300

A panelled oak court cupboard, with a plain top carved to the frieze with the date 1689, stump feet, late 17thC, 52in (132cm).
$2,250-3,000

A George III oak standing corner cupboard, with dentil cornice, a pair of panel doors above a pair of single panel doors, dummy brass hinges, restored, c1770, 43½in (110cm).
$1,200-1,500

A Dutch oak corner cabinet, with bowed outline, arched cornice, stellar inlay, a pair of panelled doors with mahogany bands, enclosing painted shelves, 18thC.
$1,050-1,350

An oak standing corner cupboard, with a pair of panel doors enclosing 3 fixed shelves, with a drawer above a pair of panelled doors, 44in (112cm).
$2,250-3,000

An oak standing corner cabinet, in 2 parts, with architectural pediment above shaped shelves enclosed by 4 moulded panelled doors, late 19thC, 37in (94cm).
$2,250-3,000

A panelled oak hanging cupboard, 17thC, 63in (160cm).
$750-1,200

A carved oak court cupboard, in 2 parts, 42in (106.5cm).
$750-1,200

An oak court cupboard, with a canopy above a central arched panel, flanked on either side by recessed panelled doors, opening to cupboard space with a narrow shelf, below a pair of panelled doors enclosing shelves, stile feet, late 17thC, 52in (132cm).
$2,250-3,000

An oak court cupboard, with moulded cornice above a frieze dated 1690 R.H., above 2 scratch carved cupboard doors, a pair of panelled doors below, stile feet, restored, late 17thC, 54in (137cm). **$3,000-3,750**

An oak and mahogany housekeeper's breakfront cupboard, with cluster columns, 4 panelled doors above 5 drawers and a small pair of doors, bracket feet, early 19thC, 86½in (220cm).
$2,250-3,000

An oak press cupboard in 3 sections, stile feet, back and feet replaced, 17thC and later, 53in (135cm).
$3,000-4,500

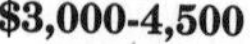

A George II oak press cupboard, including later carving, with a guilloche frieze above a pair of fielded panelled doors, on stile feet, mid-18thC, 54in (136cm).
$3,000-3,750

An oak robe cupboard, the front with panelled door carved with flower and leaf filled lozenges, surrounded by similarly carved panels, the base with 2 short and one long drawer, early 17thC, 66in (168cm).
$5,250-6,000

Purchased from W. & E. Thornton Smith, 11 & 13 Soho Square, London.

An oak press cupboard, with panelled doors carved with initials WO and 1723, above a plain 4 panelled base divided by chip carving, early 18thC, 56in (142cm).
$4,500-6,000

Purchased from Edwards & Sons, Regent Street, London, invoice dated 13th June 1923, 'Antique oak wardrobe, special price for cash £150.0.0.'

A heavily carved oak hall cupboard, in 2 parts, with stained glass leaded light insert, supported on turned columns, 36in (92cm) wide.
$750-1,200

A Charles II oak press cupboard, with guilloche carved panels above a pair of panelled doors, stile feet, late 17thC, 48in (122cm).
$3,000-4,500

An Anglo-Flemish oak cupboard, with cedar veneer, later mahogany top, stile feet, late 17thC, 39in (100cm).
$2,700-3,300

A Charles II panelled oak cupboard, in 2 parts, carved throughout with strapwork and enclosed by a single door, on stile feet, cornice moulding later, late 17thC, 66in (168cm).
$1,500-2,250

An oak cupboard, with moulded top above a frieze carved with repeating fleur-de-lys pattern, above a pair of plain panelled doors and similar panelled sides, mid-17thC, 47in (119cm).
$3,000-4,500

Purchased from Harold Wickham, 19 Chapel Place, Tunbridge Wells.

An Elizabethan style oak press cupboard, with overhanging top centred by a floral marquetry moulded panel flanked by moulded cupboards centred by bosses and flanked by cup and cover leaf carved supports, the base with a pair of 4 panel doors inlaid with floral and geometric marquetry, reconstructed, 50in (127cm).
$4,500-6,000
Purchased from Horsefield Brothers, The East Anglian Gallery, 19 Orchard Street, London, invoice dated May 12th 1915, £175.0.0. 'for Two oak Elizabethan buffets with inlay'.

A Commonwealth oak cupboard, with moulded top above a pair of doors enclosing 4 drawers, baluster turned square legs, platform stretcher, mid-17thC, 28in (72cm).
$6,000-8,250

An oak robe cupboard, the top above a panel of scrolls and leaves and a pair of 3 panelled doors, with plain panelled sides and moulded feet, c1650, 55in (140cm).
$3,000-4,500
Purchased from W. Williamson & Sons, Guildford, Surrey, invoice dated 1920, 'A very fine old panelled door all hanging wardrobe with carved cornice £75.0.0.'

A Welsh oak wall cupboard, with arched top decorated with turned roundels, initials T.E., chip carved mouldings, single plank door with butterfly hinges, c1700, 24in (61cm).
$6,000-8,250
Purchased from Leonard F. Wyburd, 87 Wigmore Street, London, invoice dated August 23rd 1926 'To antique oak cupboard £18.0.0. reduced £15.0.0.'

An oak robe cupboard, with moulded frieze above a pair of chip carved doors, each with 3 plain and one carved panel, plain panelled sides, c1650, 60in (152cm).
$6,000-8,250

An oak cupboard, with carved frieze initialled I.T., dated 1720, early 18thC, 55½in (141cm).
$1,500-2,250

An oak spindle wall cupboard, with spindle turned sides, c1640, 27in (70cm).
$5,250-6,000

Miller's is a price GUIDE not a price LIST

A Continental oak cupboard, with moulded cornice, 2 section door with fielded panels, sleigh supports, probably North European, c1700, 41¾in (106cm).
$2,250-3,000

A late 16thC style oak cupboard, the single door with 4 linenfold panels, iron strap hinges, plain panelled sides, 27½in (70cm).
$3,000-3,750

Possibly from Harold Wickham, 19 Chapel Place, Tunbridge Wells, Kent, 'Old Oak Dole Cupboard £20.0.0.'

A George II oak dresser, with raised open shelf back above 3 frieze drawers, pierced fretwork apron, turned and square supports, joined by platform stretcher, mid-18thC, 55in (140cm).
$7,500-9,000

An oak dresser, with open shelf back, later cornice, 3 frieze drawers, panelled base with 2 cupboards, stile feet, mid-18thC, 65in (165cm).
$5,250-6,000

Dressers

An oak dresser base, with plank top, on turned legs, triple panelled potboard, 17thC, 74in (188cm).
$5,250-7,500

An oak dresser, on ogee bracket feet, part 18thC, 60in (151cm).
$1,800-2,700

A Georgian oak dresser, the rack with moulded cornice, later backing, restored, 65in (165cm).
$2,250-3,000

An early Georgian oak dresser, the base with 3 drawers between 2 cupboards, block feet, rack associated, 69in (175cm).
$2,700-3,300

An oak dresser, on turned tapering legs, with pad feet, mid 18thC, 67in (170cm).
$2,250-3,000

An oak low dresser, the 2 plank top with moulded edge, 3 fruitwood crossbanded drawers, replaced turned feet, repaired, c1700, 79in (201cm).
$9,000-10,000

A George II oak dresser, with raised open shelf back and a pair of cupboard doors, 3 base drawers, cabriole legs, with pad feet, back reduced in height, 82in (208cm).
$3,000-4,500

A George III oak dresser, with simulated short drawers below 3 open shelves, arcaded apron below 3 drawers, chamfered square legs, potboard, 55in (140cm).
$5,250-7,500

An oak dresser, the associated open plate rack with moulded cornice, the base with 3 frieze drawers, square legs, mid-18thC with later parts, 65in (165cmn).
$1,500-2,250

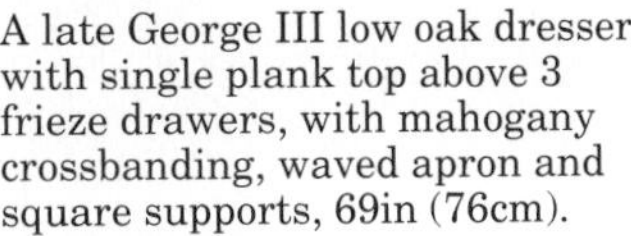

A late George III low oak dresser, with single plank top above 3 frieze drawers, with mahogany crossbanding, waved apron and square supports, 69in (76cm).
$3,000-4,500

A George III oak dresser, restored, metalwork replaced, c1800, 70in (178cm).
$4,500-6,000

A Georgian oak dresser base, with brass drop handles, stile feet, 53in (134.5cm). **$1,200-1,800**

A Georgian oak dresser base, with rosewood crossbanding, shaped apron, on square chamfered supports, 62in (157cm).
$1,200-1,800

An oak dresser, on bracket feet, c1750, 61in (155cm).
$9,000-12,000

An oak dresser base, with delft rack above, part 18thC and later, 49½in (125cm).
$1,200-1,800

An oak dresser, raised open shelf back above 3 panelled frieze drawers, baluster turned square legs, platform stretcher, part early 18thC, 96in (243cm).
$3,000-3,750

An oak low dresser, with 3 lipped frieze drawers, shaped apron, waisted front supports, early 18thC, 74in (188cm).
$3,000-3,750

An oak dresser base, with ledge back, 3 frieze drawers, shaped apron, square legs, mid-18thC, 75½in (192cm).
$2,250-3,000

An oak dresser base, with 3 panelled drawers with brass drop handles, above 2 panelled doors with iron H-hinges, later top with open shelves and moulded cornice, early 18thC, 67½in (171.5cm).
$3,000-4,500

Stools

A Charles I oak stool, with square turned legs, joined by stretchers, early 17thC, 15in (38cm).
$4,500-6,000

An oak joint stool, 17thC.
$2,250-3,000

A Charles II oak joint stool, joined by peripheral stretchers, with branded inventory initials N.D., 18in (46cm).
$3,000-4,500

A Charles I oak close stool, with moulded top and sliding seat, tapered panelled sides and front, hinged door with moulded uprights, c1630, 15in (38cm).
$3,000-4,500

A Charles I oak joint stool, with lunette carved frieze above square and columnar turned legs, joined by stretchers, mid-17thC, 18½in (47cm).
$4,500-6,000

Tables

An oak and walnut draw leaf table, with parquetry top, on spiral twist legs joined by stretchers, 19thC, 61in (155cm) closed.
$1,800-2,700

An oak farmhouse twin drop flap dining table, with a 3 plank top above a frieze with a drawer at each end, on 4 tapered legs, late 18thC, 52in (132cm) extended.
$7,500-9,000

An oak gateleg table, with oval top, frieze drawer, the baluster legs joined by square stretchers, on gently splayed square feet, late 17thC, 28in (71cm) high.
$750-900

A George I oak gateleg table, with frieze drawer, the baluster turned square legs joined by stretchers, early 18thC, 56in (142cm).
$3,000-3,750

A Louis XIV oak bench, on square and chamfered splayed legs, c1700, 53in (134cm) long.
$1,800-2,700

A William and Mary oak envelope table, with hinged top, on turned legs joined by turned stretchers, c1690, 34in (86cm).
$1,800-2,700

Purchased from Gregory & Co, who traded from 27 Bruton Street, Berkeley Square, London, as dealers in furniture, carpets and decorations.

A Flemish oak draw leaf table, with baluster turned supports joined by stretchers, on bun feet, 19thC, 53½in (136cm) closed.
$1,500-2,250

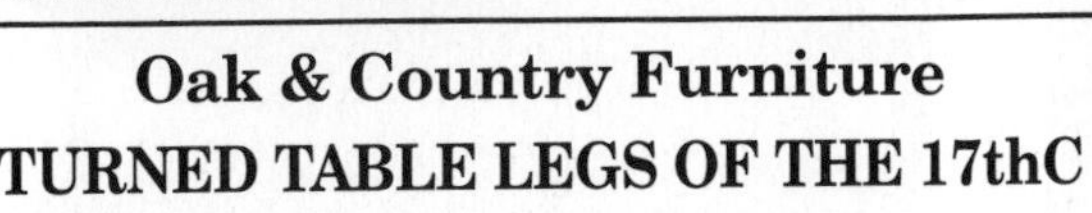

Oak & Country Furniture
TURNED TABLE LEGS OF THE 17thC

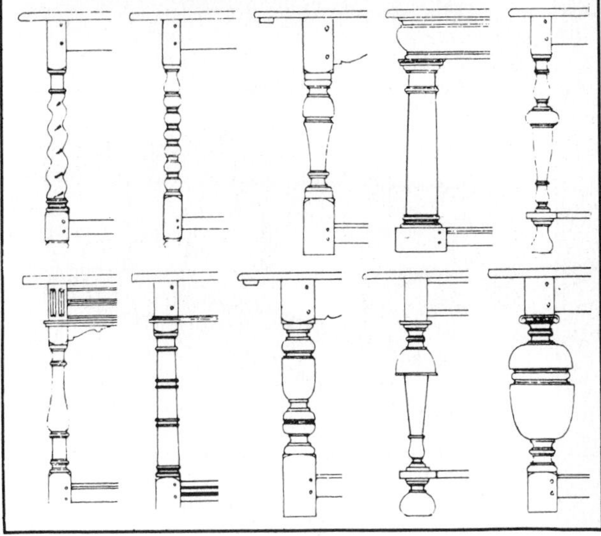

An oak twin flap table, on platform trestle base, c1670.
$10,500-12,000

A Charles II oak gateleg table, the top now with a frieze drawer, baluster turned square legs joined by stretchers, restored late 17thC, 74in (188cm) extended.
$3,000-4,500

A William and Mary oak gateleg table, with 2 drawer and arched apron, late 17thC, 42in (106.5cm) extended.
$1,500-2,250

An oak side table, with moulded frieze, on ring turned legs joined by moulded stretchers, basically 17thC and later, adapted, 51½in (131cm **$1,800-2,700**

An oak twin flap table, on squared legs joined by stretchers, early 18thC, 30in (76cm).
$1,200-1,800

An oak refectory side table, with single plank top, restored, c1700, 103in (262cm). **$7,500-9,000**

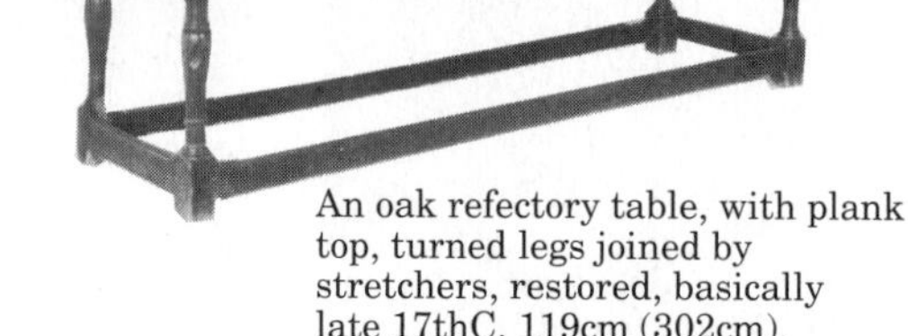

An oak refectory table, with plank top, turned legs joined by stretchers, restored, basically late 17thC, 119cm (302cm).
$5,250-6,000

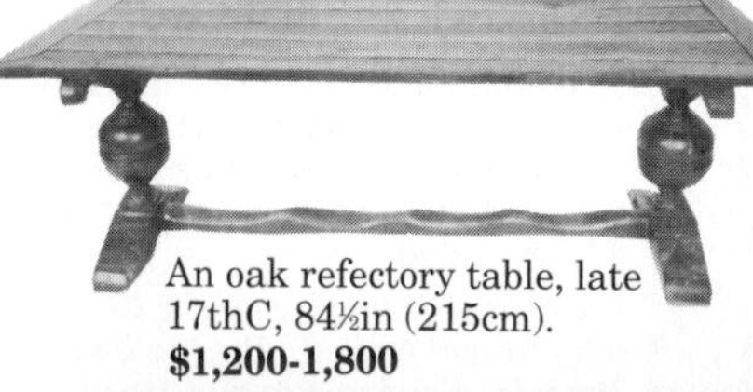

An oak refectory table, late 17thC, 84½in (215cm).
$1,200-1,800

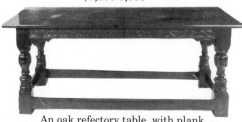

An oak refectory table, with plank top, the frieze carved with stylised interlaced S-scrolls, on ring turned baluster legs, joined by moulded stretchers, 83in (211cm). **$3,000-4,500**

An oak farmhouse kitchen table, 18thC, 82in (208cm) long. **$4,500-6,000**

An oak refectory table, on baluster turned legs joined by plain stretchers, part 17thC, 116in (294.5cm) long. **$5,250-7,500**

A William and Mary oak side table, with a frieze drawer, c1700, 30½in (77cm).
$1,500-2,250

A George III side table, with brass drop handle, shaped frieze, on turned supports and cross stretcher, 27½in (69cm).
$600-750

A William and Mary oak side table, with a frieze drawer and a shaped apron, the square and bobbin turned legs joined by stretchers, late 17thC, 34in (86cm).
$1,800-2,700

A Charles I oak stool table, with oval twin flap top with slide lopers, moulded frieze and shaped apron, on turned legs joined by plain stretchers, c1640, 24in (61cm).
$7,500-9,000

A Queen Anne oak side table, with 3 drawers, on square cabriole legs, early 18thC, 29in (74cm).
$1,500-2,250

A Flemish oak side table, the associated top above a foliate carved frieze with drawer, the baluster turned square legs headed by corbels and with stretchers, late 17thC, 36in (92cm).
$1,200-1,500

A Norfolk elm stool table, 18thC.
$3,000-4,500

A circular oak table, with a green leather top, c1920, 24in (62cm) diam.
$120-135

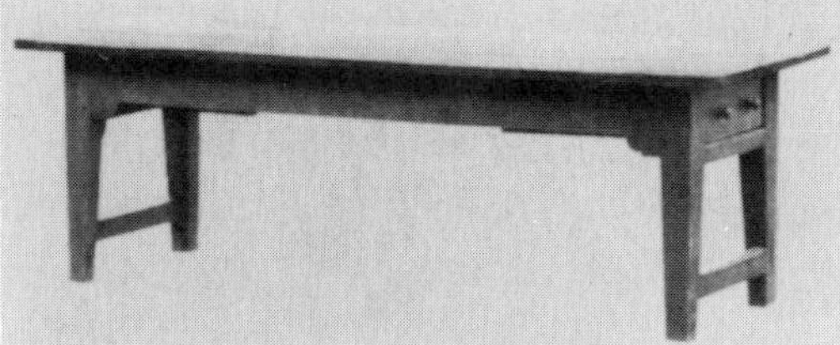

A sycamore farmhouse table, with a triple plank cleated top and 2 end drawers, late 18thC, 32in (82cm). **$3,000-4,500**

Miscellaneous

A Regency oak commode, with carrying handles, c1820.
$750-900

An oak desk-on-stand, with drawer, c1795.
$3,000-3,750

A George III yew wood plate rack, the dentil cornice above a pierced fretwork frieze, the open shelves flanked by fluted pilasters, late 18thC, 44in (112cm).
$4,500-6,000

A Charles II oak desk box, with carved frieze, c1680, 27in (69cm).
$750-1,200

A French fruitwood plate rack, with shaped frieze and conforming galleries, restored, 18thC, 27in (69cm).
$750-1,200

A Queen Anne oak box, with moulded hinged lid above 2 carved panels, divided by initials 'RW', above a long drawer carved with the date '1708', on ball feet, 24in (62cm).
$2,700-3,300

An oak screen from St Peter and St Paul Church, Seal, near Sevenoaks, Kent, designed by C. R. Ashbee, carved with Gothic tracery and a fruiting vine, acorn and oak foliage at the pediment to the arch with central carved angel, flanked by 2 linenfold panels, the central stiles carved 'To God's Glory and in Memory of Nevill Forbes, This Screen was Given AD 1931 By His Sister Janet Elizabeth Ashbee of Godden Green in this Parish', 216in (548cm), and the canopy, with arcaded concave support, open pediment with carved Gothic roundels and scrolls, joined at the top by a carved rope twist rail, the friezes carved with a band of acorns and oak foliage, and a band of entwined oak leaves, Gothic style corner posts surmounted by carved giltwood standing figures of child angels at prayer, 119in (302cm).
$1,800-2,700

A label attached to the screen is inscribed 'Prepared by Holly Bank Joinery Works Ltd, Joinery Specialists, Tunbridge Wells'. Charles Robert Ashbee (1863-1942), the celebrated architect, writer, designer and founder of The Guild of Handicraft, lived at Stormont Court, Godden Green, near Sevenoaks, hence his connection with St Peter and St Paul Church Seal (3 miles from Stormont Court).

An oak box, the sloping flap inlaid with a coat-of-arms, dated '1583' and initials 'A.M.', enclosing a later divided interior, the right hand side with a divided tray, 26in (66.5cm).
$3,000-4,500

FURNITURE

Beds

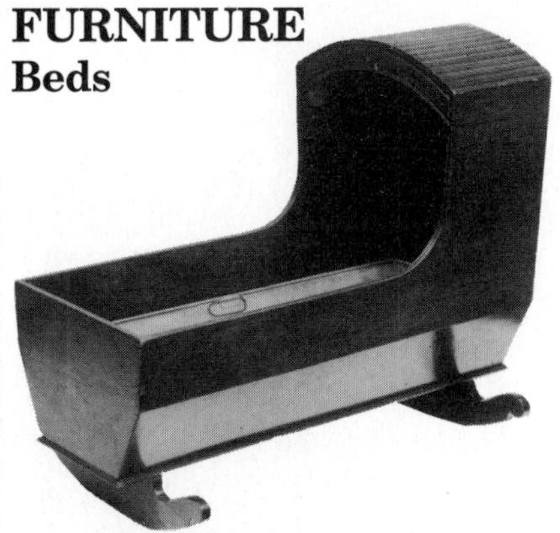

A George III mahogany cot, with fluted top domed hood, on rockers, with zinc liner for flowers.
$600-750

A French parquetry double bed, in the Louis XVI manner, the headboard with a trellis applied with a gilt-bronze pastille burner, conforming footboard with an oval classically cast plaque, and with a pair of matching side rails, Paris, c1890, 55in (139.5cm).
$4,500-6,000

A George III mahogany cradle, with arched canopy and shaped sides, on rockers, with carrying handles, 39in (99cm) long.
$450-600

A George III Sheraton mahogany tester bed.
$6,000-8,250

Tester

A tester is a wooden canopy over a bedstead which is supported on either two or four posts. It may extend fully over the bed and be known as a full tester, or only over the bedhead half and be known as a half tester.

A George III mahogany tester bedstead, with circular turned head posts and stop fluted circular turned foot posts with paw feet, 51in (129.5cm) wide.
$5,250-6,000

A beech framed campaign bed, the adjustable seat and back with cane filled panels, detachable turned feet with large brass casters, with label of Alfred Carter, 47 Holborn Viaduct, 19thC. **$375-450**

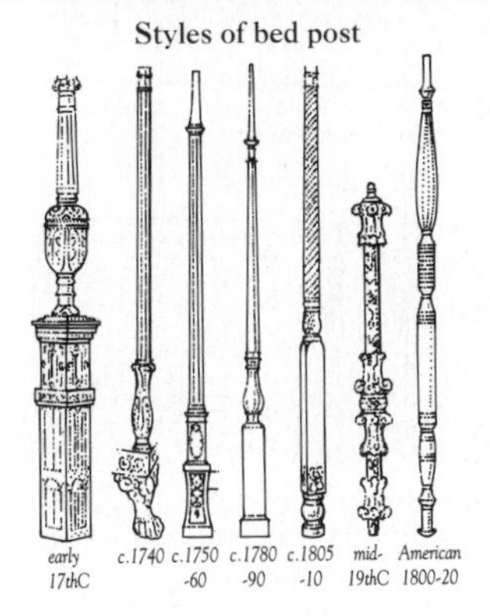

A carved mahogany four poster bed, the tester supported by floral carved cluster column and octagonal supports, with panelled square section legs, the side rail with blind fret carving, 55in (142cm).
$1,800-2,700

An Italian carved walnut bed, the headboard centred by foliage, flanked by flambeau and acanthus masks, with a conforming footboard and side rails, c1880, 59in (150cm) wide.
$4,500-6,000

Bonheur du Jour

A Louis XVI style mahogany brass mounted bonheur du jour, the superstructure with pierced gallery, on square tapering legs headed by roundels, 28in (71cm).
$1,050-1,350

A Victorian walnut and marquetry bonheur du jour, inlaid with foliate arabesques, applied with gilt brass foliate mounts, the galleried superstructure with a mirrored door flanked by 6 small drawers, the serpentine base with oval tooled leather insert, frieze drawer and cabriole legs, 48in (122cm). **$3,000-4,500**

A rosewood brass bound bonheur du jour, on turned tapering toupie feet, restored, 52½in (132.5cm).
$1,800-2,700

An Edwardian mahogany bonheur du jour, the raised back surmounted by a pierced gilt-metal gallery, bevelled mirror to the recess, flanked by cupboards enclosed by a pair of inlaid panel doors, inset leather writing surface, 2 short drawers to the frieze with brass ring handles and inlaid acanthus scrolls, raised on square tapering legs with casters, 36in (91.5cm). **$2,250-3,000**

Breakfront Bookcases

A George III 'plum pudding' mahogany secrétaire breakfront library bookcase, the key patterned cornice with fret carved swan neck pediment, the upper section with 4 astragal glazed doors, the base with a fitted drawer above 3 further drawers, flanked by 2 panelled doors and on a plinth base, 81in (205.5cm).
$10,500-12,000

A George IV mahogany breakfront secrétaire library bookcase, with moulded cornice, varnished, 89in (226cm). **$6,000-8,250**

A George III style mahogany breakfront bookcase, with broken pediment and 4 astragal glazed doors, Greek key frieze and 4 panelled and crossbanded doors below, on plinth base, 88in (223.5cm).
$4,500-6,000

A George III style mahogany breakfront bookcase, on bracket feet, 39½in (100cm).
$1,500-2,250

Breakfront Bookcases

- Breakfront bookcases were first seen in England c1740.
- In the 18thC they were usually made in mahogany although they do exist in other woods, such as satinwood.
- Early examples were often made in the solid; from c1755 many were veneered.
- They are made in several sections, and size varies enormously.
- The market for the larger ones is limited and they are therefore relatively inexpensive, although almost any genuine breakfront bookcase is an expensive item to buy today.

A mahogany breakfront library bookcase, with dentil cornice, adjustable shelves enclosed by 4 glazed astragal doors, above 4 panelled doors, on a plinth base, 74in (188cm).
$9,000-12,000

A mahogany breakfront bookcase, on bracket feet, 68in (172.5cm).
$3,000-3,750

A George IV mahogany breakfront secrétaire library bookcase, the upper section with a moulded cornice above open adjustable shelving, the drawer front and cupboard doors with flame figured veneers and panel mouldings, 96in (243.5cm).
$7,500-9,000

Bureau Bookcases

A Queen Anne style walnut bureau bookcase, with a pair of arched mirror doors, 26in (66cm).
$3,000-4,500

A George III mahogany bureau bookcase, with dentil cornice, a pair of glazed doors, sloping flap enclosing a cupboard, drawers and pigeonholes, 4 graduated long drawers below, on bracket feet, 44in (111.5cm).
$4,500-6,000

A mid-Georgian mahogany bureau bookcase, with dentil moulded cornice, geometrically moulded bracket feet, the top and base possibly associated, 38½in (98cm).
$4,500-6,000

A walnut and featherbanded bureau bookcase, the broken arch cornice with a shell finial, the fall revealing a stepped interior including a well, with 2 short and 2 long graduated drawers, on bracket feet, part early 18thC, 40in (101.5cm).
$9,000-12,000

In the Furniture section if there is only one measurement it usually refers to the width of the piece.

An early George III mahogany bureau bookcase, with architectural pediment and dentil borders, the base with stepped interior fittings enclosed by crossbanded fall, above 4 long drawers with later brass handles, on bracket feet, 38in (96.5cm).
$2,250-3,000

A Regency mahogany and ebony strung cylinder bureau bookcase, the hinged fall enclosing fitted interior with leather lined slide, above a pair of panelled doors, on bun feet, one pane of glass missing, some mouldings loose, 43½in (111cm). **$4,500-6,000**

A George III mahogany bureau bookcase.
$6,000-8,250

Dwarf Bookcases

A George IV rosewood bookcase, the stepped open front with a drawer to the base, on gadrooned top feet, 35in (90cm).
$5,250-6,000

A Victorian walnut cylinder bureau bookcase.
$4,500-6,000

A George III mahogany bureau bookcase, the fall front revealing inlaid stationery compartments, restored, c1780, 43in (110cm).
$3,000-4,500

A Regency rosewood bookcase, with later gallery, the reeded uprights terminating in turned feet with casters, 73in (185cm).
$1,500-2,250

A Regency mahogany dwarf bookcase, on later ring turned legs, 77in (196cm).
$2,700-3,300

A William IV rosewood open bookcase, with a marble top and hinged shelf friezes, 60in (151cm).
$1,800-2,700

A rosewood inverted breakfront bookcase, lacking some mouldings and veneer from the plinth, early 19thC, 72in (183cm).
$1,500-2,250

An inlaid mahogany revolving bookcase, c1900, 18in (46cm) square.
$750-1,200

A William IV rosewood graduated open bookcase, with raised scroll carved back, shaped sides, 4 shelves, plinth base, 37in (94cm).
$750-900

Library Bookcases

A Georgian style padouk and mahogany library bookcase, 88in (225cm).
$6,000-8,250

An Edwardian mahogany corner bookcase, the top with 6 glazed doors with astragal bars, base with 6 glazed doors, ogee and dentil cornice, on plinth, 34 adjustable shelves, one side 105in (266.5cm), return side 45in (114cm).
$3,000-4,500

A Continental rosewood inlaid bookcase, with ripple mouldings, plinth base, c1860, 28in (71cm).
$1,800-2,700

A mid-Victorian oak and ebonised library bookcase, on plinth base, 83in (210.5cm).
$4,800-5,700

A late Regency mahogany library bookcase, with enclosed adjustable shelves, with rounded pillar mouldings, 55in (139.5cm).
$3,000-3,750

A Recency mahogany library bookcase.
$5,250-6,000

Secrétaire Bookcases

A mahogany secrétaire bookcase, on a plinth base, c1810, 52½in (133cm).
$3,000-4,500

A George III mahogany secrétaire bookcase, with swan's neck pediment, crossbanded in satinwood with mahogany collar, the base with a secrétaire drawer, falling to reveal a fitted interior inlaid with satinwood and harewood with crossbanding to the drawer fronts, 48in (122cm).
$6,000-8,250

A mahogany secrétaire bookcase, with fret scrolled pediment, a pair of glazed doors, fitted drawer and long drawer, 2 doors enclosing trays below, early 19thC, 47in (119cm).
$9,000-12,000

A George III mahogany secrétaire bookcase, with boxwood stringing, the base with a well fitted secrétaire drawer, with marquetry urn and patera and tulip wood crossbanding, on later bracket feet, 48in (122cm).
$3,000-4,500

A George III mahogany secrétaire, with associated top, on bracket feet, 51in (129.5cm).
$3,000-4,500

A Georgian mahogany secrétaire bookcase, the upper section enclosed by a pair of astragal glazed doors beneath a dentil cornice, the base with a secrétaire drawer having fitted interior. above 3 long graduated oak lined drawers, with original swan neck brass handles, 43in (109cm).
$4,500-6,000
This lot was purchased in the early 1920s at the contents sale of Fineshades Abbey, the original catalogue being sold with the bookcase.

A mahogany secrétaire bookcase, the upper section with moulded cornice, the base in 2 sections, the top drawer with satinwood veneered fitted interior, 3 graduated long drawers below, on splayed bracket feet, early 19thC, 49½in (126cm).
$1,800-2,700

A George III mahogany secrétaire bookcase, inlaid with circular boxwood stringing and ebony, on later turned feet
$2,700-3,300

A late George III mahogany and later line inlaid secrétaire bookcase, on bracket feet, 38½in (98cm).
$3,000-3,750

A William IV mahogany secrétaire bookcase, in 2 sections, on short bun feet, 48in (122cm).
$2,250-3,000

A late George III line inlaid secrétaire bookcase, with fitted interior, part missing, 50½in (128cm).
$2,250-3,000

A William IV mahogany secrétaire bookcase, 36in (92cm).
$2,700-3,300

A mahogany bookcase, the top with chequered dentil cornice banded frieze, two glazed doors and 2 adjustable shelves, the base with fitted drawer above 2 cupboards, taper turned outset columns, shaped plinth, mid-19thC, 47in (119cm).
$2,700-3,300

A William IV mahogany secrétaire bookcase, the writing drawer revealing satin birch stationery compartments, c1830, 29½in (75cm).
$4,500-6,000

A Victorian walnut secrétaire glazed bookcase, in 2 parts, the base with fall front secrétaire, turned handles and fitted interior, 48in (122cm).
$3,000-3,750

A Victorian mahogany secrétaire bookcase, with cavetto cornice, 2 glazed doors enclosing shelves flanked by carved scrolls, above secrétaire drawer and cupboards, on plinth base.
$2,700-3,300

Bureaux

A walnut fall front bureau, with decorative crossbanding and stringing, fitted interior, replacement handles, 18thC, 33in (84cm).
$3,000-3,750

A George III mahogany bureau, with banded fall enclosing fitted interior, 4 graduated drawers, on outswept bracket feet, 35½in (90cm).
$1,500-2,250

A mahogany bureau, the fall revealing shaped stationery compartments, 4 long graduated drawers, on bracket feet, restored, c1745, 32½in (83cm).
$2,250-3,000

A walnut bureau, with herringbone banding, 18thC, 44in (111.5cm).
$3,000-4,500

A George III mahogany bureau, with crossbanded fall flap enclosing a fitted interior, brass handles and inset shield shaped bone escutcheons, on bracket feet, 42in (107cm).
$1,800-2,700

A walnut bureau, with feathered banding and fitted interior, on bracket feet, early 18thC, 40in (101.5cm).
$3,000-3,750

A mahogany bureau, the fall enclosing stationery compartments, 4 long graduated drawers, on ogee bracket feet, c1760, 38in (97cm).
$2,250-3,000

A walnut bureau, the fall front crossbanded and with double feathered bands, enclosing fitted interior, on bracket feet, 'D' section carcass mouldings, 18thC, 38½in (98cm).
$5,250-6,000

An Edwardian mahogany and marquetry bureau, with 4 drawers, on bracket feet, stamped Jas. Shoobred & Co, 33in (84cm).
$2,250-3,000

George III mahogany bureau, ith sloping fall enclosing a fitted nterior, on later bracket feet, 4in (112cm).
1,500-2,250

George III mahogany bureau, ith original cast brass swan eck handles and escutcheons, on haped bracket feet, 36in (92cm).
2,700-3,300

pine bureau, decorated in red acquer and chinoiserie, with 4 rawers below the slope, 19thC.
3,000-4,500

A George III mahogany bureau, with hinged fall enclosing fitted interior, 4 graduated drawers, on bracket feet, 35½in (90cm).
$2,250-3,000

An Anglo Dutch walnut marquetry bureau, with stepped and fitted interior, the door and drawer fronts all inlaid with marquetry, on bracket feet, 18thC, 41in (104cm).
$9,000-12,000

A George III mahogany bureau, with rosewood banded fall enclosing a fitted interior, 2 short and 3 long drawers, on ogee bracket feet, 43in (109cm).
$3,000-3,750

A South German walnut and inlaid bureau, with 3 drawers in the serpentine frieze above an inlaid slope front, enclosing a cupboard and 14 various drawers, on a later stand with turned baluster legs united by scroll stretcher, 18thC, 49in (125cm).
$4,500-6,000

A George III mahogany bureau, with sloping fall enclosing fitted interior, on later ogee bracket feet, 47½in (121cm).
$1,500-2,250

A George III mahogany bureau, with 5 drawers, on bracket feet, 36in (92cm).
$1,200-1,800

A mid-George III mahogany bureau, on later ogee bracket feet, 44in (112cm). **$2,250-3,000**

A George III mahogany bureau, with 4 graduated drawers, ornate brass handles, oak lined fall with fitted interior, on bracket feet, 38in (97cm).
$2,700-3,300

A Louis XV kingwood bureau, with shaped top edge to the fall front enclosing stepped fitted interior, 2 short and 1 long drawer, all with ebony veneered edges, on cabriole legs with engraved foliate ormolu mounts and sabots.
$3,000-4,500

A French walnut bureau de dame, inlaid with floral marquetry and a stag hunt, frieze drawer, on cabriole legs, 18thC.
$4,500-6,000

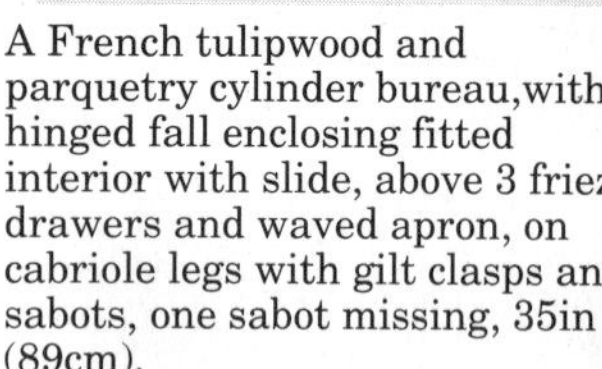

A French tulipwood and parquetry cylinder bureau, with hinged fall enclosing fitted interior with slide, above 3 frieze drawers and waved apron, on cabriole legs with gilt clasps and sabots, one sabot missing, 35in (89cm).
$2,250-3,000

Bureau Cabinets

A Louis XVI style mahogany cylinder bureau, with a three-quarter gallery above 3 short drawers, with fitted interior and green leather lined pull out slide, the apron with 5 short drawers, on fluted square tapering legs with brass fillets and ormolu mounts, 49in (125cm).
$3,000-4,500

An Italian green and cream chinoiserie bureau cabinet, decorated with figures and pagodas in foliate landscapes, on block feet joined by a stretcher, early 18thC, later decorations and scroll supports, 45in (114cm).
$4,500-6,000

A mahogany bureau cabinet, with moulded cornice, inlaid frieze and doors, adjustable shelves, the fall enclosing satinwood faced and crossbanded small and apron drawers, a cabinet flanked by pillar drawers with corinthian mouldings and gilt brass capitals, 2 short and 3 graduated long drawers, on ogee feet, basically Georgian, 46in (117cm).
$4,500-6,000

A walnut bureau cabinet, with double domed top above a pair of bevelled arched mirror doors engraved with flowerheads, above a pair of candle slides, the base with flap enclosing a fitted interior above 2 short and 2 long drawers, part c1720, 30in (76cm).
$10,500-12,000

Possibly purchased from Thomas Prior, 23a Bruton Street, Mayfair, London. Invoice dated January 3rd 1935 'To fine Old Queen Anne Double dome Bureau Bookcase with Vauxhall Bevelled plates: and an old small walnut table. £237.10.0'

A George I style black japanned cabinet, the base with enclosed fitted interior and a well, 2 long and 2 short drawers, brass drop handles and bracket feet, 33½in (85cm).
$2,250-3,000

A mahogany bureau cabinet, the associated top with broken arched pediment, 18thC and later, adapted, 38½in (98cm).
$2,700-3,300

A Georgian mahogany bureau, with additional bookcase, on bracket feet, 47in (119cm).
$1,500-2,250

A George I walnut double domed bureau cabinet.
$15,000-22,500

Display Cabinets

An Edwardian mahogany and satinwood banded display cabinet, with ledge back superstructure, on spade feet, 50in (127cm).
$1,500-2,250

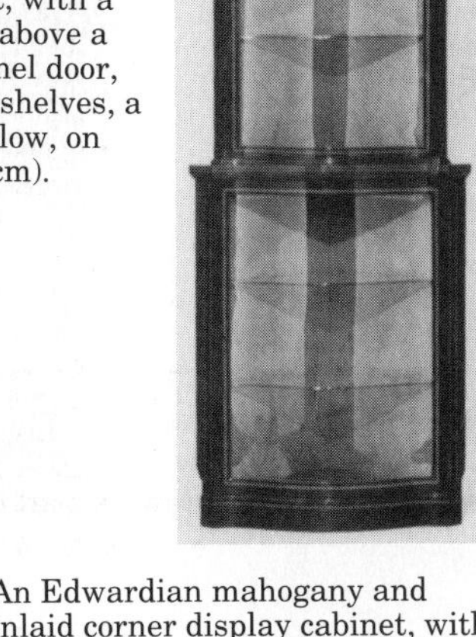

An Edwardian inlaid mahogany double corner cabinet, with a swan neck pediment above a serpentine glazed panel door, enclosing plate glass shelves, a similar panel door below, on plinth base, 31in (79cm).
$2,250-3,000

An Edwardian mahogany and inlaid corner display cabinet, with broad satinwood and chequer bands, neo-classical urns, ribbon bows, husk chains, scrolling foliage, florettes, on square section tapering legs with spade feet, 33in (84cm).
$6,000-8,250

A Regency mahogany display stand, with rope-twist cornice above 5 reeded shelves of graduated depths, interspaced with turned supports, 52in (132cm).
$1,800-2,700

A mahogany and marquetry display cabinet, late 19thC, 48in (122cm).
$2,250-3,000

An Edwardian mahogany and inlaid display cabinet, the arc back with foliate garland, on cabriole legs.
$1,050-1,350

An Edwardian mahogany inlaid and overpainted display cabinet, with projecting pediment above foliate painted frieze.
$1,200-1,800

An Edwardian inlaid mahogany display case, with lined shelves inlaid to each edge and flanked on either side by a concave panel inlaid to the centre with an oval of bell flowers and Adam style motifs, 43in (109cm).
$3,000-3,750

An Edwardian mahogany displa cabinet, inlaid with classical swags and medallions.
$1,800-2,700

An Edwardian mahogany break bowfront salon cabinet, with parquetry and diapered boxwood stringing, the shelves with green diapered cloth lining, 44in (112cm).
$1,500-2,250

A satinwood display cabinet, decorated in the manner of Angelica Kauffman, the central door tracery glazed with green swags and concave glass panels, hand painted frieze, on tapering turned legs with shaped and crossbanded undertier, 50in (127cm).
$7,500-9,000

A rosewood and gilt metal mounted serpentine vitrine, with a pair of glazed doors, lower sections of Vernis Martin panels and similar bowed side sections, on projecting curved legs with sabots, 48in (122cm).
$3,000-4,500

An Italian painted cabinet, on leaf
apped cabriole legs and claw-
nd-ball feet. **$4,800-5,700**

A French gilt metal mounted mahogany bombé vitrine, with foliate scroll gilt borders above Vernis Martin panels of 18thC figures, on cabriole legs with gilt clasps trailing to gilt sabots, 49in (125cm).
$3,000-4,500

A pair of French style display cabinets, with green velvet lined interiors and shelves, with inlaid foliate decoration and gilt metal mounts, on cabriole legs.
$4,500-6,000

A Northern European mahogany and marquetry bowfront corner cabinet, on bracket feet, 31in (79cm).
$3,000-4,500

An Edwardian mahogany and satinwood banded breakfront display cabinet, with moulded cornice, square tapering legs joined by undertier, 57in (145cm).
$2,250-3,000

An Edwardian mahogany and inlaid display cabinet, with astragal glazed door with cupboard door below, on tapered legs with spade feet, pediment associated, 25in (64cm).
$1,050-1,350

A Louis XV style vitrine, with ormolu mounts and Vernis Martin decoration, signed Albertin.
$2,700-3,300

A Sheraton revival harewood crossbanded satinwood bijouterie cabinet, with pagoda style top, fitted with a pair of frieze drawers and a cupboard with panel door, on square tapering legs with spade tips, 14in (36cm).
$3,000-3,750

An Oriental style ebonised cabinet-on-later-stand, 19thC
$2,700-3,300

Cabinets-on-Stands

A Queen Anne style cream lacquered and gilt chinoiserie decorated brass mounted cabinet, with a pair of doors depicting figures, pagodas and foliate landscapes, on silvered stand with trailing floral frieze and central female mask above pierced oak leaf apron, on cabriole legs headed by Indian masks, 33in (84cm).
$1,800-2,700

A mahogany music cabinet, with chequered and shell inlay, galleried top, the drawers with 'Stone's' patent fall fronts,on square tapered legs with spade feet, 20thC, 21in (54cm).
$600-750

An inlaid walnut secrétaire with cabinet, ormolu mounts and marble top, stamped 'Syndicate Nationale des Antiquaires', c1900
$4,500-6,000

A Louis XIV walnut cabinet, on later oak stand, with a pair of panelled doors depicting Poseidon and Diana flanking a female caryatid, above a drawer, the stand with baluster turned supports, 51in (130cm).
$1,500-2,250

A walnut cabinet-on-chest, in 2 sections, with bracket feet, 17thC 42in (107cm).
$5,250-7,500

Flemish ebony and ivory ıbinet-on-stand, the later stand ith ripple moulded border and ɔirally turned legs joined by :retchers, labelled Edwards & oberts Upholstery Warehouse, 'ardour Street, London, 45½in .15cm).
4,500-6,000

A William and Mary burr walnut and oyster veneered cabinet-on-later-stand, with spiral twist legs and block feet joined by flattened X-stretchers, 36in (92cm).
$3,000-4,500

A walnut cabinet-on-chest, with moulded cornice, above a pair of cross and featherbanded doors, enclosing drawers and pigeonholes, the moulded base fitted with a slide above 2 short and 2 long drawers, late 17thC, 34in (86cm).
$1,800-2,700
Purchased from Williamson, Guildford.

;ide Cabinets

A pair of boulle cabinets, with marble tops, richly mounted ormolu scrollwork and herm capitals, the doors and side columns with boulle and contre-boulle designs, 19thC, 32in (81cm).
$2,700-3,300

An inlaid satinwood and ebonised breakfront dwarf side cabinet, with green marbled top, the satinwood panels possibly 18thC, 73in (185cm).
$2,700-3,300

William IV rosewood breakfront low cabinet, with white marble top, 3 frieze drawers set with ırved paterae and leaf scrolls, above a pair of glazed oors, flanked by a pair of mirrored doors, each with pplied scroll carving, on plinth base, 84½in (214cm).
1,050-1,350

A Regency style concave fronted low cabinet, with a green veined marble top, above 2 doors with brass grilles and pleated silk panels with gilded borders and flanked by gilded fluted corner pilasters, on ball feet, 49½in (125cm).
$750-900

A mahogany dwarf side cabinet of broken D-shaped outline, on turned legs, early 19thC, probably reconstructed, 60½in (154cm).
$2,250-3,000

A mid-Victorian burr walnut, marquetry and gilt metal mounted dwarf side cabinet, 34in (86cm).
$1,800-2,700

A cabinet decorated by Stanley Payne, 20thC, 29in (74cm).
$1,200-1,500

Stanley Payne, designer of furniture, interiors and trompe l'oeil panels at important houses throughout England, including Locko Park, Derbyshire, Lizards Bank and Mereworth Castle, Kent.

A Victorian walnut inlaid dwarf side cabinet, with 2 shelves enclosed by a door with oval plate glass mirror panel, 26in (66cm).
$1,050-1,350

A Regency mahogany ormolu mounted side cabinet, with moulded top, the doors inlaid with ebonised lines and fitted with brass trellis, flanked by twin tapering herm pilasters inlaid with ebony lines and headed by a female Egyptian style mask, on claw feet, restored, interior slightly altered, 38in (97cm).
$2,250-3,000

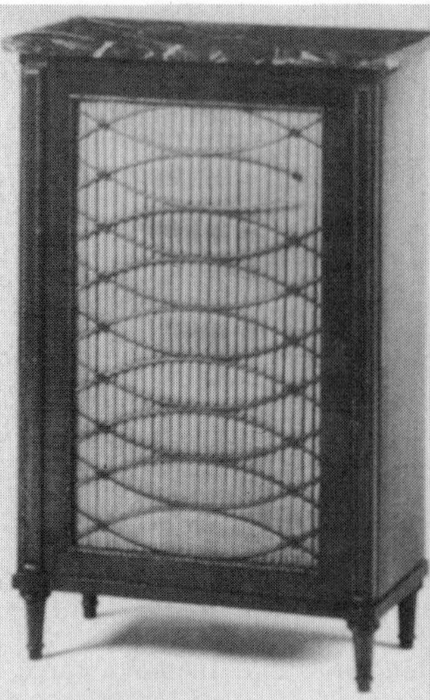

A rosewood gilt metal mounted dwarf cabinet, with mottled gree marbled top, above brass grille upholstered door flanked by channelled uprights, on later turned legs, early 19thC, probab adapted from a larger piece of furniture, 23½in (60cm).
$750-1,200

A rosewood, satinwood banded and line inlaid dwarf side cabine with recessed breakfront top above a pair of upholstered door on square tapering legs, part early 19thC, 39in (99cm).
$1,800-2,700

A French ebonised and boulle display cabinet, with single glaz hinged door, inlaid to frieze and front with gilt bronze figural an scroll decoration, late 19thC, 32i (81cm).
$900-1,500

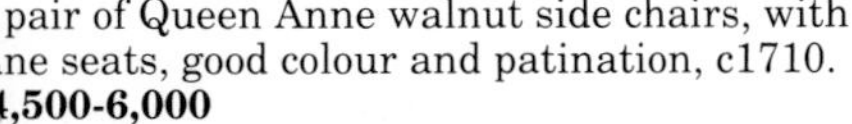

pair of Queen Anne walnut side chairs, with
.ne seats, good colour and patination, c1710.
,500-6,000

A George III oak child's box chair, English, c1800.
$1,500-1,800

An oak table chair, c1690.
$5,250-7,500

William and Mary carved
k buffet, with a drawer,
te 17thC, 37in (94cm).
.0,500-12,000

A cherrywood high chair, turned to simulate bamboo, with cane seat, c1825. **$1,200-1,500**

A matched pair of early Georgian green painted Windsor armchairs, with saddle seats, some damage and one seat replaced.
$8,250-9,750

n oak carved and panelled
ffer, English, c1690.
,000-3,750

A William and Mary oak cabinet, with 5 drawers, late 17thC, 36in (92cm).
$8,700-9,750

A baby's yew and elm Windsor chair, c1860.
$1,800-2,250

A painted beech simulated bamboo corrective chair, c1825. **$900-1,200**

matched set of 8 ash Lancashire spindle back chairs, good
lour and patination, English, c1820.
,000-9,000

A Tudor carved oak chest, with moulded hinged cover, restored, c1550, 50in (126cm).
$4,500-6,000

A George I oak desk-on-stand, English, c1720.
$2,250-3,000

A George I oak chest of drawers, veneered with walnut, original brasses, English, c1725.
$4,500-6,000

A George I oak chest of drawer crossbanded with walnut, English, c1720.
$3,750-5,250

A late 17thC oak dresser base, with 3 geometrically moulded drawers, English, c1700.
$15,000-20,000

An 18thC oak coffer, with double linen fold, guilloche and lunette carved panels, 26in (66cm).
$450-600

A 17thC oak panelled coffer, with original arcaded carved detail.
$600-900

A 17thC panelled oak court cupboard, in 2 sections.
$1,800-2,250

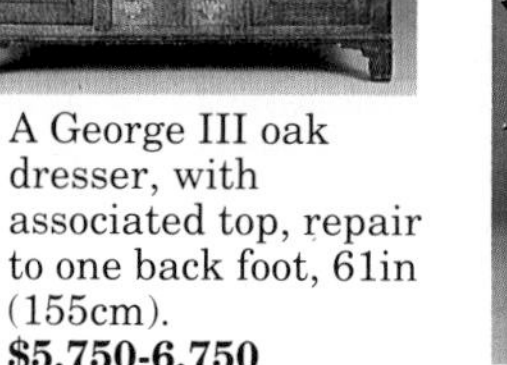

A George III oak dresser, with associated top, repair to one back foot, 61in (155cm).
$5,750-6,750

A William and Mary oak dresser base, with 3 frieze drawers, on knopped turned legs, late 17thC. **$6,750-8,250**

An oak joined press cupboard, good colour and patina, English, c1690.
$10,500-13,500

An oak dresser base, with walnut inlay, original brasses and cabriole legs, English, c1745.
$6,000-7,500

Paul Hopwell Antiques

Early English Oak

Top: A set of eight (four showing) Georgian ash wavyline ladderback dining chairs. Excellent colour, condition and patination. English c1800.

Centre: A superb 18th century dresser in oak. Excellent condition, colour and patination. N. Wales c1770.

Bottom: A rare George II oak dresser base with a superb arched moulded apron. Standing on cabriole legs with spade feet. Good colour and patination. English c1745.

Furniture restoration service available

30 High Street, West Haddon, Northamptonshire NN6 7AP
Tel: (0788) 510636

A set of 4 Charles I oak joint stools, the plank tops with moulded borders, on baluster turned and square legs joined by stretchers, mid-17thC.
$7,000-8,250

A Charles II oak centre table, on square turned legs, late 17thC.
$3,750-4,500

A Charles I carved oa credence table, with drawer, c1640.
$12,000-18,000

A George II oak lowboy, with inlay and walnut crossbanding, original condition, English, c1750. **$6,000-9,000**

A George II oak lowboy, original brasses, colour and patina, English, c1730.
$3,750-4,500

A George III burr elm tripod table, English, c1790.
$1,500-2,250

An early 18thC carved and panelled oak settle, the seat incorporating hinged lid, bearing initials and date 1706, 72in (182.5cm). **$750-1,500**

A George II yew wood 'bird cage' table, with tilt-top, mid-18thC, 33in (83cm) diam. **$4,500-5,250**

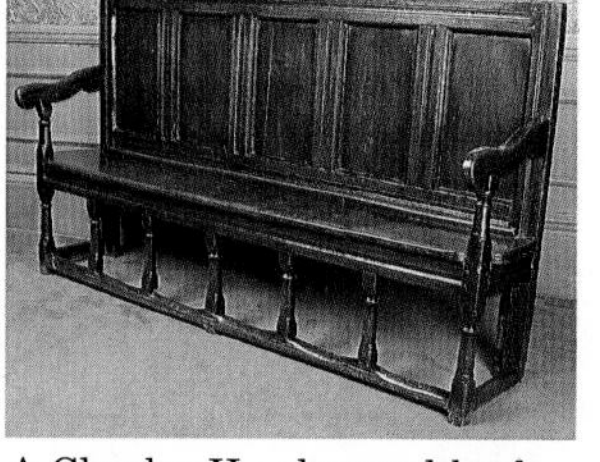

A Charles II oak panel-back settle, with 7 turned and square front legs, late 17thC, 74in (188cm). **$4,500-6,000**

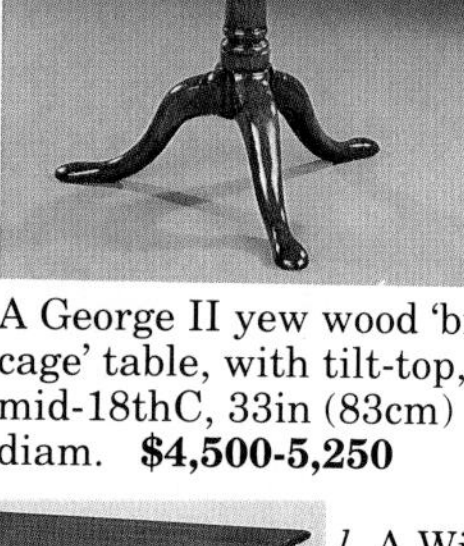

l. A William and Mary pearwood side table, inlaid with flowerheads, late 17thC.
$4,500-6,000

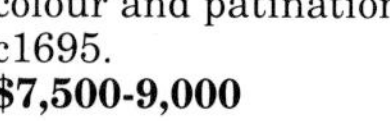

A William and Mary oak side table, with X-stretcher, good colour and patination, Englis c1695.
$7,500-9,000

An oak and ash refectory table, with 2 shaped end supports, joined by 2 later stretchers, 18th/19thC, 84in (213cm).
$6,750-8,250

A George IV oak dresser base, inlaid throughout wi rosewood and chevron bandings, on bracket feet, mi 19thC, 69in (175cm).
$4,000-5,500

.ouis XV giltwood lit d'alcove, with a olled upholstered head and footboard, mped L. Delanois, mid-18thC, 71in 30cm) long. **$6,750-8,250**

French kingwood, marquetry and ormolu- ounted bed, with pierced rocaille and C- oll cresting, late 19thC, 65in (165cm) de. **$9,000-10,500**

mahogany and giltwood bed, the overscroll adboard supported by recumbent sphinxes, rt early 19thC. **2,000-13,500**

George III breakfront mahogany rary bookcase, top with 4 glazed doors, e base with 3 drawers and 2 cupboards, 800. **$6,000-9,000**

A mahogany four-poster bed, with 2 reeded baluster columns, box spring and mattress, part early 19thC, 58in (147cm) wide. **$4,800-6,000**

A George IV mahogany bureau bookcase, the base with fitted interior, 38in (96cm). **$3,000-4,500**

A Queen Anne red japanned double domed bureau cabinet, c1700, 42½in (107cm). **$105,000-120,000**

A Queen Anne walnut double domed bureau cabinet, c1710, 43in (109cm). **$40,500-45,000**

A Queen Anne walnut secrétaire, English, 18thC. **$15,000-18,000**

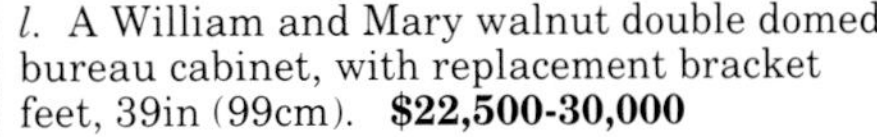

A Queen Anne gilt decorated green japanned bureau bookcase, restored, c1710. **$285,000-300,000**

l. A William and Mary walnut double domed bureau cabinet, with replacement bracket feet, 39in (99cm). **$22,500-30,000**

A Louis XV style boulle and gilt metal mounted bonheur du jour, damaged, c1860, 41½in (105cm). **$6,750-8,250**

A William and Mary walnut bureau, with fitted interior, c1700, 25in (64cm). **$7,500-10,500**

A kingwood and rosewood secrétaire à cylindre, with gilt metal mounts and marquetry, 62in (157cm). **$6,000-7,500**

A Spanish tortoiseshell cabinet, mid-17thC, with later stand, 52½in (133cm). **$6,000-7,500**

A Queen Anne child's walnut veneered bureau, c1710, 24½in (63cm). **$11,250-12,750**

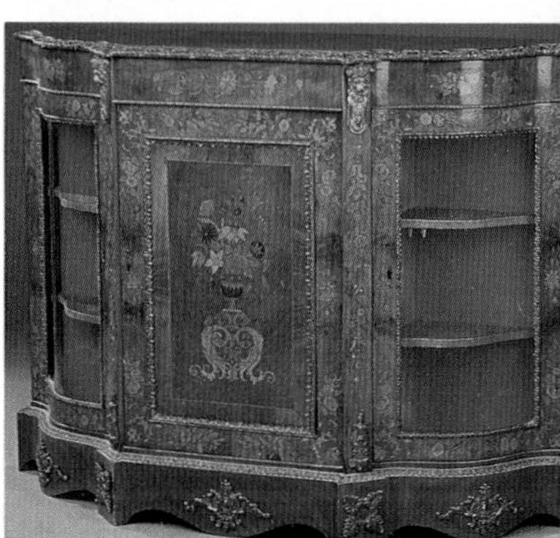

A Victorian walnut and marquetry side cabinet, with central inlaid door and gil metal mouldings, c1860, 50in (127cm). **$6,000-7,500**

An Edwardian mahogany and crossbanded writing bureau, stamped J.C. Vickery. **$4,500-6,000**

A George III mahogany bureau, possibly remodelled, c1770, 37in (94cm). **$3,750-5,250**

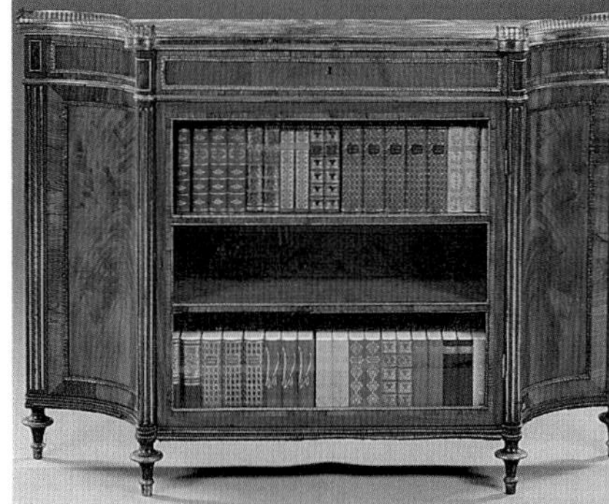

A George III mahogany and brass mounte side cabinet, in Louis XVI style, with marb top and brass gallery, c1795, 51½in (130cm **$19,500-22,500**

A George III inlaid mahogany painted and parcel gilt demi-lune side cabinet, on leaf carved legs, veneers and painted decoration of later date. **$16,500-22,500**

An ebonised and églomisé cabinet, with glass panels within ebonised astragals, backed by coloured papers, 16thC, 20in (51cm). **$4,500-6,000**

A pair of George III style painted satinwood and harewood demi-lune cabinets. **$10,500-12,000**

l. A set of 6 Anglo-Indian silver mounted armchairs, decorated with foliate motifs.
$16,500-22,500

A pair of Regency simulated bamboo bergères.
$9,750-11,250

A George III mahogany open armchair.
$675-750

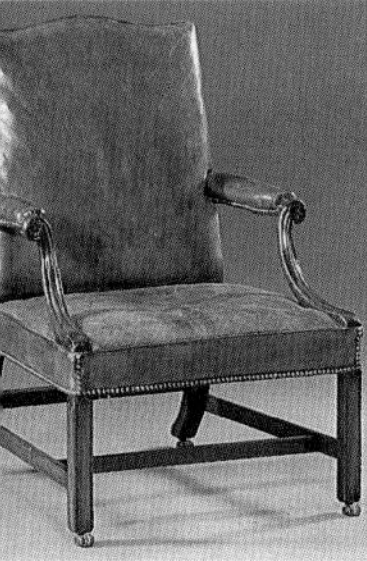

George III
ıhogany library
mchair, c1765.
,500-9,000

A pair of mahogany armchairs, c1825.
$3,750-4,500

A Regency mahogany bergère.
$6,000-9,000

A George IV mahogany library bergère, with later adjustable reading slope.
$9,750-11,250

l. A pair of Bolognese giltwood armchairs, with stamped marks, mid-18thC.
$22,500-27,000

A pair of childrens' mahogany high chairs, late 18thC.
$9,750-11,250

gentleman's reclining
mchair, by Charles
van of Leeds.
00-675

A pair of mahogany open armchairs, in Chinese Chippendale style.
$3,750-5,250

pair of George III giltwood
mchairs, in Louis XVI taste.
,750-5,250

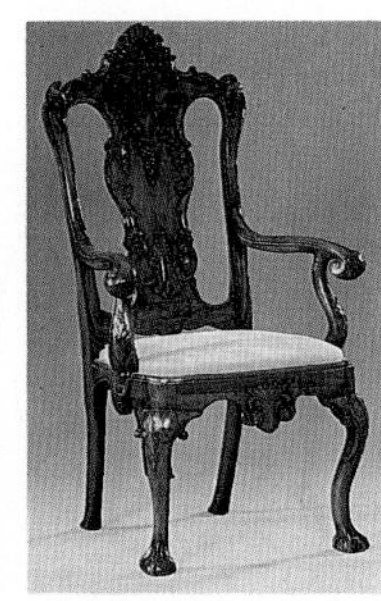

A Spanish walnut armchair, mid-18thC.
$7,500-9,000

A Queen Anne beech wing armchair, upholstered in needlework cover, c1710. **$5,250-6,750**

A Queen Anne walnut armchair, upholstered in associated mid-18thC floral crewel work, restored. **$20,250-22,500**

A George II style mahogany library open armchair, with floral needlework upholstery, on foliate headed cabriole legs and scroll feet. **$3,000-3,750**

A walnut open armchair with associated petit-point foliate needlework, restored, late 17thC. **$3,000-3,750**

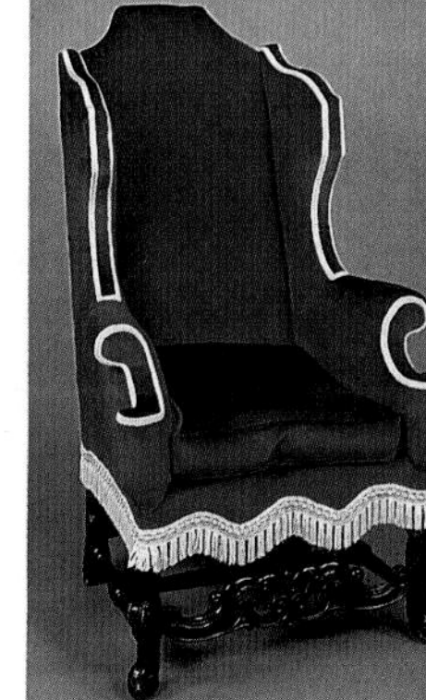

A William and Mary stained beechwood wing armchair, with velvet upholstery, on scrolled front legs and stretchers. **$4,500-6,000**

An early George III giltwood open armchair, in the manner of John Cobb, restored. **$6,750-9,000**

A Queen Anne walnut wing armchair, with needlepoint upholstery, with loose cushioned bow front seat, on carved cabriole legs, c1705. **$232,500-262,500**

A George II mahogany wing armchair, with leaf carved cabriole legs, claw and-ball feet, re-railed, c1755. **$3,750-5,250**

l. A George I walnut wing armchair, back, sides and squab cushion covered in associated floral needlework, on cabriole legs and pad feet, restored. **$6,750-8,250**

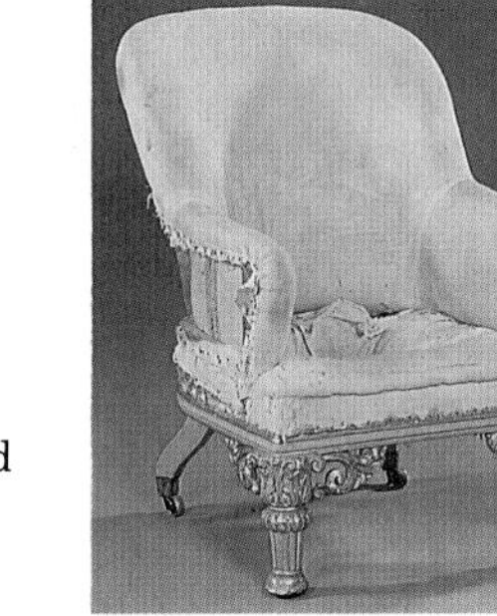

l. An English white and gilt bergère, with stuffed back and reeded leaf-capped front legs with brackets, stamped G I Morant, 81 New Bond St, mid-18thC. **$3,000-3,750**

pair of Regency
inoiserie japanned
mchairs, c1810.
,250-9,750

A set of 8 Regency cork, mahogany, boxwood and ebony lined dining chairs, with drop-in hide cushions.
$24,750-27,000

A pair of Italian painted and parcel gilt armchairs, Neapolitan or Piedmontese, each caned seat with leaf moulded frieze, c1780.
$33,000-37,500

set of 8 Regency mahogany
ning chairs, including 2 carvers,
th drop-in seats and sabre legs,
810. **$46,500-52,500**

A Restauration mahogany fauteuil de bureau, on ring turned legs, c1825.
$2,250-3,750

A set of 12 George III mahogany 'Gothick' dining chairs, including 2 carvers, with triple arched backs and cluster column legs, c1765. **$180,000-195,000**

set of 8 English mahogany
ning chairs, including 2 carvers,
810, one modern.
,250-9,750

Three early Louis XV beechwood armchairs, with caned backs and seats, c1725.
$4,500-6,000

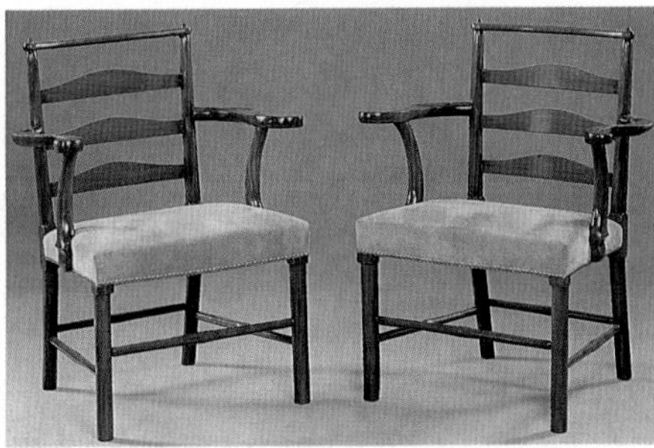

A pair of George III mahogany armchairs, with shaped ladder backs, out-scrolled arms, suede covered seats and turned legs, c1760.
$5,250-7,500

A French Empire mahogany armchair, c1810. **$1,350-2,250**

l. A set of 10 George III painted Hepplewhite dining chairs, including 2 carvers, some restoration.
$7,500-10,500

A Javanese painted and parcel gilt miniature armchair, c1730.
$4,500-6,000

A pair of George IV mahogany scoop-back chairs, c1825.
$6,750-8,250

A set of 12 William IV mahogany side chairs, with drop-in seats, repaired, c1835. **$20,000-27,000**

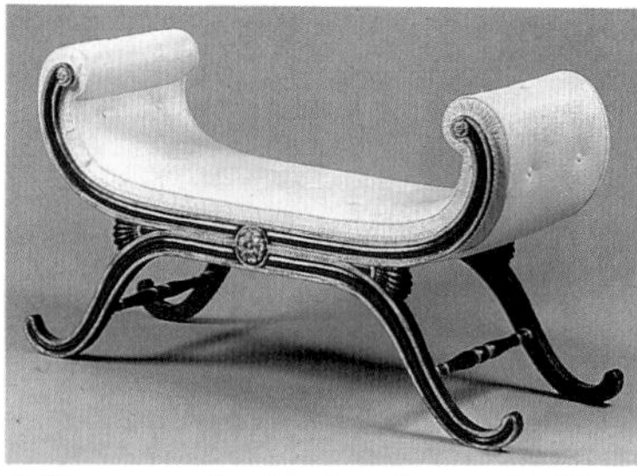

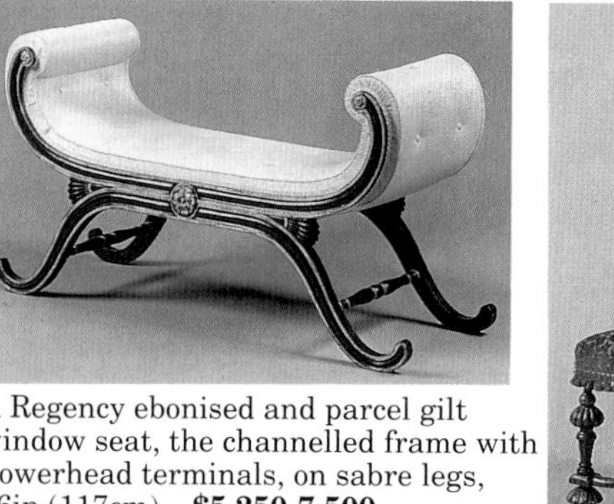

A Regency ebonised and parcel gilt window seat, the channelled frame with flowerhead terminals, on sabre legs, 46in (117cm). **$5,250-7,500**

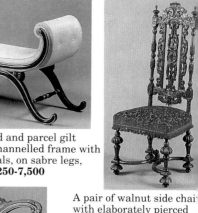

A pair of walnut side chai with elaborately pierced splats, on gadrooned shap tapering legs, mid-19thC. **$2,250-3,000**

A pair of George III mahogany dining chairs, some restoration. **$3,000-4,500**

A set of 8 mahogany dining chairs, including 2 carvers, with pierced vase shaped splats and serpentine seats. **$24,000-27,000**

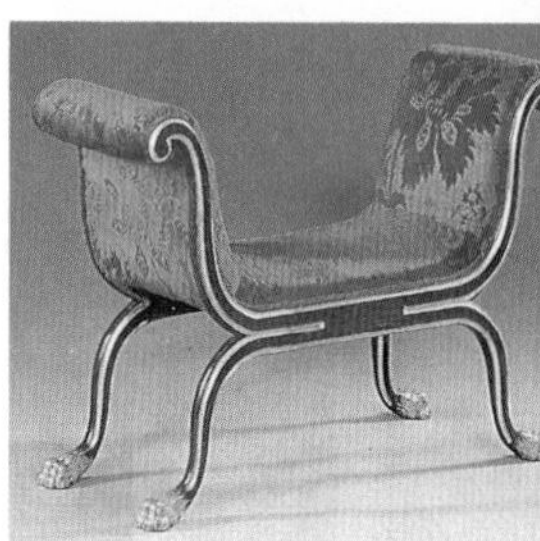

A George IV parcel gilt rosewood window seat, c182 42in (107cm). **$6,000-7,500**

A pair of George III mahogany side chairs, restored. **$3,750-5,250**

A Dutch walnut and cane Burgomaster's chair, c1700. **$2,250-3,000**

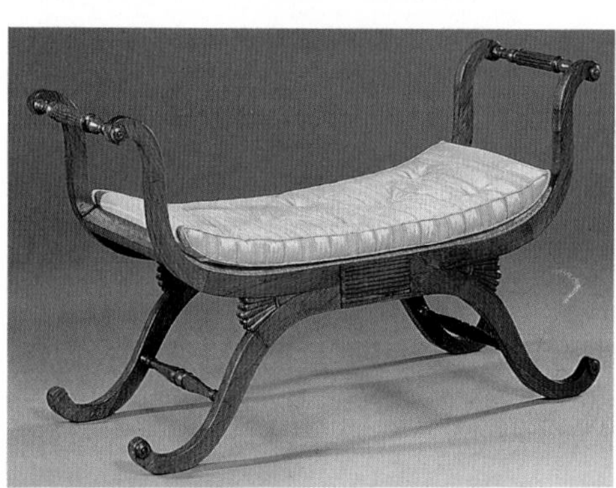

A pair of 'Scottish Grecian' rosewood window seats, attributed to William Trotter, c1815, 45in (114cm). **$22,500-25,500**

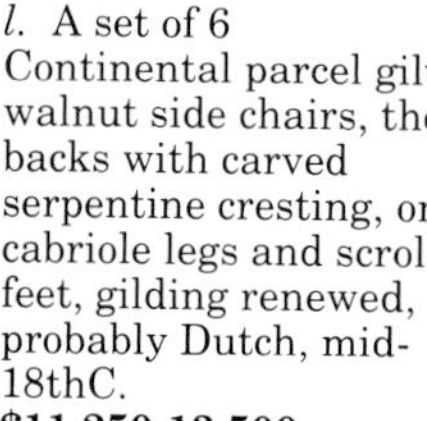

l. A set of 6 Continental parcel gilt walnut side chairs, the backs with carved serpentine cresting, on cabriole legs and scroll feet, gilding renewed, probably Dutch, mid-18thC. **$11,250-13,500**

A set of 10 Portuguese parcel gilt walnut chairs, restored, c1740. **$30,000-45,000**

William and Mary
ster veneered walnut
est of drawers, with
arwood circles, c1690.
8,500-31,500

A pair of Dutch mahogany fruitwood japanned corner cupboards, with chamfered moulded white marble tops and painted cupboard doors, 28in (71cm). **$5,250-6,750**

A George III mahogany linen press, with ivory escutcheons. **$1,500-3,000**

n English George II walnut
est of drawers, c1740.
,750-5,250

A Regency satin birch breakfront wardrobe, with ebonised stringing and moulding, with hanging space, 2 short and 2 long drawers, c1815, 91in (231cm). **$19,500-22,500**

A Louis XV provincial fruitwood armoire, c1770, 102in (259cm). **$3,750-5,250**

pair of Edwardian painted satinwood
orner cupboards, with overall
ahogany bands and boxwood and
bony lines, 25in (64cm) wide.
9,000-10,500

A William and Mary oyster kingwood chest of drawers, with pearwood stringing, c1690, 37in (95cm). **$6,750-8,250**

A William IV rosewood Wellington chest, c1835. **$6,000-7,500**

Dutch walnut cupboard, with arched
oulded cornice above a pair of panelled
oors, the lower part with one dummy
nd 2 real drawers, c1740, 66in (168cm).
7,000-8,250

l. A French Renaissance carved walnut hanging cupboard, with drawer below, c1580. **$8,250-9,750**

A George I walnut chest, the top crossbanded and inlaid, some restoration. **$12,000-13,500**

A Queen Anne inlaid burr walnut chest-on-stand, on cabriole legs, repaired, c1710.
$12,000-15,000

A George III mahogany chest-on-chest, late 18thC.
$6,000-9,000

A George III kingwood bombé commode, outlined with quartered kingwood, the shaped sides with carrying handles, c1770.
$72,000-82,500

An Italian marquetry commode, with 3 long drawers, late 18thC.
$19,500-22,500

A George III mahogany fruitwood and satinwood marquetry demi-lune commode, attributed to Thomas Chippendale, c1775.
$90,000-97,500

A Queen Anne walnut veneere tallboy, c1710, with later bracket feet. **$6,000-7,500**

A pair of George III ormolu mounted rosewood, mahogany and floral marquetry bombé commodes, restorations. **$112,500-127,500**

A Danish parcel gilt walnut commode, of serpentine bombé form, with 3 long drawers, mid-18thC, 23in (60cm) wide.
$6,750-8,250

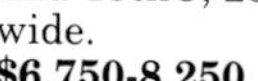

A Swedish burr elm and line inlaid breakfront commode, wit 3 fruitwood banded drawers, lat 18thC. **$7,500-12,000**

l. A North Italian burr walnut, olivewood banded and fruitwood strung serpentine commode, damaged and restored, mid-18thC, 47in (119cm).
$6,000-9,000

A Louis XV kingwood and tulipwood parquetr commode, stamped P. Roussel, mounts replaced, mid-18thC.
$48,000-52,500

A George II figured walnut Admiral's kneehole desk, featherbanded overall, on later bracket feet, 43in (109cm).
$20,250-22,500

A Regency gilt brass mounted mahogany davenport.
$6,750-8,250

A mid-Victorian burr walnut kidney-shaped desk, restorations, 52in (132cm).
$38,250-41,250

An English mahogany pedestal desk, with central hinged leather lined panel, enclosing a well, early 19thC. **$3,750-5,250**

A George II padouk and sabicu kneehole desk, with breakfront top, gilt brass handles and escutcheons, on acanthus scrolled feet with casters. **$117,000-127,500**

A Louis XVI mahogany desk, possibly German, with adjustable leather inset writing surface, c1785, 72in (183cm). **$33,000-37,500**

A William and Mary stained burr kneehole desk.
$4,500-6,000

A mahogany brass mounted desk, c1790.
$8,250-9,750

A mahogany library pedestal desk, with leather lined top and acanthus carved pedestals, 89½in (228cm).
$11,250-12,750

An inlaid rosewood davenport, c1870, 22in (56cm).
$1,800-2,250

A Victorian inlaid walnut davenport.
$1,800-2,250

r. An English mahogany pedestal desk, stamped Gillows, late 19thC, 59in (150cm).
$11,250-14,250

A Regency mahogany and ebonised secrétaire à abattant, with inverted breakfront top, restored.
$7,500-12,000

A Restauration mahogany secrétaire, marble top lacking, c1820.
$5,250-6,750

A William and Mary inlaid elm secrétaire-on-chest, on later bracket feet, c1690.
$11,250-12,750

A George II yew secrétaire tallboy, c1730, on later ogee bracket feet.
$16,500-22,500

A Swedish mahogany secrétaire, with white marble top, fluted pilasters and feet, c1800, 41in (104cm). **$6,750-8,250**

A Transitional ormolu mounted tulipwood secrétaire-on-stand.
$14,250-16,500

A Queen Anne burr walnut fall-front secrétaire, with central shaped panel opening to reveal fitted interior, featherbanded drawers below, on later bun feet, restored, c1700, 41½in (105cm).
$12,750-15,000

l. A Regency mahogany secrétaire, with adjustable leather lined reading slope. **$6,000-7,500**

A Restauration mahogany secrétaire, with grey marble top, c1820, 38in (97cm).
$4,000-5,500

A mahogany secrétaire, 19thC.
$1,800-2,250

A George III satinwood and mahogany serpentine secrétaire chest, with fitted secrétaire drawer, c1790, 59in (150cm).
$40,500-45,000

A Regency giltwood and part ebonized mirror, early 19thC.
$7,500-10,500

A George III giltwood mirror, replaced plate.
$6,000-7,500

An early George II giltwood mirror.
$18,750-22,500

A pair of George III giltwood mirrors, with elaborately carved surrounds, minor damage and repairs, c1770, 82in (208cm).
$67,500-75,000

A pair of George II style white painted and parcel gilt mirrors.
$11,250-15,000

A pair of George III style giltwood mirrors.
$14,250-16,500

A George II parcel gilt walnut mirror, with shaped carved frame, c1750.
$4,500-5,250

A George I gilt gesso mirror, restored.
$12,000-13,500

A George III giltwood mirror, with later plate.
$10,500-13,500

An Italian micro-mosaic easel mirror, early 20thC.
$3,000-4,500

A Franco-Flemish carved oak mirror, the apron centred by a shell.
$3,750-5,250

A giltwood mirror, c1765.
$3,000-3,750

A mahogany cheval mirror, on S-scroll supports, 19thC.
$975-1,500

A George III giltwood mirror.
$16,500-19,500

A Florentine giltwood mirror.
$3,750-5,250

A giltwood and painted mirror, c1815.
$4,500-5,250

A Venetian mirror, plate missing, mid-18thC.
$7,750-9,000

A Biedermeier painted, parcel gilt and walnut mirror, c1820.
$7,500-9,000

A gilt gesso mirror, with later brass candle holders. **$3,000-4,500**

A George III giltwood overmantel mirror, the central oval plate within divided plates with scrolls and acanthus leaves, c1775, 63 by 46in (160 by 116cm). **$30,000-37,500**

A George III giltwood mirror, with later shaped and divided plate, restorations, 51in (130cm) high. **$27,000-30,000**

An early George III giltwood mirror, repaired, c1755. **$27,750-30,000**

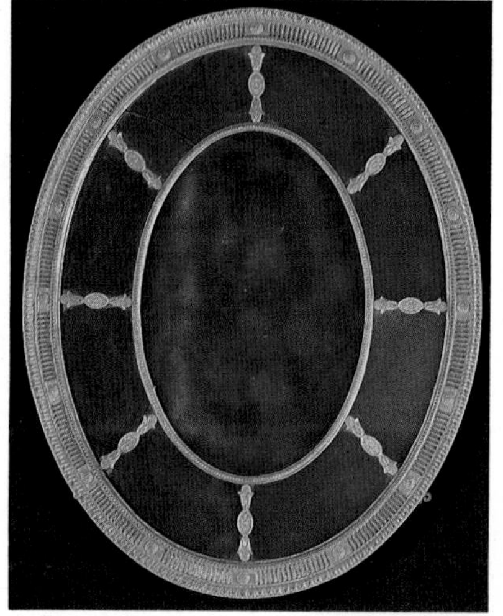
A George III giltwood mirror, border cracked, c1775, 51in (130cm) high. **$8,250-9,750**

A George II parcel gilt mahogany mirror, c1750. **$3,750-5,250**

A George III giltwood mirror, c1765. **$7,500-9,000**

A George II parcel gilt walnut wall mirror, c1730. **$6,750-9,000**

An Antwerp tortoiseshell mirror, with later plate, c1680. **$5,250-6,750**

A pair of giltwood mirrors, 19thC. **$3,000-4,500**

An 18thC mirror. **$4,500-6,000**

A Regency mirror. **$2,250-3,750**

A George II parcel gilt mahogany mirror, replaced plate, c1750, 41in (104cm) high. **$4,500-6,000**

A pair of English carved giltwood mirrors. **$2,500-3,750**

A George II parcel gilt walnut mirror, c1720. **$4,500-5,250**

A George III carved giltwood overmantel mirror, c1765. **$22,500-30,000**

George III mahogany breakfront sideboard, crossbanded with stringing and satinwood, label to back 15/Mark Rowe/ of Exeter, restored, 83½in (212cm).
11,250-12,750

A Regency burr yew and brass shelf, the back headed by small Bilston type appliqué, the 3 shelves with cast brass pillars and X-supports, c1800, 35in (90cm).
$3,750-5,250

A pair of English rosewood and marquetry shelves, 19thC.
$5,250-6,750

George III mahogany erpentine sideboard, with atinwood banding and boxwood nd ebony line inlay, 68in 173cm).
3,750-6,000

A Georgian mahogany bowfronted sideboard, with crossbanded top, on 6 tapering legs, 46in (117cm).
$3,750-5,250

A George III mahogany serpentine front sideboard, on channelled square tapering legs, restored, 68in (172.5cm). **$10,500-13,500**

Regency parcel gilt mahogany sideboard, with a arved and panelled splash rail, the frieze fitted with drawers, on pedestal supports each with a upboard, c1820, 119in (302cm).
15,750-17,000

A George III mahogany bowfronted sideboard, crossbanded and inlaid with satinwood, on tapering legs, 70in (178cm).
$7,500-9,000

A pair of George III tulipwood, mahogany and marquetry shelves, attributed to John Linnell, crossbanded with ebony and boxwood. **$19,500-22,500**

George III mahogany and ebonised sideboard, the owfront top with central frieze drawer, on square apering legs and block feet, 54in (137cm).
7,500-9,000

A late George III mahogany breakfront sideboard, with boxwood and ebony stringing, satinwood banding and oval tulipwood crossbanding, 78½in (199cm). **$4,500-6,000**

A George II mahogany double chair back settee, with leaf carved top rail, arm supports and front legs, drop-in seat, on cabriole front legs with scroll feet, c1755, 58in ((147cm).
$10,500-12,000

A George II style mahogany settee, the padded arched back with out scrolling arms and loose seat cushion upholstered in polychrome gros and petit point needlework, 70in (178cm).
$16,500-22,500

A George IV rosewood and cut brass inlaid chaise longue, with a shaped detachable back, on sabre legs with brass casters, c1820, 76in (193cm). **$9,000-12,000**

A parcel gilt decorated three-seater couch, the carved frame with central mask, on cabriole legs, 19thC. **$4,500-6,000**

An Arts & Crafts settee, designed by Charles Voysey and George Walton.
$1,500-1,800

A Louis XV walnut suite, comprising a sofa and 6 armchairs, all with loose cushions, scallop shell seat rails and cabriole legs, c1730, sofa 85in (216cm). **$75,000-105,000**

A Louis XVI revival gilt framed settee, with floral tapestry upholstery.
$900-1,200

l. A William and Mary walnut chair back settee, the high arched back with out scrolled arms, upholstered in gros and petit point needlework, distressed, 69in (175cm). **$9,000-10,500**

A George IV mahogany sofa, with triple panelled toprail, padded back, arms and bowed seat, on turned front legs, c1830, 55in (140cm).
$5,250-6,750

A Russian parcel gilt poplar sofa, the padded back with scroll cresting, pierced arms and scroll legs, c1820, 60in (152cm). **$7,500-9,000**

A mid-Victorian walnut sofa, the serpentine back, arm supports and seat upholstered in floral needlework, on part fluted shaped turned legs, 68in (173cm). **$3,000-3,750**

A pair of Louis XV beechwood sofas, with carved frames, caned backs and seats and cabriole legs, part mid-18thC, 47in (119cm). **$4,500-6,000**

A mahogany settee, with carved arms and legs, on claw-and-ball feet, constructed using 18thC pieces. **$5,250-7,500**

A George III mahogany upholstered settee, with channelled tapering cabriole legs, on scrolled and tapering feet, restorations, 75in (191cm). **$12,000-15,000**

A Regency caned mahogany sofa, with over scrolled ends, cushioned back and seat and sabre legs, c1810, 79in (200cm).
$8,250-9,750

A George II walnut settee, with shepherd's crook arms with carved handholds, on carved cabriole legs, the needlework part 18thC, restored, 54in (137cm).
$12,000-15,000

A Louis XIV carved giltwood stool, with stuffed seat, fluted and carved legs, c1690. **$7,500-9,000**

A set of Edwardian mahogany library steps, converting to a chair. **$750-850**

A pair of George III satinwood pole screens, with appliqué work banners, c1785. **$9,000-12,000**

A pair of early George III style mahogany pole screens, the banners worked in gros and petit point needlework, on carved tripod legs with claw-and-ball feet. **$3,000-3,750**

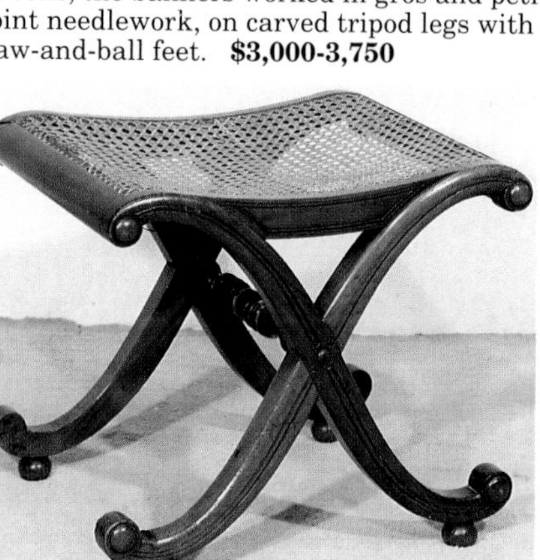

A Regency mahogany X-framed stool, with carved dished seat and turned stretcher, on bun feet, stamped Gillows Lancaster, 20in (51cm). **$2,250-3,000**

A George III mahogany tray-on-stand, modern stand, 29in (74cm). **$2,250-3,000**

An Edwardian mahogany cake stand. **$300-375**

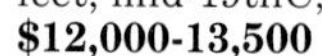

A Biedermeier walnut ottoman stool, with hinged stuffed top, tapering upholstered sides and paw feet, mid-19thC, 47in (119cm). **$12,000-13,500**

A Louis XV/XVI Transitional giltwood footstool, c1765, 21in (53cm). **$4,500-6,000**

A pair of George IV mahogany piano stools, with revolving leather seats, c1820. **$4,500-5,250**

A Victorian walnut adjustable piano stool with winding action. **$180-250**

A Victorian adjustable mahogany piano stool, 13in (33cm) diam. **$120-180**

A Louis XVI mahogany étagère, by Canabas, 29in (74cm) high. **$12,000-15,000**

A George IV specimen marble and osewood centre table, the top with 5 bands f 28 sections of coloured stones and narbles, c1825. **$75,000-82,500**

A Regency rosewood draughtsman's table, with hinged divided top, c1810, 34in (86cm). **$20,000-22,500**

A George III mahogany and plum pudding breakfast table, the tilt-top crossbanded in kingwood, 42in (107cm) diam. **$14,000-16,500**

A Regency mahogany nlaid breakfast table, 1805. **$30,000-33,000**

A George II walnut concertina-action card table, the interior baize lined, on carved cabriole legs and claw-and-ball feet, c1730, 34in (86cm). **$5,000-7,500**

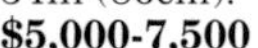

A marquetry, satinwood and rosewood D-shaped card table, restorations. **$7,500-9,000**

A George II marble topped cream and gilt console table, part c1740. **$2,250-3,000**

A George III mahogany architect's table, with hinged top, 48in (122cm). **$1,500-1,800**

A mid-Victorian walnut and marquetry centre table, 53in (135cm) diam. **$6,750-8,250**

A George III carved giltwood console table, c1760. **$29,000-31,000**

A George III mahogany architect's table, 38in (97cm). **$6,000-7,500**

An early George III carved mahogany architect's table, c1765, 56in (142cm). **$10,500-12,000**

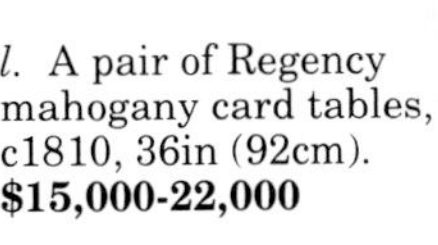

l. A pair of Regency mahogany card tables, c1810, 36in (92cm). **$15,000-22,000**

l. A George III mahogany breakfast table, with associated top and pierced Gothic arcade, later brass casters, 41in (104cm). **$4,500-6,000**

A pair of George III painted and parcel gilt demi-lune games tables, restoration and decoration of later date. **$13,500-16,500**

A George IV rosewood pedestal dining table, with 2 leaves, c1825. **$18,500-21,000**

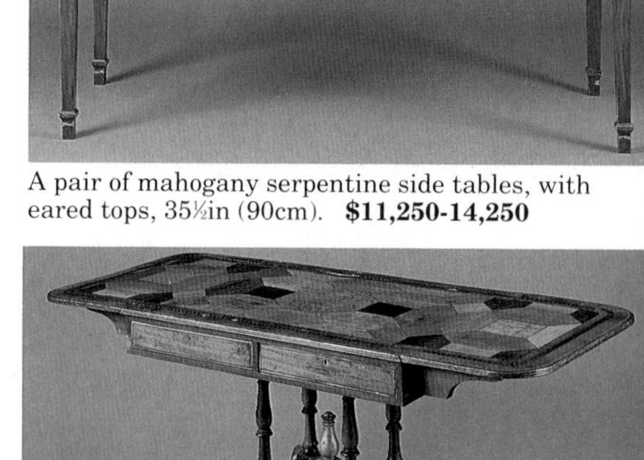

A pair of mahogany serpentine side tables, with eared tops, 35½in (90cm). **$11,250-14,250**

A Regency ebony and brass inlaid specimen wood and parquetry pedestal sofa table. **$28,000-30,000**

A Regency mahogany library table, with leather lined top, c1810, 46in (117cm). **$7,500-9,000**

A late George III rosewood sofa/games table, c1810, 57in (144cm). **$16,500-18,000**

A George III satinwood table, c1780. **$5,250-6,750**

A George III satinwood drum library table, with leather lined top, c1795, 36in (92cm) diam. **$9,750-11,250**

A George III rosewood inlaid satinwood sofa table, restored, c1805. **$14,250-16,500**

An Anglo-Chinese white metal mounted padouk dressing table, mid-18thC. **$14,250-16,500**

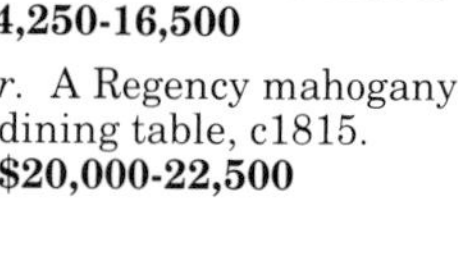

r. A Regency mahogany dining table, c1815. **$20,000-22,500**

A George III painted satinwood Pembroke table, 39in (99cm). **$6,750-9,000**

A George III fruitwood, tulipwood, satinwood nd mahogany marquetry writing table, some eneers later, restored. **$78,000-82,500**

A George III mahogany fret carved work table, restored, late 18thC, 39in (99cm). **$9,500-11,000**

An early George III mahogany supper table, with 2 flaps, c1770, 43in (109cm). **$3,500-4,500**

An early George III marble topped mahogany side able, the square chamfered legs with blind retwork and scroll brackets, c1765, 60in (152cm). **6,750-8,250**

An Anglo-Irish mahogany serving table, with moulded top and shell carved frieze, on cabriole legs with leafy scroll pad feet, c1750, 52in (132cm). **$10,500-12,000**

A Regency rosewood veneered writing and ames table, with brass banding, with sliding hequer board revealing fitted interior, 54in 137cm). **$7,500-9,000**

A George III sabicu envelope top tripod table, 27in (69cm) square. **$80,000-90,000**

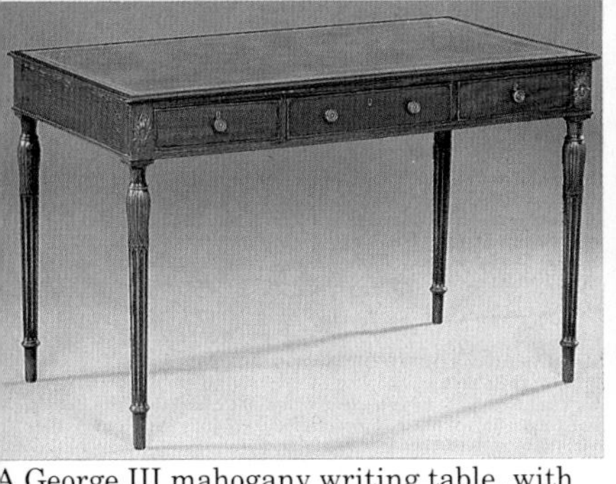

A George III mahogany writing table, with eather lined top, 3 drawers flanked by aterae, c1780, 48in (122cm). **$8,250-9,750**

A George III mahogany reading table, with adjustable hinged top, 28in (71cm). **$9,750-11,250**

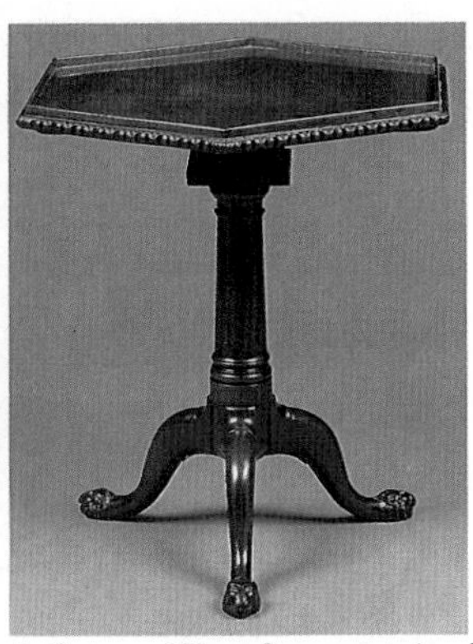

A George III mahogany tripod table, with tilt-top, top and base associated, 26in (66cm). **$6,000-7,500**

A George III wine cooler, with brass bands and loop handles, c1770, 26in (66cm).
$3,000-3,750

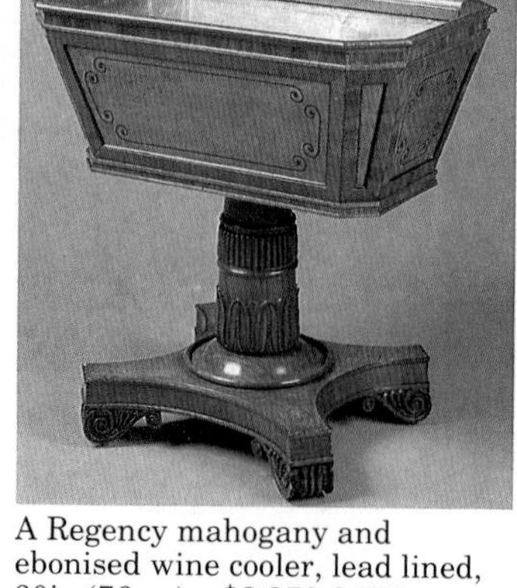

A Regency mahogany and ebonised wine cooler, lead lined, 30in (76cm). **$8,250-9,750**

A George III mahogany cellaret, with hinged top, lead lined, body inlaid with ovals, the sides with carrying handles, restored, 19½in (50cm).
$18,000-22,000

A George III mahogany brass bound wine cooler, interior refitted, c1795, 20in (51cm).
$2,250-3,000

A George IV mahogany wine cooler, with ebony stringing and brass mounted reeded legs, c1825, 29in (73cm). **$2,500-3,750**

l. A George III satinwood and mahogany cellaret, c1775, late 19thC swag inlay, 25in (64cm).
$8,250-9,750

r. A George III mahogany cellaret, with satinwood banded frieze.
$2,500-3,000

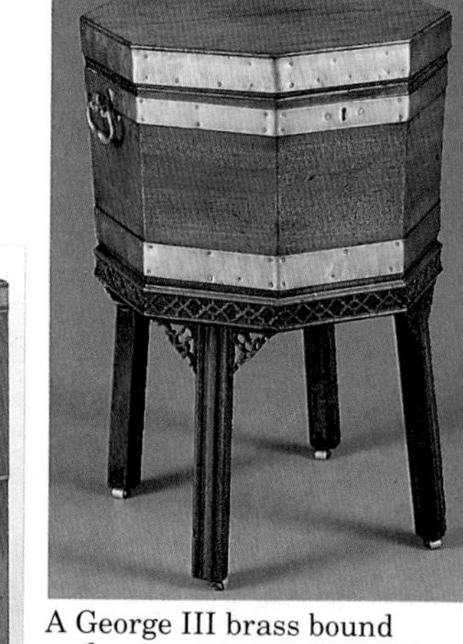

A George III brass bound mahogany wine cooler, with hinged top and lead lining, restored, 20in (51cm).
$3,750-5,250

A pair of George II brass bound mahogany wine coolers on George III octagonal stands, each with removable beaten tin lining and lion mask handles, on moulded octagonal plinth bases with hinged door to each end, one enclosing a shelf and one a cupboard, restored.
$13,500-18,000

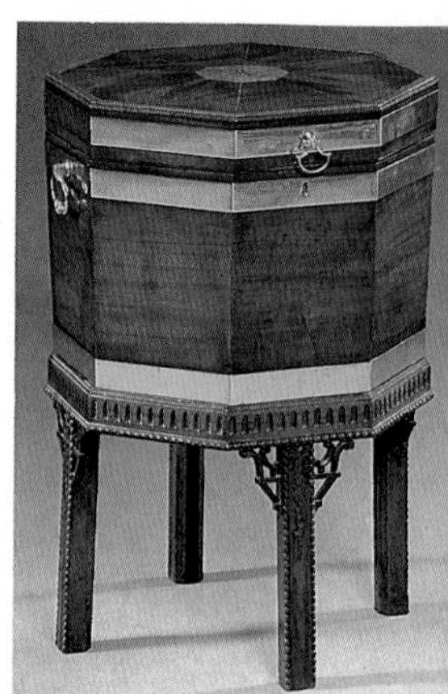

A George III mahogany cellaret, body with 3 brass bands, on later stand, c1780, 19in (48cm).
$3,000-5,000

An early Victorian serpentine giltwood dwarf side cabinet, with mirrored top above 2 mirrored shelves and back, flanked by fluted foliate carved uprights with egg-and-dart borders, on bun feet, the back stencilled 'C. Nosotti, House... Looking Glass Manufacturer 397.398 Oxford Street 399.399, established 1822', 72in (183cm).
$3,000-3,750

Charles Andrea Nosotti and Francis Nosotti are both recorded between 1829-40, at 2 Dean St. and at 298 Oxford Street.

A mid-Victorian walnut, marquetry and gilt metal mounted side cabinet, with overall amboyna bands and foliate scroll marquetry frieze, central glazed arched upholstered door, flanked by bowed open shelves and neo-Classical gilt mounts, on plinth base, 60in (152cm).
$2,700-3,300

A French gilt metal mounted marquetry side cabinet, with breccia marble top, damaged, on cabriole legs with gilt sabots, 39in (99cm).
$1,500-2,250

A Dutch colonial breakfront side cabinet, with overall ripple moulded decoration, on turned feet, mid-19thC, 67in (170cm).
$2,250-3,000

A French ebonised, brass and tortoiseshell inlaid and gilt metal mounted side cabinet, with white marble top, the doors with panels of foliate scroll designs between canted angles headed with female bust mounts, shaped aprons and block feet, mid-19thC, 43½in (111cm). **$2,250-3,000**

A French Empire period padouk wood side cabinet, with mottled black marble slab top, three-quarter pierced gilt metal gallery, on bronze patinated paw feet, 56in (142cm).
$5,250-7,500

A Dutch mahogany side cabinet, with D-shaped top above a dentil carved frieze set with a single drawer, above a pair of tambour cupboards, the apron with pierced fret decoration, on square tapering legs, late 18thC, 30in (76cm).
$1,800-2,700

Purchased from A. Mexborough Ltd, 73 High Street, Dorking, Surrey.

Chiffoniers

A Victorian mahogany chiffonier.
$1,050-1,350

A Victorian rosewood chiffonier, ornately inlaid with urn detail, the raised superstructure with bevelled glass panels above 3 cupboard doors, on turned supports.
$1,200-1,800

A 19thC mahogany chiffonier.
$1,200-1,800

A Victorian mirrored chiffonier.
$1,200-1,500

A faux rosewood chiffonier, with gilt stringing.
$1,500-2,250

Canterburies

Canterburies, originally designed for storing sheet music, but also used as plate holders to stand by the supper table, first appeared in England in the latter part of George III's reign and were predominantly in mahogany and rosewood. Sheraton attributed their name to a contemporary primate who commissioned such pieces.

From the 1820s they are found in other timbers, such as bird's-eye maple from c1825 and walnut during the Victorian period, when designs became more ornate. The relatively large number of 19thC versions now on the market are a consequence of the Victorians' passion for the piano.

Canterburies

A Regency mahogany canterbury, with slatted uprights and drawer, on ring turned tapered legs, restored, 23in (59cm).
$1,200-1,500

A Regency mahogany canterbury.
$2,700-3,300

A Victorian burr walnut canterbury, 25in (64cm)
$1,050-1,350

A George IV rosewood canterbury, 19½in (49cm).
$1,500-2,250

A Victorian figured walnut canterbury, with inlaid line and scroll decoration to the galleried top, supported on turned and fluted stems, the base with 2 divisions and ornate fretwork sides above a single drawer, on turned feet, 34in (86cm).
$2,250-3,000

A French rosewood canterbury, with turned supports and undertier, 19thC, 18in (45cm).
$1,200-1,500

Did you know?

MILLER'S Antiques Price Guide builds up year by year to form the most comprehensive photo reference library available.

›pen Armchairs

n elbow chair, with scroll carved ack rail, turned uprights and the back, part 17thC.
750-900

A George II walnut open armchair, the crest rail and arms with scroll terminals, the solid vase-shaped splat carved with leaf scrolls, flowerheads and a tassel, drop-in seat with gadroon bordered seat rail, on leaf carved cabriole legs, with pad feet.
$900-1,500

A William and Mary walnut wing chair, with leather covered back, wings and seat, turned legs with flat cross stretcher, c1680.
$4,500-6,000

Purchased from Harold Wickham, 19 Chapel Place, Tunbridge Wells, Kent, 'Old walnut frame armchair with leather seat and back, date about 17thC £30'. This chair is reputed to have been purchased at Battle Abbey after the death of the Duchess of Cleveland.

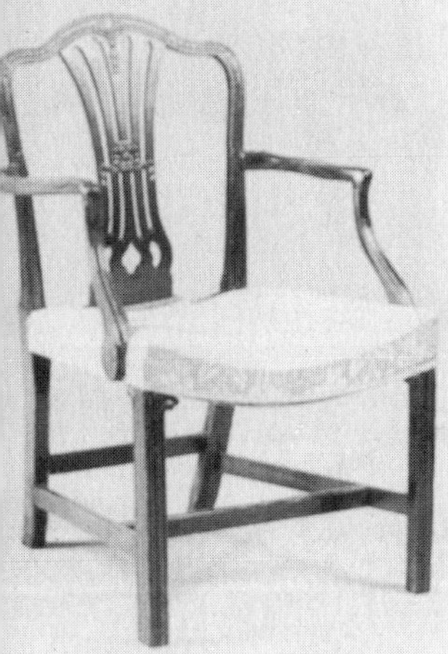

. George III mahogany open rmchair, with bowed seat overed in yellow silk damask, the vaved top rail carved with a entral anthemion and flanked by usk swags, above a pierced apering splat centred by a ribbon ie, with outswept channelled rms, on square channelled legs oined by an H-shaped stretcher, he legs extended by 2in.
1,200-1,500

A George III mahogany library armchair.
$2,700-3,300

A pair of late Victorian mahogany inlaid lady's and gentleman's armchairs.
$1,200-1,500

. pair of William IV mahogany rmchairs.
1,500-2,250

A pair of William IV mahogany reclining library armchairs, with padded adjustable seat, on turned lotus carved legs.
$2,700-3,300

A Victorian rosewood framed salon chair, with upholstered back panel, downswept sides, serpentine front, cabriole legs and brass casters.
$600-750

A pair of Regency bamboo armchairs, with pierced latticed backs and arms above wickerwork seat, on turned legs joined by stretchers, damaged, with later loose cushion.
$4,800-5,700

An Edwardian mahogany inlaid rail back armchair, with upholstered seat, on tapered forelegs. **$225-300**

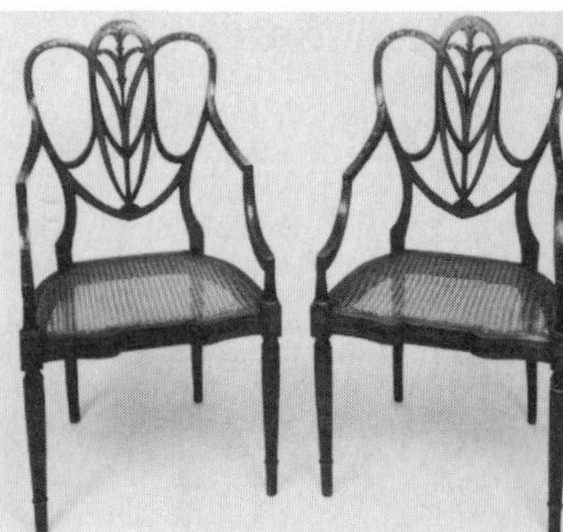

A pair of satinwood armchairs of Sheraton design, with shield- shape backs, cane seats and turned legs, with all over painted decoration of Prince of Wales feathers, drapes and flowers, 19thC. **$3,000-3,750**

An Edwardian Sheraton satinwood open armchair.
$450-600

A painted open armchair, in the manner of Sheraton, with pierced splat, cane upholstered seat and turned tapering legs, 19thC.
$450-600

A Victorian black lacquered elbow chair, with bowed cresting rail and vase-shaped splat, inlaid with mother-of-pearl and painted decoration, on cabriole legs with china casters. **$450-600**

Thomas Sheraton (1751-1806)

Thomas Sheraton was an English designer and author of several influential volumes on furniture design. He is best known for light, delicate pieces, mainly in satinwood, with restrained inlay. He also designed some very ornate pieces using paint and marquetry. Later pieces became increasingly eccentric.

A late Victorian armchair, on Queen Anne legs.
$750-900

A mahogany Hepplewhite style armchair. **$225-300**

A pair of Victorian mahogany elbow chairs, with 'paper scroll' crestings to high waisted backs, scrolled and carved arms and front supports, in need of re-upholstery.
$1,200-1,500

chestnut armchair in the rococo yle, with upholstered seat, on briole legs with claw-and-ball et joined by shaped stretchers, obably Italian or Iberian, thC. **$1,050-1,350**

A rattan armchair.
$300-375

A French giltwood fauteuil, with gold patterned upholstery, on cabriole front legs, 19thC.
$600-750

A pair of walnut framed ship's elbow chairs, with oval back panels and reversible seats, on turned front legs, early 20thC.
$225-255

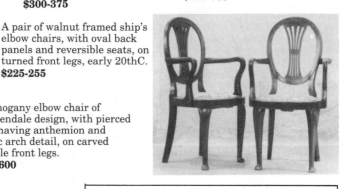

A mahogany elbow chair of Chippendale design, with pierced splat having anthemion and Gothic arch detail, on carved cabriole front legs.
$450-600

A Continental mahogany framed armchair, c1900.
$600-750

set of 4 Victorian walnut open armchairs, with rved scrolling arms, backs and carved front skirt. cabriole legs. **$3,000-3,750**

A set of 4 Continental ebonised hardwood open armchairs, each with high triple leaf carved arched cresting rail, pierced and richly carved with strapwork and foliage, over an oval medallion back, with arm pads and drop-in seats upholstered in green velour, the foliate carved open arms with C-scroll uprights extending down to panelled square baluster front legs, with brass casters.
$5,250-7,500

A William and Mary walnut wing armchair, with padded back and wings, scrolled arms and moulded legs joined by waved X-stretchers, c1700.
$5,250-6,000
Purchased from Williamson, Guildford.

A George I walnut armchair, covered in gros and petit point needlework, on cabriole legs with pad feet.
$3,000-4,500

Upholstered Armchairs

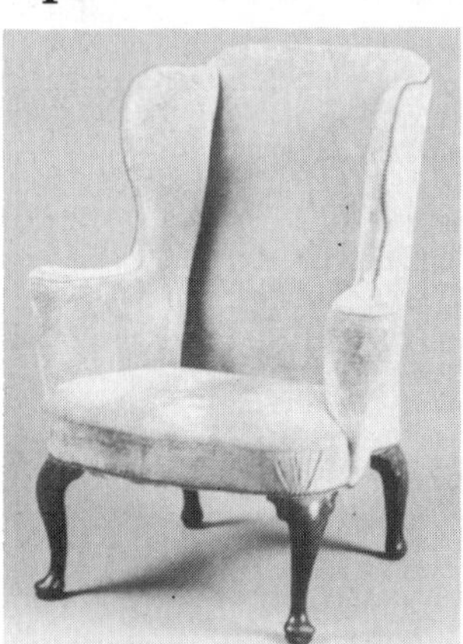
A George II mahogany wing armchair, on cabriole legs and pad feet, covered in close-nailed green velvet, largely re-railed.
$3,000-4,500

A mahogany framed bergère library chair, on turned front legs with casters, early 19thC.
$1,200-1,500

A George I walnut wing armchair the arched back, outswept arms and padded seat with floral upholstery, on cabriole legs with pad feet joined by stretchers, restored, stretchers possibly replaced.
$3,000-4,500

A Regency mahogany library bergère, with caned back, sides and seat, reeded arm supports and tapering legs.
$1,200-1,500

A George III mahogany wing armchair, covered in close-nailed red leather, on chamfered square legs joined by an H-shaped stretcher, brass caps and later casters, cross stretcher replaced.
$5,250-6,000

A Georgian bergère armchair, the mahogany frame with reeded top rail, upholstered arm pads, on fluted tapering legs with brass casters.
$2,250-3,000

A George III hall porter's chair, the arched deeply curved padded canopy covered in close-nailed pale brown striped horsehair, above a pair of cupboard doors, on square legs with block feet, restored.
$1,500-2,250

A William IV mahogany framed library armchair, with carved classical detail to the armrest supports, on reeded front legs.
$600-750

A George IV mahogany framed library armchair, with scroll and paterae crest rail, moulded arms with scroll and leaf supports, on turned and reeded legs headed by roundels. **$900-1,500**

A Regency mahogany hall porter's chair, the arched ribbed canopy, back, outscrolled arms and seat upholstered in close nailed buttoned olive green hide, the slightly bowed apron with a pair of cupboard doors, 64in (162.5cm) high.
$3,000-4,500

A George IV brass inlaid rosewood bergère chair, covered in close-nailed pale brown material, the arms carved with foliate trails and scrolls, above a scroll inlaid frieze, on reeded turned tapering legs and gadrooned ormolu caps.
$4,500-6,000
Its boldly carved 'Grecian couch' armscrolls and reeded cone legs, in the antique style, combined with brass arabesque inlay in the French manner, reflect fashionable Regency furnishings such as those introduced by the eclectic architect, Lewis Wyatt (d.1853) in the drawing room at Tatton Park, Cheshire around 1810.

A Victorian tub chair, by Lenygon & Morant, with arched padded back and seat upholstered in a stylised fern enriched rose coloured material, on turned tapering legs and casters, with chintz loose cover of exotic birds and flowers on an ivory ground, marked R-22 and inscribed at base ...28140. **$3,000-4,500**

A Victorian carved rosewood tub armchair, with button upholstery, the frame, scroll arms and cabriole legs carved with foliage and flowers, c1860.
$2,250-3,000

A pair of Victorian mahogany framed armchairs, upholstered in buttoned pink dralon, on cabriole front legs.
$2,250-3,000

A Victorian walnut open armchair, with foliate scroll arms and cabriole legs.
$750-900

A Louis XVI style beechwood bergère chair, with pale blue damask upholstery, on spiral fluted legs.
$1,200-1,800

An Edwardian mahogany library armchair, with bronze floral damask upholstery, with husk carved top rail, turned supports, on turned tapered legs.
$2,250-3,000

A three-piece bergère suite, with green velvet cushions, 1920s.
$750-900

Corner Chairs

A George II mahogany corner armchair, with horseshoe top rail above solid vase splats and columnar supports, the shaped drop-in seat above a small rear drawer, on cabriole legs with pointed pad feet, lacking adjustable candle bracket and reading rest.
$3,000-4,500

A George II walnut tub shape corner elbow chair, with outward scrolling arms, rosette carved and pierced shaped splats, drop-in upholstered seat, on a shell carved and scrolled front cabriole leg and square chamfered back legs and cross stretcher.
$750-900

Dining Chairs

A set of 7 mahogany chairs, comprising 6 single chairs and a matching elbow chair, with curved crest rails, pierced leaf and scroll decorated splats, drop-in seats, turned and reeded legs, one splat missing, early 19thC.
$1,200-1,800

A set of 4 George III mahogany and red walnut chairs, with pierced splats and nailed hide seats, c1760.
$1,800-2,700

A set of 6 George III style mahogany dining chairs, including a pair of armchairs, with drop-in seats and square chamfered legs joined by stretchers.
$1,800-2,700

A set of 8 George III Hepplewhite mahogany dining chairs, including 2 carvers, with hump backs above fretted splats, drop-in seats and square chamfered front legs.
$3,000-3,750

A set of 8 mahogany dining chairs, including 2 carvers, 19thC.
$4,800-5,700

harlequin set of 10 George III ish mahogany ladder back ning chairs, with brown leather holstered serpentine seats, on oulded square legs joined by uare stretchers.
5,250-6,000

A pair of 19thC mahogany carvers.
$750-1,200

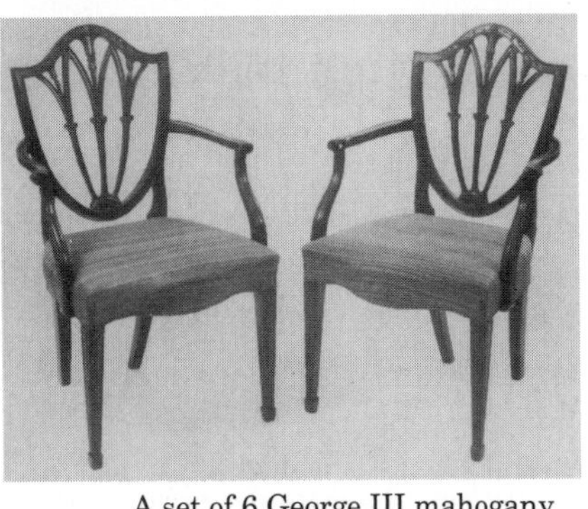

A set of 6 George III mahogany dining chairs, including 2 armchairs, the horsehair covered seats on moulded tapering legs with spade feet, restored.
$9,000-12,000

A set of 7 Regency mahogany dining chairs.
$5,250-7,500

A set of 6 Regency simulated rosewood and parcel gilt dining chairs, on sabre front legs.
$4,800-5,700

set of 8 matched George III ning chairs.
3,000-3,750

set of Georgian mahogany ning chairs, comprising one rver, and 4 singles, each with rved backrails, upholstered verstuffed seats, on turned and uted front legs.
300-750

set of 8 Regency mahogany dining chairs.
12,000-15,000

A set of 7 Regency mahogany dining chairs, comprising one carver and 6 singles, with drop-in seats upholstered in beige moquette, on turned tapered reeded legs. **$4,500-6,000**

A set of 6 Regency mahogany dining chairs, comprising 2 carvers and 4 singles.
$9,000-10,000

A set of 7 Regency mahogany dining chairs, damaged.
$4,500-6,000

One carver and 2 single Regency mahogany dining chairs, each with carved pierced backrail with central sunburst, drop-in seats and tapered reeded legs.
$2,250-3,000

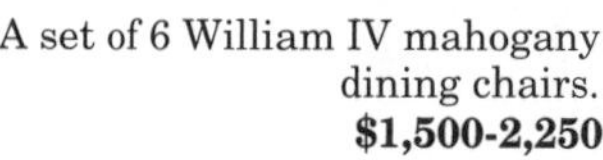

A set of 6 William IV mahogany dining chairs.
$1,500-2,250

A set of Regency mahogany dining chairs, comprising 2 carvers and 6 singles, with drop in seats, upholstered in green velvet, and bergère seats below, on tapered reeded legs.
$6,000-8,250

A set of 6 George IV mahogany dining chairs, including 2 carvers with shaped backs and back rails with 3 raised fillets, on turned and reeded front legs.
$1,500-2,250

A set of 8 Edwardian inlaid dining chairs
$3,000-3,750

A set of 8 William IV mahogany dining chairs, comprising 2 carvers and 6 singles, with drop in striped seats, on octagonal turned tapered legs.
$6,000-8,250

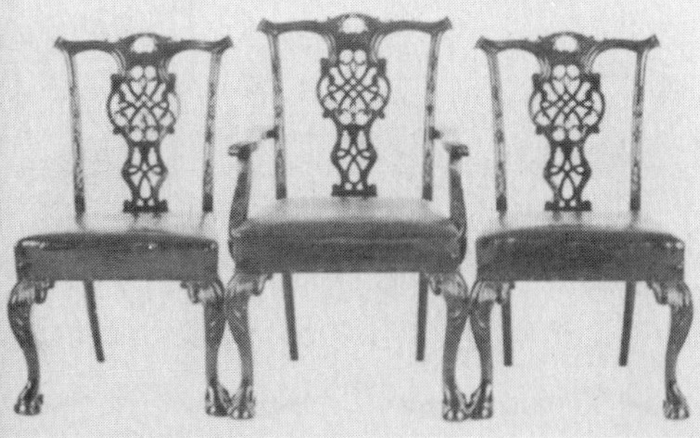

A set of 8 mahogany Chippendale style dining chairs, including 2 carvers, the cupid's bow cresting rails pierced and carved with diapering and fluting, over pierced interlaced strapwork vase-shaped splats, overstuffed seats upholstered in green American cloth, on cabriole front legs carved at the knees and claw-and-ball feet.
$3,000-4,500

A set of 7 William IV mahogany dining chairs, comprising one carver and 6 singles, each with a bowed shaped and carved cresting rail, on shaped stiles with a carved moulded mid-rail, drop-in seats upholstered in horsehair, on turned tapered legs.
$1,500-2,250

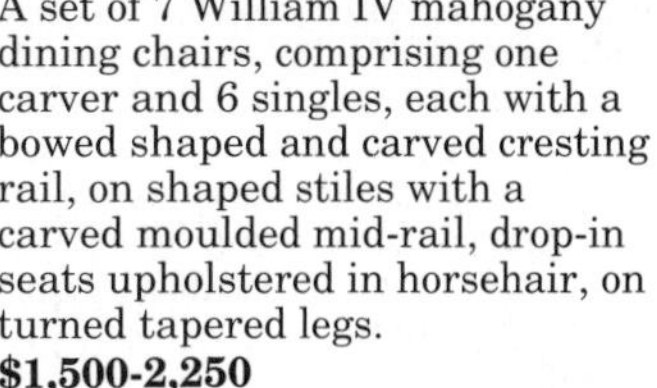

A Regency mahogany sabre legged dining chair.
$50-75

A set of 12 walnut Chippendale style dining chairs, c1910.
$12,000-15,000

A set of 8 Chippendale style carved mahogany dining chairs, including 2 carvers, with shaped acanthus carved crestings, the splats pierced and carved with florets, scrolls and foliage, drop-in seats, acanthus carved front legs, and claw-and-ball feet.
$4,800-5,700

A set of 6 Victorian mahogany balloon back dining chairs.
$1,500-2,250

A set of 6 Victorian rosewood dining chairs, with serpentine cresting rails and carved centre rails, stuffover seats with serpentine friezes and cabriole front legs.
$1,200-1,500

Thomas Chippendale (1718-79)

Thomas Chippendale, the son of a Worcestershire carver, set up as a cabinet maker in London in 1749. He was an exponent of the rococo style and his superb and delicate carving set new standards for furniture making. Besides elaborate and costly work his firm made very large quantities of relatively cheap, simple furniture of very high quality. His business, in St Martin's Lane, was carried on after his death by his son Thomas Chippendale the younger, c1749-1822.

A set of 10 mahogany Chippendale design dining chairs, including a carver, with drop-in leather seats, on square chamfered legs joined by H-stretchers.
$3,000-4,500

A set of 10 mahogany Hepplewhite style dining chairs, comprisng 2 carvers and 8 singles, with square tapered moulded legs and H-stretchers.
$5,250-7,500

A set of 12 Victorian mahogany balloon back dining chairs, comprising 2 carvers and 10 singles, with drop-in seats upholstered in red velvet, on turned tapered legs.
$5,250-6,000

In the Furniture section if there is only one measurement it usually refers to the width of the piece.

A set of 10 mid-Victorian oak dining chairs, including a pair of carvers, upholstered in petit point needlework with the Ottley crest and various coats-of-arms, pierced scrolling top rails, spirally turned uprights and legs joined by H-shaped stretchers, seat number 7 inscribed 'Lady Milton's work'.
$9,000-10,000

A set of 6 Victorian balloon back dining chairs.
$1,800-2,700

A set of 10 Victorian mahogany balloon back dining chairs, with carved and pierced decoration, the buttoned seats covered in green dralon, on scrolling legs.
$5,250-7,500

A set of 6 Edwardian mahogany dining chairs, with arched carved backs above upholstered panel, flanked by turned supports, stuffover seats, on turned and fluted legs.
$900-1,500

Hall Chairs

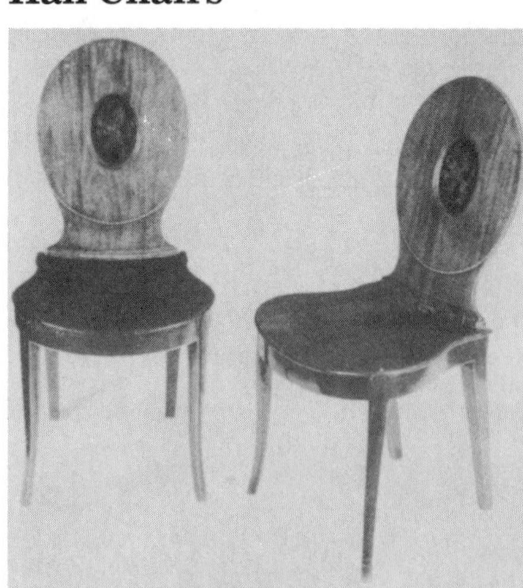

A pair of George III mahogany hall chairs, the backs with boxwood and ebony strung borders and painted crests, rounded wood seats and splayed legs. **$1,200-1,800**

A pair of Regency mahogany hall chairs, each with moulded back centred by a roundel, cane filled seats and ring turned tapering legs with later blocks. **$1,800-2,700**

A set of 4 Regency mahogany hall chairs, with solid balloon backs, painted oval reserves with the Verity crest, panel seats, on acanthus carved turned and tapering legs, one damaged. **$1,200-1,800**

Side Chairs

A Charles II chair, with upholstered back and turned supports to an upholstered seat, on ball turned frame joined by stretchers, c1660. **$1,200-1,500**

A pair of George II walnut side chairs, the veneered backs with shaped supports and crests and pierced upright burr elm splats, drop-in concave fronted seats with gros and petit point baskets of flowers, on cabriole legs carved with shells, S-scrolls and pendant husks, on shaped pad feet, some replacements, 23in (59cm). **$4,500-6,000**

A pair of 17thC beechwood side chairs, in the manner of Daniel Marot, the pierced scrolled arched top rails leaf carved, the back splats with elongated C-scrolls and pierced strapwork within moulded uprights, the upholstered seats on moulded cabriole legs joined by moulded curved stretchers. **$2,700-3,300**

A Victorian lady's chair. **$375-450**

A George III mahogany side chair, upholstered in a blue ground William Morris fabric, on moulded square legs joined by square stretchers, restored. **$1,050-1,350**

A pair of George III mahogany side chairs, with shaped leaf carved top rails, pierced splats now carved with flowerheads, drop-in seat, on blind fret-carved seat rail and moulded chamfered legs joined by H-stretchers. **$1,800-2,700**

Daniel Marot 1663-1752

Daniel Marot was born in France in 1663. He worked mainly in Holland as an architect and designer. From 1694 to 1698 he worked in England for William III. It was he who introduced grand Baroque style to England and Holland. His beds are particularly complex confections of carving and drapery and he is possibly responsible for the proportions - high backs and short legs - of William and Mary chairs.

A George I side chair, with upholstered seat, on pollard oak cabriole legs with pad feet, probably by William Marks, Fore Street, Wellington, whose label it bears.
$450-600

A pair of early George III mahogany side chairs, each with a stuffed serpentine back and seat, the seat rails carved with acanthus leaves and C-scrolls, cabriole legs front and back, with scrolled toes.
$9,000-12,000

A Victorian walnut nursing chair,with reeded frame, serpentine seat, on cabriole front legs.
$450-600

A pair of William and Mary side chairs, covered in red silk damask with tasselled borders, on boldly scrolling cabriole legs joined by concave X-shaped stretchers with a turned finial, the stiles re-supported, restorations.
$2,250-3,000

A Victorian mahogany inlaid tub chair, 22in (56cm).
$375-525

A pair of late Victorian giltwood gossip chairs, upholstered in floral trellis work repp, on simulated bamboo legs with pierced collars.
$1,200-1,500

Make the most of Millers's

Unless otherwise stated, any description which refers to 'a set' or 'a pair' includes a valuation for the entire set or the pair, even though the illustration may show only a single item.

An early Victorian carved walnut lady's chair, on cabriole legs.
$900-1,500

An Anglo-Indian scarlet lacquer and upholstered spoon back occasional chair, the frame with stylised scrolls, birds, serpents, and a deity, some damage.
$1,050-1,350

Children's Chairs

A walnut child's armchair, with arched back, serpentine splat, padded seat and cabriole legs, mid-19thC, possibly Italian.
$750-900

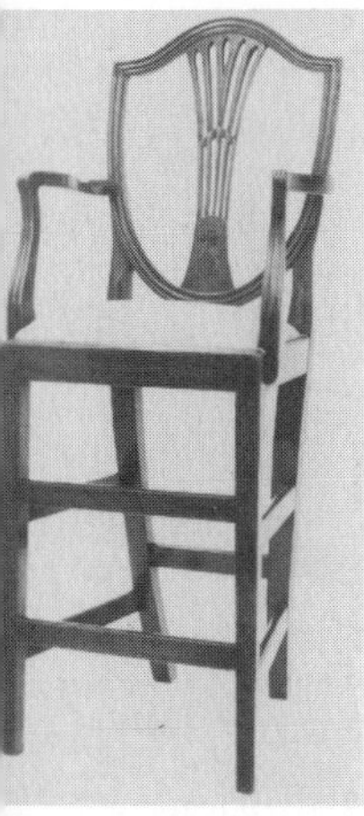

 George III mahogany child's
ıair, the moulded shield-shaped
ack and pierced splat inlaid with
ribbon suspended medallion, on
ıuare tapering legs.
2,250-3,000

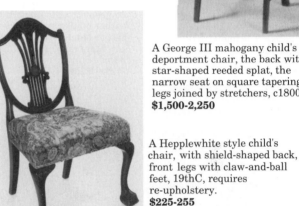

A baby chair and walker, c1920, 38in (96.5cm) high.
$135-150

A George III mahogany child's deportment chair, the back with star-shaped reeded splat, the narrow seat on square tapering legs joined by stretchers, c1800.
$1,500-2,250

A Hepplewhite style child's chair, with shield-shaped back, front legs with claw-and-ball feet, 19thC, requires re-upholstery.
$225-255

. walnut framed child's corner
'hair, with pierced back panels,
orsehair seat, on square legs
ined by stretchers, old damage,
9thC.
105-120

Miscellaneous Chairs

A Victorian beech framed commode chair.
$50-75

Chests of Drawers

A William and Mary walnut chest of drawers, with moulded edge, crossbanded inlaid top, inlaid drawer fronts with turned handles, the side panels having oval inlaid stringing, 37in (94cm).
$4,800-5,700

A George I walnut chest of drawers, the quarter veneered top with feather banded spandrels, on later bracket feet, 37½in (95cm).
$4,800-5,700

An oyster veneered chest of drawers, with 2 short and 3 long drawers, boxwood stringing, on bun feet, late 17thC, 38in (96.5cm).
$2,250-3,000

A Queen Anne walnut veneered chest of drawers, the crossbanded top geometrically inlaid with feather banding, the drawers also feather banded, on later bracket feet, some restoration, 37½in (95cm).
$1,500-2,250

A burr walnut and mahogany chest of drawers, with brass drop handles, engraved backplates, brushing slide, on bracket feet, slight damage, early 18thC.
$2,700-3,300

A George I walnut chest of drawers, the quartered top with crossbanding and thumbnail moulding, on bracket feet, 34½in (88cm).
$3,000-3,750

A George III mahogany chest of drawers, the top with inlaid boxwood line, cockbeading to the drawer fronts, 43½in (110cm).
$1,500-2,250

A George I walnut, fruitwood an pine chest of drawers, with banded top, on bracket feet, damaged, 37½in (95cm).
$1,200-1,800

A walnut chest of drawers, 18th 37in (94cm).
$1,050-1,350

A George II red walnut chest o drawers, with moulded crossbanded top, brushing slid and 4 graduated drawers, 31in (79cm).
$2,250-3,000

A George II mahogany chest of drawers, with moulded top, 2 short and 3 long drawers flanke by fluted quadrant pilasters, on ogee bracket feet, c1755, 36in (92cm).
$2,700-3,300

A Georgian style mahogany serpentine front chest of drawers, with thumb moulded edge to top, brushing slide, 4 long graduated drawers with brass handles, flanked by canted fret carved stiles, on bracket feet, 35in (89cm).
$1,500-2,250

A George III mahogany serpentine chest of drawers, with partially fitted upper drawer, with blind fretwork angle, on bracket feet.
$4,800-5,700

A George III mahogany serpentine chest of drawers, with rounded rectangular top, above a slide, on conforming bracket feet, one back foot partially replaced, 41½in (105cm).
$2,250-3,000

A mid-George III mahogany chest of drawers, on bracket feet, one damaged, 29½in (75cm).
$3,000-4,500

A mahogany chest of drawers, with boxwood string inlay, early 19thC, 38in (96.5cm).
$375-525

A George III mahogany chest of drawers, with moulded top, brushing slide, 4 graduated drawers, on shaped bracket feet, minor repairs, 33½in (85cm).
$1,800-2,700

A George III mahogany chest of drawers, with moulded top, on bracket feet, 31in (79cm).
$1,800-2,700

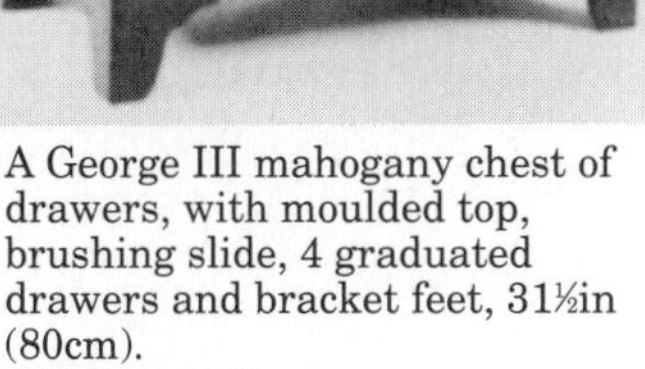

A George III mahogany chest of drawers, with moulded top, brushing slide, 4 graduated drawers and bracket feet, 31½in (80cm).
$1,500-2,250

A George III mahogany bachelor's chest, with fold-over top, 4 long graduated drawers with later brass handles, on ogee bracket feet, 29in (74cm).
$2,250-3,000

A mahogany and satinwood banded bowfronted chest of drawers, with 2 short and 3 long drawers, brass handles, splayed bracket feet, early 19thC, 42in (106.5cm).
$1,050-1,350

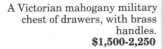

A Victorian mahogany military chest of drawers, with brass handles.
$1,500-2,250

A mahogany chest of drawers, with moulded top, a brushing slide and bracket feet, 19thC, 34in (87cm). **$1,050-1,350**

A George III mahogany chest of drawers, with later moulded top, a brushing slide, 4 long graduated drawers, on bracket feet, 30½in (77cm).
$1,200-1,500

A satinwood and tulipwood banded chest of drawers, with brushing slide, 4 graduated drawers and bracket feet, 30in (76cm).
$1,200-1,500

A George III mahogany chest of drawers, with 4 long graduated drawers flanked by canted moulded terminals, c1770, 33in (84cm). **$1,500-2,250**

A German oyster veneered and floral marquetry chest of drawers, with ebony line and holly banding, deep golden birch banding to the sides, on turned feet, plate glass top, old restoration, 18thC, 38in (96.5cm).
$4,500-6,000

A Dutch walnut and foliate marquetry upright chest of drawers, decorated with flower filled urns, birds and butterflies amongst foliage, the 2 column uprights each with gilt metal capital, flanking 5 drawers, on block feet, early 19thC, 39in (99cm).
$4,500-6,000

A Regency faded mahogany bowfront chest of drawers, with ebony stringing, 4 long drawers, lion handles, bracket feet.
$1,050-1,350

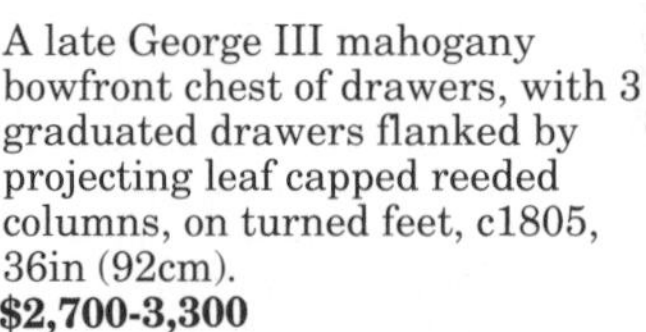

A late George III mahogany bowfront chest of drawers, with 3 graduated drawers flanked by projecting leaf capped reeded columns, on turned feet, c1805, 36in (92cm).
$2,700-3,300

A mahogany chest of drawers, with 3 deep and 2 long drawers, flanked by turned columns, on reeded legs, early 19thC.
$450-600

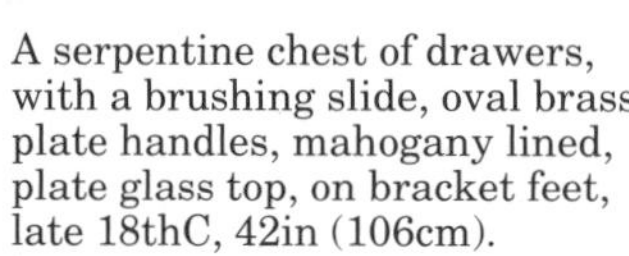

A serpentine chest of drawers, with a brushing slide, oval brass plate handles, mahogany lined, plate glass top, on bracket feet, late 18thC, 42in (106cm).
$1,050-1,350

ʼhests-on-Chests

. George II walnut tallboy, in 2 ections, the drawer fronts rossbanded and inlaid, on shaped racket feet, 42in (106.5cm).
4,800-5,700

. mid-Georgian walnut chest-on-hest, the moulded cornice above slightly concave frieze, the base itted with 3 further long raduated drawers, on a moulded linth with bracket feet, 39in 99cm).
2,250-3,000

. George III mahogany chest-on-hest, 50in (127cm).
1,200-1,500

A walnut chest-on-chest, with moulded cornice above a cushion drawer and 2 short and 3 long drawers, the base with 6 short drawers surrounded by bead mouldings, with canted corners carved with flowers, on eagle legs with claw-and-ball feet, upper part c1700, 44in (112cm).
$4,800-5,700

A George III mahogany chest-on-chest, with moulded cornice above 2 short and 3 long drawers, flanked by fluted quarter angles, with brushing slide and 3 further drawers, on bracket feet, 36½in (93cm). **$1,500-2,250**

A George III mahogany chest-on-chest, with a concave cornice, on tapering bracket feet, 41in (104cm). **$1,500-2,250**

A George III mahogany chest-on-chest, with brass drop handles and gilt metal escutcheons, the drawers with cockbeading, raised on ogee bracket feet, 46in (116.5cm).
$3,000-4,500

A George II walnut tallboy, the upper part with a cavetto cornice, the lower part with a brushing slide above 3 long drawers, all with cross and feather stringing, on bracket feet, restored, 41in (104cm).
$10,500-12,000

A Georgian style mahogany chest-on-chest, in 2 parts, on bracket feet, 19thC, 45in (114cm).
$1,500-2,250

A George III mahogany chest-on-chest, the upper part with chamfered corners and moulded key patterned cornice, the lower part with brushing slide over 3 long drawers, moulded base and bracket feet, 44in (111.5cm).
$1,500-2,250

A George III mahogany tallboy chest, with dentil moulded cornice and blind fret frieze, restored, 44in (111.5cm).
$3,000-3,750

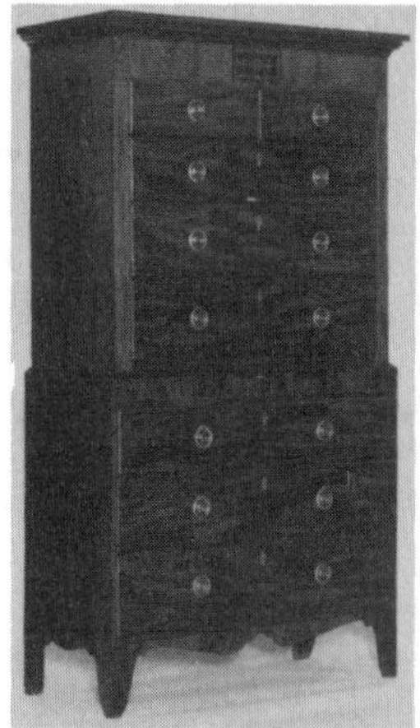

A late Regency mahogany tallboy with a flared cornice above an inlaid frieze centred by brass fleur-de-lys motifs, 2 short and 6 long graduated drawers below, with brass ring handles, on bracket feet, 44in (111.5cm).
$1,500-2,250

A George III mahogany chest-on-chest, with 2 short and 6 long graduated drawers, flanked by fluted pilasters, on bracket feet, c1770, 43in (109cm).
$2,700-3,300

A late Georgian mahogany tallboy, the top section with a dentil cornice, on bracket feet 44in (111.5cm).
$3,000-3,750

Chests-on-Stands

A Queen Anne style walnut and oak chest-on-stand, the upper section with cornice, crossbanded drawers with brass drop handles and escutcheons, matching base with 3 drawers, arched apron on cabriole legs with pad feet, 42in (106.5cm).
$1,800-2,700

A walnut and oak chest-on-stand, the later stand with bobbin turned uprights, bun feet and flattened stretchers, the chest early 18thC, 38in (96.5cm).
$1,800-2,700

A walnut chest-on-stand, with feather banding and brass handles, shaped apron, bracket feet, pine sides and top, part early 18thC, 39in (99cm).
$1,800-2,700

A George I burr walnut veneered chest-on-stand, with cross and feather banded top, 2 short drawers above 3 long drawers, on barley twist stand.
$3,000-4,500

ecrétaire Chests

George III mahogany secrétaire est-on-chest, the upper part th stepped and moulded rnice, 2 short over 2 long awers, a secrétaire drawer low with fitted interior, the se with 2 long drawers, brass ndles and bracket feet, 43in)9cm).
,250-3,000

A walnut veneered secrétaire, feather banded throughout, the cavetto cornice above 2 crossbanded quarter-veneered doors enclosing an arrangement of 12 small drawers, the base with double ovolo carcase mouldings, the top drawer fitted with pigeonholes and 4 small drawers, 3 further long drawers below, on bracket feet, restored, handles replaced, one long drawer bears small fragments of the label of John Coxed, early 18thC 43½in (110cm).
$15,000-22,500

A number of walnut veneered bureaux and secrétaire cabinets dating from the period 1700-1710 have been found labelled 'John Coxed, At the Swan in St Paul's Church-Yard, London, makes and sells Cabinets, Book Cases, Chest of Drawers, Scrutores and Looking-glasses of all sorts'. He was second in a long succession of cabinet makers at that address and by c1710 he seems to have been replaced by G. Coxed and T. Woster who continued making furniture of the same type until Thomas Woster's death in 1736. Coxed and Woster were followed at 'The White Swan' by Henry Bell and his successors.

Secrétaire Chests

The secrétaire drawer would appear to have been developed during the late George II/early George III period. As an alternative to the sloping fall of a bureau, it offers a pull-out drawer, the front of which lets down and is supported by a quadrant at each end.

Some of the finest military chests are also equipped with secrétaire drawers, to increase their utility and save transporting a desk.

A George III secrétaire chest, with 2 drawers in the frieze with centre shell inlay, the interior with 8 drawers and 8 pigeonholes, central cupboard, bracket feet.
$1,800-2,700

mahogany secrétaire chest, ith ebony stringing, the deep riting drawer opening to reveal satinwood interior of drawers, geonholes and a small pboard, over 3 long graduated awers, on splayed feet, early thC, 42in (106.5cm).
750-900

Wellington Chests

A Victorian mahogany secrétaire Wellington chest, the 7 graduated drawers with wooden knob handles, 2 being dummy drawers falling to reveal a secrétaire interior, on a plinth base, 22½in (57cm).
$2,700-3,300

A Victorian mahogany Wellington chest, with moulded top, 6 drawers behind a stile lock, on a plinth base, 26½in (68cm).
$1,800-2,700

Coffers

A Regency mahogany coffer, each side with fielded panels and fluted corners, on turned tapering legs with brass casters, 34½in (88cm).
$2,250-3,000

A Spanish carved walnut coffer, 49in (124.5cm).
$450-600

Commodes

A pair of painted satinwood serpentine commodes, each with eared top, with a pair of oval panelled doors centred by a spray of flowers, on turned legs, 39in (99cm) wide.
$9,000-10,000

A George III mahogany serpentine fronted commode, the 4 long drawers flanked by ogee moulded corners, on splayed bracket feet, c1780, 42in (106.5cm) wide.
$4,500-6,000

A Louis XV style gilt metal mounted marquetry bombé commode, with mottled red marble top, 3 frieze drawers with gilt clasps and sabots, on splayed legs, 28in (71cm).
$2,250-3,000

A French provincial petit commode, with moulded marble top, floral parquetry panels, fitted side drawer and drawer below the false drawer, on slender cabriole legs, later handles and mounts, 18thC, 21.5in (55cm).
$2,700-3,300

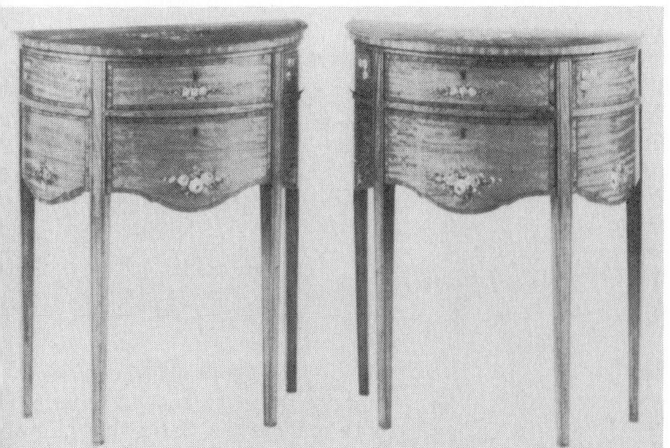

A pair of floral painted satinwood demi-lune dwarf commodes, each with 2 frieze drawers and waved apron, on square tapering legs, 25in (64cm) wide.
$3,000-4,500

A Dutch mahogany and marquetry commode, inlaid throughout with fan medallions and stringing, the projecting frieze drawer above 3 further long drawers below, flanked by brass mounted freestanding columns, and on a plinth base, early/mid-19thC, 39in (99cm) wide.
$2,250-3,000

A Louis XV style rosewood, walnut, gilt metal mounted and marquetry commode, with marble top, inlaid sans traverse with floral bouquet in cartouche surrounded by rockwork and floral mounts between projecting angles with shaped aprons, splayed legs with sabots, late 19thC, 51in (129.5cm) wide.
$3,000-4,500

An Italian walnut and marquetry dwarf commode, inlaid overall with geometric lines and feather banding, the rounded top centred by an urn of flowers above a drawer and cupboard, on cabriole legs, damaged, mid-18thC, 21½ins (55cm) wide.
$2,250-3,000

A Swedish walnut and tulipwood crossbanded and parcel gilt serpentine commode, with marble top, chased brass handles, 45½in (116cm) wide.
$1,200-1,500

A French commode, with shaped marble top, the serpentine front with wide crossbanded quartered walnut panels and ornate cast handles, escutcheons and angles, early 19thC, 48in (122cm). **$5,250-6,000**

A French provincial walnut commode, with later top, above a frieze drawer and 3 further drawers, flanked by column uprights with gilt cappings and bases, on square feet, 43½in (110cm).
$1,050-1,350

A Dutch walnut veneered commode, geometrically inlaid throughout with parquetry banding, the top with an oval shell medallion, 3 long drawers below, on tapering square legs, early 19thC, 34in (87cm).
$2,250-3,000

A Louis XVI style tulipwood and mahogany breakfront commode, with marble top, 3 drawers below with trompe l'oeil fluted decoration and central marquetry basket of flowers sans traverse, on angled square tapering legs with sabots, marble broken, 45in (114cm) wide.
$2,250-3,000

A North Italian walnut commode, the top inlaid with a star in a hexagon, all with a geometric ribbon crossbanding, on square tapering legs with simulated fluting, 48in (122cm).
$2,250-3,000

An Italian walnut inlaid and crossbanded serpentine front commode, the fascia with fielded veneers in figured walnut and fruitwood, on cabriole supports, 19thC, 70in (178cm).
$3,000-3,750

A Dutch walnut inlaid commode, with 4 wave front drawers, on carved animalier feet, restorations, 18thC, 38in (96.5cm).
$3,000-4,500

Armoires

Did you know?
MILLER'S Picture Price Guide builds up year by year to form the most comprehensive photo reference library available.

A French provincial chestnut armoire, with moulded cornice above foliate scroll carved frieze centred by an inlaid star, a pair of arched panelled doors below carved with similar foliage and waved apron, on cabriole legs, late 18thC/early 19thC.
$3,000-3,750

A French provincial blue and gilt painted armoire, with waved apron and cabriole legs, late 18thC/early 19thC, later painted, 59in (149.5cm).
$3,000-4,500

A Dutch walnut, rosewood banded and chequer strung armoire, with broken pediment and simulated dentil moulded cornice above a pair of panelled doors, flanked by fluted half column angles, with gilt capitals, above 3 drawers, on square fluted legs, early 19thC, 75in (190.5cm).
$5,250-7,500

edside Cupboards

mahogany tray top bedside
pboard, with one door, on
ender turned legs, early 19thC,
in (36cm). **$450-600**

A Victorian circular mahogany bedside cupboard, with an inset white veined marble top
$450-600

A Victorian figured walnut pedestal bedside cupboard, with a plain galleried top.
$300-375

A George III mahogany bowfronted night commode, the galleried top with hand grips, the top frieze with a dummy lock, above a tambour shutter cupboard, the pull-out pot holder with a brass swan neck handle, and serpentine edge to square pull-out legs
$1,800-2,700

orner Cupboards

George III mahogany
owfronted corner wall cupboard,
ith moulded cornice and cross
rained base, fitted with shelves
nclosed by 2 doors with H-hinges
nd escutcheons, 25in (64cm)
ide. **$1,200-1,800**

A walnut hanging corner cabinet, with arched moulded top and single quarter veneered and crossbanded door, early 18thC, 42in (106.5cm) high.
$3,000-4,500

Purchased from Arthur Edwards, 59 & 61 Wigmore Street, London. Invoice dated June 28th 1927.

A George III mahogany veneered bowfront corner cupboard, with moulded cornice above a banded frieze, the pair of doors inlaid with stringing and with brass escutcheons, enclosing shelves and 3 small drawers to the base, 28in (71cm).
$1,200-1,800

Dutch mahogany and floral
arquetry corner cupboard, the
reakfront top above a pair of
oors, on cabriole legs, 19thC,
4in (61cm).
1,200-1,800

A walnut bowfronted hanging corner cupboard, with moulded cornice and doors, inlaid with stringing, early 18thC, 25in (64cm) wide.
$2,250-3,000

Purchased from Kyrle & Co, 41 Pantiles, Tunbridge Wells. Invoice dated June 19th 1928 'An old walnut bow front corner cupboard £28.0.0'.

A late George III mahogany and line inlaid corner cupboard, with moulded cornice and pair of panelled doors and a further pair of panelled doors between canted sides, on shaped bracket feet, 45in (114cm). **$2,250-3,000**

A Georgian mahogany bowfronted hanging corner cupboard, with moulded pediment, the 2 doors enclosing 2 shelves, having brass H-hinges, over a single short drawer with brass swan neck handles and pierced backplates, 24½in (62.5cm).
$900-1,500

A rosewood, fruitwood and marquetry bowfront corner cupboard, the crossbanded top with floral and musical trophy decoration, on bracket feet, 26in (66cm) wide.
$2,250-3,000

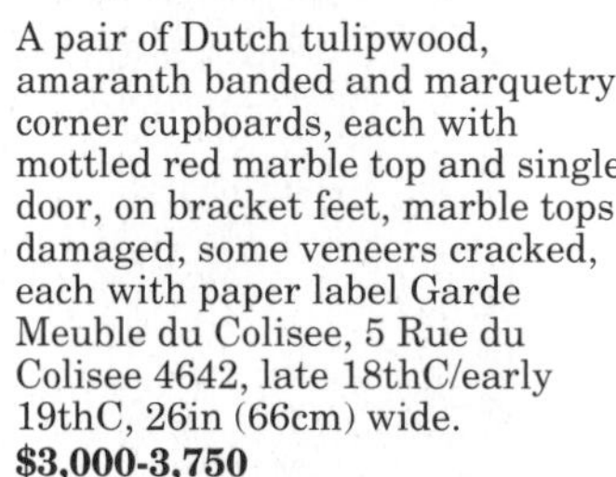

A pair of Dutch tulipwood, amaranth banded and marquetry corner cupboards, each with mottled red marble top and single door, on bracket feet, marble tops damaged, some veneers cracked, each with paper label Garde Meuble du Colisee, 5 Rue du Colisee 4642, late 18thC/early 19thC, 26in (66cm) wide.
$3,000-3,750

A Continental walnut veneered and ebonised corner cupboard, with tulipwood banding and metal mounts, probably German, late 19thC, 38in (96.5cm).
$1,500-2,250

Linen Presses

A Regency mahogany linen press, with moulded cornice, a pair of panelled doors on outswept bracket feet, one lacking veneer, doors slightly warped, 49½in (126cm).
$1,200-1,500

A late George III mahogany linen press, with chequer stringing, beaded decoration and pedimented cornice, on bracket feet, 48in (122cm).
$1,200-1,500

A late George III mahogany linen press, with moulded cornice and swept bracket feet, 54in (137cm) wide.
$1,500-2,250

A late George III mahogany linen press, with diapered fret carved broken swan neck pediment and dentil carved cornice, over slides enclosed by a pair of panelled doors, raised on ogee bracket feet, 50in (127cm) wide.
$4,500-6,000

A Victorian mahogany linen press, with a pair of panel doors above 2 short and 2 long drawers.
$1,200-1,500

A Regency mahogany linen press, inlaid with rosewood bands and boxwood and ebony lines, 51½in (131cm).
$2,250-3,000

A Regency mahogany linen press, with dentil moulded cornice above a pair of rosewood banded panelled doors, 55in (140cm).
$1,800-2,700

A George IV linen press, with pediment top above a pair of flame panelled doors.
$2,250-3,000

Wardrobes

A satinwood and tulipwood banded wardrobe, with drop pendant decorated cornice, a pair of panelled doors with long drawer below, on bracket feet, early 19thC, 50½in (128cm).
$1,800-2,700

A George III mahogany gentleman's tray wardrobe, with a moulded dentil cornice above flame mahogany panelled doors, opening to reveal 5 oak trays above 2 short and a long drawer, on double ogee bracket feet, 52in (129.5cm) wide.
$3,000-4,500

A Regency mahogany gentleman's tray wardrobe, with a moulded cornice, 50½in (128cm).
$2,250-3,000

Davenports

A Victorian burr walnut veneered davenport, with amboyna banding and boxwood stringing throughout, on scrolling front supports and bun feet, 22in (56cm) wide.
$2,700-3,300

A small mahogany davenport, with shaped carved pediment to the back section with rising lid and ink compartments, leather inset to main writing slope which rises to reveal a fitted interior, the sides with brass drop handles, 21in (53.5cm) wide.
$1,050-1,350

A mahogany davenport, with three-quarter brass gallery, leather inset sliding slope enclosing fitted interior, fitted with a slide either side and the usual arrangement of 4 drawers opposing 4 dummy drawers, on turned feet, 19thC, 20in (51cm).
$1,500-2,250

Davenports

The earliest English davenports are of plain box-like form, the upper section sliding or turning to provide knee space. The name 'davenport' appears to come from an entry in the records of the firm of Gillow, who made a small desk for a Captain Davenport to the specification that has become familiar under his name.

Until 1840 the plain Regency box-type prevailed; this has a slide top which pulls forward for ease of writing. From c1840 the type with the piano-rise top, scrolled or turned supports and a recessed case became most common. The rise, which runs on a leather belt and weights, is released by a sprung lock inside the desk, which opens to reveal small drawers and pigeonholes. Such a feature greatly enhances the value of the piece as long as it is in good working order - replacements and repairs to these mechanisms are becoming increasingly costly.

A late Victorian sycamore davenport, with three-quarter brass gallery, leather lined fall enclosing fitted interior above 4 drawers, the back fitted with a slide, on plinth base with stencilled stamp 5 times Henry Samuel, 484 Oxford Street, London, W, 21in (53cm) wide.
$2,700-3,300

A William IV rosewood davenport, with sliding slope top, having drawer interior, writing slide and 4 further drawers, on squat circular feet, 24in (61.5cm).
$2,250-3,000

A Victorian burr walnut veneered davenport, the rising stationery compartment with fret-carved front and hinged top, the projecting piano front enclosing an adjustable writing slide, the fret carved brackets above turned and knopped supports, the sides with 4 false and 4 real drawers, on turned feet with casters, mechanism faulty, 22½in (57cm) wide.
$3,000-4,500

A Victorian walnut crossbanded and string inlaid davenport, the raised back having hinged lid with fitted interior, the hinged inset leather flap revealing fitted drawers, on turned and scrolled column supports, 4 side drawers with knob handles and opposite dummy drawers, turned feet and china casters, 21½in (54.5cm) wide. **$1,800-2,700**

n Edwardian rosewood
avenport, inlaid with musical
nstruments and white stringing,
vith stationary compartment, 4
ide drawers and turned columns.
1,200-1,800

A Victorian walnut davenport.
$4,800-5,700

A mid-Victorian walnut piano davenport, with rising superstructure, adjustable leather lined slope, 4 drawers to the side and opposing dummy drawers, foliate scrolled supports and turned feet, 28in (71.5cm) wide.
$3,000-3,750

A late Victorian burr walnut davenport, with pierced gallery and leather lined sloping lid enclosing a fitted interior in bird's-eye maple, stamped Lamb, Manchester, 22in (56cm).
$1,800-2,700

esks

n early Georgian burr walnut kneehole
esk, veneered with cross and feather
anded details, with frieze drawer and 6
mall drawers around kneehole cupboard.
3,000-3,750

late George III mahogany
neehole desk, with fitted frieze
rawer, the brass plate handles
vith the words 'Trafalgar
openhagen'.
$3,000-4,500

A George III Irish mahogany kneehole desk, the moulded top enclosing a green baize lined adjustable writing slope, flanked on either side by various compartments and divisioned trays, on bracket feet, 42in (106.5cm). **$7,500-9,000**

An early George II walnut kneehole desk, the quarter-veneered top with cross and feather banding and cusped corners, fitted with a long frieze drawer and 6 short pedestal drawers flanking the recessed cupboard, on bracket feet, 34in (87cm) wide.
$9,000-10,000

A walnut and feather banded kneehole desk, with long frieze drawer and arched kneehole wit cupboard flanked by 3 drawers, on bracket feet, later top, early 18thC, 33in (84cm) wide.
$2,250-3,000

A George II mahogany kneehole desk, with moulded top above a frieze drawer, with a central cupboard, on bracket feet, part of moulding to top lacking, c1755, 32in (82cm) wide.
$1,500-2,250

A George III mahogany kneehole desk, the crossbanded top with a moulded edge, raised upon double bracket feet, 36in (92cm) wide.
$3,000-4,500

A German walnut and burr walnut veneered kneehole desk, with cast brass mounts throughout, the galleried shelf on griffin supports, shelf altered, lat 19thC, 40½in (102cm) wide.
$1,200-1,500

An Italian walnut, bone inlaid and marquetry kneehole desk, the leather lined top above 7 drawers,with overall scrolling foliage, reconstructed, part early 18thC, 44½in (112cm).
$3,000-3,750

A German walnut, elm and marquetry kneehole desk, all inlaid with architectural landscapes, on square tapering legs and bun feet joined by flattened cross stretchers, late 19thC/early 20thC, 50½in (128cm wide.
$3,000-4,500

Miller's is a price GUIDE not a price LIST

An Edwardian satinwood and painted kidney-shaped kneehole desk, with rosewood crossbanding, leather lined top, 42in (106.5cm).
$4,500-6,000

ı early Victorian mahogany
destal desk, with leather lined
p above 2 frieze drawers and 3
awers to each pedestal, on
inth bases, 42in (106.5cm).
,000-3,750

A Victorian mahogany pedestal desk, the raised back with 8 small drawers with locking pilasters, flanking a galleried shelf and a hinged writing slope enclosing a fitted well, above 8 short drawers, 54in (137cm). **$1,050-1,350**

Pedestal Desks

Pedestal desks are found in relative quantity from mid-18thC, although a few exist from the early 18thC. They enjoyed a long period of popularity and continued to be produced throughout the 19thC and into the Edwardian period. In 18thC and early 19thC they are most commonly found in mahogany and are usually veneered. They were made in a wider variety of woods in the later 19thC. Pedestal desks are usually constructed in 3 sections with 3 frieze drawers and 3 graduated drawers to the pedestals.

Walnut pedestal desks from the Victorian period are much sought after, as long as they are of good quality, and have recently risen enormously in price.

A George IV mahogany partners' desk, the pedestals with false panelled doors to each side, and fitted to each end with 2 panelled doors, one end with pigeonholes lettered A-L, the other end with the divisions removed, 60in (152.5cm).
$3,000-4,500

n early Victorian oak and ebony
edestal desk, with leather lined
p, the drawers numbered in
ass, on plinth bases, 54in
37cm).
,000-3,750

French brass mounted
ahogany pedestal desk, the
ather lined top with brass
rder, on turned toupie feet, late
thC, 60in (152cm).
,000-8,250

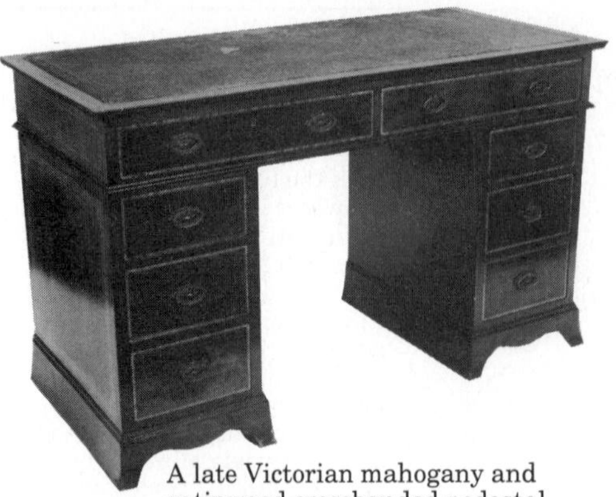

A late Victorian mahogany and satinwood crossbanded pedestal desk, with leather lined top above 2 frieze drawers and 6 further drawers, on swept bracket feet.
$2,250-3,000

A Victorian walnut pedestal des with green leather lined moulde top, replacement handles, 48½in (123cm). **$3,000-3,750**

A Victorian mahogany tambour top twin pedestal desk, 61½in (155.5cm). **$1,200-1,800**

A Victorian mahogany kneeho desk, 48in (122cm).
$1,500-2,250

An early Victorian mahogany partners' desk, with rectangul leather lined top above 8 frieze drawers, on baluster turned tapering legs, 96in (243.5cm) wide.
$1,800-2,700

A late Victorian walnut partner library desk, with leather lined top above 12 frieze drawers, and drawers and a cupboard to each pedestal, on plinth bases, 103in (261.5cm).
$7,500-9,000

\ walnut and burr walnut Vooton desk, with pierced scroll arved galleried cresting, hinged anelled front opening to reveal a itted interior and writing surface, n scroll feet, with label of Robert strahan & Co, Cabinet Makers nd Upholsterers, 24-25 Henry street, Dublin, 42½in (108cm).
5,250-7,500

A painted satinwood and rosewood banded Carlton House desk, with overall ribbon tied floral garlands, the raised superstructure with banks of drawers, flanked by hinged compartments above a leather lined surface, 56in (142cm) wide.
$4,800-5,700

An Edwardian mahogany inlaid cylinder desk, with fitted interior, pull-out writing slide, 2 small drawers, on square tapering legs with brackets, 36in (91.5cm).
$1,200-1,800

A Wooton's patent walnut desk, the top with zig-zag carved hinged frieze opening to reveal stationery slides, over 2 bowed double panelled doors, inset with a foliate strapwork decorated cast iron letter box and a simulated letter box inscribed 'Manufactured By Wooton Desk Manufacturing Company, Indianapolis, W.S. Wooton's Patent, October 6th 1874', hinged and opening to reveal a fitted interior, 43in (109cm).
$3,000-4,500

An Edwardian mahogany and marquetry pedestal desk, on tapered feet and casters, stamped Edwards and Roberts, 54½in (138cm).
$3,000-4,500

A late Victorian rosewood writing desk, in the Carlton House style, with boxwood inlay.
$1,200-1,500

A Victorian mahogany pedestal cylinder desk, the cylinder enclosing a fitted interior, each pedestal with 3 short drawers on plinth bases, 54in (137cm).
$1,500-2,250

A Sheraton revival rosewood cylinder desk, decorated in marquetry, late 19thC, 30in (76cm).
$3,000-3,750

Dumb Waiters

A George III mahogany dumb waiter, the graduated tiers supported on a turned column and triform base, with pad feet.
$1,200-1,500

A mid-Georgian mahogany dumb waiter, with ring turned baluster shaft, arched base and pad moulded feet, 47in (119cm).
$1,500-2,250

A Victorian mahogany brass mounted dumb waiter, with beaded edges on brass columnar supports, fitted with 4 drawers alternating with false drawers, 59in (149.5cm).
$4,500-6,000

This was formerly a drum table with later tiered superstructure.

Dumb Waiters

Dumb waiters are stands with 2 or more tiers of trays around a central column. They have existed in England since at least the 1720s to hold plates, desserts, wine and so on, allowing parties to continue after the servants had been dismissed.

A pair of mahogany and brass mounted dumb waiters, each circular tier with pierced Greek key gallery and joined by Corinthian column supports, on reeded column and downswept legs, 22½in (57cm) diam.
$2,700-3,300

A George III mahogany dumb waiter, the graduated tiers each raised on circular turned and gadrooned standards, on tripod cabriole legs ending in pointed pad feet, on casters.
$2,700-3,300

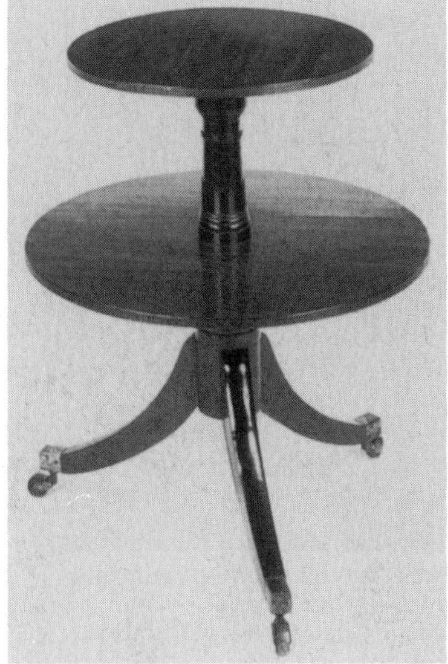

A Regency mahogany dumb waiter, with twin flap tiers on spirally turned spreading shaft, splayed tripartite base and brass caps, re-supported, 31in (79cm) high. **$1,800-2,700**

A George III mahogany dumb waiter, on turned and part spiral central column, on tripod feet, 44in (111.5cm) high.
$2,250-3,000

Mirrors & Frames

A Queen Anne walnut mirror, with divided plate and shaped moulded frame, c1715, 44in (112cm) high.
$1,800-2,700

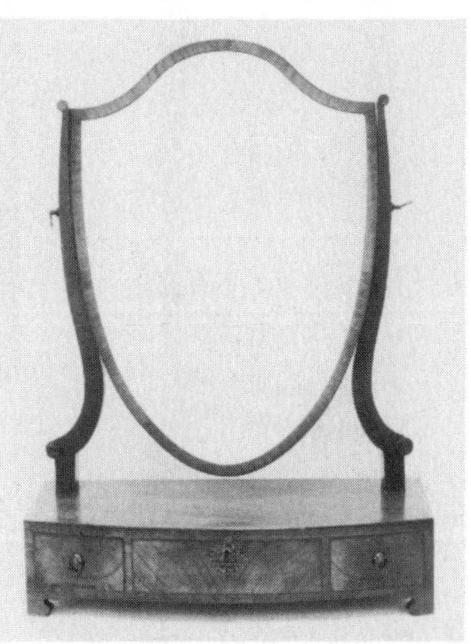

A Georgian mahogany toilet mirror.
$450-600

A walnut parquetry and giltwood toilet mirror, with later adjustable shaped arched mirror plate within a bevelled giltwood mirrored border crowned by a flaming finial, the stop fluted columnar side supports with flaming finials, the hinged flap with star parquetry enclosing a fitted interior of 4 drawers and 4 compartments centred by a scallop fronted drawer flanked by a pair of columns, the waved serpentine fitted drawer with paper scroll terminals flanked by 2 scallop shell niches, the interior with 8 compartments, on paper scroll cabriole feet, part early 18thC, 39in (99cm) high.
$3,000-4,500
With label 'My fathers Grandfather / brother John Rendall / born in the year 1740 / and his father's name was Charles', and with a handwritten copy.

A William IV dressing table mirror, with ebony inlay, c1830, 25 by 24in (64 by 61cm).
$450-600

A George III mahogany toilet mirror, the serpentine base with a single mahogany lined frieze drawer, on shaped bracket feet, restored, one foot replaced, 18in (46cm) wide.
$1,500-2,250

A George III mahogany frame cheval mirror, with boxwood stringing and turned brackets for candle arms, on splayed legs with casters, 25½in (65cm) wide.
$1,050-1,350

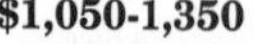

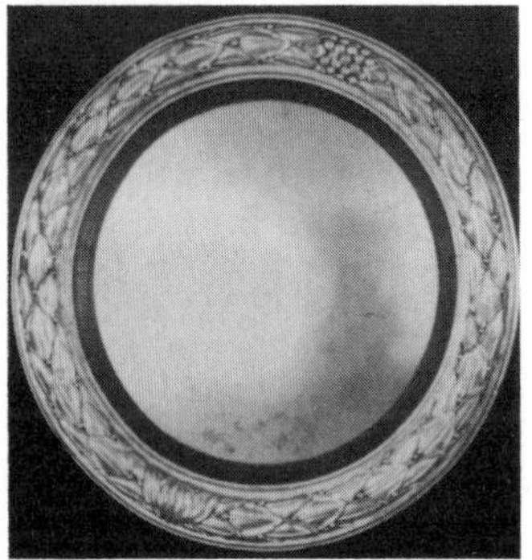

A Regency giltwood convex mirror, with reeded ebonised slip and laurel leaf surround, 33in (84cm) diam.
$4,800-5,700

A Regency giltwood convex mirror, with associated cresting of a neo-classical maiden and horse, with ribbon tied and ball decorated surround and reeded ebonised slip, with printed label 'S. Child. looking glass and manufacturer, Rathbone House ... Road Cheltenham', 47½ by 32in (120 by 81cm). **$3,000-4,500**

A George III giltwood marginal mirror, with later plate and mirrored surround with later divisions within stiff leaf and beaded surround, 59 by 42in (150 by 106.5cm). **$3,000-4,500**

A Regency mahogany and ebonised cheval mirror, with bevelled swing plate flanked by ring turned uprights with urn finials, one damaged, on dual splayed legs joined by a stretcher, 71 by 33in (180 by 84cm).
$3,000-4,500

A Regency mahogany toilet mirror, with reeded uprights, the bowed hinged base enclosing a fitted interior, lacking one finial and bun feet, 22in (56cm) wide.
$750-1,200

A William IV giltwood convex mirror, with eagle and rockwork cresting, foliate carved split moulded surround and acanthus apron, 39 by 22in (99 by 56cm).
$1,800-2,700

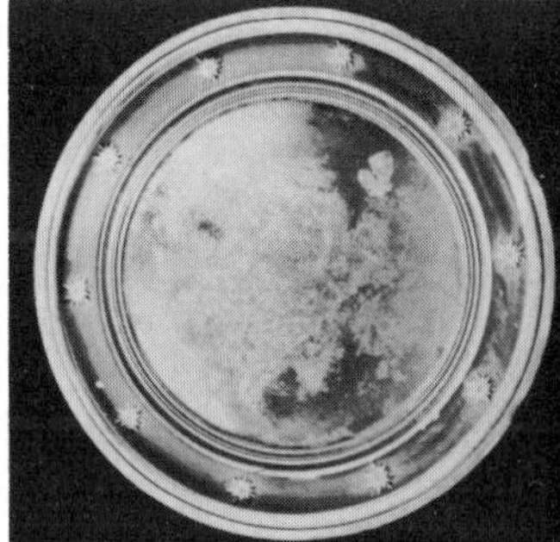

A Regency giltwood and ebonised convex mirror, the circular plate in a fluted surround banded with stars, in a moulded frame, 26in (67cm) diam.
$2,700-3,300

Almost certainly supplied to the 2nd Earl of St. Germans (1767-1849), Port Eliot, Cornwall.

An early Victorian white painted overmantel mirror, with trade label of William Froom, Looking Glass Manufacturer, Carver, Gilder, Picture Frame Maker, 13 Strand, Nr Waterloo Bridge, previously gilded, 62 by 54½in (157 by 138cm).
$750-1,200

n early Victorian mahogany ɿeval mirror, the turned prights with lotus leaf capitals ɑd scrolling feet, one candle ɔonce missing, 34in (86cm) wide.
1,200-1,800

An early Victorian giltwood overmantel mirror, by William Thrale Wright, re-gilded, lacking 2 sections of plate, one section of swag repositioned, the backboard inscribed in chalk 'Wright', with trade label, 78½ by 66in (199 by 168cm).
$2,250-3,000

Almost certainly supplied to the 2nd Earl of St. Germans (1767-1849), Port Eliot, Cornwall.

W.T. Wright is recorded in the London directories at this address from 1837-9.

A Victorian mahogany toilet mirror.
$50-75

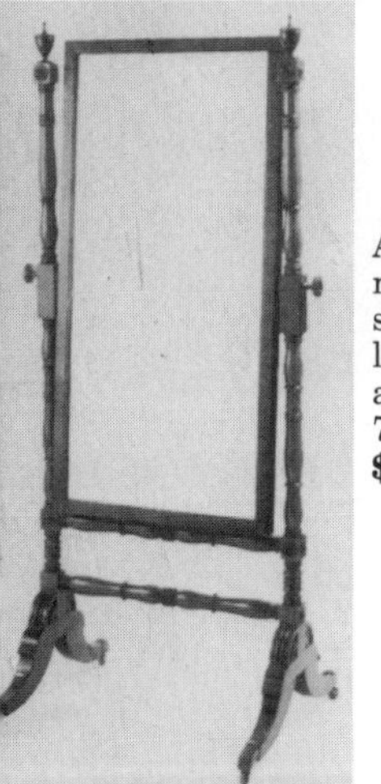

A George IV mahogany cheval mirror, the ring turned baluster stand with urn finials, on splayed legs with foliate carved brass caps and casters, 65 by 30½in (165 by 77cm).
$1,050-1,350

A mahogany framed wall mirror, tulipwood crossbanded, ebony and boxwood strung, 19thC, 37½ by 27in (95 by 69cm).
$600-750

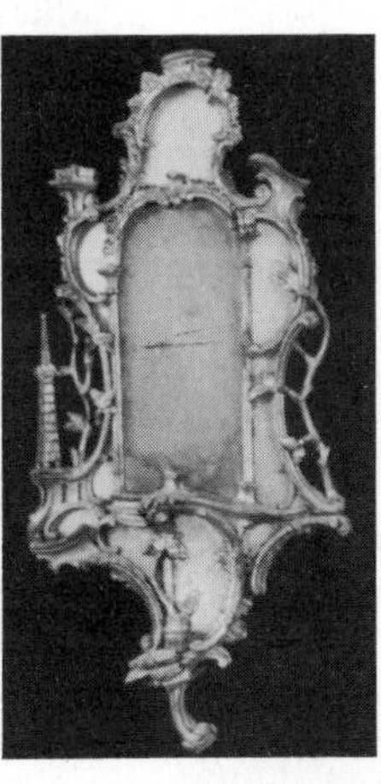

A Victorian giltwood and composition girandole, the central plate re-backed, restored, 23in (122 by 59cm).
$1,200-1,800

A pair of Regency style giltwood, composition and grey painted pier glasses, each with plate in a moulded frame between beaded uprights and below a swagged frieze and pierced cresting, centred by a gadrooned urn amidst scrolling foliage, the pierced conforming apron centred by a flowerhead, one inscribed on backing paper 'New Glass Ap 30 1891', some damage, late 19thC, 75 by 18½in (191 by 47cm).
$2,250-3,000

Did you know?
MILLER'S Antiques Price Guide builds up year by year to form the most comprehensive photo reference library available.

A Queen Anne pier glass, the 2 bevelled glass plates within a parcel gilt walnut moulded cross grain frame, with shaped arched top, 56½ by 25in (143 by 64cm).
$5,250-7,500

A walnut overmantel, late 19thC, 76½in (194cm) wide.
$1,050-1,350

A Victorian mahogany shaving mirror, the adjustable plate in a moulded frame on a telescopic action stem, the circular moulded centre section with double hinged compartments, on a turned fluted stem and moulded tripod base, with scrolled feet, c1860, 54in (137cm) high.
$2,250-3,000

Purchased from A. & S.G. Quantrell, 203 Wardour Street, London.

A mahogany swing dressing table mirror, with 3 drawers in base, 37in (94cm).
$375-525

A carved and painted dressing table mirror, c1900, 27 by 20in (69 by 51cm). **$150-225**

An Irish mirror, with blue, white and gilt glass surround, 23 by 15in (59 by 38cm).
$9,000-12,000

A rococo style overmantel mirror, the moulded gilt plaster frame with scrollwork, flowers, galleries and brackets supporting various putti, 19thC, 49 by 59in (124.5 by 149.5cm).
$2,250-3,000

A Italian carved and gilded tabernacle frame, 16thC, 26½ by 24⅜in (68 by 62cm) overall.
$2,250-3,000

An Alpine carved ebonised frame, the eared corners with basketweave moulding, ripple and wave inner and sight edges, 18thC, 69½ by 59in (176 by 150cm) overall.
$1,800-2,700

An Italian carved, gilded and painted tabernacle frame, the entablature with egg-and-dart cornice, painted classical frieze supported on a pair of Corinthian pilasters running to a base decorated with an inscription, 53½ by 39in (136 by 99cm).
$3,000-4,500

A Louis XVI style giltwood pier glass, with beaded and stiff leaf surround, surmounted by pierced ribbon tied and laurel leaf garland cresting flanked by scrolling foliage and paterae, late 19thC, 89 by 40in (226 by 102cm).
$1,500-2,250

gilt brass framed looking glass, he reeded frame applied with wags of fruiting vines and lowers, surmounted by an urn nd classical figures, probably rench, mid-19thC, 39 by 21½in 99 by 55cm). **$1,500-2,250**

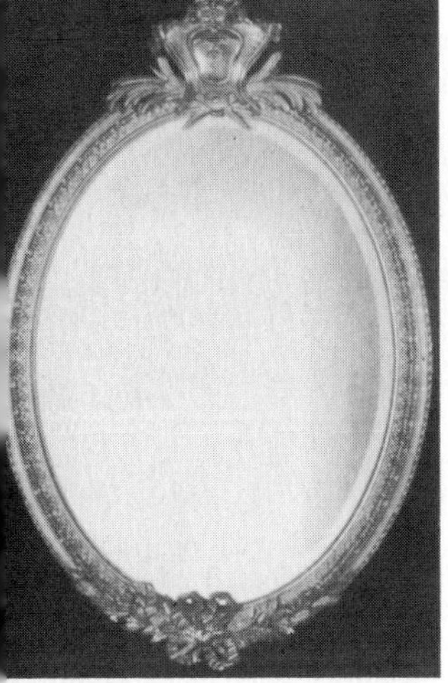

French giltwood mirror, with evelled plate, scroll cartouche resting and pierced ribbon tied pron, late 19thC, 65 by 44in (165 y 112cm).
1,800-2,700

A Dutch carved ebonised frame, with ripple and wave mouldings, 18thC, 26 by 24in (66 by 61cm) overall.
$750-1,200

A giltwood and gesso framed looking glass, surmounted by a palmette, scrolls and rocaille work, the sides similarly carved and with a conforming apron, possibly German, restored, re-gilded, 18thC, 57½ by 32½in (146 by 83cm).
$750-1,200

A Spanish green painted, silver and gilt metal mounted mirror, with arched bevelled plate surmounted by arched cresting flanked by shaped sides, all with pierced rocaille and scrolling foliage in shallow relief, 19thC, 65 by 38in (165 by 97cm).
$3,000-4,500

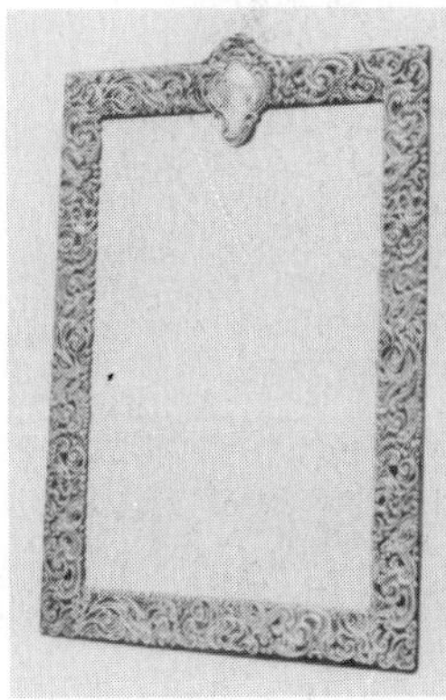

A late Victorian silver framed toilet mirror, with hallmarks for London Goldsmiths & Silversmiths Company, 1899, 22in (56cm).
$1,800-2,700

Screens

A 19thC triptych screen.
$450-600

A bamboo framed firescreen, with hand painted glass panel, 36in (92cm) high.
$50-75

A Victorian three-panel scrap screen, the edges mounted in brass studded leather, 66 by 72in (168 by 183cm).
$600-750

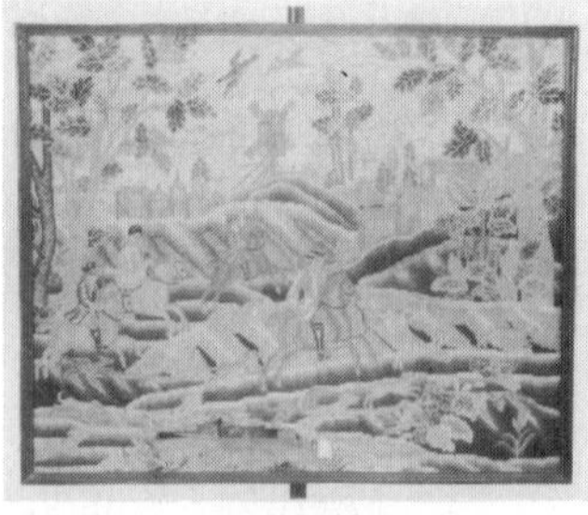

A mahogany pole screen, with baluster stem and leaf carved tripod base, early 18thC gros and petit point panel depicting a hunting scene with trees, hills and a windmill in the background, damaged, 24 by 20in (61 by 51cm). **$1,200-1,800**

A Victorian mahogany pole screen, with a Berlin woolwork floral banner within a shaped and moulded frame, on a turned and fluted column and tripod base with scroll toes.
$225-300

A four-panel leather screen, painted with figures taking refreshment outside an inn, mid-19thC.
$1,200-1,800

Settees

A William and Mary style walnut framed 2 seater settee and matching armchair, with swept and angled cresting rails over dished swept arms on fluted uprights, with pierced scroll strapwork aprons, on swelling ribbed feet, early 20thC, settee 44in (111cm).
$750-1,200

A settle, with a Chippendale style three-chair pierced splat back, shaped scrolling arms with turned supports, solid seat, velvet upholstered cushion, on square section legs, 18thC.
$1,500-2,250

Sofas & Settees

The 18thC sofa and settee were natural evolutions from the settle. There were two main developments: the fully upholstered long seat with carved show wood frame; and the upholstered seat with open-work back and arms designed as two or more joined chair backs.

The alteration or later construction of a chairback settee is usually disguised with carving applied at the joins.

An Irish George II mahogany twin chair back settee, with conforming masks and hairy paw feet, 64in (162.5cm).
$4,800-5,700

A George II walnut settee, on cabriole legs, 48in (122cm).
$2,250-3,000

A William and Mary style small settee, the upholstered back and scrolled arms to a cushioned seat, on turned legs joined by flat waved stretchers, 50in (127cm).
$3,000-4,500

Purchased from J. Martin & Sons, Tubs Hill, Sevenoaks, Kent. Invoice dated 7th February, 1923, 'To supplying a fine and rare old walnut settee with ball turned legs and under stretchers, supplying 7 yds old red silk 21in wide @ 27/6 yd £109.12.6.'

George III camel-back settee, ith outscrolled arms, pholstered and covered in ruby amask, on square supports with lain stretchers, 73½in (186cm). **4,800-5,700**

A George III white painted and parcel gilt sofa, covered in pink and white striped silk, on turned tapering fluted legs headed by lotus leaf and flowerheads, on turned feet, re-decorated, one arm terminal lacking flowerhead. **$3,000-4,500**

George III mahogany chair ack sofa, with needlework seat, n square tapering legs with pade feet, restored, 72in (183cm). **,200-1,800**

A George III mahogany settee, with serpentine back above 4 fielded panels, outscrolled arms centering a serpentine seat, raised on square moulded legs joined by plain stretchers, upholstery missing, late 18thC, 82in (208cm). **$4,500-6,000**

George III hump-back sofa, with scroll arms, on a ahogany frame, with 4 grooved square legs ined by stretchers, on brass barrel casters, 72½in 84cm). **$10,500-13,500**

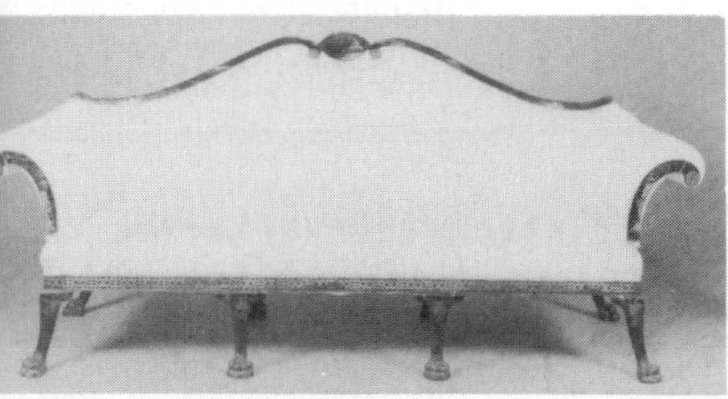

. George III style parcel gilt hinoiserie decorated ebonised ettee, painted with landscapes in ones of gold on a black ground, aised on curved supports ending n paw feet, 87in (221cm). **3,000-4,500**

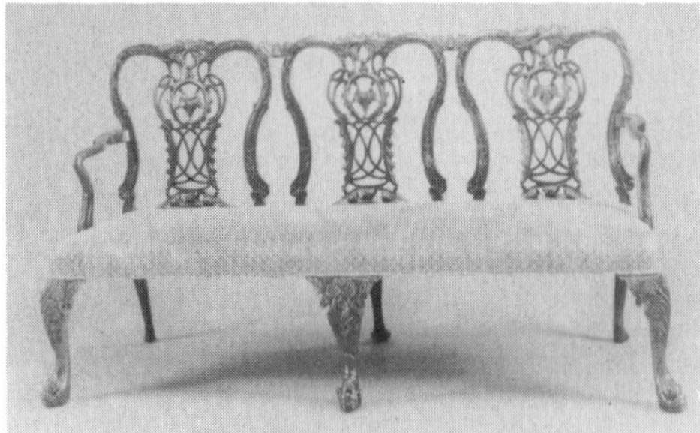

An early George III style mahogany triple chair back settee, carved with foliage and scrolls, the upholstered seat raised on foliate carved cabriole legs ending in stylised dolphin head feet, 69in (175cm).
$4,500-6,000

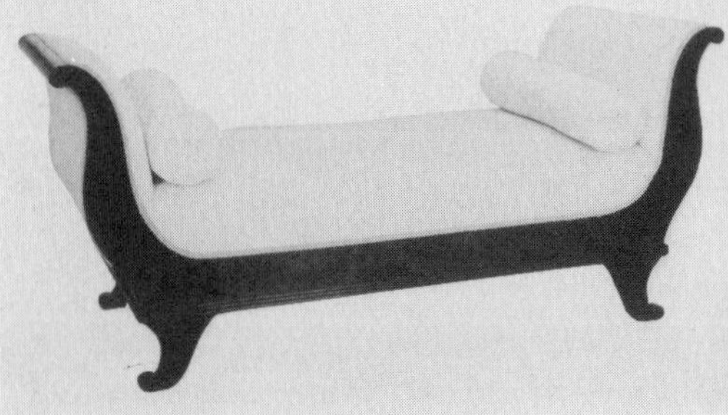

A mahogany framed scroll-end settee, on short scrolled supports with yellow cover, 19thC.
$1,800-2,700

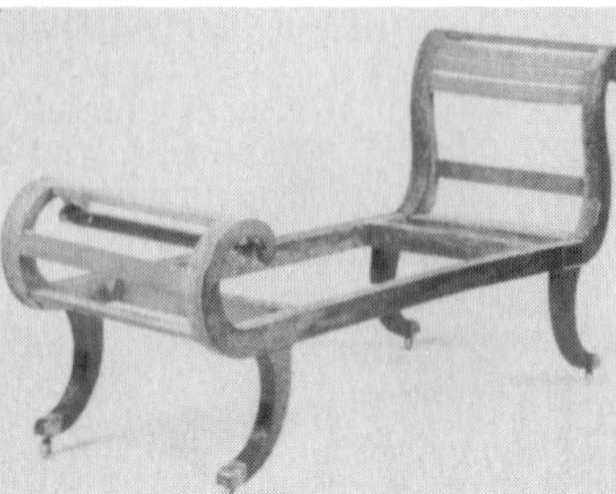

A Regency mahogany chaise longue frame with scroll ends, channelled seat rail and reeded sabre legs, 73in (186cm).
$2,250-3,000

A carved walnut two-seater settee, with fretted and foliate back panels, on turned and reeded supports, 19thC, 46in (116.5cm). **$450-600**

A Regency mahogany sofa, with fluted frame, covered in pale cream and green floral silk, on scroll tapering sabre legs with roundel terminals.
$2,700-3,300

A dark stained walnut hall bench, inset with Italian walnut and marquetry panels, the panels inlaid with engraved bone depicting a hunting scene, with figures in 16thC dress, the shaped cresting inlaid with coat-of-arms, the whole framed with carved leaf and strapwork borders and with carved mythical beast pattern arms, with coat-of-arms to front, 19thC, 63in (160cm).
$3,000-3,750

Condition and Authenticity

- The settee should be in basically good condition. However, certain signs of wear in addition to those on the seat framework are to be expected, and provide confirmation of authenticity.
- There will be a certain amount of shrinkage in the joints and where the ear pieces are applied.
- Prone surfaces and carving will show evidence of wear, especially along the seat rail.
- The carving will vary in tone - some areas will have been handled more or been exposed to more sunlight than other parts.
- Some of the polish may have worn away, possibly even down to the timber - for example, in the centre front leg and along the seat.
- Legs and feet are also vulnerable, especially the front ones. The undersides will show signs of wear difficult to reproduce artificially. Settees with relatively slender legs may show evidence of damage or repairs low down towards the feet.
- Settees of any age will almost certainly have been re-upholstered, preferably with webbing rather than springs.

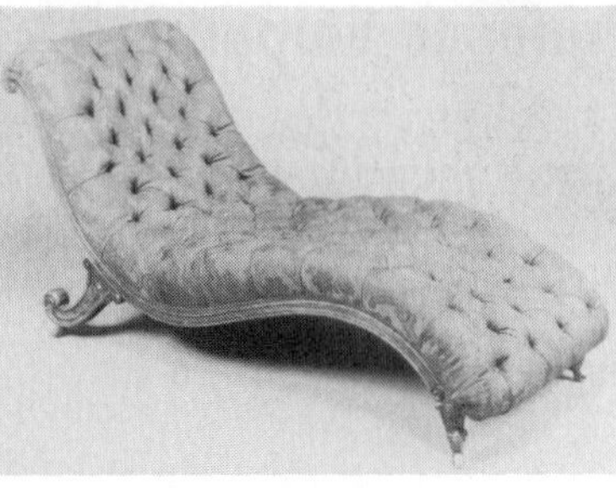

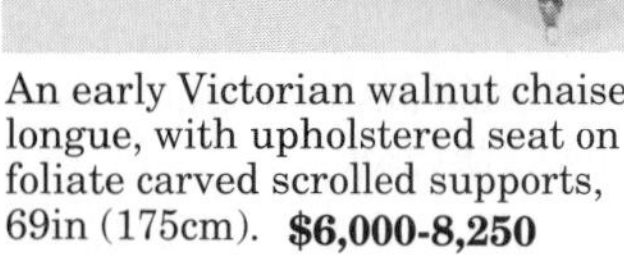

An early Victorian walnut chaise longue, with upholstered seat on foliate carved scrolled supports, 69in (175cm). **$6,000-8,250**

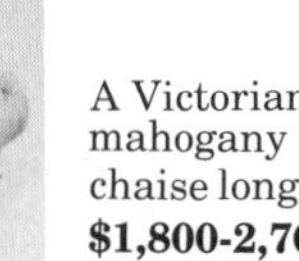

A Victorian mahogany chaise longue.
$1,800-2,700

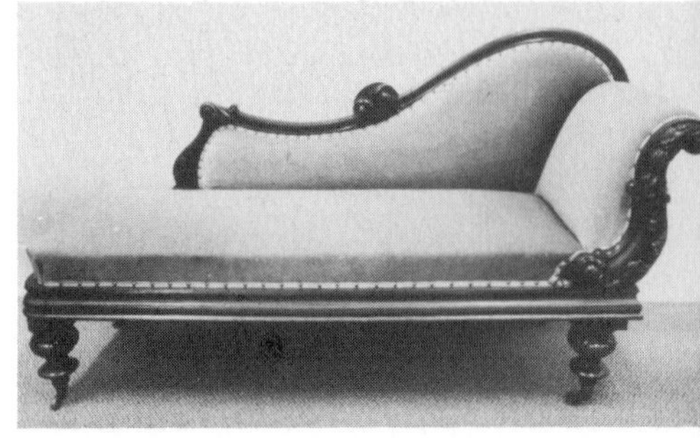

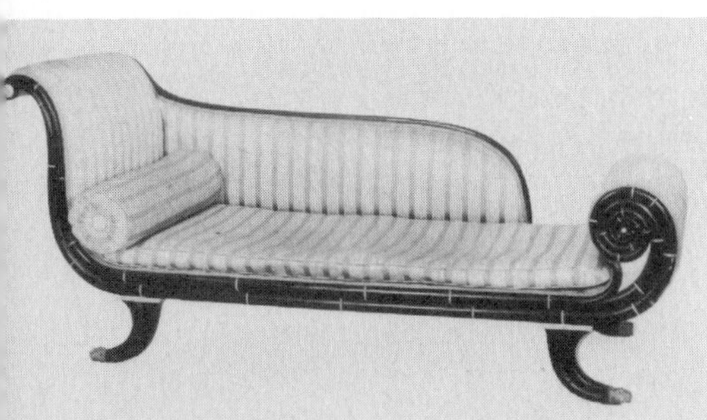

A Regency ebonised chaise ongue, with scrolled end and foot, n sabre supports.
900-1,500

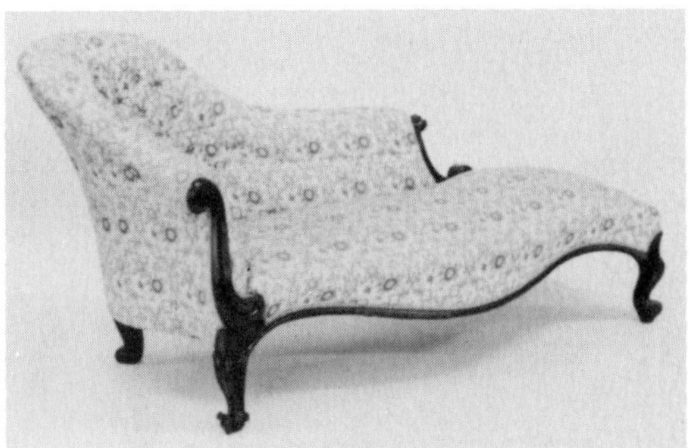

A Victorian mahogany chaise longue, with upholstered and buttoned high corner back, on a serpentine base, with carved cabriole front legs.
$750-1,200

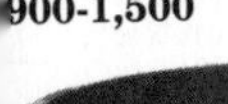

A Biedermeier mahogany framed sofa, with carved leaf scroll ornament, green and gold striped cover, c1830.
$2,700-3,300

A three-piece mahogany show frame drawing room suite, c1920.
$1,200-1,500

A pair of early Victorian giltwood ofas, upholstered in striped lamask, on turned fluted apering legs, 73in (185.5cm).
2,700-3,300

A Victorian mahogany small sofa, with carved and shaped top rail, buttoned back and serpentine upholstered seat, supported on cabriole front legs.
$750-1,200

A mid-Victorian walnut sofa, with oliate carved serpentine back and hair back end, padded serpentine eat, cabriole legs headed with loral carving and terminating in croll feet, 78½in (200cm).
1,200-1,500

A mid-Victorian walnut settee, with twin buttoned chair back ends, central circular padded section within a pierced and scroll carved frame, with serpentine padded seat and cabriole legs, headed with cabochons, replaced back legs, 74½in (190cm).
$1,500-2,250

An Edwardian two-seater settee, with inlaid and carved mahogany frame, open carved back splats, open arms, and padded tapestry upholstered seat. **$375-525**

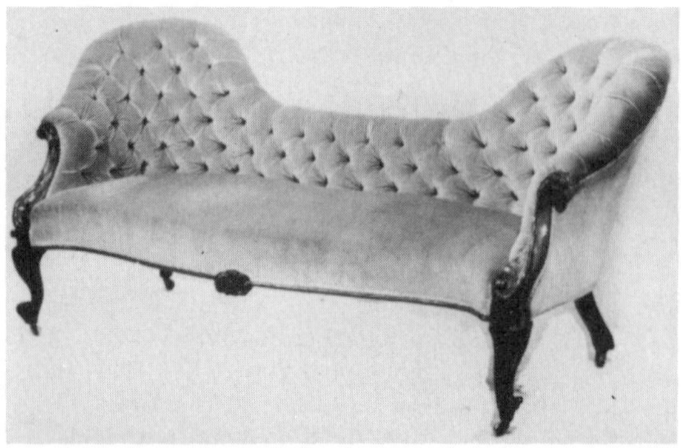

A Victorian rosewood framed sofa, with twin high backs, serpentine front, scroll moulded arms, buttoned back, covered in gold velvet, on cabriole legs with scroll feet and brass casters. **$1,500-2,250**

An early Victorian giltwood settee, covered in crimson floral damask, the arms in the form of profusely scrolling acanthus above a waved shaped foliate carved frieze, on short cabriole legs and scrolled feet, with hand written label Lowther, front left leg re-supported, 75in (190.5cm). **$4,800-5,700**

A pair of mid-Victorian stained beech chaise longues, the padded backs, arms and seats upholstered in pale russet cloth, on ring turned tapering front legs, 66in (167.5cm). **$2,250-3,000**

Miller's is a price GUIDE not a price LIST

A Victorian mahogany chaise longue, with shaped back and single scroll arm, on turned supports and casters. **$750-1,200**

A late Victorian painted satinwood sofa, on square tapering legs with bell flowers, 75in (191cm). **$2,250-3,000**

A walnut twin-back settee, with shaped arm supports, waved apron, drop-in seat upholstered in yellow velvet, on cabriole legs and pad feet, 56in (142cm). **$3,000-4,500**

A Howard sofa, with original upholstery, labelled Lenygon & Morant Ltd, Makers of Howard Chairs and Settees, stamped, 72in (183cm). **$3,000-4,500**

A Chippendale style three-piece mahogany framed lounge suite, with red striped upholstery on a carved frame with surface fretted frieze, carved mask and scroll decoration on cabriole legs with claw-and-ball feet, with Kerridges of Hailsham label. **$1,800-2,700**

A Biedermeier satin ash sofa, with undulating back, scroll ends and padded seat, on outswept legs with scroll feet, headed by rosettes, mid-19thC, possibly Scandinavian, 92in (234cm).
$2,700-3,300

A giltwood alcove sofa, the shaped bowed back with bead-and-reel ornament above bowed padded seat, on stop fluted tapering legs headed by paterae, mid-19thC, possibly French or Italian, 80in (203cm). **$1,800-2,700**

An Edwardian mahogany frame bone inlaid upholstered saloon settee, the elaborate shaped back with fan design splats, shaped arm rails and raised on cabriole.
$1,050-1,350

A two-seater settee, with upholstered back and wings, straight arms and loose cushioned seat, covered all over in crimson silk velvet.
$1,800-2,700

Sideboards

A Regency mahogany pedestal sideboard, with dipped backboard, 3 central drawers, each pedestal with 2 drawers and a cupboard, one enclosing adjustable shelves, the other with a shelf and a deep drawer, on short sabre legs, 95in (241cm). **$4,800-5,700**

A George III style mahogany sideboard and matching pedestals, inlaid throughout with satin birch bandings and stringing, sideboard 72in (183cm).
$3,000-4,500

A George III inlaid mahogany bowfronted sideboard, with tulipwood banded top, on square tapering legs with spade feet, 56in (142cm).
$3,000-4,500

A George III mahogany and inlaid sideboard, on tapered square legs, damaged, 50in (127cm).
$1,800-2,700

A mahogany, satinwood banded, line inlaid sideboard, with three-quarter galleried top above central frieze drawer flanked by deep drawers, on square tapering legs with spade feet, late 19thC, 60in (152cm).
$1,800-2,700

A George III bowfronted mahogany sideboard, with 2 cellaret drawers and a cutlery drawer, on 6 tapering supports with later flower inlay, 60in (152cm).
$3,000-4,500

A Victorian mahogany breakfront buffet, the moulded top above panelled frieze with central bowed drawer, with 2 open shelves beneath, raised on 6 square tapered spade legs, 57in (144.5cm).
$375-450

In the Furniture section if there is only one measurement it usually refers to the width of the piece.

A George III mahogany sideboard, the top with harewood crossbanding and fluted edge, on square tapering legs with block feet, restored, 58in (147cm).
$3,000-4,500

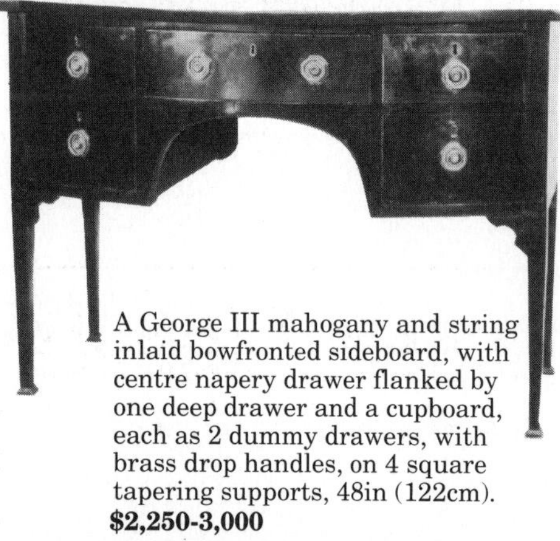

A George III mahogany and string inlaid bowfronted sideboard, with centre napery drawer flanked by one deep drawer and a cupboard, each as 2 dummy drawers, with brass drop handles, on 4 square tapering supports, 48in (122cm).
$2,250-3,000

A late Georgian mahogany breakfront sideboard, with 5 drawers, all with ebony and boxwood stringing, brass oval handles and pierced backplates, on tapering square supports, 53½in (135cm). **$2,700-3,300**

A late Georgian mahogany sideboard, with a cellaret drawer to the right and a cupboard to the left, inlaid with ebony stringing, all with a lion mask ring handles, standing on turned tapered legs, 60in (152cm).
$3,000-3,750

An Edwardian mahogany pedestal sideboard, in the Georgian style, the centre section with a napery drawer, white metal back rail, flanked by 2 pedestals each with frieze drawers and panelled cupboards, one with a cellaret, carved with scrolling foliage and shells, supported on ogee bracket feet carved with formal foliage, 96in (244cm).
$2,250-3,000

A George IV mahogany and ebonised sideboard, the inverted breakfront top with mirrored back, the frieze with 4 variously sized mahogany lined drawers inlaid with anthemia and scrolls, on ring turned tapering feet, some alteration, 81in (205.5cm).

$2,250-3,000

A Victorian breakfront mahogany sideboard, the raised panelled back fitted with an open shelf with pierced scrolling bracket supports, 3 short drawers to the frieze with lobed knob handles and 3 fielded panelled doors under, raised on bun feet, 66in (167.5cm).
$2,250-3,000

A William IV mahogany sideboard, 99in (251.5cm).
$15,000-22,500

ˌn early Victorian mahogany ıiniature sideboard, the mirrored ack with scroll carved cresting nd turned pilasters, above 3 :ieze drawers, sliding trays and ɜllaret drawers enclosed by 2 anelled doors, on plinth base, 2in (55.5cm).
750-900

An Edwardian inlaid mahogany sideboard, stamped Gillows.
$3,000-4,500

ˌ Regency mahogany bowfront ideboard, with reeded top above entral frieze drawer and arched pron flanked by a drawer, ıpboard and a deep drawer, all ʼith geometric mouldings, on ing-turned baluster legs, 72in 183cm).
2,700-3,300

ˌ Victorian mahogany sideboard, the ledge back bove top with cushion frieze drawer, on breakfront ase with raised and fluted panelled doors.
1,200-1,500

Stands

A George IV mahogany folio stand, with rounded rectangular pierced adjustable sides, solid trestle ends and bun feet, 26in (66cm).
$2,700-3,300

A mahogany torchère, on square pedestal base, c1890, 55in (139.5cm) high. **$375-525**

A late Victorian oak Gothic revival lectern, the polygonal an turned shaft with scroll capital, on octagonal base pierced with quatrefoils, on chamfered feet, 54in (137cm) high.
$375-525

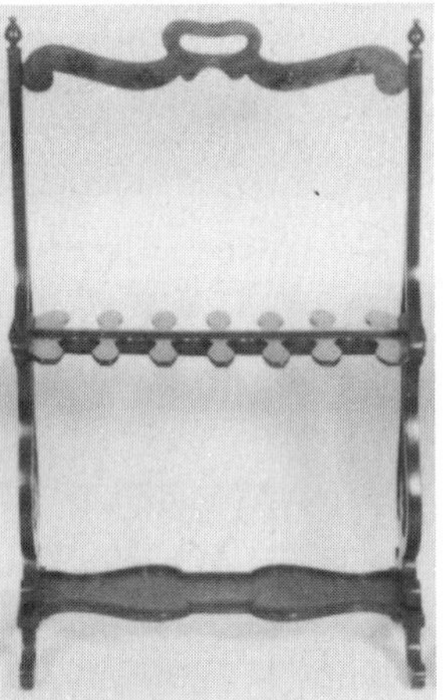

A Georgian mahogany boot stand with lyre ends, with shaped carrying rail and shaped base, raised on 4 scroll feet.
$375-525

A mahogany torchère, on a tripod stand, c1890, 43in (109cm) high.
$300-375

An early Victorian mahogany foli stand, the 2 slatted sides hinged opening to form a table, on chamfered square supports with splayed feet and china casters, 30in (76cm).
$3,000-4,500

Steps

A set of George III mahogany metamorphic library steps, folding into a stool, with padded green leather seat and hinged top opening to reveal a step with square legs, a further slide and hinged step, on square legs joined by stretchers, on brass casters, 39in (100cm) high.
$4,800-5,700

A set of George III mahogany bed-steps, with three-quarter galleried columnar top step above tambour shutter slide, the treads of stamped green leather, the sliding middle step with hinged lid, enclosing a fitted interior, with later removable lid and white porcelain pot, on turned tapering legs, restored, 30½in (77.5cm) high.
$1,800-2,700

A set of George III mahogany metamorphic library steps, folding into a stool, with close nailed padded green leather seat and hinged top opening to reveal a step with club legs and pad feet, a further sliding step and hinged step, the plain sides on square chamfered legs joined by stretchers, restored, some replacement to the step mechanism, 40in (102cm) high, open.
$4,800-5,700

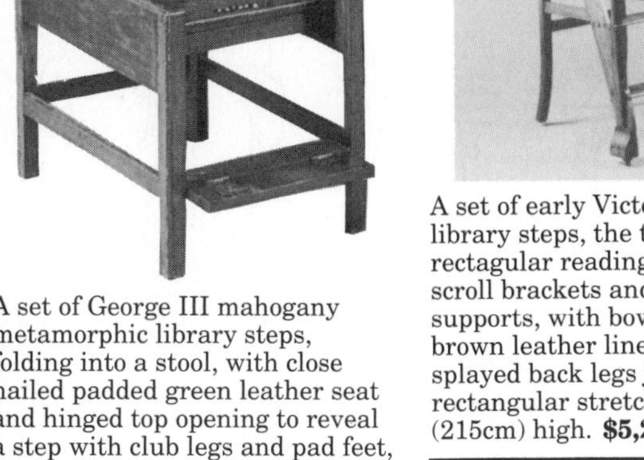

A set of early Victorian mahogany library steps, the top level with rectagular reading surface on S-scroll brackets and turned supports, with bowed handrail, 5 brown leather lined steps, on splayed back legs joined by rectangular stretchers, 84½in (215cm) high. **$5,250-7,500**

A set of Victorian oak Gothic style folding library chair/steps.
$375-525

Stools

A George III mahogany framed window seat, with raised over-scrolled sides, curved upholstered seat, on moulded square tapering legs with spade feet, 50in (127cm).
$1,800-2,700

A William IV mahogany stool, 18½in (47cm) square.
$1,050-1,350

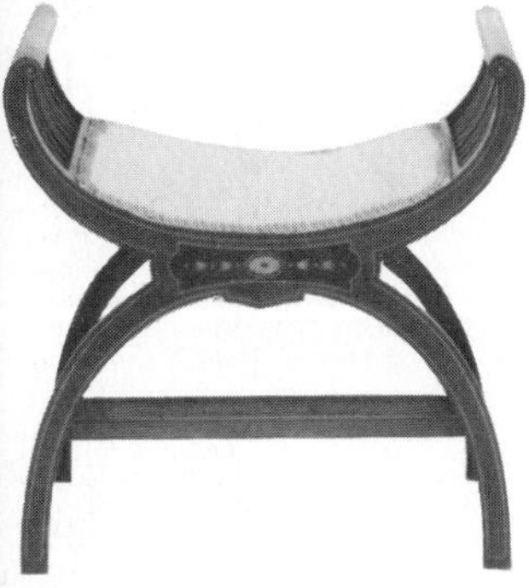

An Edwardian inlaid mahogany dressing stool of X-curvilinear form, with bell flower decoration.
$300-375

A late Regency/early Victorian giltwood curule stool, in the manner of Thomas Hope, the arm supports carved in the form of birds' heads, joined to a downward curved base by a turned stretcher and leaf carved clasps, ending in animal paw feet, minor losses to gilding, 26in (66cm).
$1,800-2,700

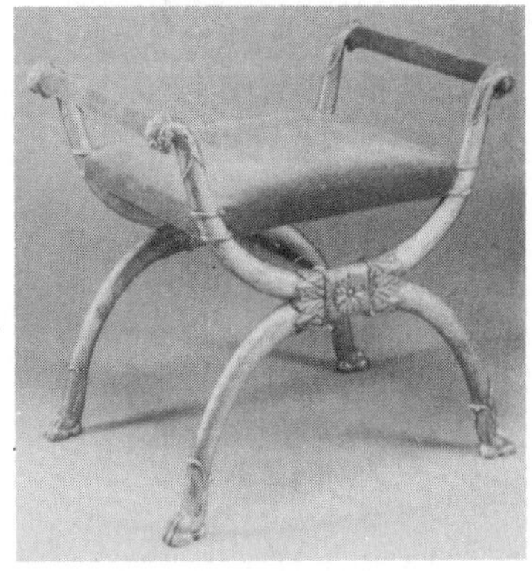

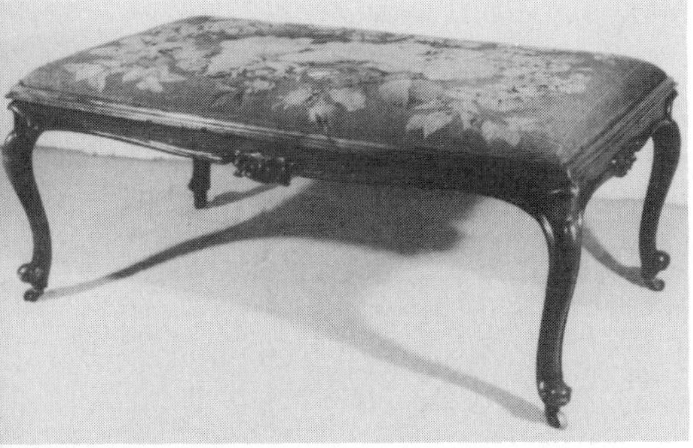

A Victorian rosewood stool, with polychrome floral woolwork top, carved scroll and flower decorated seat rail, on cabriole supports with scrolled feet and casters, 48in (122cm).
$2,700-3,300

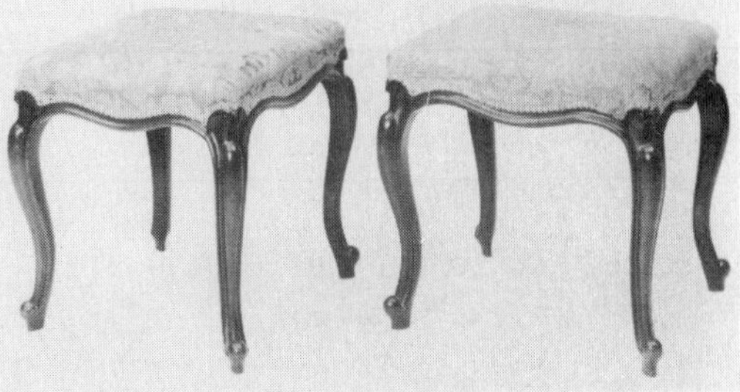

A pair of Victorian stools, with stuffed over seats, serpentine frames and cabriole legs, 19in (48cm). **$1,800-2,700**

LEGS AND FEET

Legs

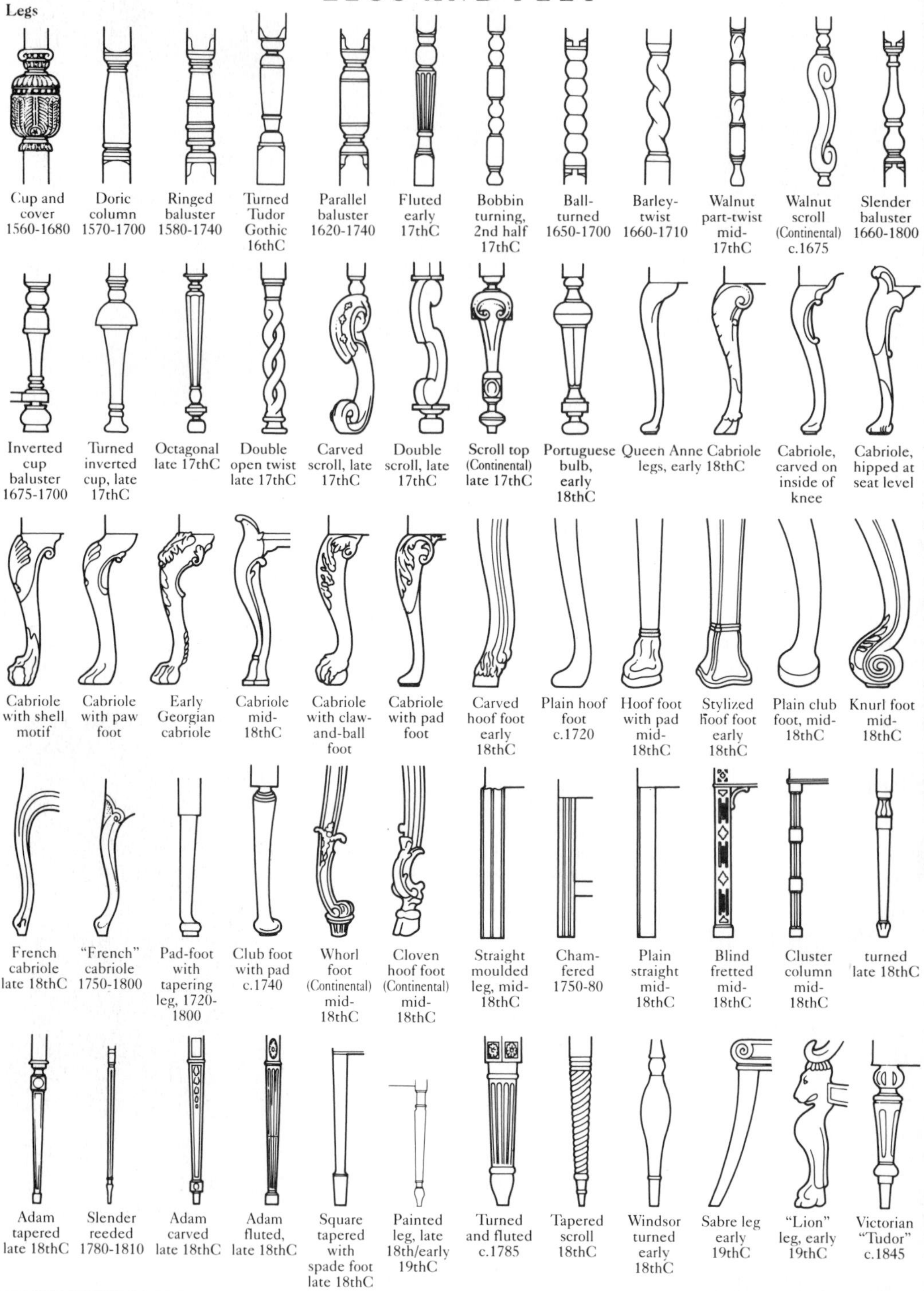

Cup and cover 1560-1680

Doric column 1570-1700

Ringed baluster 1580-1740

Turned Tudor Gothic 16thC

Parallel baluster 1620-1740

Fluted early 17thC

Bobbin turning, 2nd half 17thC

Ball-turned 1650-1700

Barley-twist 1660-1710

Walnut part-twist mid-17thC

Walnut scroll (Continental) c.1675

Slender baluster 1660-1800

Inverted cup baluster 1675-1700

Turned inverted cup, late 17thC

Octagonal late 17thC

Double open twist late 17thC

Carved scroll, late 17thC

Double scroll, late 17thC

Scroll top (Continental) late 17thC

Portuguese bulb, early 18thC

Queen Anne Cabriole legs, early 18thC

Cabriole, carved on inside of knee

Cabriole, hipped at seat level

Cabriole with shell motif

Cabriole with paw foot

Early Georgian cabriole

Cabriole mid-18thC

Cabriole with claw-and-ball foot

Cabriole with pad foot

Carved hoof foot early 18thC

Plain hoof foot c.1720

Hoof foot with pad mid-18thC

Stylized hoof foot early 18thC

Plain club foot, mid-18thC

Knurl foot mid-18thC

French cabriole late 18thC

"French" cabriole 1750-1800

Pad-foot with tapering leg, 1720-1800

Club foot with pad c.1740

Whorl foot (Continental) mid-18thC

Cloven hoof foot (Continental) mid-18thC

Straight moulded leg, mid-18thC

Cham-fered 1750-80

Plain straight mid-18thC

Blind fretted mid-18thC

Cluster column mid-18thC

turned late 18thC

Adam tapered late 18thC

Slender reeded 1780-1810

Adam carved late 18thC

Adam fluted, late 18thC

Square tapered with spade foot late 18thC

Painted leg, late 18th/early 19thC

Turned and fluted c.1785

Tapered scroll 18thC

Windsor turned early 18thC

Sabre leg early 19thC

"Lion" leg, early 19thC

Victorian "Tudor" c.1845

Bracket feet, bun feet and casters

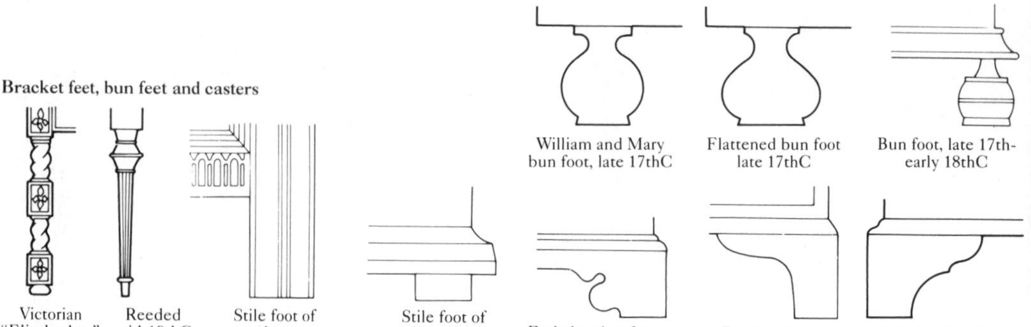

William and Mary bun foot, late 17thC

Flattened bun foot late 17thC

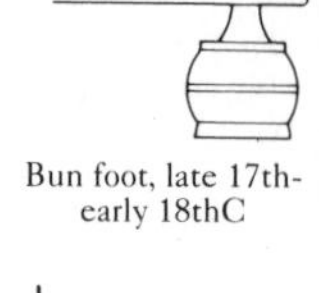

Bun foot, late 17th-early 18thC

Victorian "Elizabethan" mid-19thC

Reeded mid-19thC

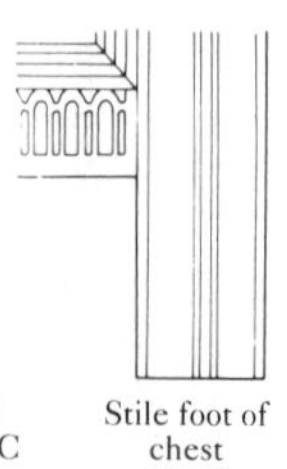

Stile foot of chest 17thC

Stile foot of coffer, 17th & 18thC

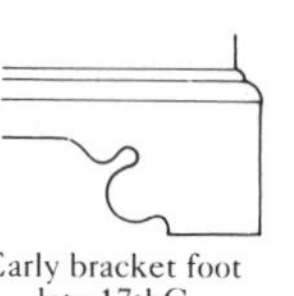

Early bracket foot late 17thC

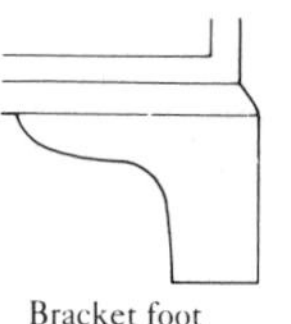

Bracket foot early 18thC

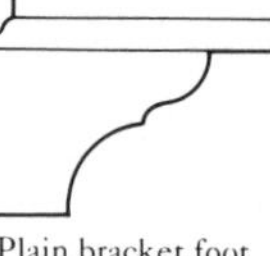

Plain bracket foot c.1725-80

Architects and Artists Tables

A George III mahogany architect's table, the hinged top with later reading support above a drawer with green baize lined writing surface including a hinged slope, on part columned canted square legs, 45in (114.5cm).
$5,250-6,000

A late George III mahogany artist's table, fitted with an adjustable leather inset slope, a lidded compartment and recesses above a frieze drawer and a slide to each side, on a plain turned column and 3 reeded splayed legs with brass terminals, the hinged top detached and of a later date, 28in (71cm).
$900-1,500

A William IV mahogany artist's table, the lifting top with hinged adjustable mechanism above 2 fitted frieze drawers on standard ends, with lappeted ornament on dual supports with bun feet joined by a turned stretcher, 24in (61cm).
$1,500-2,250

A George III mahogany architect's table, fitted with a baize lined writing slide, enclosing various compartments, on moulded square supports, centred by ring turned columns, ending in blocks, the sides fitted with circular candle holders, 36in (92cm).
$3,000-4,500

A George III mahogany artist's table, fitted with a central frieze drawer flanked by 4 short drawers, above a moulded band and a long shallow drawer, on straight moulded legs, 38in (97cm). **$750-1,200**

Did you know?
MILLER'S Antiques Price Guide builds up year by year to form the most comprehensive photo reference library available.

Breakfast Tables

A mahogany tilt-top tripod breakfast table, early 19thC.
$900-1,500

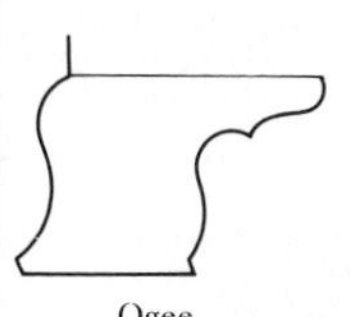

Ogee bracket foot mid-18thC

Splayed bracket foot late 18thC

Slender turned leg early 19thC

Late Regency gilt metal caster

1730-1800

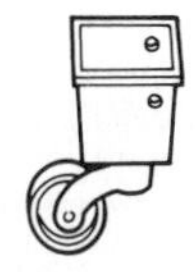

2nd half 18thC

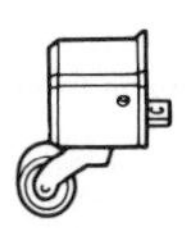

Late 18thC/early 19thC

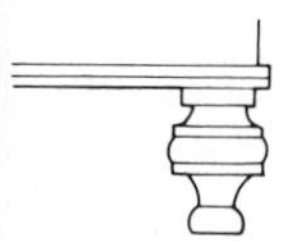

19thC-style bun foot

Leather wheel caster c.1750

Square cup caster c.1760

Tapered cup caster c.1785

Simple brass caster late 18thC

Late 18thC/early 19thC

1780-1820

1790-1830

Lion's paw 1790-1830

A mahogany breakfast table, with crossbanded top and turned column, reeded downswept legs, possibly associated alterations, early 19thC, 59½in (151cm).
$1,200-1,800

A Regency mahogany breakfast table, with ring turned shaft and splayed quadripartite base, adapted and possibly associated, 64in (162.5cm).
$4,800-5,700

A Regency mahogany breakfast table, with ebonised stringing to the crossbanded tip-up top, vase turned stem, on a similarly inlaid claw base with brass casters, 36in (92cm).
$1,050-1,350

A rosewood and brass inlaid breakfast table, with tip-up top, on faceted and baluster turned shaft with trefoil platform and gilt paw feet, the top early 19thC, 41½in (105.5cm) diam.
$2,700-3,300

A Regency mahogany drop-leaf breakfast table, with turned and reeded stem, on 4 splayed legs with leaf cast brass caps and casters, 49in (124.5cm).
$750-1,200

An early Victorian plum pudding mahogany breakfast table, with tip-up top, on lotus leaf carved shaft and gadrooned trefoil platform with scroll feet, 52in (132cm) diam.
$2,700-3,300

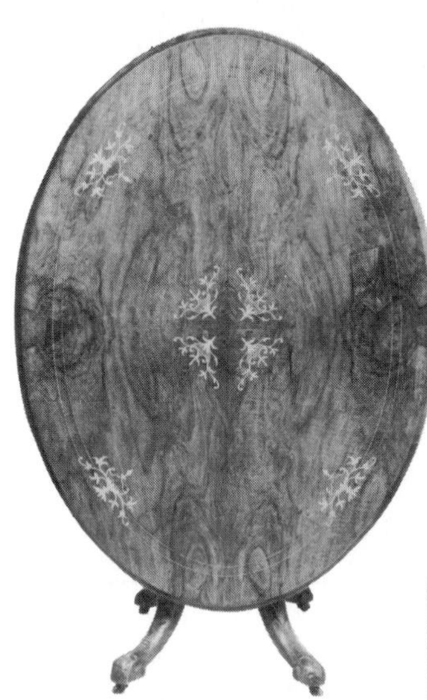

A Victorian walnut marquetry inlaid snap top breakfast table, on carved quadruple scrolling supports.
$600-750

A Regency rosewood breakfast table, with crossbanded top above beaded panelled frieze on octagonal waisted shaft, hipped downswept quadtripartite base and oak leaf cast caps, 47½in (120.5cm) diam.
$3,000-4,500

A Regency mahogany breakfast table, with reeded tip-up top, on turned column and quadripartite base with reeded splayed legs, formerly rectangular, 61in (155cm).
$1,800-2,700

A mid-Victorian burr walnut and marquetry breakfast table, with central floral bouquet and outer border of C-scroll and floral sprays, on hexagonal column and foliate carved splayed legs with scroll feet, 53½in (136cm) diam.
$4,800-5,700

A William IV mahogany breakfast table, with banded tip-up top and faceted shaft, on trefoil platform with paw feet, 49in (124.5cm).
$3,000-3,750

A George IV rosewood breakfast table, supported by C-scrolls and carved with foliage, on a triform plinth, 48in (122cm) diam.
$1,800-2,700

A William IV rosewood breakfast table, supported on a panelled and fluted column with triangular base and curving feet, 48in (122cm) diam.
$1,500-2,250

A Regency mahogany tilt-top breakfast table, on turned shaped column and quadruple splay support with brass claw terminals, 50in (127cm).
$1,500-2,250

An early Victorian rosewood breakfast table, with crossbanded top, octagonal column and concave sided platform base with turned feet, 48in (122cm) diam.
$750-1,200

Card Tables

A Queen Anne walnut card table, the semi circular cross and feather banded top lined with petit point needlework, the frieze fitted with a short drawer and 2 candleslides, on cabriole legs with pointed pad feet, restored, 24in (61cm).
$5,250-7,500

Card Tables

The earliest type of card or games table was introduced at the end of the 17thC, and was usually oak or walnut veneered, with a half round folding top and turned tapering legs united by flat stretchers. One or both of the back legs swung out to support the top.

In the early 18thC the cabriole leg was introduced, and from this date the design remained basically the same.

Pedestal versions were made during the Regency and Victorian periods.

A popular 18thC American type had a serpentine top and 5 legs, one of which swung round to support the top.

A George II mahogany fold-over concertina action card table, with green baize lining and inset token recesses, supported on circular legs with carved acanthus knees and matching pad feet, 32in (81cm). **$2,250-3,000**

An early George II walnut fold-over top card table, with rounded corners, the baize lined interior with corner candle stands and counter wells, frieze drawer, cabriole legs and pad feet, 32in (81cm).
$3,000-3,750

An early Georgian burr walnut card table, the crossbanded top enclosing counter wells with concertina action, cabriole legs headed by scallop shells and foliage, on claw-and-ball feet, restored, back legs possibly replaced, 33in (84.5cm).
$3,000-4,500

A George II red walnut card table, with a semi-circular top and a well to the panelled frieze, on cabriole legs with pointed pad feet, 33in (84cm).
$1,500-2,250

An early George III mahogany triple top tea/card table, the card section with dished counter wells, enclosing a well to the frieze, the thick back rail carved for a pen depression and ink receivers, on turned legs with pad feet, 33in (84cm).
$2,250-3,000

A George III mahogany card table, the top with a ribbon bound floret carved moulding, the concertina underframe with moulded square legs, 35½in (90cm). **$1,200-1,500**

A George III mahogany serpentine fronted card table, the lined and crossbanded folding top with a moulded edge, crossbanded apron, square tapering moulded legs headed by marquetry oval fans, 33in (84cm).
$2,250-3,000

A George III mahogany card table, inlaid overall with ebony lines, on square tapering legs, with block spade feet, ink inscription to the reverse Am/imn/0101, with typed label M. Blount 1964, 36in (92cm).
$1,800-2,700

A George III mahogany card table, with boxwood stringing throughout, the divided hinged rectangular top with satinwood ovals and crossbanding, a frieze drawer below, on tapering square legs with brass casters, 18½in (47cm). **$3,000-4,500**

A George III rosewood and satinwood crossbanded semi-circular card table, the hinged top opening to reveal the green baize lining, on square tapering legs, 36in (92cm). **$2,250-3,000**

A Victorian walnut folding swivel card table, with green baize lining, on turned columns with matching centre support, carved shaped legs with original white porcelain casters, 36in (92cm).
$1,500-2,250

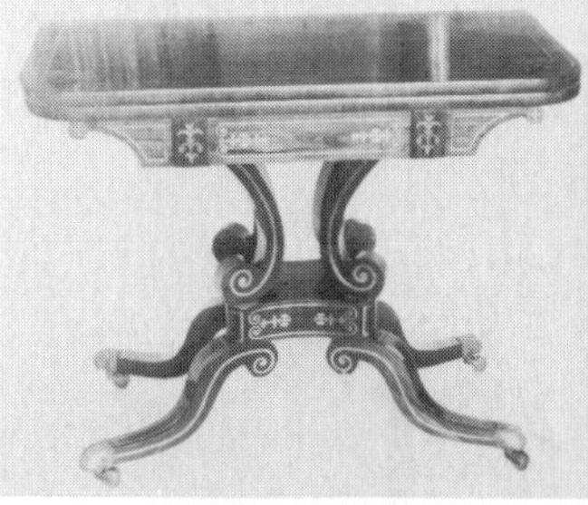

A Regency rosewood and cut brass decorative inlaid card table, 36in (92cm). **$1,800-2,700**

A Regency rosewood card table, the canted hinged green baize lined top crossbanded in satinwood, on associated turned twin baluster shaft and concave sided canted platform base, downswept legs and brass paw caps, 36in (92cm).
$1,500-2,250

A Regency mahogany fold-over card table. **$2,250-3,000**

An early Victorian rosewood card table, the veneered swivel top with a moulded edge, on casters.
$750-1,200

A Victorian fold-over serpentine shaped card table, on reeded vase column.
$1,200-1,500

A Regency simulated rosewood D-shaped card table, with banded top and baluster turned shaft with gilt collar, on splayed legs, 42in (107cm).
$1,500-2,250

A Victorian inlaid walnut card table, the hinged top raised on columnar end supports with carved splayed legs, 35½in (91cm).
$1,200-1,800

A Victorian walnut card table, by Johnstone & Jeanes, 67 New Bond Street, London, the fold-over swivel top with foliate inlaid spandrels and box stringing, with shallow moulded edge, opening to reveal a green baize playing surface, underside stamped with maker's name, 37in (94cm).
$1,500-2,250

A Victorian rosewood folding card table, with moulded edge serpentine fronted swivel top, shaped leaf and scroll decorated frieze, on tapering square column support, concave sided platform base with scrolled feet and brass casters, 36in (92cm).
$1,200-1,800

A Regency rosewood card table, with hinged swivel top, reeded panelled and roundel decorated frieze, on U-shaped support, the base and down swept legs applied with roundels, 36in (92cm).
$1,050-1,350

A Victorian burr walnut veneered card table, with fold-over top, conforming frieze, leaf carved vase-shaped stem, on splayed legs carved with fruit and flowers, ending in foliate scroll toes with casters, 40½in (102cm).
$1,500-2,250

An Italian rosewood and marquetry demi-lune card table, the top with oval panel of figures with a swing, within a ribbon tied trailing floral surround, above geometrically inlaid frieze, on square tapering legs, the top cracked, lacks baize, early 19thC, 36in (92cm).
$2,250-3,000

An Edwardian mahogany envelope card table, on 4 cabriole legs with carved shoulders, small under tier and casters, 21in (53cm).
$750-900

Centre Tables

George IV rosewood centre able, with a reeded rim, on fluted olumn support with acanthus anding, on concave triangular latform base with grooved knob erminals, on fluted bun feet, 51in 130cm) diam. **$2,700-3,300**

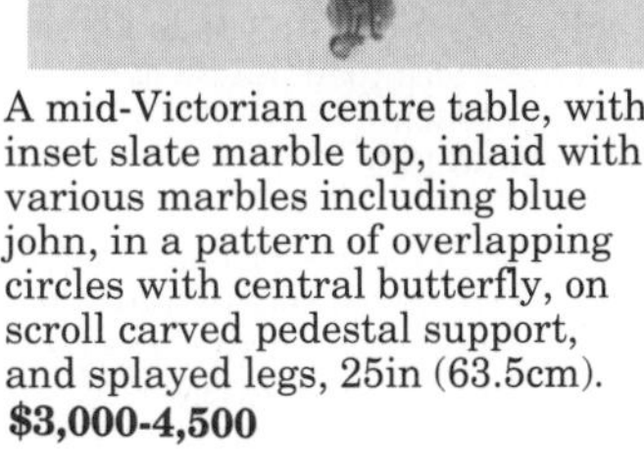

A mid-Victorian centre table, with inset slate marble top, inlaid with various marbles including blue john, in a pattern of overlapping circles with central butterfly, on scroll carved pedestal support, and splayed legs, 25in (63.5cm). **$3,000-4,500**

A George IV mahogany centre table, with wide crossbanding to the tip-up top, ring turned stem, on hipped reeded splayed legs with brass caps and casters, 49½in (125cm) diam. **$4,800-5,700**

A French mahogany and kingwood gilt metal mounted centre table, with rosewood banded top, cabriole legs headed with foliate mounts terminating in sabots, 36in (92cm) diam. **$3,000-3,750**

An Edwardian giltwood and painted centre table, the edge broadly crossbanded in rosewood, the giltwood base with a carved acanthus scroll frieze, on turned fluted legs headed by stiff leaves, 56in (142cm). **$5,250-7,500**

William IV rosewood centre table, fitted with 3 hort frieze drawers, the waisted trestle legs on crolled feet, 54in (137cm). **$3,000-3,750**

Victorian burr walnut centre table, the serpentine op on pierced and carved end supports joined by a urned stretcher, c1855, 42in (106cm). **2,250-3,000**

A French ormolu mounted kingwood and marquetry serpentine centre table, with quarter veneered top above waved frieze with central mount, on cabriole legs with gilt clasps and sabots, late 19thC, 27½in (70cm).
$1,050-1,350

A late Victorian oval marquetry centre table, the radially inlaid top with boxwood and ebony lines and tulipwood bands, with central oval trophy panel, on square tapering legs with spade feet, one drawer stamped Maple & Co., 41in (104cm).
$5,250-6,000

A French rosewood and marquetry serpentine centre table, with brass bordered top and frieze drawer, on cabriole legs with gilt sabots, late 19thC, 39in (99cm).
$1,200-1,500

A Biedermeier fruitwood and parquetry centre table, with inlaid top, on spiral twist shaft and pierced interwoven trellis base with splayed feet, Austrian or German, mid-19thC, 30½in (77cm) diam.
$5,250-6,000

A mahogany centre table, with grey veined white marble top above a concave frieze, on club legs headed by shaped angles with pad feet, 59½in (151cm).
$7,500-9,000

A South German walnut and marquetry centre table, with inlaid top, on tapering baluster supports joined by cross stretchers, 19thC, 59in (150cm). **$2,250-3,000**

Console Tables

A French giltwood console table, in the Louis XVI style, with veined white marble top, 51in (129.5cm) wide. **$2,250-3,000**

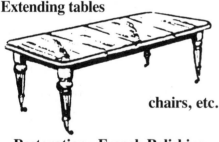

. George II style giltwood console ıble, with associated serpentine ıarblised top and support in the ırm of an eagle perched on ɔckwork, with scroll base, 19thC, 6½in (93cm).
2,250-3,000

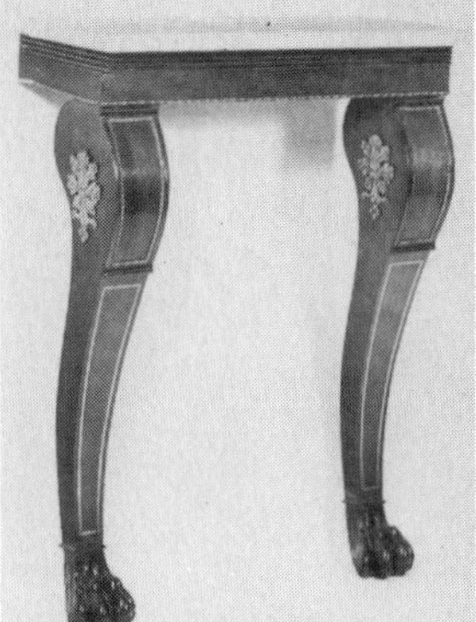

A pair of Regency gilt metal mounted rosewood console tables, with mottled white marble tops and part panelled scrolling monopodia, applied with foliate plaques, adapted, the marble of one cut, 27in (69cm) wide.
$5,250-6,000

A Louis Philippe gilt metal mounted mahogany D-shaped console table, with fossilized marble top and frieze drawer, 58in (147cm) wide.
$1,500-2,250

Miller's is a price GUIDE not a price LIST

)ining Tables

.n early Georgian mahogany 8 eater dining table, with pad feet, 1in by 56in (155 by 142cm) open.
2,250-3,000

. mahogany D-end dining table, with reeded edge to ıe top, herringbone inlaid edge to the frieze, on apering legs with ebonised ring turned details, arly 19thC, 108in (274cm) long.
4,800-5,700

. George III mahogany dining able, with 2 leaves, the edge ıoulded, on moulded square apering legs, 95½in (242.5cm) ɔng. **$4,800-5,700**

A Victorian mahogany telescopic dining table, with 3 additional leaves, supported on 8 turned legs with original casters, 120in (304.5cm) long.
$2,250-3,000

A George III mahogany twin pedestal dining table, with 2 D-shaped end sections and 2 leaves, one later, on turned baluster extra supports and splayed channelled legs with brass caps, with casters stamped with a crown B S & P patent, restorations, 2 later supporting bars, with remains of printed label Hampton & Sons Ltd/Depository, the top cut down, 99in (252cm) long extended.
$10,500-12,000

A George III mahogany dining table, with simi-circular ends and 2 leaves, on reeded square tapering legs, 93½in (237) long.
$3,000-3,750

A George IV mahogany dining table, with D-shaped pedestal ends, each on 3 sabre shape leaf capped supports, the centre portion with one hinged flap and one extra leaf, on 6 turned supports, 126in (320cm) long.
$4,800-5,700

A George III mahogany D-end dining table, with a rectangular centre section and 2 extra leaves, the top and frieze inlaid with stringing, raised on 12 square tapering supports, ending in brass casters, 111in (282cm) extended.
$3,000-3,750

A paper note attached beneath advises that 'this table was purchased from the Knatchbull-Hugheson Estate of Buckland Dinham, Somerset'.

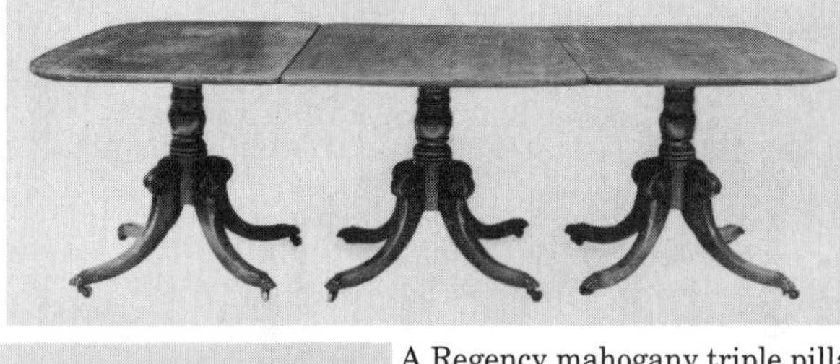

A Regency mahogany triple pillar dining table, with 2 additional leaves and steel shoes, 136in (344cm) long extended.
$12,000-15,000

A Victorian rosewood tip-up circular dining table.
$1,800-2,700

A Victorian mahogany extending dining table, the 2 central baluster supports each with 2 splayed scroll carved legs, on china casters, 94in (238cm) diam.
$3,000-3,750

A William IV rosewood tilt top dining table, on tapering column support and platform base with turned feet, 54in (137cm) diam.
$1,500-2,250

A George IV mahogany extending dining table, the frieze with ebonised stringing, on spiral reed legs and casters, c1820, 179in (430cm) long, including 2 extra associated leaves.
$9,000-10,000

. late Georgian mahogany dining able, the underframe with a oncertina action, on turned legs, 98½in (250cm) extended.
3,000-4,500

A Victorian mahogany D-end extending dining table, the oval top with moulded edge, on bulbous, carved and fluted legs with casters, with two extra leaves.
$3,000-4,500

. mahogany extending dining able, the oval top with gadrooned dge, on foliate carved cabriole egs with claw-and-ball feet, with ne extra leaf.
1,050-1,350

A mahogany D-end 4 pillar dining table, the top with moulded edge, baluster turned columns, reeded splay legs, brass terminals and casters, label inscribed Spillman & Co., Furnishers, St.Martins Lane, London WC2, 19thC, 140in (355cm). **$15,000-18,000**

Display Tables

An ebony and brass mounted display table, with glazed top and sides flanked by fluted panels, on turned and fluted tapering legs with casters, 19thC, 33½in (85cm).
$750-900

Dressing Tables

An Edwardian Sheraton revival mahogany dressing table, inlaid with satinwood, 56in (142cm).
$1,050-1,350

A French kingwood dressing table, in Louis XVI style, the hinged top decorated in cube parquetry within a feathered border, the rosewood interior with a mirror and tray, above chevron veneered sides with chased gilt metal mounts, on cabriole legs, 19thC, 22in (56cm).
$1,500-2,250

An Edwardian mahogany display table, the bevelled glazed top hinged with bevelled glazed side panels all round, moulded friezes, 4 tapering legs, 21in (53cm).
$600-750

A George III mahogany dressing table, crossbanded throughout, with under tier, block feet and leather casters.
$4,500-6,000

A Regency mahogany dressing table, the three-quarter galleried top above a mahogany lined panelled frieze drawer, on gadrooned turned tapering legs and toupie feet, with brass caps, 3 printed labels SW DRESSING ROOM, stamped GILLOWS. LANCASTER, repair to gallery, 27in (69cm).
$3,000-4,500
Almost certainly supplied to the 2nd or 3rd Barons Bolton, Bolton Hall, Leyburn, Yorkshire, c1810.

A Louis XVI style mahogany and marquetry dressing table, applie throughout with gilt brass mounts, 26in (66cm).
$1,500-2,250

A Regency mahogany dressin table, with brass handles, standing on tapering legs terminating in brass caps and casters, 42in (106.5cm).
$450-600

Drop Leaf Tables

A mahogany drop leaf table, wit ogee shaped apron, on later cabriole legs headed by acanthus knees, on claw-and-ball feet, restored, part 18thC, 38½in (97cm).
$750-1,200

A George III Irish mahogany dro leaf table, on moulded cabriole supports and scalloped pad feet, 47½in (121cm) extended.
$3,000-4,500

)rum Tables

late George III mahogany and ›ony inlaid drum table, the lined ›p above 4 numbered and 4 false ieze drawers, on a ring turned edestal, with 4 splayed legs, rass caps and casters, 48in 22cm) diam.
7,500-9,000

A drum table, by Maple & Co, the fiddle back mahogany top inlaid with a wide band of figures and signs of the Zodiac entwined with harebells and narrow boxwood and ebony line, crossbanded with satinwood, on 4 splayed legs faced in fiddle back mahogany inlaid with harebells and boxwood line, brass toes and casters, late 19thC, 42in (106.5cm). **$6,000-8,250**

A Regency rosewood and mahogany drum table, the green leather lined top above a frieze of 4 mahogany lined and 4 simulated drawers, on spreading column shaft and fluted downswept legs with hairy paw feet, stamped A. SOLOMON, associated, 41½in (105cm) diam.
$2,250-3,000

Other pieces of Regency and earlier furniture have been recorded with this stamp at the address 59 Great Queen Street. No cabinet maker corresponding to this description can be found in the London directories but an Abraham Solomon was trading in 1839 as a furniture broker. It is assumed that he stamped pieces that passed through his stock. He must be a strong candidate for having married the 2 parts of this table.

;ames Tables

A George II red walnut triple top games table, opening to reveal a tea table, a games table with guinea recesses and covered in snuff coloured suede, and a backgammon table inlaid with contrasting woods, with original backgammon square within the recess of the table, the frieze with a short drawer, on slender cabriole legs with pad feet, 33in (84cm).
$6,000-8,250

A Victorian walnut games and work table, with folding swivel top enclosing chequer and backgammon boards and a cribbage scorer, 20in (51cm) closed.
$1,050-1,350

satinwood games and tea table, ılaid with chequered stringing, ı 4 tapering legs, late 19thC, 3in (92cm). **$2,250-3,000**

An early Victorian ebony and ivory games table, the hinged chamfered moulded top with an ebony border, on spiral twist supports resting on a concave fronted platform base, with acanthus enriched scrolled cabriole feet, 25½in (65cm) square.
$3,000-4,500

Designed in the William IV 'Elizabethan' style with its columnar supports and ebony veneer, the top of this table displays a chessboard with portraits of poets within a border of picturesque landscapes. Such items were manufactured by Anthony Sandoe, Fancy Stationer and Cabinet Maker of Southampton Row, Russell Square in the 1830s.

A George III mahogany games table, inlaid overall with boxwood and ebonised lines, the sliding reversible featherbanded top lined with a chessboard and trellis pattern leather, enclosing a red leather lined interior fitted for backgammon, with one short frieze drawer and one simulated drawer to each side, on square tapering legs headed by later pierced angles, on brass caps, 41in (104cm).
$10,500-13,500

A Victorian burr walnut and inlaid work and games table, with chess, backgammon and cribbage boards. **$1,200-1,800**

A games table, with chequerboard top on black lacquered gilt decorated turned pedestal, tripod feet, 19thC.
$375-525

A Victorian figured walnut veneered games table, for backgammon, draughts and cribbage, with single drawer and sliding compartment, fold-over top with D-ends, turned supports and stretcher, 4 ogee feet with carved shoulders.
$1,200-1,800

Library Tables

A William IV mahogany library table, with green and gilt tooled leather panel, fitted with 2 drawers either end, on 4 reeded legs, 33½in (85cm).
$1,050-1,350

An Empire style mahogany library table, the top inset with gilt tooled maroon leather, draw to side frieze, on cylindrical column supports with gilt brass foliate cast capitals and acanthu sheathed cup feet, tied by a pierced shaped flat cross stretcher, 52in (132cm).
$1,200-1,800

A rosewood library table, with leather lined top, 2 frieze drawe either side and one at each end, brass and ebony inlaid frieze, on square tapering reeded legs, ear 19thC, possibly adapted, 54in (138cm).
$5,250-7,500

The distinctive dovetails of the drawers and the use of pine in th construction point to a possibly Continental origin.

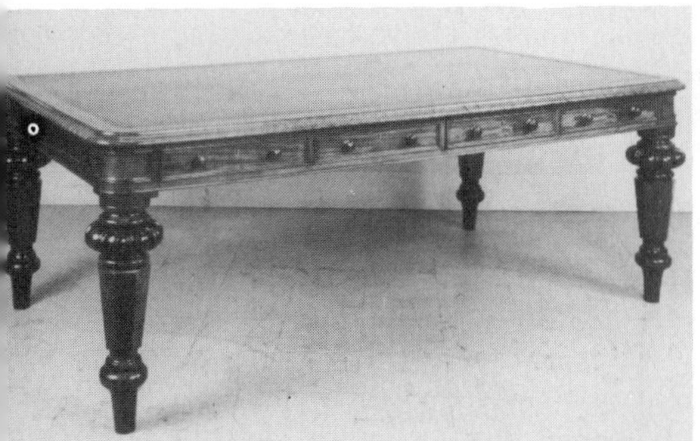

n early Victorian mahogany library table, the top ith a tooled red morocco leather writing surface, oldly moulded edge, 4 drawers on each side with urned handles, turned tapering legs chamfered and ith carved lobes, 96in (244cm).
3,000-4,500

A late Victorian mahogany partners' library table, with leather lined top, 4 frieze drawers, on turned fluted uprights and dual scroll feet joined by a stretcher, 67in (170cm). **$1,800-2,700**

Loo Tables

George IV loo table, the tilt top eneered in figured rosewood, ith a band of brass marquetry nd a gadroon edge, the rosewood eneered triform stem and base laid with brass stringing, on croll feet with casters, 50in 127cm) diam.
5,250-6,000

Nests of Tables

A nest of 4 Regency rosewood tables, with moulded tops, on turned supports joined by a curved stretcher, on trestle feet, mid-19thC, 21in (53cm).
$3,000-4,500

A nest of 4 Sheraton revival mahogany tables, each on 4 bamboo pattern supports with spreading bases, 19thC, 22in (56cm).
$1,050-1,350

Occasional Tables

A George III mahogany occasional able, with tilt-top on a spiral wist stem, 3 cabriole legs on club eet, 18in (46cm).
2,250-3,000

An early Victorian rosewood jardinière table, on baluster stem, tricorn base and 3 turned feet, 15in (38cm) diam.
$1,200-1,500

A Continental walnut occasional table, the end supports with twist detail, on scroll-over feet with twist stretchers 19thC.
$750-1,200

A Louis XV style walnut serpentine occasional table, with pierced and foliate frieze, carved cabriole supports and cross stretcher, 19thC, 38in (97cm).
$375-525

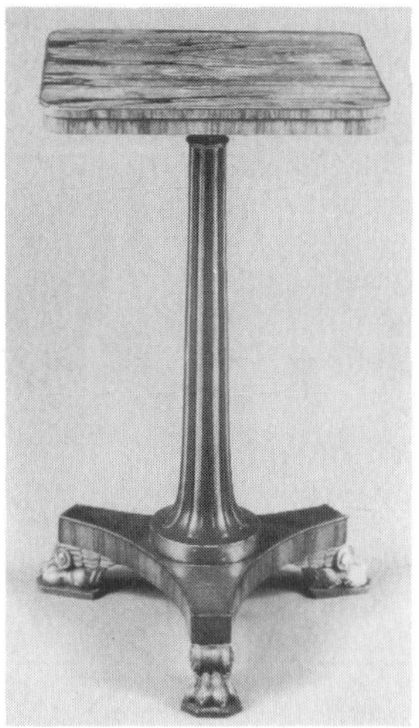

A Regency simulated rosewood and parcel gilt occasional table, with square top, reeded turned column and triform platform base, with scroll and paw feet, 18in (46cm) square.
$3,000-4,500

A rosewood occasional table, early 19thC, 15in (38cm).
$450-600

An Edwardian mahogany occasional table, with satinwoc inlay and carved frieze, c1900, 30in (76cm).
$750-900

An Edwardian inlaid mahogany two-tier occasional table, with detachable oval tray top, on lyre shaped supports with splay legs and scrolling feet, 27in (69cm).
$750-900

A Victorian rosewood occasional table, inlaid and decorated with stylised griffins, bell flowers and leaf tendrils, on reeded turned pillars, gallery platform below inlaid with batwing style paterae motif, 30in (76cm) diam.
$600-750

An Italian walnut occasional table, with inlay of St George an the dragon and geometric motif, on turned pedestal and 3 swept feet, 19thC.
$750-1,200

An Italian black slate and inlaid mosaic table, 19thC.
$10,500-12,000

Pembroke Tables

A late George III mahogany and later painted Pembroke table, with frieze drawer, overall ribbon, floral swag and musical trophy decoration with central cartouche depicting musical trophies in a floral bouquet, on square tapering legs, 42in (107cm) extended.
$3,000-3,750

A George II walnut Pembroke table, with shaped flaps, arche frieze, turned tapering legs an pad feet, c1740, 30in (76cm).
$3,000-4,500

A Regency mahogany and rosewood crossbanded Pembroke table, with corner re-entrant fleur-de-lys, frieze drawer and spiral reeded tapering legs, 42in (107cm) extended.
$1,050-1,350

George III inlaid satinwood and ainted Pembroke table, the top anded with partridgewood and ingwood, centred by a burr yew anel and edged with a painted rolling foliate border, the milarly banded frieze with a rawer, on tapering square legs ith boxwood stringing, some ecoration rubbed, 35in (89cm). **7,500-9,000**

Pembroke Tables

Pembroke tables (precursors of sofa tables) were first seen in England during the Chippendale period, when they were usually mahogany, with carved decoration; tops were either rectangular or of 'butterfly' (serpentine) outline. By the last quarter of the 18thC the oval shape had become very fashionable, and styles were lighter; veneered examples replaced those in the solid, and decoration was inlaid or sometimes painted, rather than carved. Bow-fronted tops were popular during this period. From the early 19thC Pembroke tables became less fashionable and consequently, were not as finely made as those of the 18thC.

A George III later floral painted Pembroke table, with hinged top and frieze drawer, on square tapering legs, restored, 39in (99cm). **$2,250-3,000**

A George III mahogany Pembroke table, 41in (104cm) extended. **$1,050-1,350**

A Regency mahogany and rosewood crossbanded Pembroke table, with a drawer to one end, turned pillar and platform base, with fluted scroll legs and brass claw casters, 38½in (98cm). **$2,700-3,300**

mahogany rosewood crossbanded Pembroke ble, the boxwood lined single frieze drawer ith ebony turned handles, and opposing dummy awer, 4 square tapering legs, brass toes and sters, early 19thC, 40in (102cm). **$1,200-1,500**

mahogany pedestal Pembroke table, 19thC. **450-600**

Serving Tables

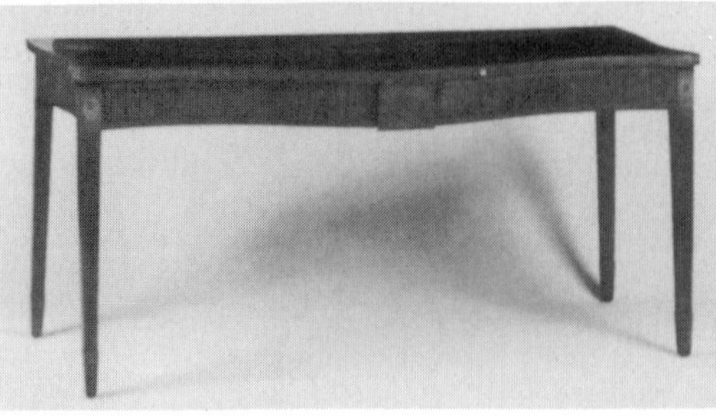

A George III inlaid mahogany serpentine serving table, restored, some inlay possibly later, 79in (201cm).
$3,000-3,750

A late George III mahogany serving table, the elongated D-shaped top with raised channelle back edge above a fluted frieze, o lotus carved gadrooned fluted turned tapering legs with laurel carved tapering feet, previously with superstructure, possibly Irish, small section of frieze moulding missing, 124in (315cm)
$12,000-15,000

A mahogany breakfront serving table, with square moulded tapering legs, 18thC with alterations, probably associated, 73½in (187cm).
$2,250-3,000

Side Tables

An oyster veneered side table, the top set with an oval banded panel, frieze fitted with a drawer, on spiral turned legs joined by flat X-stretchers, on bun feet, restored, part c1695, 38in (97cm).
$3,000-4,500
This table was possibly supplied by J.A. Moore & Co, 17 High Street, East Grinstead. Invoice dated December 9th 1921 '1 Old William & Mary Oyster veneered Table £22.10.0'.

A pair of George III mahogany side tables, with D-shaped tops, the friezes carved with classical urns and ribbon tied swags of berried foliage, on stop fluted square tapering legs, friezes possibly later carved, 46in (117cm). **$3,000-3,750**

A Georgian red walnut fold-over top side table, on slim tapering legs with pad feet, 33in (84cm).
$2,250-3,000

A George III mahogany side table, the frieze drawer with brass handle, shaped apron, on chamfered square legs, 28in (71cm).
$750-900

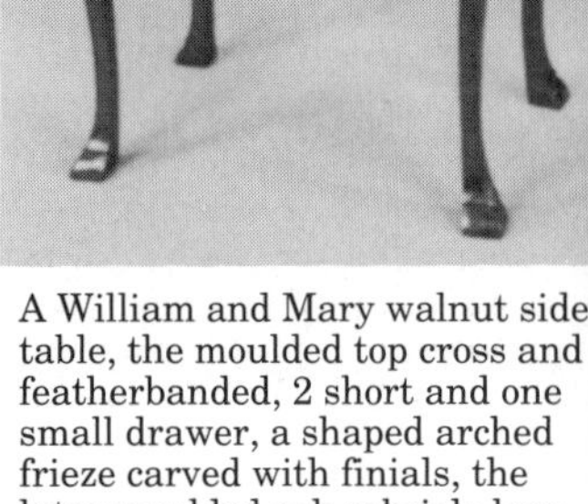

A William and Mary walnut side table, the moulded top cross and featherbanded, 2 short and one small drawer, a shaped arched frieze carved with finials, the later moulded oak cabriole legs with squared feet, c1700, 30in (76cm). **$4,500-6,000**

A George III mahogany side tabl on club legs and pad feet, 31½in (80cm).
$5,250-7,500

A George III mahogany side table, carved with blind fretwork, on square chamfered legs with similar fretwork, pierced brackets and blocked moulded feet, 38½in (98cm). **$5,250-7,500**

George III mahogany 'spider' de table, with frieze drawer, ılumnar legs joined by a turned -shaped stretcher, on turned oreading feet, restorations to retcher, 26½in (68cm).
,200-1,500

related 'spider' table, originally om the collection of Sir William urrell, Hutton Castle, erwickshire, is now at Temple 'ewsam House, Leeds.

A Regency rosewood brass strung octagonal pedestal side table, the top banded in cross grained rosewood, on a flat sided column with triple cabriole brass strung legs and brass paw feet.
$750-1,200

A mahogany serpentine fronted side table, with 2 spring loaded drawers, the carved frieze decorated with urns and swags, flanked by paterae and flutes, on chamfered tapering legs carved with ribbon ties and harebells, 48in (122cm). **$2,700-3,300**

A fiddle mahogany side table, inlaid with swags of flowers, leather top, one frieze drawer, on tapering legs, 19thC.
$1,200-1,500

A Dutch walnut and foliate marquetry side table, inlaid with mother-of-pearl and bone, on square tapered legs joined by a flattened cross stretcher, on bun feet, 18thC and later, 42½in (108cm). **$4,500-6,000**

pair of Sheraton design side tables, inlaid ith satinwood, burr yew and other woods, on apering legs. **$1,200-1,500**

mahogany side table, the associated reeded top bove a stylized foliate moulding, on cabriole legs arved with acanthus and pearl drop knees nd paw feet, reduced in depth, 57½in (146cm).
4,500-6,000

Sofa Tables

A late George III mahogany and later painted sofa table, with rosewood crossbanded top, 59in (150cm) extended.
$3,000-4,500

A George III mahogany and ebony strung sofa table, with 2 drawers on one side, 2 dummy drawers on the other, on trestle end supports and downswept legs in brass caps, 59in (150cm) extended.
$4,500-6,000

Sofa Tables

The sofa table, originally designed to stand behind a sofa, evolved from the Pembroke table in the last quarter of the 18thC, but is narrower and longer. Sofa tables usually have drawers at the front with dummy drawers behind (being too shallow for real drawers on both sides). Late 18thC examples are principally in mahogany or, to a lesser degree, satinwood or more exotic woods. The best examples are veneered, with crossbanding and inlaid stringing. Some Regency examples have fine metal mounts. Sofa tables continued to be made, in smaller numbers, until the mid-19thC, although quality declined somewhat. Victorian and Edwardian examples tend to copy earlier styles. Sofa tables from the Sheraton period are the most sought after.

Stretchers on early 19thC sofa tables are usually turned. A high stretcher is generally preferred to those positioned at the base of the supports. Late 18thC stretchers are plain.

While width is fairly constant, the depth varies somewhat from about 22-30in (56-76cm). The narrower variety usually commands higher prices.

A George III mahogany sofa table, the rounded twin flap top above a frieze with 2 drawers, inlaid with ebonised lines, columnar end supports, on downswept legs, turned feet with brass caps, repairs to 3 legs, 66in (167cm) extended. **$5,250-6,000**

A George IV rosewood and cut brass inlaid sofa table, with a pair of real and opposing dummy frieze drawers, twin turned supports, platform base, on quadruple splayed legs, with embossed brass cappings and casters, brass inlay damaged, c1820, 59in (150cm) extended.
$4,500-6,000

A George III mahogany and rosewood banded sofa table, with 2 drawers to the frieze, inlaid in harewood with geometric designs, the other side with false drawers, on reeded trestle end supports and downswept legs, terminating in brass toes, joined by an arched stretcher, 57in (145cm) extended. **$3,000-3,750**

A Regency mahogany sofa table, with crossbanded twin flap top, 2 frieze drawers, with ribbed angles, solid trestle ends joined by a turned stretcher, with splayed ribbed feet and brass caps, 59½in (150cm).
$4,500-6,000

Sutherland Tables

A Victorian walnut Sutherland table, with shaped flaps, on turned end columns, joined by turned stretcher, on scrolling cabriole legs terminating in brass capped ceramic casters, 36in (92cm).
$1,800-2,700

A Victorian mahogany Sutherland table.
$450-600

'ea Tables

George II mahogany fold-over ›a table, with moulded apron ıoulders and pad feet, 31in '9cm).
1,200-1,800

George III mahogany tea table, n moulded square chamfered ›gs headed by shaped brackets, 5in (64cm).
3,000-4,500

Regency mahogany fold-over op tea table, with reeded edge, ılaid with boxwood lines, on ›obbin turned tapering legs, 36in 92cm).
1,200-1,800

Did you know?
MILLER'S Antiques Price Guide builds up year by year to form the most comprehensive photo reference library available.

A George III mahogany fold-over tea table, the shaped frieze with single drawer and brass handle, on reeded and tapering square legs, 34in (86cm).
$750-1,200

A George III figured mahogany demi-lune fold-over tea table, on square tapered legs, 36in (92cm).
$1,200-1,500

A George II mahogany tea table, with drawer to the side, on lappeted turned tapering legs and pad feet, damaged, 29in (74cm).
$1,050-1,350

A Victorian mahogany fold-over top tea table, with plain frieze, rounded corners, on a heavily carved central column, the quatreform base terminating in scrolling feet, 36in (92cm).
$1,200-1,500

A Regency mahogany fold-over top tea table, in the manner of Gillows, on turned tapering reeded legs, 35in (89cm).
$1,500-2,250

A Regency mahogany fold-over top tea table, on turned and reeded tulip shaped central support with quatreform base terminating in paw feet, 36in (92cm).
$1,800-2,700

A Regency mahogany D-shaped fold-over tea table, on moulded square tapered column, above a quadrafoil base and paw supports, 38in (96cm).
$750-900

A Victorian faded rosewood swivel top tea table, the shaped bowfront above a vase turned column, with elaborate scroll carved quadruple cabriole base, 36in (92cm).
$1,500-2,250

Tripod Tables

An early George III mahogany tripod table, with one piece tip-up top, on baluster stem and down curved tripod base, 39in (99cm) diam.
$900-1,500

A George III mahogany tripod table, on cabriole legs and rounded pad feet, damaged, 34in (86cm) diam.
$1,500-2,250

A mahogany tripod table, with circular piecrust top, bird cage action, baluster shaft with foliat splayed base and pad feet, 29½i (75cm). **$2,700-3,300**

A Regency mahogany tripod table, with baluster shaft and splayed base, with ribbed central band and bun feet, 20½in (52cm).
$2,250-3,000

A mahogany tripod table, with spindle gallery, on associated bird cage support, with baluster shaped acanthus carved stem, on foliate carved cabriole legs and foliate pad feet, the wedge later, 23in (59cm). **$5,250-7,500**

A mahogany tripod table, with spindle galleried top, turned spreading spiral twisted urn-shaped stem on tripod base, with cabriole legs and pointed pad fee the shaft associated, restorations part 18thC, 13in (33cm) diam.
$4,800-5,700

Work Tables

A Louis XVI style satinwood and walnut work table, with pierced brass gallery, parquetry veneered top, frieze drawer with fitted interior, on square tapering legs, 19thC, 20in (51cm).
$4,500-6,000

A mother-of-pearl inlaid ebonised work table, mid-19thC, 23½in (60cm).
$450-600

A George IV maple grained an ebonised work table, the top banded in mahogany, above 3 mahogany lined drawers, 38in (97cm). **$3,000-4,500**

A George III style painted satinwood work table, restored, late 19thC, later decoration, 18in (46cm).
$3,000-3,750

George III mahogany work
ıble, inlaid throughout with
ringing and satinwood banding,
1790, 21in (53cm).
1,500-2,250

A French inlaid rosewood work table, with scrolling foliage on the lift-up top and drawer beneath, on line inlaid legs, c1840.
$2,250-3,000

An Anglo-Indian rosewood work table, the adjustable writing slope with tapering foliate carved well, on scroll uprights and dual feet joined by lotus carved stretcher, mid-19thC, 30in (76cm).
$1,200-1,500

A rosewood and mother-of-pearl work table, possibly German, inlaid throughout, the hinged top revealing a mirror and lidded compartments, c1840, 20½in (52cm).
$1,500-2,250

A Dutch walnut and floral marquetry lady's sewing table, late 18thC, 18in (46cm).
$2,250-3,000

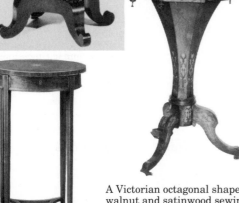

A Victorian octagonal shaped walnut and satinwood sewing table, with lift-up top, on pillar and tripod supports, 17in (43cm).
$1,050-1,350

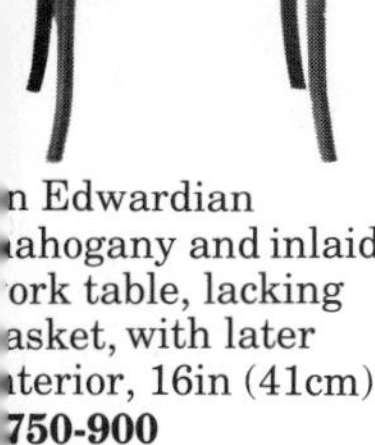

n Edwardian
ıahogany and inlaid
ork table, lacking
asket, with later
ıterior, 16in (41cm).
750-900

Napoleon III ormolu
ıounted red
ɹrtoiseshell boulle
ork table, the flap
ɔp with later
eedlework panel,
croll and shell
ıounts, on cabriole
gs with claw feet,
ßin (41cm).
1,050-1,350

Writing Tables

A Victorian walnut kidney-shaped writing table, with inset top, 2 frieze drawers, on cheval frame with turned stretcher, 48in (122cm). **$2,250-3,000**

A Louis XV style ormolu mounted mahogany and tulipwood bureau plat, the leather lined top with brass border and cabochon corner mounts, a leather lined slide at each end, on cabriole legs with gilt clasps trailing to gilt sabots, 54in (137cm).
$3,000-3,750

A North Italian laburnum rosewood and fruitwood bureau plat, the leather lined top with chevron borders and inlaid dog tooth edge above 2 frieze drawers waved apron, on cabriole legs, with paper label in ink Isabelle Fuller from Mr ? Nate, May 2nd, 1870, mid-19thC, 43in (109cm).
$2,250-3,000

A Napoleon III bureau plat, ebonised with kingwood crossbanding and inlaid lines, the top with central scroll design.
$2,700-3,300

An amboyna writing table, with ebony inlay and gilt metal beading, the top with leather inset and a drawer, on dual end supports with shaped stretcher 19thC, 48in (122cm).
$2,700-3,300

A Victorian rosewood and walnut marquetry writing table, the kidney-shaped top inset with maroon morocco cartouche shaped writing surface, 52in (132cm).
$5,250-7,500

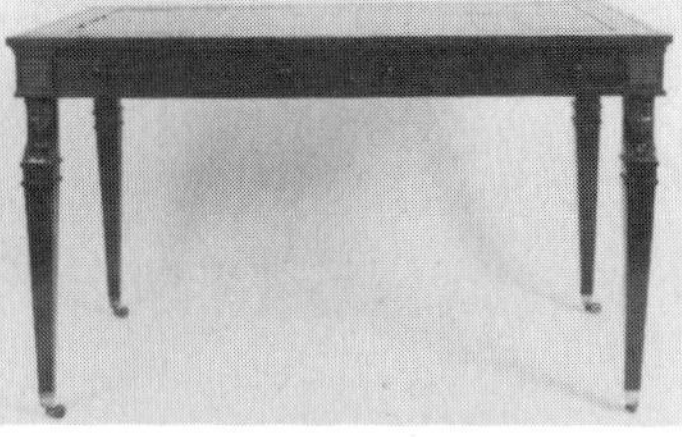

A Regency mahogany writing table, with rose pink leather top inlaid with ebony stringing, dummy drawers to the back and sides, tapering square legs with Egyptian heads below horizontally reeded panels, on brass casters, 48½in (123cm).
$6,000-8,250

An Edwardian rosewood and inlaid lady's writing table, the raised back with galleried top fitted with 2 small cupboards and mirror, 2 frieze drawers, on tapering legs, 36in (92cm).
$750-1,200

A Dutch walnut ebonised and floral marquetry writing table, with leather lined top and frieze drawer, on spiral twist uprights and bun feet joined by similar stretchers, 44in (112cm).
$2,700-3,300

Whatnots

A mid-Victorian mahogany whatnot, with 5 graduated tiers turned uprights and a drawer, on turned legs, 24in (61cm).
$3,000-3,750

Victorian figured walnut three-
ier whatnot, with fretted gallery,
n turned supports and casters,
9in (48cm). **$750-900**

A mahogany three-tier square whatnot, with turned baluster columns and conical finials, early 19thC, 16in (41cm) square.
$750-900

Did you know?
MILLER'S Antiques Price Guide builds up year by year to form the most comprehensive photo reference library available.

A mahogany butler's tray, with hinged sides and original stand, 19thC.
$750-900

Iiscellaneous

. Victorian two-tier buffet, each
ier with a three-quarter gallery,
4in (137cm). **$750-1,200**

A Victorian mahogany towel rail, 29in (74cm).
$90-105

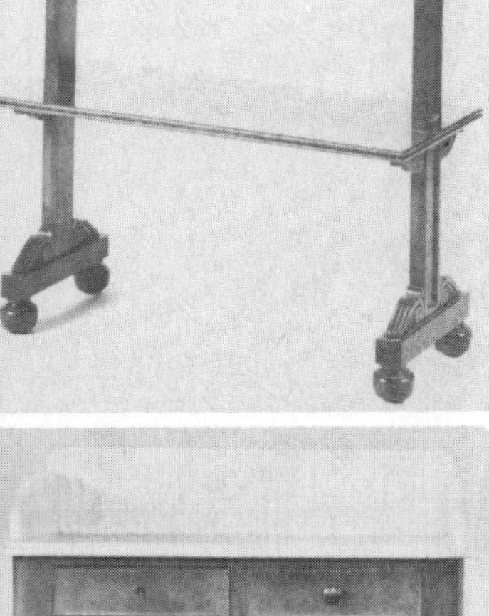

An early Victorian mahogany two-tier buffet, with channelled standard uprights with scroll brackets, on dual bun feet, 36in (92cm).
$1,050-1,350

A Victorian mahogany white and grey flecked marble tray top washstand, with 2 drawers below, on reeded turned tapering legs, 33in (84cm).
$300-375

SCOTTISH FURNITURE

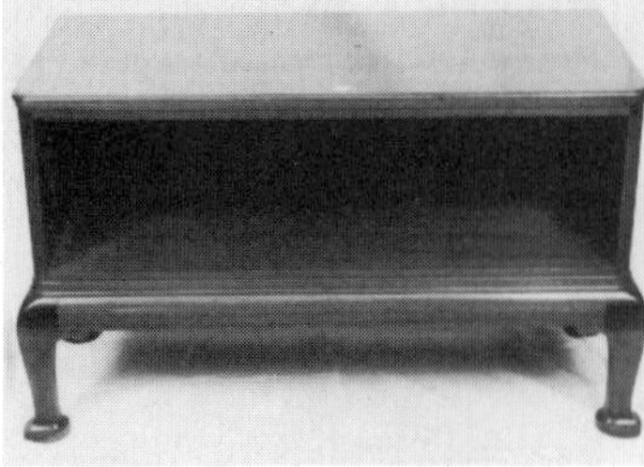

A Whytock & Reid dwarf mahogany open bookcase, c1925, 37in (94cm).
$450-600

A Whytock & Reid walnut display cabinet, with drawer in frieze, c1930, 27in (69cm).
$900-1,500

A Whytock & Reid walnut open bookcase, with panelled doors at each end, c1930, 70in (178cm).
$1,500-2,250

A Whytock & Reid mahogany two door cabinet, c1925, 33in (84cm).
$375-525

A Whytock & Reid mahogany bookcase, c1935.
$2,250-3,000

A Whytock & Reid walnut bureau, c1920, 47in (119cm).
$3,000-4,500

A Whytock & Reid two door filing cabinet, c1920, 27in (69cm).
$1,200-1,500

A Whytock & Reid walnut breakfront secrétaire cabinet c1930, 52in (132cm).
$1,200-1,500

Miller's is a price GUIDE not a price LIST

A Whytock & Reid corner cupboard, veneered in satinwood and crossbanded with tulipwood, c1950, 31in (79cm).
$1,200-1,800

A Whytock & Reid tallboy chest, with cupboards at the top, c1930, 33½in (85cm).
$750-900

A Whytock & Reid sycamore and burr ash corner wardrobe, c1920.
$750-1,200

A Whytock & Reid walnut wardrobe, c1930, 45in (114cm).
$1,200-1,500

A set of Whytock & Reid walnut dining chairs, including 2 carvers, c1910.
$2,700-3,300

A Wheeler gossip chair.
$450-600

A Shetland chair, oak with pine seat, probably made from driftwood.
$450-600

A set of Whytock & Reid walnut dining chairs, including 2 carvers, c1910.
$4,500-6,000

A pair of hall chairs, John Taylor & Sons, Edinburgh, requiring final restoration.
$600-750 when restored

A Shetland oak and pine baby's chair.
$300-375

An oak Chippendale style chair, by William Wheeler of Arncroach, Fife.
$450-600

A Shetland chair.
$450-600

A Whytock & Reid pear wood bedroom chair, c1930.
$150-180

An Orkney oak framed chair.
$375-525

A Scottish mahogany writing desk, 44in (112cm).
$600-750

A Whytock & Reid breakfront sideboard, c1920, 85in (216cm).
$2,250-3,000

A Whytock & Reid walnut sideboard, c1920, 66in (167.5cm).
$1,500-2,250

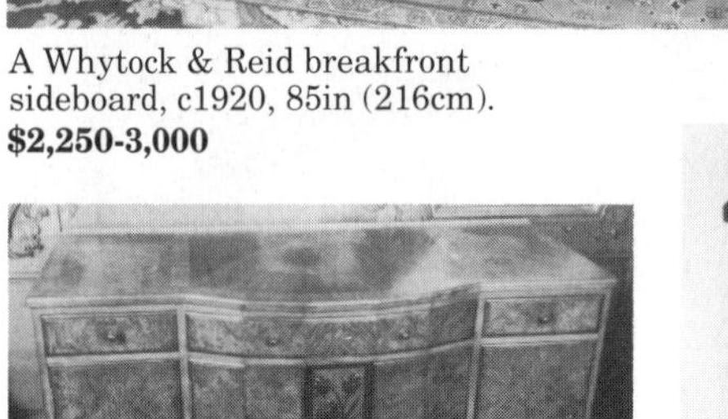

A Whytock & Reid sideboard, with carved central panel of laurel, amboyna and other woods, c1925, 54in (137cm).
$1,800-2,700

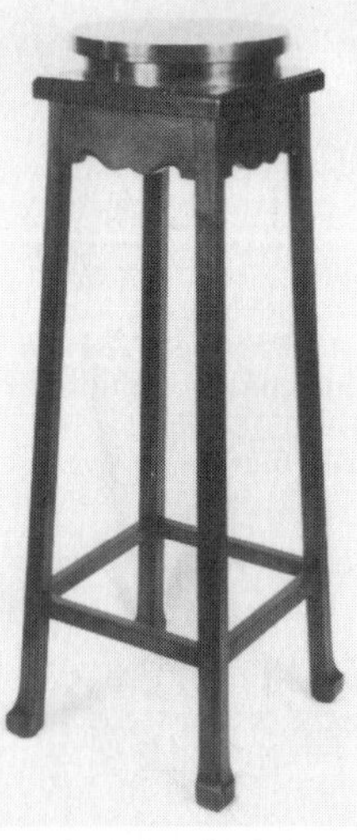

A Whytock & Reid oak stand, with walnut revolving plinth, c1930, 45in (114cm) high.
$600-750

A Whytock & Reid ash kneehole dressing table, c1930, 46in (117cm).
$1,200-1,800

A Whytock & Reid dressing table, with mirror attached, c1930, 42in (107cm).
$750-900

A Whytock & Reid walnut octagonal library table, c1925, 54in (137cm) diam.
$3,000-3,750

An early Victorian Scottish writing table, c1840, 40½in (102cm).
$1,050-1,350

SHIPPING FURNITURE

An oak side-by-side bureau secrétaire, 1930s.
$225-300

A set of 4 oak chairs, c1930.
$120-135

A set of 4 oak high back chairs, with turned legs, c1930
$120-135

A set of 4 high backed chairs, with barley twist backs and turned legs, 1930s.
$225-255

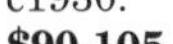

A set of 4 oak low back chairs, c1930.
$90-105

A set of 4 oak low back chairs, with turned legs, c1930.
$90-105

A set of 4 oak high back chairs, with pierced back splat and turned legs, c1920.
$225-255

An oak chest-on-stand, 1930s.
$225-300

A carved oak plant stand, with barley twist legs, c1930, 30½in (77cm) high.
$90-105

An oak cane seated stool, with barley twist legs, 1930s, 18in (46cm).
$50-75

A carved oak table, with barley twist legs, c1930, 23½in (60cm).
$50-75

An oak firescreen, 1930s, 22½in (57cm).
$50-75

An oak table, with barley twist legs, 1930s, 17in (43cm) square.
$50-75

A nest of oak tables, with barley twist legs, 1930s, largest 17in (44cm).
$180-225

An oak refectory drawleaf table, with solid top, 1930s, 36in (92cm) square.
$150-225

An oak gateleg table, 1930s, 27in (69cm) extended.
$150-225

Make the most of Millers's

Unless otherwise stated, any description which refers to 'a set' or 'a pair' includes a valuation for the entire set or the pair, even though the illustration may show only a single item.

A carved oak hall table, c1930 24in (62cm).
$375-450

An oak kneehole desk, with green and gold leather top and panelled ends, 1930s, 42in (106.5cm).
$750-900

An oak gateleg table, with barley twist legs, 1930s, 36in (92cm).
$150-225

PINE FURNITURE
Bookcases

A George II pine bookcase cabinet, some damage, 118in (300cm). **$45,000-60,000**

A George II style pine bookcase, the pierced broken scroll pediment with acanthus ornament and central urn above a pair of astragal glazed doors and a pair of panelled cupboard doors, on plinth base, 50in (127cm). **$3,000-4,500**

A George III style modern pine bookcase, with breakfront stiff leaf egg-and-dart and dentil moulded cornice, on plinth base, some carving 18thC, 90in (229cm). **$5,250-7,500**

A pine wall bookcase, c1880, 24in (61cm). **$225-300**

A George III style modern pine bookcase, on stiff leaf carved plinth base, some carving 18thC, 78½in (199cm). **$10,500-12,000**

A glazed pine bookcase, c1860, 36in (92cm).
$300-375

A pine bookcase, with glazed top cupboards, c1880, 36in (92cm).
$375-525

A pine glazed bookcase, with bracket feet added to base, c188(36in (92cm).
$300-375

Chairs

An Irish famine chair.
$225-300

A Scandinavian pine bench, painted with flowers on a brown and green ground, 19thC, 51in (130cm).
$750-900

A harlequin set of 4 Victorian slat back pine chairs.
$375-450

An Austrian pine bench, 34in (86cm).
$450-600

A set of 6 George III Irish pine and ash hall chairs, each with radiating back centred by a painted crest depicting a horse's head on a claret groun with the motto 'Ryde Through within giltwood borders, the serpentine channelled seats o square tapering legs, all stamped W.B., all with later blocks and label of Wort & Son Ltd/Depository/ Bournemouth name Commodore BGB Brooke/No. 8, minor restorations, probably previously decorated.
$6,000-8,250

Chests of Drawers

A pine chest of drawers, c1870, 40in (102cm).
$375-450

A pine chest of drawers, c1830, 36in (92cm).
$375-525

A pine chest of drawers, c1860 42in (106.5cm).
$300-375

A pine chest of drawers, with original knobs and bracket feet, c1830, 34in (86cm).
$450-600

A Federal pine bowfront chest of drawers, painted and grained all over in brown and ochre to simulate mahogany, New England, c1810, 40in (102cm).
$1,500-2,250

A pine chest of drawers, with new brass handles, c1890, 36in (92cm)
$375-450

A small pine chest of drawers, 14in (36cm).
$135-150

A Napoleon III pine and simulated bamboo tall chest, with 6 drawers, c1860, 28in (71cm).
$1,050-1,350

A satin walnut chest of drawers, c1890, 36in (92cm). **$450-600**

A pine chest of drawers, c1870, 36in (92cm).
$375-525

Cupboards

A Federal pine corner cupboard, with blue painted interior, plate grooves, scallop surround, reeded lower section with hinged door opening to a shelf, American, early 19thC, edges of shelves scalloped at later date, 52in (132cm).
$5,250-7,500

A pine wall cupboard, c1860, 21in (53cm).
$150-225

A George III pine corner cupboard, on moulded apron and block feet, 41½in (105cm).
$3,000-4,500

A pine corner cupboard, adapted from the top half of a tall cupboard, with added bracket feet and top, c1850, 36in (92cm).
$450-600

A pine estate cupboard, c1820, 96in (244cm).
$3,000-4,500

A central European pine pot cupboard, c1920, 12in (31cm).
$150-225

A pine food cupboard, c1920 36in (92cm).
$600-750

An Austrian pine linen cupboard, 19thC, 75in (191cm) high.
$1,050-1,350

A satin walnut pot cupboard, inlaid with rosewood, boxwood, holly and bone, c1890, 12in (31cm).
$300-375

A pine cupboard, adapted from a dresser base, c1870, 24in (61cm).
$225-300

A pine buffet, in 2 parts, c1780, 47in (119cm).
$3,000-3,750

A Dutch pine kitchen cupboard, with decorative cornice, 19thC, 35in (89cm).
$600-750

A pine fruitwood and tôle food cage, 18thC, 34in (86cm).
$600-750

A pine meat safe, c1860, 24in (61cm). **$90-105**

Desks

A pine desk, c1870, on later stand, 29in (74cm).
$300-375

Dressers

A Dutch pine dresser, with green textured glass doors, 19thC, 41in (104cm).
$750-900

An Irish pine dresser, c1880, 62in (157cm). **$1,200-1,500**

A pine display dresser, c1880, 76in (193cm).
$1,800-2,700

A pine dresser base, c1875, 60in (152cm).
$600-750

A pine dresser base, c1830, 60in (152cm).
$600-750

A pine Welsh dresser, with small cupboard, with glazed door to small cupboard, c1890, 48in (122cm).
$750-900

A French provincial painted hanging dresser, 19thC, 23in (59cm).
$375-450

Dressing Tables

A satin walnut dressing table, c1910, 36in (92cm).
$225-300

Settles

A pine wing-back settle, of concave form with broad plank back, early 19thC, 66in (167cm).
$900-1,500

Mirrors

Two pine framed mirrors, 14 an
16in (36 and 41cm) square.
$40-60

Stools

A round pine stool, 17½in (44cm
high. **$40-60**

A pine stool.
$50-75

[T]ables

 Regency pine tilt-top table, on entral reeded base, with 3 legs nd original wood casters, 19thC, 6in (116.5cm) diam.
600-750

 pine serving table, c1900, 36in 92cm). **$225-300**

A pine serving table, c1830, 96in (243.5cm) long. **$450-600**

A pine kitchen table, c1875, 72in (182.5cm) long.
$600-750

A pine kitchen table, cut down for use as a coffee table, c1880, 36 by 39in (92 by 99cm).
$300-375

Wardrobes

An ash wardrobe, with shoe box slides and hooks, c1895, 65in (165cm). **$600-750**

A pine wardrobe, the drawer with ceramic handles, c1890, 45in (114cm). **$600-750**

A pine mirror door wardrobe, with brass fittings, c1890, 42in (106.5cm).
$600-750

A Scandinavian pine wardrobe with 2 drawers under, c1870, 55in (140cm).
$750-900

A satin walnut wardrobe, with one drawer, c1915, 42in (106.5cm).
$450-600

An Edwardian satinwood wardrobe, c1910, 36in (92cm).
$375-525

A pine wardrobe, with rounded corners, c1880, 36in (92cm).
$750-900

Washstands

A pine washstand, c1870, 24in (62cm).
$225-300

A pine washstand, c1800, 15in (38cm).
$375-450

A Lincolnshire pine washstand, original paint, 35in (89cm).
$375-450

Dutch pine tiled back
ashstand, with marble top,
890, 48in (122cm).
00-375

A pine tiled back washstand,
c1890, 36in (92cm).
$375-450

A pine lift-up top washstand,
c1815, 36in (92cm).
$600-750

curved back washstand, with 2
rawers and 2 cupboards, c1860,
8in (122cm).
375-450

Miscellaneous

A pine box, c1880, 24in (62cm).
$150-225

A pine box, c1900, 36in (92cm).
$120-135

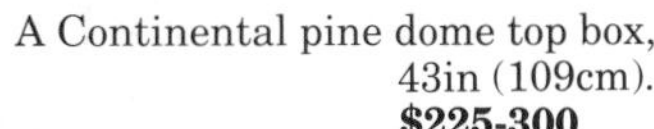

A Continental pine dome top box,
43in (109cm).
$225-300

A painted ship's box, c1880, paint restored at later date, 17in (43cm).
$150-225

A pine galley fitment, with roll front, pestle and mortar, 20in (51cm) high.
$300-375

A German Biedermeier style pine secrètaire, late 19thC, 37in (94cm).
$1,200-1,500

A pine dairy bucket, 19thC, 9½in (24cm) diam.
$50-75

A Victorian pine work box, with sectioned tray, 20in (51cm) long.
$50-75

A pine box, c1880, 42in (106.5cm)
$150-225

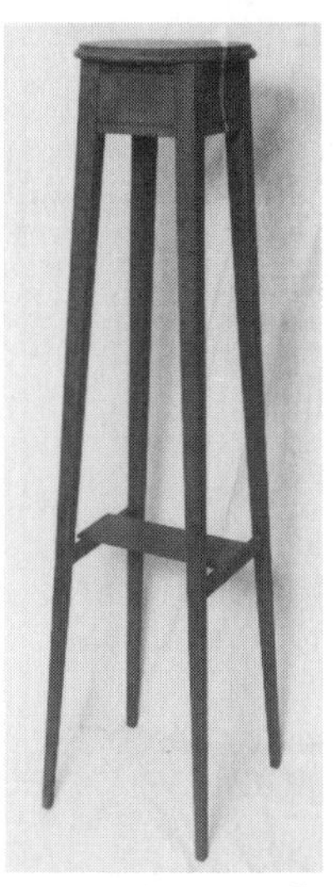

A pine plant stand, c1910, 60in (152cm) high.
$135-150

A pair of pine steps, with metal fittings, c1900, 55in (140cm) high.
$105-120

A pine towel rail, all original, c1880, 30in (76cm) high.
$135-150

A pine towel rail, with barley twist ends, c1870, 30in (76cm) high.
$135-150

A French pine decorated shelf, Alsace, c1880, 19in (48cm).
$225-300

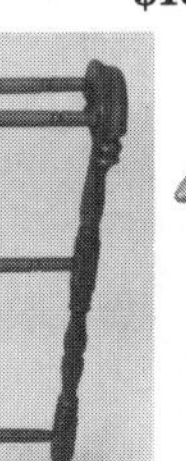

A pine towel rail, 28in (71cm).
$50-75

A Swedish carved pine coffer, c1850, 23in (59cm).
$225-300

An oak bank of drawers, lined with pine, c1930, 24in (61cm).
$450-600

ARCHITECTURAL ANTIQUES
Fireplaces

A rococo style dove grey marble chimneypiece, on a block foot, repaired, the frieze and jambs 19thC, the outgrounds, plinth blocks and shelf later, 76in (193cm).
$3,000-4,500

An early Victorian Mason's Ironstone chimneypiece, gilt and green decorated overall with flowers on a cream ground, with inset shaped reserve panels and plinth base, 62in (157cm).
$5,250-7,500

A Sicilian marble chimneypiece, the moulded shelf with re-entrant corners, above a panelled frieze, the inswept jambs each with a fluted central section, on a block foot, restored, mid-18thC, 70in (177.5cm).
$5,250-7,500

A Louis XV style liver coloured marble chimneypiece, with a serpentine moulded shelf above a panelled frieze centred by an acanthus scroll, the jambs each with a shell carved endblock, above a panelled volute pilaster, on a block foot, the side panels later, 55½in (141cm).
$1,800-2,700

A Moroccan red onyx chimneypiece, the bolection moulded surround with a central keystone, on block feet, 59½in (151cm).
$3,000-3,750

A cast iron and polished steel fire grate, the railed front above a fret pierced frieze with stylised anthemion motifs, the scroll standards with adapted urn surmounts, late 18thC, 28½in (72cm).
$2,700-3,300

A polished steel and cast iron fire grate, the railed front surmounted by spikes with ball finials, the uprights in the form of leopard head monopodia, on square plinths, early 19thC, 35in (89cm).
$5,250-6,000

A cast iron fire grate, the backplate decorated in relief with a flaming urn flanked by foliate scrolls, the basket flanked by scroll jambs with acanthus ornament, early 19thC, 36in (92cm).
$900-1,500

A Chippendale style polished steel and cast iron fire grate, on stepped plinths, 19thC, 29in (74cm). **$3,000-4,500**

A brass, polished steel and cast iron fire grate, flanked by tapering uprights with urn finials, 30in (76cm).
$5,250-6,000

A brass mounted, polished steel fire grate of brazier form, 29in (74cm).
$5,250-6,000

brass, steel and cast iron fire rate, the backplate decorated in elief with a figure in a chariot, ambrequin draped swags and rolls, fireback repaired, c1700, 5in (89cm). **$5,250-7,500**

decorative cast iron fireback, ecorated in relief with a ythological scene, surrounded y putti and fruiting foliage, minor rusting, 30½in (77.5cm). **1,050-1,350**

. pair of brass mounted cast iron re dogs of Haddon Hall type, the prights with pierced circular laques with tulips and other owers, the supports with raised croll ornament, on ball feet, 9thC, 13in (33cm). **375-450**

\ brass folding fan-shaped spark guard, 39½in (100.5cm). **$600-750**

A pair of Empire style ormolu chenets, the beaded friezes with oval paterae, the cylindrical uprights with ovoid finials, with iron billet bars, 12in (30cm). **$150-225**

A cast iron fireback, cast with the Tudor rose on a shield flanked by a supporting lion and winged greyhound, surmounted by a crown, inscribed '1571', some rusting, 27½in (70cm). **$750-900**

A brass, polished steel and cast iron fire grate, 36in (92cm). **$4,500-6,000**

An Irish gun metal, polished steel and cast iron register grate, the urns replaced, late 18thC, 36in (92cm). **$3,000-4,500**

A pair of decorative cast iron firebacks, each centred with an armorial shield flanked by scrolls and surmounted by a visored helmet and winged dragon, minor rusting, 37in (94cm).
$600-750

A French brass and wire mesh spark guard, of cartouche outline, on scroll supports, 29in (74cm).
$1,050-1,350

A pair of French Louis XVI style ormolu chenets, each with a foliate pierced frieze surmounted by a military trophy, below a balustrade gallery, flanked by twin handled urns with flaming finials, 19thC, 16in (41cm).
$225-300

A Louis XVI style brass mounted cast iron fire grate, 28in (71cm).
$375-525

A decorative cast iron fireback, 38in (96.5cm).
$1,800-2,700

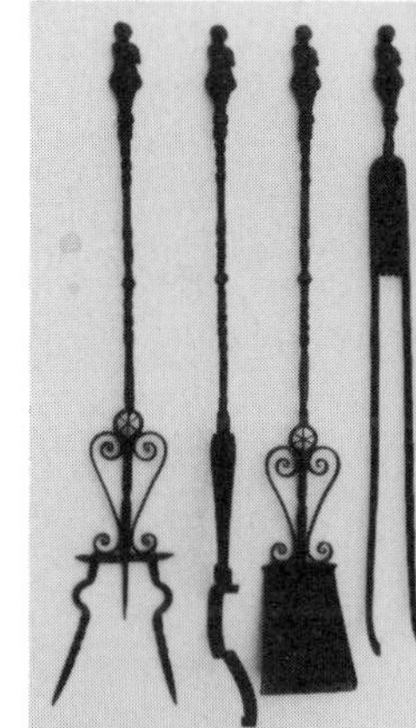

A set of 4 wrought iron fir irons, with bronze cherub handles, late 19thC.
$1,200-1,800

A set of 3 steel fire irons, the faceted pommels with knopped finials and pierced shovel, c180(
$600-750

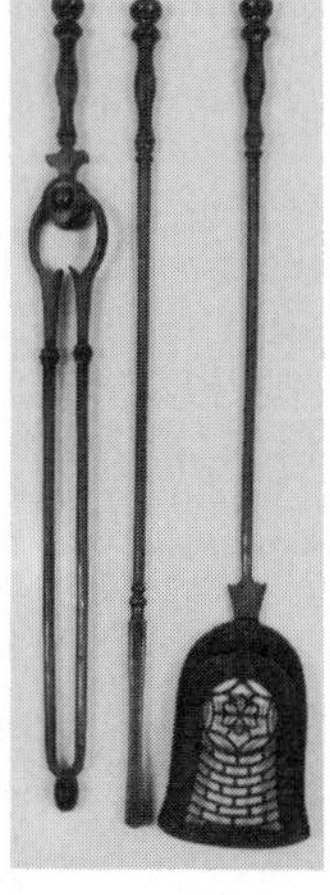

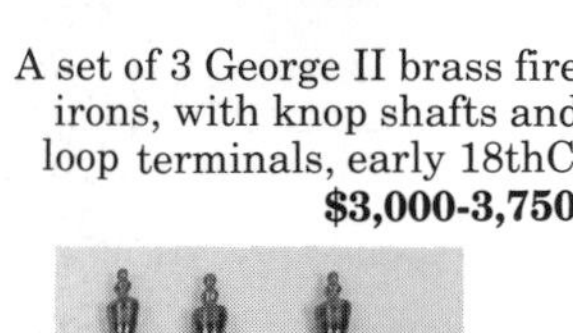

A set of 3 George II brass fire irons, with knop shafts and loop terminals, early 18thC.
$3,000-3,750

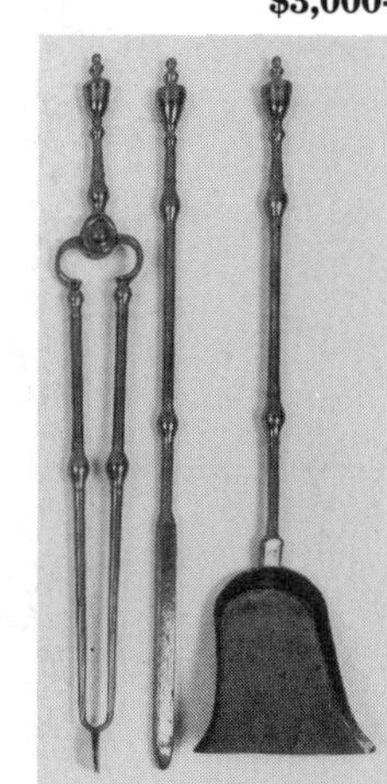

A set of 3 steel fire irons, wit urn finials, knopped shafts and shaped shovel, late 18thC.
$1,200-1,800

Staffordshire model of a hurch, c1835, 5in (13cm). **600-650**

A Wemyss Gordon plate, painted with raspberries, 8in (20cm) diam. **$450-600**

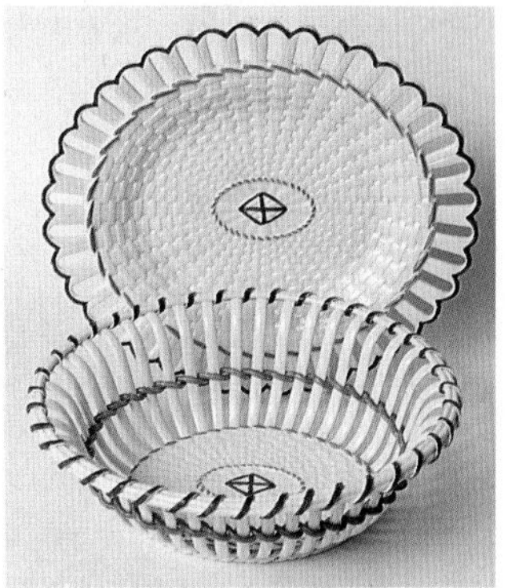

A pair of Wedgwood creamware chestnut baskets and stands, c1790. **$1,000-1,200**

Staffordshire pastille urner, c1840, 4½in 11cm). **$500-600**

A pair of Quimper plates, 11in (28cm) diam. **$100-150**

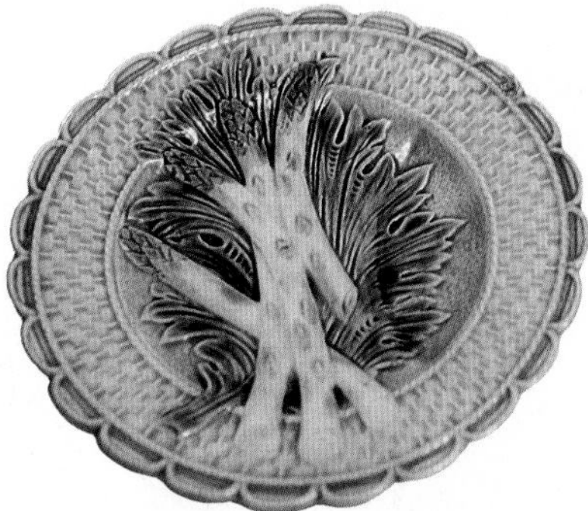

A set of 6 French asparagus plates, c1880, 9½in (24cm) diam. **$450-500**

wo Staffordshire figures, 'The ost Piece' from identical moulds 1800. **$450-500 each**

A Staffordshire pastille burner, c1835, restored, 8in (20cm). **$450-500**

A Staffordshire model of Shakespeare's house, repaired, c1850, 5in (13cm) high. **$300-350**

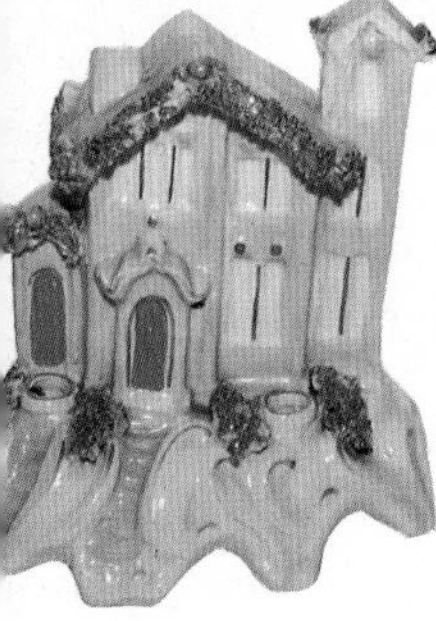

Staffordshire inkwell, estored, c1850, 4in 10cm) high. **150-200**

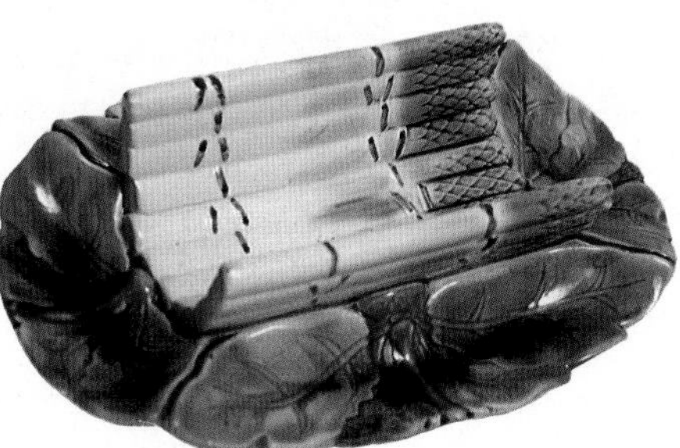

An asparagus cradle, c1880, 14½in (37cm) wide. **$200-300**

A Staffordshire pastille burner, restored chimney and flowers, c1835, 5½in (14cm) high. **$450-500**

A Staffordshire creamware arbour group, some restorations, c1765, 6in (15cm) high. **$72,000-78,000**

A majolica figure, 1868. **$500-650**

A Staffordshire saltglaz arbour group, damaged c1760, 6in (15cm). **$62,000-65,000**

A Staffordshire creamware figure of William III, damaged, c1785, 15in (38cm). **$13,500-15,000**

A Staffordshire figure, restored, c1847. **$250-350**

r. A group of Bacchus and Ariadne, c1795. **$4,500-6,000**

A pair of Royal Dux water carrier figures, 20in (51cm). **$600-750**

A Staffordshire Ralph Wood type creamware teapot and cover, restored, c1785, 11in (28cm) high. **$28,500-32,000**

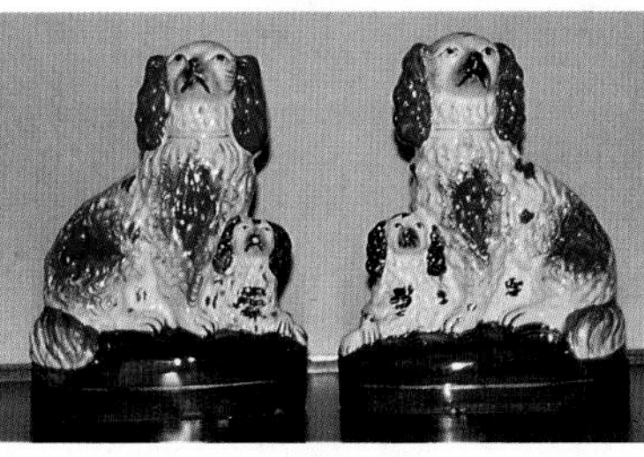

A pair of Staffordshire spaniels and pups, c1850, 8in (20cm). **$750-850**

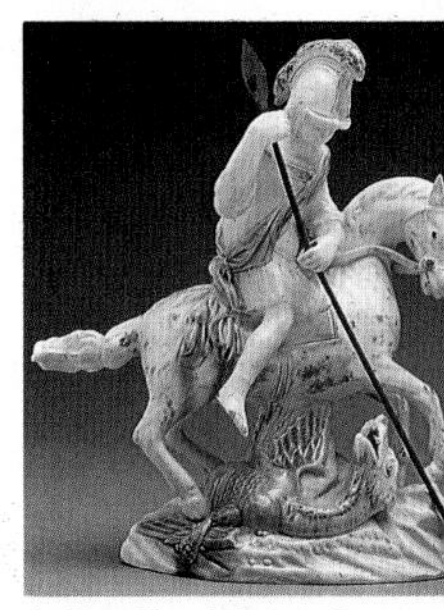

A Staffordshire figure, restored, c1780. **$2,000-3,000**

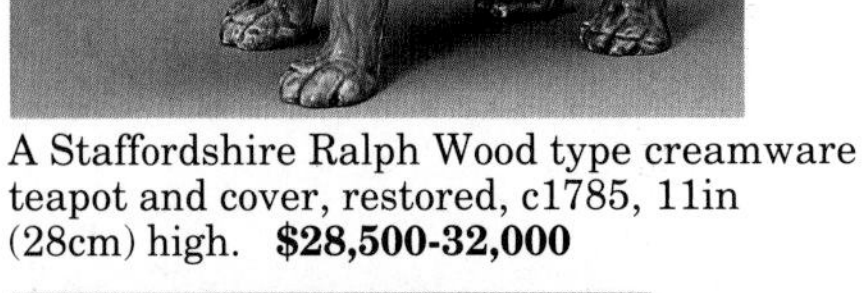

A pair of Staffordshire figures of the Duke of Connaught and General Wolseley, c1882, 12½in (32cm). **$600-700**

A Staffordshire figure of Abd-ul-Medjid, c1854, 8½in (21.5cm). **$900-950**

A pair of Staffordshire creamware models of birds, some restoration, c1755, 8½in (21.5cm) high. **$142,000-150,000**

A Staffordshire lion, in the manner of Obadiah Sherratt, on a base enamelled to simulate marble, c1820, 13½in (34cm) wide. **$1,350-2,250**

A Staffordshire creamware model of a parrot, of Whieldon type, slight flaking, c1760, 6½in (16cm). **$9,500-11,000**

A Staffordshire creamware Tob jug, c1780. **$1,000-1,500**

Two Staffordshire press moulded water buffalo, one with an oriental on its back th other with a reclining boy, c1760, 9 and 10 (23 and 25cm). **$30,000-37,500 each**

A Staffordshire Toby jug, early 19thC, 11in (28cm). **$120-150**

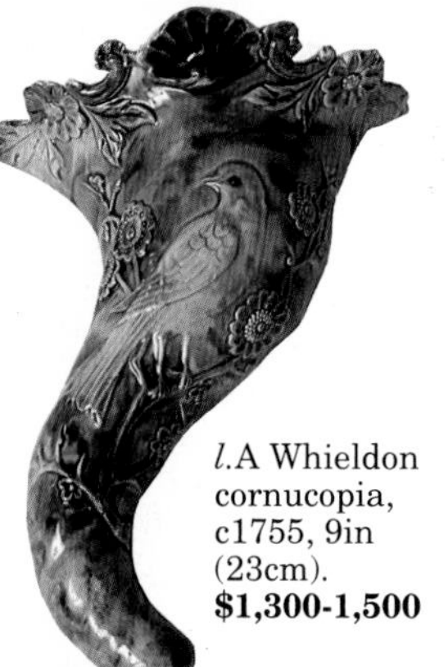

l. A Whieldon cornucopia, c1755, 9in (23cm). **$1,300-1,500**

r. A Staffordshire creamware 'Fair Hebe' jug, damaged and repaired, signed and dated I. Voyez 1788, 9½in (24cm). **$1,500-2,250**

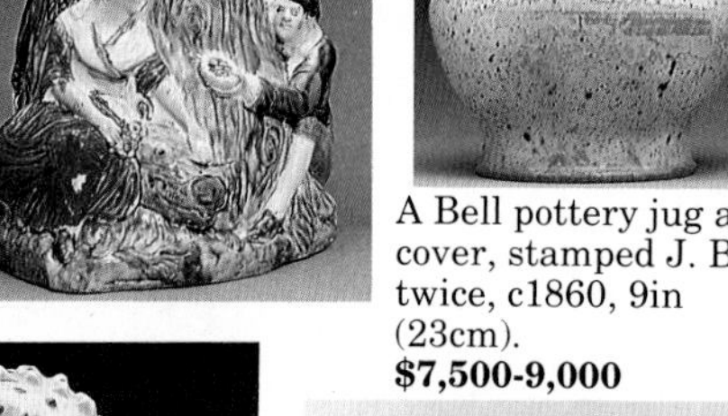

A Bell pottery jug a cover, stamped J. B twice, c1860, 9in (23cm). **$7,500-9,000**

A Staffordshire nursery jug, with Ackerman style train print, c1850, 12½in (32cm). **$1,350-1,600**

A Quimper cheese dish and cover, 9in (23cm) diam. **$150-200**

A Staffordshire saltglaze owl jug and cover, damage and restoration, c1760, 8in (20cm). **$55,000-65,000**

A Toby jug, marked Neale Co, restored, c1785, 10in (25cm). **$900-1,000**

Liverpool tankard, ith St. Nicholas hurch, c1775, 6in 5.5cm).
,250-3,000

A Staffordshire saltglaze jug, c1765.
$1,000-1,400

A tin glazed water cistern, with tap hole. c1725.
$9,000-10,500

tankard decorated with a red int, signed Joseph Johnson, verpool, c1795, 6in (15cm).
00-1,200

A Staffordshire creamware cider jug, some damage, inscribed and dated John Smallwood 1790, 11in (28cm). **$2,500-3,000**

A Staffordshire saltglaze two-handled cup, damaged, inscribed and dated H/RE 1762, 5½in (14.5cm).
$3,750-5,250

A Staffordshire saltglaze sauceboat, c1760, 8in (20cm) wide.
$3,750-4,500

Nottingham saltglaze stoneware o-handled cup, inscribed 'John & ary Rowbotham/Oct 26 1787', stored, 10in (25cm).
,250-3,250

A Staffordshire two-handled cup, c1765, 5in (12cm).
$2,250-3,000

Prattware cider jug, c1800, n (20cm).
,400-1,800

A Staffordshire solid agate pear shaped cream jug, c1750, 5in (12.5cm).
$3,750-4,500

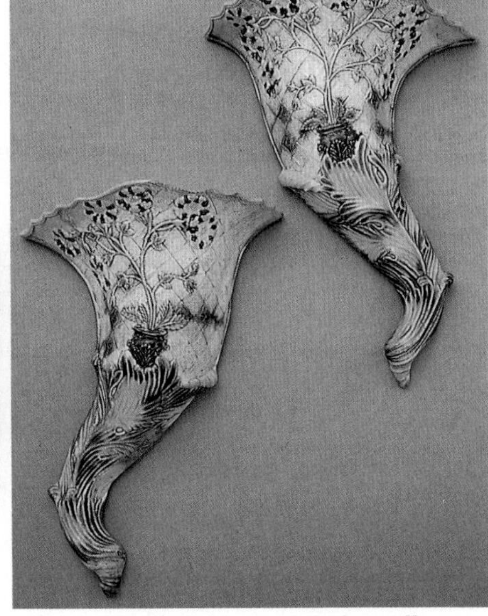

A pair of Staffordshire creamware wall pockets, of Whieldon type, some restoration, c1765, 9½in (24cm). **$7,500-8,250**

A pair of Venice broad oviform jars, each painted with a standing female saint, slight rim chips, c1580, 12½ and 13in (32 and 33cm).
$45,000-50,000

A Venice broad oviform jar, painted with a saint, damage c1570, 12in (31cm).
$25,500-28,500

A Castel Durante maiolica dish, slight damage, inscribed Gallafrone, c1520, 9in (22.5cm).
$45,000-50,000

A Faenza maiolica berretino ground armorial tondino, c1530, 9½in (24cm). **$37,500-45,000**

A Castelli plaque, painted in the Grue workshop, c1740, 8 by 11in (20 by 28cm).
$6,000-7,500

An Italian maiolica dish, by Urbino or Pisaro, with Apollo on Parnassus, 16thC, 11in (28cm). **$3,000-4,000**

An Urbino Istoriato maiolica dish, slight damage, c1550, 9in (22cm).
$9,000-12,000

An Urbania dish, painted in the manner of Hippolito Rombaldott c1680, 11in (28cm) diam, with giltwood frame. **$7,500-9,000**

An Italian maiolica altar piece, The Marches, some damage and restoration, late 16thC, 26in (66cm), mounted on wood.
$10,000-12,000

A Sicilian maiolica albarello, painted with the figure of a saint, chipped, 16th/17thC, 11in (28cm).
$2,250-3,750

A Venice albarello, inscribed 'Sandali R', with 'A D' below, damaged, c1580, 12in (30.5cm).
$4,500-6,000

A Faenza maiolica albarello, slight damage, 16thC, 9½in (24cm).
$9,000-10,500

Mason's Ironstone Bandana
are pot pourri vase, with pierced
ıd solid covers, c1845, 14in
6cm). **$800-900**

A Mason's Ironstone card rack, impressed mark, c1815. **$1,000-1,300**

A can and saucer, by C. J. Mason, pattern 878, c1815, saucer 5½in (14cm) diam. **$180-220**

Mason's Ironstone soup plate,
ıpan pattern, impressed line
ark, c1815, 9½in (24cm) diam.
120-140

A Mason's Ironstone vase and cover, c1815, 8in (20cm). **$330-380**

A hard paste porcelain teapot, by Miles Mason, slight damage, c1800, 6½in (16cm) high. **$600-660**

hand painted bone china
ate, by C. J. Mason, c1815,
½in (21cm). **$120-150**

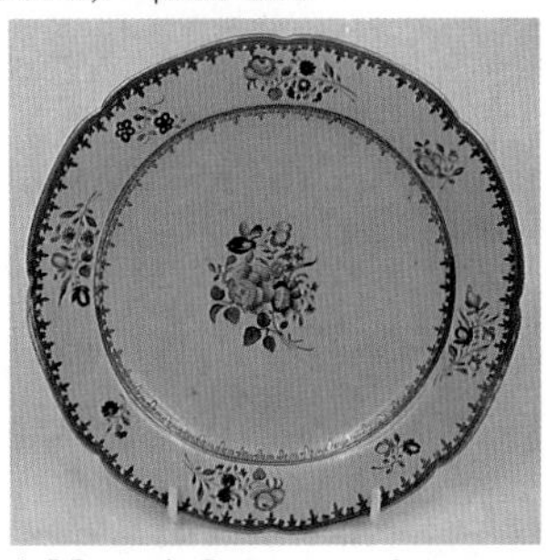

A Mason's Ironstone dessert plate, c1813, 7¼in (18.5cm). **$75-100**

A Mason's Ironstone dessert dish, slight crack, c1815, 9½in (24cm). **$250-300**

bone china cup and saucer, by
iles Mason, pattern 665, c1808,
n (12.5cm). **$200-230**

A Mason's Ironstone inkstand, impressed mark, c1815. **$800-900**

A relief moulded cup and saucer, by Miles Mason, c1818, saucer 5½in (14cm) diam. **$150-225**

pair of Mason's Ironstone wine coolers, Japan
ıttern, 9½in (24cm) high. **$1,300-1,450**

A pair of Mason's Ironstone sauce tureens, with stands, impressed mark, c1815. **$975-1,200**

A Wemyss slop pail lid, 10in (25cm) diam. **$150-225**

A Wemyss goose, 8in (20cm) high. **$750-850**

A Wemyss large tyg, painted with roses, 9½in (24cm). **$1,350-1,500**

A Wemyss honey pot, marked T. Goode & Co, 7in (18cm) high. **$750-850**

A Wemyss teapot, chocolate pot, cream jug and sugar bowl 2 to 4in (5.5 to 10cm). **$225-650 each**

A Wemyss square bees box and stand, 3in (7.5cm) high. **$375-450**

A Wemyss inkwell, 6in (15cm) long. **$300-450**

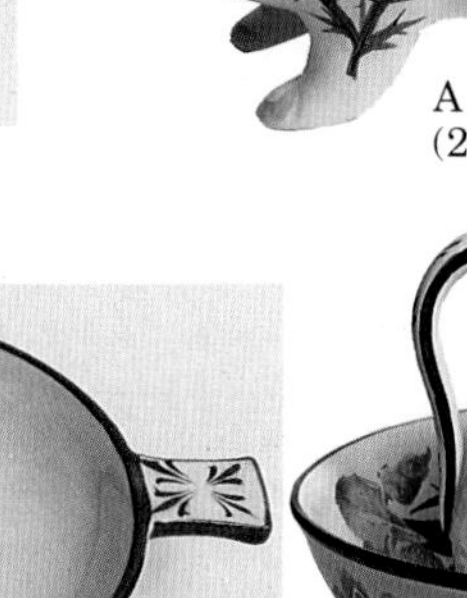
A Wemyss Plichta pig, 8in (20cm) high. **$1,000-1,800**

A Wemyss Gorden plate, 8in (20cm) diam. **$375-450**

A Wemyss jug and basin, jug 10in (25cm) high. **$2,250-3,000**

A Wemyss pomade pot, 3in (8cm) high. **$300-450**

A Wemyss quaiche, painted with raspberries, 8in (20cm) wide. **$300-450**

A Wemyss matchbox, T. Goode & Co., 2 by 5in (5 by 13cm). **$350-600**

A Wemyss biscuit barrel, 4in (10cm) high. **$350-400**

A Wemyss pig, painted with clover flowers, 11½in (29.5cm) high. **$3,000-4,500**

Lambeth delft armorial caudle cup, .maged, inscribed and dated 1657. '2,000-78,000

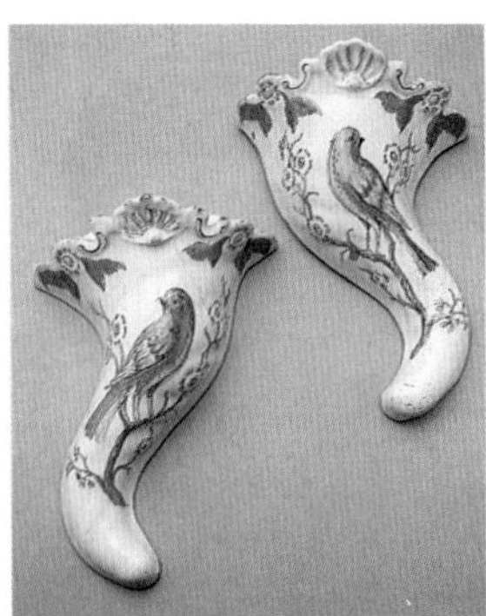

A pair of Liverpool delft wall pockets, restored, c1760, 8½in (21cm). **$4,200-4,800**

A Liverpool delft rosewater bottle, c1760. **$675-825**

A Liverpool delft puzzle jug, c1750. **$1,200-1,500**

delftware charger, obably London, 18thC, in (31cm). **:00-700**

A Liverpool delft punch bowl, the exterior decorated with Chinese houses, c1760, 20in (51cm) diam. **$10,500-15,000**

A Lambeth delft salt, damaged, c1680, 8in (20cm). **$165,000-180,000**

delftware dish with bed sides, 17thC, 12½in 1.5cm) diam. **:25-300**

The interior view of Liverpool delft punch bowl decorated with a ship flying the Union Jack *above*.

A pair of Liverpool delft wall pockets, damaged, c1770, 8in (20cm). **$9,000-10,500**

ı English delft polychrome ›wer tub, London or ·istol, damaged, c1690, 6in 5cm). **$12,000-13,500**

l. A Bristol delft bianco-sopra-bianco plate, c1760, damaged. **$600-750**
r. A Lambeth delft bowl, damaged, c1740, 9in (23cm) diam. **$3,000-3,750**

Interior of Lambeth delft armorial caudle cup, *top left*.

l. Three delft Royal portrait chargers, depicting Queen Mary, King William III and an unknown king, damaged and restored, c1690. **$10,500-12,500 each**

A Derby coffee can and saucer, painted by Richard Askew, anchor and D mark, c1775. **$6,000-9,000**

A Derby porcelain coffee can and saucer, crown, crossed batons, dots and D mark, c1796. **$12,000-18,000**

A Böttger flared beaker, slight damag gilder's mark Z, c172 **$60,000-67,000**

A coffee can and saucer, crown, crossed batons, dots and D mark, c1797. **$1,500-2,250**

A documentary slop basin, signed H, blue crossed swords and gilder's mark, c1730. **$45,000-50,000**

A Meissen flared beake damaged, blue crossed swords mark, c1725. **$25,500-28,000**

l. A Derby coffee can, painted by James Banford, marked, c1790. **$4,500-6,000**

A Derby porcelain coffee can and saucer, c1795. **$6,750-8,250**

A Derby coffee can and saucer, painted by William Pegg, crown, crossed batons, dots and D mark c1797. **$15,000-21,000**

A Derby coffee can and saucer, painted by G. Complin and W. Billingsley, marked, c1790. **$27,000-33,000**

A Chamberlain's Worcester breakfast cup and saucer, slight damage, maroon script mark, c1800. **$9,750-11,250**

A Derby coffee can an saucer, painted by Zachariah Boreman, marked, c1790. **$6,750-8,250**

l. A Derby coffee can and saucer, painted by Zachariah Boreman, crown, crossed batons, dots and D marks and inscription, c1793. **$6,750-8,250**

l. A Derby coffee can, trace marks of crown, crossed batons, dots, and D, c1797. **$7,500-9,000**

A Nymphenburg pail, damage, impressed mark, c1860. **$7,500-10,500**

A Meissen hot milk jug, c1735. **$6,000-7,500**

A Meissen salt from the Swan service, c1737.
$27,000-30,000

A Pickard tankard pitcher, with chrysanthemum, signed Reau, 16in (41cm). **$600-750**

A baluster hot water jug, crossed swords and gilder's 67 mark, c1730.
$15,000-21,000

A Chamberlain's Worcester jug, painted script mark.
$8,250-11,250

A Coalport flower pot on detachable stand, c1810, 7in (18cm).
$650-950

r. A Pickard pitcher, decorated with Falstaff, signed P. Gasper, 15in (38cm). **$1,500-2,000**

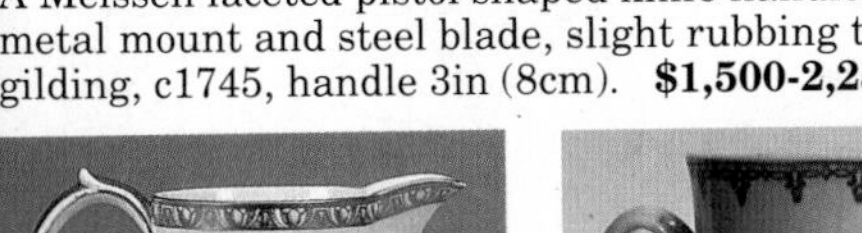
A Meissen faceted pistol shaped knife handle, later metal mount and steel blade, slight rubbing to gilding, c1745, handle 3in (8cm). **$1,500-2,250**

A Spode sporting jug, with a pointer in a landscape, and gilt initials 'J.W.' below the spout, 6in (16cm). **$2,700-3,000**

A Plymouth polychrome mug, decorated with exotic birds by Mons Souci, c1768.
$4,000-4,500

A Meissen chinoiserie table bell and stand, painted by C. F. Herold and B. G. Häuer, blue crossed swords marks, c1730, bell 5in (12cm).
$120,000-130,000

A Staffordshire porcelain lilac coloured castle, turret restored, c1840, 7½in (19cm).
$950-1,200

A Vincennes seau à verre, blue interlaced L's and dots mark, c1752, 4½in (11cm).
$5,700-6,500

A Meissen tureen and cover, with fish handles and finial, damaged and restored, blue crossed swords mark, c1728, 11½in (30cm). **$50,000-54,000**

A Paris porcelain group, probably by Jacob Petit, c1840, 8in (20cm). **$375-525**

A pair of Worcester figures of Turks, damaged, c1770, 5½in (14cm). **$13,500-15,000**

A Derby porcelain elephant and driver, by Edward Keys, crown mark over Derby in red, red 34, c1825, 5in (12.5cm) high. **$3,750-5,250**

A pair of Royal Dux figures, the man with guitar, the lady with mandolin, applied pink triangle mark, 26in (66cm). **$3,750-4,500**

A Meissen figure of Dr. Boloardo, damaged, c1744, 5½in (14cm). **$3,750-4,500**

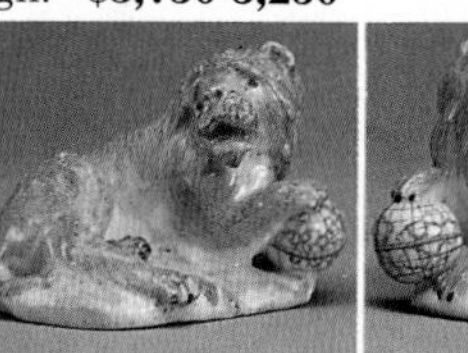

A pair of Bow lions, each with one paw on a globe, c1755, 4in (10cm). **$7,000-8,250**

A Höchst pug dog, minor cracks, c1755, 4in (10cm). **$4,000-5,250**

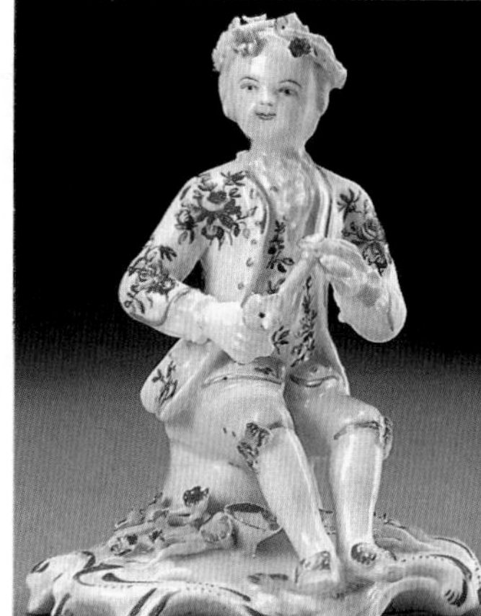

A Derby porcelain figure of 'Spring', from a set of the Seasons, patch marks, c1758, 4in (10cm) high. **$3,000-3,750**

A Meissen figure of a dancer, modelled by J.J. Kändler, restored, c1738, 7½in (18.5cm). **$55,000-60,000**

A Meissen wild boar, by J.J. Kändler, restored, c1745, 6½in (16cm). **$10,500-12,000**

Two Nymphenburg figures of an oriental and companion, by Franz Anton Bustelli, damage and restorations, impressed Bavarian shield marks, c1760, decoration later, 4½in (11.5cm). **$6,750-8,250**

A pair of Chelsea sweetmeat figures, with dogs at their feet, both holding open the lids of oval baskets, damaged and repaired, gold anchor marks, c1760, 8in (19.5cm). **$6,000-7,500**

A Derby dancing girl, patch marks, c1759, 6in (15cm). **$2,250-3,000**

A pair of Derby porcelain Mansion House dwarfs, signed J. Brown, 7in (17.5cm). **$1,200-1,500**

A Derby pair of porcelain stag and doe figures, 3 patch marks and central hole, 6½in (16.5cm). **$7,000-9,000**

A Meissen dancing peasant, c1740, 7in (17cm). **$28,000-30,000**

A pair of Meissen figures of Hungarians, by J. J. Kändler, c1745, 9in (22cm). **$12,000-15,000**

A pair of Meissen figures, marked, c1880, 19½in (49.5cm). **$3,750-4,500**

A Meissen eagle, blue crossed swords mark, c1860, 23in (59cm). **$5,250-6,000**

A Frankenthal group of 'Die Gute Mutter', by Karl Gottlieb Lück, restored, blue rampant lion mark to base, c1759, 9in (22cm) wide. **$10,500-13,500**

A pair of Chelsea groups of gallants and companions, emblematic of the Seasons, gold anchor marks, restored, c1765, 14in (35.5cm). **$13,500-15,000**

A 'Girl in a Swing' scent bottle, c1755, 3in (7cm). **$7,500-9,000**

A Meissen group of Phoebus Apollo in the chariot of the Sun, after J. J. Kändler original, c1875, 12in (30cm). **$6,750-8,250**

A Derby plate, painted by Robert Brewer, crown mark, crossed batons, dots and D in red, c1812, 9in (23cm) diam.
$2,700-3,700

A Derby shell dish, painted by William 'Quaker' Pegg, crown mark, crossed batons, dots and D in red, c1820, 9in (23cm) wide. **$7,750-8,250**

A Derby plate, painted by Fidèle Duvivier, crown mark, crossed batons, dots and D in puce, c1790, 8½in (21cm) diam.
$2,700-4,000

A Meissen blue and white plate, rim chip, blue crossed swords mark with swept hilts, c1727, 9½in (24cm) diam.
$8,250-9,000

A Coalport tray, with ampersand mark, c1865, 21in (53cm) wide.
$2,000-2,400

A Derby plate, painted by William 'Quaker' Pegg, crown mark, crossed batons, dots and D in red, c1815, 8½in (21cm).
$5,250-6,750

A Royal Crown Derby shaped dish, with pierced handles and gilt border, signed Albert Gregory, repaired, 11in (28cm) wide.
$120-150

A plate from the Camden service, the shaped rim with gilt dentil edge, painted by William Billingsley, pattern No. 185, crown mark, crossed batons, dots and D in puce, c1790, 9in (23cm) diam.
$1,000-1,200

A Meissen moulded plate with blue crossed swords mark, Dreher's //, c1735, 9in (23cm) diam.
$16,000-17,500

A Derby plate, painted by William Slater, crown mark, crossed batons, dots and D in red, c1815, gilders numeral 1 for Samuel Keys, 9in (23cm).
$2,700-4,000

A Copeland tray, c1875, 9½in (24cm).
$250-300

A Derby plate, with gilt dentil edge, crown mark, crossed batons, dots and D in red, c1820, 8in (20cm) diam.
$6,000-6,750

A pair of Derby campana vases, painted by William 'Quaker' Pegg, crown, crossed batons, dots and D, red 42, c1814, 12in (31cm). **$30,000-40,000**

A Derby Warwick vase, painted by Daniel Lucas, Bloor Circle mark, c1820, 11in (28cm). **$1,800-2,250**

A Derby vase, in the manner of James Rouse, crown, crossed batons, dots and D in red, c1820. **$2,700-3,700**

A pair of Derby frill vases, heavily encrusted with flowers, 3 patch marks on bases, c1760, 6½in (16cm). **$2,700-3,700**

A pair of spill vases, signed W.E.J. Dean, marked Royal Crown Derby England with crown in red, cypher mark for 1912, 4¾in (12cm). **$2,700-3,500**

A pair of Vienna style vases, by Wagner, blue beehive marks, No. 4075, 19thC. **$8,250-9,000**

A Meissen chinoiserie vase, in the style of C. F. Herold, blue AR mark, c1728, 11in (27.5cm). **$63,000-66,000**

An English porcelain vase, with goat's head handles, 15½in (39cm). **$1,350-1,600**

A baluster vase, probably Alcock, pattern No. 940, c1825, 11in (28cm). **$600-750**

A Derby 'Gibraltar' vase, possibly by Zachariah Boreman, marked, c1785, 14in (35.5cm). **$10,500-11,250**

A Derby 'Long Tom' vase, view by Daniel Lucas, red Bloor Derby mark, c1835, 24½in (62cm). **$3,000-4,500**

A Derby campana vase, with shipping scenes in the style of William Cotton, unmarked, c1815, 17½in (44.5cm). **$15,000-18,000**

A Meissen Kakiemon bottle, incised Johanneum, c1730, 8in (20.5cm). **$57,000-60,000**

A Derby campana vase, with view of Belvoir Castle, probably by D. Lucas. **$2,000-2,250**

Chinese export 'Hong' punch bowl, with European nd Oriental figures on the Pearl riverfront, and ags of various hongs, repaired chip, c1775, 16in 10cm) diam. **$25,500-30,000**

An earthenware basket by Kinkozan, Meiji period, 8in (20cm). **$4,500-5,250**

A Chinese moon flask, Yongzheng mark, 19thC, 19½in (49.5cm). **$20,000-21,000**

n Imari dish, decorated in nderglaze blue, enamels and ilt, c1700, 22in (55.5cm). **6,000-6,500**

A Chinese export armorial plate, c1745, 11in (28.5cm) diam. **$12,000-15,000**

A Chinese export satirical punch bowl, inscribed with rhyme Sauney's Mistake, c1785. **$13,500-16,500**

n earthenware box and cover, by Seikozan, Meiji period, 5in (12.5cm). **$20,000-21,000**

An earthenware bottle, by Yabu Meizan, Meiji period. **$2,250-2,500**

A Chinese export armorial charger, with arms of Paravicini di Cappelli, c1745, 14¾in (37.5cm). **$19,500-20,000**

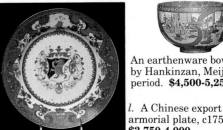

 pair of Chinese export rmorial platters, c1785, 13in (33cm). **2,500-3,000**

A Satsuma earthenware koro and cover, Meiji period, 5½in (14cm). **$4,500-5,000**

An earthenware bowl, by Hankinzan, Meiji period. **$4,500-5,250**

l. A Chinese export armorial plate, c1755. **$3,750-4,000**

A Chinese export famille rose part dinner service, comprising 72 pieces, pierced crown knop repaired, some damage, c1765, tureen stand 14in (36cm) wide. **$23,000-24,000**

A famille rose punch bowl, enamelled with mandarins and attendants, the interior with flowersprays, gilt rim, glaze crack to base, Qianlong, 15½in (39cm). **$5,500-6,000**

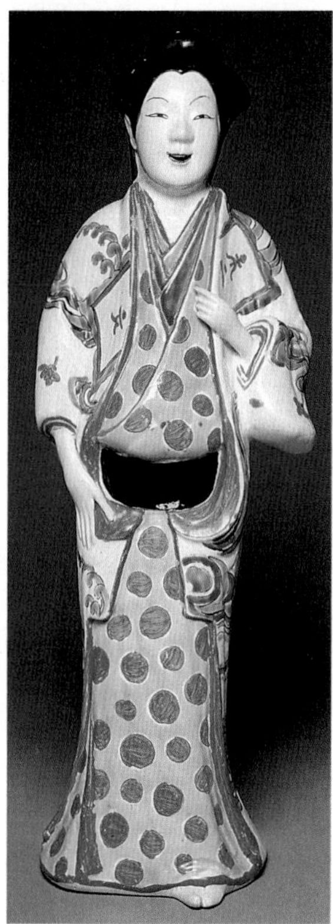

A Kakiemon figure of a bijin, restored, late 17thC, 15in (39cm).
$45,000-52,000

A Kakiemon figure of a lady, the head replaced and further restoration, late 17thC. **$30,000-33,000**

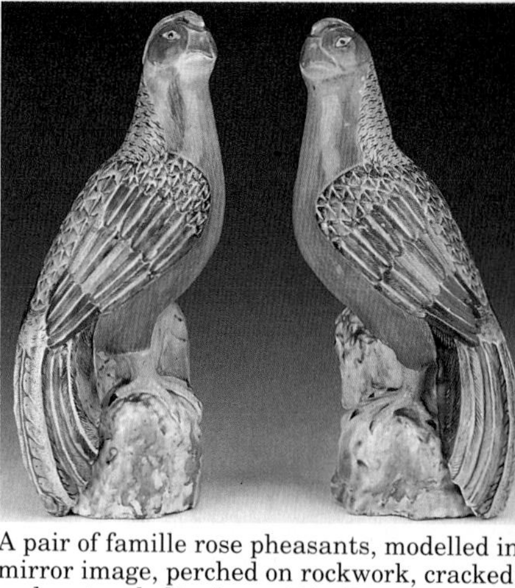

A pair of famille rose pheasants, modelled in mirror image, perched on rockwork, cracked and restored, Qianlong, 13in (33cm).
$42,000-45,000

A pale glazed Sancai horse, the saddle unglazed, restored, Tang Dynasty, 12in (31cm).
$5,250-6,750

A pair of ormolu mounted famille verte biscuit Buddhistic lions, minor restoration, Kangxi, 15in (38cm). **$37,000-43,000**

A Kakiemon model of a shishi, decorated in enamels, cracked and restored, late 17thC, 6in (15cm). **$13,500-16,500**

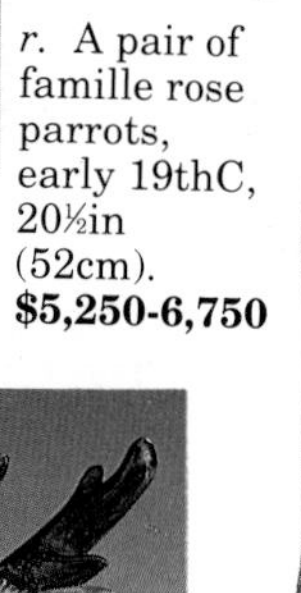

r. A pair of famille rose parrots, early 19thC, 20½in (52cm).
$5,250-6,750

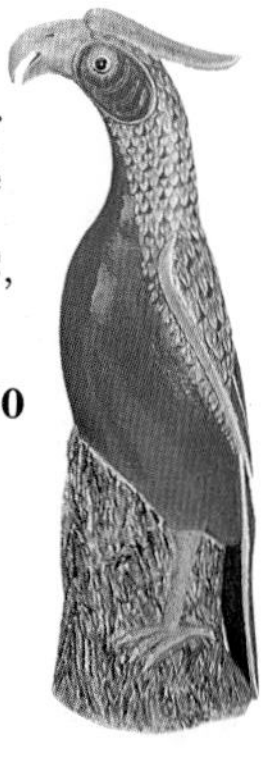

A Kakiemon model of a boy, slight damage, late 17thC, 5½in (14cm).
$21,000-22,500

A Kakiemon figure of a bijin, restored, late 17thC, 15½in (39cm).
$27,000-30,000

A famille rose figure of a recumbent stag, rubbed in places, Qianlong, 6in (15cm) long, with wood stand and box.
$13,500-16,500

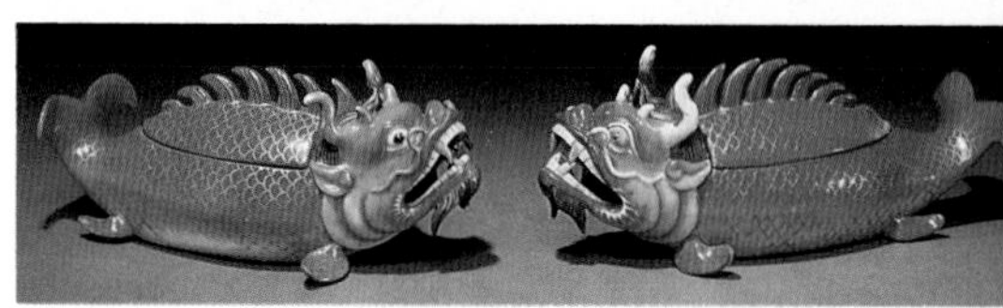

A pair of Chinese export dragon headed carp tureens and covers, restored, early 19thC, 8 and 9in (20 and 23cm) long. **$11,250-15,000**

A pair of baluster vases and covers, painted with flowers and floral trefoil lappets, gilt replacement Buddhistic lion finials, firing fault and fritted, Kangxi, 32in (82cm). **$45,000-47,000**

A pair of baluster jars and covers, one knop finial cracked, Kangxi, 15in (39cm). **$9,750-10,750**

l. Mark of Ming brush washer *below.*

An Arita dish, painted with monogram 'VOC' in the centre, late 17thC, 15½in (39.5cm). **$19,500-20,500**

An early Ming foliate brush washer pot, with flaring lobed sides, six-character mark of Xuande within a double circle, and of the period, 6in (16cm) diam. **$950,000-975,000**

A Chinese mantel garniture, comprising 3 rectangular vases, and a pair of gu-form beakers, slight damage, c1710, 12½ and 13½in (32 and 34cm). **$7,500-8,000**

A 5-piece garniture, comprising 3 baluster vases and 2 gu-shaped beaker vases, minor restorations, Kangxi, 20 and 22in (50 and 56cm). **$33,000-38,000**

An Arita octagonal tureen and cover, damage and restorations, late 17thC, 12½in (32cm) wide. **$16,500-21,000**

A finely painted early Ming dish, the centre with the Three Friends of Winter, damaged and restored, Ming Dynasty, Yongle, 13½in (34cm). **$33,000-37,500**

An Arita octagonal jar, decorated with the Three Friends, Chinese figures, a bridge, buildings and a waterfall, damaged, c1700, 20½in (51.5cm). **$10,500-12,000**

l. A pair of baluster jars and covers, each painted with quatrefoil panels, with knop finials, minor damage, Kangxi, 13in (33cm). **$6,000-9,000**

A pair of earthenware vases, decorated in enamels and gilt, signed Fujisan zo, Meiji period, 10in (25cm).
$6,000-7,500

An earthenware vase, pierced and painted in enamels, signed Kizan sei zo, Meiji period, 10in (25cm). **$7,500-9,000**

An earthenware vase, attributed to Kinkozan, Meiji period, 9½in (24cm).
$3,750-4,500

An earthenware vase, decorated in enamels and gilt, impressed seal Kinkozan zo, Meiji period, 12in (31cm).
$21,000-24,000

A pair of Satsuma earthenware vases, by Kakimoto, Meiji period.
$1,800-2,250

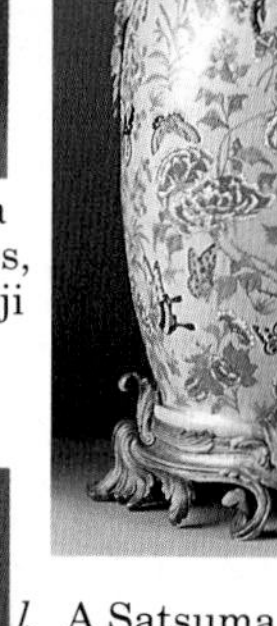

l. A Satsuma earthenware jar, signed Meiga-do Kizan, Meiji period.
$6,000-6,750

A pair of Canton ormolu mounted baluster vases, 19thC, 27in (69cm).
$10,500-15,000

A pair of Canton famille rose turquoise ground vases, chipped, late 19thC, 35in (89cm), on ebonised wood carved stands, damaged, 31in (79cm). **$11,250-13,500**

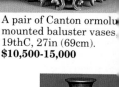

A Satsuma earthenware vase, signed Seikozan, Meiji period.
$2,250-3,000

An earthenware vase, by Kinkozan, Meiji period.
$12,000-13,500

An earthenware vase, by Kinkozan, Meiji period.
$3,000-4,500

A pair of early Kakiemon style jars, painted in enamels with flowers and fences in enamel, one jar cracked, late 17thC, 8½in (21cm).
$70,000-80,000

A pair of German blue stained glass vases, deeply engraved, one repaired, signed F. Zach, c1860, 12in (31cm).
$5,000-7,500

A pair of Bohemian blown ruby glass vases, engraved with The President's House, Washington and Battle Monument, Baltimore, c1860, 14in (36cm).
$30,000-45,000

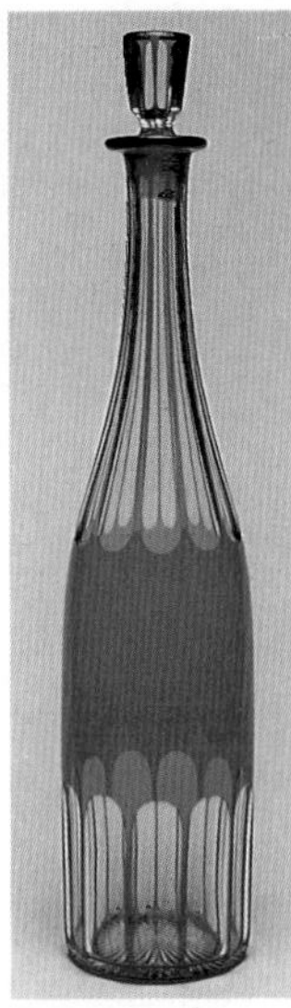

A green overlay glass decanter and stopper, c1870, 14in (36cm).
$400-450

A green, white and clear double overlay glass decanter and stopper, c1860, 16in (41cm).
$450-600

An amethyst brandy decanter, with cork stopper, c1820, 10in (25cm).
$450-550

A pair of English amethyst glass bottles, with silver mounts, c1860, 13in (33cm).
$1,200-1,500

A red flashed glass decanter and stopper, engraved with fruiting vines, c1870, 15in (38cm).
$200-250

A brown glass decanter, with metal neck and stopper, c1830, 9in (23cm).
$200-250

An enamelled decanter and stopper, possibly Apsley Pellatt, c1820, 9in (23cm).
$2,250-3,000

A Stourbridge blue glass decanter, with twisted handle and cut glass stopper, c1870, 9½in (24cm). **$300-400**

A green glass decanter, with cork stopper, engraved with flowers the Union, c1805, 10in (25cm).
$450-550

An enamelled humpen and cover, possibly Franconia, dated '1656', 13½in (34cm).
$15,000-18,000

A green export type wine glass, c1780, 6in (14.5cm).
$600-750

A pair of Stourbridge vases, with cut panels and gilt decoration, c1850, 11½in (30cm). **$1,000-1,200**

Four turquoise wine glasses, with conical bowls on stems with ball knops, c1830, 4½in (11.5cm).
$300-450

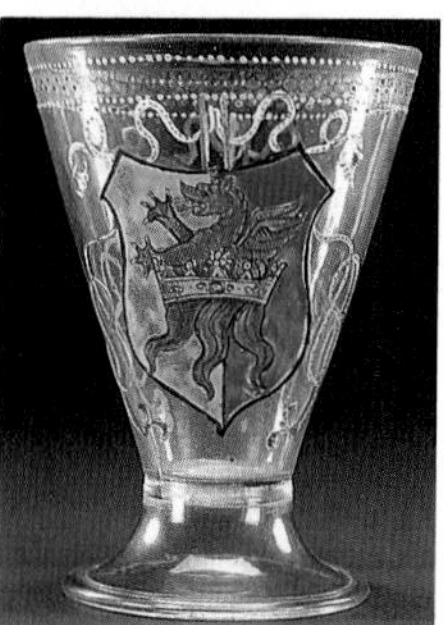
A Venetian enamelled armorial goblet, base of bowl cracked, c1500, 5in (13cm).
$24,000-25,500

An amber glass decanter, with metal stopper, engraved with water lilies, c1850. **$300-225**

A green crackle glass decanter and stopper, with gilt rim and rings, c1820, 10in (25cm).
$200-225

An amberina glass jug, c1870, 11in (28cm).
$300-400

A Netherlands turquoise flask, with 'nipt diamond waies', late 17thC, 9½in (24cm).
$7,500-9,000

A Stourbridge overlay glass goblet, c1850.
$300-400

A gold and frosted glass carafe, c1870, 10in (25cm).
$450-600

A lamp in the shape of a basket of fruit, the basket of silver plate with glass fruit, c1900, 15 by 12in (38 by 31cm). **$1,000-1,200**

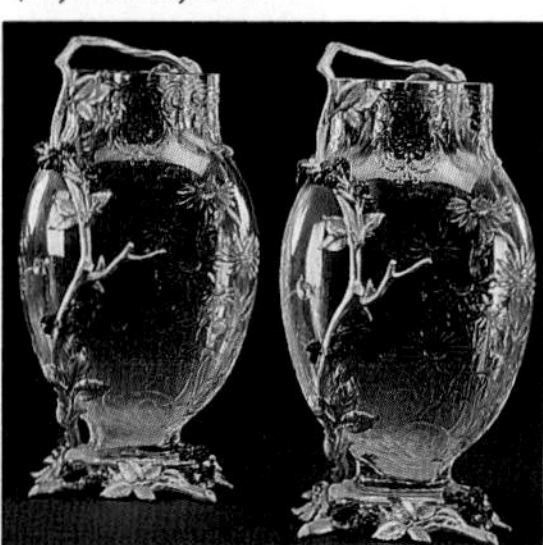
A pair of ormolu mounted vases, deeply engraved, impressed Baccarat mark, c1900, 13½in (34cm).
$6,000-7,500

A set of 9 Webb amber glasses, c1930, 8in (20cm).
$450-600

A lemonade or water set, by Richardsons of Stourbridge, comprising 2 goblets and one jug, lozenge mark for 1845.
$1,500-1,800

set of 6 cranberry glasses, 4in (10cm) high.
:25-300
set of cranberry glass cups, 2in (5cm) high.
:00-250

blue glass
ıerry decanter,
ith silver top,
.840, 14in
ɩ6cm).
350-425

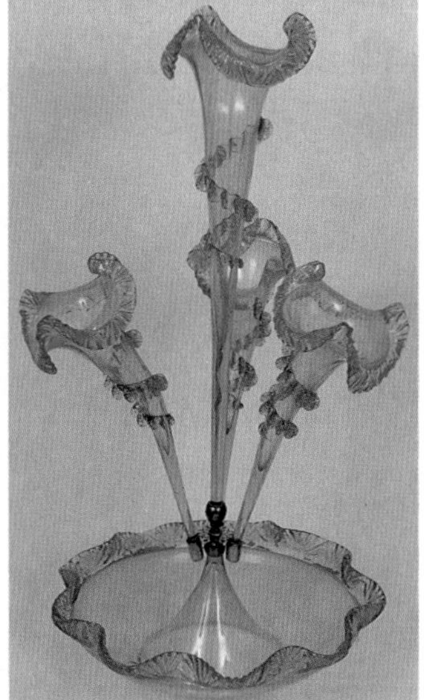

A Victorian vaseline glass épergne, 22½in (57cm) high.
$825-1,000

Nailsea cranberry
ɩass pipe, c1880, 30in
'6cm) long.
450-600

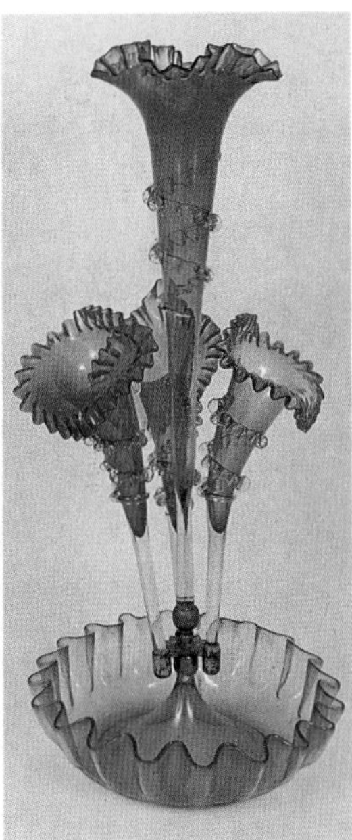

A Victorian cranberry glass épergne, 21in (53cm) high.
$600-750

A St. Louis concentric millefiori mushroom weight, mid-19thC, 3in (7cm). **$3,000-3,750**

A Baccarat pink 'thousand petalled' rose weight, mid-19thC, 3in (8cm). **$3,750-5,250**

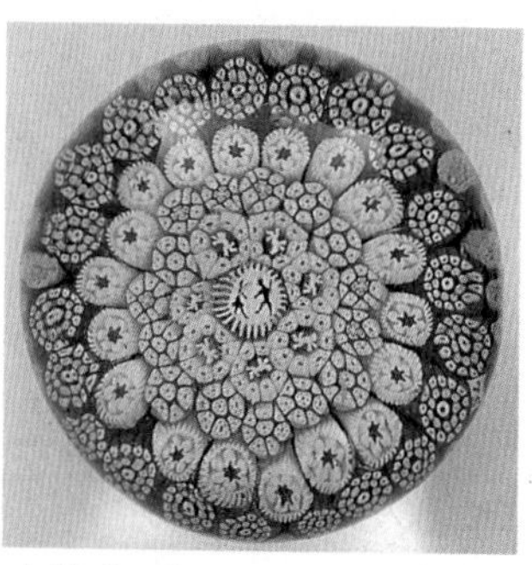

A St. Louis concentric millefiori weight, with central dancing figures, dated 1848, 3in (8cm). **$4,500-7,500**

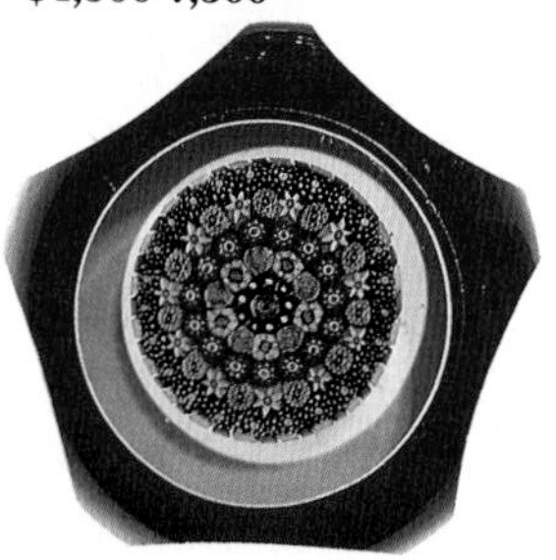

A Clichy double overlay close concentric millefiori mushroom weight. **$7,500-8,000**

A St. Louis signed close concentric millefiori weight, with central silhouette cane, mid-19thC, 3in (8cm). **$4,000-4,500**

A St. Louis fruit weight, the clear glass set with fruit on a latticinio ground, mid-19thC, 3in (8cm). **$1,400-1,800**

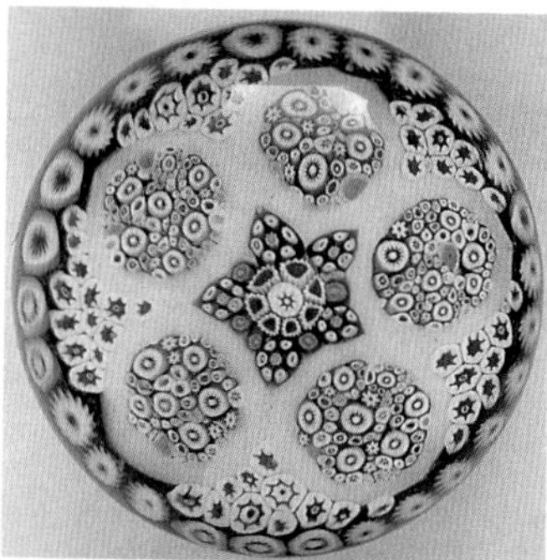

A St. Louis flat bouquet weight, mid-19thC, 2½in (6cm). **$3,000-3,750**

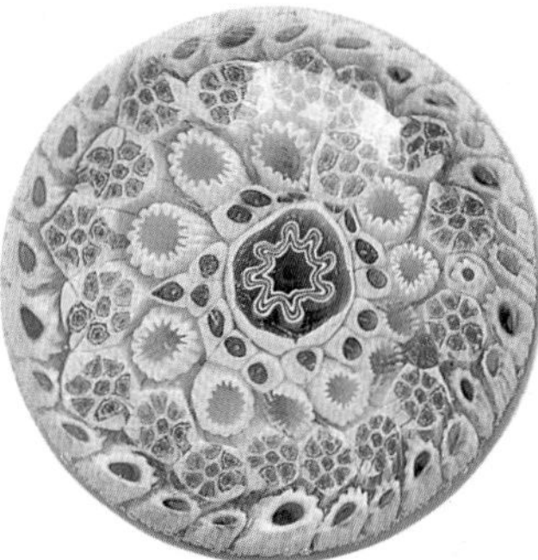

A Baccarat patterned millefiori weight, mid-19thC, 3in (8cm) diam. **$900-1,200**

l. A Bacchus patterned millefiori weight, with 5 floral clusters, mid-19thC, 3in (8cm). **$3,000-3,750**

A Clichy flat bouquet weight, sligh[t] bruise, mid-19thC, 3in (8cm). **$14,500-15,250**

A St. Louis faceted upright bouquet weight, with blue gentian[,] 3 florettes and leaves, within a spiralling torsade, mid-19thC, 3in (8cm). **$2,500-3,000**

A Baccarat garlanded yellow buttercup weight, on a star cut base, chipped, mid-19thC, 3in (8cm). **$6,750-8,000**

A Baccarat butterfly and garland weight, the butterfly with marbled wings, on star cut base, mid-19thC, 3in (8cm). **$3,750-4,500**

Bronze

An Italian bronze figure of the dancing faun, weathered green patination, the square base stamped Salvatore Errico Napoli, late 19thC, 33½in (85cm) high.
$2,250-3,000

An Italian bronze figure of Silenus, standing supporting a bowl cast with masks, now plumbed for water, weathered green patination, the circular base inscribed Fond. G. Sommer, Napoli, late 19thC, 41in (104cm) high.
$1,800-2,700

The Sommer Foundry, Naples, was active in the second half of the 19thC, where it cast reproductions after the Antique. The original model was excavated in Pompeii in 1864 and is now in the Museum of Naples. Silenus was known for his special knowledge and wisdom inspired by wine drinking.

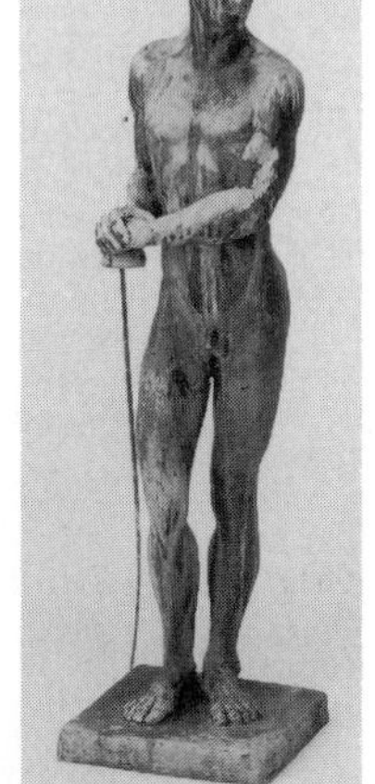

A bronze figure of a naked man, standing holding a foil, weathered green patination, on square base signed Felix Weiss and dated 1926, 41in (104cm) high.
$1,800-2,700

Bronze

Contrary to popular opinion, it is possible to produce virtually perfect copies of antique originals, and green patination, which many take to be a sign of age, is easily applied. The underside of the piece should be examined and not look too clean, and if there is wear in the patination it should be in places where it would occur naturally as the piece was handled over the years. Remember that signatures and foundry marks are as easy to fake as the piece itself.

A Japanese bronze crane, standing with head raised, slightly weathered patination, 19thC, 48in (122cm) high.
$1,050-1,350

Iron

A pair of cast iron seats, each with wooden back and geometrically pierced seat, stamped Geo Smith & Co., Sun Foundry, Glasgow, with foliate pierced end supports and indistinct diamond registration stamp, c1860, 61in (155cm).
$1,500-2,250

A wrought iron birdcage, early 20thC, 128in (325cm) high.
$2,700-3,300

A Regency wrought iron garden seat, 45in (114cm).
$1,500-2,250

A wrought iron bridge, with wooden slats, 194in (492cm). **$4,500-6,000**

A Coalbrookdale lily of the valle pattern cast iron seat, with wooden slatted seat stamped Coalbrookdale, the back with registration stamp and number, the end supports joined by stretchers, c1870, 62in (157cm). **$1,500-2,250**

A French cast iron fountain, with a water putto seated on an upturned ewer, the outswept base cast with masks, one plumbed for water, 52in (132cm) high, with associated carved stone pool surround, 84in (213cm) diam. **$3,000-4,500**

Cast Iron

Probably the most widely reproduced of all materials. If you are buying garden ornaments or furniture purported to be antique, first lift them. If they are light they are probably aluminium. If they are heavy, look at the finish. Casting marks, the little protruding spots of metal, were carefully removed in Victorian castings and any that were not would long since have been worn away. As with bronze, foundry marks are commonly faked.

A Coalbrookdale Osmundia fern pattern cast iron seat, with wooden slatted seat, the back stamped Coalbrookdale with registration stamp and number 275254, the end supports joined by stretcher, c1870, 58in (147cm **$3,000-4,500**

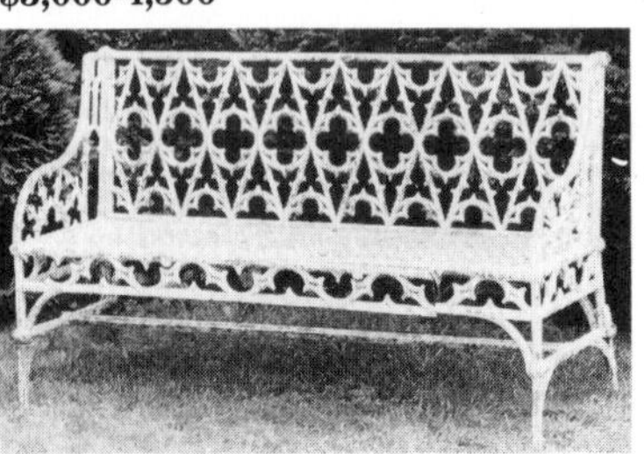

A pair of French white painted cast iron garden benches, with Gothic trellis pierced back and honeycomb pierced seat, foliate scroll sides, some damage, c1870, 57in (145cm). **$1,800-2,700**

A French cast iron urn, with scrolling handles, on square moulded pedestal, the sides cast with laurel wreaths, late 19thC, 46in (117cm) high. **$750-900**

A Victorian cast iron gate, with a central sunflower roundel, 71in (180cm) high, and a pair of cast iron panels cast with foliage, 61in (155cm) high. **$1,500-2,250**

A pair of cast iron seats, designed by Andrew McLaren, with wooden slatted seats, the back and end supports with diamond registration stamp for 8th January, 1869, numbered 15, c1870, 64in (163cm). **$4,500-6,000**

A pair of large wrought iron jardinières, with zinc liners, c1840, 45½in (115cm) diam. **$4,500-6,000**

Did you know?

MILLER'S Antiques Price Guide builds up year by year to form the most comprehensive photo reference library available.

. cast and wrought iron plant tand, with 2 curved tiers, c1840, 65in (420cm).
3,000-4,500

A set of 4 white painted cast iron garden chairs, each with pierced back and seat, stamped on the front seat rail Robert Wood, Maker, Phila, and a circular painted cast iron table, 19thC.
$6,000-8,250

. wrought iron marble top table, vith plain legs and pierced scroll pron, 53in (134cm).
600-750

A set of 4 cast iron round garden vases, with ovolo borders and leaf moulded sides, 18½in (47cm) diam. **$1,200-1,500**

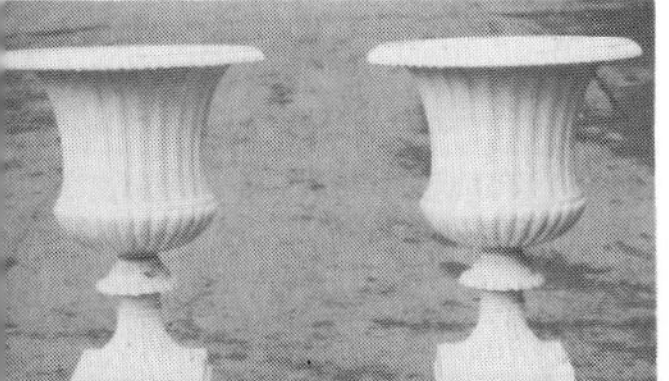

A pair of cast iron urns, 19thC, 25in (64cm) diam.
$1,200-1,500

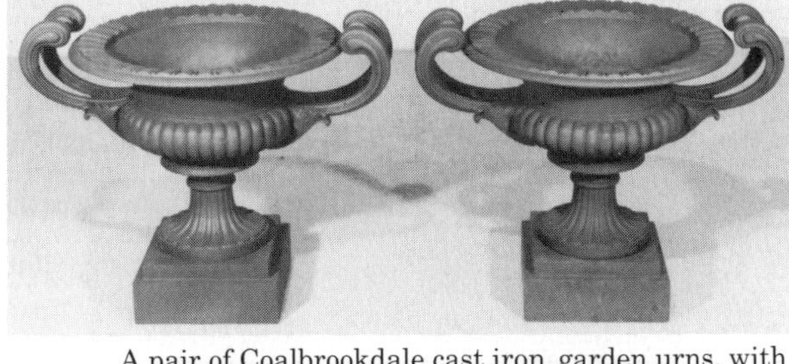

A pair of Coalbrookdale cast iron garden urns, with 2 scrolled loop handles, fluted and flared rim, gadrooned body, fluted socle base on stepped plinth, 19thC, 23½in (60cm). **$750-1,200**

Lead

. pair of lead sphinxes, possibly epicting Madame du Barry and Madame de Pompadour, on tepped bases, early 20thC, 27in 68.5cm) high.
7,500-9,000

A set of 4 lead urns, each with a oliate cast moulded rim, the body ast with a seam to each side, and with 2 scrolled dragon head andles, mid-18thC, 18½in (59cm) igh. **$6,000-8,250**

Two lead cherubs, some damage and restoration, early 18thC, the stone bases later, the figures 33 and 32½in (84 and 82.5cm).
$4,500-6,000

A set of 8 lead urns, cast with alternate female and satyr masks, beneath boldly gadrooned rim, some distortion, 18in (46cm) diam. **$3,000-4,500**

A pair of lead urns, the upper part of the body decorated with vine, above a frieze of classical figures, the lower part gadrooned, on circular spreading foot with a repeating foliate motif and egg-and-dart border, weathered, repairs, one lid later, late 19thC/early 20thC, 30in (76cm) high.
$5,250-7,500

Lead

Lead is one of the most difficult materials to identify. After a few years exposure to the elements and a little judicious waxing, new lead and old are visually indistinguishable. However, early leadwork was primarily of very high quality and the finish and detail on 18thC figures is very good, whereas modern pieces suffer by comparison. Fingers are often clumsy, hair badly detailed and faces expressionless. Also, figures in reduced scale (i.e. less than lifesize), are almost certainly late, although often misleadingly described as 18thC. Genuine 18thC lead cistern tanks which make delightful planters, should have some evidence of having been used as cisterns, usually signs of an inlet pipe around the top rim and a tap hole at the lower edge.

Marble

An Italian white marble group of 2 children, both reclining on a rocky outcrop, c1860, 36in (92cm) high. **$5,250-6,000**

A white marble urn, 24in (61cm) high, on shaped sandstone square base, c1860.
$1,800-2,700

A veined marble cistern, 18thC, 20in (51cm) high.
$2,250-3,000

Marble

There are many native British marbles, but the white marbles used in sculpture are mostly Italian. True statuary marble, the most highly prized and now virtually unobtainable, is a creamy white colour and has little or no veining. Carrara, or second statuary, is a bluer white with some degree of veining and is harder and thus more resistant to the British weather. Once the surface of the marble has broken down and become sugary, it is often beyond restoration.

Modern marbles, often dazzingly white and imported from India, can be readily identified by their crystalline nature.

When buying marble statuary, look for signs of quality carving in high relief, arms and hair carved away from the body and true proportions.

An Italian white marble fountain, the bowl internally carved with fish, the outside with foliage on baluster column and rising square base, carved with stylized dolphins and anthemion, c1870, 39in (99cm).
$4,800-5,700

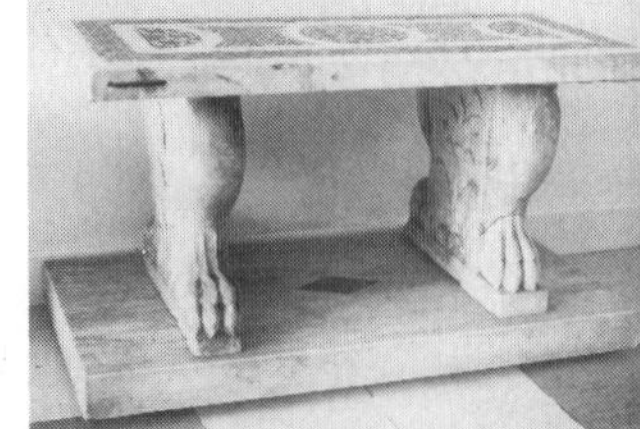

A marble and mosaic bench, inlaid with geometric tesserae fragments, on solid lion's claw monopodia base, the panelled sides carved with flowerheads, the later plinth centred by a porphyry lozenge, associated, one restored foot, 39in (99cm) high.
$7,500-9,000

Stone

Coade stone lion, late 18thC, 45 by 56in
14 by 142cm). **$15,000-18,000**

A Vicenza stone seat, with shallow arched back and on volute and carved paw supports, early 20thC, 67in (170cm) wide. **$2,700-3,300**

Reconstituted Stone

Although debased by inferior modern castings, reconstituted stone has a long and honourable history. One of the earliest types used in England was Coadestone, (named after Eleanor Coade, its inventor). Starting in 1769, the Coade factory produced an enormous number of pieces of the highest quality, and signed pieces fetch high prices.

Look for the same signs of quality as in marble carvings. The lines of cast pieces should be crisp and the material free from aggregate and air holes. As with carving, the casting should be free and confident.

A pair of carved sandstone gate pier finials of heraldic beasts, each holding a blank cartouche, on an octagonal base, weathered, minor chips, 19thC, 40in (101.5cm).
$2,700-3,300

A pair of stoneware lions, late 19thC, 29½in (75cm) high. **$3,000-4,500**

A pair of composition stone sphinxes, each wearing a headdress and reclining on rectangular base decorated in relief with hieroglyphics, early 20thC, 25in (63cm) high.
$1,200-1,800

pair of composition stone deer, te 19thC, 50 by 42½in (127 by)8cm). **$9,000-12,000**

A composition stone figure of a fisherboy, seated wearing a cap, on a rocky outcrop, mid-20thC, 51in (129.5cm) high.
$2,700-3,300

set of 4 composition stone urns, odern, 31½in (80cm) diam.
,800-2,700

A set of 4 composition stone musicians, each seated on a gate pier ball and on square pedestal, modern, 59in (149.5cm) high.
$5,250-7,500

Stone

The two stones most commonly encountered are limestone and sandstone. Common types of limestone include Portland stone (grey/white) and Bath stone (yellow). Common sandstones include York stone (dark yellow weathering to black/green) and red sandstone. Broadly speaking, limestone is preferred for statuary and sandstone for architectural elements. Beware of pieces where the surface has broken down, as they may be beyond restoration. Limestone is generally more popular than sandstone because many people do not like the black and green colour of weathered sandstone. Sandstone is also more brittle and although it will take fine detail, it is susceptible to damage.

A composition stone jardinière, the everted rim and sides with latticework decoration, on claw feet, on circular plinth, modern, 32in (81cm) high.
$750-1,200

A pair of Vicenza stone gate pier urns, the lids overflowing with fruit, Italian, early 20thC, 56in (142cm) high.
$5,250-7,500

Wood

A George II carved pine door surround, with a broken pediment above a frieze elaborately carved with acanthus leaves, the frame with foliate and egg-and-dart moulding, on block feet, some splitting, repairs, restorations, 18thC.
$2,250-3,000

Terracotta

A terracotta figure of the Venus Italica, standing looking to sinister, c1870, 65in (165cm) high.
$1,500-2,250

This is a copy of Canova's original marble statue which was completed in 1812 and placed in the Pitti Palace, Florence.

A flank of miniature pine panelling, with a moulded cornice, the chimney-breast with a rectangular picture panel, flanked to each side by an arched shelved niche, damages, losses, 20thC, 115 by 77in (292 by 195cm).
$3,000-3,750

A Pyghtle pattern wooden seat, with slatted seat and arched slatted back, c1910.
$1,050-1,350

Terracotta

Terracotta (red earth in Latin) has been used since pre-classical times. It is resistant to weathering and thus ideal for exterior statuary and planters. The most desirable colour is yellow and the least, brick red. Oil jars have become a highly popular decorative feature in gardens in recent years, but because terracotta is a fragile material, genuine ones are rare and they are still produced in considerable quantities in Southern Europe. Genuine oil jars will probably have some signs of glazing in the interior.

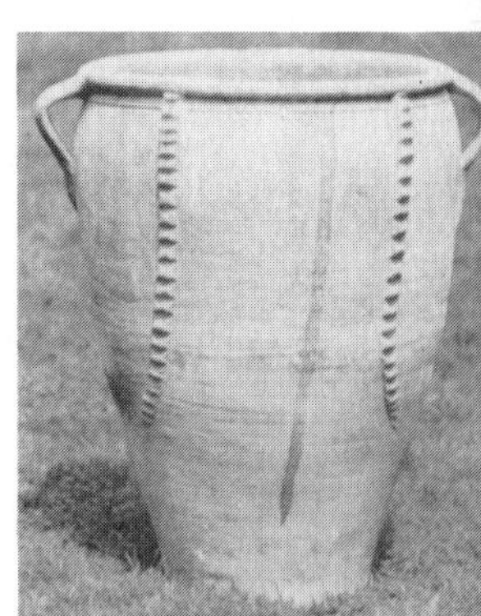

A Mediterranean terracotta oi storage jar, 29in (73cm).
$225-300

A quantity of pine panelling, wit plain fielded inset panels, including 2 door openings, each with flower-and-reel carving to the edge, including dado sections some elements associated, damages, losses, restorations, 19thC, 120 by 770in (304.5 by 1956cm).
$2,250-3,000

POTTERY & PORCELAIN

The pottery and porcelain market has undergone a period of great uncertainty over the past year. Despite a general lack of confidence, in recent months there has been a change for the better. Good prices were achieved in advance of some of the major fairs and most auctioneers began to report an improvement in the unsold percentage, down from 50%+ to between 15% and 25% on average.

Fair dealers are reporting a steady demand for 1920s and 1930s wares from Clarice Cliff, Shelley, Susie Cooper *et al* and the strength of the upper end of this market was reflected in the $20,000 obtained by Sotheby's for a Wedgwood 'Fairy' lustre ginger jar and cover.

The strongest-selling areas have been Continental ceramics. German porcelain has sold well, two of the strongest areas being early Meissen and decorative 19th century services. Above-estimate figures were achieved consistently at the lower end of the market: Bonhams achieved $2,750 against an estimate of $600-900 for a c1755 Meissen monkey band figure and a rare German faience portrait plaque thought to depict the Empress Marie-Thérèse, fetched $8,250 plus premium.

A Meissen monkey band figure of a violinist, modelled by J.J. Kändler and P. Reincke, restored, c1755, 5in (13cm) high.

My favourite rags to riches story concerned a dated English delft drug jar shown below:

An English delft drug jar of oviform shape, titled 'C. FL: Aurant', damaged, 7in (18cm).

It was purchased by the vendor as part of a lorry load of 'junk' for which he had paid $30 and he was pleased to be told that the jar, even though held together by string, was worth $450-750. He telephoned for the results after the sale and was amazed to hear that it had sold for $13,500 plus premium.

In the same sale was a piece of delft which depicted Sir Thomas Killigrew whose piratical ancestors came from my home port of Falmouth. Bidders danced the hornpipe to the tune of $67,500 plus premium.

Sotheby's totalled just over three-quarters of a million dollars for the J.P. Kassebaum Collection and the quality of the English delft was reflected in the prices. A c1640 Southwark dish sold for $63,000 and a polychrome drug jar for $75,000.

The top end of the English porcelain market performed above expectations whilst run-of-the-mill wares from all factories except Lowestoft and Caughley dropped by about 20%. As usual it was those pieces fresh to the market which performed best.

Those interested in English blue and white porcelain should beware one or two fakes which have been seen over the past few years. These seem to be copies of Limehouse shell dishes and are crudely painted with Chinese figures in gardens. The material is more akin to pottery than porcelain and the moulded detail on the reverse is poorly defined.

With these fakes, as with many others, it is necessary to examine the paste and the glaze as well as the potting technique, feel and weight. Most fakes would fool you in a photograph but if you put a fake amongst similar genuine pieces, close your eyes and go by feel alone, the false piece is immediately apparent. Of course, the ability to detect fakes and identify types of pottery and porcelain presupposes some experience in handling a variety of wares. Beginners could do worse than buy slightly damaged 19th century English pottery and porcelain. Many are highly decorative as well as being of historical interest, and the attendant research can be fascinating. Seventy-five dollars should buy a whole shelf of 19th century porcelain cups representing all the major manufacturers, and most Chinese porcelain is modestly priced, especially if damaged.

My own favourite 'buy' this year was a large porcelain dish. Though filthy, stained and held together by copper staples, it was nevertheless a marked Meissen piece c1735. Of negligible value because of the extensive damage, it is still of value as an example of the beautiful hard paste porcelain produced at Meissen. I try to avoid buying restored pieces but if I do buy one, then I remove the restoration. This is not always easy and in most cases should be left to an expert.

Christopher Spencer
April 1993

POTTERY

Baskets

A pair of David Wilson pearlware baskets and stands, c1810, 10½in (27cm). **$750-1,200**

An Italian majolica cistern, raised on 4 feet, the interior inscribed J. Battaglia, damaged, 19thC, 20½in (52cm) wide.
$750-1,200

Bowls

A creamware bowl, the exterior printed in black by Sadler and Green, with Venus Rising from the Waves, Neptune in his Chariot, The Colonists' Departure, the interior with An East Indiaman on the Port Tack, within 6 sprays of flowers and leaves, cracked, c1775, 9in (22cm) diam. **$225-255**

A Staffordshire creamware bowl, c1770.
$375-525

A Quimper silver shaped bowl, c1885, 9½in (24cm) diam.
$225-255

A pearlware cream bowl and cover, with loop handle, decorated in coloured enamels with scattered French sprigs, within blue line borders, minor restoration, early 19thC, 9in (22cm) high. **$225-255**

A creamware bowl, moulded with horizontal bands, decorated in coloured enamels, damaged, c1785, 6in (15cm) diam.
$150-225

Cottages & Pastille Burners

A Staffordshire pastille burner, c1840, 5in (13cm) high.
$150-225

A Staffordshire cottage, with blue underglaze roof and pink flowers, c1840, 4½in (11.5cm) high.
$135-150

A Staffordshire Gothic style cottage, with green, red and gilt decoration, c1870, 8in (20cm) high. **$150-225**

A Staffordshire pastille burner, the roof in underglaze blue, depicting a fox and goose, 6½in (16.5cm) high. **$150-225**

A Yorkshire pottery chapel moneybox, decorated in blue, yellow and puce, inscribed W. Ridgway - Susworth, January 14th, 1849, 6½in (17cm) high.
$1,050-1,350

vo Staffordshire cottages,
›tash Farm and Stanfield Hall,
›th wrongly titled, both with
ue roofs, orange chimneys,
een grass, and gilt decoration,
849, 6in (15cm) high.
;00-750

rongly titled items are not
ıcommon among some
'affordshire models.

Staffordshire castle ornament,
ı ochre with red doors and gilt
im, 3½in (9cm) high.
150-225

;ow Creamers

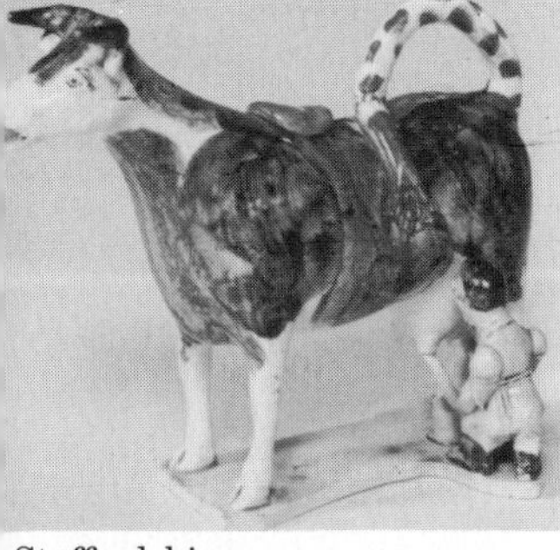

Staffordshire creamware cow
eamer milking group and cover,
›me restoration, c1775, 6½in
.6.5cm) wide.
750-1,200

ı blue and white Willow pattern
ɔw creamer, transfer printed,
1840, 7in (18cm) wide.
375-450

Cups

A Strasbourg faïence cup and cover, tin glaze decorated in coloured enamels, with figures of Chinamen in a landscape, c1775, 3in (8cm) high.
$375-525

A Victorian Staffordshire blue and white loving cup, with frogs and newts inside, 7in (18cm) high.
$225-255

Figures - Animals

A Staffordshire cockerel, decorated in Pratt colours, c1800, 7½in (19cm).
$2,250-3,000

A Brown-Westhead, Moore & Co. majolica bird group, c1870, 14in (36cm) high.
$1,500-2,250

A Victorian Staffordshire eagle, c1860, 7½in (19cm) high.
$375-450

Make the Most of Miller's

In Millers we do NOT just reprint saleroom estimates. We work from realised prices, either from an auction room or a dealer. Our consultants then work out a realistic price range for a similar piece. This is to try to avoid repeating freak results - either low or high.

A Staffordshire saltglaze solid agate model of a pug, streaked in black and with black slip eyes, c1750, 2¾in (7cm) high.

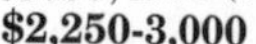

$2,250-3,000

A Samuel Alcock figure of a seated poodle with granitic decoration, impressed numerals 218, c1830, 3in (8cm) high.

$450-600

A pair of Staffordshire dogs, in white with gilding, c1860, 11in (28cm).

$225-255

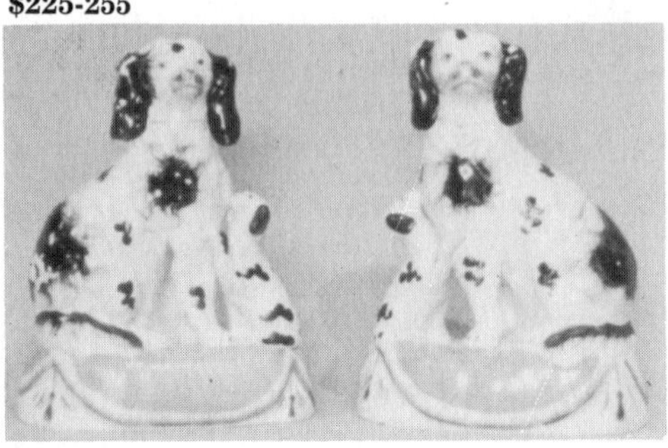

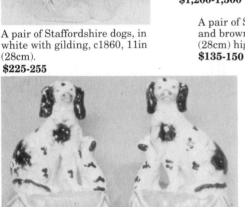

A pair of Staffordshire groups, of a spaniel and pup, c1850, 6in (15cm).

$900-1,500

A pair of Staffordshire greyhounds with a hare, tan on a green and brown base, c1860, 6in (15cm) high.

$150-225

A Staffordshire group of a cow, calf and milkmaid with a blue skirt, on a green base, c1800, 7½in (19.5cm).

$10,500-12,000

A Yorkshire group of a cow, calf and milkmaid, decorated in mulberry purple patches edged in black, c1820, 7in (17cm).

$1,200-1,500

A pair of Staffordshire lions, tan and brown colours, c1870, 11in (28cm) high.

$135-150

A Staffordshire figure of an elephant, in shades of brown on white base, trunk restored, 19thC, 8in (20cm) wide.

$450-600

A Staffordshire figure of a spaniel, seated on a rococo base, c1850, 6½in (16cm).

$375-450

A Staffordshire lion, brown on cream ground, c1810, 4½in (11.5cm).

$1,800-2,700

A pair of Staffordshire penholders, modelled as recumbent whippets, on rococo style bases, c1850, 4in (10cm).

$300-375

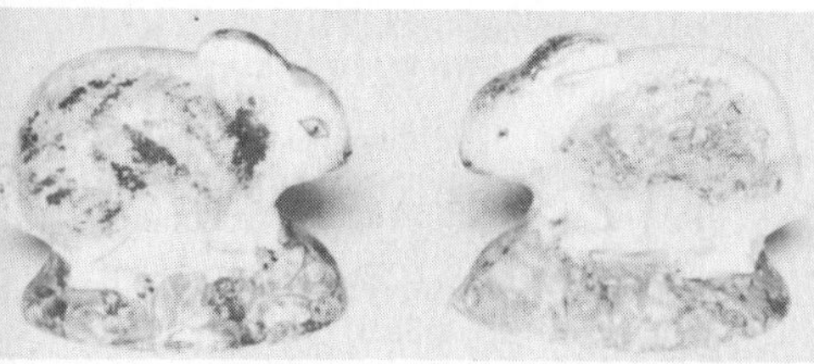

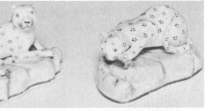

A pair of pearlware figures of hares, sponged in yellow and black, some restoration, c1800, 3½in (8.5cm) wide.
$600-750

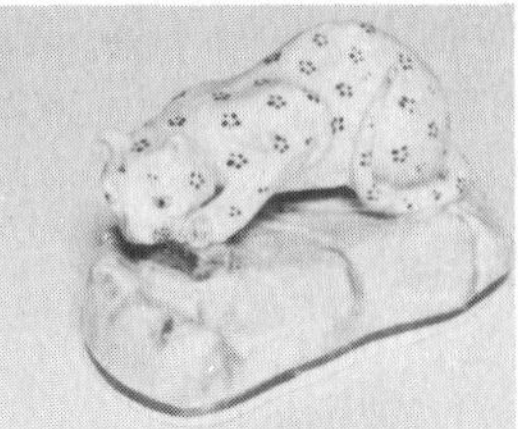

A pair of Samuel Alcock figures of leopards, impressed numerals 256 and 156, c1835, 4in (9cm) wide.
$1,050-1,350

A Prattware South American tree squirrel, Staffordshire or Yorkshire, c1800, 3in (7.5cm).
$2,250-3,000

A Staffordshire rugged sheep group on a well coloured base, with bocage, c1850, 2½in (6.5cm) high.
$225-255

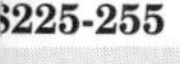

A Staffordshire figure of a Sphinx, decorated in Pratt colours, c1800, 3in (7.5cm).
$2,250-3,000

A Staffordshire zebra, with black and white stripes on a green base, c1843, 8½in (21cm) high.
$150-225

A pair of miniature Staffordshire sheep groups, white with green and yellow bocage, c1850, 2in (5cm) high.
$180-225

A Staffordshire figure of a stag, decorated in yellow and green, c1800, 5in (13cm).
$1,050-1,350

A Staffordshire sheep group with bocage, overglaze green, blue and brown, restored, Walton cartouche on the back, c1815.
$450-600

Figures - People

A Staffordshire figure of the 'Widow', in a floral dress, with a child in brown shirt and yellow trousers, on a red base with pink and yellow bocage, some restoration, c1800.
$375-525

A set of 4 Dixon, Austin & Co. pearlware figures, emblematic of The Seasons, minor flaking to enamels, Spring and Summer with slight chips to bases, impressed marks, c1820, 9in (23cm).
$2,700-3,300

A Staffordshire figure, in shades of green, pink and brown, c1830, 5in (13cm). **$600-750**

A Staffordshire group portraying the Royal children in a pony cart, the cart with separate wheel, and on an open rococo base, c1845, 7½in (19cm).
$600-750

A Staffordshire figure of a lady and child, dressed in a yellow gown, the boy in a blue jacket and striped trousers, early 19thC, 9¼in (23.5cm).
$1,050-1,350

A Staffordshire figure of Jupiter, underglaze blue and gilding, c1830-40.
$150-225

A Staffordshire figure of Little Red Riding Hood, with orange and brown overglaze, c1840.
$150-225

A Staffordshire figure of Napoleon Bonaparte, c1845, 7½in (19cm).
$150-225

A Staffordshire jug, modelled as George Whitfield, or The Nightwatchman, c1810, 9in (22cm).
$600-750

A Staffordshire figure of girl dancing with a parrot and cat, the girl wearing a blue dress with red and green check, an orange cloak, pink hat and pantaloons, c1845.
$150-225

A Staffordshire group, possibly portraying Mr. Barton and Miss Rosa Henry as 'Giaffier' and 'Zuleika' in 'The Bride of Abydos', c1847, 13in (33cm).
$750-1,200

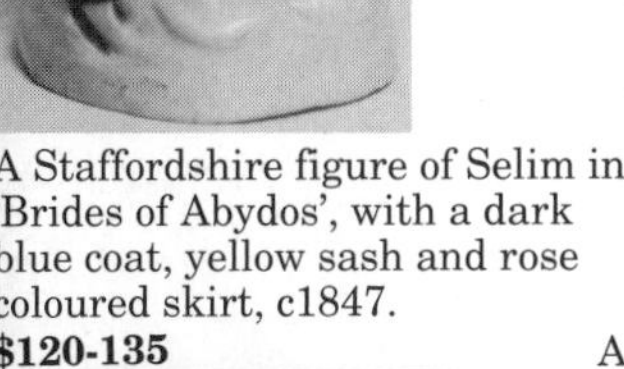

A Staffordshire figure of Selim in 'Brides of Abydos', with a dark blue coat, yellow sash and rose coloured skirt, c1847.
$120-135

A Staffordshire figure of Eliza Cook, c1849, 11in (28cm).
$300-375

A Staffordshire group of Crimean soldiers, overglaze colours, c1855, 9in (22.5cm).
$135-150

A Staffordshire pair of figures, titled The Gardener, wearing a blue coat and pink hat on yellow and green base, may represent Sir James Paxton and the Princess Royal, c1860, 9½in (24cm).
$375-450

A Staffordshire figure of the Revd. Edward Goulburn, c1850, 11½in (29cm).
$750-1,200

Miller's is a price GUIDE not a price LIST

A Staffordshire figure of 'Arabia', from a Minton original, on a yellow, green and brown base, c1850.
$180-225

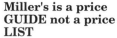

A Staffordshire equestrian figure of Lord Raglan, by Thomas Parr, c1855, 12in (31cm).
$1,500-2,250

A pair of Staffordshire figures of a sailor, titled 'England', and a Highland soldier, titled 'Scotland', c1854, 10in (25cm).
$600-750

A Staffordshire theatrical group, one wearing a blue jacket, the other a red sash, and carrying a tambourine, on cream base, c1860, 9in (23cm).
$135-150

A Staffordshire figure of St. George and the Dragon, with yellow helmet, c1860, 10in (25cm).
$225-255

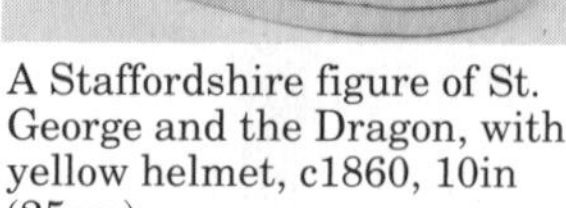

An early Staffordshire group of a shepherd and shepherdess with sheep, 5in (12.5cm).
$450-600

A Staffordshire figure of a girl by a stream, in natural colours, probably a Temperance piece, c1860.
$135-150

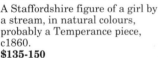

A group of French fishermen, overglazed in red, white and blue with pink shrimps, c1870, 13½in (33cm).
$135-150

A Staffordshire figure of John Milton, with a blue coat, red cloak, puce trousers, leaning on a red draped plinth, 7in (18cm).
$150-180

A Staffordshire pottery figure of a grape harvester, with pink edged jacket over a spotted skirt, carrying a basket of red grapes, on a brown base, c1880, 9½in (24cm).
$105-120

A Staffordshire pottery Millers group, the boy with pink trousers, the girl with green jacket, orange and brown mill with red door, yellow wheat sheaves, c1890, 10½in (26cm).
$225-300

A Staffordshire group, titled 'The Fortune Teller', with green and purple grape vine, some gilding and raised lettering, c1860, 12in (30cm).
$120-135

A Staffordshire pottery group of gentleman and companion, with a young girl in Highland costume, in a boat, picked out in colours, on moulded oval base, 19thC, 10in (25cm).
$225-300

A Victorian Staffordshire figure with a stag, c1860, 8in (20cm).
$225-300

A Staffordshire group of huntsmen with a clock piece, well coloured in green and orange, with pink and green head gear, 9in (23cm).
$105-120

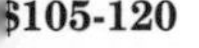

A Staffordshire Walton type figure of a woman with dog and child, in a puce gown with yellow fichu, the child with a red dress.
$1,050-1,350

A pair of Whieldon type groups, with brown, green and cream colouring, c1765, 3in (7.5cm).
$3,000-4,500

A Wood family pottery figure of a woman feeding poultry, with coloured glazes, c1785, 7½in (19cm).
$7,500-9,000

A Wood school group of a Shepherd and Shepherdess with sheep, with green, grey and black colouring, glazed, 10in (25cm).
$1,500-2,250

A pair of Wood School figures, in green, brown and cream, repaired, 8in (20cm).
$4,800-5,700

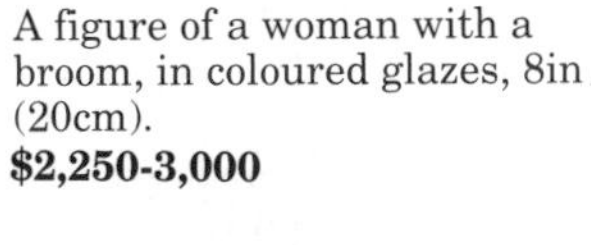

A figure of a woman with a broom, in coloured glazes, 8in (20cm).
$2,250-3,000

A Wood School figure of Van Tromp, with grey jacket, green trousers, yellow collar and cuffs, c1790, 10in (25cm).
$5,250-6,000

A Yorkshire pottery figure of a man and dog, the man with blue jacket and yellow trousers, c1800, 10½in (26.5cm).
$9,000-10,000

A Höchst faïence group, modelled as a young shepherdess seated mourning the death of a sheep, firing cracks, blue wheel and D mark, incised 49, 7in (18cm).
$900-1,500

Victorian Staffordshire Figures

Staffordshire Figures

The letters and figures at the end of each caption refer to the book *Staffordshire Portrait Figures,* by P.D. Gordon Pugh.

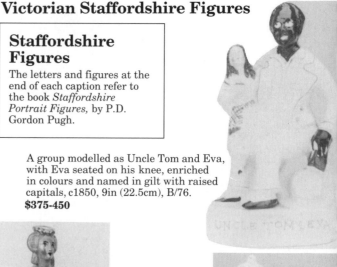

A group modelled as Uncle Tom and Eva, with Eva seated on his knee, enriched in colours and named in gilt with raised capitals, c1850, 9in (22.5cm), B/76.
$375-450

Faïence

Faïence, also spelled fayence; tin glazed earthenwares, named after the town of Faenza in Italy, but actually used to describe products made anywhere but Italy, where the same wares are called 'maiolica'.

A French pottery inkwell, the figure with pink skirt, well coloured, 8in (20cm).
$180-225

A standing group, modelled as Ready and Willing, with a soldier in an iron red jacket, tartan flag, on an oval base named in gilt capitals, c1854, 12in (30.5cm), C/190.
$1,200-1,500

A pair of Staffordshire figures, Mary Glover as 'Yourawkee' and Mrs Vining as 'Peter Wilkins', c1837, 8in (20cm), E/377.
$375-450

Flasks

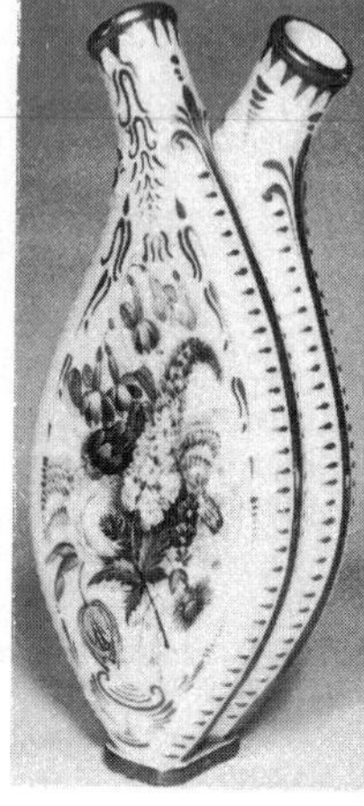

A pearlware ovoid double flask, with moulded borders, decorated in coloured enamels with sprays of flowers and leaves, picked out in gilt and with monogram 'WW', some damage, c1800, 7½in (19cm).
$300-375

'latware

. Staffordshire pearlware niniature fluted oval dish, noulded in relief with a thistle nd picked out in green, brown nd ochre, within a moulded reen border, minor rim chip, 1780, 5in (13cm).
300-375

A Quimper charger, decorated with a Breton couple with a child in polychrome enamels, c1885, 12½in (32cm).
$300-375

A Malicorne charger, painted with a country scene in polychrome enamels, with a typical floral garland border, c1890, 13½in (34cm).
$225-300

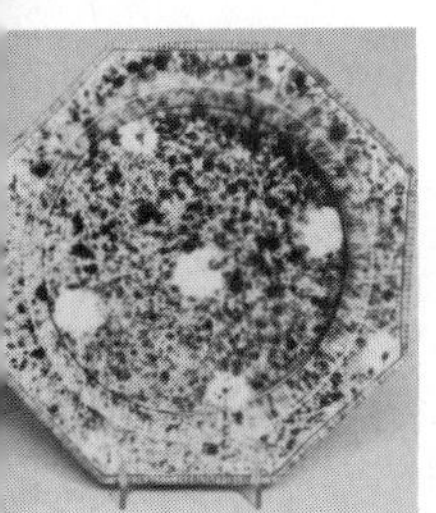

set of 6 creamware plates, with illed borders, splashed in pale lue and green on a brown ponged ground, the reverse milarly sponged, some storation, one plate with andwritten label 'Similar in ruro Museum ...', c1770, 8in 0cm).
1,050-1,350

A Dèsvres dish, decorated with figures of a Breton couple and arabesque border, c1880, 9in (23cm).
$180-225

A Nevers faïence deep dish, with polychrome enamels, impressed mark Nevers, c1780.
$225-255

. Mailing plate, North East Coast ndustries Exhibition, 1929, 11in 8cm).
750-900

. creamware dish, printed in lack, with moulded rim, c1775, 5in (38cm).
135-150

A Quimper plate, with blue, red and green decoration on cream, c1930, 6½in (16cm).
$90-105

A Quimper plate, with mistletoe motif, c1890, 9in (23cm).
$180-225

A pair of Quimper serving dishes, with figures of a Breton piper and woman in polychrome enamels, on a cream ground, c1890, 11in (28cm) long.
$600-750

A Quimper plate, decorated in yellow and blue on white, c1930.
$90-105

A Quimper fish dish, decorated in blue and red on cream, c1930.
$90-105

A Quimper plate, with yellow and blue decoration on white, c1930, 7in (18cm).
$90-105

A Quimper plate, enamel decorated with a Breton gentlewoman in coloured enamels, c1885, 9in (23cm).
$180-225

A large Quimper plate, with brown, red and blue decoration on cream, c1930, 11½in (29cm).
$90-105

A Quimper dish, with blue decoration on white, c1890, 9½in (23.5cm).
$120-135

A pottery plate, decorated with cream design on brown, c1880, 9in (22.5cm).
$90-105

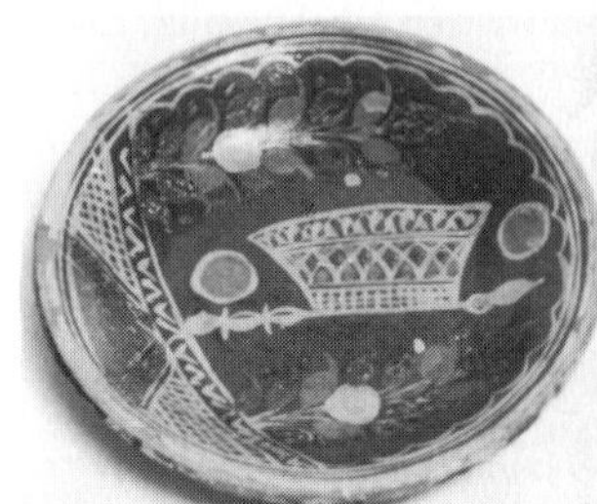

A pottery plate, with cream design on brown, c1880, 10in (25cm).
$90-105

A set of 6 majolica plates, with green decoration on cream, c1880, 8in (20cm).
$375-450

A Hispano-Moresque copper lustre dish, the raised central boss with a rabbit within a surround of spirally radiating flowers and foliage, with moulded border, pierced for hanging, rim chips, some rubbing, early 17thC, 13½in (35cm).
$2,250-3,000

n Irish blue and white pierced sh, marked, c1760, 11½in 9cm).
,250-3,000

A French majolica fish dish, in the style of Bernard Palissy, c1870, 12in (30.5cm).
$450-600

. Portuguese blue and white dish, oldly painted, the underside with adiating S-scrolls, c1640, 15in 38cm).
7,500-9,000

Jugs

A Liverpool transfer decorated creamware jug, illustrating a New York ship, 10in (25cm) high.
$7,500-9,000
These attractive jugs are more often found with inscriptions relating to English families and would be valued at £1,200-1,800.

A Minton majolica jug, c1865, 9in (22.5cm) high.
$750-900

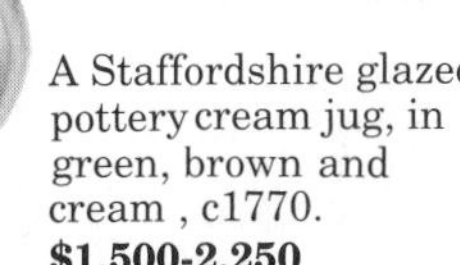

A Staffordshire glazed pottery cream jug, in green, brown and cream , c1770.
$1,500-2,250

A saltglazed enamelled jug, 3in (7cm) high.
$1,500-2,250

A Staffordshire creamware satyr's mask jug, of Ralph Wood type, picked out in manganese, with green glazed dolphin spout and handle, on round gadrooned foot, c1780, 5in (13cm) high.
$225-300

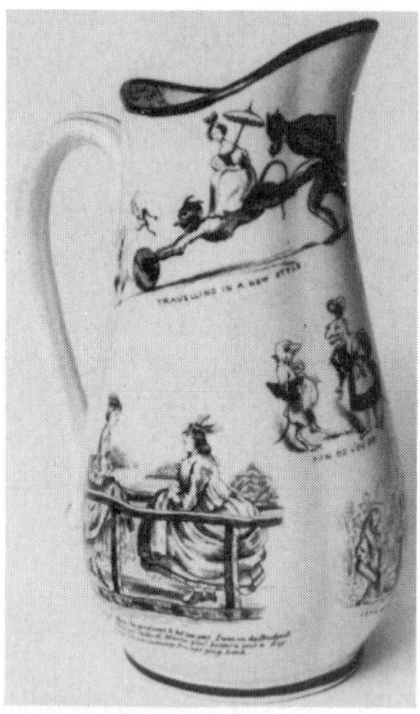

A Victorian Staffordshire printed jug, c1875, 9in (22.5cm) high.
$375-450

A Thomas and John Wedgwood saltglazed stoneware baluster-shaped jug, with notched handle, moulded with panels of figures, animals and armorials, on hexagonal foot, minor damage, c1745, 4½in (11.5cm) high.
$375-450

An English stoneware jug, with coat-of-arms on front, restored, c1840, 8½in (21.5cm).
$225-255

A pearlware barrel-shaped jug with loop handle, decorated in blue with stylised flowerheads within an interlinked and geometric band and inscribed in brown 'Danl. and Catherine Jackson 1807', hair cracks and some restoration, early 19thC, 10½in (26cm) high. **$900-1,500**

A jug, decorated with a steam train and carriage, centrally inscribed 'Joseph and Stella Addy 1843', the neck with floral sprays, brown and black borders, probably South Yorkshire, 9½in (24cm) high.
$2,250-3,000

A large pottery jug, decorated with brown spots on a cream ground, c1930, 5½in (14cm) high.
$50-75

A Savoie jug, marbelised in cream, c1880, 5½in (14cm) high.
$90-105

A Savoie pottery jug, marbelised with yellows, c1880, 4½in (11.5cm) high.
$105-120

A Savoie jug, decorated with flowers on a yellow ground, c188
6½in (16.5cm) high.
$120-135

A Savoie jug, decorated in crear
and brown, c1900, 4in (10cm) high. **$90-105**

A blue marbelised pottery jug, c1920, 6½in (16.5cm) high.
$90-105

. shaped cream jug, decorated
'ith blue spots on a cream
round, 7½in (19cm) high.
50-75

A pottery jug, decorated with cream spots on brown, c1900, 5in (12.5cm) high.
$105-120

A pottery jug, decorated with cream spots on a blue ground, c1930, 5in (12.5cm) high.
$50-75

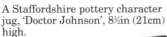

A Quimper jug, decorated in brown and orange on cream, c1930, 5in (12.5cm) high.
$105-120

A Prattware jug, decorated in brown, green and blue on a pale blue background, early 19thC, 7½in (18.5cm) high.
$750-1,200

'oby Jugs

A Staffordshire pottery character jug, 'Doctor Johnson', 8½in (21cm) high.
$135-150

A Ralph Wood Toby jug, seated holding beaker and jug, with blue coat, ochre and other glazes on green rustic base, 11½in (29cm) high. **$2,700-3,300**

A Staffordshire Toby jug and cover, a 'Planter' or 'Rodney's Sailor', wearing a deep russet coat with blue facings over a chintz striped waistcoat and black striped trousers, on a green base, 12in (30.5cm) high.
$1,200-1,800

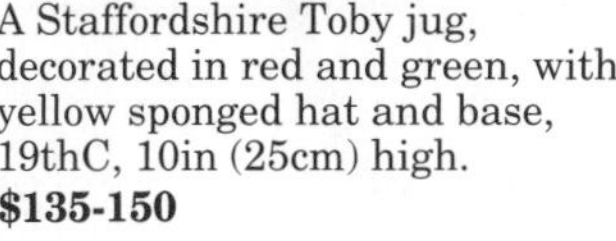

A Staffordshire Toby jug, decorated in red and green, with yellow sponged hat and base, 19thC, 10in (25cm) high.
$135-150

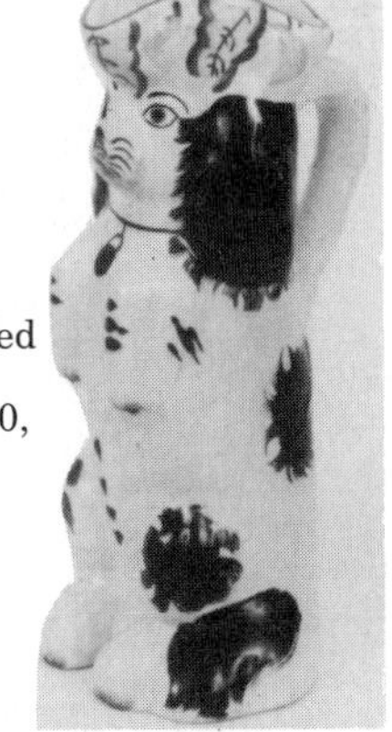

A Staffordshire dog jug, decorated with black overglaze on white, with pink and a green hat, c1850, 9½in (24cm) high.
$105-120

A sailor Toby jug, the drunken tar seated on a chest of dollars, wearing a blue jacket and striped trousers, holding a foaming mug of ale inscribed 'Success to our wooden walls' and a pipe, on a brown and green sponged base, damaged, 10½in (26.5cm) high.
$750-1,200

A Ralph Wood Toby jug, seated holding beaker and jug, the glazes predominantly brown and green, the base having canted corners, impressed 51 to base, 9½in (24cm) high.
$1,200-1,800

A Staffordshire creamware Toby jug, holding a jug and beaker of frothing ale, in black hat, wearing a blue jacket and yellow breeches, the base with canted angles, slight damage, c1780, 9½in (24cm) high.
$2,250-3,000

A Staffordshire Toby jug, possibly Wood school, with black hat, wearing green jacket, grey waistcoat, on brown seat, hat repaired, c1785, 12in (30.5cm) high.
$6,000-8,250

A Staffordshire creamware Toby jug and cover, of Ralph Wood type, in a black hat, wearing a manganese jacket and blue breeches, a pipe at his side, the base with canted angles slight damage, c1780, 10in (25cm) high.
$1,800-2,700

A sailor 'Trafalgar' Toby jug, wearing a wide brimmed tricorn hat, blue coat with white facings, red striped waistcoat, blue trousers, holding a beaker of ale (missing), and a frothing jug, seated on a mahogany chair with trunk below, inscribed 'Trafalgar' and 'Victory', on a green and brown mottled base with a pipe between his legs, some damage and restored, 12in (30cm) high.
$750-1,200

A creamware Bacchus mask jug, crowned with red, pink and green vine leaves and grapes, with a brown beard, c1880.
$180-225

A Staffordshire creamware Thin Man Toby jug, of Ralph Wood type, holding a baluster jug of frothing ale, with brown hair, green jacket, yellow waistcoat, blue breeches and brown shoes, seated on a high backed chair, hat restored, c1775, 9½in (24.5cm) high. **$4,500-6,000**

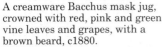

A pearlware Hearty Goodfellow Toby jug, in a black hat, pink jacket and yellow breeches, on a mound base, restored, c1830, 12in (30cm) high.
$375-525

A Prattware Martha Gunn Toby jug, decorated in blue and yellow, with a brown hat, on a cream background, c1800, 10½in (26.5cm) high.
$3,000-4,500

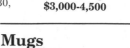

A Staffordshire Toby jug, with green jacket and yellow trousers, c1800, 10½in (26.5cm) high.
$1,500-2,250

Mugs

A Staffordshire pottery brown glazed mug, early 18thC, 5in (13cm) high. **$2,250-3,000**

A Prattware lustre mug, transf printed with Falstaff and Lady Anne Page, and a verse from 'T Merry Wives of Windsor', c1860 5in (13cm) high. **$135-150**

ᴾlaques

A pearlware plaque, in the form of a 2 storey red brick building, picked out in black and ochre, and applied with recumbent black and white dogs, the pediment inscribed 'Savings Bank', damaged and incomplete, early 19thC, 7in (18cm).
$225-300

A Continental pottery wall plaque, brightly enamelled in the Persian manner, 19in (48.5cm).
$225-300

ᴾots

A Marseille or Montpellier faïence bough pot, decorated with polychrome enamels on a yellow ground, c1770, 7in (18cm).
$300-375

An Italian maiolica albarello, probably Venetian, painted with brown, green and ochre enamels with ochre wash rim and foot, on a sgraffito blue ground, damaged, 7in (18cm). **$600-750**

A pearlware D-shaped bough pot, centrally decorated in silver lustre with vines, within a blue roundel, on a yellow basket moulded ground, within silver lustre and blue borders, cover missing, restored, inscribed in lustre on base George Boon, early 19thC, 6½in (16.5cm).
$225-300

A Montelupo large waisted albarello, boldly painted with ochre and green scrolling foliage on a blue ground, flanking a blank rectangular label, damaged, late 17thC, 12½in (31.5cm).
$1,500-2,250

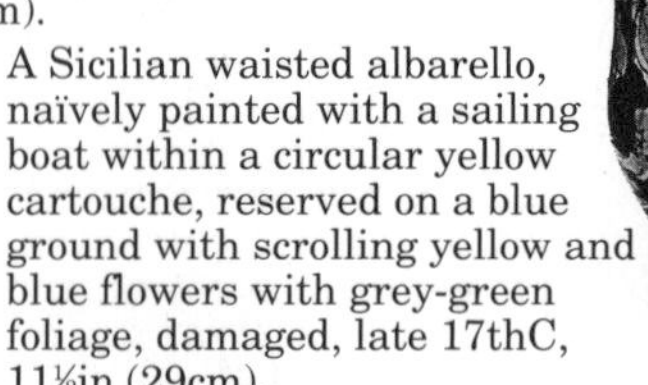

A Savoie green and brown cache pot, c1900, 7in (18cm) diam.
$50-75

A Sicilian waisted albarello, naïvely painted with a sailing boat within a circular yellow cartouche, reserved on a blue ground with scrolling yellow and blue flowers with grey-green foliage, damaged, late 17thC, 11½in (29cm).
$1,200-1,800

Services

A Wedgwood creamware botanical composite part dessert service, painted in purple and lake monochromes, in the manner of James Bakewell, with specimen flowers, rims enriched in purple and lake, comprising: 2 dishes (minor rim chips), 2 shaped slender oval dishes on 3 snail-shell feet (one with 2 rim repairs), 15 plates (all slightly damaged), the plates painted in purple with large impressed uppercase and 4 marks, some pieces with painter's marks in purple, c1770.
$3,000-4,500

A Spode's Imperial stone china part dessert service, printed in underglaze blue and over painted in pink, burnt orange and gilt with a central spray of ribbon tied flowers, within a border of buildings on islands and foliate panels, comprising 10 pieces, some damage, printed Spode's Imperial in underglaze blue and pattern No. 4176, inscribed in burnt orange.
$450-600

Tea and Coffee Pots

A Staffordshire agate ware teapot, spout slightly chipped, c1755, 4in (10cm) high.
$4.500-6,000

A Staffordshire or Yorkshire teapot, decorated in green, blue, and yellow ochre on a cream background, restored, c1800, 5in (13cm) high.
$900-1,500

A Rothwell, Yorkshire, underglaze chocolate pot, on 3 feet, 6½in (16.5cm).
$750-1,200

A Rockingham type teapot by G. F. Bowers & Co. Ceramics, with blue and polychrome floral decoration.
$150-180

A Leeds creamware teapot, with entwined strap handle, flower terminal and knop, painted in brick red enamel with 'Miss Pitt drinking tea, chipped spout and some scratches to enamel, c1770.
$750-1,200

A Staffordshire saltglazed stoneware teapot and cover, with lion knop, moulded with panels of figures, birds, animals and leaves, and with notched handle and leaf moulded spout, restored, possibly Thomas and John Wedgwood, c1745, 4½in (11.5cm).
$450-600

. pearlware baluster shaped
›ffee pot and domed cover,
ecorated in green, brown and
lue with scattered leaves,
eneath a leaf band, and brown
ne borders, early 19thC, 11½in
9cm).
150-225

A Staffordshire saltglazed stoneware teapot and cover, in the form of a 3 storey house, with notched handle and flower and leaf moulded spout, restored, perhaps Thomas and John Wedgwood, c1745, 5in (13.5cm).
$1,200-1,800

A Thomas Whieldon redware canted teapot, with serpent shaped handle, finely moulded with panels of Chinese style figures, flowers and leaves, the rim with a stiff leaf band, cover missing, damaged, c1730, 4in (10cm).
$225-255

A Staffordshire pearlware coffee pot and cover, modelled as a muzzled bear seated on his haunches, the spout formed by a dog held between his forepaws, painted in enamels in shades of brown, red, green and black, the moulded handle with chain and pin attachment, damaged, impressed J. Morris Store, c1820, 12½in (32cm).
$10,500-13,500

'iles

A Bristol manganese tile, 5in (13cm) square.
$105-120

Liverpool brown and
hite transfer ware tile,
paired, c1770, 5in
3cm) square.
105-120

A Liverpool black and white transfer ware tile, c1760, 5in (13cm) square.
$300-375

Liverpool black and
hite transfer ware tile,
765, 5in (13cm)
uare.
225-255

A Liverpool black and white transfer ware tile, c1765, 5in (13cm) square.
$225-255

A Liverpool tile, with black transfer figure on green background, 5in (13cm) square.
$225-255

A Liverpool blue and white tile, c1800, 5in (13cm) square.
$50-75

A Liverpool blue and white tile, 18thC, 5in (13cm) square.
$50-75

A London blue and white tile, mid-18thC, 5in (13cm) square.
$225-255

A London blue and white tile, 5in (13cm) square.
$90-105

A London blue and white tile, c1730, 5in (13cm) square.
$105-120

Tureens

A majolica sardine dish and cover, by J. Holdcroft.
$750-900

A Quimper beurrier or camembert dish, decorated in polychrome enamels, c1890, 8in (20cm) diam.
$180-225

A George Jones cheese dish, c1870, 13in (33cm) high.
$750-1,200

A Staffordshire blue and white Stilton cheese dome and stand, with floral decoration, 8½in (21cm).
$120-135

A Proskau partridge tureen, cover and fixed stand, the naturally modelled bird with moulded brown plumage and yellow beak and legs, a leaping green and yellow frog on one side, on a shaped circular stand applied with fruiting and flowering branches and a half fig, shaped black line rim, damaged, manganese DP mark, c1775, 9½in (24cm).
$5,250-7,500

Vases

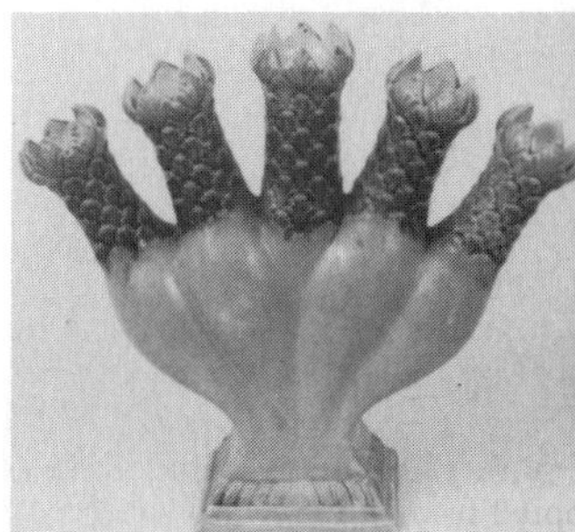

A Minton vase, c1865, 8in (20cm).
$450-600

. French faïence pot pourri vase
ıd cover, with mask handles and
ierced latticework base, painted
'ith feuille de choux around
riental style flowersprays
ainly in puce and green, mark
/22 in blue, c1800, 12in (31cm).
225-300

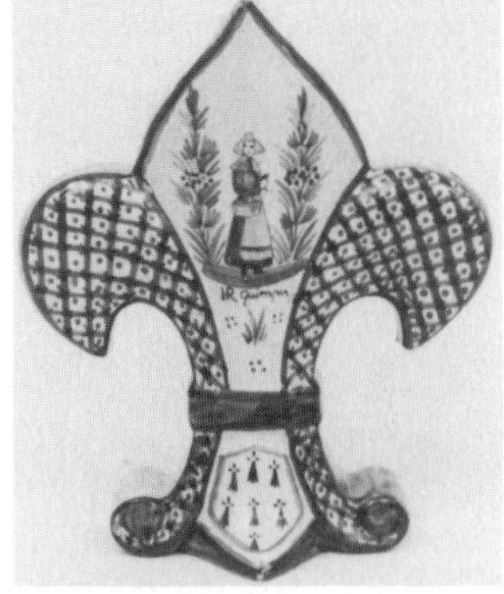

A Quimper fleur-de-lys vase, decorated in polychrome enamels, restored, c1895, 7½in (19cm).
$225-300

A Quimper vase, decorated with black and red on yellow, c1930, 9in (23cm).
$90-105

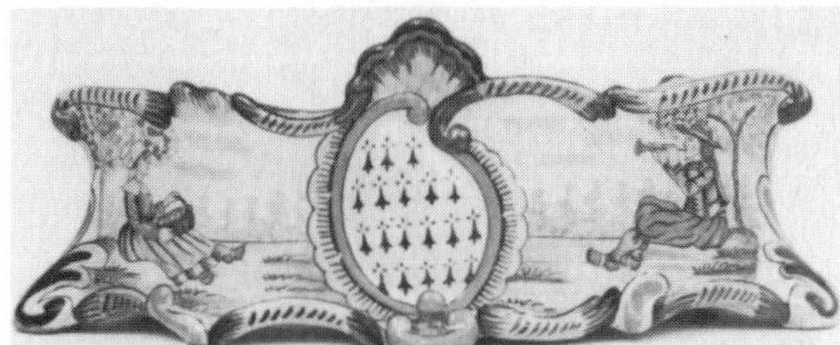

A Quimper vase, marked HR Quimper in blue, c1890, 12in (31cm) wide. **$300-375**

A creamware straight sided vase and domed pierced cover, applied with green swags and ribbons, on round base, c1785, 9in (23cm).
$450-600

Three Spanish faïence campana vases, perhaps Seville, on tapering conical stems, with fixed blue ring handles, inscribed in black 'R Alcázares', beneath a blue crown between yellow and blue bands one with a metal liner, (damaged), 19thC, 18½in (47.5cm). **$7,500-9,000**

. Minton majolica
ase, c1860, 12in
31cm).
600-750

Did you know?
MILLER'S Antiques Price Guide builds up year by year to form the most comprehensive photo reference library available.

. Quimper bouquetière or wall
ase, signed HB, c1880, 12½in
32cm).
375-450

A Malicorne wall vase, tin glaze decorated with Breton piper in polychrome enamels, with fleur-de-lys motifs, c1880, 11in (28cm).
$225-255

. Quintal creamware finger vase,
opied from Dutch tulip vases,
vith blue and white painted
ecoration, c1790, 7½in (19cm).
750-1,200

Spill Vases

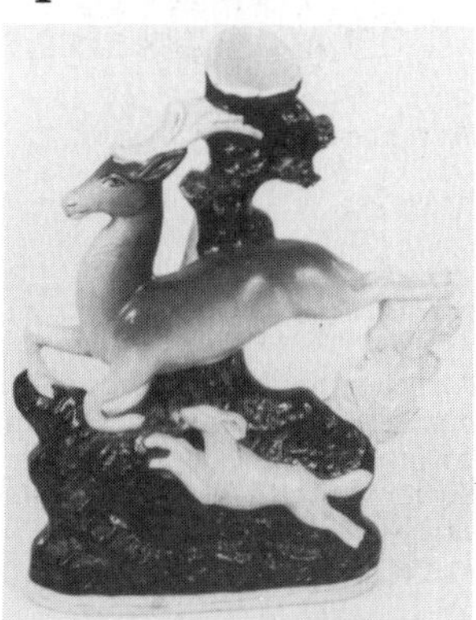

A Staffordshire Sampson Smith stag and dog spill vase, decorated in green, tan and cream, c1870, 12in (31cm).
$225-300

A Staffordshire deer spill vase, decorated in brown, yellow ochre, and green on a green base, c1800, 7½in (19cm).
$1,800-2,700

A Ralph Wood type sheep and lamb spill vase, decorated in green, yellow and cream, minor repairs, c1790, 5in (13cm).
$1,800-2,700

A Staffordshire sheep and lamb spill vase, decorated with a yello base and interior, c1845.
$225-255

A Staffordshire spill vase, modelled as the Royal children above a steam train, c1845, 9in (23cm).
$375-525

A pottery spill vase, printed in monochrome on a yellow ground within brightly coloured bands of flowers and leaves, rim chipped, early 19thC, 6in (15cm).
$150-225

Miller's is a price GUIDE not a price LIST

A Staffordshire cow and calf spill vase, decorated with overglaze tan, green and blue, c1880, 11½in (29cm).
$300-375

A Staffordshire spill vase, wit orange interior, c1850, 13½in (34.5cm). **$150-225**

Wemyss

A Wemyss honey preserve jar, 5in (13cm).
$225-255

A Wemyss mug with pigs, 'They grew in beauty side by side', by Nekola. **$1,200-1,800**

A Wemyss preserve jar, on a stand, painted with redcurrants, 6½in (16.5cm).
$600-750

A Wemyss pig, decorated with clover, 16in (41cm) wide.
$3,000-4,500

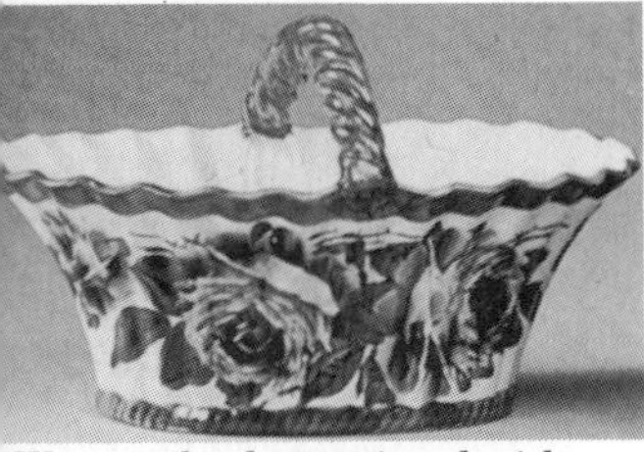

A Wemyss basket, painted with roses, impressed marks, c1900, 12in (30cm).
$600-750

A Wemyss basket, decorated with cockerels, c1910, 16in (41cm) wide.
$1,500-2,250

A Wemyss quaiche, decorated with apples, 10½in (26.5cm).
$600-750

A pair of Wemyss candlesticks, decorated with roses, 12in (30cm).
$750-1,200

A Wemyss cup and saucer, decorated with roses, cup 2in (5cm) high. **$120-135**

Wemyss Value Points

- Quality of painting - especially a large piece painted freely by Karel Nekola.
- Condition - Wemyss is, by nature, fragile and since many pieces were made for nursery use, many have been damaged, chips can be acceptable but cracks do substantially affect price.
- Other painters of note include James Sharp, David Grinton, John Brown, Hugh and Christinia McKinnon, also Karel's two sons, Carl and Joseph.
- Early pieces, particularly with a red border.
- Unusual subject matters - nasturtiums, gorse, pink flamingos.
- Beware of unmarked pieces - usually these were rejects or copies from another factory.

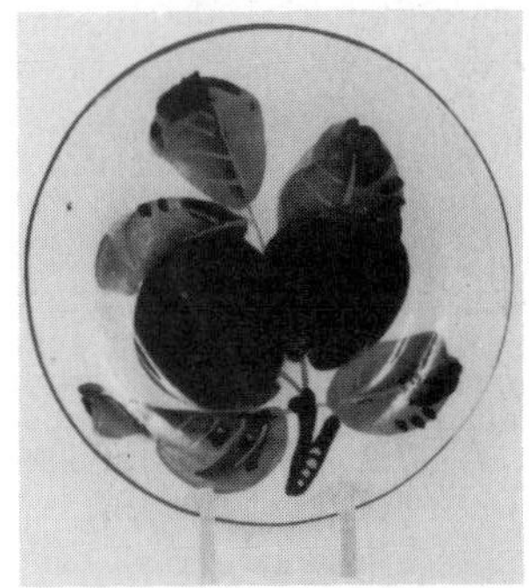

A Wemyss pickle plate, 3½in (9cm) diam.
$120-135

A Wemyss jug and basin, decorated with oranges, jug 10in (25cm) high. **$1,200-1,500**

A Wemyss pomade pot, decorated with roses, 3in (8cm). **$300-375**

A Wemyss chamber pot, painted with roses, 8½in (21.5cm) diam. **$300-375**

A Wemyss wash jug and basin, decorated with pink cabbage roses and leaves, within green line rims, painted and impressed marks and retailer's marks for T. Goode and Co, jug 5½in (14cm). **$450-600**

A Wemyss pot, decorated with redcurrants, 3in (8cm). **$120-135**

A Wemyss chocolate pot, decorated with buttercups, 5½i (14cm). **$450-600**

A Wemyss jug and basin, painted with red cabbage roses, restored, impressed and printed retailer's marks, c1900, basin 11in (28cm). **$450-600**

A Wemyss three-handled tyg painted with sweet peas, 9in (23cm). **$1,200-1,500**

A Wemyss plaque, decorated with violets, 5½in (14cm). **$375-525**

A Wemyss pot, decorated with roses. **$90-105**

A Wemyss three-handled mug decorated with raspberries. **$450-600**

A Wemyss inkwell, decorated with brown cockerels, 10in (25cm). **$450-600**

A Wemyss 'Stuart flower pot', painted with continuous swags of cabbage roses suspended from green ribbons, c1900, 6½in (16.5cm). **$600-750**

A Wemyss 'Waverley' tray, painted with a continuous border of single pink cabbage roses within a brown line rim, minor restoration to rims, c1900, 17in (44cm). **$375-450**

iscellaneous

selection of Victorian pottery
ırpet bowls.
450-600

Quimper chamberstick,
ecorated in polychrome enamels
ı tin glaze, marked H3 Quimper,
1920, 6½in (16.5cm) diam.
120-135

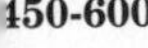

French majolica centrepiece,
1880, 15in (38cm).
450-600

A Staffordshire Prattware clock,
chip restored, c1810, 9½in (24cm).
$600-750

A Prattware pottery ornament of
a grandfather clock, damaged,
8½in (21.5cm).
$225-300

A Continental majolica glazed
jardinière and stand, decorated in
deep blue on a brown ground,
with cameo piercing, foliate and
C-scrolled detail, probably late
19thC, 42in (106.5cm).
$375-450

A set of brown
stoneware egg cups
with a stand, with
holes for spoons,
c1830, 9in (23cm).
$375-525

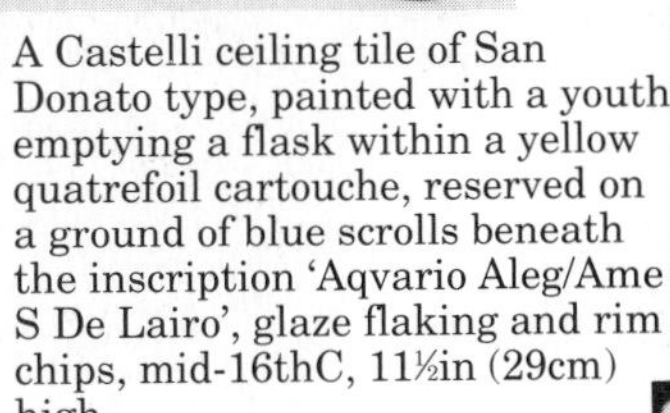

A Desvres clock, decorated in
polychrome enamels, c1890, 7in
(18cm) wide.
$225-300

A pair of door finger plates,
decorated in yellow ochre and gilt
with moulded grapevine, one
damaged, registration mark
Woods China, 1843, 10½in
(26.5cm).
$40-60

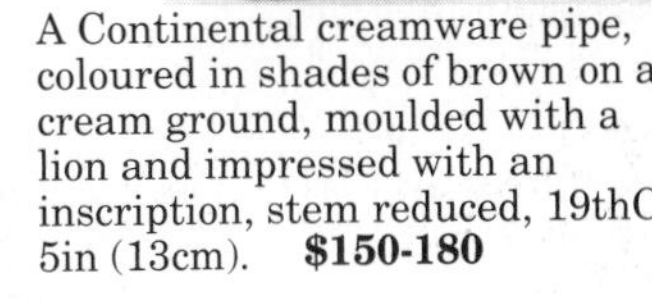

A Continental creamware pipe,
moulded with stylised foliate
ornament and sponged with a
treacle glaze on a yellow ground,
19thC, 5½in (14cm).
$150-180

A Continental creamware pipe,
coloured in shades of brown on a
cream ground, moulded with a
lion and impressed with an
inscription, stem reduced, 19thC,
5in (13cm). **$150-180**

A Castelli ceiling tile of San
Donato type, painted with a youth
emptying a flask within a yellow
quatrefoil cartouche, reserved on
a ground of blue scrolls beneath
the inscription 'Aqvario Aleg/Ame
S De Lairo', glaze flaking and rim
chips, mid-16thC, 11½in (29cm)
high.
$1,800-2,700

A Castelli ceiling tile of San
Donato type, painted with a bust
portrait of a woman wearing a
lace cap and in profile, within a
yellow quatrefoil cartouche,
reserved on a blue ground of
scrolling foliage, slight rim chips,
mid-16thC, 11½in (29cm) high.
$5,250-6,000

A Wedgwood pearlware egg stand, with central boat-shaped salt cellar and 6 pierced round egg cups, on fixed oval stand, with blue line rims, minor damage, impressed mark, 10½in (27cm).
$375-525

A pot lid, Landing The Fare, from the Pegwell Series No. 38, c1855, 4in (10cm) diam.
$120-135
No re-issue of this lid has been seen.

A creamware 'Grand Plat Ménage', the circular base with 4 fixed circular holders containing baluster jugs, surrounding a central shaped circular column, supporting 2 two-handled basket and 2 shell dishes, the upper parts supporting 4 pierced shallow trays, the scroll terminal suspending 4 pierced baskets, the whole surmounted by a detachable vase and cover on a square plinth, the finial to the domed cover modelled as a figure of Plenty, repaired, probably Yorkshire, Leeds Pottery, c1780, 24in (62cm) high.
$10,500-13,500

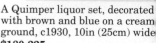

A Minton pottery stick stand, with brown top and bottom borders, small crack to base, number 3380, late 19thC, 25in (64cm).
$450-600

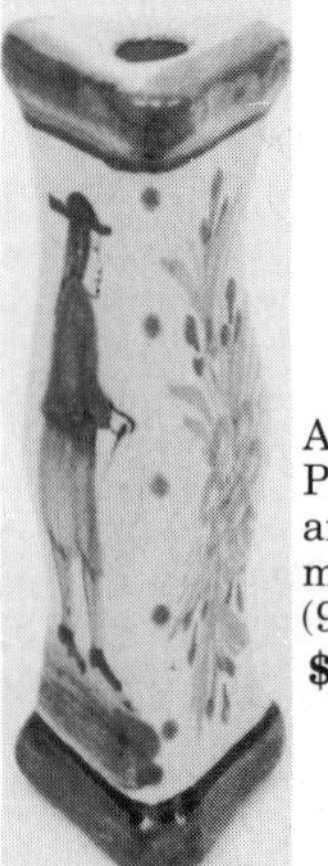

A Quimper knife rest, by Adolphe Porquier, decorated in blue, green and yellow on a pale blue ground, marked AP in blue, c1880, 3½in (9cm).
$25-40

A Desvres violin vase, Fourmaintrau-Courquin, decorated in yellow, blue, green and pink polychrome enamels, c1880, 15½in (40cm).
$375-450

A pearlware chessboard, decorated in black, within a raised blue border, 19thC, 13in (33cm) square. **$450-600**

A bonbonnière, decorated with a Breton piper in polychrome enamels, marked H. R. Quimper, c1895, 4½in (11.5cm) diam.
$135-150

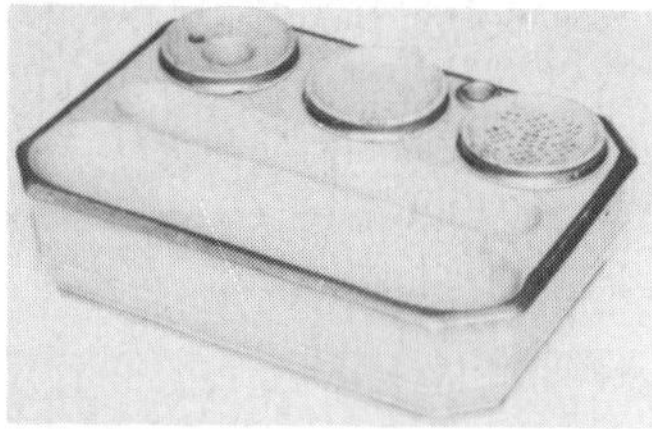

A Wedgwood drabware inkstand, fitted with an inkwell, sander, covered recess and 2 pen trays, with gilt borders, impressed mark, c1815, 8in (20cm).
$180-225

A Staffordshire redware model of a cradle, with panelled sides and turned finials, sprigged with white florets and masks, restored, 11½in (29cm).
$375-450

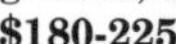

A Quimper liquor set, decorated with brown and blue on a cream ground, c1930, 10in (25cm) wide
$180-225

pair of Quimper ramekin shes, decorated with green, red d blue design on a cream ound, c1930, 3in (8cm) diam.
0-60

A Continental knife rest, decorated in orange and white, c1930, 4in (10cm).
$40-60

A Quimper tea set, decorated in brown on a cream ground, c1930.
$225-300

Quimper casserole dish, ecorated with red, green and lue on a cream ground, c1930, in (15cm) diam.
90-105

brown glazed pottery water arrier, c1880, 14in (36cm) high.
90-105

Staffordshire tea canister, ecorated in underglaze brown, 1765, 5in (13cm) high.
1,500-2,250

A pottery water carrier and lid, c1880, 14in (36cm) high.
$90-105

A Prattware screw-top box, depicting a sleeping child, early 19thC, 3in (8cm) high.
$1,050-1,350

A Staffordshire pail, with underglaze decoration, handle repaired, c1765, 3½in (9cm) high.
$750-900

A Mortlake stoneware tankard, decorated with a hunting scene in brown and cream, with a metal rim, c1785, 8in (20cm) high.
$1,500-2,250

Delft

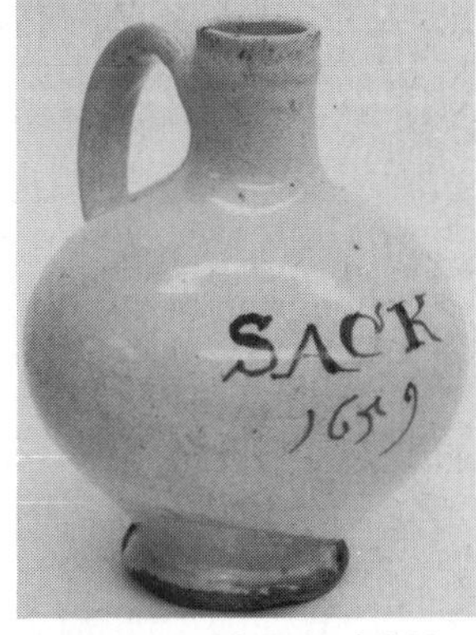

A Commonwealth period delft globe shaped bottle, with loop handle, on circular foot, titled 'Sack', and dated 1659, 6in (15cm) high.
$3,000-3,750

Did you know?
MILLER'S Antiques Price Guide builds up year by year to form the most comprehensive photo reference library available.

A Bristol delft deep bowl, the exterior boldly decorated in orange, yellow, green and blue flowers and leaves, the interior decorated in blue with a bird in flight and scattered scrolls, restored, early 18thC, 10½in (27cm) diam.
$600-750

An English delft deep bowl, the interior decorated in blue with a stylised flower spray, the exterior decorated in blue, green and brown with a Chinese style figure and flowers in a fenced garden, cracked, some rim chips restored, c1745, 10½in (26.5cm) diam.
$225-300

An English delft oviform drug jar, titled 'C. FL: Aurant:' within a cartouche surmounted by a shell flanked by 2 angels, below a winged angel's face above the initials 'I:P 1723', damaged, 7in (18cm).
$15,000-18,000

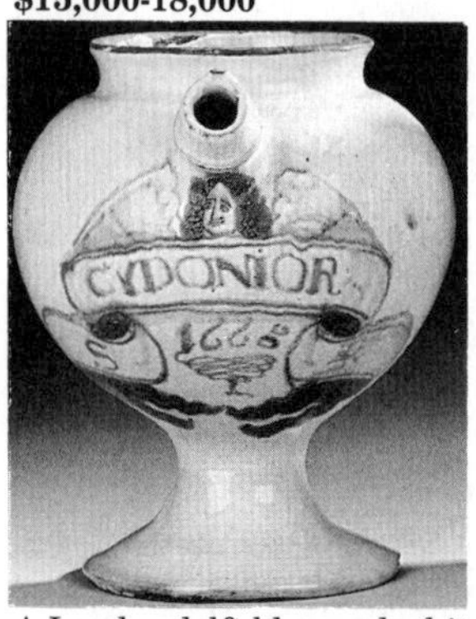

A London delft blue and white named wet drug jar, on a circular spreading foot, slight damage, 1665, 7½in (19cm) high.
$4,500-6,000

A Bristol delft blue and white wet drug jar, named 'S:Caryoph' within a strapwork cartouche, with songbirds and foliage above and a winged angel's head below, glaze flaking, c1720, 7in (18cm) high.
$600-750

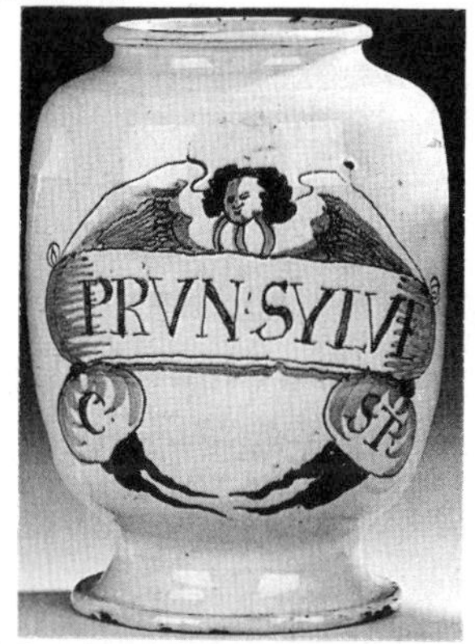

A London delft oviform dry drug jar, named 'C.Prvn:Sylvest:', surmounted by an angel's head and fluttering pennants, flaking to foot, c1680, 8¼in (21cm) high.
$1,200-1,800

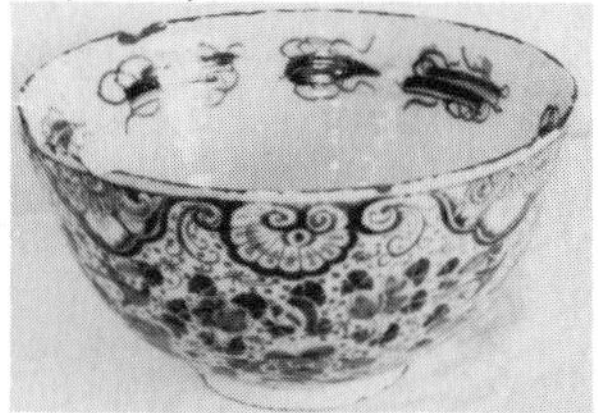

A delft blue and white punch bowl, decorated with birds and flowers, with a large flowerhead on the base of the interior, 14in (36cm) diam. **$375-525**

A delft plaque, decorated with polychrome flowers and foliage, with a blue spotted and wavy line border, 18thC, 13in (33cm) diam.
$300-375

A London delft blue and white pi tile, painted in bright blue, with the arms of The Worshipful Society of Apothecaries flanked b unicorn supporters, with motto, pierced for hanging, restored rim chip, c1700, 10in (25cm) high.
$2,700-3,300

A Lambeth delft blue and white pill tile, with the arms of The Worshipful Society of Apothecaries flanked by unicorn supporters, with motto, in manganese on a ribbon below suspending swags of foliage, pierced for hanging, restored, c1780, 10¼in (26cm) high.
$3,000-3,750

Mason's Ironstone

A pair of Mason's Ironstone candlesticks, decorated with butterflies and flowers in polychrome enamels, on a black ground, worn, c1815, 5in (13cm) high.
$450-600

A Mason's Ironstone jug, painted in typical Japan pattern in underglaze blue and iron red enamel, c1815, 4in (10cm) high.
$150-225

A pair of early Mason's Ironstone dessert dishes, decorated with Water Lily pattern, c1815, 11in (28cm).
$750-900

A Mason's Ironstone plate, decorated with dragons in green enamels, 19thC, 9in (23cm) diam.
$15-25

Mason's Ironstone ewer and asin, decorated with Elephant oot pattern in underglaze blue, on red and gilt, impressed arks, c1815, 8in (20cm) diam.
900-1,500

A Mason's Ironstone soup tureen and cover, decorated with Water Lily pattern, impressed mark, c1815, 12in (31cm) high.
$1,200-1,500

A Mason's Ironstone drainer, with Water Lily pattern, in blue, red, pink and green on a white ground, unmarked c1815, 12in (31cm) wide.
$375-525

A pair of Mason's Ironstone plates, with relief moulding and green enamelled decoration of dragons, impressed marks, 8in (20cm) diam.
$135-150

n early Mason's onstone base for a a caddy, painted in apan pattern, lacking over, c1815, 4in 10cm) square.
180-225

A Mason's Ironstone pot pourri vase, decorated with polychrome enamel and gilded, cover missing, rim repaired, c1815, 5½in (14cm) high.
$375-525

PORCELAIN

Baskets

A Chelsea basket, with pierced border, decorated in coloured enamels within a brown line rim, minor rim hair cracks, red anchor mark, c1755, 9½in (24cm).
$750-900

A Belleek basket, with handle, the trellis rim applied with flowers, 11in (28cm) wide.
$750-900

A Coalport egg basket, decorat in turquoise on white with gilt c1870, 6½in (16cm) diam.
$135-150

A Worcester t handled bask numbered 15 blue, c1760, 1 (25cm) wide.
$2,700-3,300

Bottles

A pair of Derby neo-classical turquoise ground bottles, painted en grisaille on claret grounds within gilt band cartouches, suspended by gilt tied ribbon, enriched in gilding, one vase with damage to foot and one handle with lower terminal lacking and upper terminal cracked, gold anchor marks, Wm. Duesbury & Co, c1755, 6in (15cm).
$1,500-2,250

A bottle and stopper, encrusted with white and gilt flowers and grasses between gilt line rims and flanking the Gothic initials 'LHC', perhaps Derby, c1830, 16in (40.5cm).
$2,700-3,300

Bowls

A Derby salmon ground écuel cover and stand, puce mark, gilder's No.8, c1790.
$2,700-3,300

Ecuelle

An écuelle is a French soup bowl with 2 handles; usually made with a cover and stand.

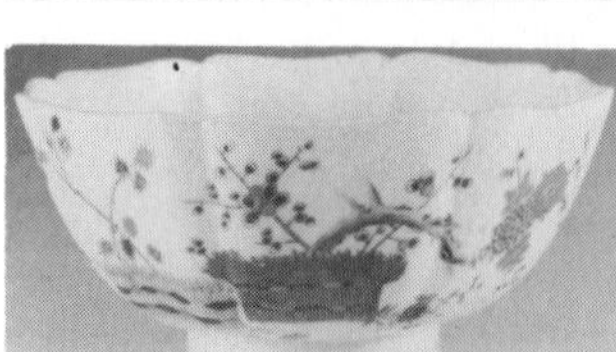

A Chelsea fluted bowl, decorated in Kakiemon style, c1750, 7in (18cm) diam.
$4,800-5,700

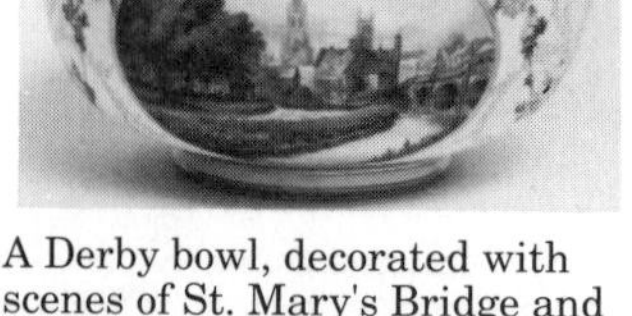

A Derby bowl, decorated with scenes of St. Mary's Bridge and High Tor, Matlock, gilt decoration on white ground, signed W. E. Moseley, c1920, 5½in (14cm).
$2,250-3,000

A Caughley blue and white finge bowl, Two Men on Bridge patter S mark, c1795.
$150-225

A Lowestoft blue and white finger bowl, 3 mark, c1770, 4in (10cm).
$180-225

A Worcester blue an white bowl, Cannon Ball pattern, c1775, 4in (10cm).
$180-225

Worcester blue and white bowl, ırds in Branches pattern, c1780, n (15cm).
;25-300

Sèvres decorated bowl and ·ver, marks in blue for 1762, ·corator marks for Therenet, 4in 0cm).
750-900

Royal Worcester bowl, ·corated with peaches and ·erries on mossy bank ground, gned Ricketts, 7in (17.5cm).
75-450

usts

Copeland parian bust of ·rincess Alexandra, in décolleté ess, signed, published June 1 ·68, the base inscribed Art nion of London May Thornycroft 1868, 15in (39cm).
,200-1,500

A Worcester fluted sugar bowl and cover, painted in colours with the Tiger in Compartments pattern, within gilt borders, the cover with flower finial, c1770, 5in (12cm). **$450-600**

A 'Sèvres' pot pourri bowl and cover, painted against a claret ground, with gilt metal mounts, pseudo Sèvres marks, late 19thC, 6½in (16.5cm). **$450-600**

A Dresden punch bowl and cover, decorated on a moulded white ground, 9in (23cm) diam.
$300-375

A pair of French porcelain busts of Louis XV and Marie Antoinette, Sèvres First Republic period 1793-1800, 5in (12.5cm).
$225-300

A First Period Worcester potted meat bowl, painted in underglaze blue with Plantation pattern, c1755, 6in (15cm) diam.
$1,200-1,500

Boxes

A Derby sugar box and cover, painted in iron red and gilt, the cover with red flower and green branch finial, finial chipped, minute footrim chips, Wm. Duesbury and Co, c1760, 4in (11cm).
$1,500-2,250

A Continental box with hinged cover, 9½in (24cm).
$450-600

Candlesticks

A Bow chamber candlestick, representing Europe and America, decorated in coloured enamels, c1760, 6in (15.5cm).
$750-900

Bow

Bow shares with Chelsea the distinction of being one of the first two porcelain factories in England, but its early history is obscure. It was founded by Thomas Frye, an Irish painter, and Edward Heylyn, a glass merchant, at Stratford Langthorne in the East End of London. In 1775 the factory was acquired by W. Duesbury, owner of the Derby porcelain factory, who removed all the moulds and tools to Derby. There they were joined by those of the Chelsea factory in 1786.

Bow Blue and White Wares

- Blue and white wares are divided into three periods which coincide roughly with changes in the appearance of the wares.
- **Early period 1749-54:** Wares often thickly potted, glaze can be blue/green in pools. Many wares painted in a pale clear royal blue which sometimes blurs. Some very well potted wares often marked with an incised R also produced.
- 'In the white' wares with applied decoration also produced.
- **Middle period 1755-65:** Darker underglaze blue. Wares more thinly potted but relatively heavy. Body more porous and prone to staining. Painter's numerals used on base and occasionally inside footrings as with Lowestoft.
- **Late period 1765-76:** Translucency poor. Marked deterioration in quality. Can resemble earthenware.

Bow Polychrome Wares

- Early period wares are decorated in vivid famille rose colours.
- The patterns used usually include chrysanthemum and peony.
- Earliest wares have a greyish body but by 1754 a good ivory tone was often achieved.
- On wares after 1760 the colours can appear dull and dirty with an adverse effect on value.
- In the late 1750s some attractive botanical plates were produced.
- After 1760 Meissen influenced floral decoration most commonly found.

A Bow candle sconce, depicting Winter, puce coat, small repair, c1765, 10in (25cm).
$1,500-2,250

A pair of Bow chamber candlesticks, c1765, 7in (18cm).
$1,800-2,700

A pair of Bow candlestick figures, modelled as scantily draped putti, enriched in blue, puce, green and yellow, restorations to nozzles, wax pans, branches and bases, minor chips to flowers and foliage and rim of one nozzle, wax pans with impressed T, c1765, 7in (18.5cm).
$600-750

A pair of Chelsea rococo style scroll moulded candlesticks, turquoise, decorated in puce and gilt, gold anchor mark, c1765, 7in (18cm).
$2,700-3,300

A Meissen candlestick, formed as cupids holding a fish which supports the candle holder, on a domed base with polychrome decoration, blue cross swords mark, 9in (22.5cm).
$450-600

A Derby candlestick group of Venus and Cupid, enriched in green and puce, some chipping to extremities, Wm. Duesbury & Co, c1765, 10in (25cm).
$900-1,050

A pair of Royal Worcester candlesticks, decorated with roses on cream ground, signed with a Hadley monogram, 6in (15cm).
$225-255

ʼandelabra

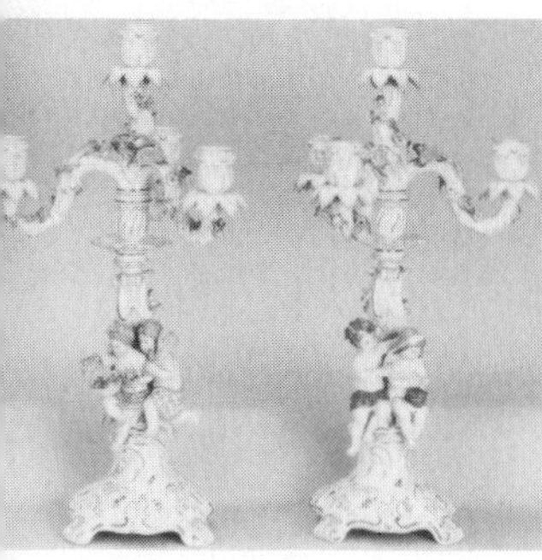

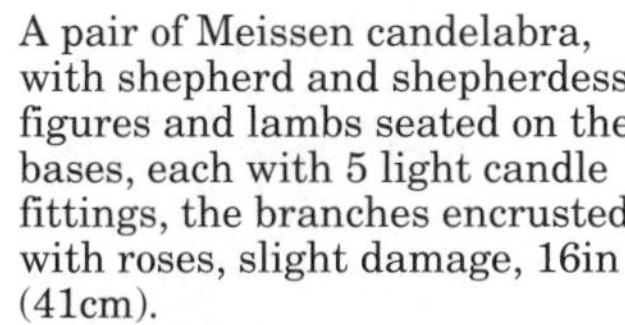

A pair of Meissen candelabra, with shepherd and shepherdess figures and lambs seated on the bases, each with 5 light candle fittings, the branches encrusted with roses, slight damage, 16in (41cm).
$1,500-2,250

pair of Meissen three-branch ındelabra of scrolling form, each pplied with models of children ›presenting the Seasons, one pplied with figures emblematic Spring and Summer, the other Autumn and Winter, painted ith scattered flowers and ısects, early 20thC, 21in (53cm).
3,000-3,750

A Plymouth centrepiece, painted with flowers and leaves within puce borders, 7in (18cm) high.
$1,500-2,250

A Royal Dux centrepiece, coloured in muted greens and pink, pink triangle mark and impressed 710, some chips, c1900, 17in (43cm).
$750-900

ʼentrepieces

pair of Royal Worcester ımports, after the originals by ımes Hadley, printed and npressed marks and registration zenges, c1880, 9in (23cm) high.
1,500-2,250

A pair of Coalbrookdale comports, with domed lids, surrounded by 3 white biscuit ware porcelain children, the whole decorated with polychrome fruit and flowers in white reserves, on gilded pink ground, Daniell printed mark, 19thC, 11½in (29cm).
$1,800-2,700

German comport, 15in (38cm).
450-600

A Continental comport, 12in high, (30.5cm). **$225-255**

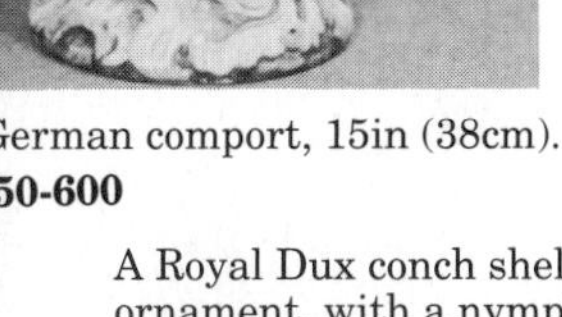

A Royal Dux conch shell ornament, with a nymph attendant, predominantly ivory, brown and gilt glazes, 15in (38cm).
$600-750

Cottages and Pastille Burners

A Staffordshire cottage-shaped pastille burner, restored, early 19thC, 4in (10cm) high.
$225-255

A pair of Staffordshire pastille burners, c1840.
$900-1,500

A Staffordshire cottage-shaped pastille burner and stand, damaged, early 19thC, 5in (13cm).
$375-450

An English cottage, with paper label from Boswell & Ward, minor chips, early 19thC, 4in (10cm).
$225-300

An English model of a Tudor mansion, naturally modelled with a figure of a woman standing at the front door, the grey walls with green vine and the roof and shaped rectangular base applied with moss, chimneypot lacking from smaller chimney, chip to main chimney stack and gables, damages to edge of base and cracks to underside, perhaps Copeland & Garrett, c1835, 7in (17.5cm).
$2,700-3,300

Pastille Burner

A pastille burner is a ceramic object for burning pastilles of compressed herbs as an air freshener, they take on numerous forms, but burners shaped as a cottage or castle, (the smoke passing through the chimney or tower) were very popular in the early 19thC.

A Staffordshire cottage ornament, c1850, 5in (12.5cm).
$150-180

Cups

A Bow coffee cup and saucer, decorated in iron red and blue with lotus pattern, outlined in gold, cell border, workman's marks, 5in (13cm).
$150-180

A Caughley blue and white cup and saucer, in the Temple pattern, with gilt decoration, c1780.
$150-180

A Caughley blue and white tea bowl and saucer, Temple pattern, c1790.
$180-225

A Caughley blue and white tea bowl, c1790.
$105-120

Caughley

A pottery was established at Caughley, near Broseley, in Shropshire soon after 1750. It began producing porcelain after it was taken over by Thomas Turner in 1772. In 1775 Robert Hancock, formerly of the Worcester Porcelain factory, joined the factory and introduced transfer printing in blue underglaze.

- Painted wares tend to be earlier than printed ones.
- Caughley body of the soapstone type often shows orange to transmitted light, but in some cases can even show slightly greenish, which adds to the confusion with Worcester.
- Glaze is good and close fitting, although when gathered in pools may have greeny-blue tint.
- From 1780s many pieces heightened in gilding; some blue and white Chinese export wares were similarly gilded in England.
- Caughley is often confused with Worcester, they have many patterns in common, for example,'The Cormorant and Fisherman' and 'Fence' patterns. Hatched crescents never appear on Caughley; they were purely a Worcester mark.

A Caughley blue and white tea cup and saucer, in Temple pattern, with gilt decoration, c1790.
$180-225

A Chaffers cup, with loop handle, colour enamelled with insects and floral sprays in a gilt Queen's pattern framework, 2½in (6cm).
$225-300

A Chaffers coffee cup, with a broad loop handle, painted in colours with a cabbage rose spray, 2½in (6cm).
$375-525

Chelsea Derby coffee cup, with
op handle, decorated with black
ıd gold husk festoons above
attered coloured florets, gilt
ntil border, gilding rubbed,
ıchor and D mark, 2½in (6cm).
135-150

Chelsea chocolate cup and
and, with puce birds on a white
ound and gilt decoration, c1760.
00-1,500

Chelsea chocolate cup and
ver, with green floral decoration
ı white ground and pink
owered finial, gold anchor mark,
1770, 3in (7.5cm).
750-900

pair of Derby tea cups and
aucers, with matching cream jug
nd sugar basin, the cups ovoid
nd ribbed with serrated gold rim,
ll with green and black rose
estoon decoration and gilt
orders, the barrel shaped jug
vith sparrow beak spout, 18thC.
225-300

A Derby vertically reeded cup and saucer, with green and gold flowered pattern, c1770, 5in (12.5cm) diam.
$750-900

A cabinet cup and stand, heavily gilded and beaded, the cup with pastoral scene, one handle restored, red mark with 78 in puce, gilder's mark on stand, c1815.
$750-900

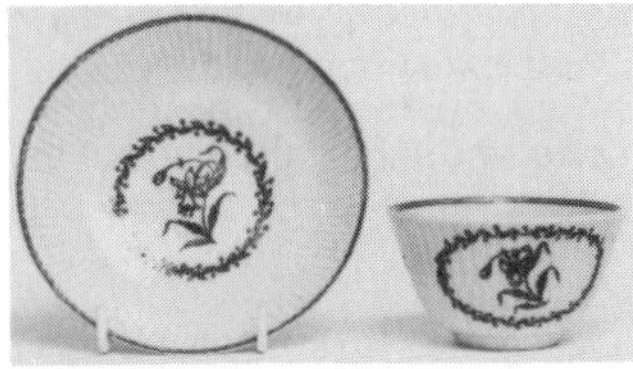

A Liverpool blue and white fluted tea bowl and saucer, c1765.
$135-150

A Christian's Liverpool polychrome tea bowl and saucer, c1778.
$300-375

A Pennington's Liverpool blue and white tea bowl, c1790.
$135-150

A Liverpool coffee cup, with plain loop handle, painted in colours with flowersprays, 2in (5cm).
$150-225

A Liverpool coffee cup, Christian's or Pennington's, with a grooved loop handle, painted in colours with chinoiserie figures in a landscape, 2½in (6cm)
$150-225

A Lowestoft ribbed coffee cup, with a loop handle, painted in green with floral sprigs and an inner scalloped border, outlined in black, 2½in (6cm) and a faceted tea bowl, gilt with trefoil leaves.
$225-300

A New Hall polychrome tea bowl and saucer, pattern 20, c1785.
$300-375

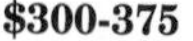

A New Hall tea bowl, 2 coffee cups and a saucer, decorated with floral sprigs and a puce diaper border, minor chips, 2in (5cm).
$225-255

A Worcester blue and white coffee cup and saucer, Prunus Root pattern, c1770.
$300-375

A Worcester tea bowl and saucer, painted in blue with Warbler pattern, and a Caughley tea cup printed in blue with sprays of flowers, damaged.
$450-600

A Worcester cup and saucer, Stormont pattern, turquoise and gilt decoration, slight damage to saucer.
$750-900

A Worcester cup and saucer, decorated with a Japan panelled and floral pattern, saucer cracked, square seal mark.
$105-120

A Worcester Barr, Flight & Barr chocolate cup and saucer, decorated by Samuel Smith, with gilt flattened loop handles, painted reserve depicting river scene with castle, on white ground with gilt vermiculated decoration, 4in (10cm).
$1,200-1,500

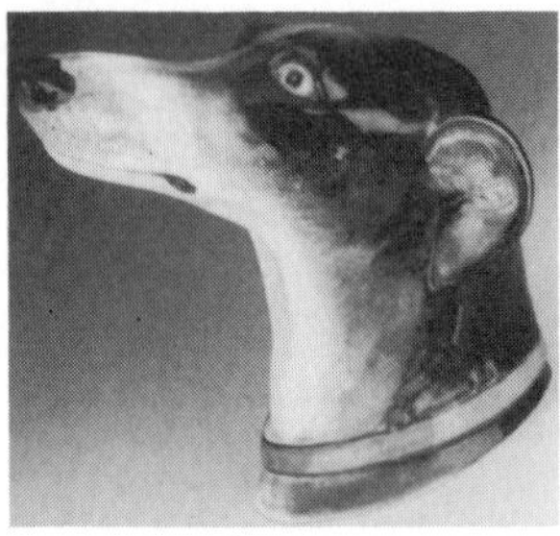

A Copeland & Garrett large stirrup cup, modelled as a hound's head with grey and black fur markings, wearing a light brown collar, edged in darker brown and with a gilt buckle round its neck, extended crack from rim to below right ear, minute rim chip, green printed mark, c1840, 7in (17cm).
$1,800-2,700

A Worcester coffee cup, tea bow and saucer, gilt with the Queen pattern, dentil rim saucer and 2 ribbed tea bowls. **$135-150**

A Worcester coffee cup, painted i colours with a version of the Sta Hunt pattern, within a gilt cartouche, inner gilt lappet border, grooved loop handle, gilt rim rubbed, small hairline crack 2½in (6cm).
$120-135

A Chantilly tea bowl and 3 saucers, painted in typical Kakiemon enamels with pairs of quails and storks among flowers, brown edged rims, chip and hair crack to tea bowl, 2 saucers repaired, hunting horns in iron red, c1730.
$600-750

Ewers

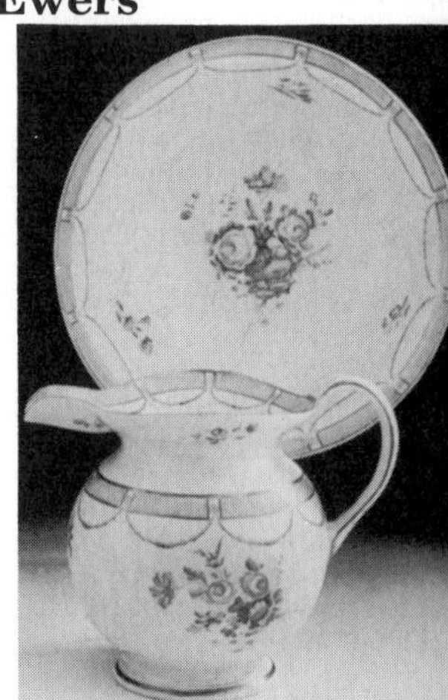

A Derby ewer and basin, painted by Edward Withers, with flowers beneath a band of turquoise panels outlined in gilt, the ewer with slight crack to base, the basin with Crown and D mark in blue, Wm. Duesbury & Co, c1780
$3,000-4,500

Worcester Persian style ewer,
4in (36cm).
1,200-1,500

Royal Worcester bone china
enaissance ewer, painted and
igned by John Stinton, puce
rinted marks, shape 1265, 11½in
29cm) high.
2,250-3,000

A Meissen blue and white ewer,
with flat domed cover, crack and
hip near base of handle, blue
aduceus mark within a double
ircle, c1735, later white metal
humbpiece, 9in (22.5cm) high.
3,000-4,500

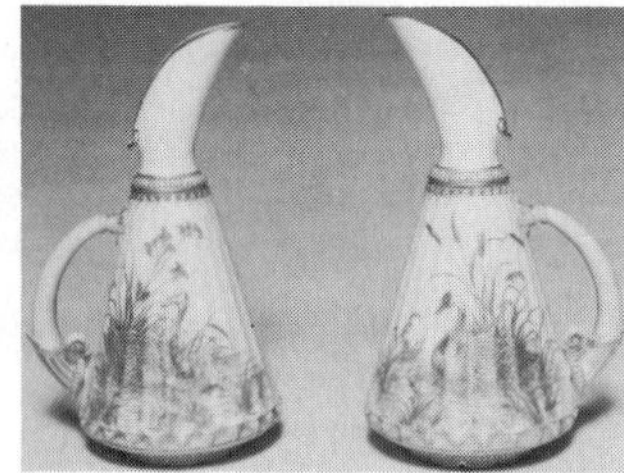

A pair of Royal Worcester ewers, decorated in gilt on an ivory ground, printed marks for 1890.
$600-750

Figures - Animals

A Bow bird, with puce, blue, black and yellow plumage, c1760, 2in (5cm).
$1,050-1,350

A Derby bird, decorated in brown yellow and black, with red and blue flowers, minor chips, c1765, 5in (13cm) high.
$1,200-1,500

A Derby model of a peacock, decorated in bright colours, on a green mound base, minor chips, c1820, 4in (10cm) high.
$450-600

Two Derby figures of goldfinches, decorated in red, yellow, black and brown, restored, c1770, 2½in (6cm). **$600-750**

A Meissen model of a green woodpecker, perched on a tree stump, chipped and restored, underglaze blue crossed swords mark, incised number 56, impressed 144, 11in (28cm) high.
$750-900

A Chamberlain's Worcester group of a striped cat and a white kitten, c1825, 3in (7cm).
$750-900

A porcellaneous figure of a cow, possibly Derby, with brown and black markings, c1820, 3in (8cm) wide.
$180-225

A Derby cow and calf group, with flowered bocage, unmarked, c1770, 4½in (11cm).
$1,200-1,500

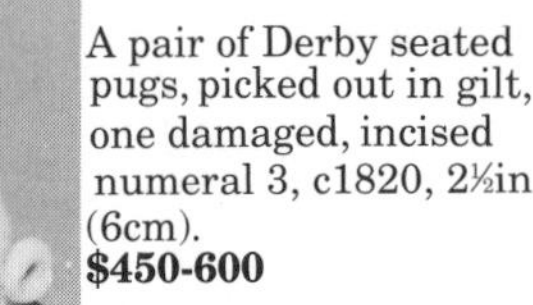

A pair of Derby type figures of hounds, 5in (12.5cm) wide.
$375-525

A pair of Derby seated pugs, picked out in gilt, one damaged, incised numeral 3, c1820, 2½in (6cm).
$450-600

A Staffordshire figure of a jockey riding a hound, 19thC, c1845, 4½in (11cm) high.
$375-525

A Meissen model of 3 hounds attacking a bull, damaged, indistinctly marked, 7in (17cm) wide.
$1,200-1,500

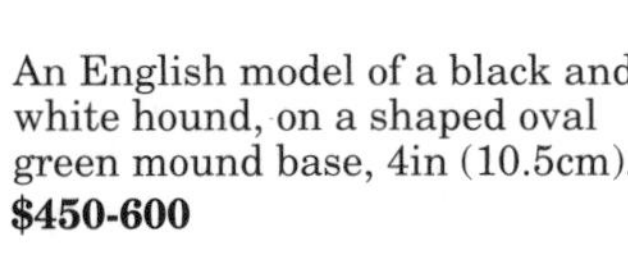

A Derby figure of a pony, some damage, crowned crossed baton mark in red, c1820, 4in (10cm).
$900-1,500

A pair of Derby figures of a stag and doe, c1765, 3in (8cm).
$750-900

A pair of Staffordshire pugs, c1860.
$750-900

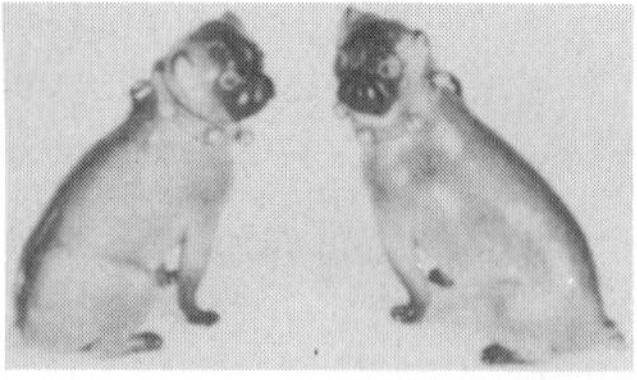

A pair of Dresden pugs, with brown coats and blue collars hung with bells, damaged, 5½in (13.5cm).
$750-900

A Royal Worcester model of H.R.H. Princess Anne on Doublet, decorated in naturalistic colours, by Doris Lindner, No. 73 of a limited edition of 750 copies, on a wooden plinth, with presentation case and certificate.
$450-600

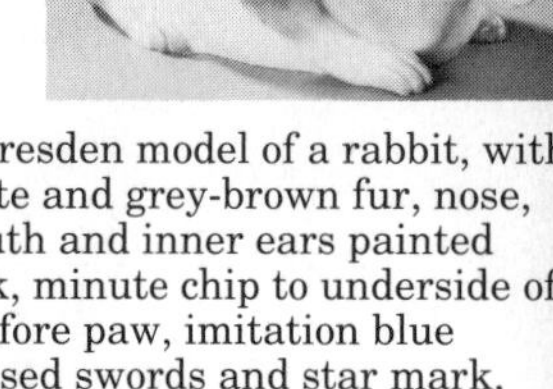

A Dresden model of a rabbit, with white and grey-brown fur, nose, mouth and inner ears painted pink, minute chip to underside of left fore paw, imitation blue crossed swords and star mark, c1880, 11in (28cm).
$3,000-3,750

An English model of a black and white hound, on a shaped oval green mound base, 4in (10.5cm).
$450-600

A figure of a mastiff, in black and fawn, on a gilt bordered base, c1820, 5in (12cm).
$750-900

A Sitzendorf monkey band, wearing 18thC wigs and costume, on scrolling gilt bases, minor chip, printed marks, 20thC, 4in (10cm) high.
$750-900

A pair of Derby figures of prowling tigers, decorated in black and brown, c1760, 2in (5cm) high.
$1,050-1,350

Figures

A Bow figure of a female gardener and a young man, c1755, 5½in (14cm).
$450-600

A Bow figure of putto and spotted dog in flowered bocage, reaching for a dove, restoration, marked, c1760, 8½in (21cm) high.
$1,200-1,500

A pair of Bow figures of Harlequin and Columbine, decorated in yellow, black, turquoise, puce and white, damaged and restored, c1762, 7½in (19cm) high.
$2,250-3,000

A Bow figure of Harlequin, decorated in pale yellow, iron red and puce on a blue ground, damaged, puce 8 and impressed T marks, c1760, 8in (20cm) high.
$2,250-3,000

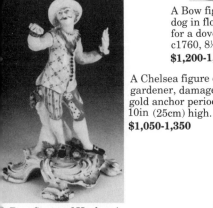

A Chelsea figure of a gardener, damaged, gold anchor period, 10in (25cm) high.
$1,050-1,350

A Chelsea putto, with restored tambourine, flesh coloured, red anchor mark, c1754, 4in (10cm).
$750-900

A Chelsea figure of a shepherd and dog, with puce coat and gold, blue and floral trousers, gold anchor period, 6in (15cm) high.
$1,200-1,500

A pair of Bow New Dancer figures, decorated in puce, blue, orange and turquoise, on scrolling copper branch, c1760, 9½in (24cm).
$6,000-8,250

A Chelsea figure of a Shepherdess, dressed in puce, green, turquoise, white, pale yellow, purple with gilding, minor chips, red anchor mark, c1756, 9½in (24cm) high.
$1,800-2,700

A pair of Derby figures of a gallant and lady, dressed as a shepherd and shepherdess, in puce, green, pale yellow, and iron red, bases enriched in gilt and turquoise, damaged, Wm. Duesbury & Co, c1760, 8½in (21cm) high
$1,800-2,700

Derby (1750-1848)

The Derby factory was founded in 1750 by a Frenchman, André Planché. In 1756, it was bought out by John Heath and his partner William Duesbury, who had until then been decorating pieces for Chelsea. In 1770, they also bought the Chelsea factory, and for the next 14 years, in a phase known as Chelsea-Derby, the two concerns operated together. In 1811, the business was acquired from Heath and Duesbury's successors by Robert Bloor, who, despite the fact that he went mad in 1826, continued to manage the declining factory until it closed in 1848. Several other factories were established in Derby in the 19thC. The most successful was the so-called 'Crown Derby' company, which survives today as the Royal Crown Derby Porcelain Company.

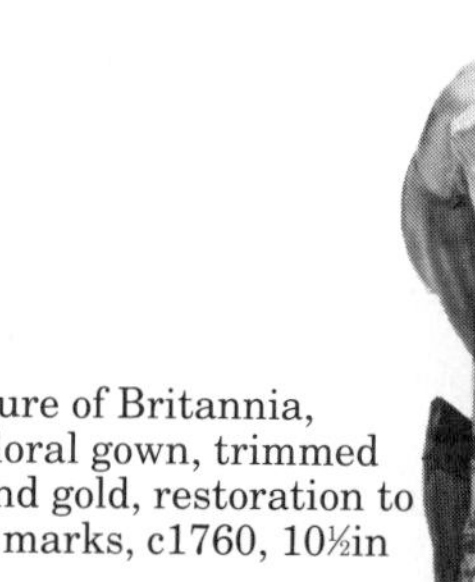

A Derby figure of Britannia, wearing a floral gown, trimmed with blue and gold, restoration to base, patch marks, c1760, 10½in (27cm).
$750-900

A Derby figure of a Scotsman, wearing blue, pale yellow, puce, white and tartan clothes, restored, Wm. Duesbury & Co, c1755, 6½in (16.5cm) high.
$600-750

A pair of Derby figures of a Jewish pedlar and companion, decorated in iron red, green, yellow and puce, damaged, Wm. Duesbury & Co, c1760, 8in (19.5cm) high.
$2,250-3,000

A Derby figure of James Quinn as Falstaff, wearing pink jacket and floral waistcoat in orange, gold and black, c1765, 8in (20cm).
$600-750

A Derby figure of Summer, in turquoise coat and pink trousers, c1758, 5in (12cm) high.
$750-1,200

A pair of Derby putti, modelled as candle holders, with pink, red and green floral decoration, blue and gilt on base, patch marks, one sconce restored, c1765, 6½in (17cm). **$1,050-1,350**

A Derby figure of Juno, Queen of the Roman Gods, wearing blue cloak and flowered dress, on rococo base, patch mark, c1765, 7in (18cm).
$1,050-1,350

pair of Derby figures of a ɔortsman and companion, ecorated in turquoise, pale ellow, puce, iron red, pink and ale blue, enriched in gilding, amaged and restored, Wm. uesbury & Co, c1770, 11in 28cm) high. **$1,500-2,250**

An English figure of Minerva, in the manner of Derby, 9in (23cm) **$375-450**

A Derby figure of Venus and Cupid, on mound base, with granitic decoration, damaged, 8in (20cm) high. **$900-1,500**

ɔur Derby figures of putti, decorated in pink, een, red, blue and puce, c1785, 4in (10cm). **80-225 each**

A Bloor Derby model of a sleeping child, after Fiammingo, applied with flowers and foliage, painted in bright colours above a gilt line, chipped, painted iron red mark, c1825, 6in (15cm) long. **$375-525**

A Derby winged figure of Father Time, wearing a gold and yellow garment, blue crossed sword mark, incised 222, c1825, 6in (15cm). **$600-750**

Derby figure of a girl, epresenting Summer, decorated red, blue, green and yellow, on reen base, incised mark 123, 1790, 6½in (16cm) high. **450-600**

A Bloor Derby model of Cupid, asleep in a flower encrusted arbour, his bow at his side, enriched in colours and gilt, red printed mark, c1830, 7½in (19cm) high. **$750-900**

Early Derby Figures

It has been suggested that Duesbury encouraged Planché to make figures because he could not get enough from Chelsea for his workshops to decorate. However, the earliest Derby figures are of a much lower standard than the Chelsea products. Representing the usual range of pastoral and allegorical subjects, they are stiffly modelled - although this may be due to the overplasticity of the clay - and they stand on simple mound bases, similar to those on the early Meissen figures of Kändler. Fortunately, most of them have been left in the white. The few that have been decorated are very primitive. For example, the mouths are often so badly painted that the lips look over large and misshapen. Under Robert Bloor the quality of the figures declined.

Most were overdecorated, with heavily rouged cheeks, sombre colours and square, octagonal or even debased rococo bases.

A Royal Worcester figure of Baccante with cymbal, after a model by James Hadley, decorated in ivory, green, gilt and blue, base incised Hadley, printed crowned circle mark, RD No. 143171, shape No. 1441, c1892. **$3,000-4,500**

A Derby figure of James Quinn as Falstaff, modelled by Farnsworth, wearing blue coat, flowered waistcoat, green trousers and red boots, restored, 8in (20cm) high. **$600-750**

A pair of Minton figures of a gardener and companion, decorated in bright colours and enriched in gilding, chipped and restored, gardener with traces of blue crossed swords mark, c1835, 7½in (19.5cm) high.
$2,700-3,300

A Plymouth figure of Winter, modelled as an old man, on a rocky mound base, chips and minor flakes, William Cookworthy's factory, c1770, 9¼in (23.5cm).
$1,200-1,500

A pair of Royal Worcester figure of a boy and girl, by James Hadley.
$1,200-1,500

A pair of Royal Worcester figures, emblematic of Joy and Sorrow, modelled by James Hadley, printed marks for 1926 and 1928, 9½in (24cm).
$750-1,200

Eight Royal Worcester figures of the countries of the world, after models by James Hadley, wearing the clothes associated with their country, glazed predominantly in ivory with painted flesh details and enriched in gilding, including John Bull, a Scotsman, an Irishman, a Chinese man, a Russian, a Negro, an Italian and a Yankee, some damage, restorations, impressed marks and model numbers, green and puce printed marks, some with registration marks, various date codes for c1880-84, 6in to 7in (15cm to 17.5cm) high.
$1,500-2,250

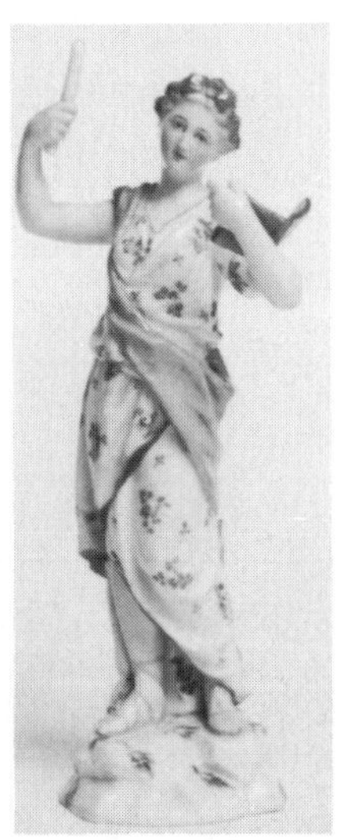

A Ludwigsburg figure of Learning, with book and scroll with flowered dress and pink drape, c1800, 7in (18cm) high.
$225-255

A Berlin figure group of children seated, one with a hurdy-gurdy, 6in (15cm).
$450-600

A Dresden figure group of 2 children with a bird and a lamb, on oval base, early 20thC, 5in (13cm).
$150-180

A Dresden figure group, enriched in colours and gilt, on an oval base, blue crossed swords mark, c1900, 12½in (32cm) high.
$2,700-3,300

A Meissen group of a sportsman and his companion, he dressed in a red coat and black breeches, she in a yellow trimmed floral dress and lilac edged hat, damaged and restored, underglaze blue crossed swords mark and impressed No. 468, 12in (31cm) wide.
$1,500-2,250

A Fulda figure of a street vendor, from the Cris de Paris series, modelled by Georg Ludwig Bartholeme, wearing black hat, yellow and white blouse, pink skirt and iron red flowered underskirt, carrying a basket of eggs, a duck in a basket surmounted by 2 birds in a cage on her back, on a domed base moulded with purple scrolls, restored, blue cross mark, c1770, 6in (15cm) high.
$12,000-15,000

Fulda

The Fulda palette consists mostly of:

- greyish blue
- green
- egg yolk yellow
- orange
- rust brown
- iron red
- puce
- black
- gilding

The Fulda factory is justly famous for its figures. Among the finest are the characters from the Commedia dell'Arte, modelled by Wenzel Neu, and the series of the Fulda court orchestra and the Cries of Paris, modelled by G.L. Bartoleme, who came from the Ansbach factory in 1770, and whose work has a lot in common with that of the famous Johann Friedrich Lück of Frankenthal.

A Meissen figure of a gallant, modelled by P. Reinicke, wearing green-lined yellow jacket, striped sash, pink breeches and yellow shoes, chipped and restored, blue crossed swords mark, c1750, 5½in (14cm) high.
$1,500-2,250

A Meissen figure of Columbine, modelled by J.J. Kändler, wearing turquoise hat, pink bodice, white dress, yellow apron, playing the hurdy-gurdy, damaged and restored, blue crossed swords mark, c1745, 5in (13cm) high.
$1,500-2,250

A Meissen figure of a boatman, modelled by P. Reinicke, wearing pink cap, pink lined green jacket, flowered waistcoat, red striped trousers with yellow sash and shoes, restored, blue crossed swords mark, c1745, 5½in (13.5cm) high.
$1,500-2,250

Twelve Meissen figures of musicians, wearing striped and flowered 18thC dress, each on a white mound with gilt C-scrolls, blue crossed swords marks, various Pressnummern and incised numbers from 60031 to 60046, 20thC, 4½in to 6in (11cm to 15cm) high.
$3,000-3,750

A late Meissen figure of a Dresden crinoline lady, wearing a yellow dress decorated with flowersprays, chipped, blue crossed swords, impressed and incised numerals, 11in (28cm).
$1,200-1,800

A Meissen group, modelled by J.J. Kändler of a gallant and his companion, he dressed in a red coat and black boots, she in a yellow lined grey jacket, full skirt and a tricorn hat, damaged, underglaze blue crossed swords mark, incised No. 507 and impressed No. 118, 11in (28cm) high.
$1,500-2,250

A Meissen group, in the manner of J.J. Kändler, damaged, underglaze blue crossed swords mark, 8½in (21cm) high.
$4,500-6,000

A composite set of 4 of the 5 Senses, after the Meissen originals, representing Touch, Smell, Hearing and Taste, all 19thC, 5in (13cm) high.
$1,200-1,500

A Samson ornament, after Chelsea, of a ballerina brightly dressed, standing on rococo base floral bocage back, restored, 12in (31cm).
$375-525

A late Meissen group of Europa and the Bull, restored, blue crossed swords, impressed and incised numeral marks, 8in (20cm) wide.
$1,050-1,350

A pair of Samson figures of a gallant and his companion, he dressed in floral panelled gold jacket and blowing a kiss, a dog at his feet, she with pink blouse and floral sprigged skirt, holding a rose, a sheep at her feet, restored, gold anchor mark, 10½in (27cm) high.
$600-750

A Volkstedt figure of a lady, wearing pink and green floral dress, with fan, 6in (15cm).
$225-300

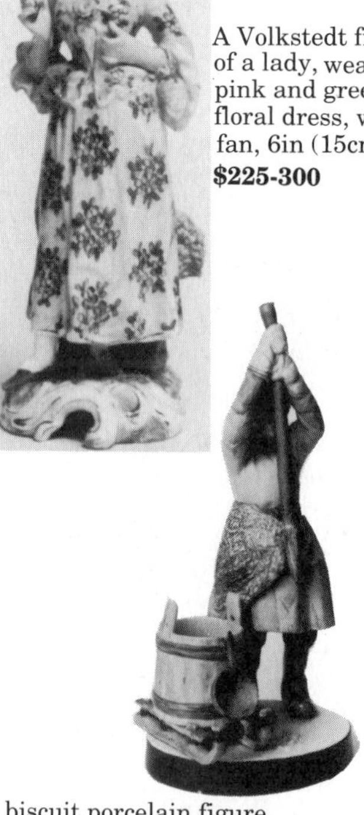

A biscuit porcelain figure, Gardner Factory, Moscow, c1860, 11in (28cm) high.
$750-900
Francis Gardner started a factory in Moscow in 1765.

A German figure group, of a seated lady with cherubs, 9in (23cm).
$600-750

Flatware

A blue and white fan-shaped dish, stained, early 19thC.
$135-150
Originally part of a set.

A Caughley blue and white spoon tray, c1780, 6½in (16cm) wide.
$300-375

A Caughley Fisherman pattern spoon tray, c1770, 6½in (16cm) wide.
$300-375

A Caughley blue and white patty dish, Fisherman pattern, c1780.
$375-450

. Caughley blue and white ;quare shaped dish, c1785, 8in 20cm).
300-375

. Caughley blue and white ɔzenge shaped dish, Temple attern, c1785.
300-375

. Caughley blue and white heart-haped dish, Weir pattern, c1785.
375-450

. Caughley blue and white ickle dish, Fisherman attern, c1785.
375-450

A Caughley blue and white shell dish, imp. nark, c1785, 7½in 19cm).
$300-375

A French lozenge-shaped spoon tray, decorated in coloured enamels with scattered flowers and insects, c1750, 6in (15cm) wide.
$450-600

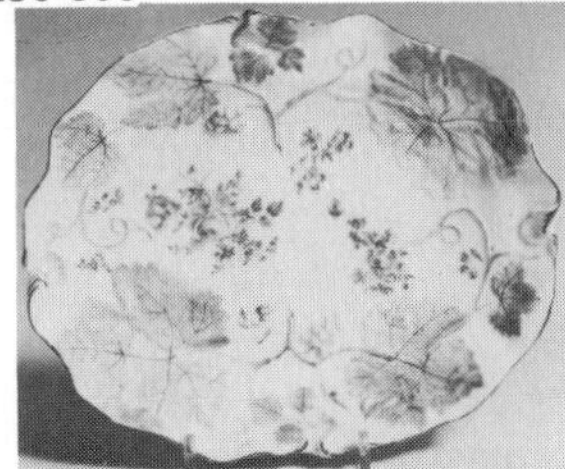

A Derby vine moulded dish, decorated in yellow, puce and green, with a brown rim and black veining, 10½in (27cm).
$1,050-1,350

A Chelsea shallow dish, cream ground with gilt border and blue, yellow, pink, mauve and green decoration, c1756, 9in (23cm) diam.
$900-1,500

A pair of Worcester dishes, c1765, 7½in (19cm) square.
$1,500-2,250

A Derby lozenge-shaped compote, with blue and gilt borders and centre panel of roses, puce mark, c1785, 11in (28cm) wide.
$450-600

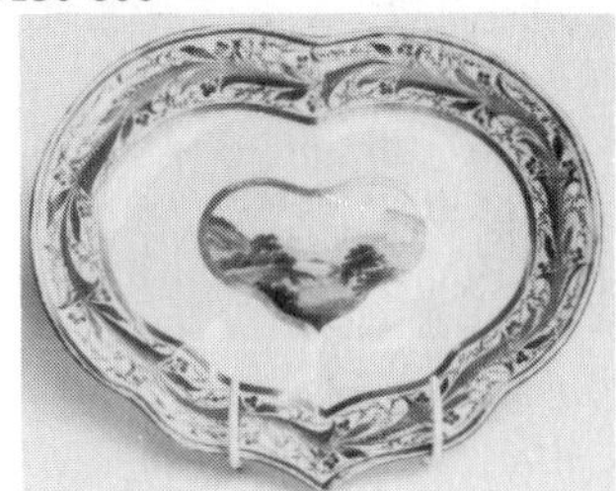

A Derby heart-shaped dish, with scene Near Matlock and gilt decoration, c1790, 10in (25cm) wide.
$450-600

A Derby lozenge-shaped dish, with salmon and gilt border, centre panel of rose and forget-me-nots, probably by Billingsley, c1790, 9½in (24cm) wide.
$375-450

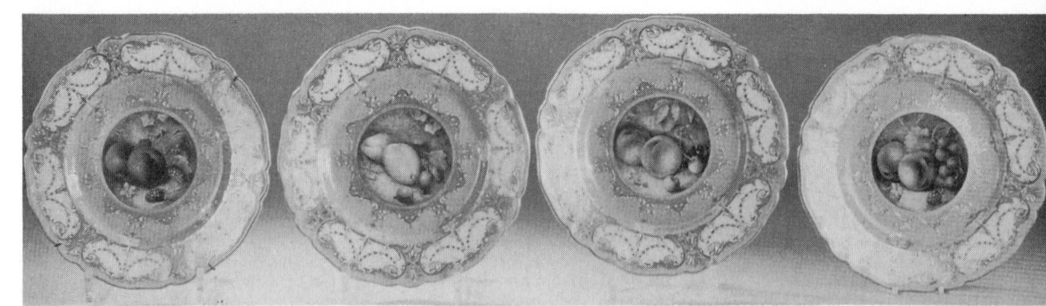

A set of 4 Royal Worcester plates, each centre painted with a panel of fruit by R. Sebright, signed, on apple green ground reserved with pink panels, enriched in gilding, puce printed marks, c1929, 9in (23cm) diam.
$1,800-2,700

A pair of Derby dessert plates, crowned crossed baton mark, c1815-20, 8¼in (21cm).
$750-900

A Worcester blue and white leaf pickle dish, c1785.
$225-300

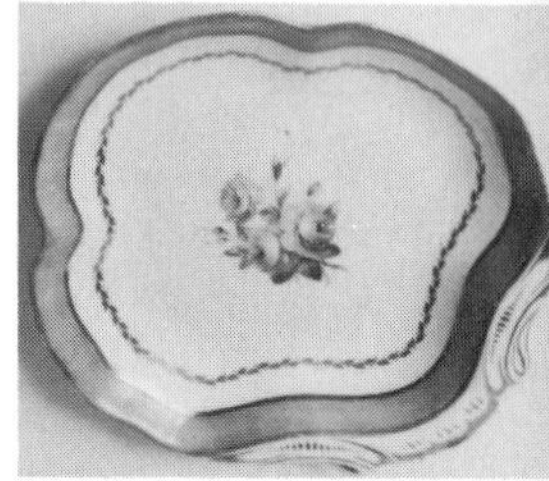

A pair of Derby fruit dishes, green and gilt, c1810, 9½in (24cm) wide.
$750-900

A Derby shallow dish, decorated in red, yellow, blue, and pink, with gilt rim, possibly painted by M. Webster, workman's mark, c1810, 9½in (243cm) wide.
$750-900

A pair of Fürstenberg dinner plates, the centres painted in colours with landscape vignettes, one with rim chip, blue F marks, c1770, 10in (25cm) diam.
$750-900

A Derby cabinet plate, with coloured scene near Derby, border of gilt on blue ground, c1830, 9in (23cm) diam.
$450-600

A shaped oval carving dish, with well, printed in blue, mid-19thC, 19½in (49cm) wide.
$150-180

A Nantgarw plate, with moulded border of blue and red bird scene and gilt edge, imp. mark, c1820, 8¼in (21cm) diam.
$900-1,500

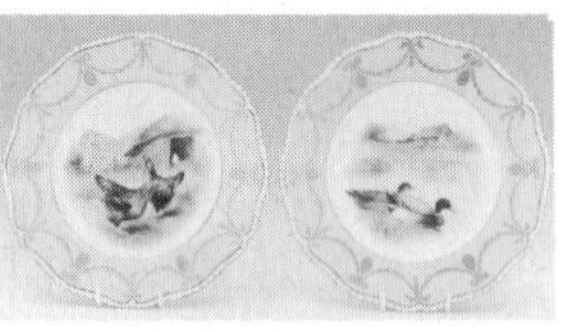

A pair of Royal Worcester cabinet plates, painted in colours by C. Johnson, signed, inscribed Rouen Ducks and Cockins (sic) in puce, printed mark in brown and green, 10in (25cm) diam.
$375-450

A Paris porcelain plate, decorated with a spray of flowers within a gilt border, 19thC, 9½in (24cm) diam.
$375-450

A Sèvres lobed dish, decorated by Theodore, on pink ground, restored, mark in blue for 1773, 11½in (29cm) wide.
$1,200-1,500

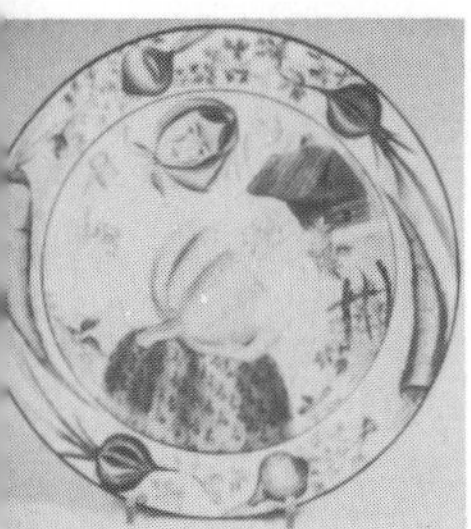

Russian propoganda plate, ecorated in coloured enamels, nperial factory mark in green nd blue overglaze State orcelain factory mark dated 921, 12in (31cm) diam.
3,000-3,750

Vienna porcelain plaque, epicting Columbus, signed H adler, 19thC, 19½in (50cm) am.
,700-3,300

A Royal Vienna dish, painted with a central medallion of Orpheus at the gate of the Underworld, on a pink ground within a gilt border, blue beehive mark, late 19thC, 13½in (34cm) diam.
$1,200-1,500

A Royal Vienna plate, painted with a scene of Classical figures within an interior representing Venus presenting Helen to Augustus, within a blue and gilt border with landscape panels and scrolling foliate ornament, inscribed to reverse, blue beehive mark, late 19thC, 15in (38cm) diam. **$900-1,500**

A pair of Continental dishes, with 'Sèvres' marks, painted with fête galante scenes within well, gilt hatched scroll borders with musical trophies on royal blue grounds, one signed Poitovin, 17in (43cm) diam.
$4,500-6,000

Goblets

Vienna goblet and cover, ainted by E. Beringer with Landliche Musik and 'agdfanfare', decorated in dark uce and blue border, on a single lade knopped stem and swept ircular foot, the waisted ylindrical cover with cone finial, rinted beehive mark in nderglaze blue and inscribed in urnt orange, signed, 15in (38cm) igh.
900-1,500

A Vienna goblet and cover, the waisted cylindrical bowl painted in colours with 'Amor Am Pranger and Tanrende Nimyalien', gilt decorated pink and claret borders, on a single blade knopped stem and swept circular foot, waisted cylindrical cover with bud finial, damaged and repaired, printed beehive mark in underglaze blue and inscribed in iron red, 15in (38cm) high.
$750-900

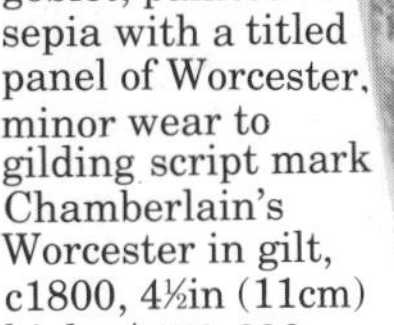

A Chamberlain's Worcester flared goblet, painted in sepia with a titled panel of Worcester, minor wear to gilding script mark Chamberlain's Worcester in gilt, c1800, 4½in (11cm) high. **$450-600**

Inkwells

A pair of Stevenson & Hancock Derby inkstands and covers, in the form of oil lamps, with elongated handles and flowers in relief on white and gilt ground.
$300-375

A Derby desk tidy, with panels of river scenes and blue and gilt decoration, restored, c1815, 12in (31cm) wide
$750-900

A Paris inkstand, painted with bouquets of flowers within gilt scroll borders on green ground, on 4 scroll feet, and another inkstand with 3 wells within a tray with moulded borders, both with underglaze blue marks for Jacob Petit, 19thC. **$750-900**

Jars

A Worcester blue and white Fence pattern tea jar, c1765, 4in (10cm).
$750-900

Jugs

A Chelsea sparrow beak creamer, painted with sprigs of different coloured flowers, red anchor mark, c1755. **$1,200-1,500**

A Caughley blue and white Fisherman pattern sparrow beak jug, with gilt decoration, 5in (12.5cm).
$375-450

A Caughley blue and white Temple pattern cream jug, c1785.
$150-180

A Caughley blue and white sparrow beak jug, c1780, 4in (10cm).
$375-450

A Pennington's jug, of baluster shape with a spurred scroll handle, painted in blue with a windmill, named 'J; Shaw, 1798' on reverse below a printed blue floral border extending part way around the rim, flower moulded spout, riveted cracks, 9½in (24cm) high. **$3,000-4,500**

An H & R Daniel blue ground oviform jug, one side painted with a view of Teddesley Hall, enriched in gilding, c1835, 9in (23cm) high.
$5,250-6,000

Edward John Walhouse of Hatherton, Stafford, inherited Teddesley Hall, Staffordshire, on the death in 1812 of his great uncle Sir Edward Littleton, 4th Bt., assuming the surname and arms of Littleton. In 1812 Edward Littleton married Hyacinthe Mary Wellesley, the natural daughter of Richard, Marquess Wellesley and niece of the Duke of Wellington. He became M.P. for Staffordshire in the same year, entering Earl Grey's cabinet as Chief Secretary for Ireland in 1833. On his honourable resignation in 1835 following a cabinet leak, he was created Baron Hatherton and it would seem, therefore, most likely that this jug was specially commissioned to celebrate his enoblement.

Teddesley Hall, built for Sir Edward Littleton by William Baker in 1757 was demolished in 1954.

According to family tradition King George III (known as Farmer George) visited Teddesley Hall and, whilst the party in his honour was in progress, he donned his coachman's uniform in order to see for himself the state of the local agriculture. Meeting the woman tossing hay he said 'why are you not up at the house celebrating the King's visit?' to which she replied 'we can't wait for Kings whilst the weather is good and the harvest must be taken in.' The King apparently took off his coat and helped her.

A Liverpool polychrome sparrow beak jug, c1780.
$375-450

A Longton Hall strawberry leaf moulded jug, picked out in green and puce, small restoration, c1755, 3in (8cm). **$900-1,500**

A New Hall polychrome creamer, c1785. **$150-180**

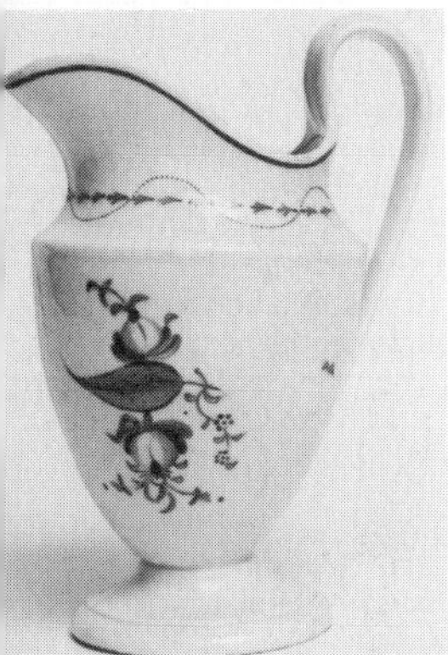

A New Hall polychrome helmet-shaped creamer, pattern 122, c1790, 4½in (11cm).
$225-300

A Worcester polychrome sparrow beak jug, probably by Rogers, 3in (8cm).
$450-600

A Vienna pear shaped hot water jug, painted on one side with 2 hearts tied with ribbon to a tree above the inscription 'Tou jour en vigueur', the other side with a ship above the inscription 'Ciel Favorable', underglaze blue beehive mark, 7½in (19cm) high.
$900-1,500

A miniature washstand basin and jug, brightly decorated within gilt borders, early 19thC, the jug 3in (8cm).
$375-450

A Samuel Alcock Burslem Royal patriotic jug, of baluster form with moulded dragon head handle and acanthus form spout, the body printed en grisaille with 2 scenes, one depicting the Seige of Sebastopol, the other a weeping mother and children, green painted and gilt lined borders, hair crack to handle, printed factory mark and registration diamond, c1854, 8in (20cm) high.
$225-255

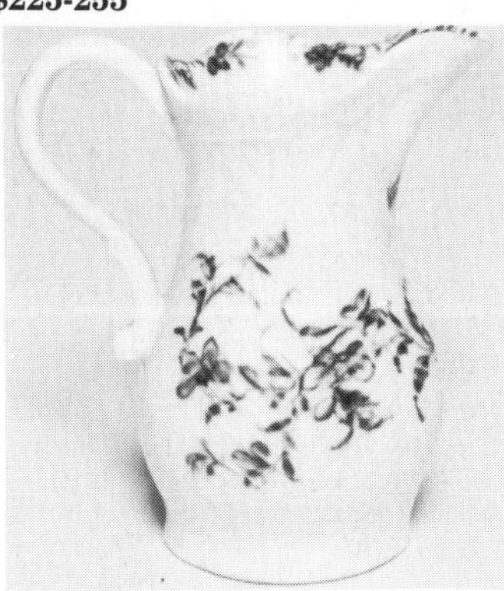

A Worcester herringbone moulded small baluster shaped jug, decorated in blue, hair crack, c1758, 3½in (9cm).
$450-600

Mugs

A Derby barrel-shaped mug, decorated with bamboo and exotic birds in green, yellow and red, c1758, 6½in (16cm) high.
$2,250-3,000

A First Period Worcester blue and white mug, painted with rural views, hatched crescent mark, 5in (13cm) high.
$450-600

A Worcester mug, with reeded loop handle, printed in black with the Milkmaids pattern, after Robert Hancock, c1760, 3in (8cm).
$600-750

A pair of late Georgian mugs, painted with gilt initials and polychrome floral sprays, 3½in (9cm) high.
$90-105

A Derby barrel-shaped mug, with pink, blue and green floral decoration, c1770, 3½in (9cm) high.
$1,200-1,500

A Böttger Goldchinesen two handled beaker and a saucer, gilt at Augsburg with chinoiserie figures taking tea and a steaming lantern and kettle, with dragons and birds in flight, the saucer with lustre 3 1/3 and Dreher's /, c1725.
$2,700-3,300

Plaques

A Derby flower painted plaque, probably by Steele, c1800, 11½ by 9½in (29 by 24cm).
$3,000-3,750

A Berlin plaque, painted with Princess Louise after Richter in the manner of Wagner, 12½ by 7½in (32 by 19cm), in gilt metal mounted glazed blue velvet lined leather easel case.
$4,500-6,000

Pots

A Böttger cream pot and cover, of squat baluster form, with moulded scroll handle and 3 paw feet, painted by J.G. Mehlhorn, within a shaped gilt scroll and Böttger lustre and red scrolling foliage cartouche, the cover similarly painted, gilt rims, some damage and restoration, gilder's 10 to base, c1725, 4½in (11.5cm) high.
$7,500-9,000

A Derby bough pot and pierced liner, painted with an oval panel of Trent near Ingleby, Derbyshire, liner cracked and chipped, blue painted mark, 8in (20cm) wide.
$750-1,200

A Worcester garniture of 3 yellow ground cache pots and stands, with scenes of Oxford and Keswick, c1810.
$3,000-3,750

Sauceboats

A Derby sauceboat and stand, copy of a Bow design decorated in green, blue, red and gilt, sauceboat incised 2 mark, c1795, 8in (20cm) high.
$1,200-1,500

A Caughley blue and white butter boat, c1770.
$225-255

. Lowestoft blue and white auceboat, c1790. **225-300**

A pair of Worcester shell moulded cream boats, of 'Dolphin Ewer' form, decorated in puce, orange, yellow and green, c1765, 3in (8cm) high. **$3,000-4,500**

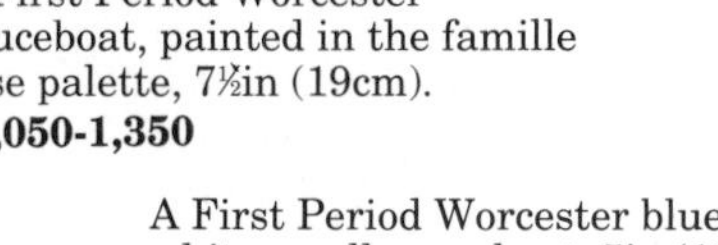

A First Period Worcester sauceboat, painted in the famille rose palette, 7½in (19cm). **$1,050-1,350**

. Worcester cos lettuce shaped auceboat, decorated in coloured namels, restored, c1755, 7½in 19cm) wide. **$375-450**

A First Period Worcester blue and white small sauceboat, 5in (13cm) wide. **$450-600**

ervices

Belleek white lustre tea set, ith gilt borders, comprising: 4 ıps and saucers, cream jug, ıgar basin and teapot, late ıark. **450-600**

A part tea and coffee service, probably Coalport, Anstice, Horton and Rose, each piece painted with a Japan pattern, No. 561 in Imari colours, comprising: a tea plate, 2 saucer dishes, 6 tea cups, 10 coffee cups and 11 saucers, some damage. **$1,800-2,700**

An English tea and coffee service, painted in overglaze enamels and gilt in the Imari palette of iron red, black and green with a Japan pattern, comprising 21 pieces, some damage, marked for Swansea and with red printed mark, pattern No. 259, c1820. **$1,200-1,500**

. Coalport yellow ground part tea nd coffee service, painted in epia, possibly by William illingsley at Mansfield, with ındscape scenes within oval gilt and cartouches, the borders eserved and gilt with a foliate and beneath gilt rims, omprising: an oval teapot, cover nd stand, 2 saucer dishes, one eacup, 10 coffee cans and 5 aucers, some damage, c1800. **2,700-3,300**

An H & R Daniel part dessert service, decorated in coloured enamels and gilt, comprising 14 pieces, pattern No. 3835 in gilt, c1825. **$1,050-1,350**

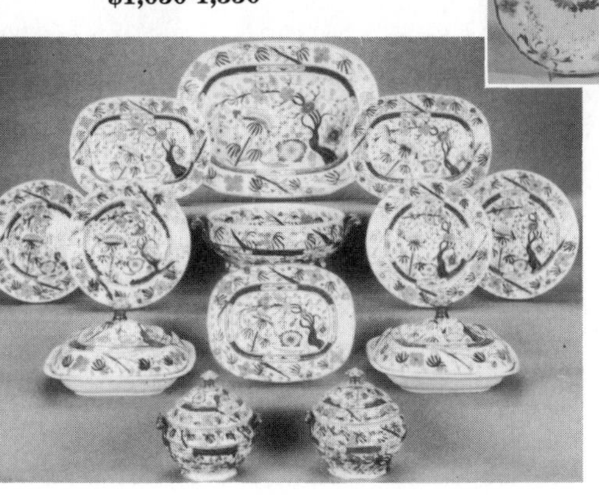

A Coalport composite Imari pattern part dinner service, painted in iron red, blue, green, yellow and enriched in gilding, with peony and prunus sprays, comprising 119 pieces, some damage, c1810 and 1825. **$3,000-4,500**

A Coalport crested green ground part dessert service, painted in iron red and gilt with a crest, above the motto 'Constantia et Vigilantia' on a ribbon cartouche, the borders reserved and painted with loose bouquets within shaped oval gilt scroll cartouches flanked by gilt flowering foliage, within shaped white and gilt milled rims, comprising 45 pieces, some damage, c1820.
$12,000-15,000

An early Victorian Japan pattern part tea service.
$180-225

A Derby Imari pattern part dessert service, the centres painted with stylised bulbs and foliage, the borders with radiati panels of diaper and whorl pattern reserved with blue and gilt quatrefoil medallions of flowers and mythical beasts, comprising 26 pieces, some damage, blue square seal marks c1785 and later.
$2,700-3,300

A Derby Imari pattern part dessert service, painted in underglaze blue, iron red and green, enriched in gilding, damaged, iron red crown, crossed batons and D marks, Robt. Bloor & Co, c1820.
$2,700-3,300

A Coalport dessert service, comprising: 18 pieces, each painted with a specimen rose, signed F. Howard, with blue and gilt borders, printed marks, pattern No. X6093/0.
$2,250-3,000

A Staffordshire part tea service, painted with bouquets within gi scroll and feuilles-de-choux cartouches, the borders gilt with flowersprays, weeds and shells within zig-zag rims, comprising 18 pieces, gilding rubbed, c1850.
$750-1,200

A Rockingham part tea and coffe service, painted with a small landscape vignette and mushroor borders, comprising 17 pieces, puce marked, pattern No. 1198.
$1,800-2,700

A Minton botanical part tea and coffee service, painted in a bright palette with loose bouquets of specimen flowers beneath a band of gilt foliate ornament and gilt rims, comprising 17 pieces, damaged, blue interlaced L's enclosing M marks, pattern No. 786, c1812.
$7,500-9,000

A Minton green bordered part dessert service, the borders with swags of stylised foliage and blue cornflowers within gilt oval scroll medallions, comprising 31 pieces, damaged, pattern No. 7687, c1860.
$1,500-2,250

. Berlin tea service, of ogee shape ith deep blue ground reserving ilt edged panels painted with owers, comprising 26 pieces, nderglaze blue Pfennigmarke nd printed red KPM and orb iarks, c1860.
2,250-3,000

A Grainger & Co. Worcester fruit service, the deep underglazed borders with jewelled turquoise and pearl on gilt bordered rims with gilt jewelled surround to the central painted roundel, various views, English coastal and landscape, comprising 13 pieces.
$1,200-1,500

A Meissen part tea service, painted with various hunting scenes within wooded landscape vignettes resting on ombrierte gilt rocaille and scroll half cartouches, comprising 11 pieces, damaged, blue crossed swords marks, various Pressnummern, c1750.
$6,000-8,250

. Chamberlain's Worcester part essert service, each piece ioulded with the Union border in ow relief on a pale sage green round, the centres painted with floral specimen, comprising 14 ieces, some damage, red painted cript mark with 155 New Bond t address, 2 dishes possibly ater, c1820.
900-1,500

A Meissen part tea and coffee service, with green branch handles, painted in purple camaieu with deutsche Blumen on a Dulong pattern ground, comprising 33 pieces, damaged, blue crossed swords marks, some with various Pressnummern, the spoon trays impressed k, c1750.
$6,000-8,250

A Nantgarw part dessert service, the centres painted with loose bouquets, the wells with gilt diaper pattern within shaped cartouches, the borders with flowersprays and lightly moulded with scrolls and flowerhead enriched with gilding within lobed gilt rims, comprising 19 pieces, damaged, impressed Nantgarw C.W. marks, c1820.
$10,500-13,500

\ Paris Rihouet Lerosey tête-à-ête in the Sèvres style, with ɔanels of exotic birds within gilt 'oliate borders on a turquoise ground within gilt dentil rims, comprising 7 pieces, inscribed in ;ilt, 19thC. **$12,000-15,000**

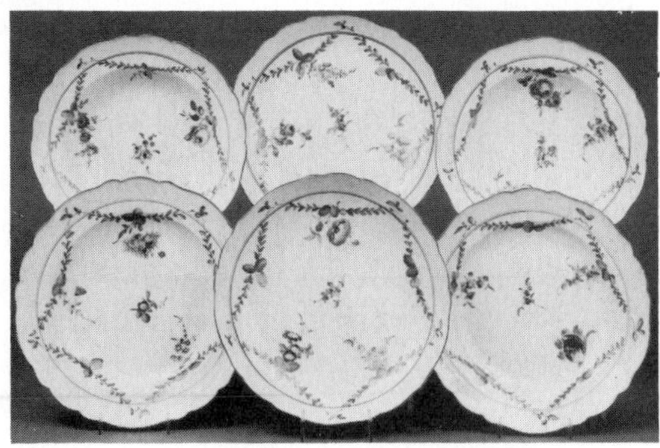

A Meissen part dinner service, painted with sprays of flowers suspended from swags of foliage and a puce line within shaped puce line rims, comprising 31 pieces, damaged, blue crossed swords and dot marks, various Pressnummern, c1770.
$6,000-8,250

A Berlin dinner service, each piece painted with scattered flowersprays within a spirally moulded border and waved gilt rim, comprising 102 pieces, underglaze blue sceptre mark and painted KPM and orb mark, 19thC.
$6,000-8,250

A Paris celadon ground part dessert service, boldly painted with pairs of birds on branches above garlands of bright foliage, comprising 14 pieces, damaged, c1880.
$225-300

Tankards

A Royal Copenhagen tankard, commemorating the coronation of King Edward VII and Queen Alexandra, the silver cover with the emblems of England, Scotland and Ireland, with inset medal and lion rampant thumbpiece, the body painted with a monogram, symbols, swags of flowers and 9 August, 1902, 7½in (19cm) high.
$750-900

A Worcester Barr Flight and Barr tankard, marked, c1805, 7½in (19cm) high.
$1,800-2,700

Tea & Coffee Pots

A Derby coffee pot and cover, decorated with chinoiserie figures in red, yellow, blue and green, cover restored, c1760, 10in (25cm) high.
$1,800-2,700

A Plymouth blue and white teapot and cover, tin mark, c1770, 6in (15cm).
$900-1,500

Three Worcester pieces: *l.* a blue and white teapot and cover, with pointed knop, loop handle and floral pattern, crescent mark, 4½in (11cm). **$450-600**
c. a blue and white sparrow beak cream jug and cover, with floral knop and pattern, crescent mark, 6in (15cm). **$300-375** and
r. a blue and white fluted barrel teapot and cover, with floral knop, reeded spout and E-shaped handle, fruit and wreath pattern, 4in (10cm).
$300-375

A Royal Worcester teapot, cover and stand, on a peach ground, decorated with sprigs and bouquets of flowers, c1900.
$225-300

A Meissen chinoiserie coffee pot and cover, with gilt short spout and scroll handle, painted in the manner of J.G. Höroldt, damaged blue crossed swords mark, Dreher's mark of 11, gilder's 26, c1730, the cover 19thC, 9in (22cm) high.
$3,000-3,750

A Worcester polychrome teapot and cover, with chinoiserie decoration, c1770.
$900-1,500

. Meissen teapot and cover, of quat baluster form, the curved pout with bearded mask erminal, the loop handle with noulded foliage terminals, ainted in the manner of A.F. von öwenfinck in purple camaieu vith Orientals, the domed cover imilarly painted and with nopped spire finial and brown ne rim, damaged, blue crossed words and KPM mark, 1724, the ecoration c1740, 5in (12.5cm) igh.
3,000-4,500

A Meissen chinoiserie teapot and cover, of squat baluster form, with moulded gilt edged scroll handle and faceted purple and gilt scroll spout, painted in the manner of J.G. Höroldt, with an Oriental taking tea and his companion beside a fence and shrubs within panelled Böttger lustre and scroll cartouches, flanked by trailing indianische Blumen and scattered insects, the later copper gilt mount cover with iron red monochrome vignettes, blue crossed swords and KPM mark, gilder's 11, c1724, 4½in (11cm) high.
$4,500-6,000

Tureens

A Doccia oval fluted two-handled tureen, cover and stand, painted with scattered flowersprays including pink roses, blue convolvulus and orange daisies, the scroll handles enriched with gilding and mask terminals, the cover with a white convolvulus finial, damaged and repaired, c1765, stand 9in (23.5cm) wide.
$3,000-4,500

/ases

pair of Coalport vases and overs, each painted with peaches nd grapes, signed F.H. Chivers nd F. Howard, the blue grounds ecorated in gilt, damaged, rinted mark and gilt numerals 7540, 16½in (42cm).
2,250-3,000

A pair of tulip shaped vases, perhaps Derby, c1820, 6in (15cm).
$1,200-1,500

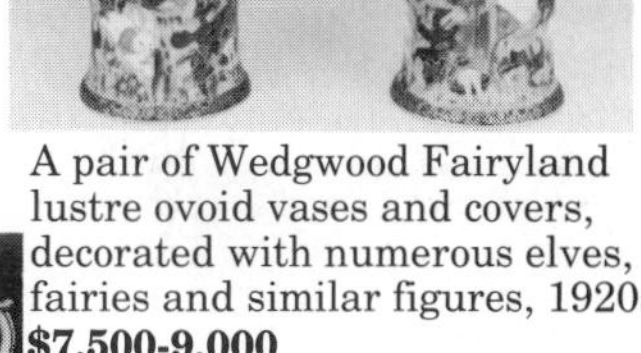

A pair of Wedgwood Fairyland lustre ovoid vases and covers, decorated with numerous elves, fairies and similar figures, 1920s.
$7,500-9,000

A garniture of Minton scroll footed vases, encrusted with flowers, mid-19thC.
$450-600

. Derby spill vase, with a hunting ound surrounded by gilt lecoration, c1820, 4½in (11cm).
1,200-1,500

A Spode flared vase, painted on a lilac and gilt cell pattern ground, red painted mark, 6in (15cm) high.
$900-1,500

A Royal Worcester vase and cover, painted by John Stinton, with green ground and coral bands, moulded with stiff leaves and Renaissance style scrolls, damage, printed puce marks and numeral 1572, date for code 1906, 10½in (26.5cm).
$2,250-3,000

A garniture of Worcester Flight Barr and Barr two-handled vases, each painted in the style of Baxter, damaged, painted puce marks, 12 and 11in (31 and 28cm) high. **$6,000-8,250**

A pair of Worcester Barr Flight and Barr topographical vases, painted with Forge Bridge, Westmoreland, within gilt panel between beaded rims, the interic painted with crowns above monograms EC, on square bases damaged and repaired, painted and impressed marks, c1810, 5½ (14cm) high.
$750-1,200

A pair of Royal Worcester two-handled pedestal pot pourri vases and covers, painted by Harry Ayrton, signed, printed mark in black, No. H314 in black and initialled PW in black, 7in (18cm) high.
$2,700-3,300

A Grainger's Worcester vase, turned base to a baluster centre and elongated neck, peach blue ground with decoration of swallows and scrolls, 10½in (26cm).
$225-255

A pair of Victorian vases and stands, deep blue ground, with gilded handles and reserve cameos of shepherds and shepherdesses, 24in (61cm).
$225-255

A pair of Dresden Helena Wolfsohn vases and covers, painted in colours with 18thC courtiers and peasants seated in open landscapes within blue panels, decorated in polychrome enamels with bunches of summe flowers, within gilt cailloute borders, damage and restoration 20in (50cm) high.
$2,700-3,300

A Meissen Augustus Rex vase, damaged, blue AR mark, Dreher's XII to foot rim, c1730, the decoration later, 11½in (29cm) high. **$9,000-12,000**

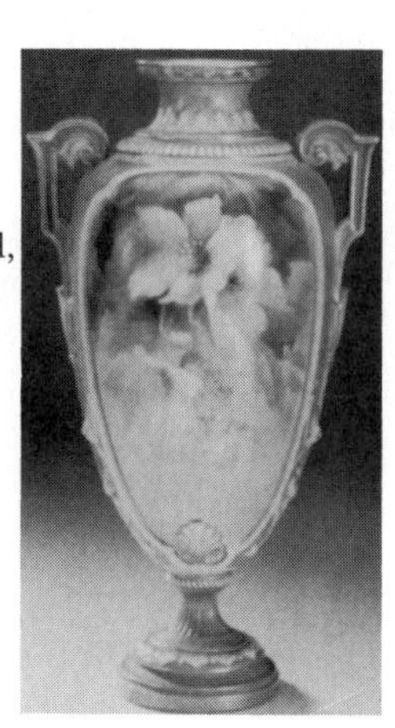
A Royal Worcester two-handled vase, painted by Roberts, signed, with panels of flowers against a green ground, repaired, green printed marks, 12in (31cm).
$375-525

A Royal Worcester pot pourri vase and cover, painted by W. Powell, signed, with 2 storks by rocks against a blue ground, green printed marks, 7½in (19cm).
$1,200-1,500

An amphora, c1850 11in (28cm) high.
$375-450

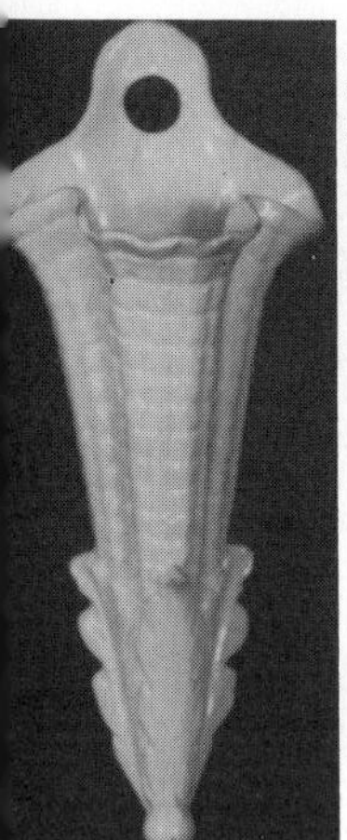

A pair of Victorian wall pockets, John Mortlock, London, c1875, 8½in (21cm) long.
$150-180

A pair of Paris flared beaker vases, with beaded borders, in Spode style, decorated in colours with central panel of flowers and leaves, on a flower scattered green and gilt leaf ground, 9½in (24cm) high.
$900-1,500

Miscellaneous

Three Royal Worcester wall brackets, allegorical of the Seasons, Spring with chip, Summer with restoration, crack to reverse, c1870, 9½in (24cm) high.
$900-1,500

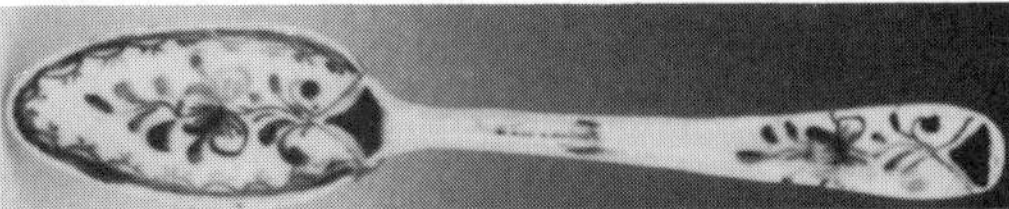

A Lowestoft blue and white mustard spoon, the handle painted with a flowerspray and the bowl with a flowerspray within a foliate loop border, c1765, 4½in (11cm) long.
$2,700-3,300

Caughley blue and white emple pattern spittoon, c1785, in (10cm) high.
1,200-1,800

A set of 3 French tea canisters and covers, in an inlaid rosewood casket, possibly Giey-sir-Avjon, one container slightly chipped, incised marks, c1840, 5in (13cm).
$900-1,500

A Minton jardinière, with blue gilt and bird decoration.
$450-600

Derby salt and stand, ecorated in gilt on a salmon round, slightly rubbed, red ark, c1825.
120-135

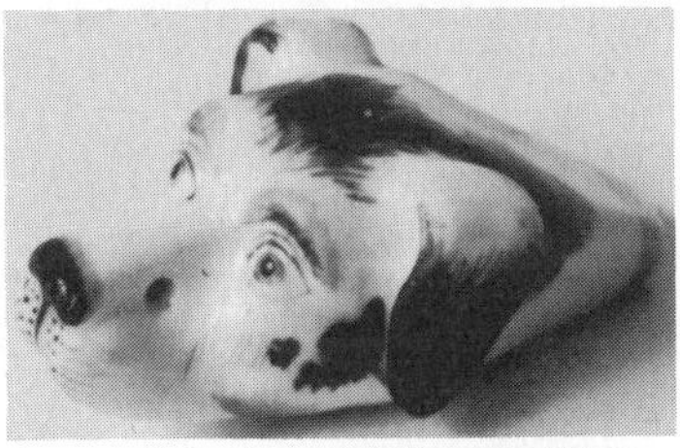

A porcelain dog whistle, possibly Derby, c1820, 2in (5cm) long.
$225-300

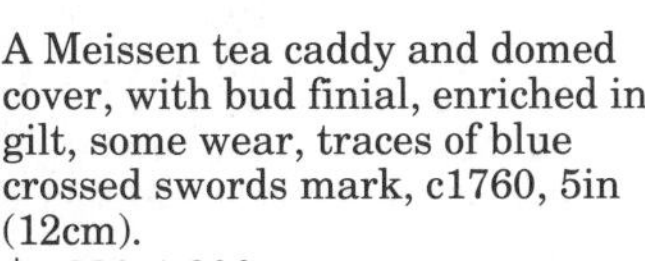

A German pipe bowl, moulded with scrolling foliage, painted with spiralling panels of ribbon tied floral sprays between borders of stylised rope twists, enriched in gilt, 18thC, 1½in (4cm) high.
$750-900

A Meissen tea caddy and domed cover, with bud finial, enriched in gilt, some wear, traces of blue crossed swords mark, c1760, 5in (12cm).
$1,200-1,800

A porcelain framed wall mirror, the rococo frame moulded with scrollwork and encrusted with flowers, the corners and surmount applied with putti, German, damaged, late 19thC, 49 by 27½in (124.5 by 70cm).
$2,250-3,000

SCOTTISH CERAMICS

A Seaton Pottery bacon bowl, c1896, 16½in (42cm) diam.
$450-600

A J & M P Bell, blue and white punch bowl, Triumpha pattern. 10in (25cm) diam.
$150-180

A Bough commemorative bowl, Coronation George VI and Queen Elizabeth 1937, marked E.A. Bough CXX 1937 P, 8½in (21cm) diam.
$750-900

A Bough muffin dish, 9in (22cm) diam.
$300-375

A Mak' Merry cup and saucer, painted by a lady artist in green and white, 6in (15cm) diam.
$150-180

A Mak' Merry mug, painted by a lady artist, 4in (10cm) high.
$150-180

A Methven pottery plate, 11in (28cm) diam.
$135-150 each

A Mak' Merry powder bowl, painted by a lady artist, 4in (10cm) diam.
$225-300

A Strathyre plate, decorated by Mary Ramsay, 10in (25cm) diam.
$225-300

A J & M P Bell blue and white transfer printed meat dish, Triumpha pattern, 19½in (49c wide.
$300-375

A Glasgow Prattware Wellingtc plaque, 9in (23cm) diam.
$225-300

A Mak' Merry mug, painted by lady artist, 5in (12cm) high.
$135-150

A Mak' Merry mug, painted by lady artist, 5in (12cm) high.
$150-180

A Mak' Merry jug, decorated in brown, orange, blue, yellow and red, 7in (18cm) high.
$300-375

pine bowfront chest of drawers, with 2 ort and 3 long drawers, shaped frieze d squat ball feet, 19thC.
450-900

A Danish pine bureau bookcase, c1860, 84in (213cm) high.
$2,250-3,000

A pine bureau bookcase, c1790, 42in (106.5cm) wide.
$3,000-3,500

pine chest of drawers, with 2 short and 2 long gesso ecorated drawers, English, 19thC, 40in (101.5cm) wide.
600-900

A Scandinavian chest of drawers, c1880, 52in (132cm).
$600-750

n Irish glazed bookcase, 1830, 84in (213cm) high.
1,250-1,350

A pine 5 drawer chest of drawers, 41in (104cm).
$375-475

A painted pine chest, with serpentine fronted top and 8 drawers, early 19thC, 30in (77cm) wide. **$2,000-2,250**

A Danish pine wardrobe, c1880, 40in (101.5cm) wide.
$650-750

An Irish food cupboard, c1850, 78in (198cm) high.
$1,200-1,300

A pine pillar wardrobe, c1880, 50in (127cm) wi
$800-900

A pine food safe, c1900, 25½in (65cm) high.
$60-75

An Irish glazed food cupboard, c1870, 50in (127cm) wide.
$1,500-1,900

An Irish pine cupboar c1820, 90in (228.5cm).
$1,200-1,500

A pine linen press, c1860, 46in (116.5cm) wide. **$900-1,000**

A pine display cabinet, c1840.
$1,800-2,000

A Georgian country pine corner cupboard, with shaped open shelves, 26in (66cm) wide.
$750-1,000

A pine 2 door folding bed cupboard, Irish, early 19thC, 50in (127cm) wide.
$1,000-1,300

An Irish pine housekeeper's cupboard, early 19thC.
$1,200-1,800

A glazed food cupboar c1850, 53in (134.5cm) wide.
$1,500-1,800

A miniature pine clockmaker's chest of 17 drawers, 18thC, 18in (46cm).
$225-375

A nest of 48 drawers, c1880, 74in (188cm).
$1,200-1,500

A pine 4 door cupboard, on bracket feet, English, 18th 52in (132cm).
$1,000-1,350

A European pine wardrobe, 58in (147cm) wide. **$1,000-1,350**

A single pine wardrobe, with gesso decoration, 19thC, 34in (86cm).
$750-1,200

An Irish pine cupboard 19thC, 32in (81cm).
$900-1,200

ine panelled sideboard, h 3 cockbeaded drawers ıer side of central ›board doors, 19thC, 96in 3.5cm) wide.
200-1,800

A pine sideboard, with panelled ends, 7 drawers and recessed cupboard, 19thC, 70in (177.5cm).
$900-1,300

A pine high backed panelled settle, with 2 drawers under seat, solid sides with arms, on sledge feet, 18thC, 48in (122cm) wide.
$750-1,000

A pine serpentine sideboard, with carved back, 19thC, 66in (167.5cm) wide.
$1,000-1,800

A Welsh pine high backed settle, with 2 drawers under seat, early 18thC, 52in (132cm). **$600-900**

An Irish pine dresser, with pierced and fretted frieze to top of delft rack, base of 2 panelled doors with double canted mouldings, on sledge feet, early 19thC, 50in (127cm). **$1,500-2,250**

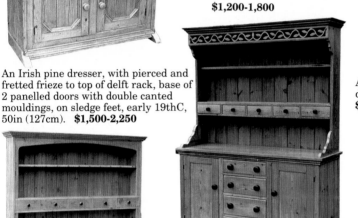

An English pine shaped gallery back serving dresser, early 19thC, 60in (152cm) wide.
$1,200-1,800

A Cornish dresser, with 2 glaze doors, 19thC, 48in (122cm) wide
$1,000-1,500

A pine dog kennel dresser, with arched top to delft rack incorporating 5 small drawers, base of 3 drawers over 2 cupboards and kennel, 19thC, 60in (152cm) wide. **$1,200-1,800**

A pine dresser, the open delft rack with pierced fretted frieze and 5 spice drawers, over base of 4 central drawers with 2 doors either side, 19thC, 60in (152cm) wide.
$1,500-2,250

An Irish pine dresser, base with drawers and 4 doors, 19thC, 50in (127cm) wide. **$1,350-1,800**

A Welsh pine glazed top panelled dresser, base with 4 drawers and 2 cupboards, 19thC, 60in (152cm) wide.
$1,500-2,000

An Irish pine dresser, from Limerick, c1800, 66in (167.5cm). **$2,250-3,000**

A dresser base, with 3 drawers, 18thC, 63in (160cm).
$1,800-2,200

A pine dresser, the breakfront top with astragal glazed door to either side, 2 drawers and 2 doors in base, 19thC, 60in (152cm).
$1,800-2,400

pine secrétaire, c1860, 42in
[06.5cm) wide.
1,500-2,000

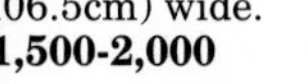

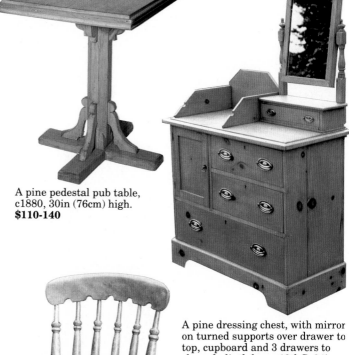

A pine pedestal pub table,
c1880, 30in (76cm) high.
$110-140

A pine dressing chest, with mirror on turned supports over drawer to top, cupboard and 3 drawers to shaped plinth base, 19thC, 34in (86cm) wide. **$450-600**

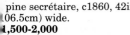

pine gallery back
ashstand, with shelf and
rawer under, on turned legs,
9thC, 24in (61cm).
225-300

A Welsh high backed turned spindle armchair, early 19thC.
$225-375

A pine picture frame, c1870, 35 by 31in (89 by 79cm). **$120-140**

Scandinavian pine dressing
nest, c1900.
375-400

A dairy table, c1850, 28in (71cm) wide.
$150-170

An pine mule chest, with 2 drawers, early 19thC, 32in (81cm). **$225-375**

A Restauration gilt bronze fender, the central pole held by seated cherubs, c1830, 48½in (123cm) wide.
$5,250-6,750

A pair of gilt bronze chenets, in the form of a plinth surmounted by an oil lamp and faced by mythological attributes, c1820, 9in (22cm) high.
$2,250-3,000

A pair of Louis XV gilt bronze chenets, formed of rococo scrollwork surmounted by seated figures of Neptune and a lady, mid-18thC, 15in (38cm) high. **$6,000-7,500**

A fender, basket grate and set of 3 fire irons, all in steel and brass, 19thC.
$2,250-3,000

A pair of bronze, gilt bronze and steel fire irons, with handles in the form of leafy scrolls, c1820, 28in (72cm) long.
$2,250-3,000

A set of Regency steel fire iro
and a pair of en suite andiron
all with unusual gadrooned u
finials, c1820.
$5,250-6,000

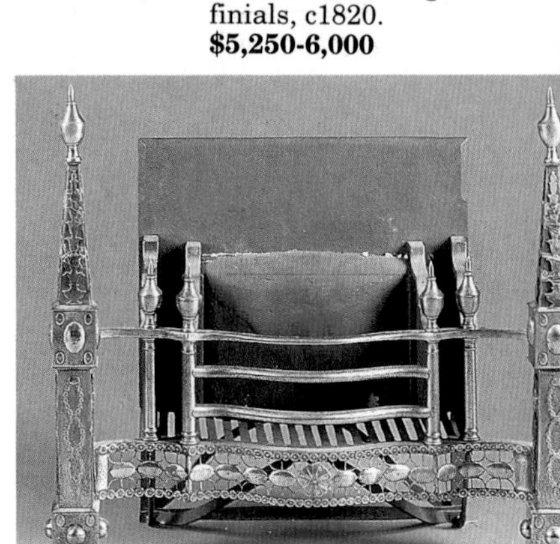
A George III steel fire grate, later framing an backplate, 43in (109cm
$4,500-7,500

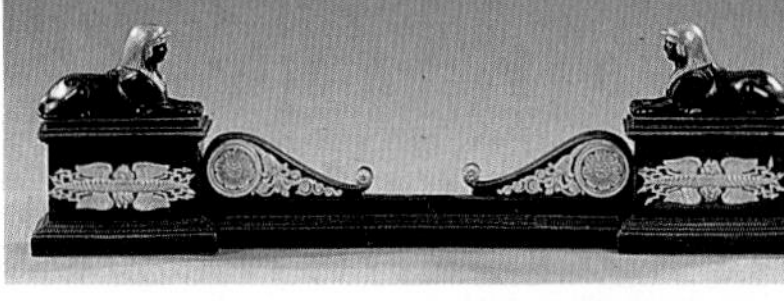
l. A Restauration bronz and gilt bronze fender, c1825. **$5,250-6,750**

r. A Restauration bronze and gilt bronze fender, plinths surmounted by lions, c1825, 60in (152cm).
$3,000-3,750

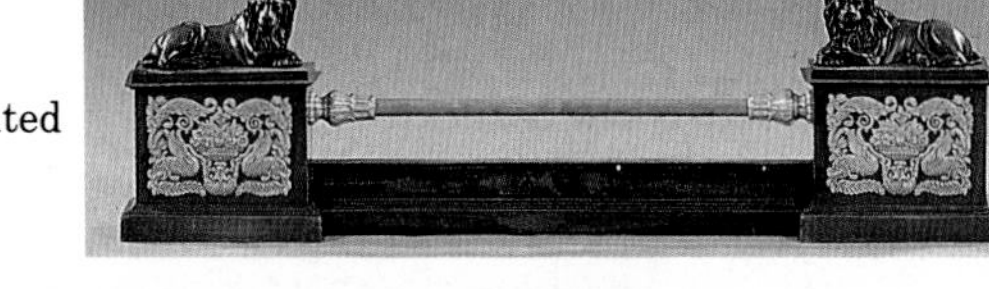

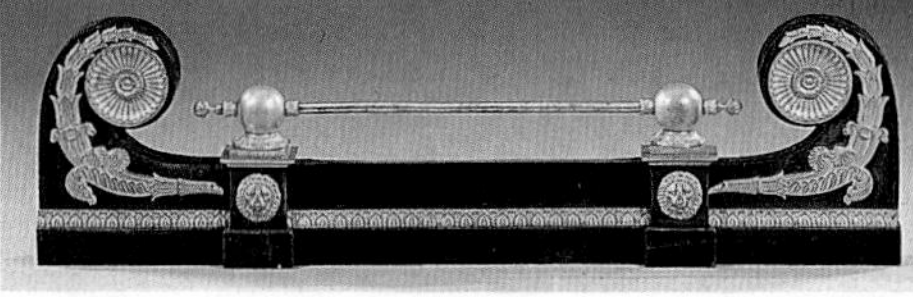
l. A Restauration bronze and gilt bronze adjustable fender, with giant scrolls at each end, c1825.
$3,000-4,500

A pair of Louis XVI gilt bronze chenets, each surmounted by 2 swag draped urns, c1775.
$3,000-3,750

A pair of Louis XVI bronze an gilt bronze chenets, each with lion on a draped plinth, c1785, 17in (43cm). **$18,000-19,500**

pair of carved stone rmorial hounds, each with aised tail, on rope twist ase, 18thC, 34in (86cm).
4,500-6,000

n Italian travertine narble urn, on associated luted and moulded foot, 1870, 45in (114cm) high.
3,750-6,750

pair of bronze urns, on ising fluted circular foot and square base, c1850, 7½in (70cm) high.
14,500-16,500

marble and bronze bust f Minerva, with later ronze helmet, 17th/18thC, 0in (101.5cm).
12,750-14,250

A white marble figure of a muse, stamped S.T.O. Galletti, Roma, 1864, 62½in (159cm) high.
$15,000-18,000

An Italian Carrara marble fountain, early 20thC, 71in (180cm).
$13,000-15,000

An impressive marble figure, entitled 'Il Vincitore', the powerful looking man with flowing hair seated naked on a rocky outcrop, holding a sword, titled and signed C.Corti, 19thC, 75in (190.5cm). **$25,500-27,000**

An Italian white marble figure of a seated discus thrower, the naked athlete with robe draped over one leg, on an oval shaped base, c1870, 50in (127cm) wide. **$12,000-15,000**

A medieval Pyrenean marble well head, on associated canted square base, 28in (71cm) high.
$6,750-8,250

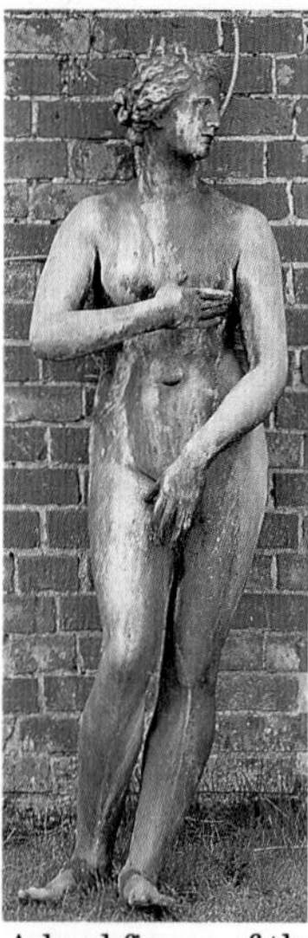

A lead figure of the Medici Venus, mid-18thC, 61in (155cm) high. **$6,000-7,500**

A carved stone figure of Nelson in military uniform, by Robert Forrest, minor chips, on carved base, c1836, 88in (223.5cm) high. **$25,500-27,000**

An Italian rosso marble trough, with a guilloche band to the top, the sides carved with stylised animals, a coat-of arms on one end, weathered, probably 18thC, 62in (157cm) wide. **$9,750-11,250**

A white marble figure of Hercules, inscribed 'Valore, P.B.', 18thC, 76in (193cm) high. **$18,000-19,500**

An Italian white marble group of Venus and Cupid, late 19thC, 46in (116cm). **$10,500-12,000**

A lead figure of Uffizi Mercury, mid-18thC, 68in (173cm) high. **$4,500-6,000**

A white marble figure of Pan, 66in (168cm), on a stone pedestal inscribed 'Pan, Florence, 1906'. **$18,000-19,500**

A marble seat, with seated grotesque lion arms and volute carved supports, early 20thC, 71in (180cm). **$4,500-6,000**

An Italian carved pink Verona marble trough with Bacchic reliefs of grapevines and winged putti on the sides, on carved Istrian marble double griffin supports, some damage, 19thC, 88½in (225cm). **$18,000-19,500**

A Portland stone curved bench, with volute carved arms and supports, early 19thC, 114in (290cm). **$7,500-9,000**

l. Detail of bronze sundial, *below*.

pair of rosso Verona marble urns, with lobed wer section, early 8thC, 37in (94cm), on ssociated stone bases. **13,500-15,000**

The Hampton Court Moor, by John Van Nost, c1701, 42in (106cm), bronze dial signed Dan. Delander, early 18thC. **$52,500-60,000**

A carved gritstone figure of the Faun with Pipes, standing next to a tree, draped with a lion's pelt, Low Countries, early 18thC, base monogrammed 'V.M.', on a plinth, 130in (330cm). **$15,000-18,000**

A pair of Italian monumental white marble urns, the frieze carved with Bacchanalian dancers, on a square plinth, some damage, 20thC, 63in (160cm) high. **$25,500-27,000**

A pair of marble urns, each campana body carved with Bacchic putti, with double grotesque mask loop handles, the fluted socle on a square base, early 19thC, 19in (48cm). **$10,500-12,000**

pair of white marble lions, with dentil oulded ears and stylised mane, on ectangular bases, early 19thC, 24in (61cm) igh. **$12,000-13,500**

An Italian white marble bath, with carved rings and a lion's mask, on paw supports, 19thC, 74in (188cm). **$10,500-12,000**

A pair of Napoleon III brass and bronzed models of The Marly horses, on contre partie boulle bases, with mask spandrels and edges with foliage, one indistinctly signed Coustou, 27in (69cm) wide. **$12,000-13,500**

A bronze figure of a dog, in naturalisti pose.
$900-1,000

A brass alms dish, Nuremberg, c1550, 16½in (42cm) diam.
$600-700

An English copper coffee pot, c1800, 8½in (21cm).
$175-275

A copper ale jug, c1830, 13in (33cm).
$320-380

A Restauration bronze and gilt bronze wall bracket, with a cas Bacchanalian mask above leaf and berry carving, c1820, 9in (23cm) high. **$3,750-4,000**

An English bronze cooking pot, c1650, 12in (31cm) high.
$400-600

An English bronze mortar, c1670, 5½in (14cm) high.
$225-300

A Flemish brass alms dish, c1690, 18in (46cm) diam.
$500-600

An English brass kettle, c1860, 8½in (22cm) high.
$160-200

A copper ale jug, c1820, 10in (25cm) high.
$225-275

bronze Bacchanalian roup, signed Clodion, 9thC, 21in (53.5cm), on a iltwood plinth.
2,250-2,750

A gilt bronze group of 2 cherubs, after Charles Cumberworth, on a floral encrusted base and green onyx plinth, 19thC, 10½in (26.5cm) high.
$750-900

A bronze figure of a Grenadier, entitled Grenadier 1st Guards 1815, signed J. E. Boehm Scr, 18in (45cm), on a plinth.
$1,300-1,500

pair of gilt bronze rns, the plinths faced ith plaques of assical scenes, 1820, 10½in (26.5cm).
1,800-2,200

A bronze and gilt bronze bust of Napoleon, 19thC, 11in (28cm).
$2,500-3,000

A Neapolitan bronze figure of Venus, signed M. Olmodio, 19thC, 26in (66cm).
$1,500-1,800

A pair of Restauration bronze, gilt bronze and marble tazzas, c1830.
$3,500-4,500

A pair of Restauration bronze, gilt bronze and marble tazzas, c1830.
$4,000-5,000

A pair of bronze busts of Voltaire and Rousseau, c1825, 9½in (24cm).
$2,000-3,000

bronze bull standing on a promontory, with rich ark brown patination, signed by Isidore Bonheur, 9thC, 12in (31cm), on a marble plinth.
3,750-4,500

A pair of gilt bronze and red marble tazzas, with snake handles and rectangular plinths, mid-19thC, 14in (36cm) high.
$5,250-6,000

Three Staffordshire commemorative patriotic patch boxes, early 19thC, 2in (5cm). **$3,000-3,750**

A pair of enamel tea caddies, the lids inscribed 'Green' and 'Bohe', painted with floral bouquets, metal mounts, some restoration, Birmingham, c1760, 4½in (11.5cm) high. **$3,500-4,500**

A Staffordshire enamel patch box, the lid painted with a grey tabby cat, c1780. **$5,250-6,000**

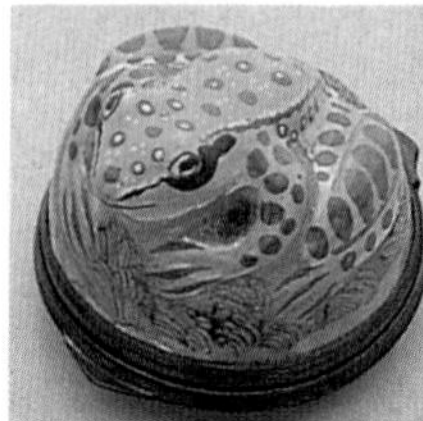

A Staffordshire enamel frog bonbonnière, c1780 2in (5cm) diam. **$6,000-6,750**

An enamel writing casket, the interior with compartments for inkwell, sander and writing equipment, restored, Bilston, c1770. **$3,000-3,750**

An enamel parrot and fruit bonbonnière, Bilston, c1765. **$4,500-5,500**

An enamel etui, Bilston, c1765, slight damage. **$1,000-1,350**

An enamel bodkin case, Bilston, c1770, 5in ((13cm) long. **$1,200-1,500**

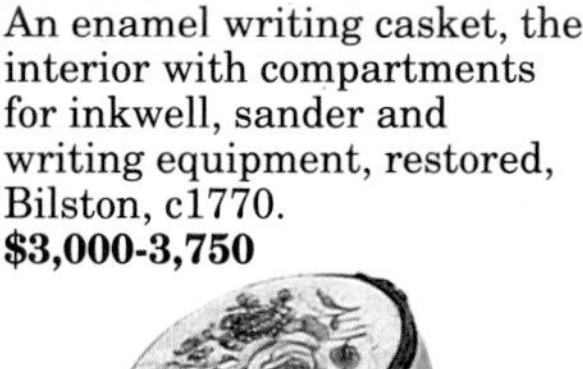

An enamel spaniel patch box, with original steel mirror, restored, Bilston, c1770. **$2,500-3,500**

An enamel bonbonnière, c1765, 4in (9.5cm). **$2,250-3,000**

A Staffordshire enamel hare bonbonnière, restored, c1780, 2in (5cm). **$2,250-3,000**

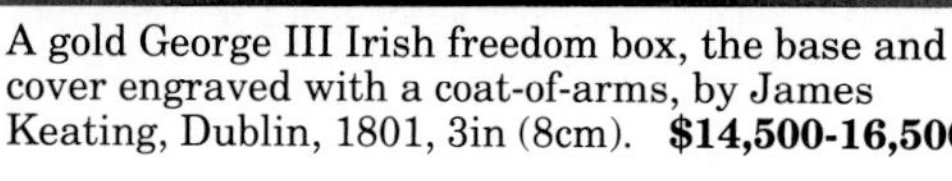

A gold George III Irish freedom box, the base and cover engraved with a coat-of-arms, by James Keating, Dublin, 1801, 3in (8cm). **$14,500-16,500**

A Staffordshire enamel 'watch' pendant patch box, c1780. **$750-900**

An enamel snuff box, Bilston, c1760, 2½in (6cm) wide. **$3,800-4,800**

r. A multi-coloured gold powder box, the lid chased with a bouquet, probably Swiss, c1830, 3in (7cm) wide. **$2,500-3,500**

A marble bust of a Moorish pageboy, early 18thC.
$10,500-12,000

A French ivory figure of the young Christ, early 17thC, 6½in (16cm) high. **$7,500-12,000**

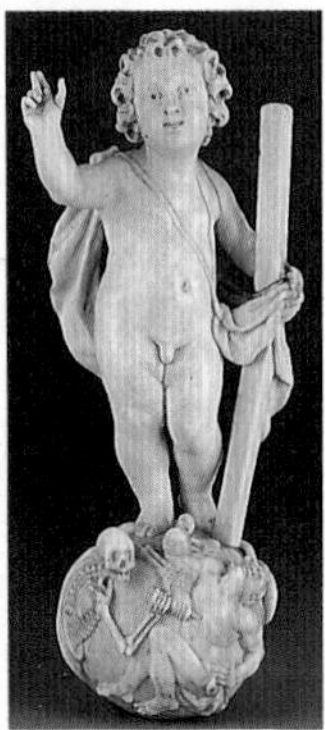

A German ivory figure of the Christ child, 17thC.
$13,500-16,500

Danish marble figure ' a hunter, damaged , id-19thC.
20,000-22,500

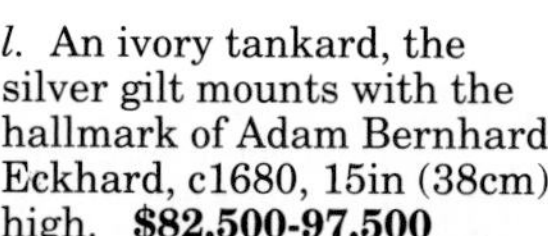

An Italian marble cistern, 18thC, 24½in (62cm) high.
$8,250-9,750

r. A pair of Swedish porphyry urns, with everted rims, waisted socles, and square bases, c1800, 19in (48cm) high.
$12,000-15,000

l. An ivory tankard, the silver gilt mounts with the hallmark of Adam Bernhard Eckhard, c1680, 15in (38cm) high. **$82,500-97,500**

marble figure of ıe birth of Venus, ırly 20thC.
15,000-22,500

A South German ivory tankard, early 18thC, with later silver mounts, 15in (38cm). **$24,000-30,000**

l. A Dresden ivory figure of a pedlar, early 18thC.
$33,000-37,000

A pair of Louis XV ormolu mounted porcelain Buddhas, mid-18thC, 12½in (31.5cm).
$30,000-37,500

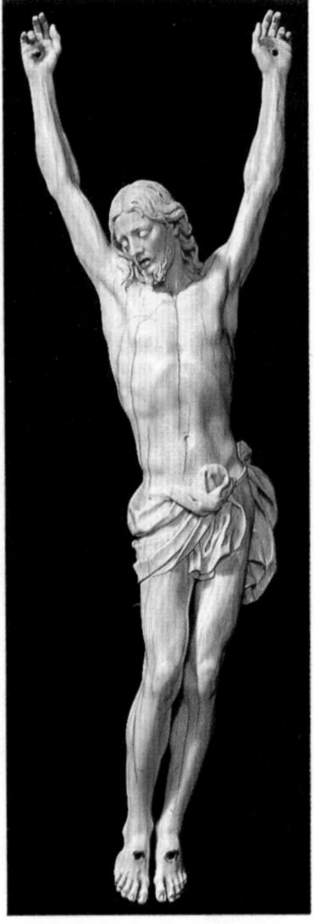

A Flemish ivory crucifix figure, mid-17thC, 17in (43cm) high.
$18,000-22,000

A silver presentation cradle, by T. & J. Bragg, Birmingham 1904, on a wooden plinth, 16in (41cm) high. **$2,250-3,000**

A Norwegian silver peg tankard, on 3 claw-and-ball feet, engraved with initials within a ribbon tied palm leaf cartouche, c1700, 8in (20cm) high. **$6,500-7,500**

A George II silver tea kettle-on-stand, with lamp. **$2,250-2,750**

A George III silver four-piece tea and coffee set, the coffee jug on lamp stand with reeded and paw supports, the milk jug and sugar basin with leaf capped handles and gilt interiors, the coffee jug Matthew Boulton, Birmingham, other 3 pieces Thomas Robins, London, all c1809, 95oz 18dwt. **$6,800-8,200**

A Belgian silver mustard pot, c1735, 7in (17cm) high. **$11,250-12,000**

A George II silver beer jug by John Barbe 1738, 8in (20cm) high. **$7,000-9,000**

A set of 12 George III silver dinner plates, by John Crouch and Thomas Hannam, engraved with a crest, 1800, 10½in (26cm) diam, 254oz. **$10,500-12,000**

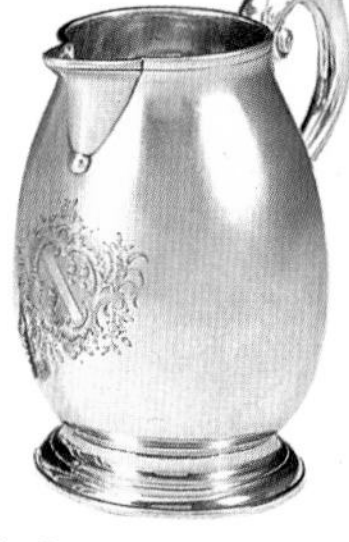

A George III silver ale jug, by William Grundy, London 1766, 8in (20cm). **$6,000-7,500**

A Victorian silver tea urn, by Edward Barnard & Sons, London 1844, 18in (45.5cm) high, 143oz 2dwt. **$4,500-6,500**

A George IV silver teapot, with cast rose finial, on 4 mask and paw feet, by Paul Storr, London 1825. **$3,000-3,750**

A George III silver tankard, 1787, 8in (20cm). **$3,000-3,750**

r. A George III silver box, by Phipps & Robinson, London 1809, 3in (7cm) high, 5oz 14dwt. **$4,500-5,500**

ın American silver six-piece tea and offee set by A. Rogers, Boston, 5250gr. **3,500-4,500**

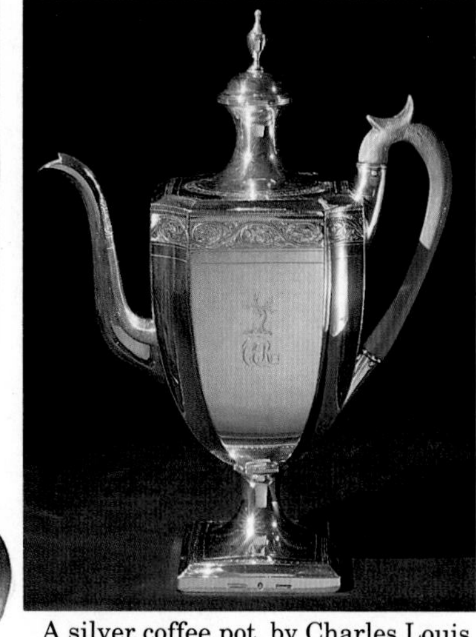

A silver coffee pot, by Charles Louis Boehme, Baltimore, c1804, 14in (36cm) 41oz. **$23,000-26,000**

George II silver fruit basket, by amuel Herbert & Co, London 1752, 4in (36cm) long, 56oz 18dwt. **10,500-12,000**

A silver peg tankard, on 3 claw-and-ball feet, by Nicolai Willemsen Horstman, Trondheim, c1720, 9in (22.5cm). **$13,500-15,000**

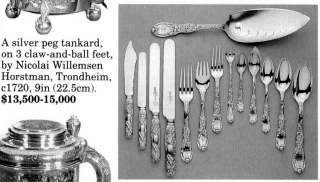

A 196 piece silver flatware set, with chrysanthemum pattern, initialled 'ECMC', in wood canteen with brass handles, by Tiffany & Co, New York, c1890, 347oz excluding knives. **$20,000-22,500**

silver and enamel presentation nuff box, the lid chased in high elief with the coat-of-arms of ichmond, maker's mark I.P., ondon, c1782, 4in (10cm) wide. **5,500-6,000**

A Norwegian silver peg tankard, c1640, 9in (23cm), 1185gr. **$19,500-22,500**

l. A silver bowl, by George Ridout, New York, c1750, 7in (18cm) diam, 16oz 15dwt. **$16,500-18,000**

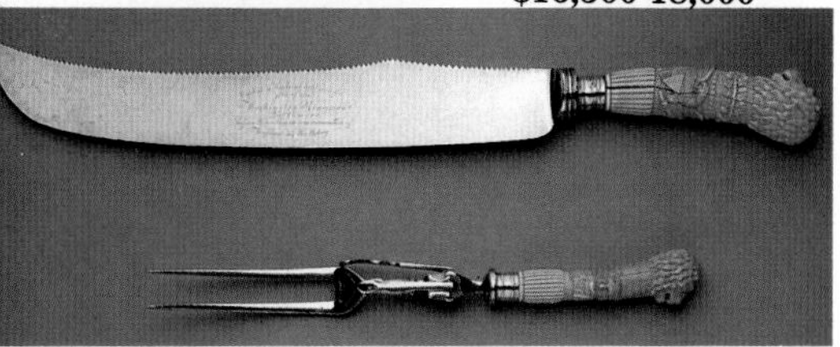

pair of silver mounted carved ivory and steel arvers, the ivory handles carved with busts of George Vashington, the American Eagle and Seal, the mounts . Rodgers, Sheffield 1827. **$15,000-16,500**

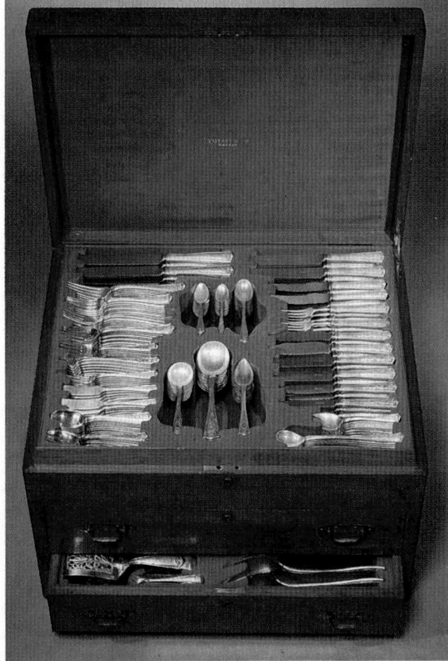

A silver flatware set, comprising 347 pieces, in Winthrop pattern, by Tiffany & Co, New York, c1930, 407oz 10dwt, in 3 drawer fitted mahogany chest. **$18,000-21,000**

A pair of silver two-handled melon fluted soup tureens, covers and liners, by Robert Garrard, 1843, 15in (38cm) wide. **$25,000-30,000**

A George I silver punch bowl and ladle, the punch bowl by Richard Bayley, London 1724, **$18,000-21,000**, the ladle by John Gibbons, London 1726. **$3,000-3,750**

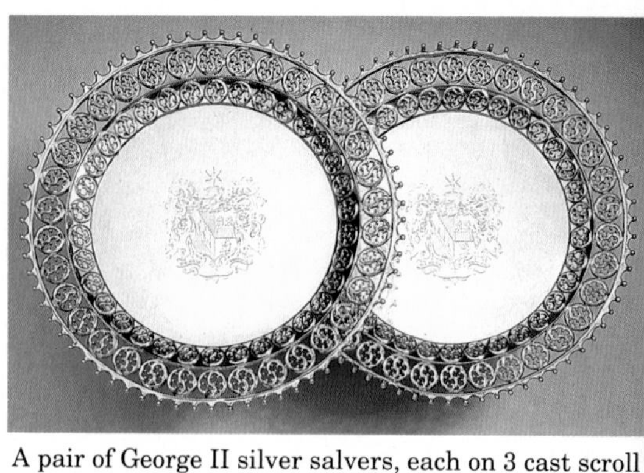

A pair of George II silver salvers, each on 3 cast scroll panel supports, by Edward Wakelin, London 1755, 9in (23cm) diam, 35oz 7dwt.
$34,000-37,000

A set of 4 George III candlesticks, by William Cafe, 1760. **$19,500-22,500** and a set of 4 George I plain candlesticks, by David Willaume, 1726. **$28,000-30,000**

A pair of George III silver wine coolers, the friezes depicting the Triumph of Silenus, maker's mark IP, 1804. **$24,500-30,000**

A George III soup tureen and cover, by Paul Storr, 1804.
$23,000-30,000

A silver wine cistern, on 4 scrolled supports, lion mask and drop handles, gilt interior, by Hunt & Roskell, London 1875. **$17,000-22,500**

A silver tankard, by Benjamin Burt, Boston, USA, c1799.
$10,500-13,500

A silver tea kettle, stand, lamp and tray, by John Emes, 1802, 14in (36cm), 96oz. **$3,750-5,250**

l. A silver two-handled soup tureen and cover, by Craddock and Reid, c1824, 18in (46cm).
$14,250-16,250

A pair of George III silver wine coasters, by Thomas Daniell, London 1786, with mahogany bases. **$3,750-4,500**

Two matching George II silver salvers, both London, one John Jacob, 1744, the other Richard Rugg, 1756, 7in (18cm) diam. **$2,250-3,000**

A Belgian vase shaped mustard pot, c1735, 8in (20cm). **$9,500-10,500**

Three silver sconces, by C. R., Dublin, c1694, 11in (28cm). **$22,000-24,000**

A George III centrepiece, by Benjamin Smith, 1818, 14in (35.5cm), with clear glass bowl. **$5,250-6,750**

A George II silver two-handled cup and cover, by Richard Gurney & Co., London 1745. **$3,800-4,800**

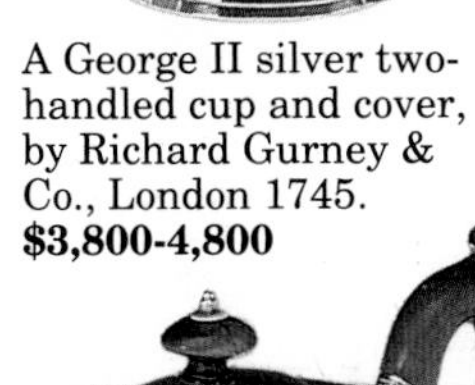

A George III silver teapot and stand, by Hester Bateman, London, c1789. **$4,500-5,500**

A silver gilt dessert service, by Holland, Aldwinckle & Slater, London 1880. **$6,500-7,500**

A Georgian silver cow creamer, London 1764, maker's marks erased, 4oz. **$4,500-5,500**

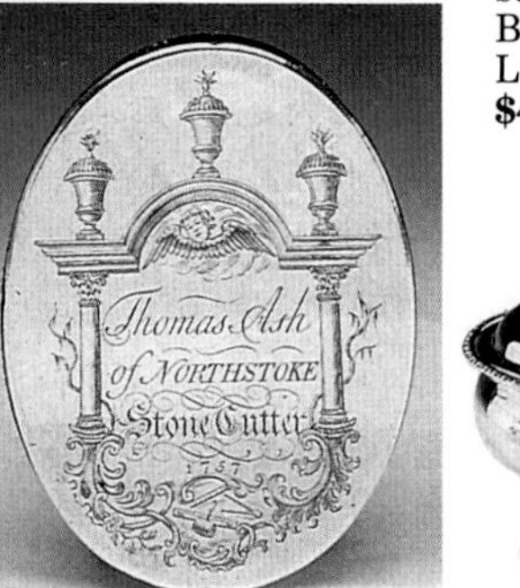

A silver tobacco box, with detachable cover engraved with arms of Henley of Somerset, maker's mark RW, English, c1715, base inscribed c1757, 4in (10cm), 4oz 18dwt. **$7,500-8,500**

Two George III silver preserve tureens, London 1762 & 1763. **$3,500-4,000**

A Queen Anne plain beer jug, by David Willaume I, 1706, 11in (28cm), 42oz. **$12,750-15,000**

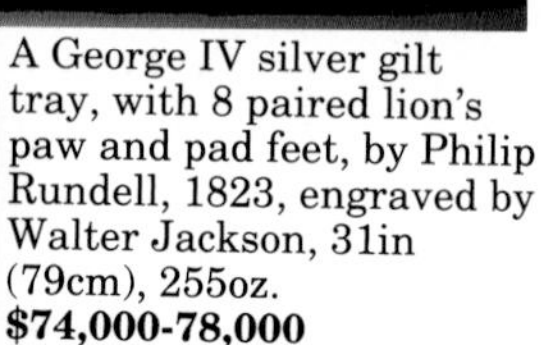

A George IV silver gilt tray, with 8 paired lion's paw and pad feet, by Philip Rundell, 1823, engraved by Walter Jackson, 31in (79cm), 255oz.
$74,000-78,000

An Upper Rhenish polychrome and giltwood relief of the Harrowing of Hell, distressed, c1500, 23in (59cm) high.
$7,000-9,000

A carved, painted and gessoed American Eagle, by Wilhelm Schimmel, Pennsylvania, c1880, wingspan 22½in (57cm).
$38,000-45,000

A polychrome and giltwood relief of Christ being Presented to the People, with guild mark of Antwerp, c1560, 19in (49cm) high. **$10,000-12,000**

An oak figure of St. Adrian, by Circle of Adriaen van Wesel, Utrecht, late 15thC, 35in (89cm).
$27,000-30,000

A silver wine cooler, collar and liner, by Paul Storr, 1825, 11½in (29cm) high, 157oz.
$19,500-22,500

A Flemish/French carving of St. Martin on horseback, some original polychrome decoration, c1500, 33in (84cm). **$11,500-12,500**

l. A pair of silver gilt mounted frosted glass wine coolers, by Samuel Jackson, 1825, 10½in (26cm) high.
$10,000-12,000

r. A silver gilt four-light candelabrum centrepiece, by Edward Barnard & Sons, 1846, 27½in (70cm) high.
$9,000-10,500

ᴀ terracotta Newsboy architectural plaque, by H.A. ,ewis, South Boston, Massachusetts, USA, c1885, ·1in (155cm) square. **$15,000-18,000**

A pair of silver and enamel cornucopiae, each with classical scenes, by Hermann Böhm, Vienna, c1875, one base chipped, 10in (26cm) high. **$11,250-12,750**

'he copper firemark of the ℨath Sun Fire office, c1830, 'in (18cm) high. **160-200**

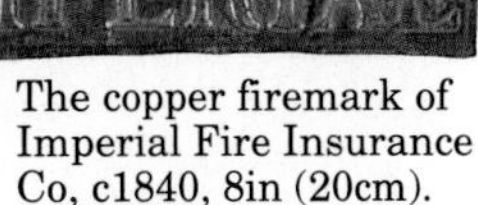

The copper firemark of Imperial Fire Insurance Co, c1840, 8in (20cm). **$120-150**

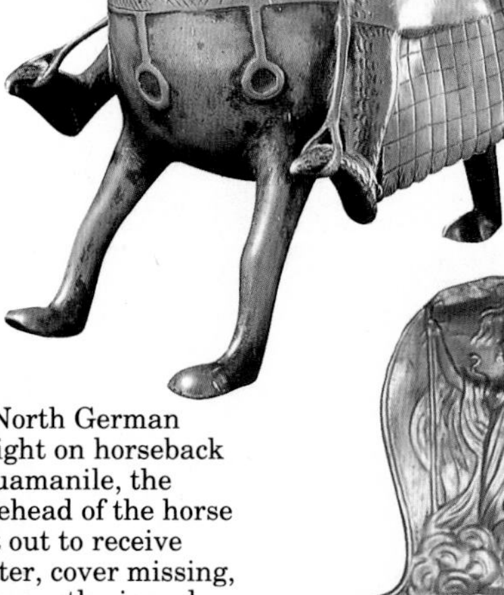

A North German knight on horseback aquamanile, the forehead of the horse cut out to receive water, cover missing, the mouth pierced as a water spout, damaged and repaired, c1200, 12in (31cm). **$998,000-1,120,000**

A Lobmeyr enamelled vase, JLL trademark in white enamel, c1880. **$8,500-10,500**

ᴀn ormolu centrepiece, lepicting George IV as a Roman ℇmperor, by Rundell, Bridge & ℜundell. **$185,000-195,000**

GUARDIAN

The copper firemark of the Guardian Fire & Life Assurance Co., c1840, 9in (23cm). **$90-120**

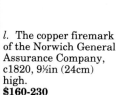

l. The copper firemark of the Norwich General Assurance Company, c1820, 9½in (24cm) high. **$160-230**

The firemark for The British Fire Office, c1830, 8in (20cm) high. **$110-120**

Samuel John Stump (1785-1863), miniature of Richard Miles, signed on the obverse, and in full on the reverse, 7in (18cm) high.
$1,800-3,000

William John Thompson (1771-1845), miniature of an officer, signed and dated on reverse, January 3rd 1810, ormolu frame, 3in (7cm) high. **$1,800-2,200**

John Linnell (1792-1882), miniature of a lady, signed and dated 1828, in gilt metal frame, 5in (13cm) high.
$1,800-2,200

r. Fernando Giachosa (fl. c1842), miniature of a gentleman, signed and dated 1842, in gilt metal frame, 5½in (14cm) high.
$900-1,200

Dutch School, oil on copper, miniature of a gentleman, in carved giltwood frame, c1640, 2in (5cm) high.
$1,800-2,200

The English School, oil on copper, miniature of a gentleman, in wood frame, c1635, 5in (12cm) high. **$1,000-1,200**

Circle of Nicolas de Largillière, oil on copper, miniature of a lady, c1710, 2in (5cm). **$750-950**

English School, oil on copper, a pair of miniatures of a lady and a gentleman, turned wood frames, c1660, 3½in (9cm) high.
$900-1,000

John Wright (died 1820), miniatur of Captain George Scott, signed on the reverse and dated 1812, in gilt metal mount, 3in (7cm) high.
$3,500-4,500

Jan van Alcen, oil on copper, miniature of a lady holding a blac spaniel, in carved giltwood foliate frame, c1710, 4½in (11cm) high.
$1,400-1,800

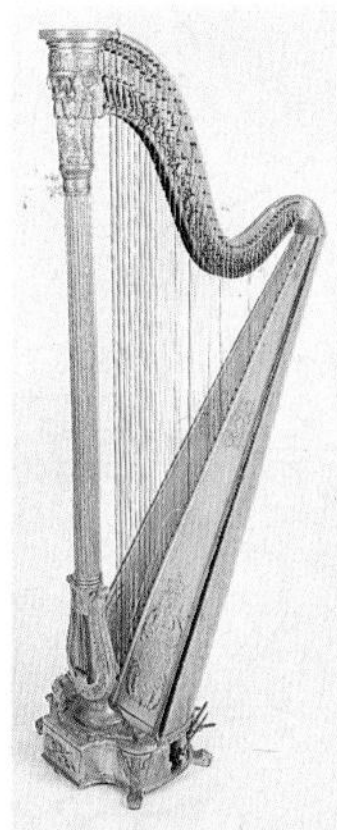

An early Victorian parcel gilt grained and composition harp. **$3,500-4,500**

l. A chamber organ by Hugh Russell, London, 1780, 45in (114cm). **$21,000-22,500**

A two manual harpsichord, by Jacob & Abraham Kirckman, with extensive marquetry strapwork, case veneered with panels of burr walnut with boxwood stringing, London, 1776, 37in (94cm) wide. **$100,000-120,000**

A single manual harpsichord, with mahogany case, burr walnut, boxwood stringing and kingwood crossbanding, Jacob Kirckman, London, 1765. **$40,000-52,000**

A two manual harpsichord, with mahogany case, veneered with burr walnut, decorative stringing and tulipwood crossbanding, Jacob & Abraham Kirckman, London, 1772, 37in (94cm). **$27,000-37,000**

l. A single manual harpsichord, Johan Daniel Dulcken, Antwerp, 1745. **$70,000-97,000**

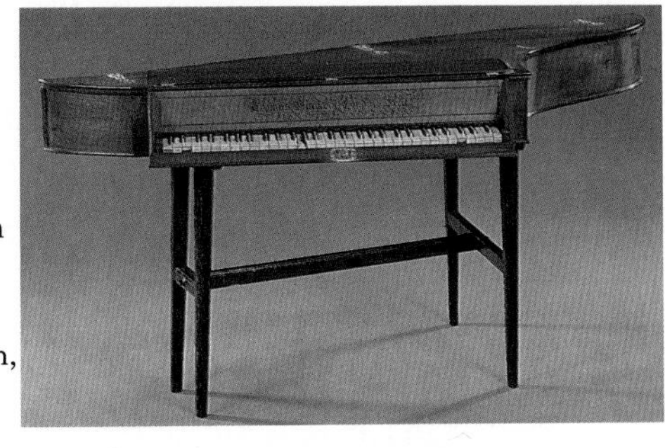

r. A spinet, with mahogany case, by Thomas Hitchcock the Younger, London, c1725. **$19,500-22,500**

A pine carved and gilded rooster weathervane, on hand-forged cast iron rod, in metal base, damage and repairs, Maine, USA, late 18thC, 93in (236cm) high. **$66,000-82,000**

A moulded copper and zinc flying horse weathervane, attributed to A.L. Jewell & Co., Massachusetts, USA, late 19thC, 36in (92cm) long **$8,250-11,250**

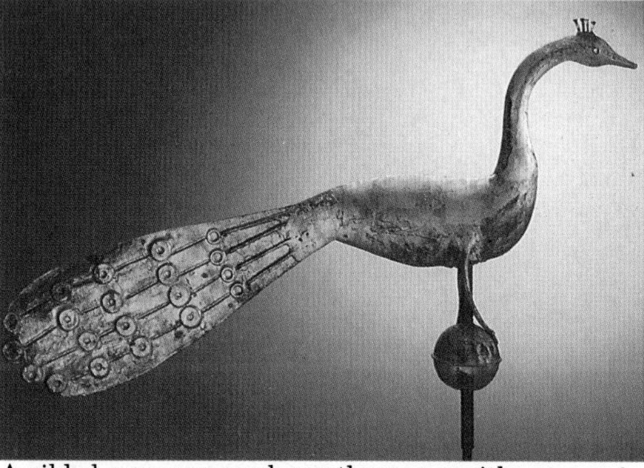

A gilded copper peacock weathervane, with repoussé tail and wrought iron legs, mounted on a rod with an orb, attributed to A.L. Jewell & Co., Massachusetts, USA, late 19thC, 25in (64cm). **$9,750-12,000**

A moulded and painted copper centaur weathervane, some paint flaking, attributed to A.L. Jewell & Co., late 19thC, 26in (66cm) long. **$16,500-22,500**

A gilded elephant weathervane, mounted on a rod, on a black metal base, restored, attributed to J.W. Fiske, New York, late 19thC, 22in (56cm) long. **$28,000-30,000**

A group of copper rooster weathervanes, American, late 19thC, 20 to 30in (51 to 76cm) long.
top and bottom l. **$3,000-3,750 each**
top r. **$9,000-10,500** *bottom r.* **$1,000-1,200**

l. A copper rooster weathervane, English, c1850. **$450-500**

pair of C W McMay plates, Mr
ıd Mrs Burns, early 20thC, 10in
5cm) diam.
135-150

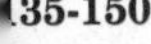

A Mak' Merry jug, 6in (15cm) high. **$300-375**

A Lockhart & Co ewer, with transfer printed blue and white Etruscan pattern, 13½in (34cm) high.
$150-180

jug, painted by Elizabeth Mary
'att, impressed mark, 6in (15cm)
ıgh.
225-300

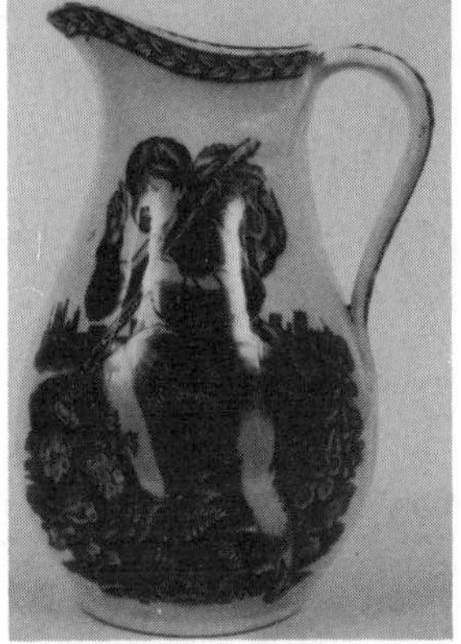

A Glasgow jug, Dick Whittington, design registered 1869, 8½in (21cm).
$120-135

A J & M.P. Bell & Co tureen and cover, in Holly Wreath pattern, c1860, 9½in (24cm) diam.
$150-225

'Glasgow Style' Ceramics

The Glasgow Society of Lady Artists was formed in 1882 and rapidly became the focus of artistic activity amongst the lady amateurs of the city.

The club settled permanently at No. 5 Blythswood Square in 1893 and this became a lively social centre from which men were excluded.

A Kircaldy Toby jug, 10in (25cm) high.
$180-225

A Mak' Merry teapot, painted blue, green and white by a lady artist, 4in (10cm) high.
$375-450

A Mak' Merry ginger jar and cover, painted pink and blue, by a lady artist, 4½in (11cm) high.
$300-375

Bough breakfast set,
ɔmprising: teapot, milk jug, cup
nd 2 saucers, marked C.C.A.
375-450

A puzzle jug, possibly Musselburgh, c1820, 6in (15cm) high.
$750-900

A pair of Dunmore vases, decorated in yellow and brown, 15in (38cm) high.
$375-450

GOSS & CRESTED CHINA

A Swan bathing machine, Staplehurst.
$15-25

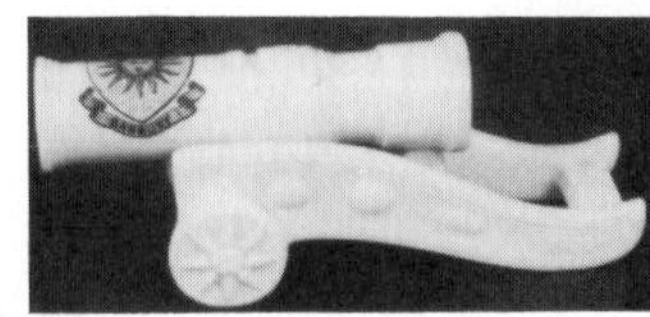

A Goss Mons meg, Banbury.
$50-75

A Carlton Blackpool Tower and Big Wheel ashtray.
$7.50-15

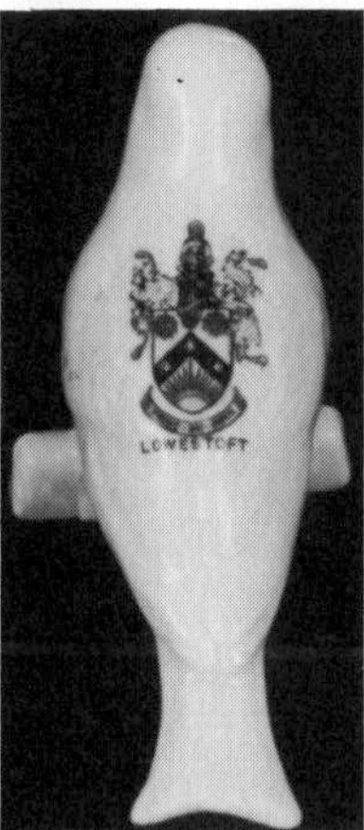

A canary, Lowestoft.
$15-25

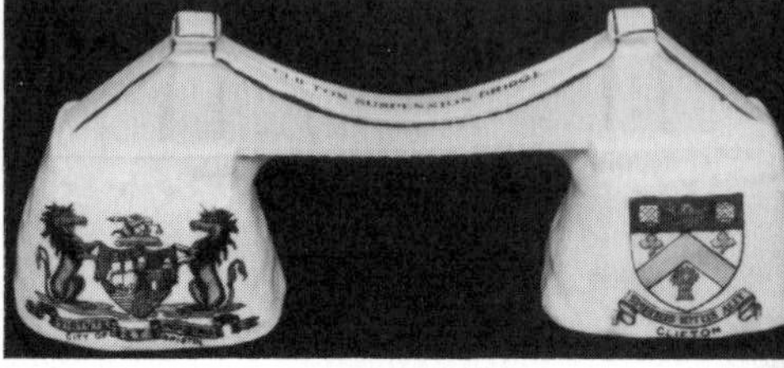

An Arcadian Clifton suspension bridge.
$120-135

An Arcadian Rochester Castle.
$90-105

A Grafton sugar bowl, Staplehurst.
$15-25

A Kingsway Scotch bottle, Dartmouth.
$15-25

A pictorial clog, Newton Abbo
$7.50-15

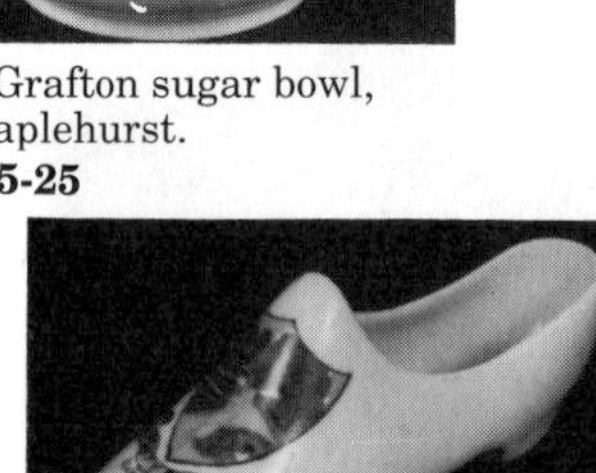

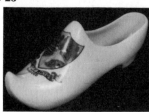

An Arcadian sabot, Llangoed.
$7.50-15

A pictorial candlestick, Guildford.
$7.50-15

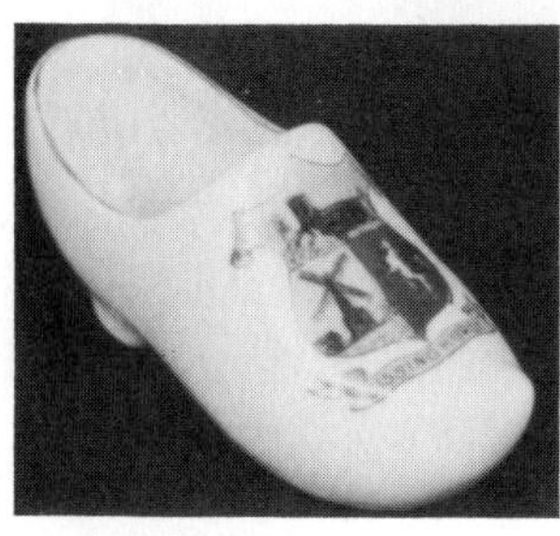

A sabot, Sissinghurst.
$7.50-15

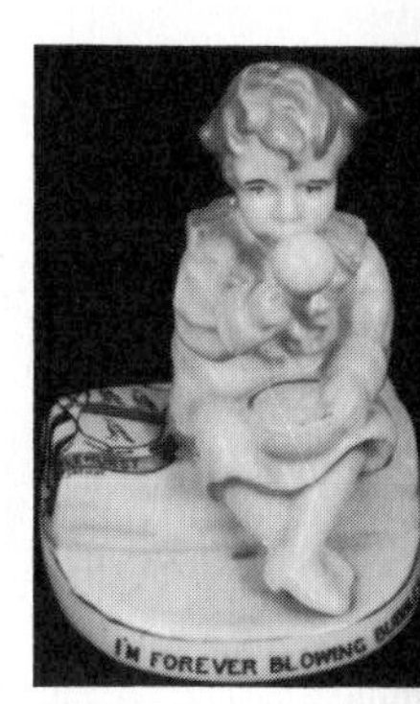

A Carlton Bubbles figur Staplehurst.
$90-105

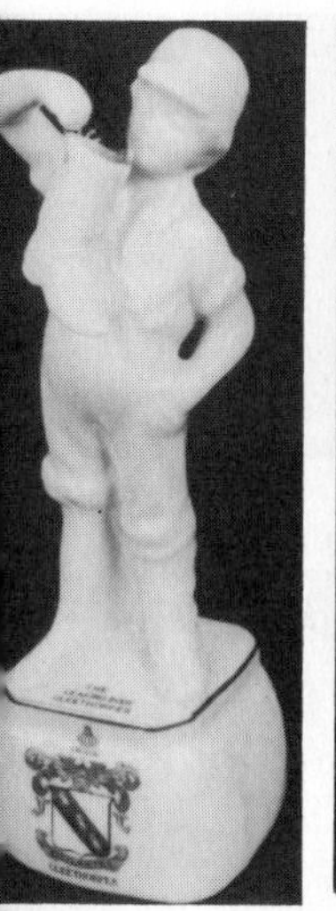

Grafton leaking boot figure, leethorpes.
90-105

A Lifeboatman memorial, Dymchurch, German, 3562.
$25-40

A Goss melon cup, forget-me-not 'M'.
$7.50-15

An Arcadian jug, Harrogate.
$7.50-15

A Willow crested china Queen Victoria statue, Windsor, 6½in (16cm).
$25-40

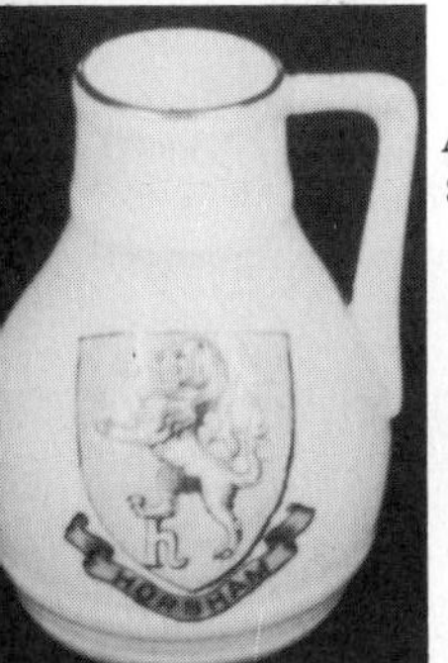

A Goss pitcher, Horsham.
$7.50-15

A Goss butterfly vase, with 3 Scottish crests.
$90-105

A Willow crested statue of Newton, Grantham, 6½in (16cm).
$40-60

Goss candle snuffer, Hastings.
7.50-15

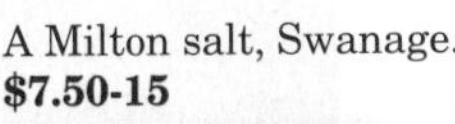

A Milton salt, Swanage.
$7.50-15

Goss teapot stand, Exmouth.
7.50-15

A vase with 1930s beauty, 'Glamour', by Gemma.
$7.50-15

A German decorative vase, Hove.
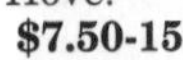
$7.50-15

An Arcadian thimble, Pegwell Bay.

$25-40

A Devonia crested Armada memorial, Plymouth, 8in (20cm).
$40-60

A Goss vase with flags of allies.
$120-135

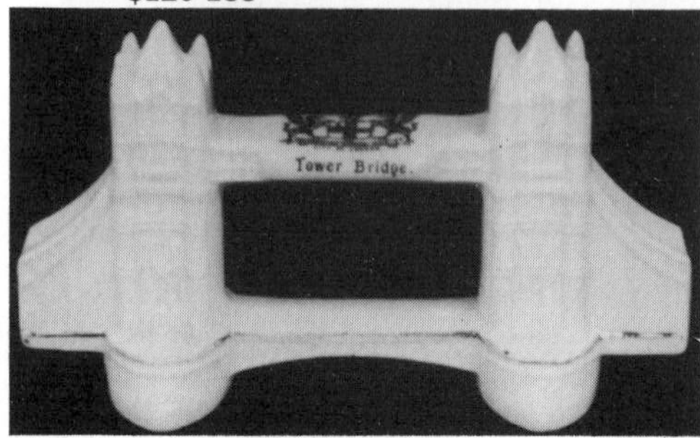

An Alexandra crested china Tower Bridge, City of London, 5½in (14cm) wide.
$40-60

A Carlton crested china Boer War memorial, Hull.
$40-60

A Willow crested Highland Mary statue, Middlesbrough.
$40-60

A vase, Sissinghurs
$7.50-15

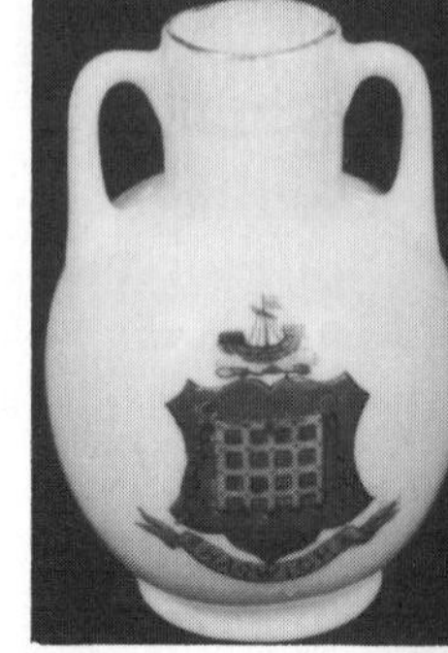

A Savoy pitcher, Harwich
$7.50-15

A crested memorial, City of London, Nelson's column, 6½i (16cm).
$90-105

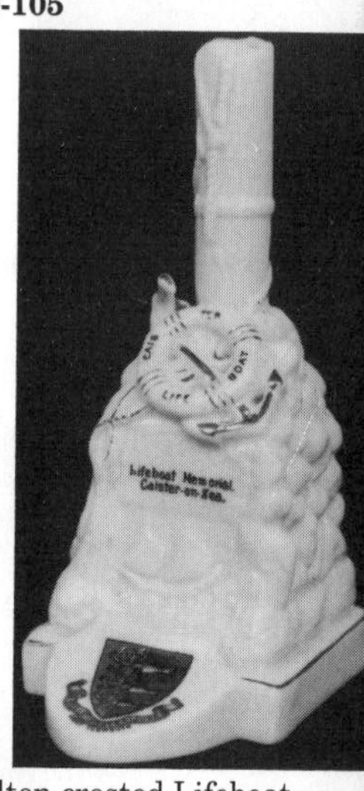

A Carlton crested Lifeboat Memorial, Caister-on-Sea, 1903 7in (18cm).
$50-75

RIENTAL CERAMICS

Chinese dynasties and marks

Earlier Dynasties

Shang Yin, c.1532-1027 B.C.
Western Zhou (Chou) 1027-770 B.C.
Spring and Autumn Annals 770-480 B.C.
Warring States 484-221 B.C.
Qin (Ch'in) 221-206 B.C.
Western Han 206 BC-24 AD
Eastern Han 25-220
Three Kingdoms 221-265
Six Dynasties 265-589
Wei 386-557

Sui 589-617
Tang (T'ang) 618-906
Five Dynasties 907-960
Liao 907-1125
Sung 960-1280
Chin 1115-1260
Yüan 1280-1368

Ming Dynasty

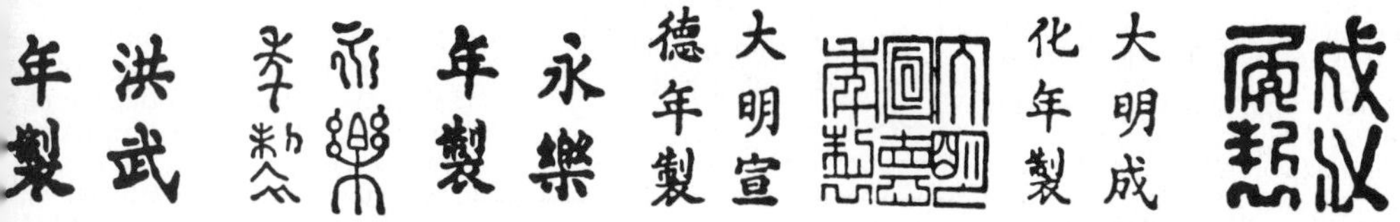

洪武年製

ngwu (Hung Wu)
1368-1398

永樂年製

Yongle (Yung Lo)
1403-1424

大明宣德年製

Xuande (Hsüan Té)
1426-1435

大明成化年製

Chenghua (Ch'éng Hua)
1465-1487

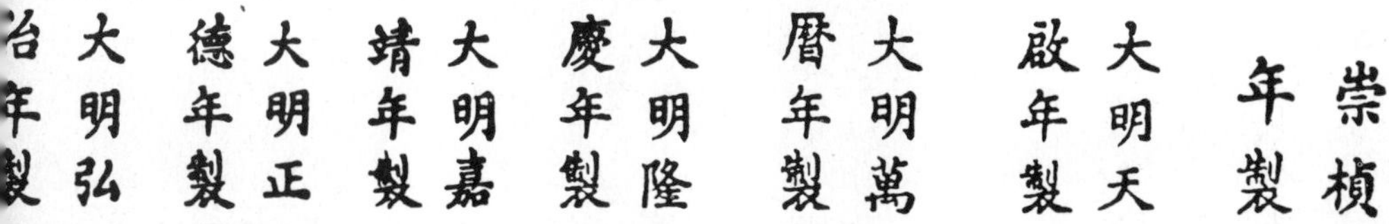

大明弘治年製

Iongzhi
ung Chih)
88-1505)

大明正德年製

Zhengde
(Chéng Té)
1506-1521

大明嘉靖年製

Jiajing
(Chia Ching)
1522-1566

大明隆慶年製

Longqing
(Lung Ching)
1567-1572

大明萬曆年製

Wanli (Wan Li)
1573-1620

大明天啟年製

Tianqi
(Tien Chi)
1621-1627

崇禎年製

Chongzhen
(Ch'ung Chêng)
1628-1644

Qing (Ch'ing) Dynasty

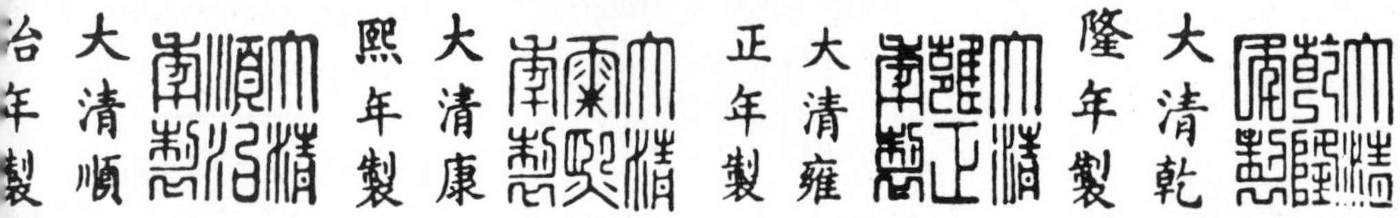

大清順治年製

Shunzhi
(Shun Chih)
1644-1661

大清康熙年製

Kangxi (K'ang Hsi)
1662-1722

大清雍正年製

Yongzheng (Yung Chêng)
1723-1735

大清乾隆年製

Qianlong (Ch'ien Lung)
1736-1795'

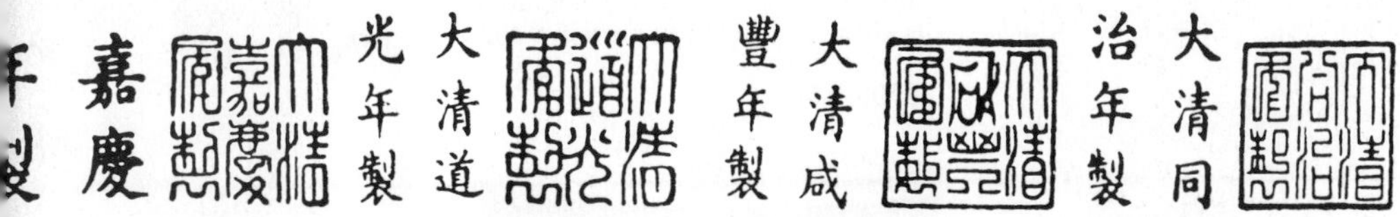

嘉慶年製

Jiaqing (Chia Ch'ing)
1796-1820

大清道光年製

Daoguang (Tao Kuang)
1821-1850

大清咸豐年製

Xianfeng (Hsien Féng)
1851-1861

大清同治年製

Tongzhi (T'ung Chih)
1862-1874

大清光緒年製

Guangxu (Kuang Hsu)
1875-1908

大清宣統年製

Xuantong
(Hsuan T'ung)
1909-1911

洪憲年製

Hongxian
(Hung Hsien)
1916

CHINESE CERAMICS

Bottles & Canisters

A Canton blue and white canister, painted in slightly runny underglaze blue, hair crack to neck and star crack to base, the base inscribed in black No.120, 19thC, 11in (28cm).
$1,200-1,800

A pair of Chinese blue and white bottles, one with chips to shoulder and neck, Kangxi, 10½in (26.5cm).
$2,700-3,300

Miller's is a price GUIDE not a price LIST

A Canton blue and white caniste painted around the sides in slightly runny underglaze blue, with a continuous Willow patter scene, some damage, the base inscribed No.118, now fitted wit a cylindrical metal liner, 19thC, 14in (36cm).
$1,800-2,700

Bowls

A Chinese Imari bowl, painted and gilt, cracked, rim chips, glaze scratches, 18thC, 16in (40.5cm) diam.
$1,800-2,700

A procelain ormolu mounted bowl and cover, decorated in underglaze blue, on ormolu stand with rococo scroll feet, linkd by floral swags, 11in (28cm) high overall.
$225-255

A Chinese blue and white bowl, painted to the exterior with a band of scrolling flowers and foliage above a band of stylised lotus leaves to the foot, Daoguang seal mark and of the period, 5½in (14cm) diam.
$900-1,500

A blue ground porcelain bowl, seal mark, Tao-Kuang, on hardwood stand, 6in (15cm) diam.
$1,200-1,500

A yellow ground porcelain bowl, seal mark, Tao-Kuang, 6in (15cm diam, with hardwood stand.
$3,000-4,500

Drinking Vessels

A Cantonese mug, with strap handle, painted and gilt with insects among scattered flowersprays, some gilt rubbing, 6½in (15cm).
$300-375

pair of Chinese Imari tankards, ith loop handles, domed covers nd interior drainers, painted and ilt with alternating panels of tus flowers and leaves and uatrefoil panels of daisies on ylised foliage grounds, 18thC, ½in (21.5cm).
3,000-3,750

A Chinese export Jesuit ware coffee cup, c1770, 2¾in (7cm).
$105-120

A Chinese Imari mug, with loop handle and lotus flower terminal, painted and gilt with shaped panels of peonies, on a ground of scrolling lotus flowers and leaves, 18thC, 6in (15cm).
$900-1,500

Miller's is a price GUIDE not a price LIST

igures

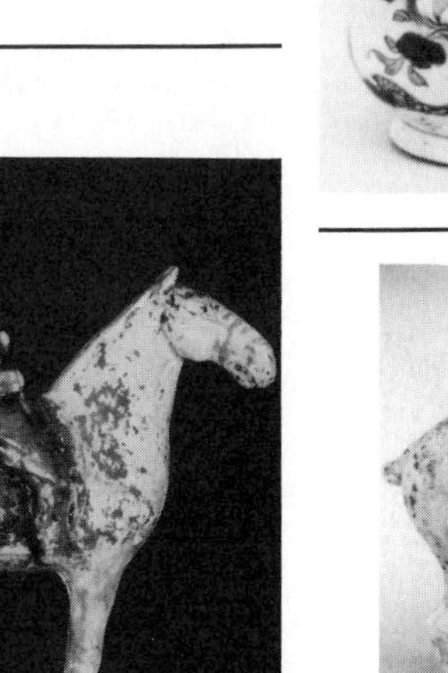

Chinese buff pottery model of n equestrian rider, wearing a unic with open lapels, some red nd black pigments remaining, ang Dynasty, 16in (40.5cm).
1,800-2,700

A Chinese painted buff pottery figure of a saddled horse, some restoration, Tang Dynasty, 12in (30.5cm).
$1,500-2,250

A Chinese red pottery model of a winged earth spirit, seated on its haunches, some red pigment remaining, restored, Tang Dynasty, 18in (46cm).
$375-525

latware

Chinese famille rose saucer ish, 18thC, 10½in (26.5cm) iam..
375-525

A pair of Nanking blue and white sauceboat stands, c1760, 8in (20cm) wide.
$375-525

A Chinese export armorial plate, hair crack, c1760, 9in (23cm) diam.
$375-525

A pair of Chinese blue and white fluted dishes, with barbed rims, two minute cracks, Chenghua six-character marks, Kangxi, 8in (20.5cm) diam.
$750-1,200

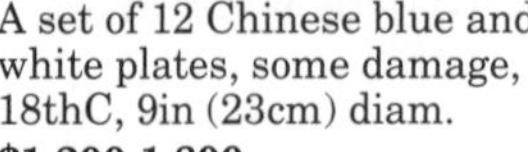

A set of 12 Chinese blue and white plates, some damage, 18thC, 9in (23cm) diam.
$1,200-1,800

A Chinese export blue and white meat dish, with central decoration, late 18thC, 16in (40.5cm).
$375-525

A porcelain dish, with everted rim, painted in the centre with sailing boats on a river between rocks and pagodas, 14in (35.5cm).
$375-525

A pair of Chinese silver-shaped dishes, each painted in iron red and gilt, with peonies, chrysanthemum and scrolling foliage, within a piecrust rim, chips, 18thC, 12in (30.5cm). and a similar dish.
$750-1,200

Three Chinese blue and white dishes, rim chips and fritting, Qianlong, 15in (38cm).
$1,200-1,800

A Cantonese deep dish, painted and gilt to the centre on a key fret pattern ground, 14½in (37cm).
$1,200-1,800

A pair of Chinese blue and white dishes, one cracked, both chipped, Daoguang seal mark and of the period, 7in (18cm) diam.
$750-1,200

A Chinese export famille rose soup plate, painted and gilt with a central coat-of-arms within a scattered flowerspray and spearhead border, some gilt rubbing, c1765, 9in (23cm).
$300-375

The arms are probably those of Jenkinson.

Make the Most of Miller's

In Millers we do NOT just reprint saleroom estimates. We work from realised prices, either from an auction room or a dealer. Our consultants then work out a realistic price range for a similar piece. This is to try to avoid repeating freak results - either low or high.

ars

Chinese blue and white aluster jar, with flaring neck and vin moulded ring handles, angxi seal mark, 12in (30.5cm).
750-900

A pair of Chinese Imari pierced jars, painted and gilt with peonies, lotus, chrysamthemem and further flowers, both damaged, no covers, Kangxi, 6½in (16cm).
$750-900

A Cantonese jar and related domed cover, with Buddhist lion finial, painted and gilt with alternating panels of dignitaries, birds and butterflies among flowers on a trellis pattern ground, neck of vase cracked and small chip to cover, gilt rubbing, 40in (101.5cm).
$1,800-2,700

A Chinese ochre and cream glazed pottery jar, with a short everted neck, drilled for electricity, glaze degraded, chips and flakes, Tang Dynasty, 11in (28cm).
$750-900

'ureens

Chinese blue and white tureen ıd stand, the related domed ›ver with pomegranate finial and ɔar's head handles, some chips, ;ianlong, stand 15in (38cm) wide.
1,200-1,800

A Chinese blue and white tureen and cover, decorated with deer in a landscape setting, late 18th/early 19thC, 13in (33cm) wide.
$1,200-1,800

A Chinese export porcelain tureen, cover and stand, decorated in famille rose, the cover with flower finial, some damage, late 18thC, stand 16in (40cm) wide.
$4,500-6,000

/ases

Clobbered

In the late 18thC it was the practice in Europe to enhance the value of simple blue and white porcelain from China with overglaze enamelling - now called 'clobbering'. Most clobbering was done in Holland but a small amount was done in London decorators' workshops.

A pair of Chinese clobbered bottle vases, painted with jardinières of flowers and precious objects hanging from silk tassels below bands of scattered flowersprays and geometric patterns, one with chip and cracked neck, the porcelain Kangxi, 12in (30.5cm) high.
$750-900

Two Cantonese vases, one with Buddhistic lion handles, painted and heavily gilt, the other with lion mask handles, 14in (35.5cm) high.
$750-900

A Chinese celadon glazed baluster vase, with flaring neck, incised and decorated with scrolling flowering stems, 16thC, 18in (45.5cm) high.
$1,200-1,800

Two Chinese Yingqing funerary vases, the crackled glaze of pale bluish tone, minor damage, Song Dynasty, 13in (33cm) high.
$1,200-1,800

A pair of Chinese Kraak-porselein vases, late Ming, 4½in (11cm) high.
$180-225

Make the Most of Miller's

CONDITION is absolutely vital when assessing the value of an antique. Damaged pieces on the whole appreciate much less than perfect examples. However a rare, desirable piece may command a high price even when damaged.

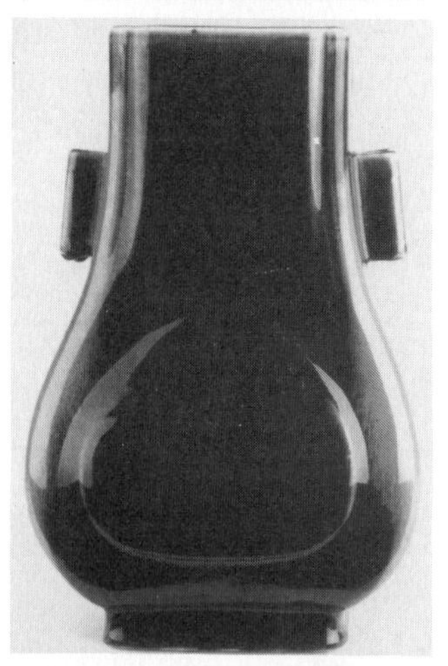

A Chinese flambé glazed hu vase, with moulded petal shaped panels to either side, slight restoration to foot of vase, Qianlong seal mark and possibly of the period, 12in (30.5cm) high, fitted box.
$900-1,500

A pair of Cantonese vases, in bright colours of pink, blue, green and yellow, late 19thC, 13in (33cm).
$1,200-1,500

A pair of Cantonese vases, with stepped waisted bases and drop-in domed liners, painted and gilt with alternating panels of dignitaries on terraces and birds and butterflies among flowers, on green scroll grounds, gilt rubbed, 13in (33cm) high.
$1,200-1,500

Miscellaneous

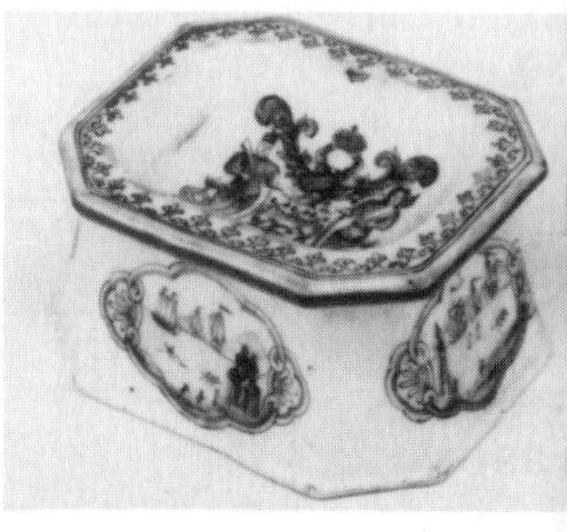

A Chinese export salt, painted in famille rose enamels, en grisaille and gilt with a central coat-of-arms and the motto 'All Worship Be To God Only' above seascapes to the sloping sides, firing fault, chip to the underside of rim, c1775, 3in (8cm) wide, and a famille rose teapot and domed cover, Qianlong.
$1,200-1,800

The Arms are those of the Fishmongers Company.

A pair of famille rose beakers, 3in (7cm) high, and a matching saucer dish.
$450-600

A pair of miniature paint pots, with lids, blue with underglaze blue landscape and figure decoration, four-character mark to base, Chien-Lung, 3in (7cm) diam.
$225-300

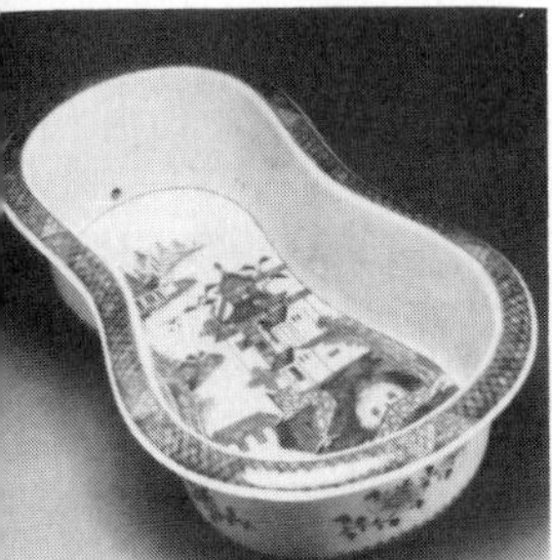

A Chinese export blue and white bidet, some glaze crackling, cracks to base and lower body, incised Z mark above the drainage hole, 24in (61.5cm).
$750-900

A buff pottery neck rest, impressed on one side with a floral roundel and pierced with a waisted oval on the other, covered in a finely crackled straw coloured glaze streaked in green and brown, some rim chips, possibly Liao Dynasty.
$450-600

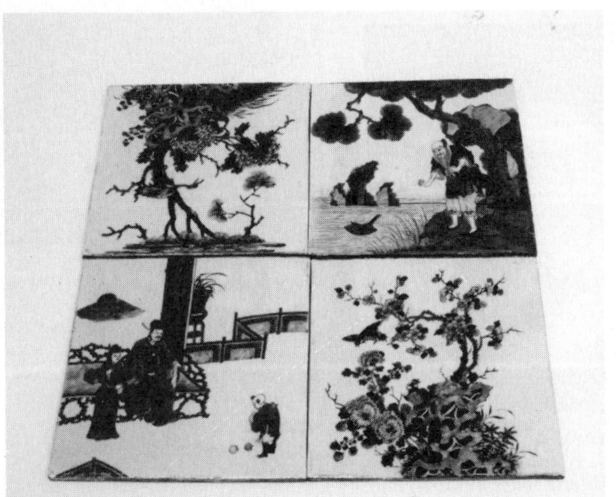

A collection of 16 Chinese underglaze blue tiles, 19thC, each 12in (30.5cm) square, with carved hardwood 4-fold screen in which they were originally housed, distressed condition.
$750-900

A Chinese blue and white ice bucket, with moulded leaf base, twin handles and foliate rim, painted with sprays of flowers and scrolling leaves, crack to base, chips to rim, Qianlong, 6½in(16.5cm) high.
$3,000-4,500

A globular teapot and flat cover, painted gilt with stylised kiku flowerheads among further flowersprays and leaves, 18thC, 4in (10cm) high.
$450-600

Make the Most of Miller's

Every care has been taken to ensure the accuracy of descriptions and estimated valuations. Price ranges in this book reflect what one should expect to pay for a similar example. When selling one can obviously expect a figure below. This will fluctuate according to a dealer's stock, saleability, at a particular time, etc. It is always advisable to approach a reputable specialist dealer or an auction house which has specialist sales.

JAPANESE CERAMICS
Bowls

A Kakiemon bowl, painted in iron red, enamels and gilding with floral sprays, the everted rim with florets on a red ground, all within a brown edged rim, slight cracks, late 17thC, 4¾in (12cm).
$1,200-1,800

A Satsuma earthenware bowl, richly painted and moulded with the Buddha surrounded by numerous Buddhist deities and a dragon in a landscape, the interior with a formal floral border, signed Choshuzan saku, Meiji period, 13¾in (35cm).
$2,700-3,300

Make the Most of Miller's

CONDITION is absolutely vital when assessing the value of an antique. Damaged pieces on the whole appreciate much less than perfect examples. However a rare, desirable piece may command a high price even when damaged.

A Nabeshima blue and white bowl, the lightly moulded petal lobed form with flared rim, decorated in underglaze blue with foliate designs, foot rim chipped, rim crack, early 18thC, 4¾in (12cm).
$3,000-4,500

An Imari bowl, the moulded swirl sides painted on the interior with branches of fruit, the exterior with flowers and scrolling foliage, in underglaze blue, red, yellow and green enamels, Edo period, 18thC, 7in (18cm) diam.
$750-900

Flatware

A Kakiemon dish, decorated in iron red, enamels and gilding, with a tiger beside bamboo and prunus, chipped and cracked, late 17thC, 9½in (24cm).
$2,700-3,300

An Imari saucer dish, painted with figures and dogs in a garden within a border of radiating panels of birds and foliage, gilding slightly rubbed, 18thC, 13¾in (35cm).
$1,800-2,700

Imari

Most Japanese porcelain was manufactured in and around the town of Arita, in the province of Hizen. The factories of Arita were within eight miles of the port of Imari, the market town of the district, and the place to which all porcelain was carried before being shipped to Nagasati for export to Europe.

The term 'Imari' survives to describe a certain type of decoration on Arita wares, namely underglaze blue, with on-glaze iron red and gold decoration.

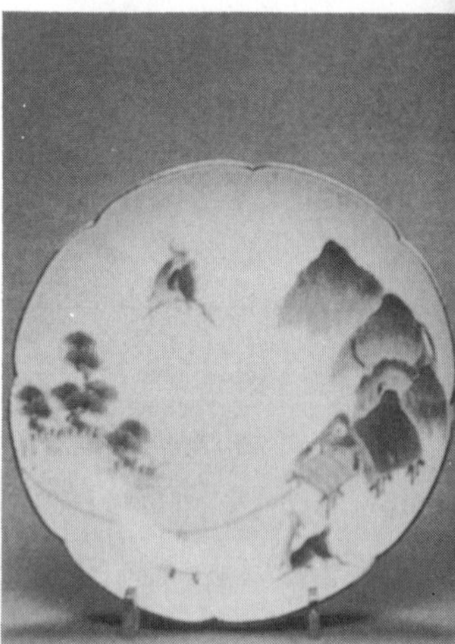

A pair of Arita blue and white dishes, painted in underglaze blue within the brown edged rim with running deer, a thatched cottage, a pine grove and a hanging bird scarer, running Fuku mark, 18thC, 7½in (19cm).
$1,800-2,700

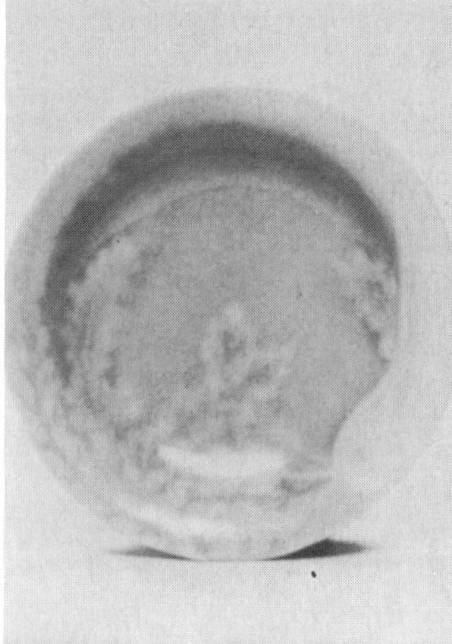

A set of 5 Nabeshima dishes, the body of irregular form, moulded in slight relief and coloured with underglaze celadon and white with a daikon, 18thC, 5in (12.5cm), with wooden box.
$3,000-4,500

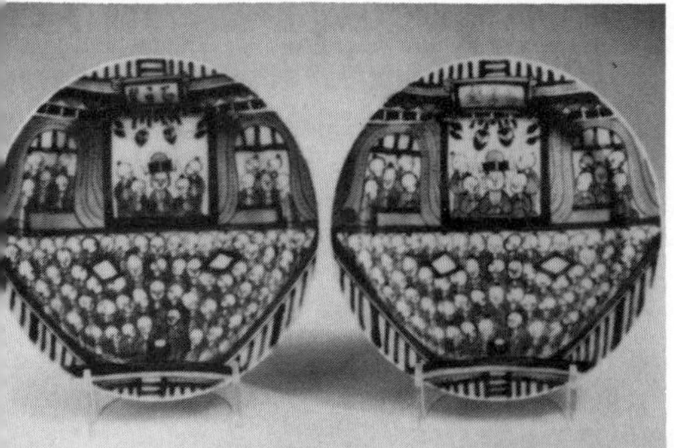

A pair of Arita blue and white plates, painted with the One Hundred Boys pattern, c1700, 6½in (16cm) diam.
$1,800-2,700

An Imari charger, painted and gilt, underglaze blue Chenghua 6-character mark, 18in (46cm) diam.
$900-1,500

An Imari salver, in blue, rust and green pallet, 19thC, 17in (43cm).
$450-600

An Imari dish, Meiji period.
$450-600

A pair of Imari dishes, decorated in underglaze blue, iron red and gilt, some pitting from firing, marked Fuku cho shun, 19thC, 18in (46cm).
$7,500-9,000

An earthenware dish, decorated with irises, birds and leaves, within a gilt ground flower and diaper border, 13½in (34cm).
$225-300

Figures

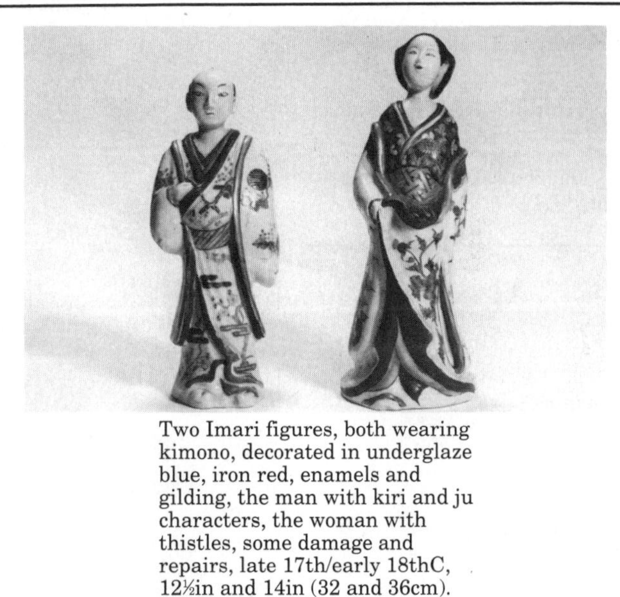

Two Imari figures, both wearing kimono, decorated in underglaze blue, iron red, enamels and gilding, the man with kiri and ju characters, the woman with thistles, some damage and repairs, late 17th/early 18thC, 12½in and 14in (32 and 36cm).
$5,250-6,000

An Arita celadon cockerel censer, covered overall with a green glaze, the feet applied to the separate base, beak and tail with restored chip, late 17th/early 18thC, 8½in (21cm).
$1,800-2,700

An Arita polychrome group of a cockerel, hen and chick, perched on rockwork, hole punched in base, c1700, 6in (15cm).
$1,800-2,700

An Arita jar, painted in underglaze blue, the shoulder and everted neck with repeated formal motifs, one chip and patch of overpaint, late 17thC, 15in (38cm).
$1,050-1,350

An Imari jar and cover, painted i underglaze blue, iron red and gil gilt rubbed and the cover damaged, late 17th/early 18thC, 24in (62cm).
$3,000-4,500

An earthenware model of a crane, painted in black, brown and red enamels, impressed seal mark Tozan, Meiji period, 5in (12.5cm).
$1,500-2,250

An Arita blue and white baluster jar and domed cover, cracked and restored, late 17th/early 18thC, 27½in (70cm).
$2,700-3,300

An Arita jar, late 17th/early 18thC.
$900-1,500

Jars

An Arita blue and white jar, painted in underglaze blue with panels of ho-o and peonies, reserved on a foliate ground, the shoulders with leaf-shaped panels of stylised flowers, late 17thC, 12in (31cm).
$1,800-2,700

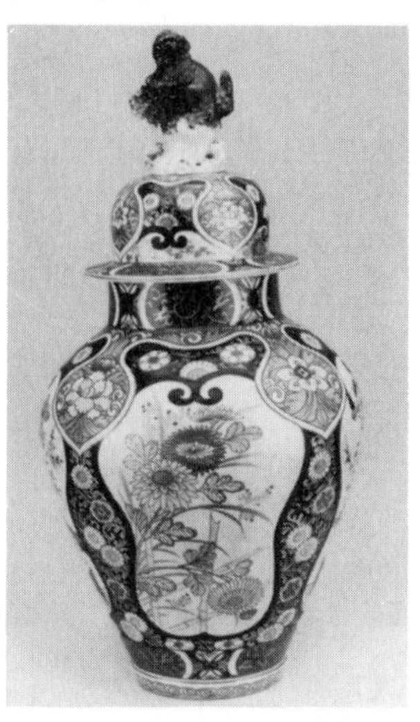

An Imari baluster jar and domed cover, with shishi lion finial, painted and gilt, cracked, c1700, 25½in (65cm).
$1,200-1,800

An earthenware jar and cover, decorated on a brown glaze in gilt and oxidised silver with still life, landscape and birds, signed Kinkozan zo, Meiji period, 4in (10cm).
$1,200-1,800

'ases

n Arita blue and white bottle ıse, with slightly everted rim, ıinted with flowering prunus ·anches, crack to base, c1700, ½in (29cm).
,200-1,500

n Arita baluster vase, painted in nderglaze blue, coloured ıamels and gilt, minute chip to ·ot, slight gilt rubbing, c1700, 8in (45cm) high.
3,000-4,500

. pair of Arita blue and white aluster vases and domed covers, ith shishi lion finials, painted ith ho-o among flowering trees nd grasses issuing from pierced ›ckwork, both damaged, 12in 30.5cm), and a globular jar, late 7thC.
900-1,500

An Arita bottle vase, painted in underglaze blue with flowers and grasses, late 17thC, 11in (28cm).
$3,000-3,750

An Arita vase, painted in greyish underglaze blue, reserved on a floral ground, the shoulder and everted neck with repeated formal motifs, late 17thC, 15½in (40cm).
$2,700-3,300

A pair of Imari baluster vases, painted and gilt, crack to rim of one, no covers, gilt rubbing, 17th/18thC, 13in (33cm) high.
$3,000-3,750

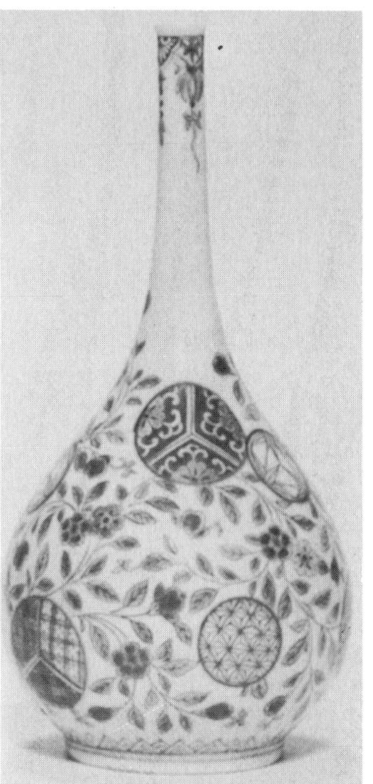

An Imari bottle vase, painted in underglaze blue, iron red, green, yellow, aubergine, black and gilt, with medallions of different sizes amidst scrolling foliage, late 17th/early 18thC, 8½in (22cm).
$1,800-2,700

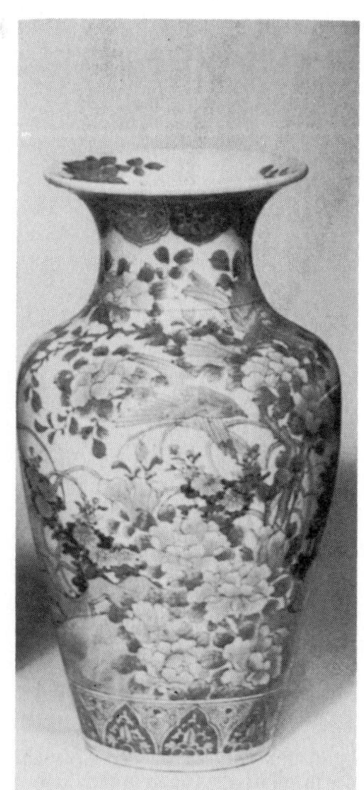

A pair of Arita blue and white baluster vases, both cracked, 19thC, 19in (48cm) high.
$750-900

A pair of Imari vases and covers, painted in underglaze blue, iron red and gilt with 3 panels depicting hydrangea, weeping cherry and peony, one vase dented and with glaze defects in firing, foot chipped and hair cracks, the other and both covers restored, late 17th/early 18thC, 28in (71cm).
$5,250-6,000

A pair of earthenware vases, one damaged, c1900, 31in (79cm).
$1,800-2,700

A vase and cover, decorated in Imari style, in underglase blue, iron red and gilt, the cover with shishi knop, star crack on base, marked Fukagawa sei with rebus, Meiji period, 21in (53cm).
$2,250-3,000

An earthenware vase, decorated in enamels and gilt with two heart shaped panels over a midnight blue ground, signed Kinkozan zo, Meiji period, 15½in (40cm).
$3,000-3,750

A porcelain vase, decorated all-over beneath the glaze with red scrolling karakusa on a celadon green ground, signed in underglaze blue Kozan sei, 10in (25cm).
$3,000-3,750

A vase, painted in the Imari style, in underglaze blue, iron red and gilt, reserved on a ground of ho-o amongst scrolling peony, marked Fukagawa sei with rebus, 15in (38cm).
$1,800-2,700

An earthenware vase, painted in enamels and gilt with panels of figures on a ground of rinzu and kiku design, slightly rubbed, signed Kinkozan zo kore, Meiji period, 4in (10cm).
$1,500-2,250

A Satsuma earthenware vase, decorated in enamels and gilt, reserved on a midnight blue ground, signed Yasuda zo beneath a Satsuma mon, Meiji period, 10in (25cm).
$1,050-1,350

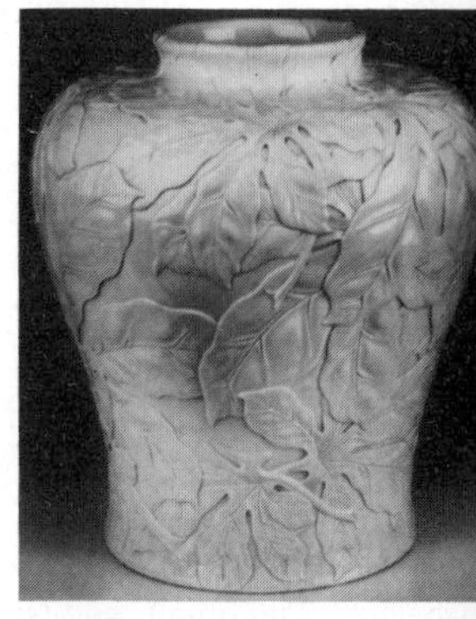

A cream glazed baluster jar, with flattened shoulders and short everted neck, moulded in relief with maple leaves, 13in (33cm), wood stand.
$2,250-3,000

A pair of late Kutani vases, painted in pink, grey and blue enamels, within gilt and polychrome borders at top and bottom, Meiji period, signed Nihon Yokohama Imura sei zo, 18in (46cm).
$3,000-3,750

A pair of Imari vases, each painted and gilt with stylised flowerheads and hexagonal panels on a ground of dense flowerheads and leaves above a band of stiff leaves to the foot, 24in (61cm).
$1,200-1,500

A pair of Imari bottle shaped vases, 11½in (29cm).
$750-1,200

A pair of Imari bottle vases, one with body crack, 12in (30.5cm).
$375-525

Miscellaneous

An Arita polychrome and underglaze blue cistern and domed cover, on tripod lappet feet, painted and gilt, with metal tap, knop missing from cover, gilt rubbed, crack to base, old restoration to body, 17th/18thC, 12½in (32cm).
$1,200-1,500

A pair of Imari double gourd vases, with narrow necks, painted and gilt with boys at play among flowerheads and scrolling foliage, some gilt rubbing, 12in (30.5cm).
$1,200-1,500

An earthenware tea set, comprising: a teapot, sugar bowl, milk jug and 12 cups and saucers, painted in enamels and gilt with figures following pursuits of the 12 months, one cup with repaired handle, marked Seizan and rei, Meiji period.
$2,700-3,300

An Arita ewer, decorated in blue and iron red, late 17thC, and a Chinese copy, 18thC, 3½in (9cm).
$750-900

An Imari urn, moulded and painted in underglaze blue and enamelled in iron red, lilac, turquoise and puce, the neck stitched and restored, late 17th/early 18thC, later carved and pierced wood cover, 18in (46cm) high.
$1,800-2,700

GLASS

Last year I wrote that prices of most glass had stabilised and that I didn't think they would rise too rapidly in the year ahead and indeed this has turned out to be the case. In fact, some of the more mediocre items have come back somewhat, particularly drinking glasses. Only about 13% of a collection of Lowlands 'façon-de-Venise' and other Continental clear, mostly engraved, glass was unsold, and only about 23% of the pieces made prices above the higher estimates. Lastly, in a sale of Continental colour glass, post-1840, about 50% was unsold.

The saleroom handouts, the press, trade reviews, and so on, often make much of the high prices realised on articles sold today, but bought many years ago at what appear to have been bargain prices. However, largely because of inflation, all is not what it appears to be. Late last year, taking inflation into account, I compared the performance of twenty-one English glasses that came up for sale in a London saleroom. For all of these, I had marked catalogues indicating what price the glasses had fetched when previously offered for sale some years ago.

Statistically the sample, shown in the following table, is very small: indeed, people's confidence would be very low if any predictions were to be made on this small sample; nevertheless it is of some value as a pointer to the effects of inflation over the years. I have tried to show this by adding to the initial purchase price the effect of inflation over the intervening years until the piece was sold again late in 1992.

The best performers were a Silesian stem goblet engraved with a bacchus astride a wine cask, and a Royalist goblet showing the Fall of Man - Adam and Eve - in diamond point. However, the average collector without a deep pocket can ill afford to sport $15,000 and $30,000 respectively on glasses such as these, nor $11,000 on an opaque twist glass engraved with a figure of a privateer that sailed out from Bristol during the second half of the 18th Century to do battle with the French.

In the table, prices realised were the hammer prices as, in most cases, there was no buyer's premium when these glasses were first sold (bought). Neither, for that matter, were there any printed estimates (and I don't want to get involved in the selling commission that has to be deducted from the realised price, thus reducing the profit margin).

So, buy glass, not for investment, but because you love it!

R. G. Thomas
May 1993

	Date First Sold (a)	Price Realised (b)	Price Realised in 1992 (c)	Apparent % inc. (c)-(b) (d)	Price (b) adj'd for inflation (e)	Real % inc. (e)-(b) (f)
1) Baluster Wine Shoulder Knop	3.66	$200	$750	243	$2,000	loss
2) Baluster Wine Drop Knop	3.66	$150	$750	385	$1,500	loss
3) Bacchus Goblet	3.68	$300	$15,000	5,263	$2,500	508
4) Jacobite Fiat Dram Glass	3.68	$375	$1,500	265	$3,500	loss
5) 4 Knop Opaque Twist Wine	4.67	$75	$1,000	1,150	$750	42
6) Engraved Composite Stem Wine	12.67	$75	$750	817	$750	5
7) Colour Twist Firing Glass	12.67	$375	$2,500	530	$3,500	loss
8) Sunderland Bridge Rummer	6.85	$300	$300	loss	$600	loss
9) Opaque Twist Beilby Wine (fruiting vine)	12.68	$150	$1,350	847	$1,000	15
10) Nelson Commem. Rummer	3.68	$75	$750	809	$700	5
11) Baluster Mushroom Knop Wine	2.79	$750	$3,500	362	$2,000	74
12) Royalist Goblet 'Fall of Man'	10.74	$4,500	$30,000	549	$22,500	34
13) Jacobite Opaque Twist Wine 'Success To The Society'	4.80	$900	unsold		$1,800	
14) Opaque Twist Firing Glass	1.75	$75	$500	483	$375	27
15) Lynn Opaque Twist Wine	6.74	$150	$500	233	$750	loss
16) Privateer Opaque Twist Wine	3.78	$2,500	$11,250	341	$7,500	34
17) Privateer Opaque Twist Wine	12.67	$750	$10,500	1,300	$6,500	62
18) Ratafia Opaque Twist Wine	3.77	$75	$750	700	$300	155
19) Lilac Colour Twist Wine	3.77	$600	$3,800	550	$1,800	108
20) Blue Colour Twist Wine (much better glass than 19)	1.75	$75	$2,250	2,400	$375	445
21) Composite Stem Candlestick	2.79	$800	$4,500	445	$2,250	107

Bowls

A Venetian bowl with spiral gadrooning, an applied translucent blue trail to the folded rim and the ribbed foot, c1500, 11½in (29cm) diam.
$3,000-3,750

A salad bowl, with an everted rim cut with cross cut diamonds, the faceted bowl on a domed fluted plinth, 12in (30.5cm) wide.
$2,700-3,300

An Irish bowl, the body cut with small diamonds in between flute cut pillars, fan cut handles and notched rim, c1825, 5¾in (14.5cm) diam.
$900-1,500

A Venetian grey tinted bowl, 'nipt diamond waies' on the underside above a spreading ribbed foot with folded rim, c1500, 12in (31cm).
$4,500-6,000

A Venetian bowl, the sides applied with a blue trail above the ribs and under the folded rim, the spreading ribbed foot with thick applied blue trail around the rim, early 16thC, 10in (25cm).
$4,500-6,000

A glass bowl, cut with spirally fluted and diamond bands, early 19thC, 11in (28cm) diam.
$375-525

Decanters and Bottles

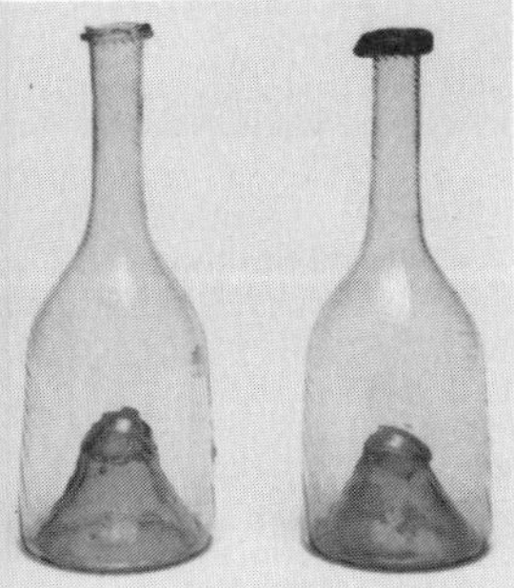

A pair of South German 'forest' glass cruet bottles, c1680, 5in (12.5cm).
$120-135

A decanter, the body engraved with egg-and-tulip decoration, with scale cut neck and lunar sliced lozenge stopper, c1780, 9½in (24cm).
$375-525

A glass decanter and stopper, c1800, 10in (25cm).
$375-525

A pair of square spirit bottles, with flute cutting and a band of diamond cutting, star cut bases and cut mushroom stoppers, c1810, 6¾in (17cm).
$225-255

A Masonic decanter, the plain mallet shaped body engraved with Masonic symbols within floral sprays and monogram 'J.B.', with bevelled lozenge stopper, c1780, 9in (23cm).
$1,200-1,800

Three spirit decanters, with plain bodies and lozenge stoppers, c1800, 6½ to 7½in (18 to 19cm).
$180-225 each

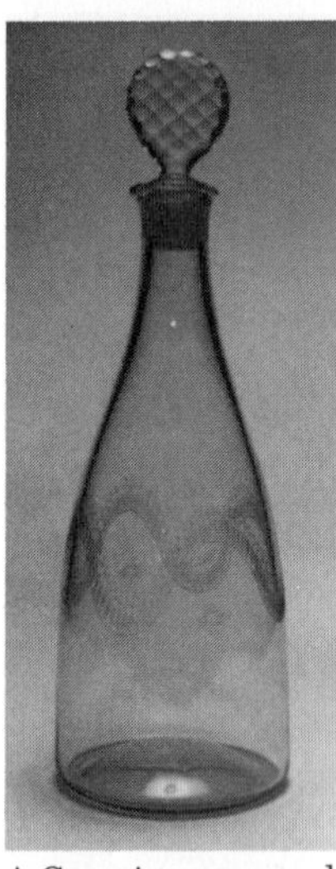

A Georgian engraved decanter, with stopper, c1770, 11½in (29cm).
$750-900

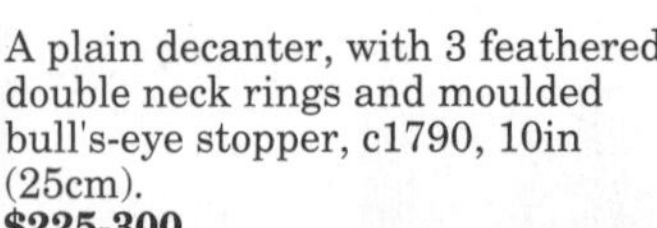

A plain decanter, with 3 feathered double neck rings and moulded bull's-eye stopper, c1790, 10in (25cm).
$225-300

A pair of decanters, the cylindrical bodies with prism, flute and small diamond cutting, diamond cut neck rings and cut mushroom stoppers, c1810, 8½in (22cm).
$900-1,500

A Gothic revival cut glass rosewater decanter in an ormolu mount, c1870.
$375-525

A glass decanter, c1780, 10½in (26.5cm).
$375-450

A Scottish glass decanter, engraved by Millar, c1870, 12½in (31.5cm).
$750-900

A set of 3 octagonal sided spirit bottles, with a band of blaze cutting round the top of the bodies, flute cut necks, pouring lips and cut ball stoppers, in plated stand, c1810, 6½in (16.5cm).
$450-600

A magnum carafe, with ovoid body and flute, prism and diamond cut body, 3 cut neck rings, star cut base, c1825, 10½in (26.5cm).
$1,050-1,350

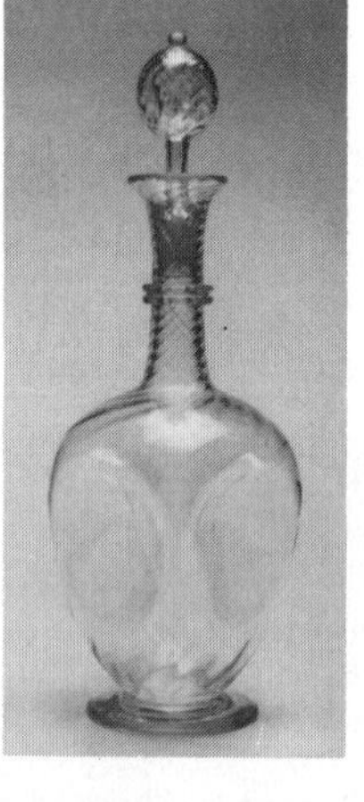

A glass decanter and stopper, c1890, 12½in (31.5cm).
$375-450

A pair of Victorian decanters, with diamond cut bodies and flute cut necks, cut ball stoppers, c1860, 9½in (23.5cm).
$225-300

A pair of Victorian decanters, with globular bodies cut with printies, flute cut necks and diamond cut ball stoppers, c1880, 23in (59cm).
$300-375

A pair of decanters, the ovoid bodies with flute and small diamond cutting, diamond cut neck rings and mushroom stoppers, c1810, 9in (23cm).
$1,050-1,350

A pair of glass bottles, 12½in (32.5cm).
$25-40 each

A pair of decanters, the ovoid bodies with base fluting, a band of small cut diamonds and flute cut necks, and 3 annulated neck rings with target stoppers, c1810, 9in (22cm). **$1,200-1,800**

l. A cylindrical decanter, with facet cut body and neck rings, with hexagon cut stopper, c1840, 9in (22cm) high.
$225-300

c. A spirit sized diamond and flute cut decanter, with plain flat neck rings and mushroom stopper, c1810, 8in (20.5cm).
$150-225

r. A cylindrical decanter, with panel cut body, 3 neck rings and cut hexagonal stopper, c1840, 8½in (21cm).
$225-255

A pair of pillar cut glass decanters, c1820, 9½in (24cm).
$1,200-1,800

A pair of Stourbridge ogee shaped decanters and stoppers, probably Richardson, finely wheel engraved with star cut bases, 14½in (37cm).
$1,200-1,800

Drinking Glasses

ALE GLASSES

A pair of double series opaque twist ales, with spiral gauzes outside central columnar gauze, and hammered bowls, c1765, 7in (18cm).
$750-900

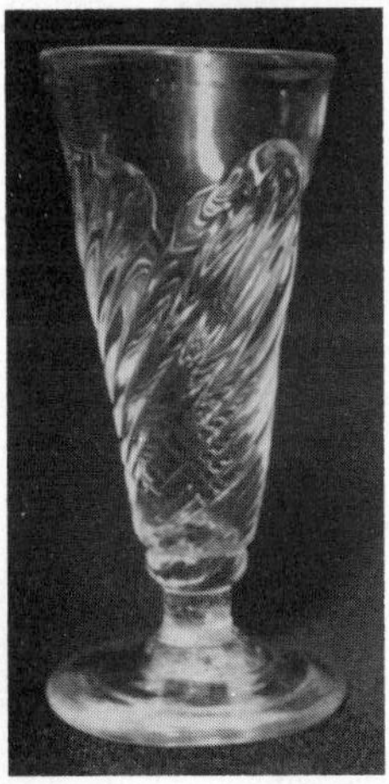

A dwarf ale glass, the conical body with flammiform moulded wrythen decoration, on a knopped stem and plain conical foot, c1750, 6½in (16.5cm).
$225-255

A dwarf ale glass, with a conical bowl engraved with monogram 'JM' within a garter cartouche and floral sprays, on a short knopped stem and plain foot, c1810, 5in (13cm).
$105-120

Two ale glasses, with drawn facet cut stems and plain conical feet, c1770,
l. Diamond facet cut, 7½in (18.5cm).
r. Engraved with hops and barley, with hatched border round rim, 7½in (18.5cm).
$375-525 each

Three ale glasses, with deep funnel bowls on stems with double series opaque twists, on plain conical feet, c1760, 7½ to 8in (19.5 to 20cm).
$300-375 each

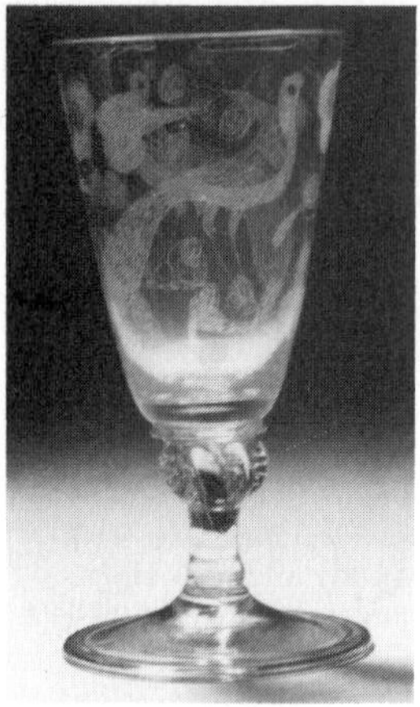

A diamond engraved ale glass, supported on a merese above a short shoulder knopped stem with pincered propeller ornament and folded conical foot, c1695, 5in (12.5cm).
$3,000-4,500

Four dwarf ales, with wrythen moulded conical bowls, on plain conical feet, c1810, 4½ to 5in (1 to 12.5cm). **$90-105 each**

Three dwarf ale glasses, the conical bowls engraved with hops and barley, on short knopped stems, c1810, 4½ to 5in (12 to 13cm).
$90-105 each

An ale glass, with a deep funnel bowl engraved with barley ears and vines, on air-twist stem, c1745, 8in (20cm).
$750-1,200

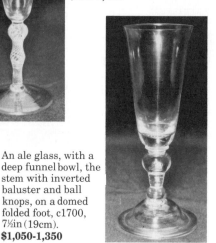

An ale glass, with a deep funnel bowl, the stem with inverted baluster and ball knops, on a domed folded foot, c1700, 7½in (19cm).
$1,050-1,350

CHAMPAGNE

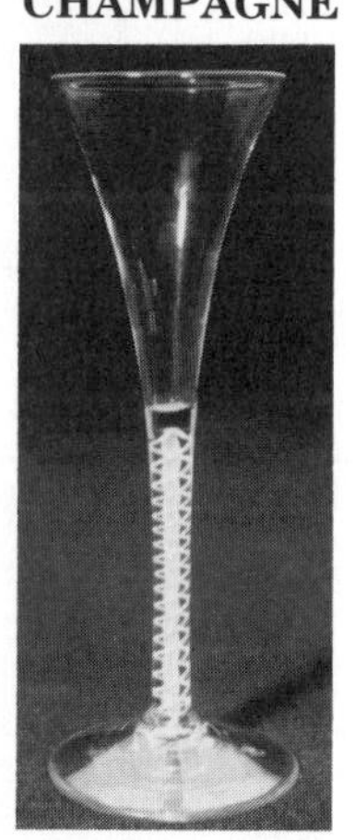

A flute, with trumpet bowl on slender stem with double series opaque twist, on a plain conical foot, c1760, 7½in (18.5cm).
$750-900

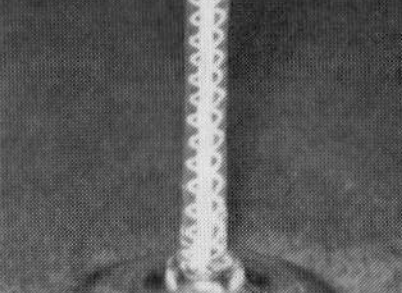

A flute, c1760, 7½i (18.5cm).
$750-900

BEAKERS

A conical beaker, the body engraved with Masonic symbols and initials 'JW' on the reverse, c1800, 5in (12.5cm).
$750-900

A Bohemian glass beaker, with enamelled coat-of-arms of the Holy Roman Empire, 19thC, 8in (20cm).
$225-300

A pair of panel cut champagne flutes, with everted lip and faceted knop.
$225-300

A balustroid champagne glass, with a double ogee bowl, the stem with a beaded knop between 2 plain sections above a domed foot, minor chip, c1730, 5in (12.5cm).
$450-600

An air-twist firing glass with a bell bowl, the stem filled with spiral threads above a thick foot, c1750, 4in (10cm).
$450-600

Firing Glasses

Firing glasses are always short stemmed. They are dram glasses or small wines made with a specially strong, thick foot for use at meetings. When a toast was drunk the members would strike the table simultaneously with their glasses, the noise was said to resemble the firing of a musket.

FIRING GLASSES

A colour-twist firing glass, the stem with an opaque gauze core entwined by a pair of translucent green and a pair of opaque spiral threads, on a thick foot, c1770, 4½in (11cm).
$2,700-3,300

An opaque twist toastmaster's glass, the stem with a gauze corkscrew core within a pair of 6-ply spirals, on a conical foot, c1765, 5½in (14cm).
$1,200-1,800

An opaque twist toastmaster's firing glass, the deceptive bowl with a band of diagonal tool marks, the short stem with a gauze core within 2 spiral threads, on a terraced foot, c1765, 4in (10cm).
$900-1,500

A baluster toastmaster's glass, the deceptive straight sided funnel bowl supported on an inverted baluster stem enclosing an elongated tear, on a folded conical foot, c1710, 4½in (11.5cm).
$750-900

GOBLETS

A goblet, with deep round funnel bowl, on a stem with inverted baluster knop and air tear, on a folded conical foot, c1700, 6in (15.5cm).
$1,050-1,350

An engraved balustroid goblet, the stem with a central ball knop between plain sections above a domed foot, 1720, 7in (18cm).
$750-1,200

A set of 6 goblets, with ogee bowls and stems with double series opaque twists, on plain conical feet, c1760, 6½in (17cm).
$3,000-4,500

A balustroid goblet, the trumpet bowl on a stem with shoulder ball and central cushion knops, on a folded conical foot, c1720, 8in (19.5cm). **$1,050-1,350**

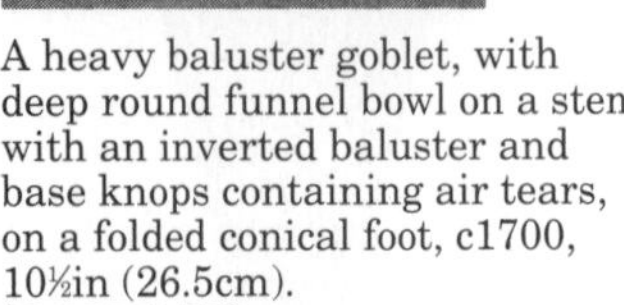

A heavy baluster goblet, with deep round funnel bowl on a stem with an inverted baluster and base knops containing air tears, on a folded conical foot, c1700, 10½in (26.5cm).
$3,000-3,750

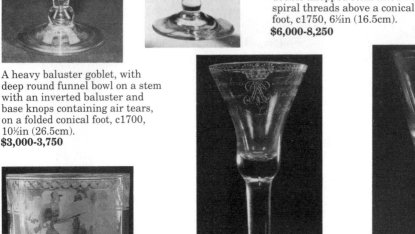

A baluster goblet, the bell bowl supported on a triple annulated knop above an inverted baluster stem terminating on a basal knop, on a conical foot, c1730, 6½in (16cm).
$450-600

A Jacobite portrait air-twist goblet, the bowl with a bust portrait of Prince Charles Edward, inscribed above 'Audentior ibo', supported on a double knopped stem filled with spiral threads above a conical foot, c1750, 6½in (16.5cm).
$6,000-8,250

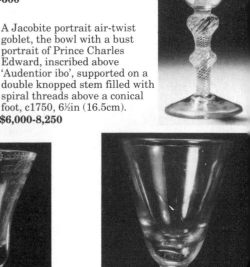

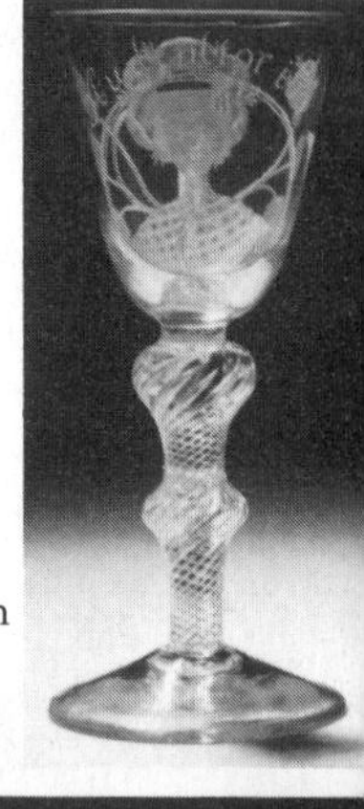

A pair of Davenport goblets, each with etched straight sided bowl, set on a knopped stem and conical foot, inscribed Patent on the base, one with minor footrim chip, 6in (15cm).
$6,000-8,250

A baluster goblet, the bell bowl with an air tear, on a stem with annulated shoulder knop and base ball knop, on a folded conical foot, c1720, 7in (18cm).
$1,500-2,250

The Gregson of Tilliefour Old Pretender goblet, of Jacobite significance, the waisted bell-shaped bowl with solid base enclosing a small tear, finely engraved in diamond point with a crown surmounting the cypher 'JR' direct and reversed, intertwined with the figure 8, inscribed on either side 'Send Him soon home To Holyruood Houfe And that no Sooner Than I do Wifh', and inscribed below 'Vive La Roy' flanked by ornate scrolls, a border of scrollwork around the rim, set on a plain stem and conical folded foot, c1745, 9½in (24cm).
$60,000-75,000
This important glass belongs to the same series as the Amen Glasses, and is engraved in similar style. It will be noticed that Holyrood has a superfluous 'U' (erased). Whilst the majority of the 40 known Amen glasses have trumpet bowls only 3 examples are known with bell shaped bowls; one, the Steuart Amen, can be found in the collection of the National Museums of Scotland, the other, the Ferguson Amen, is in the Cinzano Collection, and are listed 36 and 38, respectively, by Charleston and Seddon.
The last Amen glass sold at Sotheby's 'The Spottiswoode Amen' glass, on 25th March 1991.

A heavy baluster goblet, the round funnel bowl with air tear in base, the stem with angular and base ball knop and elongated air tear, on a folded conical foot, c1720, 7½in (19cm).
$1,500-2,250

A Bohemian engraved goblet, with inscriptions, supported on a wrythen knop and baluster stem enclosing translucent red threads and flanked by collars, the conical foot with scroll ornament and stylised stiff leaf border, c1720, 10in (25cm).
$1,800-2,700

A Bohemian engraved goblet, set on a triple hollow knopped stem flanked by mereses, on a wide conical folded foot, c1700, 9in (23.5cm).
$1,800-2,700

A Jacobite goblet, engraved with a heraldic rose flanked by open and closed buds, above a double knopped air-twist stem and conical foot, 9½in (24cm).
$2,700-3,300

A Bohemian goblet, with wide conical folded foot engraved with leaf band, c1700, 10½in (27cm).
$2,700-3,300

The Confederate Hunt goblet, of Jacobite significance, the bucket bowl engraved with a rose, bud and thistle, inscribed, set on the remains of an opaque twist stem replaced by a turned wood foot with a metal band, c1760, together with a card disc listing the names of the Cycle Club, dated 1825, 9½in (24cm).
$7,500-9,000

In the guise of a hunting goblet honouring the lady patronesses, this commemorates the election of Lady Williams Wynne as Lady Parramount (the 3rd baronet's widow, born Frances Shakerley) and of the cycles held by the well known Jacobite families of Mytton, Owen, Shakerley and Williams in the years mentioned. Wenman and Dashwood were well known supporters of the Jacobite cause and Sir Watkin Williams Wynn, MP for Denbigh, was known as 'father' of the Cycle Club. It is interesting to note that ladies of these families were elected Lady Patronesses in the middle of the century because some 30 years later, when the club jewel was instituted in 1780, there was no Lady Parramount but the then Lady Williams Wynn was elected Lady Patroness and held that office for some years.

A Dutch engraved ship goblet, set on an annulated knop and octagonal pedestal moulded stem, the shoulder studded with diamonds, basal collar and folded domed foot, c1720, 8in (20.5cm).
$3,000-4,500

A Dutch 'Friendship' goblet, the bell bowl finely engraved in the manner of Jacob Sang and part polished with a three-masted ship with 'The Plough' forward, inscribed within 2 bands, one with a snake biting its tail, 'Dusleyde ons Vriendschap', c1748, 7½in (19.5cm).
$3,000-4,500

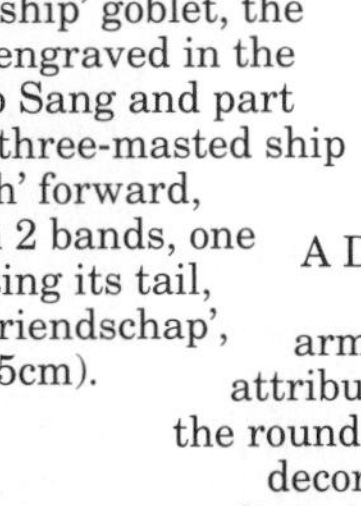

A goblet, point engraved by Lawrence Whistler in 1951, the deep cup bowl stipple and point engraved with a riverscape view within an oval panel flanked by cornucopiae spilling out flowers, fruit and a flight of swallows, inscribed below, foot inscribed Leslie. Sep 14, 1951, c1850, 5in (13cm).
$2,700-3,300

A Dutch stipple engraved armorial goblet, attributed to Alius, the round funnel bowl decorated in both diamond point and stipple techniques with the crowned arms of Princess Frederika Sophia Wilhelmina, c1745, 7½in (19cm).
$4,800-5,700

A Dutch 'Kraamvrouw' goblet, the reverse with inscription, set on a beaded knop flanked by an angular knop and plain section with basal knop, conical foot, attributed to Jacob Sang, c1750, 7½in (19.5cm).
$6,000-8,250

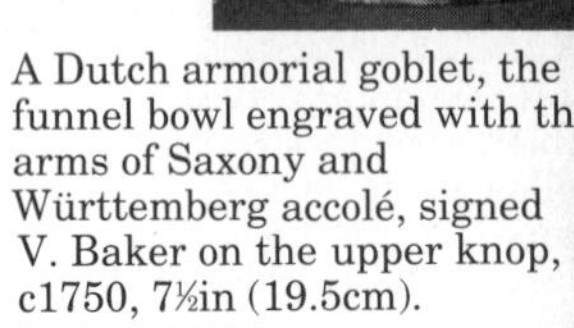

A Dutch armorial goblet, the funnel bowl engraved with the arms of Saxony and Württemberg accolé, signed V. Baker on the upper knop, c1750, 7½in (19.5cm).
$2,250-3,000

A Dutch engraved whale hunting goblet, the funnel bowl inscribed 'T Welvaaren van de Groenlansche Vissery', c1745, 7½in (19cm).
$6,000-8,250

A Dutch armorial goblet, the funnel bowl engraved with the arms of Anne, daughter of George II, c1750, 7½in (19.5cm).
$3,000-4,500

An Anglo-Dutch armorial goblet, of crizzled lead glass, the bucket bowl engraved with the arms of William of Orange as Stadholder of the Netherlands flanked by military trophies, the reverse with a crowned lion of the Province of Holland, the base with 'nipt diamond waies' above a pair of hollow quatrefoil knops flanked by mereses, wide conical folded foot engraved with a foliate band, c1685, 7¼in (18.5cm).
$15,000-18,000

A Dutch diamond engraved goblet, the funnel bowl engraved with the figures of Justice and Liberty within an oval panel flanked by drapery and the inscription, the reverse also inscribed and date 1795, set on a faceted baluster stem and conical foot with scallop rim, 7in (17.5cm). **$3,000-4,500**

The inscription refers to the French occupation of Holland in 1795 and translates as 'French wine makes men happy but the French people give freedom to slaves'.

A Saxon engraved armorial goblet, the reverse inscribed, set on a faceted knop and teared inverted baluster, wide conical folded foot, Berlin or Dresden, c1725, 10½in (26.5cm).
$3,000-3,750

A Silesian goblet, engraved in the manner of Christian Gottfied Schneider, on cut baluster stem and faceted conical foot with stiff leaf border, c1740, 7½in (19cm).
$12,000-15,000

A German engraved armorial goblet, set on a faceted cushion knop and inverted baluster with basal knop, conical foot with leaf band, probably Bohemian, c1730, 8½in (22cm).
$4,500-6,000

A Dutch armorial goblet, the funnel bowl finely engraved and part polished, set on a teared angular knop above a teared inverted baluster flanked by ball and basal knops, conical foot, probably by Jacob Sang, c1760, 8¼in (21cm).
$7,500-9,000

A Silesian engraved goblet, the double ogee bowl set on a faceted inverted baluster with collar and conical foot with hound's tooth rim, c1720, 8½in (22cm).
$10,500-12,000

A Dutch goblet, the funnel bowl engraved and part polished, set on a multi-knopped stem comprising a teared inverted baluster below 2 beaded cushion knops, the rim of the bowl and the conical foot engraved with a narrow ovolo band, the pontil area finished as a daisy, possibly Jacob Sang, c1745, 9in (23.5cm).
$10,500-12,000

A Silesian goblet, the funnel bowl engraved with a continuous scene, inscribed 'Vivat Negotium', set on a faceted inverted baluster and conical foot engraved with a scroll, Warmbrunn, c1730, 6½in (17cm).
$6,000-8,250

A Dutch light baluster goblet, the funnel bowl engraved with a prancing horse below the inscription 'Aurea Libertas', set on an inverted baluster with beaded shoulder flanked by an angular knop and basal knop, conical foot, probably Jacob Sang, c1755, 7½in (19cm).
$3,000-4,500

A Dutch armorial light baluster goblet, the funnel bowl engraved with the arms of Princess Frederika Sophia Wilhelmina of Prussia, set on a beaded knop flanked by an angular knop and plain section with basal knop, conical foot, possibly Jacob Sang, c1750, 7in (17.5cm).
$2,700-3,300

GOBLETS & COVERS

A Bohemian engraved amber flash goblet and cover, on a stem and spreading foot with scalloped rim, the cover with everted scalloped rim and engraved with a band of fruiting vine, with tall spire finial, slight chips, c1865, 24in (61cm).
$4,500-6,000

A Silesian engraved 'Friendship' goblet and cover, the domed cover and faceted finial similarly engraved, c1750, 10in (25cm).
$2,250-3,000

A German goblet and cover, engraved with a crest with the initials 'S_GF', inscribed, set on a faceted knop and hollow inverted baluster, the faceted domed foot with floral garland, domed cover with faceted finial, possibly Saxon or Hesse, 1768, 16in (40cm).
$3,000-4,500

A Silesian 'Friendship' goblet and cover, the double ogee bowl engraved, set on a faceted inverted baluster stem with basal knop, conical foot engraved with leaf scrolls and domed cover with faceted finial, c1760, 8½in (21.5cm).
$2,250-3,000

A Saxon engraved goblet and cover, with inscription, on faceted teared inverted baluster stem, folded conical foot, the domed cover with faceted spire finial and engraved with leaf fronds, c1740, 11in (28.5cm).
$3,000-4,500

A Bohemian double goblet and cover, gadrooned and engraved, the smaller domed cover with floral finial, c1690, 14½in (37.5cm).
$4,800-5,700

Three bucket rummers, with plain bodies and knopped stems, on plain conical feet, *l.* c1815, 6½in (16.5cm), **$135-150**, *c.* c1810, 5½in (14cm), **$105-120** *r.* c1810, 6 (15.5cm), **$105-120**

A pair of rummers, the incurved bowls with a band of moulded blaze decoration, with cushion knopped stems, on plain conical feet, c1830, 5in (12cm).
$150-225

RUMMERS

An ovoid bowl rummer, engraved with a band of vesica and star decoration, on a plain conical foot, c1800, 5in (13cm).
$150-225

A rummer, the ovoid body finely engraved with Masonic symbols, the initial 'G' on the reverse side, with capstan stem, on a plain conical foot, c1810, 6in (15cm).
$375-525

An engraved rummer, inscribed 'May Farming Flourish', the reverse inscribed 'A Trifle From Yarmouth' above the initials 'R S.', on a short stem, spreading stepped foot and square base, attributed to William Absolon, slight damage, early 19thC, 6in (14.5cm).
$750-1,200

A pair of rummers, the ovoid bowls on stems with collars and square domed lemon squeezer, feet, c1810, 6½in (16cm).
$225-255

Three bucket bowl rummers, with short stems and plain conical feet, c1830, 5 to 5½in (12.5 to 13.5cm).
$225-300 each

An Irish lipped mixing rummer, with panel cut bowl below a band of fine diamonds, on knopped stem, 6½in (16cm).
$150-225

. rummer, the bucket bowl
ngraved with a coursing scene,
n a short stem with ball knop, on
plain conical foot, c1830, 6in
15.5cm).
900-1,500

A large bucket rummer, with flute cut base, the bowl engraved with Masonic symbols and the initials 'J. E. D.' on the reverse, on a ball knopped stem and plain conical foot, c1810, 7in (18cm).
$750-900

TUMBLERS

Two Lobmeyr engraved tumblers, after designs by Michael Powolny, engraved and acid etched, with a scalloped border to rim and an elf playing the mandolin within a similar cartouche and scattered flowersprays, c1914, 3½in (9cm).
$2,700-3,300

VINE GLASSES

A wine glass, with base ribbing to trumpet bowl, on a stem with a multiple spiral air-twist, plain conical foot, c1750, 6½in (16cm).
$750-900

A pan top bowl wine glass, on a stem with a multiple spiral air- twist, folded conical foot, c1750, 6in (15cm).
$750-900

Jacobite wine glass, the
umpet bowl engraved with a
acobite rose, one bud and star,
n a multiple spiral air-twist
em, plain conical foot, c1750,
½in (16.5cm).
1,500-2,250

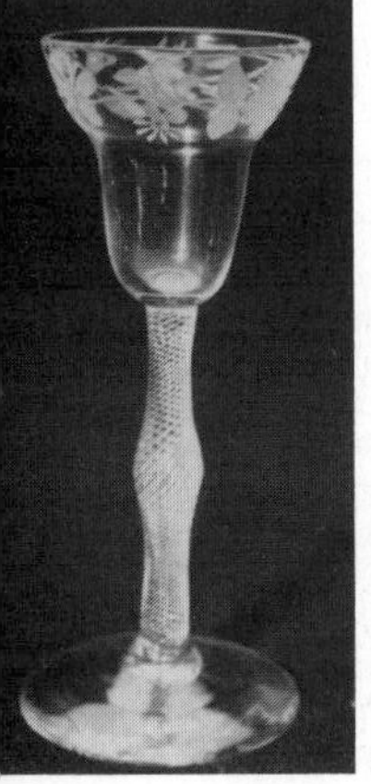

A wine glass, with pan top bowl engraved with honeysuckle, rose and carnation, on a stem with a multiple spiral air-twist and swelling knop, plain conical foot, c1750, 7¼in (18.5cm).
$750-900

A set of 4 tumblers, conical bodies with flute, prism and small diamond cutting, c1820, 4in (10cm). **$300-375**

A Williamite colour twist wine glass, the bowl engraved with an equestrian portrait of William III with feathered hat inscribed above 'The Glorious Memory of King William', the reverse inscribed 'Boyne 1st July 1690', set on an opaque twist stem including a pale yellow and grey thread, conical foot, late 18thC, 6in (15cm).
$6,000-8,250

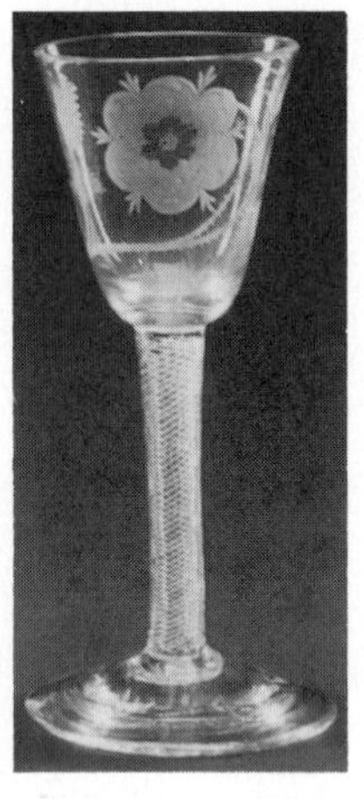

A pair of Jacobite wine glasses, set on a multi-spiral air-twist stem and conical foot, c1750, 6in (15cm).
$1,200-1,500

A Jacobite air-twist wine glass supported on a double knopped stem filled with spiral threads above a conical foot, c1750, 7in (17.5cm).
$750-900

An incised twist wine glass, the large round funnel bowl with honeycomb moulded base and band of floral engraving, coarse incised twist stem, on plain conical foot, c1750, 6in (15cm).
$1,050-1,350

A Jacobite mercury twist wine glass, of drawn trumpet shape, the stem with 2 entwined corkscrew spirals above a conical foot, small chips, c1750, 6in (15cm).
$1,500-2,250

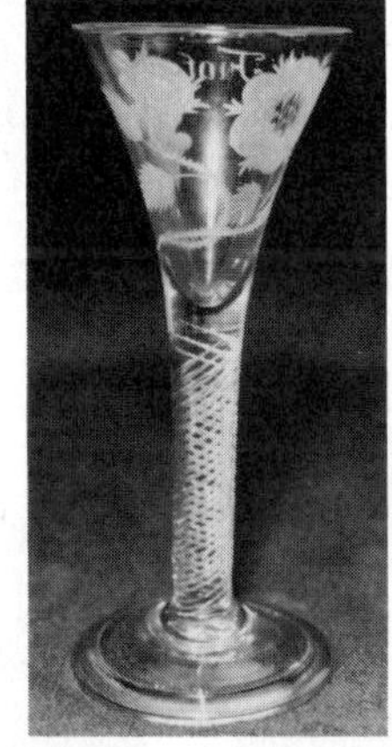

A Jacobite wine glass, the trumpet bowl engraved with Jacobite rose, 2 buds and 'Fiat', drawn multiple spiral air-twist stem, on folded conical foot, c1750, 7in (17cm).
$2,700-3,300

A Lynn wine glass, with 3 horizontal ribbed rings to bowl, double series opaque twist stem and plain conical foot, c1760, 5½in (14cm).
$1,200-1,500

A wine glass, with engraved and polished ogee bowl, stem with an entwined opaque laminated corkscrew core including 2 translucent blue threads, on a conical foot, c1765, 6in (15cm).
$1,500-2,250

Two wine glasses, with round funnel bowls, double series opaque twist stems, plain conical feet, c1760, 6½in (16cm).
$375-450

A 'Privateer' wine glass, the funnel bowl inscribed 'Prosperity to the London', in a ribbon above a spray of fruiting vine, the reverse with an insect, on spiral air-twist cable stem and conical foot, 6in (15cm).
$2,700-3,300
The London, a galley of 170 tons, 18 guns and 60 men, was declared on 16th December 1742 with John Mitchell as the commander and John Noble as sole owner.

A set of 9 wine glasses, with ovoid bowls and stems with double series opaque twists, on plain conical feet, c1760, 6½in (16cm).
$3,000-4,500

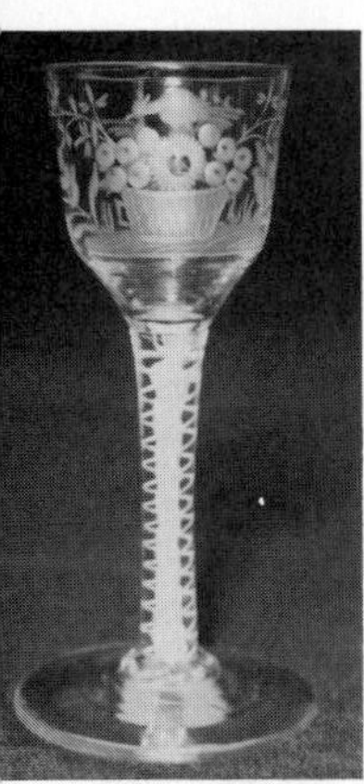

A wine glass, the ogee bowl engraved with a basket of flowers and 2 birds in flight, on a stem with a double series opaque twist and plain conical foot, c1760, 6in (15cm).
$750-900

A wine glass, with an ogee bowl, the stem with an opaque gauze corkscrew core entwined by 2 translucent dark red spiral threads, on a conical foot, c1765, 6in (15cm).
$2,700-3,300

A Beilby opaque twist wine glass, with bell bowl enamelled in white with a border of fruiting vine beneath a gilt rim, the stem with a gauze corkscrew core entwined by 2 spiral threads, on a conical foot, c1770, 7in (17cm).
$1,800-2,700

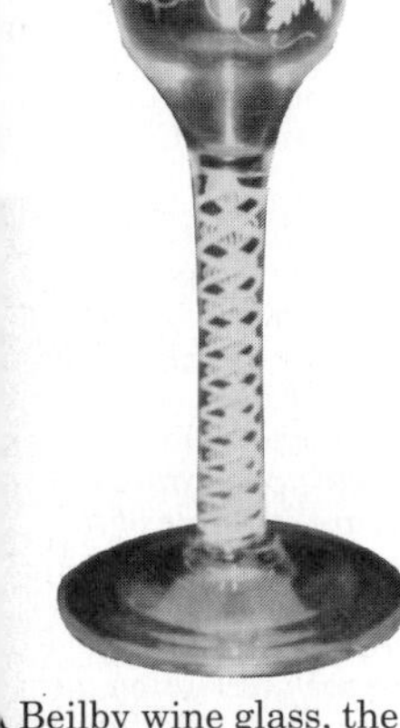

Beilby wine glass, the gilt immed ogee bowl with opaque vhite band of fruiting vine, on a tem with double series opaque wist and plain conical foot, 1775, 6in (15cm).
3,000-3,750

A wine glass, the wide round funnel bowl engraved with fruiting vine, on a double series opaque twist stem and plain conical foot, c1760, 5½in (14cm).
$450-600

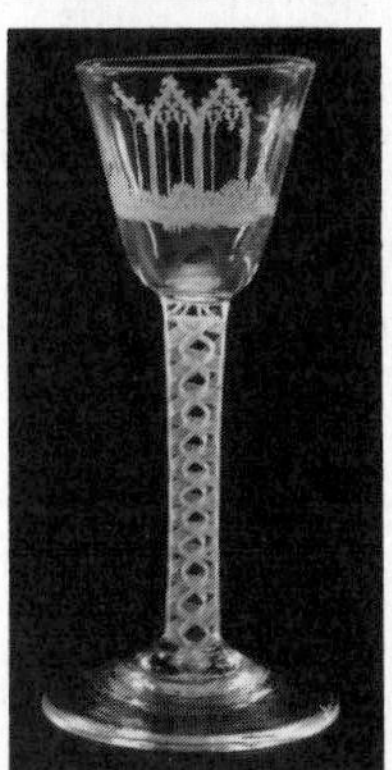

A Beilby enamelled 'Gothick' wine glass, the funnel bowl painted in opaque white enamel with a ruined Gothic cloister flanked by 3 cypresses and a tree, on a double series opaque twist stem and conical foot, 6in (15cm).
$10,500-12,000

This would appear to be the only known example of a Beilby wine glass in the Gothick style.

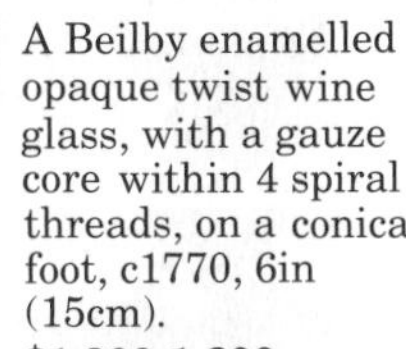

A Beilby enamelled opaque twist wine glass, with a gauze core within 4 spiral threads, on a conical foot, c1770, 6in (15cm).
$1,200-1,800

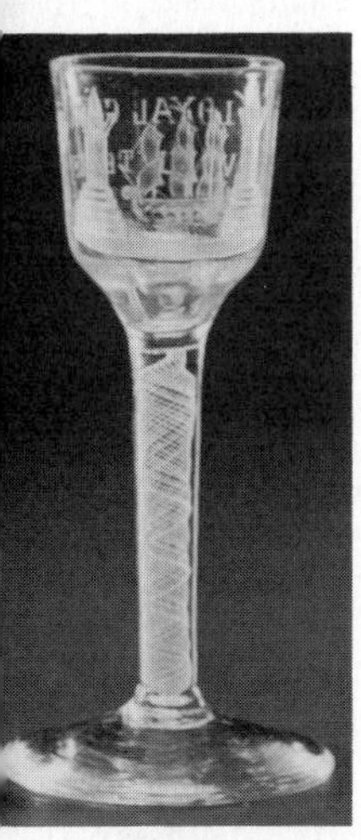

An Irish Volunteer opaque twist vine glass, the ogee bowl ngraved with the Arms of Cork, he reverse inscribed 'Loyal Cork Volunteers' flanked by leaf prays, set on an opaque twist auze stem and conical foot, 1800, 6in (15cm).
2,700-3,300

The Loyal Cork Volunteers were a eomanry corps formed in 1796.

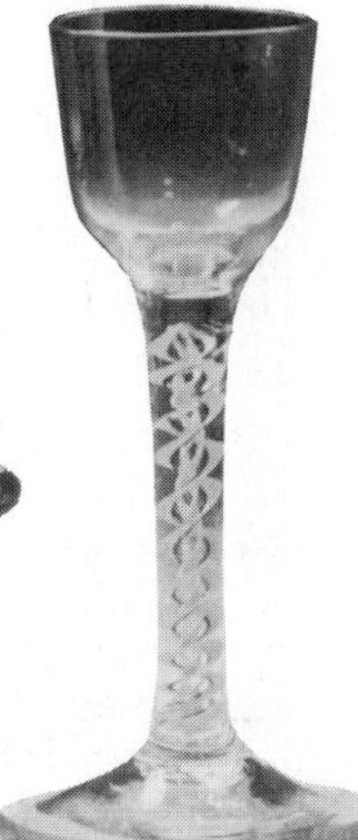

A wine glass, with ogee bowl, stem with twisted opaque ribbon core within 2 corkscrew spirals with translucent red inner edges, on a conical foot, c1765, 6in (15cm).
$1,800-2,700

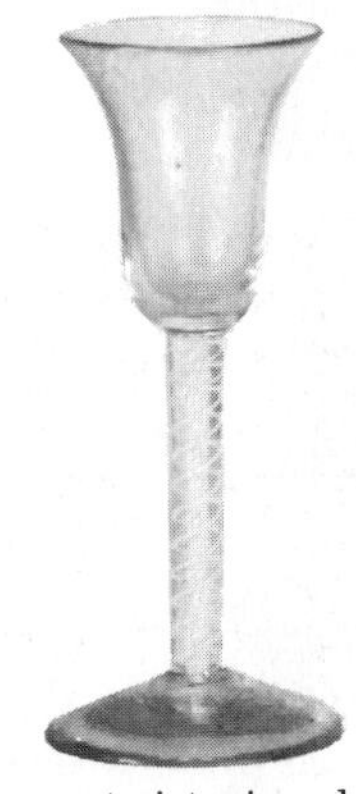

An opaque twist wine glass, with a bell-shaped bowl, the stem with a spiral gauze and 2 thread twist, 6in (15cm). **$180-225**

Two wine glasses, with trumpet bowls and drawn plain stems containing mercury corkscrew air-twists, on plain conical feet, c1750, 6 and 7in (15 and 18cm).
$450-600 each

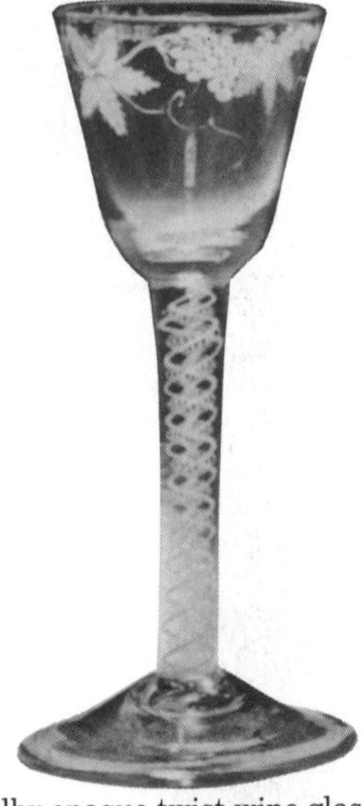

A Beilby opaque twist wine glass, the funnel bowl enamelled in white, the rim with traces of gilding, the stem with a gauze corkscrew core within 2 spiral threads, on a conical foot, c1770, 6in (15cm).
$1,200-1,500

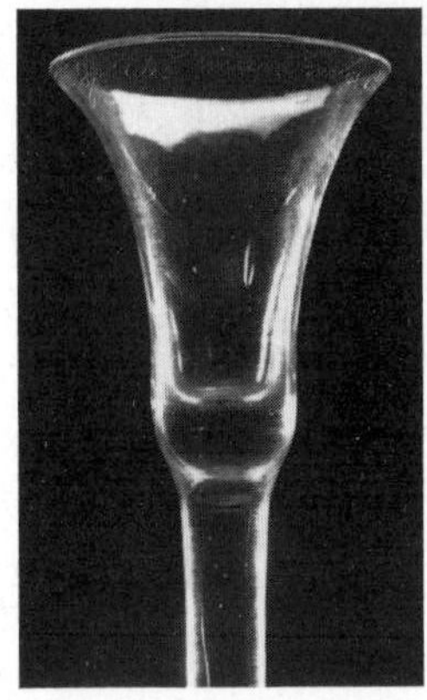

A disguised Jacobite wine glass, the bell-shaped bowl inscribed in diamond point around the rim 'God blefs Prince Charles, & down with the Rump', set on a plain stem and conical foot, the foot inscribed 'P.C.' and later engraved with initials 'RB' and 'P. Charles,' c1745, 6½in (16cm).
$5,250-7,500
Whilst other glasses simply engraved in diamond point with Jacobite sentiments are known to exist - together with the group of Amen glasses which are more elaborate in their appearance - this item is a rare example of its type. The inscription is a known Jacobite sentiment and has been used elsewhere. It has been suggested that the inscription on the foot may be a later addition. The lightness of the engraving on the rim of the bowl suggests that it was intended to be disguised.

A composite stemmed wine glass, with trumpet bowl and stem with multiple spiral air-twist section above a plain section with inverted baluster air beaded knop, c1745, 7in (17cm).
$1,050-1,350

A baluster wine glass, supported on a collar above a wide angular knop and swelling knop enclosing a tear, on a folded conical foot, c1710, 5½in (13.5cm).
$750-900

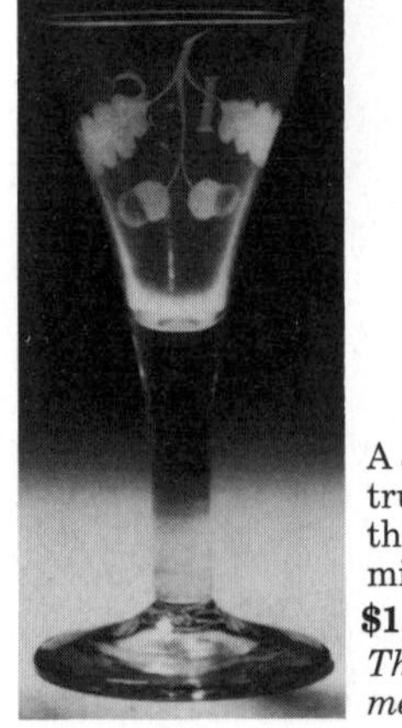

A composite stemmed wine glass, the stem filled with air-twist spirals set into an inverted baluster knop, above a domed foot, c1750, 6in (15cm).
$450-600

A Jacobite wine glass of drawn trumpet shape, the reverse with the initials 'I.S', on a conical foot, mid-18thC, 6½in (16.5cm).
$1,050-1,350
The initials are regarded as a memorial to James Stuart.

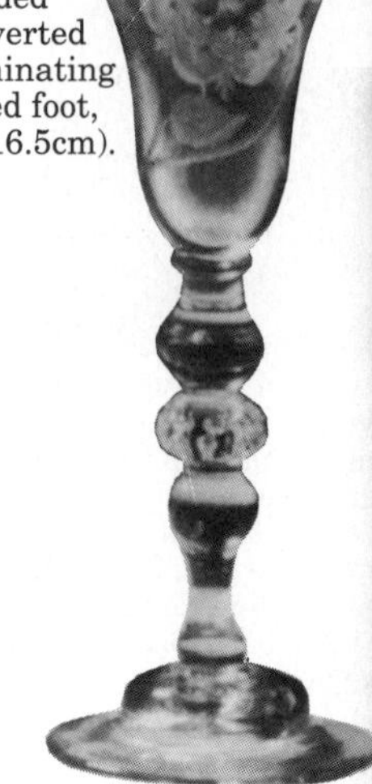

A Jacobite light baluster wine glass, the stem with a beaded knop between true and inverted baluster sections and terminating in a basal knop, on a domed foot, slight chips, c1745, 6½in (16.5cm).
$750-900

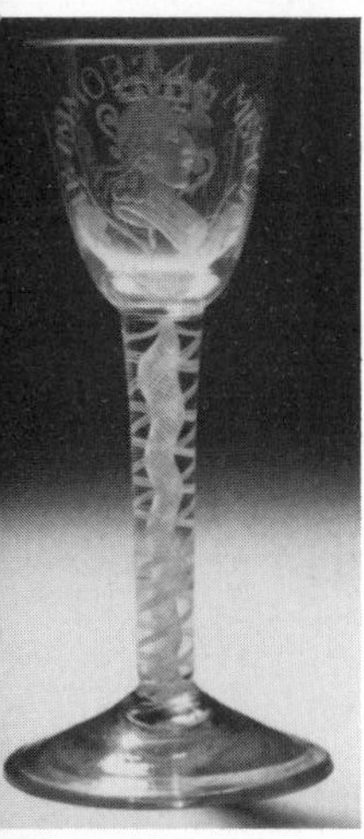

A baluster wine glass, the bell bowl supported on a 7-ringed annulated knopped stem, in graduated sizes terminating in a basal knop, on a folded conical foot, c1715, 6in (15cm).
$2,700-3,300

A Jacobite wine glass, the trumpet bowl engraved with Jacobite rose, 2 buds and star, c1750, 6½in (16cm).
$1,800-2,700

Williamite portrait opaque vist wine glass, the funnel bowl ngraved with a portrait of 'illiam III in profile to the right ithin the inscription 'The nmortal Memory', the reverse ith a crowned Irish harp flanked y fruiting vine, on a double eries stem and conical foot, hipped, late 18thC, 6in (15cm).
4,500-6,000

A baluster wine glass, with cushion knop above a beaded knop, flattened knop and drop knop terminating in a basal knop, on a domed foot, c1720, 6½in (16.5cm). **$750-900**

A baluster wine glass, the bell bowl supported on a triple annulated knop above an inverted baluster section and basal knop, on a folded conical foot, c1720, 6in (16cm).
$600-750

A baluster wine glass of 'kit kat' type, trumpet bowl, with solid shank and air tear, inverted baluster and ball knops, on plain domed foot, c1720, 7in (17cm).
$1,050-1,350

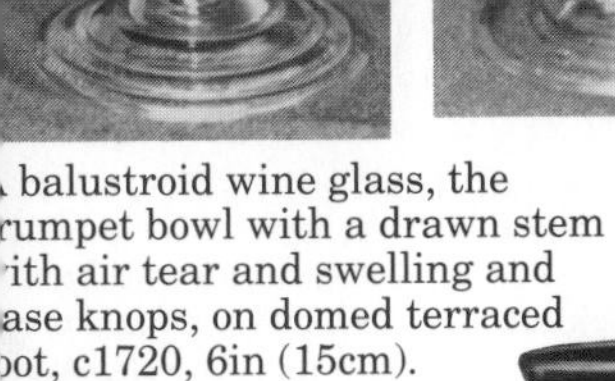

balustroid wine glass, the rumpet bowl with a drawn stem ith air tear and swelling and ase knops, on domed terraced oot, c1720, 6in (15cm).
600-750

A pair of wine glasses, with trumpet bowls, engraved with fruiting vine, on plain drawn stems with plain conical feet, c1750, 7in (17cm).
$750-900

A pedestal stemmed wine glass, supported on an octagonally moulded tapering stem enclosing an elongated tear, above a folded conical foot, c1730, 6in (15cm).
$450-600

A baluster wine glass, the bell bowl on a stem with inverted baluster and base knops with air tears, on folded conical foot, c1720, 6½in (16cm).
$750-900

A baluster wine glass, the stem with a slender plain section terminating in a spreading knop above a cushion knop, on a folded conical foot, c1720, 7in (18cm).
$750-900

A baluster 'kit kat' type wine glass, the trumpet bowl on a long drawn section with air tear, inverted baluster knop, on folded conical foot, c1740, 7in (17cm).
$900-1,500

A Williamite wine glass, the trumpet bowl finely engraved with King William and ribbon tribute above 'To the Glorious Memory of King William', with diaper type engraved border round rim, on a cylinder knop stem and ball knop, on folded conical foot, c1710, 6in (15cm).
$3,000-4,500

A baluster wine glass, with a bel bowl, the stem with a triple annulated knop above a plain section and enclosing a tear, terminating in a basal knop, above a folded conical foot, c172 6½in (16cm).
$450-600

A baluster wine glass, the bell bowl with air tear in base, on a stem with an annulated shoulder knop and folded domed foot, c1720, 6in (15cm).
$600-750

Two balustroid wine glasses, with trumpet bowls, drawn stems with air tears and ball knops and plain domed feet, 7 and 7½in (17 and 18cm).
$750-900 each

A balustroid wine glass, the trumpet bowl engraved with a band of fruiting vine, inverted baluster and base knop stem, on plain domed foot, c1740, 7in (17cm).
$900-1,500

A balustroid wine glass, the be bowl with air tear in base, on a stem with annulated and base knop with central air tear, on folded conical foot, c1725, 6in (15cm).
$1,050-1,350

A heavy baluster wine glass, the conical bowl with solid section and air tear, on a stem with collar and large ball knop with air tear, small base knop, on domed folded foot, c1710, 6in (15cm).
$1,500-2,250

An engraved opaque twist wine glass, the quadruple knopped stem with a gauze core within 2 ribbon spirals, on a conical foot, c1765, 7in (17cm).
$1,200-1,800

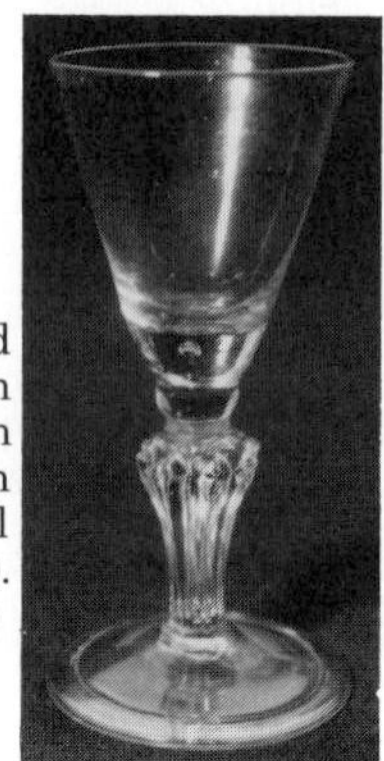

A wine glass, the pointed round funnel bowl with solid base section, on an 8-sided moulded Silesian stem and folded conical foot, c1740, 5½in (14cm).
$450-600

A wine glass, with deceptive bowl engraved with fruiting vine, on a drawn stem with diamond facet cutting and swelling centre knop, heavy disc firing foot, c1770, 5½in (14cm).
$1,050-1,350

A Dutch engraved wine glass, by Jacob Sang, Amsterdam, engraved with a 3 masted ship, the reverse inscribed 'Het Land's Welvaaren', set on a beaded inverted baluster flanked by an angular knop and a basal knop, conical foot, the pontil engraved in diamond point J: Sang Fec: 1762, 7½in (18cm).
$15,000-18,000

A pair of Dutch engraved wine glasses, each with funnel bowl inscribed 'De Negotie' and 'De Zee-haart' within a scroll cartouche, supported on a knopped baluster stem, and conical feet, 7in (17cm).
$2,700-3,300

A set of 4 facet stem wine glasses, with round funnel slice cut everted rim bowls, on hexagon facet, centre knop, cut stems and scalloped feet, c1780, 6in (15cm).
$2,700-3,300

A pedestal stem wine glass, the thistle bowl engraved with a band of foliate decoration, with solid base on a 4-sided pedestal stem, on folded conical foot, c1725, 6½in (16cm).
$1,200-1,500

MISCELLANEOUS DRINKING GLASSES

A pair of cordial glasses, the ovoid bowls with a band of hatched decoration, hexagon facet cut stems and plain conical feet, c1770, 5in (12.5cm).
$750-900

Three gin glasses, with trumpet bowls, knopped balustroid stems and folded conical feet, c1725.
l. and r. **$180-225 each**
c. **$900-1,500**

A Davenport port glass, with flared bucket bowl, rim etched leaf and ovolo band within line borders and hatching, set on a graduated triple knopped stem and solid domed foot, c1810, 4in (11cm).
$3,000-3,750

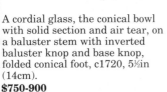

A Jacobite dram glass, engraved with a 6-petalled rose, a bud and a half opened bud, the reverse with the motto 'Fiat' beneath a star, supported on a cushion knop enclosing a tear above a thick terraced foot, c1745, 4in (9.5cm).
$2,700-3,300

A cordial glass, the conical bowl with solid section and air tear, on a baluster stem with inverted baluster knop and base knop, folded conical foot, c1720, 5½in (14cm).
$750-900

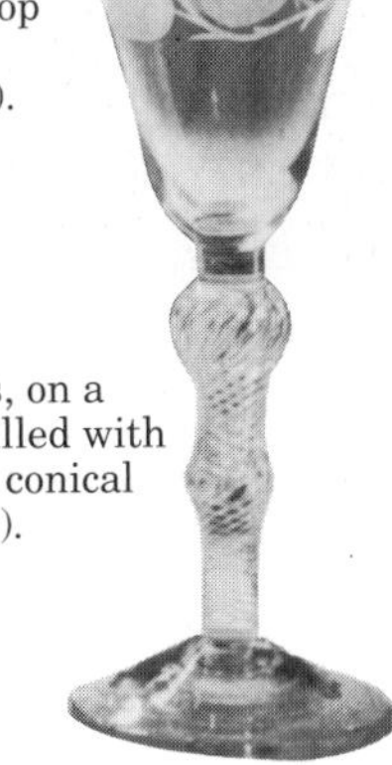

An air-twist cider glass, on a double knopped stem filled with spiral threads, above a conical foot, c1750, 7½in (18cm).
$2,700-3,300

Jars

A pair of George III glass urn shaped jars and covers, cut with diamond and spiral bands, 12in (31cm).
$750-900

A pair of cut glass jars and covers, possibly Irish, cut with bands of diamonds and flutes, set on a collared faceted stem, with square pedestal foot, star cut base, the domed cover similarly cut, c1800, 13½in (34cm).
$2,700-3,300

A garniture of 3 cut bonbonnière, comprising a cut bowl and cover with mushroom finial, the everted rim decorated with fans and diamonds above a globular bowl, knopped stem and square cut base 12in (31cm) and 2 smaller bowls and domed covers, damaged. **$600-750**

Jugs

An ovoid bodied water jug, the body with flute cut base and band of diamonds, notched rim and cut strap handle, c1810, 8in (20cm).
$750-900

A clear glass cream jug and sugar basin, with translucent blue rims, c1800, 4 and 3in (9.5 and 7.5cm).
$900-1,500

An Irish water jug, the body with panels of cut raised diamonds, flute and prism cutting, deep scalloped rim, cut strap handle, c1810, 7in (18cm).
$1,050-1,350

A water jug, the body with leaf and fan cut decoration, bridge flute cut above and below, prism cut neck, notched rim, plain strap handle, c1825, 7½in (19cm).
$750-900

A coin tankard, the waisted body with trailed neck and base gadrooning, plain conical foot, applied loop handle, silver coin in base, c1780, 5¼in (13.5cm).
$1,050-1,350

An ale or beer jug, the baluster body engraved with hops and barley and 'R.I.T', applied foot ring and plain handle, c1780, 7in (17cm).
$1,050-1,350

A water jug, the body cut overall with small diamonds, flutes and prisms, notched cut rim, applied strap handle, star cut foot, c1830, 6½in (16cm). **$750-900**

A jug and glass set, engraved with leaf design, by Osler of Birmingham, c1860, 5in (13cm).
$300-375

A pair of claret jugs, with flute cut ovoid bodies, 3 annulated half neck rings and strap handles, c1840, 9½in (24cm).
$750-900

A cut glass jug, c1830, 13in (33cm).
$1,050-1,350

A glass jug, engraved with a classical design, c1860, 11in (28cm).
$225-255

A glass jug, with vine engraving, c1860, 10in (25cm).
$375-525

A glass claret jug, c1880, 13½in (34cm).
$375-450

A glass claret jug and stopper, with engraved crest, c1880, 18in (46cm).
$1,500-2,250

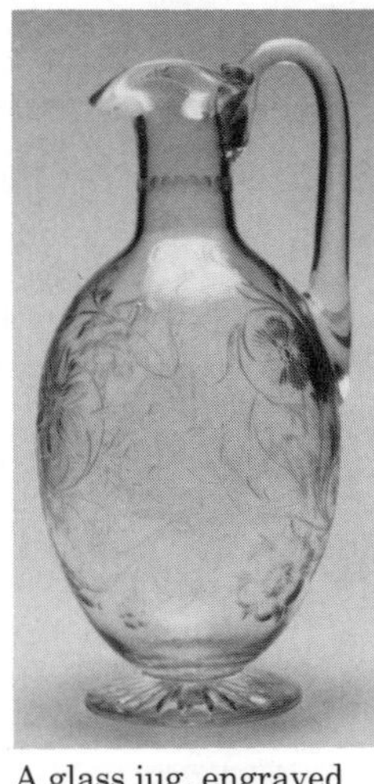

A glass jug, engraved with flower design, c1880, 10½in (27cm).
$750-900

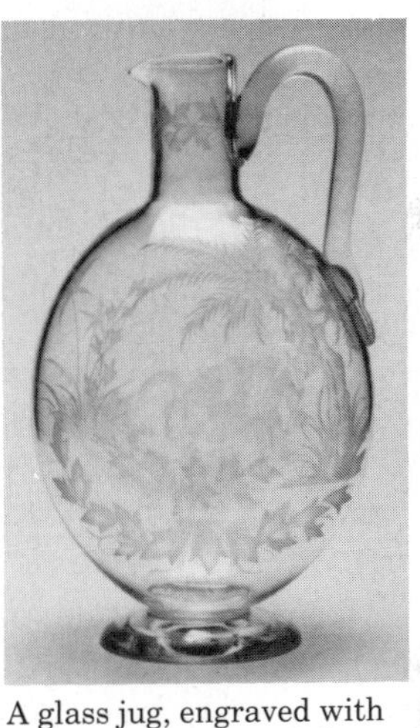

A glass jug, engraved with a swan and cygnet, 9½in (24cm).
$900-1,500

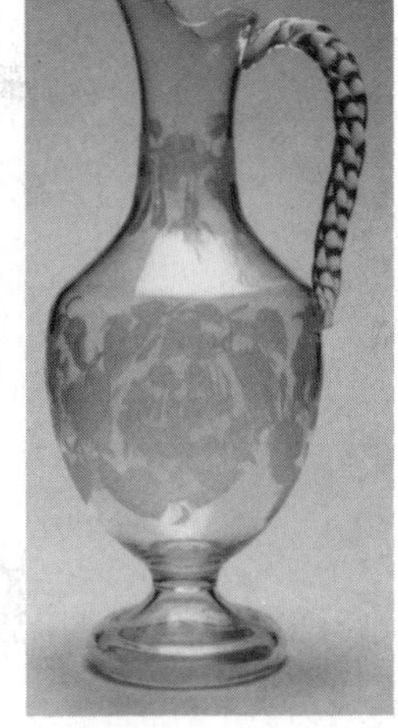

A glass jug, acid etched with fuchsia, c1870, 12in (31cm).
$375-450

Miller's is a price GUIDE not a price LIST

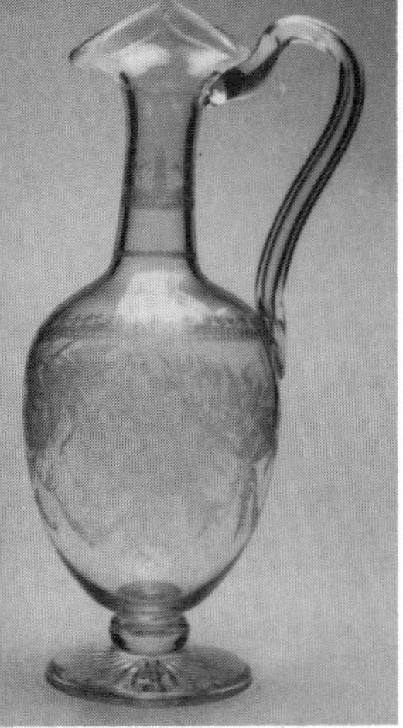

A glass jug, engraved with foliage, c1870, 11½in (29cm).
$1,200-1,500

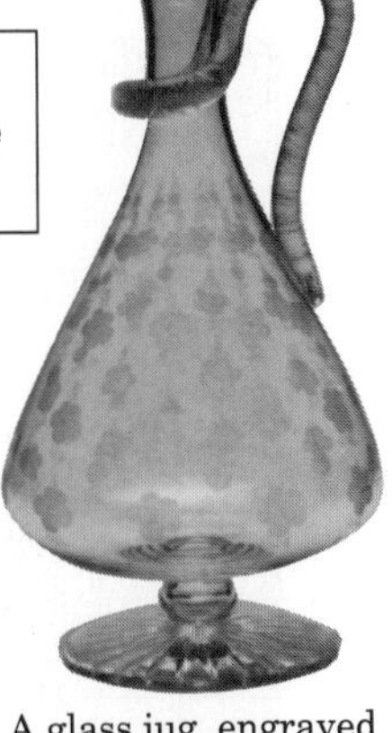

A glass jug, engraved with flowers, c1880, 10in (25cm).
$450-600

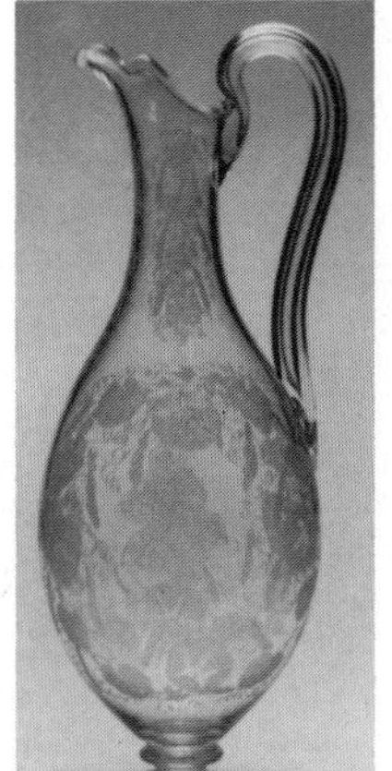

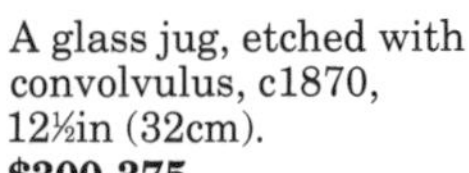

A glass jug, etched with convolvulus, c1870, 12½in (32cm).
$300-375

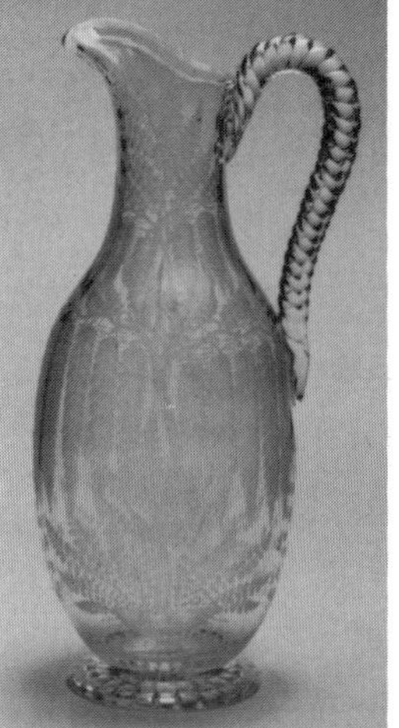

A glass jug, engraved with decorative tree, c1870, 10½in (27cm).
$450-600

A Stourbridge jug and 2 stem glasses, finely engraved in the manner of Joseph Keller, the jug with faintly ribbed neck and star cut base, jug 11½in (29cm), glasses 6½in (16cm).
$2,700-3,300

A glass jug, with green stripe decoration and silver rim, c1900.
$450-600

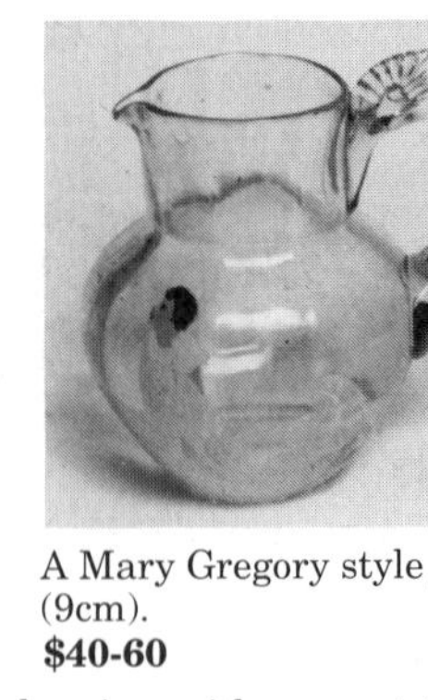

A Mary Gregory style jug, 3½in (9cm).
$40-60

Scent Bottles

A cameo ruby ground scent bottle, overlaid in white and carved with a trailing prunus branch, with silver mount to the neck and hinged silver cover, probably Stevens and Williams, 3½in (9cm).
$375-525

A George IV Coronation scent flask and stopper, Apsley Pellatt, inset with a central sulphide medallion of George IV in the guise of a Roman Emperor, the reverse with a medallion depicting the Coronation and dated July 19th 1821, the sides and base with hobnail cutting, flame stopper, 5½in (14cm).
$3,000-3,750

Services

A part Sunderland cut glass armorial service, each piece heavily cut with large diamonds, fan shapes and horizontal step cutting, star cut bases, the decanters and rinsers engraved with a lozenge cartouche enclosing a crest of a cubit arm holding in the hand a dagger upwards, comprising 26 pieces, some damage, probably Wear Flint Glass Co., c1820, damaged, 9in (23cm).
$3,000-4,500

A green glass dessert service, each piece decorated with a gilt Greek key pattern border, centred by a gilt foliate medallion, comprising 16 pieces, some damage, c1870.
$450-600

Tazzas

A tazza, with upturned rim, on moulded Silesian stem and domed folded foot, c1750, 9in (23cm) diam.
$375-525

A French 'Gorge de Pigeon' ormolu mounted tazza, c1835, 8½in (21cm) wide.
$2,700-3,300

A tazza with an everted rim, on pillar moulded basal knopped stem and domed and folded base, 16in (41cm) diam.
$1,200-1,500

. patch stand, the flat platform ith everted rim, bobbin knopped tem and folded conical foot, 1740, 2in (5cm) diam.
375-525

A façon de Venise diamond point engraved tazza, Low Countries, 17thC, 14½in (37cm) diam.
$7,500-9,000

A sweetmeat stand, with saucer platform gadroon moulded stem with 2 ball knops, folded conical foot, c1740, 3in (7.5cm).
$375-450

A tazza, with galleried rim, on a turned knop shaft and spreading circular base, 9in (23cm) diam.
$1,200-1,500

'ases

. blue tinted glass gilt and ilvered vase, with large carp on ne side, one chasing an eel, the ther with a frog leaping amongst ly pads, flanked by seaweed and owering grasses, within stylised croll borders, attributed to Jules Barbe, possibly Thomas Webb, tourbridge, c1890, 10in (25cm).
4,800-5,700

'he decoration on this vase bears strong resemblance to the work f Jules Barbe, particularly the haracteristic tooled gilding.

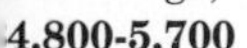

A Cranberry glass stem vase, in silver plated mount, c1910, 9in (23cm).
$135-150

Three hyacinth vases:
l. green c1820, 7in (18cm)
$150-180
c. blue, c1860, 5½in (14cm)
$135-150
r. blue, c1870, 7½in (19cm).
$105-120

. pair of engraved vases, on star ut bases, Thomas Webb and ons, Stourbridge, chipped, igned W. Fritsche, 1924, 16in 11cm).
2,250-3,000

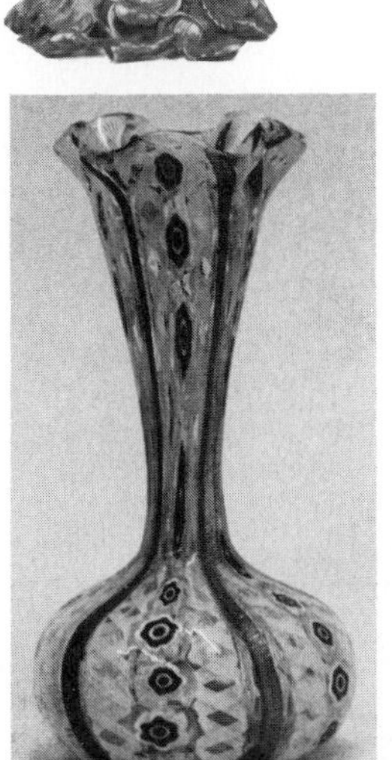

A millefiore and latticino vase, 5in (13cm). **$105-120**

A pair of Bohemian ovoid overlay glass vases, 19thC, 4½in (11cm).
$1,500-2,250

Two Italian millefiore vases, the red, white and green glass overlaid in clear, 8 and 11in (20 and 28cm).
$3,000-4,500

Miscellaneous

Two lace maker's lamps:
l. a hollow baluster stem, on conical folded foot, with drip pan and handle, c1760, 9in (23cm).
$375-525
r. incised twist stem, c1755, 3½in (9cm).
$300-375

A pair of lace maker's lamps, with globular reservoirs, knopped stems and applied loop handles, each on dished folded foot, 19thC, 5in (13cm).
$300-375

A flytrap, on 3 feet, 19thC, 6½in (16cm).
$50-75

A pair of diamond cut butter coolers, with covers and stands, the dishes 5in (13cm) diam.
$600-750

A pair of Irish George II style cut glass six-light chandeliers, drilled for electricity, minor restoration and replacement, 58in (147cm) high. **$7,500-9,000**

A cruet bottle, the body with prism and diamond cutting, stepped star cut foot and silver lid, marked London, 1830, 5½in (13.5cm).
$150-225

A pair of round glass urns, cut with diamond and lozenge shape bands, early 19thC, 5in (12cm).
$300-375

An oil lamp, with 3 wick orifices on a plain stem with folded conical foot, c1750, 6in (14.5cm).
$1,200-1,800

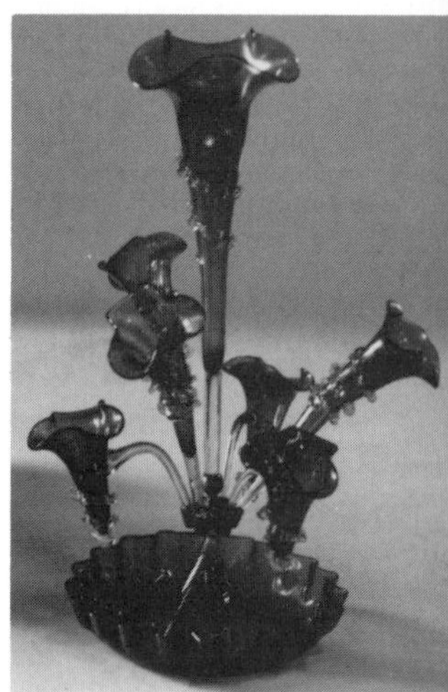

A Victorian Cranberry glass épergne, entwined with clear glass shell design, 22in (56cm).
$450-600

A set of 3 salts, the bodies with cut leaf and sliced decoration, notched rims and oval moulded scalloped lemon squeezer feet, probably Irish, c1800, 3in (8cm).
$450-600

A 'Nailsea' blue and white rolling pin, 16in (41cm).
$150-180

CLOCKS

'HE STATE OF THE MARKET

'hankfully, the clock market has survived his particular 'annus horribilis' (and the two receeding), in remarkably good health, and he time-honoured, if hackneyed, phrase 'if 's reasonable and honest, it'll fetch its price' as generally held true. Clocks offered at uction with estimates and reserves that ccurately reflected their various merits or efects, have found contented buyers. Iowever, where the market has suffered in arallel with other areas of the Fine Arts vorld, is in the lack of fine-quality clocks ffered for sale. This appears to be true of all ategories of clock except, sadly, the biquitous French gilt spelter mantel clocks - especially those with bits of decoration nissing! - and the depressingly ordinary arriage timepieces of the 1910s, in articular those with presentation nscriptions.

Comparing prices and generalising about he ups and downs of the market can be azardous and misleading, although the narket does appear to be stable. Clock ealers and retailers, especially those with menable bank managers, have still been nuch in evidence at auction and still keen to uy that special item with which to tempt lients to part with their money. The buying as perhaps been a little more discerning, elective and cautious, but the more accurate nd better-informed valuations and ataloguing have ensured that the unsold ates at auction have not increased unduly. n addition, most auction rooms can, I'm ure, claim some highlight for their year, vith an example of a piece of exceptional nerit fetching an exceptional price. Indeed, ; would be very sad for the clock world if his were not so, and if the knowledgeable nd wealthy collector chose not to disregard he general economic gloom and buy fine xamples when they became available.

:URRENT GOOD BUYS

f you are entering the market as a ommitted purist wishing to buy an example f the finest clock of whatever type you esire, I am not aware of any ways of getting 'right' clock at a bargain price. If, however, ou are seeking an attractive and functional ddition to your furnishings, examples of nost types of clock made from the 1850s nwards can be bought at a reasonable price, specially if you are prepared to make a few ompromises.

With the fairly stable prices over the past 'ear for most types of clock, a new buyer can nter the fray reasonably assured that their inancial commitment will not prove a isaster and in view of the dearth of good locks, it is unlikely that the market will be looded with stock, causing a consequent lump in prices. The variety of readily available clock types is very great and to suggest good buys in all categories is almost impossible, but if 'good buys' implies a possible bargain with investment potential, I would make the following few suggestions.

SIGNATURES

Most clocks are signed by the clockmaker. The signature can help to date a clock, but does not guarantee that a clock was made in the stated period, or by the man whose name it bears. During the 19thC, it was common for the clock to be signed by the retailer rather than the maker. The position of the signature varies with the type of clock, but usually appears on the dial and/or backplate.

- Cases were made separately, and are almost never signed.
- Occasionally, a fake signature has been added, usually to a clock that was not signed by its maker. One way to detect this is to feel the engraving; old engraving feels smooth, whereas new work can feel sharp.

Bracket/table clocks

If you desire a bracket or table clock and don't mind an ebonized case rather than a walnut or fruitwood one, the prices for such clocks from the first quarter of the 18thC are, in my opinion, very reasonable. As long as the component parts are original, a very acceptable example of the English clockmaker's art can be bought for well under $15,000 and reasonable, unsigned examples can be found for $4,500-6,000.

If you have a large Gothic-style house, for around $1,500-2,250 you could buy a late Victorian bracket clock with a fine-quality

A Victorian ebonised chiming bracket clock, the 5 pillar triple chain fusee movement with anchor escapement chiming on 8 bells, with hour strike on gong, securing brackets to case, 28½in (72.5cm).
$1,800-2,700

triple train fusee movement. Cases are usually of carved oak, well-figured walnut or beautifully inlaid mahogany, or they can be ebonized; the clocks are invariably of good quality and exhibit fine workmanship, but may be too large for many buyers' tastes and accordingly are reasonably priced. A similarly cased example with a less highly regarded German movement will be well under $1,500. These clocks are not rare and so selective buying could be rewarding.

The mahogany and rosewood cased bracket clocks of the 1820s, unless they have the high quality of the McCabe's or a similar specialist maker, are again readily affordable at under $1,500. They are usually found in honest original condition, perhaps because in this price range they may be deemed not worth tinkering with.

Carriage clocks

Many homes house a carriage clock and most of these are of the basic timepiece or half-hour strike type in a plain gilt brass case with a French movement. Unless the case is of special merit in some way, the value of these clocks is unlikely to increase; they were made in huge numbers by many manufacturers over a long period and should be bought for functional or decorative purposes only. For investment potential, it is hard to beat the earliest French or English examples of the 1830s, although their quality has been acknowledged for a long time and good bargains of this type are very rare. Porcelain panels, polychrome enamel decoration, carving and elaborate mouldings all raise value enormously but be wary of damage to the decorative cases because it is often far easier and cheaper to repair the movement than to restore chipped porcelain or enamel.

Garnitures

Among the most affordable types of clock, the typical late 19thC French garniture appears in myriad styles and in various materials.

A Napoleon III ormolu and porcelain mounted striking mantel clock garniture, with milestone shaped clock case, Roman dial painted with classical figures, the centre painted with putti, the going barrel movement with anchor escapement and strike on bell, the painted porcelain urns on foliate cast ormolu bases, 13in (33cm).

$1,200-1,800

Gilt spelter examples can be bought for well under $750, the movements are always of the standard bell-striking drum type and the value lies purely in their decorative appeal. They are readily available, but are not very practical, as spelter is easily damaged, but if you want a good show for the money, these clock sets are the ones to go for.

Lantern clocks

Lantern clocks have suffered more alterations, modifications and 'improvements' than most other types of clock. An apparently late 17thC example can be bought for $1,500-3,000, but these very basic timepieces are seldom in original condition and should be given the closest scrutiny before purchase, especially if they are intended as an investment.

Longcase clocks

The appeal of the mellow sound of a handsome longcase clock is still strong and, with few exceptions, these clocks prove reliable sellers at auction. The range of styles and prices is wide, but there are still bargains to be found. The large Edwardian longcases with wonderful quality gong-striking movements in equally fine mahogany cases are still in the $3,500-5,500 range, but they are generally over 8 feet tall and therefore have limited appeal. At the other end of the scale, and if you don't mind winding your clock every day, a country oak 'cottage' 30-hour longcase can be bought for under $1,500. These generally have a fairly crude case and movement but have great character and some have an attractively decorated brass or painted dial.

Most of the longcase clocks on the market are furnishing clocks - bought for their visual appeal and compatibility of style and period with the house. Like lantern clocks, they are liable to have been tampered with: 'modernised' in style, cut down to remove case rot or to reduce the height or, most common of all, to have had the original movement replaced. This is generally not done to deceive but to return a useful piece of furniture to active service. If you are in the market for a totally original London-made longcase, then the price will be high and likely to remain so; if it's an attractive piece of decorative furniture that also tells the time, look around and you are bound to find a characterful addition to your household at a very reasonable price.

Mantel clocks

The mantel clock is second in popularity to the carriage clock, and as most European countries have produced them in large numbers since the mid-19th century, the choice is wide. In France from 1780 to 1880 they appeared in large numbers in a wide range of highly decorative cases with figural decoration. As a rule, those of the 1830s-50s are a little more subtle and of better quality and, as with the garnitures, the movements are of a fairly standard type and not therefore of great importance. The abundance of these clocks dictates a modest price, with ormolu examples readily vailable at $750-1,500, but quality and ondition do vary, so bide your time and shop round. Clock buyers can also be patriotic in heir buying and a very imposing American our-glass clock of c1900 can be bought in the JK for about half the price of its French ounterpart.

porcelain mounted ormolu mantel clock, Vincenti ell striking movement No. 6190, with blue orcelain dial centred with an armorial crest, the laborate case inset with 2 similarly decorated orcelain plaques and enclosed by 6 pillars with orcelain finials and female term plinths forming e feet, French, c1860, 12½in (31.5cm).
1,800-2,700

Wall clocks

Wall clocks can sometimes be bought nexpensively. The plain mahogany dial lock of the late 18thC, with a pretty, signed ilvered dial and original verge escapement ow fetches upwards of $2,250, but there are many slightly later examples with anchor scapements that are still priced at a few undred dollars. Cream painted dials and arger diameter clocks (15in plus) are enerally less expensive. The most bundant wall clock is the 'Vienna' type, made initially in the 1820s in Vienna but

An English mahogany dial clock, with fusee movement and Roman enamel dial, signed Jump, London.
375-450

atterly in Germany. The early examples with crisp white enamel dials had precision nd movements of long duration and can easily fetch $4,500 plus. The type made in large numbers by Gustav Becker (and others) later in the century can be bought for as little as $450. The movements are good, if not special, and the cases can be of excellent quality and detail and may feature a wide range of coloured woods, giving a large choice. The later spring-driven examples are very poor successors to the earlier weight-driven clocks and should be avoided, although they are very inexpensive.

Skeleton clocks

Skeleton clocks are very much an acquired taste, and some very good Victorian examples languish in the $300-600 range. The more elaborate types of the 1860s and 70s, signed by the likes of Condliff of Liverpool, and with superbly crafted movements and cathedral-style frames, seldom fetch less than $3,000. If you buy a skeleton clock with a broken or missing dome, remember that a suitable replacement might cost as much as the clock itself, but the exposed movement really will need protection from dust. There are some rather unconvincing modern skeleton clocks available, but the thin gauge and poorly finished brass work are usually obvious giveaways.

FAKES AND FORGERIES

Thankfully, the clock market is not bedevilled by fakes and forgeries to any great degree but a substantial purchase must be made with caution and guidance. The obvious trick of 'signing' movements or dials with the name of a famous clock maker has and does occur but it is rare - and it must be remembered that from the 1830s, many clocks, both bracket and longcase, bore the name of the retailer or workshop that assembled or finished off the clock but did not make the movement.

Most of the important and sought-after clockmakers had some individually distinctive method of construction or style of decoration by which their clocks can be identified. In many cases the workshop records of these makers are available and some of the makers assigned number or letter sequences to their productions, making detective work straightforward.

Complete fakes - recently made clocks deliberately purporting to be antique clocks - are virtually unheard of: a clock's construction is so complex that it would be near-impossible - and certainly not financially viable - to try to reproduce convincingly. But, as always, there are exceptions. Brass lantern clocks with chapter ring signatures of late 17thC style were produced at the turn of this century, but the metalwork is generally cruder than on the originals. The 'marrying' of one movement to another case, is widespread, especially in longcase clocks, but is not usually done to deceive. With a basic feel for what 'looks right' and with some knowledge of how various casemakers made their cases, any alteration to the mounting blocks to accept a replacement movement is fairly evident.

TRANSPORTING A CLOCK

The spring from which the pendulum is suspended is fragile, and may break when the clock is moved. Spring-driven clocks with a short pendulum, such as English bracket clocks or most 19thC French clocks should be held upright when carried. When transporting a bracket clock, take out the pendulum (if detachable), or pack the back with tissue paper. When transporting a longcase clock, remove the weights and pendulum. The hood should be taken off, and the dial and movement packed separately.

WOODS

Buyers tend to choose the wood that best blends with their other furniture; however, if they were more readily available, walnut bracket and longcase clocks would be the most sought-after for the richness of the wood's grain and its sumptuous colour. It's mahogany, of course, that we see most of but the varying types of mahogany veneers in use from the mid-18thC display a rich variation of colour and figuring. Oak has its country followers and was generally used for the cheaper clocks. Satinwood is very rare in comparison and was used for a short period for veneers in the late 18thC and early 19thC and later for decorative inlay work. Satinwood clock and barometer cases are very desirable and accordingly expensive.

Rosewood cases, sometimes with brass inlay, do not fare as well as I think they ought to, possibly because they are associated with the 1820-40 period when clock styles were rather uninspiring, but a good grained well-polished rosewood case can look marvellous: perhaps these clocks will have their day soon. Generally the least popular cases are those with ebony veneers.

REPAIRS AND RESTORATION

This is a problem area for the clock market because of the cost involved and the continuing debate over what is an acceptable degree of renewal/replacement. There are no short cuts to getting a good job done and, especially with an early and potentially good clock, the bill for repairs involving the making up of parts, can be large. All clock afficionados will agree that lasting damage can be done by a cheap, botched job. If you can't, or won't, afford the necessary repairs, don't buy the clock in the first place. Always ask for a detailed report from the workshop as to why the clock is misbehaving or not running and what their remedy and charges might be.

Few repair jobs on clock movements are straightforward and unforeseen problems do arise so try to be a little understanding when the final bill arrives. Most clock workshops survive on personal recommendation and reputable dealers who do not have their own workshop will usually have some they have been using happily for years.

The restoration of clock cases can lead to nearly as many problems, and may be just as expensive, but the client should dictate the degree of 'finish' that is wanted, bearing in mind the rest of the furniture. It is far wiser to go to a workshop with a definite idea of what you envisage, than to leave it in their hands and be disappointed by the job and horrified by the price.

The problem of over-restoration and the extent to which replaced parts are acceptable, confront Vetting Committees at all the major Antiques Fairs and the breadth of disagreement even among acknowledged experts is considerable. The old maxim of buying the best item that you can afford from a reputable source makes a lot of sense in the clock market. Very few 18thC clocks will have survived in working order without refurbishment, and their cases will have suffered damage from heat and humidity, so the skill is to buy the most sympathetically restored clock.

HINTS AND TIPS

• You can certainly buy advantageously at auction but the motto 'caveat emptor' is particularly relevant to the clock buyer.
• The potential cost of necessary repair and restoration must never be overlooked and unless you are buying a late 19thC clock, parts may well have to be made up.
• Don't assume that the difference in price between the immaculate bracket clock in the local antique shop and the 'bargain' bracket clock you buy at auction will be enough to restore yours to showroom condition.
• If you are considering an expensive early clock it is well worth buying the services of a reputable dealer for a few hours to view the clock with you.
• The major auction rooms have some highly knowledgeable staff who will be able to point out problem areas and there is always the opportunity of returning the clock if it is not as was catalogued. However, they obviously cannot guarantee that all the clocks on offer are 'goers'.
• Unless you are a skilled craftsman with specialist tools available, steer clear of undertaking mechanical work, but by all means do some gentle case polishing. Treat dials and chapter rings very gently and leave the oiling of the movement for the clock's occasional service, as too much oil will stop the movement rather than keep it out of the workshop.
• Buy a clock that you'll enjoy looking at and listening to and tread especially carefully if you are buying with short to medium term investment in mind.

James Lowe
May 1993

CLOCKS
Bracket Clocks

\n ebonised fruitwood bracket lock, the 8-day twin fusee novement with foliate engraved ackplate, the arched brass dial vith silvered chapter and strike ilent rings, moon phase and date pertures, matted centre and ierced foliate spandrels, signed Vill'm Allan, London, late 18thC, 8½in (47cm) high.
$3,000-3,750

\ Victorian English walnut eneer chiming bracket clock, the vhite painted dial signed F.Dent, 31 Strand, London, triple fusee, signed anchor movement chiming on 8 bells with hour gong, 31in 79cm).
$2,700-3,300

A George III ebonised striking bracket clock, the silvered engraved dial signed George Allan London, within the Roman and Arabic chapter ring, the 5 pillar twin chain fusee movement with anchor escapement and strike/trip repeat on bell, foliate engraved backplate, similarly engraved securing brackets to case, 18½in (47cm) high.
$1,800-2,700

A George III stained walnut cased repeating bracket clock, by Robert Atkins of London, the baluster 4 pillar movement with crown wheel escapement, striking and repeating the hours at will on a single bell, the backplate engraved with scrolling strapwork and leaves, 20in (51cm) high.
$4,800-5,700

A bracket clock, in ebonised case with gilt metal mounts and chiming action, by George Davis, Halifax, 19thC, 24in (61cm).
$600-750

A brass bound mahogany chiming bracket clock and bracket, the 7½in (19cm) enamel dial signed Ellicott London, and set on a gilt brass plate with strike/silent lever in the corner, the signed 6 pillar, 3 train fusee movement stamped A. & J. Thwaites 395 on the front plate, with later half deadbeat escapement, bell striking and quarter chiming on 8 bells, the backplate engraved, with a brass bound mahogany bracket incorporating a key drawer in the sliding front, clock 18½in (47cm), bracket 10in (25cm).
$22,500-30,000

A George III mahogany bracket clock, the silvered dial with subsidiary strike/silent regulation in the arch, the date dial inscribed Grant Fleet Street London, No. 422, the twin fusee movement with anchor escapement bell striking and pull repeat, the backplate signed and numbered within a floral and foliate engraved cartouche, 14½in (37cm).
$4,500-6,000

A George III mahogany bracket clock, with silvered arch dial, signed Willm. Dorrel, London, 17½in (44cm).
$2,700-3,300

A Victorian walnut Gothic design bracket clock, with 3 point castellated and finial surmount above cluster columns and an arcaded, carved and moulded base, the glazed arched door enclosing a silvered brass dial, signed C.F. Loof, Parade, Tunbridge Wells, the 3 train key wind fusee movement striking on 8 bells and single gong.
$4,500-6,000

A George III bracket clock, in mahogany case, the brass and silvered arched dial with an automaton farrier's shop in the arch, and signed on a silvered plaque Tinker and Edmondson, Leeds, 8-day striking double fusee movement with anchor escapement and 5 pillars and engraved backplate, c1800, possibly associated, 22½in (57cm).
$3,000-3,750

An ebonised bracket clock, the square 6½in (17cm) brass dial inscribed Jonathan Lowndes, Pall Mall, London, the double fusee movement with stop work, crown wheel escapement, striking the hours on a single bell and chiming the quarters on 2 graduated bells, 18thC, 16in (41cm).
$3,000-3,750

An ebonised mantel or bracket clock, the silvered dial with foliate scroll engraved spandrels, and inscribed Kleyser & Co. 66 High St. Southwark, London, the bell striking fusee movement with pull repeat, 19thC, 12½in (31cm).
$1,200-1,500

A rosewood bracket clock, with 5in (12.5cm) convex painted dial, signed James Marlow, Liverpool, 2 train movement striking on single bell, architectural case with quartered columns and white string inlay, glazed door to back, supported on 4 brass bun feet, 14in (36cm) high.
$750-900

A William IV walnut bracket clock, the brass dial with a subsidiary regulation dial in the arch, engraved with scrolling foliage and flowers and inscribed F. Graham, Newcastle, 8-day bel striking movement, lacking 3 brass ball feet, 13½in (34cm).
$750-1,200

A George III mahogany bracket clock, the 6¾in (17cm) dial signed Jno. Matthews Leighton, with lea spandrels and a strike/silent dial in the arch, c1800, 15½in (39cm) high.
$3,000-3,750

A George III mahogany bracket clock, with silvered dial, strike/silent ring in the arch and month dial, 8-day hour strike on a bell with lock pendulum, signed Benjamin Reed, Plymouth to the dial and brass backplate, with brass handle and ogee bracket feet, 16½in (42cm) high.
$2,250-3,000

A George III faded mahogany striking bracket clock, the 7in (18cm) dial signed on a silvered plaque, John Rycutt, London, the matted centre with false pendulum aperture and date, silvered chapter rings, foliate spandrels with strike/silent in the arch, the 5 pillar fusee movement with verge escapement with plain signed backplate, 18in (46cm).
$4,500-6,000

A Neuchatel black japanned quarter striking bracket clock and bracket, with 7in (17.5cm) enamel dial, central alarm hand, engine turned gilt bezel, square plated gong striking movement with pin wheel escapement, the strike work mounted on the backplate, pull wound alarm sounding on a bell above, the waisted case decorated with gilt flowers on a black ground,with gilt mouldings, feet and finial, conforming similarly decorated bracket, Swiss, c1790, clock 23in (58.5cm), bracket 10in (25.5cm).
$1,200-1,800

An ebonised quarter chiming English bracket clock, the 7½in (19cm) silvered dial with ogee arch, foliate engraving with subsidiary chime/not chime in the arch, the 3 train fusee movement chiming on 8 bells, separate hour bell, c1850, 19½in (49cm).
$1,500-2,250

A George III ebonised musical and automaton bracket clock, the 7in (17.5cm) dial signed Thos. Gardner, London, subsidiary dials for chime/not chime and tune selection, the similarly signed 3 train movement with later anchor escapement, bell striking and playing one of 4 tunes on 8 bells with 11 hammers, 19½in (49cm).
$10,500-12,000

A rosewood and brass inlaid English bracket clock, the painted dial set within a pierced and engraved mask and signed T. J. Wood, Barbican, London, the 5 pillar bell striking fusee movement with anchor escapement, and signed backplate, c1850, 16in (41cm).
$4,800-5,700

A bracket clock, by John Taylor, London, with 8-day double fusee striking movement, brass and ormolu decorated dial, ebonised case with moulded domed top, brass handle and finials and moulded base, 10½in (26cm) high.
$3,000-3,750

A French tortoiseshell and brass boulle bracket clock, the 9½in (24cm) cast dial with enamel cartouche numerals, the bell striking movement with outside count wheel, cast foliate pendulum bob, the Louis XV style waisted case with gold painted metal mounts and matching bracket, 35in (90cm) high.
$3,000-3,750

A French chiming boulle bracket clock and bracket, with 12-piece cartouche dial, 2 tier movement No. 862 with wing, scythe and hour glass trade mark, anchor escapement and chiming on 8 bells and a gong, the straight sided case veneered with brown shell, inlaid with brass and outlined with gilt brass mounts, conforming wall bracket, c1870, clock 24½in (62cm), bracket 12in (31cm).
$3,000-3,750

An English mahogany bracket clock, the painted convex dial signed Yonge, Strand, London, the twin fusee movement with gong striking, c1830, 15½in (39cm) high.
$1,800-2,700

An ebonised bracket or table clock, signed John Pepys, London, with striking brass movement, anchor escapement and engraved backplate, on brass ball feet, pendulum and key, 18thC, 16in (41cm) high.
$3,000-3,750

A Victorian oak chiming bracket clock, dial with silvered chapter ring, matted centre, subsidiary rings in arch for regulation, chime/silent and chime on 8 bells/Westminster chime, the triple chain fusee movement with anchor escapement and chiming on 8 bells with hour strike on gong, 24in (61cm) high.
$1,200-1,800

Did you know?

MILLER'S Antiques Price Guide builds up year by year to form the most comprehensive photo reference library available.

An inlaid and ebonised bracket clock, the white enamel dial with gilt brass engraving, flowers and scrolling foliage, the wire gong striking 8-day movement with side winding, 19thC, 16in (41cm).
$4,500-6,000

An English ebonised and brass inlaid bracket clock, signed below the chapter ring Gillett & Co., Croydon, the gong striking movement with twin fusees, with presentation inscription dated October 1892, c1890, 27½in (70cm). **$900-1,500**

A George III bracket clock, the 8-day movement with a verge escapement and an engraved backplate, bob pendulum, the brass and silver dial with subsidiary month and strike silent regulation, the lunette inscribed John Scott, London, the centre with bob aperture and calendar, gilt brass rococo corner spandrels, 15½in (39cm).
$5,250-6,000

Carriage Clocks

A French carriage clock, with white enamel dial inscribed 'Prize Medal 1851', 8-day lever movement with strike and repeat on a bell with full sweep seconds hand, the dial and movement signed Miroy Frères Btes, Paris and R. d'Angouleme du Temple, 10, No. 2724, mid-19thC, 8in (20 cm).
$900-1,500

A French brass cased carriage clock, with 8-day lever movement striking the hours on a gong with repeat and alarm, in need of some restoration, late 19thC, 7½in (19cm). **$750-900**

A gilt brass grande sonnerie striking carriage clock, with bi-metallic balance to silvered lever platform, strike/repeat/alarm on 2 gongs and with 3 position selection lever in base, the white enamel Roman dial with blued spade hands, alarm rings below, Anglaise style case with engraved dedication to top, brown leather travelling case, 6½in (16cm).
$1,800-2,700

A French porcelain mounted grande sonnerie engraved gorge carriage clock, the movement with ratchet tooth lever escapement and striking on 2 gongs in a gilt brass gorge case, engraved overall with leaves and masks, and inset with three 'Sèvres' panels, the front painted with the dial and a rural landscape within opal, gilt and gros bleu borders, each side painted with a maiden and a putto, representing Summer and Autumn within similar borders, a strike control lever in the base and a leather covered travelling case, c1870, 6in (15cm).
$1,500-2,250

A French gilt brass repeating carriage clock, the white enamel dial with gilt mask, the gong striking movement with maker's stamp, lever platform escapement, Brocot No. 330, c1870, 6½in (16cm).
$1,200-1,800

A gilt brass striking carriage clock, with bi-metallic balance to silvered lever platform, strike/repeat on gong, the backplate with stamp for Drocourt, white enamel Roman and Arabic dial with blued spade hands and retailer's signature J.W.Benson, 25 Old Bond St., London, corniche case, 6in (15cm)
$750-1,200

A French carriage clock with barometer, the 4in (10cm) annular dial with visible lever escapement and paste set bezel, gong striking movement No. 13850, with a leather covered travelling case, c1900, 9in (23cm).
$1,800-2,700

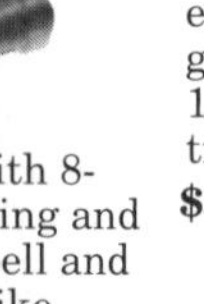

A French carriage clock with 8-day lever movement, striking and repeating the hours on a bell and with half hour passing strike, lacking the handle, not working, 19thC, 5½in (14cm).
$600-750

A gilt brass oval striking carriage clock, with stamp for Drocourt, white enamel Roman chapter disc, with pierced blued hands, signed by retailer Dent, 33 Cockspur Street, London, with original brown leather travelling case, 5½in (14cm).
$2,250-3,000

An English carriage clock, in the manner of Thomas Cole, silvered engraved dial with Roman chapter, the fusee movement with maintaining power, plain steel balance and lever escapement, signed Hunt & Roskell, 156 New Bond St., London, No. 10044, the engraved case with outset pillars on a cast foliate base on claw feet, 4½in (11cm).
$3,000-3,750

Garnitures

A French ormolu and enamel three-piece clock garniture, the dial and case enamelled with flowers in colours on a black ground, bell striking 8-day movement, the conforming side pieces each in the form of a cherub figure supporting 3 candle sconces, clock 14in (36cm), sconces 15in (38cm).
$1,500-2,250

A French gilt metal and pink and grey striated marble garniture de cheminée, the movement striking on a single bell, with gilt metal putto pendulum, flanked by a pair of two-handled urns, clock 24in (61cm), vases 17in (43cm).
$750-900

A clock garniture, in black and russet slate, the clock with seated bronze Egyptian figures representing night and day, surmounted by a bust of a pharoah, the twin obelisks with detailed motifs and ancient symbols, Myers printed to clock face, clock 17½in (44cm) obelisks 15½in (39.5cm). **$1,200-1,500**

Lantern Clocks

A brass lantern alarm clock, the 5½in (14cm) chapter ring set on a leaf and flower engraved plate, signed John Snow Ano Do 1630, the reverse also signed John Snow 1630, with central alarm disc and single hand, the posted movement with reconverted balance and verge escapement, outside count wheel and replaced alarm work mounted on the iron backplate, the frame with slender one-piece corner columns with turned feet and finials, later frets with restoration, part 17thC, 15in (38cm).
$5,250-6,000

A Continental grande sonnerie lantern clock, the 10in (25cm) dial with engraved centre, 3 train weight driven movement with verge escapement and cow tail pendulum, inside count wheel for the quarters, nag's head detent to release the double 6-hour striking train with outside count wheel, the frame with iron corner posts, turned feet and finials, the bells mounted above, frets lacking, mid-18thC, 20in (50cm) high.
$3,000-3,750

A brass lantern clock, with 7in (17.5cm) silvered chapter ring, the centre signed Wm. Goodwin, Stowmarket, single hour hand, the posted movement with anchor escapement, outside count wheel, the case with turned finials, ball feet and dolphin frets, iron hanging hoop and wall spikes, c1710, 15½in (39cm), with modern oak wall bracket.
$3,000-3,750

A brass lantern clock, the circlet dial with Roman numerals and signed R. Raymeni, Clare, the pierced cresting with interlaced adorsed dolphins and foliage, on bun feet, 13½in (34cm).
$1,050-1,350

A brass lantern clock, the circlet dial with Roman numerals, the case with pierced flowerhead cresting, the sides with engraved bands, on turned tapering feet, 14½in (37cm) high.
$1,050-1,350

Longcase Clocks

A George III mahogany and oak longcase clock, with 12in (31cm) painted dial, faded signature Barry, Lichfield, with seconds dial, calendar aperture, painted floral spandrels and arch, 4 pillar rack, striking movement, 86in (219cm).
$1,800-2,700

A Bristol longcase clock, 8-day movement, 12in (31cm) white enamel dial, rocking Father Time to arch, Roman numerals, subsidiary seconds dial, date aperture faintly signed Aquila Barber, Bristol, in an inlaid brocken arch top case, with bracket feet, 19thC, 92½in (235cm).
$3,000-3,750

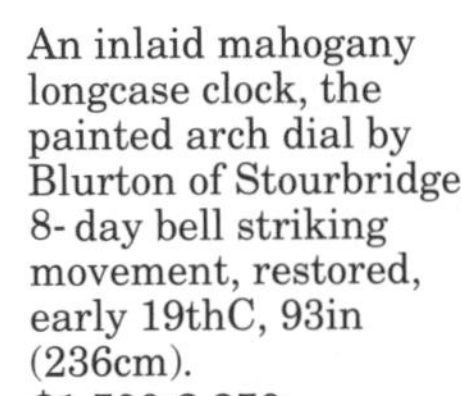

An inlaid mahogany longcase clock, the painted arch dial by Blurton of Stourbridge, 8- day bell striking movement, restored, early 19thC, 93in (236cm).
$1,500-2,250

A George III mahogany longcase clock, the 12in (31cm) painted dial signed Bentley & Beck, Royal Exchange, London with subsidiary seconds and calendar dials, rack and bell striking movement, c1810, 87in (221cm).
$4,500-6,000

A mahogany longcase clock, the 13in (33cm) break arch dial with subsidiary seconds dial, the silvered chapter ring with date scale, the moonphase arch signed J. N. Benson, Whitehaven, 8-day movement with false plate, bell striking, the restored case with arched hood, reeded canted corners and fielded panel base, c1780, 88½in (224cm).
$2,700-3,300

A George III longcase clock, by Bertler & Eggert of Bristol, with 8- day movement striking on a bell, painted dial with automaton 'swans in a lake' in the arch, the main dial painted with Admiral Lord Nelson in triumphant pose, 87in (221cm).
$2,700-3,300

A mahogany longcase clock, with silvered dial, Roman numerals, seconds and date dials engraved with floral sprays, strike silent dial to the arch, inscribed Bouffler, London, 8-day striking movement, the arched hood surmounted by brass pineapple finials, flanked by fluted pilasters, a panel door to the trunk with fitted panel base, on bracket feet, 19thC, 93in (236cm).
$2,700-3,300

An oak and mahogany longcase clock, the arched painted dial signed Thos. Dickinson, Boston, with 8-day striking movement, early 19thC.
$1,500-2,250

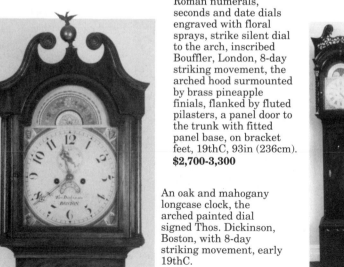

A George III mahogany longcase clock, with 8- day movement, double pediment to the hood, above brass dial showing the moon and high tide at Bristol, the centre with calendar aperture, subsidiary seconds dial, by Caleb Evans, Bristol, on ogee bracket feet, c1770, 96in (243.5cm).
$10,500-13,500

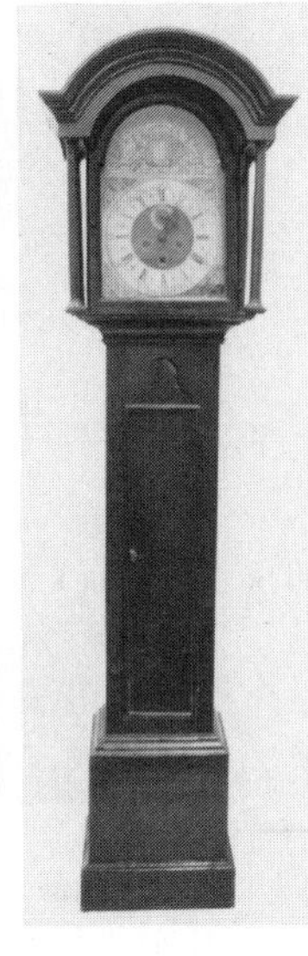

An early George III oak longcase clock, by Thomas Bridge, Wigan.
$3,000-3,750

A mahogany longcase clock, the 13in (33cm) brass break arch dial with silvered chapter ring, subsidiary seconds and date dials on a foliate engraved centre, moonphase in the arch and signed Peter Clare, Manchester, the 8-day movement with bell striking, c1790, 92½in (235cm).
$4,500-6,000

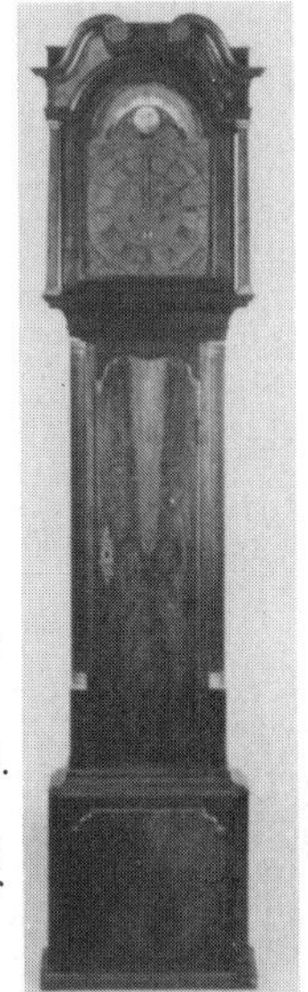

A black lacquer longcase clock, the brass 12in (31cm) break arch dial with subsidiary seconds dial and date aperture, signed in the arch William Barron, London, 8-day movement with bell striking, internal count wheel, the case with flat top and arched trunk door, the whole chinoiserie decorated, c1740, 84½in (215cm).
$1,200-1,500

A George III oak longcase clock, with 8-day striking movement, silvered chapter ring and Roman numerals, decorated with applied gilt spandrels and a boss to the arch, engraved Geo. Clapham, Brigg, 86in (218.5cm).
$900-1,500

A George III mahogany longcase clock, the brass arch dial with a painted moonphase dial in the arch and signed Clifton, Liverpool, 8-day striking 4-pillar movement, with second hand and date indicator, 90in (228.5cm).
$2,700-3,300

John Clifton of Liverpool is recorded as a maker of longcase clocks 1777-90. He died in 1794.

A George III black and gold lacquer longcase clock, the 8-day 5 pillar movement with an arched brass dial, with equation pointer and moon phases, subsidiary seconds dial and calendar, cast corner spandrels, inscribed Frances Durrell, London, the hood with brass finials, arched top waist door and base with an Oriental port scene, 92in (233.5cm).
$3,000-4,500

An inlaid mahogany longcase clock, the 12in (31cm) painted break arch dial with subsidiary seconds dial, curved calendar aperture and lunar disc and calendar in arch, signed Wm Bullock, Bradford, together with a later dwarf stand, mid-19thC, 93in (236cm).
$2,700-3,300

An oak and mahogany longcase clock, with arched painted dial, inscribed Border, Sleaford, 8-day striking movement and broken swan neck pedimented hood flanked by reeded columns, 19thC.
$1,200-1,500

A mahogany longcase clock, the enamelled face having subsidiary date and seconds dials, painted figure spandrels and a rolling moon in the arch, 8-day striking movement, maker B. French, Upwell, early 19thC, 90in (228.5cm).
$1,500-2,250

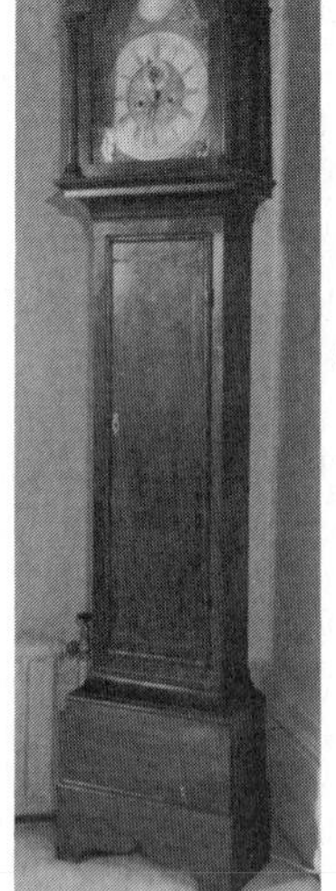

A figured walnut longcase clock, by Robert Potts of Patrington, the arched brass dial with silvered chapter ring and seconds hand, 18thC, 88in (223.5cm).
$4,500-6,000

A George II oak and mahogany longcase clock, by Charles Edward Gillett, Manchester, 8-day movement with inside pinned locking plate, c1760, 86½in (220cm).
$6,000-8,250

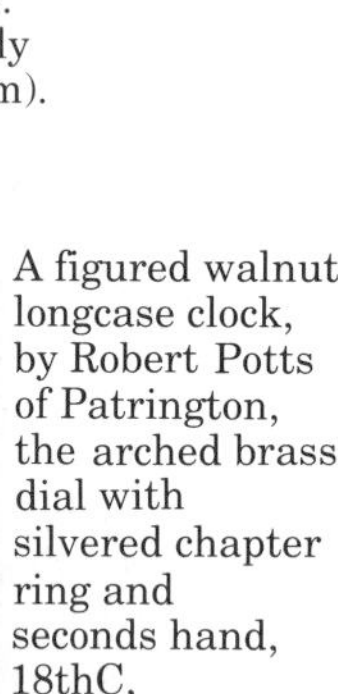

A George III oak and mahogany longcase clock, the 12in (31cm) painted dial signed Jn° Hargraves Jun, Sleaford, date sector and subsidiary seconds dial, painted spandrels and decorated arch, the 4 pillar rack striking movement with fluted canted corners to the trunk, the hood with swan neck pediment and flanked by fluted pilasters, 85in (216cm).
$1,050-1,350

A George II mahogany tavern longcase clock, with 20in (51cm) green painted wood dial, signed Finch, London, gilt numerals and hands, 5 pillar weight driven movement with deadbeat escapement, the case with architectural broken pediment, waisted trunk enclosing a similarly painted fielded panel inscribed 'Donum convivii vice Jacobi Hill. Hujus Societatis Gardiani Anno 1744', 94in (238cm).
$9,000-12,000

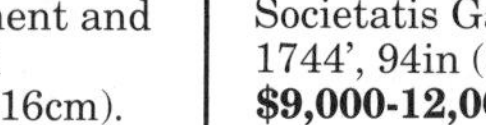

A mahogany white dial longcase clock, by Shepley of Manchester, early 19thC.
$3,000-4,500

A George III mahogany longcase clock, the silvered arch dial with moon phase engraved with landscapes and 'High Water at Bristol Key', flowers at the corners, subsidiary seconds dial and full sweep date indicator, signed Pan. Higdon Brewham, the 8-day 3 train movement striking the hours on a bell and chiming on 8 bells, hand missing, 96in (243.5cm).
$2,250-3,000

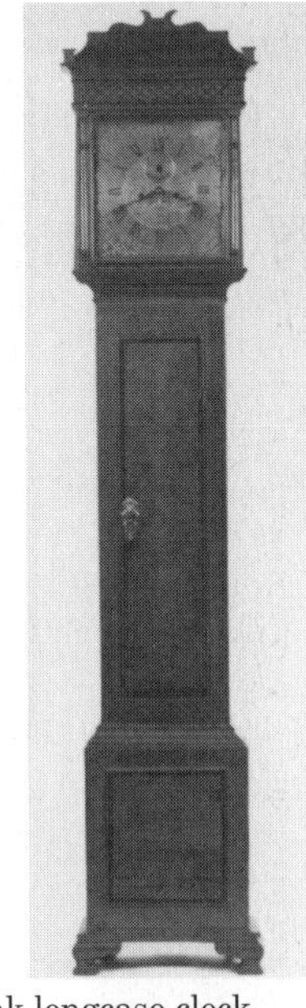

A George III mahogany longcase clock, the 12in (31cm) dial with double screwed well chased foliate and C-scroll spandrels, seconds dial, calendar aperture, strike/silent dial in the arch and signed Jn° Holmes, London, on a silvered plaque, 5 pillar rack and bell striking movement with maintaining power and pendulum with roller suspension, c1775, 90in (228.5cm).
$12,000-15,000

A George III mahogany longcase clock, with 14in (36cm) silvered dial, seconds dial and calendar sector, signed Thomas Willshire, Bristol, the arch with moon and tidal disc indicating 'High Water at Bristol Key', rack and bell striking movement, replaced bracket feet, c1790, 102in (259cm).
$3,000-4,500

An oak longcase clock, with 8-day movement, the 12in (31cm) square brass dial with urn pierced spandrels, circular chapter ring with Roman numerals, floral engraved centre with date indicator and seconds hand, with key, by Richard Houton, Oversley Green, mid-18thC, 87in (221cm).
$2,700-3,300

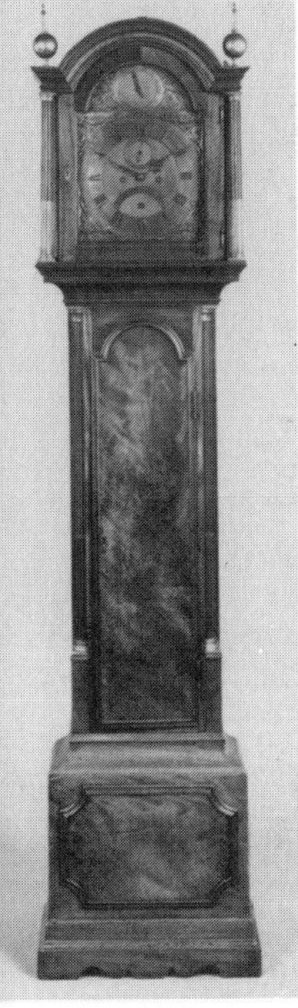

A George III mahogany longcase clock, 3 ball-and-spire finials, the dial signed Frans. Hobler, London on an arched plaque in the matted centre with calendar aperture and large diameter subsidiary seconds ring, brass chapter ring with pierced blued hands, foliate spandrels, strike/silent ring in arch, the 5 pillar rack striking movement with anchor escapement, 91in (231cm).
$5,250-6,000

A George III oak and crossbanded mahogany longcase clock, the dial signed Hindley, York, on the silvered chapter ring, the matted centre with small diameter seconds ring and central silvered alarm disc, pierced blued hands, foliate spandrels, date ring to arch, the movement with 4 baluster pillars, deadbeat escapement, maintaining power applied to the centre wheel, rack strike and alarm on bell with pull trip repeat cord, restored, 79in (200.5cm).
$3,000-3,750

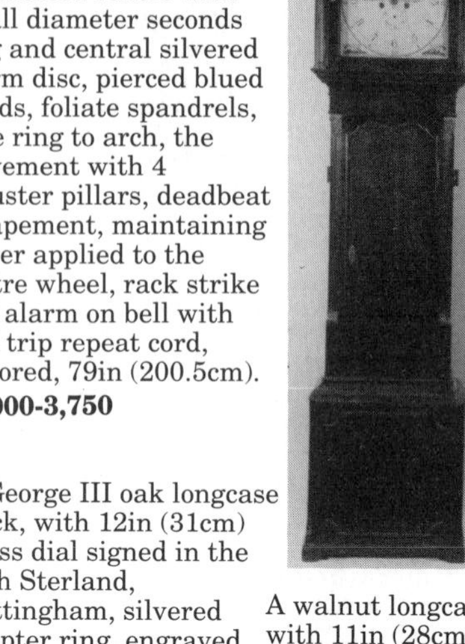

A George III mahogany and oak longcase clock, with 14in (35cm) painted dial, signed W. Nicholas, Birmingham, with seconds and calendar dials, painted shell spandrels and decorated arch, 4 pillar rack striking movement, 89in (226cm). **$1,200-1,800**

A George III oak longcase clock, with 12in (31cm) brass dial signed in the arch Sterland, Nottingham, silvered chapter ring, engraved silvered centre with subsidiary seconds and date aperture, 4 pillar racking striking movement, 8-day movement, plain case, 86in (218.5cm).
$1,500-2,250

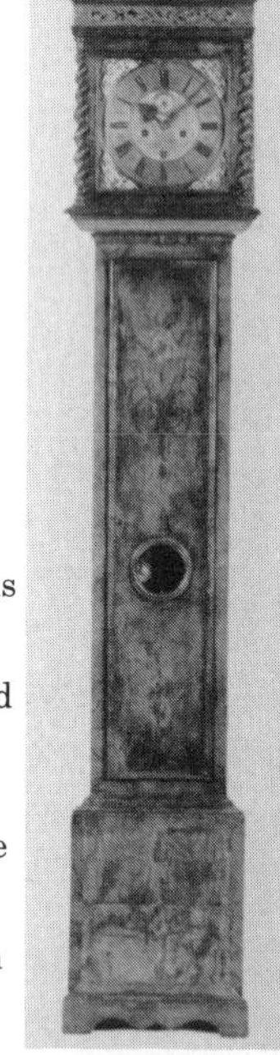

A walnut longcase clock, with 11in (28cm) dial, cherub and leaf spandrels divided by engraved leaves, seconds dial, calendar aperture, signed Robt Pattison, Greenwich, movement with 5 well turned latched pillars and inside countwheel, flat topped case, repoussé brass cornice fret, c1700, 85½in (217cm).
$7,500-9,000

A George III mahogany longcase clock, the dial signed Francis Shuttleworth, Salisbury, in the arch above the painted moonphase, brass chapter ring and dial centre with subsidiary seconds ring and calendar aperture, pierced blued hands, floral spandrels, the 5 pillar rack striking movement with anchor escapement and now striking on gong on backboard, 88in (223.5cm).
$2,250-3,000

A carved oak longcase clock, with square hood and ogee cornice, fluted side columns with acanthus brass capitals, 8-day movement, 12in (31cm) square brass dial with pierced urn spandrels, circular chapter ring with Roman numerals, engraved Oriental design to centre, seconds hand and date indicator, with key, maker George Henett, Marlborough, mid-18thC, 84in (213cm).
$750-900

A George III mahogany longcase clock, the dial signed E Courter Ruthin in the silvered centre, with subsidiary seconds and date ring, silvered chapter ring, pierced blued hands, the added arch with strike/silent ring, the 4 pillar rack striking movement with anchor escapement, adapted and composite, 81in (206cm).
$2,700-3,300

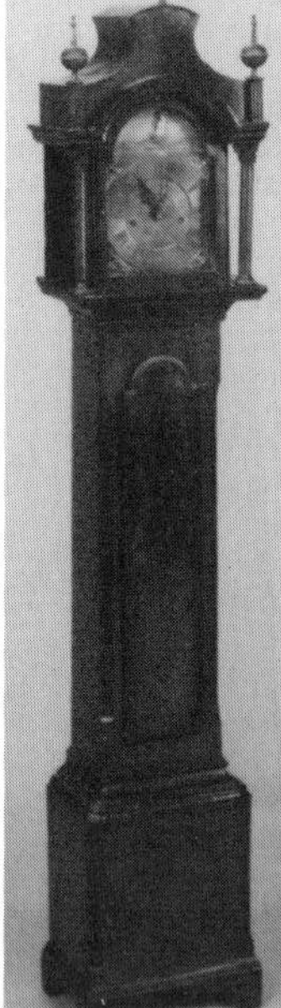

An 18thC style fruitwood longcase clock, the dial bearing the signature Tompion London, with an automaton ship in the arch, the 2 train 8-day bell striking movement with anchor escapement, c1880, 69in (175cm).
$4,500-6,000

Queen Anne burr valnut longcase clock, by ho. Tompion London, he concave moulded case n plain foot with ectangular trunk door, he flat top hood with rass capped three-uarter columns and ierced wood sound fret, he 11in (28cm) dial igned Tho. Tompion, ondon, on a silvered eserve in the matted entre with subsidiary econds ring and alendar aperture with in hole adjustment, bolt-nd-shutter maintaining ower with lever by III, ierced blued hands, ilvered chapter ring vith lozenge half and uarter hour divisions, ouble screwed Indian nask and scroll pandrels and foliate ngraved border, latches o the dial feet and to the substantial pillar novement, punched 542 t base of the backplate, ertical rack strike on ell above, anchor scapement with gilt teel rod, pendulum with alibrated rating nut, the novement secured hrough the seat board vith hooks on to the base illars and with securing racket to the backboard, he case with restoration, 0in (203cm).
45,000-60,000

A George III mahogany longcase clock, with break arch hood, shaped trunk below the blind fret, reeded quarter trunk columns and panel base, 8-day movement with rack striking bell, by William Lassell, Toxteth Park, Liverpool, c1720, 90in (228.5cm).
$9,000-12,000

A George III mahogany longcase clock, by William Taylor, Whitehaven.
$5,250-6,000

A mahogany longcase clock, signed T. Pyke, Bridgwater, Somerset, with white dial, 8-day movement, corners painted with representations of the Empire and in the arch a rampant eagle with banner 'Tempus Fugit', original pendulum, weights and winder, 89in (226cm).
$7,500-9,000

A mahogany longcase clock, the silvered dial with subsidiary seconds and inscribed Weslake, Southwark, bell striking 8-day movement, early 19thC, 81in (205.5cm).
$2,700-3,300

A walnut marquetry musical longcase clock, with 12in (31cm) dial with calendar aperture, seconds dial, mask and leaf spandrels, tune change lever at III, signed on the chapter ring Willm. Hulbert, Bristol, the substantial 3-train 5 pillar bell striking movement playing one of two tunes every 4 hours, on 9 bells with 17 hammers, the flat top case with formerly rising hood, ebonised pilasters and inlaid with trailing flowers around the door, formerly with a lenticle, similarly decorated plinth, the sides japanned black, c1705, 85in (216cm).
$7,500-9,000

A mahogany longcase clock, with 13in (33cm) painted break arch dial, signed Jno Roberts, Bath, subsidiary seconds dial and date aperture, moonphase in the arch, sea shell spandrels, the dial plate and date and moonphase rings stamped Wright, Birmingham, the 8-day movement with bell striking, c1835, 88in (223cm).
$3,000-3,750

A chinoiserie lacquer longcase clock, with 8-day movement striking on a bell, the arched brass and silvered dial with seconds, strike/silent dials and calendar aperture, by William Webster, Exchange Alley, London, 18thC, 104in (264cm).
$2,250-3,000

A walnut longcase clock, with 12in (31cm) arched brass dial, matt centre signed on a tablet Robt. Henderson/London, silvered chapter ring with Roman numerals, arabic 5 minute intervals, seconds dial, calendar aperture, pierced gilt brass spandrels and strike/silent dial in the arch flanked by dolphins, the 4 pillar movement with anchor escapement, rack striking on a bell, weights, 99in (251.5cm).
$7,500-9,000

A red walnut longcase clock, with brass dial of month duration, by Simon Thorne, Tiverton, c1730, 92½in (234cm).
$12,000-15,000

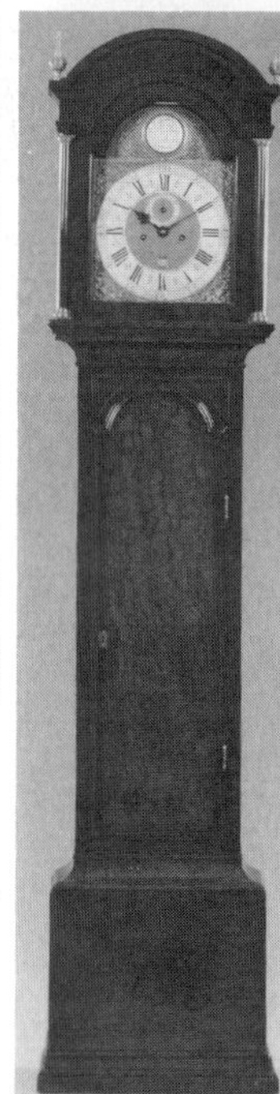

A George II walnut longcase clock, with 12in (31cm) arched dial, silvered chapter ring, subsidiary seconds, date aperture, signed on a silvered disc in the arch Wm. Kipling, London, bell striking movement with anchor escapement c1730, 86in (218.5cm).
$9,000-12,000

A Regency mahogany and ebonised longcase clock, the silvered dial with Roman numerals and seconds ring, signed Widenham, No 13 Lombard Street, London, below a classical gabled pediment, 83in (210.5cm).
$5,250-6,000

A mahogany longcase clock, the brass dial with later break arch, the silvered chapter ring signed Thomas Wightman, London, moonphase in the arch, the altered 8-day movement with bell striking, pinned internal countwheel, in later case, 99in (252cm).
$2,700-3,300

An oak longcase clock, the brass 14½in (37cm) break arch dial signed Sutton, Stafford, subsidiary seconds dial, moon phase in the arch with altered motion work, the 8-day movement with bell striking, c1785, 85½in (217cm).
$1,500-2,250

A Charles II walnut and floral marquetry longcase clock, the hood with ebonised twist columns and later blind fret, the 10in (25cm) square dial signed Char. Gretton in Fleet Street beneath the silvered chapter ring, the matted centre with ringed winding holes, decorated calendar aperture and subsidiary seconds ring, pierced blued hands, foliate winged cherub spandrels, the 6 ringed pillar movement with outside countwheel strike and anchor escapement, associated and restored, 78in (198cm).
$15,000-22,500

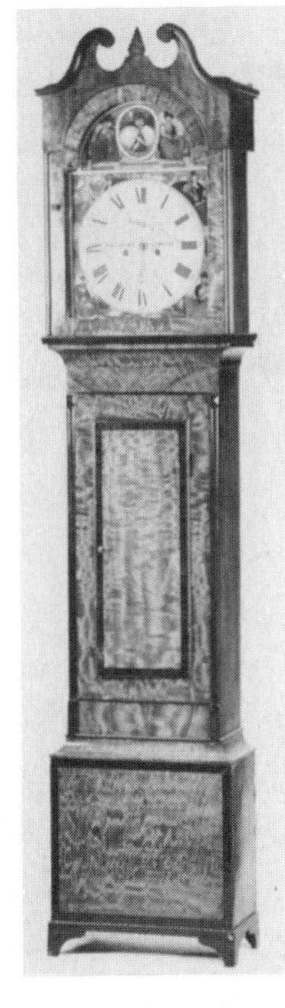

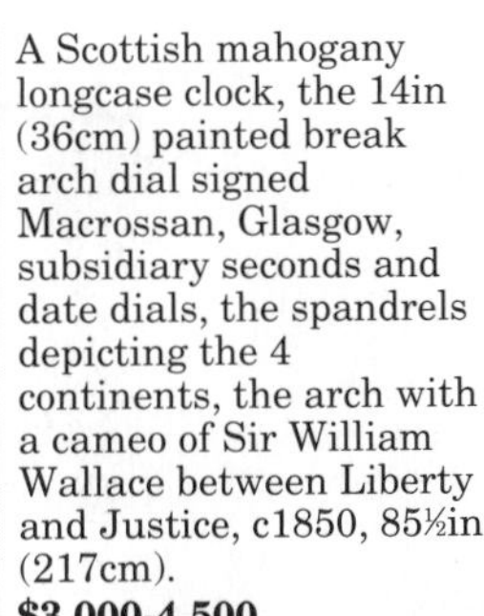

A Scottish mahogany longcase clock, the 14in (36cm) painted break arch dial signed Macrossan, Glasgow, subsidiary seconds and date dials, the spandrels depicting the 4 continents, the arch with a cameo of Sir William Wallace between Liberty and Justice, c1850, 85½in (217cm).
$3,000-4,500

A Regency period mahogany longcase clock, with painted dial and moon phase, 8-day with rack striking sounding the hours on a bell, satinwood inlay to the door and base, c1815.
$6,000-8,250

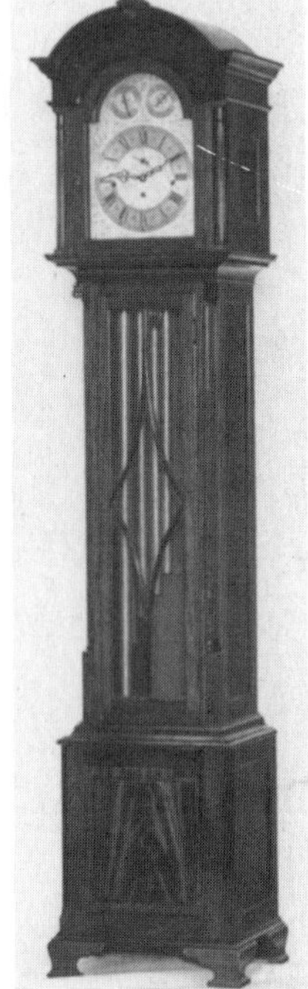

A mahogany longcase clock, with silvered dial, engraved with acanthus scrolls and Roman numerals to the chapter ring, chimes silent and selector dials to the arch, fitted month duration movement striking on nine gongs, 84in (213cm).
$2,700-3,300

A George II oak longcase clock, with 8-day movement, brass dial, the silver calendar dial framed by dolphin spandrels and signed Archd. Strachan, c1760, 84in (213cm).
$6,000-8,250

A longcase clock, c1755.
$1,200-1,500

A Scottish longcase clock, the 8-day movement striking on a bell, a circular painted dial with subsidiary second and calendar dials, inscribed Geo. White, Glasgow, the mahogany veneered case with a domed hood, fret outline surmount, the door with a brass bezel, ebony stringing to the banding, reeded pilasters, the trunk with moulded outline door flanked by roundel capped pilasters, the base on bracket feet, early 19thC, 86in (218.5cm).
$1,050-1,350

l. A late Georgian longcase clock, green and gilt Japanese lacquered case, with a swan neck pediment above the arched hood, circular engraved brass face, 8-day movement by C. Woller, Birmingham, flanked on either side by columns with brass capitals, 88½in (224cm).
$1,800-2,700

r A George III mahogany and oak cased longcase clock, the hood with a swan neck pediment set with a central finial above the arched glazed door, enclosing an arched painted dial with 8-day movement, second and date hand and with gilt spandrels against a blue ground, by Emmanuel Burton of Kendal, flanked by turned columns above the shaped oak and mahogany banded trunk door, with reeded quarter column corners and conforming base.
$1,800-2,700

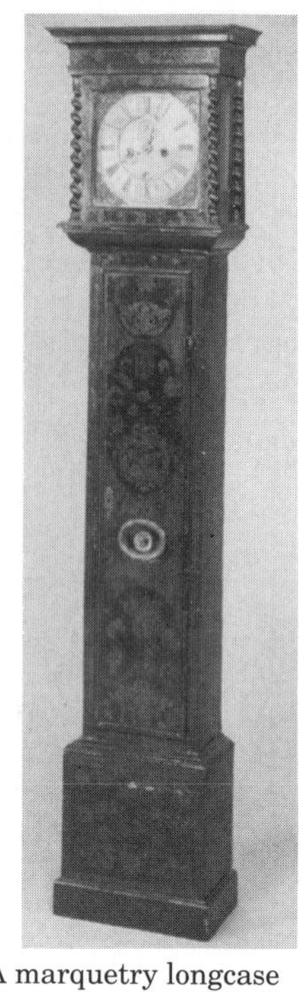

A marquetry longcase clock, the 11in (28cm) dial signed Ben Wright, Londoni fecit, with seconds dial, calendar aperture and cherub and leaf spandrels, the 8-day latched movement with inside countwheel, in a flat topped case with formerly rising hood flanked by spiral columns, c1695, 81in (205cm).
$9,000-12,000

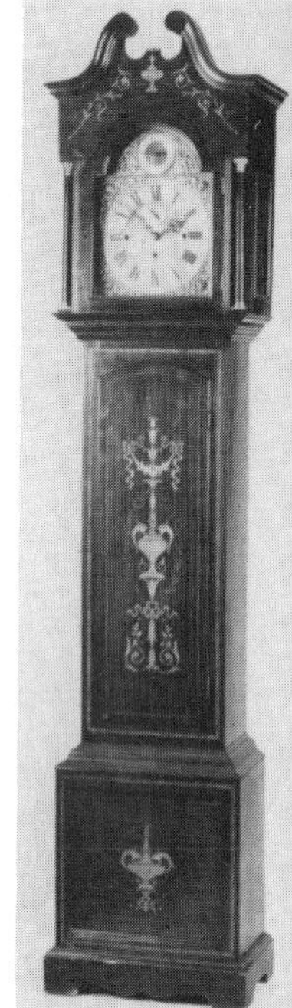

A mahogany and inlaid chiming longcase clock the 12½in (32cm) brass break arch dial with silvered chapter ring, subsidiary seconds dial chime/silent dial in the arch, the 8-day 3 train movement chiming on nest of 8 bells and striking the hours on a gong, c1900, 94in (238cm).
$3,000-3,750

A mahogany and inlaid chiming longcase clock, the 12in (30.5cm) break arch dial with silvered chapter ring, subsidiary seconds dial, chime/silent and selector dials in the arch, the heavy 3 train 8-day movement chiming on 8 tubular bells,and striking on a further tubular bell, 98½in (250cm).
$4,500-6,000

A mahogany chiming longcase clock, 110in (280cm).
$7,500-9,000

A mahogany longcase clock, signed in the arch Edwd. Woodyear, Salisbury, c1830, 82½in (209cm).
$1,200-1,500

A George III lacquered longcase clock, the case redecorated with raised gilt chinoiserie to the plinth with later foot, similar decoration to the arched trunk door and to the hood with pagoda top and surmounted by gilt ball finials, the dial signed R. Todd Scarborough in the silvered chapter ring, subsidiary seconds in the matted centre with calendar aperture, later blued hands, foliate spandrels, the arch now with rocking ship automaton, the 4 pillar rack striking movement with anchor escapement, composite and restored, 91in (232cm). **$1,800-2,700**

A Scottish mahogany longcase clock, the 13in (33cm) painted break arch dial signed Jas. Young, Dundee, subsdiary seconds and date dials, the spandrels and arch depicting various Scottish battles, the false plate stamped Laudale & Tod, Edinburgh, the 8-day movement with bell striking, c1825, 83in (211cm). **$2,700-3,300**

l. A longcase clock, by Michael Wilde of Wakefield, with 8-day movement, reeded flower painted dial, in oak case with brass finials, 93½in (237cm). **$1,200-1,500**
c. A longcase clock, by Hudson & Son, Otley, with 8-day movement, having arched dial with painted landscape decoration, 19thC, 93½in (237cm). **$1,050-1,350**
r. A longcase clock, by A. Ferguson Mauchline with 8-day movement, arched painted dial with agricultural scenes in oak, 91½in (232cm). **$1,050-1,350**

A George III mahogany longcase clock, the dial with silvered chapter ring, the engraved centre with subsidiary seconds and calendar rings, pierced blued hands, cherub spandrels, and painted arch with automaton rocking ship, the 4 pillar rack striking movement with anchor escapement, the boxwood inlaid case with chamfered angles to plinth, lacking foot, 88in (224cm). **$1,800-2,700**

Lyre Clocks

A Louis XVI gilt, bronze and white marble calendar lyre clock, the annular enamel dial with central calendar and centre seconds, the bell striking movement with pin wheel escapement and large sunburst pendulum enclosing the movement, with grid iron rod and knife edge suspension, the lyre crisply cast and chased with leaf, bead and guilloche decoration raised on an oval marble plinth, c1785, 22½in (57cm).
$12,000-15,000

A late Victorian mantel clock, the satinwood case painted with neo-classical decoration of ribbons, wreaths, thyrsi and urns.
$750-900

An ebonised mantel clock, with perpetual calendar and equation of time by William Jones, Gloucester, painted white dial with subsidiary dials below for day and month, centre equation of time sector and revolving moon phase, the single fusee movement with an anchor escapement in a drum top with canted corners, straight case and stepped base with oval side gilt handles, 19thC.
$3,000-3,750

Mantel Clocks

A gilt bronze mantel clock, with 3¼in (8cm) engine turned dial, the slender vertically aligned fusee movement signed Thomas Hawley, Strand, London, the suspension with horizontal adjustment, the waisted case with foliate scrolls, English, c1830, 14in (35cm).
$2,700-3,300

A silvered and gilt bronze Gothic revival mantel clock, the 4½in (11.5cm) gilt dial pierced with tracery and signed Le Plastriers, Paris, the movement also signed and with silk suspension, striking a gong in the mahogany plinth base, the ornate case surmounted by a bell tower, pierced and gilt pendulum, c1835, 26in (66cm).
$1,050-1,350

A gilt bronze, bronze and marble mantel clock, the enamel dial signed J. B. Marchand A Paris, bell striking movement, the gilt case flanked by the seated figure of a woman in classical dress and a young scholar with a book, the white marble plinth profusely decorated with gilt bronze mounts, c1850, 24in (61cm).
$3,000-3,750

A French ormolu and silvered bronze musical and automaton mantel clock, with glass dome, c1840, 17in (43.5cm).
$2,700-3,300

A French ormolu mantel clock, 19thC, 17in (43in).
$750-900

. walnut mantel clock, with ngraved silvered dial signed :harles Frodsham, Clockmaker to I.M. The King and Queen, 115 Iew Bond Street, No. 2111, the novement with anchor scapement, pendulum and key, 9thC, 10in (25cm).
1,800-2,700

A bronze mounted red marble mantel clock, with 3in (7.5cm) silvered dial signed Vulliamy London, pierced heart hands, rubbed, engine turned centre and ormolu serpent bezel, similarly signed fusee movement No. 599, with circular plates, half deadbeat escapement, rise and fall regulation and steel rod pendulum with similarly numbered bob, c1820, 11½in (29cm).
$3,000-4,500

A French Empire mantel clock, the 8-day movement striking the hours and half hours, and with white enamel dial, 16in (41cm).
$2,250-3,000

A French Empire gilt bronze mantel clock, in the form of Phoebus in his chariot, on marble base, some damage.
$4,500-6,000

A rosewood mantel clock, the 3½in (9cm) silvered dial with shaped top, signed Wright, London, the fusee movement with anchor escapement, c1825, 12½in (32cm).
$1,800-2,700

A French ormolu mounted boulle mantel clock, with 7½in (19cm) cartouche dial, bell striking movement with outside countwheel, the case inlaid throughout with pierced brass decoration, inverted bracket top, surmounted by Minerva, c1870, 42in (107cm).
$4,500-6,000

A Paris porcelain twin train mantel clock, the cartouche shaped blue ground case heightened in gilt and painted and modelled with vignettes of flowers, flanked by figures of seated children, on a shaped plinth, the movement with countwheel strike, on a giltwood and gesso stand, 19thC, 20in (51cm). **$1,200-1,800**

A Louis XVI gilt bronze mounted white marble mantel clock, the 5in (12.5cm) enamel dial signed A Paris, bell striking movement with circular flat bottomed plates, later spring suspension and sun mask pendulum, c1790, 24in (61cm).
$4,500-6,000

A French gilt bronze mounted re boulle mantel clock, with 5½in (14cm) 24 piece cartouche dial, bell striking Japy Frères movement, No. 3644, waisted cas veneered with red shell inlaid with brass, c1870, 18in (46cm).
$1,200-1,800

A French ormolu and Meissen mantel clock, the drum shaped case with enamel dial, supported within a floral bouquet of applied flowerheads, mounted with winged figures of children, the shaped platform pierced and chased with rocaille, 19thC, 13½in (34cm). **$900-1,500**

A 'Sèvres' mounted ormolu mantel clock, with bell striking J. B. Delettrez movement with Brocot escapement signed for Thomas Agnew & Sons, the porcelain dial painted at the centre with a putto within tooled gilt and rose pink borders, French, c1870, 19½in (49.5cm).
$5,250-7,500

A French ormolu mantel clock 20in (51cm).
$750-900

A French ormolu and Belgian black marble twin train mantel clock, surmounted by a bronze goup of a young woman and child personifying Summer, the circular dial with Roman numerals, 19thC, 27in (69cm).
$1,050-1,350

A French green onyx and champlevé enamel 4-glass mantel clock, the 3½in (9cm) gilt dial with enamel surround and centre, the gong striking movement stamped Japy Frères, Brocot suspension, c1905, 13½in (34cm).
$900-1,500

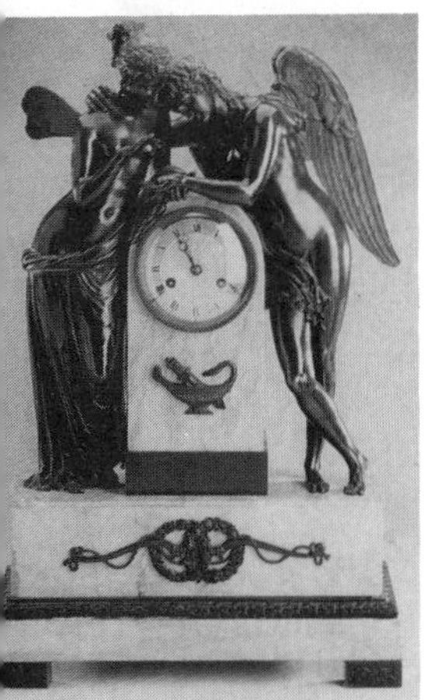

French bronze and marble antel clock, the gilt dial with ntral engraving, the bell riking movement with outside untwheel and silk suspension, e domed case flanked by figures Cupid and Psyche, above a ctangular base with bronze ounts and feet, c1830, 22in 6cm). **$2,700-3,300**

A French/English tortoiseshell and silver mantel clock, with enamel dial signed for J.C. Vickery Regent St. London, 8-day movement with lever escapement, rectangular case with domed cresting and turned finial, the front inlaid with finely cut silver and with silver mouldings, feet and back, hallmarked 1913, shell cracked on cresting, 8½in (21cm). **$1,800-2,700**

A French gilt metal and white marble mantel clock, with circular white enamel dial and Roman numerals, the case set with a classical portrait plaque, a cherub to either side and surmounted by goats and a basket of flowers and fruits, late 19thC, 16in (41cm). **$750-900**

A black slate and decorative porcelain cased mantel clock, with decorative ormolu mounts, circular dial and French striking movement, resting on paw supports, 19thC, 20in (51cm). **$375-525**

A grande sonnerie repeating and alarm boulle mantel clock, with silvered foliate engraved dial, signed Chatourel à Paris, similarly signed 4 train gong striking movement with fusee and train for the gong, standing barrels for the strike and alarm, verge and balance escapement, Austrian, c1810, 9½in (24cm).
$3,000-3,750

A French gilt brass and faience mantel clock, bell striking Japy Frères movement, No. 7857, the ogee arched case inset at the front and sides with faience polychrome panels and raised on a plinth with elephant head feet, c1880, 15in (38cm).
$1,050-1,350

A French/Austrian gilt bronze mounted cut glass mantel cloc[k] the enamel dial with gilt engin[e] turned bezel, later French 8-da[y] lever movement, cylindrical cu[t] glass case surmounted by an eagle on a ball with gilt bronze base, damaged, 19thC, 15in (38cm).
$900-1,500

A French gilt bronze and green onyx mantel clock, the keyless movement with gilt dial signed Sorley, Paris, and mounted with a 6in (15cm) diam magnifying sphere, the sphere supported between the outstretched wings of an eagle, seated on a rocky base above a turned support with a square base, c1900, 18in (45cm).
$3,000-3,750

A mahogany repeating mantel clock, the 7¾in (19cm) painted convex dial signed Stroud, Pentonville, the twin fusee movement with anchor escapement and bell striking, English, c1825, 16in (41cm).
$4,500-6,000

A Louis XIV tortoiseshell and brass boulle mantel clock, the 4½in (11.5cm) enamel dial signed Sibelin A Paris, the movement now with anchor escapement and lacking striking train, back plate signed Les Frères Sibelin A Paris, c1710, 16in (40cm).
$4,500-6,000

Portico Clocks

A French gilt ormolu portico clock, with engine turned gilt dia[l] Roman chapter surrounded by a[n] acanthus leaf cast bezel, round bell striking 8-day movement, putti on a swing pendulum, 4 column case with acanthus capitals on a stepped decorated base on 4 feet, 19thC, 18in (46cm).
$1,050-1,350

;keleton Clocks

. Victorian chiming skeleton 'ock, with 9in (23cm) pierced ilvered chapter ring, 3 train ısee and chain movement with nchor escapement and chiming n 8 bells with a further hour bell, ull chords for repeat and trike/silent elaborate leaf cast ·ame with 7 substantial ring ırned pillars, white marble linth and glazed brass cover, 5in (63cm).
12,000-15,000

A month going skeleton clock, the 4½in (11cm) silvered and engraved dial signed E. Saxby, Maker, Lambeth, London, and enclosing subsidiary seconds and calendar dials, the fusee and chain movement with 6 wheel train, half deadbeat escapement and 5 spoke wheels, the frame with ball and spire finials, 2 lacking, and raised on a wood plinth with a glass dome, 9½in (24cm).
$1,200-1,500

An 8-day brass skeleton clock, designed as a Gothic steeple with flying buttress supports, having pierced circular dial with Roman numerals, double fusee movement, striking hourly on large Gothic gong, ebony and zinc compensated pendulum, on lacquered 2 tier circular plinth with glass dome, with key, c1850, 29in (74cm) overall.
$1,200-1,500

Miller's is a price GUIDE not a price LIST

An English skeleton clock with passing trike, with 6¼in (16cm) silvered chapter ring, fusee and chain novement with 6 spoke wheels and anchor escapement, the 5 pillar, well pierced scroll frame with top mounted bell, white marble plinth, with original glass dome, c1860, 20in (51cm).
$1,200-1,500

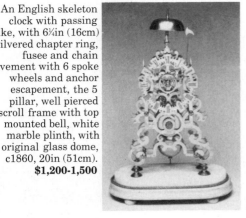

An English skeleton clock, the 3¼in (8cm) silvered and engraved chapter ring signed for Sowter, Oxford, fusee and chain movement with half deadbeat escapement and Gothic arched frame raised on a circular ebonised plinth, cracked glass dome, c1850, 9in (23cm).
$1,200-1,500

Table Clocks

An English mahogany table clock, with 6½in (16.5cm) brass break arch dial signed Rich. Collins, Margate, silvered chapter ring, date aperture and false pendulum aperture, strike/silent dial in the arch, the twin fusee bell striking movement with verge escapement, the bell top case with glazed side panels, c1790, 19in (49cm).
$3,000-3,750

A mahogany brass inlaid table clock, with 8in (20.5cm) convex painted dial, strike/silent above XII, 5 pillar bell striking fusee movement with anchor escapement signed James McCabe, Royal Exchange, London, the backplate and the pendulum bordered with engraving, Gothic arched case with repoussé brass side handles, Gothic frets and inlaid at the front with brass flowerheads, leaves and stringing, c1810, 19in (48cm).
$1,800-2,700

A Queen Anne ebony veneered basket top table clock, the 7in (18cm) dial with cherub spandrels, one replaced, calendar aperture and strike/not strike lever above XII, 6 pillar bell striking fusee movement signed Jacobus Hassenuis Londini, on the leaf and tulip engraved backplate, with verge escapement and formerly with quarter repeating, the moulded case with a repoussé brass basket, carrying handle, finials and mounts for the front door, c1705, 13in (33cm).
$5,250-6,000

An ebonised musical table clock, with 8in (20.5cm) foliate engraved silvered dial signed Johnson, London in the arch below a tune selection dial, the bell top case with flambeau finials, scale side frets and bracket feet, c1790, 20in (51cm).
$4,800-5,700

A Continental walnut quarter repeating and alarm table clock, the case with deeply arched cresting, the door flanked by spiral colums and key drawer below, 20in (51cm).
$7,500-9,000

3lack Forest Clocks

ʌ carved walnut cuckoo and quail able clock, from the Black Forest, ɟermany, with 5½in (14cm) dial igned for Camerer Kuss & Co., ɾith carved bone hands, 3 train ɹsee movement with wood plates nd 3 bellows connected to the rticulated wood birds, the chalet ase profusely decorated with arved vine leaves, c1875, 23½in 60cm).
1,500-2,250

A carved beech cuckoo and musical wall clock, from the Black Forest, Germany, with a 7in (18cm) dial, 3 train brass plated weight driven gong striking movement operating the cuckoo bellows and a 2-tune 6cm cylinder mechanism at every hour, the case well carved with conifers, a deer, a nest of young birds and surmounted by an eagle, a pair of doors above the dial opening to reveal the cuckoo and a seated musician, slight damage to carving, c1890, 34½in (87.5cm).
$2,700-3,300

A stained beech quarter striking cuckoo wall clock, from the Black Forest, Germany, with a 6¾in (18cm) dial, 3 train brass plated weight driven movement stamped D.R.P. No. 219355, striking the quarters on 4 rod gongs with a further gong and cuckoo for the hour, leaf carved chalet case with stag's head cresting, a pair of nesting birds below and a door opening to reveal the automaton carved wood cuckoo, c1900, 33½in (85.5cm).
$1,200-1,500

A large carved beech trumpeter clock from the Black Forest, Germany, with 8¼in (21cm) dial, the case with polychrome painted decoration overall, hands replaced, slight damage, c1875, 42½in (108cm).
$3,000-3,750

A trumpeter clock, from the Black Forest, Germany, with 5½in (14cm) dial with bone ɹands, the 2 train wooden posted movement operating the trumpeter every hour, the bellows and 3 trumpets mounted above the movement, the Gothic case with fretted side doors and carved base, a door below the dial opening to reveal the bugle player, c1890, 25in (64cm), with 2 fir cone weights and carved pendulum.
$1,500-2,250

Wall Clocks

A Victorian mahogany cased station wall clock, the circular dial on a carved scroll wall mounted fixed bracket, the white dial with Roman numerals, inscribed John Bennett, 65 and 64 Cheapside, enclosing a fusee movement striking on a single gong, 36in (92cm).
$600-750

A Continental polychrome wood wall timepiece, the dial painted with a circus scene, with Roman numerals, 19thC, 8in (20cm).
$300-375

A shop interior wall clock and bracket, with 17½in (45cm) cream painted dial with black Roman numerals inscribed Fredjohns Ltd., Jewellers, Wimbledon, in medium oak case with turned columns and dentil cornice, the matching large bracket with han set day, date and month perpetual calendar, late 19thC, 62in (157cm).
$1,500-2,250

A Victorian mahogany cased drop dial wall clock, the case embellished with grape and vine leaf decoration, with a painted white dial inscribed Pratt, Norwich, timepiece movement.
$600-750

A mahogany wall clock, with 14in (36cm) circular painted dial, the false plate stamped Wilkes & Son, the 8-day bell striking movement with small diameter barrels, c1825, 61in (154cm).
$900-1,500

Miscellaneous

An English mahogany dial clock, with fusee movement and painted Roman dial, signed T Fox Canterbury.
$300-375

An American inlaid walnut dial clock, c1860.
$600-750

A French/English silver digital flick clock, the hours and minutes indicated by rotating cards, the 8-day movement with platform lever escapement, the circular case with hammered finish, on bun feet, hallmark Birmingham 1905, 7in (18cm).
$900-1,500

marine chronometer by
rodsham, 3-tier rosewood
neered box lined with satinwood,
nged flush brass handles,
rtouches, corners and
ringing, c1841, 4in (10cm) diam.
,700-3,300

A French novelty timepiece alarm, the spelter case in the form of a bearded old man with articulated arm, wearing a wide brimmed hat, inset with a circular pink enamel dial, on a stepped rectangular platform, 10in (25cm).
$600-750

A Greenwich Time clock, not in working order, 37in (94cm).
$1,800-2,700

An English rosewood dial clock, inlaid with mother-of-pearl, with twin fusee striking movement, c1850.
$1,800-2,700

egulators

A Vienna regulator, the walnut and ebonised case with broken arched pediment above a circular white enamel dial with Roman chapters, twin train movement and gong strike, 19thC, 48in (122cm).
$1,500-2,250

A Victorian mahogany wall regulator, with 12in (31cm) painted dial, signed Jas. Gowland, London Wall, concentric minute ring, subsidiary seconds and hour dial, movement with tapering pillars, high count train, Harrison maintaining power, short ebony rod pendulum, in a well figured case with concave base, 44in (112cm).
$3,000-3,750

A Vienna regulator wall clock, 19thC.
$750-1,200

A Caledonian railway signal box wall regulator clock, the white enamelled dial signed Caledonian Rail Co. Jas. Ritchie & Son, Edinburgh, Roman numerals, blued hour and minute hands, the 4 pillared movement with dead-beat escapement, Harrison's maintaining power, wood rod pendulum, in truncated mahogany wall case with circular sliding hood, 62in (158cm).
$2,250-3,000

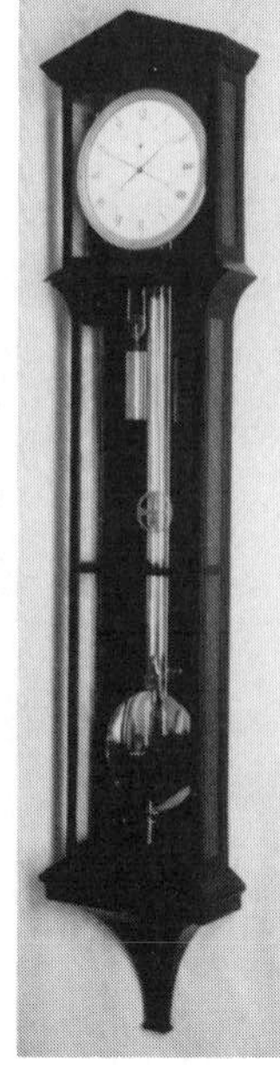

A Viennese regulator, signed Lehrner Kaschan, with glass enclosed movement and Huyens winding method, compensated pendulum with knife edge suspension, c1830, 60in (152cm).
$30,000-45,000

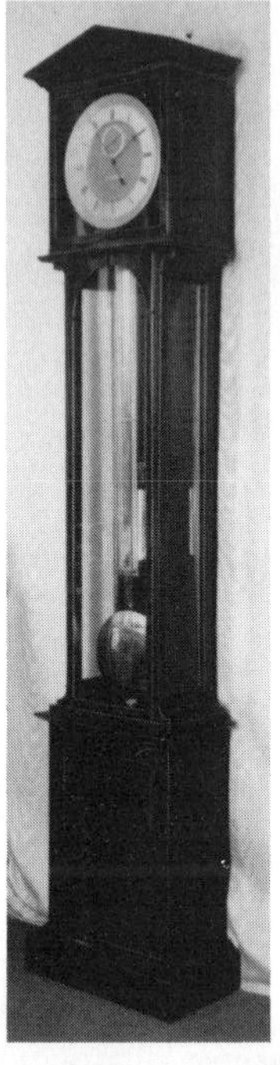

A year-going Viennese floor standing regulator, with brass encased movement and end stops, seconds beating grid-iron pendulum, in a mahogany veneered case with maple stringing, c1830, 72in (182.5cm).
$30,000-45,000

A month-going Viennese regulator in a mahogany six-light roof top case, with lift off lower door, steel pendulum, c1835, 43in (109cm).
$7,500-9,000

A grande sonnerie striking Viennese regulator, by Glink, the two-piece dial with pie-crust bezel, in a figured ash veneer case with carved decoration, c1850, 45in (114cm).
$7,500-9,000

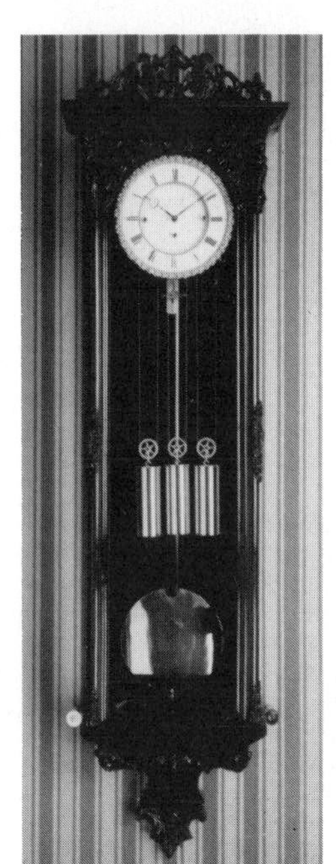

A grande sonnerie striking Viennese regulator, in a rosewood veneered case with maple stringing and carved decoration, the two-piece enamel dial with pie-crust bezel, c1850, 47in (119cm).
$9,000-12,000

Watches

n 18ct gold pair case verge ocket watch in a plain outer ase, the signed frosted gilt fusee ovement with pierced cock and ot to the edge of the top plate, iamond endstone and square aluster pillars, by Willm. dcock, London, mid-18thC, .7cm).
1,050-1,350

An 18ct gold and enamelled key wind open faced fob watch, the movement signed E. P. Biddle, Merthyr Tydvil, M4317, London 1869, and another.
$450-600

An English 18ct gold open faced pocket watch, gilt dial, Roman chapter and floral centre fusee lever movement, signed F. W. Benson, 58-60 Ludgate Hill, London, inscribed cuvette 'Presented to Supt. D. Dunham by the Inhabitants of Slough and the Vicinity in recognition of zeal and ability displayed by him in the capture of the Denham murderer, May 24th 1870, H. M. London 1870', 5.5cm. **$750-1,200**

An open faced silver verge watch, silver dial with applied gilt Roman numbers with subsidiary second dial, foliate border, polished case with ribbed band, signed Robt. Neill Belfast, No. 8148, hallmark London 1820, 5.5cm.
$225-255

A 15 by 22mm Watchface Ticka camera, with polished chrome body engraved 'Ticka. Patented in most countries. Houghtons Limited London', lens cap attached to body by a chain, Time and Instantaneous shutter, enamel watch face with Roman numeral figures, metal watch hands, interior with printed cardboard label 'Ticka' an ever ready waistcoat pocket camera. Patented throughout the world.
$3,000-3,750

large triple cased silver 3 train uarter striking and repeating larm verge coachwatch, the uter case with shagreen and ilver pinwork, the intermediary ase finely chased and engraved vith plain inner case, the silver ilt engine turned dial with raised Roman numerals, subsidiary econds and central alarm disc, old moon hands, signed on raised ectors, the signed frosted gilt novement under signed dustcover vith monometallic balance and liamond endstone, now lacking underdial work for much of the triking, repeating and alarm work, by Bentley & Beck, London, No. 1039, 5½in (14cm).
3,000-3,750

A French desk timepiece, the enamel dial with Arabic numerals within deep blue reserves, subsidiary seconds, keyless lever movement inscribed France, contained in a spherical glass case with blue and white paste set bezel, c1900, 9cm.
$1,200-1,800

A silver pair cased doctor's dial watch, maker's mark VR in an oval, signed Twyford, London 1009, hallmarked Birmingham 1827, 5.4cm diam.
$900-1,500

A silver pair cased verge watch, with white enamel dial with 'John Robinson' written around the inside of the border, inscribed Born at Birkby, May 15th 1794, and with Masonic symbols, H. M. London 1789, signed Geo Robinson, London, No. 7594, 6cm.
$450-600

A lady's gold and enamel keyless hunter pendant watch, by Vacheron & Constantin, Geneva, in a chased and engraved case with enamelled monogram to the front cover, the white enamel dial with Arabic numerals and subsidiary seconds, the signed and frosted gilt bar movement with bimetallic balance and lever escapement jewelled to the third, No. 358557 under signed cuvette, 3.3cm.
$1,050-1,350

A gold, enamel and seed pearl quarter repeating verge pocket watch, by Dominice & Blondel, Paris, the engine turned 2 colour gold back with seed pearls and enamel ring set to the rim, the bezel similarly decorated, the gold engine turned dial with Arabic numerals on white enamel cartouches, white enamel minute ring, blued steel moon hands, the signed fusee movement with pierced bridgecock repeating on 2 gongs operated by the pendant, 3.9cm.
$1,800-2,700

A gentleman's 18ct gold keyless wind open faced pocket watch, the gilt freesprung lever movement signed Clerke, 1 Royal Exchange, London, plain cuvette, the signed white enamelled dial with black Roman numerals, subsidiary seconds and blued steel hands, the case back monogram engraved, London 1900.
$750-900

A gentleman's 18ct gold key wind open faced pocket watch, the gilt fusee movement with a verge escapement, the backplate marked London No. 2227, slow/fast regulator, large rose diamond endstone, dust cover, plain inner case, the gilt dial with gilt Roman numerals, subsidiary seconds and gilt hands, the case with a milled rim, London 1820.
$1,200-1,800

A repoussé silver pair cased quarter repeating, quarter striking calendar chaise clockwatch with alarm, by Johann Michael Baur, Friedberg, the movement now with lever escapement and spring barrel, compensation balance, blued steel spiral spring and regulator, signed on the backplate Johann Michael Baur, applied decoration to the pillars lacking, silver champlevé dial, Roman numerals, outer Arabic minute ring, inner revolving alarm disk, signed J. M. Baur, c1750, 13.2cm.
$10,500-12,000

A gentleman's 18ct gold keyless wind open faced pocket chronograph, with an unsigned gilt three-quarter plate jewelled lever movement No. 99771, plain cuvette, the white enamelled dial with black Roman numerals, subsidiary seconds, centre stop seconds and with blued steel hands, the case back crest, motto and initial engraved, London 1887.
$750-1,200

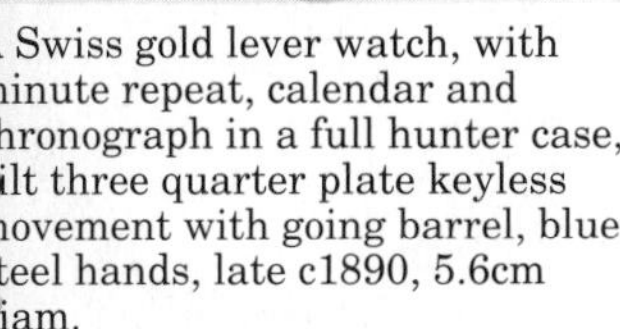

. Swiss gold lever watch, with ninute repeat, calendar and hronograph in a full hunter case, ilt three quarter plate keyless novement with going barrel, blue teel hands, late c1890, 5.6cm iam.
3,000-4,500

An English silver pair cased verge, with an engraved gilt metal dial and enamelled chapter engraved gilt centre, edge inscribed 'Keep me clean and use me well and I to you the time will tell', signed Thos Holmes, Cheadle 786, maker's mark VR, hallmarked Birmingham 1826, 5.5cm diam.
$600-750

A Swiss quarter repeating verge, in an 18ct gold open face case, full plate gilt fusee movement, pierced and engraved bridge cock with polished steel endstone, plain 3 arm gilt balance with blue steel spiral hairspring, silver regulator dial with blue steel indicator, push pendant quarter repeating on 2 steel gongs, engine turned gilt dial, with white enamel chapters for the Arabic numerals and minute markings, blue steel Breguet hands, signed and numbered gilt cuvette, c1810, 2in (5cm) diam.
$1,200-1,800

. Swiss repeating watch, in a old open face case, gilt novement with 2 resting barrels aving polished steel stop work, ylinder escapement, plain brass alance with spiral spring, steel scape wheel, plain cock, steel oqueret and regulator, pendant uarter repeating on 2 steel ongs, lateral slide in the band to ctuate the musical mechanism, ngraved gold dial with engine urned centre, Roman numerals, lue steel Breguet hands, c1810, .7cm diam.
3,000-4,500

A silver pair cased verge, full plate fusee movement with round pillars, pierced and engraved round cock, table covering only part of the 3 arm steel balance, silver regulator disc, white enamel dial with Arabic numerals, gold hands, silver oval pendant and bow, signed J. Johnson, maker's mark TG, hallmarked London 1813, 5.3cm diam.
$150-225

Wristwatches

A World War II German airman's wristwatch, the frosted gilt movement signed A. Lange & Sohne, the black dial with outer minute ring and inner hour ring, luminous hands and sweep centre seconds, the interior of the snap on back engraved with maker's details and reference numbers, the movement stopping on pulling out the winder, 5.5cm.
$1,200-1,800

An Omega gold electronic chronometer Constellation calendar wristwatch, in circular case with milled bezel, the gilt textured dial with raised baton numerals, date aperture, sweep centre seconds, case with screw on back with maker's mark, with integral flexible gold bracelet and buckle.
$900-1,500

A 9ct gold automatic wristwatch, by Jaeger-LeCoultre, in a circular case with concealed winder, the matt silvered dial with alternating dagger and Arabic numerals, subsidiary dials for running seconds and power reserve indication, with signed movement, 3.5cm.
$750-1,200

A Continental gentleman's Chopard bracelet watch, the square dial with applied baton markers, signed L. U. Chopard and Cie, repeated on the movement and case, flexible bracelet.
$450-600

A gentleman's Rolex Cellini 18ct gold wristwatch, with signed 19 jewel movement, the case and dial with repeat signatures, the white dial with Roman numerals, leather strap.
$750-900

A lady's bracelet watch, the dial with diamond, baguette diamond and baguette synthetic sapphire bezel, the diamond articulated shoulders with diamond and faceted metal bracelet.
$900-1,500

A gentleman's 18ct gold wristwatch, by Piaget, the yellow dial with Roman numerals, the strap with maker's 18ct gold buckle.
$750-900

A gentleman's 18ct gold Chopard Automatic bracelet watch, the dial with baton markers and date aperture with integral textured brick link bracelet, the clasp with Kutchinsky mark.
$750-900

A Rolex Oyster 9ct. gold octagonal wristwatch, the white enamel dial with Arabic numerals and red 5 minute divisions, sweep centre seconds, the case with screw down winder and screwed back with maker's mark, No. 29107, the signed ultra prima movement timed to 6 positions.
$2,700-3,300

A 1920s platinum wristwatch, by Movado, the silvered dial with raised Arabic numerals and subsidiary seconds, the hinged back with maker's mark and integral dust ring, the signed movement jewelled to the centre.
$750-1,200

A Rolex gold Quarter Century Club wristwatch, in a tonneau case, the brushed silvered dial inscribed Eaton, sweep centre seconds, case with screw down winder and screwed back with maker's mark No. 6222, signed movement with 17 jewels No. 32737. **$1,200-1,800**

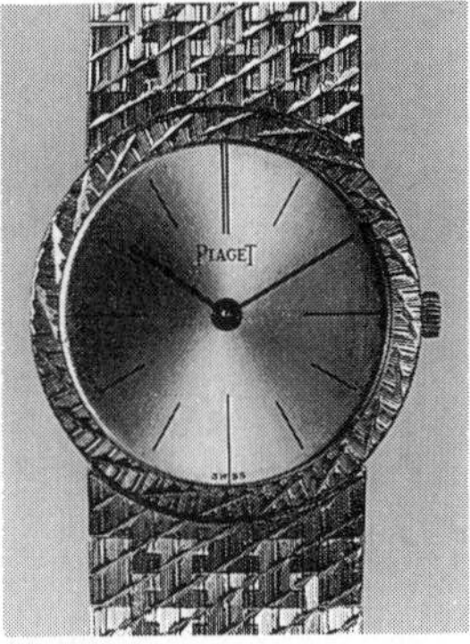

A gentleman's 18ct white gold and diamond set wristwatch, the bezel set with diamonds, the gilt dial with diamond set quarter hour marks, the back secured by 6 screws, with maker's black leather strap and diamond set white gold buckle and matching pair of cufflinks, in presentation box. **$2,700-3,300**

A lady's 18ct gold wristwatch, with champagne baton dial, fine nickel fully jewelled lever movement, signed Piaget, on a brick link engraved bracelet, c1980.
$600-750

A gentleman's Continental Audemars Piguet slim wristwatch, the signed circular 17 jewel movement adjusted to temperatures and 4 positions, the dial with baton markers.
$1,200-1,800

A gentleman's Rolex Oyster 18ct gold and diamond perpetual day date superlative chronometer officially certified bracelet watch, the champagne dial with diamond and baguette diamond markers, day and date aperture and sweep centre seconds, with a diamond bezel, the Rolex bracelet with deployant clasp.
$7,500-9,000

A gentleman's steel Rolex Oyster Perpetual GMT Master superlative chronometer, officially certified, the brown dial with dot markers, sweep centre seconds, 24 hour hand and cyclops glass to the date aperture, the revolving bezel in blue and bronze.
$750-900

A gentleman's Continental Rolex Oyster perpetual day date, superlative chronometer, officially certified, the dial with dart markers, day and date apertures and sweep centre seconds, with textured bezel and shoulders, with a Rolex Continental textured brick link bracelet attached.
$4,500-6,000

Miscellaneous

A bronze and onyx French novelty timepiece, the spherical goliath pocket watch held by a bronze eagle perched on a gilded rock supported on a green onyx fluted column, c1900, 16in (40cm) high.
$1,200-1,800

BAROMETERS
Stick Barometers

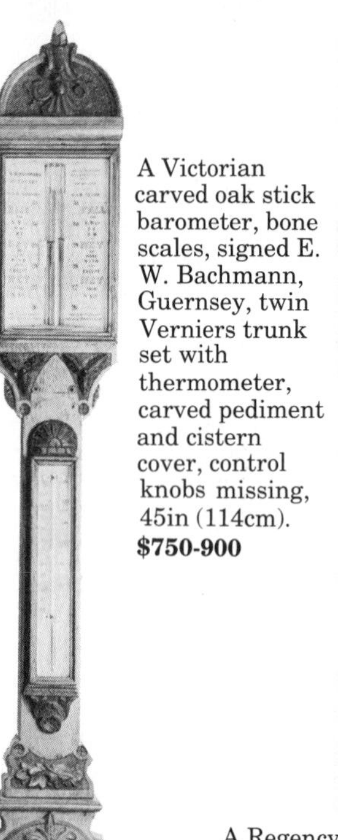

A Victorian carved oak stick barometer, bone scales, signed E. W. Bachmann, Guernsey, twin Verniers trunk set with thermometer, carved pediment and cistern cover, control knobs missing, 45in (114cm). **$750-900**

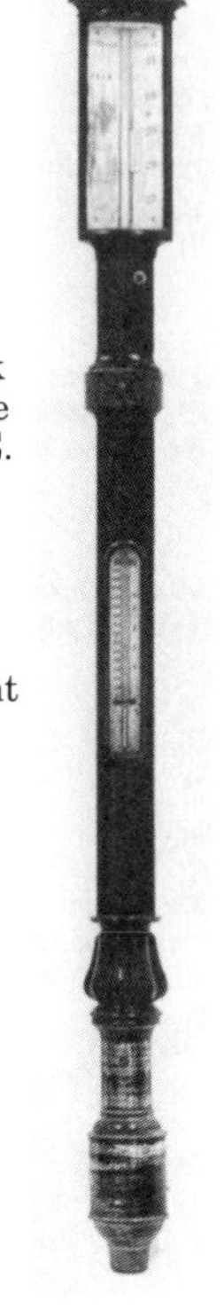

A Regency rosewood ship's barometer, by J. Bassnett of Liverpool. **$3,000-3,750**

A Regency rosewood ship's barometer, by Crichton, London. **$750-900**

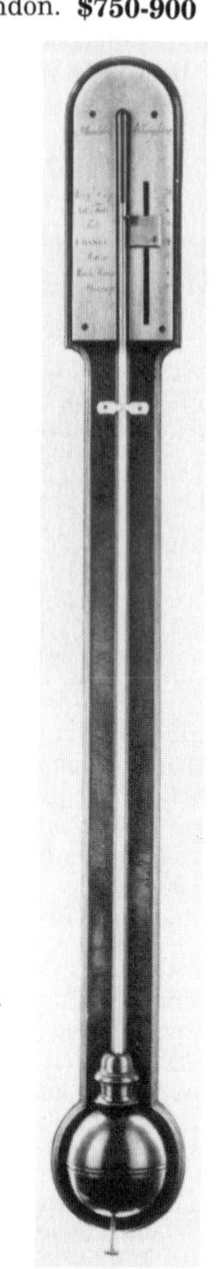

A mahogany stick barometer, with round top and hemispherical cistern cover, by Baddely, Albrighton, c1790. **$3,000-3,750**

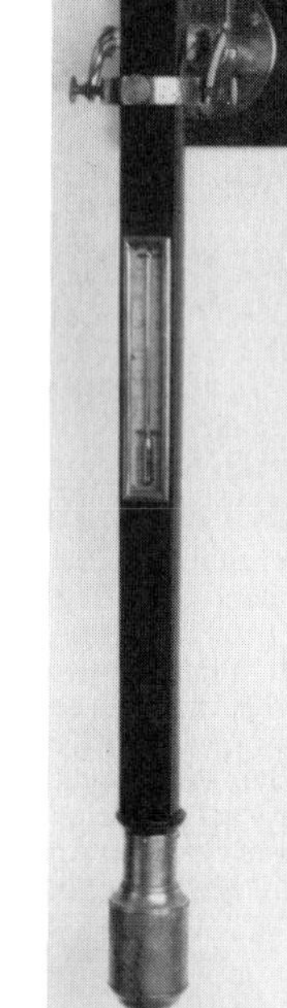

A mahogany marine barometer, by Spencer Browning, London, with brass trimmed ivory plates, replaced gimbals, c1835. **$3,000-3,750**

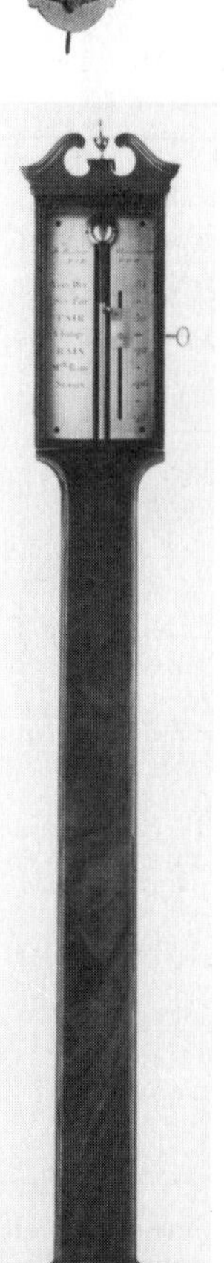

A mahogany stick barometer, with glazed door and swan's neck pediment, by F. Molton, Norwich, c1815. **$3,000-3,750**

A Victorian mahogany stick barometer, with sliding verniers for barometer and thermometer, the trunk with turned cistern cover, signed M.Sadler, Aston St. Birmingham on the ivory plate. **$750-900**

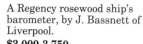

A George III mahogany and chequer banded stick barometer, the silvered dial with thermometer scale signed P. Gally Cambridge, the tube with hemispherical well cover, the top with broken arch pediment, 38½in (97cm). **$1,200-1,500**

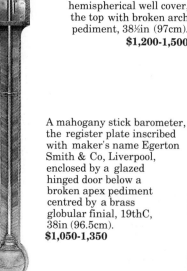

A mahogany stick barometer, the register plate inscribed with maker's name Egerton Smith & Co, Liverpool, enclosed by a glazed hinged door below a broken apex pediment centred by a brass globular finial, 19thC, 38in (96.5cm). **$1,050-1,350**

A Georgian mahogany and ebonised stick barometer, the bowfronted case with swan's neck pediment and ivory urn finial above a silvered dial, the trunk with thermometer and adjusting dial, the base with urn shaped reservoir, signed Thos Harris & Sons, British Museum, London, 41in (104cm).
$3,000-3,750

A George III mahogany bowfronted stick barometer, bone scales, with vernier and trunk set thermometer, case with moulded pediment, signed G. & C. Dixey, Opticians to the King, 3 New Bond St., London, cistern cover missing, 39in (99cm)
$3,000-3,750

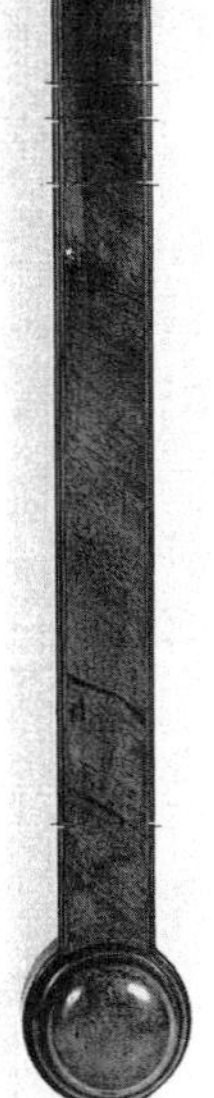

A walnut stick barometer, with silvered dial and vernier, signed J. King & Son Bristol, glazed door and turned cistern cover, 18thC.
$450-600

A mahogany marine barometer, with hinged door opening to reveal the recessed register with vernier, the door mounted with an alcohol thermometer, the scale signed A. Maspoli, 79 Lowgate, Hull, slim gimballed case with moulded cresting and brass cistern, dated1835, later mahogany wall bracket, 36in (91.5cm).
$3,000-3,750

Augustus Maspoli, 1826-55, Opt. math & Phil. Hull, 49 Salthouse Lane (1826-31), 79 Lowgate, (1835-55).

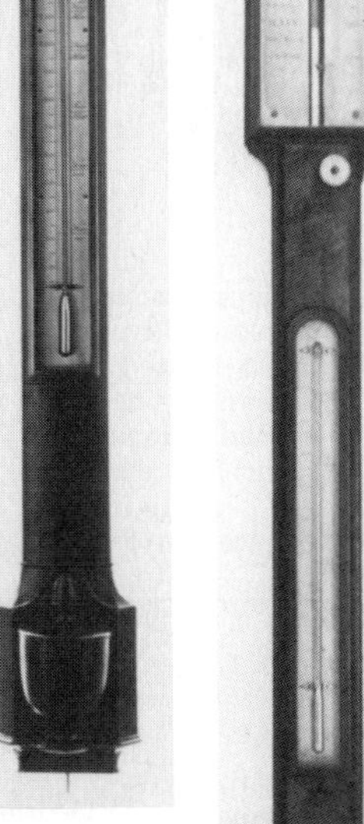

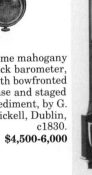

A flame mahogany stick barometer, with bowfronted case and staged pediment, by G. Tickell, Dublin, c1830.
$4,500-6,000

A mahogany stick barometer, the register with vernier scale and signed Jo. Smith, Royal Exchange, London, the case with inset thermometer, ebonised moulded edge, shallow domed cistern cover and surmounted by later scroll crestings, register plate originally silvered.
$3,000-3,750

A mahogany stick barometer with boxwood and ebony chequer strung border, swan's neck pediment with urn finial, and silvered register plate with vernier scale, 38in (96.5cm).
$450-600

Miller's is a price GUIDE not a price LIST

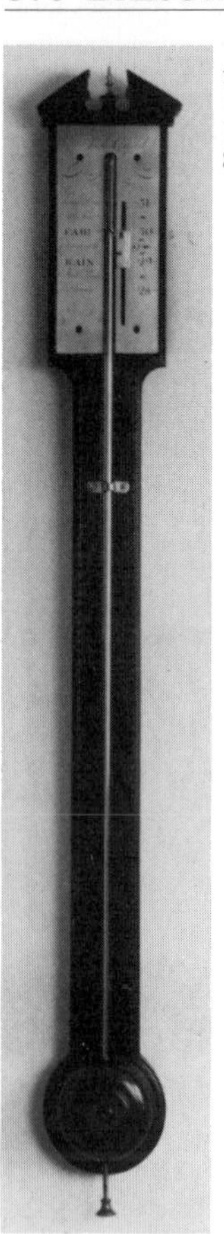

A mahogany inlaid stick barometer, with break arch pediment, by Lock, Oxford, c1800.
$1,800-2,700

A George III mahogany stick barometer, the concealed tube with silvered plates and vernier, the case with swan neck cresting, cistern cover, bordered with ebony stringing and inset with a mercury thermometer, signed Jas. Powell, Worcester, c1800, 39in (99cm).
$1,500-2,250

A walnut stick barometer, the concealed tube with silvered plates and simple vernier, the case with broken arch cresting, brass ball and spire finials and turned cistern cover, case altered, c1730, 39½in (100cm).
$2,250-3,000

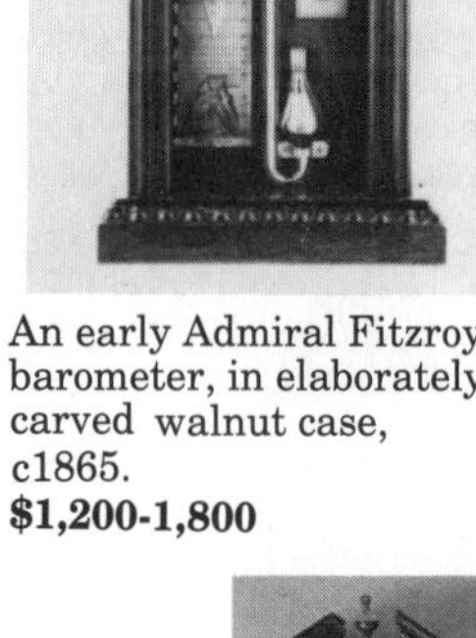

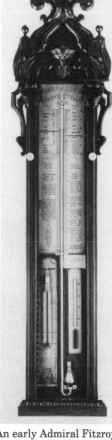

An early Admiral Fitzroy' barometer, in elaborately carved walnut case, c1865.
$1,200-1,800

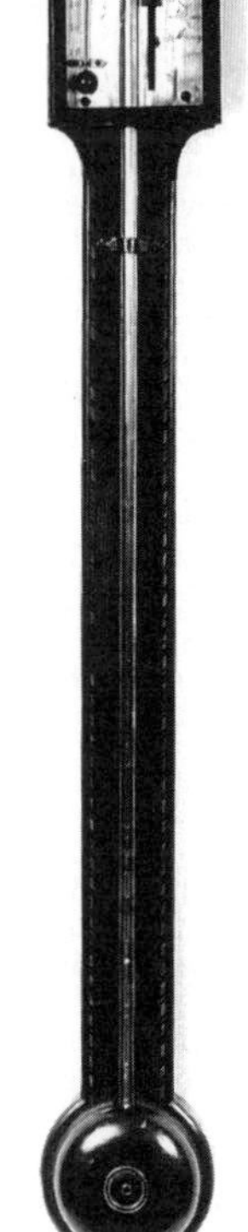

A French provincial stick barometer, the polychrome pine board painted with a scale and flowers, the domed top inscribed Barometre Simple, mercury tube replaced, late 18thC, 37in (94cm).
$600-750

A George III mahogany and chequer strung stick barometer, with thermometer scale, inscribed J. Vitory Zaneta, 98 Market St. Lane, Manchester, 39in (99cm).
$1,050-1,350

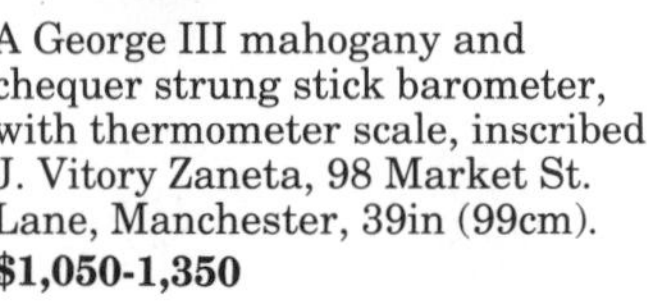

A George II mahogany stick barometer, by B. Peverelly, London.
$1,050-1,350

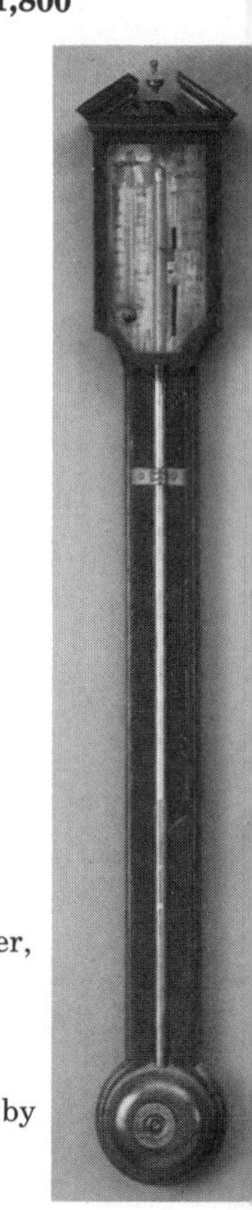

A George III mahogany and chequer banded stick barometer, the silvered dial with thermometer scale signed I.M. Ronketti, the tube with hemispherical well cover, the broken arch pediment centred by a brass finial, 38in (96.5cm).
$1,200-1,800

Wheel Barometers

A Victorian walnut wheel barometer, silvered dial signed L. Casartelli, 20 Duke St., Liverpool, trunk with thermometer, raised carved border, 45in (114cm).
$750-900

A Victorian rosewood wheel barometer, with swan's neck pediment, circular silvered dial, hygrometer and thermometer scales, the dumpy level plate signed Abraham, Optician Bath, 43in (109cm).
$750-900

A mahogany inlaid barometer, by J. Gatty, London, c1800.
$2,700-3,300

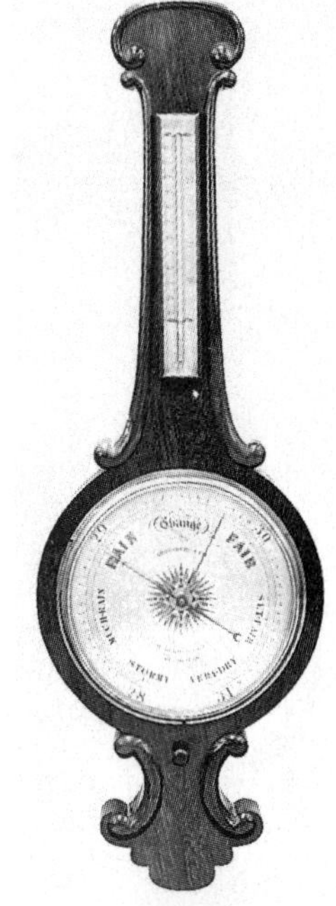

A rosewood wheel barometer and thermometer, by Aronsberg & Co, with silvered register plate, contained in a banjo case with C- scroll carving to the borders, pediment and base, 19thC, 44in (111cm).
$600-750

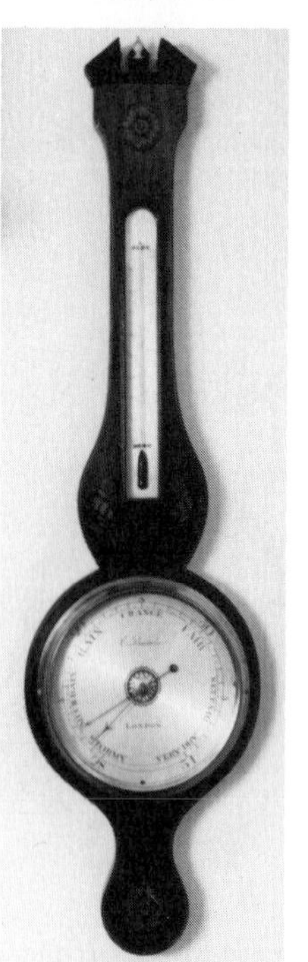

A mahogany shell inlaid wheel barometer, with architectural pediment, signed M. E. Bianchi, London, c1815.
$1,050-1,350

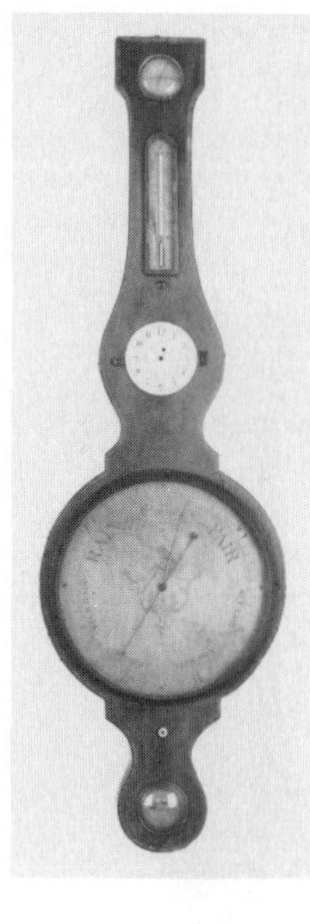

A George III wheel barometer, with silvered register plates to the dry/damp dial, thermometer and spirit level engraved F. Faveria & Co, Lincoln, contained in a mahogany banjo case, set with a convex white enamelled dial with black Arabic numerals, with a verge watch escapement, ivory turner, brass bezels, the whole crossbanded and strung with ebony and box, 46in (116.5cm).
$3,000-3,750

A mahogany Sheraton style inlaid wheel barometer, with rope stringing, by Mojana, Edinburgh, c1820.
$3,000-3,750

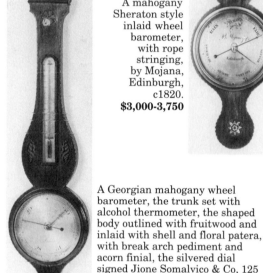

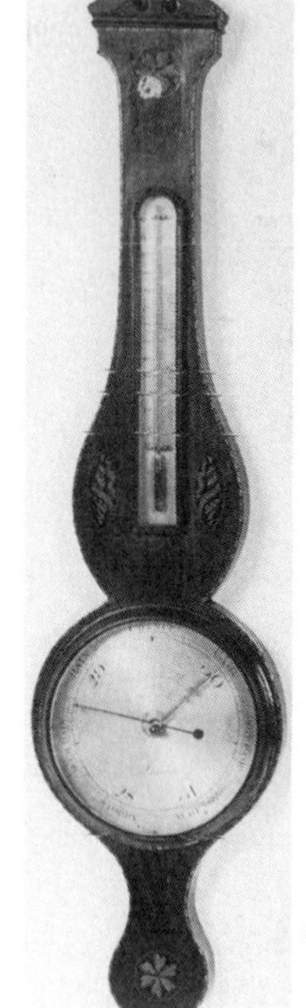

A Georgian mahogany wheel barometer, the trunk set with alcohol thermometer, the shaped body outlined with fruitwood and inlaid with shell and floral patera, with break arch pediment and acorn finial, the silvered dial signed Jione Somalvico & Co, 125 Holb[n] Hill, London.
$450-600

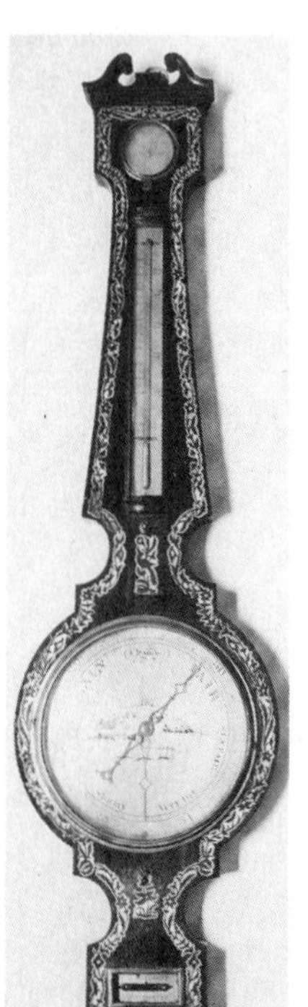

A rosewood and mother-of-pearl inlaid wheel barometer, the silvered dial engraved in the centre with buildings in a landscape, hygrometer and mercury thermometer, the bubble level signed J. Predrary, Manchester, the case with swan's neck pediment, c1860, 39½in (100cm).
$450-600

A Georgian mahogany wheel barometer, with 10in (25cm) silvered dial, mirror, thermometer and hygrometer above and level below, the shaped body outlined with fruitwood stringing with swan's neck pediment and urn finial, signed Lione & Co, 7 Charles Str[t], Hatton Garden.
$375-525

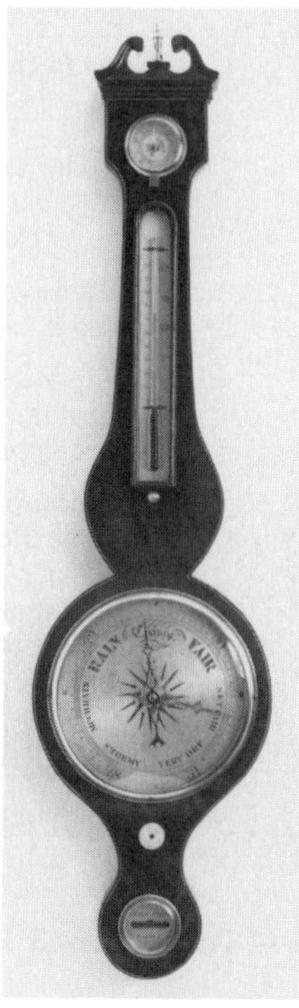

A mahogany four-dial wheel barometer with ebony and boxwood stringing, c1830.
$1,050-1,350

A rosewood barometer, c1860.
$450-600

A mahogany and ebony strung round top wheel barometer, by P. L. D. Martinelli, London, c1790.
$2,700-3,300

A Georgian mahogany wheel barometer, the trunk set with thermometer, the shaped body with fruitwood stringing, floral and shell paterae and break arch pediment, the 8½in (21cm) silvered dial signed Piotti, Hull.
$750-900

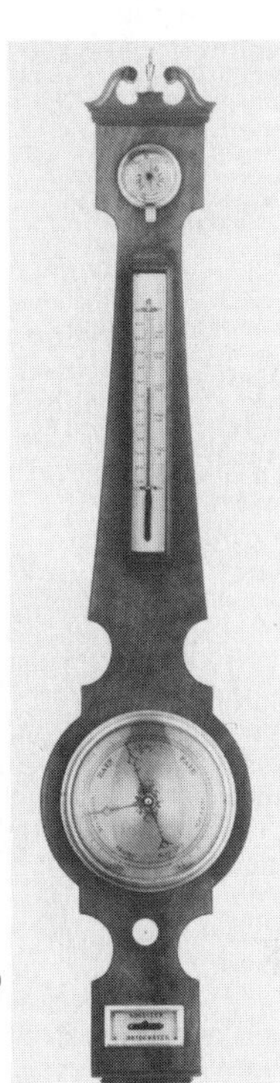

A mahogany wheel barometer, with square base, by Rossiter, Bridgwater, dial 6in (15cm), c1845.
$1,200-1,500

A mahogany five-dial wheel barometer, with ebony and boxwood stringing, c1845.
$750-900

Barographs

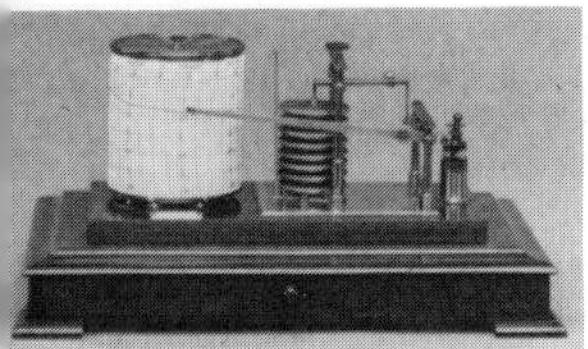

A mahogany barograph, the chart drum driven by a French timepiece movement with cylinder escapement, the pen controlled by a stack of 8 vacuum flasks set on a mahogany plinth with ink bottle to the side and chart drawer, glazed cover, with a quantity of unused charts and the original instruction booklet, by Short and Mason, London, c1920, 14in (36cm) wide.
$1,200-1,500

A lacquered brass barograph/barometer, with recording drum, key, mechanism, ink bottle, ink needle and circular weather indicator, in fitted mahogany case with chart drawer and bevelled glass cover, 14in (36cm) wide.
$2,700-3,300

A barograph, with moulded oak case and bevelled glass, c1880.
$750-1,200

An oak cased barograph, with drawer, bevelled glass and silvered brass aneroid dial, c1890.
$1,200-1,500

A Cyclo-Stormograph barograph, with concealed movements and bearing supporting forecasting chart, in an oak case, by Short & Mason, c1930.
$750-1,200

SCIENTIFIC INSTRUMENTS

Dials

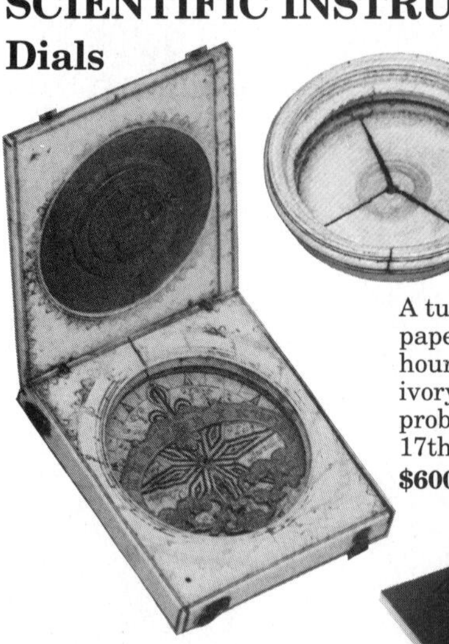

A turned ivory compass dial, with paper compass rose, gilt brass hour ring and hinged gnomon, in ivory case with screw lid, probably South German, late 17thC, 2in (5.5cm) diam.
$600-750

An ivory diptych dial, the upper outer face engraved with pin gnomon dial, upper inner face inset with silver coloured metal volvelle, with tidal calculator and moon phase dial, lower, inner face with string gnomon dial and analemmatic magnetic dial, the base inset with silver coloured metal disc engraved with calendar scales, by Charles Bloud, Dieppe, late 17thC, 3 by 2½in (7 by 6cm).
$1,050-1,350

A Stockert paper card dial, in turned boxwood case with domed cover, a horizontal dial, the dial plate calibrated IIII-XII-VIII, over paper card dial with compass rose, blued steel needle, folding gnomon in fitted mahogany case, with a part dial signed Johann Willebrand in Augsburg 48, and 2 miniature pewter sundials and a square brass plate engraved with scales.
$450-600

An equinoctial sundial, with paper card dial, hour scale, half meridian circle, gnomon, latitude arc divided 10-70°, on turned wooden stand, attached to paper card base with compass box, in paper card carrying box, signed Philips' Sun-Dial, Made in Germany, 9in (23cm) high.
$750-1,200

Miller's is a price GUIDE not a price LIST

A brass pocket sundial, the underside engraved CF within a shield reserve, the engraved rectangular plate signed Nan-Ler and stamped with the fleur-de-lys mark, the mother-of-pearl dial enclosing a coat-of-arms with coronet supported by putti, with folding gnomon, 18thC, 2in (5cm).
$375-450

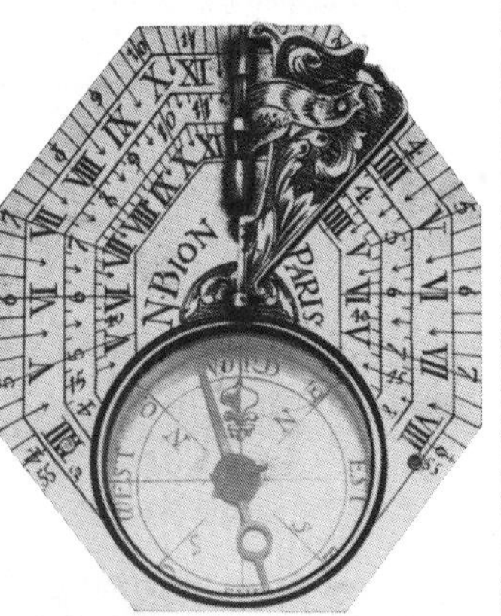

A French silver Butterfield dial, engraved with 4 hour scales, inset compass well and with hinged gnomon and bird pointer, the base with 24 towns and latitudes, signed N. Bion à Paris, 18thC.
$1,500-2,250

A Korean brass string gnomon horizontal dial, the base plate pierced and moulded with flowers and foliage, with enamelled hour dial and compass rose, bubble level, folding plummet, on 3 adjustable screw feet, with semi-precious stone caps, 4½in (11.5cm) long.
$375-525

A brass portable sundial, mounted on a walnut quadrant, the turned stem on a moulded circular base, early 19thC.
$4,800-5,700

Chinese brass sundial, with ıtitude arc and pointer, sprung nomon on sliding bar, 2 hour uadrants and folding frame, 3in cm) long.
750-900

A gilt brass universal equinoctial dial, signed Joahann Schrettegger in Augsburg, with inset compass well and mounted with folding latitude ark, hour ring and gnomon, in original case with printed list of latitudes and instructions, late 18thC, 2in (5cm).
$750-900

lacquered brass universal quinoctial dial, with folding pring loaded gnomon, divided II-XII-VIII, folding latitude arc ngraved 10°-80°, inset silvered ial with bubble and cross bubble, ngraved quadrantly, with edge ar needle and clamp on 3 velling screws, signed on the our ring Cary London, 4½in 1cm) diam.
900-1,500

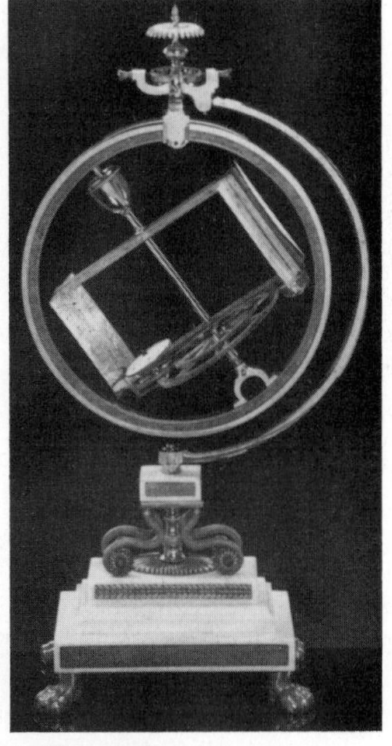

A gilt and silvered brass mechanical equinoctial dial, the heavy engine turned gilt brass meridian ring engraved with quadrant, fixed steel rod in the polar axis about which a rectangular frame revolves with silvered plates engraved with the months of the year and zodiac signs, and with an equation of time scale mounted above 3 gear wheels connected to white enamel watch dial, the whole pivoted from gimbals above and surmounted by flower petal finial on white marble base, with gilt brass mounts, raised on 4 lion paw feet, signed F. Sauter, Stockholm, c1805, 18in (46cm).
$60,000-75,000

F. Sauter is recorded as a clockmaker in Stockholm in 1808, and 3 clocks by him are in museum collections. Phillip Matthias Hahn (1739-1790) clock and watch maker of Ostmettingham made a number of similar equinoctial dials. Their use was to check the accuracy of clock and watch movements.

lobes

pair of terrestrial and celestial lobes by Newton, Son & Berry, hancery Lane, London, raised on urned baluster columns with ripod supports terminating in rass capped feet and casters, arly 19thC, 34in (86cm) high.
3,000-3,750

6in terrestrial table globe-on-tand, the coloured gores laid on phere within brass meridian, the orizontal ring applied with alendar and zodiac scales, on urned mahogany stand with tretcher, some damage, 19thC, ½in (24cm) high.
1,200-1,800

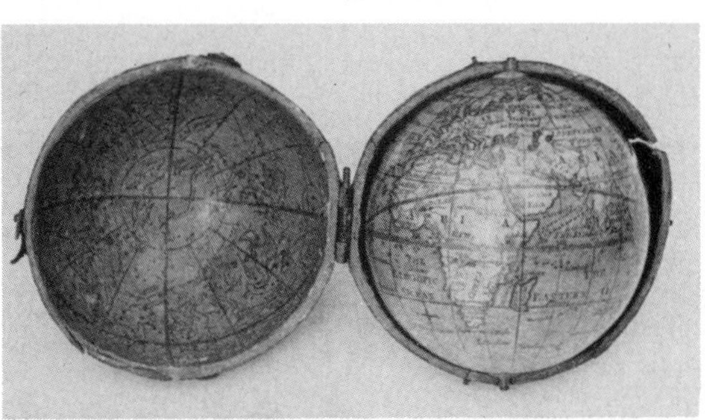

A 3in pocket terrestrial globe, applied with label printed Darton & Co, 55 Gracechurch Street, London, 1809, the sphere applied with hand coloured gores and mounted within fishskin covered case.
$3,000-3,750

A 2¾in pocket terrestrial globe, the sphere applied with hand coloured gores, printed 'A Correct Globe with the new Discoveries', contained in fishskin covered case with print of the heavens applied to the interior with label 'A Correct Globe with y New Constelations of Dr Halley & C., late 18thC.
$3,000-4,500

A Newton's 3in terrestrial globe the sphere applied with coloured gores, in turned wood case with domed lid, restored, 19thC.
$1,050-1,350

A Newton's 3in terrestrial globe, mid-19thC.
$900-1,500

A 3in pocket terrestrial globe, the coloured gores and trade label printed 'Harris, 77 Cornhill, London', in fishskin covered case with print of the heavens applied to inner surfaces, early 19thC, 3in (7.5cm).
$4,500-6,000

A pair of Malby's terrestrial and celestial table globes, the celestial dated 1850, the terrestrial dated 1848, bearing the Agent's label of Hodge and Smith, Grafton Street, Dublin, the stands with short turned and lobed tapered legs joined by a turned X-stretcher, 9in (22.5cm) diam.
$3,000-4,500

A 12in terrestrial table globe, with 12 coloured paper gores, showing the voyages of Capt. Gore and Capt. Cook, the brass meridian circle divided quadrantly, paper horizon ring on 4 tapered pillar legs, united by stretchers, marked London C. Smith & Son, 172 Strand, globe damaged.
$2,700-3,300

An 18in celestial globe-on-stand, by A.W. Bardin, the sphere mounted in brass meridian with horizontal ring above, on mahogany tripod base, globe cracked, part of horizontal ring scale missing, stand repaired, missing compass stretchers, c1800, 41in (104cm) high.
$2,700-3,300

Miller's is a price GUIDE not a price LIST

Iicroscopes

brass monocular compound
icroscope by Henry Crouch,
ith coarse and fine focusing, in
ahogany case with 3 oculars and
objectives, early 20thC, 12in
0.5cm).
00-750

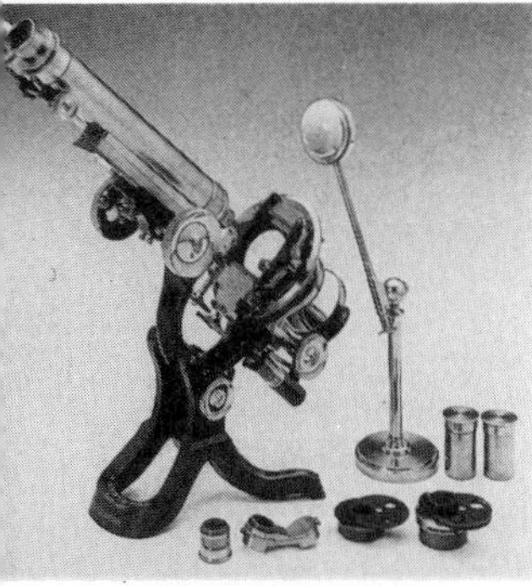

brass compound binocular
icroscope, signed J. Swift & Son,
ondon, with fine and coarse
cusing, circular stage and
nodised brass tripod base, in
ahogany case with 2 oculars, 2
jectives, bench condenser, sun
age wheel of stops and other
cesories, c1880.
,050-1,350

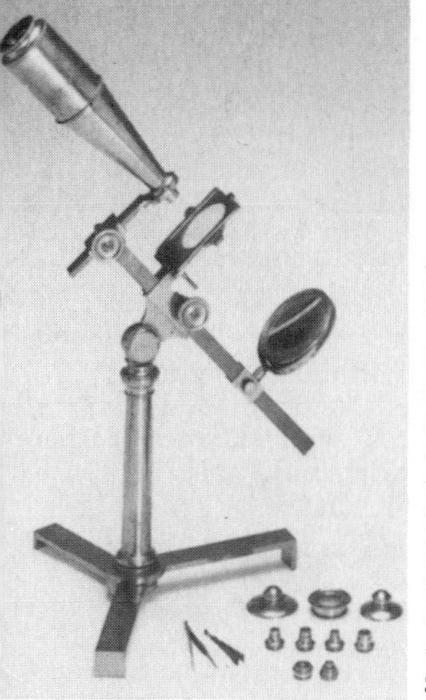

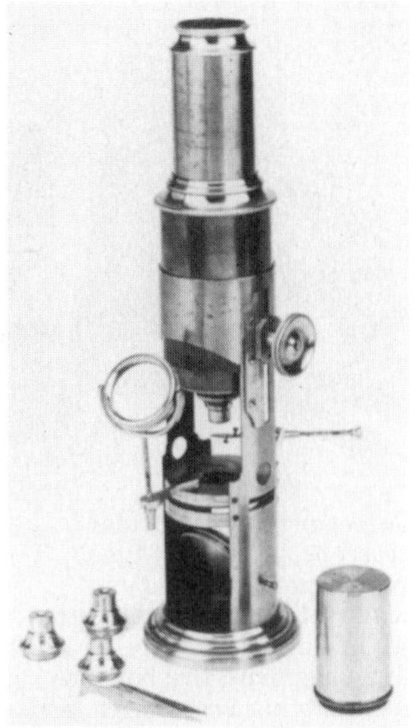

A lacquered brass Martins type drum microscope, with draw tube rack pinion focusing, single eyepiece, spring stage, concave mirror, fitted mahogany case with accessories, including numbered objectives 1-6, lieberkuhn, stage forceps and magnifier, in fitted mahogany case, 11in (28cm) wide.
$450-600

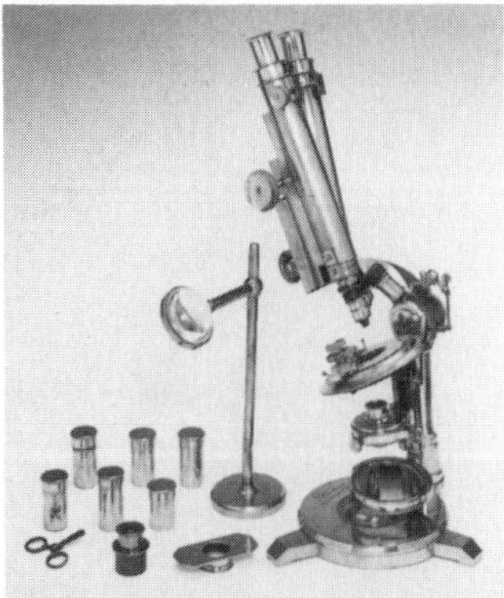

A brass compound binocular microscope, signed W. Watson & Sons, 313 High Holborn, London, No. 1466, the tubes with triple turret nosepiece, rack and pinion focusing and dual adjustment to the eyepieces, 20in (51cm) high, in mahogany case with set of 5 oculars and 2 eyepieces, analyser and bench condenser, late 19thC.
$2,250-3,000

A brass compound monocular microscope, signed on the foot Watkins, Charing Cross, London, the bar limb construction with rack and pinion focusing to the stage, plano/concave reflector, column support with folding tripod base, 19in (49cm) high, in mahogany case with 7 objectives, 2 lieberkuhns, live box, tweezers and other accessories, the lid applied with trade label, and case of specimen slides, early 19thC.
$1,500-2,250

A simple botanical microscope, the ebony base mounted with reflector and brass column, fitted with stage and 2 simple lenses, 4in (10cm), in fishskin covered case, with 2 slides and set of stage forceps, early 19thC.
$600-750

A lacquered brass monocular microscope, signed Smith & Beck, 6 Coleman St., London 1337, in fitted mahogany case with accessories.
$1,050-1,350

A lacquered brass monocular microscope, with detachable body tube and locking collar, rack and pinion and fine screw focusing, square faced rackwork in rectangular housing, square stage, concave mirror, Y-shaped foot, signed M. Pillischer, London, No. 769, with accessories in fitted mahogany case, 7in (17.5cm).
$300-375

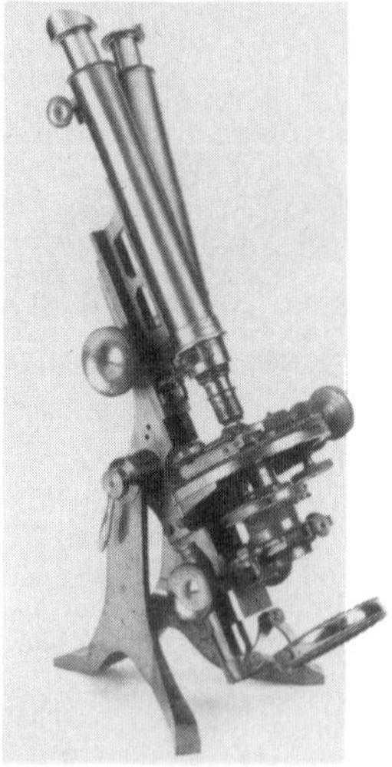

A lacquered brass binocular microscope, signed on the foot Ross London 4061, and on the binocular body tube Wenhams Binocular by Ross London, in fitted glass fronted case with carrying handles and accessories, with 2 part filled cases of accessories by various makers including an iris by R. & J. Beck, a large prism on sliding collar signed George S. Wood Late Abraham & Co, Optician Liverpool, polariser, camera lucida by Powell & Lealand, Ross London, H. Crouch, London and others, late 19thC, 21in (53cm) high.
$450-600

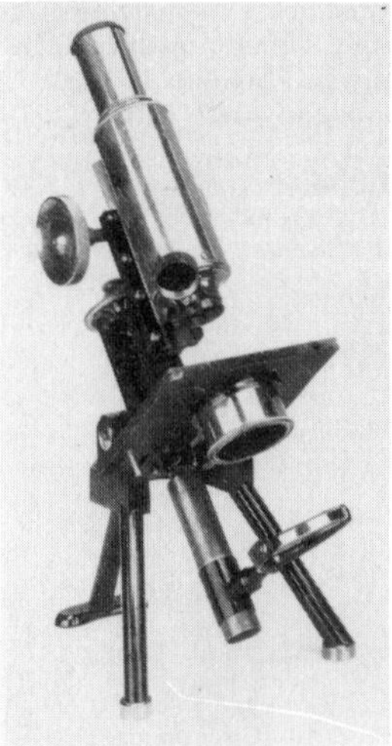

A lacquered brass microscope, signed E. Leitz Wetzlar, No. 19488, with draw tube focusing, fine focusing screw, square stage, knuckle joint, sub stage condenser, plano-concave mirror, on Y-shaped foot, in case with accessories, 13in (33cm).
$300-375

A brass travelling microscope illuminating lamp, signed J Swift's registered, with an on/off fuel screw, paraffin basin, telescopic adjustment on folding tripod stand in brass case, 9in (22.5cm).
$600-750

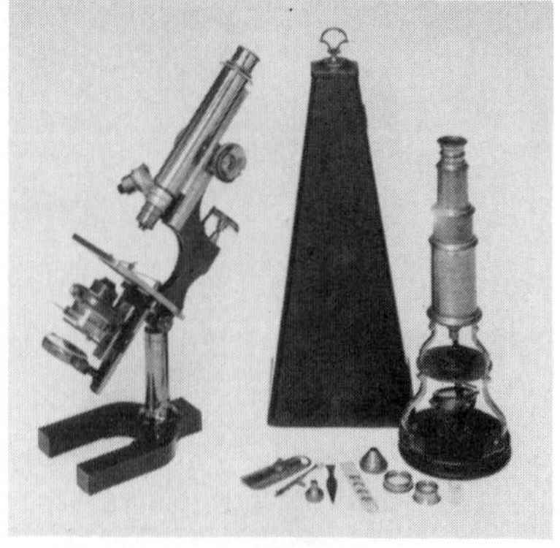

A Culpeper type monocular microscope, with draw tube focusing, circular stage and concave reflector, on mahogany base, 10¼in (26cm), in pillar case with 2 objectives, live box, fish plate and other accessories, and a W. Watson & Sons brass compound monocular microscope, with focusing by rack and pinion and milled screw, double nosepiece, sub stage condenser, 13in (33cm), 19thC.
$1,200-1,500

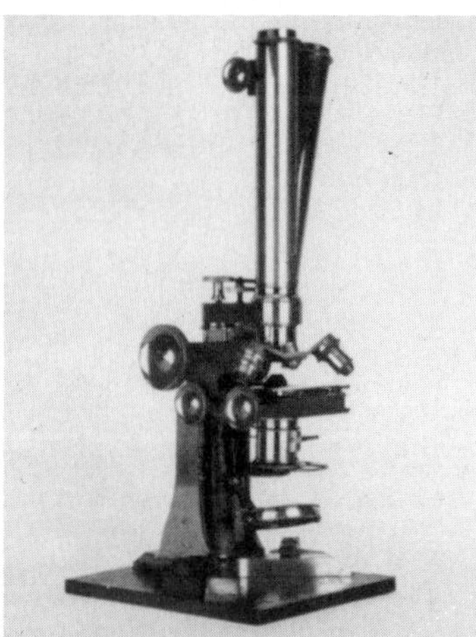

An oxidised and lacquered brass monocular microscope, signed J. Swift & Son London, with rack and pinion and fine focusing screw, double nosepiece, square stage, plano-concave mirror on sliding collar, on raised tripod foot, in fitted mahogany case wit accessories, .
$375-525

A lacquered brass binocular microscope, signed J Swift, 43 University St., London WC, with eyepiece rack and pinion and fin focusing screw, the body tube attached to limb by screw, with main rack and pinion focusing, triangular rack work, square mechanical stage, sub stage condenser, plano-concave mirror on Y-shaped foot, in fitted mahogany case with accessories, late 19thC, 12in (31cm).
$600-750

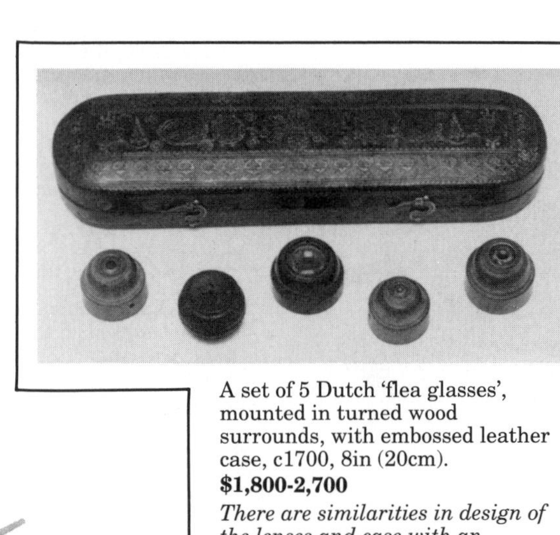

A set of 5 Dutch 'flea glasses', mounted in turned wood surrounds, with embossed leather case, c1700, 8in (20cm).
$1,800-2,700
There are similarities in design of the lenses and case with an example made by Johan van Musschenbroek.

cased collection of pproximately 1,000 microscope pecimen slides, professionally ounted, in mahogany cabinet ith 29 drawers and brass arrying handle, late 19thC, 20in 51cm).
1,500-2,250

A lacquered brass Martins type drum microscope, signed W. E. & F. Newton, 3 Fleet St. Temple Bar London, with rack and pinion focusing, single nosepiece, circular spring stage, with mirror on circular foot, with 6 numbered lenses and other accessories in fitted mahogany case with trade label. **$750-900**

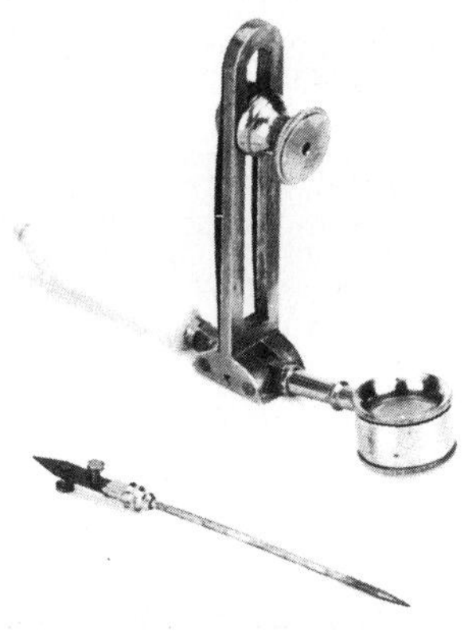

A simple microscope, with turned bone handle, live box, stage forceps in red leather covered case, 3in (7.5cm) wide.
$375-525

Telescopes

brass reflecting telescope-on-tand, signed James Short ondon 149/1032=7, focusing to he secondary reflector by milled nob, screw and shaft, tube 11in 28cm) long.
1,500-2,250

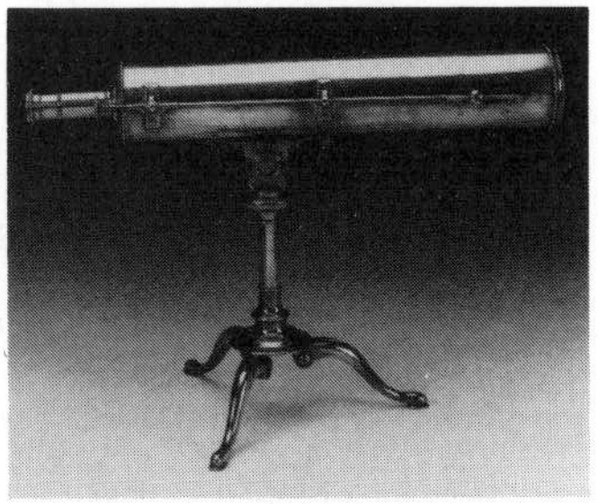

A 3in brass reflecting telescope-on-stand, engraved on the eyepiece tube B. Martin, Fleet Street, London, New Metals by Jones 1797, Rep by Newton & C° 3 Fleet Street 1884, the Gregorian reflector with adjustment to the secondary reflector by long shank and screw mechanism, 18in (46cm), the tube supported by a bracket above column and folding tripod base, c1770.
$2,250-3,000

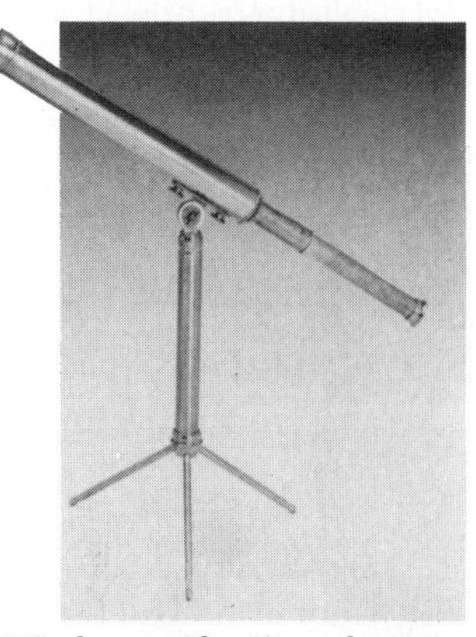

A 1½in brass refracting telescope, with 2 draw tubes, supported by bracket above tripod base, by Aitchison, early 20thC, length of tube 15in (38cm), with alternative eyepiece.
$750-900

1½in single draw brass elescope, signed Ramsden, ondon, with adjustable eyepiece, nternal ray shade and dust slide, ody tube focusing, pillar mount, ocated by slide, shagreen body ube covering, damaged and acking tripod stand, 18thC, 4½in 11cm), in mahogany case.
450-600

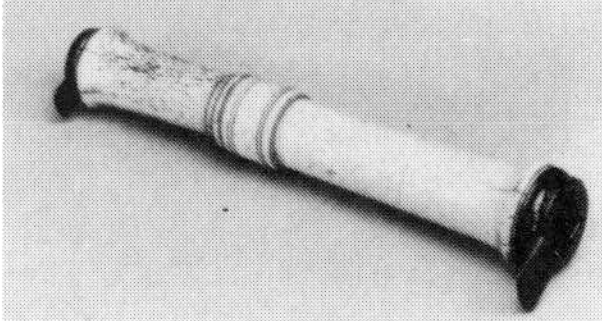

A turned bone telescope in 2 parts, with lacquered brass dust covers and slides, 18thC, 6½in (16cm). **$450-600**

A 2¾in Gregorian reflecting telescope, signed around the collar James Short London, 242 over 1061 9.6, the tube with milled wheel focusing, complete with eyepiece, cover, on column support which screws into the lid of the mahogany case, 16½in (42cm).
$3,000-3,750

A 3in lacquered brass refracting telescope, with rack and pinion focus, on tapered pillar support and folding tripod stand, with additional lenses, in pine case bearing the trade label of J.W. Bailey, London, 19thC.
$750-1,200

A terrestrial collapsing globe, labelled 'By the Queens Royal Letters Patent Betts's New Portable Terrestrial Globe compiled from the latest and best authorities, London, John Betts, 115 Strand', the 8 coloured lithographed gores printed on linen, stitched over a black japanned umbrella type frame with brass coloured caps, contained in original wooden box with advertisement on verso of lid, c1860, 15in (38cm) diam.
$750-900

Two small field telescopes, one signed J King, Bristol, with 6 brass draws, horn bound tube, extended length 13in (33cm), in case with collar and screw and alternate eyepiece, the other with 2 sets of 2 draws, extended length 8in (20cm), in case with collar and screw.
$450-600

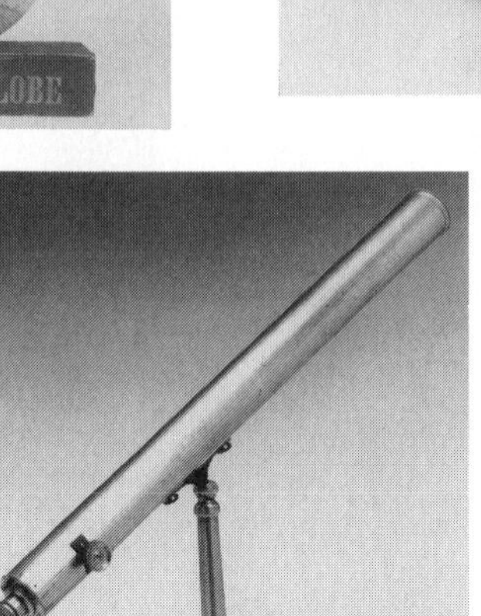

A 3in brass refracting telescope-on-stand, signed Clarkson, London, the brass tube mounted on tapering brass column and folding iron base, in pine case with 2 oculars, early 20thC, length of tube 38½in (97cm).
$900-1,500

A brass and rosewood three-draw telescope, with folding tripod stand, and an additional eyepiece, in fitted mahogany case, by Newton & Co, 3 Fleet Street, Temple Bar, London, hinge damaged, 19thC, 30in (76cm) extended.
$750-900

Surveying

A surveying compass, signed J. Bedington Maker with twin folding sighting vanes, silvered dial, in fitted mahogany case, early 19thC, 7in (18cm) wide.
$300-375

A lacquered brass surveying level, signed and with trade label Troughton & Simms Opticians and Mathematical Instrument makers to the honourable board of Ordinance London, in fitted mahogany case with accessories, 19thC, 16in (41cm) wide.
$375-525

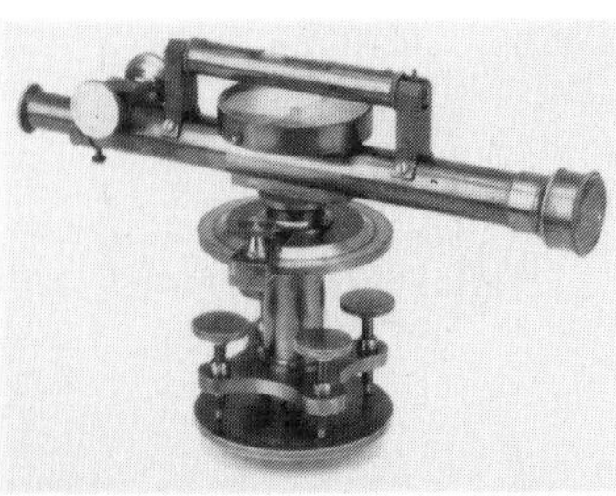

A French oxidised and lacquered brass surveying level, 12in (31cm) wide.
$300-375

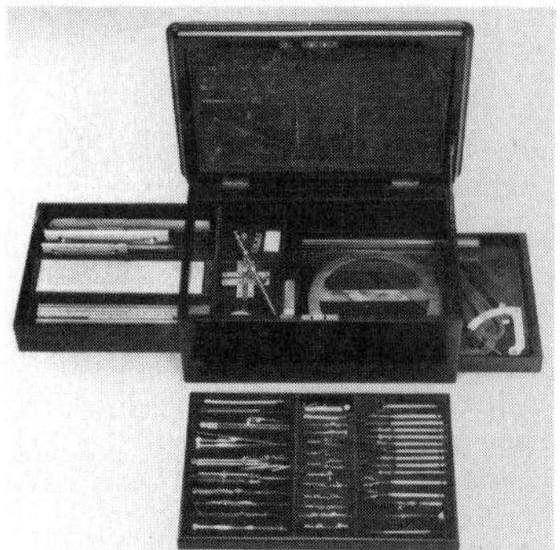

A set of ivory and nickel drawing instruments, mid-19thC, 21in (53cm) wide.
$1,200-1,800

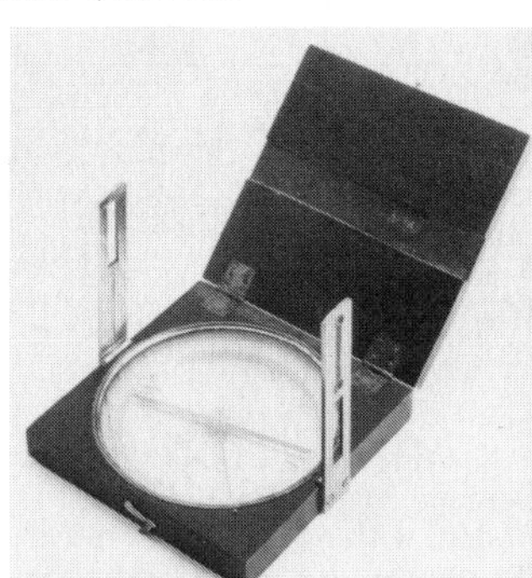

A surveying compass, signed Cole, Maker, Fleet Street, London, with twin folding sighting vanes, silvered dial divided 10-360°, with edge bar needle and clamp, in fitted mahogany case, mid-18thC, 6in (15cm) wide.
$375-525

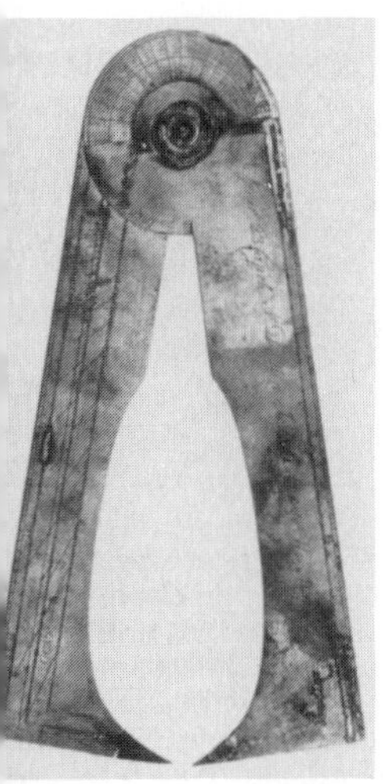

pair of gunner's brass callipers, gned Spear 22 Capel St. Dublin ıst. Maker to His Majesty's rdinance, the scales for Iron uns Proof Service and Brass uns Proof Service with 2 iron ɔinters, 7in (17.5cm) long.
00-750

n ebony and brass octant, signed an ivory plaque on the cross rm Spencer Browning & Co, ondon. Made for P. Atkey owes, the ivory arc from 0°-105°, nely divided by 'S.B.R.', with rass index arm, ivory vernier, agnifier, tangent screw and amp, the body with telescope vepiece, and 2 mirrors with ıades in fitted mahogany case, ith accessories, early 19thC.
750-900

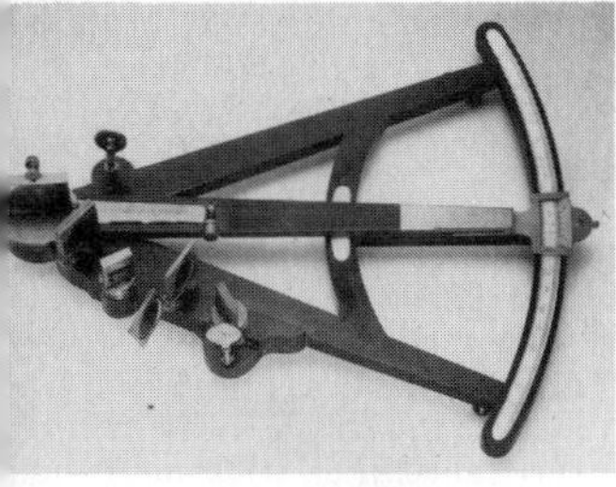

. Benjamin Martin Hadley's uadrant, signed on the brass ıdex arm Martin Inv et fecit ondini, with ebony frame and vory scale, vernier, maker's laque and pencil holder, fore and ack sights, and 2 sets of coloured lters, c1770, 16in (41cm) radius.
3,000-4,500

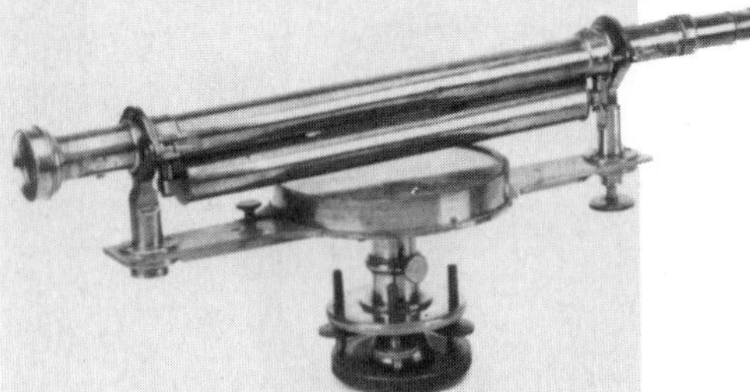

A brass surveying level, signed on the silvered dial Cary London, with rack and pinion objective focusing, over graduated bubble level, the limb with compass box with edge bar needle and clamp, the dial divided quadrantly, with levelling screw on staff mounting in fitted mahogany case, 19thC, 14½in (37cm).
$300-375

A lacquered brass 'Douglas' reflecting protractor, signed Cary London Patent 185, the scale rule combined with a 0°-120° part circle, the hinged arm with sliding vernier quadrant, fitted with pin hole sight and mirrors, in fitted mahogany case with trade label for William Harris & Co. 6½in (16cm).
$600-750

The patent was designed by Sir Howard Douglas in 1811 and was used on a plane table.

A brass three-ring sextant, signed Williams & Son Cardiff, with silvered scale from -5°-145°, brass index arm with vernier, magnifier, tangent screw and clamp, 7 coloured shades, mirror and telescope eyepiece, in fitted case, 19thC.
$600-750

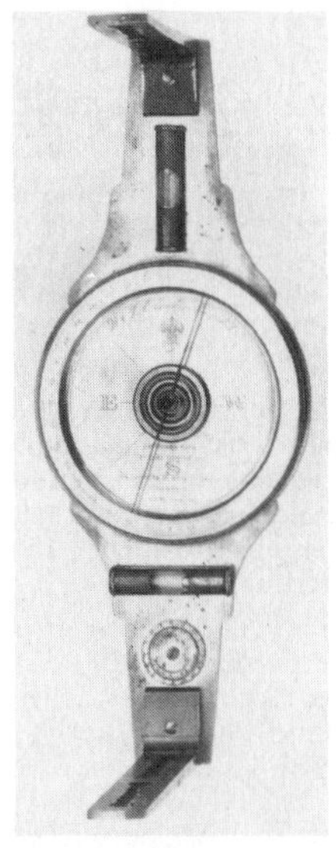

A brass surveying compass, signed on the dial W. & L.E. Gurley, Rio de Janeiro, in fitted mahogany case, 19thC, 14in (35cm) wide.
$375-525

An oxidised and lacquered brass theodolite, signed on the silvered compass dial Chadburn & Son, Liverpool, with fitted mahogany case, 19thC, 15in (38cm) wide.
$1,050-1,350

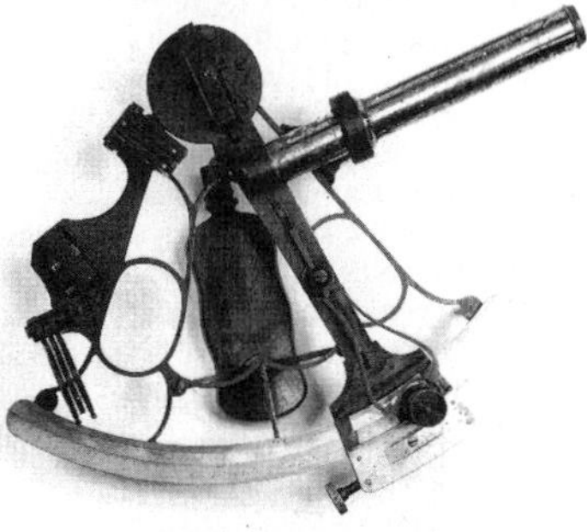

A sextant, signed Kelvin and James White Ltd, Glasgow, 6370, the silvered scale divided from -5°-155°, the index arm with vernier magnifier, tangent screw and clamp, the frame with telescope eyepiece, 2 mirrors each with 3 shades, in fitted mahogany case containing additional eyepieces and dust caps, late 19thC.
$900-1,500

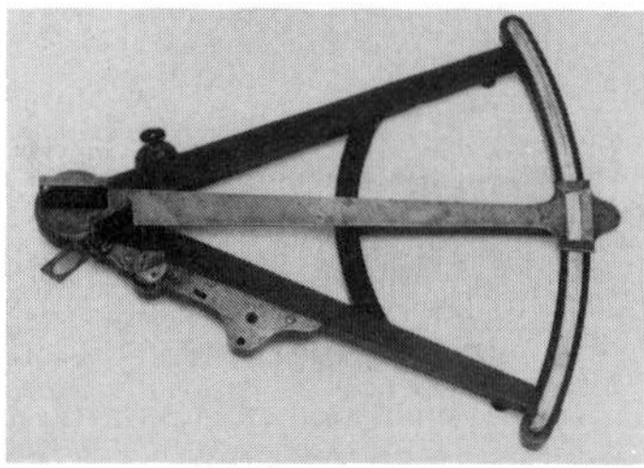

A Spencer Browning & Rust ebony Hadley's quadrant, with ivory scale, brass index arm, peep hole sight and one set of coloured filters, late 18thC, 15½in (39cm) radius.
$1,050-1,350

A black enamelled transit theodolite, signed E. R. Watts & Son Ltd, London 53511.
$300-375

An azimuth theodolite, signed T. Heath, fecit, the telescope mounted with sights above racked 240° arc, compass rose and horizontal circle of degrees arc, on staffhead mount with 4 levelling screws, some damage, mid-18thC 16½in (42cm).
$10,500-12,000

This model was illustrated as the frontispiece to John Hammond, The Practical Surveyor, 1731 edition.

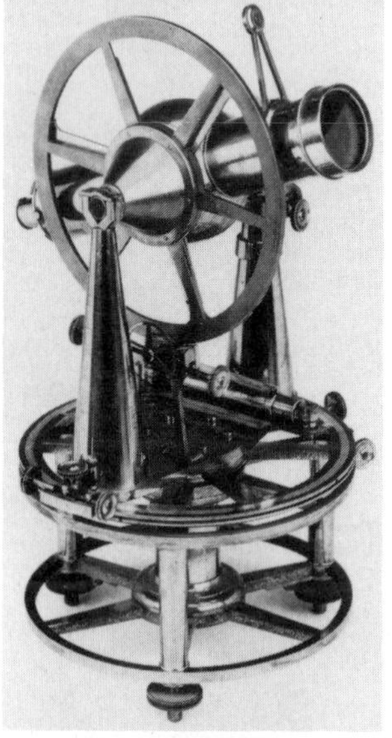

A lacquered brass transit theodolite, signed Thomas Jones, Charing Cross, London, the telescope with right angle eyepiece on sliding plate, the 8in diam. vertical circle with silvered scale divided 10-360°, with triple vernier scale, wheel clamp, tangent screws, supported by twin conical trunnions, over the 9in diam. horizontal circle with graduated bubble level, silvered scale divided 10-360°, triple vernier scales, tangent screw and clamp on circular table mount, supported by 3 outer pillars and central tapered trunnion, with 3 levelling screws, early 19thC, 17in (43cm) high, in a substantial fitted mahogany carrying case with brass fittings.
$10,500-12,000

A grey enamelled transit theodolite, signed W.F.S. 44301 B 18261, the telescope with focus, clamp, eyepiece micrometer, fine focusing and cross hairs, the silvered vertical circle with twin vernier and magnifiers, with graduated bubble, mounted over the enclosed silvered horizontal circle with twin verniers and magnifiers, the cross bubble over 3 screw tripod mount, in fitted case, 13½in (34cm) high.
$750-900

A blue enamelled transit theodolite, The Eltham, signed Stanley, London, 50409, on an A frame support over a similarly mounted horizontal circle, with cross bubble over 3-screw tripod mount, in fitted case with accessories, 13in (33cm).
$450-600

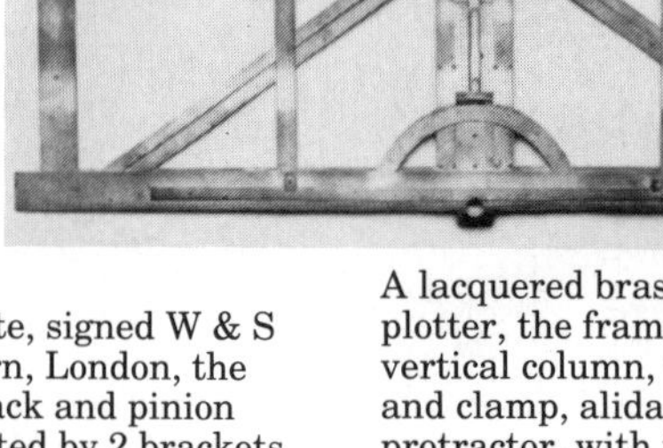

A lacquered brass trigonometric plotter, the frame with central vertical column, with main slide and clamp, alidade and protractor, with further scales and movement, on plush covered board, 19thC, 36in (91cm) wide.
$450-600

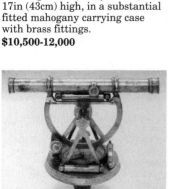

A brass theodolite, signed W & S Jones, 30 Holborn, London, the telescope with rack and pinion focusing, supported by 2 brackets above racked arc, compass and horizontal circle of degrees with verniers and 2 spirit levels on staff head mount, early 19thC, 9in (22.5cm) high, in mahogany case.
$900-1,500

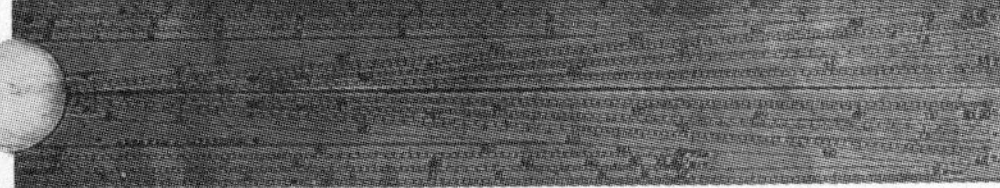

A boxwood and brass sector, signed Cole Maker at Ye Orrery in Fleet Street, London, engraved with scales, 18thC, 13in (33cm) wide.
$750-900

A boxwood and brass sector, signed Abraham Liverpool, with engraved scales, 19thC, 12½in (32cm). **$375-450**

A lacquered brass combination surveying instrument, signed Baker and Hooper, with alidade, twin folding sighting vanes, trough compass, parallel rules, protractor and bubble level, in fitted mahogany case, 12in (30.5cm), and a brass parallel rule protractor.
$1,800-2,700

Medical & Dental Instruments

A hand blown dark green carboy, with cork stopper, 40in (101.5cm).
$750-1,200

Four globular green glass hand blown carboys, 2 dark green and 2 lime green, with cork stoppers, 2 with partial remains of labels, 14in (36cm) high.
$750-1,200

\ wooden door, with glass panel, llustrating a green carboy, and nscribed in red Dispensing Dept, he glass 36½ (93cm) high.
375-450

Thirty-three clear glass wet drug rounds, with painted gilt, red and black labels, including 'Smalts', various sizes.
$375-450

\ pair of apothecary's glass jars, ach with domed lid, painted on nner surface and applied with ilt labels 'Peruvianbark' and Rhubarb', mid-19thC, 20in 51cm).
750-1,200

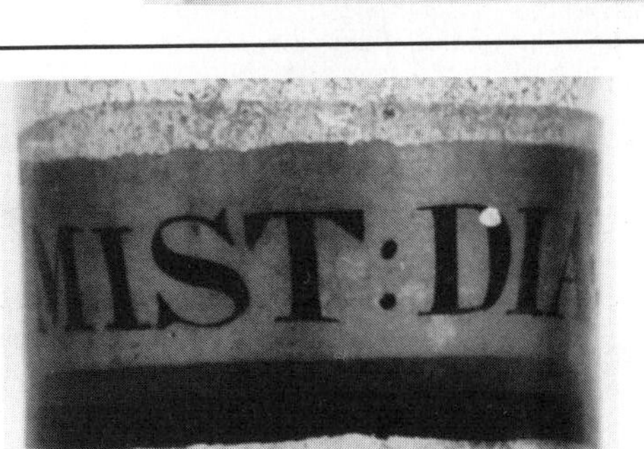

Twenty-six clear glass drug rounds, with painted labels in black, red and gilt, including 'MIST:DIAR'.
$450-600

A brass bound mahogany medicine chest, opening to interior fitted with 10 glass bottles, 2 drawers containing a set of scales and weights, glass pestle and mortar and small bottles, mid-19thC, 8¼in (21cm) wide when closed.
$1,050-1,350

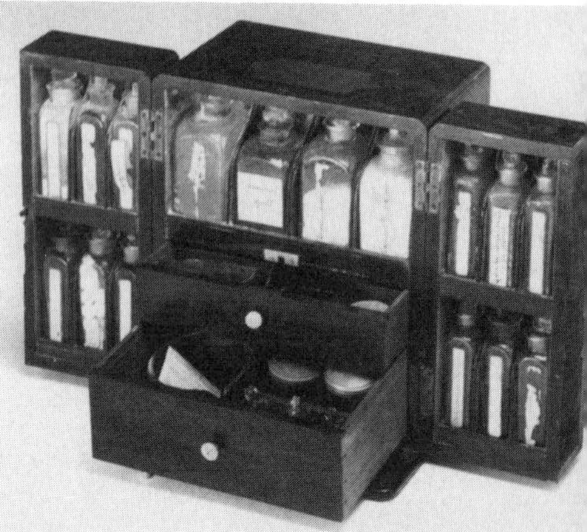

A mahogany medicine chest, the fitted interior with glass bottles, mortar and pestle, measuring flask, set of scales, compartment at the back containing 4 further bottles, 19thC, 10½in (27cm).
$3,000-3,750

Twelve Bristol blue drug rounds, 3 with pouring spouts, 3 with stoppers missing, with titles including 'SYR:SENNAE' and 'SULPH:VIVUM', various sizes and labels.
$450-600

TINCT. ALOES

Twenty-nine clear glass wet drug rounds, of various sizes and designs, including 4 ribbed bottles, with gilt, red and black labels marked 'For Poison', the others with gilt and black shield labels variously inscribed, including 'TINCT LIMONIS'.
$450-600

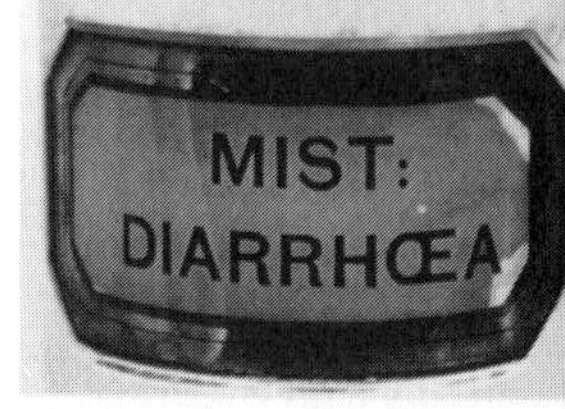

Twenty-two clear glass drug rounds, with gilt, white, red and black octagonal shield labels, various sizes, including large drug round with label for 'PEAR DROPS', with cut glass stopper.
$750-900

Thirty clear glass drug rounds, with painted black and gilt labels, including 'FER:et', 'AM:CIT' and 'F:CALUMBIA', various sizes and stoppers.
$900-1,500

A pewter 'Gibson' spoon, indistinctly signed MAW, Aldersgate, mid-19thC, 5in (13cm).
$375-450

Fifteen ribbed green glass drug rounds, variously inscribed on yellow and black labels, including 'LIE:HYDRARG:PERCH' (poison)
$900-1,500

A silver gilt linctus dropper, the stylised fish head with glass eyes, and tongue pierced to form the dropper, the body of turned horn concealing the reservoir, with silver tail, hallmarked London 1857, 6in (15cm) long.
$2,700-3,300

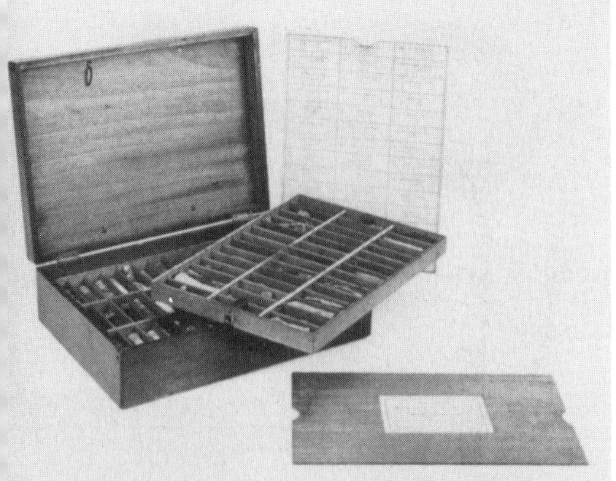

mahogany medical cabinet, ith 2 numbered content cards id 3 numbered trays, containing ots, herbs, plants and minerals, in (38cm) wide.
00-375

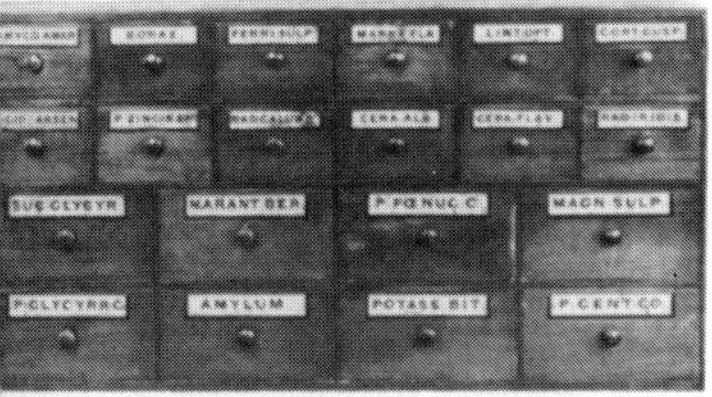

mahogany chemist's drug run, ith drawers, each with painted bel, 48in (122cm).
,200-1,500

n eyeglass, in turned 'scissor' ood frame, with 2 strengths of lter, late 18thC, 3in (7.5cm) ide.
450-600

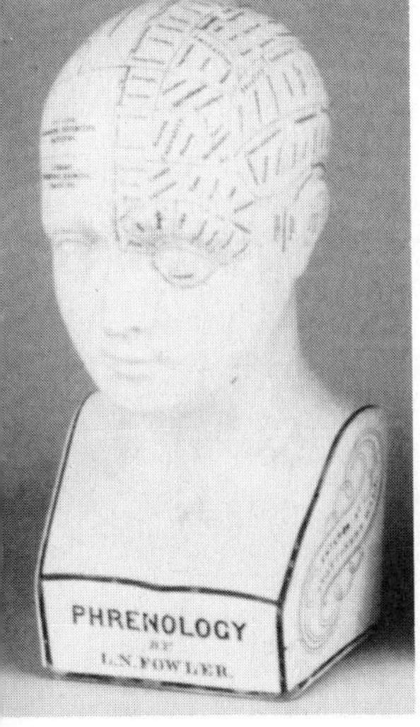

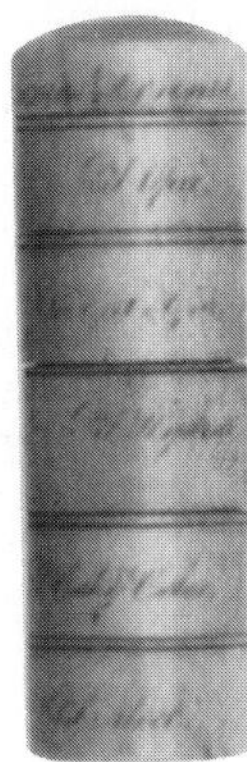

An ivory pill tower, with labelled sections, inscribed James Dennis, 3in (7.5cm) high.
$450-600

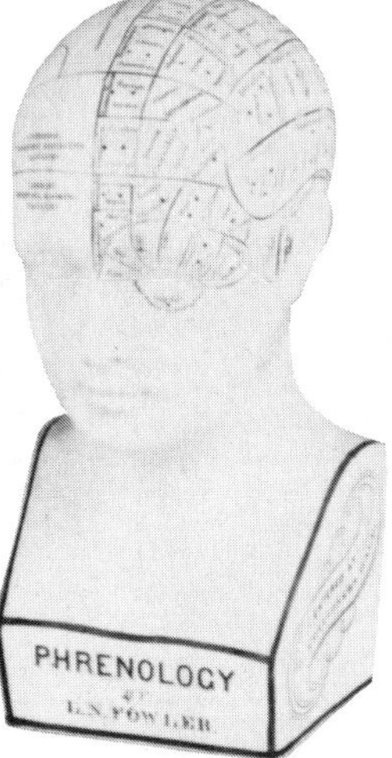

A porcelain phrenological bust, the cranium divided in areas controlling Time, Ideality, Sublimity and other actions and emotions, marked in blue and black, signed L.N. Fowler, 337, Strand, London, 19thC, 11½in (29cm).
$1,200-1,500

A pair of leather framed spectacles, the crudely cut leather frames with inset 1⅛in (3cm) lenses, one cracked.
$450-600

Apparently these spectacles were found in the drawer lining of an 18thC chest of drawers.

A porcelain phrenological bust, the cranium divided in areas controlling emotion, marked in blue and black, signed L. N. Fowler, 337 Strand, London, late 19thC, 11½in (29cm).
$3,000-3,750

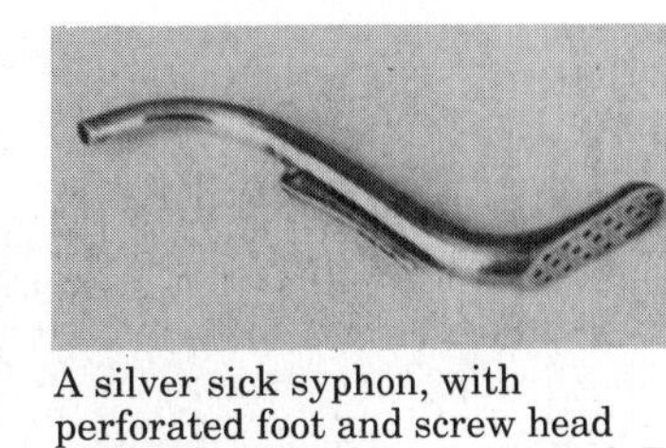

A silver sick syphon, with perforated foot and screw head attachment, with maker's mark T. & E. Phipps, London 1802, 5in (13cm) long.
$300-375

A mahogany velvet lined domestic medicine chest, signed Springweiler & Co., Makers, London, case damaged, 9½ by 8in (24 by 20cm).
$750-900

An articulated human skeleton, dismantled, in carrying case with trade label 'Established A.D. 1815, Millikin & Lawley, dealers in surgical Instruments, Microscopes and Osteology, 165 Strand, London WC2 (Five doors East of King's College)', 22in (56cm) wide.
$225-255

A pair of silver oval lens spectacles, with segmental bridge, folding sides with pear drop ends, in fitted silver mounted tortoiseshell case, 5½in (13.5cm).
$225-255

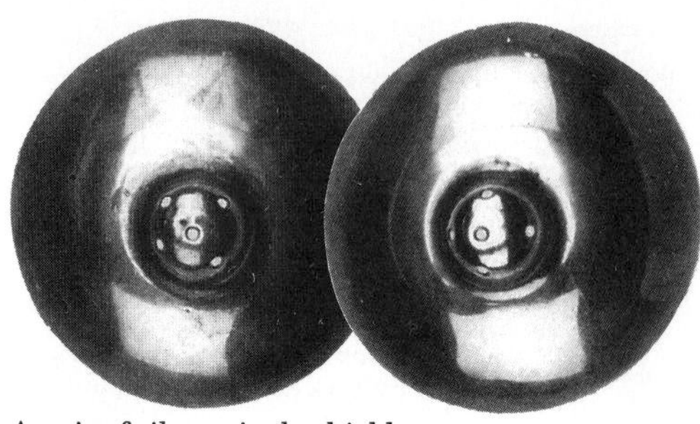

A pair of silver nipple shields, signed Weiss, mid-19thC.
$375-525

A pair of round lens, Martins Margins temple nose spectacles, with arched bridges, straight sides with loo ends, in a paper card case.
$450-600

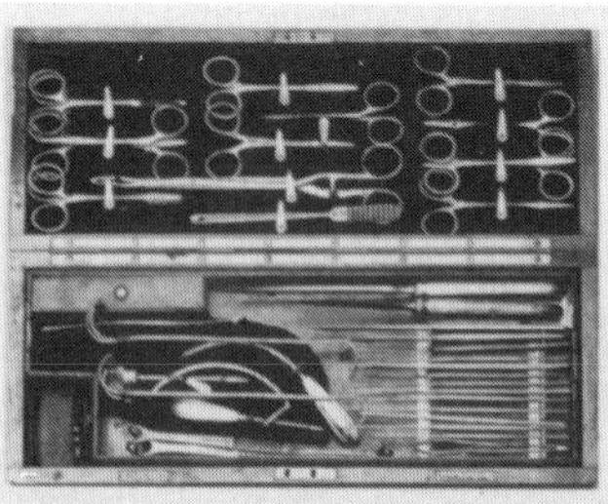

A WWI field surgeon's instruments case, the lid with forceps, lift-out tray with Liston knives, lancets, 2 trocar and cannulae, trephine, the lower case with trephine and handle, bone saw and small bone saw, 2 silver trachaeotomy tubes and spools, bullet probe, needles and other instruments in velvet lined brass bound mahogany case, with protective metal casing, signed Meyer & Meltzer London.
$1,200-1,500

A pair of silver round lens blue tinted spectacles, with segmental bridge, jointed sides with pear drop ends, in fitted shagreen cas and a pair of blue tinted D-end spectacles, with segmental bridg thin blued steel frame, with red leather case.
$300-375

A percussion hammer with turned finial, tapered ivory handle, damaged, a pentagon end dura cutter with octagonal ebony handle c1860, a goat's foot elevator and another instrument of similar pattern.
$300-375

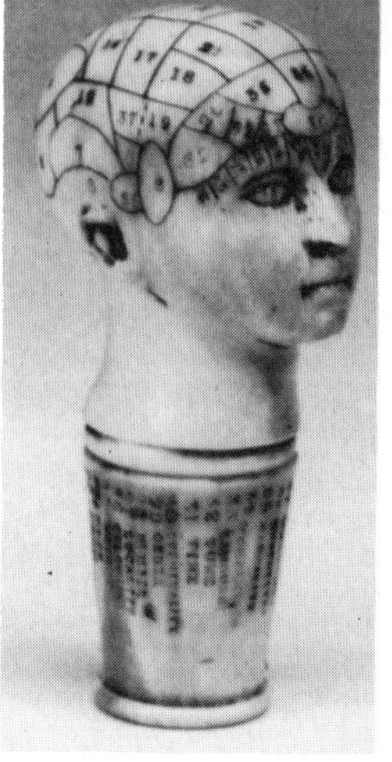

An ivory cane handle, shaped as a phrenology bust, incised with numbered areas on the cranium relating to numbered sentiments inscribed on the neck, including areas for Wonder, Hope and Weight, with detachable neck, mid-19thC, 2½in (6cm).
$1,200-1,800

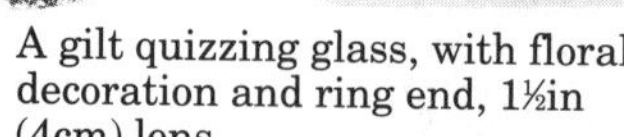

A gilt quizzing glass, with floral decoration and ring end, 1½in (4cm) lens.
$150-225

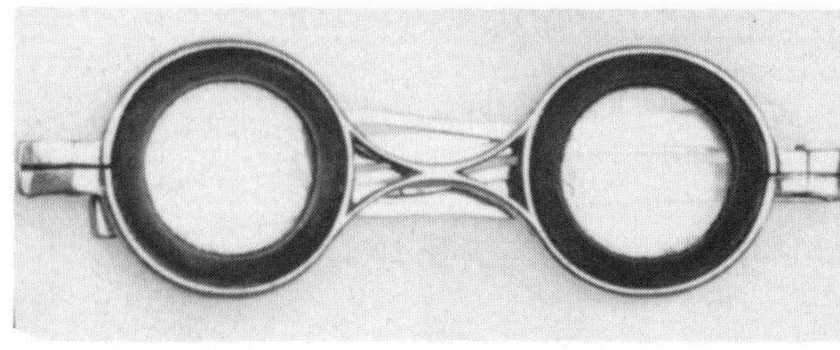

A rare pair of silver Martins Margins, with round lens, X-frame, horn inserts, folding side with large pear drop ends, one altered, dated.
$600-750

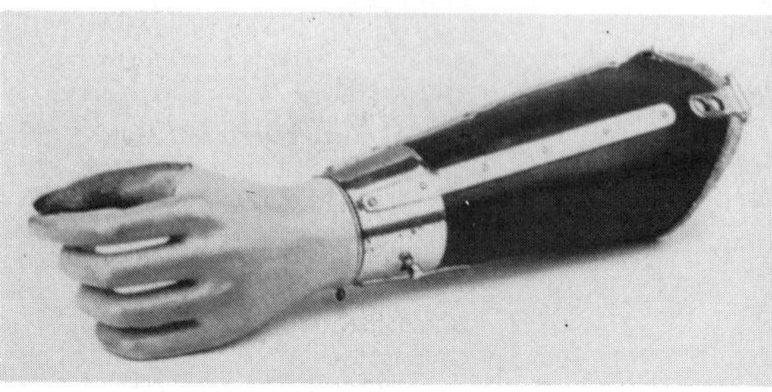

A leather and metal braced artificial arm, the composition and wood hand with articulated thumb, rotating detachable wrist with locking levers, cord straps, signed Steeper, 15in (38cm) long.
$375-450

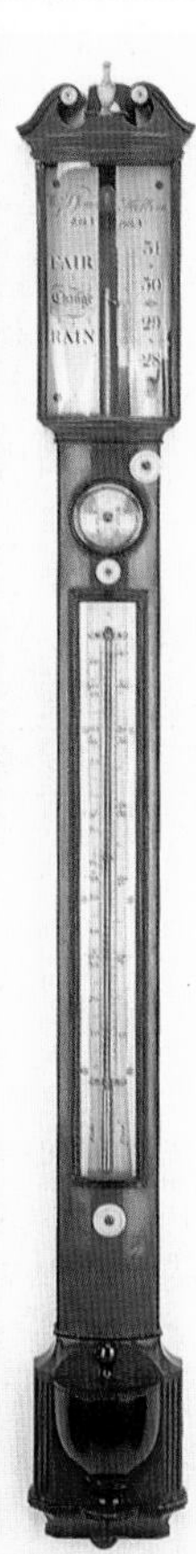

Georgian
ahogany and
onised stick
rometer, by W.
J. Jones, 40in
01.5cm).
,000-6,750

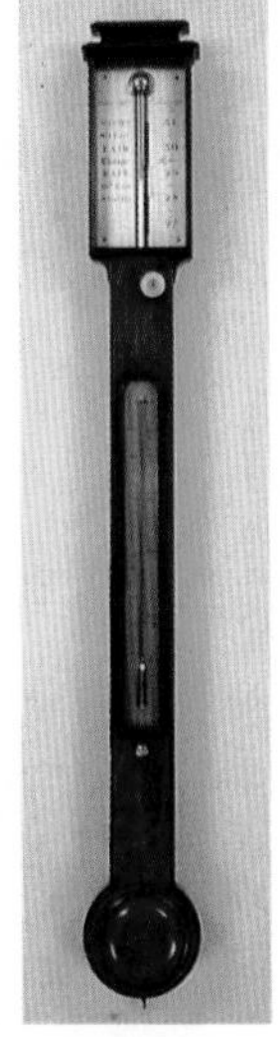

A mahogany cistern stick barometer, signed Zerboni & Co., c1825.
$3,000-3,750

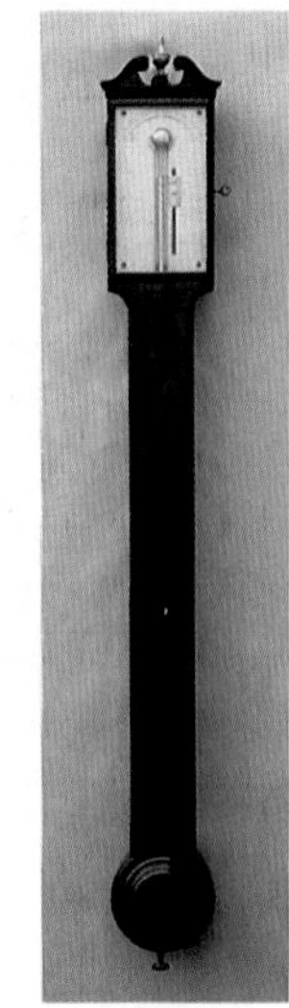

A mahogany stick barometer, by George Adams, London, c1785.
$3,750-4,500

A mahogany shield-shape wheel barometer, by A. Alberti, Sheffield, 8in (20cm) dial, c1825.
$1,800-2,250

A satinwood inlaid mahogany wheel barometer, signed Vittory & Merone, Manchester, c1785.
$4,500-6,000

An inlaid mahogany round top wheel barometer, by James Gatty, London, c1780.
$3,750-4,500

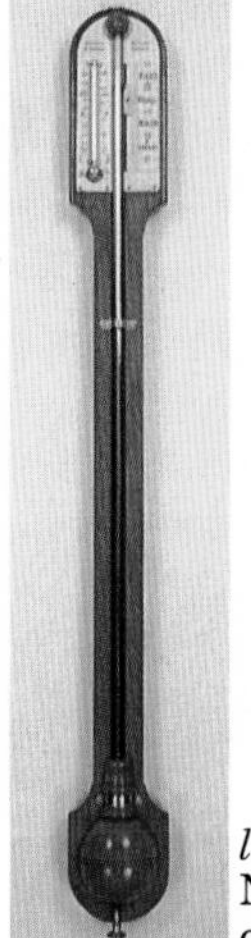

l. An oak stick barometer, by Negretti & Zambra, London, c1870. **$1,000-1,300**

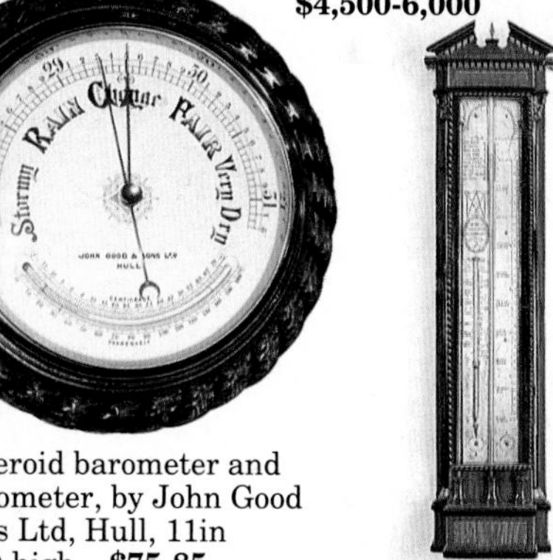

An aneroid barometer and thermometer, by John Good & Sons Ltd, Hull, 11in (28cm) high. **$75-85**

A Dutch ebonised barometer, signed Geb Lurafco te, late 18thC.
$5,250-6,000

brass inlaid
ahogany and
sewood wheel
rometer, by
ollond, London.
,750-4,500

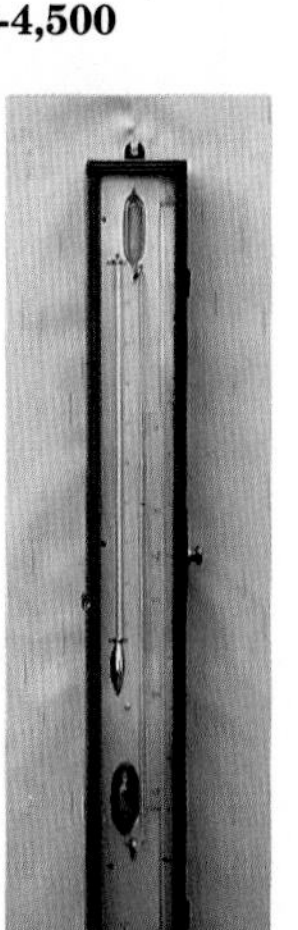

A sympiesometer, No. 372, by A. Adie, Edinburgh, c1822.
$3,000-3,500

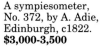

A rosewood cased wheel barometer, with hygrometer, thermometer, mirror and spirit level, c1840. **$2,200-2,800**

A leftward pointing Masonic mahogany 'signpost' barometer, by Giobbio, Trowbridge, c1800.
$7,500-9,000

A Victorian inlaid mahogany musical bracket clock, 19thC, 25½in (65cm).
$2,250-3,750

A Regency 8-day bracket clock, E. Thorp, Stockwell, c1820. **$3,750-4,500**

A Victorian ormolu mounted walnut bracket clock.
$6,000-6,750

A Regency mahogany 8-day bracket clock, by Edward Lee, c1810, 15½in (39cm).
$4,500-5,250

A Regency 8-day bracket clock, by Perigal, London, the ebonised case with brass mounts, 11in (28cm). **$5,250-6,000**

A Victorian 8-day grande sonnerie bracket clock, with mahogany brass mounted case, 27½in (70cm).
$2,250-3,000

A George II walnut timepiece, signed Thomas Faldo, Shefford, mid-18thC, 17in (43cm).
$5,250-6,000

A Charles II ebonised striking bracket clock, by William Cattell, 12in (30.5cm).
$10,000-11,250

A George III bronze mounted mahogany musical bracket clock, by Adam Travers, London, restored, 18thC, 25½in (65cm).
$9,750-11,250

A Louis XV boulle bracket clock, dial and movement signed Panier à Paris, c1730, 40in (102cm).
$5,250-6,750

A Regency 8-day rosewood brass inlaid bracket clock, by William Turner, 5 pillar movement striking hours on a bell.
$3,000-3,750

A Regency mahogany 8-day bracket clock, by James Wilson, striking the hours on a bell, c1810. **$4,500-5,000**

A satinwood carriage clock, with enamel dial signed Hʸ. Marc A Paris, bell striking movement No. 18562, with ratchet tooth lever escapement, c1850, 6in (15cm). **$1,000-1,250**

A red boulle carriage clock, with enamel dial signed Hʸ. Marc A Paris, bell striking movement No. 18839, with lever escapement, c1850, 6in (15cm). **$2,500-3,000**

A gilt brass and enamel striking carriage clock, stamped E.M. & Co., 6½in (16cm). **$3,000-3,750**

A gilt brass porcelain mounted striking carriage clock, signed Howell James & Co., 5½in (14cm). **$1,500-2,250**

A gilt brass striking carriage clock, with automaton singing bird, stamped Japy Frères, 11½in (30cm). **$7,500-9,000**

A French repeating carriage clock, with 8-day heavy plate movement, the brass masked dial plate engraved and inset with enamel chapter ring, separate alarm dial, original carrying case and winding key, c1875. **$5,250-6,000**

A gilt brass striking ar musical carriage clock for the Chinese market stamped Japy Frères, 7½in (18.5cm). **$2,500-3,500**

A Victorian gilt brass carriage chronometer, signed E. White, 20 Cockspur Street, London, No. 1449, 9½in (23.5cm). **$9,000-9,750**

A brass carriage clock, complete with leather covered case, early 20thC, 5in (13cm). **$150-250**

A gilt brass grande sonnerie striking calendar carriage cloc with stamp for Drocourt, signe by Tiffany & Co., New York, with leather case, 8½in (21.5cn **$15,000-17,000**

walnut and arquetry ngcase ock, by eorge Tyler, 705, 83in 11cm).
1,250-2,000

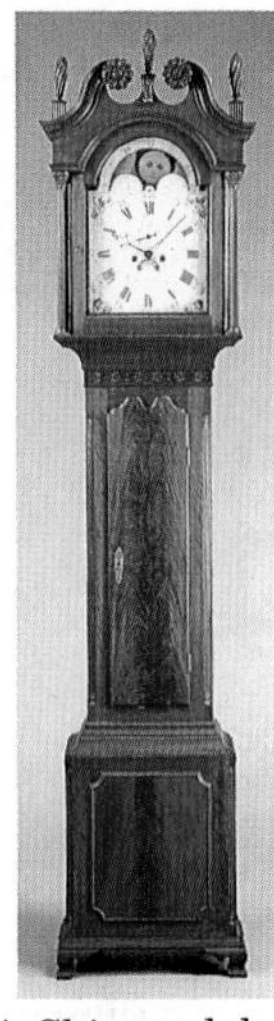
A Chippendale carved walnut longcase clock, by Jacob Hostetter, c1810, 104in (265cm).
$27,000-30,000

A mahogany and shell inlaid longcase clock, by Sainsbury, Bridgwater, c1810, 84in (213cm).
$6,000-6,500

A George III oak and mahogany longcase clock, c1795.
$3,500-3,800

A Federal inlaid mahogany longcase clock, by Aaron Willard, c1800, 100in (254cm).
$38,000-44,000

An 8-day round dial longcase clock, Charles Merrilies, c1825.
$4,500-5,250

n oak longcase clock, by . Buchan, Perth, with 8-ay movement, moon phase nd high water indication, 1790, 83in (210cm).
4,500-5,500

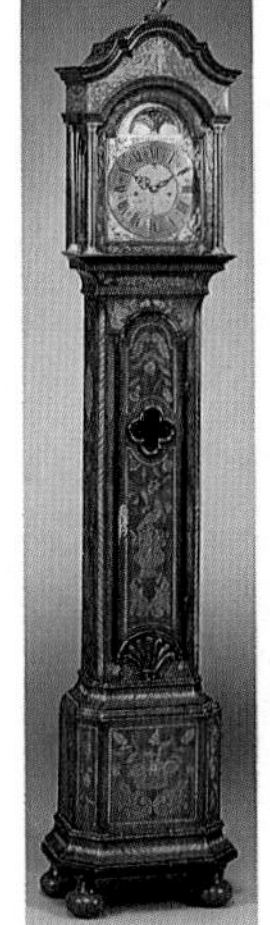
A Dutch rococo inlaid walnut longcase clock, Johannes Logge.
$12,000-13,000

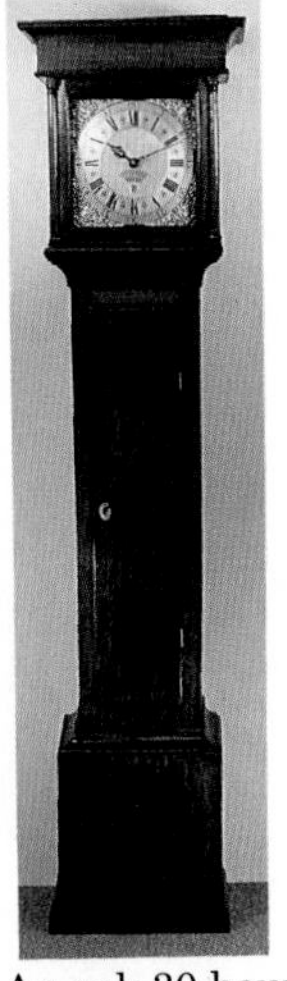
An oak 30 hour longcase clock by Nickall, Wells, 18thC.
$3,000-3,500

A flame mahogany strung and inlaid longcase clock, by Cox, Devizes, late 18thC, 90in (228cm).
$7,500-8,000

. flame mahogany longcase lock, by Bellzoni, haftesbury, the arch having lion with moving eyes, arly 19thC, 83in (210.5cm).
5,500-6,000

A mahogany and boxwood strung longcase clock, by Pitt, Tetbury, early 19thC, 86in (218.5cm).
$3,250-3,750

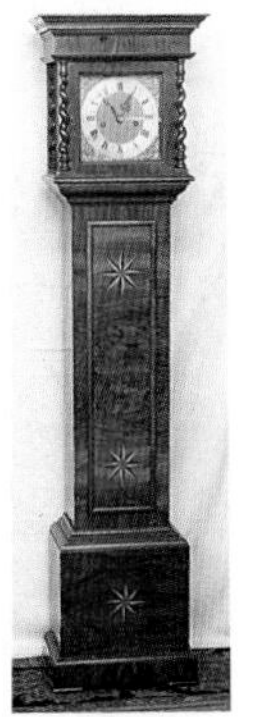
A figured walnut case longcase clock, with brass dial and silvered chapter ring, early 20thC.
$900-1,000

A mahogany 8-day longcase clock, by R. Summerhays, Ilminster, striking the hours on a bell, c1840.
$4,500-5,000

A London mahogany longcase clock, c1790.
$10,500-12,000

A mahogany longcase clock, by Morse & Tanner, Malmesbury, 8-day striking movement, c1840, 90in (228cm).
$3,750-4,250

A mahogany longcase clock, by Chas. Price, Wiveliscombe, with 8-day repeating movement, 86in (218.5cm).
$3,000-4,500

A mahogany longcase clock by Howse, Marlborough, c1830, 82in (208cm).
$3,000-3,500

An oak and mahogany 8-day longcase clock, by Harlett and Dursley, striking hours on a bell, c1810, 78in (198cm).
$3,750-4,500

l. A George III dark green japanned longcase clock, by William Rout, 18thC.
$3,750-5,250

A longcase clock by Robert Seagrave, 8-day movement, c1770, 97in (246cm).
$12,750-14,250

A longcase clock by Aynesworth Thwaite.
$3,750-4,500

A Scottish mahogany longcase clock c1790.
$6,750-7,500

An oak longcase clock, by Maurice, Haverfordwest, late 18thC, 83in (211cm).
$3,000-3,500

A George II gilt decorated scarlet japanned longcase clock, signed Henry Fish, 18thC, 98in (249cm).
$14,250-15,500

An oak and mahogany longcase clock, by Richard Herring, with Adam and Eve automata, c1810.
$3,750-5,250

A mahogany ar oak 8-day longcase clock, by Thomas Johns, c1830.
$3,750-4,500

A Chippendale carved cherrywood longcase clock, dial signed Isaac Brokaw, case attributed to Matthew Egerton, c1800, 67in (170cm).
$24,750-27,500

A mahogany 8-day longcase clock, maker's label Etham Canham, Croydon, c1840.
$4,500-5,500

A mahogany 8-day longcase clock, by Whitehurst, Derby, c1810.
$4,500-5,000

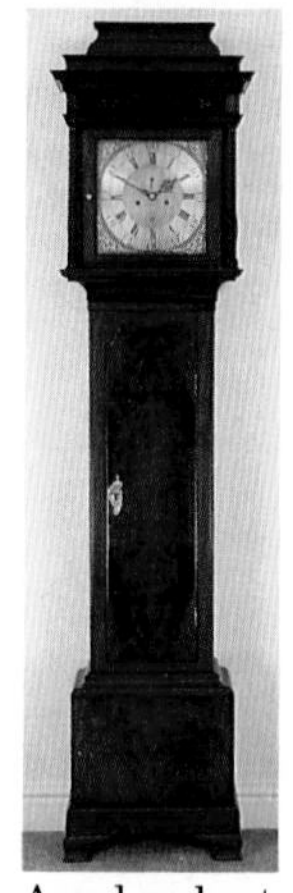

A red walnut veneered 8-day longcase clock, Nathaniel Brown, Manchester, c1770.
$9,000-9,500

A mahogany 8-day longcase clock, by Ashton, Brigg, c1810 89in (226cm).
$4,500-6,000

An oak 8-day longcase clock, by John Pearson, Louth, c1810, 82in (208cm).
$3,000-3,750

A mahogany 8-day longcase clock, by John Crichton, Dundee, c1795, 82in (208cm).
$5,250-6,000

A William III walnut and marquetry longcase clock, the dial signed Josh. Alsope cast Smith Field, 5 ringed pillar movement with anchor escapement, 85in (216cm).
$15,500-18,000

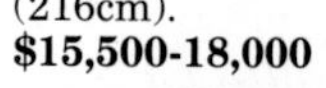

An oak 30-hour longcase clock, by William Cuff, Shepton Mallet, striking the hour on a bell, c1770, 82in (208cm).
$3,000-3,500

A Scottish 8-day longcase clock, by William Young, c1840 83in (210cm).
$6,000-7,500

A mahogany longcase clock, by Boucher, Bristol, late 18thC.
$7,500-8,000

l. An oak longcase clock, by John Way, Newton St, Loe, c1750, 78in (198cm).
$4,500-6,000

r. A walnut 8-day longcase clock, by Richard Street, London, striking the hours on a bell, c1720, 98in (249cm).
$15,000-16,000

Directoire
rmolu mantel
ock, enamel dial
gned Laurent A
aris, c1795, 14in
6cm).
1,800-2,200

A Regency ormolu mounted black marble mantel timepiece, signed Vulliamy No. 466. **$7,500-9,000**

A mantel clock, late 19thC, 14in (36cm). **$1,000-1,200**

French gilt and silvered
rass perpetual calendar 4-
lass mantel clock, 14in
36cm). **$5,250-6,750**

A carved wood parcel gilt mantel clock, enamel dial signed Callerström Stockholm, c1810. **$3,750-5,250**

A French gilt brass mantel clock, with porcelain dial and urn surmount. **$450-600**

An Empire ormolu striking mantel clock, dial signed Simon à Paris, 17in (43cm). **$3,750-4,500**

A bronze, gilt bronze and marble mantel timepiece, with enamel dial, 4 pillar fusee drum movement, backplate signed Vulliamy London 298, c1797, 17½in (44cm). **$13,500-18,000**

l. A satinwood veneered mantel timepiece, with glass panelled sides, top and back, on brass bun feet, silvered dial signed Parkinson and Frodsham, Change Alley, London, early 19thC, 8in (20cm). **$1,800-2,500**

An Edwardian inlaid mahogany mantel clock, with 8-day striking movement, by Clerke, Royal Exchange, London, 15in (38cm). **$750-1,000**

A mahogany 8-day fusee drop dial wall clock, the 8in (20cm) painted dial signed McCabe, c1820.
$2,250-3,000

A mahogany table clock, with verge escapement, by John Hanckles, London, c1765, 15in (38cm).
$10,500-11,500

A Limoges mounted silvered table clock, with bell striking Japy Frère movement, stamped Dufaud Paris, c1885, 27in (69cm). **$8,250-9,750**

A mahogany table clock, by Hunter & Son, c1795.
$2,250-3,250

An ebonised table clock, signed Geo. Phil[p]. Strigel, c1780.
$4,500-5,250

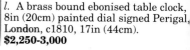

l. A brass bound ebonised table clock, 8in (20cm) painted dial signed Perigal, London, c1810, 17in (44cm).
$2,250-3,000

A gilt bronze clock, Hemmel à Paris, part mid-18thC.
$3,000-4,500

A lantern clock by Kingsnorth of Tenterden, complete and original, 18thC.
$1,800-2,250

A mid-Victorian porcelain and gilt white metal mounted clock garniture, French.
$2,250-3,750

A mahogany table clock, signed Frodsham, London, c1840, 14in (36cm).
$2,750-3,500

A walnut quarter repeating table clock, by Joseph Windmills, c1720, 18½in (47cm).
$15,000-18,000

A French Empire gilt portico clock. **$900-1,050**
A French rococo ormolu mantel clock, 19thC. **$900-1,05**
A French gilt spelter mantel clock, 19thC, 23in (59cm) high. **$300-350**

A French Empire ormolu and bronze pendule au negre, with enamel dial, bell striking silk suspension movement, c1810, 13½in (34.5cm) high.
$12,000-15,000

Biedermeier period ienna Regulator wall ock, 8-day duration ıovement, signed on the ackplate, by Hoser.
3,750-4,250

. rosewood table clock, trike/silent lever above 60, igned Barwise, London, 1840, 18in (45.5cm).
3,750-4,500

A Vienna Regulator clock, in ebonised case, 19thC, 40in (101.5cm).
$375-450

. Viennese lantern tyle regulator, 1810, 30in (76cm).
30,000-33,000

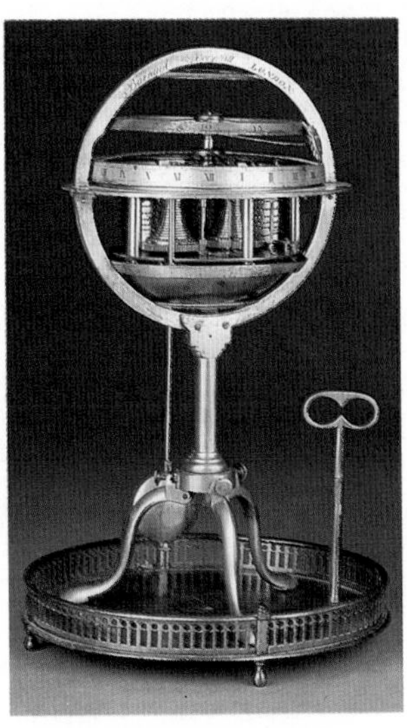

A spherical striking skeleton clock, the meridian ring signed Barraud, Cornhill, London, 12in (30.5cm) high.
$9,750-11,250

A gold quartz centre seconds calendar wristwatch, inscribed Santos de Cartier, with 18ct bracelet.
$6,750-7,500

An 18ct white gold Officer's Campaign wristwatch, by Patek Philippe, one of 150 made in white gold, with original packaging.
$15,000-16,500

An 18ct gold and diamond automatic world time calendar 'Voyager' wristwatch, by Ebel, with 18ct 'Discovery' bracelet.
$10,500-11,250

A Rolex pink gold triple calendar and moonphase automatic wristwatch, c1950.
$10,500-12,000

An 18ct gold sweep seconds wristwatch, by Patek Philippe, the cloisonné enamel dial with map, c1955.
$61,000-67,000

An 18ct gold Rolex Day/Date automatic centre seconds calendar wristwatch, with 18ct President bracelet, signed, c1980.
$5,250-6,000

A gold wristwatch, by Patek Philippe, signed, c1950.
$4,500-5,250

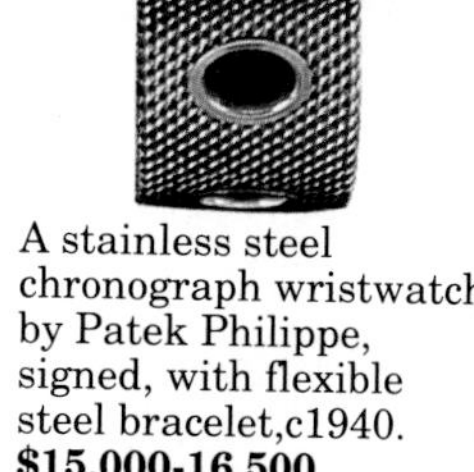

A stainless steel chronograph wristwatch by Patek Philippe, signed, with flexible steel bracelet,c1940.
$15,000-16,500

A gold Rolex Oyster perpetual Day/Date chronometer wristwatch.
$5,500-6,500

An 18ct white gold lady's bracelet watch, by Patek Philippe.
$2,250-3,000

A gold automatic wristwatch by Blancpain, with date aperture.
$3,000-3,750

A gold Rolex Oyster perpetual Day/Date chronometer wristwatch.
$3,750-4,500

An 18ct gold Officer's Campaign wristwatch, enamel dial with Breguet numerals, one of 2,000 produced by Patek Philippe.
12,000-15,000

An 18ct gold wristwatch, No. 2801668 3760/1, the signed movement with 18 jewels, by Patek Philippe, with woven gold bracelet.
$3,000-3,750

An 18ct gold wristwatch, with black onyx dial and cabouchon winder, by Patek Philippe, with white gold bracelet.
$1,800-2,200

An 18ct gold lady's wristwatch, with pink coral dial, movement with 18 jewels, by Patek Philippe.
$3,000-3,750

An 18ct gold lady's wristwatch, 18 jewels, by Patek Philippe, with white gold bracelet.
2,500-4,000

A platinum and diamond set lady's wristwatch, by Patek Philippe.
$2,250-3,000

A tantalum and pink gold Royal Oak calendar quartz wristwatch, by Audemars Piguet.
$4,500-5,250

A Cartier gold Baignoire wristwatch, with cabouchon winder, by Cartier, with leather strap.
$8,250-9,750

An 18ct gold lady's Polo quartz wristwatch, by Piaget.
$3,750-5,250

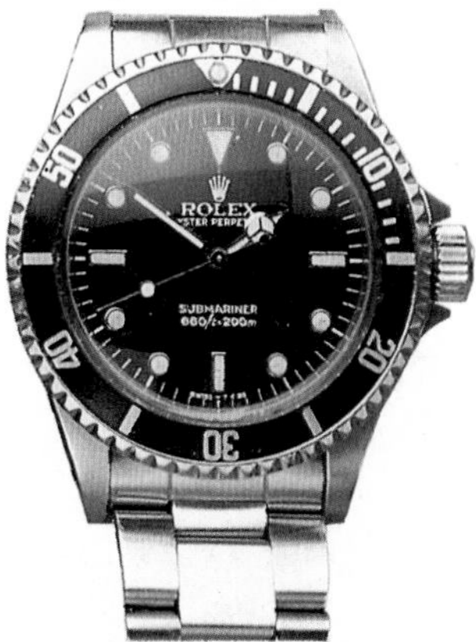

An 18ct lady's white gold and diamond wristwatch, by Patek Philippe.
4,000-5,000

A two-colour gold and diamond automatic centre seconds calendar wristwatch, by Cartier.
$6,000-7,500

An 18ct gold diamond, coral and onyx wristwatch, by Patek Philippe.
$5,500-7,500

A Rolex stainless steel Oyster Perpetual Submariner wristwatch, with lever escapement and 25 jewels.
$800-900

A gilt metal watch, by Pascal Hubert, c1700. **$5,500-7,000**

An 18ct gold Rolex Prince Imperial keyless jewelled lever dress pocket watch, signed movement, import marks for Glasgow 1932.
$1,800-2,200

An 18ct gold keyless open face split second chronograph pocket watch, gilt movement jewelled to the centre, Ch. Ed. Lardet, Fleurier, 5.2cm. **$1,800-2,500**

A silver pair case hour striking verge watch, Jn. Ellicott, No. 2408, Londo hallmark for 1743.
$2,500-3,000

An 18ct gold hunter cased double dial calendar watch, with cover winding and moon phases, by B. Haas Jne, Paris & Geneve, c1885. **$18,500-21,000**

A silver pair case verge watc signed David Le Stourgeon, London, 18thC.
$3,000-3,750

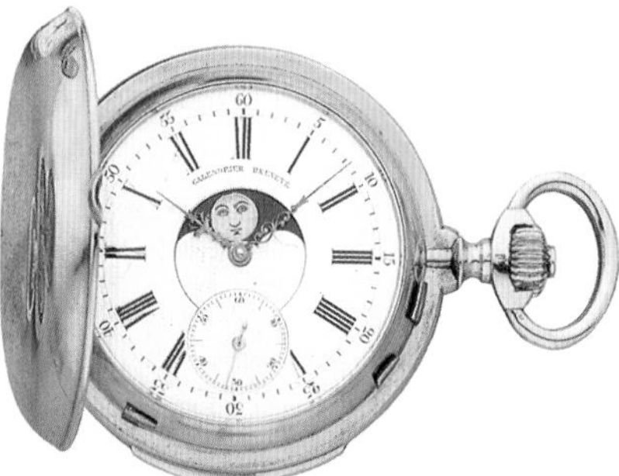

An 18ct gold hunter cased minute repeating double dial watch, with moon phases, c1900, 5.6cm.
$8,250-9,750

A gold and enamel pair case pocket watch, with gilt and enamel chatelaine, by Jno. Wightwick, London, hallmarked London 1775.
$6,000-6,750

An 18ct gold open faced lever watch, with Burdess's patent winding, by Adam Burdess, hallmarked 1875, casemaker' initials RY.
$2,500-3,000

A silver and inlaid tortoiseshell pair cased verge watch, Michael Johnson, c1700.
$2,500-3,000

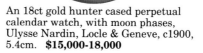

An 18ct gold hunter cased perpetual calendar watch, with moon phases, Ulysse Nardin, Locle & Geneve, c1900, 5.4cm. **$15,000-18,000**

A silver gilt pair case verg chronograph watch, signe John Brown, London.
$1,000-1,200

A gold, enamel and split pearl open face watch, with signed movement by Pouzait & Godemar, Geneve, No. 3194, c1790, 5.2cm.
$3,000-3,750

A gold and enamel open face pocket watch, for the Chinese market, by Vaucher Fleurier, the monometallic 'bat's wing' balance with duplex escapement. **$11,250-12,750**

A gold, enamel and split pearl quarter repeating open face watch, dial and movement signed, by Gregson, Paris, c1790, 5cm.
$3,750-4,500

A gold triple case verge pocket watch, by Lam. B. Vrythoff, No. 704, early 18thC, 5.5cm.
$2,500-3,250

A gold repoussé pair cased verge watch, outer case by John Valentine Haidt, No. 221, hallmarked 1727, later dial, later, rolled gold key, 4.8cm.
$5,250-6,000

A gold quarter repeating verge watch, with later gold fob and agate intaglio, signed on the cuvette mask Courvoisier & Comp. No. 42434, c1830, 5.4cm. **$1,800-2,250**

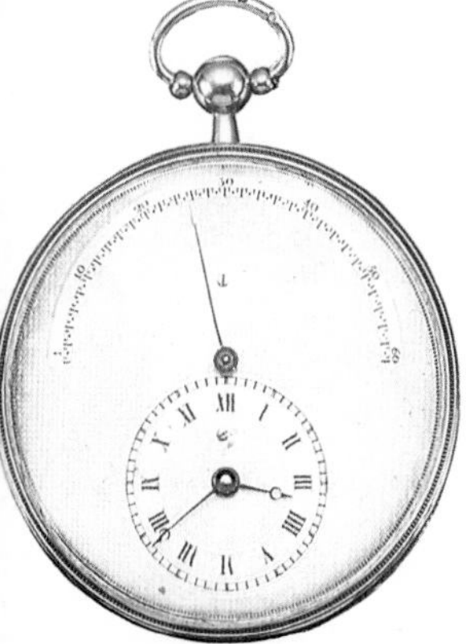

A Continental gold open face retrograde seconds cylinder pocket watch, 5.4cm.
$5,250-6,000

A gold open face minute repeating chronograph watch, Patek Philippe, c1915.
$20,000-22,500

r. An 18ct gold pair case duplex watch, the cases marked for Chester 1835.
$12,000-13,500

l. A gold open face minute repeating perpetual calendar watch, with moon phases, Patek Philippe, c1939.
$38,000-45,000

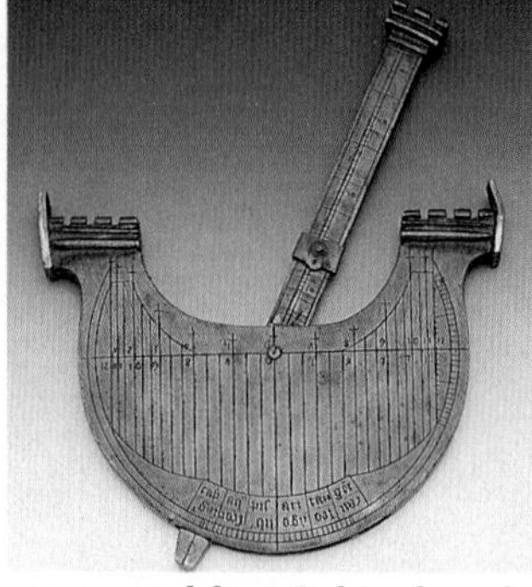

A universal rectilinear brass dial, constructed from 2 ship-shaped brass plates, made in the late medieval 'Little Ship of the Venetians' style, possibly 18thC, 6in (15cm). **$62,000-67,000**

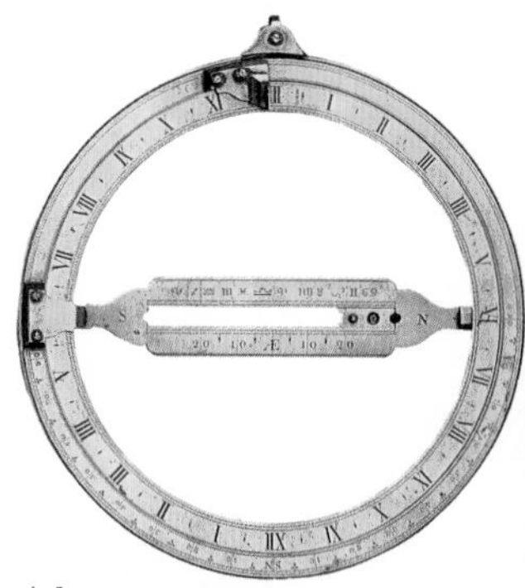

A lacquered brass universal equinoctial ring dial, unsigned, 18thC, 9in (22cm).
$2,250-2,500

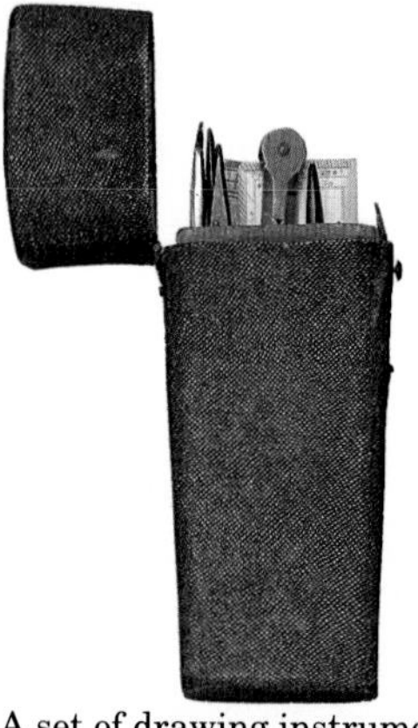

A set of drawing instruments, by W. & S. Jones, in fishskin case, early 19thC, 7in (17.5cm). **$250-300**

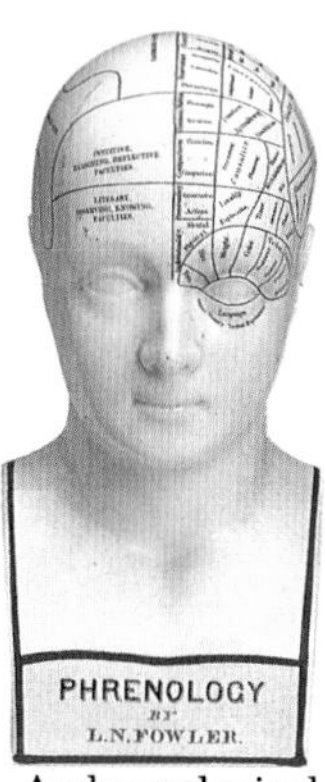

A phrenological porcelain bust, late 19thC, 12in (31cm).
$2,500-3,000

A pair of Regency brass bound mahogany celestial and terrestrial globes, by J. W. Cary, restored, 18in (46cm) diam, 45in (114cm) high.
$19,500-22,500

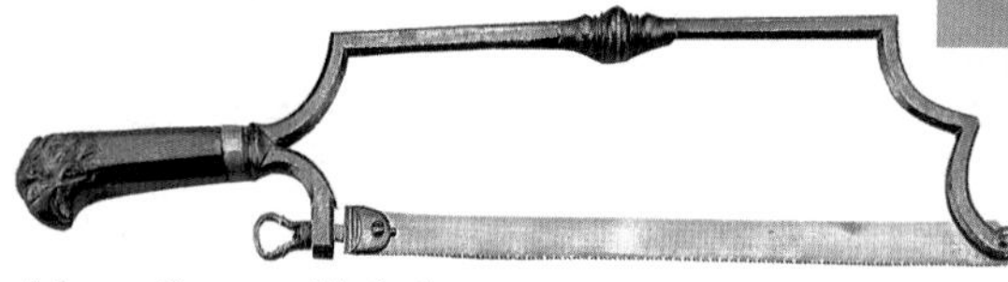

A large German blade bone saw, with carved eagle's head wood handle, wrought iron frame and blade, early 18thC, 23in (59cm) long. **$1,800-2,000**

l. A lacquered brass universal equinoctial compass dial, engraved Troughton & Simms, London, 19thC, 6in (15cm), in a fitted mahogany case.
$800-950

A celestial library globe, by W. and J. M. Bardin, mounted on a mahogany tripod stand, restored, 18in (46cm) diam.
$4,500-6,000

A mahogany domestic medicine chest, containing 12 bottles, glass slide, drawer for 5 bottles, scales and weights, and other items, 8in (20cm) high.
$1,200-1,400

A pair of Newton's globes, with printed and coloured paper gores, on carved mahogany stands, both globes and stands damaged, c1870, 22in (56cm). **$12,000-15,000**

Historic Televisions
& Video Recorders
Michael Bennett-Levy
Photography Ivor Tetteh-Larty

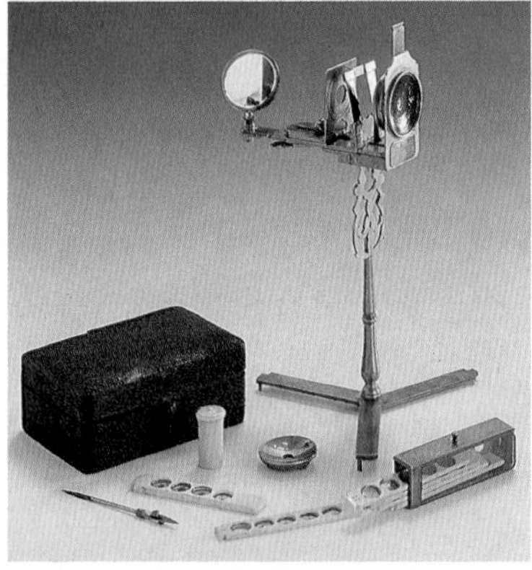

A brass simple microscope, stamped 108 and signed Geo. Lindsay Inv[r] & Fec[t] on silver plaque below the eyepiece, with accessories, c1745, 6½in (16.5cm). **$10,500-12,500**

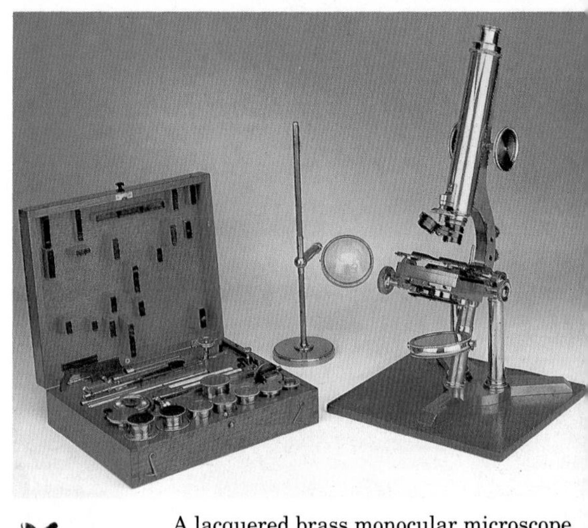

A lacquered brass monocular microscope, signed J.A.s Smith, London, with cased se of accessories, mid-19thC, 17½in (44.5cm). **$2,500-3,500**

A brass circumferentor, signed G. Adams London, stamped T. Rawling, late 18thC, 14½in (37cm), in a fitted mahogany case. **$1,500-2,250**

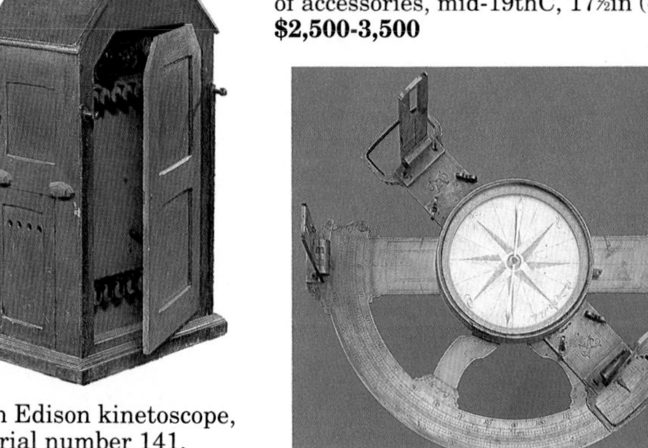

An Edison kinetoscope, serial number 141, maker's label, with 5 film loops, American, c1894, 49in (124.5cm). **$33,000-37,500**

A brass graphometer, signed and dated Benneke a'Berlin 1792, late 18thC, 14in (36cm). **$4,400-5,200**

A brass scale, signed R. Burton, 18thC 14in (36cm). **$300-500**

A lacquered brass solar microscope, signed B. Martin London, in a velvet lined case, c1775, 10½in (26.5cm). **$1,350-1,600**

A brass surveying instrument, simple theodolite/circumferentor with central compass dial, on central tripod mount, signed Thos. Wright, 12in (31cm) diam. **$800-950**

A brass compound monocular microcscope, signed Pastorelli, Optician, London, English, late 19thC 18in (46cm) and accessories. **$1,800-2,400**

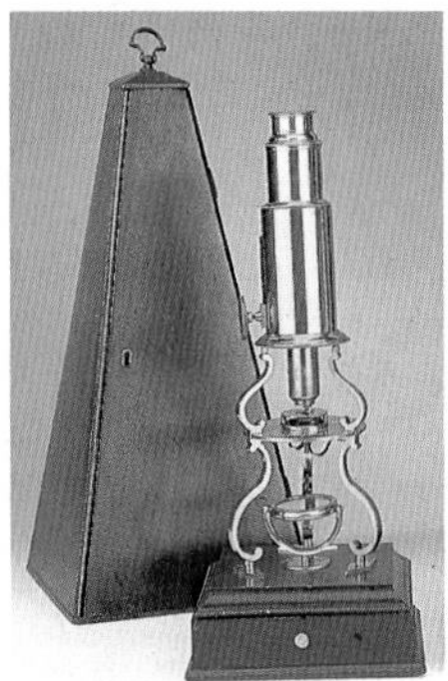

A brass 'Culpeper' type monocular microscope, signed J. Abraham Bath, in a mahogany case, late 18thC, 17in (43cm) high. **$1,200-1,800**

l. A monocular/binocular compound microscope, signed A Ross, London, No. 1768, binocular signed Wenham's binocular, by Baker, London, late 19thC, 18½in (47cm) and accessories. **$3,750-4,750**

\ Meissen silver gilt mounted
ınuff box, the base with
leutsche Blumen, c1755, 1½in
3.5cm). **$7,500-8,250**

\ Fürstenberg silver mounted snuff
ox, the interior of the base richly
;ilt, slight damage, c1770, 3in (8cm).
;5,250-6,000

ι Meissen sugar box, painted by J. G.
Höroldt, with chinoiserie decoration,
ılue KPM mark, c1724, 5in (12cm).
;22,500-24,000

\ gold and bloodstone box, the lid
ıltered and now containing jewels,
ın inner lid with a later two-tune
nusical mechanism, 4in (9.5cm).
1,800-2,400

A Böttger chinoiserie sugar box and cover, painted in the manner of J. G. Höroldt, showing figures taking tea and smoking, slight damage, c1725, 5in (12.5cm) wide.
$24,750-25,750

A silver mounted shagreen nécessaire, probably French, the interior including a crest-engraved silver seal, c1750, 3in (8cm). **$2,500-3,250**

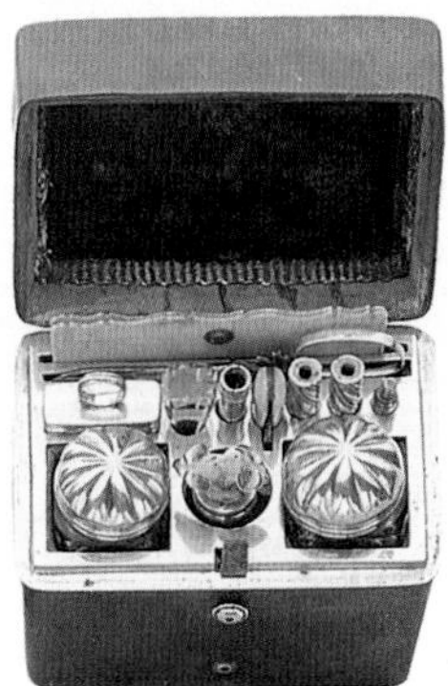

A silver mounted shagreen nécessaire, probably English, mid-18thC, 3in (7.5cm).
$2,250-3,000

An enamel bonbonnière, painted as a frowning pug's head, with gilt metal mounts, Birmingham, c1760, 2½in (6cm).
$3,750-4,500

A pair of Victorian brass bound and rosewood veneer dressing cases, by Thomas Jeyes Edwards, the fittings with silver lids, c1846. **$3,750-4,250**

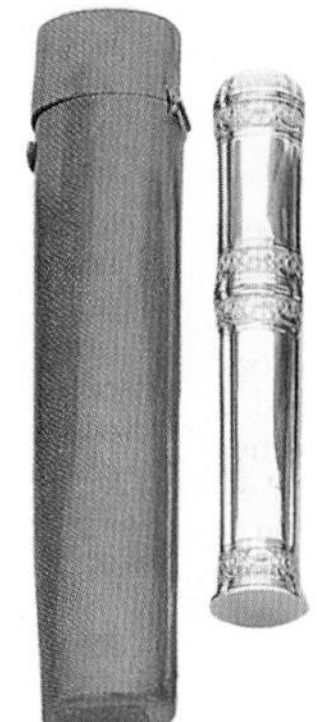

A two-colour gold etui, charge and discharge marks of Jean Baptiste Fouache, Paris, rubbed, 1774, 4in (10cm), in associated shagreen case.
$2,250-3,000

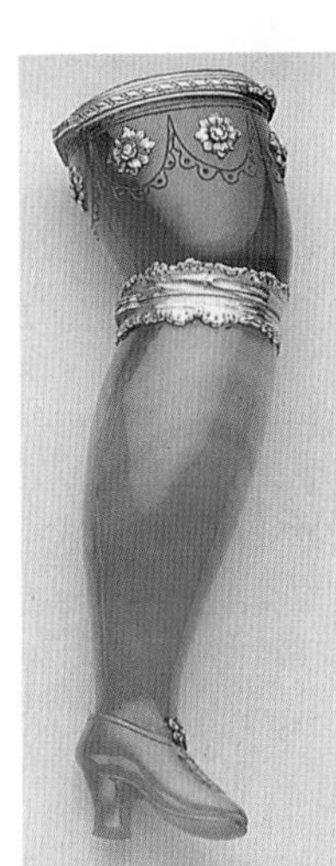

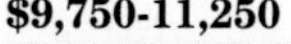

A hardstone jewelled and gold mounted bonbonnière, late 19thC.
$9,750-11,250

A George III brass bound hardwood dressing case, engraved with the initials 'ED' below an earl's coronet, William Price, London, c1813, 15½in (39cm). **$2,500-3,000**

l. A Parker 15 eye dropper pen, with No 5 nib, c1910.
$2,500-3,000

r. An 18ct gold Parker Vacumatic pen, c1939.
$2,000-2,250

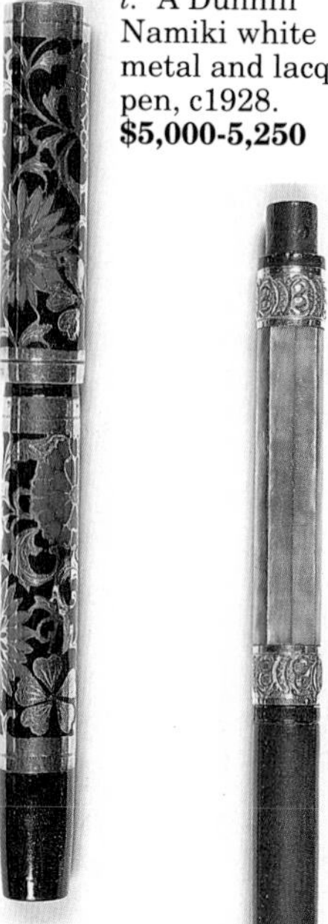

l. A Dunhill Namiki white metal and lacquer pen, c1928.
$5,000-5,250

r. A Waterman 622 eye dropper pen, with mother-of-pearl overlay, c1910.
$650-750

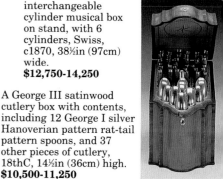

A Nicole Frères interchangeable cylinder musical box on stand, with 6 cylinders, Swiss, c1870, 38½in (97cm) wide.
$12,750-14,250

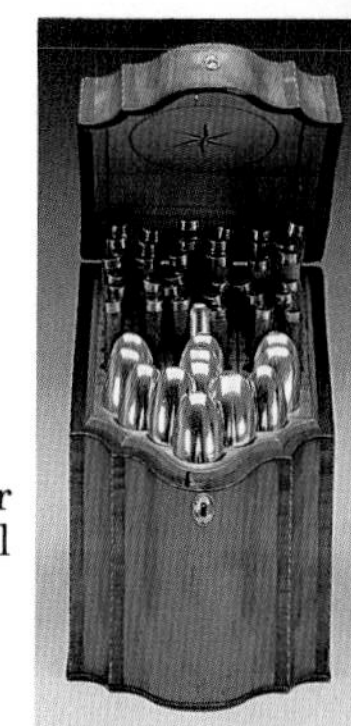

A George III satinwood cutlery box with contents, including 12 George I silver Hanoverian pattern rat-tail pattern spoons, and 37 other pieces of cutlery, 18thC, 14½in (36cm) high.
$10,500-11,250

A shaped plated and engraved biscuit box, with hinged lid, on 4 paw feet, 8in (20cm) high. **$200-300**

A Swiss tortoiseshell singing bird musical box, the enamelled cover with piqué silver and gold inlay, with bird shaped key, c1860, 4in (10cm) wide. **$3,750-5,250**

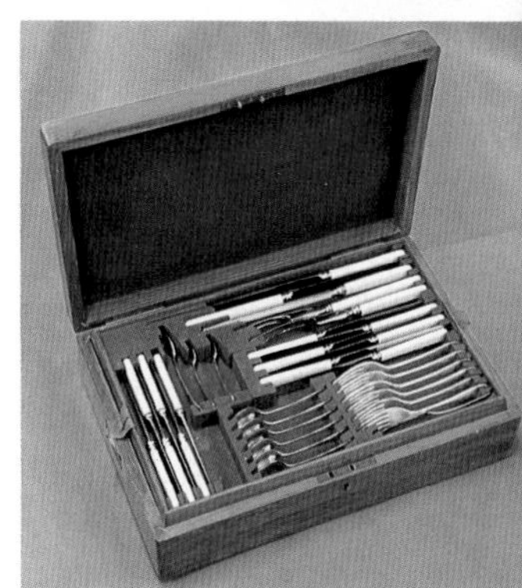

An oak canteen of plated cutlery, by Martin Hall & Co, Sheffield, including carvers, ladles, basting spoon, butter knife.
$300-400

A coromandel wood and gilt brass mounted jewel casket, with velvet lined interior, on lion's paw feet, c1810, 16in (41cm) wide. **$4,500-5,250**

A rosewood work/writing compendium.
$750-850

A gilt bronze mounted velvet covered casket, probably Florentine, the exterior stamped with fleurs-de-lys, with ogee shaped sides with handles, 18thC, 26in (66cm).
$6,000-6,750

A pair of bronze and gilt bronze table candelabra, damaged, c1810, 21½in (54.5cm).
$4,500-7,500

An Empire gilt bronze surtout, and pair of candelabra, signed Thomire à Paris, c1810, 24 and 25in (61 and 64cm) high. **$45,000-52,500**

A pair of Louis XVI gilt bronze wall lights, c1780, 22in (55cm).
$11,250-12,750

A pair of Empire bronze, gilt bronze and marble candelabra, c1810, 37½in (95cm). **$14,250-15,750**

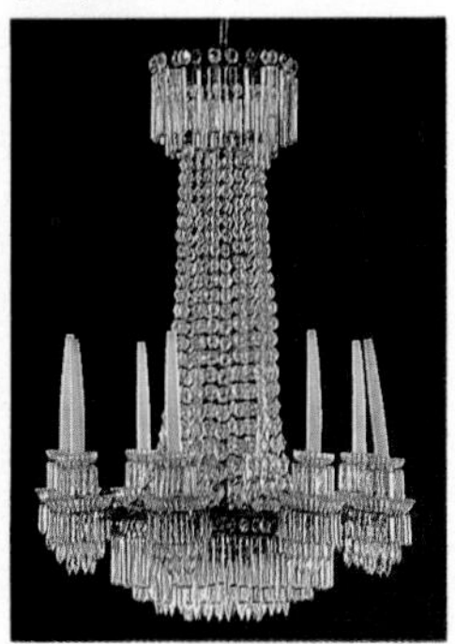

A glass chandelier, with 8 pendant hung nozzles and drip pans, c1815, 39in (99cm) high.
$12,000-12,750

A pair of Empire ormolu and bronze four-light candelabra, each with draped female figures supporting twin torches, on stepped griotte marble plinth bases centred by mount of Cupid and Psyche, 31in (79cm) high.
$22,000-24,750

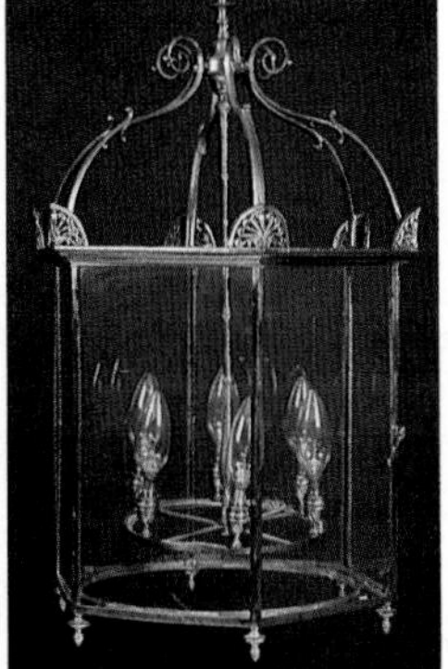

A Regency brass hexagonal hall lantern, with six-light platform, 34in (86cm) high.
$12,000-13,500

A pair of glass chandeliers, each with 6 S-scroll arms, some replacements, late 18thC, 46in (116.5cm).
$40,000-48,000

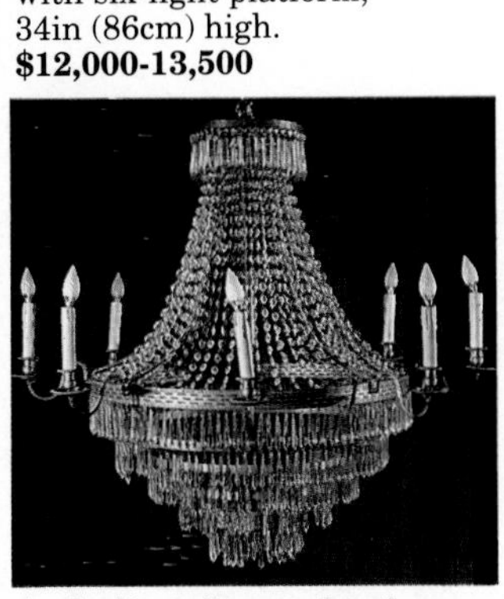

An Italian gilt metal and cut glass eight-light chandelier, fitted for electricity, c1800, 42in (106.5cm). **$3,000-4,500**

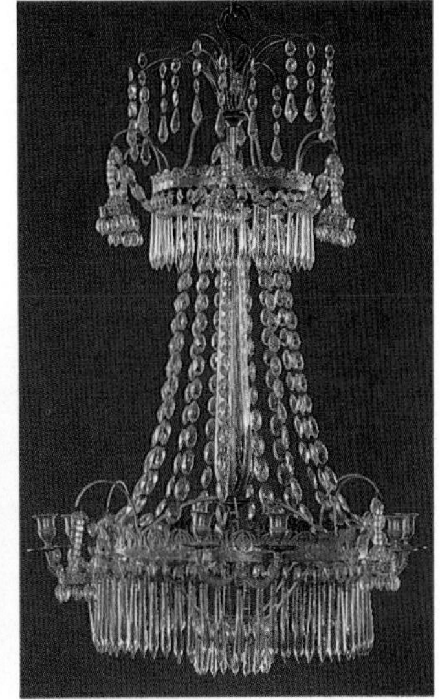

A Swedish glass and gilt bronze chandelier, c1790, 36in (92cm) high. **$15,000-18,000**

A pair of bronze and parcel gilt oil lamps, with brass burning mechanisms by Hinks & Sons, c1840, 28in (71cm). **$2,500-3,000**

A pair of gilt bronze candelabra lamps, now with steel shafts and tôle shades, c1800, 31in (78cm). **$9,000-12,000**

A Restauration gilt bronze chandelier, with 8 candle branches, c1820, 24½in (62cm). **$12,750-13,500**

A set of 4 Restauration palais-royal gilt bronze and mother-of-pearl candelabra, on circular bases, c1820, 14½in (37cm). **$9,750-11,250**

A German gilt metal 16-light chandelier, with central baluster surmounted by a double-headed eagle, 19thC, 41in (104cm) high. **$4,500-5,000**

A pair of Restauration gilt bronze candelabra, c1825, 39in (99cm). **$10,500-12,000**

A pair of Louis XVI gilt bronze wall lights, c1780, 14½in (37cm). **$2,250-3,000**

A hexagonal brass and stained glass hall lantern, c1850, 32in (81cm) high. **$10,500-11,250**

r. A French brass library lamp, mid-19thC, 27in (69cm). **$1,250-2,250**

l. A pair of gilt bronze wall lights, c1785, 14½in (37cm). **$3,000-4,500**

A brass and stained glass hall lantern, restorations, mid-19thC, 26½in (67cm **$19,500-21,000**

A Restauration bronze gilt bronze and tôle lamp, c1820, 28in (71cm) high. **$6,000-7,500**

A pair of twin light ormolu mounted candelabra, c1900, 22½in (57cm). **$3,000-3,500**

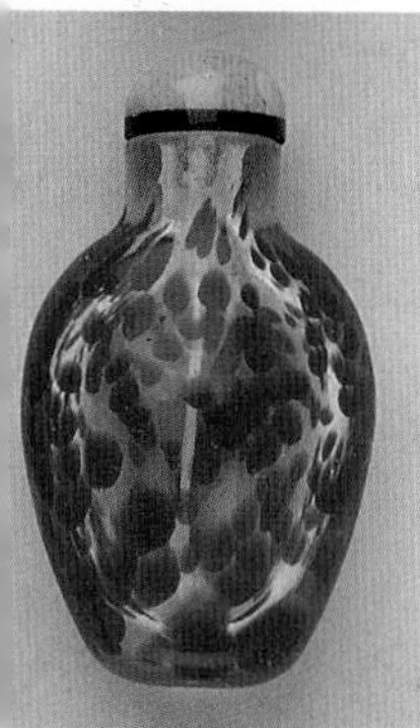
glass snuff bottle, e clear glass body appled with bright ue, 18thC.
750-900

An enamelled glass snuff bottle, by Ye Bengqi, with four-character Qianlong mark on base.
$18,750-21,750

A carved glass overlay snuff bottle, decorated in green with an egret, c1800.
$10,500-12,000

A Japanese ivory okimono of a fisherman, on a carved wood base, c1900, 16½in (42cm).
$2,000-3,000

glass overlay snuff ttle, decorated with a asshopper, c1810.
,750-4,000

A pair of Japanese carved ivory groups, depicting a toy vendor and a fruit seller, signed, late 19thC, 12in (31cm).
$300-450

An ivory netsuke of a hare, signed Yoshinaga, early 19thC.
$2,500-3,000

gold ground moulded rcelain double snuff bottle, th gold stoppers, showing dies with lanterns, c1825.
,000-3,750

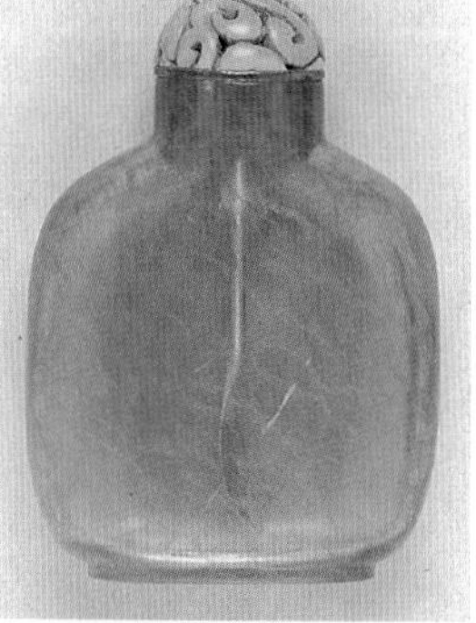
An amethystine glass snuff bottle, c1830.
$3,000-3,750

An amber snuff bottle, carved with a bear and eagle in combat, the reverse with an eagle on a flowering prunus, c1850.
$3,750-4,500

A Japanese coloured and carved ivory figure of an old sage, late 19thC, 6½in (16cm).
$1,500-1,800

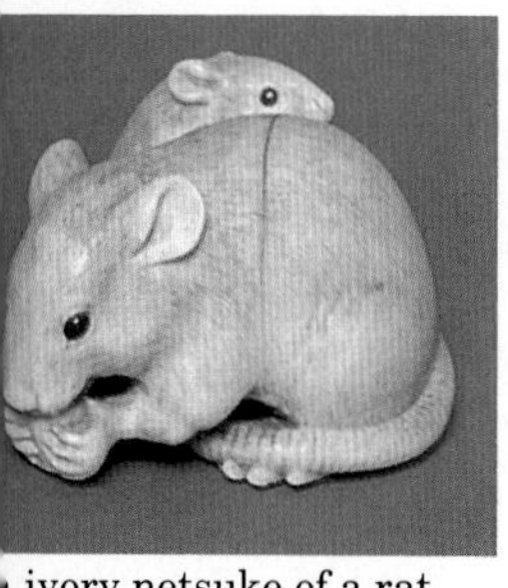
ivory netsuke of a rat d young, the mother lding a candle, signed atomo, 19thC.
,250-9,000

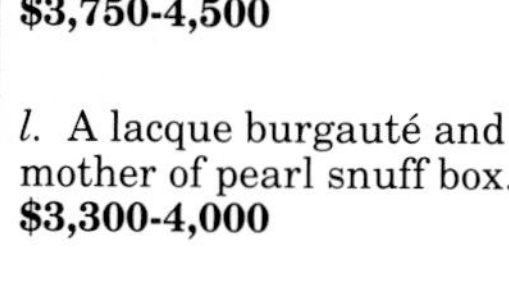
l. A lacque burgauté and mother of pearl snuff box.
$3,300-4,000

An ormolu mounted Japanese lacquer casket, with paw feet, lacquer 18thC, assembled early 19thC, 17in (43cm) wide.
$28,500-31,500

A Tibetan gilt bronze figure of a deity, holding a dhorje, 17thC, 6in (15cm).
$3,000-4,500

A wooden figure of Buddha, with traces of gilt an coloured floral decoration, early Ming dynasty, repaired, 38½in (97cm). **$45,000-52,500**

A polychromed gilt wood figure of Guanyin, traces of pigment, gilding and gesso, some damage, Song dynasty, 37½in (96cm).
$135,000-138,000

A kojubako, signed Kajikawa, with red tsuba seal, 19thC, 5in (12.5cm).
$9,000-10,500

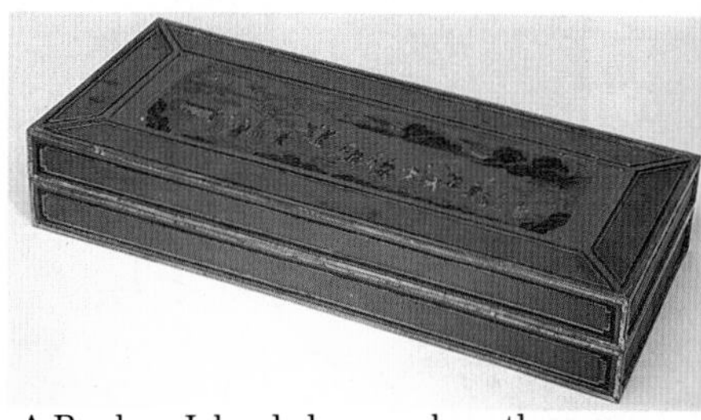

A Ryukyu Islands lacquer box, the cover decorated with a Chinese court procession an pavilion in a landscape, some restoration, 17thC, 29in (74cm). **$6,000-9,000**

A Japanese lacquer kodansu, with silver mounts, mid-19thC.
$3,000-3,750

A bronze and gilt okimono of a seated Temple Guardian, signed Miyao zo, late 19thC, 28½in (72cm) and another.
$17,000-19,000

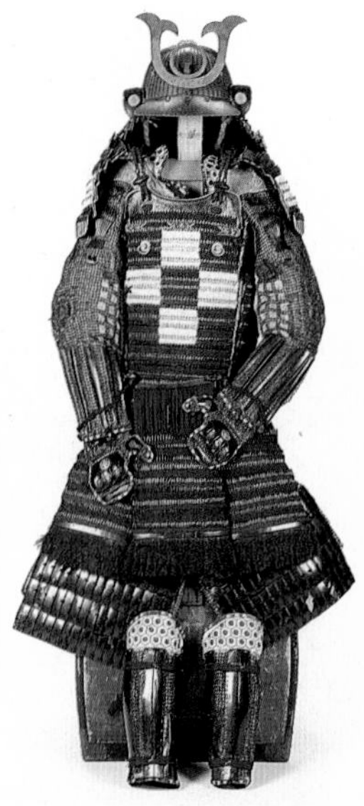

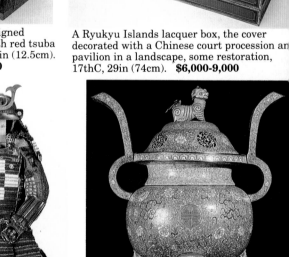

A Kon-ito-shira odishi domaru, probably Myochin, 18th/19thC.
$13,500-15,000

A Canton enamel temple tripod incense burner and cover, with a Buddhistic lio finial, on monster mask legs, small restorations, Qianlong seal mark and o the period, 43½in (110cm) high.
$17,000-19,000

set of 6 dental scalers, with
ırned octagonal bone handles,
eel heads, in fitted velvet lined
ather case, mid-19thC, 5in
3cm) wide.
00-375

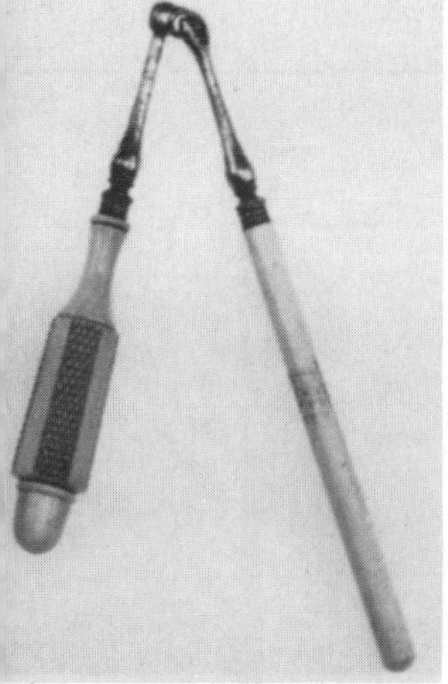

dental double hand drill,
ceted hollow bone handle, with
rill bits, screw-on cap, octagonal
condary bone handle, signed
aw, London.
,200-1,500
his hand drill was designed by
audius Ash, c1850.

Three beechwood monaural stethoscopes, 19thC, 5½ to 7in (14 to 17.5cm).
$375-525

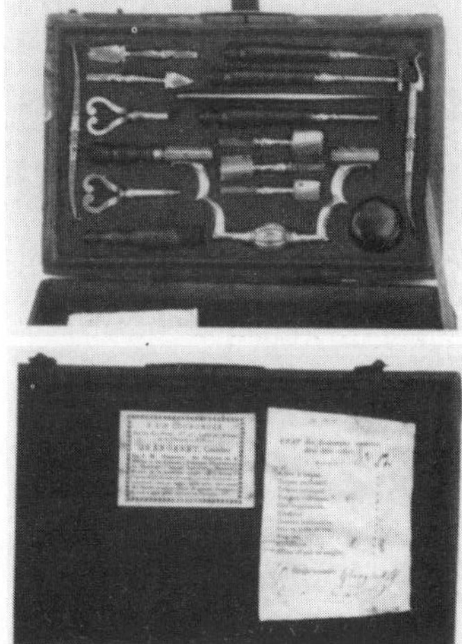

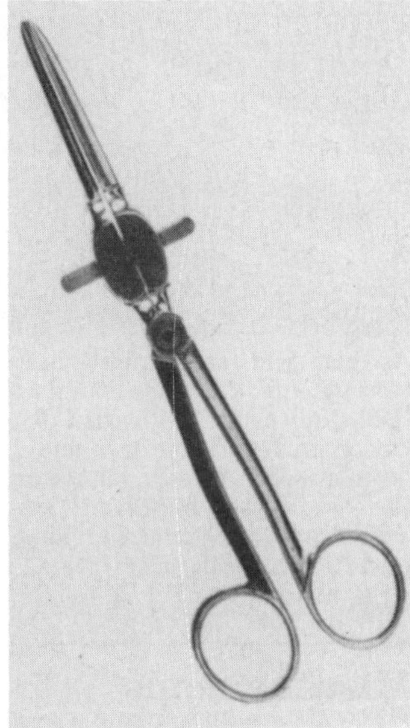

A pair of steel surgical forceps with parallel action jaws, knuckle joint, triangular section blade with serrated face, flat blade with smooth tortoiseshell face, central parallel plate lock, 19thC, 6½in (16.5cm).
$150-180

A French ebony and polished steel trepanning set, signed on instruments Grangeret Paris, the case inscribed Chirurgie Militaire, with a lenticular signed Hospice De Limoges, in a wool lined leather covered brass bound wood case, with brass clasps and carrying handle, large brass escutcheon stamped 'C.210', c1800, 13 by 8½in (33 by 21cm).
$5,250-6,000

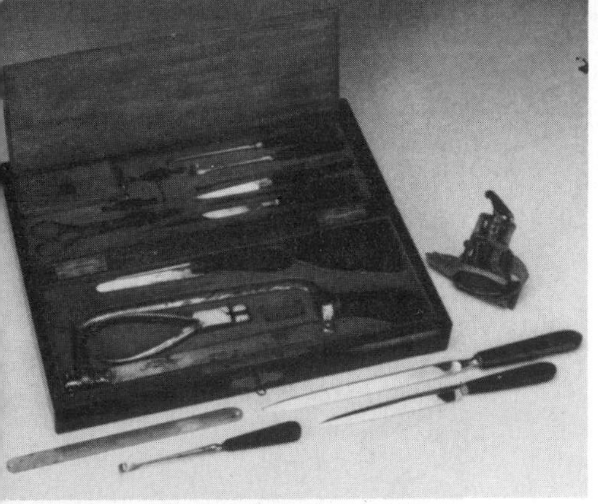

set of Charriere amputation
ıstruments, the mahogany case
ith recessed brass carrying
andle engraved 'Dr. Heynen',
rench, mid-19thC, 16in (41cm)
ide.
,800-2,700

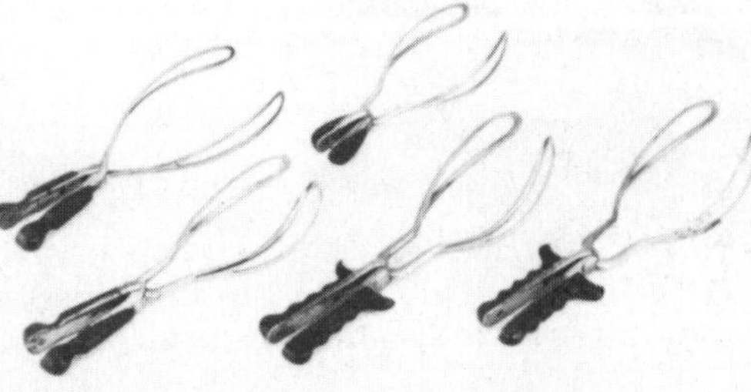

A set of 5 obstetric forceps, 2 with cross hatched ebony handles, one with smooth ebony handle, and 2 with shaped hand grip ebony handles, in cloth carrying pouch, signed Place & Co., Place & Thistlewaite, J. & W Wood, Manchester, and Wood, Manchester. **$750-1,200**

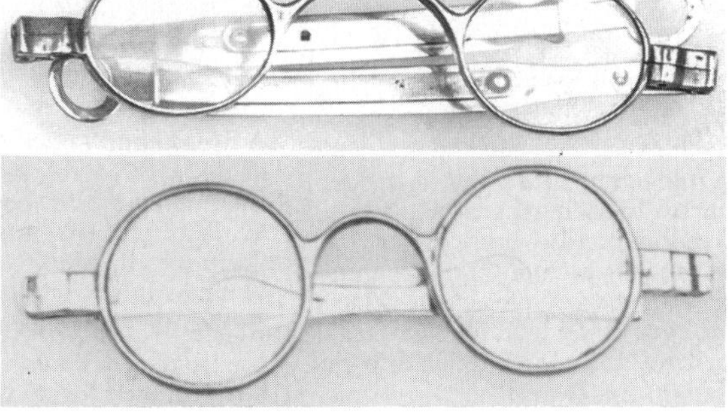

A pair of silver round lens spectacles, with segmental bridge, folding sides with pear drop ends, in case, etched D 24: and a pair of silver oval lens spectacles, with segmental bridge and telescopic sides with small ring ends, in case. **$375-450**

A Weiss field set of amputation instruments, the brass bound mahogany case fitted with 4 Liston knives, Hayes saw, and large amputation saw, signed on the case 'Weiss's Improved Air Tight Case, 62 Strand, London, mid-19thC, 14½in (37cm) wide.
$1,050-1,350

A chequer grip bone handled tooth key, with cranked shaft and claw.
$225-300

An ebony handled double tooth key, with blued claws and cranked shaft with spare claw, signed Young, 18thC.
$225-300

Miscellaneous

A brass guinea scale, with folding scale and sliding weight, signed A. Wilkinson, Ormskirk, Lancashire, the lid with monogram JW, 5in (13cm) wide.
$375-450

Three rare male contraceptive devices, of animal membrane, each with erotic illustration, indistinct inscription, with silk ties, mid-19thC, 8½in (21cm) long.
$4,500-6,000 each

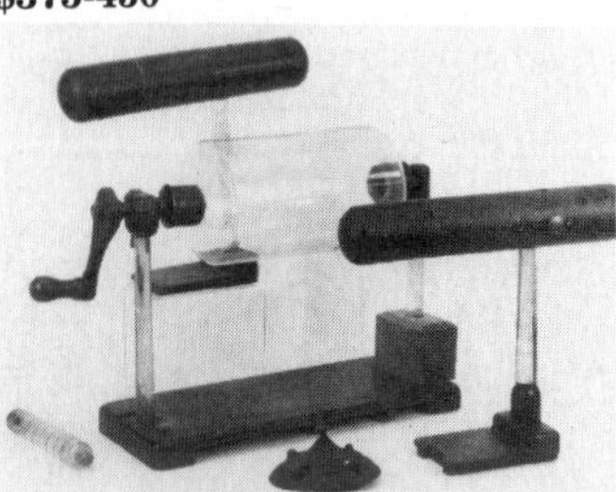

N A I R N E's

Patent Medical Electrical Machine,

(*For Ready Money only*)

AS many Perſons wiſh to try the Effect of Electricity, Mr. NAIRNE has contrived this Machine, whereby any Perſon, *without the Aſſiſtance of another*, may try its Effects in all the various Methods practiſed by the moſt eminent Medical Electricians.

This Machine is alſo applicable to every other Purpoſe of Electricity.

Made and Sold by NAIRNE & BLUNT, ...tical, Philoſophical and Mathematical Inſtrument-...kers, No. 20, *Cornhill*, oppoſite the *Royal Exchange*, *London*.

A mahogany and painted wood barrel friction generator, with winding handle, brass collectors with glass insulators, in original fitted wood travelling case with maker's trade label, by Edward Nairne, 18thC, 22in (55cm) wide.
$1,800-2,700

A brass candlestick pattern postal scale, with spring scale, on moulded circular foot, signed R. W. Winfield, Birmingham, January 13, 1840, No. 170, 6in (15cm) high. **$750-1,200**

Robert Walter Winfield registered the design on 13 January, 1840, and it lasted for 25 years.

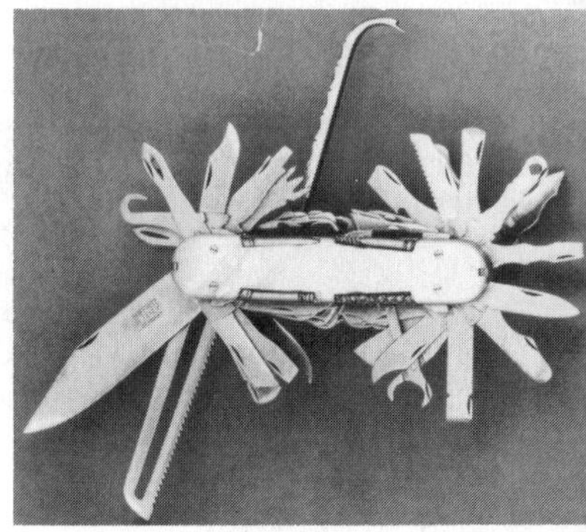

An exhibition multi-blade pocket knife, with 96 blades and mother-of-pearl scales, the main knife blade marked Hoffritz N.Y. Germany and Stainless, the other blades including scissors, files, saws, gimlet and corkscrew, 5in (13cm) long folded.
$2,700-3,300

:AMERAS

n A. Adams & Co., 6 by 9cm opical Minex camera, Folding [odel no. 8090, with polished ·ak body, tan leather focusing ɔod and bellows and a Ross, ɔndon Xpres 5½in f/4.5 lens no 4581, an Adams tropical focusing ɔod, 6 tropical darkslides, an dams tropical rollfilm back, and magazine plate back.
7,500-9,000

J.H. Dallmeyer, London, 5 by ;in Carfac collapsing camera, ith a Dallmeyer Stigmatic ·ries II No. 3 15cm f/6 lens in a al set Compound shutter, 3 ·uble darkslides, and a allmeyer Hingeless Film Pack lapter, in maker's leather case.
50-600

ie Carfac collapsing camera was lvertised in the British Journal ıotographic Almanac from 1912-14. The film pack adapter came standard.

J. Lancaster & Son, quarter-ate wood body Rover camera, ith a brass Lancaster patent ee-Saw shutter and leather ıter case.
300-375

A 2½ by 6in (6 by 15cm) panoramic falling plate camera No. 5627, with wheel stops, 3 speed shutter and waistlevel finder.
$300-375

This camera was probably made or imported by W. Butcher & Sons, London.

A J.H. Dallmeyer, London, 16-on-127 rollfilm Dual camera No. D154, with a Dallmeyer Dalmac Anastigmat f/3.5 3in lens No 143852, in a rimset Compur shutter, in maker's fitted leather case.
$1,050-1,350

A Gandolfi 10 by 8in mahogany and brass studio camera, with black leather bellows, extended baseboard and universal plate back, with accessories.
$1,800-2,700

This camera was made for John Dixon Studios of London and Paris in the late 1960s. The camera was commissioned from Gandolfi with an extended baseboard so that an 18in lens could be used for close-up work.

An A.P.M. Ltd., 4¼ by 3¼in 119 rollfilm Apem reflex camera, with a Ross, London, Telecentric f/6.8 13cm lens No. 75540.
$300-375

A W. Butcher & Sons, London, quarter plate mahogany body Royal Mail camera, with 15 lenses and push-pull shutter.
$1,200-1,800

An A.J. Melhuish, London, 10 by 8in (25 by 20cm) Kinnear pattern camera, with brass rear standard, applied label Melhuish's Patent, mahogany baseboard and front lens standard, red leather square cut bellows, mahogany and brass single wet plate darkslide, and a brass bound dividing lens with internal brass lens cap and rack and pinion focusing, signed McLean, Melhuish & Co. London.
$3,000-4,500

Arthur James Melhuish was listed as a photographer from 1860 until 1894. He was active as a photographic inventor before this, inventing the first roll holder for sensitised calotype paper in 1854. He died in 1896.

A George Hare, London, whole plate brass and mahogany field camera, No 7356, with red square cut bellows, focusing screen section stamped Plates, a brass bound J. H. Dallmeyer No. 7 Stigmatic Series II lens, No. 63013, maker's label George Hare, Manufacturer, 26 Calthorpe St, London, and 3 mahogany double darkslides.
$600-750

An H. Park, London, 10 by 12in mahogany and brass tailboard camera with maker's plate, signed H. Park, Manufacturer, 5 Station Buildings, Acton St., Kingsland, London NE, in a fitted canvas case, 6 mahogany double darkslides in a matching canvas base, 2 spare lens panels, a brass bound lens and a Ross No. 6 Wide Angle Symmetrical 8in lens.
$600-750

A Bloch, Paris, 45 by 107mm stereo Physiographe camera, with a pair of C. P. Goerz Doppel-Anastigmat lenses Nos. 119093 and 119095, and film magazine, in maker's original leather case.
$1,800-2,700

A London Stereoscopic Co., rollfilm tropical The King's Own De Luxe Model B camera, No. B.407, with polished teak body, brass binding, black leather bellows, a Zeiss patent 11½in (29cm) lens No. 13049, in a Compound shutter and a brass plate 'The London Stereoscopic Co. 3 Hanover Square, W.British Manufacture', in maker's brown leather case.
$1,800-2,700

A Houghtons Ltd., quarter plate tropical Sanderson camera, No. 17166 with teak body, a C.P. Goerz Dagor Series III 125mm f/6.8 lens, No. 280254, in an Ensign Sector shutter and 3 double darkslides.
$600-750

A J. F. Shew, London, quarter-plate mahogany body patent Eclipse camera, with red leather bellows, brass bound Shew lens and inset plaque signed J. F. Shew & Co. Sole Makers Newman St. London, Eclipse Apparatus Patent, No. 4102.
$375-525

A Lizars Challenge Dayspool tropical camera, Scottish with Spanish mahogany body, red leather bellows, Beck f4 No.2 Anastigmat lens and leather carrying case, c1905.
$600-750

A McKellen, Manchester, whole plate, brass and mahogany Double Pinion Treble Patent fie camera No. 857, with red leathe square cut bellows, a T. S. & W. Taylor, Leicester, 8½ by 6½in (21 by 16cm) Rectilinear 11.1in lens and Waterhouse stops, and maker's label 'McKellen's Doubl Pinion Treble Patent, Spring Gardens, Manchester', and one double darkslide.
$375-525

An H.J. Redding & Gyles, London, half plate mahogany body Luzo camera, No. 1022, wit brass fittings, internal bellows, 2 waistlevel finder, focusing arm, shutter and maker's plate Luzo, Trade Mark H. J. Redding & Gyles, Sole Makers, 3 Argyll Place, London W.
$1,200-1,500

The half-plate version of the Luz was advertised from 1893-1900.

A quarter-plate smooth black leather covered Una hand and stand camera, with a Ross Homocentric 5in f/6.3 lens, No 69159, in a Compound shutte and 6 double darkslides, in maker's fitted leather case.
$750-1,200

Thornton-Pickard Mfg. Co. Ltd., by 4in mahogany and brass und Type C aerial camera, No ', internal roller blind shutter, p mounted plate changer and a ylor, Taylor & Hobson Cooke viar anastigmat Series II 10in .5 lens.
,000-4,500

Chicago Ferrotype Co., 1in am Wonder Cannon ferrotype mera, with rechromed body, rect vision finder, a Laack f/4.5 mm lens, pneumatic shutter d spare buttons.
,500-2,250

Ernemann Kino ematographic camera, Model No. 907315, in a mahogany se, with Ernon f/3.5 5cm lens,). 94503, hand turned echanism and 2 film cassettes, 910.
00-750

A Thornton-Pickard Mfg. Co. Ltd., mahogany and brass fitted Merito Optical lantern, with red leather bellows, brass bound lens, metal chimney, electric illuminant and plate Thornton-Pickard Merito Optical Lantern, Pat. No. (1908) 17027, Altrincham.
$225-300

An Ernemann-Werke A.G., 4½ by 6cm Ermanox Reflex camera No. 1297448, with an Ernemann Ernostar Anastigmat f/1.8 10.5cm lens, No. 179654.
$2,700-3,300

A Levy-Roth 35mm Minnigraph camera, No. 1713, with a Minnigraph f/3 lens.
$750-1,200

A Nippon Kogaku, Japan, Exakta-mount Nikkor-Q.C. camera, f/3.5 13.5cm lens, No. 257451, lens hood, caps and 'red spot' mounting indicator, in maker's leather case.
$600-750

A New Ideas Mfg.Co., New York, 35mm metal body Tourist Multiple projector, No. 308, with lamphouse, internal projection mechanism, 2 film spools and lens, on a wood baseboard.
$750-1,200

A Goltz & Breutmann Dresden 45 by 107mm Stereo Mentor camera, No. 12444, with a pair of Carl Zeiss Tessar f/4.5 9cm lenses, Nos. 541675 and 541610, 3 double darkslides and a Mentor filmpack, in maker's leather case.
$375-525

A Simons & Co. 35mm Sico camera, No. 38, with polished teak body, and a Rüdersdorf A. G. Sico anastigmat f/3.5 6cm lens, No. 6837, in a dial-set Compur shutter, in a leather case.
$3,000-4,500

A Minolta 35mm CLE camera, No. 1019659, with a Leitz Summicron-C f/2 40mm lens No. 2564166, instruction booklet, a Minolta M-Rokkor 90mm f/4 lens No. 2015886, a Minolta M-Rokkor 28mm f/2.8 lens, No. 1013909, a Minolta Auto CLE flash unit and instruction booklet, and a release, in a fitted case.
$1,800-2,700

A Hasselblad, Sweden, 6 by 9cm Svenska Express falling plate camera, No. 4767, with inset retailer's label J. L. Nerlien, Aktsk, gilt stamped Hasselblads Svenska Express.
$300-375

A Cie de Française de Photographie, Paris, 10 by 12c metal body Photosphere camer No. 692, with shutter, lens, removeable finder, and 3 doubl darkslides, in a fitted leather case.
$1,800-2,700

A Leica outfit, in a Leitz fitted outfit case.
$2,700-3,300

The engraving on the camera indicates British military use.

A Morsolin, Turin, 35mm Argu camera, No. 130, with alloy an black leather covered body, collapsible optical finder, helic focusing and an E. Koristka Equator anastigmat f/6.3 5cm lens, No. 80722.
$4,500-6,000

This camera is, to date, the onl known example of the Argus camera and dates to 1921.

A G. A. Krauss, Stuttgart, 35mm Peggy I camera, No. M. 165/3, with a Carl Zeiss Jena Tessar f/3.5 5cm lens, No. 1292504, in a Compur shutter, in maker's leather ever ready case.
$450-600

A Rolleiflex No.1 original model, with 75mm f3.5 Tessar lens, cased.
$90-105

A LeicaFlex SLII black camera, with 50mm f2 Summicron R lens.
$900-1,500

Miller's is a price GUIDE not a price LIST

A screw-fit Thambar 9cm f/2.2 lens, No. 226272, with centre spot filter, lens hood and caps, in maker's original box.
$3,000-3,750

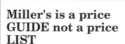

;ubminiature & ›etective Cameras

 Houghtons Ltd, London, silver ıcka watch camera, opening key issing, hallmarked 1907, with ·utter cover, in maker's plush ned case.
ı,800-2,700

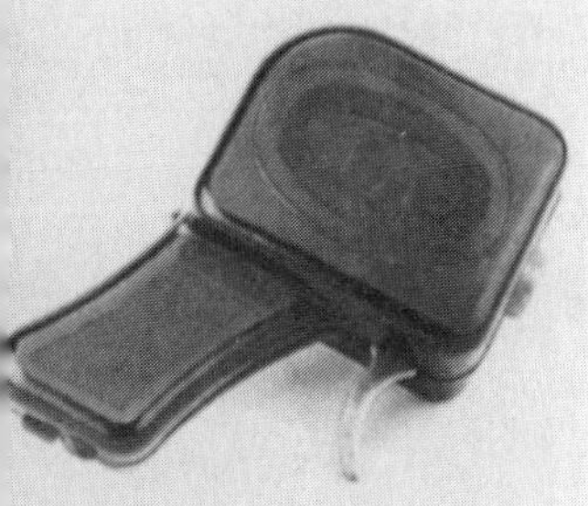

ɴ Erac Selling Co., London, 6mm plastic body Erac pistol ımera, casing cracked, with an ıternally contained metal-body ımera.
180-225

. Marion & Co., London, 2 by 2in un-metal Metal Miniature amera, with rack and pinion ocusing lens, slide shutter and 13 ingle metal slides, in maker's tted oak box.
3,000-3,750

A set of Coronet Camera Co., Birmingham, coloured Midget cameras in black, brown, green, red and blue, each with metal fronts, 2 in original leather case and one in original box.
$900-1,500

A Coronet Camera Co., 16mm brown body Midget camera, Birmingham, mounted on an umbrella.
$300-375

A K. Kunik 16mm red-body Mickey Mouse camera, with paper Mickey laid on to shaped metal advertising stand.
$375-450

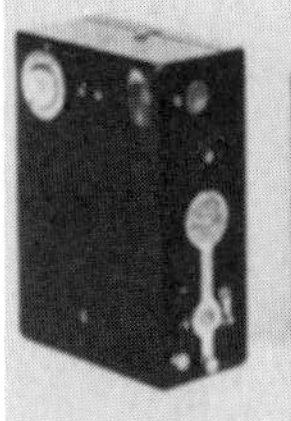

An Expo Camera Co., New York, 1¼ by 1in Expo Police camera with black metal body, with nickel fittings, waist level finder, interior transfer and instruction booklet 'Direction book for Expo Police Camera', in maker's original box.
$750-900

A Shincho Seiki Co. Ltd, 16mm plastic body Darling-16 camera, with instruction leaflet, in maker's box, in original shipping carton.
$600-750

A Konrad Köhnlein, Germany, 14 by 18mm Wiko camera, with plastic moulded casing, nickelled fittings, removable back plate, focal plane shutter and a Laack, Rathenow Meniske f/11 3cm lens.
$900-1,500

A Steineck Camera-Werk metal-body Steineck ABC watch camera, with a Steinheil VL f/2.5 12.5mm lens and red leather wrist strap and guarantee card, in maker's presentation case.
$1,050-1,350

A Showa Optical Works Ltd, 14 by 14mm Gemflex twin lens reflex camera, No. 6066, with back plate marked Made in Occupied Japan, a Gem viewing lens and a Gem f/3.5 25mm taking lens, maker's leather ever-ready case, instruction leaflet marked Miura Trading Co. Ltd. Tokyo and films, in maker's box. **$750-900**

A Doryu Camera Co., 16mm Doryu-2-16 pistol camera, No. 10012, with frame finder, cross-hatched wood hand grip, and a Hokutar 17mm f/2.7 lens.
$9,000-12,000

A Le Coultre et Cie Compass outfit, comprising a Compass II camera, No. 2674 with a CCL3B Anastigmat f/3.5 35mm lens and focusing back in a Compass blue leather slip case, 'Instructions on the use of the Compass Camera and II', and various accessories.
$3,000-4,500

A Magic Introduction Co., New York, 2in diam. metal-body Photoret camera, in maker's wooden box.
$375-450

A 5 by 3½in decoratively engraved yellow metal finger ring camera, with single speed shutter, four- click iris diaphragm and internal film holder.
$9,000-12,000

An E. Schmid 35mm metal-body Biflex 35 camera, No. 1107, with green-crackle finish, nickel fittings, and a Biflex-Trivar f/2.8 2cm lens, No. 1019, in maker's leather case stamped Biflex.
$3,000-4,500

A San Giorgio, Italy, 16mm Parva camera, No. 201608, with brushed chrome body, shutter speed P, 40, 100, 150, direct vision finder, internal blind shutter, and a San Giorgio Essegi 2cm f/3.5 lens.
$9,000-12,000

This is the rarest Italian-made camera, and one of the rarest subminiatures, only 9 examples of which were made in 1947.

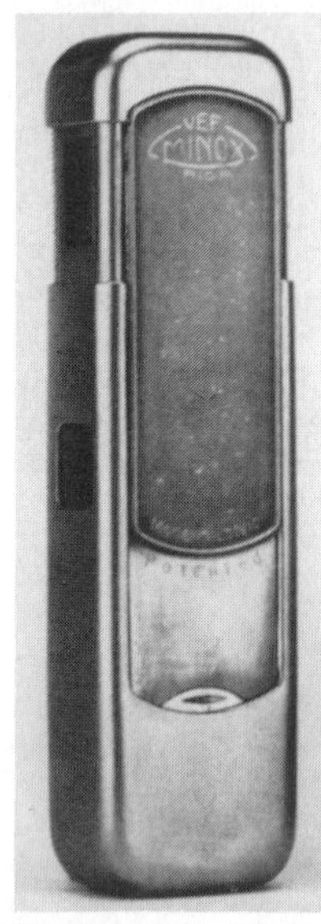

A V.E.F., Riga, 8 by 13mm original Minox camera, No. 13219, with a Minostigmat 15mm f/3.5 lens. **$600-750**

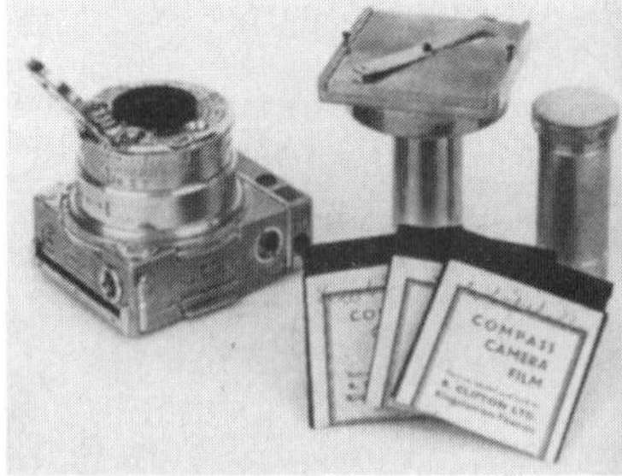

A Le Coultre et Cie, 35mm Compass II camera, No. 1590, with a CCLB Anastigmat f/3.5 35mm lens, in maker's blue leather purse, a Clifton alloy film processing tank, Compass film sheaths, and a Compass Camera Ltd. 'Something new under the Sun' booklet.
$1,800-2,700

A Tokyo Optical Co., 14 by 14mm Tone camera, with direct vision and waist level finders and a helically focusing Tone Anastigmat c/3.5 25mm lens, in maker's ever-ready case, in original box stamped Made in Occupied Japan. **$150-225**

Viewers

A wood body stereoscopic Kromax colour viewer with brass fittings, rear mirror, stereoscopic slide holder, internal green filter, inset label Barnard & Gowenlock's Kromax, Registered, top mounted red and purple filters.
$750-1,200

Bonds 'Kinora' viewer, with and turned mechanism and xidised viewing hood, on ahogany base, c1910, together ith 18 reels in maker's cartons, me with Holder Brothers, Hull tailer's label.
,500-2,250

British Mutoscope & Biograph o. Ltd, mahogany body Kinora ewer, No. 1094, with decorated ody, plain metal column, turned ood base, clockwork mechanism, aker's plate and 3 Kinora reels.
3,000-4,500

mahogany body stereoscopic romskop viewer, No. 538, with eflector, coloured filters and tailer's label 'The Kromskop. ve's Patent'.
,050-1,350

A wood body hand held stereoscope, with a pair of brass bound eyepieces, hinged lid and inset label Carpenter & Westley, 24 Regent Street, London, 6 stereo diapositives, and 3 stereographs.
$150-180

A Bonds 'Kinora' viewer, with hand turned mechanism and oxidised viewing hood, on mahogany base with stringing, c1910, together with 6 reels.
$600-750

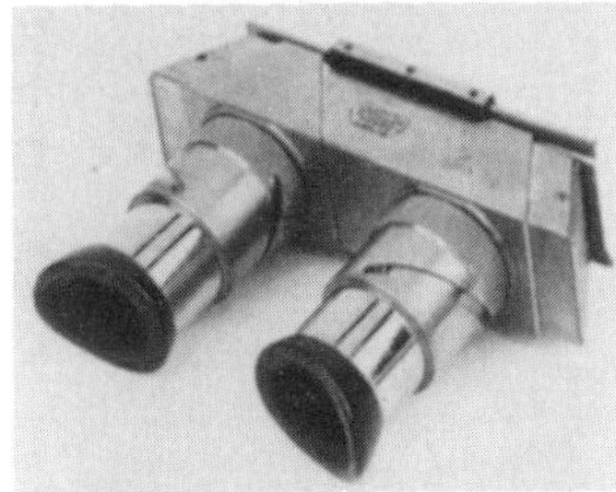

A Votra nickel-body stereo viewer.
$600-750

A mahogany and brass biunial magic lantern with brass bound lens section, a pair of three-draw rack and pinion focusing lenses, chimney, maker's plaque J. H. Steward, Optician to the British and Foreign Govs., 406 Strand, London, a pair of Triumph electrical illuminants, in a fitted wood case with internal accessory drawer holding a brass bound kaleidoscopic projecting lens, signed C. & F. Darker, spare Triumph light, brass gas piping and brass gas regulator.
$4,800-5,700

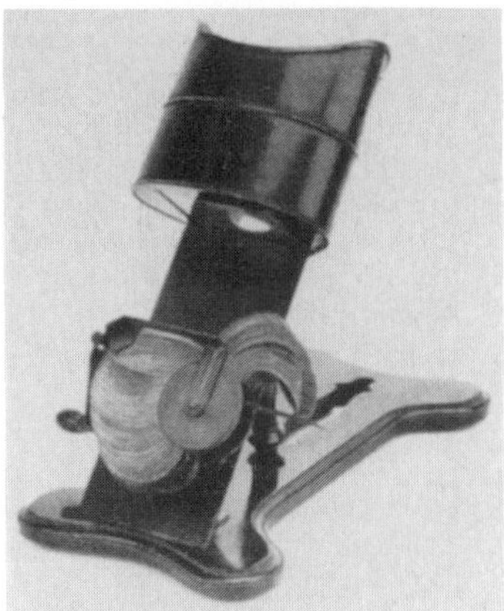

A Kinora Ltd, mahogany body viewer, with metal eyeshade, hand-crank mechanism and 14 reels, each in a box, and an unboxed reel showing ballet dancers. **$1,050-1,350**

A London Stereoscopic Co., cardboard body New Jewel Kaleidoscope, with turned wood eyepiece, rotating brass section, on a decorative metal stand.
$1,050-1,350

A Chappuis, London, wood body patent Reflecting Stereoscope, with screw focusing eyepiece section, hinged lid with label, on a barleytwist stand.
$1,050-1,350

This stereoscope was the subject of British patent No. 1558 of 3 June 1857 to Paul Emile Chappuis.

A W. Butcher & Sons, Blackheath, wood body Reflectoscope lantern viewer, with 3¼in diam. viewing lens, slide aperture, mirror and 2 rear opening doors, c1890.
$375-450

A wood body hand cranked projection shutter, with applied paper labels Cinématographe. Fabrication Française. Déposé E.V.L. Déposé.
$600-750

This device is attached to the front of a metal lantern and the lantern lens attached to the front on the mechanism.

An E. Reynauld, Paris, miniature Le Praxinoscrope, with black drum, applied trade label, turned wood base and 4 picture strips, 5in diam.
$600-750

A metal cased Filoscope with printed kinetic photographic subject, titled 'The Derby 1896', with title sheet, information sheet and picture sheets No. 3-187.
$450-600

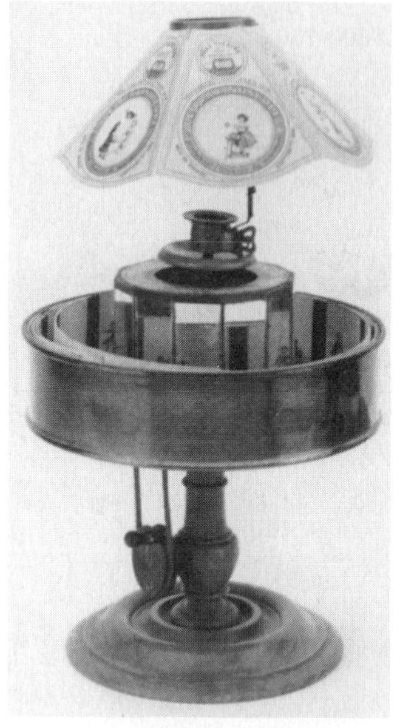

An E. Reynauld, Paris, hand cranked pulley-operated 8in diam. Le Praxinoscrope, with candle holder, shade on a turned wood base and 6 picture strips.
$1,050-1,350

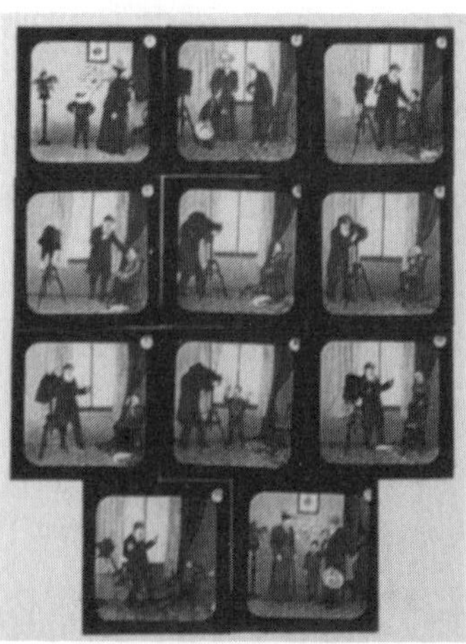

Nine coloured transfer lantern slides, showing a photographer in his studio with a young sitter, 3¼ by 3¼in (8 by 8cm).
$450-600

A cardboard body hand cranked Ciné Mickey film strip projector, with battery operated bulb light source and 6 film strips featurin Mickey Mouse, in boxes, in maker's box with applied printe label and legend Dessins Animé en couleurs d'après Walt Disney.
$300-375

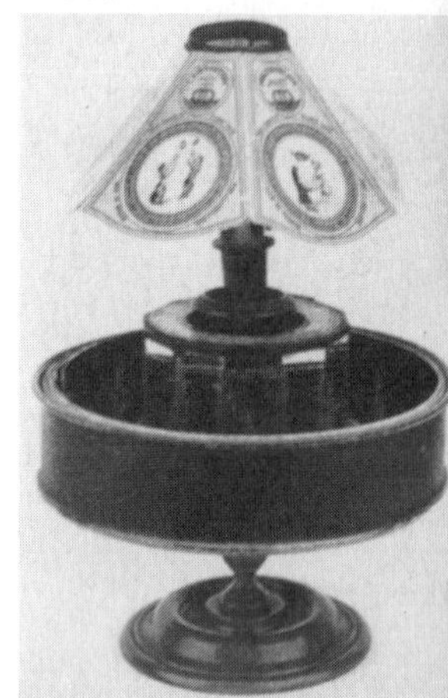

An E. Reynauld, Paris, 9in dian Le Praxinoscope, with candle holder, later shade and 6 pictur strips, on a wood base.
$1,050-1,350

A five-part peep view, the front section printed in German, French and English, 'The Royal iron rail-road between Nurember and Furth', 7½ by 5¼in (19 by 13.5cm).
$1,200-1,500

A London Stereoscropic Co. Wheel of Life zoetrope, on a turned wood stand, and with 12 picture strips, 12in diam.
$750-900

An Ernst Planck hot-air powered child's Praxinoscope, with spirit burner, condensing piston, connecting pulleys and 6in diam. mirrored drum, on a wood base with EP label, and 11 Praxinoscope picture strips, in maker's box.
$6,000-8,250

A French Polyorama Panoptique, the paper covered body with lens in shaped wood mount, paper bellows, push-pull focusing and hinged lid and back, mid-19thC, and 13 coloured night and day slides, 8in (20cm) wide.
$1,200-1,500

An Ernst Planck metal body projecting Praxinoscope lantern, with integral spirit burner, chimney, hand crank, shutter mechanism, standard slide holder and slides, in maker's wood box.
$1,500-2,250

A French zoetrope, with cardboard bodied drum, on turned ebonised wooden stand, with 5 double sided picture strips, 10in (25cm) high.
$450-600

Miscellaneous

A collection of daguerreian equipment.
$6,000-8,250

KODAKS

A red and gilt coloured glass shop sign advertising Kodak, in a wood frame, 12 by 48in (30 by 122cm).
$225-300

A brass body darkroom lamp, with contained paraffin burner, red glass window, spare glasses and methylated spirit bottle, in a fitted wood box.
$450-600

A lacquered brass microscope slide projection attachment, by W. C. Hughes, London, with slide stage, rack and pinion focusing and Watson lenses, in maker's fitted wood box.
$300-375

An Edwardian photographic tinting set, with instructions, 6in (15cm) wide. **$50-75**

A lacquered brass lantern slide illuminator attachment, with right angle reflector, 6 wood mounted slides, each with 3 slide preparations and a wood mounted live box in a fitted wood case.
$300-375

SILVER

A REVIEW OF THE YEAR

In many ways the antique silver market today reflects, as it has done historically, the economic state of the nation. At present as we move out of recession, buyers, private and trade, are manifestly nervous. For the last two or three years there has been a definite feeling throughout the trade that although the obviously better quality items are in demand and, therefore, will sell well; those pieces of an inferior nature or in bad condition will fare comparatively badly.

At auction, buyers are also bidding for fewer lots in each sale than they used to, which has meant that the commercial pieces, whether 18thC, 19thC or modern, have generally dropped in value. Modern silver can today be purchased at auction for less than $7.50 an ounce which is considerably less than the heady days of the early 1980s when the spot price for silver exceeded $30 an ounce.

A Victorian two-handled campana shaped champagne cooler, with detachable cast coat-of-arms, by John Hunt and Robert Roskell, 1865, the base stamped Hunt & Roskell late Storr & Mortimer, 16½in (41.5cm) high, 214oz.
$10,500-13,500

Although there are obvious weaknesses in the market, the prices for those pieces which are in demand have remained strong and even increased over the past twelve months. Antique silver has traditionally been bought by knowledgeable collectors and it is true to say that they have been starved within recent months of truly first rate and unusual items. We have seen perhaps greater demand than ever before for those few pieces in each sale that can be included in this category, be they the novelty pieces of the Victorian era made by such well known people as William Comyns or the firm of Sampson Morden; the exotic pieces from the Regency period which exhibit the strength and grandeur of the period or the fine pieces of the early 18thC, influenced and often made by the Huguenot goldsmiths. So long as they exhibit quality, distinctive design and good condition they will all sell well.

A George II melon shaped tea kettle, stand and lamp, engraved with a coat-of-arms within a rococo cartouche and twice with a crest, by Elizabeth Buteux, 1731, Britannia Standard, 16½in (41.5cm), 114oz.
$22,500-30,000

Following the relative success of the Dowty Collection of silver made by Paul de Lamerie, and sold by Christie's in New York in April 1993, it would seem that the maker's name is perhaps not as important overall as the quality of the piece involved. Although certain pieces in the collection showed a true strength of line and ornament, the condition of many of the pieces was just not quite fine enough to stimulate excessive interest. Also, many of the pieces had been on the market within the last 20 or 30 years. In recent years a gap of such a length would not have inhibited many buyers, but today the most keenly sought after items are those that have descended through a particular family or collection and have therefore never been offered for sale before. These are the items, so long as they are in good condition, that will generate strong if not frenzied bidding and ultimately prices that on many occasions will far exceed their auction estimates.

In many ways the market can be said to be healthier than it has been for perhaps the last ten years. Many people, particularly collectors, take the view that the prices for second or even third rate items had run out of control and that the fall by possibly as much as 50% in the price of these items in monetary terms reflects their inferior quality. Certainly, dull Georgian

A Victorian breakfast dish, with pierced oval strainer and plain liner, by Walker & Hall, Sheffield 1888, 13in (33cm), 70oz.
$2,700-3,300

candlesticks and dull Georgian salvers have decreased in value by between 20% and 50%. Those collectors who have kept a true eye on quality need not panic, however, for the value of their collections are without doubt increasing. The division between items truly worthy of a serious collector and those just below par is becoming wider and serious buyers are currently determined to stand off. If a piece is not absolutely 100% right then they will leave it and wait for another day. This, of course, has made estimating extremely difficult. As a valuer, I run the risk of disappointing clients when advising that a piece may only be worth 70% to 80% of its value two or three years ago. Some owners still find it hard to believe that prices can go down as well as up. 'Caveat emptor' is often quoted in the antiques world but this normally applies to fakes and forgeries. It can and should just as easily be applied in monetary terms as well. In any event, as most auctioneers will tell you, antiques, silver or otherwise, should be bought because you like them and not as investments. Finally, some people may like to think that because items are virtually half the price they were three or four years ago then they must be worth buying. This is not necessarily the case and it is worth bearing in mind that just because the piece is 'cheap' it is not necessarily worth buying.

Best Buys at the Moment

We have again reached the state where Georgian coffee pots and candlesticks can be purchased at auction for less than their brand new equivalent. So long as they are in good condition and with clear marks they must be more attractive to the eye, bearing in mind their patina and also their design, than most modern equivalents. Table services also fall into this category.

Pieces made in the early 18thC seem to be the most popular with collectors at present. This period is characterised by simplicity and lack of ornament. Good condition Queen Anne or George I pieces are finding a ready market. However, quality items from this period seem to be in extremely short supply and because they are popular with both English and foreign collectors, they will probably be in demand for many years to come. The main reason for the continued interest in this particular area is not that it is particularly attractive or illustrates the heights of goldsmiths talents, it is probably due to the fact that most pieces are potentially useful. Candlesticks, teapots, cream jugs, sugar basins and so on can and should all be used and most will fit in with today's modern interiors. Many also consider it to be the typical 'British' style. It is also an area which the new collector can learn and understand relatively quickly.

The antiques market is to a large extent dictated by fashion and this, of course, cannot be anticipated with any great accuracy by me or anyone else; suffice to say that price should be of secondary importance to quality. If you ask a surveyor or property developer which are the three most important considerations when buying land or property they invariably will reply: 'position, position, position'. The three most important factors when buying antique silver would in my opinion be: 'quality, quality, quality'.

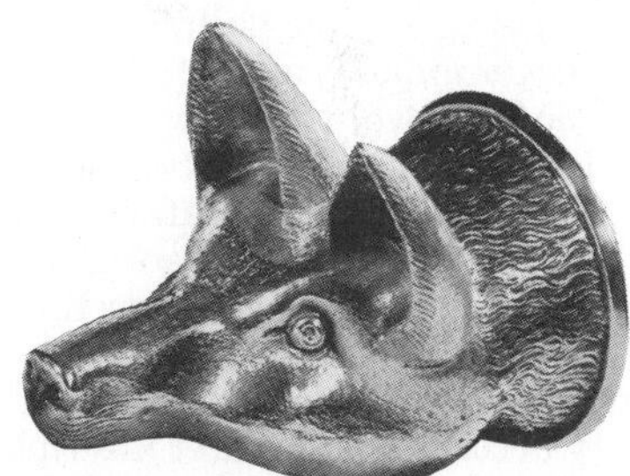

A George IV fox mask stirrup cup, the neck realistically chased to simulate fur and with moulded rim, by Edward Farrell, 1823, 5in (12cm) high, 5oz.
$4,800-5,700

Fakes and Forgeries

The hallmarking laws in England are extremely strict - and rightly so. From the earliest times silversmiths have on occasion tried to dodge the relevant hallmarking laws. Even the great names such as Paul de Lamerie were guilty of offences. Other pieces have been faked deliberately, while some have simply been altered at a later date. All these categories and others are covered by the hallmarking act and if a piece contravenes the act then it is illegal to offer it for sale whether privately or at auction.

Thankfully, most fakes and forgeries are relatively easy to detect. However, some are more difficult and on occasions even the experts disagree. To adjudicate in such instances the Goldsmiths' Company has the power to retain an item after the Committee has made its decision in order to carry out whatever is necessary to the piece before being returned to its owner. The hallmarking system which has been in operation in England since the 14thC, allied to the Antique Plate Committee, ensures that virtually no sub-standard, faked or forged silver reaches the open market.

A Russian sweet dish, the gilt interior with 6 compartments, Moscow 1842, 6in (15cm), 10oz.
$450-600

The laws governing the hallmarking on gold and silver make it unlawful for the owner to do whatever they wish with the article. However, so long as the laws are not broken, the repair and restoration of antique silver is perfectly valid and there is no law forbidding either the decorating or the removal of decoration from a piece previously hallmarked. From the collector's point of view later decoration or a later inscription will greatly reduce the interest and almost certainly the value. If such decoration is not too deep it can be removed relatively easily without damage being done to the piece and a skilled craftsman can, of course, restore the surface colour. However knowledgeable people become, all pieces of antique or antique silver must be looked at with an ever increasingly suspicious eye.

A Dutch tobacco box, engraved with the scene of the Israelites with the Arc of the Covenant, the base with the scene of the angel releasing St Peter from gaol, each with biblical reference above, the sides with a townscape and the initials 'GF', by Evert Bot, Amsterdam 1774, 5½in (14cm) long, 231gr.
$6,000-8,250

So long as one buys from a reputable auction house or dealer mistakes should not be made, and honest advice can be obtained free of charge. If a collector has the time to establish a rapport with a particular auctioneer or dealer, much information can be gained and without doubt this alliance will be of mutual benefit.

Cleaning and Restoration

When silver is in general daily use it should only need washing with hot water and soap, drying with a clean duster and then perhaps further rubbing with a soft chamois leather. There is no substitute for elbow grease as long as the marks are not rubbed away as they have been by so many butlers over the years. When silver is heavily tarnished a silver polish can of course be used, but sparingly. When not in use silver can be wrapped in acid-free tissue and kept in an airtight room or in sealed plastic bags. Cleaning silver does, of course, increase the appeal to some collectors, but it should be done sparingly and with a caressing hand rather than a forceful one. When restoration is called for, find an expert! Too many pieces have been ruined by enthusiastic amateurs. Trying to repair something oneself will almost certainly end in frustration and probably tears. In conclusion, restoration, provided it is within the hallmarking laws, is perfectly legitimate.

A George III coffee pot, with ebonised handle and button, by Thomas Wallis and Jonathan Hayne, London 1811, 8in (20cm) high, 28oz.
$750-1,200

Makers and Marks

Within the last year or so it has become apparent that buyers are perhaps less interested in the maker of a piece than the overall impression that this piece creates. It has perhaps been a fallacy for some collectors to concentrate on certain makers and, of course, the great names such as Paul de Lamerie, Paul Storr, Paul Crespin and Robert Garrard and so on, come to mind. But as we learn more about the actual workshop practices of these famous names we realise that only a small proportion of those pieces bearing the particular maker's marks would actually have been made by the silversmith in question. The maker's mark, or more correctly the sponsor's mark, means just that. Marks in general are as important today as they have been for many years. The great thing about English silver is the unbroken line of a hallmarking system since the 14thC. In its most basic sense these marks form a guarantee which has given buyers great confidence for centuries and still continues to do so. Hallmarks are of immense interest not only to collectors but also to students of English silver. It is true to say, however, that many important pieces are devoid of any marks, for whatever reason. Unmarked pieces should not be dismissed out of hand but should be given the same consideration, perhaps more, than fully hallmarked pieces.

In conclusion, the world of antique silver, and, of course, the wider spectrum of antiques in general, is ever changing and always stimulating. There is an enormous amount to learn about this particular subject and if a collector is hungry for knowledge, it will soon be accumulated. One's thirst for knowledge, however, should never be fully quenched. The dealers or collectors who suggest that they know it all, are to be treated with considerable suspicion.

Stephen Clarke
June 1993

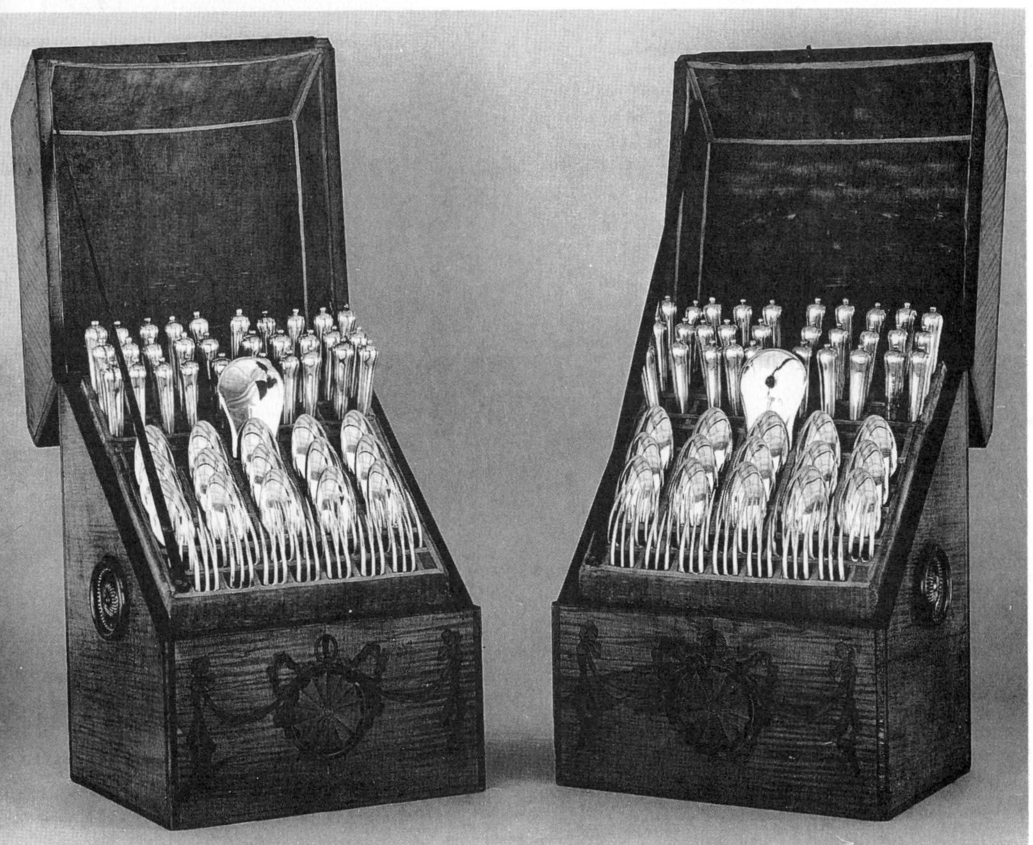

A German dessert service, with reeded borders, the knives with bun finials, comprising: 30 table forks and spoons, 30 table knives with silver blades and 2 pastry spoons, c1800, in a pair of Louis XVI satinwood cutlery boxes, with sloping hinged lids inlaid with a fan pattern, the fronts inlaid with a fan pattern hanging from a knot of ribbon flanked by swags, with gilt metal ring handles, boxes 14½in (36.5cm) high, 4880 gr.
***Est.* $7,500-9,000**

SILVER
Baskets

A Victorian comport, finely pierced and embossed with floral swags and gadroon rim, Sheffield 1900, 14oz.
$750-1,200

A George III basket, with bead cast overhead handle with circular box hinges, the bead cast border enclosing pierced oval foliate panels, the central oval section bright cut engraved with swags of pendant husks enclosing a crest and the motto 'Data Fata Sequutus', on an arcade pierced oval foot enclosing 2 roundels pierced with an urn, by William Plummer, London 1781, 13½in (34cm) wide, 851gr.
$1,800-2,700

A heavy gauge metal sugar basket, with square base, overhead swing handle, pierced and engraved formal designs, maker's mark P.F., assayer's mark F. Fabricius, Copenhagen 1794, 7½in (19cm).
$750-1,200

A George II cake basket, with chased scroll swing handle, pierced bowl and engraved base with coat-of-arms, ornate scroll border, 4 scroll feet with female masks, by James Luff, London 1742, 72oz.
$10,500-13,500

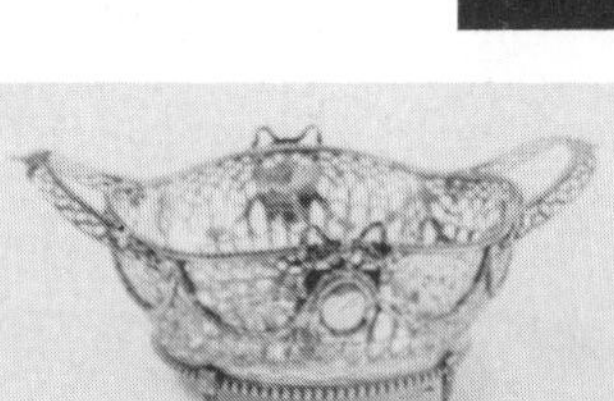

A two-handled circular pierced fruit basket, by Mappin and Webb, London 1912, 11½in (29cm), 23oz.
$750-1,200

A George III cake basket, with presentation inscription and engraved with central coat-of-arms, the body with fruiting vine and wheatear decoration, spiral swing handle, maker A.S., London 1762, 33oz.
$1,050-1,350

Miller's is a price GUIDE not a price LIST

A pair of boat-shaped sugar baskets, with loop handles and gilt interiors, the oval stem feet with engraved crest and motto, b Samuel Roberts Jr, George Cadman & Co., Sheffield 1798, together with a pair of thread edge ladles, by Richard Crossley, London 1794, 14½oz.
$1,800-2,700

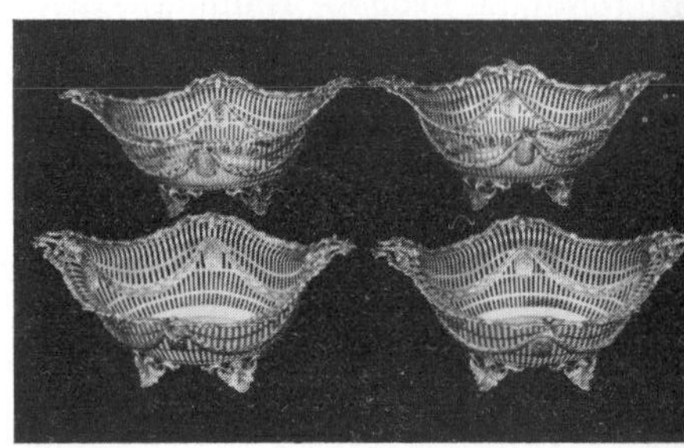

A composite set of 4 baskets, with rococo scroll and flowerhead cast and pierced everted border, over pierced arcading chased with swags of laurel, enclosing foliate rosettes, and raised on 4 acanthu leaf and scroll cast and pierced feet, by Thomas Bradbury, one pair Sheffield 1896 the other Sheffield 1918, 2,675gr., together with 2 original shallow clear glas dishes.
$5,250-7,500

Beakers

A beaker, with wrigglework girdl lip bearing traces of gilding, thread band above gadroon circular foot, gilt interior, maker's mark HN or NH, probably Swedish, c1700, 6½in (16cm), 8oz.
$750-1,200

owls

A pair of silver pedestal bowls, with leaf rims, shell and ring handles, on circular bases, Birmingham c1930, 7in (18cm) diam, 40oz.
$600-750

An Edward VII rose bowl, monogrammed and with presentation inscription, the shaped rim with shell and scroll edging above sides chased with flowers and scrolling foliage on matted ground above a reeded and fluted lower body and spreading base, W.H. Sparrow, Birmingham 1907, 10½in (26cm) diam, 33.2oz, together with a metal grille and ebonised wood plinth. **$1,050-1,350**

set of Continental bowls, the penwork sides with embossed ibbon tied swags of flowers and ands of paterae and leaves, ibbon tied reeded rims and eaded edge to the bases, blue lass liners, the dessert bowl with acant oval cartouches, urmounted by doves and rophies, on leaf chased legs and ast foliage scroll stretcher with a air of doves, import mark ondon 1906, 7½in (19cm) diam, he pair of sweatmeat bowls on vinged panel feet, 5in (13cm), 2oz.
1,800-2,700

oxes

silver trinket box, 1927, 3in 7cm) diam.
225-255

A silver money box, engraved with The Three Blind Mice, 1905, 3½in (9cm).
$600-750

A silver trinket box, the cover chased with a putto offering a flower to a classical maiden, foliate chased sides, Chester 1901, 4in (10cm).
$300-375

A George III silver tea caddy, engraved with armorials, slide-on base and cylindrical cap with berry finial, by Samuel Taylor, London 1766, 5in (12.5cm) high, 8oz 2dwt.
$1,500-2,250

The arms are those of Bois or Williams, Co. Brecknock.

A silver and tortoiseshell trinket box, 1912, 3in (7cm) diam.
$375-525

A silver snuff box, with reeded sides, mother-of-pearl base and cover carved with a man's head, Birmingham 1825, 3in (7cm).
$300-375

A silver cigarette case, c1905, 4 by 3in (10 by 8cm).
$375-450

This cigarette case belonged to a Russian officer.

A George V tea caddy, with gadroon edging, chased and foliate festoons, on 4 shell feet, the detachable cover with strawberry finial, London 1911, 5in (13cm), 11½oz.
$750-900

An Edwardian visiting card case, the fascia and reverse with chased scene, within foliate stamped and repoussé border, probably by Joseph Gloster, Birmingham 1905, 3 by 3½in (7 by 9cm).
$300-375

A silver articulated fish spice box with engraved scalework, green paste eyes, hinged head, Continental, 7½in (19cm).
$225-300

Candelabra

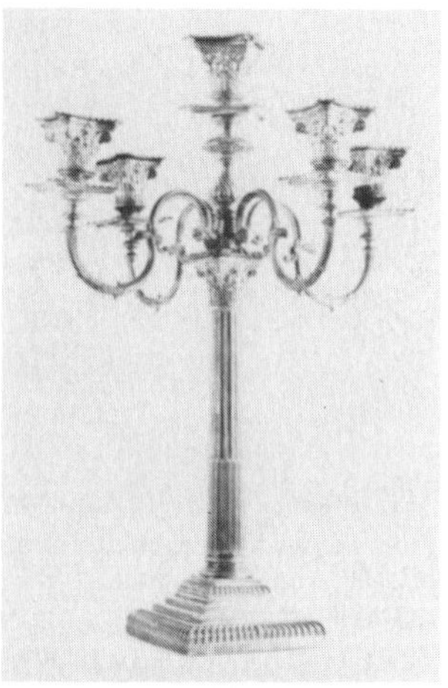

A silver Corinthian column 5 branch candelabrum, by Hancocks & Co., London 1898, 17in (43cm).
$1,500-2,250

A George IV four-light candelabrum, on spreading circular base and tapering cylindrical stem, with reeded scroll branches, circular drip-pans, vase shaped sockets, detachable nozzles, fluted and beaded borders, the base and central nozzle engraved with Pegasus, by Matthew Boulton and Plate Co., Birmingham 1827, 3 nozzles, Sheffield 1807, 25in (64cm), 77oz.
$3,000-4,500

A William IV six-light candelabrum centrepiece, on shaped triangular base with shell and scroll feet each surmounted by book and Royal crown, the base chased and applied with acorns, oak leaves and wheat ears and with fluted baluster stem, scroll branches, foliate drip pans and vase shaped sockets, detachable nozzles, by Robert Garrard 1836, 28in (71.5cm), 228oz.
$6,000-8,250

The arms are those of Maunsell with Cokayne in pretence, for Thomas Philip Maunsell (1781-1866), of Thorpe Malsor, Northamptonshire and his wife, Caroline Elizabeth, 3rd daughter and co-heir of The Hon. William Cokayne. He was MP for North Northamptonshire 1835-1857.

Candlesticks

An almost matching pair of early George II candlesticks, the cylindrical sockets issuing from inverted octagonal baluster stems on domed lobed circular bases engraved with a crest and armorial, by James Gould, London 1732 and 1733, 6½in (16.5cm), 794gr.
$3,000-3,750

A pair of dressing table candlesticks, with mask and scroll moulded concave square bases, swag and leaf pillar stems, Corinthian sconces with detachable nozzles, Sheffield 1910, 6in (15cm).
$750-900

A pair of silver column candlesticks, with embossed flowers and gadrooning, Sheffield 1895/1896.
$1,200-1,500

pair of silver Edwardian neo-assical design candlesticks, ɔpoussé with rams' heads, urns ıd pendant swags, the etachable sconces with beaded orders, on square tapering ɔlumns and square bases, irmingham 1908, 12in (31cm).
1,200-1,500

;offee & Chocolate Pots

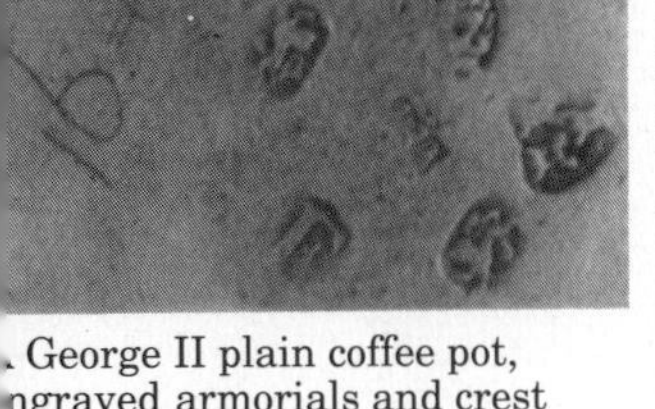

. George II plain coffee pot, ngraved armorials and crest f Charlton of Hesleyside, Iorthumberland, impaling 'emberton of Aislaby and tanhope, Co Durham, the riginal recipient of the crest was Villiam Henry Charlton of Iesleyside, the domed cover with ırned finial and wood scroll andle, maker William Beilby, Iewcastle mark 1745, 17oz gross.
;1,800-2,700

A Queen Anne style coffee pot and matching milk jug, the domed lids with bobbin finials, the beech side handles with applied silver decoration, London 1915, 8in (20cm), 49oz.
$1,200-1,800

A George III coffee pot, the hinged stepped domed cover with urn finial, acanthus leaf sheathed spout, single spur fruitwood handle, on a swept foot with beaded borders, possibly by John Lambe, London, 1783, 811gr. gross.
$2,250-3,000

An Irish coffee pot, the hinged lid with domed cover and baluster finial and scrolled spout, on a spreading circular base, maker's mark RI Dublin, 11½in (29cm).
$900-1,500

A coffee pot, the domed cover with urn finial and scroll thumbpiece, the fluted spout with hinged cover, oblique baluster turned wood handle, the 3 feet headed by cartouche shaped panels, repaired, probably by Antoine Lucas, Paris 1776, 8in (20cm), 17½oz. **$1,800-2,700**

A William IV coffee pot, tapered cylindrical and embossed with flowers and scrolls, rose finial, lightly crested, Edward Barnard & Sons, London 1832, 7½in (19cm), 645gr.
$1,200-1,500

A Dutch coffee jug, on beaded circular foot, the domed cover with bud finial, wood scroll handle, probably Amsterdam 1883, import marked 1894, 7½in (18.5cm), 13oz.
$900-1,500

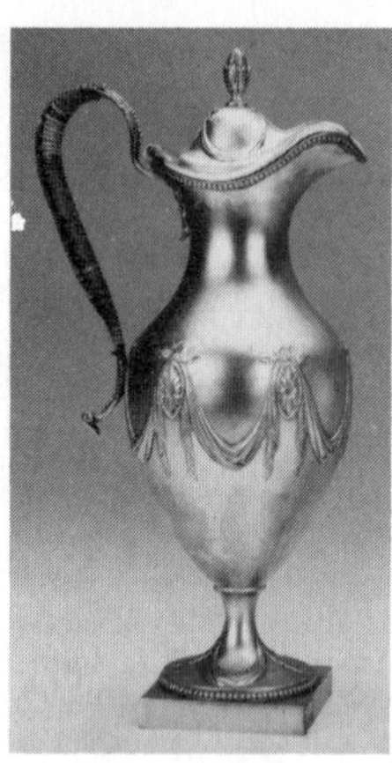

A George III coffee pot, repoussé with ribbon tied drapes centred by rosette medallions, with cast beaded borders, the hinged high domed cover with stiff leaf cast finial, with bead and acanthus leaf sheathed woven wicker S-scroll handle, on a drape repoussé socle and square foot, maker's mark indistinct, London 1776, 751gr gross.
$1,800-2,700

Cruets

A cruet, in fitted case, c1880, 2in (5cm).
$300-375

A Victorian milk churn cruet, 1½in (4cm).
$120-135

A Victorian silver cruet stand, engraved with scrolls and possibl containing the 7 original bottles, centre carrying handles, by G. Angell, London 1850.
$1,200-1,500

Cups

A two-handled challenge cup and cover, with leafage scroll frieze, London 1912, 32oz.
$375-450

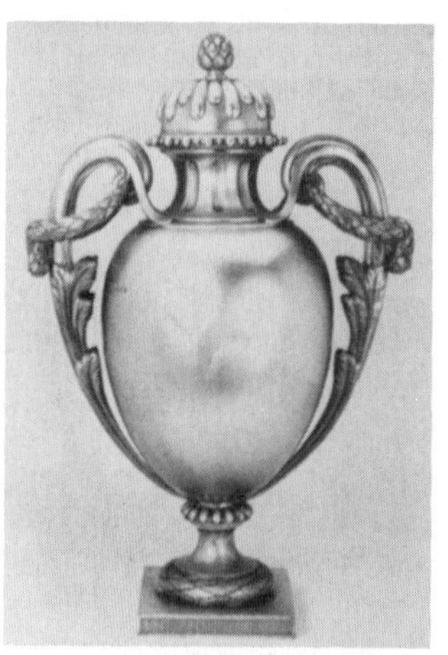

A two-handled partly fluted cup and cover, on square base and with lobed and foliate chased stem, the fluted and leaf capped scroll handles hung with laurel wreaths, beaded rim and bud finial, by Daniel and John Welby, 1914, 27in (68cm), 343oz.
$9,000-12,000

A George III two-handled partly fluted cup and cover, applied with a band of Vitruvian scrolls and with husk capped scroll handles, the waisted domed cover chased with a band of foliage and with circular cartouches and applied above with drapery swags, on square base, by Thomas Heming, 1770, 14½in (37cm), 76oz.
$5,250-7,500

The arms, crest and monogram are those of Flood for John Flood, Esq., (1745-1807), of Flood Hall, Thomastown, Co. Kilkenny, son of John Flood of Farmley (1696-1774), M.P. for Kilkenny, who married Elizabeth Aldworth, daughter of Richard Aldworth and his wife Elizabeth, daughter of Lord Doneraile. After much litigation John Flood (1745-1807) succeeded to the estates of his cousin The Rt. Hon. Henry Flood (1732-1791) who had intended his estate to endow Dublin College for the encouragement of the Irish language.

A George II two-handled cup and cover, on domed foot, the body with applied rib, leaf capped double scroll handles and domed cover with vase shaped finial, the cup engraved with a coat-of-arms within a rococo cartouche, by Thomas Tearle, 1741, 11in (27.5cm), 41oz.
$5,250-7,500

The arms are probably those of a lady of the Wastell family.

Miller's is a price GUIDE not a price LIST

Cutlery

ix William and Mary silver dog-
ose spoons, 3 by Pierre Harache,
694, one unmarked, 1694, all
ondon, and 2 with maker's mark
f Daniel Garnier of London,
1694, the terminals later
onogrammed and engraved with
he date 1694, rat-tail bowls,
70gr. **$1,500-2,250**

A composite King's pattern table service, in fitted oak box, comprising: 24 tablespoons, table forks, dessert spoons and forks, 18 teaspoons, 6 salt spoons, 4 sauce ladles and a pair of basting spoons and soup ladle, each engraved with a crest, by William Eaton, Robert Peppin and George Adams, 1821, 1824, 1832 and 1841, 338oz. **$7,500-9,000**

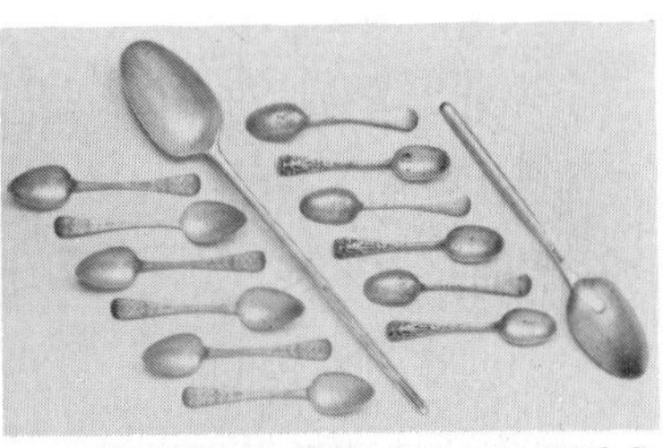

A selection of silver flatware, 18thC. **$1,200-1,500**

A set of thread edge Old English pattern cutlery, comprising: 12 tablespoons, table forks, dessert spoons, dessert forks and teaspoons, crested, makers Thomas Alfred, Walter Brinsley Slater and Henry Arthur Holland, London, 1895/96, 85oz. **$1,500-2,250**

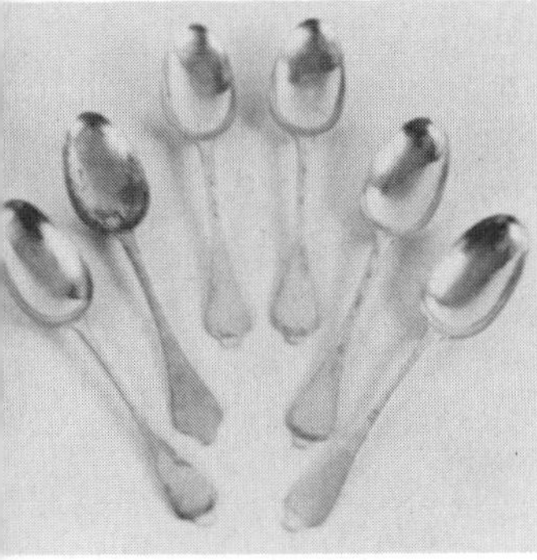

ix Queen Anne rat-tail dessert
poons, trefoil handles, maker
robably Henry Greene, London
706, 9oz.
375-525

An early Victorian fiddle pattern fish slice, engraved with an initial, with fish and seaweed pierced and engraved blade, maker's mark RW, London 1843, 164gr. **$225-300**

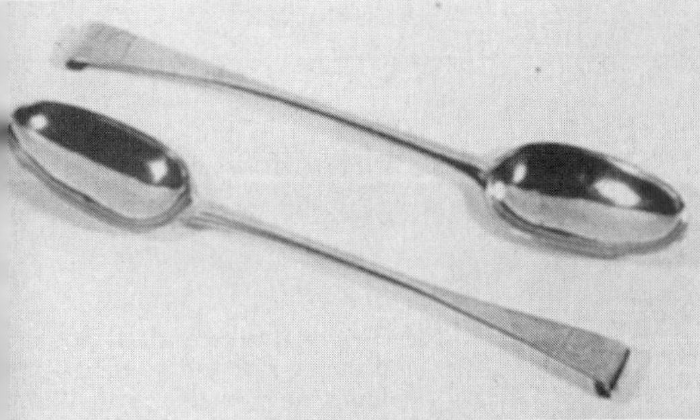

'wo Irish serving spoons with
own scrolled handles, each
ngraved with a crest, maker's
ark, probably John Laughlin,
1770. **$1,050-1,350**

An early Victorian composite fiddle, thread and shell pattern part table service, comprising: 12 tablespoons and forks and a pair of basting spoons, engraved with motto and crest, maker's mark EE, London 1854/56, 2863gr. **$1,050-1,350**

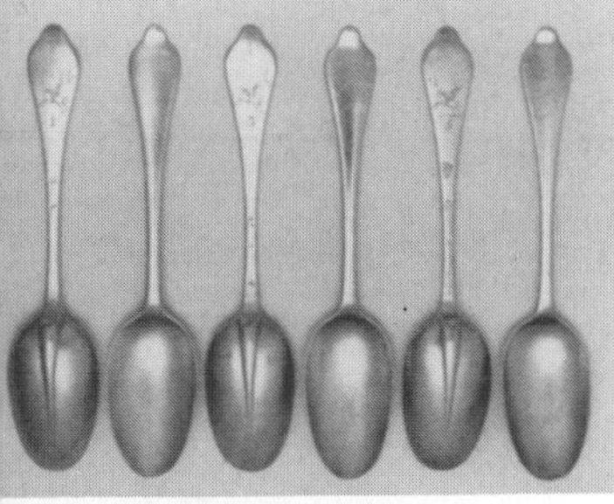

set of 30 Queen Anne dog-nose
attern table spoons, each
ngraved with numbers 1-30,
'egasus and initials, by Joseph
3arbut, 1706 and 1708, 76oz.
;7,500-9,000

Dishes

A pair of entrée dishes, on heater bases, with gadrooned borders and rocaille shell lugs at the extremities, armorial engraved domed covers with artichoke finials, the bases with leaf wrapped loop side handles and panel supports, c1870, 14in (36cm). **$1,200-1,500**

A George III entrée dish, with foliate moulded and gadrooned edges, the handle cast anthemion, scrolls and shells, engraved armorial and crest, maker's mark W.T., London 1801, 13in (33cm). **$1,200-1,500**

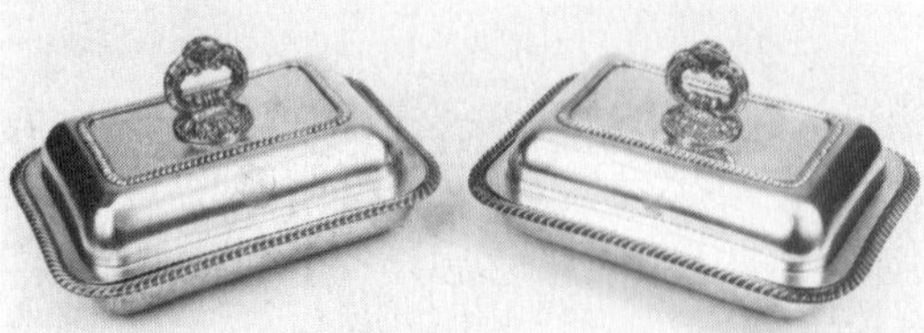

A pair of George IV entrée dishes, with gadrooned edges, the covers engraved with a crest, with foliate, shell and scroll handles, maker's mark J.K. and Co., one handle apparently unmarked, also inscribed Payne and Son, Bath, Sheffield 1824, 11½in (29cm), 106¾oz.
$2,250-3,000

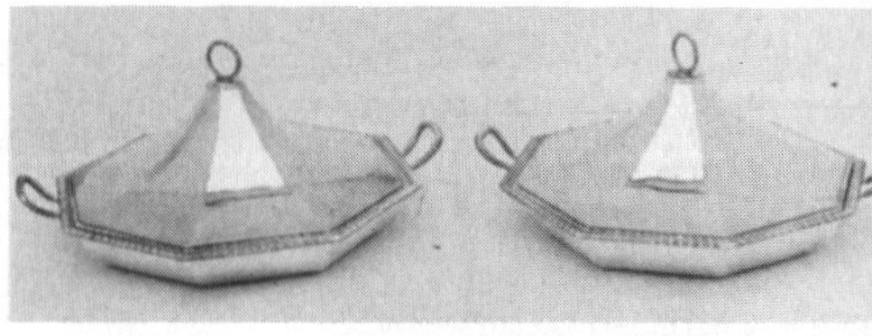

A pair of George III entrée dishe and canopy covers, with gadrooned rims and handles, London 1767, 60.5oz.
$3,000-4,500

A pair of George IV entrée dishes, set with acanthus leaf handles and shaped gadrooned borders, maker I.H., 1825, 10½in (27cm), 95oz.
$2,250-3,000

A Victorian entrée dish, with hot water compartment, loose tray and cover, supported on 4 scroll feet mounted with prowling cats, the cover finial in the form of a wedge of cheese with mice, makers Robert Garrard, London 1843, 113oz.
$12,000-15,000

Goblets

A pair of George III campana shaped goblets, engraved with armorials and with reeded lower bodies, on plain spreading bases, by John Edwards, London 1808, 707gr.
$1,500-2,250

A pair of ovoid goblets, gilt line with flared feet, engraved with crest and embossed with palm leaves and beaded foot rims, by William Grundy, London 1776, 6½in (16cm), 17oz.
$1,500-2,250

Ewers

A Victorian Cellini pattern hot water ewer, with chased decoration, Stephen Smith, London 1880, 11½in (30cm), 28½oz.
$1,200-1,800

Inkstands

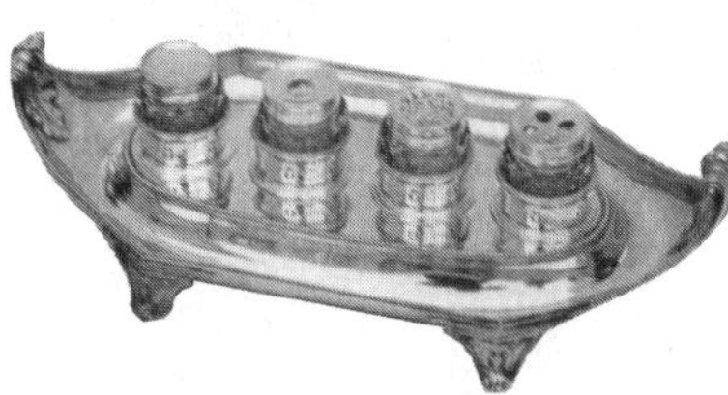

A George III boat-shaped inkstand, with 4 silver topped bottles, with beaded rim on pierced and beaded scroll feet, maker's initials W. P., London 1781, 39½oz.
$4,500-6,000

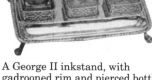

A George II inkstand, with gadrooned rim and pierced bottl holders, on claw feet, by William Robertson, London 1759, 20½oz.
$2,700-3,300

A standish with double inkwells, clear glass liners, hinged lids, rectangular tray, decorated with cast beading, London 1898, 8½ by 5½in (22 by 14cm).
$900-1,500

A Victorian inkstand, with canted corners, 2 glass receivers flanking a wafer box, gadrooned edges, scroll panel feet, maker John Newton, Mappin, London 1888, 4oz excluding receivers.
$1,500-2,250

Jugs

A cream jug, London 1776, 4in (10cm) high.
$375-450

A cream jug, London 1802, 4½in (10.5cm) high.
$300-375

A cream jug, by Messrs Bernard, London 1900, 5in (12.5cm) high.
$300-375

A cream jug, London 1843, 4in (10cm) high.
$300-375

A cream jug, Sheffield 1911, 3in (7.5cm) high.
$225-255

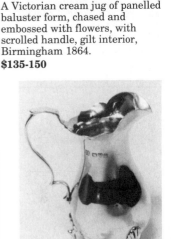

A Victorian cream jug of panelled baluster form, chased and embossed with flowers, with scrolled handle, gilt interior, Birmingham 1864.
$135-150

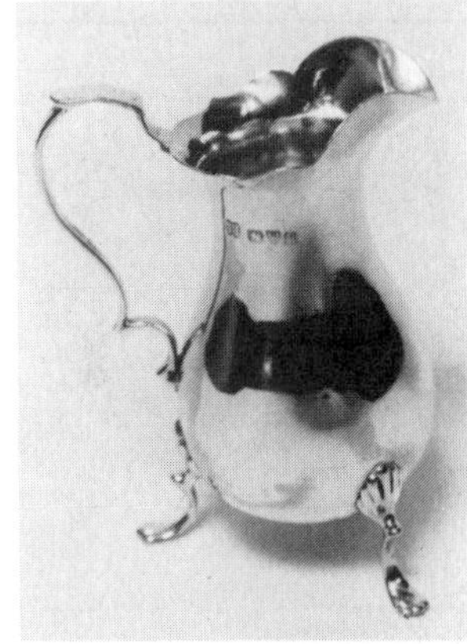

A cream jug, Sheffield 1902, 3in (7.5cm) high.
$150-225

A cream jug, Chester 1900, 4in (10cm) high.
$120-135

Mugs & Tankards

A William IV christening mug, monogrammed and with acanthus decorated lower body and spreading base with leaf capped scroll handle, by Charles Fox, London 1836, 4½in (11cm), 7oz.
$450-600

A George III pint mug, with later rustic scene chased and inscribed, scroll handle, London 1807, 4½in (11.5cm), 9oz.
$750-900

Two reeded tankards, with bracket handles, the hinged domed covers engraved with a crest, by Samuel Wastell, 1723 and Gurney and Cooke, 1746, 26oz.
$9,000-12,000

A silver mounted tankard, the part faceted barrel encircled by later hoops engraved with masks, husks and a Latin inscription, dog tooth bordered foot, the domed lid chased with stylised foliage, lion and armorial engraved shield finial, scroll handle with mask decoration, probably German, 17thC, 9in (22cm).
$6,000-8,250

Make the Most of Miller's

In Millers we do NOT just reprint saleroom estimates. We work from realised prices, either from an auction room or a dealer. Our consultants then work out a realistic price range for a similar piece. This is to try to avoid repeating freak results - either low or high.

A George II tankard, London 1731, 24½oz.
$2,700-3,300

A George II quart lidded tankard, engraved with crest, maker Thomas Whipham, London 1751, 31oz.
$3,000-3,750

A Charles II tankard, with scroll handle, hinged slightly domed cover and double lobed thumbpiece, engraved with a coat-of-arms within a plume cartouche, on moulded foot, the base with initials, maker's mark TL, 1676, 7in (18cm), 36oz.
$15,000-18,000

Salts

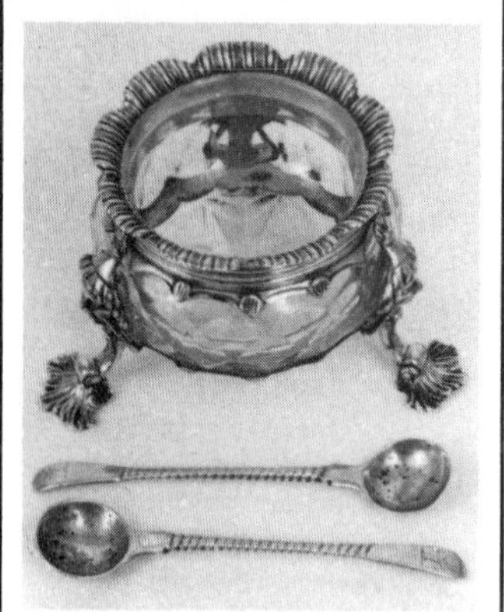

A Scottish silver and cut glass salt, with mark, c1750, 3in (8cm) diam.
$750-1,200

A pair of oval salts, shell and gadroon rims, on cast bases, similar twisted wire handles, one salt fully marked, the other maker's mark only, by John Jones, London 1766.
$600-750

Sauceboats

A sauceboat, Sheffield 1940, 2½in (6cm).
$135-150

A George II sauceboat, with bold card cut rim, scrolled handle, standing on animal feet, London 1737.
$600-750

A pair of Victorian cast sauceboats, the upper rims and feet moulded in rococo style, leaf moulded scroll handles, maker's Goldsmiths & Silversmiths Co., London 1896, 7in (18cm), 30¾oz.
$1,050-1,350

Salvers

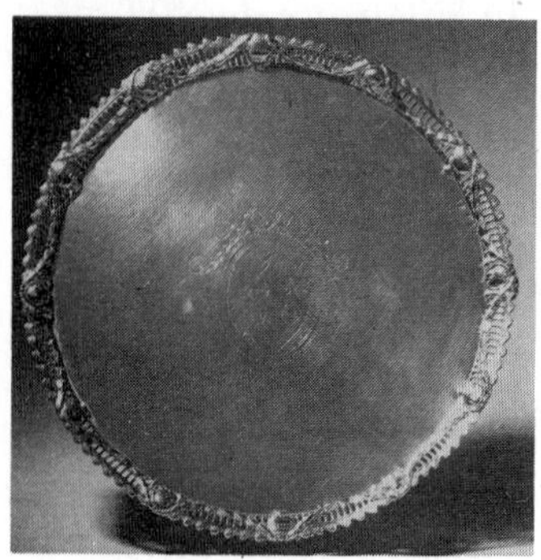

A George III salver, on 4 pierced bracket feet, the border pierced and chased with classical medallions, urns and husk swags and with waved rim, by John Carter, 1774, 16in (40cm) diam, 64oz.
$5,250-7,500

The arms are those of Grant impaling another.

Services

A silver plated coffee set and tray, c1900. **$300-375**

A three-piece tea set, comprising: teapot decorated with chased flowerheads and foliage to ribbed body and foot, hinged lid surmounted by a bird of paradise, and with scroll and acanthus handle, London 1833, and identically decorated two-handled sucrier and milk jug, London 1836, each piece monogrammed, 49oz. **$1,800-2,700**

A Victorian four-piece tea and coffee service, the pear shaped panelled body repoussé with foliage and scrolls, hatched vacant and monogrammed cartouches, the teapot and coffee pot with moulded swan neck spouts, the hinged covers with finials, the milk jug and sugar basin with gilt interiors, all with leaf scroll handles, on leaf and shell panel feet, makers Josiah Williams & Co., Bristol 1878, 72oz. **$2,700-3,300**

A Georgian matched three-piece tea service, with foliate handles, on circular collet feet, teapot by John McKay, Edinburgh 1819, sugar and cream by Charles Fox, London 1824/1837, 40oz. **$1,050-1,350**

A three-piece tea service, with crested and chased foliate and scroll decoration above reeded girdles, with leaf capped scroll handles on rim bases, Joseph and John Angel, London 1835, 1836 and 1839, 1,055gr. **$750-1,200**

A William IV three-piece tea set, melon fluted with diaper and scroll engraved shoulders and cast scroll handles, the milk jug of inverted pear shape, all on leafy bracket feet, with a pair of Old English pattern sugar tongs, London 1836, 50oz. **$1,200-1,500**

A four-piece tea service, comprising teapot, hot water jug, sugar basin and cream jug, each engraved with repeating floral motifs, maker's mark S.S. and stamped Goldsmiths Alliance Limited, Cornhill, London 1869, 80oz. **$2,700-3,300**

An Indian three-piece tea set, comprising: circular teapot with gimped rim, elephant finial, spout and handle, and with lobed sides with embossed figure decoration, matching sugar bowl and cream jug, 19thC, 1680gr. **$1,200-1,500**

A four-piece tea and coffee set, part fluted and festoon and ribbon chased, ring bases, gadroon rims, the pots with composition handles and buttons, Sheffield 1905/06, 68oz. **$1,200-1,500**

A five-piece silver tea set comprising: teapot, hot water pot, sugar bowl, cream jug and tray, with shell, leaf and gadrooned bands, ivory knops and handles, Edward Viner, Sheffield 1936, 162oz. **$3,000-4,500**

A seven-piece fluted circular tapered tea and coffee service, engraved with shells and foliate scrolls on rim feet, comprising: a teapot with ivory scroll handle and fluted knob, a coffee pot with ivory scroll handle and fluted knob, a hot water jug with scroll and pendant spout, ivory scroll handle and fluted knob, a sugar bowl with 2 scroll handles, a pair of sugar tongs and a plain oval tray, the border carved with shells, foliate scrolls and scale reserves and turned ivory handles, Birmingham marks.
$4,500-6,000

A composite late George III four-piece tea service, repoussé and engraved with scenes after Tenier, comprising: tea kettle with fruiting vine, carved ivory handle, on stand with burner raised upon acanthus leaf feet, teapot with hinged domed cover, with cast and applied bird and leaf finial and raised upon 4 paw feet with lion mask terminals, two-handled sugar basin with rustic and figure cast handle, raised upon 4 stylised scallop shell feet with grotesque mask terminals, and a similar milk jug, by Edward Farrell, London 1819/21, 6681gr.
$7,500-9,000

A mid-Victorian four-piece tea and coffee service, each with ornate scrolling handle, profusel chased with scrolls, lines and leaves, on curving scrolled feet, probably Richard Hennell, London 1858, 70oz.
$2,700-3,300

A Victorian tray with scalloped rim and beaded border, enclosing a chased panel decoration to the centre of flowers, leaves and scrolls, the whole supported on 4 ornate pierced scroll feet, maker J.E.W. and J. Barnard, London 1869, 21in (53cm) diam, 100oz.
$3,000-4,500

An Edwardian five-piece silver gilt dessert servic comprising: a garniture of 3 cake tazzas, and 2 dishes on scroll feet, with pierced scroll decoratio below applied borders, engraved with initials, London 1902, 8 to 10in (20 to 25cm), 78oz.
$1,800-2,700

A seven-piece tea service, comprising: a tea urn, stand and lamp, teapot, hot water jug, two-handled sugar bowl and cover, milk jug, slop bowl and two-handled tray, the kettle stand on 4 lion's paw and anthemion feet, with detachable lamp with domed cover, the teapot, hot water jug and cream jug each with eagle's head spout and wood handles with swan and rosette terminals, the teapot and hot water jug each with hinged slightly domed covers and pine cone finials and with stylised foliage borders, the tray with similar border and entwined swan handles and engraved with a monogram, by Bointaburet, Paris, 19thC, the tea kettle and stand 17in (43cm), the tray 30in (76cm).
$7,500-9,000

A late George V four-piece tea service, comprising: plain globular teapot and cover, matching sugar basin, cover, milk jug and rounded cylindrical hot water jug and cover, the covers with spherical ivory finial and all with ivory loop handles, by Mappin and Webb, Sheffield 1934, 1177gr., and a matching tray, with applied ivory loop handles, by Mappin and Webb, Sheffield 1935, 19in (49cm) wide over handles, 2,194gr.
$4,500-6,000

An early Victorian three-piece tea set, embossed and chased with rococo flowers, scrolls, shells and cartouches, scroll handles, open rococo panel feet, the teapot and sugar bowl, by Charles Fox, milk ewer by Charles T. & George Fox, London 1840 and 1843.
$1,800-2,700

Scent Bottles

A silver scent bottle, London 1900, 2½in (6.5cm).
$225-300

A silver engraved scent bottle, 2½in (6cm).
$225-300

Make the Most of Miller's

CONDITION is absolutely vital when assessing the value of an antique. Damaged pieces on the whole appreciate much less than perfect examples. However a rare, desirable piece may command a high price even when damaged.

Teapots

A Regency compressed teapot, embossed and chased with foliage, shells and scrolls to a scale ground, having a cast moulded spout, the sides with a crest and coat-of-arms to the cartouches, the domed hinged cover with an artichoke finial, wood scroll handle, on a circular foot, by Rebecca Emes & Edward Barnard, London 1818, 24oz.
$600-750

A George III teapot, with bands of engraving and initialled laurel cartouches, with a swan neck spout, the domed hinged cover with an oval ivory finial, ivory scroll handle, by Alice & George Burroughs, London 1804, 16½oz.
$600-750

A George III silver teapot, chased with leafage and blooms flanking cartouches, acanthus decorated spout and lid, ivory handle, by Alice & George Burroughs, London 1816, 5½in (14cm), 845gr.
$1,050-1,350

A George III tea kettle, of repoussé design with swing handle, spirit burner and heavy plated stand, London 1810, 56oz.
$1,800-2,700

A George III teapot, with ivory finial, bright cut engraved with floral draped oval cartouches and formal bands, replacement scroll handle, by Crispin Fuller, London 1793, 11½in (29.5cm), 11¾oz.
$750-1,200

A George III silver teapot, with lightly engraved anthemion girdle, ivory handle and finial, by John Emes, London 1801, 3¾in (9.5cm), 360gr.
$750-1,200

A Regency teapot, partly ribbed with a reeded band, later engraved with later initials, scroll spout and handle with classical mask appliqué, the hinged cover with a melon finial, on a circular spreading foot, London 1814, 25½oz. **$600-750**

Tureens

A George II two-handled sauce tureen and cover, engraved with coat-of-arms with gadroon edging, scroll handles and shell and scroll feet, the cover with acanthus finial, by Sebastian and James Crespell, London 1768, 8in (20cm), 612gr.
$1,200-1,500

A George III partly fluted soup tureen and cover, on spreading foot, with lion's mask, drop ring handles and gadrooned rim, the domed cover with detachable unmarked crest finial, engraved with 2 coats-of-arms and inscription, by Peter, Ann and William Bateman, 1802, 15in (38cm), 90oz.
$9,000-12,000
The inscription reads 'The 1st Troop of East Essex Volunteer Cavalry', and 'to T. T. Cock Esq. their Captain 30th Aug 1802'. The arms are those of Cock with another in pretence and the arms of the County of Essex.

A two-handled sugar vase and cover, with twin loop handles, London 1905, 13oz.
$375-525

Miscellaneous

A French oval jardinière with clear glass liner, 4 matching circular dessert stands, and a pair of matching silver mounted pear shaped claret jugs, each on hoof, column and ram's mask feet, each pierced and chased with foliate scrolls, ribbons and floral swags, engraved with a monogram within an oval cartouche between applied doves, cherubs and flaming torches, the jugs with similar mounts and with leaf capped double scroll handles, hinged domed covers with vine tendril finials, c1880, jardinière 14½in (37cm).
$7,500-9,000

A Charles II Provincial two-handled porringer, chased with a broad band of stylised foliage and engraved with presentation inscription, possibly Southampton c1666, 3in (7.5cm), 4.5oz.
$5,250-7,500

A Scandinavian cast table bell, the terminal cast in the form of a baby and dog eating a bunch of grapes, marked 830S, by KBS, 7in (18cm).
$600-750

A silver cow creamer, marked, 4in (10cm) long.
$750-1,200

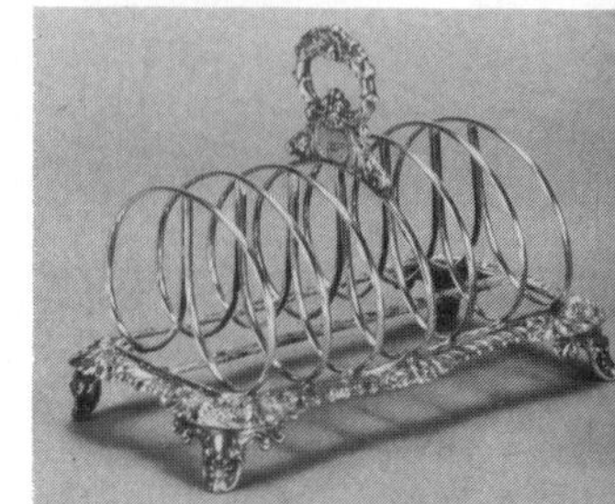

A William IV silver toastrack, with gadroon, shell and foliate border and central handle, by Edward Barnard & Sons, London 1835, 7in (18cm), 355gr.
$750-1,200

A George III sugar caster, with repoussé fruit, vine, shell and scroll decoration and cupid playing a lyre, on a circular foot, London 1809, 9in (23cm), 16½oz.
$750-1,200

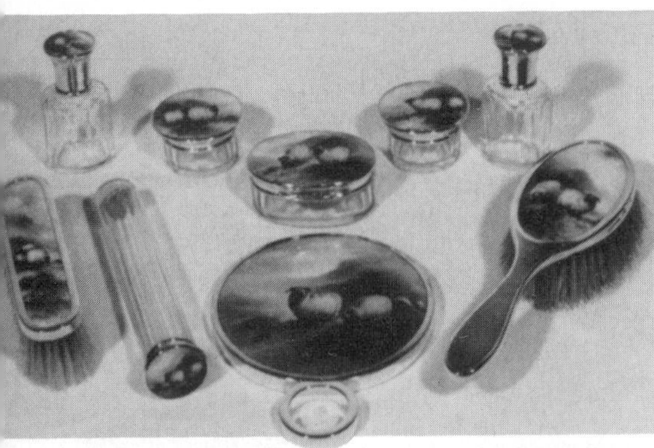

\ silver and porcelain mounted art dressing table set, painted with highland sheep decoration, omprising: a hand mirror, lothes brush, hair brush, a pair of scent bottles, and 4 trinket jars, igned E. Barker.
3,000-4,500

An Edwardian replica of The Warwick Vase, the body chased and applied with masks, lion's pelts, foliage and trailing vines, with vine tendril handles and ovolo rim, on a swept circular foot and square base, by Elkington & Co. Ltd., Birmingham, 1904, 6,000gr, 10½in (27cm), with plated liner and wirework double grille.
$7,500-9,000

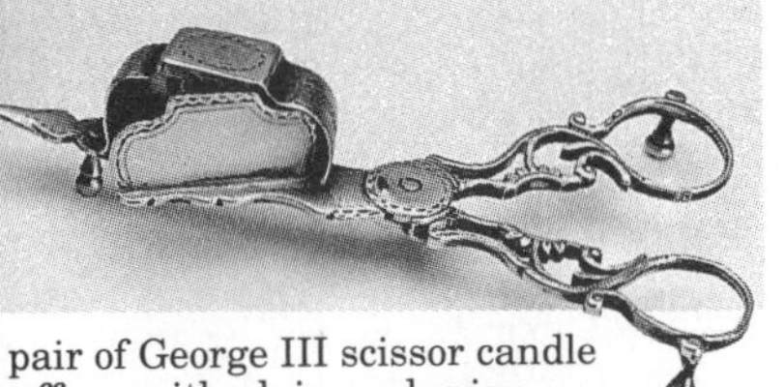

A novelty silver tea strainer, in the form of a tennis racket, Birmingham 1907, 6½in (16cm).
$375-525

\ pair of George III scissor candle nuffers, with plain oval grips, penwork scroll shanks, circular ox hinge and plain stem, with right cut engraved decoration, ntaglio duty mark, London 1785, 0gr. **$375-525**

A pair of Victorian tazzas, the centres engraved with a crest, shaped gadroon borders, clear glass liners, on pierced panelled stem feet, London 1870, 9in (23cm) diam, 46.5oz.
$3,000-4,500

\ pair of French hollow cast nodels of strutting pheasants, with detachable heads, on aturalistically cast circular bases, import marks for London 1900, 16in (40cm) high, 4,169gr.
4,800-5,700

A silver egg snipper, c1917, 4in (10cm) long.
$375-525

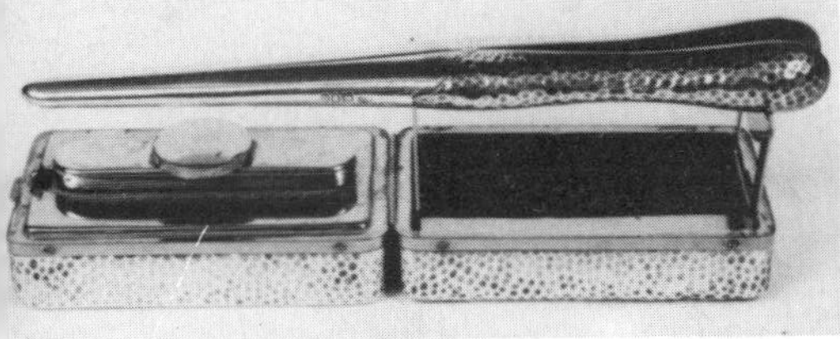

\ silver glove stretcher on a stand, with methylated spirit heater, c1900, 9in (22.5cm).
150-225

A silver articulated fish vinaigrette, 3½in (9cm).
$135-150

A silver hat pin holder, 1906, 5in (12.5cm).
$150-180

WINE ANTIQUES

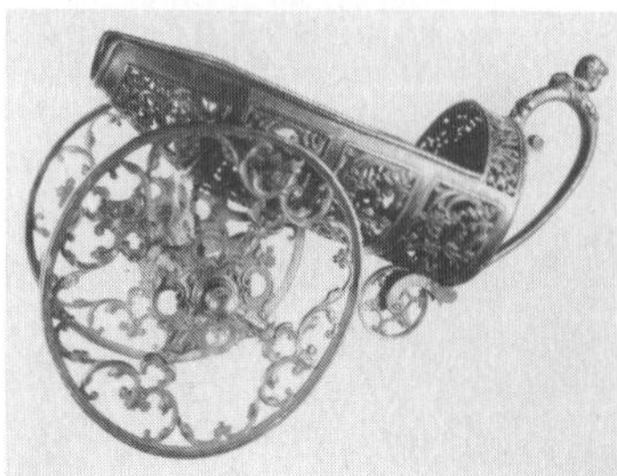

A bronzed finish port or wine bottle cradle, with 2 front wheels and a single back wheel, c1850.
$375-525

An onion shaped green glass wine bottle, English, c1710.
$120-135

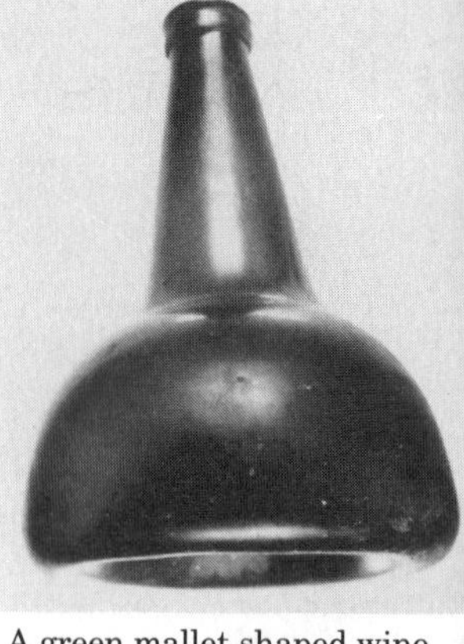

A green mallet shaped wine bottle, with string rim construction, deep kick-up wit definable pontil mark, Dutch, c1725. **$105-120**

One dozen bottles of Vintage 1948 port, W. & J. Graham & Co, excellent levels, embossed wax seals.
$1,500-2,250

A George III mahogany carrier, for 6 bottles, 13½in (34cm) wide.
$1,050-1,350

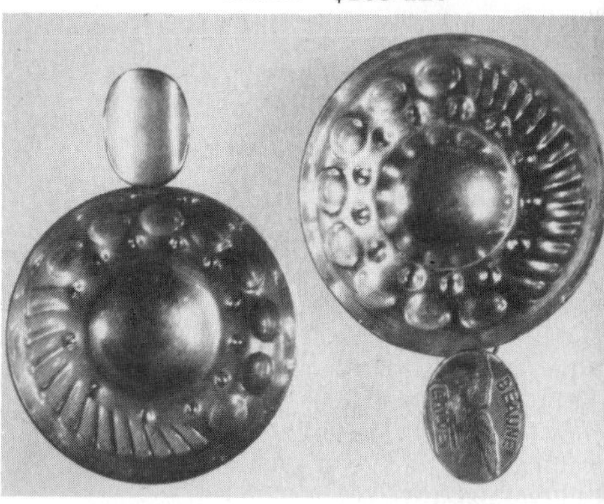

Two silver plate wine tasters, or tastevins, one advertising Calvet of Beaune. **$40-60 each**

A set of 3 Sheffield plate decanter stands, the shaped panelled everted sides with moulded foliage scroll borders, turned wood bases with bosses and baize, early 19thC.
$750-900

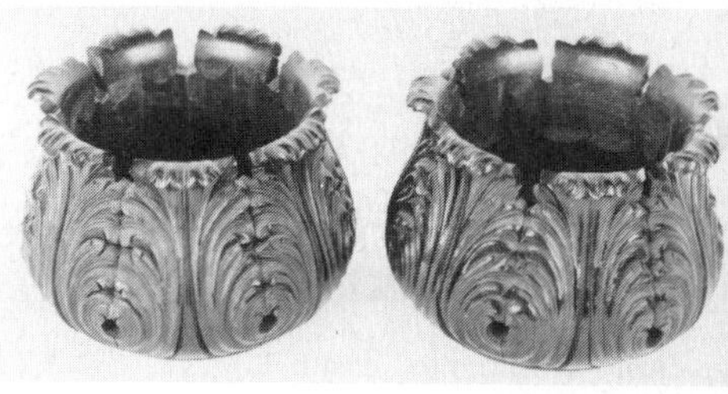

A pair of mahogany jardinières/ wine coolers, 19thC, 14in (36cm diam.
$1,800-2,700

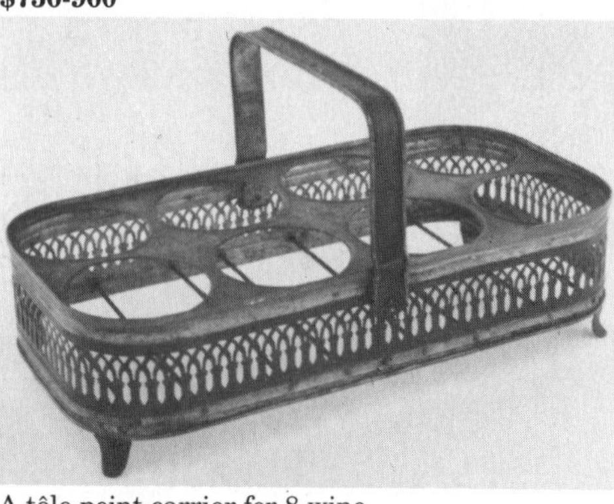

A tôle peint carrier for 8 wine bottles, with swing handle, 19thC, 15in (38cm).
$375-450

Four white pottery wine cellar bi labels, with black enamel names, top half unglazed for writing dates, c1850.
$40-60 each

double-action brass barrel homason type corkscrew, with one handle and applied brass laque showing the Royal coat-of-rms, c1840.
150-225

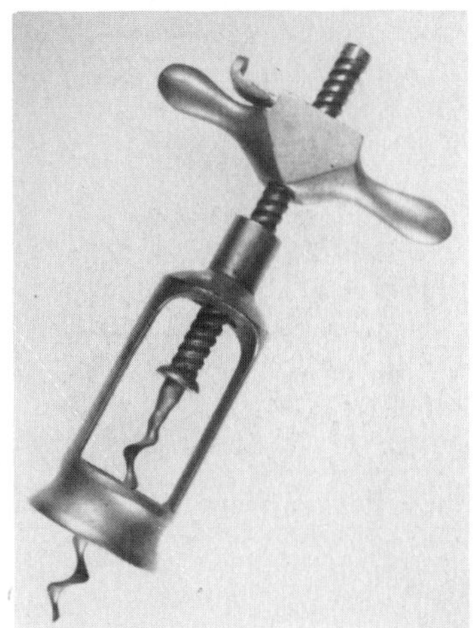

A French all steel open frame corkscrew, by J. Perille.
$120-135

A London rack corkscrew, with open barrel and side wind handle, c1870.
$50-75

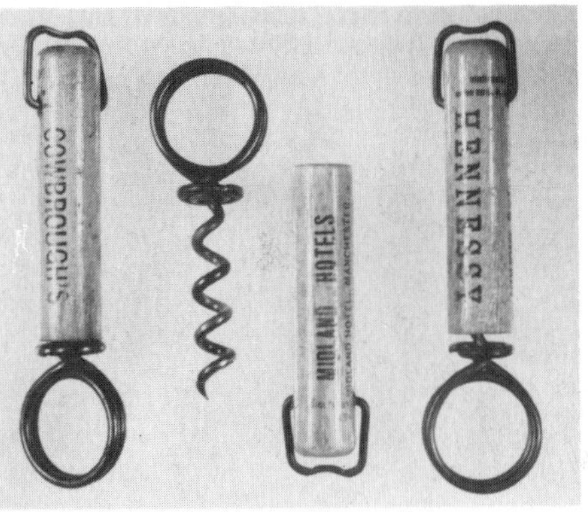

Three American twisted wire corkscrews, with original wood sheaths and black lettering advertisements.
$7.50-15

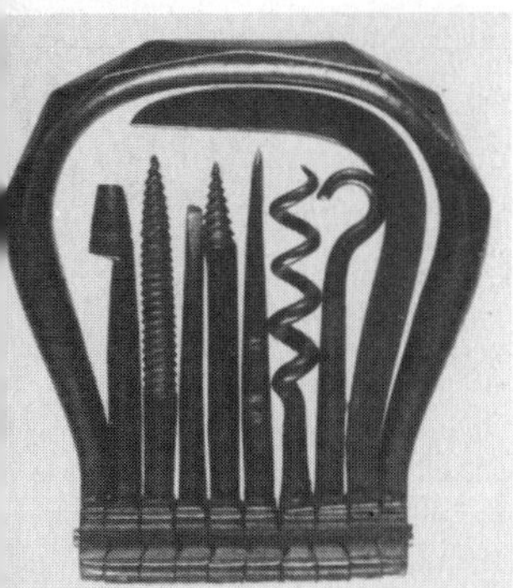

An all steel combination 8-tool bow corkscrew, with faceted handle, incorporating a helical worm corkscrew.
$120-135

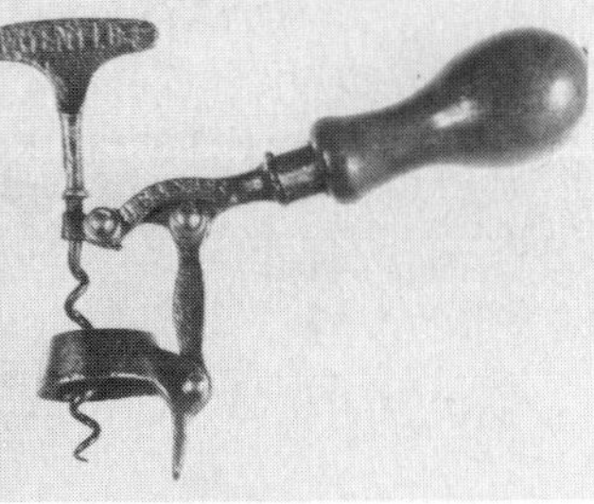

A steel single lever corkscrew, marked 'Patent Lift' 'JB & Sons', with turned wooden handle.
$750-900

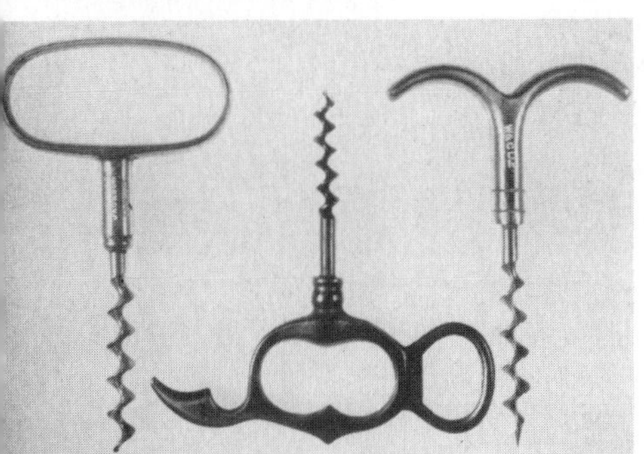

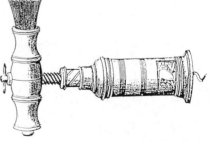

Three all steel corkscrews, cellarman's marked Farrow & ackson. **$7.50-15**
combination corkscrew/bottle pener/wire cutter.
25-40
n 'Eyebrow' stamped with naker's initials.
7.50-15

A Thomason 1802 patent type corkscrew, the barrel embossed with grapes, pears, barley, flowers and foliage, bone handle, c1820.
$375-525

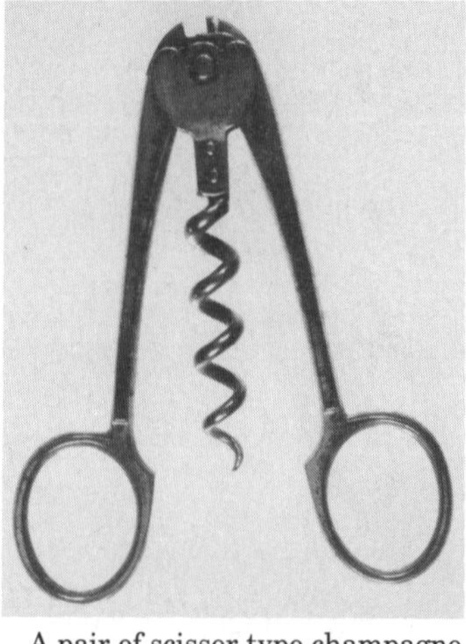

A pair of scissor type champagne wire nippers combined with corkscrew, c1860.
$50-75

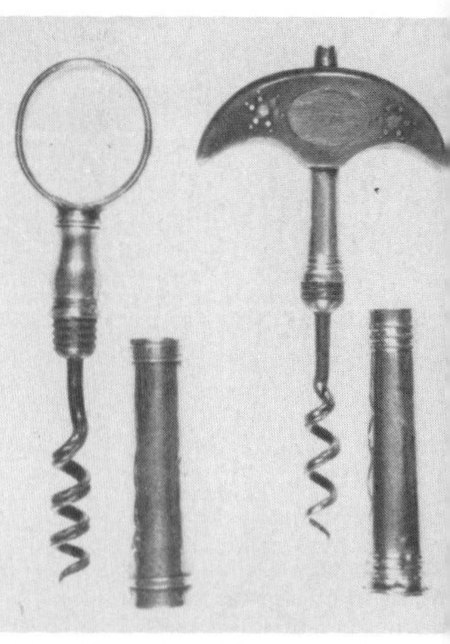

Two Georgian silver pocket corkscrews, one with finger ring handle, the other stained green ivory, both with silver sheaths, b Joseph Taylor.
$300-375 each

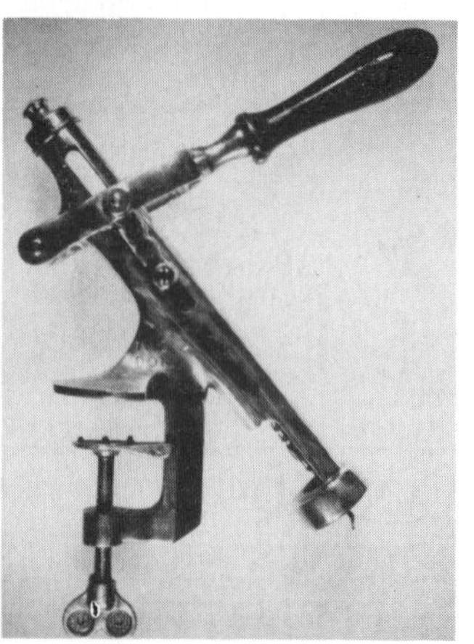

A Victorian cast brass publican's bar cork drawer, named 'The Don'.
$150-225

A Victorian cast iron publican's bar cork drawer, named the 'Hektor'.
$150-225

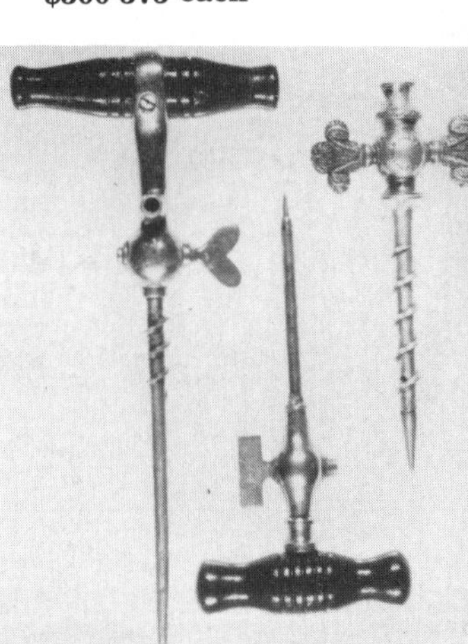

A selection of champagne tap one with fleur-de-lys handles, marked by S. Maw & Son, London, c1880.
$25-40 each

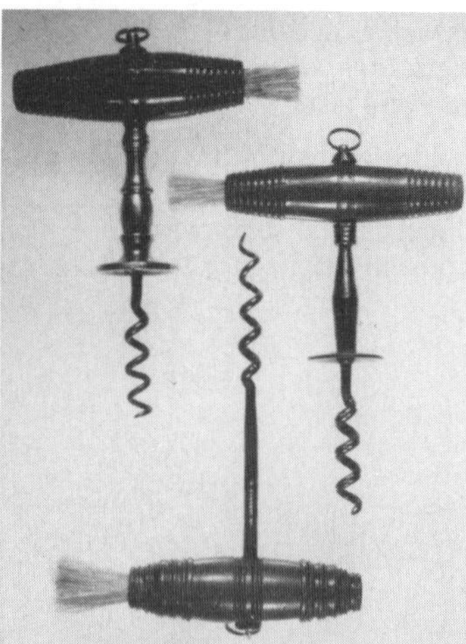

Two Henshall Button type corkscrews, with turned walnut handles, c1840.
$25-40 each

A turned rosewood T-bar corkscrew, with dusting brush, c1840.
$40-60

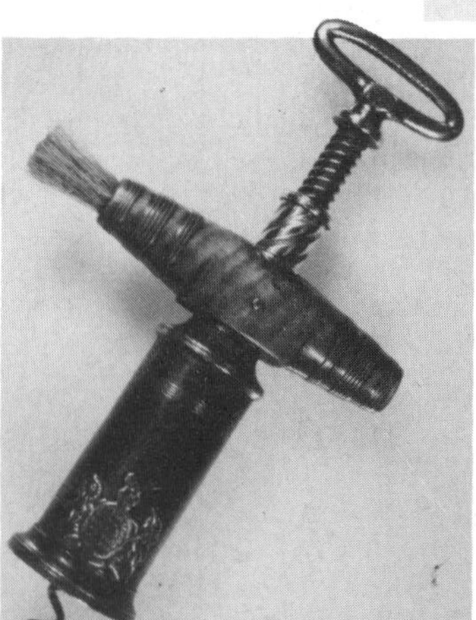

Sir Edward Thomason's Varient corkscrew, c1815.
$375-450

Did you know?

MILLER'S Antiques Price Guide builds up year by year to form the most comprehensive photo reference library available.

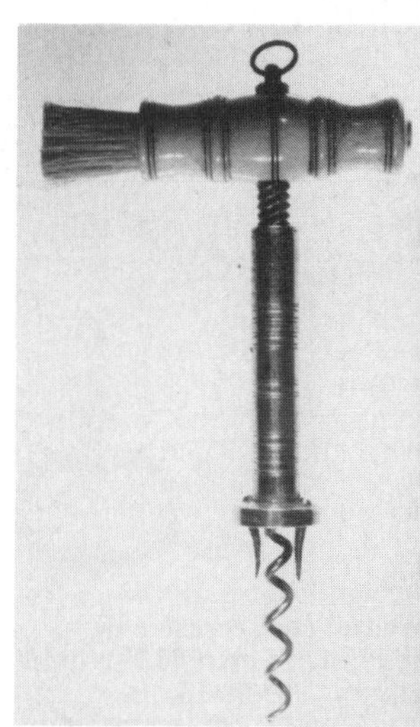

A corkscrew, with brass barrel inscribed 'Robert Jones & Son, Birmingham, Registered No. 42 8th Octr 1840', with bone handl
$300-375

William IV mahogany cellaret, ıth domed hinged lid and pering body, on circular reeded em and 4 lotus-scroll legs, 830, 26in (66cm) wide.
,800-2,700

George III mahogany and brass ound wine cooler, on base with 4 uare moulded tapering legs, ith scroll brackets, 21in (53cm) ide.
5,250-7,500

n early Victorian mahogany arcophagus wine cooler, the aised hinged lid with fruit and canthus cresting enclosing a lead ned fitted interior, panelled ides and paw feet, 27½in (70cm) ide.
3,000-4,500

A George III mahogany brass bound table wine cooler, with raised overscrolled handles and later copper liner, 17in (43cm).
$1,200-1,800

A Georgian mahogany and brass bound wine cooler, 24in (61cm).
$1,800-2,700

A George III brass bound mahogany wine cooler, the hinged top enclosing a later lead lined interior, the tapering body with carrying handles to each end, on a stand with simple moulded lip, on channelled splayed square legs headed by scroll angles, 2 handles broken, 22in (56cm).
$2,700-3,300

A George III octagonal brass bound mahogany wine cooler, the hinged top banded in tulipwood enclosing a lead lined and divided interior, brass carrying handles, on a stand with fluted frieze, moulded square section supports and brass casters, 19in (48cm).
$5,250-7,500

A George III mahogany wine cooler, the hinged top with moulded edge, with brass loop handle, lead lined interior, the body with brass banding and baluster tied loop handles, the stand with fluted frieze, 4 panelled square supports with pierced angle brackets and leather casters, 19in (48cm) wide.
$5,250-7,500

A mahogany cellaret, the hinged top constructed as a 6-compartment bottle rack, enclosing a fitted interior, c1770, on later stand with shaped shell applied apron, carved cabriole legs with lion's paw feet, 20in (51cm) wide. **$1,500-2,250**

A Regency mahogany sarcophagus cellaret-on-stand, crossbanded throughout and inlaid with ebony lines, brass lion's mask and ring handles, on lion's paw feet.
$5,250-7,500

METALWARE

Brass

A brass bucket, with swing handle and incised ribbing, 9½in (24cm) diam.
$600-750

Two Flemish brass candlesticks, with capstan base and pierced squat nozzle, solder repairs and drilled, early 17thC, 4in (11cm).
$600-750

A Dutch brass Heemske candlestick, c1680, 8in (20cm).
$300-375

A Victorian brass chamberstick, 7in (18cm) high.
$600-750

A helmet shaped embossed brass coal scuttle, some damage, 19in (48cm). **$135-150**

A pair of brass candlesticks, wi stems engraved and embossed with classical bands of foliate decoration, French, early 19thC 11in (28cm).
$375-525

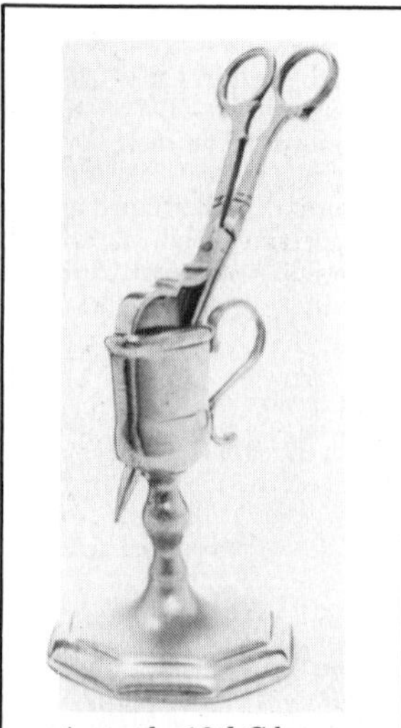

An early 18thC brass upright scissor snuffer and holder, with octagonal base.
$450-600

A brass alms dish, embossed with the pastoral lamb and an inscription, with everted rim and geometric decoration, 16in (41cm) diam.
$600-750

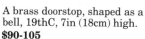

A brass doorstop, shaped as a bell, 19thC, 7in (18cm) high.
$90-105

Bronze

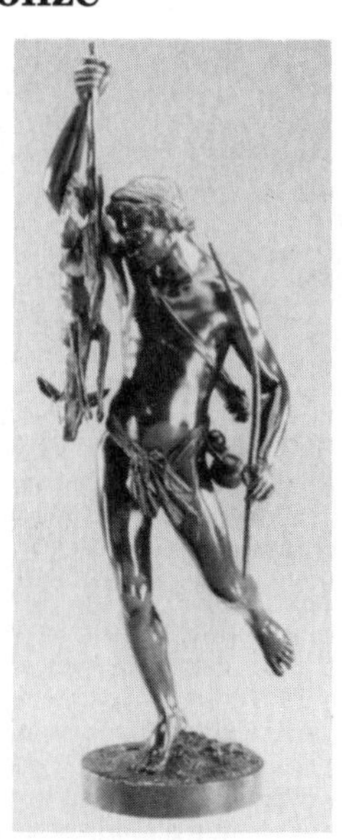

A classical bronze figure holding doe, The Huntsman, signed Jean Jacques Pradier, brown patination, c1870, 21in (53cm).
$1,200-1,800

A bronze bust of a girl, inscribed 'L. Gahagan fecit, Dublin 1843', 13½in (34cm) high.
$750-1,200

A gilt bronze figure group, 19thC, 15½in (40cm) high.
$750-1,200

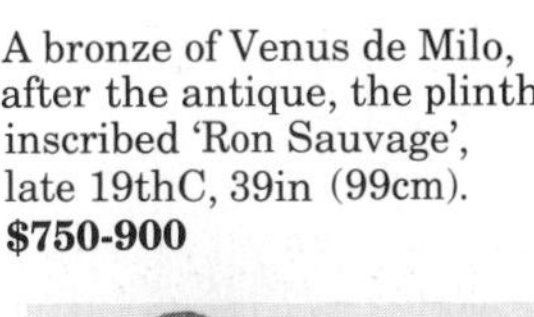

A bronze of Venus de Milo, after the antique, the plinth inscribed 'Ron Sauvage', late 19thC, 39in (99cm).
$750-900

A bronze group of a young peasant boy, restraining a dog with a whip about its muzzle, the base signed and dated 'E. Truffot, '87', and entitled 'Berger Jupille', 19thC, 28in (71cm) high.
$2,700-3,300

A bronze figure of Silenius, 19thC, 24in (62cm) high.
$750-1,200

A bronze mother and child group, variegated pale brown and green patination, signed Louis Dominique Mathet, c1890, 18in (46cm).
$1,500-2,250

A bronze Neapolitan figure, by Albert Carrier, on a mahogany base, figure 39in (99cm).
$10,500-13,500

This figure is signed A. Carrier and stamped 737 indicating this was an early work prior to 1874, after which time he signed his full name.

A bronze plant holder, in the ·rm of a girl standing over and eering into a well, George Van erStraeten, signed, 26½in (67cm) igh.
,200-1,500

A bronze figure of a young lady olding a torch aloft and a wheel ı her left hand, Alphonse Henri 'elson, signed, 40in (102cm) igh.
1,800-2,700

A bronze and alabaster figure of a snake charmer, Rudolf Franke Nautschutz, inscribed on footrim, c1900, 11½in (29cm) high.
$1,800-2,700

A pair of bronze and gilt metal blackamoors, holding ceremonial staff and arm aloft, wearing plumed headdresses and floral tunics, on quatrefoil stepped bases, 18thC, 17in (43cm).
$1,200-1,500

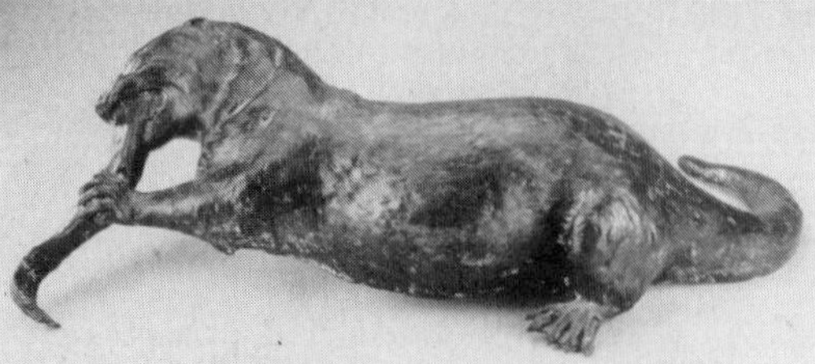

A bronze otter with fish, brown patination, English School, 20thC, 30in (76cm) long.
$1,200-1,800

A bronze model of a setter, dark brown patination, on rounded base, signed Eugéne de Gaspary, early 20thC, 6in (15cm).
$750-1,200

A bronze model of a goat, on a naturalistic base, signed P.J. Mêne, 5½in (14cm) long.
$1,050-1,350

An Austrian cold painted bronze figure of a rabbit, late 19thC, 6in (15cm).
$750-1,200

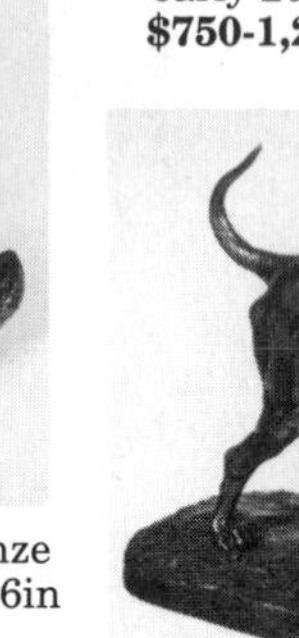

A patinated bronze model of a hound, branded W, on naturalistic base, signed P.J. Mêne, 1843, 9in (23cm) long.
$1,050-1,350

A bronze group of a boar hunt, from a model by Pierre Jules Mêne, on naturalistic ground, signed P.J. Mêne, on a shaped green marble plinth, 19thC, 23in (59cm) high.
$2,700-3,300

A bronze group, 'Vainqueur du Derby', signed P.J. Mêne and dated 1863, 16½in (42cm) high.
$4,800-5,700

A bronze cowboy on horseback, mid-brown patination, signed John Skeaping and numbered 4/10, mid-20thC, 10in (25cm).
$2,700-3,300

A bronze polo player on horseback, dark brown patination, signed Lorne McKean and dated 1970, numbered 4/7, 11½in (29cm).
$2,700-3,300

A bronze figure of a cat, 'Young Barry', by Tom Merrifield, one of an edition of 95, 11in (28cm) long.
$1,200-1,800

A bronze jump jockey on horseback, mid-brown patination, signed John Skeaping, dated 1968 and numbered 8/10, 11½in (29cm) high.
$4,800-5,700

pair of bronze figures of a triever and a pointer, carrying a ıeasant and a hare, 13in (33cm) ng.
'50-1,200

n Austrian cold painted bronze, odelled as a North American ains Indian, wearing a war ›nnet, buckskin trousers and inged moccasins, sitting on the lge of a canoe and holding a ıddle aloft, attributed to ergman, 10½in (26cm) long.
,050-1,350

bronze urn, the frieze with acchanalian scene, within ıdrooned and acanthus borders, ıe handles mounted with seated uns playing pipes, on a reathed and stepped base,)thC, 14½in (37cm) high.
2,700-3,300

A pair of classical bronze columns, surmounted by Mercury and Ceres after Giambologna, each stepped fluted column with gilt bronze mounts, on sienna and black marble bases, 19thC, 37½in (95cm).
$4,800-5,700

A pair of French bronze ornamental ewers, the bodies chased with foliage, the friezes raised with figures of amorini emblamatic of the Arts and Sciences, the handles modelled with cherubs, 23in (59cm) high.
$1,050-1,350

Two gilt bronze Chamberlain's keys, one with opposing C-scrolls centred by the monogram for Frederik V of Sweden, surmounted by a crown, 19thC, 5in (13cm).
$1,200-1,500

An animalier bronze group, after Antoine Louis Barye, 'Jaguar devouring a Hare', the naturalistic base signed Barye, 21in (53cm) long.
$2,700-3,300

A bronze urn with beaded and foliate border, entwined snake and foliate handles, the lower body lobed and cast with flowers and leaves, on flared foot with band of overlapping leaves, early 19thC, on later wooden base, 10in (25cm) high. **$750-1,200**

A Regency gilt and bronze inkstand, in the form of a snake wreathed boat, with negro oarsman.
$750-1,200

A Venetian bronze pastille burner, the pierced lid and sides with roundels and Gothic tracery enriched with punched decoration and grotesque masks, with central hinged door cast with Cupid, on 3 lion couchant feet, 16thC, 9½in (24cm).
$9,000-12,000

Copper

A medium size oval copper kettle and lid.
$135-150

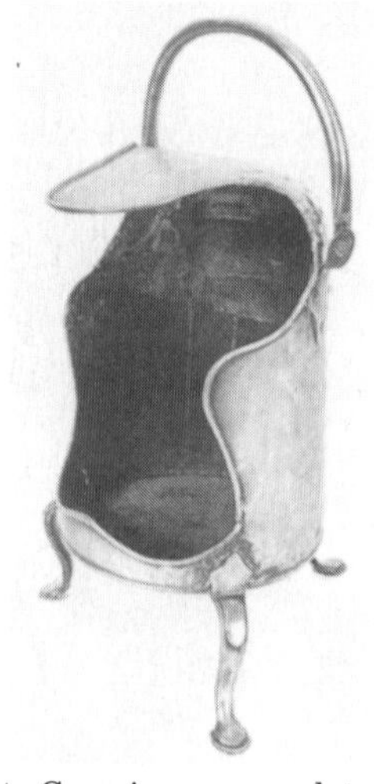

A late Georgian copper plate bucket, with domed fold-over lip to the top and cut away side panels, overhead swing handle, 3 cabriole legs with pad feet, repaired, 25in (64cm) high.
$300-375

An early Victorian copper kettl
10in (25cm) high.
$225-300

A copper tea urn, c1830.
$450-600

A copper kettle, with brass and copper handle, 10in (25cm) high.
$150-180

A copper warming pan, c188
31in (79cm) long.
$225-255

Gold

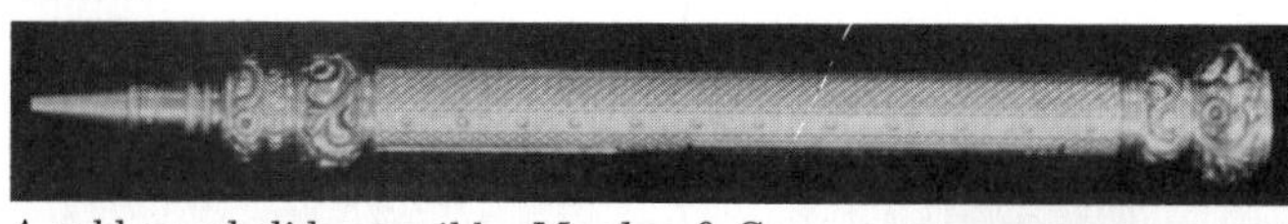

A gold cased slide pencil by Mordan & Co, with engine turned decoration, the terminal and slide chased with scrolls with chalcedony seal top, 5in (12cm).
$450-600

Iron

A pair of 19thC cast iron recumbant lions, 9½in (24cm) long. **$375-450**

A pair of American cast iron dogs, painted black, one tail replaced, 19thC, 50in (127cm) long.
$5,250-6,000

Two French iron tapering cylindrical birdcages, late 19thC.
$450-600

A branding iron, c1880, 13i
(33cm) long.
$50-75

A pair of American cast iron Hessian andirons, late 19thC
$1,800-2,700

An American polychrome cast iron swing-frame toilet mirror, the oval plate with pierced border supported by female figures standing on palm fronds, the leaf chased base modelled with the Union flag, 19thC, 21in (53cm) high.
$600-750

Lead

A lead Christian medallion, cast in low and high relief, with a Madonna and child, the edge banded by a rosary, inscribed 'Namban ji-seki hakkutsu', probably 16th/17thC.
$4,500-6,000

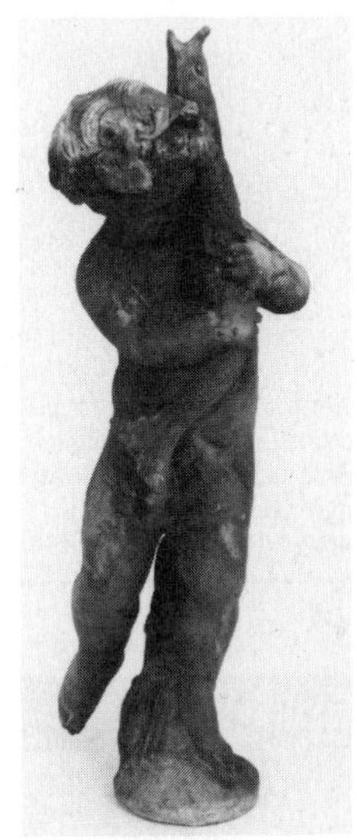

A lead fountain figure, in the manner of Verochio, 37in (94cm) high. **$600-750**

Pewter

. pewter wine cup, 19thC, 4½in 1cm).
50-75

A pewter pepper pot, c1800, 4in (10cm).
$50-75

A pewter tankard, with ram's horn thumbpiece, touch in base of a bird, possibly that of Adam Banck, early 18thC, 7½in (19cm).
$750-900

A pewter straight sided flagon, with hammered body, scroll thumbpiece and domed cover, damaged, c1700, 11½in (29cm).
$375-450

A French pewter flagon, with flat lid and bar thumbpiece, above bulbous body, c1700, 12in (31cm).
$750-900

A Swiss pewter Glockenkanne, with a band of relief cast grape vines, screw-on ring top and cylindrical front spout, late 18thC, 14in (36cm).
$600-750

A collection of American pewter coffee and teapots, minor repairs, 1820-60, 7 to 11½in (18 to 29cm) high.
$2,250-3,000

A collection of American pewter coffee pots and a teapot, c1830-70, minor repairs, 6½in to 12in (16 to 31cm) high.
$1,800-2,700

A collection of American coffee pots, a teapot and creamer, earl 19thC, some minor repairs, 4 to 11½in (10 to 29cm) high.
$1,800-2,700

Steel

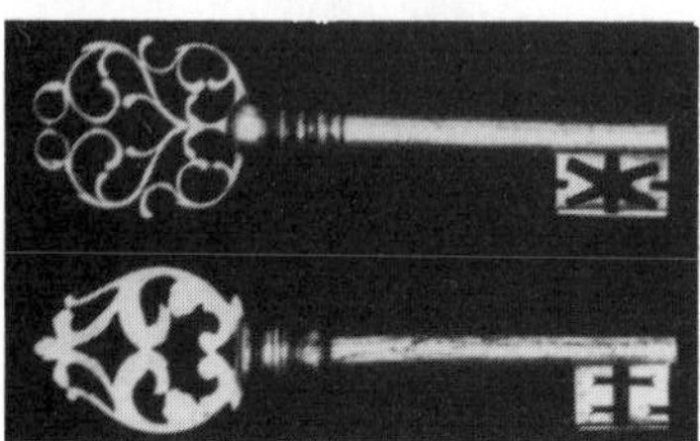

Two steel keys, pierced and interlaced with plain cylinder pipes, the bits intricately pierced, c1700, 6in (15cm).
$1,800-2,700

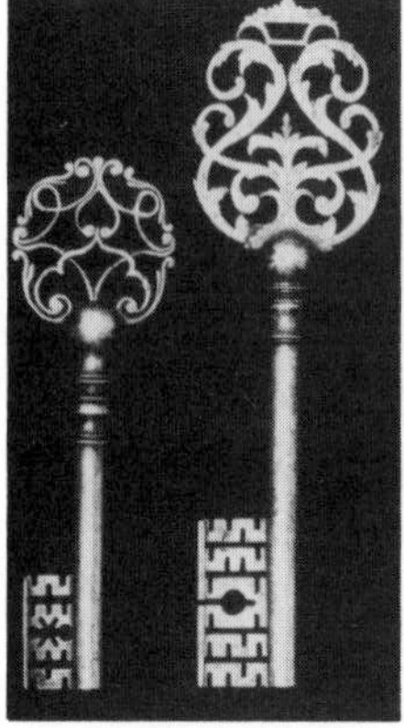

Two steel keys, late 17thC, 6in (15cm).
$1,800-2,700

Two Venetian steel keys, 17thC, 5in (13cm).
$3,000-4,500

ENAMEL

An enamel pot pourri pot, painted with floral groups, the base with dragonfly, domed ribbed gilt metal cover, 2½in (6cm) diam.
$225-255

Wirework

A Victorian wirework cylindrical birdcage, with pierced metal bands, 18½in (47cm) high.
$375-525

A wirework basket of shell flowers, on a shell covered walnut veneered base, with glass dome, damaged, 19thC, 17½in (44cm) high.
$375-525

HORN

A horn beaker, engraved with rural and town scenes and inscribed 'Willm. Munford, Normanstone, August 7th 1787', and initialled 'NL', 5in (13cm).
$600-750

IVORY

An engraved ivory veneered workbox, in the form of a house the hinged roof cover with compartmented interior, Anglo-Indian Vizagapatam, c1800.
$4,800-5,700

A Continental carved ivory recumbent lion, 19thC, 5½in (14cm) long.
$600-750

A set of 6 European ivory figures of dogs, including a pair of mastiffs, a pair of greyhounds, and a pair of setters, each with black and white glass eyes, seated on chamfered cushion plinths, stained to simulate leather, and originally surrounding a centrepiece, 4in (10cm) high.
$10,500-13,500

An Italian carved ivory group of the Madonna and Child, on an ebony and ivory plinth, raised in relief with an entwined monogram and the Scene of the Annunciation, early 19thC, 15in (38cm) high.
$2,700-3,300

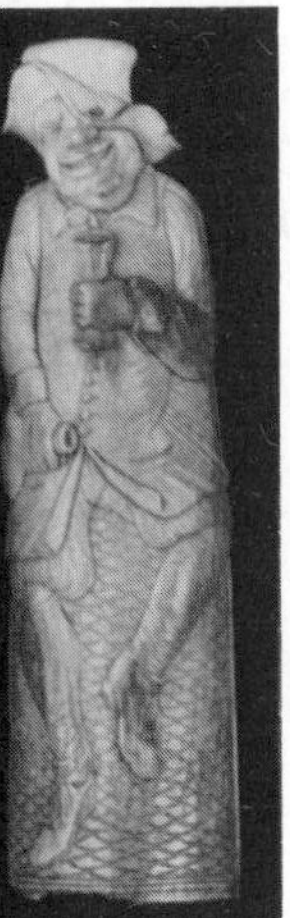

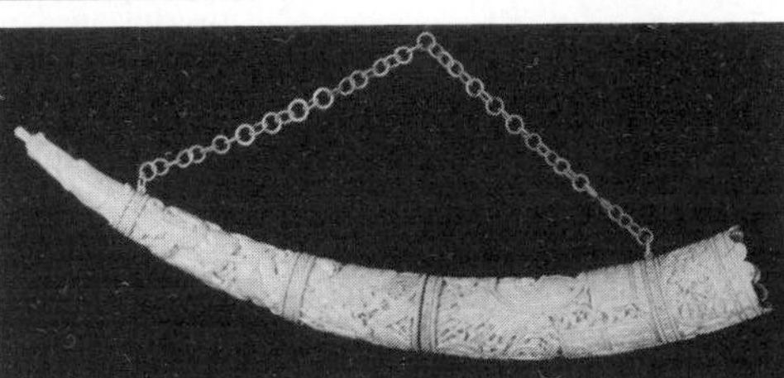

A carved ivory oliphant, with three-quarter length portrait, inscribed beneath Ioannes Sobiesky III D.G. Rex. Poloniae. ETM.D.Lith.MDCLXXXIII, with ivory interlocked chain, broken, 19thC, 32in (81cm).
$10,500-13,500

A French School ivory relief plaque of Venus attended by amorini, mid-19thC, 6 by 4½in (15 by 11cm).
$2,700-3,300

Dutch ivory tobacco rappoir, of laughing man wearing a floppy at covering one eye, holding a up in his left hand, a flask in his ght, as he dances down a paved reet, 18thC, 7in (18cm).
3,000-4,500

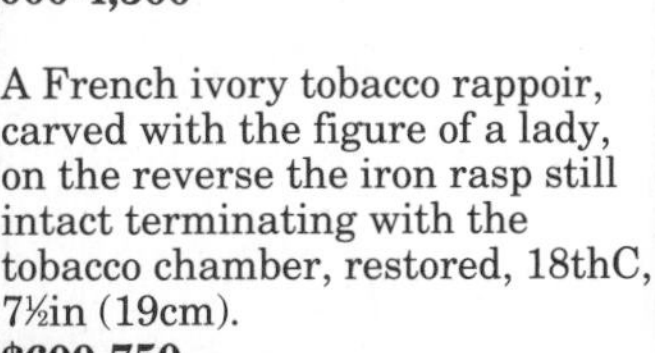

A French ivory tobacco rappoir, carved with the figure of a lady, on the reverse the iron rasp still intact terminating with the tobacco chamber, restored, 18thC, 7½in (19cm).
$600-750

A French ivory carving of a lady, her dress tied with a flowing ribbon, an embroidered cloak over one shoulder, on turned ivory pedestal base, 8½in (21cm).
$1,800-2,700

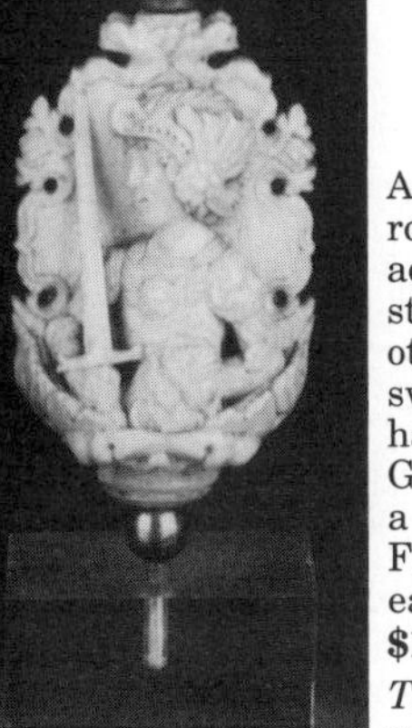

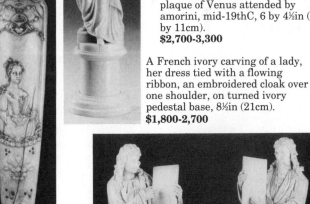

An ivory bead from a chaplet or rosary, the figures set in stylised acanthus leaves, Lucretia stabbing herself with a sword, the other side with David holding a sword in his right hand, in his left hand he holds the head of Goliath, set in high relief against a pierced and carved cartouche, Flemish or Northern French, early 16thC, 2⅜in (6cm).
$10,500-12,000

This bead bears a very close resemblance to one in the Victoria and Albert Museum.

A pair of ivory figures of 2 Evangelists, one young, Mark, the other bearded and old, both clad in long flowing drapery, long flowing hair and holding tablets, German or Austrian, c1800, on later wood stands, 8½in (22cm).
$5,250-7,500

A Flemish ivory statue of St. Sebastian, wearing a loincloth tied to the trunk of a tree, looking downwards in despair, a quiver and arrows resting beside the trunk of the tree to symbolise his fate, on shaped black marble base, 17thC, 9in (22cm).
$5,250-7,500

A pair of ivory reliefs of Louis XIII of France and Henri IV of France and Navarre, with inscriptions beneath them, in tooled leather case decorated wit gilded fleur-de-lys and palmette border, centred by the letter H, the letter H stamped in each corner, Dieppe, 19thC, 8 and 9in (20 and 22cm) high.
$7,500-9,000

An ivory photograph frame, carved with dragons, scrolls and flowers, on bun feet and with strut, containing a porcelain plaque of 2 children in a leafy glade, 5in (13cm).
$375-450

A French School ivory carving of 2 figures in 18thC costume standing before a gate, 'The Young Courtiers', c1880, 5½in (14cm).
$2,250-3,000

A bust of a lady with flowing hai on a dwarf marble socle, early 19thC, 26in (66cm).
$5,250-7,500

MARBLE

A sculpted white marble bust of a classically robed statesman, the reverse signed and dated 'W. Behnes, Sculp London. 1840', on a waisted socle, 32½in (82cm) high.
$1,200-1,500

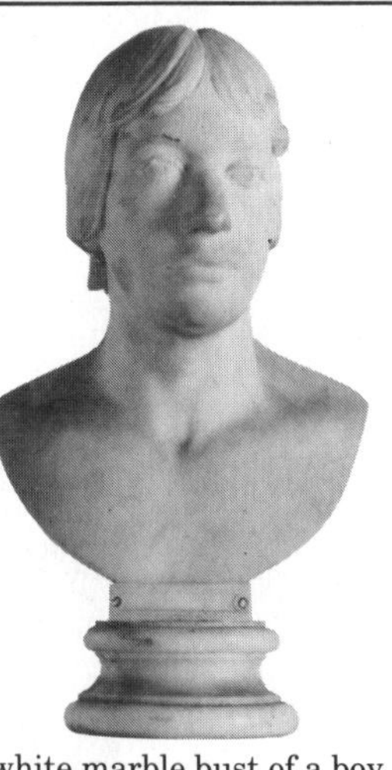

A white marble bust of a boy, early 19thC, 21in (54cm) high.
$900-1,500

An Italian sculpted white marble bust of a drunken peasant, clutching a wine bottle, late 19thC, 20in (51cm).
$3,000-4,500

An Italian white marble bust of a girl, wearing a lace shawl, on a green marble plinth.
$3,000-4,500

ɴn Italian sculpted marble bust of . lady, signed and dated on the everse 'A. Costolifece. 1838. 'irenze', on a waisted socle, .9thC, 30in (77cm) high, on ɪssociated white painted wood ▪edestal.
2,250-3,000

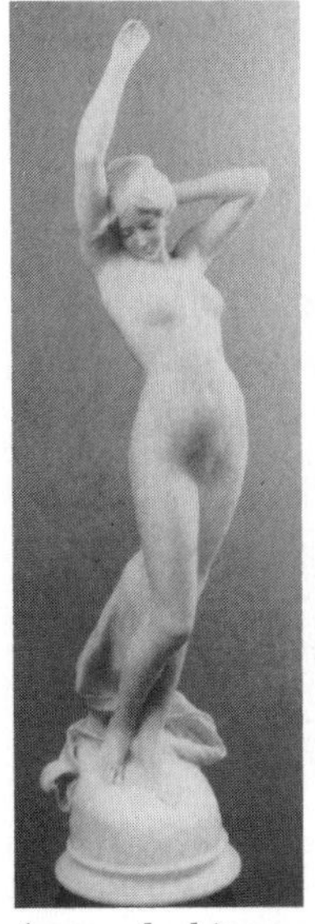

A carved white marble figure of a girl, one finger repaired, by Affortunato Gory, Paris, 40in (102cm).
$4,500-6,000

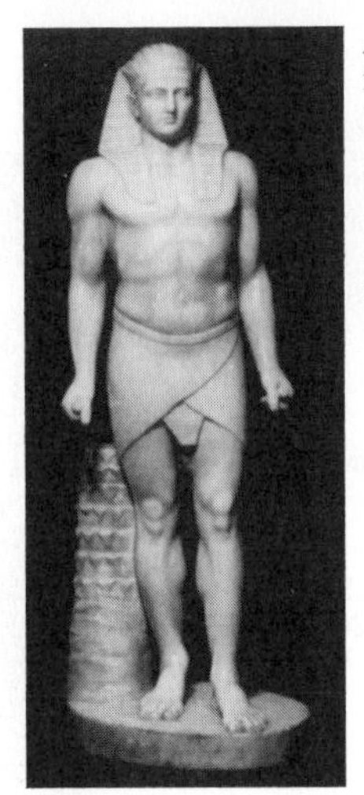

An English white marble figure of Antinous, after the antique, wearing an Egyptian headdress and kilt, holding rolled bolts of linen in each hand, early 19thC, 31in (79cm) high.
$4,500-6,000

A Carrara marble group of the Rape of The Sabines, after Giambologna, on square rockwork base, damaged and repaired, 25in (64cm) high.
$600-750

)RMOLU

ʌ pair of French ormolu twin ɪght wall appliqués, the branches vith chased berried foliage, with ʻibband backplates, 22in (56cm).
;1,800-2,700

A pair of French ormolu candlesticks, in the manner of Sebastian Antoine Slodtz, the nozzles, inverted baluster stems and circular bases chased with rocaille, mid-19thC, 9½in (24cm).
$900-1,500

A pair of French ormolu chenet, each with a putto and flaming brazier, with acanthus ornament, on shaped plinths, 17in (43cm).
$1,800-2,700

ʌ pair of French ormolu candle sconces, 19thC.
;225-300

Miller's is a price GUIDE not a price LIST

PLASTER

A late Victorian white painted plaster bust of William Bell Scott, the base inscribed R.G. Davies, 23in (59cm) high.
$375-525

A Victorian white painted plaster relief portrait medallion of William Bell Scott, by Alexander Munro, in a gilt surround, the case 21in (53cm).
$2,250-3,000

TERRACOTTA

A terracotta tobacco jar, in the form of a pug, c1870, 9½in (24cm) high.
$1,050-1,350

A terracotta cat money box, c1880, 9in (23cm) high.
$225-300

A terracotta tobacco jar, c1880 7in (18cm) high.
$750-1,200

WOOD

An Austrian walnut model of an owl, with hinged head, glass eyes and twin inkwells in base, beak chipped, late 19thC, 13½in (34cm).
$1,200-1,500

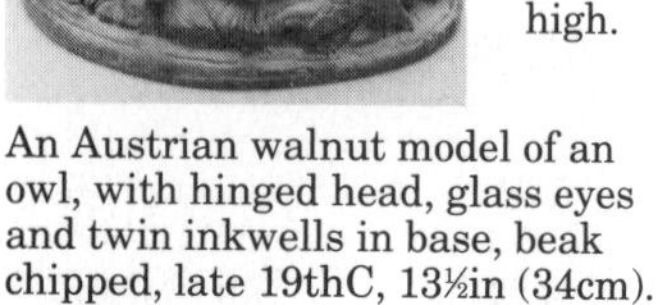

A carved wooden elephant, with articulated trunk, 11½in (29cm) high. **$600-750**

A pair of Italian polychrome and giltwood angel candlesticks, with detachable wings, damaged and restored, c1500, 17½in (44cm).
$15,000-18,000

A pair of Flemish oak figures of angels, kneeling on wave carved bases, with traces of polychrome decoration, late 17thC, 38in (97cm).
$5,250-7,500

A carved begging dog, stamped J. Bergen & Co, Interlaken, c1880, 33in (84cm) high.
$10,500-13,500

An inlaid oval tray. late 19thC, 16 by 26in (41 by 66cm).
$300-375

A pair of painted wood dummy board figures of Queen Elizabeth and Sir Walter Raleigh, 19thC, 38in (97cm).
$1,200-1,500

A naïve carved oak figure representing Victory, standing on a rocky outcrop with 2 lions prowling at her feet, damaged, 19thC, 23½in (60cm) high.
$300-375

…n Austrian walnut carving of an …agle, with spread wings and …lass eyes, late 19thC, 21in …3cm).
…1,200-1,500

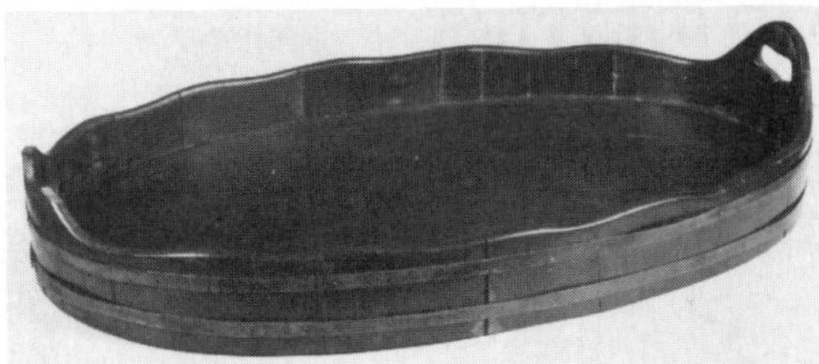

A George III mahogany oval tray, 22in (56cm).
$300-375

A George III carved fruitwood urn, of neo-classical form, with pineapple finial, the stop fluted body carved with a band of pendant husk chains, on circular plinth, 26in (66cm).
$1,800-2,700

l. A Georgian wooden pug tobacco jar, 6in (15cm).
$1,800-2,700
r. c1870. **$1,050-1,350**
c. An inkwell, c1870, 5in (13cm).
$750-1,200

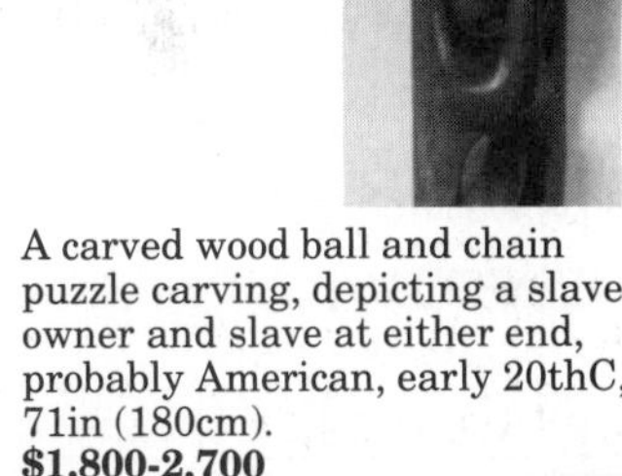

A carved wood ball and chain puzzle carving, depicting a slave owner and slave at either end, probably American, early 20thC, 71in (180cm).
$1,800-2,700

… maple mazer, engraved …Blacksmiths Hall', 15thC, with …ater gilt rim, 6½in (16cm) diam.
…1,050-1,350

A Dutch marquetry tray, 19thC, 22in (56cm) long.
$300-375

A carved and painted pine flying Canada goose, in the style of Ira Hudson, painted black with white markings, mounted on a rod, possibly Maritime Provinces, early 20thC, 40in (102cm) long.
$3,000-4,500

…A polychromed limewood relief of …St. George and the Dragon, South …German, early 16thC, in later …rame, 26in (66cm) high.
…9,000-12,000

A George III mahogany and brass bound plate bucket, 17in (43cm) high.
$750-1,200

A set of Victorian turned wood egg cups-on-stand, c1890, 9in (23cm) wide.
$300-375

A pair of Black Forest relief carved panels, of hunting trophies and weapons surrounded by branches and foliage, 19thC, 34in (86cm).
$750-1,200

ANTIQUITIES
Glass

A Hellenistic iridescent amber coloured core-formed glass amphoriskos, with twin glass handles attached to the shoulder and rim, decorated with opaque red spiral trailing combed into a festoon pattern with horizontal lines above and below, repaired, 2nd-1st Century B.C., 7½in (19cm).
$6,000-8,250

A red glass head with black wig, from a composite shabti, circa 1400 B.C., 2.5cm high.
$2,250-3,000

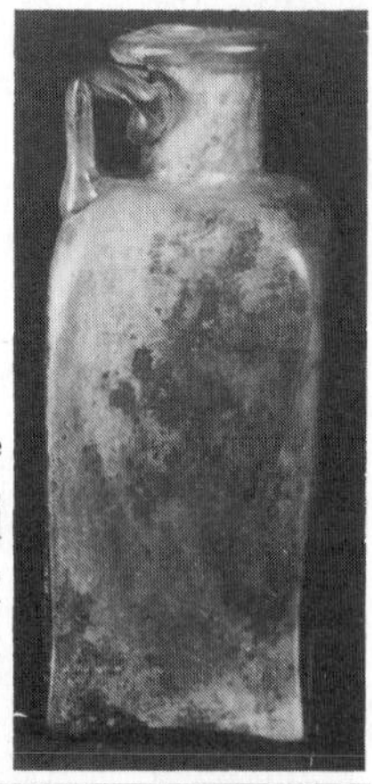

A Roman turquoise squared glass bottle, with thick disc rim and wide strap handle, 2nd Century A.D., 8½in (21.5cm).
$900-1,500

A Roman dark green glass two-handled flask, the base with pontil mark, Rhineland, 3rd-4th Century A.D., 5⅝in (14.3cm).
$5,250-6,000

An Egyptian limestone relief showing 2 estate workers, with traces of pigment, some restoration, mounted in wood frame, Dynasty VI, 2323-2150 B.C., 26in (66cm).
$6,000-8,250

Limestone

An Egyptian limestone relief fragment, carved with the head of Rameses II, wearing the blue crown, with coiled uraeus and the eyes with pronounced cosmetic lines, New Kingdom, 19th Dynasty, Reign of Rameses II, circa 1290-1224 B.C., 13in (33cm) high.
$15,000-22,500

An Egyptian limestone stela, representing Lady Tawaret-Hotep worshipping the god Osiris, her son behind, the text above reads 'The Lady of the House, Chief Songstress of Isis, Tawaret-Hotep and her son Ipuy, whom she loves make this offering to Osiris, Lord of Eternity, Prince of Everlastingness', Anubis recumbent above 19th/20th Dynasty, circa 1320-1085 B.C., 16⅝in (42.5cm), mounted.
$3,000-4,500

Antiquities

- Objects made before 600 A.D. in Europe and pre-Columbian in America are generally classed as antiquities.
- Most countries have strict laws governing the excavation and export of antiquities.
- Objects legitimately on the market come from collections formed in the 18thC and 19thC. Nevertheless, there is much stolen material on the market.
- If in doubt seek museum assistance.
- Cleaning should always be undertaken by experts.

Marble

A Roman deeply carved white marble acanthus leaf column capital, 3rd-4th Century A.D., 5in (13cm).
$900-1,500

A Roman marble votive peach, a section of the flesh cut away to reveal the stone within, circa 2nd Century A.D., 2in (6cm).
$3,000-4,500

. Roman marble female ead, with a tang for ısertion into a large gure, circa 1st Century ..D., 16in (41cm).
30,000-45,000

A Roman marble female figure, standing with her chiton and himation wrapped around her, head missing, circa 1st Century A.D., 17in (43cm).
$3,000-4,500

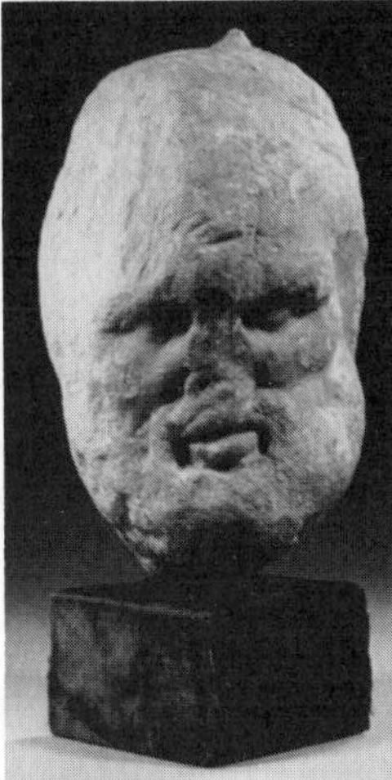

A Greek marble head of Seilenos, gazing downwards, bearded and wearing a fillet, mounted, 3rd Century B.C., 10in (25.5cm).
$2,700-3,300

A Roman marble bearded male head, balding and with furrowed brow, the pupils of the eyes depressed, first half of 3rd Century A.D., 11½in (30cm).
$3,000-4,500

Ietalware

ın Etruscan bronze mirror, finely ngraved with a mythological cene, 5th-4th Century B.C., 5in 13.5cm) diam., in a fitted late 8th/early 19thC green shagreen eather decorated case.
3,000-4,500
'aid to have been the property of 'rincess Pauline, sister of Iapoleon I.

A Roman bronze appliqué head of a gorgon, with tongue lolling out and frowning expression, wearing a stephane, mounted, circa 1st Century A.D., 2in (4.5cm).
$2,700-3,300

A Roman bronze appliqué, modelled in high relief with the figure of a legionary wearing armour and holding a shield, the 2 horses behind him, circa 1st Century A.D., 4in (9.5cm).
$6,000-8,250

A Canaanite bronze duck-bill fenestrated socketed axe head, 8th-7th Century B.C., 3½in (9cm), mounted. **$375-525**

A Roman bronze standing figure of Mercury, with a winged hat (petasos), holding the purse in his left hand, nude except for the chalmys draped over his left shoulder, circa 2nd Century A.D., 5½in (13.5cm), mounted on perspex base.
$2,250-3,000

A Greek bronze figure of a reclining lion, probably from a votive fibula or garment clasp, with projections under the body for attachment, part of the tail missing, circa 520 B.C., 1½in (3.5cm).
$6,000-8,250
Such brooches were too heavy for mortal use and were probably offerings to a god or goddess.

A Roman bronze dagger hilt in the form of an eagle's head, with naturalistically modelled features and incised feathers, 1st-2nd Century A.D., 3in (8cm).
$1,200-1,800

A Greek geometric bronze figure of a horse, with long thin legs, a tang at the back on which its tail rests, the base with a raised rectangular and central band surrounding the 2 lines of openwork zig-zag lines, Laconia, 8th Century B.C., 3in (7cm).
$7,500-9,000

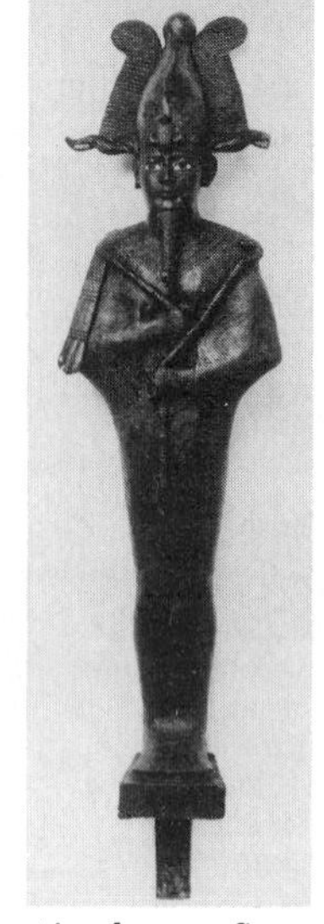

An Egyptian bronze figure of Osiris, standing on a trapezoidal base, his hands emerging from his cloak and grasping the crook and flail, wearing a broad finely engraved collar, braided beard with curled tip and the atef-crown with ram's horns and sun-disc, his face with slightly smiling mouth, straight nose and large eyes with pupils reserved against silver or electrum, 26th Dynasty, 664-525 B.C., 19in (48.5cm).
$22,500-30,000

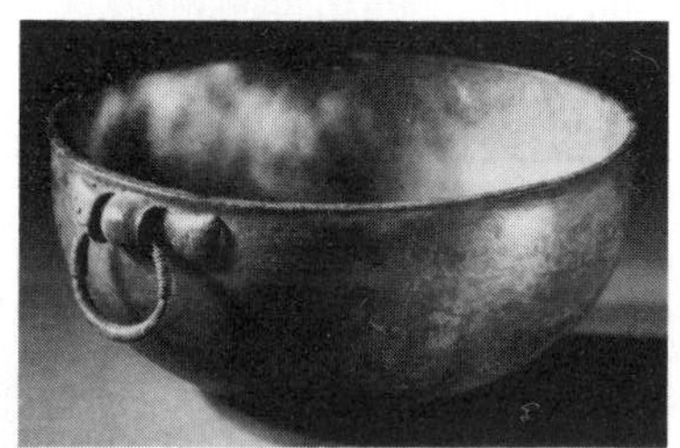

An Egyptian bronze bowl, with single loop handle, New Kingdom, circa 1567-1085 B.C., 7in (18cm).
$1,800-2,700

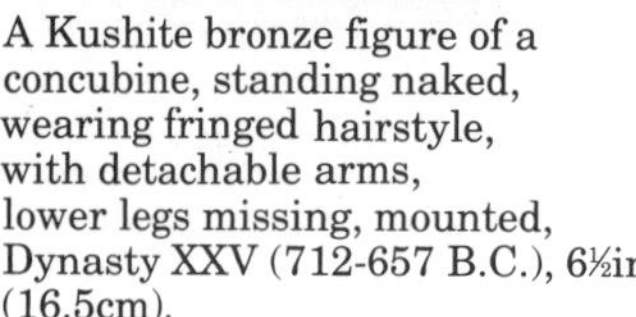

A Kushite bronze figure of a concubine, standing naked, wearing fringed hairstyle, with detachable arms, lower legs missing, mounted, Dynasty XXV (712-657 B.C.), 6½in (16.5cm).
$2,700-3,300

A Greek geometric bronze figure of a bull, with small boss-like eyes, 8th Century B.C., 2in (5.5cm).
$2,700-3,300

An Egyptian bronze figure of Amun, wearing a pleated royal kilt with narrow belt, with braided beard and the headdress of Amun with engraved plumes, with traces of gilding, Late Period, 26th-30th Dynasty, circa 664-342 B.C., 9in (23cm).
$9,000-12,000

A late Roman bronze lamp and stand, the ridged staff supported by 3 clawed feet, the shaft surmounted by a lamp, the curled foliate handle terminating in 2 ducks' heads, the hinged lid of floral design, circa 5th Century A.D., 14½in (37cm).
$2,700-3,300

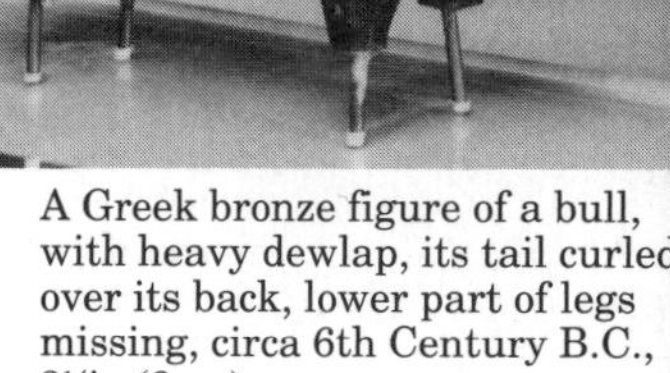

A Greek bronze figure of a bull, with heavy dewlap, its tail curled over its back, lower part of legs missing, circa 6th Century B.C., 3½in (9cm).
$3,000-4,500

Pottery

An Apulian red figure bell krater, one side showing a draped female being pursued by a naked male, the other with 2 youths, Greek/Southern Italy, 4th Century B.C., 15in (38.5cm).
$3,000-4,500

A Villanovan Impasto pottery urn and lid, the lid surmounted by a figure of a bull with high curving horns, repaired, circa 8th Century B.C., 15½in (39.5cm).
$3,000-4,500

An Apulian red figure Pelike, decorated with male and female figures, Greek/Southern Italy, 4th Century B.C., 13½in (34.5cm).
$1,800-2,700

A black glazed pottery fish plate, Greek/Southern Italy, repaired, 4th Century B.C., 10½in (26.5cm) diam.
$1,800-2,700
From the Perrone-Phricas Group

An Apulian red figure bell krater, one side decorated with a winged Eros and a draped female, the other with 2 draped men conversing, Greek/Southern Italy, 4th Century B.C., 11½in (29cm).
$3,000-4,500

A Bronze Age Jordanian pottery amphora, decorated with red painted frieze of stylised palm trees and snakes, with cross hatching above and below, 1500-1400 B.C., 16in (40.5cm).
$1,800-2,700

A buff pottery Daunian storage jar, decorated with painted tendril and leaf decoration, 10½in (26.5cm).
$1,200-1,500

An Apulian red figure volute krater, one side decorated with a naiskos scene, white painted masks on the handles, Greek/Southern Italy, 4th Century B.C., 24½in (61.5cm).
$7,500-9,000

A Cypriot pottery amphora, the decoration in dark brown with added red paint with a frieze of concentric circles, also on the neck, circa 700-600 B.C., 23in (58cm).
$3,000-4,500

An Attic black figure neck amphora, one showing Herakles wrestling with a Cretan bull, the other showing Dionysus holding a kylix, attended by a maenad, late 6th Century B.C., 10in (25cm).
$3,000-4,500

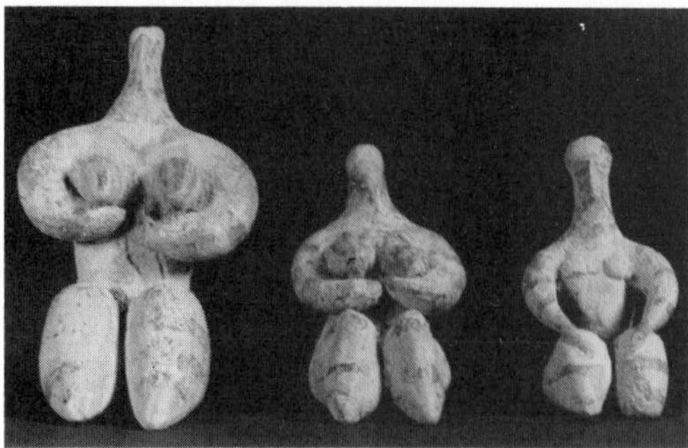

A pottery seated Mother Goddess figurine, her arms curved beneath prominent breasts, brown painted linear decoration, 3½in (8.5cm), and a similar smaller female and male, Syria, Tel-Halaf, 6th millennium B.C.
$2,700-3,300

An Attic black figure lip cup, one side showing two athletes, circa 540 B.C., 5½in (14cm) diam.
$4,500-6,000

A pre-Dynastic pottery jar, the body decorated on each side with a boat and an antelope, repaired, Naqada II, circa 3200-3000 B.C., 5½in (14cm) high.
$5,250-6,000

A Canosan pottery funerary head vase, polychrome decorated in pink, blue and white, 3rd Century B.C., 14½in (37cm).
$2,250-3,000

Seals

An Ur III haematite cylinder seal, depicting a Lamma goddess introducing a worshipper to a seated goddess, crescent in the sky, circa 1900-1700 B.C., 1in (3cm). **$450-600**

A Cypriot rock crystal cylinder seal, decorated with a winged solar disc, a leaping bovine creature, recumbent sphinxes, a bird of prey, and a scorpion, circa 1600-1400 B.C., 1in (2.5cm).
$15,000-22,500

Few examples of this 'primitive' style of seal have survived, and this example is unusually elaborate.

A Syrian or Anatolian steatite cylinder seal, carved with 2 figures facing each other, with a small figure between them, Syria or Asia Minor, circa 2500 B.C., 2in (5cm).
$4,500-6,000

An Akkadian blackish-green serpentine cylinder seal, with contest scene, carved with a bull-man in conflict with a lion, a bearded naked hero in conflict with a water buffalo, and a bull in conflict with a bearded hero wearing a kilt and flat cap, with inscription 'Ur-Enlil, scribe', Mesopotamia, circa 2400-2200 B.C., 1½in (4cm).
$30,000-45,000

A Neo-Assyrian or Neo-Babylonian chalcedony cylinder seal, decorated with a god, a worshipper, antelopes, a stylised sacred tree, and various animals, Mesopotamia, circa 800-600 B.C., 1½in (4cm).
$6,000-8,250

Terracotta

A Roman terracotta campana relief, the polychrome fragment moulded in high relief showing 2 facing young satyrs, 1st Century B.C., 7in (18.5cm).
$2,700-3,300

A Boeotian terracotta figure of Aphrodite, with traces of red paint on hair, large rectangular vent, repaired, 350-330 B.C., 10in (25.5cm). **$750-1,200**

A Roman terracotta frieze fragment with Dionysiac scene, moulded in high relief, the upper border with egg-and-dart frieze, circa 1st Century A.D., 16in (40cm).
$5,250-7,500

A terracotta figure of a woman playing castanets, wearing a chiton and himation, on integral base, rectangular vent, 4th-2nd Century B.C., 8in (20cm).
$1,050-1,350

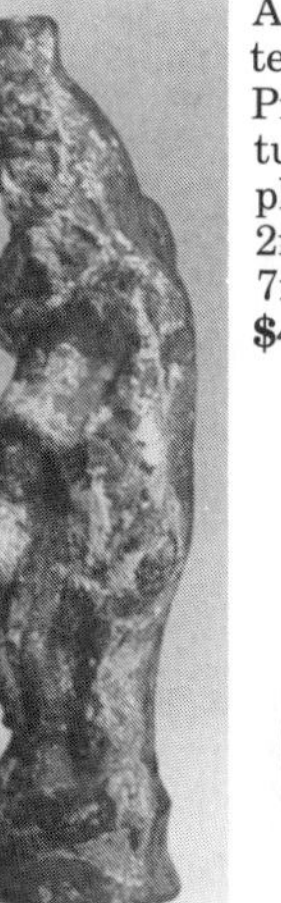

A Romano-Egyptian terracotta figure of Priapus, holding up his tunic to expose his erect phallus, repaired, 2nd-1st Century B.C., 7in (17.5cm).
$450-600

An ancient Near Eastern terracotta chariot, in the form of a ram, the 4 wheels re-attached with perspex rods, circa 2nd Millennium B.C., 7in (17cm).
$2,250-3,000

A Mycenaean terracotta figurine of 'Phi'-type, with stylised beaked head, moulded breasts, decorated with vertical striations in dark brown, Mycenaean III A.B., 1400-1200 B.C., 5in (12.5cm), mounted.
$1,800-2,700

A Boeotian terracotta figure of a dancing woman, wearing a chiton and a himation, her hair parted in the middle, large rectangular vent, repaired, circa 350 B.C., 10in (25.5cm).
$1,200-1,500

A Hellenistic terracotta female head, with an ornate crown of rosettes, a pendant round the neck, circa 2nd-1st Century B.C., 4in (10cm), mounted.
$600-750

A Canosan terracotta trefoil oinochoe, on a separate pedestal, with added red and yellow decoration, 16in (40cm)
$1,800-2,700

A Hellenistic terracotta head of a male, possibly Silenus, with luxuriant beard and stern expression, possibly an architectural fitting, circa 2nd-1st Century B.C., 4in (9.5cm), perspex mounted.
$450-600

Wood

An Egyptian wood painted panel, from the inside of a wood sarcophagus, pink, black, white and blue painted decoration, repaired, Late Period, after 600 B.C., 46½in (118.5cm).
$750-1,200

A wood funerary mask, with eyes and eyebrows painted in black, with an ochre headdress, 9⅝in (24.5cm), and 2 stylised wood masks, all Late Period, (712-332 B.C.). **$1,200-1,500**

A Viking whalebone plaque, with openwork and incised ornamentation of a pair of inward turning animal heads, a decorated border below, 15in (38cm), mounted on a wooden board; and a tapering bone dress pin with central eye, 5⅝in (14.5cm), in 2 parts, 9th-10th Century A.D.
$2,700-3,300

Plaques similar to this example have been found in rich women's graves, mainly from Norway; they were possibly used for smoothing linen cloth. This example was given to the present owner by Diana Knowles who lived at Orleigh Court in Lyon. An old label on the back of the board says that the plaque was found during the renewing of flagstones in the Great Hall at Orleigh Court by Thomas Davie in 1780, from what was believed to have been a Viking burial. It seems more likely that the plaque came from Scandinavia where Diana Knowles had a romantic attachment.

Miscellaneous

A white hardstone inlay of a profile king's head, with originally inlaid eyebrow and beard lines, Late Period/Ptolemaic, 2in (4.5cm), display mounted.
$3,000-4,500

A Canopic quartzite jar, the stopper carved as a jackal headed Duamutef, Late Period, after 600 B.C., 15in (38cm).
$3,000-3,750

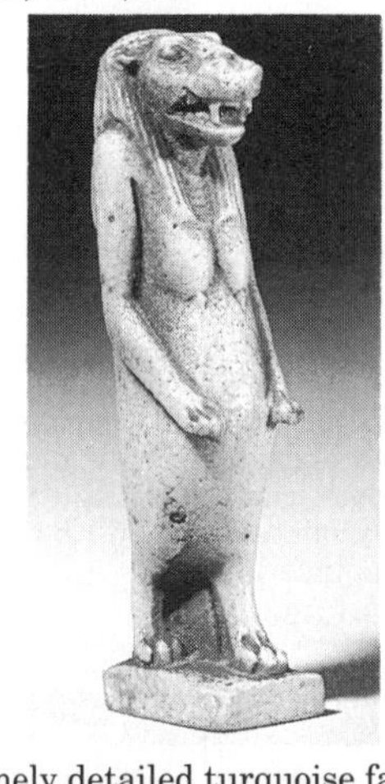
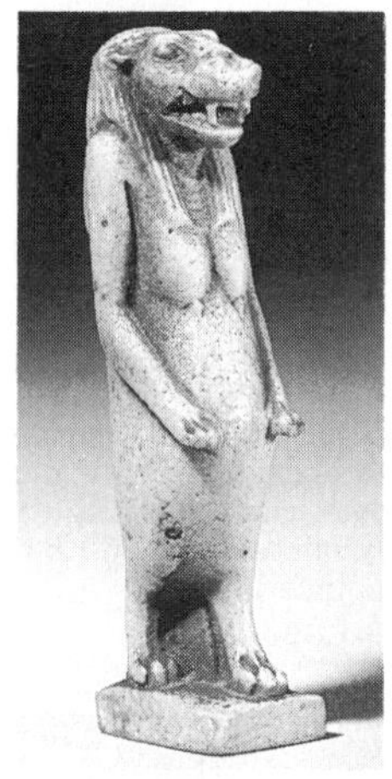

A finely detailed turquoise faience amulet of Tueris, the hippopotamus headed goddess standing with her left foot forward, her hands to her belly, on integral rectangular base, with suspension loop, 6th-4th Century B.C., 2in (5.5cm). **$750-1,200**

An alabaster pilgrim flask, minor chip at rim, Dynasty XIX-XX, (1307-1070 B.C.), 4in (10.5cm).
$1,200-1,800

A Greek bone spectacle fibula, composed of 2 conjoined flat discs, decorated with incised circles, divided by a plate with 2 smaller incised circular discs, traces of iron (pin missing), repaired, and a similar fibula, circa 8th-7th Century B.C., 2½in (6.5cm).
$750-1,200

'OOLS

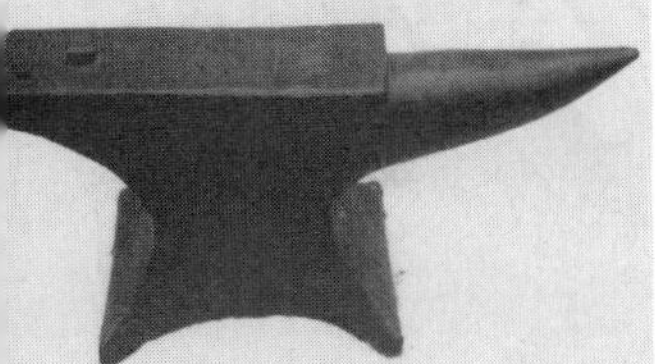
farrier's anvil, 26in (66cm) ide.
135-150

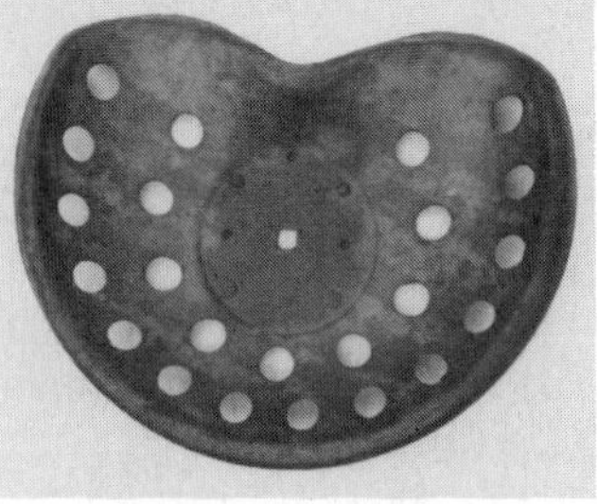
A metal tractor seat.
$50-75

A steel, brass and stained wood jack plane, by Norris, London, 14in (36cm).
$600-750

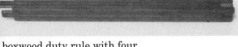

boxwood duty rule with four ides, by Edward Roberts, c1770, 2in (31cm).
225-255

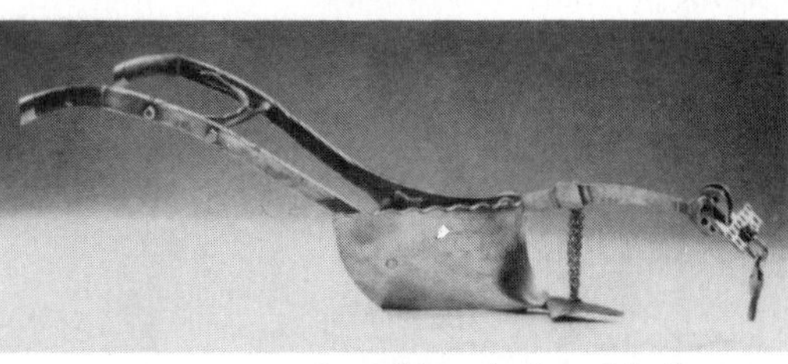
A working steel model of a plough, mid-19thC, 34in (86cm).
$600-750

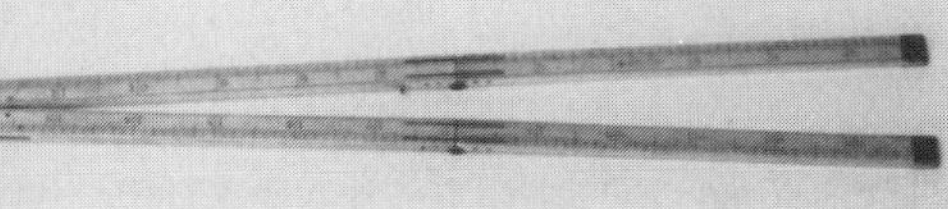
four-fold ivory rule, 19thC, 24in 1cm).
135-150

A Customs and Excise boxwood combined barrel gauging and slide rule, by Dring & Fage, c1900, 36in (92cm).
$135-150

set of plasterer's moulds for rnices, etc., on ceilings.
7.50-15 each

A collection of boxwood moulds for making composition ornaments for picture frames, furniture, etc., 19thC, 4½ to 13in (11.5 to 33cm).
$50-75 each

pair of blacksmith's bellows, om a set of 4, 29in (74cm).
135-150 each

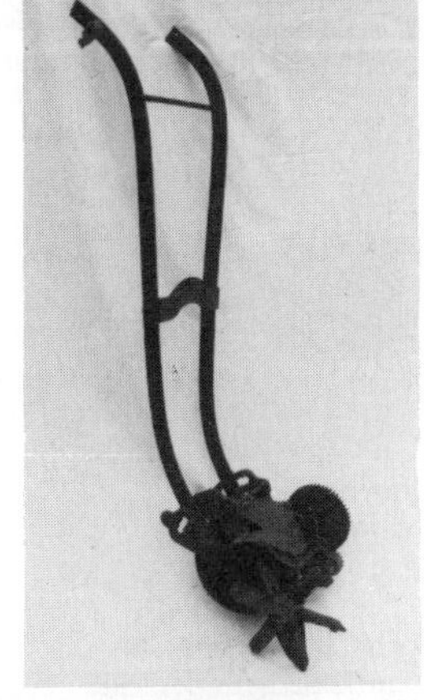
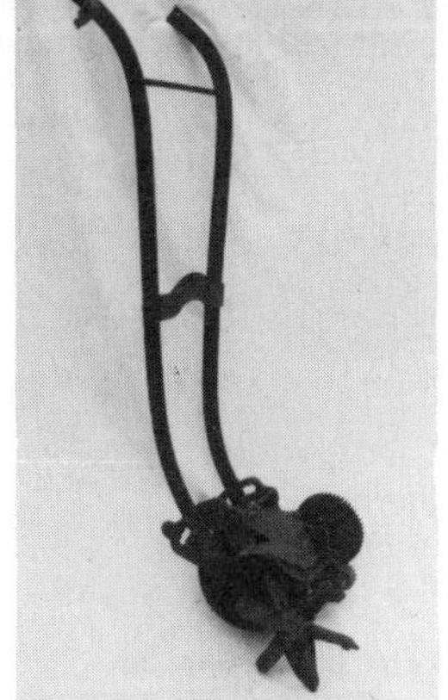
An lawn edge trimmer, 43in (109cm). **$50-75**

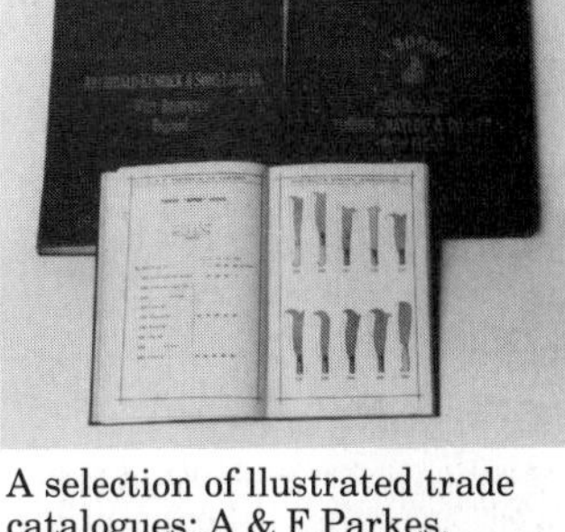
A selection of llustrated trade catalogues: A & F Parkes, Birmingham; 'Heavy Edge Tools' 1910. **$135-150**
Turner Naylor & Co., 'Tool Catalogue' 1928. **$105-120**
A. Kenrick & Sons 'Hardware Catalogue' 1926.
$135-150

white line marker, 35in 9cm) high.
50-75

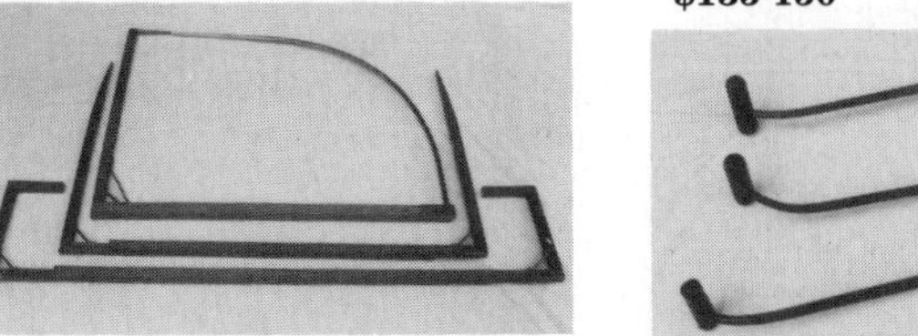
A set of 3 boxwood barrel measuring gauges, by Dring & Fage, c1900, 31in (79cm) closed.
$600-750

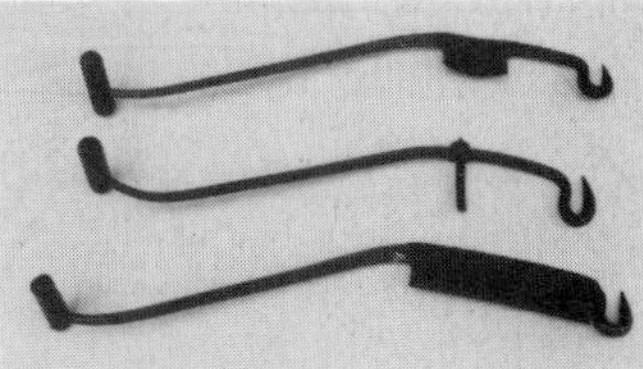
A set of 3 clogger's knives, 19thC, 42in (106.5cm).
$375-450

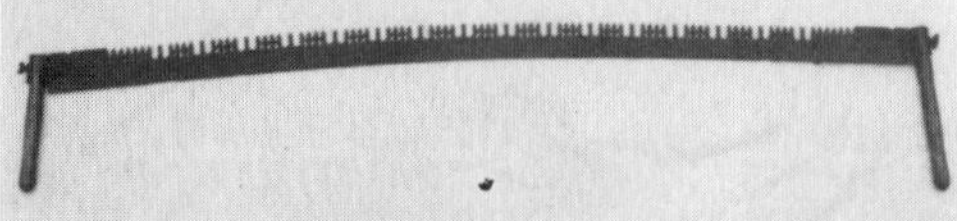

A Yankee saw, 75in (190.5cm).
$7.50-15

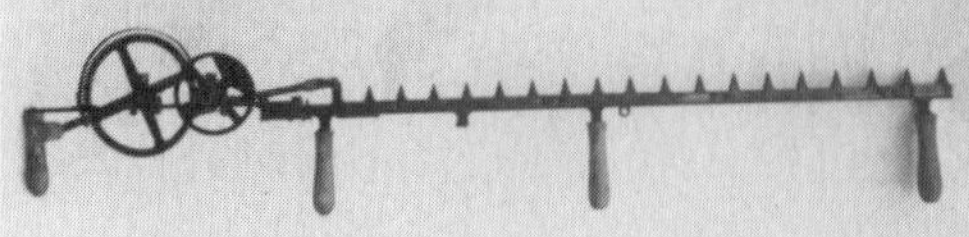

An 'All British Little Wonder' hedge clipper, by John Hansen, 63in (160cm).
$50-75

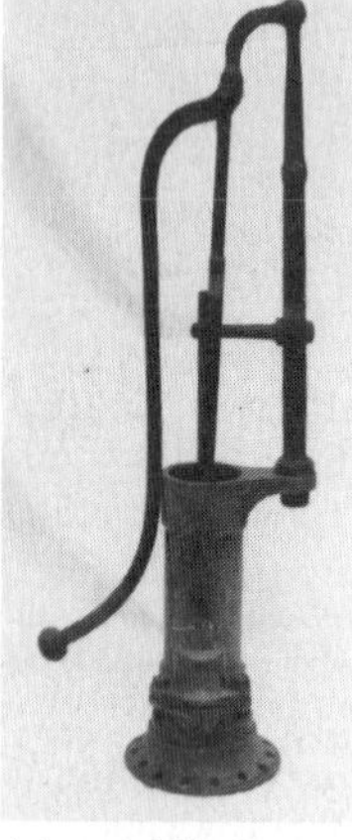

A brass bilge pump, 34in (86cm).
$120-135

A Salter's spring balance, 16in (41cm).
$50-75

A fruitwood grain shovel, English, 19thC, 42in (106.5cm).
$50-75

A set of Victorian maplewood theatre printers' blocks, largest 9in (23cm).
$7.50-15

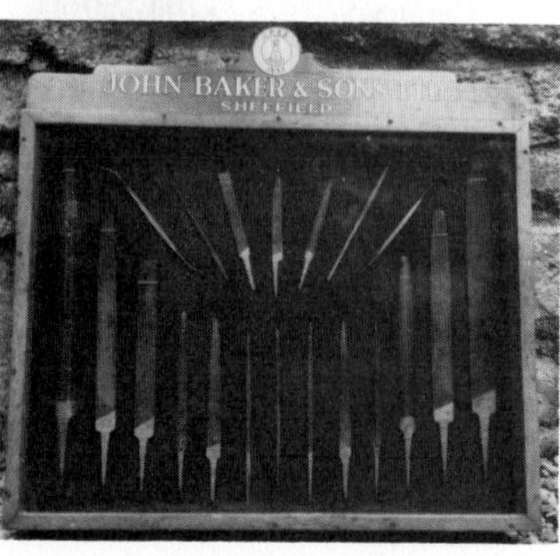

A manufacturer's display case of files, John Baker & Sons Ltd, Sheffield, early 20thC, 19 by 24in (48 by 61cm).
$300-375

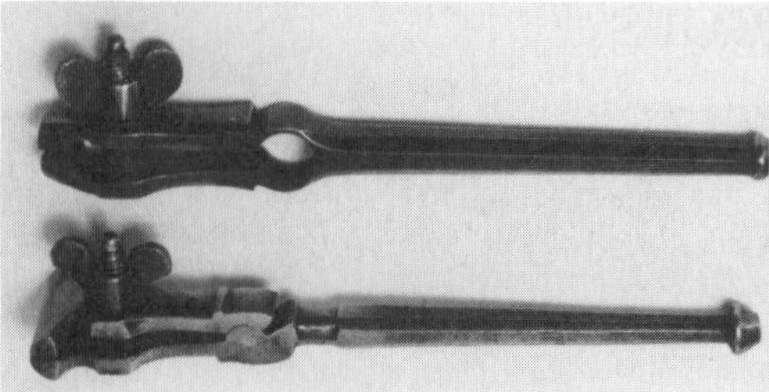

Two pin vices, 19thC, 4½in (11.5cm
$40-60

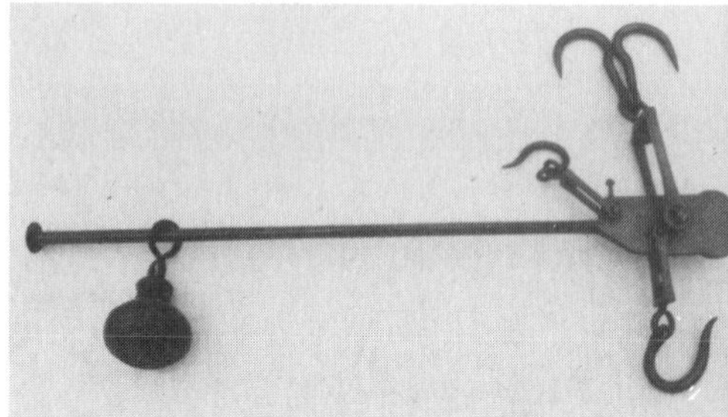

A steelyard, 33in (84cm) lon
$50-75

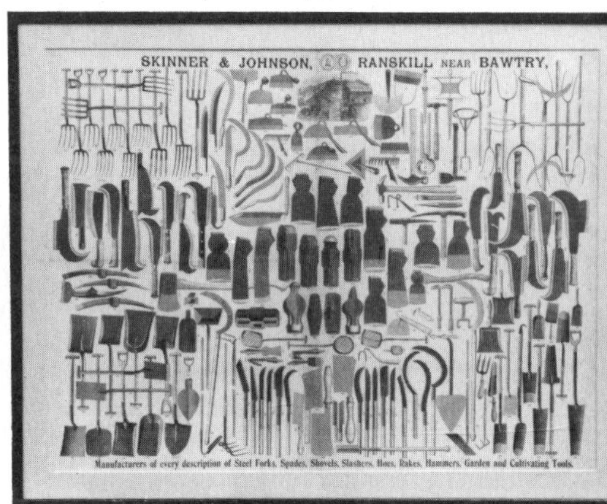

A framed advertisement for Skinner & Johnson, Ranskill, showing heavy edge tools, c1900 20 by 27in (51 by 69cm).
$150-180

A sash fillister plane, by John Green of York, c1790, 9in (23cm).
$150-225

A small size dovetailed steel smoothing plane, by Mathieson o Glasgow, late 19thC, 7in (18cm).
$90-105

An ebony and brass bevel, lat 19thC, 9½in (24cm).
$7.50-15

TREEN

An Oriental game in the form of a wooden fish, c1880, 20in (51cm).
$135-150

A turned wooden jar with a lid, 5in (13cm) diam.
$90-105

A wooden jar, 6½in (16.5cm) diam.
$50-75

A carved wooden figure of an eagle, c1880, 20in (51cm).
$375-450

A painted wooden plate from Brittany, 10in (25cm) diam.
$15-25

A carved oak musical box, c1880, 10in (25cm).
$225-255

A wooden shoe tree, c1880, 11in (28cm). **$15-25**

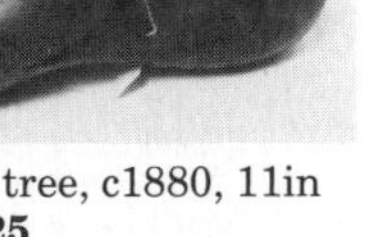

A wooden model of a caravan, 16in (41cm) long.
$225-300

Two carved wooden shoe trees, c1880, 8 and 9in (20 and 23cm).
$25-40

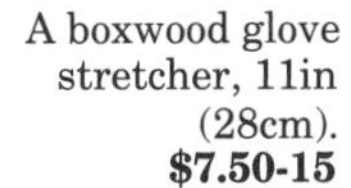

A boxwood glove stretcher, 11in (28cm).
$7.50-15

KITCHENALIA

A shallow wooden bowl, c1880, 19in (48cm) diam.
$90-105

A wine basket, c1900, 11 by 14in (28 by 36cm).
$50-75

A French wine bottle carrier, c1880, 15in (38cm).
$50-75

A two-handled wooden bowl.
$50-75

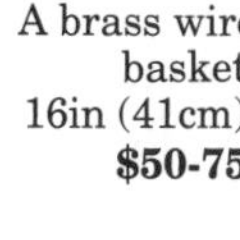

A brass wire basket, 16in (41cm).
$50-75

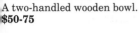

A Victorian beech bread board, carved with 'Our Daily Bread', 11½in (29cm).
$25-40

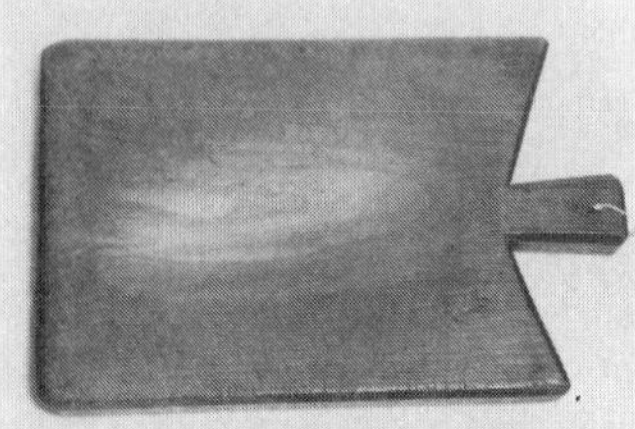

A French fruitwood chopping board, 19thC, 16 by 11in (41 by 28cm).
$50-75

A French fruitwood chopping board, 19thC, 14 by 9in (36 by 22.5cm).
$50-75

A Victorian octagonal ash bread board, carved with wheat pattern, 10in (25cm).
$25-40

Two domestic wooden bowls, c1880, 26 and 24in (66 and 61cm).
$50-75 each

A wooden shallow bowl, c1880. 20in (51cm).
$50-75

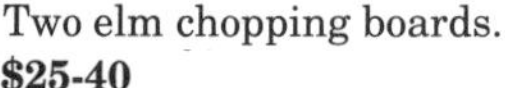

A rectangular pine cheese board, 23in (59cm).
$25-40

Two elm chopping boards.
$25-40

A turned fruitwood dairy platter English, 19thC, 14½in (37cm).
$90-105

A turned fruitwood dairy bowl English, 19thC, 14½in (37cm).
$135-150

A Victorian beech bread board, carved with 'Bread', 12in (30.5cm).
$25-40

A cheese board or a pot stand, 9in (22.5cm) diam.
$25-40

Three salt glazed bowls, 10 to 20in (25 to 51cm) diam.
$25-40 each

. Victorian bread knife, with
eech handle, carved with a
lower pattern, 12in (31cm).
25-40

A Victorian bread knife, with pearwood handle carved with wheat pattern, 12in (31cm).
$25-40

n Edwardian bread knife, with
eech wood handle, with 'Bread'
arved on handle, by H. Samuel,
heffield, 12in (31cm).
40-60

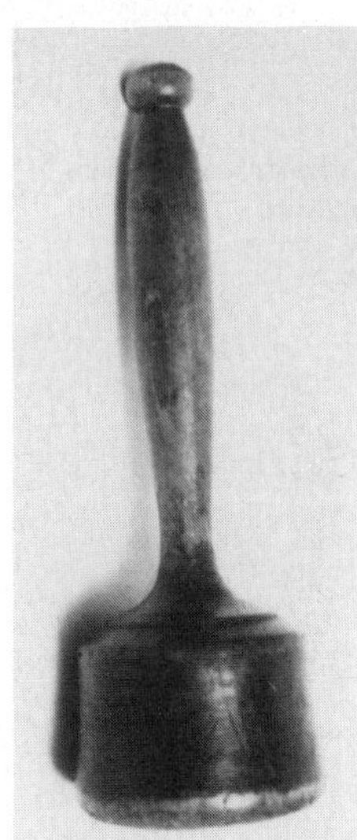

A wooden pestle, 8in (20cm).
$7.50-15

A fruitwood pestle, 9in (22.5cm).
$7.50-15

. bread knife, with beech handle
arved with ivy leaf pattern,
1910, 12in (31cm).
25-40

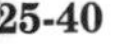

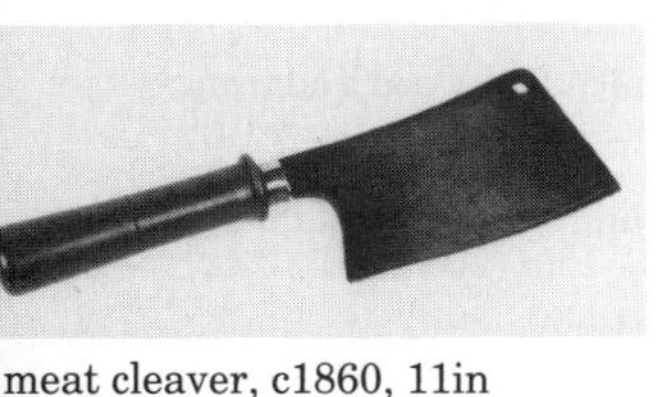

. meat cleaver, c1860, 11in
28cm).
25-40

A fruitwood pestle, 15in (38cm).
$7.50-15

A wooden rice pestle, 12in (31cm).
$25-40

. Spanish pine pestle and mortar,
in (18cm).
150-225

A barrel butter churn, 20in (51cm).
$105-120

A round pine cheese board.
$40-60

Three wooden butter seals, 4in (10cm) diam.
$40-60 each

A sycamore butter skimmer, 19thC, 8½in (21cm) diam.
$50-75

A butter seal, 4½in (11cm) diam.
$25-40

A butter mould, engraved with Prince of Wales' feathers, 19thC, 4in (10cm) diam.
$40-60

A French fruitwood and iron mounted spice grinder, lacking feet, 18thC, 9in (23cm).
$900-1,500

A French fruitwood spice grinder, with tin top and fruitwood handle, 19thC, 9in (23cm).
$225-255

A Dutch coffee grinder, c1880, 13in (33cm).
$50-75

A French fruitwood and iron mounted spice grinder, with shouldered body and one drawer, steel and wood winding handle, 18thC, 10in (25cm).
$900-1,500

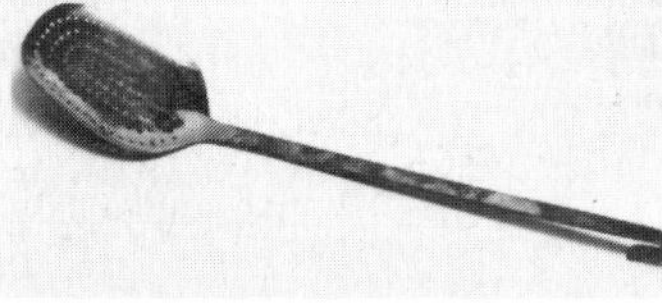

A copper draining spoon, c1880, 20in (51cm).
$50-75

A copper ladle or pan, c1880, 14½in (37cm).
$50-75

A blue enamel strainer and slice, 7½ (18.5cm) diam and 8in (20cm) long.
$7.50-15 each

A butter pat, 4in (10cm) diam
$25-40

A butter mould, engraved wit wheat ears, 19thC, 4in (10cm)
$40-60

A brass pan, with steel handle c1860, 9in (23cm) diam.
$105-120

A copper saucepan, c1880
$105-12

A copper lid, c1880, 14½in (37cm) diam.
$50-75

A copper fish kettle, 15in (38cm).
$375-450

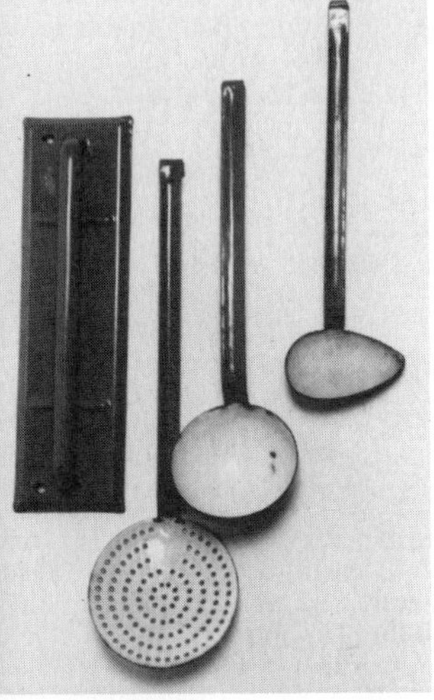

A German set of enamel kitchen spoons with rack, 19thC.
$50-75

A copper draining spoon or ladle, c1920, 10in (25cm) diam.
$40-60

A carved rolling pin, 11in (28cm).
$50-75

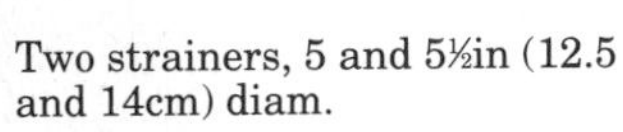

A copper urn with lid, 10in (25cm) diam. **$225-255**

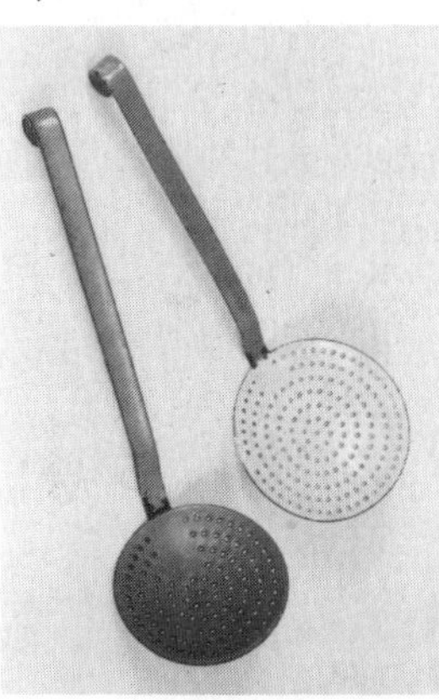

Two strainers, 5 and 5½in (12.5 and 14cm) diam.
$7.50-15

A Victorian painted beech rolling pin, 15in (38cm).
$15-25

A Victorian china rolling pin, Nut Brown pattern, 17in (43cm).
$25-40

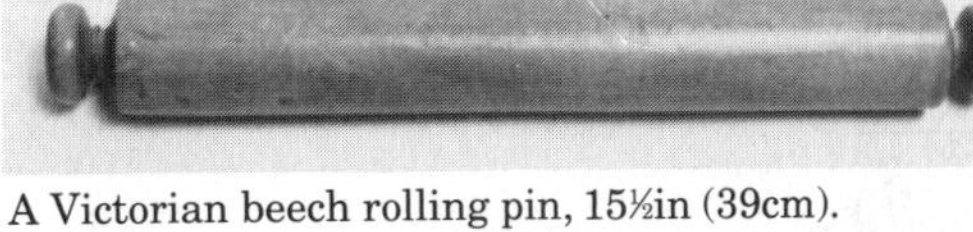

A Victorian beech rolling pin, 15½in (39cm).
$7.50-15

A Victorian beech rolling pin, with moving handles, 17in (43cm).
$7.50-15

A selection of iron weights, 1½ to 6in (3.5 to 15cm).
$7.50-15

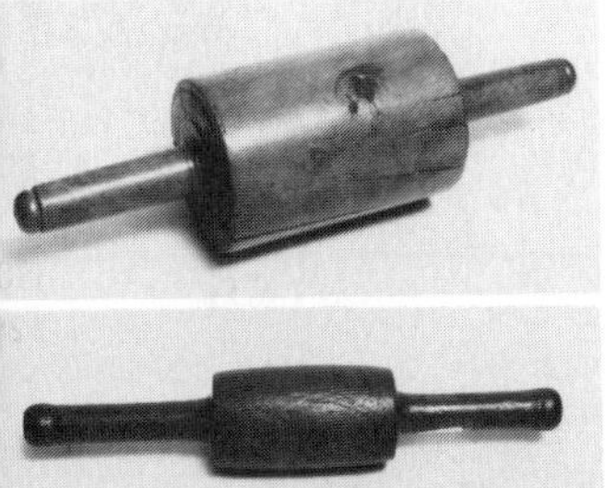

Two wooden rolling pins, 15 and 12in (38 and 31cm) long.
$7.50-15

A large brass pan, 12in (31cm) diam.
$90-105

A set of shop scales, 20in (51cm) wide.
$225-300

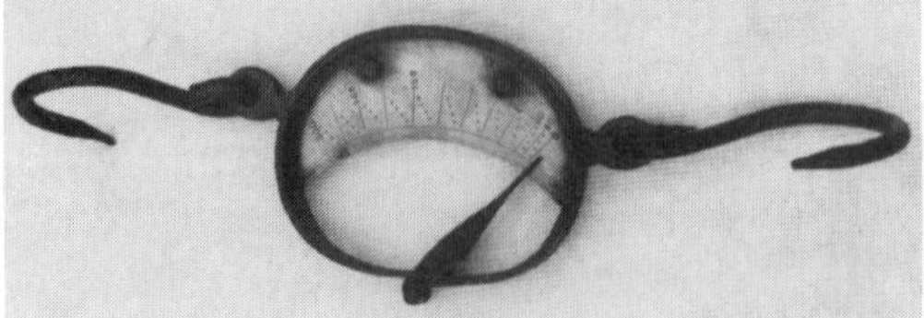

A Victorian balance, 11in (28cm).
$105-120

Two English wooden gravy spoons, 19thC.
$50-75 the pair

A brass spring balance, c1900, 24in (61cm) high.
$120-135

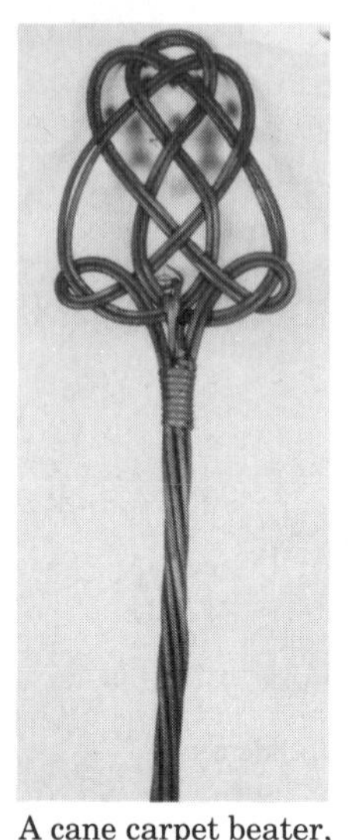

A cane carpet beater, 27in (69cm).
$7.50-15

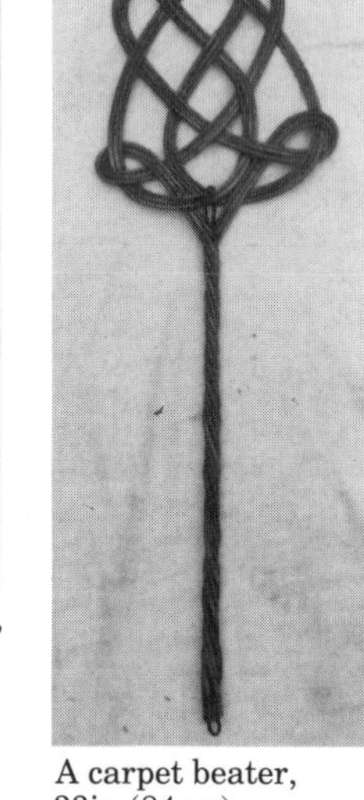

A carpet beater, 33in (84cm).
$25-40

A brass funnel, c1880, 6in (15cm diam.
$25-40

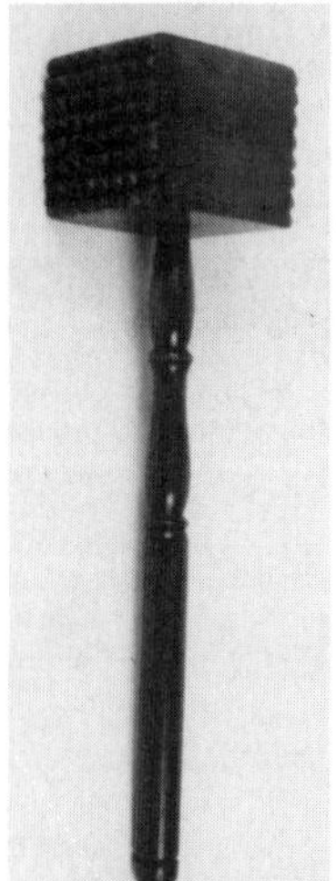

A sycamore steak beater, 19thC, 14½in (37cm).
$25-40

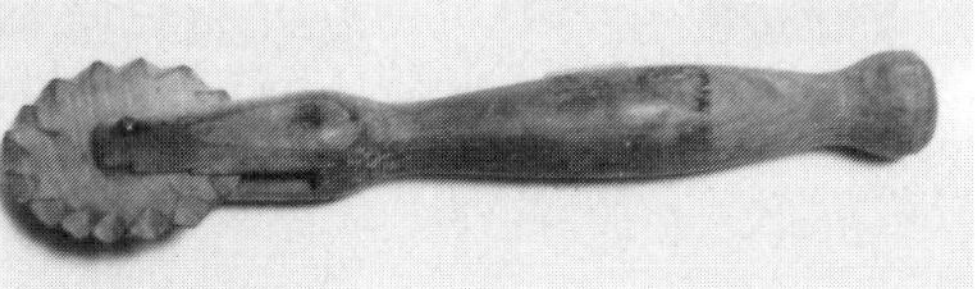

A Victorian wooden pastry cutter, 8in (20cm).
$25-40

A French chestnut water jug and mortar, 19thC, 7in (18cm).
$120-135

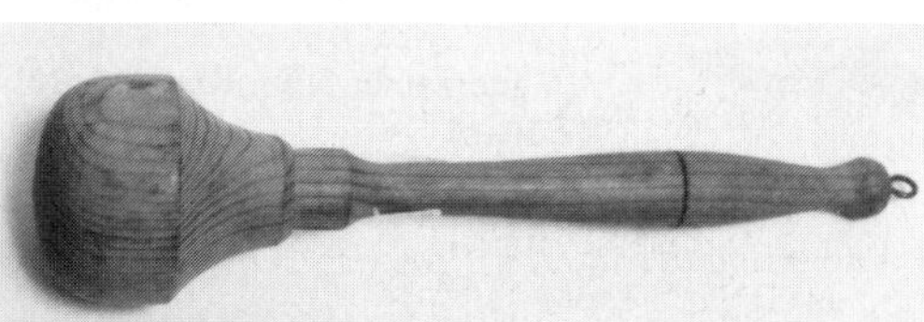

A Victorian wooden salmon priest, 10in (25cm).
$25-40

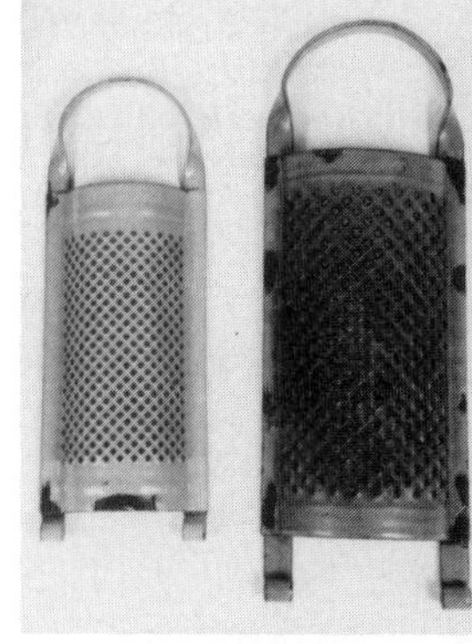

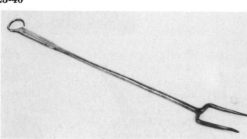

Two enamel graters, 9 and 10½in (22.5 and 26cm).
$7.50-15 each

A steel flesh fork, 18thC, 21½in (54.5cm).
$50-75

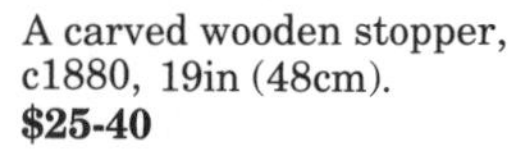

A carved wooden stopper, c1880, 19in (48cm).
$25-40

An iron game rack, 18in (46cm).
$50-75

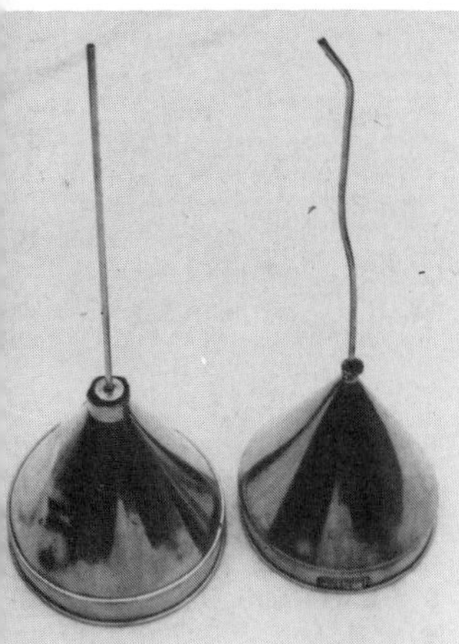

'wo copper beer or cider funnels,
3in (59cm) long.
50-75 each

A staved sycamore and fruitwood jug, bound with 3 riveted copper bands with copper lip and spurred sycamore loop handle, with triple kicked terminal, possibly Scottish, 19thC, 9in (23cm) over handle.
$150-225

A blue enamel coffee pot, 10in (25cm).
$7.50-15

A sycamore ladle, 19thC, 12½in (32cm).
$25-40

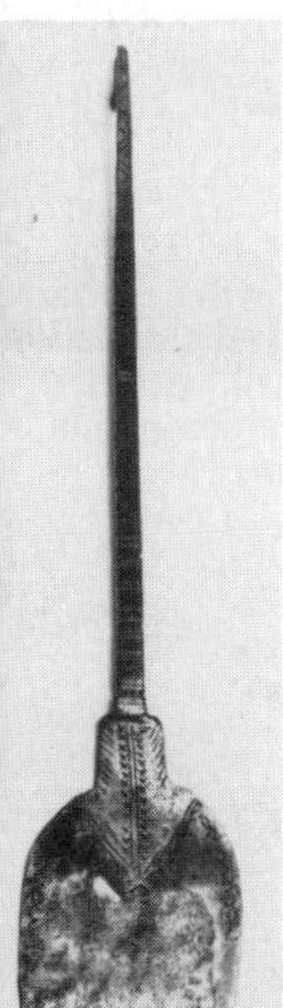

A flat metal spoon, c1880, 19in (48cm).
$25-40

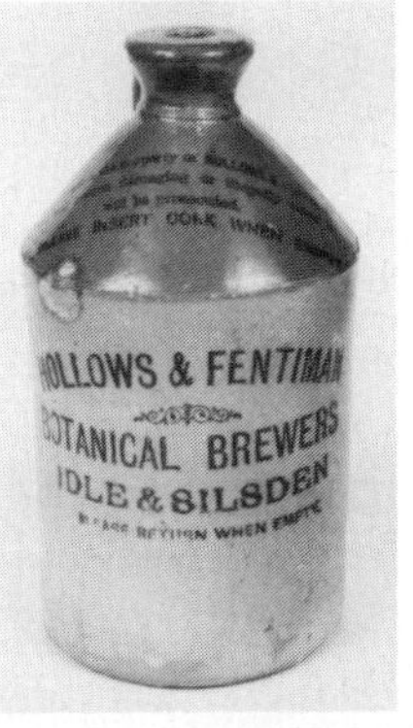

A wicker covered glass jar, 18in (46cm).
$25-40

A brewer's jar, 11in (28cm).
$25-40

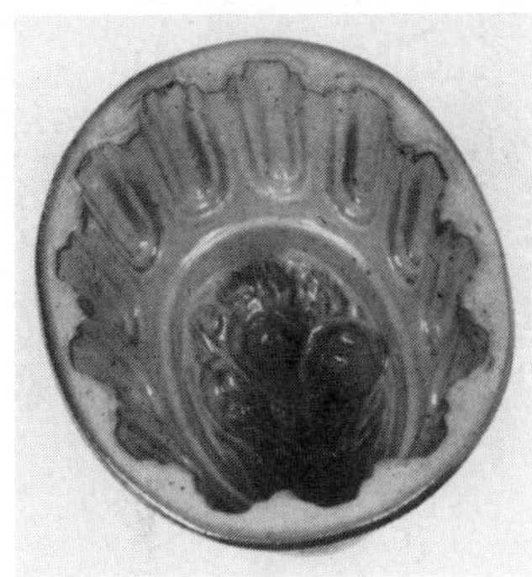

A stoneware salt glazed jelly mould, with pears design, 19thC, 6in (15cm).
$25-40

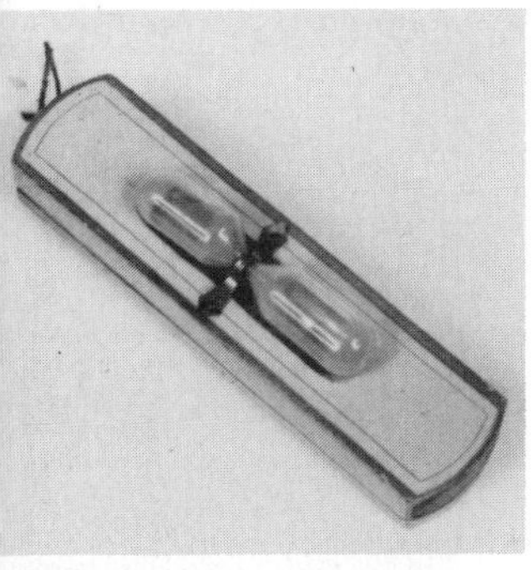

wooden hanging egg timer, on a ream and green base, c1920, 6in 15cm).
7.50-15

An enamel bread bin, 11 by 11in (28 by 28cm).
$25-40

Did you know?
MILLER'S Antiques Price Guide builds up year by year to form the most comprehensive photo reference library available.

A French carved wood novelty bottle opener, 21in (54cm).
$375-525

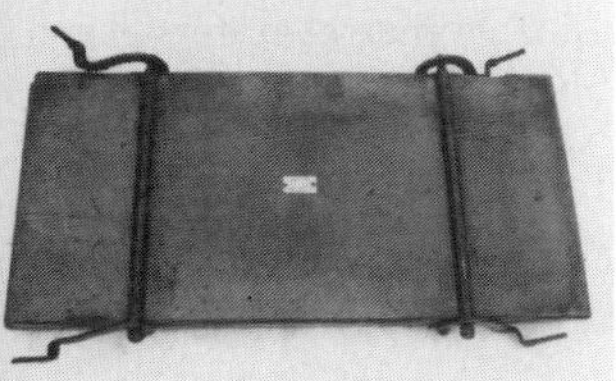

A trouser press, 12 by 26in (31 by 66cm).
25-40

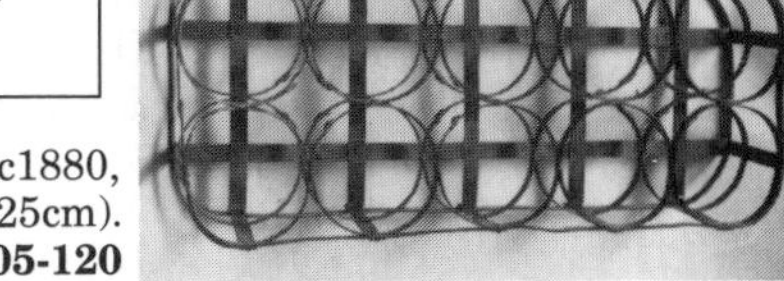

A wine bottle rack, c1880, 22 by 10in (56 by 25cm).
$105-120

A fruitwood carved wooden pulley, 3in (8cm).
$15-25

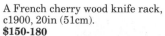

An iron grill, 13in (33cm) wide.
$50-75

Four drink flasks in a wire basket, c1880, 10in (25cm) high 9in (23cm) square.
$135-150

A boxwood 4-tier cylindrical spice box, for Mace, Cloves, Nutmeg and Cinnamon, damaged, 19thC, 10in (25cm).
$150-225

A Norwegian carved and painted wood mangle board, with lion handle and foliate decoration, 1803, 28½in (72cm).
$1,800-2,700

A French cherry wood knife rack, c1900, 20in (51cm).
$150-180

A flat iron, c1900, 6½in (16cm).
$15-25

A Welsh oak spoon rack, early 19thC, 14in (36cm) high.
$135-150

An ash and iron mounted cider barrel, early 19thC, 9in (23cm).
$150-180

A Doulton keg, 16in (41cm) high.
$40-60

Three spirit barrels-on-stand, c1880, 11in (28cm).
$300-375

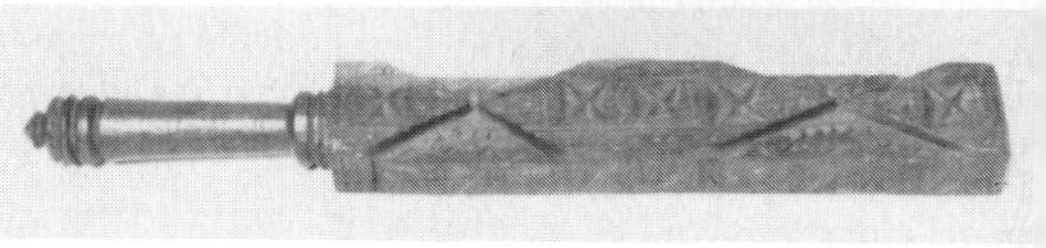

A wooden carved laundry beater, 21in (53cm).
$25-40

BOXES

Card Cases

A Tunbridge ware card case, c1840, 3 by 4in (8 by 10cm).
$375-525

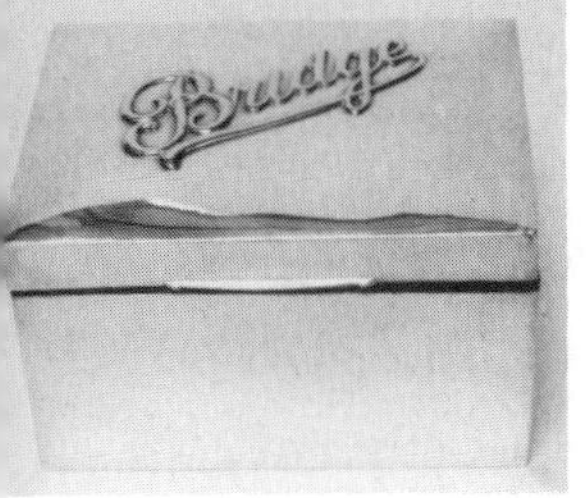

A silver card box, Birmingham 1915, 3 by 4½in (8 by 11cm).
$150-225

A Victorian card case, pierced and embossed all-over with flowers and foliate scrolls, by Nathaniel Mills, Birmingham 1842, with leather case, 4in (10cm).
$375-525

A Victorian card case, stamped with waved fluting, George Unite, Birmingham 1890, 4in (10cm).
$300-375

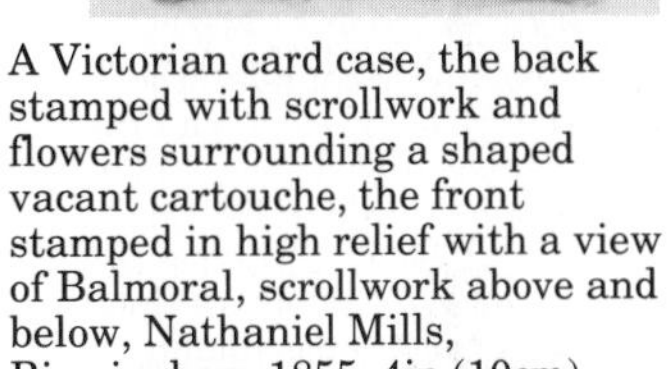

A Victorian card case, the back stamped with scrollwork and flowers surrounding a shaped vacant cartouche, the front stamped in high relief with a view of Balmoral, scrollwork above and below, Nathaniel Mills, Birmingham 1855, 4in (10cm).
$600-750

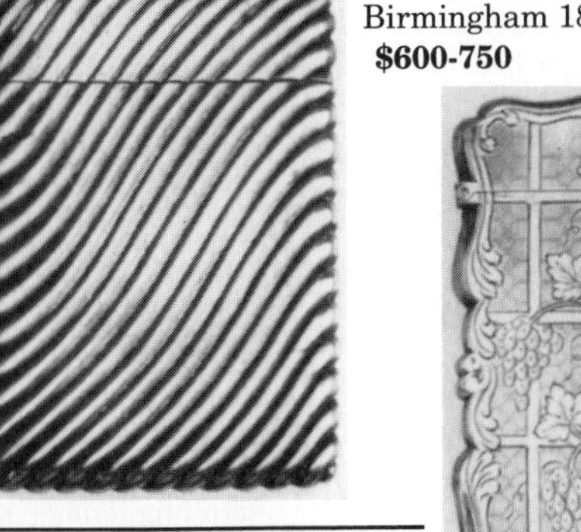

An early Victorian card case, each side engraved with trailing fruit laden vines on trelliswork, on an engine turned ground, Nathaniel Mills, Birmingham 1848, 4in (10cm).
$375-525

Dressing Boxes

A Victorian rosewood dressing case, with brass edge mouldings, inlaid string lines and flush brass side handles, Bramah lock, mauve morocco leather lined interior fitted with an easel mirror and blotter in the lid, inscribed in gilt 'Edwards, Manufacturer to Her Majesty, 21 King St, Bloomsbury, London', 2 lift-out trays, 12 various hob cut glass bottles and boxes, the silver covers engine engraved and engraved with pierced flowers, scrolls and foliage, each with monogram within a central roundel, London 1838 and 1845, maker Thomas Diller, the lift-out instrument tray containing 11 steel and silver instruments some with mother-of-pearl mounted handles, damaged, 14 by 10in (36 by 25cm).
$2,250-3,000

A Regency brass mounted mahogany dressing box, the hinged lid with 'CCI' monogram, leather lined interior, with silver mounted cut glass bottles and brass label Manufactured by Bailey & Blue, Cockspur Street, London, the base with a drawer, recessed carrying handles, 20½in (52cm) wide.
$1,200-1,500

A gentleman's rosewood dressing box, with brass inlay, c1830.
$600-750

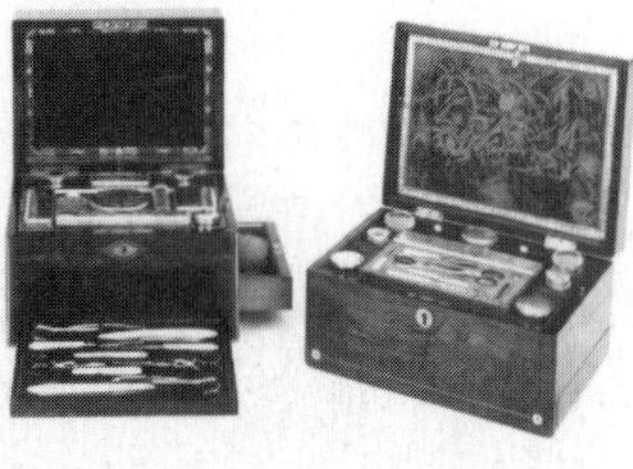

A selection of Victorian dressing boxes, with leather lined interiors, 2 with side drawers, 11 to 12½in (28 to 31cm) wide. **$225-255**

A Victorian coromandel wood dressing case, inlaid with brass string lines, edge beads and a Gothic monogram 'HM', flush brass handles at the sides, the black morocco and velvet lined interior with a brass bound mirror and stationery pocket in the lid, the hinge inscribed 'G. Betjemann and Sons, makers, 36 and 38 Pentonville Road, London', lift-out tray with 14 hob cut glass bottles and boxes, the silver gilt covers engraved with formal designs, scrolling foliage and green and white enamel Gothic 'HM' monograms, hallmarked London 1863 and 1869, makers John and William Pittway and William Neal, the base drawer with lift-out tray containing 14 silver gilt and gilded metal instruments, some with mother-of-pearl handles and a mother-of-pearl 6in (15cm) rule, 4 monogrammed ivory backed brushes, Bramah locks, 16½ by 12in (42 by 31cm).
$5,250-7,500

Jewellery Boxes

A French carved walnut jewellery casket, in the form of a coffer, the velvet lined interior with a tray and compartments, c1870, 7 by 12½in (18 by 31cm).
$600-750

An ebonised and gilt metal mounted jewel cabinet, of architectural form, with inset enamel plaques having painted figure decoration, 2 doors enclosing 2 small drawers, turned columns and lion' paw feet, 6in (15cm).
$750-1,200

A Regency bombé shaped jewel casket, covered in red morocco, with chased brass mounts, 10in (25cm).
$600-750

A silver, tortoiseshell and piqué jewel casket, in the form of a Louis XVI style cylinder bureau, the tortoiseshell panels inlaid with musical trophies and scrolling foliage, maker William Comyns, London 1905, 6in (15cm) wide.
$750-1,200

Knife Boxes

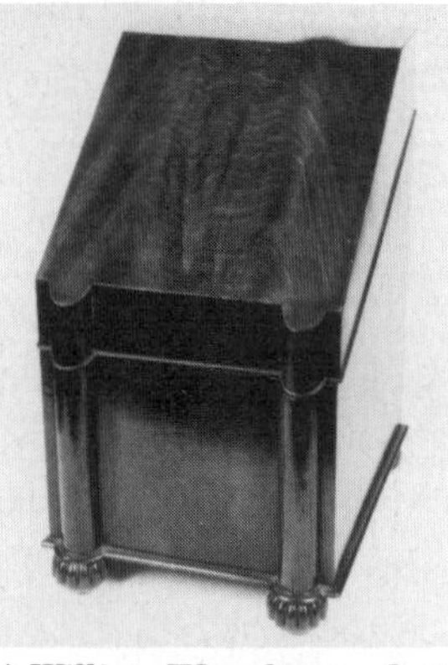

A William IV mahogany knife box, interior replaced, c1830, 17in (43cm) high. **$225-255**

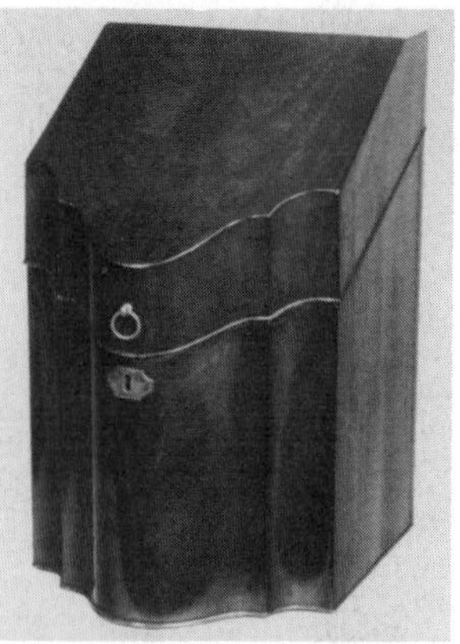

A George III serpentine knife box, with hinged sloping top, the reverse inlaid in ebony and boxwood with a stellar medallion and enclosing a fitted interior, 10in (25cm).
$1,800-2,700

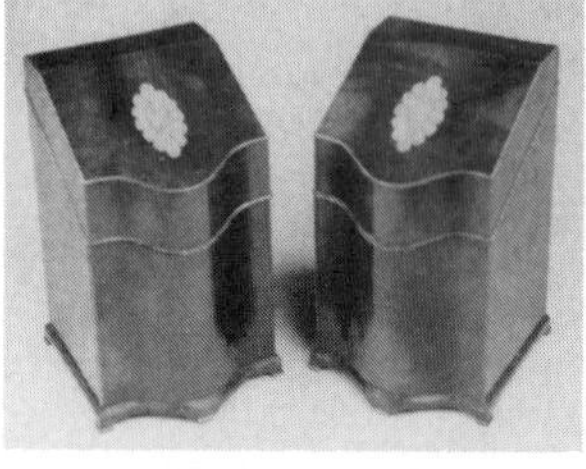

A pair of George III mahogany knife boxes, with satinwood inlaid medallions and chevron borders, cutlery divisions replaced, c1790, 15½in (39cm) high.
$1,800-2,700

Salt Boxes

A French carved walnut salt box, with serpentine hinged cover and apron drawer, 19thC, 8in (20cm) wide.
$750-1,200

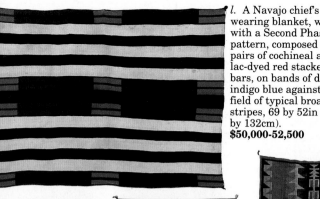

l. A Navajo chief's wearing blanket, woven with a Second Phase pattern, composed of 12 pairs of cochineal and lac-dyed red stacked bars, on bands of deep indigo blue against a field of typical broad stripes, 69 by 52in (175 by 132cm).
$50,000-52,500

A Saltillo serape, 94½ by 56in (239 by 142cm).
$19,000-20,000

Late Classic Navajo ınket, 62½ by 49in 59 by 124cm).
,000-12,000

A Navajo Germantown rug, with Fred Harvey tag, 79 by 61in (200 by 155cm).
$6,750-8,250

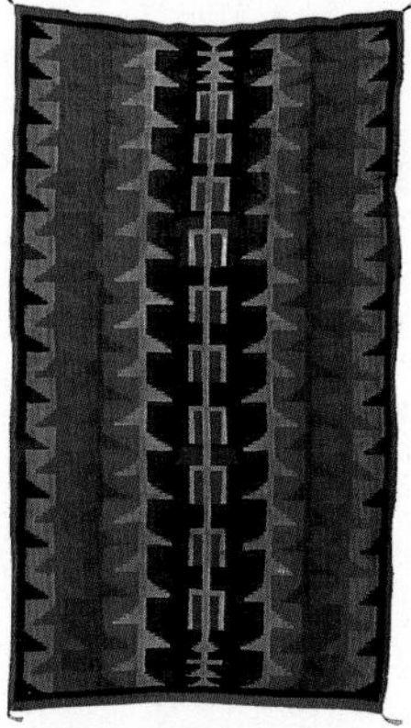

A Navajo Germantown rug, 92 by 52in (231 by 132cm).
$2,250-5,250

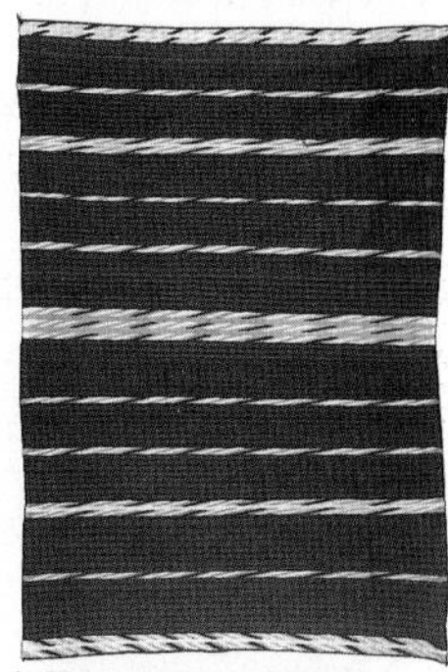

A Transitional Navajo blanket, 71 by 48in (180 by 122cm.
$13,500-15,000

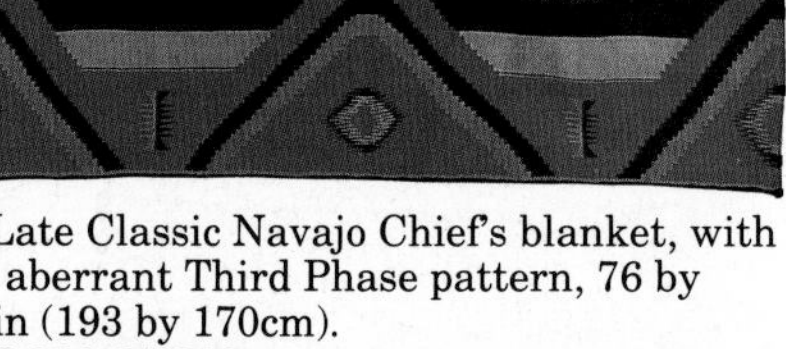

Late Classic Navajo Chief's blanket, with aberrant Third Phase pattern, 76 by ın (193 by 170cm).
8,000-21,000

A Navajo Germantown rug, 85½ by 46½in (217 by 118cm).
$6,750-8,250

A Navajo Germantown rug, with an aberrant Chief's pattern, 63 by 44in (160 by 111.5cm).
$10,500-13,500

Late Classic Navajo Chief's blanket, with a ird Phase pattern, 65½ by 57in (166 by 4.5cm). **$13,500-15,000**

A Classic Navajo wearing blanket, with Second Phase pattern, 70½ by 53½in (179 by 136cm).
$42,000-45,000

A Great Lakes quilled buckskin pouch, slightly flaring shape, animal hair suspended from imitation pocket flap, 7½in (19cm) long. **$22,500-27,000**

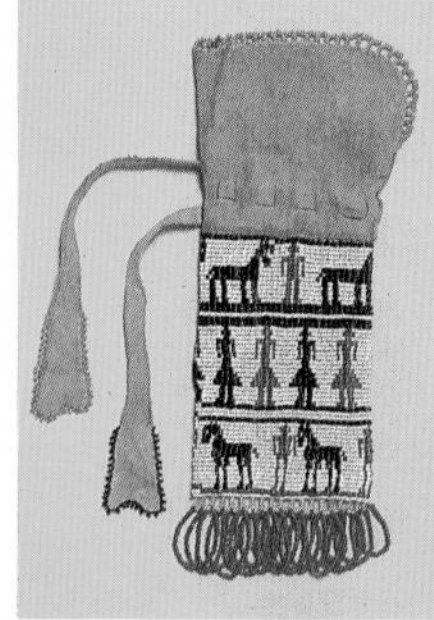

A Wasco pictorial beaded hide pouch, overlaid with a panel of glass seed beads, attributed to Taswatha, (Ellen Underwood). **$5,250-6,000**

An Eastern Athapaskan beaded a[nd] fringed hide woman's costume, probably slave, 1870s, tunic 30in (76cm), skirt 37½in (95cm) long. **$19,500-21,000**

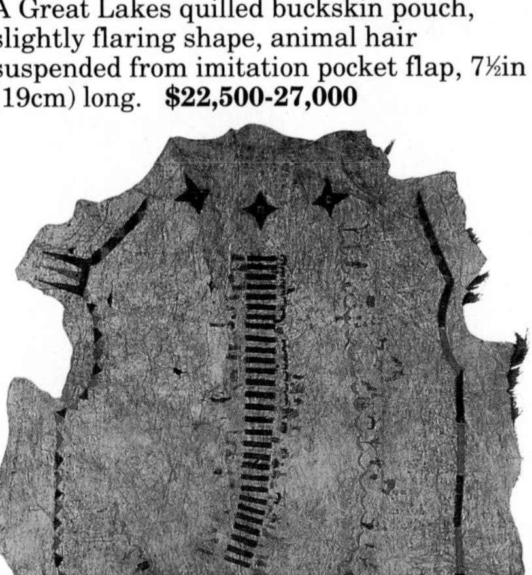

A Kiowa buffalo hide winter count, with central panel of parallel bars, flanked by outlined figures, animals, a house and a baby carriage. **$9,000-12,000**

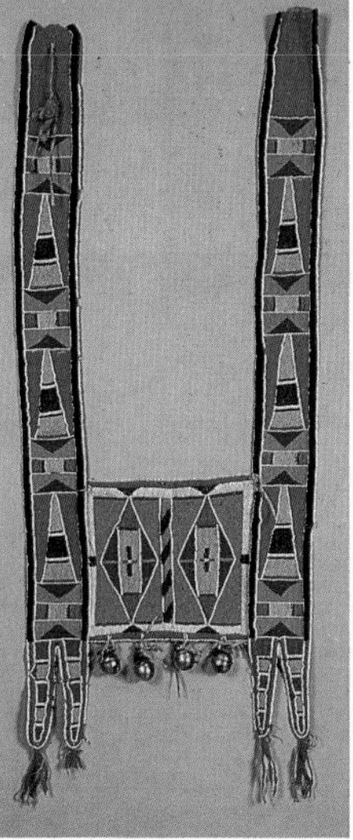

A crow beaded and fringed cloth and hide martingale, trimmed with red and blue trade cloth and large metal bells, 40in (101cm) long. **$9,000-12,000**

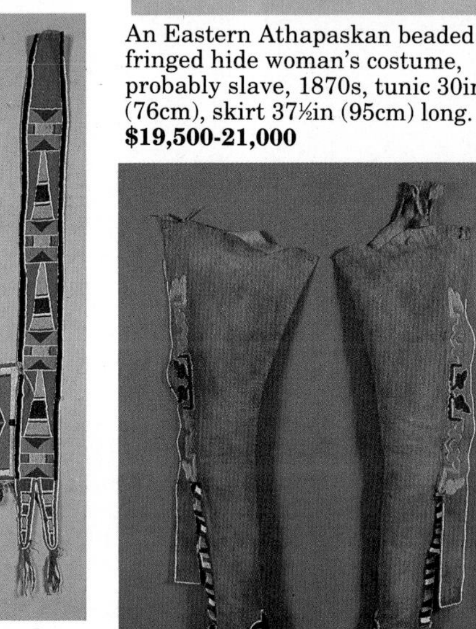

A pair of Oto beaded hide front sea[m] leggings, the 2 pendant flaps edge[d] with white beads, 35in (89cm) long. **$16,000-18,000**

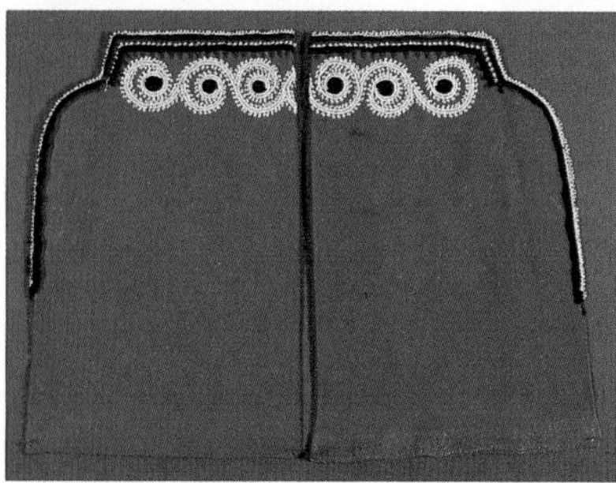

A pair of Eastern Athapaskan beaded cloth leggings, stitched in glass seed beads, trimmed with black hemtape, 13½in (34cm) long. **$3,000-4,500**

A Pomo beaded and coiled oval gift basket, with a beaded handle on the rim, 9in (23cm) long. **$9,000-12,000**

A Great Lakes quilled buckskin tobacco bag, 20in (51cm) long. **$67,500-75,000**

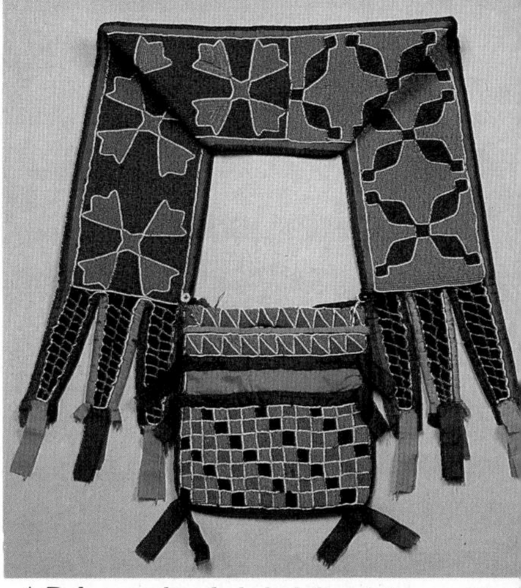

A Delaware beaded cloth bandoleer, with si[lk] backed shoulder strap spot stitched on the front, and pocket pouch, 29in (74cm) long. **$21,000-27,000**

uni polychrome jar, with a frieze
triated rainbird motifs, indented
e, 12in (30.5cm) diam.
)00-10,500

An Acoma polychrome jar, 10½in (26.5cm) diam.
$1,350-1,500

A Zuni polychrome jar, with indented base, 12½in (31.5cm) diam.
$6,000-9,000

iopi polychrome seed jar, with
rt cylindrical neck, 11in (28cm)
m.
)00-3,750

A Zuni silver turqouise and coral pendant, by Dan Simplicio, c1935, 4½in (11cm).
$3,750-4,500

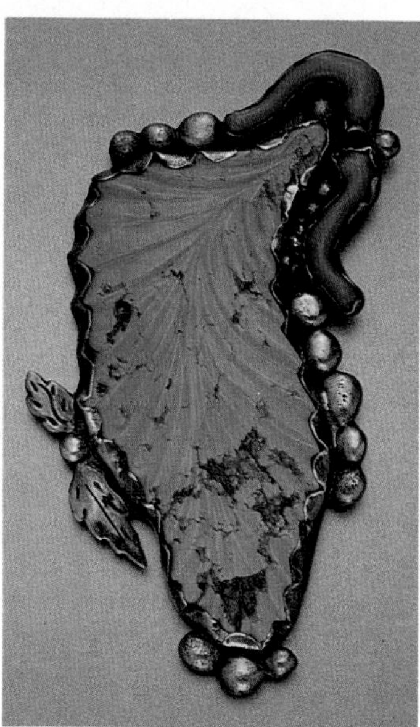

A Zuni silver turquoise and coral pendant, hand carved by Leekya Desyee, silverwork by Dan Simplicio. **$3,500-4,500**

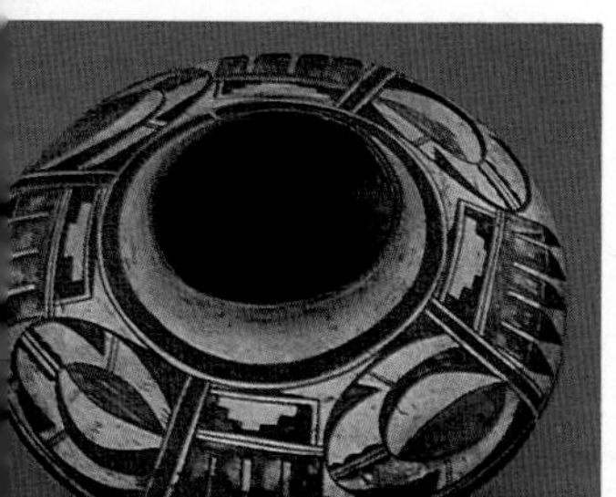

Iopi polychrome seed jar, of
nated form with short cylindrical
k, 10in (25cm) diam.
250-3,000

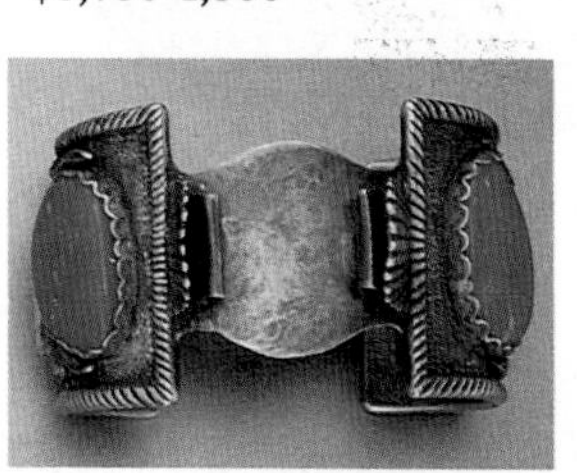

A Zuni silver, turquoise and coral watch band bracelet, by Dan Simplicio, 3in (7.5cm) wide.
$600-900

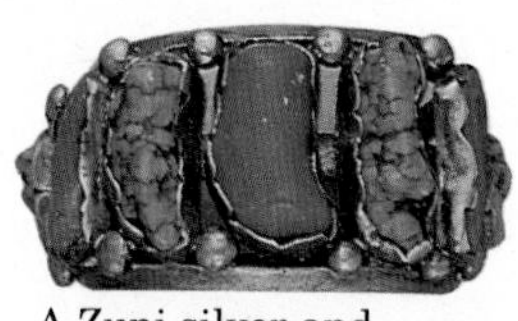

A Zuni silver and turquoise man's bracelet, by Dan Simplicio, c1935, 2½in (6cm) wide.
$6,750-7,500

Iopi polychrome bowl, with flaring sides
tapering rim, 11½in (28.5cm) diam.
300-1,400

An Ildelfonso blackware plate, signed Marie+Santana, 12in (31cm) diam.
$4,500-5,250

A North West Coast male figural group, inscribed, 16in (41cm).
$9,000-10,500

A Chumash coiled tray, woven in naturally variegated and blackened juncus stem, 17in (43cm) diam.
$45,000-52,500

A Washoe polychrome coiled degikup, tight woven in willow, redbud and blackened bracken fern root, woven by Lena Dick, c19 8in (20cm) diam. **$5,250-6,000**

A San Ildefonso blackware plate, signed Marie+Santana, 16in (41cm) diam. **$10,500-13,500**

A Zuni black on red jar, with indent base and slightly domed tapering ne 12in (31cm) diam.
$7,500-9,000

A Mohave/Yuma polychrome pottery cradle doll, secured to a bark cradle board, trimmed with white beads and feathers, 19in (48cm) long.
$10,500-13,500

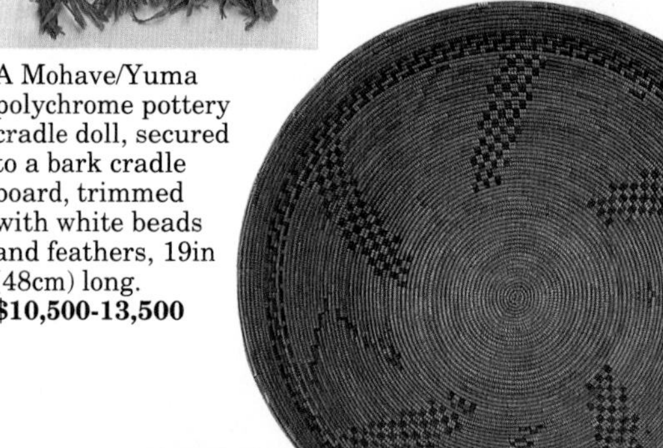

A Chumash coiled bowl, 16in (41cm) diam. **$13,500-16,500**

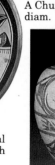

A Great Lakes catlinite effigy pipehead the shank of tapering faceted section flattened on the underside with flaring bowl, 5in (12cm). **$18,000-21,000**

A Kawaiisu polychrome coiled seed jar, woven in willow, red yucca and brackenfern root, 10in (25cm) diam.
$9,000-12,000

A Polacca polychrome pictorial plate, probably Nampeyo, with perforated projection for suspension at the top, 10in (25cm) diam.
$7,500-10,500

l. A Zuni polychrome jar, with indented base and short tapering neck, 14in (36cm) diam.
$9,000-12,000

...narble torso of a deity, ...eco-Roman, circa 1st ...ntury A.D., 8½in (21cm) ...h.
...,500-15,000

A Roman marble head of Apollo, 2nd Century A.D. after a Greek original of the early 4th Century B.C., 11in (28cm) high.
$216,000-231,000

A marble figure of a satyr, circa 1st Century A.D., after a Hellenistic sculpture of the 3rd Century B.C., his short tail fragmentary, 16in (41cm) high.
$36,000-42,000

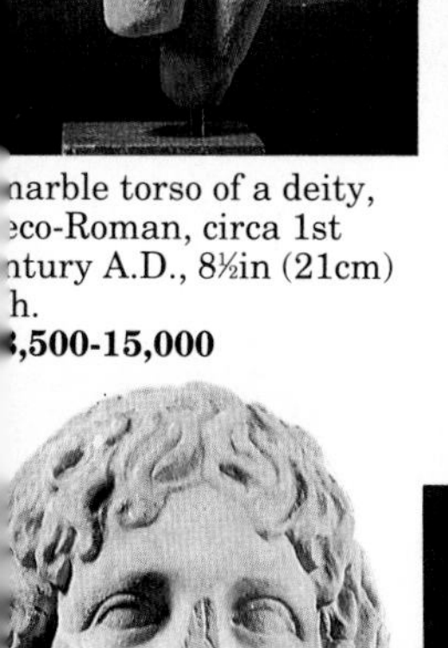

...Greco-Roman marble ...ad of a young man, ...aired, mounted, 2nd- ... Century B.C., 12in ...cm) high.
...4,250-16,500

A Roman marble funerary stela, with inscription, 1st Century A.D., 34in (86cm) high.
$37,000-39,000

A late Hellenistic or early Roman marble head of a goddess, 2nd Century B.C./1st Century A.D., 7in (18cm).
$5,250-7,500

A Greco-Egyptian marble head of a Ptolemaic queen, early 3rd Century B.C., 6in (15cm).
$10,500-15,000

A Cycladic marble hanging jar or kandila, with inward tapering collar and flaring pedestal foot, minor chips, Bronze Age, circa 3000-2800 B.C., 10in (25cm) high. **$15,000-18,000**

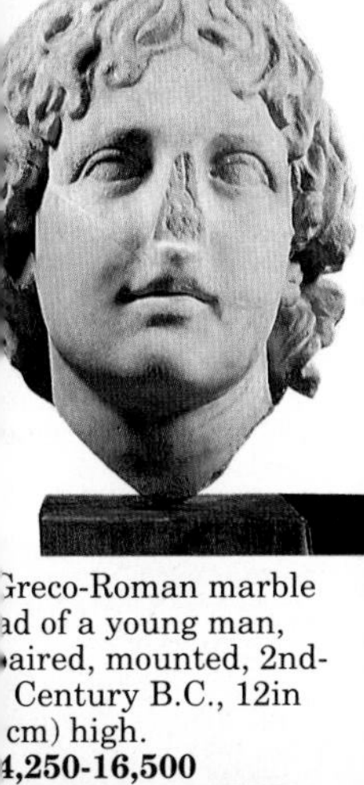

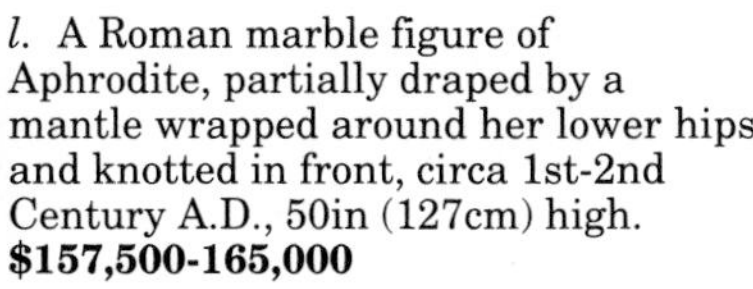

l. A Roman marble figure of Aphrodite, partially draped by a mantle wrapped around her lower hips and knotted in front, circa 1st-2nd Century A.D., 50in (127cm) high.
$157,500-165,000

A Roman marble torso of a philosopher, 2nd Century A.D., 18in (46cm) high.
$22,500-24,000

A Roman marble figure of the goddess Hygeia, circa 2nd Century A.D., 22in (56cm).
$15,000-16,500

An Attic red-figure Lekythos, attributed to the Brygos Painter, c480-470 B.C., 14in (35cm). **$9,750-12,750**

An Apulian red-figure pyxis, attributed to the Baltimore Painter, circa 340-320 B.C., 3½in (8.5cm). **$1,000-1,300**

A Lucanian red-figure bell krater, attributed to the Pisticci Painter, cir 430 B.C. **$7,500-9,000**

A Cypriot red polished ware three-bodied jug, early Bronze Age, 22in (56cm). **$5,250-6,750**

A Roman pottery jar, found and made in Cologne, circa 3rd Century A.D. **$1,000-1,200**

A Roman pottery hunting cup, from Cologne, circa 1st-2n Century A.D. **$3,750-4,500**

An Attic red-figure Nolan amphora, attributed to the Phiale Painter, circa 450-425 B.C., 13in (32cm). **$11,250-12,750**

A Roman pottery hunting cup, found and made in Cologne, circa 1st-2nd Century A.D, 5in (12cm). **$6,000-7,500**

A Lucanian red-figure bell krater, with a laurel wreath around the exterior rin by the Anabates Painter, 4th Century B.C., 11in (28cm). **$4,500-6,000**

A Greek/South Italian black glazed hydria, circa mid-4th Century B.C., 13in (32.5cm) **$6,750-7,500**

An Apulian red-figure bell krater, one side with an Arimasp fighting a griffin, the reverse side with restive horse, circa 35(340 B.C., 9½in (24cm). **$6,000-9,000**

Apulian pottery basin, the erior with a quadriga driven by a nged Victory,above a woman's ad between scrolling foliage, 26in cm) diam. **$9,750-11,250**

A Paestan red-figure amphora, attributed to one of the Forerunners of Paestan, circa 350 B.C., 17in (43cm). **$8,250-9,750**

An Assyrian alabaster relief fragment, Kalah, circa 884-859 B.C., 4in (10cm) high. **$37,500-40,500**

quartzite upper part of a abti of Akhenaten, eyes painted, shabti late Dynasty III, circa 1340 B.C., from royal tomb of Akhenaten Tell el-Amarna, 5in (13cm). 3,000-72,000

An Attic black-figure hydria, circa 530 B.C., 14½in (37cm). **$27,000-30,000**

A Paestan pottery oinochoe, 4th-3rd Century B.C., 15in (38cm). **$9,750-12,000**

Attic black-figure amphora, attributed the Swing painter, circa 530-525 B.C., in (38cm) high. **5,000-27,000**

An Apulian red-figure column krater, attributed to the Baltimore painter, circa 340-330 B.C., 25½in (65cm). **$12,000-15,000**

A group of Egyptian glazed faience figures, circa 1196-525 B.C. **$3,000-7,500 each**

A group of seven large turquoise glazed composition amulets, all mounted on wood stand, slight damage, 712-332 B.C., 1 to 2½in (3 to 6.5cm). **$4,000-6,000**

A turquoise figure of Ptaichos, 664-525 B.C., 2⅓in (6cm). **$3,750-4,500**

A green glazed composition figure of t[h]e Baboon of Thoth, circa 6th Century B.C. **$12,750-15,750**

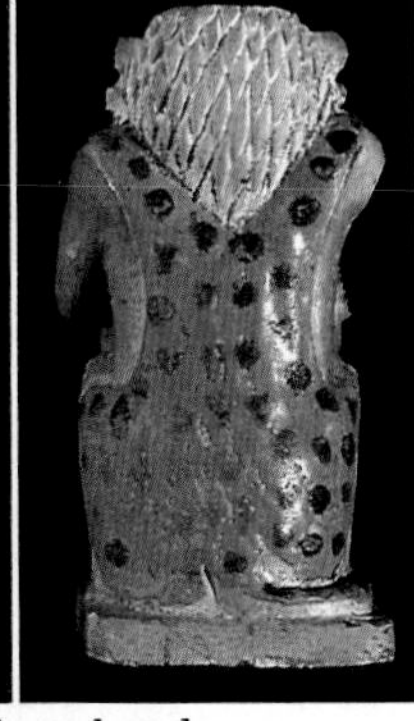

A turquoise and yellow glazed composition Bes jar, slight damage, probably 525-404 B.C., 2⅓in (6cm) high. **$15,000-16,500**

A glazed composition shabti for Tawosret, 1397-1360 B.C. **$25,500-27,000**

A wooden figure, Middle Kingdom, circa 1800 B.C., 5½in (14cm). **$5,250-6,750**

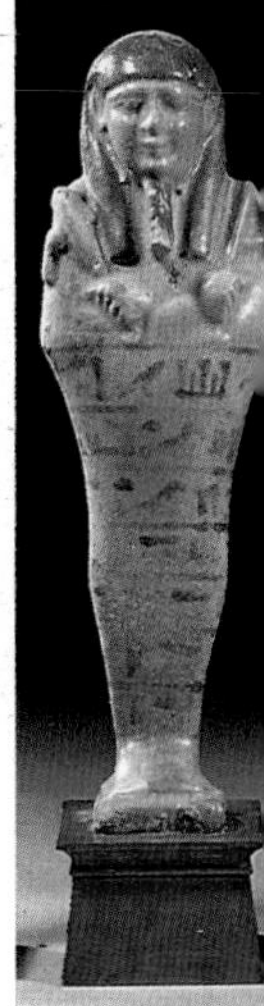

A glazed compositio[n] shabti, 4th Century B.[C.] **$1,500-1,8[..]**

A basalt figure of an official, inscribed, Middle Kingdom, 1786-1650 B.C., 5½in (14cm). **$13,500-18,000**

A shabti of the Imy Khent priest, 4th Century B.C. 7in (17.5cm). **$3,000-3,750**

A figurine of a naked child wearing a collar, 305-30 B.C. **$3,000-4,500**

A shabti, with 10 bands of text, 570-526 B.C. **$2,250-3,000**

A shabti of a priest of Neith, 6th Century B. **$3,750-4,500**

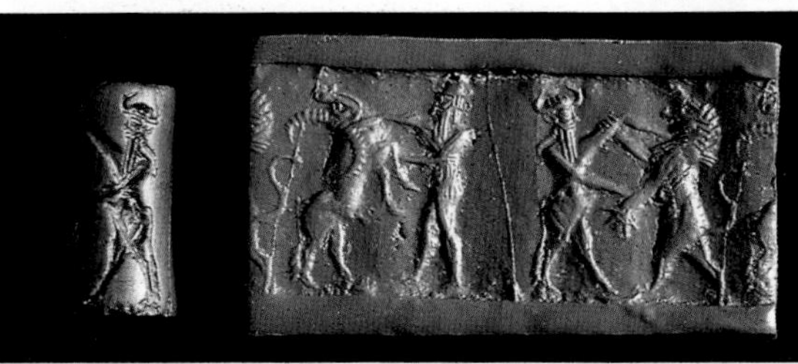

An Akkadian green jasper cylinder seal, showing a contest scene, c2334-2193 B.C., 1⅛in (3cm) high. **$6,000-6,750**

ronze figure of the God
iris, 26th Dynasty, 664-
5 B.C., 16in (41cm)
thout tenon.
6,500-29,000

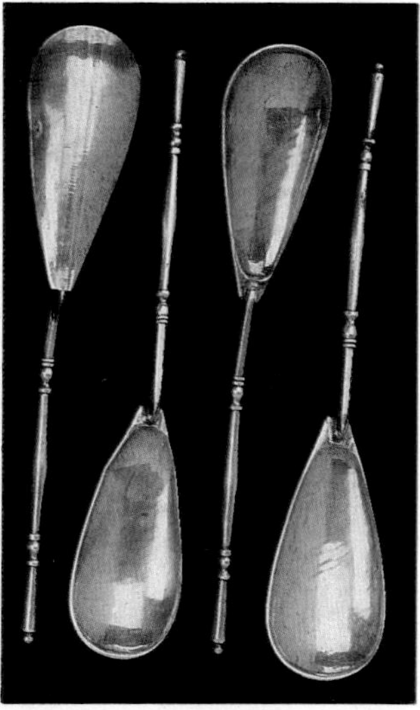

A set of 9 identical late antique silver spoons, Eastern Mediterranean, 7th Century A.D. **$24,000-30,000**

A Hellenistic silver bowl, applied with the head of Medusa, circa 2nd Century B.C., 7in (18cm) diam. **$18,000-22,500**

A Roman bronze chariot fitting, circa 1st Century B.C./1st Century A/D., 5 by 5½in (13 by 14cm). **$23,000-25,000**

ronze figure of a god, Hittite
l Kingdom or earlier, circa
0-1700 B.C., 10½in (26cm) high
h hatchet.
2,500-90,000

A Hellenistic silver figure of Apollo, circa 2nd-1st Century B.C., 8in (20cm). **$144,000-150,000**

A Greek bronze helmet, Magna Graecia, circa 4th Century B.C. **$11,250-14,250**

A Greek silver oinochoe, with
cessed base, everted rim with egg-
d-dart decoration, circa 3rd
arter 4th Century B.C., 9in
3cm). **$67,500-75,000**

A Greek bronze figure of a bull, circa early 5th Century B.C., 4in (10cm). **$18,000-22,500**

A Celtic bronze terret ring, found on common land in Dartford, England in 1991, late 1st/mid-3rd Century A.D., 2½ by 2½in (6 by 6cm).
$28,500-31,500

A bone, wood and bronze dagger, c1750 B.C., 10½in (26.5cm).
$14,250-15,750

A bronze figure of the goddess Neith, traces of inscription, mounted, damaged, Late Peric 712-332 B.C., 9in (22.5cm).
$8,250-9,000

l. A Roman bronze figure of Apollo, circa 3rd Century A.D., 9in (23cm).
$8,250-9,750

A Roman bronze figure of Aphrodite, 2nd-3rd Century A.D., 5½in (14cm).
$6,000-7,500

A bronze figure of Osiris, mounted, Late Period 712-332 B.C., 13½in (34cm).
$9,000-10,500

A Roman bronze figure of dancing lar, mounted, rig hand repaired, 1st Centu A.D., 6in (15cm).
$15,750-18,000

A Celtic bronze figure of a dancing man, mounted, damaged, circa 1st Century B.C., 6in (15cm).
$12,000-15,000

r. A Hellenistic silver bowl, the foot decorated with central rosette, circa 2nd Century B.C., 6½in (16cm). **$6,750-7,500**

ı Etruscan terracotta
ead of a youth, circa
te 5th Century B.C.,
½in (29cm).
,250-6,750

A Coptic textile fragment, Egypt, circa 5th-6th Century A.D., 16 by 12½in (40 by 31.5cm).
$9,000-10,500

A Coptic textile tapestry weave fragment, Egypt, circa 5th Century A.D., 17 by 13½in (43 by 34cm).
$10,500-13,500

n Etruscan terracotta
tive female head, 4th-
d Century B.C., 12in
1cm).
,000-4,500

An Egyptian opaque red glass heart amulet, New Kingdom, 19th Dynasty, Reign of Rameses II, 1279-1213 B.C., 1½in (4cm). **$6,750-7,500**

An Egyptian cartonnage mummy mask, Ptolemaic Period, circa 304-30 B.C., 10½in (27cm).
$7,500-9,000

A Boeotian terracotta figure, repaired, circa 450 B.C., 14in (36cm).
$6,000-7,500

n Etruscan
lychrome painted
rracotta antefix, circa
0 B.C., 7in (18cm).
,750-4,500

A female Boeotian terracotta figure, repaired, circa 400 B.C., 13in (33cm).
$3,000-4,500

A terracotta figure of Aphrodite, 3rd Century B.C., 10in (25cm).
$3,000-3,750

An Egyptian cartonnage mummy mask, Ptolemaic Period, circa 304-30 B.C., 14½in (37cm).
$10,500-12,000

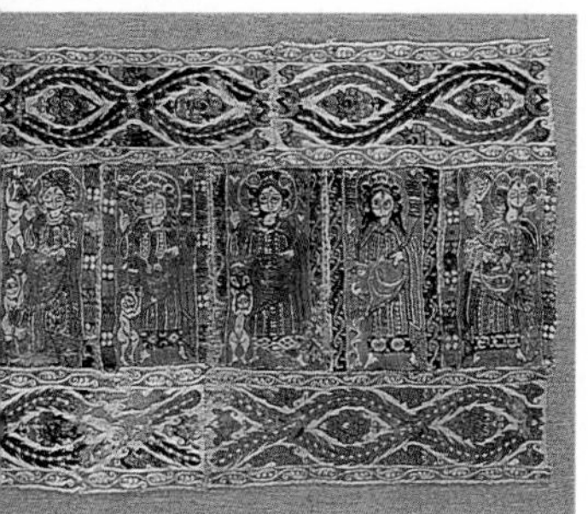

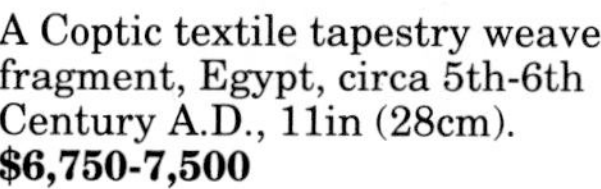

A Coptic textile tapestry weave fragment, Egypt, circa 5th-6th Century A.D., 11in (28cm).
$6,750-7,500

A Boeotian terracotta figure, early 3rd century B.C., 12in (31cm).
$7,500-8,000

A Boeotian terracotta figure of a woman, repaired, circa 330 B.C., 11½in (29cm).
$3,000-4,500

An Egyptian limestone relief fragment, Deir el-Bahri, Rei of Neb-hepet-re Mentuhotep, Middle Kingdom, 11th Dynasty, circa 2049-1998 B.C., 5½ by 7in (14 by 18cm).
$11,250-12,000

A wooden figure of an apis bull, ears pierced for possible attachment, mounted, 6th-4th Century B.C., 3½in (9cm). **$11,250-12,000**

A Roman green mould-blown glass inscribed beaker, circa 1st Century A.D., 3in (7.5cm).
$42,000-45,000

A Boeotian terracotta female protome, circa 420 B.C., 9½in (24.5cn
$6,000-6,750

A Roman iridescent pale blue glass skyphos, 1st-2nd Century A.D., 6in (15.5cm) wide.
$3,750-4,500

A translucent glass cinerary urn and knopped cover, circa 2nd Century A.D., 12½in (32cm) high.
$4,500-6,000

A Roman iridescent gla snake thread sprinkler flask, 3rd-4th Century A.D., 4½in (11.5cm).
$6,000-7,500

A wooden funerary boat with occupants, showing the bust of the deceased under the canopy, Middle Kingdom, 2040-1640 B.C., 23in (58cm) long.
$8,250-9,000

Roman Imperial porphyry bath support, with concave resting ırface on top, each end carved in bold relief with lion's heads merging from foliage and supported on lion's paws, one side ırved in shallow relief, the other with a raised blank panel, nd Century A.D., 58½in (148cm). **$217,000-247,500**

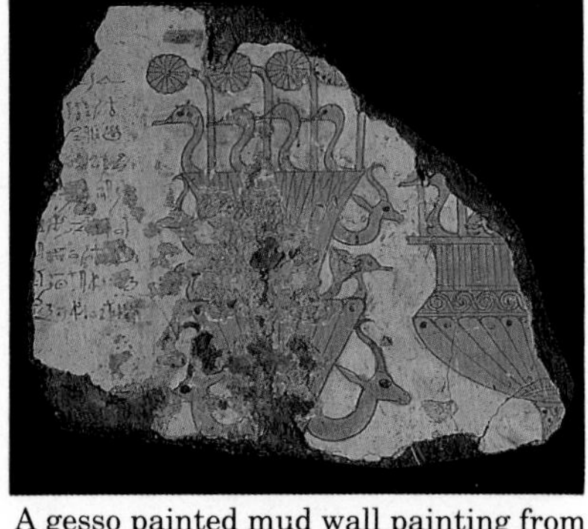

A gesso painted mud wall painting from the tomb of Sebekhotep, from Thebes, circa 1410 B.C., 13in (33cm) high. **$23,000-26,000**

n Attic white-ground Lekythos agment, near the Thanatos ainter, decorated with an rmed warrior, circa 440 B.C., in (18cm). **$31,500-34,500**

A Picenian red sandstone torso of a warrior, Abruzzo, circa mid-6th Century B.C., 22in (55cm). **$232,500-240,000**

A gesso painted mud wall painting from the tomb of Sebekhotep, from Thebes, circa 1410 B.C., 13in (33cm) high. **$37,000-38,000**

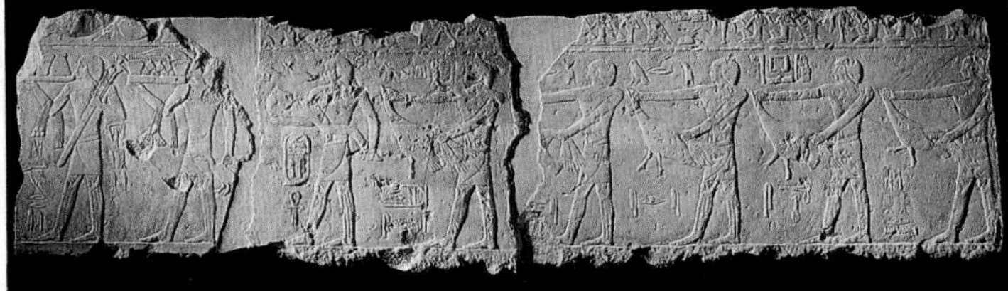

An Egyptian limestone relief fragment, from the tomb of a high official, from (?) Saqqara, Old Kingdom, circa 2355-2325 B.C., 77in (195cm). **$46,500-50,000**

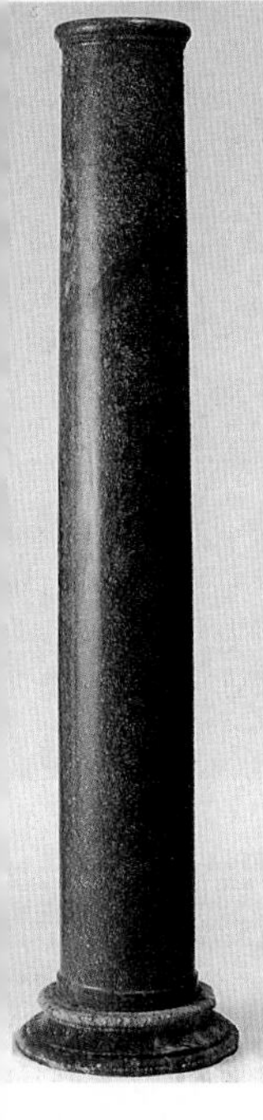

A painted limestone bas-relief fragment, depicting a procession of offering bearers, probably from Saqqara, 2465-2150 B.C., 15in (38cm). **$12,000-13,500**

Two Roman Imperial porphyry columns, each slightly cylindrical with contoured base and torus moulding at the top, circa 2nd Century A.D., 89 and 87in (226 and 220cm). **$255,000-262,500**

r. The upper part from the lid of an Egyptian anthropoid wood sarcophagus, Late Period, circa 712-30 B.C., 22in (56cm). **$37,500-39,000**

A Jimini wood face mask, with projecting mouth, and a pair of horns, 11½in (30cm).
$6,750-7,500

A British West African cock mask, with carved teeth, 30in (76cm). **$6,750-7,500**

A wood mask called 'Lapun', from Yasa Village, Manam Island, 10in (26cm). **$1,800-2,500**

Four miniature Dan masks, 2 with large almond shaped eyes, the other 2 with worn features, 4 to 4½in (10 to 11.5cm).
$1,000-1,200

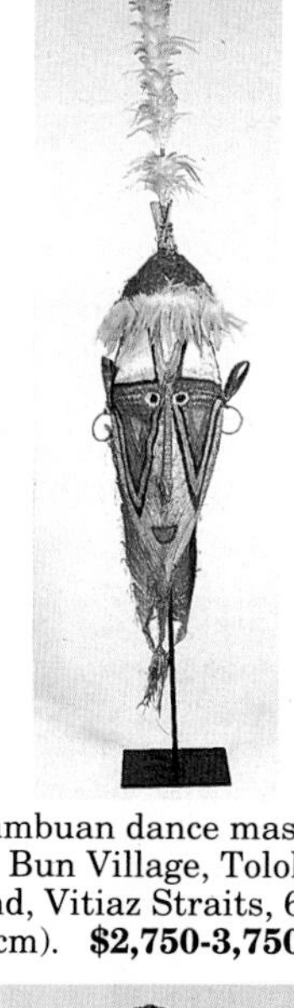

A Tumbuan dance mask, from Bun Village, Tolokiwa Island, Vitiaz Straits, 63in (160cm). **$2,750-3,750**

A cane mask covered by tapa fibres, possibly from Orokolo Bay, Papuan Gulf, Elema People, 21in (54cm).
$1,800-2,500

A basketry helmet mask, from the Abelam People, Wosera Area, 15in (38cm). **$600-900**

A basketry mask with green sea snail shell, from Yangoru People, Menbauru Village, 11½in (29cm).
$450-600

Four miniature Dan masks, one with ornate coiffure above slit eyes, one with smooth coiffure, two with weathered features, 3in (8.5cm). **$1,000-1,100**

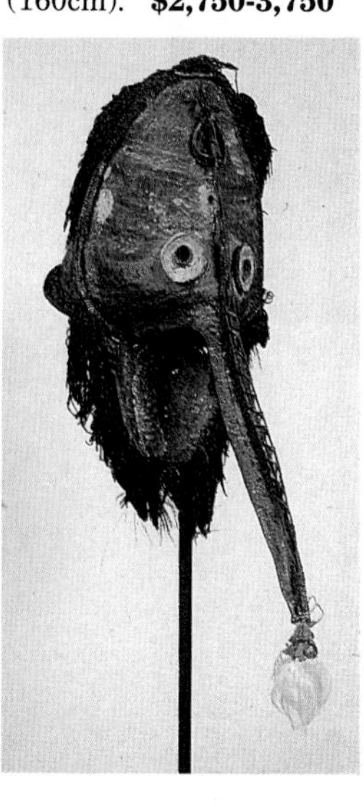

l. A Tumbuan dance mask, from Kraimbit Village, Blackwater River, decorated with human hair, and a boar's tusk, 45in (114cm).
$2,000-2,250

n Oceanic Manam
slands mask, 25in
34cm).
4,500-6,000

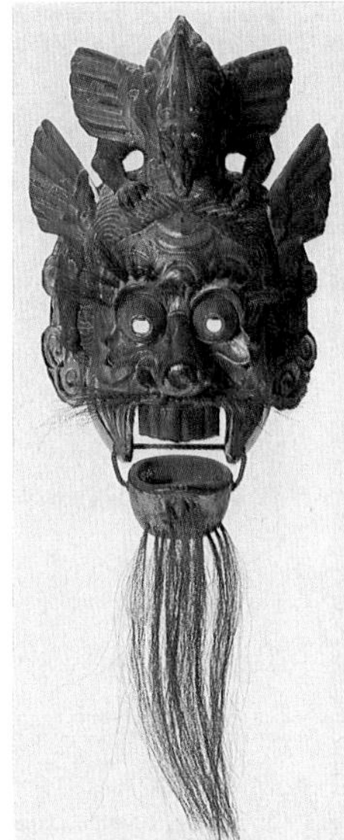

An Oriental lacquered wood Bugaku mask of Ryo-O, Edo period, slight damage, signed, 15in (39cm).
$7,500-9,000

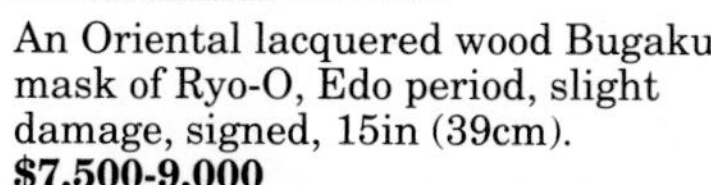

An Izi elephant mask, ogbodo enyi, for the most senior of the 4 male grades, north eastern Ibo, 23in (58cm).
$12,000-15,000

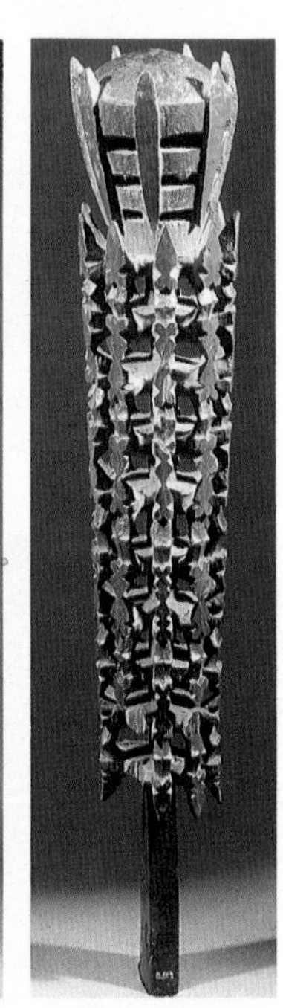

An African Nalu mask, banda or kumbaduba, 71in (180cm).
$3,750-4,500

A Mitiaro staff god, toa wood, c1800.
$99,750-105,000

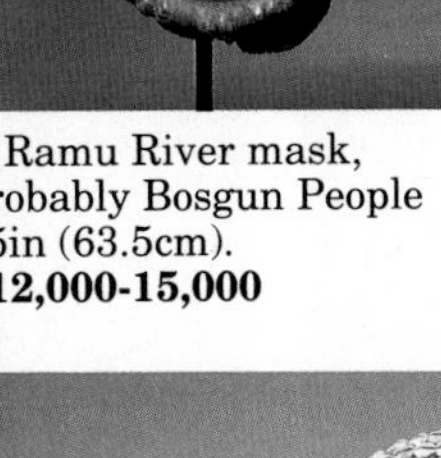

Ramu River mask,
robably Bosgun People
5in (63.5cm).
12,000-15,000

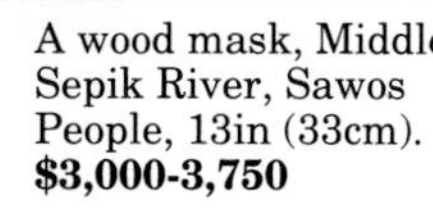

A wood mask, Middle Sepik River, Sawos People, 13in (33cm).
$3,000-3,750

A Dan mask, from Ivory Coast, 13½in (34.5cm) from chin.
$21,000-22,500

A Cameroon grasslands helmet mask, slight damage, 26½in (67in).
$46,500-52,500

A Songe male figure, on a circular base, 22in (56cm).
$9,750-10,500

A Baga bird, with 3 small birds carved on its back, on a single support, 18in (45cm).
$15,000-15,500

A Lower Sepik River figure, inscribed, 12½in (32cm).
$12,750-13,500

A Hornbill figure from East Sepik Province, 7½in (19cm).
$400-450

A female figure from Asimpa Village, Okapa Sub-district, Eastern Highlands, 31½in (80cm) high.
$5,250-6,000

An Akan terracotta female figure, with an elongated ringed neck, 14½in (36.5cm).
$4,500-5,250

A figure of a pig, from the Trobriand Islands, with cylindrical body, flattened head with ears and snout, all-over incised decoration, 21½in (55cm) long.
$1,000-1,200

A figure of a pig, probably from the Trobriand Island, 14in (35cm) long. **$1,350-1,500**

A seated figure from the Massim area, 3½in (9cm) high.
$400-650

A pair of Yoruba male twin figures, ibeji, with strands of beads round their waists and necks, 10in (26cm).
$6,000-7,500

A Yoruba female twin figure, ibeji, 11½in (29cm).
$3,500-3,750

Fijian female figure,
th arms joined at hips,
in (35cm).
5,000-18,000

A Kota brass covered reliquary figure, 21in (54cm) high.
$172,000-180,000

A Senufo male figure, 14in (35cm).
$24,000-27,000

A Kuba figure of a king, ndop, with a parrot carved on the base, 29in (74cm).
$11,250-12,000

Bankoni terracotta
;ure of a hunter, 13th/
th Century, 16in (40cm).
0,500-12,000

A Baule male figure, on an Inagaki base, 17in (43cm).
$11,250-12,000

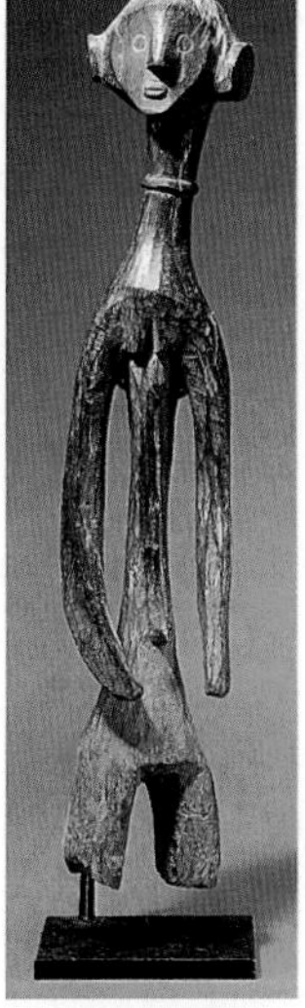

A Mumuye female figure, 33in (84.5cm).
$9,750-11,250

A Baga dance crest, carved as a seated female equestrian figure, with loin cloth and a bag over each shoulder, restored, 34½in (88cm) high.
$31,500-34,000

Maori nephrite Hei
ki, 4in (11cm).
5,500-17,000

A Senufo male figure, 40in (100cm).
$3,000-4,500

l. A Venda female figure, on block like feet, 18in (45cm).
$7,500-9,000

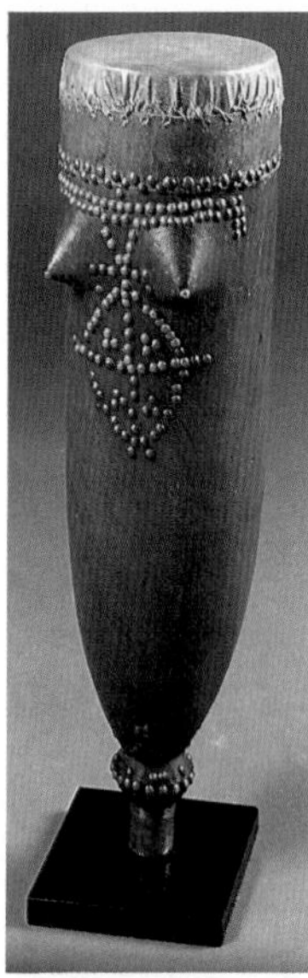

An Angolan Tshokwe drum, formed from an old metal fitting, 29in (74cm) high.
$18,000-21,000

A Yoruba drum, perhaps from Ijebu-Igbo, Ijebu area, 14½in (37cm).
$17,000-19,000

A Benin ivory box, with a frieze of human figures, 3⅜in (8.5cm) high.
$7,500-9,000

A collection of African baskets, including Rotse round and rectangular baskets, a Kuba box, and a Rwanda container.
$5,250-6,000

Two Santa Cruz Island neckrests, both carved in the shape of a bird, one with exaggerated angular body with label on base, 15in (38cm) and 17½in (45cm) long.
$2,250-3,750

A Sulka shield, with incised stylised masks, 47½in (120cm).
$6,000-7,500

A Luba Shankadi neckrest, composed of female caryatid figure, 7in (17.5cm).
$15,500-17,000

A finger drum, Milne Bay Province, Trobriand Islands, one end with raised concentric circles, the other with 2 pierced ridges for attachment, 13in (33cm). **$1,000-1,200**

A Maori feather box, wakahuia, the container with a tiki head rising from a long tapering neck at each end, 21¼in (54in) long.
$24,000-25,500

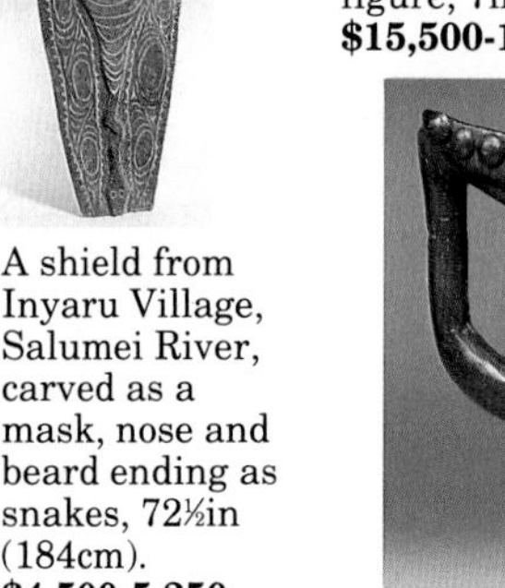

A shield from Inyaru Village, Salumei River, carved as a mask, nose and beard ending as snakes, 72½in (184cm).
$4,500-5,250

l. A Luba wood neckrest, a carved seated female figure on a circular base, 6⅛in (15.5cm).
$6,750-7,500

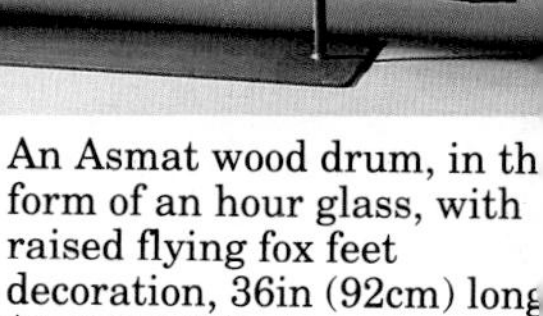

An Asmat wood drum, in the form of an hour glass, with raised flying fox feet decoration, 36in (92cm) long.
$1,500-2,250

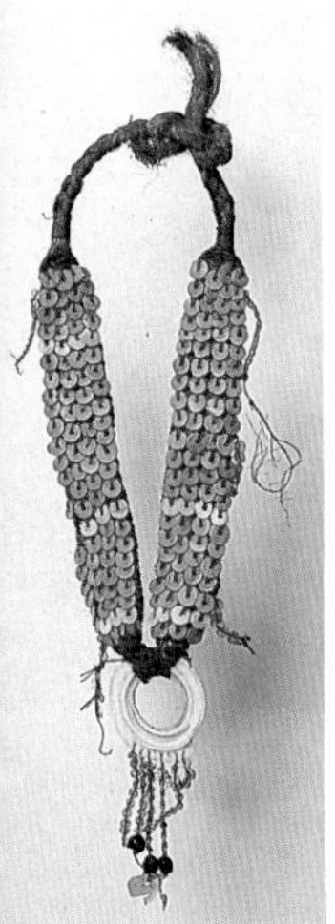
A necklace, from Panaete Island, Deboyne Islands, 21½in (55cm).
$750-1,200

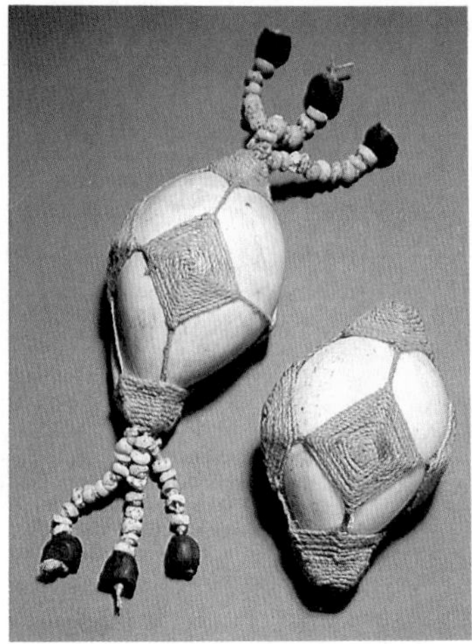
A pair of cowrie shell wristlets, Northern Province, Cape Nelson, Ako Village, 3 and 3½in (8 and 9cm). **$300-375**

A comb from Louisade Island, 8in (20cm).
$4,500-6,000

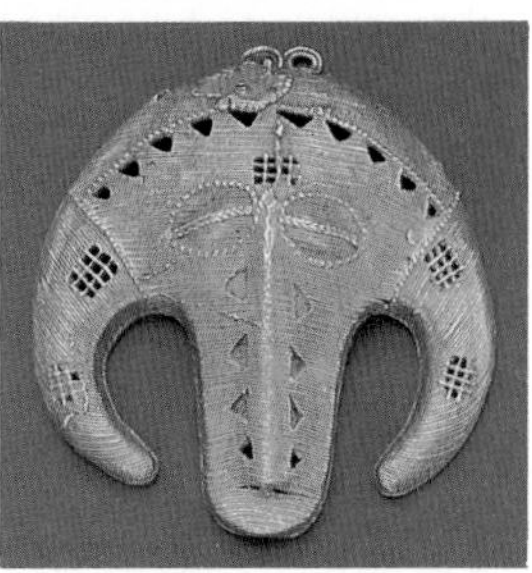
An Ashanti gold pendant, cast in the form of a ram's head, 3½in (8.5cm) diam.
$2,250-3,750

A fibre costume, Asmat people, 41½in (105cm).
$3,000-4,500

A New Ireland ceremonial dance headdress, inscribed, 26in (66cm).
$4,500-6,000

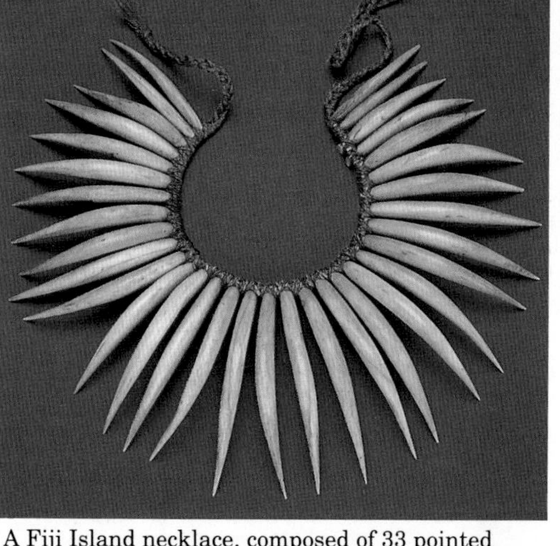
A Fiji Island necklace, composed of 33 pointed sperm whale teeth pendants, threaded on a braided sennit band, naturally aged patina, inscription on the teeth reading 'M.C. 5491, Umlauff', 24in (61cm) long.
$7,500-9,000

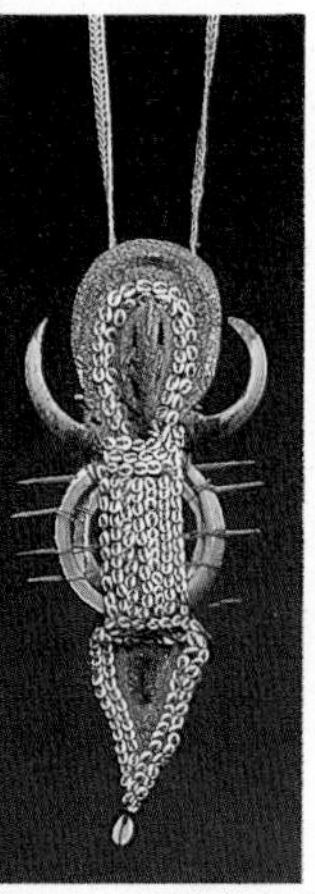
A fibre pendant, Abelam People, 12½in (32cm).
$1,000-1,500

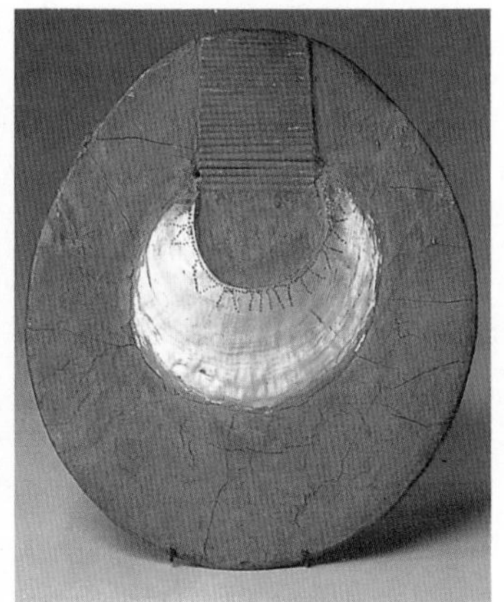
A Kina shell wealth pendant, Mount Hagan area, the oval shape board inset with an incised kina shell, deep red patina, 16in (40cm) high.
$2,000-2,500

A turtle shell arm band, Siassi style, 6in (15cm).
$750-900

r. A Bambara male antelope headdress, 33in (84cm).
$4,500-6,000

A canoe prow, Irian Jaya, North Coast, Tabala Nusu Village, the rectangular shaft terminated by a bird, supported by a wood bridge, 14½in (37cm). **$1,000-1,350**

A canoe paddle terminal, from Lower Sepik River, Porapora River, 10in (25cm). **$600-900**

A canoe prow, from Gawa Island, Marshall Bennett Islands Group, decorated with typical bird motif, remains of white and red pigment weathered patina, 71½in (182cm) long.
$6,000-9,000

A Sepik hook, stone carved, encrusted black patina, 29½in (75cm).
$15,000-18,000

A canoe prow decoration, Woodlark Island, Yanaba Island, 23in (59cm).
$2,000-2,250

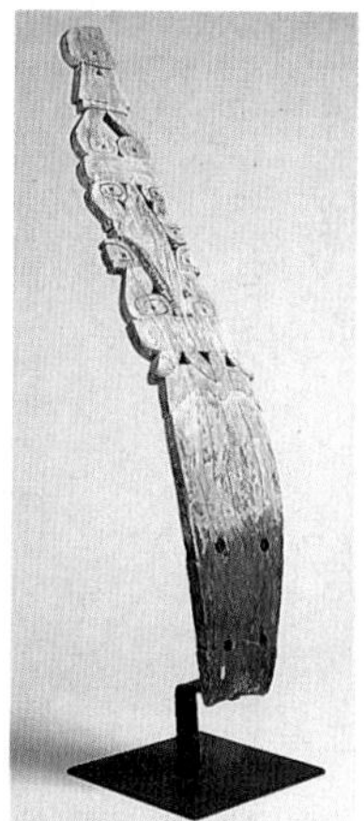

A canoe prow, from Rivo Village, Astrolabe Bay.
$1,500-1,800

A suspension hook, from southern Sepik River tributary, 34in (86cm).
$7,500-9,000

A canoe bailer, from Wotam Village, coastal Sepik River region, 18in (46cm) long.
$1,000-1,350

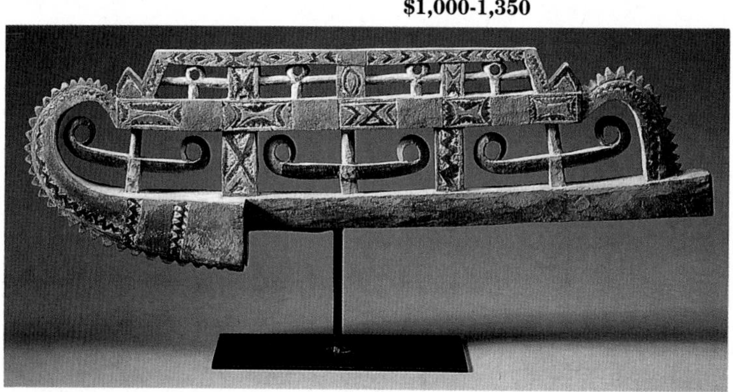

A canoe prow ornament, from Apan Village, Ponam Island, possibly made by Pan-Ou Sangul who died in 1960, 33½in (85cm). **$3,750-4,500**

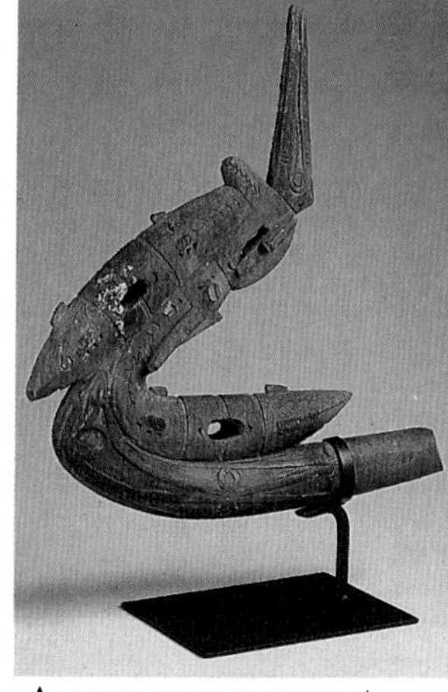

A canoe prow ornament, from WarapuVillage, Sissano Lagoon, 15in (38cm) long.
$1,500-1,800

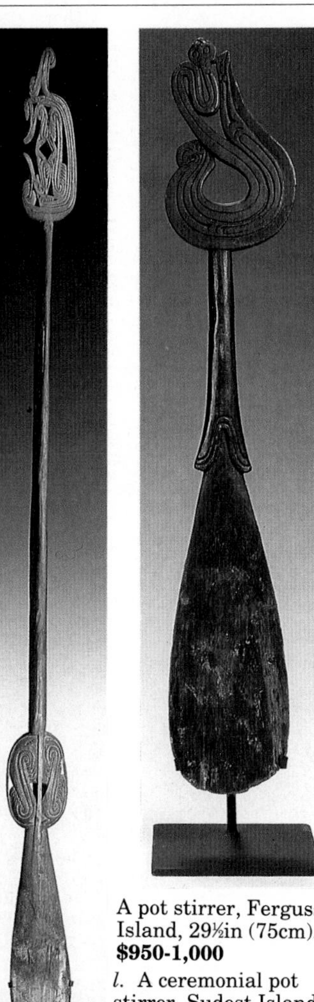

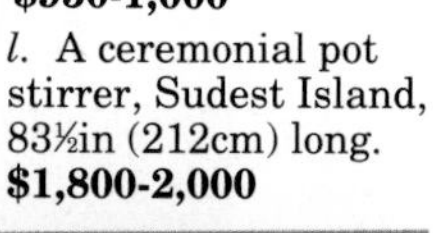

A pot stirrer, Fergusson Island, 29½in (75cm). **$950-1,000**

l. A ceremonial pot stirrer, Sudest Island, 83½in (212cm) long. **$1,800-2,000**

A Betel Nut mortar, from Kwaio people, Sinalangu Harbour, West Kwaio, Central Malaita, 10in (25.5cm). **$950-1,000**

A Huon Gulf canoe-shape feasting bowl, from Gilinit Village, Itni River, 44½in (113cm). **$3,000 3,750**

A wood bowl, from Vitiaz Straits, with boar's tusk, reptile and bird's head motifs, 11in (28cm). **$650-750**

A Huon Gulf bowl, from the Arawe people, Kandrian Area, 17in (44cm). **$750-900**

wood bowl, from the Boiken eople, showing carved reptilian gure, 2 lugs at each side, 18in 46cm) long. **$750-900**

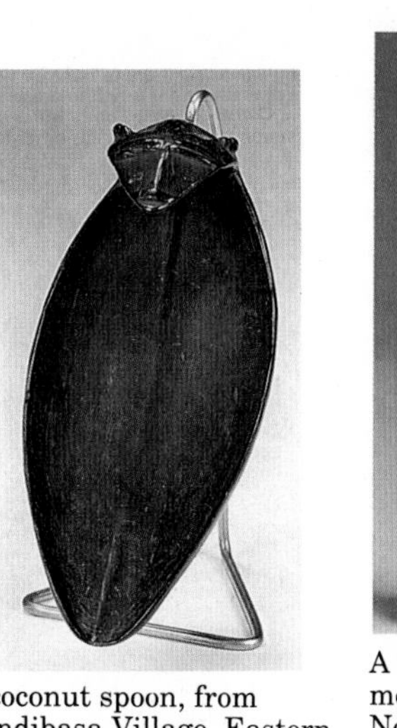

A coconut spoon, from Pundibasa Village, Eastern Highlands Province, 6in (15cm). **$3,750-4,500**

A betel nut mortar, from North Malaita Region, 8in (21cm) high. **$1,200-1,500**

A lime spatula, from the Tawala people, Ununu Village, Milne Bay, 18in (45cm) long. **$900-1,200**

food bowl, from Kadovar Island, the cup ending with 2 figures with hands esting on their knees, and 2 figures on the outside, 30in (77cm). **1,400-1,800**

A Huon Gulf men's house gable hanger, Dampier Straits, 11in (28cm).
$1,800-2,250

A spear launcher, Middle Sepik River, with cylindrical shaft with central flattened appendage, carved end, incised decoration, 43in (110cm).
$950-1,000

A stool, from Saparu Village, Yuat River, supporting a male and female figure, all-over red paint, 15in (38in).
$2,250-3,000

A stool, from Krinjambi Village, Lower Sepik River, the base supporting a bent figure, curved back supporting the stool, 17in (44cm). **$1,500-2,250**

A wood stool ,from Boitalu Village, Kiriwina Island, Trobriand Islands, 22in (56cm) high.
$2,500-3,000

An axe handle, from the Dani People, Highlands, Balim Valley, the large rounded end with an inset sharpened wedge shaped stone blade, 30in (76cm) long.
$1,800-2,250

A wood taro mortar, from Tuam Island, Dampier Straits, with dark brown patina, 14½in (37cm) long.
$1,200-1,500

A Dogon ceremonial stool, dense weathered wood, aged patina with natural erosion, 15in (38cm) high.
$1,800-2,750

A pounder, Sharcoal Village, Kairiru Island, 34½in (87.5cm) high.
$1,200-1,500

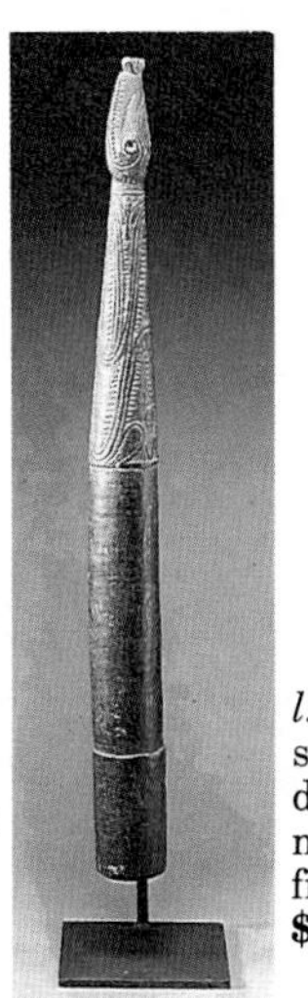

l. A Garamut slit gong stick, Upper Sepik River, decorated with stylised masks and a reptilian head figure, 28½in (72cm) long.
$750-1,500

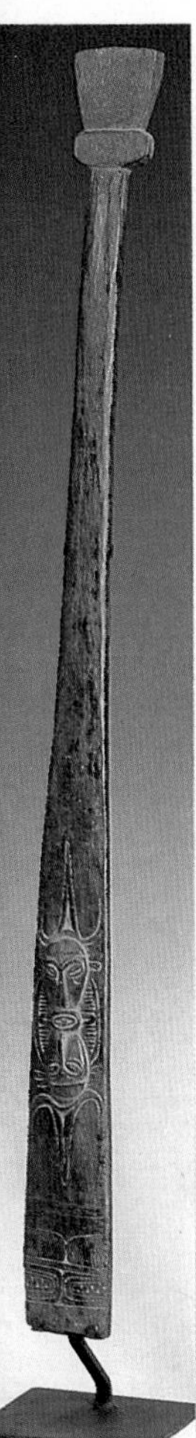

Tumbuan
nce club, from
lengi Village,
in (105cm)
ng.
,250-3,000

A Mitshogo iron bell, surmounted by a wooden handle, with the neck of a female head, 16in (41cm) high.
$9,000-10,500

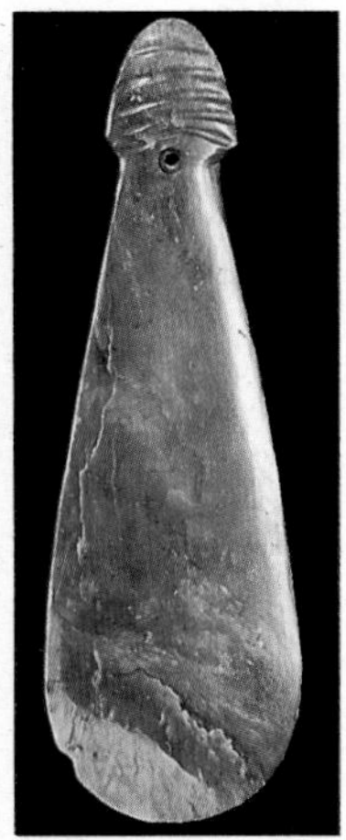

A Maori jade club, patu, 11½in (29cm) long.
$3,750-5,250

A coconut shell container, from Marshall Lagoon, Central Province, the lid linked to the bowl with strings, 4in (11cm) high.
$600-900

A Kongo ivory hunting horn, with almond shaped mouthpiece, 15½in (39.5cm).
$5,500-6,500

A skirt making board, from Trobriand Islands, 27in (68cm) long.
$750-900

A betel nut mortar, from Kadovar Island, with oval base supporting 2 seated figures, 5in (13cm) high.
$2,500-3,000

A fish net float, from the Arawe People, 24in (61cm).
$300-375

A pair of charms, from the Papuan Gulf, carved from 2 dwarf coconut shells, 4 and 3in (10 and 8cm) long.
$1,200-1,500

fish net float,
om Dabali
illage, Rogeia
land, with a
otif of a
ocodile eating
bird, 14in
5cm) high.
150-250

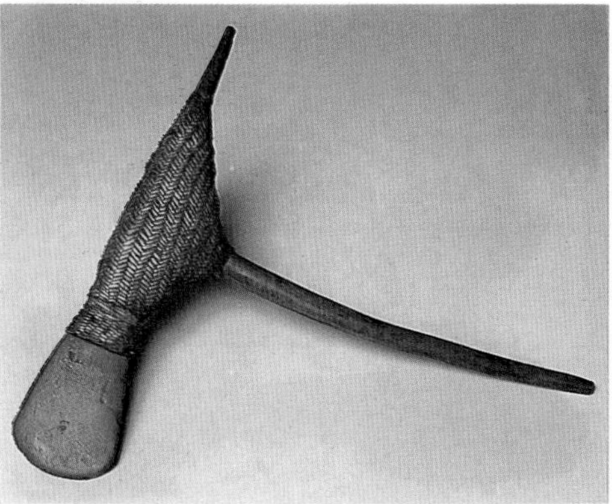

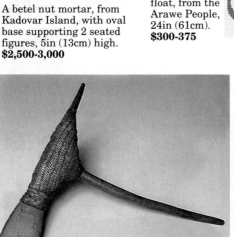

An adze, from Western Highlands Province, the handle ending with a tightly woven cane attachment holding a stone blade, 20½in (52cm). **$600-900**

A lime gourd, from Trobriand Islands, the calabash container with a cowrie shell attachment, 11in (28cm).
$600-750

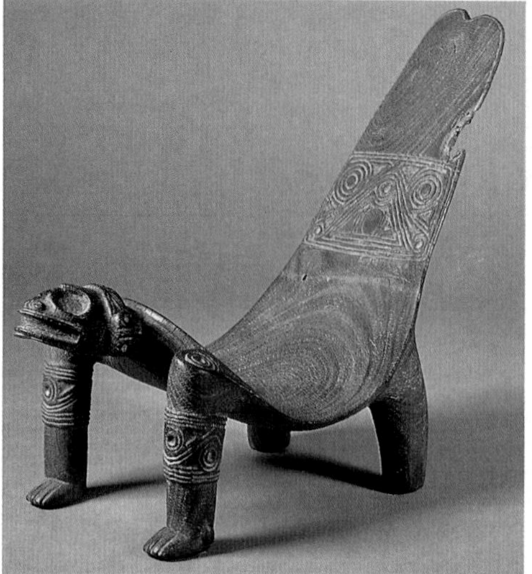

An Arawak Duho, in the form of a mythological creature, with incised scrolled adornment, 1100-1400 A.D., 16in (41cm).
$9,750-11,250

A Maori ceremonial panel, 74in (188cm).
$6,750-7,500

A pair of Maori house panels, Ba of Plenty Region, both with a standing Tiki figure, c1870, 54½i (138cm). **$9,750-12,750**

An Owo rectangular seat, on 4 legs with central strut, elaborately carved, glossy patina, 25½in (65cm) wide.
$6,750-7,500

A Raratonga Island staff god section, carved with 4 groups (miniature figures, dark brown patina, 35in (89cm).
$165,000-168,000

A house post, Sawos People, Pangambit Village, 73in (185cm).
$3,750-4,500

A Marquesan Club, U'u, th head with miniature mask the base of shaft slightly flared, 54in (137cm).
$37,500-45,000

A Songye prestige stool, the support carved as a female figure, some native metal repairs, 23in (59cm) high.
$202,000-210,000

nuff & Cigarette oxes

ivory and silver snuff box, rved and decorated with gold qué scrolls and rope-twist rework, stylised flowers and rquoise and coral jewelled coration, plain silver sides with drooned borders, 18thC, 4 by in (10 by 9cm).
50-600

Continental silver gilt cigarette se, one side engine turned, the enamelled with a wooded verside scene, import marks for ondon 1930, 3in (8cm).
00-375

George IV gilt lined snuff box, ith reeded concave sides, the se engine turned within a cast liate border, the lid applied with plaque cast with a scene of bbotsford House surrounded by double foliate border, Thomas haw, Birmingham 1822, 3in cm).
450-600

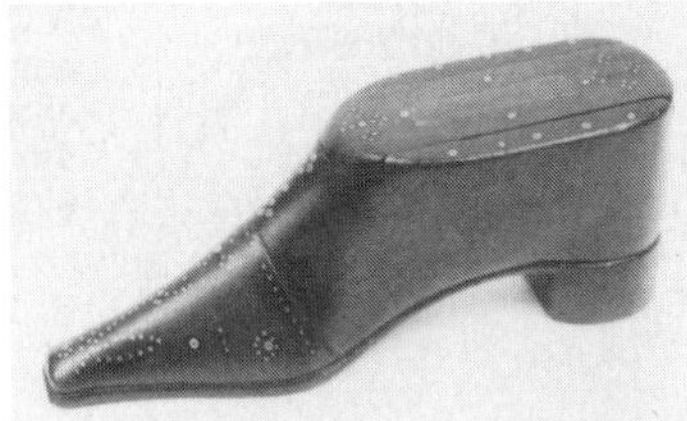

A studded shoe snuff box, c1860, 5½in (14cm).
$375-450

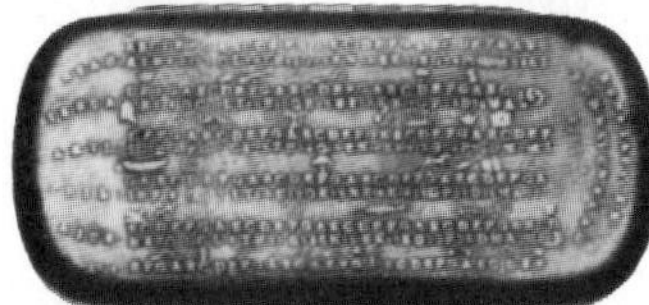

A brass calendar tobacco box, raised with inscription 'Runstafwen Forswewskad 1787 4/1', both sides with calendar scales and signs of the zodiac, 5in (13cm) long.
$135-150

A brass calendar tobacco box, with worn raised inscription, 5in (13cm) long.
$40-60

A Russian gilt line cigarette case, the back profusely shaded polychrome cloisonné enamelled with flowers and scrollwork, the front enamelled with a duck shooting scene within a floral and scrollwork border, 4in (10cm).
$1,200-1,800

A gold mounted pressed tortoiseshell snuff box, the cover pressed with a cartouche of a gentleman serving a glass of wine to a lady, the rest decorated with foliage, the sides and base with flaming torches, scrolled gold thumbpiece, early 19thC, 3½in (9cm).
$450-600

A Scottish penwork snuff box, formed from a knurled and spurred piece of wood, the sides decorated with thistles, the lid with a dancing woman and skeleton beyond, inscribed, early 19thC, 4in (10cm).
$1,500-2,250

A papier mâché snuff box, black lacquered with humorous engraved hand painted design applied to the lid, probably French, c1865, 3½in (9cm).
$600-750

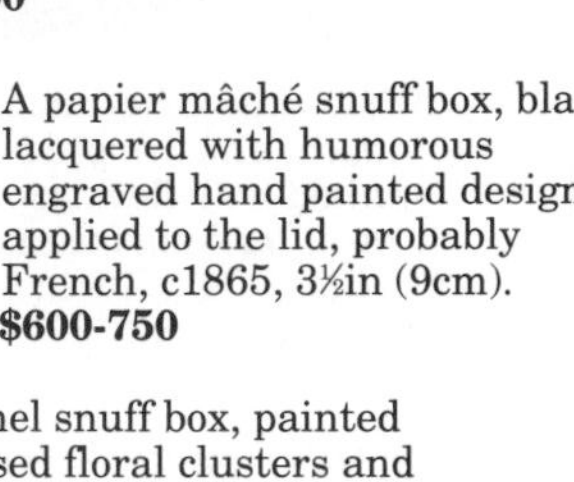

An enamel snuff box, painted with raised floral clusters and scrolls on a green linen ground, 19thC, 2½in (6cm).
$225-255

An Austro-Hungarian snuff box, with cut corners, the sides and base enamelled in blue, the lid enamelled with a scene of dancing couples within an engraved floral and scrollwork border, 3½in (9cm).
$450-600

A Queen Anne tobacco box, the lid engraved with an extensive coat-of-arms, Edward Cornock, c1707, 4in (10cm).
$750-1,200

Stationery Boxes

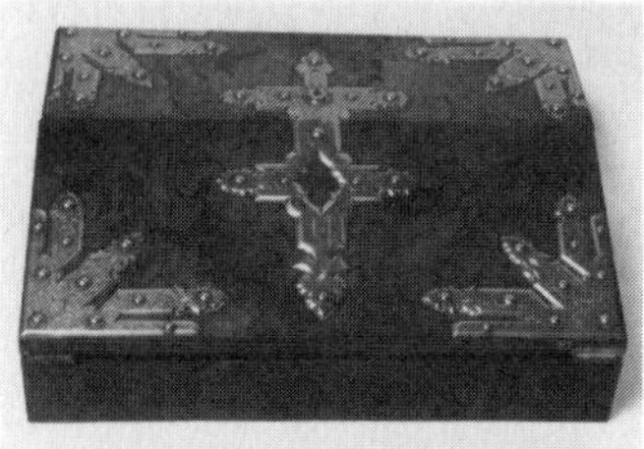

A brass on walnut writing slope, c1870.
$600-750

A papier mâché stationery box, with writing slope, c1880, 14½ by 11½in.
$750-900

A coromandel writing box, with oak fitted interior and sliding action ink tray, brass fittings, Santiago Lopex, c1880, 16 by 11 (41 by 28cm).
$750-1,200

Tea Caddies

A Regency rosewood tea caddy, the lift-up top opening to reveal a well fitted interior, the right hand canister when removed revealing a trade label 'T. Dalton, Dressing Case, Fancy Cabinet Manufacturer and general dealer in fancy articles, Wholesale and Retail, Great Ormond Street Queens Square, London', 13½in (34cm) wide.
$375-450

A George III sycamore and marquetry tea caddy, the top inlaid with a fan patera, the front with a rose spray, 6½in (16.5cm) wide.
$600-750

A Georgian green tortoiseshell t[ea] caddy, the segmented dome top opening to reveal 2 green tortoiseshell lidded compartments, the tapering bod[y] raised upon plated ball feet, 7in (18in).
$2,250-3,000

A George III sycamore and marquetry tea caddy, the front inlaid with floral sprays and roses, lacking interior, 6in (15cm) wide.
$375-525

A tortoiseshell veneered bowfront tea caddy, on ball feet, c1800, 4½in (11cm) wide.
$750-900

A papier mâché tea caddy, decorated with scrolled flowers, mother-of-pearl inlay, hinged lid of ogee outline, with a border of inlaid mother-of-pearl with scen[ic] design of lake and distant house supported on ball feet, divided interior with lids, 19thC, 9in (23cm).
$450-600

Georgian satinwood and lipwood crossbanded tea caddy, th dyed boxwood shell paterae coration and silvered brass loop ndle, 7½in (19cm) wide.
50-900

George III satinwood and ebony ing inlaid sarcophagus shaped a caddy, with green velvet lined terior, brass lion's mask ndles and brass paw supports, ½in (31.5cm).
50-600

A George III tea caddy, painted in Etruscan style, with a continuous band of figures, bead and key borders and the lid with anthemion on a green ground, the interior with 2 lidded divisions, 8in (20cm) wide.
$750-1,200

A George III tortoiseshell and ivory tea caddy, with oval silver escutcheon to the front, lacking interior, 6in (16cm) wide.
$1,050-1,350

A Tunbridge ware tea caddy, with rosewood parquetry and other woods, with stepped lid, enclosing 2 similarly worked compartment covers.
$450-600

A tortoiseshell tea caddy, with 2 lidded divisions, 19thC, 7in (17cm).
$450-600

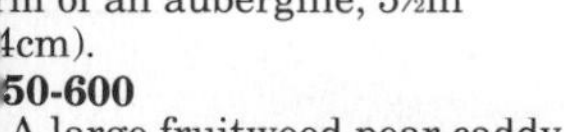

A hardwood tea caddy, in the rm of an aubergine, 5½in 4cm).
50-600

A large fruitwood pear caddy, le with crack and stalk missing, thC, 6½in (16cm).
,050-1,350

A George III mahogany neered tea caddy, inlaid tinwood and floral marquetry th canted corners, 4½in (11cm).
75-525

A rosewood tea caddy, with original glass jars and mixing bowl, c1820, 12in (31cm) wide.
$1,500-2,250

Miller's is a price GUIDE not a price LIST

tortoiseshell tea caddy, with goda top, c1820, 8in (20cm) gh.
50-1,200

A tortoiseshell and ivory inlaid tea caddy with mother-of-pearl floral decoration, hinged lid revealing 2 fitted compartments, on bun feet, 19thC, 6in (16cm) wide.
$1,500-2,250

A melon shaped tea caddy, with gilt and lacquer decoration, original pewter liner and lid, c1840, 5½in (14cm).
$750-900

A tortoiseshell tea caddy, c1810.
$750-1,200

A George III mahogany tea caddy, 7in (18cm) wide.

$135-150

A red lacquer tea caddy wit pewter liners and lids, c183
$750-900

A red lacquer tea caddy, c1840, 5in (13cm) wide.
$450-600

An inlaid tea caddy, c1790.
$600-750

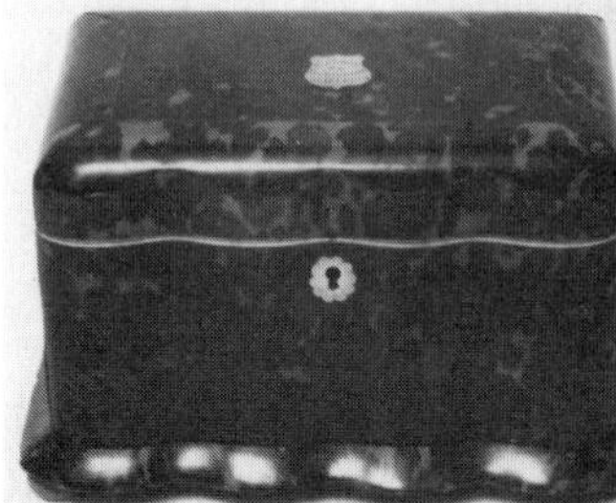

A tortoiseshell tea caddy, 18? 5in (13cm).
$750-1,200

An inlaid harewood tea caddy, late 18thC, 5½in (14cm).
$900-1,500

A mahogany hexagonal shaped tea caddy, 4½in (11cm).
$375-525

A George I walnut tea cadd
$600-750

Miscellaneous

An American painted and decorated pine utility box, all in muted tones of yellow and brown within sponge decorated, gilded and ebonized borders, the interior of the lid with theorem painting of a fruit and flower filled basket in colours, 19thC, 13in (33cm) wide.
$2,250-3,000

A French carved walnut candle box, the rising panel with a fish trophy, 19thC, 14½in (36cm) high.
$900-1,500

A Spanish Moorish oak casket, overlaid with iron pierced with scroll designs, the coffered hing top with an iron loop handle, locks to the top and the base, th interior with a double compartment to one side, 17thC 10½in (26.5cm) wide, excluding handle.
$1,200-1,800

ı Indian ivory inlaid rosewood ble cabinet, the sloping flap .th a floral spray and a border of terlaced foliage, enclosing a ırt fitted interior, the sides with rrying handles, 18thC, 23in 9cm) wide.
ı,200-1,800

A painted and decorated pine bride's ribbon box, probably Continental, late 18th/early 19thC, 19in (48cm) long.
$3,000-4,500

ı Indian ivory mounted horn .sket, applied with ivory bands ›corated with flowers and anches, pierced ivory panels on e sides and cover, lined with darwood and containing a ıantity of carved natural and ained ivory counters, 19thC, ;in (12cm).
ʒ00-750

A stencilled and painted theorem box, with hinged lid opening to a compartmented interior with slide, the top and sides stencilled with fruit filled comports and flowers in silver, white and red on a black ground, American, probably New England, mid-19thC, 10in (25cm) wide.
$2,250-3,000

An Afro-American painted and decorated yellow pine slave's trunk, the hinged lid opening to a divided well, the sides fitted with carrying handles and decorated with geometric motifs and polychrome, 19thC, 24in (61cm) wide.
$1,800-2,700

An enamel box, painted with floral clusters within white cartouches on a royal blue ground, 19thC, 2⅛in (5.5cm) high.
$225-300

A Viennese enamelled box with serpentine front, the 2 compartments with engraved brass rims and decorated panels, painted with scenes of courtship, 3½in (9cm) wide.
$600-750

A Spanish embossed leather casket, the tooled leather cover decorated with birds, beasts and scrolling foliage, mounted with pierced iron hinges and lock, the walnut interior inlaid with grotesques and foliage, late 17th/early 18thC, 14½in (37cm) wide.
$1,200-1,500

Make the Most of Miller's

In Millers we do NOT just reprint saleroom estimates. We work from realised prices, either from an auction room or a dealer. Our consultants then work out a realistic price range for a similar piece. This is to try to avoid repeating freak results - either low or high.

A painted and grained pine trunk, with black painted iron lock and handles, the lid with grain painted initials 'H C.', the whole painted and grained in shades of reddish brown, now mounted on a Chinese style black painted wood stand, probably New England, 19thC, 24in (61cm) wide.
$300-375

A Spanish domed top trunk, covered in leather stamped with scrolling borders and an elaborate medallion, with pierced wrought iron hasp and loop handles, 17thC, 36in (91.5cm) wide.
$3,000-3,750

A burr walnut and brass bound writing box, 19thC, 19½in (50cr
$300-375

A tortoiseshell box, with embossed and pierced silver mounts and escutcheon, Birmingham 1892, 8in (20cm).
$600-750

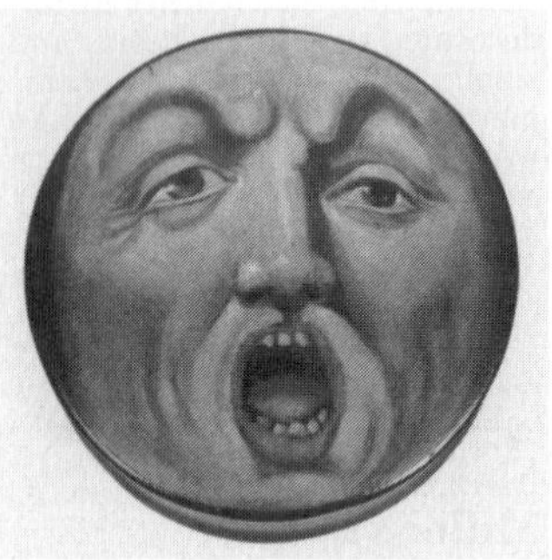

A Georgian papier mâché box with a painting of a face, c1830, 4in (10cm) diam.
$450-600

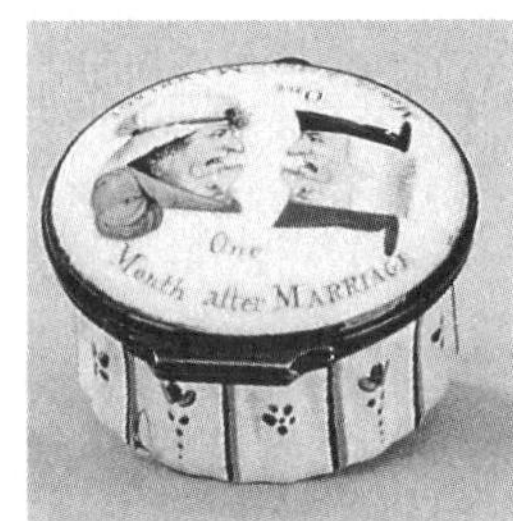

An enamel marriage motto box, the fluted sides painted with flowers, the cover with 2 satisfi faces and the motto 'One Month before Marriage', and when reversed, 2 dissatisfied faces an the motto, 'One Month after Marriage', 2in (5.2cm) diam.
$600-750

A William and Mary oyster veneered walnut lace box, the crossbanded top with inlaid geometrical pattern, 21in (53cm) wide.
$750-1,200

A pine lodging box, scumb decorated in red, 19thC, 35½in (90cm).
$375-450

A Chinese export camphor wood trunk, brass bound, covered in velum and painted with bands of flowers on a green ground and with brass stud decoration, 19thC, 39½in (100cm).
$1,050-1,350

A painted and decorated pine utility box, opening to an interi with a deep well, the top and sides painted with a red, white and yellow lace and floral motif on a sapphire blue ground with the initials 'M.W.', probably Ne England, early 19thC, 12in (31cm) wide.
$2,250-3,000

IUSIC

Iusical Boxes

tortoiseshell singing bird box, e case with compartment at the ck and operating slide at the ont, the gilt brass oval lid graved with leaves and a bird, e fully operating movement th brightly feathered bird with oving wings and beak, late thC, 3½in (9cm), in original ather case.
,500-2,250

Fortissimo Comb musical box, aying 12 airs, accompanied by 9 tional bells with bee strikers, ckel plated cylinder,tune dicator and tune sheet, with ossbanded rosewood veneered se, with inlaid star shaped rtouches to front and lid, by A. Bremond, No. 13547, one oth, 3 tips off treble comb, the linder 30in (76cm) wide.
,000-4,500

Bremond bells in sight cylinder usical box, the 10½in (27cm) linder playing 6 airs, ccompanied by 6 saucer bells ntained in marquetry and alnut veneered case, one tooth comb broken, No. 15639, c1870, 0½in (52cm).
1,500-2,250

A Swiss bells, drum and castanets in sight cylinder musical box, the 13in (33cm) cylinder playing 12 airs, accompanied by 6 bells with butterfly strikers with zither attachment and tune indicator in veneered case with stringing to front and lid, 2 teeth replaced, c1890, 26in (66cm).
$2,700-3,300

A bells in sight musical box, playing 8 airs accompanied by 9 optional bells, in burr walnut veneered case with tune card, some teeth missing, No. 17519, late 19thC, 23in (59cm) wide.
$1,800-2,700

A Swiss two-per-turn cylinder musical box, by Nicole Frères, the cylinder playing 10 popular airs as listed on tune sheet, contained in marquetry inlaid case, No. 35733, mid-19thC, 18in (46cm).
$3,000-4,500

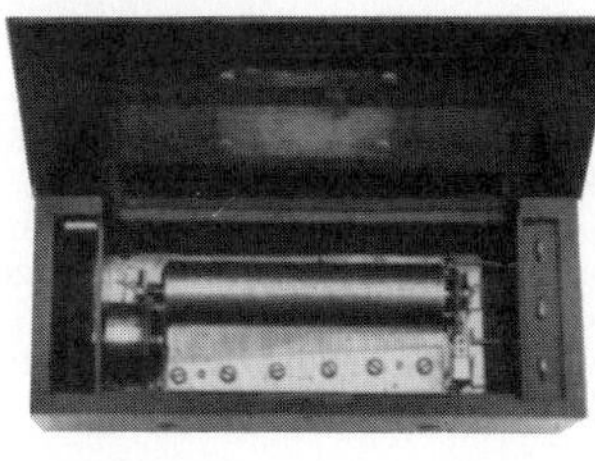

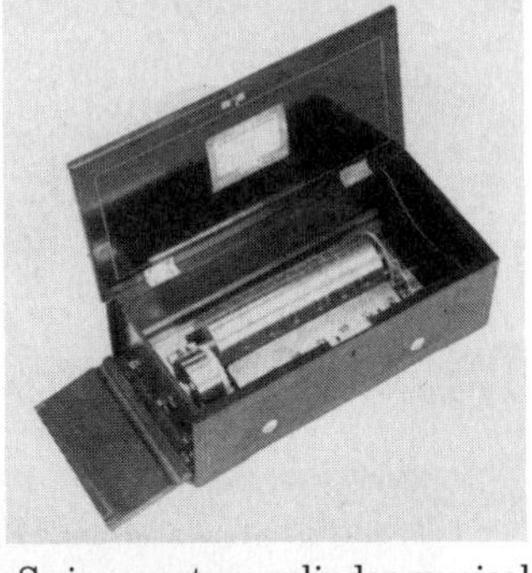

A Swiss overture cylinder musical box, by Nicole Frères, the key wind movement with 9 by 3in (23.5 by 7.5cm) cylinder playing 3 overtures, with tune card in grained case with inlaid lid, No. 29696, c1850, 17½in (44.5cm) wide. **$5,250-7,500**

A Swiss Langdorff and Fils bells in sight cylinder musical box, the 13in (33cm) cylinder playing 12 dance and popular airs, accompanied by 4 bells struck by seated mandarins with nodding heads, the tune card in grained case with veneered front and inlaid lid, c1875, 24in (61cm).
$1,800-2,700

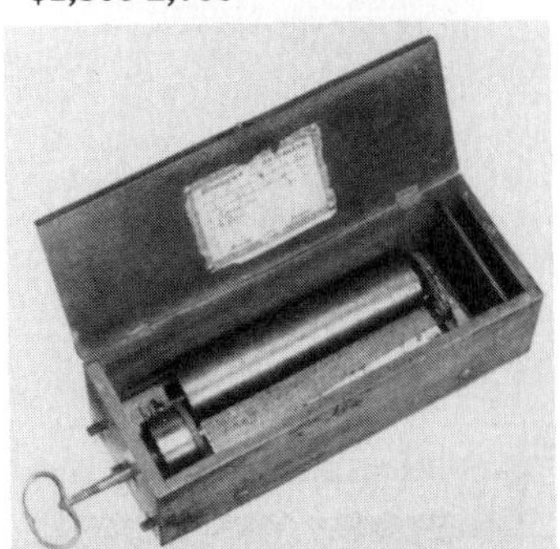

A Swiss key wound cylinder musical box, by Nicole Frères, playing 4 operatic airs as listed on tune card, the comb signed F. Nicole, in fruitwood case with exposed controls, No. 15328, c1830, 13in (33cm).
$1,800-2,700

A lever-wind musical box, by Nicole Frères, No. 41754, tune sheet numbered 41753, playing 4 waltzes, with inlaid lid, 16in (41cm), the cylinder 8in (20.5cm).
$1,800-2,700

Three silver singing bird boxes.
$2,250-3,000 each

A musical box of mandoline overture type, probably by Hellier of Berne, Switzerland, playing 6 operatic airs by Belline, Mayerbee, c1820.
$4,500-6,000

A Nicole Frères cylinder musical box, No. 959, playing 12 airs, as listed on sheet and contained within a marquetry, walnut veneered and strung case, late 19thC, 21in (53cm).
$2,700-3,300

A six air lever-wound cylinder musical box, by Ducommun Girod, with 10½in (27cm) cylinder playing popular airs, in walnut veneered case.
$2,700-3,300

A musical box by Sherstone & Sherstone, in burr maple case with satinwood stringing and crossbanding, with 13in (33cm) cylinder mechanism, and 5 spare cylinders.
$1,500-2,250

A Symphonion, the 19in (48cm) upright disc musical box with diametric combs, coin mechanism, oak motor cover with Riley, Birmingham, transfer and walnut case, of typical design with glazed door and Symphonion title, with 10 discs, lacks coin drawers, 52in (132cm). **$3,000-4,500**

A Nicole Frères key-wound cylinder musical box, playing 6 hymns, the 10½in (27.5cm) cylinder in inlaid case with song sheet, No. 34237.
$1,050-1,350

A mandoline musical box, by P.V.F., playing 6 airs, teeth grouped in fours, in feather banded bird's-eye maple case with brass carrying handles, No. 14374, 19½in (49cm), the cylinder 11in (28cm). **$1,500-2,250**

A Swiss musical box, in a burr walnut case with kingwood and boxwood stringing, the 11in (28cm) drum playing 6 airs, by M. & Co., 21in (53cm).
$1,500-2,250

A Swiss singing bird box, in tortoiseshell case, movement in working order, the metal base plate engraved with a coat-of-arms and the motto Perseverando, with original leather case, the cover stamped Marie, the inner velvet lining impressed with a coronet and the letter M, c1860, 4in (10cm).
$1,200-1,800

German 19⅛in (49cm) ·mphonion disc musical box, ·th twin comb movement and ·in mechanism, in walnut case ·th coin drawer, together with · discs, one tooth missing, c1900, ·in (91.5cm).
·,500-6,000

An upright 19⅝in (50cm) Polyphon disc musical box with 2 combs, coin mechanism and dark stained case with glazed door, coin drawer and replacement pediment, on contemporary stand with moulded panel, 75½in (192cm) high.
$7,500-9,000

An upright 19⅝in (50cm) Polyphon disc musical box, with double combs, coin slot mechanism and drawer, in typical case with pediment and glazed door, 51in (129.5cm) high. **$6,000-8,250**

A Gloria 18½in (47cm) table disc musical box, with angled double combs, one with extra treble sections, in walnut case with fretted top boards, monochrome print in lid and inlaid rosewood panel to top, with 24 discs, 3 teeth missing.
$1,800-2,700

A German 19⅝in (50cm) Polyphon disc musical box, the periphery movement playing on 2 combs, contained in walnut veneered case with marquetry inlaid lid, with winding handle at the side, together with a collection of approximately 60 metal discs, case distressed, c1900, 26in (67cm) wide.
$5,250-6,000

A German 19⅝in (50cm) Polyphon disc musical box, with double comb movement, in walnut case with coin drawer and motor cover, together with 20 discs, lacks pediment, c1895, 38in (96.5cm) high.
$6,000-8,250

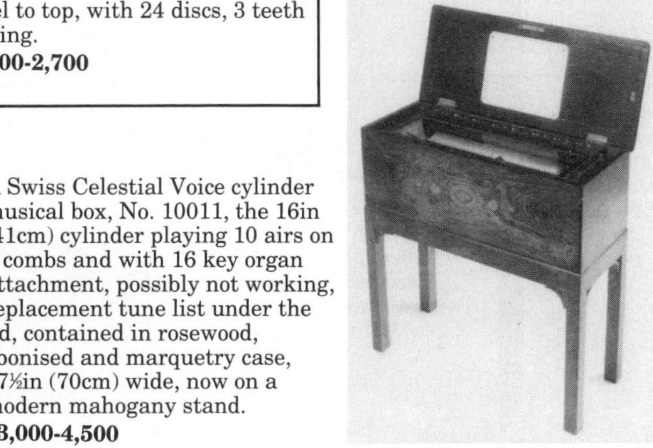

A Swiss Celestial Voice cylinder musical box, No. 10011, the 16in (41cm) cylinder playing 10 airs on 2 combs and with 16 key organ attachment, possibly not working, replacement tune list under the lid, contained in rosewood, ebonised and marquetry case, 27½in (70cm) wide, now on a modern mahogany stand.
$3,000-4,500

A German 15½in (39.5cm) Polyphon disc musical box, the single comb movement contained in a purpose built replacement case of serpentine form, on carved cabriole legs, together with 8 discs, c1895, 22½in (57cm) wide.
$1,200-1,800

Musical Instruments

A walking stick clarinet, by Charles Felchin, the body in 4 boxwood joints, each carved to give the appearance of a rough hewn branch, carved en suite with the joints, the circular covers recessed into knots, rosewood mouthpiece, the mouthpiece cover with ebonised knob, brass ferrule, stamped Felchin à Berne, c1830, approximate sounding length 22in (56cm).
$9,000-10,000

A six keyed boxwood and ivory clarinet, branded Milligan, London, on the joints, the sounding length 23in (59cm).
$375-525

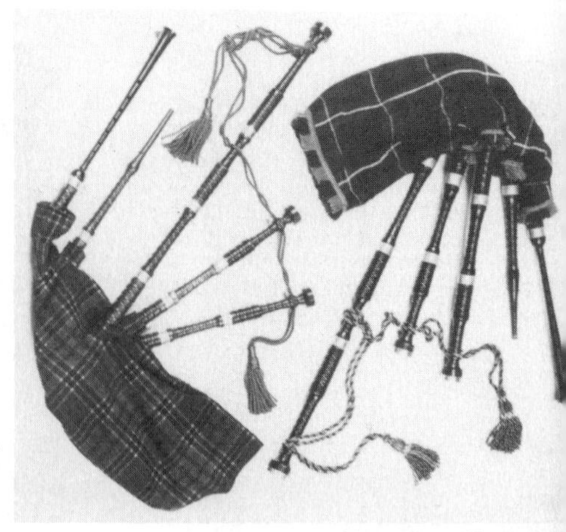

Two sets of bagpipe
$450-600

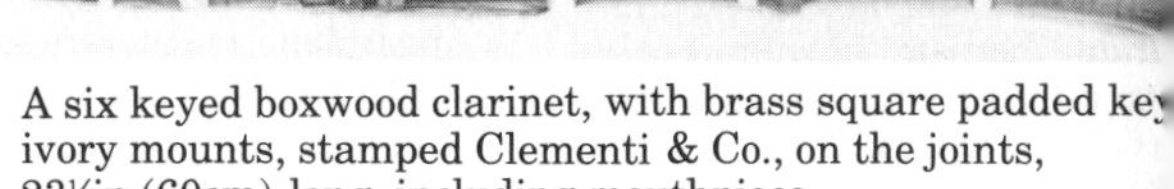

A six keyed boxwood clarinet, with brass square padded ke ivory mounts, stamped Clementi & Co., on the joints, 23½in (60cm) long, including mouthpiece.
$375-525

A six keyed boxwood and ivory flute, branded Clementi & Co., on the joints.
$375-450

A one keyed boxwood flute, by Button & Whittaker, the sounding length 14in (36cm), and a one keyed boxwood piccolo, the sounding length 10½in (27cm).
$300-375

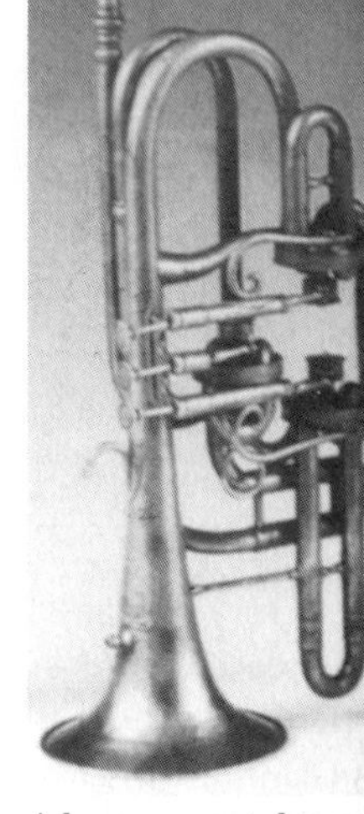

A brass cornet, by Gisborne, in a box.
$375-450

A one keyed boxwood flute, the single key of brass with trapezoid cover, one later horn mount, 2 corps de rechange, one reconstructed around the G hole, stamped I.A. Crone between a crown and a star, late 18thC, sounding lengths 22in (56cm) and 22in (55.5cm).
$7,500-9,000

A brass cornet, by Kohler London, with 3 patent piston action rotary valve in original box with additional crooks and tuning slides.
$3,000-4,500

A concertina, by C. Wheatstone, London, with fretted nickel plated ends and 56 buttons, in the original box.
$1,050-1,350

An eight keyed flute in rosewood, by Martin Frères, Paris, branded with a bee, the sounding length 22½in (58cm).
$450-600

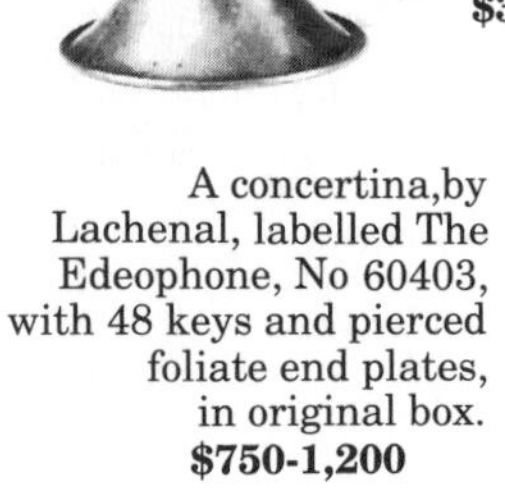

A concertina,by Lachenal, labelled The Edeophone, No 60403, with 48 keys and pierced foliate end plates, in original box.
$750-1,200

A boxwood 1847 patent Böhm-system flute, with brass mounts and keywork, the latter comprising 11 open and 4 closed, with dimpled key cups, brass sheathed tuning slide and tenons, brass mounted boxwood crutch, the crutch socket now absent, engraved Boehm & Mendler, München on the sheathing of the upper joint tenon, in leather bound case, sounding length 23in (58cm).
$9,000-10,000

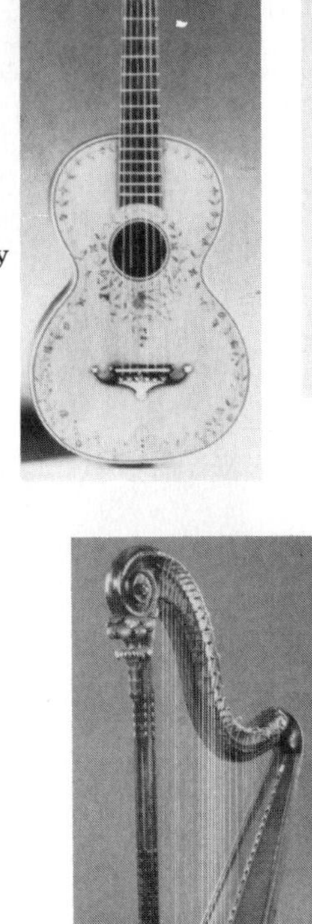

A guitar, with floral mother-of-pearl inlay, unlabelled, probably French, in a case, c1840.
$600-750

A portable 3 octave harmonium, by Debain, with burr walnut case, ormolu mounts and gilt tripod base with pedal, 23in (59cm) wide.
$1,050-1,350

A ladies guitar, labelled Panormo/1828, London, the length of back 17½in (44.5cm), in a case.
$1,800-2,700

A single action pedal harp, the body of 7 sycamore ribs, the later soundboard of plain pine, the arm with later glazed panels on the right side, crochet system controlled by 7 pedals, 37 strings, with cloth cover, School of Georges Cousineau, Paris, 64½in (163.5cm).
$3,000-4,500

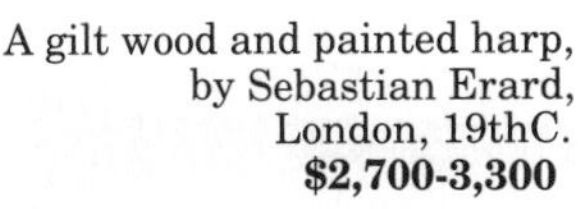

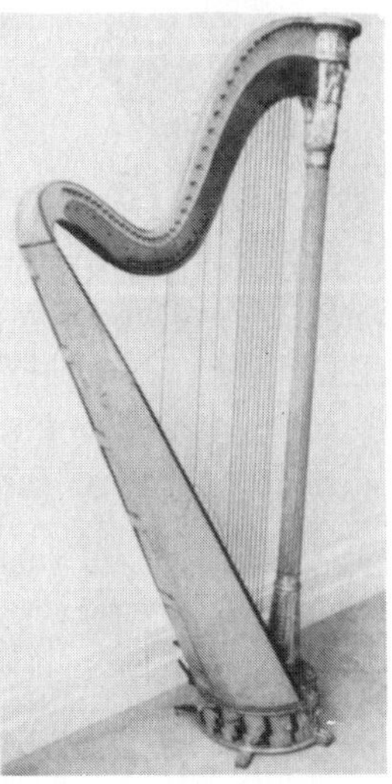

A gilt wood and painted harp, by Sebastian Erard, London, 19thC.
$2,700-3,300

An Austrian lady's guitar, with mother-of-pearl foliate decoration, labelled Nach dem Modell des Luigi Legnani, von Nikolaus Georg Ries in Wien, 1833.
$750-900

A French guitar, labelled Lacote e Luthiers, Paris, the back and ribs of rosewood, the front and soundhole edged with mother-of- pearl decoration to the bridge, brass machine head with ivory handled turners, length of back 17in (43cm).
$1,800-2,700

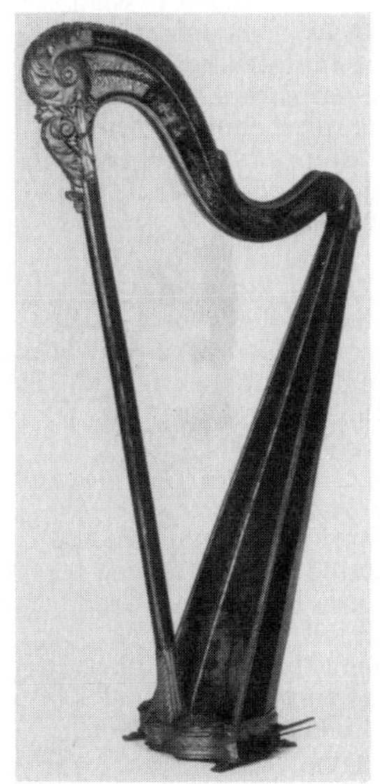

A pedal harp, the body of 7 staves laquered black, the soundboard painted with musical trophies and a rural scene, the arm with chinoiserie decoration and gilded mouldings, crochet action, 7 pedals and 38 strings, stamped H. Naderman à Paris at the top of the soundboard, 64½in (163.5cm).
$9,000-10,000

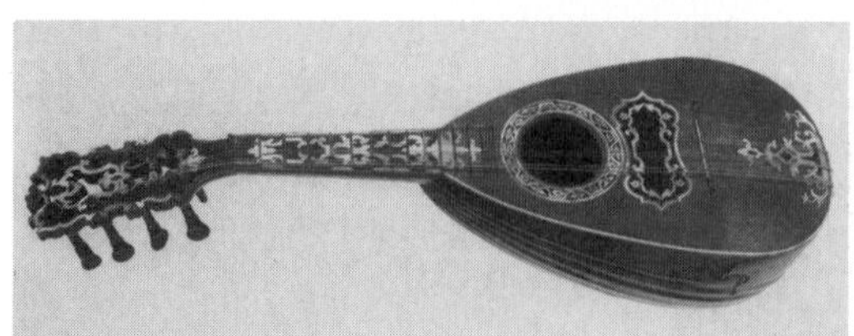

A Neapolitan mandolin, the back with tortoiseshell overlaid ribs, each divided by bone and ebony stringing, shaped tortoiseshell capping strip, the table inlaid at the top, bottom and around the sound hole with mother-of-pearl and tortoiseshell with inset scratch plate, the shaped head, neck and fingerboard overlaid with tortoiseshell and with scrolling mother-of-pearl inlay, 4 double courses of strings, 14 frets, labelled Antonius Vinaccia fecir (sic) Januarii; Neapoli 1764, 22½in (57cm), in 19thC fitted wooden case.
$4,500-6,000

A tenor saxophone, engraved C.G. Conn Ltd. Elkhart Ind. USA, No. M243763, in a fitted case, inscribed Berkeley of London.
$375-525

An alto saxophone, engraved René Guenot, Paris, on the bell, in a case, together with a soprano saxophone, similarly engraved, in a case.
$600-750

A gold laquered alto saxophone, engraved The Regent, The British Band Co. Ltd., 295 Regent St., London, W1 on bell, in fitted case.
$750-900

A tangent action square piano, the faciaboard and cheeks of satinwood with holly and stained fruitwood stringing with mahogany crossbanding, the later nameboard with 3 veneered panels, the case of mahogany with wide stringing in various woods, octave keyboard, with ivory naturals and ebony accidentals, the tangent action with underdampers, the soundboard extending over the keyshafts, the harp stop controlled by a later brass lever, on frame stand with shelf stretcher, English or Irish, c1780, 60in (153cm) long.
$7,500-9,000

The absence of this piano's original nameboard is particularly frustrating. The action is very neatly engineered and executed. The casework and the construction of the keywell is somewhat suggestive of an Irish origin and the work of William Southwell. On the other hand features such as the flat facings to the keys are found on pianos by Joseph Merlin. Both these makers are renowned for their ingenuity and could have been responsible for the unusual action.

A two keyed stained boxwood oboe, with ivory mounts, the reed socket mount later, brass keys with circular covers, the C key with fishtail touchpiece, twinned G holes, stamped Parker, London, on each joint, 22½in (57cm).
$2,250-3,000

A treble alto recorder in the manner of Stanesby, with boxwood body and well defined ring markings, England, 18thC, 20in (51cm) lonh.
$1,200-1,800

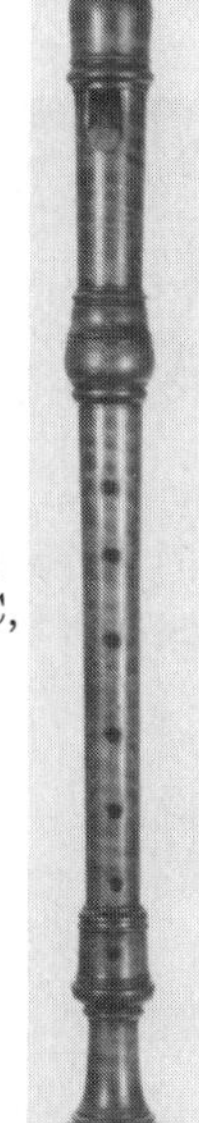

A baritone sarrusophone, the body, keywork, crutch and crook of silver plated brass, stamped Maino & Orsi, Prof Romeo Orsi, Prenatal Privilegiata Fabrica d'Instrument Musicali, Milano-Italia, Exportanzione Mondiale, c1855, 84½in (214.5cm) long.
$10,500-12,000

A Victorian parcel gilt satinwood upright piano, the piano by Erard the cabinet by L. W. Collman, the case fitted with gilt bronze leaf tips, flowerheads and a pair of candelabra, carved with foliage, columns and a lyre and incised decorations, with panels fitted to simulate grill work, 61in (155cm) wide.
$5,250-7,500

straight strung underdamped pright piano, by John roadwood & Sons, No. 92412, in mahogany case with satinwood ılaid front panel within a gilt urround, the turned and fluted upports applied with husks, 1905. **$900-1,500**

A Blüthner boudoir grand piano, No. 70246, dark stained case on ebonised tapering square legs with brass casters, 76in (193cm), with a modern mahogany box top duet stool.
$2,250-3,000

An ormolu mounted kingwood and tulipwood crossbanded grand piano, by Erard Paris, the case banded with ormolu and raised on 3 legs with scroll feet and lyre shaped pedal bracket with acanthus scroll feet, the keyboard cover signed, with a hinged folding lid, the satin birch interior signed Par Brevet de Invention/ Seb. et Pre Erard/13821, rue de Huil/Paris, No. 83420, lacking the 3 mounts heading the legs, late 19th/20thC, 60in (152cm) wide.
$30,000-45,000

The firm of Erard was established in the 1770s in Paris by Sébastien Erard, born Strasbourg 1752. The firm continued to be in family hands until 1873, when it was managed by Amedée Blondel and called Erard et Cie.

A grand piano, by John Broadwood & Sons, the 6 octave keyboard with ivory naturals and ebony accidentals, English grand action, 2 pedals controlling forte and una corda stops, mahogany music deck and pedal lyre on 3 baluster legs, inscribed and bearing the serial No.8555 on the reverse of the nameboard and Murray on the keyframe, London, 1820, 102in (259cm).
$3,000-4,500

A violin and 2 bows, in case, the instrument with carved lion's head scroll with mother-of-pearl eyes, indecipherable label, 14½in (37cm).
$375-450

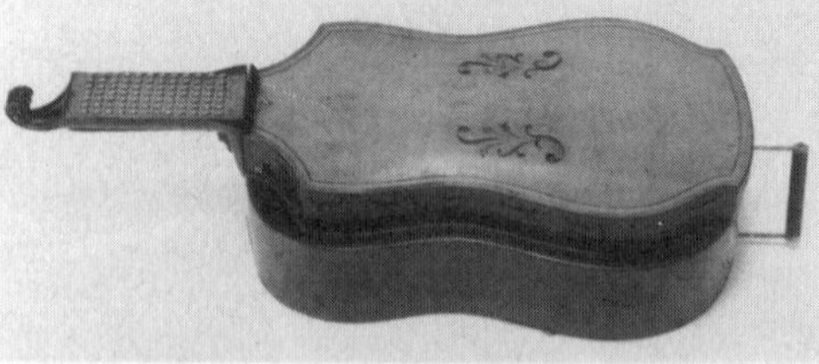

A mélophone, with rosewood body in 2 sections, the lower section containing the bellows with brass stringing, piston action bellows lever with ebony handle, the upper section covering the key mechanism, the sides pierced by numerous C-holes, the top of sycamore edged with fruitwood and ivorine purfling, the fingerboard with 89 nickel buttons, a vent lever beneath the neck, in original wooden case, some brass stringing detached, labelled Exposition 1839, A. Brown, Paris, Rue des Fossés du Temple, 20, 30in (77cm) long, excluding handle.
$2,250-3,000

A violin, in case, by Nicolas Emmatus Cremona, 1636, 14½in (37cm).
$300-375

Gramophones

An E.M.G. Mark IX hand made gramophone, with double spring Paillard motor, 2 spring EMG soundbox, oak case and swan neck papier mâché horn, 22in (56cm) diam., with a Davey fibre cutter, a fibre drying canister and an HMV speed tester.
$2,700-3,300

A coin operated gramophone, with Clark-Johnson soundbox, wood travelling arm and oak case with coin mechanism, slot for record storage, Gramophone Company and Recording Angel transfers, Angel mark branded on base, brass horn and internal counter with ratchet wheel missing, c1898, 26in (66cm) wide.
$7,500-9,000

An H.M.V. Junior Monarch oak horn gramophone, with single spring motor, in oak case with Blackenstein's, London, retailer's label, with Parlophone soundbox, dated on base 1907, the horn 22in (55cm) diam.
$1,800-2,700

A pathéphone, model F, with single spring motor, 10in (25cm) turntable, Multitone disc reproducer, accelerating start lever, scrolling back bracket, in walnut case with 16½in (42cm) pink flower horn, some surface rust to horn, French, c1910, with 47 Pathé and Diamond records.
$375-525

A Klingsor gramophone, with pierced hinged door enclosing string covered horn aperture, Klingsor sound box and single spring motor in lower compartment covered by fold down flap, in mahogany case on bracket feet, German, 20thC, 29in (74cm).
$750-1,200

A Pathé gramophone, in inlaid mahogany case, with rising top, on square tapered legs, early 20thC.
$375-450

Columbia disc Graphophone, odel BNWM, with double spring otor, in mahogany case, No. 6 undbox and black flower horn. **'50-900**

'honographs

German Puck phonograph, the ecoratively cast iron base with ounted horn, in the form of a hell with a gnome perched on the dge, lacks reproducer and tone rm, c1902, 18in (46cm) long. **750-1,200**

n Edison red Gem phonograph, Iodel D, No. 318449D, with K eproducer, maroon Fireside horn, rane and 34 wax amberols. **1,800-2,700**

\n Edison Gem phonograph. **$375-450**

A Lumière pleated diaphragm gramophone, by His Master's Voice, Model 510, in quarter veneered mahogany cabinet with cabriole legs and gilt fittings, 43in (109cm). **$3,000-4,500**

A German child's horn gramophone, with wooden base, 5½in (14cm) turntable and orange metal horn with red interior, c1920. **$150-225**

Polyphons

A Polyphon, in a walnut case with hinged lid and a raised panel of floral marquetry, the interior with a print of dancing putti, with the original handbook and 46 discs, late 19thC. **$3,000-4,500**

A Nicol Frères penny-in-slot Polyphon, playing 20in (50cm) diam. discs, carved and inscribed Polyphon on the moulded cornice, over an arched glazed door, a money drawer to the base with foliate cast iron slot and winding handle apertures, 38in (96cm) wide, together with 26 discs. **$3,000-4,500**

An HMV model VIIA mahogany horn gramophone, with triple spring motor, rocking turntable, Denison brake, Exhibition soundbox, No. 455966, J.B. Cramer, Liverpool agent's plaque, and mahogany horn, c1913, the horn 22in (55.5cm) diam. **$1,800-2,700**

A walnut polyphon, c1900. **$5,250-7,500**

Receivers

Two Fada receivers, in yellow Bakelite cases with red tuning knobs, 1940s. **$600-750 each**

A Marconiphone V2 receiver with 2 valves, 2 wavelength plates and one Regenerator Unit, lacking front panels, and a Marconiphone A2 amplifier with 2 valves and front panels with defective lid hinge, a Sterling Primax speaker with defective diaphragm, and 2 headphone earpieces in a crystal set box.
$750-1,200

l. An Ekco Type A22 AC mains receiver, in circular black Bakelite case with circular dial, case cracked, 1945, 13in (33cm), and an Ekco Type ES 31 extension speaker in brown Bakelite case with cream grille.
$450-600
r. An Ekco Type AD75 AC mains receiver, in circular brown Bakelite case, 14½in 37cm) diam.
$450-600

A Burndept Ethodyne 7 valve Super Heterodyne receiver, Standard model, in mahogany case with controls on front, hinged half lid, with BBC transfer and aerial socket with inset compass on fixed lid, 31in (79cm) wide, with 2 frame aerials, and instruction book dated 1.9.25.
$1,050-1,350

Miscellaneous

A Swiss carved wood musical coat hook, in the form of a fox in hunting outfit, containing a 4 air cylinder movement, one feather to hat broken, late 19thC, 17in (43cm).
$750-1,200

A Swiss musical rocking ship automaton, with a ship and water wheel on oval ebonised wood base, under painted glass dome, late 19thC, 15½in (39cm).
$750-1,200

A Swiss carved wooden musical coat hook, in the form of a dog in hunting outfit, containing a 4 air cylinder movement, late 19thC, 16½in (42cm).
$1,050-1,350

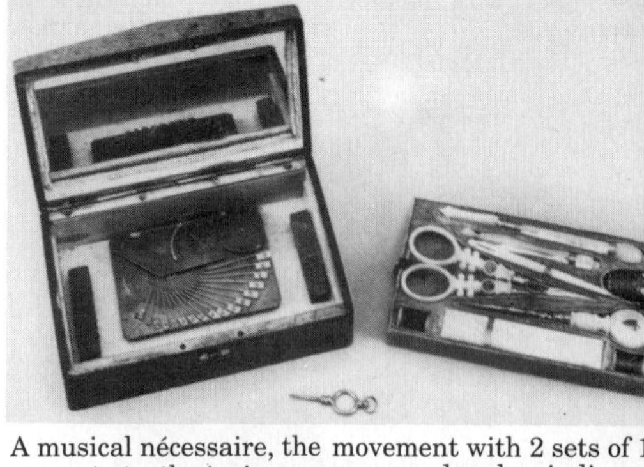

A musical nécessaire, the movement with 2 sets of 1 separate teeth, 4 wing governor and male winding key, in burr wood case, with mother-of-pearl inlay, internal mirror and silver hinge and lock plates, containing implements and later white metal thimbl c1810, 5½in (13.5cm) wide. **$5,250-7,500**

BOOKS & BOOK ILLUSTRATIONS

ɩ group of Pennsylvania German 'rakturs, comprising a song book ıscribed 'for Rakel Bischop 1835', ınother song book inscribed 'for ːlizabeth Reinert 1811', a leather ound hymnal with a bookplate y Christian Strenge, and a ːerman printed bible with a ːoral Scherenschnitten of flowers nd leafage.
4,500-6,000

Three shaped books, 'The Little Drummer Boy', London, Paris and New York, printed in Germany or Raphael Tuck & Sons, tall rregularly shaped 8°, 10½ by 5in 26 by 12cm), 'The Next Door Children and other stories', London and New York, printed in Bavaria for Ernest Nister and E.P.Dutton, no date but 1897 or earlier, tall irregularly shaped 8°, 10 by 4½in (25 by 11cm), and Miss Dollikins', London, Ernest Nister, printed by him in Nuremberg, no date, irregularly shaped 4°, 5 by7in (12 by 18cm), llustrations by C.S.Flint, some coloured, original wrappers depicting and shaped like a dolls' house, backstrip somewhat split.

An antique illuminated book binding, 'This is the receipt and Expenditure for the space of one year of the general customs of the Illustrious Commonwealth of Siena', in glazed display case, 16 by 26in (41 by 66cm).
$4,500-6,000

Two volumes of Le Monde des Automates, by Edouard Chapuis,
$750-900

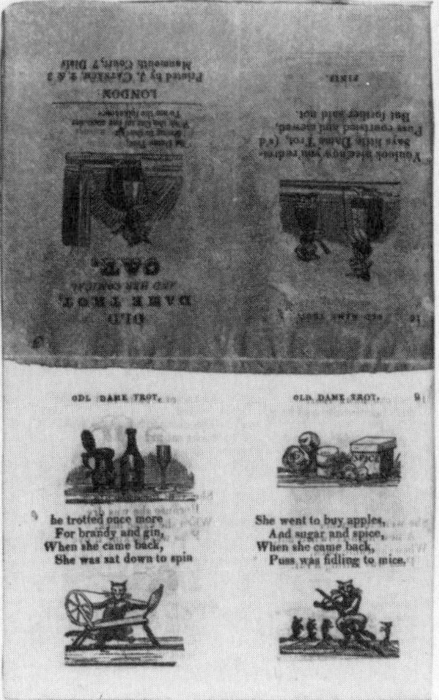

Les Jouets, by Leo Claretie, Histoire-Fabrication, 6 coloured plates, 300 line engravings, 325 pages, coloured embossed cover, quarto, late 19thC.
$300-375

Four volumes by Samuel Richardson, entitled Pamela: or, Virtue Rewarded, London: For C. Rivington.
$3,000-3,750

'A collection of 30 farthing histories' by publisher James Catnach and others, 30 works, 16 pages each title in one volume, first and last page of each work with an overall coloured wash, each leaf creased for folding, numerous woodcut illustrations, c1830, 7½ by 5in (19 by 12cm).
$4,500-6,000
Very rare in this form, titles include 'Old Dame Trot and her comical cat', 'The London Cries', 'The Death and Burial of Cock Robin', 'The Butterfly's Ball and the Grasshopper's Feast', 'The History of Sir R. Whittington and his cat'. Halliwell was perhaps the greatest of the early chapbook enthusiasts, and published works on broadside ballads and the nursery rhymes of England. Sotheby's sold part of his library over 4 days, after his death in July 1889. His inscription is as applicable today as it was when he wrote it, 'Pieces of this kind are exceedingly well worth keeping as illustrative of the lower popular child literature and after a time they always become immensely rare'.

Two volumes by Tobias Smollett, entitled Travels through France and Italy, For R.Baldwin, 1766.
$7,500-9,000

Four volumes by Tobias Smollett, entitled The Adventures of Peregrine Pickle, London: For the Author and sold by D. Wilson, 1751, First Edition, Rothschild 1910.
$1,200-1,800

A selection of illustrations, by Ernest Howard Shepard, 1879-1976:

'Now we'll go right up to the house, and sing our bewitching carols under the drawing room windows', pen and black ink heightened with white, 7 by 6in (17 by 15cm).
$3,000-4,500

This is an original illustration for Kenneth Graham's 'Bertie's Escapade', J. B. Lippincott Company, 1949, p.13.

'It had HUNNY written on it', and 'It *is* honey, right the way down', two vignettes on one sheet, pencil, unframed, 6½ by 8⅓in (16 by 21cm). **$9,000-10,000**

The finished version of the latter drawing appears in 'Winnie The Pooh', by A. A. Milne, Methuen Co. Ltd., 1926, p.59.

'Politeness', a pencil, pen and black ink unframed illustration, signed and inscribed, dated January 1959, 7 by 4in (18 by 10cm).
$3,000-4,500

This illustration is a later version for 'When We Were Very Young', by A. A. Milne, Methuen & Co. Ltd., 1924, p.41.

'Pooh and Owl visiting in Owl's Parlour', a pen, blue ink and coloured chalks illustration, 4½ by 7in (11 by 18cm).
$10,500-12,000

This illustration is a later colour version for 'Winnie The Pooh', Methuen & Co. Ltd., 1926, p.49.

'So he started to climb out of the hole', signed with initials, a pencil, pen and black ink initialled illustration, 3½ by 4½in (8.5 by11.5cm).
$15,000-18,000

See A. A. Milne's 'Winnie The Pooh', Methuen & Co. Ltd., 1926 p.25.

'So Pooh pushed and pushed and pushed his way through the hole' a pencil, pen and black ink illustration, 3½ by 4½in (8.5 by 11.5cm).
$15,000-18,000

See A. A. Milne's 'Winnie The Pooh', Methuen & Co. Ltd., 1926, p.23.

'Fairy Star's Annual', by M. Joyce Davies, gouache on card, initialled in ink, 20 by 7in (25 by 17cm).
$120-135

'Our Girls' Yarns', by M. Joyce Davies, gouache on card, signed in ink, 6 by 7in (15 by 17cm).
$150-225

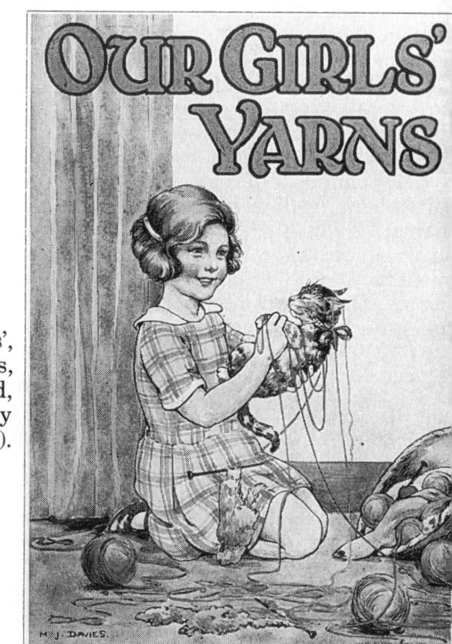

complete set of artists drawings r one episode of 'Detective Tilly, hrymes Done Here', Anon, rincess Picture Library, and the iginal proof for the cartoon, 1½ by 8½in (30 by 21cm).
120-135

'Schoolboy Yarns', by E. E. Briscoe, gouache on card, initialled in ink, 15 by 10½in (38 by 27cm).
$150-225

'Away We Go', by Barbara Spurr, gouache on card, signed in ink, 15 by 11in (39 by 28cm).
$375-450

Did you know?
MILLER'S Antiques Price Guide builds up year by year to form the most comprehensive photo reference library available.

'Walking the Dog', by Barbara Spurr, gouache on card, and 4 others, 15 by 11½in (38 by 11.5cm).
$105-120

Modesty Blaise, The Scarlet Maiden: 2', Romero, by Peter 'Donnell, ink on board, laid on nasterboard, 21in (53cm).
375-450

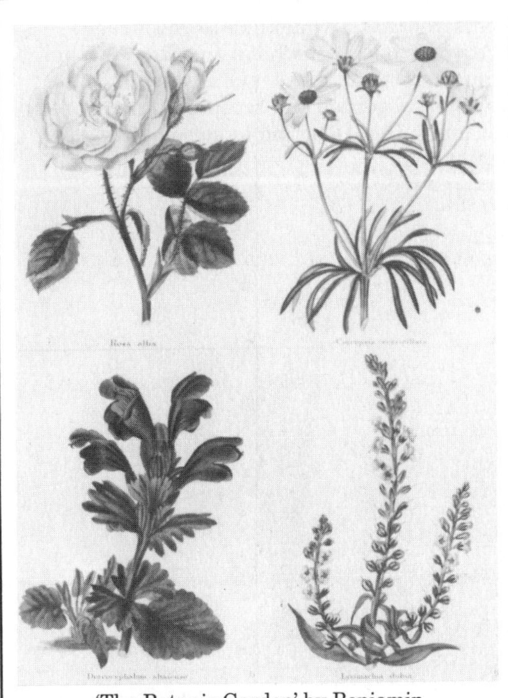

'The Botanic Garden' by Benjamin Maund, volumes 1-6, of 13, 144 hand coloured plates, 6 additional engraved titles, dedication in volume 4, quarto, half mauve calf, gilt tooled spine, green labels, marbled boards, some water staining and browning.
$1,800-2,700

DECORATIVE ARTS 1870 TO THE PRESENT DAY

INTRODUCTION

It would be impossible to write this overview of the Art Nouveau and Art Deco market without mentioning the word recession, although I'm sure that by this stage of the guide you are heartily sick of it, if indeed living through it has not been bad enough. Art and antiques are not inflation- or recession-proof: prices can go down as well as up, so the main criterion for buying or collecting anything should primarily be that you like it and enjoy living with it. If over the long term it also proves a good investment, then all well and good, but this should not be the primary concern. Disappointments are more likely to occur if it has been.

To make sure you don't overpay, preparation and homework are essential before making a purchase. This can be done through regular viewing of auctions, by seeking advice from specialists and through contact with reputable dealers. The whole field of Decorative Arts from 1870 to the present day offers such a wonderful array of styles, designs, materials, colours and contrasts to the collector or interested spectator that I would like to encourage everyone to look at what's on offer; whether your taste be for glass, metalwares, silver, jewellery, bronzes and sculpture, furniture or ceramics, there's bound to be something to tempt you.

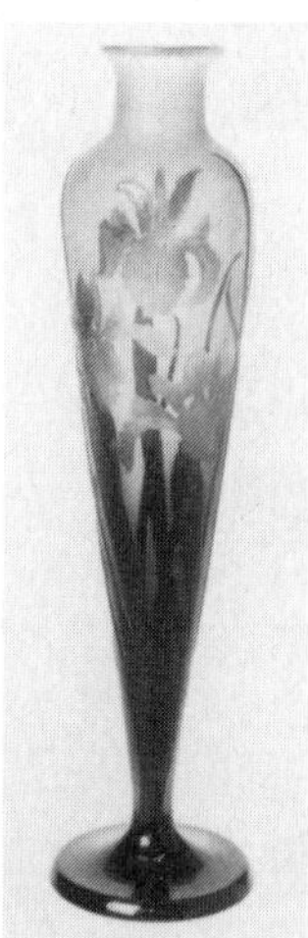

A Gallé cameo glass vase, the amber tinted body overlaid with pale blue and amethyst glass, acid etched with tall iris blooms and foliage, intaglio signature Gallé, 17in (43cm) high.

$3,000-4,500

Over the past year even traditionally strong areas have suffered: French glass by Gallé, Daum, Lalique and the like, were hit by the recession despite the fact these are well known makers and justifiably sought after because of the quality of their work and the primary position that they hold in the history of late 19thC and early 20thC applie arts. Other areas may appear to have fared better, but bear in mind that while fashion and speculation may produce some wonderful prices at the peak there can also be grave disappointments when the peak car no longer be sustained. So I am pleased to report that genuine interest has resurfaced in the traditionally solid areas: a Gallé vase that was unsold at the beginning of last year with an estimate of $18,000-22,500, was auctioned at Phillips in London at the beginning of this year with the same estimate and realised $27,000, bearing out the general rule that good and rare examples, within an established area of collecting, maintain their levels better.

Dr Christopher Dresser was a popular figure who is recognised for some very unusual and far-sighted designs and for being one of the first industrial designers.

A Linthorpe pottery circular dish, designed by Christopher Dresser, painted in bright and naturalistic enamelled colours with white chrysanthemums against a brown stippled grounc impressed Linthorpe, facsimile signature and HT for Henry Tooth and 'BL' monogram for painter, 11½in (29cm).

$225-300

Once appreciated on a primarily academic level and collected by a minority, he became the rising star of the late 1950s and has beer popular ever since. That is not to say he is not worth the money, only that such a meteoric rise commercially was not backed by a solid, long-established body of collectors Fashion and speculation managed to get in there somewhere.

Moorcroft and Doulton ceramics have come through relatively unscathed, perhaps because they have been popular for many, many years and appeal to a wide range of collectors. They are also not too expensive, relative to, say, French Art Glass and Impressionist pictures, and therefore not susceptible to Fashion and Speculation.

Vhat a relief, I hear their collectors cry! One final thing I would like to draw your ttention to is how reasonable some of the urniture from the Aesthetic Movement, othic Revival and Arts and Crafts Movement can be. Yes, the important names vill always make important prices, but there re many others who made good quality urniture in solid woods that is cheap in omparison with the mass-produced, hipboard furniture that appears in many High Street Stores.

OME LEADING MAKERS:

oetz (1836-1939)
n 1840 Johann Loetz bought a glassworks at Klostermühle and introduced new ranges, tarting with effects simulating hardstones uch as onyx and cornelian. In 1890 he egan experimenting with iridescent effects nd in 1895 and 1896 he took out patents to rotect these metallic blue and gold finishes. So was born the Loetz iridescent glass that as since attracted so many collectors. The irm continued to experiment, bringing in nore colours and more controlled decorative chemes. They also employed many leading lesigners including Koloman Moser, Michael Powolny, Josef Hoffmann, Otto Prutscher nd Dagobert Peche from the Wiener Verkstätte.

iberty & Co
Arthur Lasenby Liberty (1843-1917) founded is firm in 1875, having previously worked or the Farmer and Rogers' Great Cloak and Shawl Emporium. His shop in Regent Street old imported blue and white china, silks, abrics and textiles. Very soon this led to a urnishing and decorating department. Liberty's reputation for fabrics was stablished then and continues to this day.

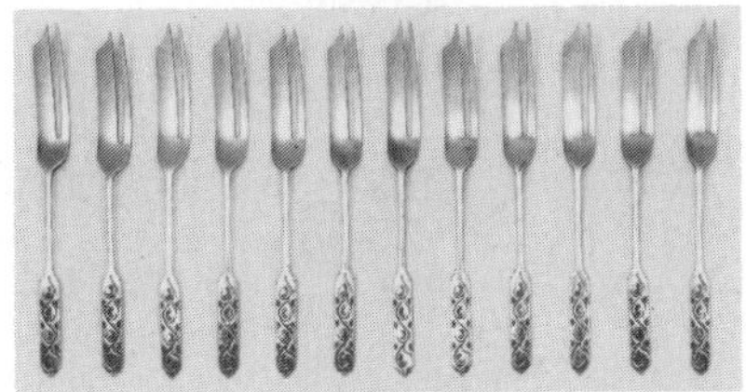

A set of 12 Liberty & Co. silver cake forks, the handle of each with blue green enamel details, stamped maker's marks L&Co., England, Birmingham hallmarks for 1928, 175grams, in fitted case.
$900-1,500

As well as furniture and textiles, the firm lso made jewellery, pewter and silver. Arthur Liberty was astute enough to achieve he hand-finished look advocated by the Arts nd Crafts movement, while taking dvantage of the technological advances of he age. Many of the leading figures and vorkshops found it difficult to stay in usiness and compete with this approach: Liberty's thrived.

In the late 1890s they introduced a range of pewter and silver wares entitled 'Tudric' and 'Cymric'. The pieces were executed by the Birmingham firm of W. H. Haseler to the designs of Oliver Baker, Bernard Cuzner, Jessie M. King, Rex Silver and, of course, Archibald Knox, whose Celtic designs were synonymous with the term Art Nouveau.

Nelson (1859-1942) and Edith Dawson
Nelson Dawson trained both as an architect and a painter and in 1881 he decided to add another string to his bow and took up metalwork. He subsequently studied enamelling under Alexander Fisher, one of the great enamellers of his age. In 1893 he married Edith Robinson to whom he taught the art of enamelling and together they produced many fine pieces of jewellery.

Nelson Dawson was one of the founder members of the Artificers Guild in 1901 and was Art Director until 1903. His wife had to give up enamelling because of ill health caused by the poisonous fumes given off by the enamels in the kiln. Nelson gave up all metalwork by 1914 and devoted the rest of his life to his painting.

George Jack (1855–1942)
George Jack was an American architect and furniture designer. He came to London in 1875 and worked for Philip Webb at his practice. Because of Webb's connections with Morris & Co, George Jack became involved with designing furniture for that firm as well, and eventually became Morris & Co's chief furniture designer. Many of his designs made use of walnut or mahogany; they were of simple outline but often incorporated fine, elaborate, floral marquetry panels. He was a member of the Art Workers Guild and took over Webb's architectural practice in 1900.

Chryselephantine Sculpture

Small figures in bronze or ivory became increasingly popular from the turn of the century, but during the 1920s and 30s the favoured technique was chryselephantine - a novel combination of bronze and ivory. The more ivory the piece contains, the more expensive it is likely to be.

Most featured women, often dancers, athletes and 'modern' subjects. These often had a bronze torso or body, cold painted in suitable colours, an ivory face, and sometimes, ivory arms and legs. They are usually mounted on stepped marble onyx bases. Some of the leading sculptures were by D. H. Chiparus, Ferdinand Preiss, Bruno Zach, P. Philippe and C. J. Colinet.

Franz Xavier Bergman
Bergman bronzes are often signed 'Nam Greb', which as you have probably already deduced is 'Bergman' spelt backwards. While he is known for his bronzes of Middle Eastern figures and groups, his female figures of a more erotic nature are particularly sought after. Very often they have a mechanical device of a coat that opens or a dress that pulls up to reveal the naked woman beneath.

Tiles

There is always a ready market for the attractive tiles of this period. The end of the 19thC saw a revival of tile making. The entrepreneurial Victorians patented machinery to mass produce the tile body and later a machine that could apply printed decoration. Not all these tiles were bad of course, but it is fair to say that as time went on, in many cases the quality decreased. Hand decorated tiles were still available but they were a lot more costly. William De Morgan (1839-1917) was a master tile designer. A friend of Burne-Jones and William Morris, he was a leading figure in the Arts and Crafts Movement and one of the great ceramists of his age. But it is not just his designs that are good. It is the quality and use of colour that strikes most people. He spent a long time carefully working over the correct chemical balance to achieve the vibrant effects. The painters he employed were very skilled in applying the thick pigments necessary to produce the depth of colour. His tiles were expensive in their day, just as they are now, but they are also among the best around.

A set of 12 William De Morgan ruby lustre tiles, comprising: 6 depicting galleons and 6 decorated with sprigs of foliage, each 6 by 6in (15 by 15cm).
$1,800-2,700

Royal Doulton Chang Wares
Royal Doulton's experiments with transmutation glazes culminated in the mid-1920s in the amazing Chang wares. These are characterised by a heavy body covered, dripped and draped in thick running glazes of white and vibrant colours, with a crackle finish. The range included vases of various sizes, snuff bottles, lamps, bowls and dishes. Production ceased in 1940 and never resumed.

Rookwood (1880-1967)
This American Pottery founded by M. L. Nichols in Cincinnati, Ohio in 1880, produced a range of wares using various glaze techniques, and motifs drawn from inspirations as diverse as Japan, plant life, the animal kingdom and American Indians.

Müller Frères (c1900-1933)
The Müller family included nine brothers and one sister. Having been apprenticed to many of the good glass making factories of the late 19thC, including Gallé, they established their own glass decorating workshop in about 1895 in Luneville. Decorating was their forte and they produce cameo glass from the most simple kind to th most complex and subtle, using multi-coloured layers with detailed wheel carving. In 1906 two of the brothers were asked to design a range of cameo glass for the Belgian glassworks of Val Saint-Lambert. They produced over four hundred different models these pieces are signed VSL.

The outbreak of the First World War (during which one of the brothers was killed forced them to close the Factory. After the war they bought the Hinzelin glassworks at Croismare and concentrated on commercial, mass produced glass for ceiling shades and bowls, mostly of opaque white glass with moulded Art Deco patterns or plain shapes in multi-coloured flecked glass. The Depression of the late 1920s and early 1930s forced them to close down for good in 1936.

A Müller Frères yellow and brown cameo glass mushroom lampshade, depicting an Arab leading a camel beneath palm trees, with the pyramids and the sphinx beyond, on a cold painted bronze base by L. Carvin, cast as a seated lioness, licking her right paw, with her 2 cubs playing round about her feet, on a naturalistically cast base, signed, 18½in (47cm) high.
$3,000-3,750

Harold Stabler (1872-1945)
A designer and craftsman, Stabler studied at Kendal Art School switching from cabinet making to metalwork. and later became head of metalworking at the Keswick School of

ndustrial Arts (1898-1899). In 1906 he aught metalwork at the Sir John Cass 'echnical Institute in London and later ecame its head (1907-1937). He and his vife Phoebe were partners in Carter, Stabler nd Adams at Poole for whom they designed. Ie was commissioned to design tiles for the nderground station at St Paul's in London, vhere they can still be seen.

ibyl Dunlop (1889-1968)

)unlop was a jewellery designer working etween the wars. The origins of her echnique, particularly in the use of abochon stones and wire-metalwork, are rmly grounded in the Arts and Crafts style. Some of her work was a happy marriage etween the Arts and Crafts style of the 890s and the new Art Deco influence of the 920s and 1930s. This sounds incongruous, et somehow she managed to make it work. ;he was Scottish born but was based in ondon, selling her work from her shop in Kensington Church Street. Most of her ewellery is unsigned, her name appearing nstead on the boxes in which the pieces vere presented.

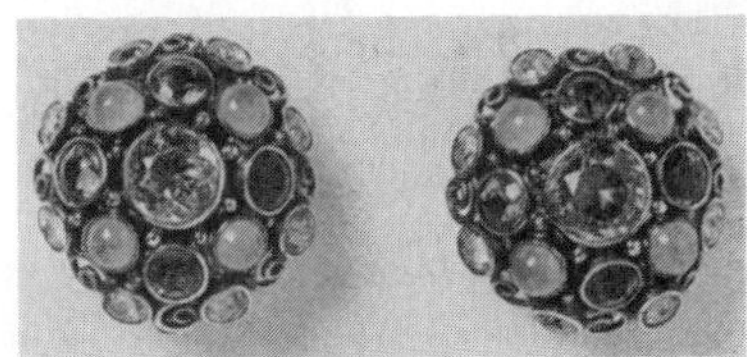

A pair of Sibyl Dunlop gem set earclips, with entral aquamarine flanked by chrysoprase abochons, further aquamarines and tourmalines, 'in (2.5cm) diam.
$1,800-2,700

Alvar Aalto (b1898)

Alvar Aalto was a Finnish architect whose vork, particularly his designs in the strong et versatile bent and laminated wood, had a reat influence on the designers of the 1930s. He founded the firm Artek in Helsinki in 1931 which produced and promoted his urniture and furnishings. Some pieces bear a long, narrow, white tag stamped Finmar - he English firm through which some pieces vere sold.

A Finmar birch chest of drawers, designed by Alvar Aalto, the drawers with solid pulls, raised on rched supports, Finmar label, 32in (81.5cm).
$600-750

Clarice Cliff (1900–1972)

Clarice Cliff, ceramic designer and decorator, studied at Burslem School of Art. She became an apprentice at A. J. Wilkinson Pottery, with its Newport subsidiary, where she went on to be its leading designer and Art Director until the War. She married Colley Shorter, the owner of the pottery, in 1940. Her best and most sought after designs are stylish and dramatic, the colours bold and bright. They reflect the freedom and openness of the twenties, in contrast to the Edwardian Age that the First World War had swept away.

As Artistic Director she also commissioned leading artists of the period to design for her, among them were Dame Laura Knight, Frank Brangwyn and Paul Nash.

A Goldsheider figure, with printed marks, 16in (40cm) high.
$450-600

Goldscheider

Friedrich Goldscheider started his ceramics factory in Vienna in 1885. He was succeeded after his death by his wife and sons. Early productions are traditional in subject matter, with a finishing process that simulated a bronze patina. The firm's Art Deco figures, many designed by leading sculptors of the period such as Lorenzl and Dakon, are very stylish, glossy and bold. They are best known for their masks, which are colourful, unusual and very collectable.

Fiona Baker
June 1993

ARTS & CRAFTS
Furniture

An Arts and Crafts oak armchair, attributed to William Birch.
$450-600

An Arts and Crafts oak chest, attributed to Heals, with 3 long drawers beneath an enclosed cupboard, the doors set with fielded chestnut panels, with exposed joints throughout.
$1,050-1,350

A William Birch oak armchair, attributed to E. Punnett, the back inset with 2 rush panels, above a rush seat and 4 rectangular section legs with H-shaped stretcher.
$750-1,200

An Arts and Crafts oak reclining armchair, attributed to William Birch, the ladder back with turned uprights, having an adjustable rod support, shaped armrests, turned front and square back supports united with stretchers, with William Morris fabric cushions.
$1,050-1,350

A pair of Arts and Crafts oak reclining chairs, c1920.
$900-1,500

A pair of oak reclining chairs with 2 cushions, c1920.
$300-375

An Arts and Crafts mahogany display cabinet, in the style of J. S. Henry, the angled glazed doors separated and bounded by planks inlaid with stylised floral pattern in fruitwood, supported above a pointed pedestal base by 3 groups of 2 frontal columns and a solid back.
$1,200-1,500

A Fradgley Arts and Crafts three-piece salon suite, comprising: a two-seater settee and a pair of armchairs, inlaid with ebony stringing and fruitwood stylised floral inlay.
$2,250-3,000

An Arts and Crafts oak dining table, the top made from 3 pieces of wood, 84½in (214cm) long.
$1,200-1,800

n Arts and Crafts oak dining
ble, 54in (137.5cm) wide.
,800-2,700

n Arts and Crafts inlaid oak ecrétaire, possibly Scottish, laid with ebony and pewter, ith stylised flower motifs within bony and ivory inlaid borders, win drawers below, on square upports united by stretchers, rass pulls and further chequer lay, 41in (104.5cm) wide.
1,200-1,500

late Victorian oak washstand, ttributed to E. & J. Jones of)swestry, with tiled galleried aised back, Cararra marble top, bove 3 frieze drawers on ring urned tapering legs, c1870, 48in 122cm) wide.
1,200-1,800

dward Jones of Leeds and)swestry, took over the firm of ohn Kendall & Co. in 1864, in artnership with John Marsh.)uring the following decade, the ame appears variously as dward Jones, Marsh & Jones, nd Marsh, Jones & Cribb. The rm was associated with the esigners Charles Bevan and ruce Talbot.

An Arts and Crafts ash table, 31in (79cm) high.
$300-375

An Arts and Crafts gateleg table, in dark stained oak, the 2 end legs formed as shaped planks with a club motif, 47in (120cm) extended.
$750-1,200

A carved oak Arts and Crafts plant stand, c1890, 35½ (90cm) high.
$300-375

An Arts and Crafts oak corner cabinet, the door having 4 panels inset with copper, possibly Newlyn, depicting stylised acorns and squirrels, with copper shaped strap hinges, 24in (61cm) wide.
$900-1,500

An Arts and Crafts Glasgow School oak settle, 46½in (117cm) wide.
$600-750

A late Victorian Arts and Crafts mahogany and ebonised wardrobe, by Christopher Pratt & Sons, with dog tooth cornice above mirrored door, flanked by 2 foliate carved panelled doors on stile feet, with brass fittings, with paper label, 66in (167cm) wide.
$1,500-2,250

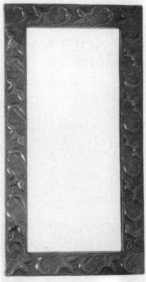

An Arts and Crafts copper mirror, possibly by Pearson or Newlyn, the glass mounted in a wooden frame, faced with copper and heavily embossed with stylised flowers and leaves against a hammered ground, 25½in (65cm) wide.
$750-1,200

An Arts and Crafts copper faced mirror, with inwardly bevelled sides embellished with foliate motifs in relief and with hammer textured surface, the corners applied with brass banding, with bevelled glass, 18½in (47.5cm) wide. **$450-600**

A Cotswold oak pedestal desk, 49½in (125.50cm) wide.
$750-900

An oak sideboard, by Heals, with fielded panels throughout, on a trestle base, with inset Heals label, 44½in (113cm) wide.
$750-900

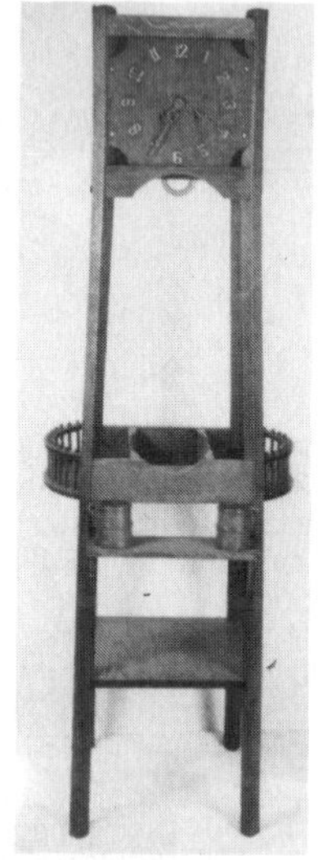

An Arts and Crafts oak clock on a stand, American, 67in (170cm) high.
$375-525

A set of Gordon Russell walnut dining chairs, comprising: 6 upright chairs and 2 carvers, eac having a lattice back with centra panel inlaid with burr panels an ebony crossbanding, with drop ir seats, metal label The Russell Workshops, Broadway, Worcestershire. **$5,250-7,500**

A Cotswold School oak dressing table, made by A. Moody, with central easel mirror, 42in (107cr wide, and a matching bedside cabinet, inscribed in pencil underneath cabinet Made by A. Moody, Leicester, 1931.
$750-900

ART NOUVEAU
Furniture

A mahogany line inlaid breakfront wardrobe, by Heals & Sons, with 2 oval panelled doors and 2 short drawers above 4 long drawers, flanked by 2 quarter veneered cupboard doors, on toupie feet, with label, 85in (116cm) wide.
$1,200-1,800

A French mahogany, thuyawood and parcel gilt cabinet-on-stand, the arched top with scroll carved cornice above vernis Martin painted door and drawer, flanked by cartouche panels above pierced scroll apron and concave undershelf on splayed legs, late 19th/early 20thC, restored, 42in (107cm) wide.
$2,700-3,300

An oak sideboard, by Liberty & Co., with mirrored shelved superstructure above 2 short drawers and 2 cupboard doors o block stile feet, with plaque and paper label, 60in (152cm) wide.
$750-1,200

'Colluden' oak sideboard, by
iberty & Co., the superstructure
ith central shelving, door
issing, flanked by an open
ıelf on either side, with copper
rapwork hinges and door
ırniture, 80in (203cm) wide.
,200-1,800

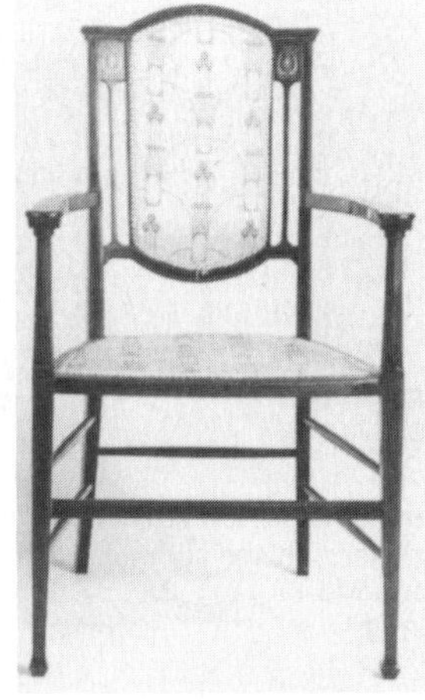

A mahogany salon suite, probably by J. S. Henry, comprising: a 2 seater settee, 2 armchairs and 6 side chairs, inlaid with stylised flowers in fruitwoods and lightwood stringing, the seats and backs upholstered with a Secessionist style fabric.
$3,000-3,750

A hexagonal coffee table by Heals, with an undershelf and supported on 6 legs of triangular section with rounded fluted sides, 28½in (72cm) wide.
$600-750

set of six oak framed dining
ıairs by Johnson of Renfrew.
750-1,200

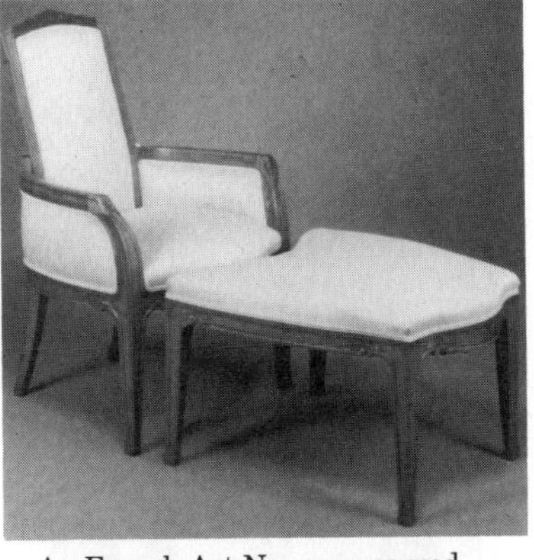

An French Art Nouveau carved walnut armchair and foot stool, the serpentine seat front and seat rail conforming to the shaped foot stool, upholsterd in beige silk, c1900, 53in (135cm).
$6,000-8,250

An Art Nouveau walnut armchair, probably Bath Cabinetmakers, with a pair of matching side chairs, the pierced backs inlaid with lightwood stringing and a floral motif highlighted with mother-of-pearl, the central splat carved with stylised flowers, on square section tapering legs, the seats upholstered with a Secessionist style fabric.
$750-1,200

French Art Nouveau walnut
vriting table, the rectangular top
bove a shaped and carved apron,
et with a pair of drawers, on
noulded legs rising to carved
vhiplash scroll brackets, 39in
100cm).
750-1,200

An Art Nouveau mahogany display cabinet, probably by J. S. Henry, with a glass fronted door above a bow fronted cupboard, with overhanging cornice, on legs with claw feet, the carcase inlaid with stylised floral designs in fruitwoods, 64in (163cm) high.
$1,200-1,800

A set of mahogany dining chairs, designed by G. M. Ellwood for J. S. Henry, comprising: 2 carvers and 6 upright chairs, each having a circular panel at the top inlaid with pale wood, pewter and brass foliate motifs, with vertical slatted back, upholstered lower back and seat with compressed ball feet, square back legs. **$10,500-12,000**

Glass

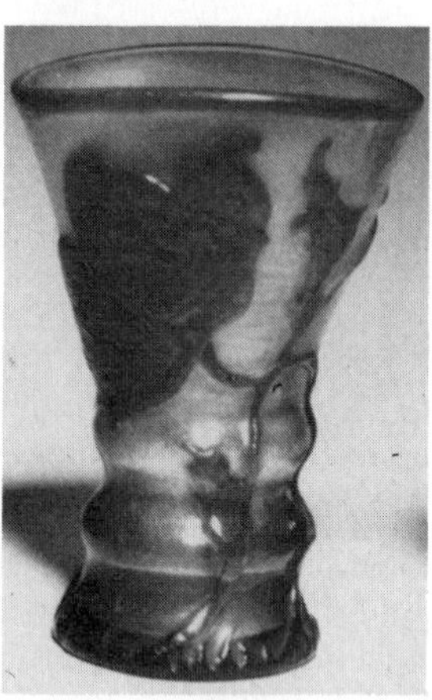

A Gallé acid etched carved and polished vase, of ribbed cylindrical form with flared neck, clear glass overlaid in orange with flowers and foliage, cameo signature Gallé, small chip to underside of base.
$750-1,200

Six various Austrian Art Nouveau hock glasses, in the style of Koloman Moser.
$300-375

A Daum acid etched and enamelled landscape vase, th grey tinted glass decorated in shades of grey, pink and gree with rainswept winter trees, enamelled factory mark.
$750-1,200

A Gallé acid etched and carved cameo vase, overlaid in white then lemon yellow, intaglio cut with a seahorse and various shells beneath dense tall slender seaweed, with 5 pointed leaves forming a band round the shoulder, cameo mark Gallé, 7½in (18.5cm).
$3,000-4,500

A Loetz lavender blue glass bowl, attributed to a design by Michael Powolny, on 3 feet, decorated with applied black vertical banding, 8½in (21cm) diam.
$750-900

Iridescent Glass

A Loetz iridescent vase, with short cylindrical neck, the pink glass decorated with golden diagonal combed festoons, 8½in (21cm).
$1,500-2,250

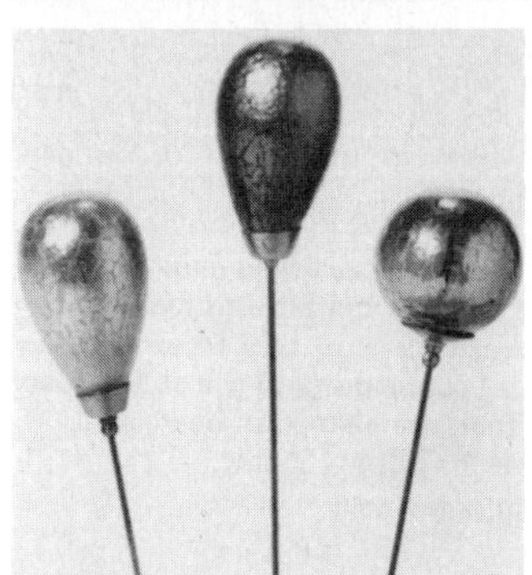

Three Loetz glass topped hatpins, one with peacock blue splashes, the other with mauve blue splashes against yellow and the third with iridescence of greenish hue.
$375-450

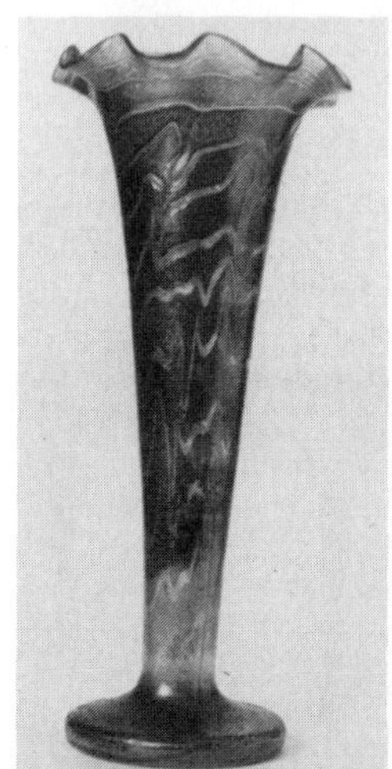

A Loetz iridescent glass vase, with wavy rim, rising from a spreading circular base, with random undulating banding an exhibiting tones of mauve, viole and green tinged golden iridescence, 27½in (70cm).
$1,050-1,350

A Sam Herman spherical vase, the milky glass decorated with abstract trails in blue and yellow under an iridescent finish, original paper label, 13½in (34cm).
$450-600

ronze

double-sided bronze vase, 11½in
9cm) high.
750-1,200

An Art Nouveau bronze easel mirror, in the manner of Georges de Feure, the bronze frame decorated in relief and openwork with leaves and florets on sinuous stems, 21½in (54cm).
$1,050-1,350

An Austrian cold painted bronze elephant lamp, with coloured glass inserts, by Bergman, 16in (41cm).
$2,250-3,000

silvered bronze figure, with
mb, signed, 34in (86cm) long.
3,000-4,500

A French Art Nouveau bronze vase, designed by Paul Follot, of slender tulip form with fluted sides and 4 elegant loop handles extending from the neck, on square base, artist's signature cast in the bronze, 20½in (52cm).
$3,000-4,500

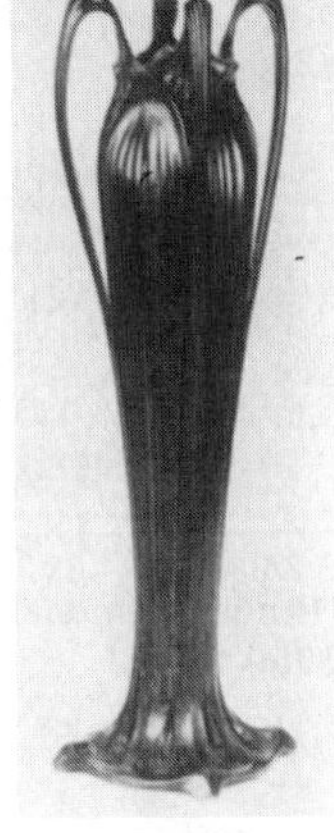

opper

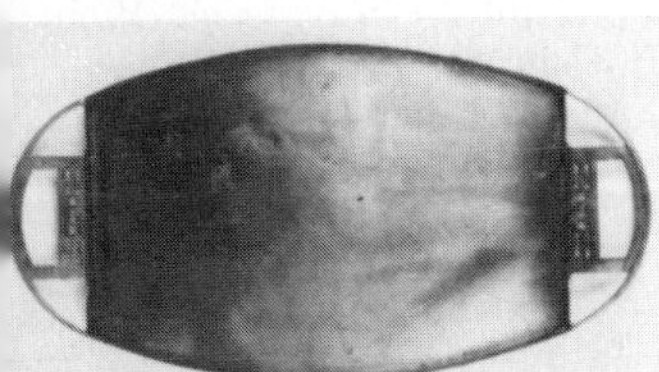

copper and brass tray, by
ustave Scrurrier Bouvy, c1905,
3in (59cm) wide.
375-450

A pair of Art Nouveau copper candlesticks, attributed to W.E.J. Benson, 10½in (26cm).
$375-525

A W.M.F. copper and brass egg coddler, c1909, 10in (25cm).
$150-225

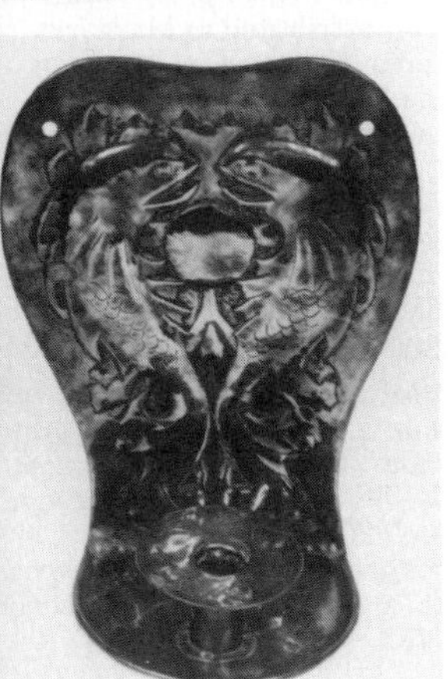

Newlyn School copper wall
conce, 11in (28cm).
225-255

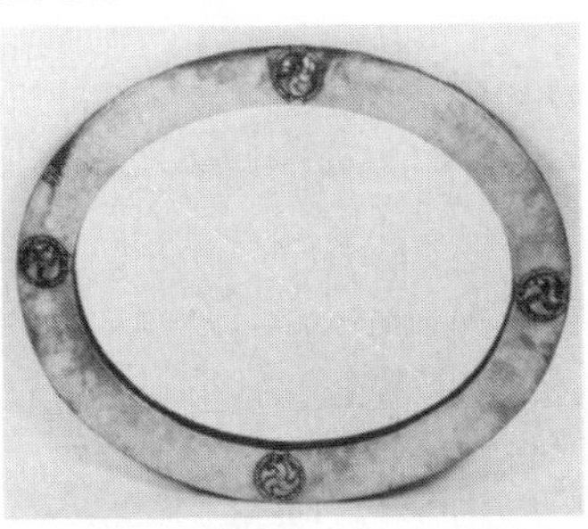

A Liberty & Co. copper mounted mirror, the frame fitted with 4 scrolling bosses and beaten finish throughout, with Liberty label, 24in (62cm) wide.
$300-375

A copper wall mirror, attributed to John Pearson, the glass mounted in a wooden frame faced with copper and embossed with birds in flight, trees, plants and a winding path, 14½ by 18½in (37 by 47cm).
$450-600

Pewter

A Liberty & Co., English pewter biscuit barrel and cover, embellished with stylised buds and tendrils, having swing handle and domed cover, stamped marks and numbered 01167, 5in (13cm) high.
$225-300

A Liberty & Co, Tudric jardinière, with pink enamelled insets.
$750-1,200

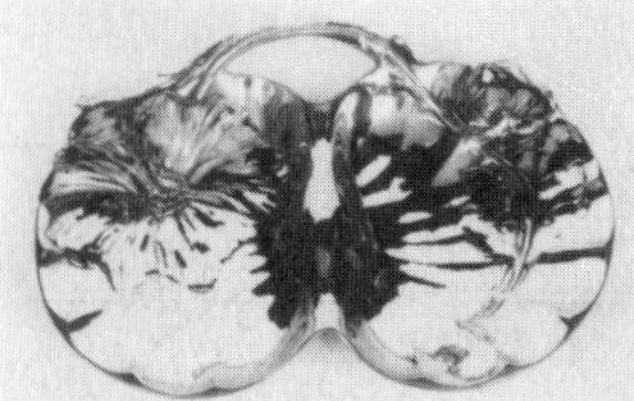

A Kayserzinn pewter dish, 11in (28cm) wide.
$375-525

A Kayserzinn lidded pewter jug, 9in (23cm).
$375-450

An Art Nouveau pewter desk blotter, 6in (15cm).
$225-300

Liberty

Liberty & Co., was the principal outlet for Art Nouveau designs in England.

Arthur Lasenby Liberty (1843-1917) founded his furniture and drapery shop in 1875. Later he commissioned designs exclusive to his store, including Cymric silver and Tudric pewter, which gave rise to a distinctive 'Liberty Style'.

A Liberty & Co., Tudric pewter clock, with embossed copper face above a blue and green enamelled plaque, flanked and mounted by stylised scrollwork, impressed Tudric 0367, with key, 6½in (16cm) high.
$750-1,200

A W.M.F. pewter lamp, c1900, 14in (36cm).
$1,500-2,250

A pair of Liberty Art Nouve pewter vases, 10in (25cm).
$750-900

A Liberty & Co., English pewter salad bowl, designed by Rex Silver, with an openwork design of interwoven entrelacs extendir to form 2 small handles, marked English Pewter Made by Liberty & Co., numbered 0318, with original green glass liner, probably by Whitefriars, 10½in (27cm) diam.
$1,800-2,700

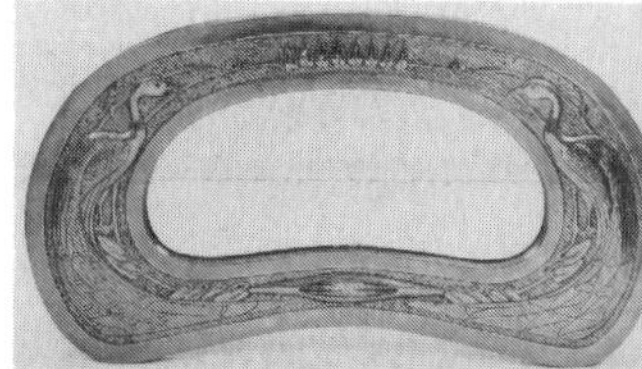

A Glasgow School pewter wall mirror, attributed to Margaret Gilmour, mounted in a wooden frame faced in pewter and embossed with a peacock at eithe end, united by branches with stylised leaves, enamelled with a blue/green panel, reserved against a textured ground, 12 by 24½in (31 by 62cm).
$1,200-1,800

Similar use of enamelling can be seen on a wall clock by Margaret Gilmour, illustrated in 'Glasgow Girls - Women in Art and Design 1880-1920', and similar style leaves are shown in 'The Glasgow Style' by Gerald and Celia Larne No. 182.

A Liberty pewter and enamel clock, c1903, 11in (28cm).
$1,500-2,250

An Art Nouveau pewter mirror, 22in (56cm).
$1,500-2,250

A W.M.F. Art Nouveau plated pewter mirror, the surround cast in relief with the figure of a maiden in long flowing drapery, her hair adorned with flowers, stamped factory marks, 14½in (37cm).
$1,200-1,800

A Liberty pewter tea set and tray, c1910, tray 17in (43cm) wide.
$750-1,200

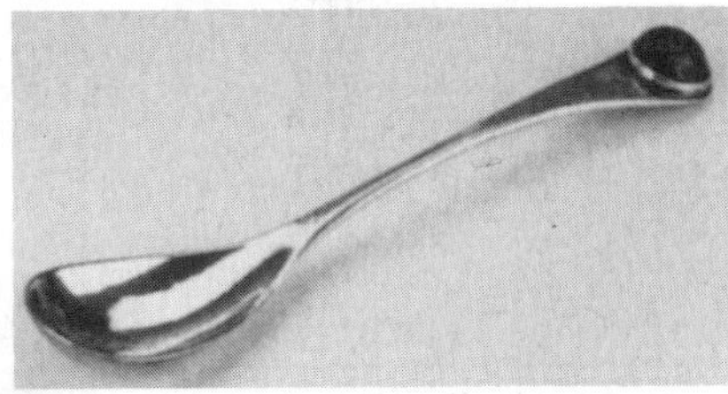

A Guild of Handicraft silver jam spoon, designed by C.R. Ashbee, set with turquoise, engraved 'Lorna', stamped G of H Ltd with London hallmarks for 1904, 50gr.
$375-450

ilver

W.M.F. silver plated dessert rvice, with unusual box, 13in 3cm).
,200-1,500

An A.E. Jones hammered silver rose bowl, decorated with a repoussé frieze of Tudor roses amid foliage, mounted on wood plinth, stamped maker's marks A. E. J. with Birmingham hallmarks for 1909, 9in (23cm) diam, 990gr.
$3,000-3,750

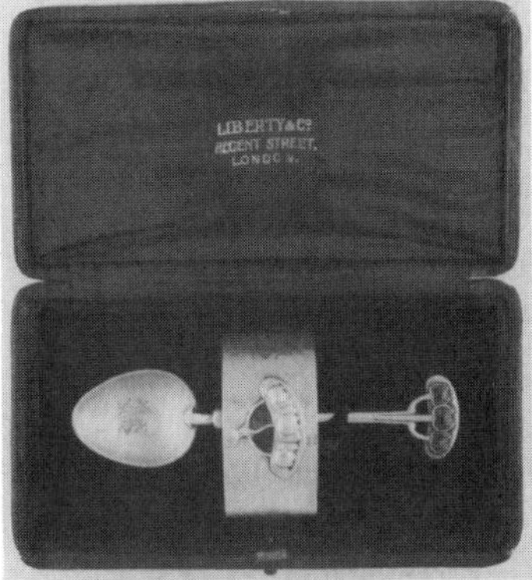

A Liberty & Co., silver and enamel christening set, comprising a teaspoon and matching napkin ring, in original box, both with moulded floral design, heightened with blue and green enamel, maker's mark for Birmingham 1908, 4in (11cm).
$375-450

A pair of Liberty & Co., Cymric silver candlesticks, design attributed to Archibald Knox, maker's mark for Birmingham 1909, one repaired.
$2,700-3,300

An Elkington Art Nouveau bowl, of pierced oval outline, with curved handles supported on 2 C-shaped stems above an oval domed base, stamped 'E. & Co.', with Birmingham hallmarks for 1910, 7in (17cm).
$600-750

A C.R. Ashbee hammered silver bowl, with pierced design of stylised fruit laden branches, stamped 'CRA' with London hallmarks for 1899, 8in (19.5cm) diam, 430gr.
$1,800-2,700

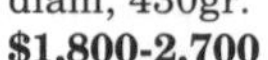

A Liberty & Co., silver rose bow designed by Bernard Cuzner, engraved with Golden Wedding dedication on one side, marked & Co, for Birmingham 1916, separate grille top for flower display, 6½in (16.5cm) diam.
$2,250-3,000

A Tiffany & Co., silver child's mug, the body decorated in low relief, with etched detailing, with a scene of children preparing a number of small dogs to jump through a hoop, stamped Tiffany & Co. 410SE, maker's 7590, Sterling Silver 925-1000 M, 3in (7cm).
$375-450

An Art Nouveau preserve jar and spoon, George Lawrence Connell, with plain glass jar, hammered openwork trefoil frame and tripod handle to cover, Birmingham 1909, the spoon with heart shaped bowl and enamelled interlace motif terminal, spoon 1912, 5in (13cm), 12oz.
$2,250-3,000

A Georg Jensen silver vase and cover, of baluster form, on a sma circular foot, the lip moulded wit leaves, the overhanging cover with moulded piecrust edge, set with 4 cabochon amethysts in flower buds, impressed marks fo Georg Jensen and import marks for 1924, 8¼in (21cm) high.
$4,500-6,000

Georg Jensen (1886-1935)

Georg Jensen was a Danish designer of silverware and jewellery, whose workshop was established in 1904 in Copenhagen. Famous for his prize winning rose lidded teapot.

An Art Nouveau silver photograph frame, stamped in relief with entrelac scrolls, with enamelled hearts and ovals in mottled blue and green, on later wood mount and easel support, Birmingham 1904, 8in (20cm).
$600-750

A Guild of Handicraft hammered silver beaker, designed by C.R. Ashbee, with repoussé and engraved decoration of stylised flowers and leaves, stamped G of H Ltd with London hallmarks for 1904, 4in (11cm), 210gr.
$750-900

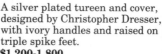

A silver plated tureen and cover, designed by Christopher Dresser, with ivory handles and raised on triple spike feet.
$1,200-1,800

This piece has been well used and is missing a spoon, which would have increased the value considerably.

ı Edward VII Art Nouveau ıotograph frame, decorated with ylised foliate motifs and hiplash on a textured ground, J. Hall, Birmingham 1903, 12in 0cm), a 2-division frame, ırmingham 1901, 3in (7.5cm) ıd a plain frame, Birmingham 914, 7½in (18.5cm).
'50-1,200

A Georg Jensen 155 piece Acorn pattern table service, with stamped marks.
$9,000-10,000

W.M.F. silver plated ntrepiece, c1905, 33in (84cm) gh.
,000-4,500

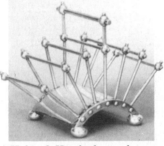

A Hukin & Heath electroplated toast rack, designed by Christopher Dresser, convex base on 4 bun feet, wire frame with 7 supports joined by small spheres, the central support raised to a handle, stamped H&H 2556 with date lozenge for May 1881, 5in (13cm) high. **$600-750**

A Hukin & Heath plated spoon warmer, designed by Christopher Dresser, with open top, sealed hot water reservoir, straight ebonised handle and 4 spiked feet, maker's marks and 2693, 6in (15.5cm) long. **$750-1,200**

W.M.F.

W.M.F. is short for the Austrian Württembergishe Metallwarenfabrik, one of the principal producers of Art Nouveau silver and silver plated objects in the early 20thC.

A Hukin & Heath electroplate division letter rack, designed by Christopher Dresser, with adjustable supports, the arched base on 4 bun feet, surmounted by rod and ball supports, stamped marks, 5in (13cm) high, and a cut glass and electroplate condiment set. **$750-900**

Christopher Dresser (1835-1904)

Christopher Dresser was an influential English pottery, metalware and glass designer who was inspired by Japanese art. He worked for Tiffany as well as the pottery firms of Ault, Linthorpe and Pilkington.

ewellery

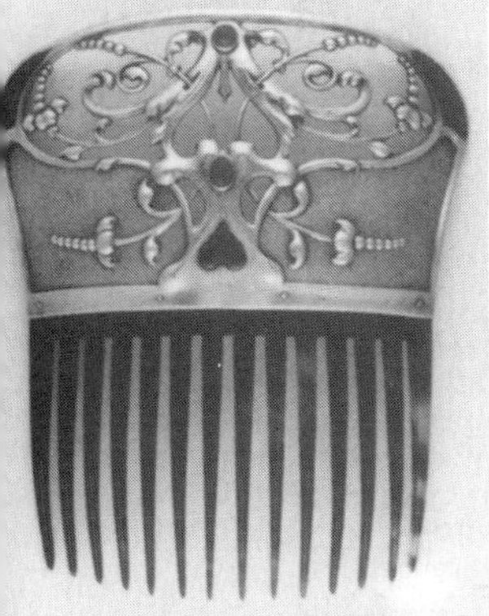

The pink, a type of carnation, was the Guild of Handicraft, Essex, House logo.

A Guild of Handicraft white metal cloak clasp, designed by C.R. Ashbee, each circular piece with repoussé decoration of pinks.
$750-900

An Art Nouveau hair comb, with embossed openwork scrolling foliage set with blue stained chalcedony cabochons and blue enamelling, probably Scandinavian, 5½in (14cm) wide.
$450-600

A Guild of Handicraft white metal and enamel waist clasp, designed by C.R. Ashbee, each circular piece with pierced floral decoration and set with turquoises, the centre with green/blue enamel.
$1,200-1,800

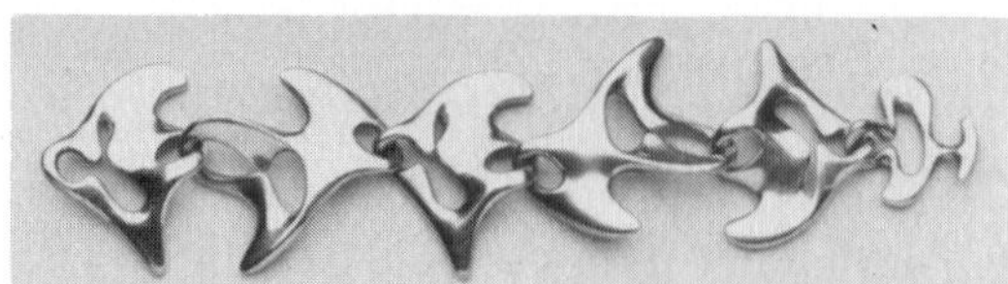

A Georg Jensen silver bracelet, designed by Henning Koppel, formed by 5 amoebic-like openwork plaques linked together, Danish maker's marks and London import marks for 1960, 8½in (21cm) long.
$750-1,200

A Liberty & Co., silver cloak clasp, with foliate design set wi seed pearls, stamped L & Co wi Birmingham hallmarks for 190
$450-600

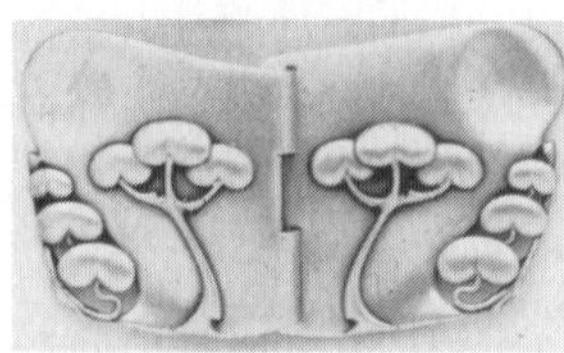

Two Liberty & Co., silver waist clasps, one from a design for a bell push by Arthur Penny, each section of stylised honesty decorated with a central turquoise, marked LCCUD Cymric with Birmingham hallmarks for 1903, and another stamped L & Co Ltd., with Birmingham hallmarks for 1899.
$1,050-1,350

A Liberty & Co., Glasgow Style silver and enamel waist buckle, with openwork decoration of stylised foliage with enamel details, stamped L & Co with Birmingham hallmarks for 1902.
$1,200-1,800

A white metal and enamel brooc by Ernestine Mills, with polychrome foil enamel decoratic of a bird perched on a branch of flowering prunus, signed with 'EM' monogram, and a set of 6 enamel buttons, by Beatrice Cameron, in green, turquoise an purple scrolling foliate cloisonné enamel decoration, in original fitted case, damage to enamel.
$750-1,200

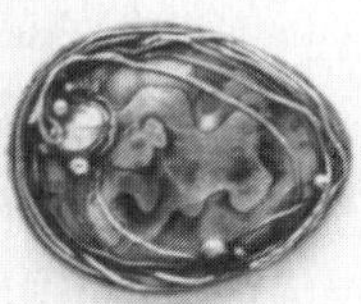

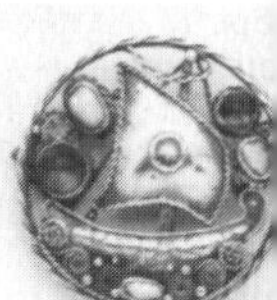

Three white metal brooches, by Mary Thew, one brooch with blister pearl and chrysoprase, one with abalone sh with wirework decoration set with blister pearl, anothe with openwork decoration of a sailing vessel, set with baroque pearls, citrine and amethyst and the hatpin set with agate. **$1,050-1,350**

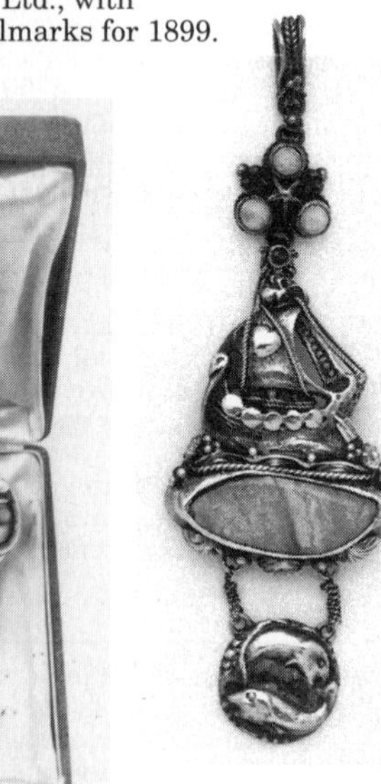

An Artificers Guild yellow and white metal pendant, by J.H.M. Bonnor, of a Viking ship in full sail, with wirework details and decoration of sea creatures, suspended from a loop with the North Star, set with enamel, opals and garnet, with monogram J.H.M.B. **$1,200-1,800**

An Art Nouveau hair comb, the gilt floral openwork head set with 3 opals within curvilinear frame to the blonde tortoiseshell comb, the reverse with stamped signature, in maker's case stamped Ch Dubret, 83 Rue de la Liberté, Dijon.
$1,050-1,350

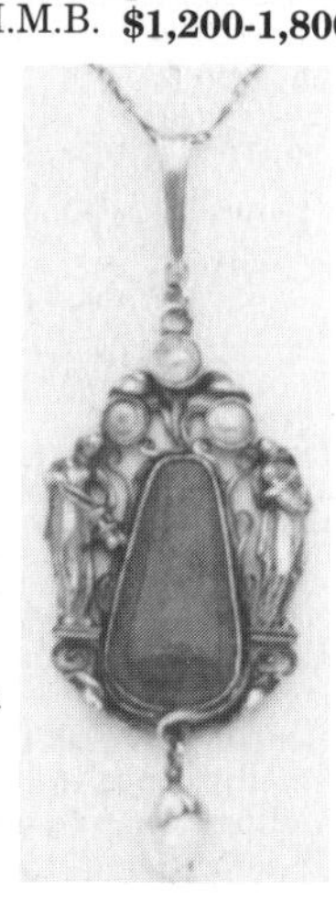

A yellow and silver pendant on a chain, by Joseph A. Hodel, the wirework foliate design set with a black opal, baroque pearls and 2 modelled and cast yellow metal maidens, stamped Hodel.
$2,700-3,300

A white metal and enamel pendant, by Nelson and Edith Dawson, the central floral enamelled medallion mounted i an octagonal frame, suspended from an earlier wirework bow se with crystal, and crystal drop, inscribed ND.
$1,500-2,250

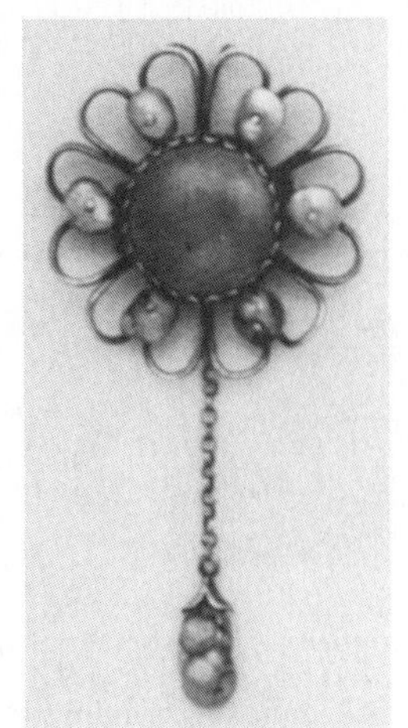

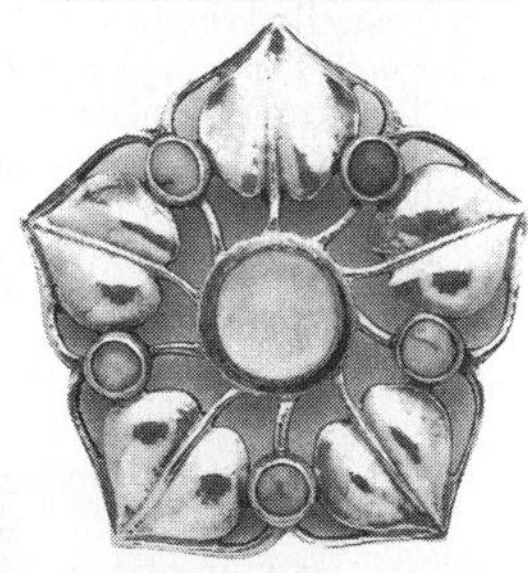

Two Guild of Handicraft white metal brooches, one designed by C.R. Ashbee with openwork repoussé decoration of stylised foliage, set with moonstone and turquoise, stamped marks G of H Ltd., and one with wirework design in the form of a flower set with baroque pearls and turquoise enamel and a pear drop.
$1,050-1,350

Three white metal brooches, by Bernard Cuzner, one with pierced and chased design of birds amid foliage, one with pierced decoration of leaves and berries, set with a central amazonite, and another with wirework heart shaped design set with a central Ruskin Pottery circular plaque, all with maker's mark.
$1,050-1,350

A Guild of Handicraft white metal brooch, designed by C.R. Ashbee, in the form of a winged insect with an articulated body, its body formed by an opal, in original case.
$1,200-1,500

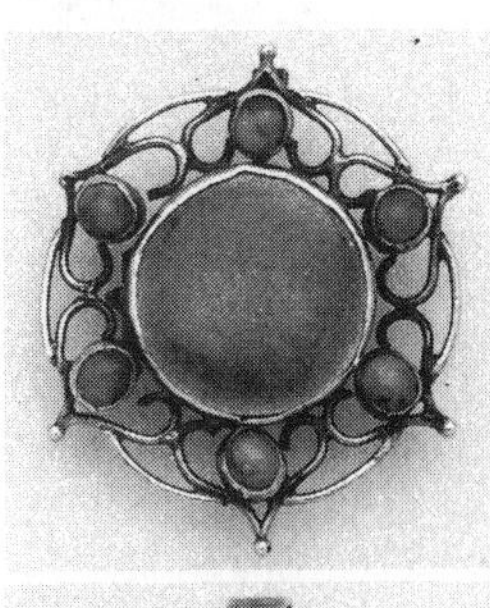

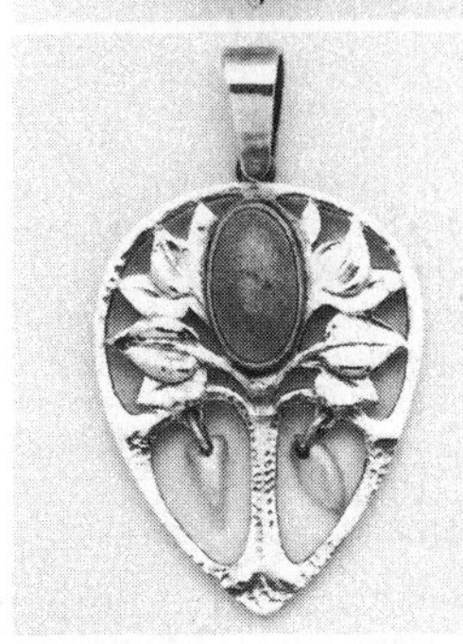

Two Guild of Handicraft brooches, one designed by C.R. Ashbee, with an openwork design in the form of a tree, with repoussé details set with turquoise enamel and baroque pear drops, in its original fitted case, engraved LC, and another with a wirework scrolled design, set with turquoises and turquoise enamel.
$1,050-1,350

A Liberty & Co., silver and enamel waist clasp, designed by Jessie M. King, with circular openwork decoration of stylised flowers and birds with blue/green enamel details, stamped L & Co with Birmingham hallmarks for 1906.
$2,250-3,000

A white metal and cloisonné enamel buckle and 2 white metal brooches, all by Nelson and Edith Dawson.
$1,050-1,350

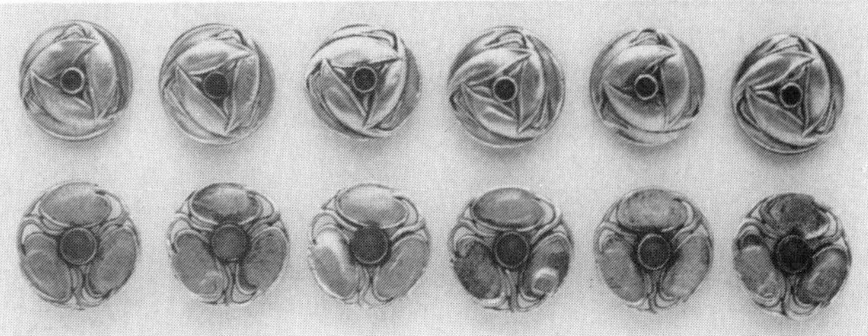

Two sets of 6 Guild of Handicraft white metal buttons, each of stylised foliage motif, set with agate and chrysoprase, one set in original fitted case.
$750-1,200

Ceramics

A Linthorpe pottery bowl, designed by Christopher Dresser, with silver rim, impressed mark and signature, 10in (25cm) diam.
$300-375

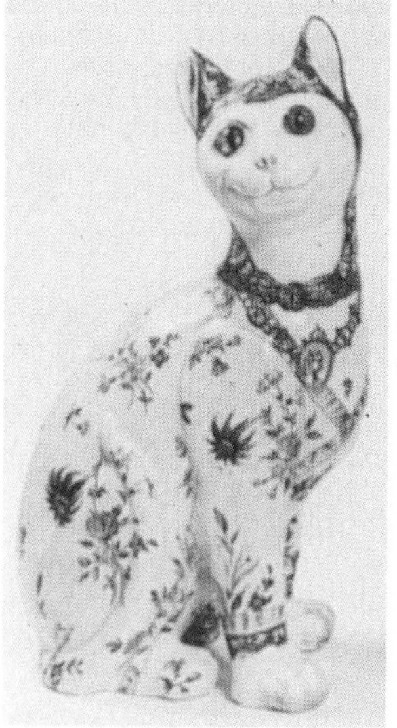

A Gallé faience cat, painted with polychrome floral sprays on a yellow ground, wearing a pendant with dog medallion and grey and white floral scarf, green glass eyes, some damage, unmarked, 13in (33cm) high.
$750-900

A pair of Brannam pottery vases, by James Dewdney, decorated in sgraffito with oval panels of birds perched on flowering boughs, in red slip against stippled white beneath a blue translucent glaze, incised C.H.Brannam, Barum J.D. 1888, R to necks, 14½in (37cm).
$375-450

A Carlton Ware charger, 13in (33cm).
$150-180

A Bretby figure of a fisher boy, standing on a rocky mound, c1895, 35in (89cm) high.
$750-900

Emile Gallé (1846-1904)

- Emile Gallé was the father of the French Art Nouveau movement and founder of a talented circle of designers based around Nancy.
- He is perhaps more important for technique than design. In 1884 he advertised his 'new colourations' or kinds of translucent glass; in 1889 he developed cameo glass; in 1897 he introduced 'marquetry in glass'.
- After his death, factories continued to produce his wares, signed Gallé but marked with a star, until the 1930's.

An Art Nouveau hanging plaque, 9in (23cm) diam.
$300-375

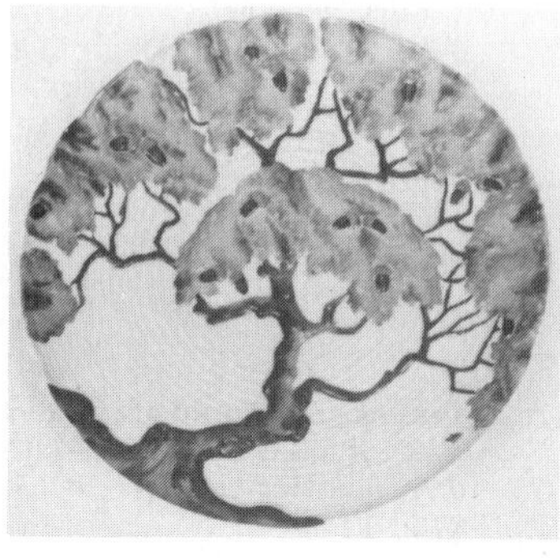

A Linthorpe pottery ewer, designed by Christopher Dress the red body covered with a streaked milky green/brown glaze, facsimile Dresser signature, 'HT' monogram for Henry Tooth and numbered '5(8½in (21cm) high.
$750-900

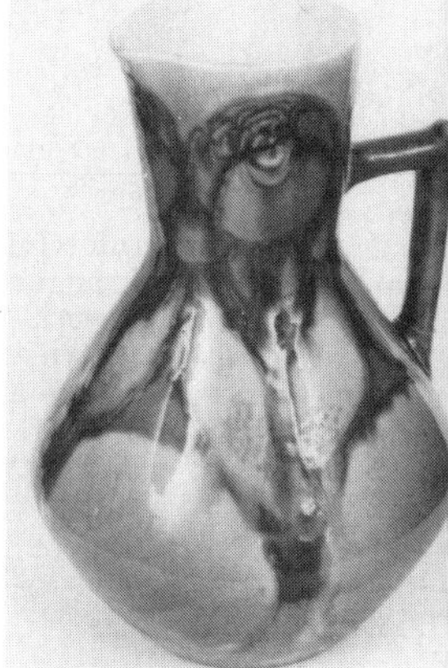

A Minton Secessionist jug, wi green, yellow and grey glaze, 11½in (29cm) high.
$150-225

A Brannam pottery slipware vas the red body overlaid with white slip, decorated with sgraffito panels of birds amid flowering shrubbery, flanked by formal flower and leaf motifs, beneath a pale honey glaze, signed C.H.Brannam, Barum, N. Devon dated 1881, R on neck, 15in (38.5cm) high.
$1,050-1,350

Brannam pottery slipware vase, th red body overlaid with white p, decorated with 3 sgraffito nels of armorial style beasts d foliage, flanked by foliate and ometric panels and borders, neath a honey glaze, signed C. annam, Barum, N. Devon and ted 1881, R on neck, 15in 3cm) high.
50-1,200

this early date it is highly ausible that C.H. Brannam mself threw and decorated this ece.

A Bretby 'jewelware vessel', 16in (41cm) high. **$225-300**

A pair of Fenton Sutherland Art Ware vases, by Frank Beardmore & Co., with pink, green and yellow decoration, 12½in (31.5cm).
$750-1,200

A pair of Ault brown and black earthenware vases, c1930, 10½in (26cm).
$105-120

Watcombe Pottery terracotta a set, designed by Christopher esser, with bands of ridged coration, comprising: a teapot d cover, milk jug, sugar basin, p with saucer and tray, with pressed W, teapot 3in (8cm).
00-1,500

A stoneware face jug, both sides of the jug modelled with the face of a mildly amused, overweight and ageing male, with strap handle, incised 10.12.1909 R.W. Martin & Brothers, London & Southall, 7in (18cm) high.
$1,050-1,350

An Austrian wall plaque by Boss, 6½in (16cm). **$225-300**

tapering sided jug, incised with gentleman and companion in edieval costume, flanked by owing flowers and leaves on a own ground, incised mark, R.W. artin, London and Southall, and ted 15th July 1881, 8½in 1cm).
375-525

A Hadcote vase, with raised slip design in turquoise, made for Liberty & Co., 7in (18cm) high.
$225-255

A pair of Martin Brothers stoneware candlesticks, each on sloping footed square base, incised with panels of water birds, surmounted by twisted columns incised with foliage and the monogram PA, glazed in shades of green and blue, incised factory marks, damaged, 8in (20cm).
$375-525

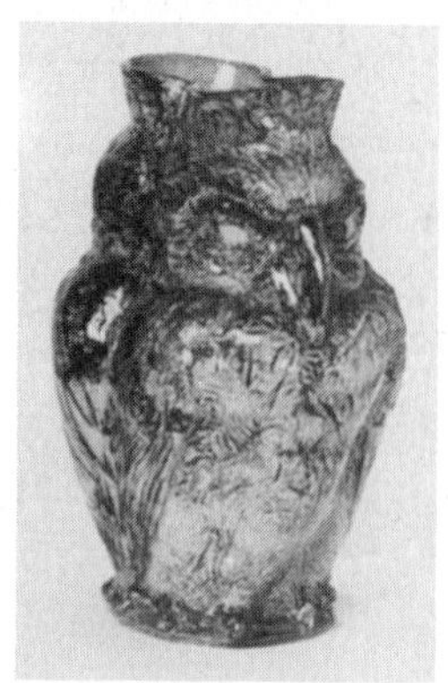

A stoneware double bird vase, one half of the vessel formed by the body of a bird with 'shifty' expression, the other squinting, their plumage picked out in browns, ochre, beige, blue and black, signed on base R.W. Martin & Brothers, London & Southall, dated 3-1892, 8½in (21cm) high.
$3,000-4,500

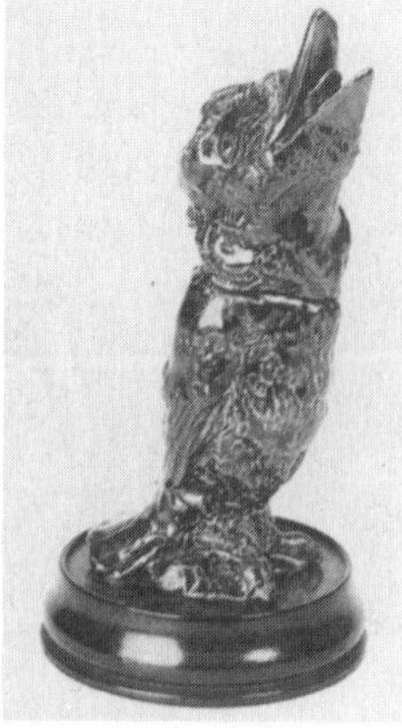

A stoneware bird, with removable head, resembling a duck with beak parted to reveal a tongue, the creature glazed dark brown and resting on a circular wooden base, signed on neck and near base Martin Brothers, London & Southall, indistinct date, 8in (20cm) high. **$1,200-1,800**

A C.H. Brannam sgraffiato handled vase, fish motif wit trailed organic Art Nouveau forms, 5in (13cm) high.
$300-375

Martin Brothers

The pottery firm owned by the Martin Brothers was active in London between 1873 and 1914. It was best known for its grey stoneware, often in grotesque shapes or with incised decoration.

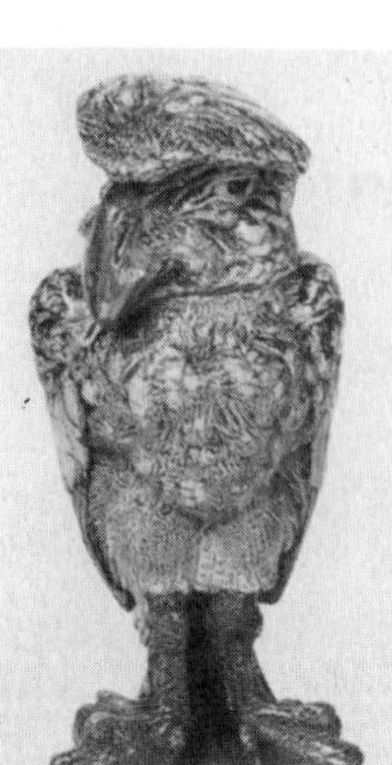

A stoneware bird, with removable head, modelled with broad beak, heavy head plumage resembling eyebrows, in browns, ochre and beige with areas of pale blue, signed on neck and base R.W. Martin & Bros, London & Southall dated 3-1901, 12in (31cm) high.
$7,500-9,000

A stoneware flask, finely incise on one side with an amusing fa of the Sun, the reverse side showing a bearded Man in the Moon amid stars and comets, signed Martin Bros, London & Southall, and dated 11-1891, 6½ (16.5cm) high. **$1,800-2,700**

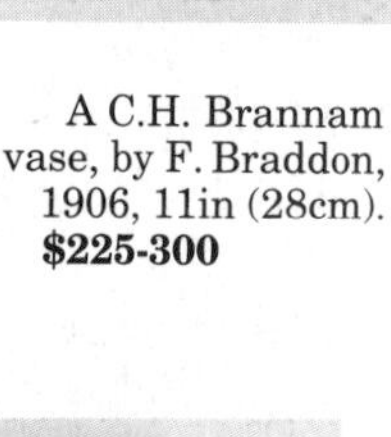

A C.H. Brannam vase, by F. Braddon, 1906, 11in (28cm).
$225-300

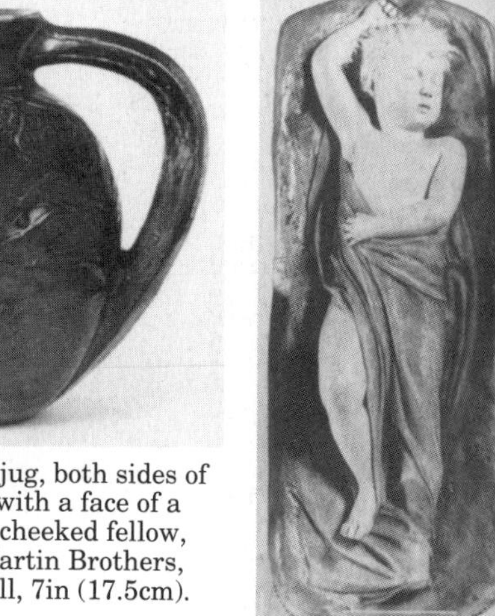

A stoneware face jug, both sides of the jug modelled with a face of a grinning, chubby cheeked fellow, incised 3-1891, Martin Brothers, London & Southall, 7in (17.5cm).
$750-1,200

A Minton secessionist jardinière and stand, tube lined with stylised vertical floral banding in mauve and pale blue enhanced with sinuous green tendrils on a blue ground, marked Minton Ltd., No. 72 to each base, slight repair to rim of jardinière, 40in (102cm).
$1,200-1,800

A stoneware effigy, modelled as young boy sleeping with a drape over his body, in blue, brown an cream, incised 'He rests, He sleeps, nor dreams of any harm' Edwin Bruce Martin, R. Wallac Martin S.C., original plaster cas modelled in Wandsworth Road, about 1862. **$1,200-1,800**

loorcroft

Walter Moorcroft Orchid design
p and saucer, c1949.
25-255

A William Moorcroft orchre Poppy clock case, with original movement, c1920, 5in (13cm) high.
$1,500-2,250

A MacIntyre Moorcroft teapot and stand, with seaweed design, c1902.
$1,050-1,350

Moorcroft MacIntyre Florian
ppy design vase, c1904, 3½in
cm) high.
50-600

Wm Moorcroft (1872-1946)

William Moorcroft was a Staffordshire artist-potter known especially for his 'Florian' and 'Aurelian' ware. From 1898 he worked for MacIntyre's and set up independently in 1913.

A MacIntyre Moorcroft Pomegranate design tea kettle, c1912.
$1,500-2,250

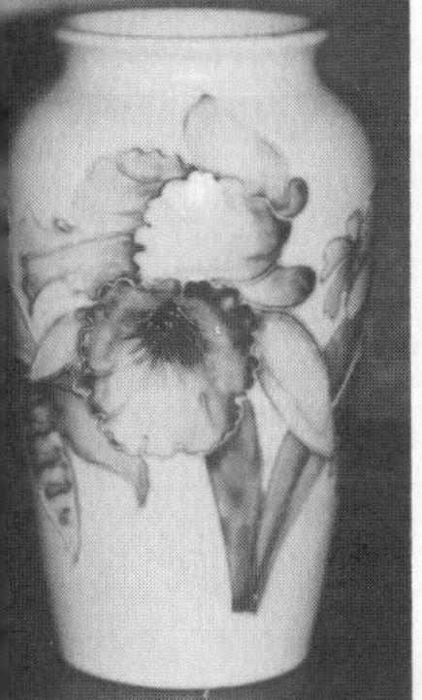

A William Moorcroft saltglaze Orchid design vase, c1930, 7in (18cm) high.
$600-750

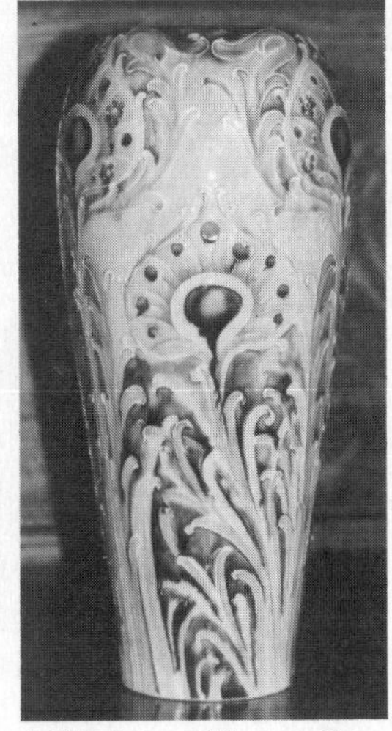

A MacIntyre Moorcroft Peacock design vase, on a celadon ground, signed W. M. Des, c1900, 10in (25cm).
$2,700-3,300

A MacIntyre Moorcroft blue Florian vase, highlighted with gilt, incised W. M. Des, c1898, 9in (23cm) high.
$1,500-2,250

A Moorcroft ovoid footed bowl with inverted rim, decorated with fish and water weeds, in shades of green, blue and yellow, impressed factory marks, signed in green, 6in (15cm) high.
$1,200-1,500

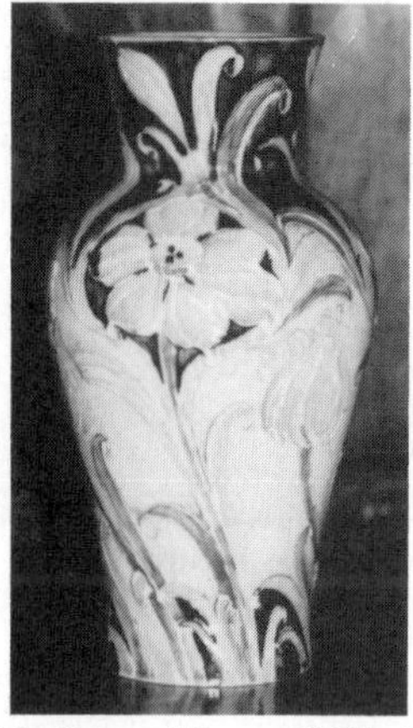

A MacIntyre Moorcroft Florian vase, with blue and yellow flowers, c1903, 6in (15cm) high.
$1,200-1,500

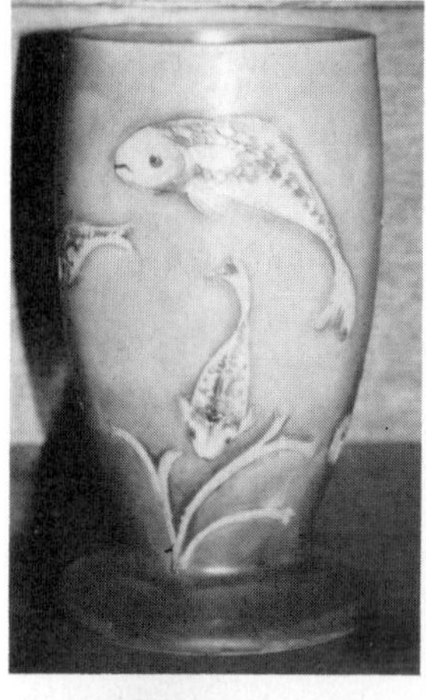

A William Moorcroft saltglaze Fish design vase, c1928, 9in (23cm) high.
$1,200-1,800

A MacIntyre Moorcroft Florian Ware Poppy pattern jug, with simulated bamboo moulded handle, EPNS mount, hinged cover and thumbpiece, damaged, printed mark in brown, initialled WM in green, early 20thC, 8½in high.
$600-750

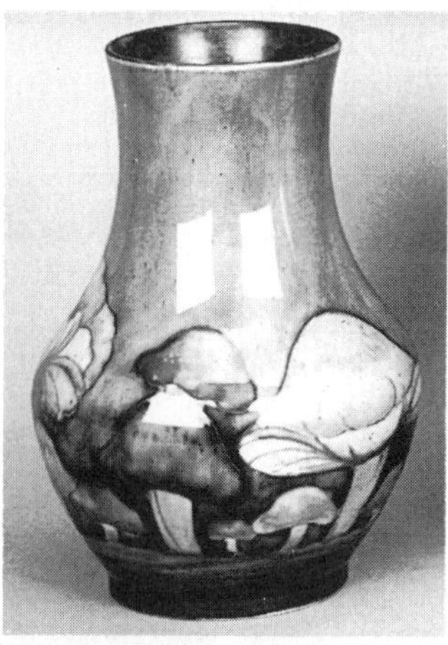

A Moorcroft Claremont pattern vase, designed by William Moorcroft, the swollen cylindrical form with flared neck and everted rim, blue and green mottled green with yellow, pink, green and blue mushrooms, restored, impressed Moorcroft, Made in England, and green signature W. Moorcroft, c1920, 6½in (17cm) high.
$600-750

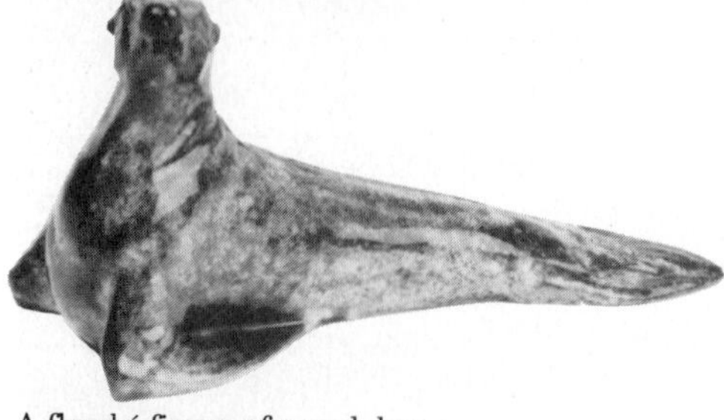

A flambé figure of a seal, by William Moorcroft, 8in (20cm) long.
$1,500-2,250

A MacIntyre Florian Iris pattern vase, designed by William Moorcroft, on flared foot, flared cylindrical form with everted rim, blue ground with raised slip decoration of cartouches of green and yellow irises, brown printed MacIntyre Florian Ware stamp, green signature W. Moorcroft Des, c1900, 6½in (17cm) high.
$750-900

A MacIntyre Claremont patter bowl, designed by William Moorcroft, the green and blue streaked ground with decoratio of crimson, blue and green mushrooms, printed marks Ma for Liberty & Co, registered No. 420081, with green signature W Moorcroft, c1903, 8½in (21.5cm)
$1,500-2,250

A MacIntyre Moorcroft tobacco j and cover, on a celadon ground with red flora, c1903, 5in (13cm) high.
$1,200-1,500

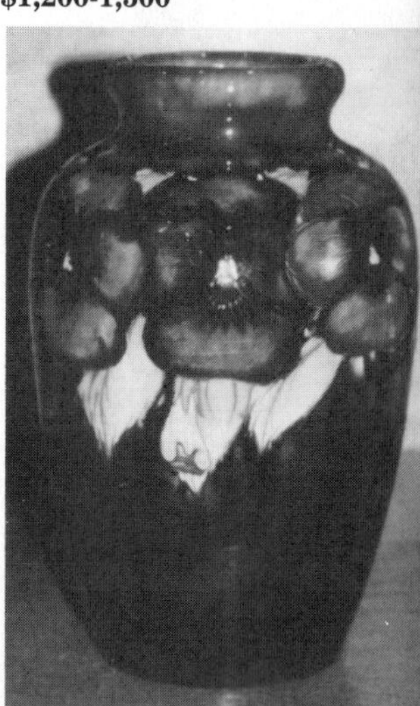

A William Moorcroft Pansy desig vase, on blue ground, c1925, 9in (23cm) high.
$450-600

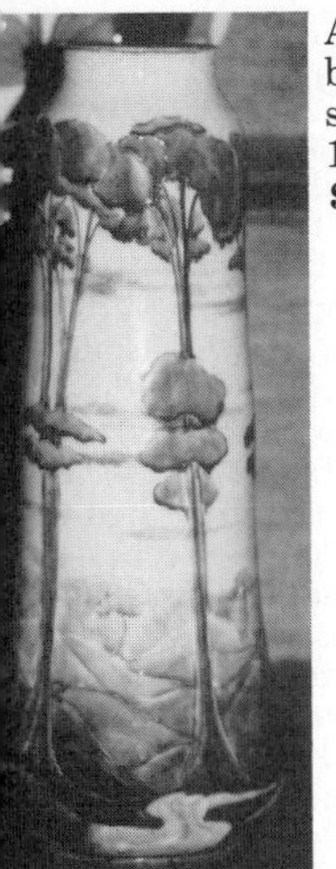

A MacIntyre Moorcroft Florian blue Landscape pattern vase, signed W. Moorcroft Des, c1903, 12in (30.5cm) high.
$2,250-3,000

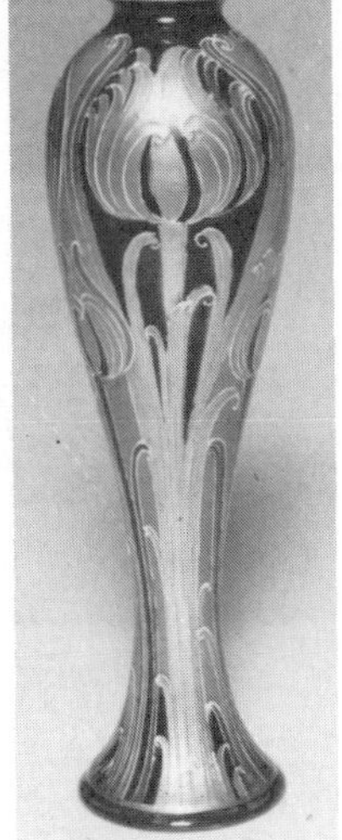

A Moorcroft MacIntyre Florian Ware vase, tube lined in white and decorated in green and gilt on a blue ground, printed mark and pattern No. M2019, 9in (23cm) high.
$750-900

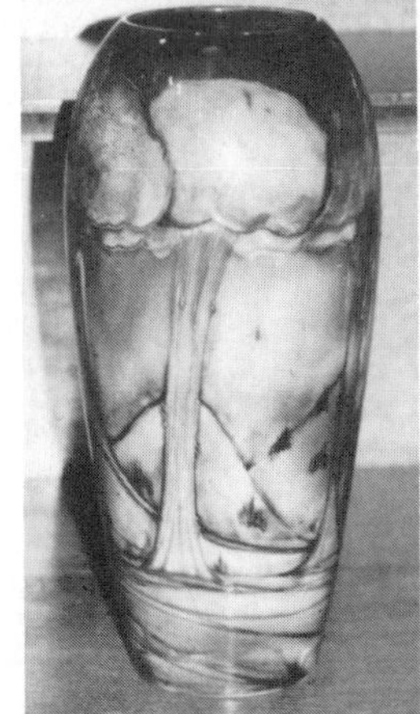

A William Moorcroft Flambè Landscape vase, c1928, 12in (30cm) high.
$4,500-6,000

A Walter Moorcroft Bougainvillea design vase, on a green ground, c1955, 10in (25cm) high.
$600-750

A William Moorcroft Toadstool design vase, 7in (18cm).
$450-600

Walter Moorcroft Fuchsia sign vase on a green ound, c1949, 12in 1cm) high.
'50-1,200

A Walter Moorcroft Hibiscus design vase, on ivory ground, c1955, 8in (20cm) high.
$225-300

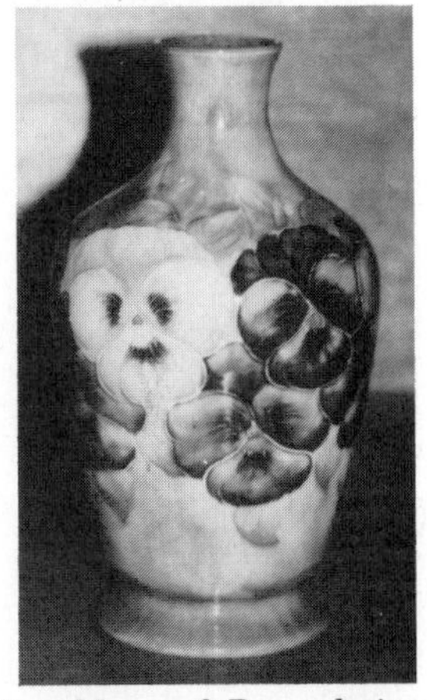

A William Moorcroft Pansy design vase on pale green ground, impressed Burslem, signed in green, c1913, 5in (13cm) high.
$750-1,200

A Moorcroft Cornflower vase, decorated with blue flowers and leaves, reserved against a very pale blue ground, impressed marks, signed in full in blue, with paper label, 12½in (31.5cm) high.
$900-1,500

A MacIntryre Florian peacock pattern vase, designed by William Moorcroft, blue ground with raised slip decoration of blue, green and yellow stylised peacock eyes, with brown printed MacIntyre Florian Ware stamp, Reg. No. 347807, green monogram W.M. des., c1900, 3½in (9cm) high.
$900-1,500

A Moorcroft MacIntyre Florian Ware vase, decorated with cornflowers and butterflies, outlined in white slip and coloured in shades of blue, factory mark with W.M. Des, painted in green with M757, 8½in (20cm) high.
$1,050-1,350

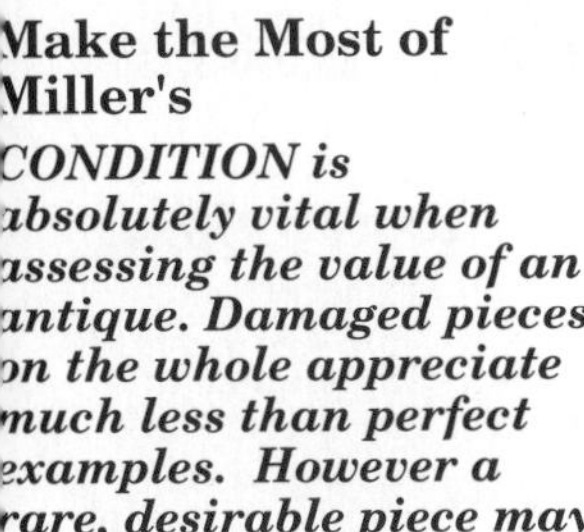

Make the Most of Miller's

CONDITION is ıbsolutely vital when ıssessing the value of an ıntique. Damaged pieces on the whole appreciate much less than perfect examples. However a rare, desirable piece may command a high price even when damaged.

Doulton

A Royal Doulton figure, 'Coppelia', numbered HN 2115 7in (18.5cm).
$375-525

A Royal Doulton pilot figure of an Elizabethan lady courtier holding a rose, 10½in (22cm).
$1,050-1,350

Doulton

A London pottery firm established in 1815, but important for its Art Pottery only from 1860s, when it revived brown stoneware and salt glaze ware. Its leading potter was Tinworth and it had links with the Martin Brothers. In the 1870s the Barlow sisters decorated ware with animals and scenes. In the 1880s and 1890s, many different artists made or decorated fancy ware 'siliconware' or enamelled china. In 1902 Doulton received the Royal Warrant. Royal Doulton figures were introduced in 1913, since when more than 2,000 designs have been produced, many of which are highly collectable.

A Royal Doulton figure, 'Clemency', HN 1633, 7½in (19cm).
$300-375

A Royal Doulton pilot figure of a young lady in a red dress, standing by a sundial, 7in (18cm).
$1,200-1,800

A Royal Doulton figure, 'Sonia' number HN 1692, 6½in (16.5cm).
$450-600

A Royal Doulton miniature character jug, 'Pearly Girl'.
$3,000-4,500

A Royal Doulton miniature character jug, 'Pearly Boy'.
$3,000-3,750

A Royal Doulton pottery Old King Cole musical mug, with yellow crown, fitted with Thorens Swiss movement, No. D6014, 8in (20cm) wide. **$750-1,200**

A Royal Doulton figure of a newsboy, HN 2244, 8in (20cm).
$225-300

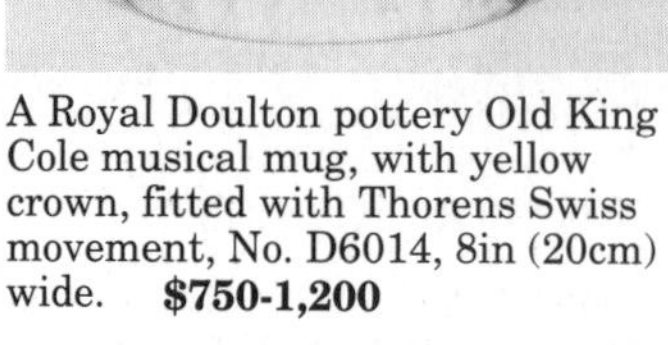

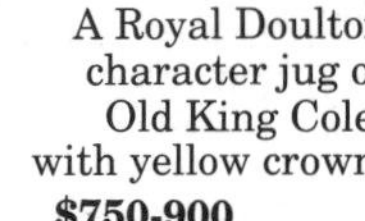

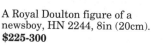

A Royal Doulton character jug of Old King Cole, with yellow crown.
$750-900

Royal Doulton pilot figure of a otanist, 6½in (16cm).
750-1,200

A Royal Doulton loving cup, moulded in relief with the Three Musketeers, in polychrome, No. 395 from an edition of 600, printed marks, 10in (25cm).
$450-600

A Royal Doulton character jug, ''Ard of 'earing', No. D6588.
$750-900

Doulton bust of Churchill, one f only 3 made, c1940, 8½in 21cm).
1,800-2,700

A Doulton jardinière, signed by George Tinmouth, c1880, 12in (30.5cm) high.
$750-1,200

A Doulton Lambeth biscuit barrel, by Florence Barlow, with plated swing handle and lid, the mottled brown body with incised acanthus scroll and star decoration, incised 'FEB' mark to base.
$225-300

Two Doulton stoneware candlesticks, by George Tinworth, signed, c1900, 8in (20cm) high.
$1,500-2,250

A Royal Doulton earthenware suffragette inkwell, 3in (7.5cm).
$375-450

A Royal Doulton soap dish, specially designed and manufactured by the factory for the proprietors of Wright's Coal Tar soap, c1920, 6in (15cm) wide.
$150-225

A Royal Doulton fish ashtray, in green, blue, brown and grey, 6in (15cm) wide.
$150-225

A Doulton bull dog, 'Old Bill' in a steel helmet with a rucksack, khaki glaze. **$450-600**

A pair of Royal Doulton pottery vases, brown ground with raised blue and light brown floral and leaf pattern, 12½in (32cm).
$225-300

A Royal Doulton Art Deco coffee ware, cream ground with a yellow, green, blue and orange C-scroll pattern, slight damage and losses.
$135-150

A pair of Doulton faience vases, c1880, 11½in (29cm) high.
$600-750

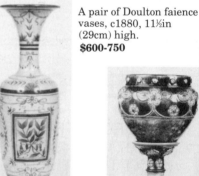

A Royal Doulton earthenware 56 piece dinner service, designed by Sir Frank Brangwyn, comprising; 52 pieces, cream ground with green geometric panels with green, yellow and blue foliage motifs, minor damage, printed marks Designed by F. Brangwyn R.D., Royal Doulton, England c1930, and 'Harvest', a 23 piece part tea service, designed by Sir Frank Brangwyn, incised and impressed decoration of fruit with foliage and sheaves of corn, polychrome on a cream ground, various printed Royal Doulton marks, minor damage, c1930.
$3,000-3,750

A Doulton Lambeth vase, by Hannah Barlow, with green ground and mid band of ponies, 13in (33cm) high.
$600-750

A Royal Doulton glazed stoneware jardinière and stand, deep blue and mottled green glazed ground, impressed lion, crown and circle mark, incised monogram MB, early 20thC, minor damage, 42in (106cm).
$1,050-1,350

A pair of Doulton faience vases, by M. M. Arding, ochre base, blue ground, c1883, 11in (28cm).
$600-750

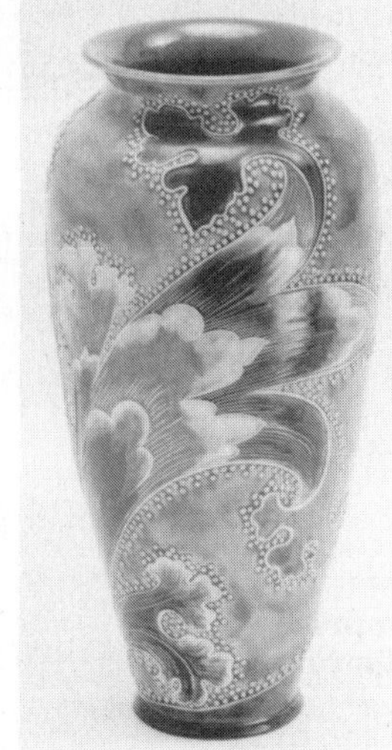

A Doulton Lambeth stoneware vase,with decorated seaweed fronds in the Art Nouveau style in blue, green and white on shaded brown and green ground, initialled MVM for Mark V. Marshall, 17in (43cm) high.
$375-525

A pair of Doulton faience vases, by A. Euphemia Thatcher, assisted by Elizabeth Shelley, c1800, 11in (28cm) high.
$600-750

A Royal Doulton Chang vase, 13½in (34cm).
$1,050-1,350

Doulton Series Ware vase, The lue Children, with blue and hite gilt rim, introduced in 1890, 1920.
600-750

A Doulton faience moon flask, painted by Hannah Barlow, c1900, 11½in (29cm) high.
$1,200-1,800

Miller's is a price GUIDE not a price LIST

A Doulton faience vase, by Mary Butterton, dated 1879, 22in (56cm).
$750-1,200

Doulton faience vase, painted y Mary Butterton, with 3 ircular panels of white peonies n a yellow ground, on a reserve f overlapping palmettes in hades of brown and yellow, the eck with a band of butterfly ving design, painted monograms, lamaged, 24in (61cm) high.
750-900

A pair of Doulton Lambeth vases by Frank Butler, 14in (36cm) high.
$1,050-1,350

Miscellaneous

A French wrought iron and glass Art Nouveau light fitting, signed.
$1,050-1,350

ART DECO
Furniture

An Art Deco cherrywood framed sofa, with carved back rail and cornucopia arm supports, in original patterned silk cover.
$750-1,200

Miller's is a price GUIDE not a price LIST

An Art Deco Hille birch veneer sofa and chair, upholstered in muted pink fabric with small dots, with chair en suite, 66½in (171cm).
$5,250-6,000
Ex Elton John collection.

An Art Deco macassar ebony bedroom suite, comprising; a double bed, 63in (160cm) wide, bedside cabinets, 20in (50cm), an large wardrobe, 75in (109cm) high.
$2,250-3,000

An Art Deco gilded armchair and stool, in the manner of Maurice Dufrene, upholstered in green velvet/dralon, with a matching footstool and cushions. **$1,200-1,800**

An Art Deco three-piece cloud back suite, upholstered in cream coloured leather, on casters.
$3,000-3,750

A pair of Art Deco armchairs, the reclining back and seat upholstered in original beige/brown fabric, each arm enclosing a magazine rack and bookshelves with diamond motif frieze at the front, stamped at the back W. Hudson 2842.
$450-600

An Art Deco three-piece suite, possibly designed by Paul Follot in walnut, comprising: canape and 2 bergères, with yellow gold patterned velvet upholstery, eac piece with shaped upholstered cushion. **$5,250-7,500**

n Art Deco three-piece red
ather upholstered cloud suite,
mprising a sofa and 2
mchairs each with scallop
aped backs and curved sides,
e sofa 66in (167.5cm) wide.
,250-3,000

n Art Deco cocktail cabinet, in
neered light walnut, the 2
nelled doors enclosing fitted
nk mirrored interior, on slender
rved floral and acanthus
pports, by Epstein, 46in
16.5cm).
750-1,200

French Art Deco console, in
rought iron, marble and wood
irrored console, in the style of
aul Kiss, the rectangular mirror
ate within a simple hammered
amework, with lower D-shaped
ack marble shelf with a single
pport composed of stylised
oral devices, raised on a
oulded wooden plinth, c1925,
2in (183cm). **$5,250-7,500**

An Art Deco burr walnut cocktail cabinet, the central cupboard with twin fluted doors enclosing shelves, flanked by stepped side cupboards enclosing shelves, on arched supports on a solid ebonised base, 47½in (119.5cm).
$2,250-3,000

From the estate of Eileen Agar, born 1904, died 1992, the surrealist and artist.

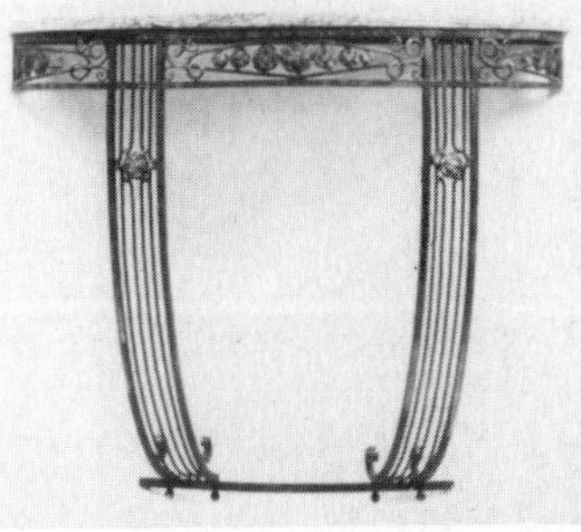

A French Art Deco calamander table, part veneered, the oval top supported on 4 stocky legs with a cross stretcher between, the legs and feet carved with Oriental scrolls, 59in (150cm) long.
$1,050-1,350

An Art Deco inlaid walnut fire screen, 34½in (87cm) wide.
$225-255

An Art Deco D-shaped console table, in wrought iron with partly painted marble top, in the manner of Edgar Brandt, 42in (106.5cm) wide, and a matching overmantel.
$1,050-1,350

An Art Deco bird's-eye maple dining room table, with a glass cover, on 2 U-shaped supports on solid feet, united by a stretcher, 78in (198cm) long.
$1,500-2,250

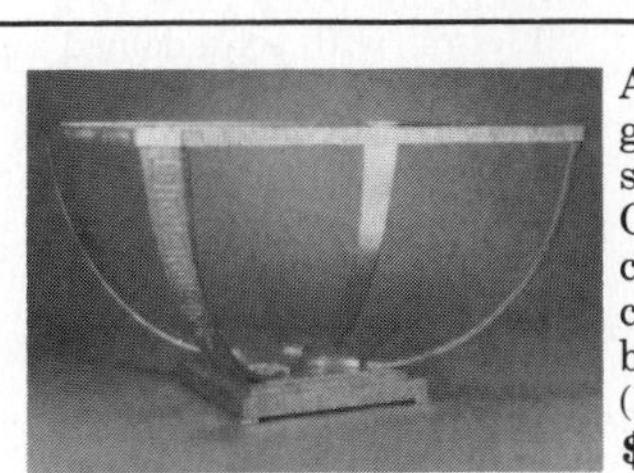

An Art Deco style gilt metal and glass dining table, the inset square top, the frieze cast with Greek key motifs, raised on 4 curved legs similarly cast conjoined to a stepped square base, raised on 4 feet, 48in square (123cm) square.
$5,250-7,500

A French Art Deco black lacquered display cabinet, with vertical sides splaying sideways towards the top, on a footed pedestal base, finished with horizontal metal banding.
$1,500-2,250

An Art Deco walnut cabinet, c1930, 30½in (77cm) high.
$375-525

An Art Deco mahogany chest of drawers, with marble top, c1930, 27½in (70cm) high.
$450-600

An Art Deco walnut sideboard, c1930, 57½in (145cm) high.
$600-750

An Art Deco ebonised occasional table, c1930, 26in (66cm) high.
$225-255

An Art Deco macassar ebony and fruitwood fire surround, the top with curved overlapping sections forming a swag design, 54in (136.5cm) high.
$750-1,200

Lalique

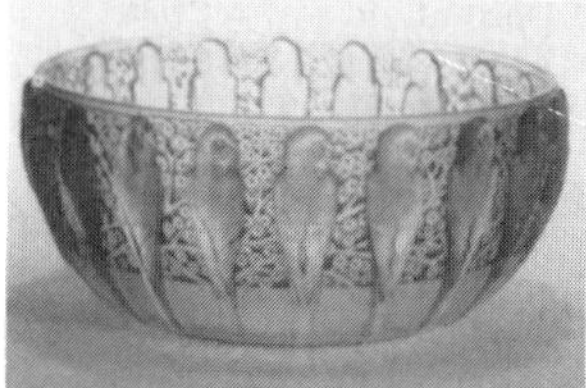

A Lalique opalescent glass bowl, 'Perruches', with steep sides and moulded in high relief with a frieze of budgerigars, heightened with blue staining, signed R. Lalique France, 9½in (24cm).
$2,700-3,300

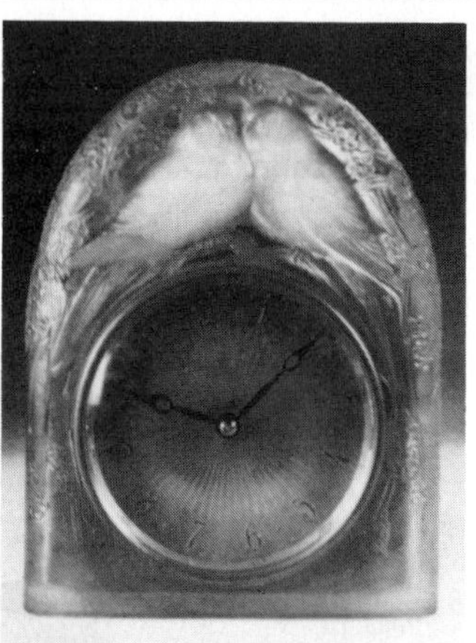

A Lalique opalescent glass clock, 'Deux Colombes', moulded in relief with a pair of doves among prunus blossom, moulded R. Lalique, 9in (22.5cm) high.
$2,700-3,300

A Lalique black glass circular box and cover, 'Pommier du Japon', moulded on the top with branches of prunus blossom, the sides finely ribbed, moulded on the base R. Lalique and Arys, 3½in (8.5cm) diam.
$1,500-2,250

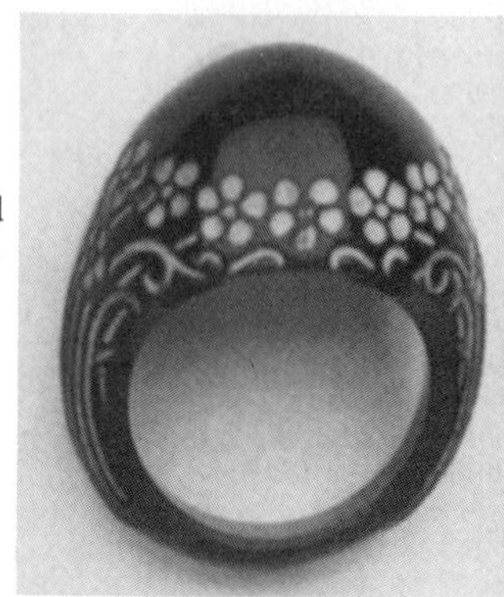

A Lalique black glass ring, 'Fleurs', with solid domed top and intaglio moulded with florets and stems picked out with white enamelling, unsigned.
$750-900

A Lalique clear glass car mascot, 'Faucon', moulded as a falcon, its talons clasping a circular base, moulded R. Lalique, 6½in (16cm).
$1,500-2,250

René Lalique

René Lalique (1860-1945) was the foremost jeweller of the Art Nouveau period and became the leading glass designer of the Art Deco period, making a wide range of objects, including car mascots, perfume bottles, vases, tableware and plates, clocks, jewellery, lighting and figurines.

Some of his glass was incorporated into furniture. Most wares were machine made for the mass market, although the perfume bottles were relatively expensive in their day as they often carried scent by top perfumiers.

 Lalique black glass seal, 3leuet', on solid base and noulded with cornflowers, eighted with green staining, vith metal base engraved with nonogram, signed on edge R. alique, 2in (4.50cm) high.
375-525

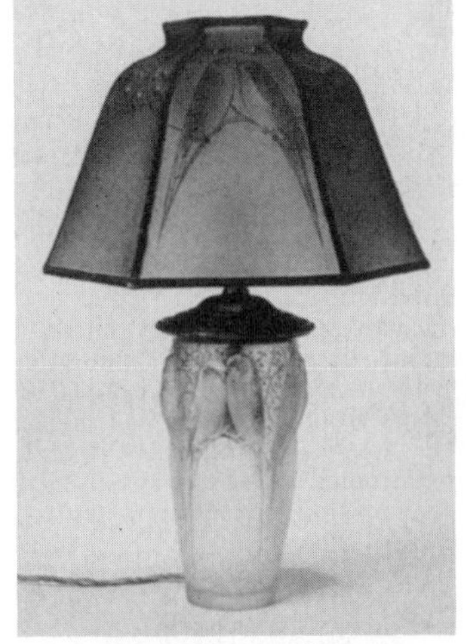

A Lalique opalescent glass vase, 'Ceylan', moulded in relief, with 4 pairs of lovebirds perched amid prunus blossom, heightened with blue staining, etched R. Lalique France, complete with original mica shade of octagonal outline painted with lovebirds amid berried boughs, and with detachable electrical mount, 20in (50cm) high.
$1,500-2,250

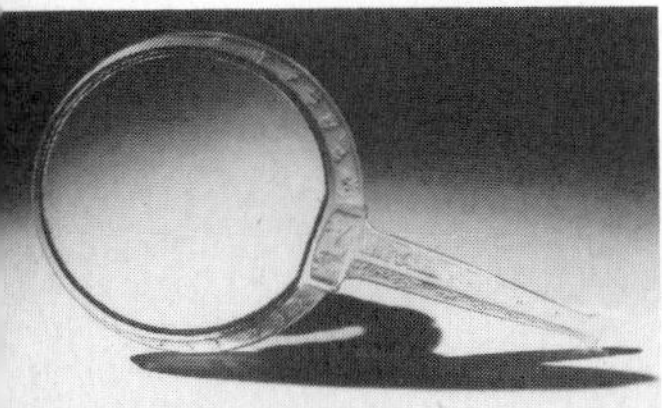

 Lalique hand mirror, 'Narcisse Couché', moulded with panel lepicting narcissus gazing into a ool, with foliate panels forming he surround, later signed R. alique, 11½in (29.50cm) long.
2,250-3,000

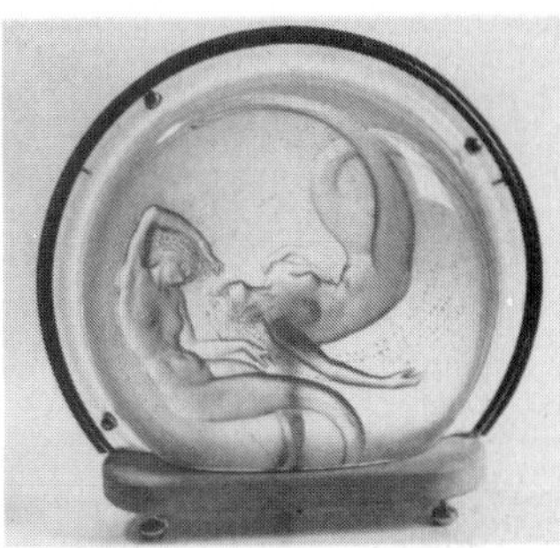

A Lalique opalescent glass plafonnier, 'Deux Sirènes', converted into a table lamp, comprising an oval marble base of 4 chrome bun feet, surmounted by semi-circular shade in chrome metal mount, minor rim chips, 15½in (39.5cm) high.
$750-1,200

A Lalique glass vase for washing grapes, 'Ricquewihr', of broad cylindrical shape, in clear glass decorated with horizontal banding moulded with grapes and vines, heightened with brown staining, marked Lalique in block letters, 5in (12.5cm) high.
$450-600

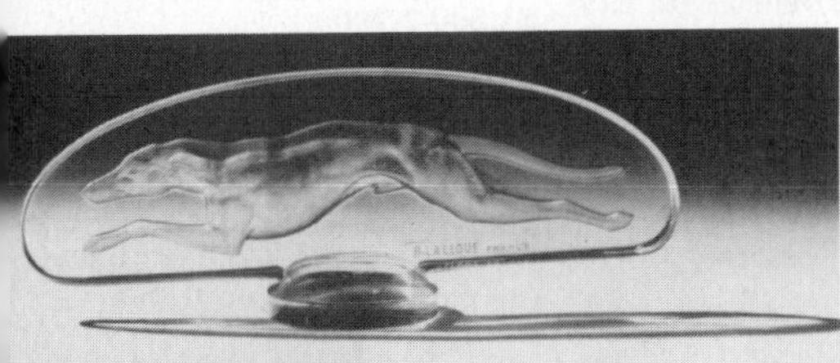

A Lalique car mascot of oval outline, 'Lévrier', intaglio moulded with a figure of a racing greyhound, moulded R. Lalique France, 7½in (19cm) long.
$1,500-2,250

A set of 6 Lalique conical wine glasses, 'Strasbourg' the stems moulded in relief with 2 naked figures gripping hands, stencil etched R. Lalique, 6in (15cm) high.
$600-750

A Lalique clear glass oval fruit lish, 'Saint Gall', with folded over im, the underside moulded in elief with swags of bubbles, and 4 matching candlesticks with letachable nozzles, acid stamped R. Lalique, damaged.
$750-900

Lalique Scent Bottles

- Lalique's earliest scent bottles were commissioned by François Côty.
- The most inventive forms are in greatest demand.
- Sealed bottles with original contents are always at a premium.
- More than one stopper was designed for some bottles.
- The underside of the stopper should carry a number corresponding to that on the bottle base.
- Some very small scent bottles carry the initials 'R.L.' instead of a full signature.

A Lalique frosted glass vase, 'Aigrettes', moulded on the upper section with the interwoven bodies and long tail feathers of exotic birds in flight, heightened with some blue staining, signed on base R. Lalique France, 10in (25cm).
$4,800-5,700

A Lalique opalescent glass vase, 'Bacchantes', of flared form, heavily moulded in relief with a band of naked maidens, their arms and bodies entwined, etched R. Lalique France to base, 9½in (24.5cm).
$7,500-9,000

A Lalique glass scent bottle, 'Origan', made for D'Héraud, the square vessel moulded on one side with the face of a girl with goat's horns protruding from her head, the reverse has the title 'Origan' heightened with brown staining, with original box, 2½in (6.5cm).
$750-1,200

A Lalique smoked glass two-handled vase, the handle moulded with flowerheads and foliage, moulded Lalique mark, 5½in (14cm). **$750-900**

A Lalique frosted glass vase, 'Nefliers', moulded in relief with slender leaves and blossom of a medlar tree, heightened with pale mauve staining, signed on base R. Lalique, 5½in (14.5cm).
$600-750

A Lalique frosted vase, 'Archers', moulded in relief with a frieze of naked male archers, with birds in flight above, heightened with a greyish staining, signed R. Lalique France and No. 893, 10½in (26.5cm).
$3,000-3,750

A Lalique polished and frosted glass vase, 'Sauterelles', moulded with grasshoppers perched on curving stems, heightened with green and blue staining, etched R. Lalique France,10½in (26.5cm) high.
$2,700-3,300

A Lalique opalescent jade green glass vase, 'Ormeaux', of spherica form with narrow neck and everted rim, moulded in relief with overlapping leaves, chips to rim and pontil, etched R. Lalique No. 985, 6½in (16.5cm).
$1,800-2,700

A Lalique spherical frosted glass scent bottle and stopper, 'Dans la Nuit', moulded in relief with stars, the reserve stained blue, in original box, moulded R. Lalique, 3in (8cm) high.
$375-450

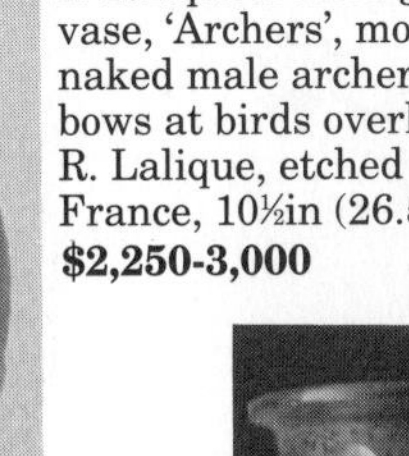

A Lalique frosted glass oviform vase, 'Archers', moulded with naked male archers aiming their bows at birds overhead, moulded R. Lalique, etched R. Lalique France, 10½in (26.5cm) high.
$2,250-3,000

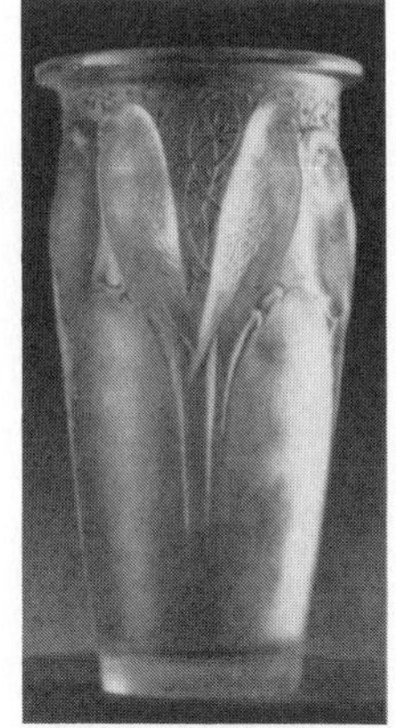

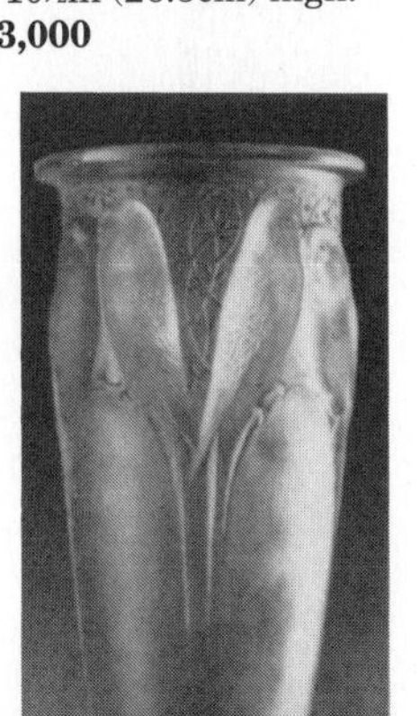

A Lalique blue opalescent cylindrical vase, with raised budgerigar decoration, engraved R. Lalique, France, 9½in (23.5cm) high.
$2,250-3,000

A Lalique enamelled globular vase, 'Baies', moulded overall in shallow relief with thorny branches and berries interwoven and heightened with black enamel, moulded R. Lalique on base, 10½in (27cm).
$9,000-12,000

Lalique smokey grey glass vase, ırchers', moulded with naked ıale archers aiming their bows at ırds overhead, moulded R. alique, 10½in (26.5cm) high.
2,700-3,300

A Lalique vase, moulded with 6 birds perched among berry laden branches, incised R. Lalique, No. 986, France mark, 5½in (14.5cm) high.
$1,500-2,250

letal

n Art Deco cold painted bronze gure, possibly by Lorenzl, cast as dancing girl in ruff collar, she ands with arms posed, painted ı red, gilt and silver colour, on ı oval onyx base, 10in (24.5cm) igh.
600-750

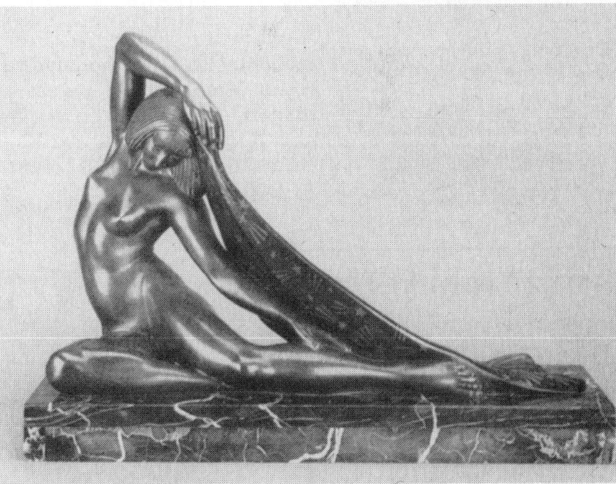

A bronze figure, cast from a model by Raymonde Guerbe, of a nude maiden sitting poised with a flowing drape decorated with silver stars, mounted on a black and white striated marble base, signed in the bronze Raymonde Guerbe, 15½in (39cm) high.
$3,000-4,500

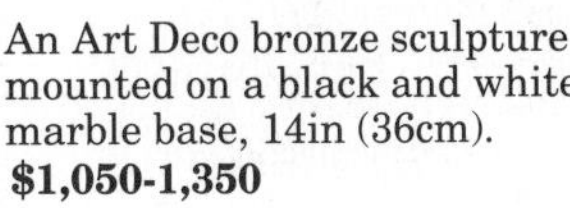

An Art Deco bronze sculpture, mounted on a black and white marble base, 14in (36cm).
$1,050-1,350

An Art Deco bronze figure of a dancing girl, cast from a model by Lorenzl, poised on one leg she kicks her other leg forward, her arms in dance pose, on a marble plinth, signed Lorenzl, 17in (43cm) high.
$1,200-1,800

A bronze figure, cast from a model by Lorenzl, incised Lorenzl, 11in (30cm).
$600-750

An Art Deco oval plated dish, with young female figure surmount.
$225-255

A French Art Deco silver plated tea set and tray, c1930, teapots to 7in (15 to 18cm) high.
$1,500-2,250

A gilt bronze figure, cast from a model by M. Guirand Rivière, of a young female athlete, wearing a turban, on a stepped black marble plinth, incised signature M. Guirand Rivière, 9½in (24cm).
$1,200-1,500

Four George V Art Deco two-handled sweetmeat dishes, with ivory handles, on spreading base Goldsmiths and Silversmiths Co Ltd, Britannia Standard, Londo 1935, 543gm.
$1,050-1,350

Bronze and Ivory

A bronze and ivory figure, 'Sonny Boy', by Ferdinand Preiss, 8½in (21cm). **$1,200-1,500**

An bronze and ivory figure, 'The Necklace', by F. Preiss.
$2,250-3,000

A bronze and ivory figure of a dancing girl, cast and carved from a model by F. Preiss, silvered, on marble base, signed, foundry mark, 9in (23cm).
$3,000-4,500

bronze and ivory figure, ancing Girl', carved and cast om a model by Bruno Zach, gned, mounted on a black arble base, 15in (39cm).
,800-5,700

painted bronze and ivory figure, ast and carved from a model by erdinand Preiss, as a young girl earing a pleated dress with ruff ollar, and red conical hat, on arble base, signed, 6in (15.5cm).
750-900

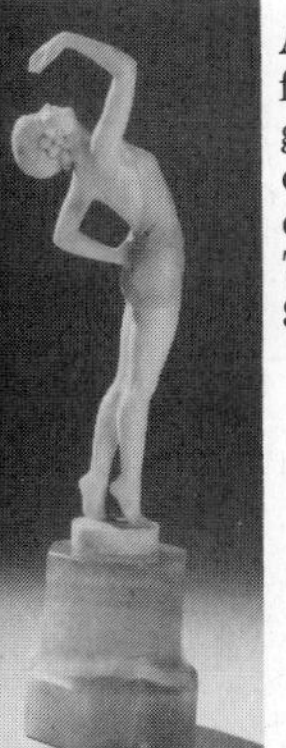

A carved ivory figure of a dancing girl, by F. Preiss, on an octagonal onyx base, signed, 7in (17.5cm).
$3,000-4,500

An Art Deco bronzed spelter and simulated ivory figure by Menneville, of a seated girl reclining on an onyx veneered base, 13in (33cm).
$1,200-1,500

An Art Deco bronze and ivory figure of a young Dutch boy, by J. Bertrand, in the style of L. Sosson, 5½in (14.5cm), on a square plinth, with incised signature.
$300-375

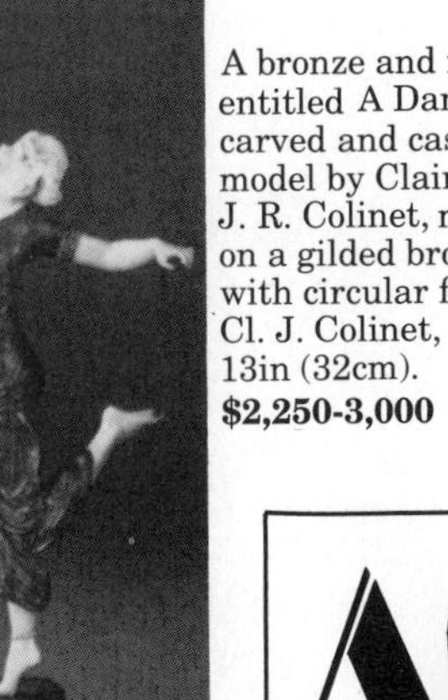

A bronze and ivory figure, entitled A Dancer, carved and cast from a model by Claire J. R. Colinet, mounted on a gilded bronze base with circular foot, signed Cl. J. Colinet, 47C, 13in (32cm).
$2,250-3,000

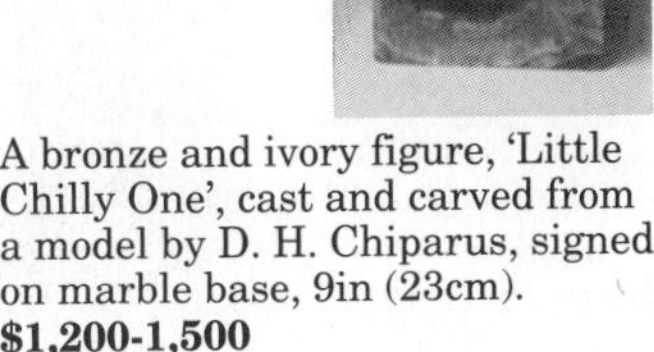

A bronze and ivory figure, 'Little Chilly One', cast and carved from a model by D. H. Chiparus, signed on marble base, 9in (23cm).
$1,200-1,500

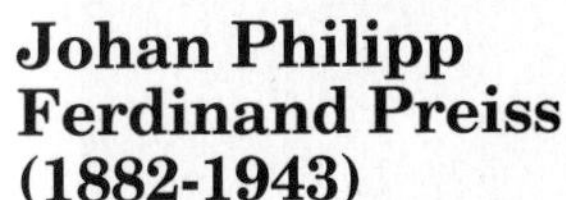

Johan Philipp Ferdinand Preiss (1882-1943)

J. P. F. Preiss was a leading Art Deco sculptor, producing ivory and bronze figures of children and athletes, including works for the Berlin Olympics of 1936. Figures embossed with a 'PK' monogram were produced by the company he founded with Kassler in Berlin in 1906.

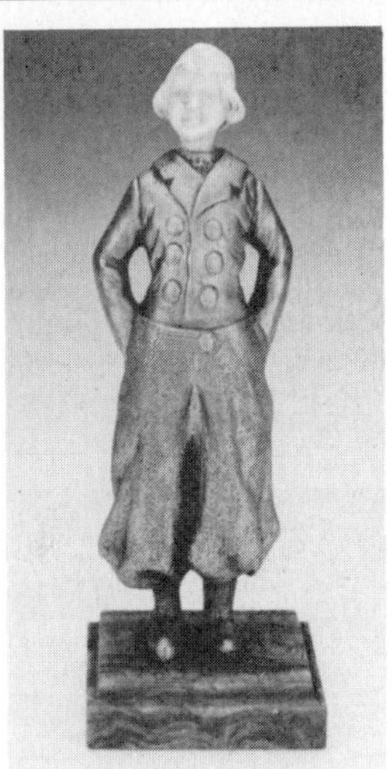

A bronze and ivory figure, 'Cabaret Girl', cast and carved from a model by Ferdinand Preiss, cold painted in silver, turquoise and gilt, triangular base stamped with founder's monogram PK, onyx stand, 15in (38cm).
$5,250-7,500

A cold painted bronze and ivory figure of a young woman in a medieval costume, cast and carved from a model by Demetre Chiparus, signed, 10in (25.5cm).
$1,800-2,700

A bronze and ivory figure, cast and carved from a model by Lorenzl, of a young girl in a spo tunic, impressed signature, 8in (21cm).
$375-450

A bronze and ivory figure of a lady in Renaissance costume, by Endstorfer, signed, AR foundry stamp, brown patination, 9in (23cm).
$750-900

A gilt bronze and ivory figure of a standing girl, by L. Barthelemy, c1900, on an onyx plinth, damaged, 12in (31cm).
$750-1,200

A bronze and ivory figure of a lady with a fan, by Emil Meier, signed with AR foundry stamp, a green marble base, brown patination, c1905, 9in (23cm).
$600-750

Ceramics

A Goldscheider polychrome painted ceramic figure of a negro dandy, naturalistically painted, impressed factory marks, damaged, 20½in (52cm).
$2,250-3,000

l. A Goldscheider pottery head of a woman in a brown headscarf, partly concealing orange curly hair, on a green base in the form of a dress collar, printed Made in Austria, 8in (20cm).
$150-225
r. A Goldscheider pottery face mask, of a girl with curly turquoise hair and yellow dress collar, on an ebonised wooden base, painted and stamped factory marks, 12in (30cm).
$1,050-1,350

A Goldscheider pottery model of a dancing girl, by Lorenzl, wearing a mauve, blue and black skirt, the cylindrical column on a circular base, signed Lorenzl, painted factory marks and impressed 581828, 9½in (23.5cm).
$1,050-1,350

A Goldscheider pottery figure by Kostial, of an Eastern dancer wearing mauve pantaloons with flared skirt, artist's signature, factory marks, impressed 5549 48 8 to base, 17½in (44.5cm).
$1,500-2,250
This figure is based on a design by Umberto Brunelleschi.

A Goldscheider pottery figure of a dancing girl, after Lorenzl, with a peacock design dress in mottled blue and green glazes, on a domed circular base, transfer printed and impressed marks, 15in (38cm).
$750-1,200

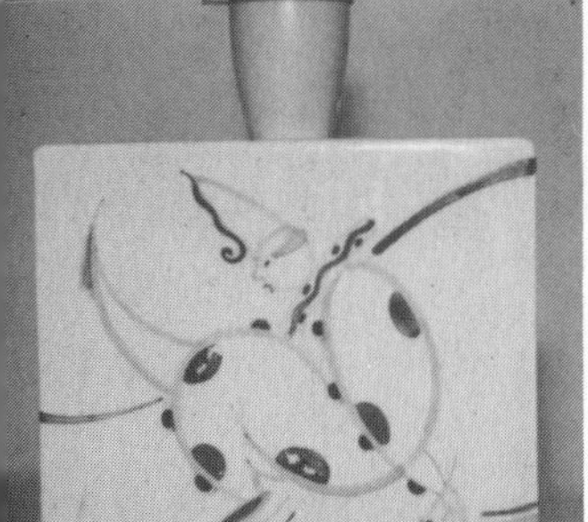

A Susie Cooper Art Deco table lamp base, 5in (12.5cm).
$1,050-1,350

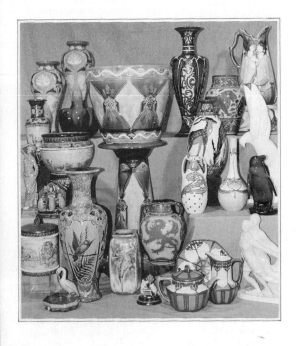

An Art Deco pottery ornament by Vago-Weiss, of a leaping ibis, 18in (46cm).
$135-150

A Poole fruit bowl with fruit design, in brown and coral, impressed mark, c1926, 13in (33cm).
$50-75

A Poole Pottery historic plaque, entitled 'Poole Whaler, 1783', inscribed on reverse 'This dish was made and painted at the Poole Pottery in the year 1932, ship drawn by Arthur Bradbury, painted by Margaret Holder', 14½in (37cm).
$450-600

A Carlton Ware ginger jar and cover, decorated with coloured enamels in a chinoiserie pattern featuring a repeating scene of an Oriental couple in traditional costume amid pagodas, birds and trees, in orange, blue, green, mauve and yellow against a brown ground heightened with gilt, marked W & R Carlton Ware on base, 12in (31cm).
$450-600

A Gouda jardinière, Marga design, c1921, 6½in (16.5cm) high.
$225-255

A Poole Pottery 'Festival of Britain 1951' presentation bowl, deep with broad everted rim painted with rose, shamrock, thistle and daffodil symbolising unity in the British Isles during Festival year, the centre with Poole's coat-of-arms in red, green, mauve, blue and yellow, 17in (43.5cm).
$750-900
Probably designed by Claude Smale, this piece would have been part of the small output of presentation pieces granted to the pottery under licence during festival year, and possibly unique in representing the town of Poole itself.

A French Art Deco crackle glazed ceramic group, modelled as a lady wearing a full ball gown of cream and gold, with Harlequin standing behind her in black, silver and cream, marked C. H. France, and G. Deblaze, 14in (36cm).
$375-450

A French porcelain golfing flas and stopper, signed E. Marqui and P. Bastard, Editeur, Paris France, on base, 11in (27.5cm)
$300-375

A Carlton Ware Rouge Royale ginger jar and cove oviform with domed cover, covered in a lustrous mottled maroon red glaze with gilt and polychrome enamel decoration of pagodas and scenes of Oriental life, printed factor marks, 10½in (26.5cm).
$600-750

A Poole Pottery historic plaque, entitled 'Waterwitch, built by Meadus, Poole 1871, 207 tons, Master Captain C. H. Deacon, drawn by Arthur Bradbury, 1932', painted by Ruth Paveley, 14½in (37cm).
$300-375

Carlton Ware pottery Glamour
a-for-two set.
!25-300

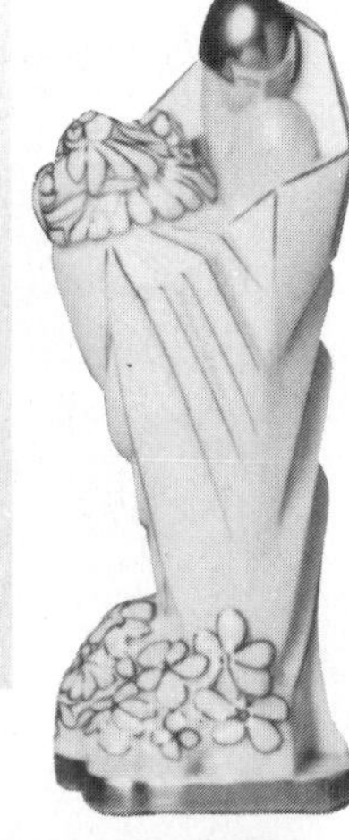

A Robj Art Deco porcelain figural lamp, modelled as a woman with gold bobbed hair, standing swathed in a long white robe and holding a large bunch of flowers, with a depression for aromatic oils, with flowers at her feet, painted with gilt highlights, printed Robj, Paris, Made in France, 13in (33cm).
$600-750

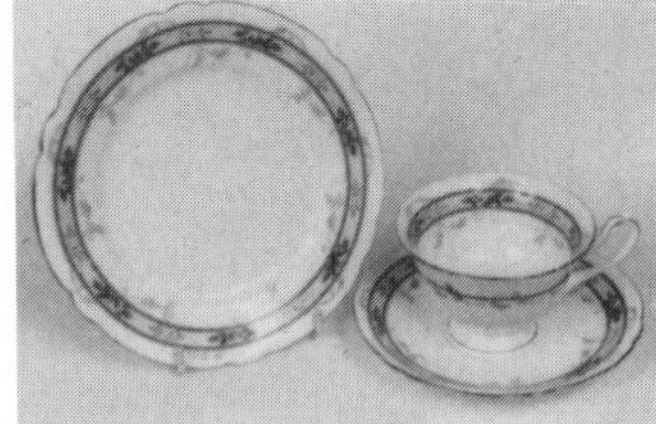

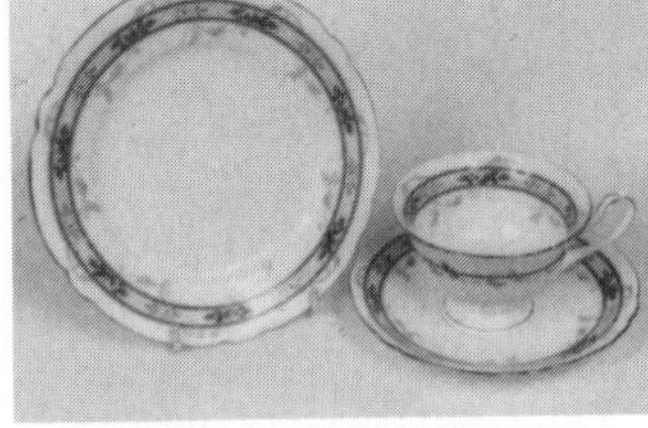

A Shelley Gainsborough Trio, Classical design, c1918.
$40-60

Make the Most of Miller's

In Millers we do NOT just reprint saleroom estimates. We work from realised prices, either from an auction room or a dealer. Our consultants then work out a realistic price range for a similar piece. This is to try to avoid repeating freak results - either low or high.

A Poole Pottery cream vase, c1925.
$50-75

A Shelley Regent Trio, Yellow Phlox design, c1933.
$40-60

A Shelley Vincent Trio, Dorothy Perkins (yellow rose) pattern, no. 11168/2, c1920.
$40-60

A Shelley lustre vase, by Walter Slater, painted in colours and gilt on a petrol blue ground with a Japanese beauty carrying a lantern, walking beside a river bank flanked by willows, a bridge in the distance, beneath a moonlit sky, printed factory marks and facsimile signature, 15½in (39.5cm).
$600-750

A Royal Dux figural vase, the twin-handled vessel formed as a tree trunk with green leaf and mistletoe embellishment, supporting to one side the standing figure of an Art Nouveau maiden in long flowing green dress, pink triangular mark to base, 26in (65.5cm) high.
$1,050-1,350

A Poole Pottery vase, the design attributed to Truda Carter, painted in pink, grey, orange, pale green and white with zig-zags, stylised leaves and flowers, reserved against a pale pink ground, impressed Poole, England, 10in (25.5cm) high.
$225-300

A Gouda vase, Rembrandt design, c1927, 6½in (16cm) high.
$135-150

A Poole Pottery tin glazed doorstop, designed by Harold Stabler, modelled as a galleon in full sail, in blue, green, yellow and white, 21in (53cm) high.
$750-1,200

A Dutch Arnhem Factory vase, Isolda design, green background, c1920, 14in (36cm) high.
$225-300

A Shelley Art Deco coffee service, decorated in orange and black, comprising a coffee pot, sugar bowl, cream jug, 6 cups and saucers, pattern no. 11792, coffee pot 7½in (19cm) high.
$450-600

A Charlotte Rhead dressing table set in the Trellis pattern, in shades of orange, yellow, green and coffee lustre on a cream ground, comprising: a tray, powder bowl and cover, 2 squat candlesticks, and 4 other items, printed factory marks.
$375-450

A Shelley China Mode shaped part tea service, lightly printed black and overpainted in bright blue, green, black and orange, comprising: 4 tea cups, 4 saucers, 6 tea plates, sugar basin and milk jug, printed mark in green, registered No. 756533, pattern No. 11755, inscribed in burnt orange.
$375-450

Miller's is a price GUIDE not a price LIST

A Gouda vase, Bochara design, c1920, 9in (22cm) high.
$225-255

A Gouda vase, Kalman design, c1929, 8in (20cm) high.
$120-135

A Gouda jug, Peter design, c1923, 11in (28cm) high.
$150-180

A Gouda vase, Westland design, c1927, 12in (30.5cm).
$225-255

A Gouda vase, Ali design, c1924, 6½in (16cm) high.
$150-180

A Gouda wall vase, Paula design, c1920, 6in (15cm) high.
$150-180

A Carter Stabler Adams Poole Pottery dish, a variation on Truda Carter's spotted deer, the centre painted in colours with a spotted deer amid flowering branches, impressed pottery marks, 15in (37.5cm).
$450-600

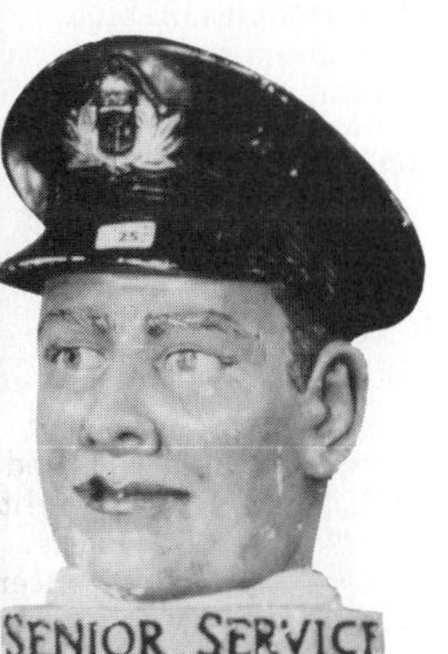

An Art Deco pottery flat backed bust of a sailor, advertising Senior Service cigarettes, 14in (35cm).
$105-120

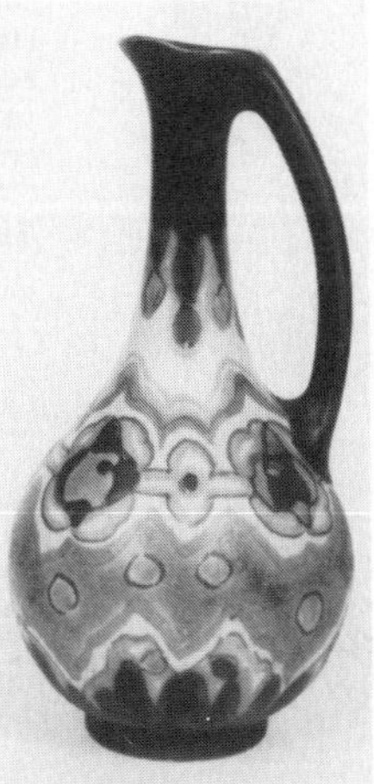

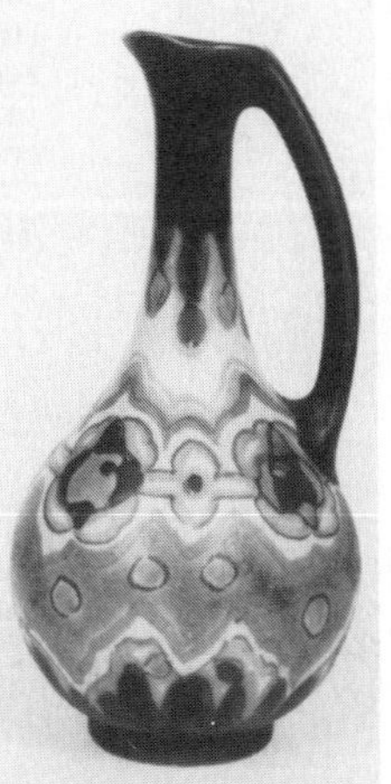

A Gouda jug, Costia design, c1926, 7½in (18cm) high.
$50-75

A Gouda bowl, Collier design, c1922, 8in (20cm) diam.
$180-225

Clarice Cliff

Three Clarice Cliff coasters, Delicia Pansy, Cabbage Flower and Orange Roof Cottage patterns, and 2 ashtrays in Rhodanthe and Aurea, painted in colours, printed factory marks.
$450-600

A Clarice Cliff Bizarre pattern Age of Jazz figural group, modelled as a two-dimensional dancing couple, he in black tie and she in a bright green gown with red, yellow and black decoration, raised on a stepped rectangular base, factory marks and facsimile signature to base, 7in (18cm) high.
$5,250-7,500

Age of Jazz figures like this dancing couple are much sought after. These have a two-dimensional effect but are in fact freestanding plaques.
Not all novelty items by Clarice Cliff are as highly collectable: for example Cliff Toby jugs have never been in strong demand.

A Clarice Cliff Appliqué Bizarre pattern plate, in Eden design, painted in colours with yellow, red and black banding, lithograph mark, 9in (23cm).
$4,800-5,700

This pattern is previously unrecorded in the Appliqué range

A Clarice Cliff geometric Lotus jug, the ribbed tapering cylindrical body painted with a band of orange, blue and yellow triangular motifs, between orange and green bands, gilt printed mark, 11½in (29cm) high.
$900-1,500

A Clarice Cliff Newport pottery Bizarre pattern Stamford shape part tea service, each piece painted with a small rectangular panel enclosing cottage with orange roof, yellow door, and window amongst rolling hills with poplars beyond, on a cream ground within a wide green band, comprising: teapot and cover, tea plate, sugar basin, milk jug and conical tea cup with solid triangular handle, printed mark in black, inscribed 5954 in brown, damaged.
$375-450

A Clarice Cliff Bizarre cat, depicted with a cheerful countenance, painted orange wi black spots and sporting a green bow tie, printed factory mark an facsimile signature, 6in (15cm) high.
$750-900

A Clarice Cliff Geometric patter comport, painted with a central star motif supporting 4 segmented triangles, in blue, yellow, red, green and purple on cream ground, printed marks, 7i (18cm) diam.
$225-300

A Clarice Cliff geometric Lotus jug, decorated with green, blue and orange triangular motifs, betwee orange and green bands, black printed factory mar 11½in (29cm) high.
$1,050-1,350

Clarice Cliff Blue Autumn
ttern coffee pot, with sinuous
ee painted in blue, green and
llow above red grass, a cottage
lf hidden by purple cottages on
e reverse, printed Fantasque,
zarre, Clarice Cliff, 7½in
9cm) high.
75-450

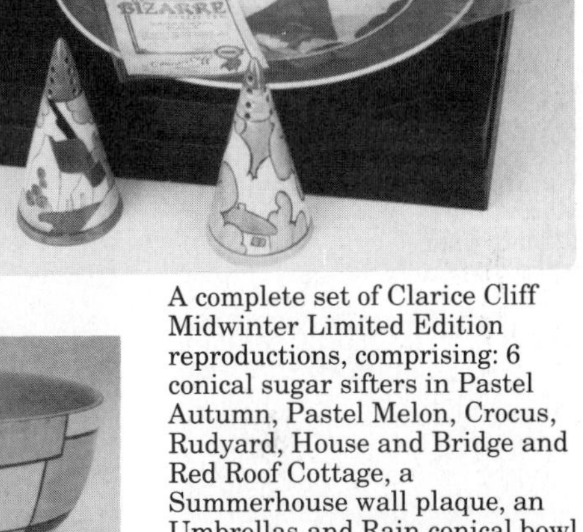

A complete set of Clarice Cliff Midwinter Limited Edition reproductions, comprising: 6 conical sugar sifters in Pastel Autumn, Pastel Melon, Crocus, Rudyard, House and Bridge and Red Roof Cottage, a Summerhouse wall plaque, an Umbrellas and Rain conical bowl and a Honolulu baluster vase, all in original boxes, printed factory marks.
$3,000-4,500

A Clarice Cliff Newport pottery Bizarre pattern bowl, decorated with geometric shapes in shades of blue, green and mauve enclosing 2 leafy branches, printed mark in black, 9½in (24cm) diam.
$300-375

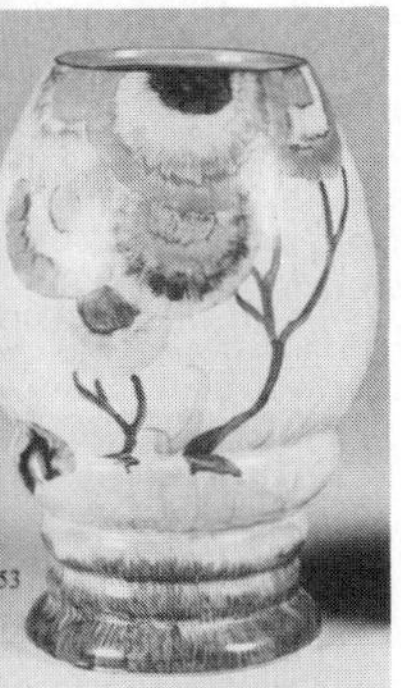

A Clarice Cliff Bizarre vase, painted in the Rhodanthe design, oviform on ribbed foot, printed marks, 8in (20cm) high.
$375-525

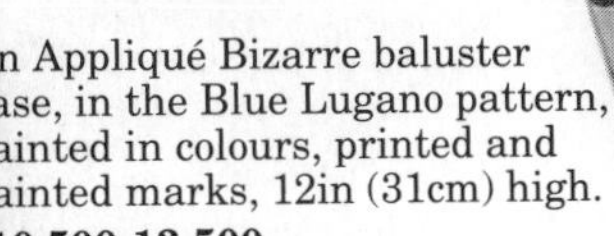

n Appliqué Bizarre baluster
ase, in the Blue Lugano pattern,
ainted in colours, printed and
ainted marks, 12in (31cm) high.
10,500-13,500

A Clarice Cliff Isis vase, in the Lumberlost pattern, having red and white floral clusters with brown and green bushes nearby, under a canopy of red flowering trees, factory marks and facsimile signature to base, 10in (24.5cm) high.
$450-600

Two Clarice Cliff Circus plates, designed by Laura Knight, one centred with a horse and trainer performing in the ring, enclosed by audience and clown border, in mauve, yellow, brown, black and green, another with a girl astride a horse, in same colours, with factory marks and facsimile signatures to base, both 9in (23cm) diam.
$600-750 each

An original artwork for a Clari Cliff advert, depicting several young ladies drinking coffee fro a Tankard coffee set, gouache o paper, 22 by 28in (56 by 71 cm)
$1,200-1,500

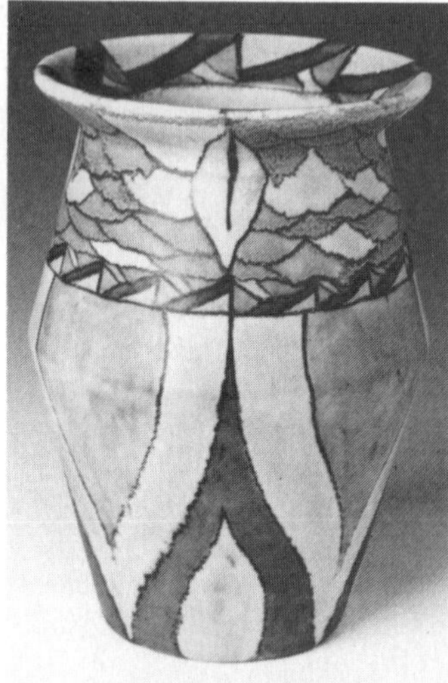

A Clarice Cliff Inspiration, Persian pattern vase, shape 342, painted with abstract shapes in vertical and horizontal bands in turquoise, blue, orange and brown, factory marks and facsimile signature with Persian to base, 8in (20cm) high.
$750-1,200

A Clarice Cliff Bizarre, Orange Secrets pattern vase, oviform wit horizontally ribbed neck, painted in vivid colours with cottages on rolling hillside, having orange banding, factory marks and facsimile signature to base, 8in (20cm) high.
$750-900

A Clarice Cliff Bizarre Honolulu patterned jug, Fantasque, hand painted by Newport pottery, 11½in (29cm) high.
$1,200-1,800

A Clarice Cliff conical coffee set, in the Rising Sun design, painte in orange, mauve and yellow blooms with blue grapes against an orange and white sunburst ground, comprising: a coffee pot and lid, 6 cups and saucers, a milk jug and sugar bowl, factory marks and facsimile signature to base, coffee pot 7in (17cm) high.
$750-1,200

A Clarice Cliff Isis vase decorated in Green Japan design, with a summerhouse by a lake, an exotic orange and green leaved tree nearby with purple and black foliage, beneath a yellow sky, factory marks and facsimile signature to base, 11½in (29cm) high.
$750-1,200

A Clarice Cliff Bizarre cup, saucer and plate in the Broth pattern, painted in colours with orange banding, rubber stamp mark.
$300-375

iscellaneous

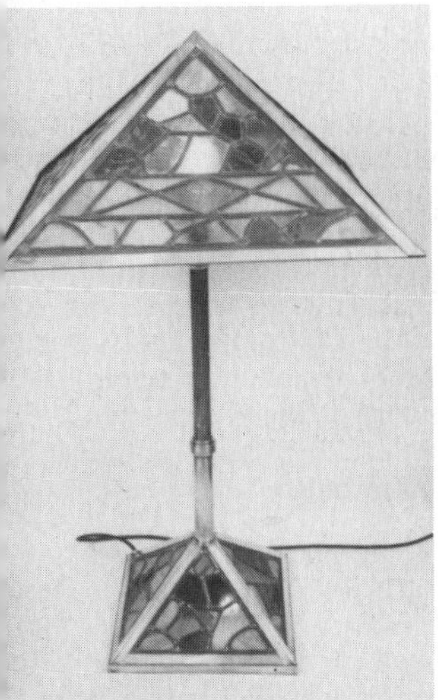

silver plated and coloured glass
t Deco table lamp, fully
escopic and adjustable, c1920,
in (84cm).
,800-2,700

Martin Art Deco chromed metal
d glass chandelier, the square
andard supporting 6 fixtures,
ch set with frosted and clear
ass rods, with conforming
iling cap, c1930, 28in (71cm).
,500-6,000

 Art Deco lacquered cigarette
se, with central geometric band
coquille d'oeuf silver coloured
nding and red bands all against
black ground, marked PSA and
chor in square and numbered
, probably French, 4½ by 3⅓in
1.5 by 8.5cm).
600-750

A pair of Art Deco bronze wall lights, of stepped rectangular section, with slatted gallery at the top, with frosted glass panes, 16in (41cm) high.
$1,050-1,350

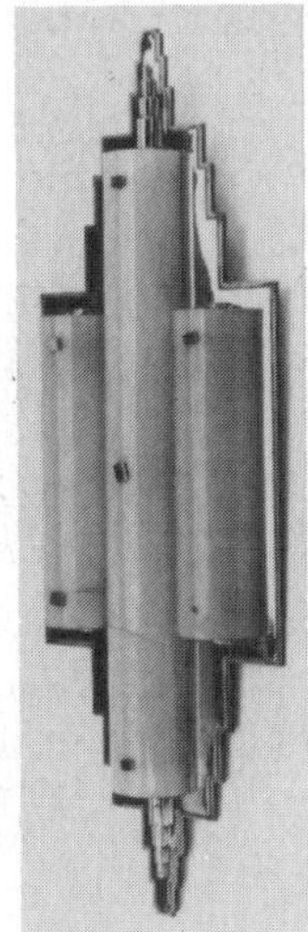

A set of 6 Art Deco cinema wall lights, each with rectangular chrome backs surmounted by tubular peach plastic shades, with stepped 'skyscraper' terminals at either or both ends, depending on size, comprising 2 small, 2 medium and 2 large, damaged, 22½, 42 and 67in (57, 107 and 170cm) long, a set indicator board, 6 cinema reels and a film splicer.
$1,500-2,250

Did you know?
MILLER'S Antiques Price Guide builds up year by year to form the most comprehensive photo reference library available.

An Art Deco chrome and Bakelite calendar clock, 10in (25cm) wide.
$150-225

A set of Art Deco enamelled cufflinks, dress buttons and studs, each showing in black and white the formalised figure of a man and the letter 'M', in fitted case, and a pair of dress clips, each fashioned as a woman wearing a tiered dress, the dresses being in simulated coral.
$600-750

An Art Deco woollen carpet, machine woven, in strips, with a repeating geometric foliate design in cream, green, blue and shades of red, 81 by 122in (205 by 310cm).
$1,050-1,350

An Art Deco brass light fitting with multi-coloured glass shades, probably by Loetz.
$750-1,200

A GUIDE TO COLLECTING SCOTCH WHISKY

Collecting Scotch whisky is a hobby enjoyed by many enthusiasts most of whom never touch a drop from the more expensive bottles in their collections but who appreciate the bottles for their age, originality of design, shape, condition and design and colouring of the label.

All of the above factors contribute towards the essence of the best collections in the world, some of which are housed overseas. The export market has seen many bottles which have never been available at home, hence the high quality of foreign collections.

No two bottles are the same where older examples are concerned. Above all the 'Golden Nectar' was produced for consumption, but it never ceases to amaze that bottles which actually manage to survive from the last century are still in excellent condition to this day. Some brands have disappeared without trace whilst other which do materialise have never been heard of before.

Some of the best collections in this country are owned by the distilleries themselves. They are continually looking for bottles to replenish their archives; usually brands which are no longer produced or early examples of samples which were not kept with the future in mind.

Martin Green
June 1993

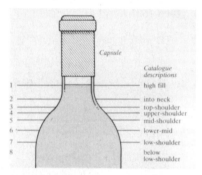

A stoneware flagon of Heather Dew Blended Scotch Whisky, blended and bottled by Mitchell Brothers Ltd, Glasgow, imported by Foreign Vintages Incorporated New York, glazed stoneware flagon reads 'The Greybeard, Federal Law Forbids Sale or Re-Use Of This Bottle', driven cork, paper seal accompanied by stopper cork, 86.8°.
$300-375

Two bottles of James Eadie's Special Old Scotch Whisky, trademark 'X', James Eadie, Burton-on-Trent, driven corks, lead capsules embossed 'Fine Old Scotch Whisky', one label slightly stained and torn.
$225-300 each

A bottle of Chivas Regal 25 Yea Old, shoulder label reads Purveyors to His Majesty King George V and to Her Majesty, imported by Fred L. Meyers & Son, The Sugar Wharf, Kingstc Jamaica, B.W.I., driven cork, le capsule, low shoulder level, ear 20thC.
$750-1,200

One bottle Dalmore whisky, 'distilled by McKenzie Brothers, Dalmore Distillery, Ross-shire, bottled by State Management Stores, Invergordon', this whisky bottled after a short period of maturation, the colour of the spirit has taken on a tiny hint of oak, driven cork, lacking capsule, mid-shoulder level, single malt, c1930.
$900-1,050

A bottle of Heirloom Finest Scotch Whisky, bottled by Rutherford & Kay, Edinburgh, London and Birmingham, 3-piece moulded glass bottle, driven cork, embossed lead capsule, unlabelled, level 4cm from base of capsule, c1880.
$2,250-3,000

One bottle of Robert Brown Specially Selected Very Old whisky, 17 Hope Street, Glasgow, reproduction label applied to front of bottle, driven cork, embossed lead capsule Robert Brown on top, 'Same as Supplied to His Royal Highness The Prince of Wales' around neck, 3-piece moulded glass bottle, top shoulder level, late 19thC.
$750-1,200

This was recovered from the wreck of the S.S. Wallachia that sank in 1895. The S.S. Wallachia, a single crew steamer, was originally owned by Taylor and Cameron of Liverpool and used on the Black Sea run until bought by William Burrell & Son of Glasgow in 1893, after which she regularly made trips to the West Indies.
On 29th September 1895 at 10 a.m. she left Queen's Dock, Glasgow, in very foggy weather, bound for Trinidad and Demerara carrying a general cargo which included whisky. At around 4pm the fog began to thicken once more and the Wallachia grounded off Innellan Pier but quickly refloated on the rising tide.
As the ship made her way down river, the captain was startled by the appearance of a very large steamer off his starboard bow, which collided with the Wallachia shortly after. Following these events she sank with a huge explosion and has remained off the North Ayrshire coast ever since.
The above bottle was recovered, at great risk, during a recreational dive in 1978, under 2 feet of silt.

Glass

Early bottles were often hand blown or made in three pieces joined together while the glass was molten. Look for slight bubbles and imperfections in the glass which is usually clear or green in colour, bottles which do not stand perpendicular and those which are not conventionally shaped.

A bottle of The Old Blend White Horse Whisky, By Appointment to His Majesty The King, White Horse Distillers Ltd, Lagavulin Distillery, Islay and Glenlivet District, excellent label, driven cork, lead capsule, accompanied by original tie-on neck label and tissue wrapping, lower mid level, bottled 1926.
$750-1,200

One bottle of John Begg Blue Cap whisky, by appointment to the Late King George V, Royal Lochnagar Distillery, Balmoral Stopper cork, lead capsule embossed 'Take a peg of John Beg', into neck level, c1940. **$450-600**

A bottle of Glenfingal Fine Old Scotch Whisky, sole proprietors John M. Scott & Co, Leith, driven cork, lead capsule, upper shoulder level, and a miniature stone jug of Sterling Whisky, for Auld Lang Syne, with wax seal.
$600-750

A bottle of Gilmour Thomson's Royal Blend, as supplied to His Late Majesty, King Edward VII, label reads 'This rare old blend is distinguished by having a bouquet as in fine old matured wines, Gilmour Thomson & Co. Ltd, Glasgow', screw cap, lead capsule, lower mid-shoulder level, c1920.
$750-900

A glass decanter of Dalmore whisky, with remains of sample label, 'distilled by McKenzie Brothers, Dalmore Distillery, Ross-shire, sample drawn June 190?', this sample drawn shortly after distillation, the whisky is natural spirit colour, glass stopper protected by wax paper seal, level 3cm from base of stopper, c1900.
$450-600

A bottle of Very Old Blended Glenlivet, Churtons Ltd, Liverpool and Glasgow, a whisky of distinction as supplied to The Lords, label bears Certificate of Analysis by the late Granville H. Sharpe, F.C.S., label bin soiled and torn, but legible, stopper cork, lead capsule, upper shoulder level, c1900.
$1,050-1,350

Two bottles of Glen Garry Very Old Scotch Whisky, prize medal blend, Purveyors to The House of Lords, John Hopkins & Co. Ltd, Distillers, Tobermory, Isle of Mull, applied lower label printed with Statement of Analysis by Public Analyst for the City of Glasgow and the counties of Lanark and Renfrew, 3-piece moulded glass bottles, driven corks, paper capsules printed on top 'Glen Garry Very Old Scotch Whisky', one into neck level and one high fill, 1917.
$750-1,200

The Tobermory (Ledaig Tobermory) Distillery Isle of Mull, was founded in 1798 by John Sinclair, ownership changed in 1827 to that of Sinclair and McLachlan and then reverted back to John Sinclair from 1833-37. The distillery was re-established in 1878 and changed hands twice until ownership became that of John Hopkins & Co. who were the owners between 1890 and 1916 when taken over by United Distillers who operated under the same name. The distillery fell silent between 1930 and 1972 and it is now owned and operated by Tobermory Distillers Ltd.

The Single Malts

The single malts available today for everyday drinking have been matured for between 8 and 15 years in the cask. Anything older is usually more special. On the whole, most distilleries have released onto the market a particular brand which is very special. Primarily produced for commemorative purposes or the collectors market, it is also enjoyed by serious malt drinkers.

A bottle of Glenfiddich Special whisky, bottled at the distillery and guaranteed by William Grant & Sons Ltd, shoulder label slightly torn, stopper cork, lead capsule, into neck level, pre-1930.
$750-1,200

A bottle of Milton Duff 13 Years Old Scotch Whisky, distilled and blended by George Ballantine & Son Ltd, Dumbarton and Elgin, stopper cork, lead capsule, single malt, 85°.
$450-600

A bottle of Strathmill Fine Old Scotch Whisky, by Appointment to H.M. King George V, bottled and guaranteed by W. & A. Gilbey Ltd, driven cork, wax capsule, into neck level, 30° under proof, c1910.
$3,000-4,500

A bottle of The Fife Whisky 8 Year Old, named after His Grace The Duke of Fife, K..S., by Special Permission, 3 gold medals, P. MacKenzie & Co. (Distillers) Ltd Edinburgh and Liverpool, driven cork, lead capsule embossed 'The Fife Whisky', level 3.5cm from base of capsule.
$450-600

A House of Lords Fine Old Scotch Whisky, "Lion Brand" Special Quality, Stephen W. Young & Co, Bonnington, Edinburgh, hand blown bottle, driven cork, lead capsule embossed on top 'Old Scotch Whisky', Certificate of Analysis applied to rear of bottle, dated 9th June 1899.
$1,800-2,700

Labels

The condition and legibility are highly important; look for date, name of bottler, company name, crest and logo. Some labels are very colourful depicting printed scenes of distilleries or views of Scotland, others can be very plain bearing only the basic details of the whisky.

Where single malts are concerned look for the name of the distillery. The words 'Liqueur Scotch Whisky', 'Rare Old Liqueur Scotch Whisky', 'Fine Old Scotch Whisky', etc., denote that the whisky was moderately mature when bottled.

Where blends are concerned look for the words 'Rare' or 'Fine Old Blended Scotch Whisky'. Some of the malts used in the blend may have spent between 3 and 25 years or more in the cask.

bottle of Glen Grant whisky, ttled by Archd. Campbell, Hope King Ltd, stopper cork, lead psule, single malt, proof rength.
00-750

A half bottle of Royal Arms Rare Old Blended Scotch Whisky, by Royal Warrant to His Majesty King George V, R.A. Scotch, J.G. Thomson & Co. Ltd, Leith, stopper cork, embossed lead capsule, damaged, level 4cm from base of capsule, c1910.
$150-225

A bottle of Talisker Over 8 Years Old Pure Malt Whisky, high strength, stopper cork, lead capsule, single malt, 80°.
$450-600

bottle of King's Quality Rare d Blended Special Liqueur, By ppointment, purveyors to the yal Household during three igns J.G. Thomson & Co. Ltd, ith, stopper cork, lead capsule nbossed 'Royal Arms Rare Old otch Whisky', level 2.5cm from se of capsule, c1940.
450-600

A bottle of Long John Special Reserve Scotch Whisky, Long John Distilleries Ltd, Glasgow, British Analytical Control Certificate dated 1925 applied to rear of bottle, tin screw cap bears patent number 36949/1932.
$900-1,500

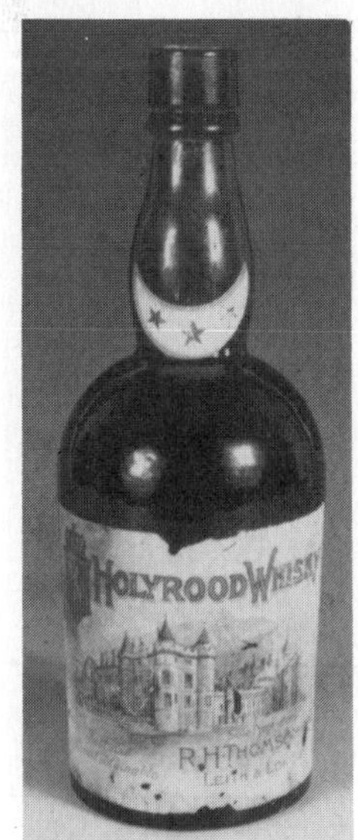

A bottle of Holyrood Whisky, R.H. Thomson & Co, Leith and London, 3-piece moulded glass bottle, driven cork branded 'Holyrood Whisky R.H. Thomson & Co', lacking capsule, into neck level, late 19thC.
$750-900

Capsules, Corks and Seals

Early capsules were usually made of lead or a metal based substance and fitted to the bottle after the cork had been driven in. Some are embossed with the company name logo or crest and/or name of the brand or distillery.

If the bottle does not have a driven cork it may have a stopper. In order to distinguish this, look for a slight indentation running around the neck underneath the capsule where the edge of the stopper meets the neck of the bottle.

The earliest form of seal, applied after the cork had been driven, was made of melted wax and often embossed with the name of the producing company, brand name of the whisky or a crest.

Other types of seals were introduced in the 1920s by some companies, for example, spring loaded caps made of tin or metal protected by lead were very common. Screw caps were also introduced at this time, similar to those which can be found on everyday drinking whiskies today.

A bottle of Old Orkney Real Liqueur Whisky, McConnell's Distillery Company Ltd, Stromness Distillery, Orkney, label torn but legible, stopper cork, lead capsule embossed 'Old Orkney Whisky, Real Liqueur', into neck level, c1915.
$1,800-2,700

The Stromness Distillery, Orkney, was founded by John Crookshanks in 1817 and was family owned until 1852 when ownership became that of John Sinclair until 1867, when ownership was passed to MacPherson Bros. Circa 1900 the distillery was renamed Man O'Hoy. The distillery was owned by J. & J. MacConnell Ltd, Belfast, until 1910. MacConnell's Distillery Ltd, London were the owners from 1915 until 1940, however the distillery has been silent since 1928.

A bottle of The Perth Royal Fin Old Highland Whisky, bottled b Matthew Gloag & Son, Perth, screw cap, lead capsule, lower-mid level, pre-war strength, c1930.
$600-750

A bottle of Logan's Extra Age O Scotch Whisky, by Appointmen to His Majesty The King, screw cap, lead capsule embossed 'Lai O'Logan De Luxe', level 3.5cm from base of capsule, c1940.
$375-525

20thC Whisky

Since the 18thC, some 860 malt and grain distilleries have existed, only a small proportion managing to survive.

A bottle of The Old Blend White Horse Whisky, By Appointment to His Majesty The King, White Horse Distillers Ltd, Lagavulin Distillery, Islay and Glenlivet District, screw cap, lead capsule, top shoulder level, bottled 1935.
$750-1,200

A bottle of Tamdhu 23 Years Old Pure Highland Malt Scotch Whisky, by the Highland Distilleries Co. Ltd, Tamdhu- Glenlivet Distillery, Knockando, stopper cork, lead capsule, into neck level, single malt, 83°, distilled 1950, bottled 1973.
$600-750

A pencil and watercolour heightened with bodycolour, 'Slainte', by Hugh Dodd, signed, 20thC, 15 by 10in (38 by 25cm).
$750-900

GHTERS

o French Dunhill 'unique' ket lighters, one with shagreen ered body, the lettered snuffer n engraved with registered mber 73741, the base signed red Dunhill, Paris, the other h white enamel striped oration to body, with lacement metal snuffer arm.
00-750

A Dunhill lucite bodied desk lighter, modelled on either side with scenes of a Kingfisher.
$750-1,200

A Cartier French lighter, with reeded body and integral wind shield, signed Cartier, Paris.
$600-750

A Dunhill 18ct gold engine turned lighter, with applied monogram J.C., London hallmarks for 1929.
$600-750

A Dunhill silver plated lighter, with wind shield to wick. **$150-225**

NDIAN & SOUTH EAST ASIAN ART

vory

North East Indian ivory figure Durga, Bengal, Berhampur, the ulti-armed goddess poised to ay the buffalo demon ahisha, her lion vehicle leaping Mahisha as he emerges from e neck of the decapitated uffalo, c1850, 8¼in (21cm).
4,800-5,700
his figure is from a larger shrine at would have been made by embers of the Bhaskara caste. nother more complete shrine is the Victoria and Albert useum and was exhibited at the reat Exhibition of 1851, escribed then as 'modern'.

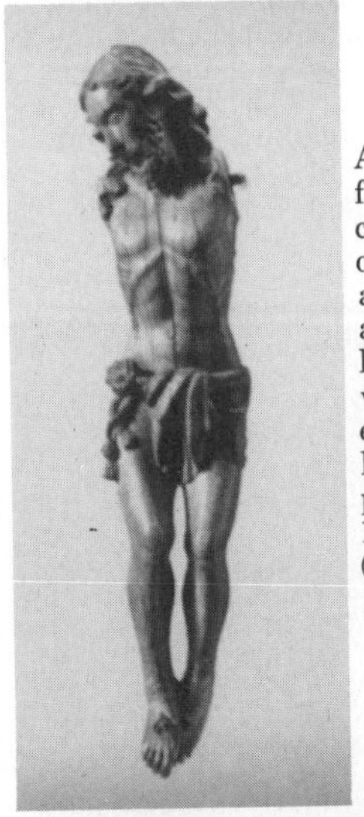

A Goanese fragmentary ivory crucifix, the figure of Christ wearing a twisted rope belt and short loincloth, his bearded face with anguished expression, with long centrally parted wavy hair, 17thC, 8in (20cm) high.
$3,000-4,500

A Goanese ivory figure of a Saint,17th/18thC, 9½in (24cm) high.
$5,250-7,500

A North Indian ivory two-panel screen, Mughal, each panel composed of several inset pierced openwork plaques with reticulated geometric designs and reserved lobed medallions and arabesques, with borders of scrolling foliate vine, c1800, 20in (51cm) high.
$4,800-5,700

Metal

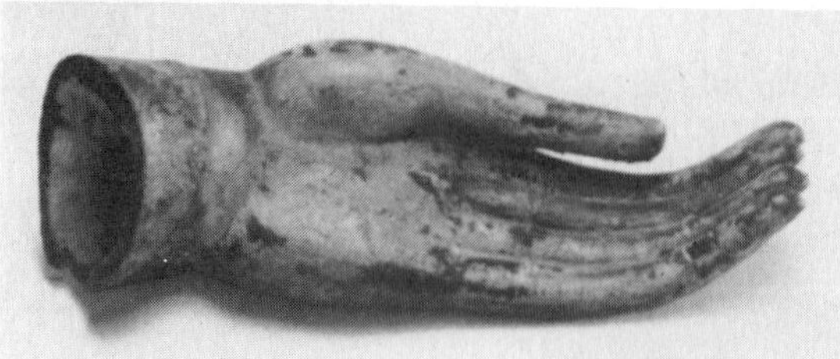

A monumental Thai bronze hand of Buddha, Ayuthia style, with incised fingernails, the hem of Buddha's robe in relief on the wrist, remains of gilding and lacquer, 16th/17thC, 23½in (60cm) long. **$9,000-10,000**

A Tibetan gilt bronze group of the Adibuddha Vajradhara in Yab-yum, wearing turquoise inset beaded jewellery and five-leaf crowns, 17thC, 9in (23cm).
$7,500-9,000

A Thai silver mask of the crowned Buddha, Lopburi/Haripunjay style, his face with bow shaped mouth, outlined lips, his ears with elongated pierced lobes, wearing a jewelled crown with tall triangular foliate projections, 13thC, 7½in (19cm) high.
$2,250-3,000

A Thai bronze head of Buddha, his face with serene benevolent expression, with elongated pierced ear lobes, hair arranged in rows of small curls with remains of gilding, 17thC, 9½in (24cm).
$3,000-4,500

A Tibetan silver figure of a Karmapa Lama, seated with his legs loosely crossed on an inscribed gilt bronze lotus throne, with remains of cold gilding, wearing monastic robes finely incised with floral and cloud motifs, 17thC, 3½in (9cm).
$3,000-4,500

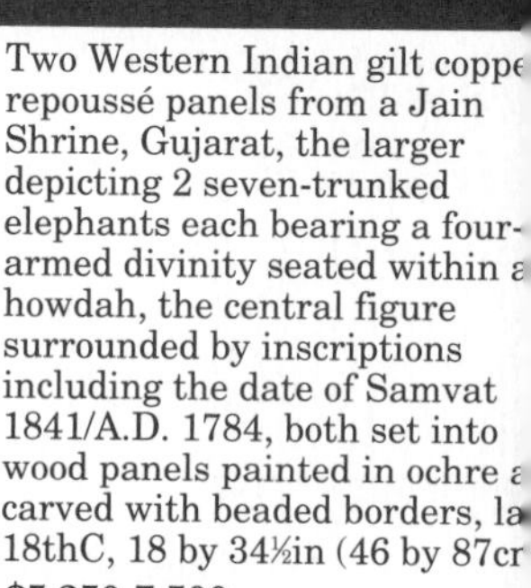

Two Western Indian gilt coppe repoussé panels from a Jain Shrine, Gujarat, the larger depicting 2 seven-trunked elephants each bearing a four-armed divinity seated within a howdah, the central figure surrounded by inscriptions including the date of Samvat 1841/A.D. 1784, both set into wood panels painted in ochre a carved with beaded borders, la 18thC, 18 by 34½in (46 by 87cr
$5,250-7,500

A Tibetan gilt bronze figure of Buddha Sakyamuni, seated in dhyana-sana on a lotus throne his hair arranged in small tigh curls and pigmented blue, the domed usnisa surmounted by a cintamani, 17thC, 12½in (32cm high.
$4,500-6,000

A pair of Indian silver overlaid wood elephants, Rajasthan, wearing blankets decorated with quatrefoil flowers, 14in (36cm) long.
$4,500-6,000

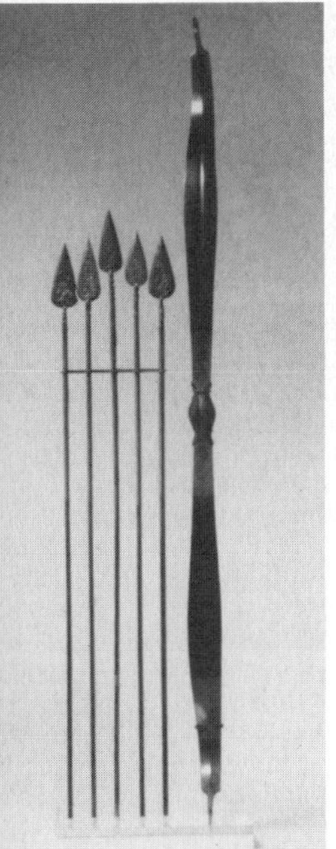

North Indian damascened steel ɔw and 5 steel tipped arrows, ⁄ughal, the bow grip's central ɛction covered in leather, the leaf ıaped arrow tips carved both ıdes, 18thC, bow 41in (104cm) ıng.
6,000-8,250

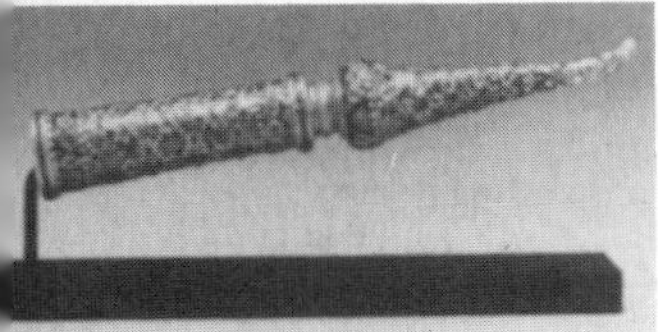

ɪn Indian enamelled gold and em-inset Hookah mouthpiece, ɪajasthan, enamelled overall in merald green, red, light blue, lack and white, in patterns of ense flowering plants and inset ith ruby and diamond chips, arly 19thC, 7½in (19cm).
5,250-7,500

. pair of Indian silver overlaid ood elephants, Rajasthan, each tanding and richly caparisoned ith elaborate textiles decorated ith quatrefoil flowers within a ross hatched design, strands of ells on their ankles, and visaged edallion on their foreheads, 26in 66cm) long.
7,500-9,000

A Nepalese copper repoussé figure of Samvara with his Consort, 17thC, 33½in (85cm) high.
$5,250-7,500

A Central Javanese bronze figure of Vajraraga, 10thC, 6in (15cm) high.
$2,700-3,300

An Indian parcel gilt watered steel striking device, in the form of an elephant attacking a spotted mythological animal wearing a gilt decorated harness, the striking blade incised with an inscription, 19thC, 4in (10cm) long.
$1,050-1,350

A North Indian bronze figure of the Bodhisattva Padmapani, Kashmir, standing in tribhanga on a lotus with his right hand in abhaya mudra, remains of blue pigment in his hair, the double aureole incised with flame motifs, 10th/11thC, 9in (23cm).
$3,000-3,750

Stone

A North East Indian grey stone stele of Vishnu, Pala Dynasty, standing in samapada on a lotus and flanked by his 2 consorts Lakshmi and Sarasvati, his remaining 3 hands holding the padma, gada, and cakra, and wearing a pleated dhoti, long floral garland, belt suspending beaded festoons, beaded mediation strand, jewelled collar, and conical crown, 12thC, 29½in (75cm) high.
$7,500-9,000

An Eastern Indian black stone stele of Kali, Pala Dynasty, 11thC, 19in (48cm).
$1,800-2,700

A Pala black stone stele of Surya, Eastern India, probably Bengal, 12thC, 29in (74cm) high.
$9,000-12,000

A North East Indian black stone stele of the Crowned Buddha, Pala Dynasty, probably Bihar, t death of Buddha depicted above, lines of Pali script incised on the reverse, 10thC, 14in (36cm) high
$5,250-7,500

Sandstone

A Thai sandstone head of Buddha, Ayuthia style, his face with serene meditative expression, 17thC, 11½in (29cm) high.
$3,000-4,500

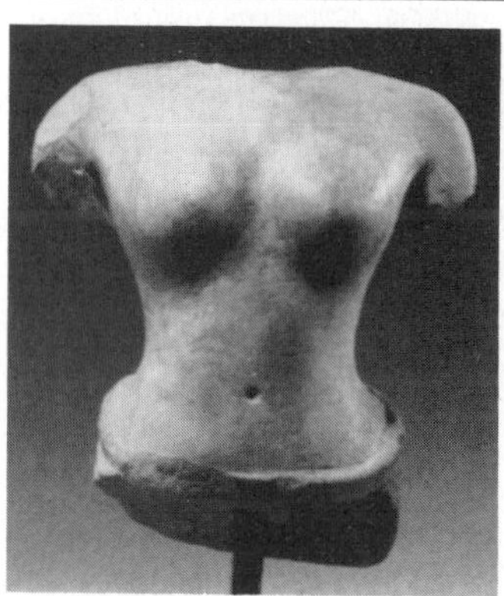

A Khmer grey sandstone torso of a Goddess, Angkor Wat style, with wide hips, narrow waist, breasts with incised nipples, wearing a vertically striated sarong held by a belt decorated with rosettes, 12thC, 12½in (32cm) high. **$4,800-5,700**

A Thai sandstone head of Buddha, Ayuthia style, his face with serene meditative expression, remains of black and white pigment on the surface, 16in (41cm) high.
$4,800-5,700

A Central Indian buff sandstone bust of Vishnu, Uttar Pradesh, 10thC, 14½in (37cm) high.
$1,800-2,700

A mottled red sandstone Jali screen, Mughal, with openwork reticulated pattern of hexagons centering 6-pointed stars, 18thC, 55 by 21in (140 by 53cm).
$7,500-9,000

A Central Indian red sandstone Capital, in the form of Narasimha, the lion-headed avatar of Vishnu, 12thC, 11½in (28.6cm) high.
$3,000-4,500

grey sandstone bust of Buddha, obably Angkor Borei, his face ith smiling benevolent pression, 7thC, 9in (22cm) high.
,800-5,700

buff sandstone stele of the ddess Ambika, seated on the ck of her recumbent lion hicle, a child seated on her lap asping her necklace, 8thC, 33in 4cm) high.
,800-5,700

A central Indian buff sandstone stele of Ganesha, the elephant headed divinity dancing in a lively attitude, flanked by diminutive musicians, apsaras above his head, 11thC, 31in (79cm) high.
$4,800-5,700

A Central Indian red sandstone head of a divinity, probably one of 4 faces from a large mukhalinga, the 3rd eye indicated vertically on his forehead, wearing a large beaded ear ornament, 10thC, 20½in (52cm).
$3,000-4,500

This head is possibly one of 2 missing faces from a Shivalinga published by Leroy Davidson in the 1968 exhibition entitled Art of the Indian Subcontinent from Los Angeles Collections. It is difficult to determine whether the head is that of Aghora or Tatpurusha. Stylistically, the similarities of overall scale, the rendering of such details as the beaded necklace, earring, coiffure, and facial features show the close relationship to the above mentioned example.

A Gupta mottled red sandstone relief fragment, Mathura Region, 5thC, 24½in (63cm) high.
$4,800-5,700

A Khmer grey sandstone head of Buddha, Bayon style, from the figure of the Buddha sheltered by Muchalinda, 12thC, 6½in (16cm) high.
$5,250-7,500

A central Indian red sandstone relief fragment, carved with a mithuna couple in erotic embrace, 12thC, 18½in (32cm) high.
$4,800-5,700

A Central Indian buff sandstone stele of Ganesha and his consort, 10thC, 24½in (63cm) high.
$3,000-4,500

Miller's is a price GUIDE not a price LIST

Wood

A South Indian wood figure of a goddess, 19thC, 53in (135cm) high.
$3,000-3,750

A Nepalese wood Hayagriva Shrine, 18thC, 26½in (67cm) high.
$6,000-8,250

A South Indian gilded wood figu of a goddess, 19thC, 39in (99cm high.
$1,800-2,700

A South Indian wood headdress, North Kerala, 18th/19thC, 34½in (87cm) wide.
$2,250-3,000

Miscellaneous

A Sawankhalok glazed pottery figure of a war elephant, Sukhothai, 14th/15thC, 13in (33cm) high.
$4,500-6,000

A North Indian pale green jade mirror, Mughal, traces of gilding, 18thC, 8in (20.5cm) high.
$3,000-4,500

An orange terracotta relief of Buddha Amitabha, Dvaravati style, 8th/9thC, 17in (44cm) high
$4,800-5,700

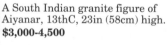

A South Indian granite figure of Aiyanar, 13thC, 23in (58cm) high.
$3,000-4,500

ICONS & RUSSIAN ART

A Greek triptych of the Deisis, above Five Chosen Saints, the doors painted in 3 registers with various Saints, late 18thC, 13½in (35cm) high.
$1,500-2,250

n icon of the Mother of God of azan, in parcel gilt oklad with namelled halo, 19thC, 12¼in 31cm) high.
,500-2,250

An icon of St George, with scenes of his martyrdom, 19thC, 34in (86cm) high.
$4,500-6,000

An icon of the Hodigitria Mother of God of Tikhvin, 19thC, 35in (88cm) high.
$3,000-4,500

n icon of the Mandylion, ealistically painted, in silver gilt klad and halo, 19thC, 14½in 37cm) high.
900-1,500

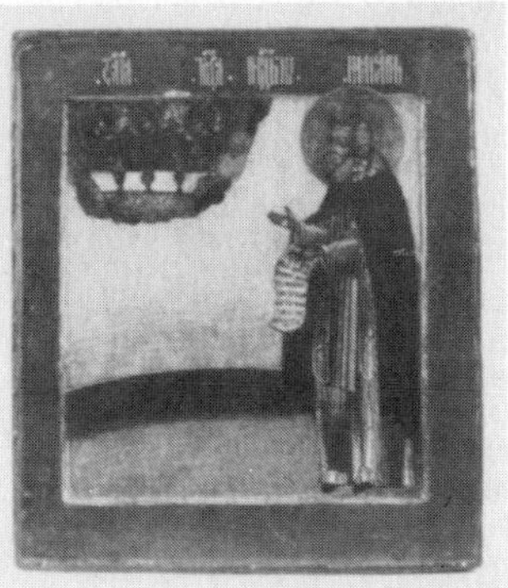

An icon of St Makarii, late 18thC, 12¼in (31cm) high.
$1,200-1,500

An icon of St George and the Dragon, early 19thC, 28in (71cm).
$7,500-9,000

ANS

fan with plain ivory sticks, the and painted paper leaf ortraying Bacchus and Ariadne a golden chariot drawn by hite horses, the border with asselled swags, early 18thC, 11in 28cm). **$750-900**

A pierced ivory brisé fan, Englsih, slight damage, c1790, 9½in (24cm).
$1,200-1,800

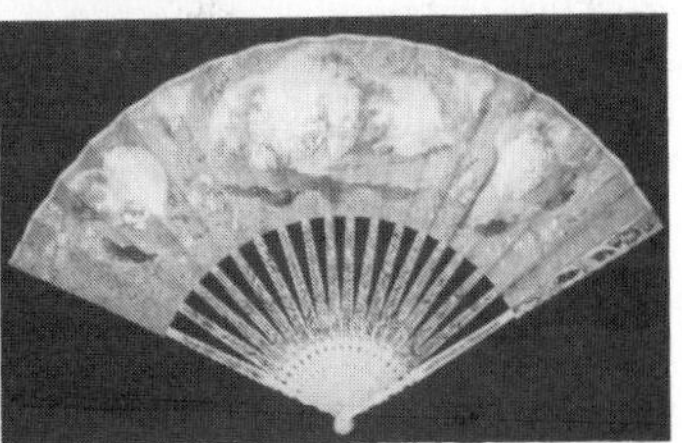

Two fans, one with paper leaf painted with a flute player entertaining 2 ladies, with vignettes either side, the ivory sticks and guards pierced and painted; and another painted with buccolic gallants, bone sticks and guards, c1770.
$300-375

fan, the leaf painted with a nun eading a prayer book inscribed Pastor Fido, the ivory sticks arved and pierced, English, 1740, 11in (28cm), in ontemporary fan box.
600-750

A printed fan, Les Cuisines Républicaine de 1795.96 ... &c., the leaf with an engraving of street vendors and their clients, with a frieze of pale blue wash with a Greek key fret pattern, with wooden sticks, French, 9in (23cm).
$750-1,200

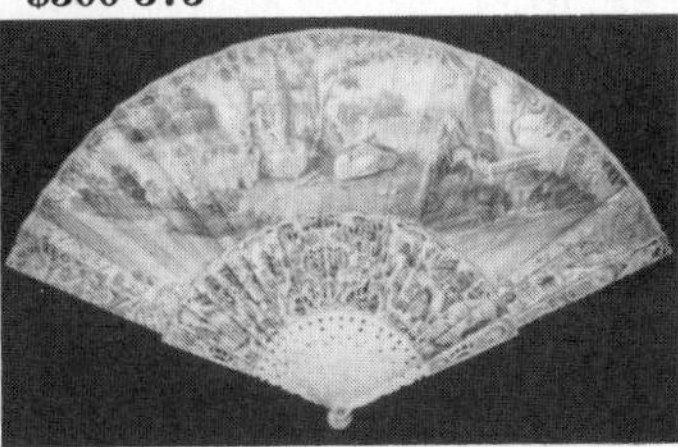

A fan, the paper leaf painted with a group by a lake, the ivory sticks and guards foiled, pierced and painted and applied with mother-of-pearl figures, c1750.
$450-600

l. An Italian fan, the chicken skin leaf painted with The Castel San Angelo and Pompeian decoration, the reverse with 3 butterflies, the ivory sticks carved, pierced and gilt, slight damage, c1775, 11in (28cm), in contemporary box.
$1,200-1,800
c. A carton brisé fan, a chromolithograph of portraits of beautiful women including Mary 'Perdita' Robinson, Madame Vigee le Brun, Marie Antoinette and La Comtesse du Barry in heart shaped frames of forget-me-nots, published by Raphael Tuck & Sons Ltd., inscribed from Marcella, late 19thC, 7in (18cm).
$600-750
r. An ivory brisé fan, decorated with birds and flowering trees in gold, silver and black hiramakie and takamakie, with some kirigane, the guardsticks decorated with vines, butterflies and birds in Shibayama work, Japanese, slight damage, c1880, 11.5in (29.5cm).
$3,000-4,500

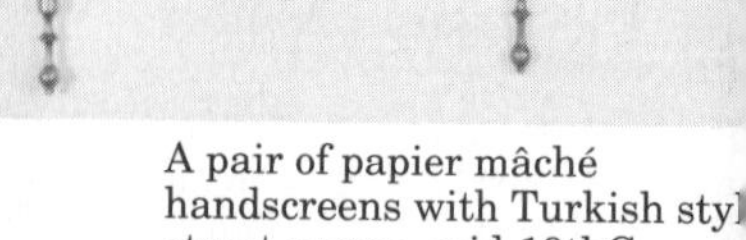

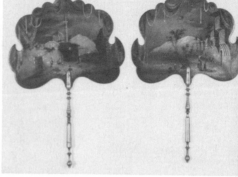

A pair of papier mâché handscreens with Turkish styl street scenes, mid-19thC.
$375-525

A printed fan, the leaf a hand-coloured etching of an allegory of a Peace Treaty, probably the Treaty of Aix 1747 with the monarchs of the countries involved seated around a table, with heralds at a balcony holding a scroll inscribed Articles of Peace, and classical portraits beyond numbered for a key and an orange tree in the foreground, the reverse with a woman carrying a basket on her head, standing by ruins, the ivory sticks carved and pierced, English, slight damage, c1747, 11in (28cm).
$1,800-2,700

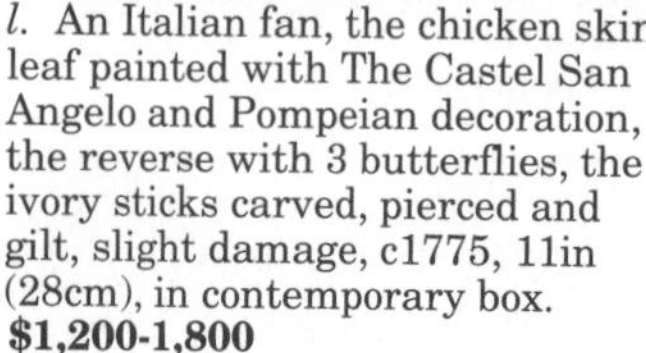

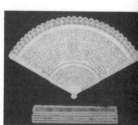

A Chinese Export ivory brisé fa finely fretted and carved with central shield displaying monogram SG, with bridges, boats, flowers and boats surrounding, c1790, 10½in (26.5cm), in hand stitched card box. **$750-1,200**

A painted fan, after Reni, the paper leaf painted with Aurora strewing flowers before the chariot of the sun, ivory sticks and guards pierced and gilded, c1780.
$300-375

A Chinese gilded black lacquer brisé fan, displaying a meandering vine laden with grapes surrounding a central cartouche with initials 'DAR', and 2 others, the guards with foliage, early 19thC, 10½in (26.5cm).
$375-525

A Canton tortoiseshell brisé fan, carved and pierced with figures and a building, the guardsticks decorated with gilt metal filigree butterflies and waterlilies, slight damage, mid-19thC, 9½in (24cm), in a fitted lacquer box.
$1,050-1,350

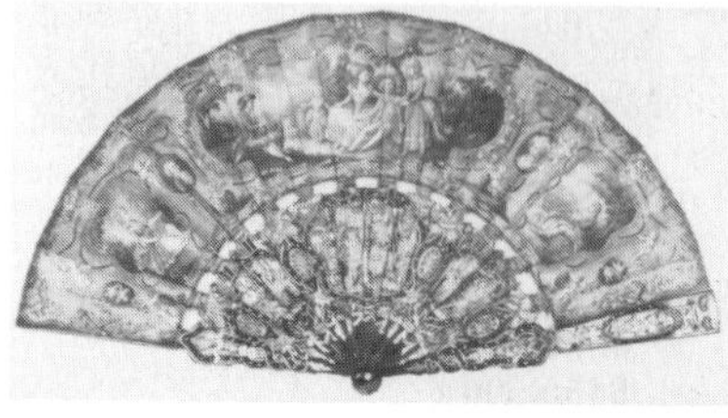

A fan, the silk leaf painted with an elegant family in a park, 2 portrait miniatures, and putti holding escutcheons with monograms CB or GB, the reserves embroidered with spangles, the tortoiseshell sticks carved, pierced and gilt, c1775, 10in (25cm). **$1,800-2,700**

A fan, the leaf of Brussels lace, the mother-of-pearl sticks finely carved and pierced with trophies of love and an oval vignette of a lady playing the piano signed J. Vaillan, the upper guardstick with a crest and the motto Deus Nobis quis contra, the lower guardstick with a gentleman musician, c1880, 11in (28cm), in a box.
$600-750

A fan, the black gauze leaf painted with circus scenes, signed Donzel, with ebony stick, the guardsticks carved with clowns with ivory heads and hands, c1890, 12½in (32cm).
$600-750

A French machine lace trimmed fan, on mother-of-pearl sticks, inscribed Faucon, Paris, late 19thC, 12½in (32cm).
$135-150

A Victorian chromolithographed novelty Valentine card, in the form of a fan, with 12 compartments, the heads containing oval medallions of full length ladies in various poses in floral frames, with roundels beneath containing a continuous verse, with elaborately gilt designs on the handles, c1890, 17in (43.5cm) wide.
$750-1,200

A Chinese Export fan, having carved bone sticks and guards, the painted paper leaf portraying ladies and scholars, applied ivory faces and silk costume, similar to the reverse, c1870, 11in (28cm).
$450-600

A French fan, the gauze leaf decorated with gold metal sequins and spangles, in formal foliate pattern within a border, having mother-of-pearl inlay to the blond tortoiseshell sticks and guards, c1900, 11½in (29cm).
$225-255

A fan, the paper leaf painted with a shepherd and his flock surprising a social gathering in the woods, the ivory sticks and guards pierced and gilded with figures, c1750.
$600-750

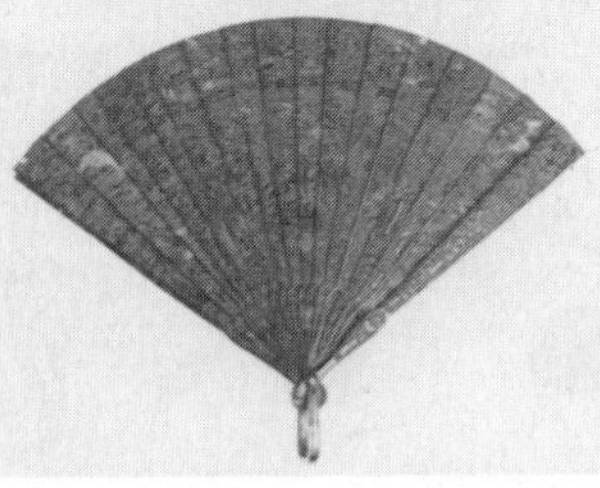

A Chinese tortoiseshell brisé fan finely fretted and carved with an interior scene to the central cartouche, figures in a pavilion garden with willow trees, one guard stick depicting a dragon, the other replaced, mid-19thC, 7¼in (18.5cm).
$375-450

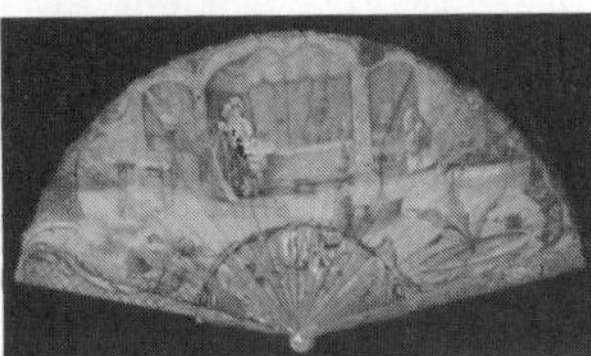

A fan, the mother-of-pearl sticks pierced and gilded with cherubs in Art Nouveau style, c1890, 10½in (27cm), in a satin box by Duvelleroy, and 2 others.
$1,800-2,700

A lace trimmed fan, signed F. Houghton, on carved mother-of-pearl sticks, late 19thC, 13½in (34.5cm).
$375-525

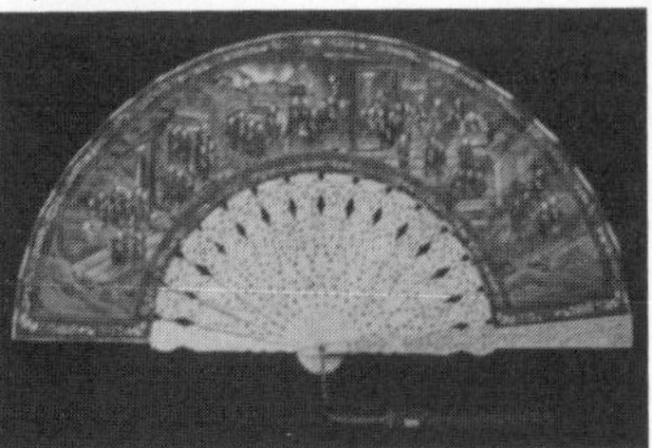

A gilt metal filigree brisé fan, enamelled in blue and green with vignettes of a pagoda and other buildings, slight damage, mid-19thC, 7½in (19cm).
$1,050-1,350

A fan, the paper leaf painted with a group by a lake, the ivory guards and sticks pierced and painted with a servant and his mistress, c1740.
$750-1,200

A French fan, the lace leaf applied with a chicken skin panel, blond tortoiseshell sticks pierced and gilded, one guard applied with an ivory putto, with Duvelleroy case, and 2 others, 19thC.
$600-750

A fan, the leaf of needlelace, Point d'Alençon, displaying a sheaf of corn and harvesting tools to the centre, flanked by horses held by reclining Cupids, trees and birds between, within a formal border of finely detailed blossom on a trellis, possibly made in Burano, mounted on plain tortoiseshell sticks, mid-19thC, 10½in (26.5cm).
$1,200-1,800

OPERA GLASSES

A pair of A. Coiffier opera glasses, signed on the mother-of-pearl eyepieces A. Coiffier ing[r] Opticien Paris, gilt brass draws and tubes bound in white enamel with coloured flowers, in blue velvet case, French, late 19thC.
$750-1,200

A pair of Carl Zeiss opera glasses, in gilt brass with mother-of-pearl covered body, German, c1930.
$300-375

A pair of oval framed opera glasses, with brass draws and tortoiseshell bound tubes; and pair of blue enamel opera glass with mother-of-pearl mounted eyepieces, early 20thC.
$750-1,200

A pair of opera glasses, with turned ivory eyepieces, gilt brass draws and blue enamelled tubes, in leather case, French, late 19thC. **$600-750**

A pair of blue enamel opera glasses, signed by retailer Salom & Co., Opticians, 137 Regent Street, London, with mother-of-pearl mounted eyepiece, gilt brass draws and enamel binding, in a case, French, late 19thC.
$600-750

Two pairs of opera glasses, one with mother-of-pearl bound tubes and handle, signed Voigtlander & Sohn, the other in white enamel with mother-of-pearl mounted eyepieces, German and French, early 20thC.
$750-900

A pair of champlevé opera glasses, with gilt brass draws an shaped tubes bound with blue champlevé enamelling, in leathe case, French, late 19thC.
$750-1,200

WALKING STICKS & CANES

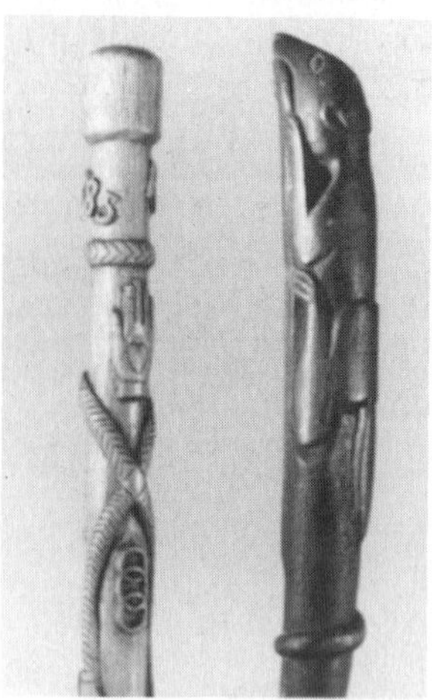

Two American carved wood folk art canes, *l.* initialled RWH, dated 1885, with a tapering shaft, relief carved with entwined snakes, small birds, tassels, a heart and hand and other symbols relating to I.O.O.F., *r.* the handle carved in the form of a mongoose being devoured by a large snake entwining the tapering shaft, age cracks, c1900, 35 to 38in (89 to 96.5cm).
$750-1,200

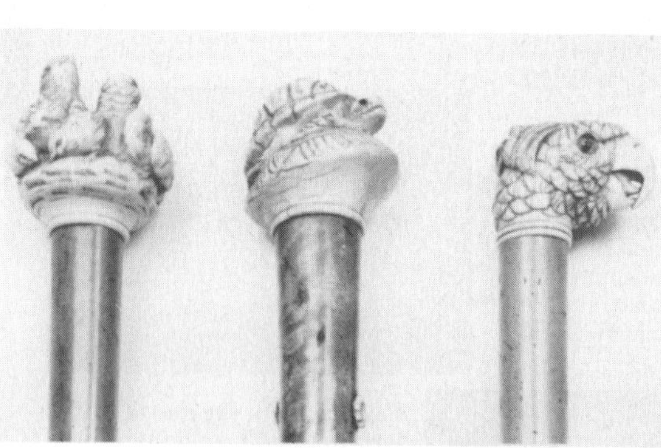

Three umbrella handles, all with ivory terminals, carved with *l.* a grouse and young, *c.* a figure of a tortoise, *r.* a head of a parrot with blue glass eyes.
$225-300 each

Miller's is a price GUIDE not a price LIST

An American carved wood cane, the tapering shaft carved in relief with figures of a donkey, horse, birds, potted plants, hammer, horseshoe and snake, the handle carved in the form of a stylised man's head, initialled MM, c1900, 35in (89cm).
$1,200-1,800

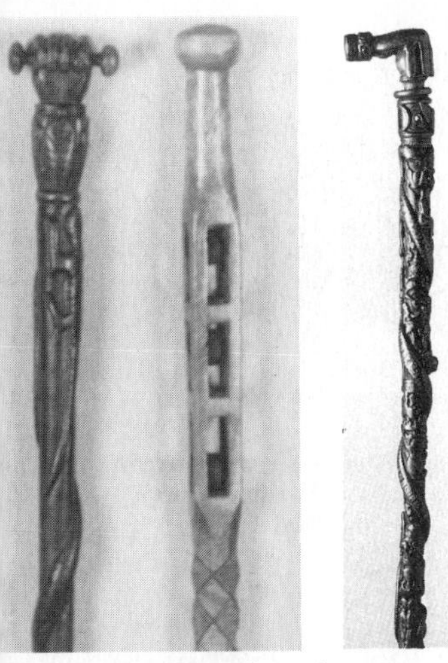

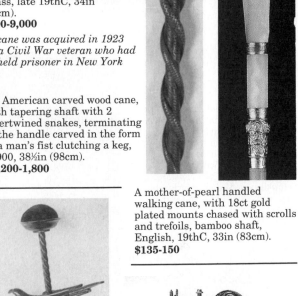

wo American carved wood canes: carved with a handle in the rm of a man's fist clenching a arbell, the sleeve and collar with ylised palm leaves and incised ith the date 1902, the tapering naft carved with lizards and ntwined with a snake, *r.* with a neapple carved shaft enclosing 3 uzzle balls, c1900, 36in (92cm).
1,200-1,800

A finely carved wood walking stick, with angular handle in the form of a man's hand grasping a ball finial, the shaft with spread winged American eagle, relief carved Biblical figures and animals, the length entwined by the Serpent bearing the inscription 'As in Adam all die, even so in Christ Jesus all shall be made alive', the base encased in brass, late 19thC, 34in (86.5cm).
$7,500-9,000

This cane was acquired in 1923 from a Civil War veteran who had been held prisoner in New York State.

An American carved wood cane, with tapering shaft with 2 intertwined snakes, terminating in the handle carved in the form of a man's fist clutching a keg, c1900, 38½in (98cm).
$1,200-1,800

A mother-of-pearl handled walking cane, with 18ct gold plated mounts chased with scrolls and trefoils, bamboo shaft, English, 19thC, 33in (83cm).
$135-150

EWING

Princess of Wales sewing achine, c1860.
150-225

A hemming bird, the decorated clamp having needle compartment with acorn knop, the bird with plumage markings, English, c1800, 5½in (13.5cm).
$150-225

A cast iron Newton Wilson Cleopatra chain stitch sewing machine, No. 11506, with gilt decorations, English, hook missing, c1870, in a later wooden case.
$5,250-7,500

US Patent Office model of atent No. 24881 (1859), Joseph . Morton, Improved Loop-Check Thread-Holder for the Wheeler Wilson or other similar sewing achines, with brass holder for ristle loop-check, steel model of Vilson rotating hook and wood ame, 5½in (14cm), with original atent Office label and photostat f specification.
375-525

A French bodkin case, decorated in Vernis Martin style with winged putti with garlands of flowers amidst clouds, silver collar, 19thC, 5in (14cm) long.
$375-525

A Wilcox & Gibbs sewing machine, c1890.
$90-105

A Gresham Imperial sewing machine, c1870.
$375-525

A Wanzer sewing machin British, c1895.
$90-105

A turned rosewood sewing clamp, the vase top of Tunbridge ware, having removable lid with blue velvet pin cushion impressed with lyre motif and mirror to the inside, 5½in (13.5cm), and a Tunbridge ware box containing templates, a Mauchline thimble box, and 6 steel buttons, early 19thC.
$375-450

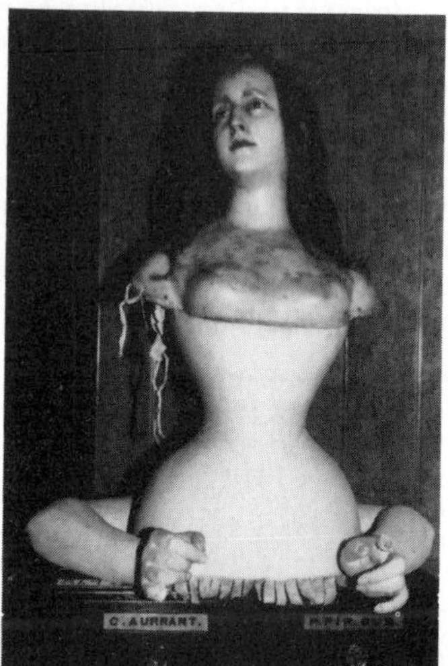

A wax milliner's bust, 31in (79cm).
$450-600

A Royal Shakespeare sewing machine, No. 143974, with gilt decorations, on rectangular cast iron base, with tools and instructions in maker's wooden case.
$900-1,500

TEXTILES
Costume

Costume : Condition

- Condition of costume is critical since stitching, fastening and laundering details are an important part of the appeal to the collector.
- Beware of areas that have obviously been treated, cleaned or repaired, in case important evidence has been lost.
- Ancient repairs or alterations, however, can add interest to a piece.

A gentleman's pale green silk suit, with a figured pin stripe, faced and lined with pink silk, woven à disposition with borders, buttons and pockets of trailing ribbons and pink roses, comprising: breeches, waistcoat and coat, c1770.
$6,000-8,250

A pair of young girl's hoops, composed of an oval hoop with 2 supporting bands, covered with padded glazed linen, with pocke holes and draw-string waist, mi 18thC.
$9,000-10,000

A little girl's crushed strawberry watered silk dress, the short sleeved bodice having horizontal pleats to the stomacher front with silk button trim, fringed robings and tabs to waistline, full skirt, hook fastening and ribbon bow to the back, c1870, and another.
$600-750

An aesthetic silk Paisley design gown, lined in red with covered buttons, deep pleat to back and cord tie. **$300-375**

An Italian silk and metal thread embroidered velvet cope, the orphreys centred by a figure of Saint Andrew on the front and the Madonna and Child on the back, scrolling strapwork interspersed with masks above and below, clusters of foliate scrolls decorating the remainder of the panels, 16thC, 48in (121cm), and another.
$2,700-3,300

An open robe of dark ground chintz, printed with lily-of-the-valley and other flowers, bodice slightly altered, late 18thC.
$2,250-3,000

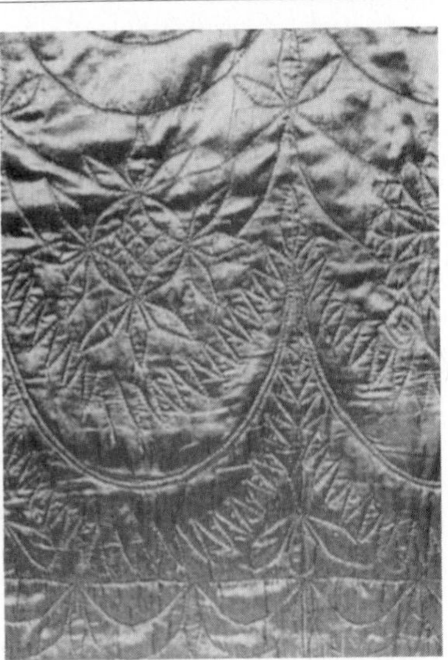

A lady's quilted pale delphinium blue silk petticoat, designed with swags of ribbon and flowers to the hem, unpicked at the waist, pocket to one seam, English, c1740.
$300-375

A gold thread embroidered velvet chasuble, the elaborately embroidered orphreys worked with scrolling foliage and flower-filled urns interspersed with roundels incorporating busts of saints and a nobleman, surrounded by gold thread borders, 49in (125cm), and an Italian gold thread embroidered red velvet shawl, 16thC.
$1,500-2,250

A chain mail mini dress composed of metal squares with chain links, some studded, labelled Paco Rabanne, Paris, Made in France, c1968.
$7,500-9,000

l. A child's ribbed tartan silk dress, with wide flared skirt, short sleeves and black velvet buttons to the front fastening and tabs to the hemline, with label 'from M. Clack and Co., 15, 17 Ludgate Hill, London, Ladies and Childrens' Outfitters', with another of Royal blue velvet, English, c1850.
$600-750
r. A small boy's black velvet suit, the high buttoned jacket having braid binding, breast pocket and pocket flaps, the breeches having fall front and braid trim, c1880.
$300-375

A gentleman's waistcoat of ivory satin, woven à disposition with chocolate cut and ciselé velvet floral border and pockets, the ground woven with ciselé harebells, with tinsel buttons, c1740.
$750-900

A sleeveless evening black silk dress, crêpe woven with undulating wires, with deep back décollétage and matching high collared shoulder cape in the manner of a matador's mantle, lined with scarlet silk, labelled in seam Schiaparelli, London, indestinctly inscribed on reverse with client's name, late 1930s.
$5,250-7,500

A pair of gentleman's silk canvas braces, embroidered with stylised flowers in shades of lavender and green, lined lavender silk, the kid straps having three-pronged brass adjustment buckles, c1840, 3 later waistcoats, an opera hat and 2 others.
$225-255

A beaded jacket, the black beaded ground floral decorated with silver coloured beads and diamanté, c1920s.
$225-255

A Chinese semi-formal blue silk robe, embroidered in coloured silks and gilt threads with 8 roundels worked with dragons chasing flaming pearls amongst cloud scrolls, over a sea-wave border worked with religious symbols, the cuffs with smaller roundels and a sea-wave border lined with blue silk, late 19thC.
$2,250-3,000

A Chinese semi-formal red silk robe, embroidered in coloured silks, with 8 roundels, each worked with cranes framed by cloud scrolls, over a sea-wave border, the wide sleeves with double sleeve bands worked with smaller roundels, c1870.
$1,050-1,350

A Chinese court blue silk robe, embroidered in coloured silks and gilt threads, the top section with 4 dragons chasing flaming pearls amongst cloud scrolls and symbols over a sea-wave border, the waist worked with dragons, the skirt with 12 dragon roundels above larger dragons and a turbulent sea-wave border, with horseshoe cuffs, lined with blue silk, mid-19thC.
$2,250-3,000

A Chinese theatrical yellow silk coat, embroidered in coloured silks and gilt threads, lined with white cotton, late 19thC.
$1,200-1,500

A Japanese ivory silk damask kosode, woven with saya patterns over embroidered in coloured silks and gilt threads, lined with crimson silk, late 19thC.
$2,250-3,000

An olive green velvet school cap, with a silver tassel, c1920.
$50-75

A pair of leather riding boots with trees.
$180-225

A Japanese maiwai indigo cotton costume, painted in coloured inks, with deep sleeves, lined and altered, late 18thC.
$1,200-1,800

A pair of hobnail boots.
$15-25

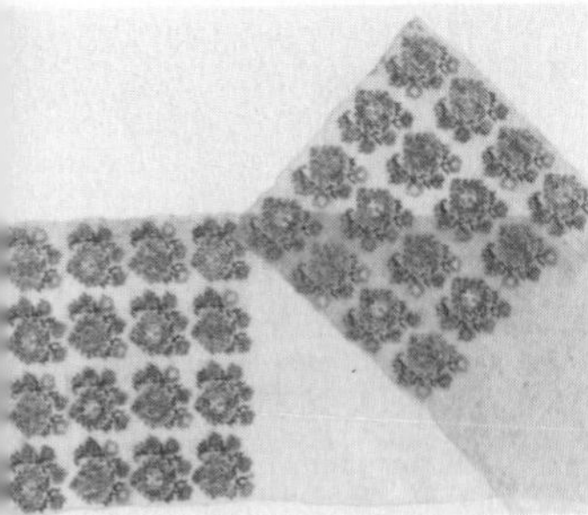

. Turkish striped linen sash, mbroidered at either end with 4 ows of flowers, early 19thC, 62in 157cm).
450-600

. gentleman's ivory quilted cotton at, tamboured with sprays of owers and perching birds, 'ersian, c1800.
750-1,200

A shield-shaped needlework purse, embroidered in coloured silks and silver gilt threads, one side with a stag, the other with a unicorn, both within a scrolling frame, lined with green silk, Continental, mid-18thC, 4in (10cm).
$1,050-1,350

A Victorian beaded bag, with vorked flowers to an ivory round, drawstring top and tassel o the base, c1860, and a purse, 1840.
135-150

A pair of leather riding boots, no formers, c1930.
$50-75

A printed cotton handkerchief, depicting the Declaration of the Independence of the United States of America, July 1776, with the protagonists listed, within a rust coloured border, the outer frame of dark brown scrolling motifs, c1840, 31in (79cm) wide.
$1,050-1,350

A Chinese lady's informal green kossu silk robe, woven in many colours, with butterflies amongst branches of flowers, the sleeve bands of blue kossu silk woven with floral roundels, lined with pink silk damask, late 19thC.
$1,050-1,350

A Chinese dragon blue kossu silk robe, woven in coloured silks and gilt threads, lined with blue silk, repaired, mid-19thC.
$1,050-1,350

A Victorian carriage parasol, with collapsible handle and brown silk cover, bone ring and top finial, some damage, 26in (66cm).
$50-75

A shield-shaped needlework yellow silk purse, embroidered in coloured silks and silver gilt threads, one side with the monogram CVI possibly for the Emperor Charles VI surmounted by a crown, the other side with Imperial Arms of Austria, both surrounded by small flowers, lined with pink silk, Continental, c1740, 4½in (11cm).
$1,500-2,250

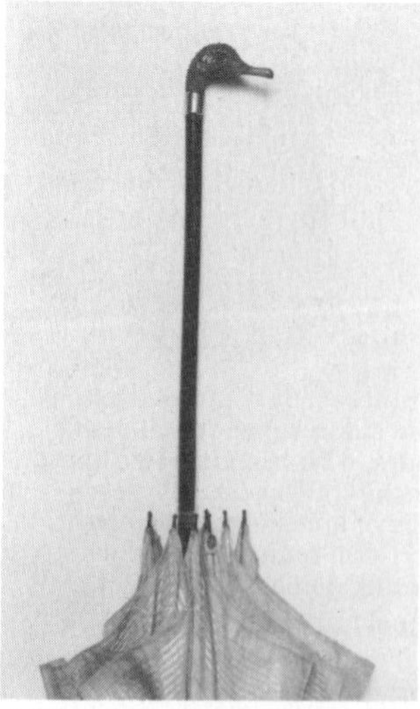

A Victorian parasol, with a cream cotton cover, the handle carved with a duck's head, gold coloured band, 36in (91.5cm).
$105-120

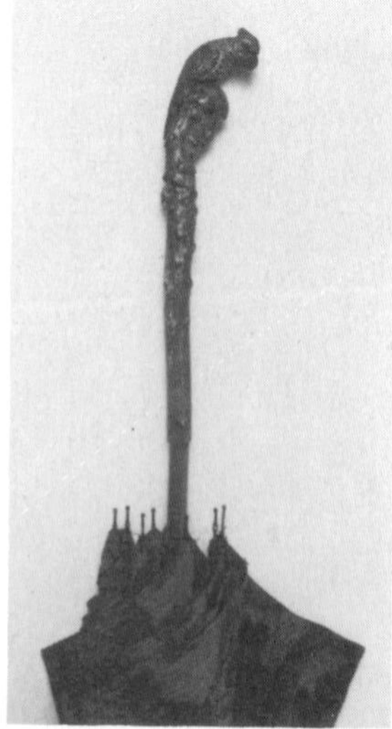

A Victorian parasol, with a heavy cotton cover, briar handle carved with a parrot, 35in (89cm).
$105-120

A parasol, the shade of lilac silk with gilt and blonde silk lace overlaid, the ivory handle carved with posies of roses, with gold fittings, including a vacant cartouche surmounted by a crown, the finial an orb, encircled with a belt enamelled with Greek key pattern, opening to reveal a chain rosary with 6 coral stations and a crucifix set with rubies, in a fitted velvet case.
$3,000-4,500
This carries a declaration to the effect that the parasol is said to have belonged to the Empress Eugenie of France. The quality of the workmanship would certainly suggest a Royal commission.

Embroidery & Beadwork

An Italian silk embroidered table cover, 17thC, 112 by 69½in (285 by 177cm).
$1,800-2,700

An oval needlework picture, embroidered in coloured silks, with a young girl holding a parrot and a bird cage, with roses and tulips on either side of her, framed by a border of delicate trailing flowers, 18thC, 13 by 12in (33 by 31cm).
$1,050-1,350

A whitework picture depictin Judith presenting the head o Holofernes, the figures with etensive raised work and embroidered with seed pearls early 17thC, 5 by 3½in (12.5 b 8.5cm).
$9,000-12,000

A needlework picture, embroidered in coloured silks, gilt and silver gilt threads, the back inscribed 'worked in silver lace, the value of the silver full five shillings', also with typed label with provenance Penllyn Castle, Glamorganshire, c1660, 7 by 10in (17.5 by 25cm).
$3,000-4,500

An Italian gold thread embroidered silk coverlet, on crimson silk ground with metal thread edging, 18thC, 75½ by 59in (192 by 150cm).
$1,800-2,700

A beadwork picture, worked in coloured beads, with a lady and gentleman in a landscape, their hair of metal thread and their costume trimmed with lace, mi 17thC, framed and glazed, 10 b 13in (25 by 33cm).
$2,700-3,300

needlework picture, worked in loured silks and gilt threads ith the bust of Charles I within raised work frame, and putti d large raised flowerheads in e corners, against an ivory silk ound, framed and glazed, nglish, late 17thC, 15 by 11in 8 by 28cm).
,700-3,300
ith an ink label on the back: 'orked by Mrs Holder, who died '00'.

A mid-Georgian needlework picture, depicting a Biblical scene in gilded and ebonised frame, 33 by 24½in (84.5 by 62cm)
$600-750
This needlework picture was a gift from Dante Gabriel Rossetti to Alice Boyd and William Bell Scott.

An English silk and metal thread stumpwork embroidered coverlet, highlighted with gold sequins, 2 sides with meandering flowering vines, c1650, 57 by 44in (145 by 112cm).
$4,800-5,700

n Italian beaded and crewelwork anging, centred with a bust of a aint surrounded by a band of eads in a floral pattern,18thC, 7¾ by 33½in (147 by 85cm).
3,000-4,500

An oval embroidered picture worked in coloured silks with a lady sitting in a landscape holding a basket of flowers, late 19thC, 7 by 8½in (17.5 by 21.5cm), in a china ebony and tortoiseshell frame.
$1,800-2,700

ace

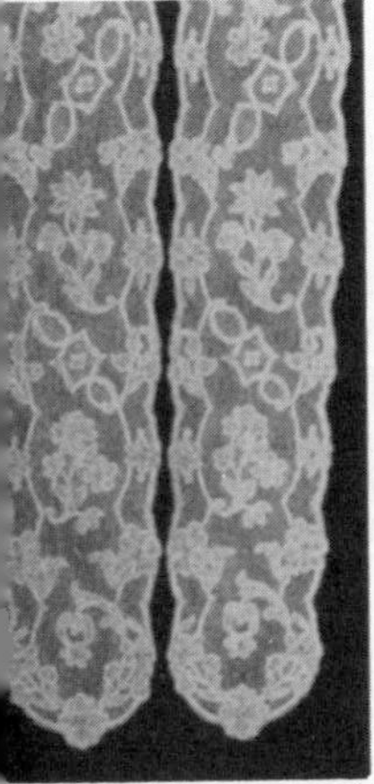

pair of Mechlin bobbin lace ppets, with flowersprays gainst a vrai droschel ground vithin a floral border, Flemish, 1755, 21¾in (55cm).
600-750

A flounce of Maltese silk bobbin lace, displaying medallions surmounted by coronets and thistles, with fleur-de-lys and foliage to the scalloped border, late 19thC, 156in (396cm) long.
$375-525

A flounce of Belgian needlelace, Point de Gaz, with pendant bouquets of flowers between floral columns linked by scrolls with elaborate fillings, multi-petalled roses to the border, trailing vines above, late 19thC, 224in (570cm) long.
$3,000-4,500

A flounce of Point de France needlelace, worked with urns and other formal devices, c1720, 140in (431.5cm) long.
$7,500-9,000

Samplers

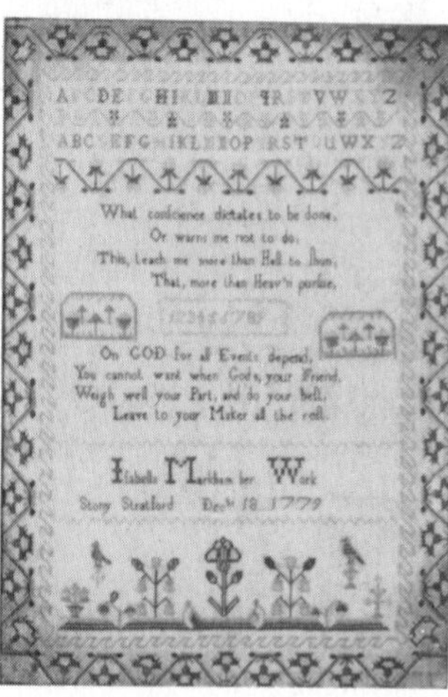

A sampler by Isabella Markham, 1779, worked in brightly coloured silks, with 2 verses and rows of the alphabet, bluebells and other flowers, within a border of stylised carnations, 12 by 17in (31 by 43cm), framed and glazed.
$1,050-1,350

A sampler by Louisa Pegden, aged 12, with a griffin, birds, flowers, Adam, Eve and deer, c1830, 17 by 13in (43 by 33cm).
$1,050-1,350

A silkwork sampler by Sarah Johnson, 1843, 16 by 12in (41 by 31cm).
$450-600

A sampler by Hannah Mills, worked in silk, 1818, 16 by 13in (41 by 33cm) **$600-750**

A needlework sampler, showing the family record of the Bacon-Sawyer family, by Rebeckah Bacon, aged 11 years, Jaffrey, Cheshire County, New Hampshire, dated 1828, in blue, green, yellow and pink silk, with borders of floral vines, some fading, 16½ by 17½in (42 by 44.5cm).
$4,500-6,000

It is interesting to note that the upper inner corner of flowers is unfinished. The original silk thread and needle are left in the linen backing. Rebeckah was the youngest of the 4 children born to Jacob Bacon (1786-1866) and Betsey Sawyer (1782-1854) and by 1816 they were living in Jaffrey, New Hampshire. At the age of 30, Rebeckah married Fabyon Rice, her second husband.

A sampler by Mary Green, aged 11, with 3 verses, a farm, sheep and flowers c1830, 18½in (47.5cm) square.
$1,050-1,350

A sampler by Eliz Wilkins, 1813, worked in brightly coloured silks, of Paradise with Adam and Eve and the serpent, also 2 houses with gardens in front and a lion tied to a tree, within an elaborate border of naturalistic flowers, 20½ by 22in (52 by 56cm), framed.
$1,050-1,350

A sampler displaying Caleb and Joshua, a large pot of flowers and random small trees and birds, a pious verse above, within a stylised floral border, worked in silk cross stitch on linen, Jane Lofthouse's Work Age 11 1834, English, 19¾ by 19¼in (50 by 49cm), framed in rosewood.
$900-1,050

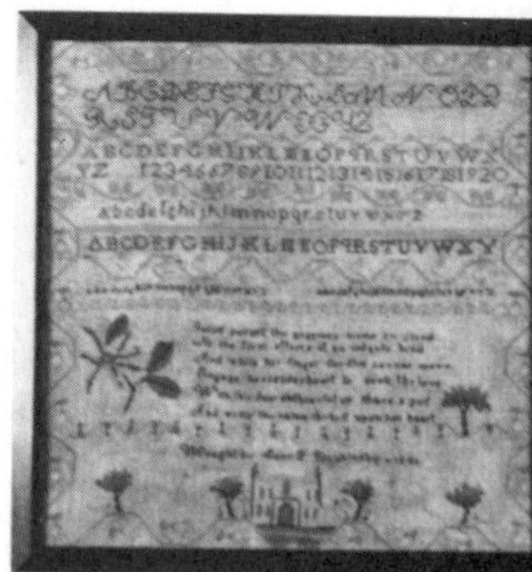

A needlework sampler, made by Lucy P. Blankinship, probably Massachusetts, dated 1841, in green, brown, blue and red silk, with bands of letters and numerals, above a pious verse, within a border of rosebuds, some fading and discolouration, 16¼in (41.3cm) square.
$300-375

An early Victorian child's needlework sampler, by Martha Bitterson, aged 9, dated 1845, worked with a verse, buildings, sportsmen, birds, butterflies and trees within a strawberry border, 16½ by 17½in (42 by 45cm).
$1,200-1,500

A needlework sampler, signed Ellen E. Odenwelder, probably Pennsylvania, worked in lavender, rose, orange, green, blue and white wool, c1850, some discolouration and fabric loss, 22 by 24½in (56 by 62.2cm).
$1,500-2,250

A needlework sampler, probably Pennsylvania, worked in red, white, pink and brown wool, on a loosely woven linen ground, mid-19thC, some fabric loss and discolouration, 17in (43.2cm) square, in a period frame.
$2,250-3,000

Tapestries

A pair of tapestry curtains, woven in coloured wools and gilt threads, with a medieval design of coats-of-arms against a lattice work ground, the borders with stylised flowerheads amongst strapwork, late 19thC, 120 by 50in (304.5 by 127cm).
$1,500-2,250

A Victorian woolwork door hanging tapestry, depicting Elizabethan figures and animals in a wooded glade, 82 by 52in (208 by 132cm). **$450-600**

A Brussels historical tapestry from the story of Anthony and Cleopatra, after designs by Justus van Edmont, from the workshop of Geraert Peemans, Cleopatra dangling a baroque pearl over a tazza, her attendant and Anthony seated beside her at a banqueting table, the servant holding up a cake, swags of flowers above centred by a scrollwork cartouche incorporating 'SVPRA PORTAM' highlighted with metal thread, Brussels town mark and weaver's mark GPM on lower selvage, late 17thC, 79in (201cm) wide.
$15,000-22,500

This is a reduced variant of the weaving Cleopatra Dissolving the Pearl, from the set of 8 or more woven by Jan van Leefdael and Geraert van der Strecken, comprising the story of Anthony and Cleopatra.

An Aubusson Verdure tapestry, early 18thC, 91 by 121in (232 by 307cm).
$10,500-13,500

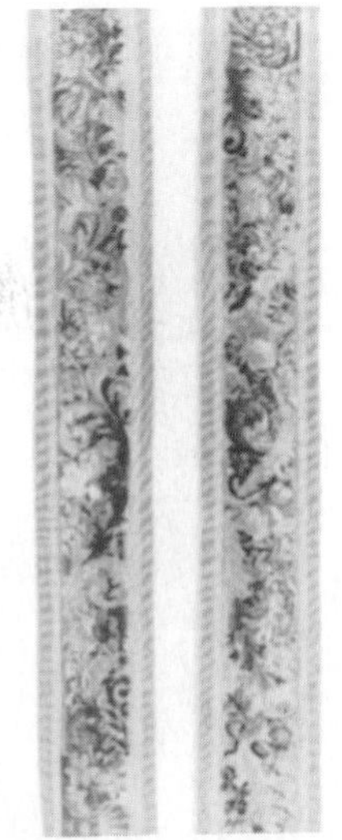

A pair of Franco-Flemish tapestry border panels, 18thC, with later selvage, 93 by 11¼in (236 by 28.6cm).
$1,050-1,350

An Aubusson tapestry fragment, after a design by Joseph Vernet, depicting 2 men leaning against barrels by the seaside, cliffs on the background, signed in reverse on the barrel: DONI, dated 1776, 78 by 54in (198 by 137cm).
$5,250-6,000

A Flemish tapestry covered four-fold screen, each with lower section of red velvet, c1700, each panel 67in by 18in (170 by 45.7cm).
$5,250-7,500

A French genre tapestry, 19thC, 78 by 87in (197 by 222cm).
$7,500-9,000

An Aubusson Biblical tapestry, 17thC, 111 by 164in (282 by 386cm).
$15,000-18,000

An Aubusson entre fenêtre tapestry, with a putto holding a crowned orb, shell motifs in upper sections, with spiralling laurel leaves along the sides, 111 by 30½in (282 by 77.5cm).
$3,000-4,500

A Flemish Biblical tapestry, depicting ladies and a gentleman in courtly dress, beneath canopies, late 17thC, 148 by 151in (333 by 384cm).
$15,000-18,000

A Flemish tapestry covered three fold screen, the back with crimson coloured brocade, c1600, each panel 81 by 21in (205 by 53.3cm).
$7,500-9,000

A French architectural tapestry, with weaver's mark H&GG on lower right selvage, 19thC, 99 by 63in (252 by 159cm).
$9,000-12,000

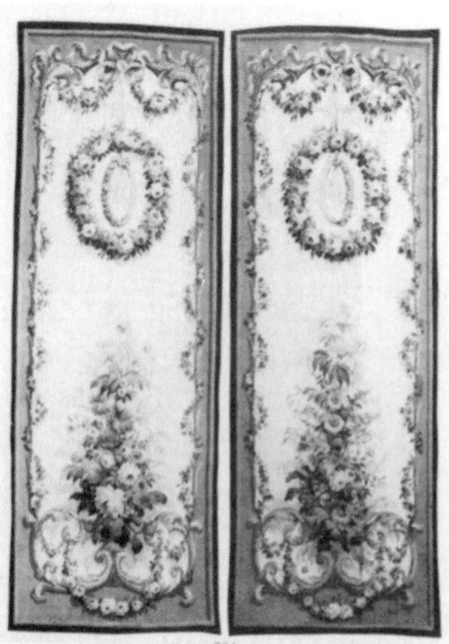

A pair of Aubusson entre fenêtre tapestries, 19thC, each panel 122 by 44in (310 by 112cm).
$9,000-12,000

American Quilts

A pieced and appliquéd cotton Tree of Life quilt, composed of slate, green, blue, red, yellow and orange, mounted on a white cotton ground with outline and circle quilting, probably Pennsylvania, 20thC, 80 by 88in (203 by 224cm).
$3,000-4,500

A crewelwork quilt, with later chintz border, parts of the original border at each corner, old repairs, c1760, 90 by 82in (229 by 208cm).
$600-750

pieced and appliquéd cotton iris ıilt, made by Caroline C. Drake, ›mposed of dark and light ›vender and green, with alloped borders trimmed with een, signed on the back, merican, dated 1939, together ith an all white cotton arseilles spread made for a four-›ster bed, 88 by 80in (224 by)3cm).
,200-1,800

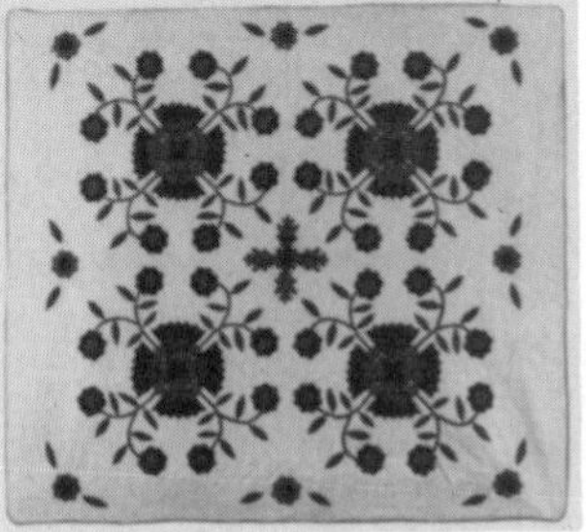

A pieced calico and cotton quilt, composed of red, yellow, grey and brown, printed and solid calico patches arranged in the Rose of Sharon pattern, the white cotton field with oak leaf and diagonal line quilting, American, late 19thC, 80 by 84in (203 by 213cm).
$1,800-2,700

A pieced cotton diamond-in-the-square quilt, composed of pastel tones of pink, green, lavender, coral, on a white cotton field heightened with diamond and pretzel quilting, probably Pennsylvania, c1930, 80 by 76in (203 by 193cm).
$750-1,200

A pieced, appliquéd and trapunto cotton quilt, composed of red, green, yellow and blue printed and solid calico patches, within red sashings, all mounted on a white cotton ground with fine line quilting, some fading, probably Pennsylvania, c1860, 92 by 92in (234 by 234cm).
$3,000-4,500

A pieced cotton Moravian quilt, composed of variously printed and solid calico and cotton patches arranged in a church pattern, some of the patches tied with silk ribbon and heightened with embroidery, minor stains and fabric loss, probably Pennsylvania, late 19thC, 84 by 76in (213 by 193cm).
$1,800-2,700

›merican Hooked ugs

pictorial hooked rug runner, he America's Cup, worked in lue, purple, yellow, green, beige nd pink fabric, probably New ngland, early 20thC, 212 by 26in ;39 by 66cm).
4,800-5,700

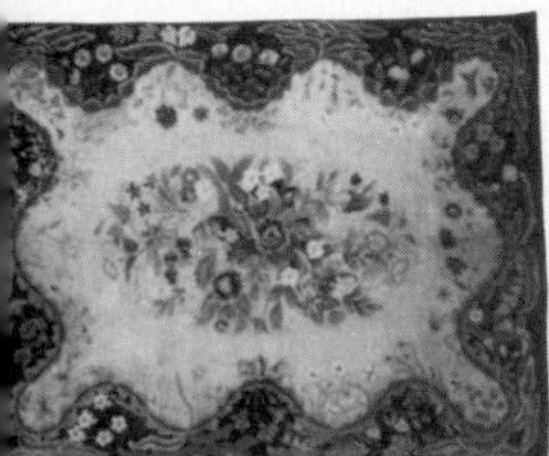

ɴ American pictorial floral ooked rug, worked in tones of reen, brown, coral, rose, yellow nd beige fabric, with a large oval entral bouquet of spring flowers, ndulating black borders with prays of flowers and leafage, 1940, 72 by 96in (183 by 244cm).
3,000-4,500

'ound in Ipswich, Massachusetts.

An American pictorial hooked rug, worked with beige, green, black, lavendar, minor stains, early 20thC, 32 by 55in (81 by 140cm).
$1,200-1,800

An American pictorial hooked rug, worked in brown, blue, dark green and red fabric, 20thC, 38 by 27½in (97 by 70cm).
$600-750

An American pictorial hooked rug, worked in tones of blue, brown, beige, red, green and yellow fabric, c1880, 36 by 60in (92 by 152cm).
$1,800-2,700

Miller's is a price GUIDE not a price LIST

RUGS & CARPETS

A Bakhtiyari rug, with trees and flowering bushes on a dark field, one main meandering flower and leaf border and 6 narrow borders, slight wear, 120 by 64in (305 by 163cm).
$750-1,200

A Kashan prayer rug, Central Persia, the madder mihrab with a hanging lamp and a flowering vase within indigo palmette and vine border, 81 by 52½in (206 by 133cm).
$1,050-1,350

A Kashan garden rug, Central Persia, the indigo field with a madder medallion and spandrels within an indigo palmette and vine border, 78 by 53in (198 by 135cm).
$1,500-2,250

Make the Most of Miller's

In Millers we do NOT just reprint saleroom estimates. We work from realised prices, either from an auction room or a dealer. Our consultants then work out a realistic price range for a similar piece. This is to try to avoid repeating freak results - either low or high.

A Ghashghai rug, South West Persia, the ivory boteh field within madder boteh and bracket border, 76 by 59in (193 by 150cm).
$600-750

A Tabriz rug, North West Persia, the indigo foliate field within a madder palmette and vine border, 77 by 51in (196 by 130cm).
$1,200-1,500

An Agra carpet, the shaded mauve field with overall stylise palmettes in ivory, crimson and mauve surrounded by crimson stylised large palmettes, serrat leaves and floral tendrils borde between an ivory link lozenge stripe, slight wear, 153 by 119in (389 by 302cm).
$10,500-12,000

A Ghashghai rug, South West Persia, the indigo boteh field within an ivory boteh border, 92 by 57in (234 by 145cm).
$1,500-2,250

A Kazak rug, the field with 4 rectangular medallions containing serrated floral motifs in brick red, ivory, blue and yellow, inner hooked flowerhead stripe between an ivory stepped flowerhead border and outer barber pole stripes, 77 by 45in (196 by 114cm).
$1,200-1,800

. Caucasian soumac, with 3 dark lue lozenge shaped medallions ith smaller star motifs on a red eld with small latchhook iedallions and scattered with owers, several narrow borders ith flowers, worn, 170 by 112in 432 by 285cm).
$1,050-1,350

A Megri rug, West Anatolia, the field with an indigo and sage panel filled with medallions, within pale saffron and ivory gul borders, 81 by 55in (206 by 140cm). **$1,200-1,800**

An Afshar rug, the field with overall flowering vine stripes in ivory and indigo, damaged, 110 by 61in (279 by 155cm).
$2,250-3,000

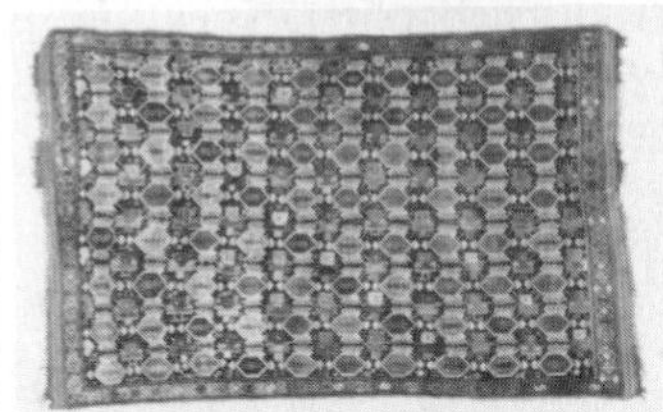

A Qashqai rug, the indigo field with diagonal rows of stylised lozenges linked with angular floral motifs surrounded by small stars and S-motifs in blue, yellow, green and ivory between similar rust border, an outer zig-zag stripe, small repairs, 77 by 45in (196 by 114cm).
$3,000-3,750

. Shirvan washed rug, Jorth East Caucasus, the ndigo field with 2 columns f 5 octagonal guls within aned diagonal border, 81 y 54in (206 by 137cm).
$1,200-1,800

A Gendje Kazak rug, Central Caucasus, the polychrome diagonal caned boteh field within madder gul border, 90 by 49in (229 by 125cm).
$1,500-2,250

A Kashan carpet, with a central nany petalled flowerhead nedallion on an ivory field, the whole closely in-filled with scrolling flowers and leaf tendrils n pinks, blues, greys and greens, bright blue scroll corners with pink ground spandrels, one main vory ground flower filled border and several narrow borders, 250 by 150in (635 by 381cm).
$6,000-8,250

MINIATURES

A Cleric, by Thomas Forster (born c1677), signed and dated 1709, in turned wood frame, 4½in (11cm) high.
$1,050-1,350

A George III miniature portrait of Mary Lewin (neé Hale), by John Smart, signed with initials and dated 1784, wearing a black and white feathered hat, white dress trimmed with white lace and gold braid, the reverse with glazed panel enclosing a gold monogram on blue silk, 2½in (6cm), papier mâché outer frame.
$7,500-9,000

A miniature painting on enamel, Lord Ashburton, by Henry Spicer, 1794, 3½by 3in (9 by 8cm).
$750-1,200

A Lady, English School, early 19thC, 2in (5cm). **$300-375**

A Lady, English School, with curled hair, white dress and black shawl, c1815, 3in (7.5cm).
$600-750

A Gentleman, English School, with powdered hair, wearing a blue jacket, yellow waistcoat and frilled cravat, cloud and sky background, c1790, 2½in (6.5cm) gold frame. **$375-525**

A German nobleman, wearing light armour and blue jacket, w orders and medals, c1775, 2½in (6cm) unmounted.
$1,200-1,800

A silhouette of a young lady, by John Miers, with lace fichu and ribbon tied hair, on plaster, in verre églomisé border and turned ebonised frame, the reverse with Miers trade label No. 11, creased c1795.
$1,200-1,800

Queen Caroline, English School in elaborate feathered bonnet, pink wax, turned wood frame, c1820, 7½in (19cm) high.
$750-1,200

A Poet, possibly German, c1840, 1½in (4cm).
$375-525

. Lady, English School, c1830, ith black hair, an embroidered hite dress and ermine stole, ith distant landscape ackground, 5in (13cm), carved rmolu frame, with leather ravelling case.
750-1,200

. miniature of a lady, wearing a hite bonnet, black dress with lue ribbon, the reverse with hair ocket under glass, the gilt metal rame carved flowers and foliage, arly 19thC, 1½in (4cm), with riginal fitted red morocco overed case.
600-750

. Gentleman, by H. Hull, signed, vith powdered hair, wearing a rown jacket with striped vaistcoat and white stock, pale loud and sky background, c1795, ½in (6cm), gold and pearl set rame on velvet stand.
750-1,200

A Gentleman, by James Scouler, wearing a blue jacket and waistcoat, with grey background, initialled, c1765, in ebonised frame, 2in (4.5cm).
$225-255

A Gentleman, by Joseph Boze (1745-1825), wearing a blue coat and waistcoat, white cravat, the reverse with hair device and initials BA in seed pearls, gold frame, 3in (7cm).
$1,800-2,700

Professor Pernthaller, by Alois von Anreiter (1803-1882), wearing a black suit, purple waistcoat, white shirt, black cravat, holding a book, a quill and inkstand on a table beside him, signed and dated 1856, gilt metal mount, within folding tooled leather case, 5in (13cm).
$1,200-1,800
Professor Pernthaller was the governor of Emperor Maximilian I of Mexico. Maximilian born in Vienna in 1832 accepted the Crown of Mexico in 1864.

A painting on card of a young man, English School, c1800, 4 by 4in (10 by 10cm). **$150-225**

A Young Girl, by Andrea Piazza, with short brown hair and wearing a pink dress, shown on grass with clusters of flowers and distant landscape background, signed, c1825. **$600-750**

A Princely Family, Continental School, in a formal garden, wood frame, c1790, 5in (13cm).
$2,700-3,300
The identification of this family is open to question. The father wears the blue sash of the St. Esprit and the lady dressed in green to his left the Star Cross Order Badge. It has been suggested that it may portray the family of Duke Ferdinand of Bourbon-Palma (1751-1802), husband of Archduchess Maria-Amelia, or Duke Hercules III of Modena (1727-1803) with his grandchildren; but we are unable to substantiate this.

Two miniatures, A Gentleman, by J. Bogle, 1778, initialled and dated, wearing a green jacket, in gilt frame and a Gentleman, c1770, wearing a scarlet jacket, 1½in (3.5cm) gold clasp frame.
$450-600

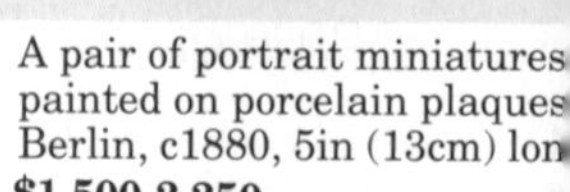

A pair of portrait miniatures painted on porcelain plaques Berlin, c1880, 5in (13cm) lon
$1,500-2,250

A dog, by Luiji Banen, with signed initials, c1900, 3in (8cm).
$50-75

King Charles I, by John Faber (c1655-1721), in black cloak, with the star and ribbon of the Garter, tall black hat, pen on parchment, signed and inscribed, in turned wood frame, 5in (13cm).
$3,000-3,750

An inscription on the reverse of the drawing reads 'Portrait of King Charles First as he sat on his trial in Westminster Hall, January 23 1648, a drawing with the Pen by J. Faber'.

A Lady, believed to be Miss Orton, by Thomas Hazlehurst (1740-1821), wearing white dres with blue sash, long curly hair, signed with initials, gilt metal frame, 3in (8cm).
$900-1,500

A label on the reverse of the miniature states that the sitter died aged 30 in 1806.

A Gentleman in Greek costume, wearing a scarlet beret with gilt tassel, and blue jacket, c1850, 2¾in (7cm), in ormolu frame.
$225-300

Sarah Cox, by James Ferguson (1710-1776), wearing a dress with lace border and cuffs, lace bonnet, foliate border, plumbago turned wood frame, 3in (8cm).
$750-1,200

An Officer, by H. Johns (active c1792), wearing blue uniform with red facings and gold frogging, yellow waistcoat, wearing the Order of Maria Theresa, signed and dated 1792, gilt metal frame, 2½in (6cm) diam.
$750-1,200

A Russian Officer, with grey hair and side whiskers, wearing black jacket with red collar and gilt epaulettes, grey background, c1810, 2¾in (7cm), in later gilt frame.
$750-1,200

Gentleman, English School, in e manner of A. Daniel, with ue jacket and short cropped fair ir, c1800, 2½in (7cm), plain gilt ame.
,050-1,350

Lady, by James Leakey (1775-65), wearing a white dress with hu, black bandeau in her dark ir, the reverse with lock of hair ithin blue glass border, gold ame, 2½in (6cm).
00-1,500

French enamel miniature of apoleon, wearing a green tunic ith medals and a sash, the onze and ormolu easel frame ased with foliate scrolls, and th applied bay laurel fronds ntred by a sunflower, with raldic eagle and riband rmount, early 19thC, 9 by 6in 3 by 15cm).
750-900

A Gentleman, by Thomas Hazlehurst (1740-1821), wearing blue coat with black collar, white waistcoat and cravat, signed with initials, the reverse with monogram B-J on plaited hair panel, gold frame, 3in (7cm).
$2,250-3,000

A Lady, English School, in the manner of Cosway, with powdered hair, wearing a low cut white dress, cloud and sky background, the reverse with memorial panel, gold and pearl set frame, 3in (8cm).
$750-1,200

A Gentleman, by Peter Paillou, signed and dated, with curled brown hair, wearing a pale blue jacket, white shirt and cravat, pale cloud and sky background, 1798, 2½in (6cm), plain gold frame, with hair reverse.
$750-1,200

Two miniatures, A Gentleman, English School, c1790, with ribbon tied blonde hair, wearing a green jacket and white ruffled shirt, plain gold frame with hair, seed pearl and enamel reverse, 3in (7cm), with red leather case, and A Lady, English School, c1900, with grey hair, wearing a white bonnet and black dress, seated in an armchair, 3in (7cm).
$450-600

A Stobwasser lacquer box top, entitled The Chalybeat, painted with a young lady wearing a scarlet cloak and low cut white dress, c1800, in later ebonised frame, 4in (10cm).
$450-600

A Young Girl, English School, with curled brown hair, wearing a coral necklace and blue and white dress, brown background, c1840, papier mâché frame, 2½in (7cm).
$600-750

A Lady, by Richard Cosway, R.A., (1742-1821), on card, pencil heightened with body colour, minor damage, framed, 5½in (14cm).
$750-1,200

This drawing is typical of Cosway's late, highly mannerist stained or tinged portrait drawings. These are mainly drawn in graphite but have watercolour for the face. It can be compared to the bust length drawing of 'A Lady revealed by Cupid or an Angel' in the Huntingdon Library, San Marino and the three-quarter length portrait drawing of 'Madame Recamier' which was engraved by A. Caron in 1802.

Prince Starhemberg, by J.M. Khaetscher (active c1710), in breastplate, lace jabot, long powdered curling hair, enamel on gold, signed on reverse, damaged, gilt metal frame, 1in (3cm).
$750-1,200

This may be a portrait of Franz Ottokar or his son Conrad Sigismund, Prince Starhemberg.

A Gentleman, by Franz Schrotzberg (1811-1889), wearing black coat with velvet collar, brown waistcoat, black shirt and cravat, signed and dated 1837, gilt metal mount, 4in (9cm).
$750-900

A pair of bronzed silhouettes, by J. Miers, he with hair in a pigtail, high collared jacket and lace jabot, she with a bonnet and ruffed dress, gilt mounts, ebonised frames with Miers' 12th Double Letter trade label, 3in (8cm).
$1,200-1,800

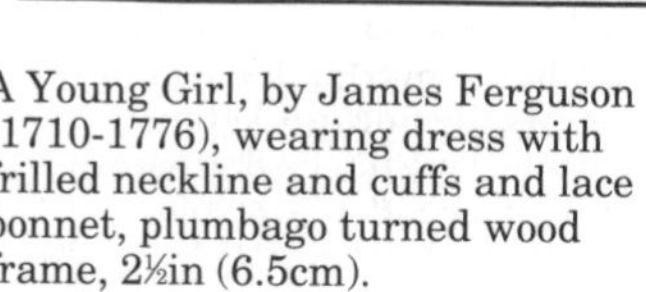

A Young Girl, by James Ferguson (1710-1776), wearing dress with frilled neckline and cuffs and lace bonnet, plumbago turned wood frame, 2½in (6.5cm).
$1,200-1,800

A Lady, English School, early 19thC, in gold frame, 3in (8cm).
$300-375

A Gentleman, School of Gaspard Smitz, wearing black doublet, sleeves slashed to reveal white shirt, lawn collar with tassels, oil on copper, gilt metal frame with beaded outer border, c1660, 2in (5cm).
$750-1,200

David with the Head of Goliath, 19thC, in a silver gilt and paste set frame, 3in (7cm).
$600-750

. Clarice Cliff Lotus jug, in
ıe Blue 'W' pattern, 12in
31cm) high.
2,500-2,700

A charger, painted by Clarice Cliff, from one of the Brangwyn panels (No.7) designed for the House of Lords, 1925, first exhibited at Olympia 1933, 17½in (44cm) diam. **$3,000-3,750**

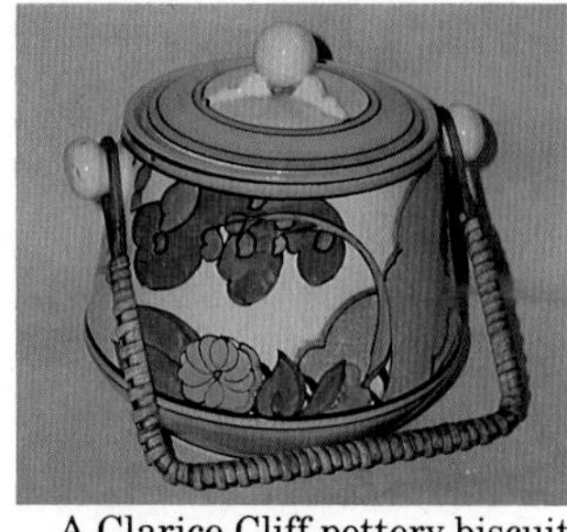

A Clarice Cliff pottery biscuit barrel.
$375-525

. Doulton Burslem vase,
y Fred Sutton, a
ortrait artist, c1900,
1½in (29cm) high.
900-1,200

A Royal Doulton figure of a Sealyham terrier, HN 1030, 9in (23cm) long.
$75-100

An Art Nouveau vase, in Chryso design, from Regina factory, Gouda pottery, c1920, 11½in (29cm) high.
$450-525

A Clarice Cliff Applique Orange Lucerne single handled Lotus jug, printed marks.
$8,250-9,000

. Doulton Lambeth vase,
esigned by Hannah Barlow
nd Eliza Simmons, c1891,
0in (51cm) high.
3,300-3,800

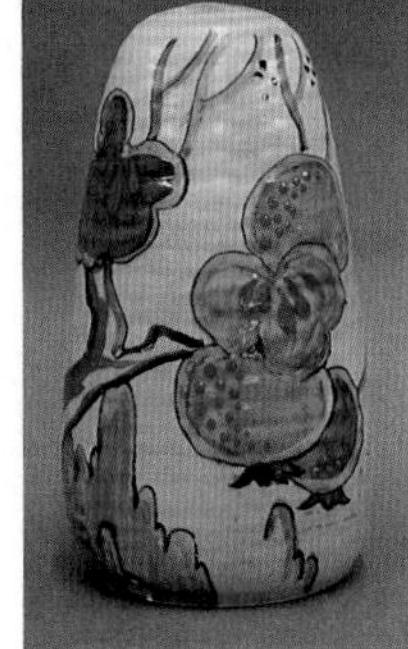

A Clarice Cliff Inspiration pattern caster, 5in (13cm) high.
$90-120

Two Minton majolica cockerel and matching hen planters, designed by David Henck.
$2,250-3,000

A Gouda pottery charger, in Syncap design, c1927, 12in (31cm) diam.
$225-300

A Doulton Luscian ware vas by H. Piper, c1895, 8in (20cr high.
$375-525

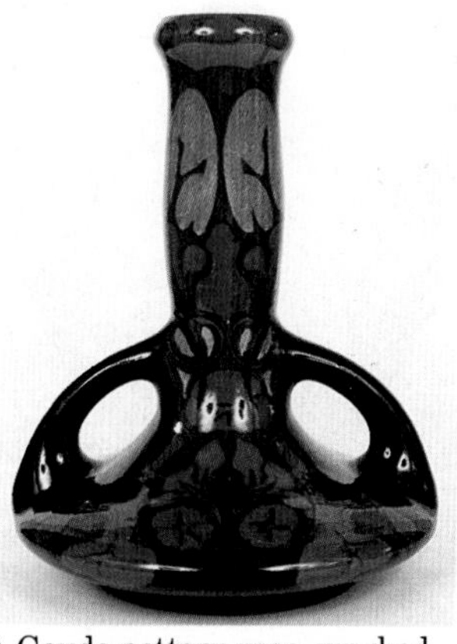

A Gouda pottery vase, marked Zuid (Holland), c1920, 10in (25cm) high.
$375-500

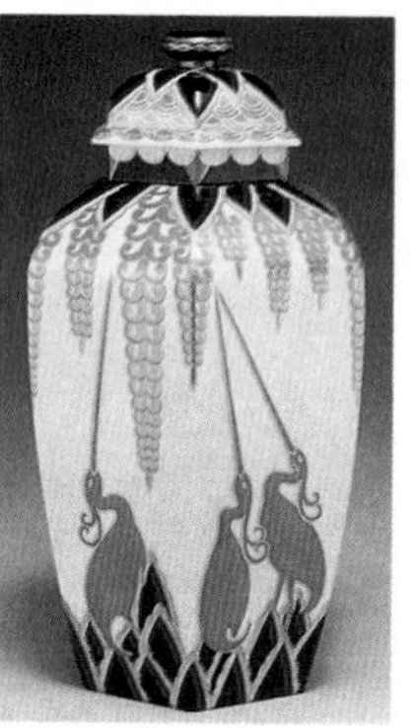

A Kurt Wendler porcelain ginger jar and cover, Rosenthal, c1920.
$1,350-1,500

A Carlton Ware butter dish, c1940, 10½i (26cm) wide. **$1,200-1,500**

Ex Elton John Collection.

A Doulton ball teapot, decorated with flowers and butterflies, c1916, 5½in (14cm) high. **$200-250**

A Gouda pottery vase, from Goedewaagen factory, c1915, 4½in (11cm) high.
$120-180

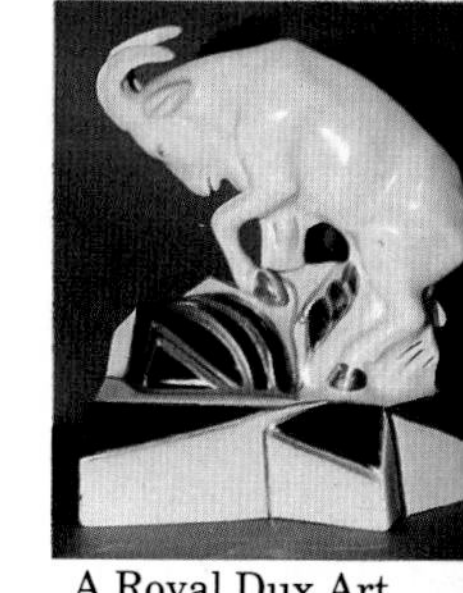

A Royal Dux Art Nouveau blue and gi decorated figure of a ram, 7in (17cm) high
$150-200

A selection of four Royal Doulton figures, 'Veronica', HN 1517, 8in (20cm) high, 'Aileen', HN 1645, 6in (15cm) high, 'Prue' HN 1996, 7in (17cm) high, and 'Easter Day' HN 2039, 7½in (18cm) high.
$150-225 each

A Foley Intarsio clock, designed by Frederick Rhead, c1900, 9in (23cm high.
$525-675

A Carlton Ware spill vase, decorated with an exotic bird in gilt lustre on a blue ground, 6in (15cm) high.
$120-150

A Foley Intarsio vase, designed by Frederick Rhead, c1900, 11in (28cm) high.
$600-750

A Shelley Intarsio vase, designed by Walter Slater, c1912, 10in (25cm) high.
$525-600

Villiam de Morgan two-ndled vase, Merton Abbey riod, c1885, 41in (104cm) high.
,000-10,500

Art Nouveau vase, Rozenburg ctory, La Hague, c1897, 7in 7cm) high.
75-750

A pair of Florian Ware Art Nouveau tapered vases, with floral decorations on blue ground, signed, early 20thC, 8in (20cm) high. **$1,250-1,500**

A Dutch pottery jug, Arnhem factory, c1926, 10½in (26cm) high.
$300-375

Shelley lustre vase, gned Walter Slater, c1920, in (38cm) high.
50-900

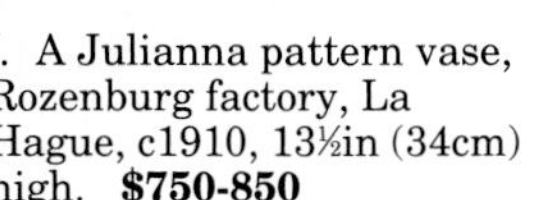

A Foley faience trio, designed by Frederick Rhead, centrepiece 8in (20cm) high.
$825-1,000

l. A Julianna pattern vase, Rozenburg factory, La Hague, c1910, 13½in (34cm) high. **$750-850**

A Zsolnay iridescent glazed ceramic figural jardinière, signed Zsolnay-Pecs and Made in Hungary, 7in (17cm) high.
$4,000-5,000

A pair of Moorcroft MacIntyre pottery floral skittle vases, inscribed W. Moorcroft MacIntyre Burslem, 12in (30.5cm) high.
$3,000-3,750

A Moorcroft oviform jardinière, with inverted rim, with 2 bands of peacock feathers, restored, signed in green, 8in (20cm) high. **$1,400-1,800**

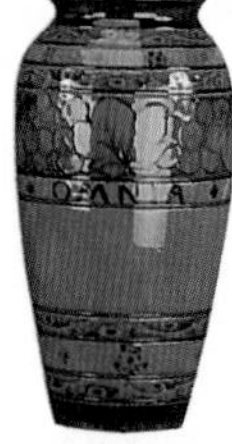
A Moorcroft flambé vase, signed, 10in (25cm) high.
$1,000-1,200

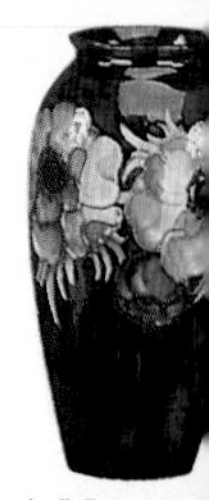
A Moorcr vase, impressed mark, sig
$300-400

A Moorcroft jardinière, decorated with a band of foliage, damaged, signed, 8in (20cm) diam.
$600-750

A Moorcroft twin-handled pedestal fruit bowl, the interior with pansy, restored, signed, 8in (20cm) diam.
$375-450

A William Moorcroft band Pomegranate design vase, c1928, 17in (43cm) high.
$3,000-3,750

A Moorcroft bowl on Tudric pewter foot, the interior with a band of pansies, the exterior with a band of buds and foliage, stamped marks, 8in (20cm) diam.
$375-450

A Moorcroft vase, decorated in the Moonlit Blue pattern, impressed factory mark, signed in blue, 10in (25cm) high. **$1,400-1,800**

A Moorcroft vase, restored, marked, 12in (31cm) high.
$1,400-1,800

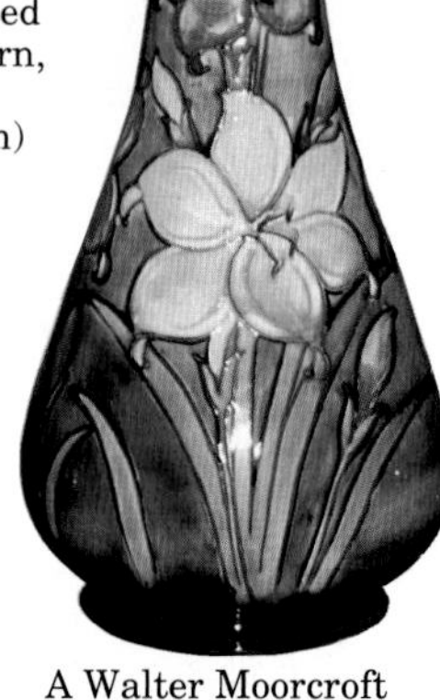
A Walter Moorcroft African Lily design vase, c1955, 12in (31cm).
$550-700

A Moorcroft bowl, in Claremont pattern, Liber mark, signed, 10in (20cm) diam. **$1,000-1,200**

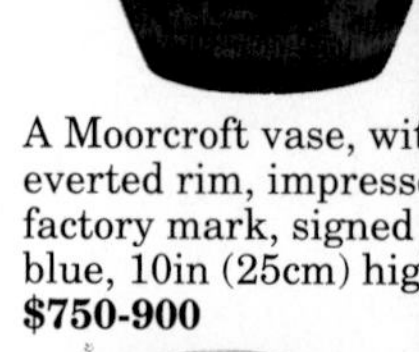
A Moorcroft vase, wit everted rim, impress factory mark, signed blue, 10in (25cm) hig
$750-900

A Walter Moorcroft Clematis design vase, c1955, 5in (13cm) high.
$300-450

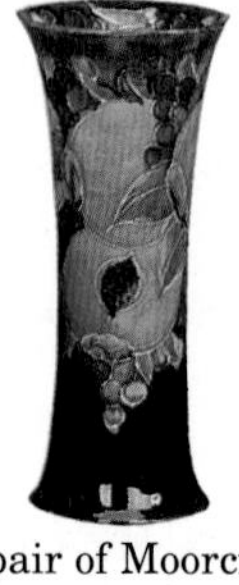
A pair of Moorcroft Pomegranate pattern vases, factory mark, signed, 10½in (26cm) high.
$700-825

A Moorcroft MacIntyre jardinière, marked.
$1,200-1,400

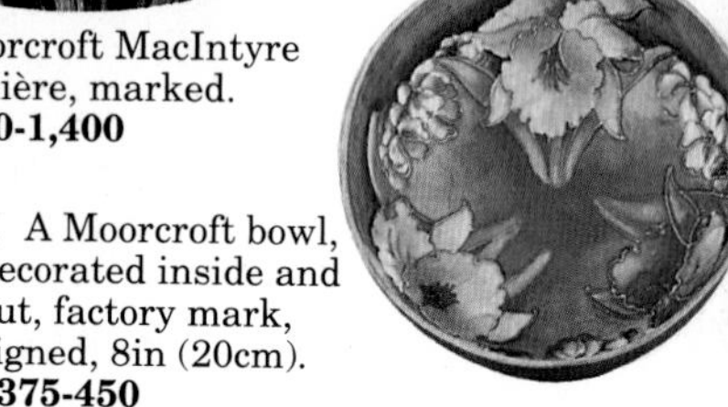
r. A Moorcroft bowl, decorated inside and out, factory mark, signed, 8in (20cm).
$375-450

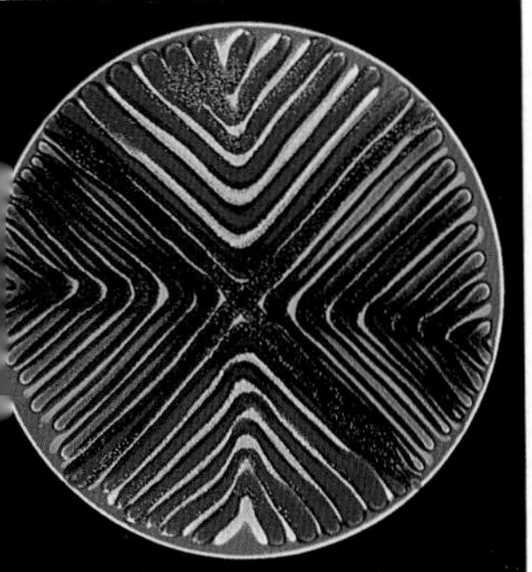

Poole Pottery Studio bowl, ape 5, artist unidentified, 60s, 14in (36cm).
00-700

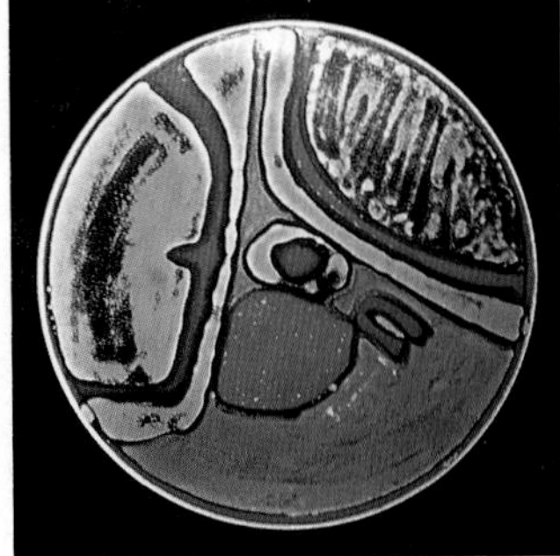

A Poole Pottery Studio plate, shape 4, artist unidentified, 1960s, 10in (25cm).
$300-400

A Poole Pottery Studio bowl, shape 57, by Carol Cutler, 1960s.
$300-400

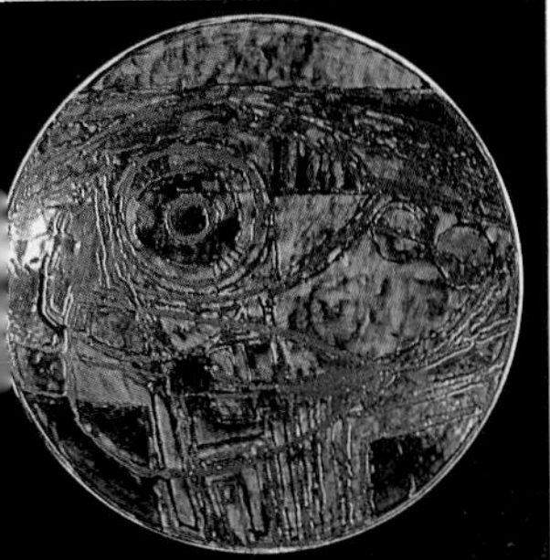

Poole Pottery Studio charger, Tony Morris, Studio stamp, 60s, 14in (36cm).
00-450

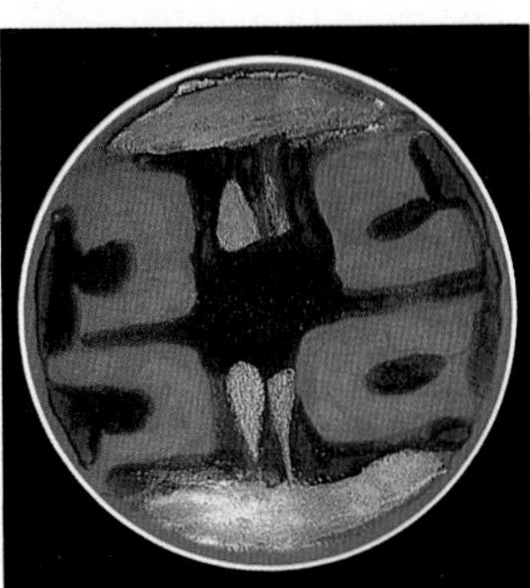

A Poole Pottery Studio plate, shape 4, 1960s, 10in (25cm).
$300-400

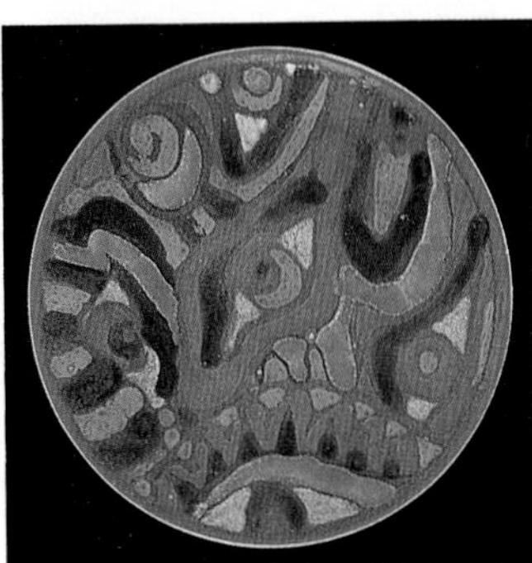

A Poole Pottery Studio plate, the pattern 'Watching through half-closed eyes, colours and shapes moved and mingled', 1960s, 14in (36cm). **$400-500**

Poole Pottery Studio plate, lower power-peace', Angela 'yburd, 1960s, 10in (25cm).
150-200

A Poole Pottery Studio plate, Ethnic design by Tony Morris, 1960s, 12in (31cm).
$400-450

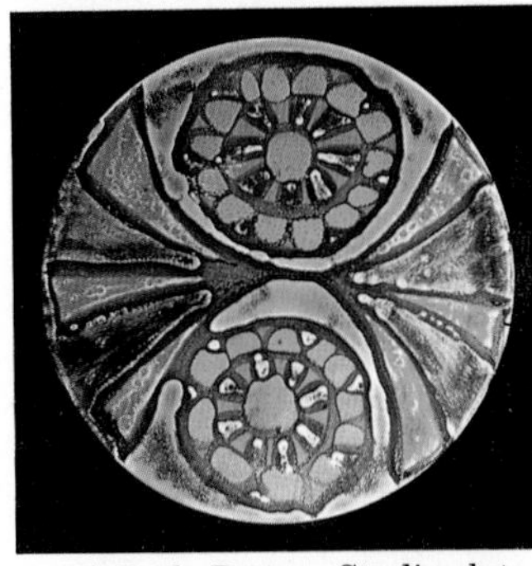

A Poole Pottery Studio plate, shape 4, 1960s.
$300-400

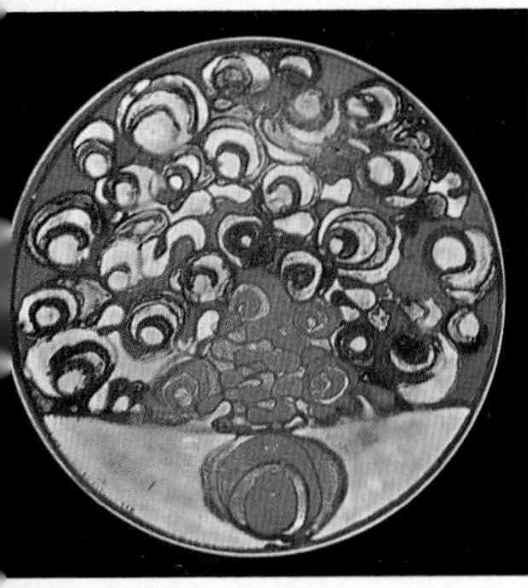

Poole Pottery Studio charger, hape 54, artist unidentified, 960s, 16in (41cm).
800-900

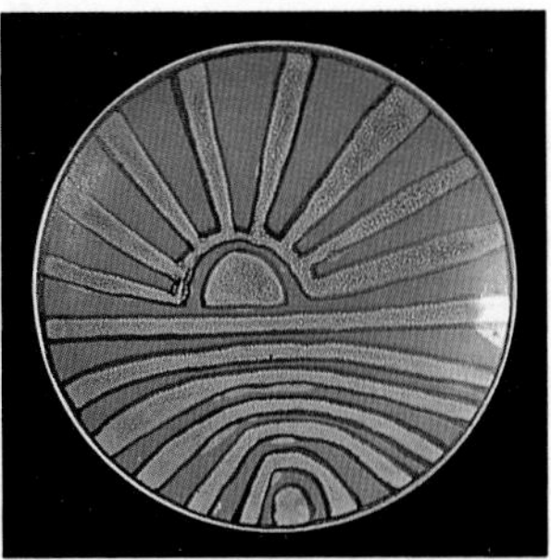

A Poole Pottery Studio plate, 1960s, 8in (20cm).
$300-400

A Poole Pottery charger, marked Studio, probably Tony Morris, 1960s, 14in (36cm).
$500-600

A Steuben Aurene blue iridescent glass vase, inscribed Steuben Aurene 2479, c1910, 12½in (31.5cm) high.
$2,250-3,000

A Loetz glass bowl, the design attributed to Koloman Moser, decorated internally with bubbles and silver iridescence, 11in (28cm) diam. **$3,750-4,500**

A Steuben Aure glass covered jar inscribed, c1910 14in (36cm) high
$2,250-3,000

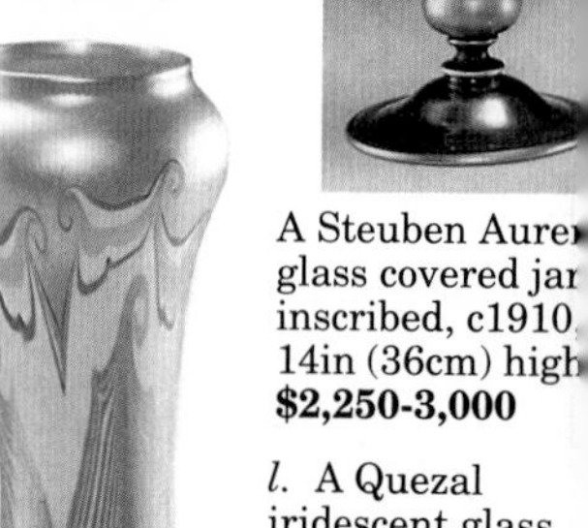

l. A Quezal iridescent glass vase, signed Quezal/937, c1920, 11in (28cm) high.
$2,250-3,000

A Tiffany Favrile iridescent glass vase, signed and numbered E1630, 9in (23cm) high. **$1,400-1,800**

A Daum cameo glass and wrought iron lamp and shade, the shade supported on 3 iron arms, the yellow glass overlaid and etched with brown and orange, etched Daum Nancy, 17½in (44cm). **$6,000-7,500**

A Loetz iridescent glass footed bow supported on a pad foot by a twiste stem, 8½in (21cm) high.
$4,500-6,000

l. A Tiffany Favrile glass vase, inscribed L.C.T. and H1753, c1897, 5in (12.5cm).
$1,200-1,400

A G. Argy-Rousseau pâte de verre coupe, Fers de Lance (Bloch Dermant 30.04), moulded F. Argy-Rousseau, 1930, 7in (17cm) diam.
$12,000-14,500

A Daum wheel carved cameo glass vase, inscribed Daum Nancy, c1900, 10½in (26cm) high.
$7,500-9,000

A Tiffany Favrile glass vase, with thic rolled rim, inscribed Louis C. Tiffany 865N, c1919, 13in (33cm) high.
$16,500-19,500

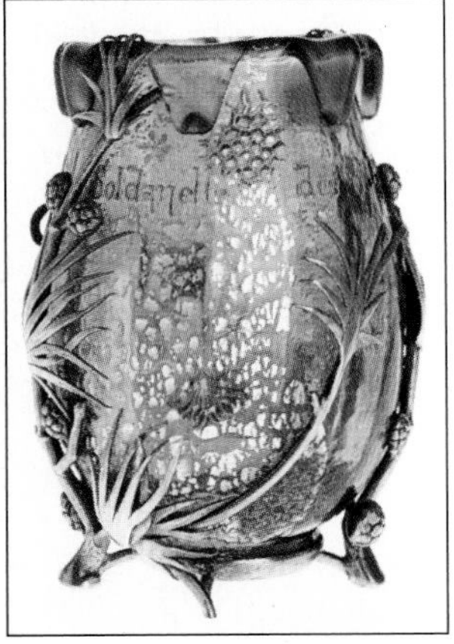

"La Soldanelle des Alpes", a Gallè gilt-mounted vase de Tristesse, 14.5cm high. Sold for £19,800

A Moorcroft "Persian" pattern two-handled vase, 24cm high. Sold for £2,750

A George Hunt enamelled and carved ivory pendant, 11.5cm. Sold for £3,080

"Cleopatra", a bronze and ivory figure by Bruno Zach, 35.5cm high. Sold for £4,840

A group of Liberty & Co. "Tudric" pewter ware. Prices ranging from £330-£1,100

An important Gothic Revival walnut armchair, designed by J.P Seddon, probably for the 1862 International Exhibition in London. Sold for £17,600

19TH & 20TH CENTURY DECORATIVE ARTS AT PHILLIPS

The pieces shown here illustrate the wide range of items that we have successfully sold in recent auctions.

Our Decorative Arts Department has the combined experience of nearly 40 years in the auction world, making us ideally suited to give professional advise on buying and selling at auction.

For further information please contact
Keith Baker or Fiona Baker.

Tel : (071) 629 6602

Britain's Nº 1 *best*-Seller

101 New Bond Street, London W1Y 0AS

A Lalique green glass vase, 'Sauterelles', moulded with grasshoppers on curving blades of grass, 10½in (27cm) high.
$3,000-4,500

A Lalique vase, 'Baies', moulded with interlinked branches and berries, 10½in (27cm) high.
$1,300-1,800

A Gallé gilt mounted 'Vase de Tristesse', 'La Soldanelle Des Alpes', incised Emile Gallé, 5½in (14cm) high.
$27,000-30,000

A Lalique frosted glass table lamp, 'Six Danseuses', signed on foot R. Lalique France, 10½in (26cm) high.
$7,500-9,000

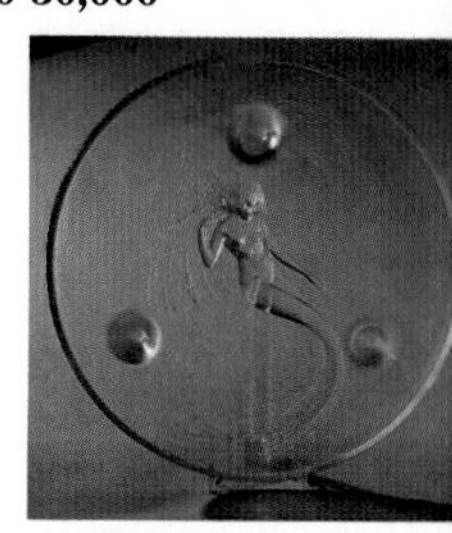

A Lalique opalescent glass shallow dish, 'Sirene', moulded signature, etched No. 376, 14½in (37cm) diam. **$3,750-5,250**

l. A Lalique silver and opalescent glass goblet, embellished in relief with pine cones and needles, stamped on foot rim Lalique and No. 20, 7½in (19cm) high.
$24,000-27,000

A Lalique espallion glass vase, moulded in relief with fern fronds, etched signature R. Lalique, France, No.996, 7½in (19cm).
$3,000-4,500

A Lalique toilet water jar and stopper, amber tinted and figure embossed, early 20thC, 3½in (9cm) diam.
$300-350

A Lalique powder bowl and domed lid, amber tinted and figure embossed, early 20thC, 4in (10cm) diam.
$400-500

A Lalique glass vase, 'Gui', with moulded signature, 6½in (16cm) high.
$600-900

A Lalique opalescent glass vase, 'Bacchantes', heavily moulded in high relief with a frieze of naked female figures, signed R. Lalique France on base, 10in (25cm) high.
$11,500-12,500

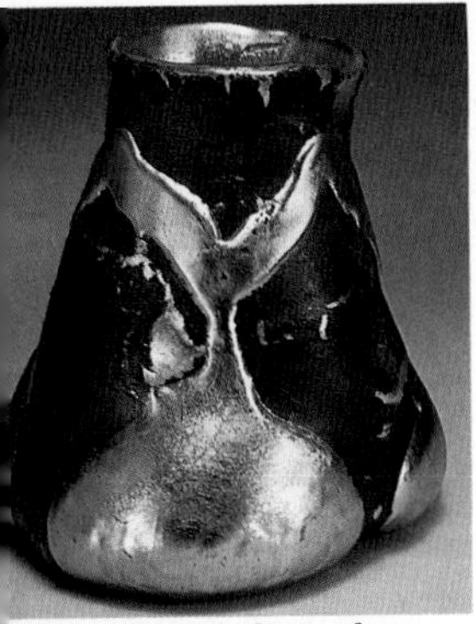

Tiffany Favrile lava glass se, inscribed L.C. Tiffany/ vrile/Exposition/Special, and 54N, 7in (17cm) high.
7,000-30,000

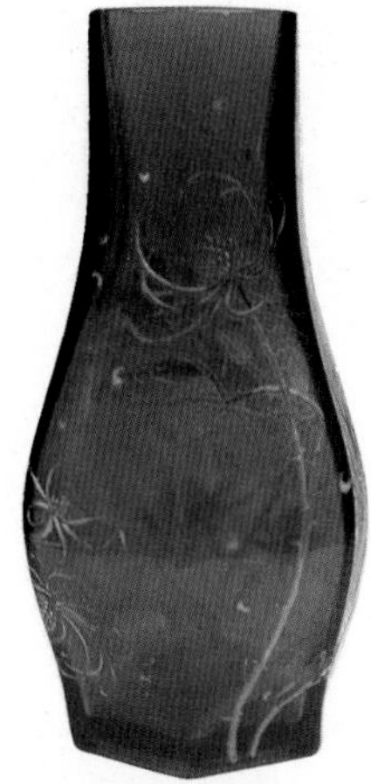

A carved enamelled and gilded glass vase, by Gallé, with gilt signature Emile Gallé, c1890, 8½in (21cm) high. **$3,000-3,500**

A Daum cameo glass vase, signed Daum Nancy, c1900, 13in (33cm) high.
$3,000-3,750

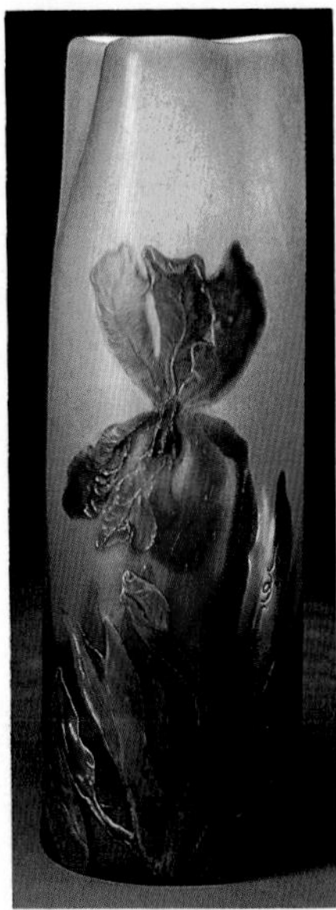

A Gallé marquetrie sur verre wheel carved cameo glass vase, c1900, 9in (23cm) high.
$60,000-67,500

Daum vase, with etched d enamelled winter ıdscape, c1900, 5in (12cm) gh. **$2,500-3,000**

l. A Gallé four-layer cameo glass charger, signed Gallé, c1900, 14½in (37cm) diam.
$9,000-10,500

A blown and cut glass sculpture, 'Troubled Waters', by Ray Flavell, signed, 1992, 10in (25cm) high.
$6,000-6,750

A Gallé cameo vase, decorated internally, signed, c1890, 9½in 24cm) high.
$6,000-7,500

Gallé cameo glass table ımp, signed in cameo on base nd shade, Gallé with star receding, 24in (62cm) high.
18,000-22,000

A Daum cameo glass vase, internally decorated, signed, c1900, 10½in (26cm).
$6,000-7,500

A Daum enamelled cameo glass vase, signed Daum/Nancy, c1910, 20in (51cm) high.
$5,250-7,500

A Gallé four-layer cameo glass vase, signed, c1900, 7in (17cm) high.
$2,250-2,500

A Tiffany Favrile glass and bronze poinsettia border lamp, c1910.
$25,000-27,000

A Tiffany Favrile glass and bronze peony floor lamp, shade impressed Tiffany Studios/New York 1505, base Tiffany Studios/New York/387, c1910, 65in (165cm) high . **$90,000-105,000**

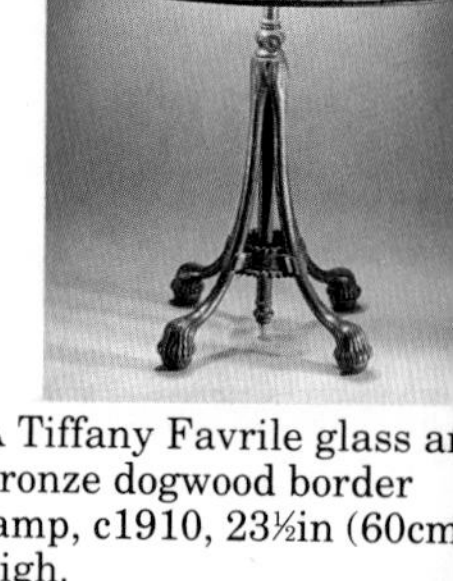
A Tiffany Favrile glass and bronze dogwood border lamp, c1910, 23½in (60cm) high.
$24,000-27,000

A Tiffany Favrile glass and bronze poinsettia border lamp, c1910.
$21,000-24,000

A Tiffany Favrile glass and bronze lily lamp, c1915, 19½in (49cm) high.
$14,000-16,000

A Tiffany Favrile glass and bronze cyclamen lamp, c1910.
$27,000-30,000

A Tiffany Favrile glass and gilt bronze lily lamp, c1925, insribed and impressed marks, 23in (59cm) high.
$45,000-52,000

l. A Tiffany Favrile glass and bronze lotus lamp, c1915, 25in (64cm) high.
$35,000-37,000

A Tiffany Favrile glass and bronze turtle-back tile standard lamp, c1915, 67½in (171cm) high.
$27,000-30,000

A Tiffany Favrile glass and bronze turtle back tile geometric chandelier, shade impressed Tiffany Studios New York, c1915, 20in (51cm) diam.
$17,000-20,000

A Tiffany Favrile glass and bronze wisteria lamp, on a tree trunk base, base impressed Tiffany Studios/New York/26854, c1915, 26in (66cm) high.
$168,000-180,000

A Tiffany Favrile glass and gilt bronze turtle-back tile geometric lamp, c1915, 26in (66cm) high.
$14,000-16,000

A Tiffany Favrile glass and bronze dragonfly lamp, c1910, impressed marks, 21in (53cm) high.
$30,000-33,000

A bronze figure, by Tom Bennett, 'Reflections'.
$3,750-5,250

A cast iron figural group, 'Diana and Hound', Wilhelm Hunt Diederich, inscribed, c1925, 25in (64cm) high.
$9,000-12,000

. Bruno Zach painted bronze gure of a girl, 'A Riding Crop', n oval marble base, signed, 4in (86cm) high.
20,000-22,000

A French bronze figural lamp, by Leo Laporte-Blairsy, inscribed, No. 57283/26, c1900, 12in (31cm) high.
$9,000-10,500

A French gilt bronze figural lamp, inscribed E. Wante, c1900, 12½in (32cm).
$6,000-7,500

A bronze figure, 'Dancing', by Tom Bennett.
$1,500-3,000

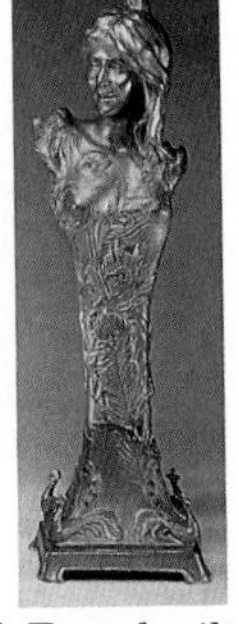

A French bronze figural group, 'Leda and the Swan', Paul Silvestre, mounted on a rectangular base, inscribed P. Silvestre, Susse Fes Edits Paris, impressed foundry stamp, c1925, 31in (79cm) long.
$5,250-6,750

A French gilt bronze bust, 'Peacock Girl', Leopold Savine, inscribed, c1900, 15½in (39cm).
$1,200-1,500

A painted wrought iron chandelier, Gilbert Poillerat, c1930, 66in (167.5cm).
$7,500-9,000

A silvered and gilt bronze figure, 'Spirit of Flight', Frédéric Focht, inscribed, slight damage, c1925, 34in (86cm) long.
$12,000-14,000

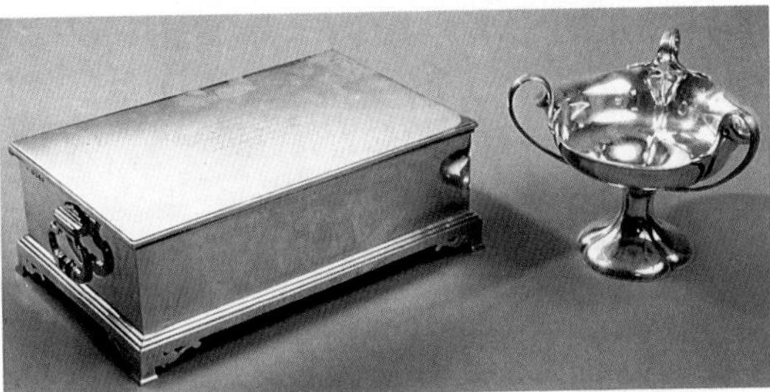

A cigar casket, with 2 carrying handles, London, 1934, 95oz, 11½in (29cm) long. **$900-1,200**
An Edwardian fruit dish, with 3 reeded handles, London 1904, 14oz, 8in (21cm). **$450-550**

A bronze and ivory figure, 'Actress', Demètre H. Chiparus, stamped, inscribed, c1925, 17in (43cm). **$9,000-10,500**

A silvered cold painted bronze, 'Charm of the Orient', A. Godard, c1930, 19in (48cm). **$6,500-8,500**

A bronze and ivory figure, 'The Tennis Player', cast and carved from a model by Ferdinand Preiss, unsigned, 11in (28cm). **$6,500-8,500**

A cold painted bronze and ivory figure, 'Testris', Demètre H. Chiparus, c1925, 17in (43cm) high. **$13,500-18,000**

A silvered gilt cold painted bronze and ivory figure, 'Nimble Dancer', Demètre H. Chiparus, c1925, 18½in (47cm). **$7,500-10,500**

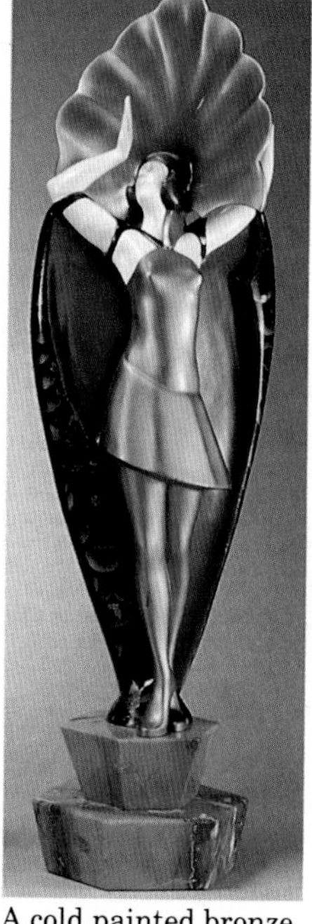

A cold painted bronze and ivory figure of a dancer, inscribed Roland Paris, some losses to paint, c1925, 23in (58cm) high. **$10,500-15,000**

A silvered bronze and ivory figure of a woman, 'Dourga', Demètre Chiparus, losses to hands, base inscribed, c1925, 24½in (62.5cm) high. **$7,500-10,500**

A cold painted bronze and ivory figure, 'Balancing', Ferdinand Preiss, c1925, 15in (38cm) high. **$8,500-10,500**

A cold painted bronze and ivory figure, 'Lighter than Air', Ferdinand Preiss, c1925, 13½in (35cm) high. **$5,500-8,500**

A cold painted bronze and ivory figure, 'Spring Awakening', Ferdinand Preiss, c1925, 14in (37cm) high. **$16,500-21,000**

Antique Galleries
26 Broad St., Pendleton, Salford
Manchester, M6 5BY, Tel: 061 737 5938
Photography by Brian Linney
AUDREY STERNSHINE Specialist in Art Nouveau & Art Deco.

A patinated bronze and ivory figure, 'Ankara Dancer', C.J.R. Colinet, c1925, 25in (63cm).
$45,000-52,000

A patinated bronze and ivory figural group, 'The Girls', Demètre H. Chiparus, mounted on onyx base, minor losses, inscribed, 20½in (51cm) high.
$150,000-180,000

A bronze and ivory figure, 'Hindu Dance Demètre Chiparus, c1925.
$15,000-16,500

A painted bronze and ivory figural group, 'The Sisters', mounted on brown onyx base, Demètre H. Chiparus, c1925, 29in (74cm).
$75,000-90,000

A carved bronze and ivory figure, 'Cleopatra', Bruno Zach, 14in (35.5cm) high.
$6,750-8,250

Three bronze and ivory figures of femal athletes: *l.* 'Oars Woman', *c.* 'Javelin Thrower', and *r.* A Skater, by Ferdinan Preiss, c1925, 12½in (32cm) high.
$6,000-9,000 each

A cold painted bronze and ivory figural group, 'Finale', Demètre H. Chiparus, c1925, 16½in (41cm) high.
$40,000-45,000

A gilt and silvered bronze and ivory figure, 'Semiramis', Demètre Chiparus, c1925, 26½in (67cm). **$80,000-85,000**

l. A bronze and ivory figure, 'The Archer', Ferdinand Preiss, c1930.
$30,000-37,500

A Maurice Dufrène silver plated 4-piece tea and coffee service and tray, manufactured by Gallia, retailed by La Maitrise, c1925. **$4,500-6,000**

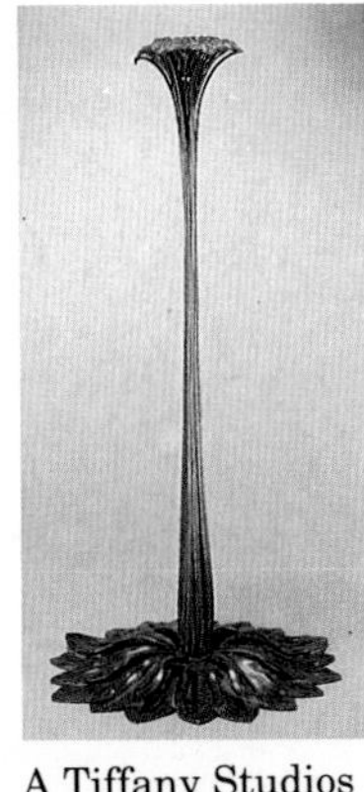

A Tiffany Studios bronze candlestick, 'Saxifrage', c1910. **$20,000-22,000**

A bronze figure, 'The Mushroom Fairy', by Gilbert Bayes. **$3,000-3,500**

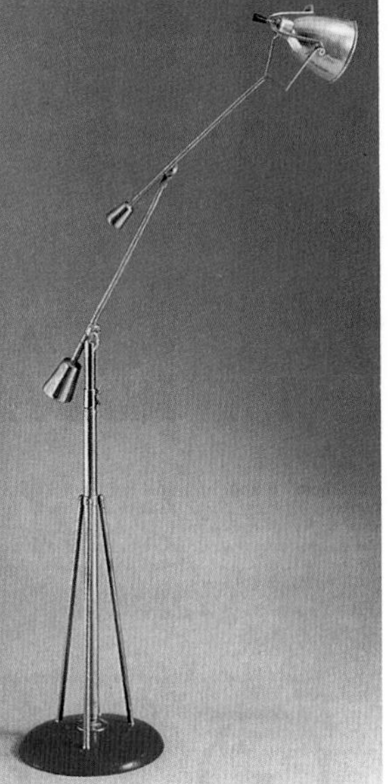

A floor lamp, by Edouard-Wilfrid Buquet, c1925, 67in (170cm) high. **$15,000-16,500**

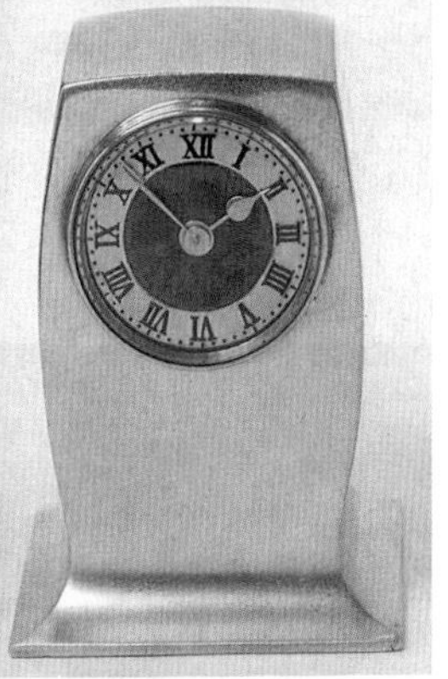

A pewter timepiece, the copper dial enamelled, impressed 0760, made by Liberty & Co., 4½in (11cm). **$750-850**

A silver picture frame, by William Hutton, maker's mark with London hallmark for 1904. **$2,250-3,000**

A silver and enamel photograph frame, William Hutton, hallmark 1903. **$3,000-4,500**

A Danish silver 3-piece coffee set and tray, Georg Jensen Silversmithy, designed by Johan Rohde, 1930. **$8,000-9,500**

l. A Dutch bronze antelope clock, c1920, 11in (28cm) high. **$1,700-2,500**

r. A Cornelius van der Hoef silver plated tea service. **$2,000-2,500**

A silver and enamel timepiece, by Liberty & Co., maker's mark for Birmingham 1905, 4in (9.5cm) high. **$1,800-2,200**

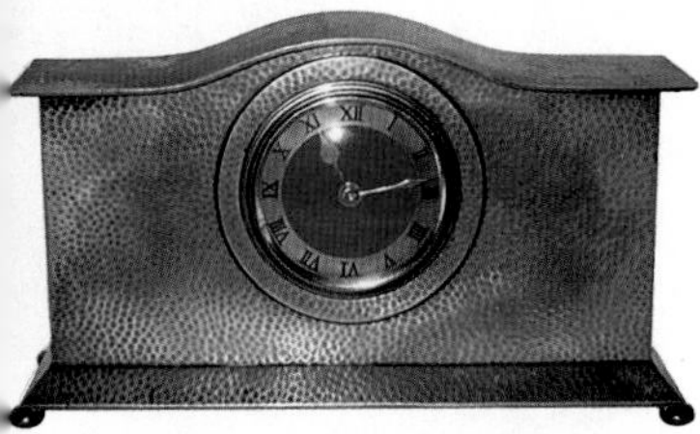

A Tudric pewter mantel timepiece, for Liberty & Co., c1930. **$350-500**

A Danish silver 7-piece tea and coffee set and matching rectangular tray, by Georg Jensen Silversmithy, numbered 2, 2B, 2D, Blossom pattern, all except tongs engraved with names and date 1924, all marked, 188oz 10dwt. **$20,000-25,000**

A silver plated brass tea infuser, by Hans Pryzrembel, c1930.
$900-1,000

A silver tea infuser, by Christian Dell, c1925, 6in (15cm).
$900-1,000

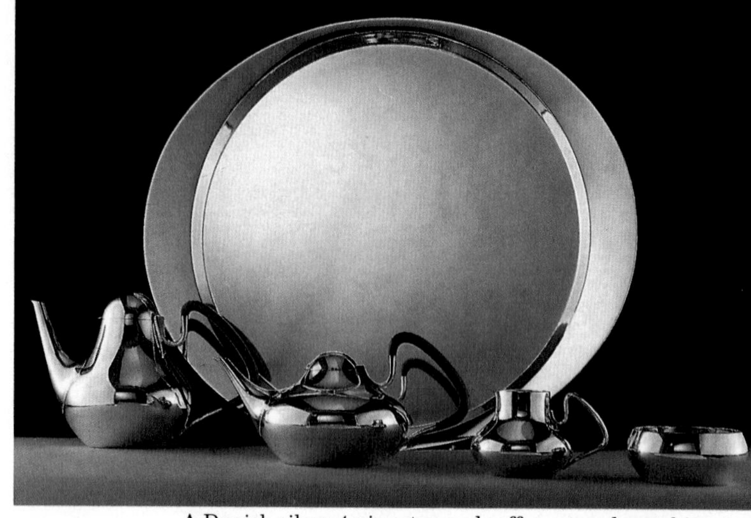
A Danish silver 4-piece tea and coffee set and matching tray, designed by Henning Koppel, numbered 1017, by Georg Jensen Silversmithy, marked on bases, 20in (52cm) wide, 151oz 10dwt.
$12,000-15,000

A Peter Behrens brass electric tea kettle, by A.E.G. Berlin, c1909, underside stamped 3592/14.
$600-700

A Peter Behrens brass tea kettle, impressed maker's mark, c1908.
$900-1,200

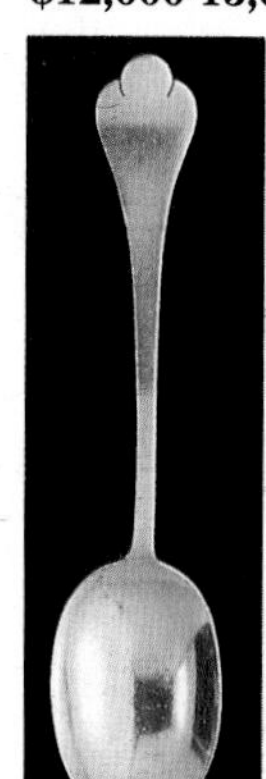
A Charles Rennie Mackintosh electroplated spoon, designed for Miss Cranston's Willow Tea Rooms, Glasgow, c1904, impressed mark Miss Cranston's.
$1,000-1,200

A silver plated metal, painted wood and glass punch set, by Wüttembergische Metallwarenfabrik, c1930, stamped factory mark.
$4,500-6,000

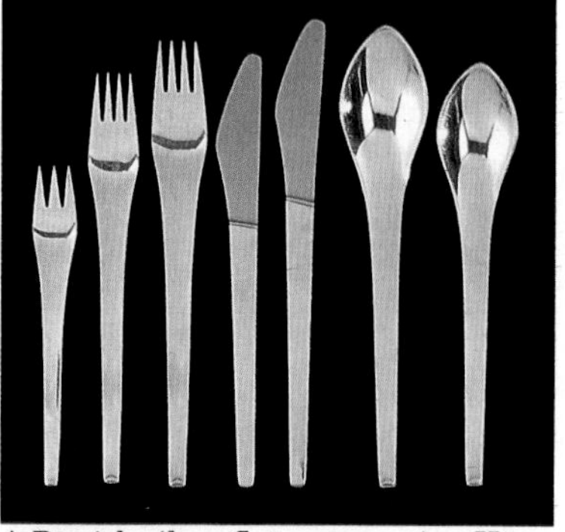
A Danish silver flatware service, Hans Hansen Silversmith, comprising 42 pieces, designer's monogram on knives, blades marked Hans Hansen/Denmark, c1955.
$2,500-3,500

A Peter Behrens chromium plated metal electric tea kettle, impressed A.E.G., Berlin, element lacking, c1909.
$700-850

An enamelled silver centrepiece, the satellites fitted with optional candle holders, the central dish with optional silvered bronze floral arranger, inscribed Jean Goulden/CXXII/1930 and stamped maker's mark, 45in (89cm) wide.
$40,000-45,000

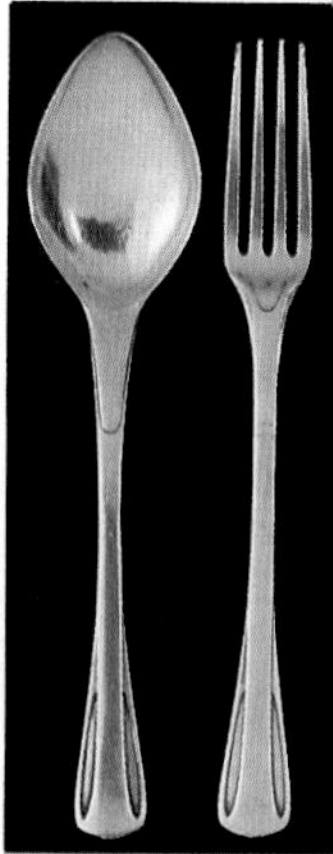
Six pieces of Joseph Maria Olbrich silver plated tableware, by Christofle, 1903
$600-750

French Art Nouveau
armoire, c1900, 105in
(267cm) high.
$7,500-9,000

A Wendell Castle dressing table and stool, Arc monogram, signed Claude Graham III, c1985.
$6,000-7,500

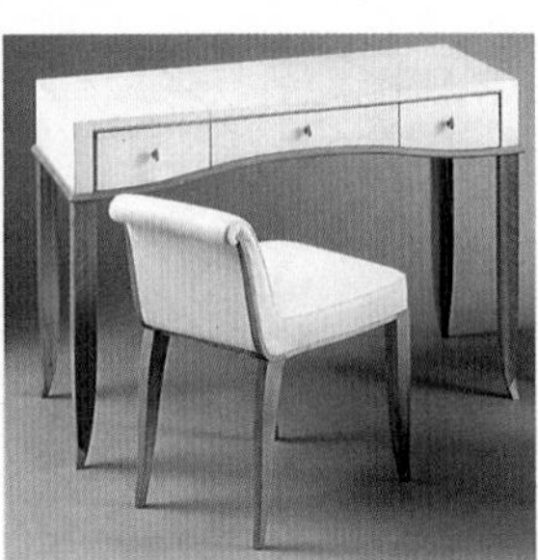

A fruitwood coiffeuse and chair, by Paul Dupré-Lafon, c1945.
$12,500-13,500

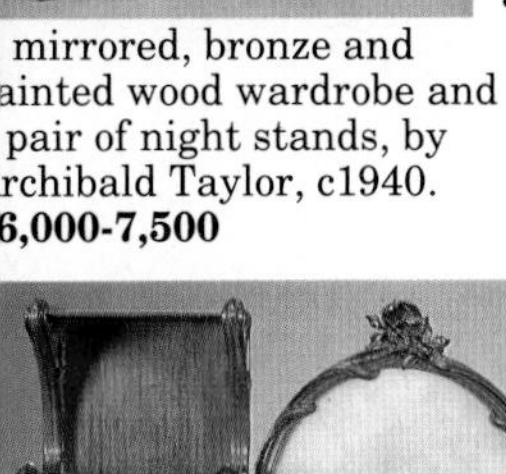

mirrored, bronze and painted wood wardrobe and pair of night stands, by Archibald Taylor, c1940.
$6,000-7,500

A Scottish mahogany hammered copper and leaded glass firescreen, c1900.
$3,000-3,750

A Majorelle mahogany bed and a pair of nightstands, c1900.
$24,000-30,000

An Art Nouveau mahogany, fruitwood marquetry and mother-of-pearl cabinet, School of Nancy, c1900. **$16,500-19,500**

An Austrian Biedermeier style painted wood corner étagère, c1920.
$4,500-5,200

A Marsh & Jones inlaid linen press, attributed to Charles Bevan, 89½in (227.5cm).
$3,700-5,200

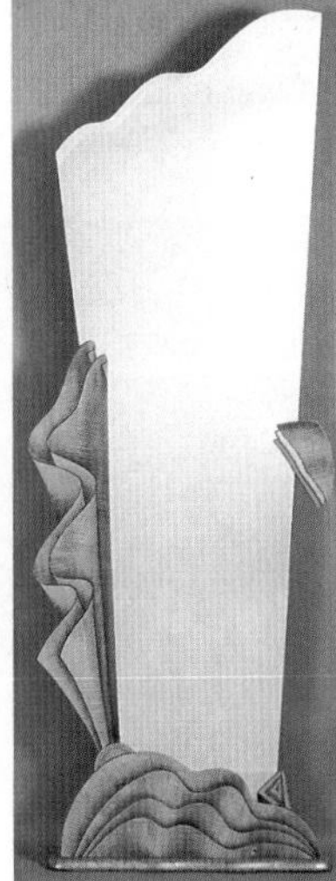

A mirror, by John Cederquist, 1990,
$4,500-5,200

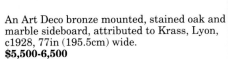

An Art Deco bronze mounted, stained oak and marble sideboard, attributed to Krass, Lyon, c1928, 77in (195.5cm) wide.
$5,500-6,500

A painted steel and leather side chair, by Frank Lloyd Wright, c1904.
$5,250-6,000

A laminated and carved oak settee, by Wendell Castle, signed and dated 66, 56in (142cm) long.
$12,000-15,000

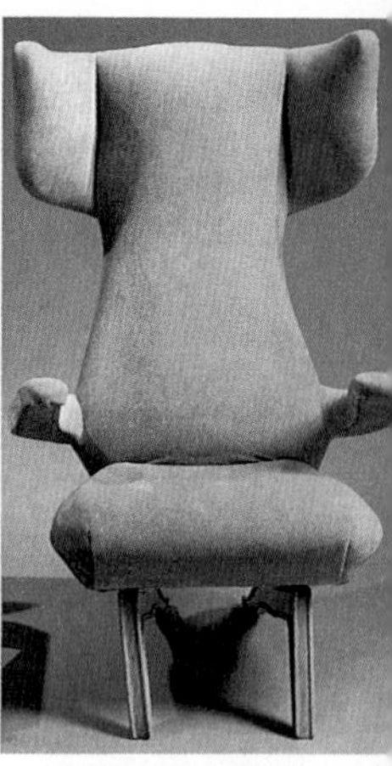

A maple upholsterec wing chair, by Franc Campo and Carlo Graffi, c1953.
$9,000-10,500

A pair of oak side chairs, designed by Peter Behrens, with rush seats.
$5,250-6,000

A stained mahogany side chair, by Richard Riemerschmid, manufactured by B. Kohlbecker & Sohn, Munich, 1903.
$2,500-3,500

A mahogany and leather armchair, by Henry van de Veld designed for the Haby Salon, Berlin, 1901.
$13,000-15,000

A pair of French palmwood upholstered side chairs, c1930.
$3,750-5,250

A black metal and ponyskin chaise longue, by Le Corbusier, Pierr Jeanneret and Charlotte Perriand, manufactured by Embru Corporation, Switzerland, c1932. **$10,500-13,500**

l. An ash and painted canvas armchair, by Wharton Esherick, signed Hedgerow/to Jasper MCMXXXVII Wharton. **$10,500-13,500**

A pair of French mahogany upholstered club chairs, c1935.
$3,750-5,250

A Bruno Paul maple armchair, restored, manufacturer's monogram, Munich, 1901.
$21,000-25,000

A pair of Josef Hoffmann stained bentwood and brass side chairs, by J. & J. Kohn, Austria, c1901.
$8,250-11,250

A set of eight Carlo Mollino oak and brass side chairs, made by Appelli, Turin, Italy, c1952.
$18,000-22,500

An Aesthetic Movement ebonised and inlaid open armchair, c1870.
$3,000-3,750

A painted deal 'Berlin' chair, designed by Gerrit Rietveld in 1923, branded label, made by Gerard van de Groenekan, c1960.
$10,500-16,500

A Josef Hoffman bentwood 670 'Sitzmachine', manufactured by J. & J. Kohn, c1905.
$33,000-38,000

A pair of French upholstered club chairs, attributed to André Arbus, c1945.
$5,250-6,750

A 'Red/Blue' beech and deal chair, by Gerrit Rietveld, designed in 1918, executed in 1919.
$38,000-45,000

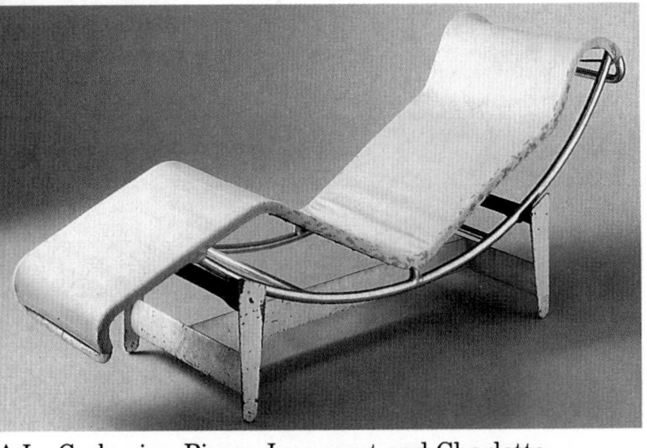

A Le Corbusier, Pierre Jeanneret and Charlotte Perriand, white painted metal and canvas chaise longue, manufactured by Thonet, designed c1928, 63cm (160cm). **$52,000-60,000**

An Otto Wagner stained beechwood and aluminium stool, by Thonet, c1904.
$24,000-30,000

A granite conference table, designed by Marcel Breuer, c1966, 120in (304.5cm) long.
$7,500-10,500

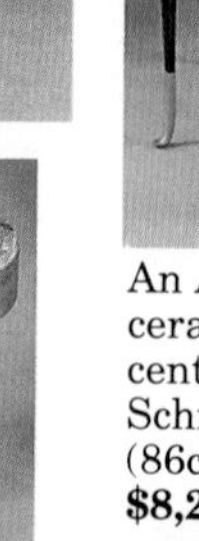

An Adolf Loos mahogany ceramic tile and brass centre table, by F.O. Schmidt c1900, 34in (86cm) diam.
$8,250-9,500

An Austrian marble, brass and black painted wood centre table, c1910.
$7,500-9,000

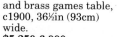

A marble and wrought iron coffee table, by Raymond Subes, marble repaired, c1930.
$7,500-9,000

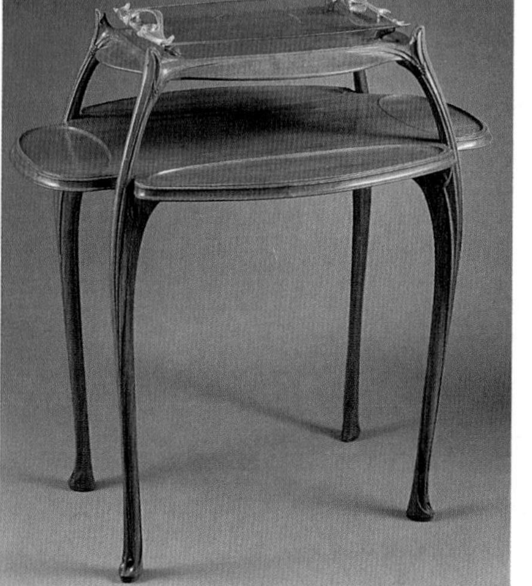

A two-tier mahogany, gilt bronze and glass tea table, by Hector Guimard, signed and inscribed, c1903.
$187,500-200,000

An Austrian stained oak and brass games table, c1900, 36½in (93cm) wide.
$5,250-6,000

An architectural teak wood model, by Marcel Breuer, c1960 10½in (26.5cm) high.
$3,750-5,250

A French gilt bronze and glass centre table, c1935, 47in (119cm).
$8,250-9,750

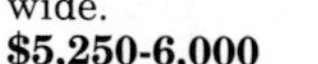

A Joseph Hoffman 'hour glass' stained wood table, c1905, 23½in (60cm).
$5,250-6,750

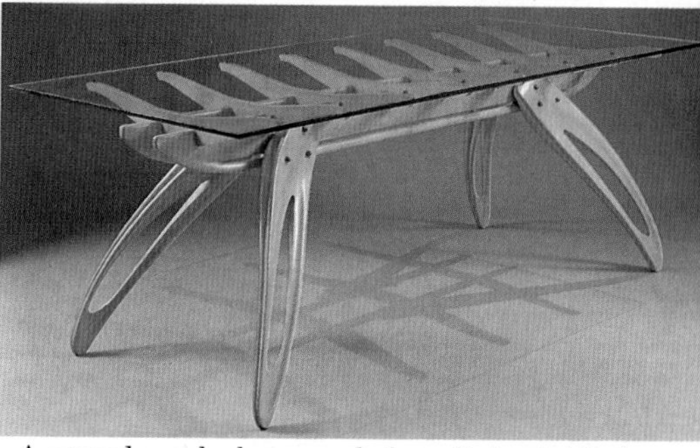

A carved maple, brass and glass dining table, by Franco Campo and Carlo Graffi, c1953, 84in (213cm) long.
$45,000-55,000

A nine-piece nickel and chromium plated metal, painted wood and leather dining room suite, by Ludwig Mies van der Rohe, comprising: table sideboard, serving table and 6 side chairs, c1931.
$18,000-24,000

An ebonised and gilded oak dining table, by Ernest Boiceau, c1935, 102in ((259cm).
$14,000-18,000

painted vellum, tooled copper, brass and wood desk nd side chair, by Carlo Bugatti, the chair signed, 1902.

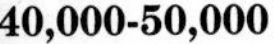

40,000-50,000

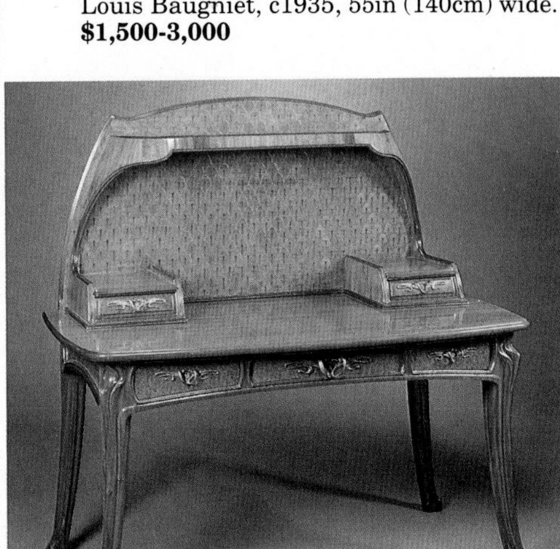

A stained oak and beech desk, by Marcel Louis Baugniet, c1935, 55in (140cm) wide.
$1,500-3,000

French rosewood, mahogany and leather desk, 1935, 75in (190.5cm) wide.
8,250-9,750

A Majorelle inlaid mahogany desk, c1900, 57½in (146cm).
$18,000-24,000

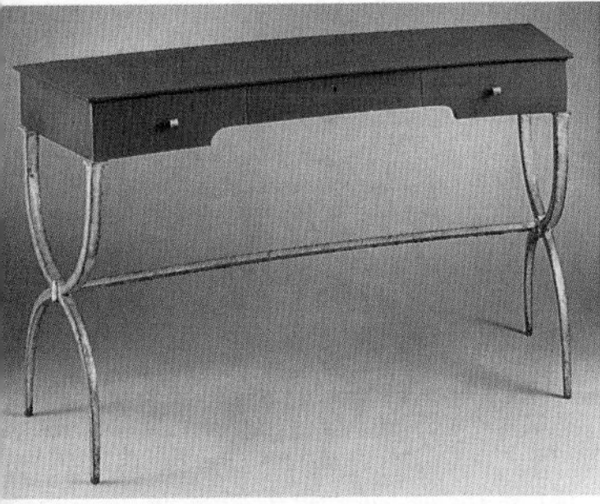

green lacquered wood and gilt iron lesk, by André Arbus, c1940, 51in 130cm) wide.
13,000-16,000

An Arts and Crafts writing desk, with folding flap, 33in (86cm).
$300-450

An armchair, by Ludwig Mies van der Rohe, c1927.
$6,750-9,500

French oak partners' desk and leather upholstered armchair, c1930, 82½in (209cm).
7,500-9,000

A pair of French mahogany and leather armchairs, c1930.
$6,750-8,250

A bentwood half barrel chair,c1904.
$4,500-5,250

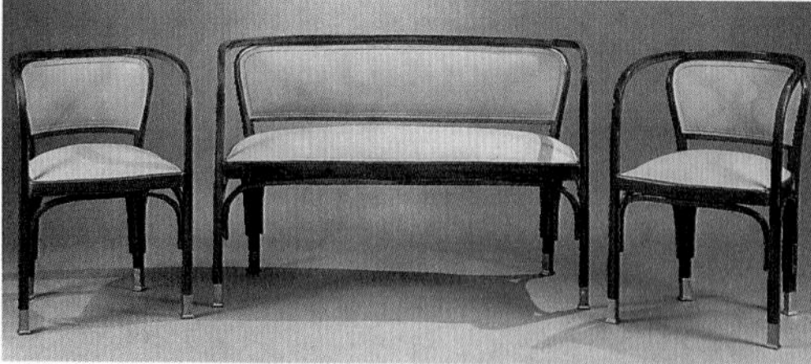

A Gustav Siegel leather upholstered stained bentwood and brass seating group, made by J. & J. Kohn, c1905, settee 48in (122cm) wide.
$10,500-12,500

An Austrian burr maple settee, upholstered in khaki twill, c1920, 55in (140cm) wide.
$6,500-7,500

A French Art Deco parcel gilt mahogany five-piece salon suite, upholstered in silk moiré, c1925, settee 50in (128cm) wide.
$7,500-9,000

A pair of Jacques Adnet black lacquered wood upholstered 'cube' club chairs, upholstered in beige canvas, c1930.
$13,500-16,500

A Josef Hoffmann leather upholstered bentwood 'Buenos Aires' three-piece seating group, made by J. & J. Kohn, c1904, settee 52in (133cm).
$16,000-17,000

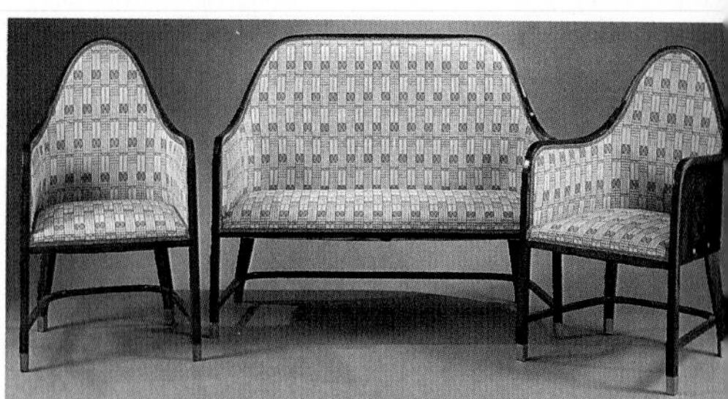

A Joseph Hoffmann upholstered stained bentwood and brass seating group, c1901, settee 47in (120cm) wide. **$15,500-16,500**

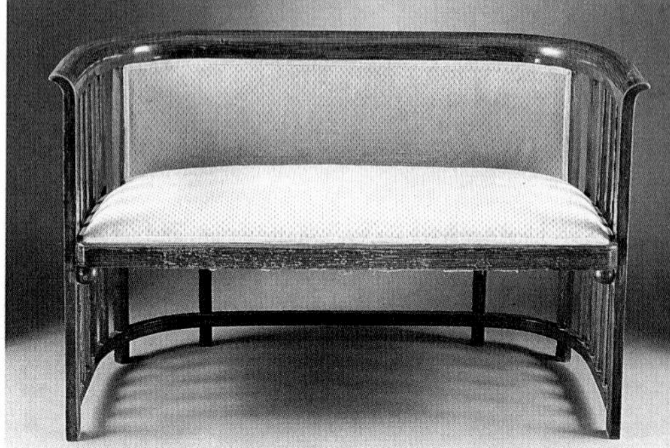

A Josef Hoffmann faux-grained bentwood settee upholstered in velvet, with branded label, c1905 47in (120cm) wide. **$4,500-6,000**

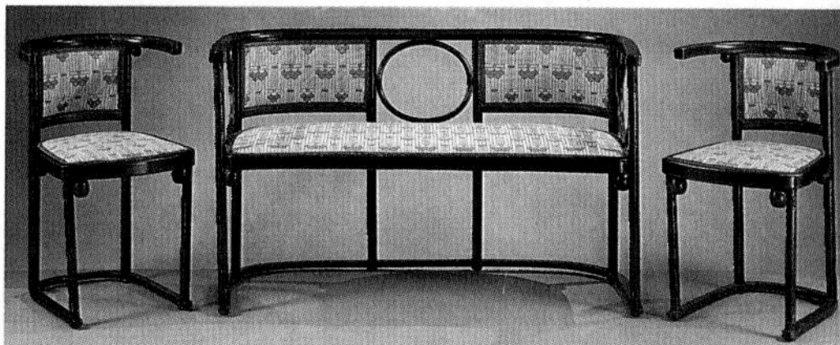

A Josef Hoffmann 'Fledermaus' stained bentwood upholstered seating group, probably made by J. & J Kohn, c1905. **$5,250-6,000**

A pair of Ebène de Macassar and chromed steel upholstered armchairs and footstool, in the style of Pierre Chareau, c1930. **$6,750-7,500**

A French bronze mounted stained oak draw-leaf dining table and four chairs, attributed to Krass, Lyon, c1928, 117in (297cm) extended.
$6,000-8,000

A white metal brooch by Henry Wilson, the domed seven-sided form of cast stemwork with a central flowerhead and pale turquoise enamel detail.
$450-600

An Arts and Crafts circular clip brooch, attributed to Sybil Dunlop,with gold leaves, tourmalines and mother-of-pearl.
$500-700

Guild of Handicraft white and yellow metal ooch, designed by C. R. Ashbee, set with ster pearls, pearls, sapphires, 2 paste placements, tourmalines and moonstones.
2,000-13,500

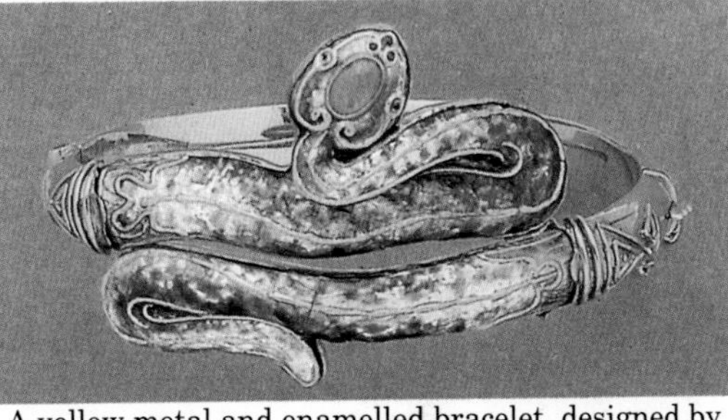

A yellow metal and enamelled bracelet, designed by James Cromer Watt, formed as a snake, of blue-green enamel, set with opal, stamped monogram JCW. **$3,750-4,500**

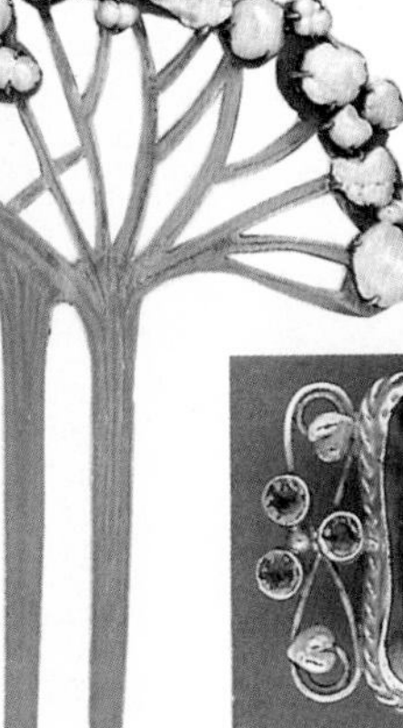

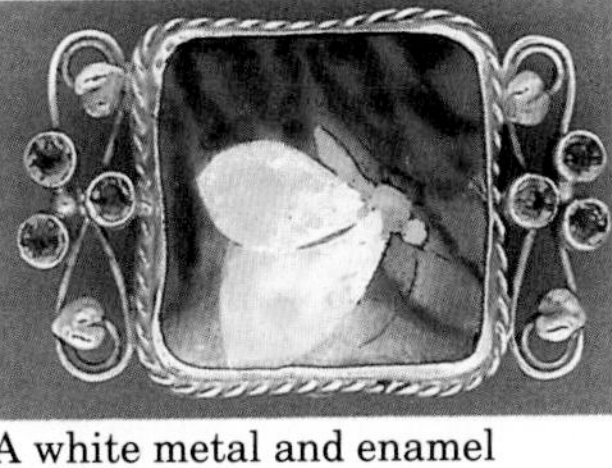

A white metal and enamel brooch, set with citrines, stamped G. Hunt 1922, and another set with amazonite.
$1,000-1,200

A yellow metal, enamel and rock crystal brooch, by Henry Wilson or Henry G. Murphy, set with opals and a central cabochon amethyst.
$2,500-3,000

horn hair comb, by Fred T. artridge, set with baroque pearls white metal, formed as an mbellifer, slight damage, signed artridge.
1,200-1,500

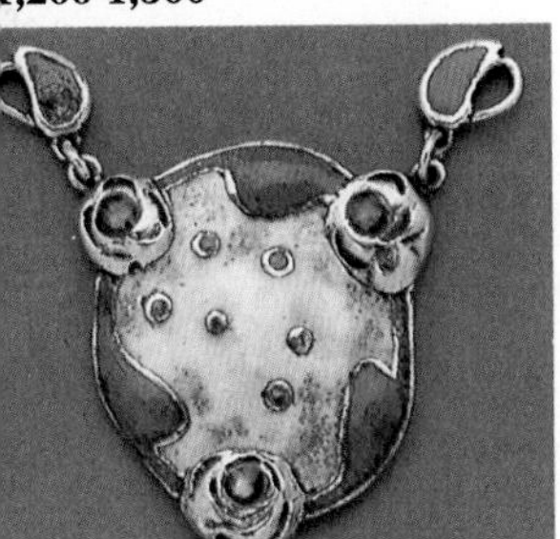

green and mottled white namel pendant, designed by ir Frank Brangwyn for La Maison de l'Art Nouveau, aris, with monograms F.B., V.B.
4,000-6,000

Medusa, a yellow metal, ivory and enamel brooch, by George Hunt, set with opals and pearls, stamped Medusa, G.H.
$3,750-4,500

A Liberty & Co. yellow metal and enamel ring, by Archibald Knox.
$3,750-4,500

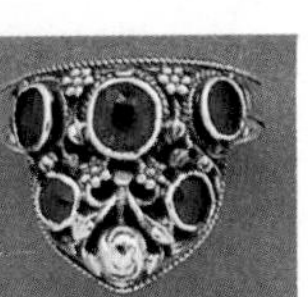

A yellow metal and sapphire ring, by Henry Wilson, with pierced decoration.
$3,000-4,500

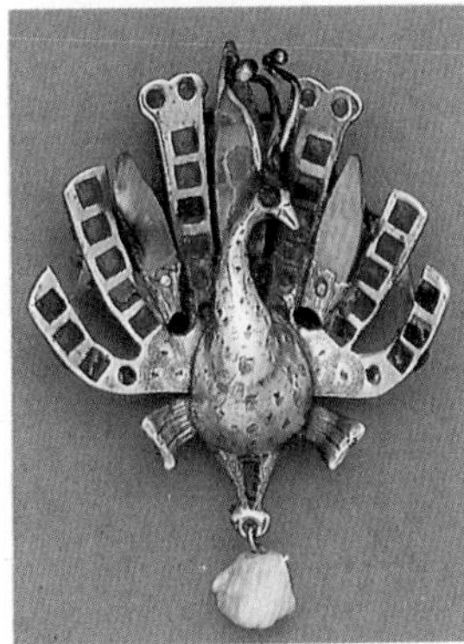

A Guild of Handicraft silver peacock brooch, designed by C. R. Ashbee, set with enamel, abalone and a ruby, stamped, maker's marks, London hallmarks for 1907.
$2,500-3,000

Book of Hours, use of Paris, in Latin, illuminated manuscript on vellum, 202 leaves, c1415, 7 x 12in (18 x 30cm).
$125,000-130,000

Book of Hours, in Latin, illuminated manuscript on vellum, 228 leaves, ?Paris, c1430.
$230,000-240,000

Antiphonal of Marguerite de Baconel, in Latin, illuminate manuscript on vellum, 178 leaves, South Flanders, c154 8 x 5½in (20 x 13.5cm).
$15,000-18,000

Book of Hours, use of Rome, in Latin, some rubrics in French, illuminated manuscript on vellum, 112 leaves, 7 x 5in (17 x 12cm).
$10,000-11,250

In Fairyland, A Series of Pictures from Elf-World, by William Allingham, illustrated by Richard Doyle, 1870. **$450-600**

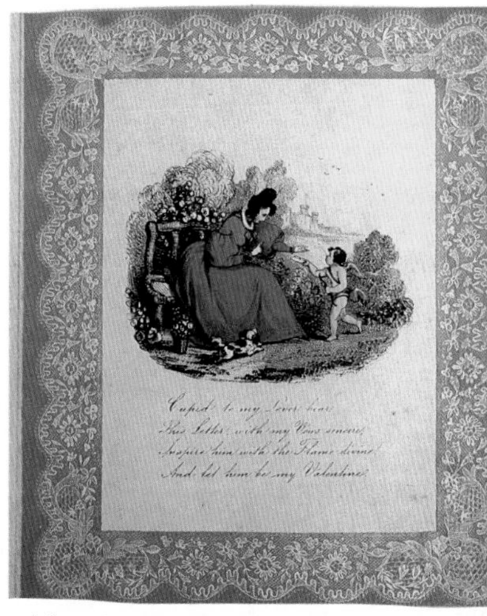

A hand coloured lithograph, depicting a woman seated on a bench instructing Cupid, who is holding a valentine card, watermarked Fellows 1836, 9½ x 8in (2 x 20cm). **$90-120**

Four hand coloured lithographed illustrations for children's stories, by Wilhelm Hey, Grimm Brothers, J. Lohmeyer & F. Flinzer, C. Offterdinger, illustrator.
$600-700

Transformation Books - Fred Weatherley & Others, Pleasant Surprises for chicks of all surprises, pop-up plates, and others.
$1,800-2,300

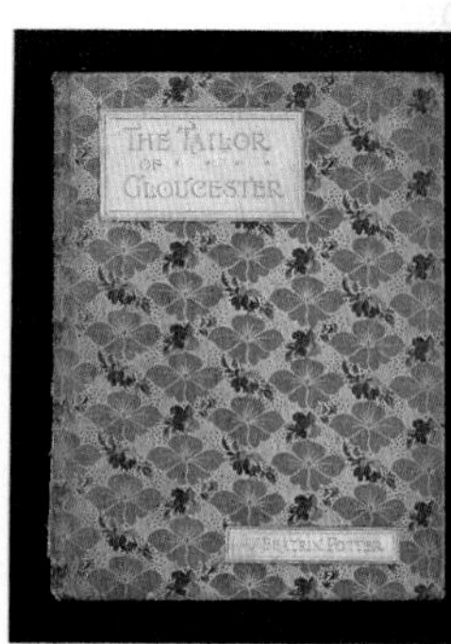

The Tailor of Gloucester, by Beatrix Potter, Frederick Warn & Co.,1903, coloured frontispiece and 26 plates, first edition.
$650-750

DOLLS

:EVIEW OF THE MARKETPLACE

ı 1992 and during the first half of 1993 we ave seen a major fall in the price of French ébés, largely because of the lack of demand om Japan. The yen has fallen to such an xtent that pretty Brus, Jumeaus, Steiners nd other French dolls from the 1880s and 890s are now fetching almost a third less ıan they would have done two years ago, so erhaps now is a good time to start investing ı the finest pressed bisque-headed dolls.

English wooden dolls of the 17thC and 8thC have still to regain their peak of 1989. fine quality late 17thC doll in original lothes sold for $39,000 in May 1993, hereas a slightly earlier doll also in original lothes, fetched $95,000 in May 1989. Again re appear to be in a situation where it is robably wiser to buy, if you can find a good iece, than to sell.

Conversely, wax dolls seem at last to be oming into their own. There are some elightful early English beeswax dolls from he 18thC and 19thC that are of very good uality and feature fine modelling. They are sually fashioned as babies, wearing ontemporary high-waisted, low-necked baby obes. In June a 13½in doll in wax, with eyes perated by a wire, but with the wax broken t the neck, fetched $400 at auction. A later Inglish poured-wax doll in the manner of Iadame Montanari, again dressed in ontemporary clothes, fetched $2,000 last eptember.

German bisque-headed character dolls are till very much in demand. A 21in mould Io. 107, made by Kammer and Reinhardt nd advertised as 'Carl', fetched $50,000 in ondon in June 1993. It is some time since his mould in a large size has appeared on he London market, which partly explains he high price of the doll. Similarly, Googlies re still much sought after: an 11in Ernst Ieubach, mould No. 319, designed by H. chalkau, sold for $4,500. This face is narvellously expressive with a rather pprehensive look. In the same sale, a 13in Kestner mould No. 221, with a happy xpression went for $5,250.

Character dolls of another kind, also made n Germany in around 1910, include the nine teiff school children with their teacher which were sold in September 1992 for 19,500. Still in immaculate condition with heir desks, books and classroom equipment, hey even had little black cotton 'tabliers' - he overalls worn by school children all-over 'rance.

Dolls modelled after famous people or film haracters are always interesting, articularly if in original clothes. A 17½in Dean's cloth doll dressed as Amy Johnson omplete with flying suit, gloves, whistle, oggles and earphones went for $600 with hree soft toys. Composition Shirley Temples are always popular. Those still in their original box and with original accessories command a premium.

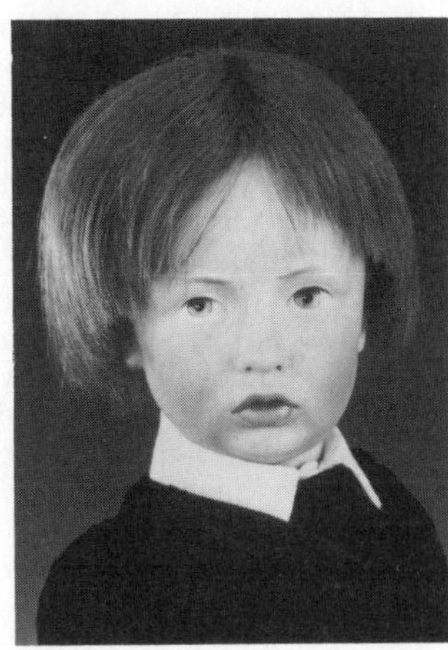

A rare German bisque-headed character doll - 'Carl'.
$45,000-60,000

Cloth dolls are holding their prices well in all areas. A boxed set of Chad Valley's Snow White and the Seven Dwarfs reached $2,250. In this set the Dwarfs were the smaller 6½in high version. Lenci dolls of all types in near mint condition are still highly collected, a nice group in September selling for between $300 for a late 16in 149 series doll, to $1,000 for a rare 11in character Red Riding Hood doll in original box, with two other smaller unimportant Lencis. In the same sale a 20in Du Mein stockinette doll by Kathe Krüse went for $1,400, while the sleeping Traumachen version fetched $1,650 in June 1993.

Marks

Some, but not all dolls, have marks which can provide various information, such as the maker, the country of origin, the mould number, the size and any trademark. The marks are not always immediately visible, and you may have to look very carefully to find them - for example, under the hair at the back of the neck, or on the back of the shoulder. Some dolls have stamps or labels attached to the body.

STARTING A COLLECTION

The obvious advice one could give to a novice collector is to acquire some knowledge. This is not much help when you are just beginning, full of enthusiasm, to collect and are mystified as to why some dolls fetch thousands of pounds, while others go for just a few pounds. Museums, while useful, tend not to identify items closely enough and certainly do not price them. Even if dolls are well identified, it is difficult to tell from descriptions whether they are rare, very rare or ordinary. Even if dolls are listed as rare, this does not necessarily mean they are valuable. Rarity is not equal to value; quality, condition and looks also enter into the equation.

If you are lucky enough to make friends with a knowledgeable dealer who does not mind helping you, then you will be able to ask advice and profit from their years of experience. But you must remember that dealers have to earn a living and any purchases you may make, although of good quality, will be at retail prices and you must not expect to be able to recoup your outlay in the short term. A good dealer will always tell you about the defects of a doll, and this is particularly important to an inexperienced buyer who may otherwise not look for such things as hairline cracks, new wigs, redressing, overpainting or mismatched bodies.

A bisque-headed lady doll, impressed 1159, Halbig S & H 9½in hat with Au Nain Bleu label, 24in (61cm) high.
$2,700-3,300

See as many dolls as possible, and perhaps note down what takes your fancy, with prices if available. Go to doll fairs, museums, specialist auctions and dealers and visit any collectors who are willing to show you their dolls. Then go to the public library and get out as many books on dolls as you can. All books are useful, even the coffee table type which contain more illustrations than information, and they can at least direct you towards a certain maker or type of doll.

WHAT TO COLLECT

Having decided how much money you want to spend on building your collection, you will need to consider what sort of collection you want. You may decide to collect by medium - - for example, wood, wax or pressed bisque; or you could cut across the substance divide and buy dolls from a particular period, such as the first quarter of the 19thC, the 1860s, or even character dolls made between 1909 and 1914, or you could collect black, Oriental, male or even paper dolls.

Remember that if you choose a cheaper type such as paper, 20thC composition, hard plastic or celluloid, you will be able to make more purchases during the year out of a given amount of money and your collection will grow faster. On the other hand, saving up for and planning the purchase of one magnificent doll that is going to thrill you every time you look at her, may be more to your taste. It's very much a matter of personal preference, and also perhaps on the space you have to display your buys.

A bisque shoulder-headed topsy-turvy doll, one head in black bisque, the other in white, impressed 6½, heads 5 and 4in (12.5 and 10cm).
$1,050-1,350

You must also bear in mind that dolls are very vulnerable, both to damage and to the attentions of burglars. Make sure your collection is properly insured, and kept out of the way of dust, damp and moths. I personally don't think it a good idea for the collection to be visible to every caller to the house. A cupboard with doors, a glass case on an upstairs landing or in a spare bedroom, or even a curtain across an alcove, are some possible locations. I think it is sad if dolls are always kept completely hidden away in boxes although I know this is perhaps the best way to preserve them. Remember that daylight does terrible things to original clothes - fading colours and rotting silk.

BUYING FROM FAIRS AND DEALERS

If you are not near a reputable dealer, go to a doll fair. Unless you already feel confident about buying, it is probably wisest not to rush in and purchase in the first few minutes as you will not know whether you are getting a bargain or not. Go round the stalls comparing dolls and prices, you may be surprised at the difference in value of what seem to be identical dolls. You may indeed have spotted a bargain, but it is more likely that the higher priced doll is in better condition, has original clothes or even an original box. If a doll has not been played with, even if it is relatively ordinary, then this can double or treble the value.

If you have lost your heart to a doll - in my iew, the only reason for buying - then think arefully before parting with your money. Iow much of the doll is original? Does it ave any serious defects? (Damage to the isque or china will almost always hold down he value when attempting to resell.) Have ou seen similar dolls at the same sort of rice? Has the dealer been honest about any hanges that he or she may have made (new hoes, a wig, ribbons, repairs, etc)? Have you ead about this doll and is it from a good aaker? You must also consider the quality, earing in mind that moulds were often eused many times, and after a while roduced dolls with much less crisp odelling than those made when the mould as new. Also, impurities sometimes got ato the clay or glaze, resulting in spotting or itting on the bisque.

Finally, are the clothes acceptable? Dolls re most valuable when their clothes are riginal, in other words, what the doll was earing when it left the toy shop. lternatively, clothes may be contemporary ith the doll - perhaps made by the child ho owned the doll originally. Or the clothes ay be new, but made of old materials. A ealer should tell you which of these is the ase. What I would not advise is paying xtra for a doll dressed in modern fabrics in fanciful style, covered in frills, ribbons and ows of tricel or viscose. Natural fabrics only lease, apart from rayon which is acceptable or '30s dolls, and nylon or nylon taffeta for 0s and '60s dolls.

*bisque-headed character doll, impressed K*R114 6, needs restringing, very small chip on neck socket, 8in (46cm) high.*
6,000-8,250

When you have decided that the doll is hat you want and the price is fair, ask the ealer to give you a receipt and to write own important points about the doll, or note hem down yourself. You may think you will emember, but written details, such as the me, place and cost of the purchase, will be seful and amusing for you years later when ecalling your first ventures into the world of dolls. It is also very necessary when you want to sell or upgrade your collection.

BUYING AT AUCTION

Auction houses are of course a good place to buy dolls, but you need to be careful and have some idea of what you are doing before raising your catalogue in a packed saleroom. It is advisable to read the catalogue, especially the small print at the beginning and the disclaimer. Some salerooms try to mention all damages, others only do so on the illustrated lots. If in doubt ask for a condition report and state what you want to know: condition of bisque and body, age of accessories, and so on. Estimates in catalogues can occasionally be misleading, may not be definitive and may prove inaccurate. Check against previous prices paid for similar dolls, or against prices of similar dolls in the same sale. If you think you have found what you want and the estimate appears to be fair then you can either attend the sale and bid yourself, get a friend or porter to do it for you, or leave a bid on the book. This means filling in a form giving your maximum price for the lots you wish to buy. The auctioneer will then bid on your behalf up to your maximum figure against any reserve or other bids he may have on the book or in the room. Of course, most people tend to leave bids in round numbers, so by leaving one bid extra say at $650 instead of $600 you may just outbid the others. Bidding on the book does have its advantages, you are quite anonymous, so that it is possible to avoid embarrassment if you and your best friend both want the same doll. It also prevents your enthusiasm running away with you, and will stop you paying more than you meant to for an item in the heat of the moment. A lot of collectors and dealers buy in this way, it saves time, they can view at leisure, decide what they want and then come in to pay and collect at a later date to suit themselves. I always advise people who are unable to make up their mind if they can afford something that they want, to leave a small bid just in case it succeeds. If they do not bid at all then they have no chance of acquiring the item. The secret is to hit on a price above which you feel the doll is too expensive for you. That way you will have few regrets and may make some good purchases.

If you are a successful bidder remember to collect your purchase promptly and to check the doll carefully before signing the release order. Once you have signed for your doll the auctioneers will not refund your money or take the doll back. It is also important when viewing to read the saleroom announcements. Do not forget the buyers' premium and VAT at the current rate is charged on the premium. Sometimes VAT is charged on the hammer price as well, this is normally indicated by an asterisk or a dagger beside the lot number in the catalogue.

SOME POPULAR DOLL TYPES

Wax Dolls: Wax is a fascinating material in itself, as it was used commercially in so many different ways over such a long period. There are 18thC and early 19thC dolls made of beeswax; some of the earliest true baby dolls were made of beeswax in England in around 1800. There are also the slightly later papier mâché heads which were dipped in wax to give a thin translucent coating over the brightly painted features. The Germans used to pour wax onto a mould, and then after it had dried, a liquid plaster-type composition was poured in to reinforce it. Some of these dolls have finely moulded features and even collars and bodices, but look out for cracks because the reinforcing material does not marry well with the wax and damage usually results. The cream of wax dolls are, of course, the poured English waxes of the last half of the 19thC and beginning of the 20thC. Having no reinforcing material they are more likely to survive intact, and when they are in good condition they are among some of the loveliest dolls ever made.

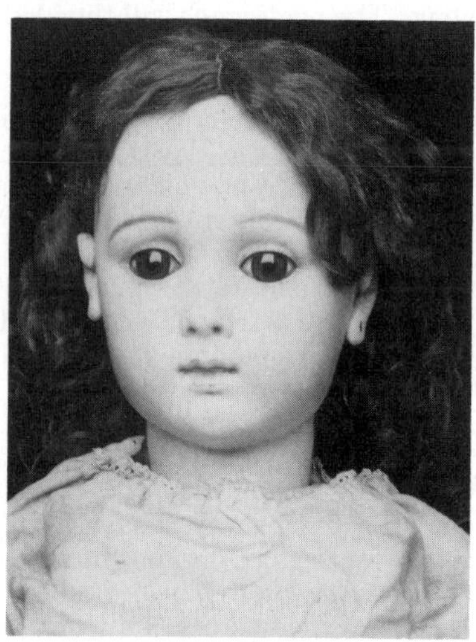

A Jumeau Triste pressed bisque-headed bébé, impressed 15, body stamped in blue Jumeau Medaille d'Or Paris, 31in (84cm) high.
$9,000-12,000

Pressed Bisque Dolls: Pressed bisque-headed dolls were made like rolling out pastry and pressing it by hand into a two-piece mould. Dolls of this kind can be identified by the unevenness of the inside of the heads and with a filled ear cavity, unlike later poured-bisque heads where the clay was turned into slip by the addition of water, and was poured in and out of the moulds leaving an even layer of clay adhering to the inside of the mould. The later method was obviously far quicker, but these dolls sometimes lack the delicacy of those made by hand.

Barbies and other 20thC Dolls: A relatively new collecting phenomenon is the Barbie craze. It is hard to be neutral about Barbie. You either love her American sophistication and her beautifully-made '60s fashionable clothes and accessories, or you despise her precocious vulgarity. It is hard to imagine creating such well-made costume for a mass-produced doll as those that were made in Japan between 1959 and 1967 with hand-knitted jerseys and cardigans, some even with collars and cuffs of a different typ or yarn, such as mohair.

All these early clothes were lined, which has helped to preserve their shape. The materials were of good quality and the details on the accessories adds period charm to the outfits. In fact it is this period aspect which I consider to be at the heart of Barbie's appeal. She is always so much a girl of her time and, through her clothes, friends and accessories, an indicator of the mainstream fashions of her day. Condition again is all important, a mint and boxed doll fetching many times the price of a played-with, stained doll who has had a haircut. Al Barbie's outfits have names, from 'Swingin' Easy' a dancing costume, to 'Dog 'n' Duds' fo taking the poodle for a walk. Then there are 'Woolly PJs', 'Platter Party', 'Me 'n' My Doll', 'Miss Astronaut', 'Slumber Party' and 'Fraternity Dance', to name but a few.

Finally, there are also the English and American hard plastic dolls, introduced in the '50s; and composition Mama dolls, made between the wars, with voice boxes. Again, for these dolls to have real value they must be in original clothes.

Whatever you decide to collect, it is important to realise that prices can go down as well as up: fashions change, currencies fluctuate, and the market can get flooded with a certain type of doll which fulfils buyers' needs for a number of years, so that demand, and therefore prices, fall. Doll collecting is still very much an expanding field, and is suitable for all incomes and tastes. More research is being done all the time and new areas of collecting are constantly being found. Buy a doll you love and can live with, and you will not go far wrong.

Olivia Bristol
June 1993

An important Check Before you Buy

Examine the individual parts of a doll to make sure that the limbs are in good condition and are original, and check that the body belongs with the head and is not a 'marriage' of parts: some dolls were given replacement bodies if the original one was damaged.

OLLS
'ax

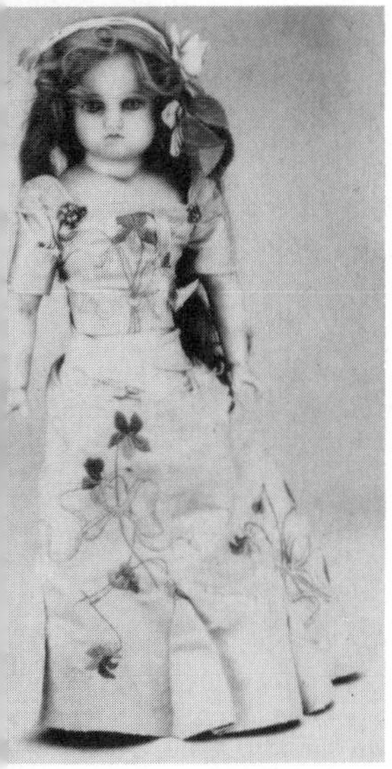

wax over composition headed ll, with blue eyes, blonde ohair wig, stuffed body with ıx limbs, dressed in ntemporary cream silk ıbroidered gown with train, uising to wax on arms, with ıno & Otto Dressel mark, 17in 3cm) high.
750-1,200

A poured wax headed doll, with blue inset eyes, light brown hair in ringlets, stuffed body with wax limbs, dressed in original tucked lawn frock, trimmed with lace and blue silk sash, underclothes, socks and blue kid slippers, 24in (61cm) high.
$2,250-3,000

A wax doll, with lace trimmed pantaloons, flannelette petticoats, leather shoes and straw hat, 19thC, 19½in (50cm) high.
$50-75

A poured wax headed doll, with blue eyes, inset brown hair, stuffed body with wax limbs, in contemporary pink and white frock and whitework bonnet, damage to feet, 18in (46cm) high.
$750-1,200

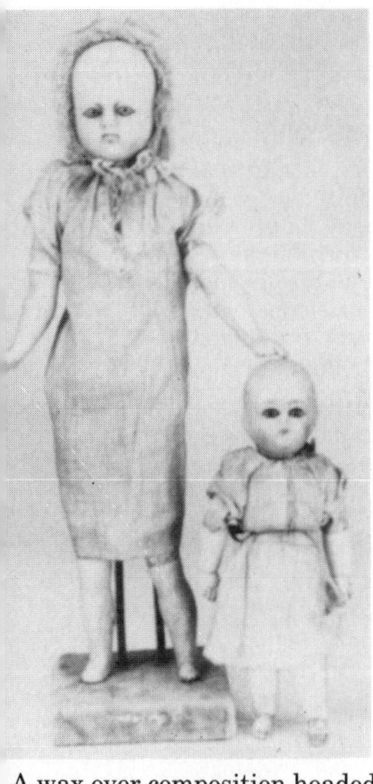

A wax over composition headed ıby doll, with fixed bright blue ·es, stuffed body, waxed limbs ıd original shift and bonnet, ›nneberg, late 19thC, 13in 3cm) high. **$375-525**
A dipped wax shoulder headed ıufling, with painted curls, blue eeping eyes, 'floating joints', uffed body portion and original ıift, Sonneberg, mid-19thC, 7½in 9cm) high.
750-1,200

Bisque

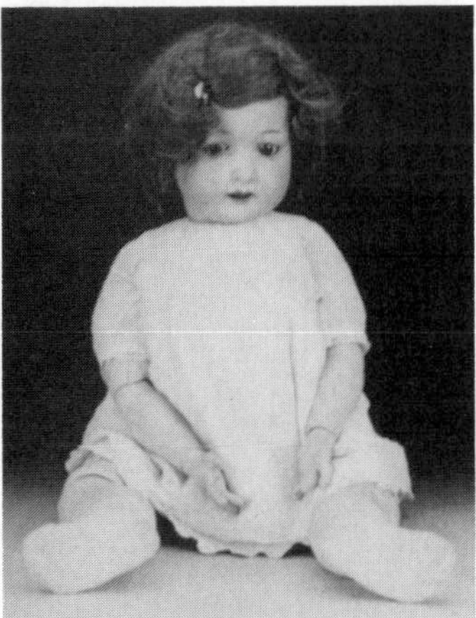

A Heubach Kopplesdorf bisque socket head character doll, with light brown short wig, painted features, closing blue glass eyes, open mouth with 4 upper teeth and moving visible tongue, dimpled chin, on a composition body with jointed limbs, wearing a white muslin dress over flannel petticoat, back of head impressed Heubach 267.11.Kopplesdorf. B.R.M. Thuringia, 27½in (70cm) high.
$600-750

l. A bisque headed character doll modelled as an Oriental, with dark eyes, pierced ears, black mohair wig, and jointed wood and composition body, dressed in green silk, impressed SH 1199 DEP 6, 14½in (37cm) high.
$1,200-1,800
r. A bisque headed character doll modelled as an Oriental, with dark eyes, black mohair wig, straight limbed composition body, in original cotton print suit and cardboard coolie hat, impressed AM 4/0, 11½in (29cm) high.
$375-525

A bisque headed three-faced doll, smiling, sleeping and crying, the stuffed body with jointed limbs, remains of contemporary frock and parasol, with patent stamp, 14in (36cm) high.
$1,050-1,350

A bisque swivel headed Parisienne, with blue inset eyes, pierced ears, cork pate, blonde mohair wig, kid body with individually stitched fingers, dressed as a child in original blue silk frock and feather trimmed hat, underwear, striped socks and high buttoned boots, 12½in (31cm) high.
$1,800-2,700

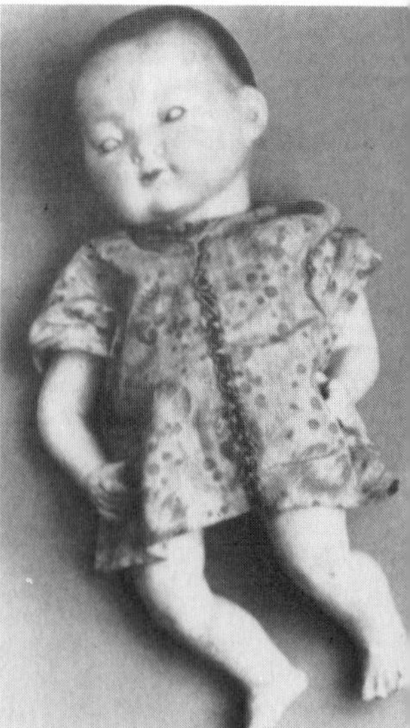

A bisque headed character baby doll modelled as an Oriental, wi brown sleeping eyes, 5-piece boc and original shift, impressed A ELLAR in a star M 3K.
$750-900

l. A bisque headed character do jointed wood and composition body, impressed K*R 109, 10½in (26cm) high.
r. A bisque shoulder headed Parisienne, with gusseted kid body, impressed C 1S.
$1,800-2,700

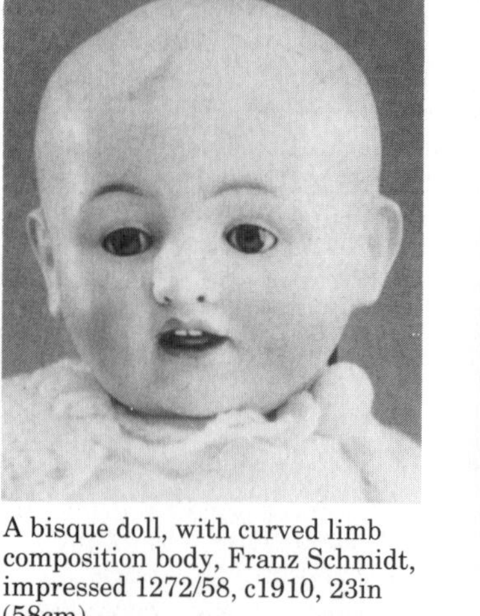

A bisque doll, with curved limb composition body, Franz Schmidt, impressed 1272/58, c1910, 23in (58cm).
$750-900

A Schmitt et Fils bisque doll, with 8 ball jointed wood and composition body, in original dress and red shoes, crack to face, impressed crossed hammers in shield, 7, c1860, 14½in (37cm).
$1,200-1,800

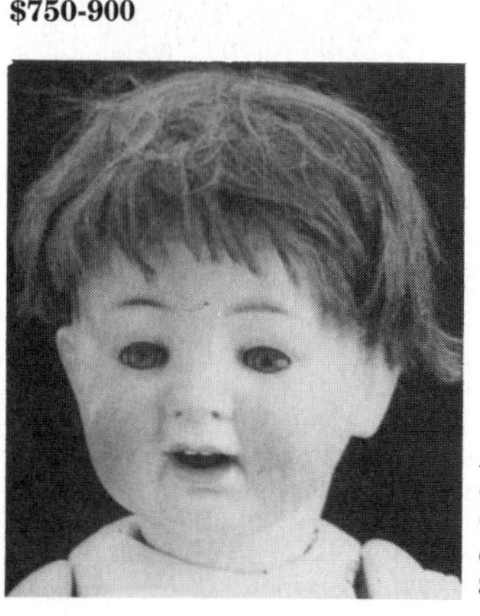

A bisque character doll, with curved limb composition body, C.M. Bergmann, impressed 7, c1910, 14½in (37cm).
$600-750

A bisque shoulder headed marotte, with original pink and white satin streamers and stra hat, impressed 4700 SH PB in a star 12, 11in (28cm) high.
$750-900

A bisque shoulder headed doll, ıpressed 1010, by Simon & ꞏalbig, 11in (28cm) high.
450-600

l. A bisque shoulder headed ɔll, impressed 1010, by Simon & ꞏalbig, 14in (36cm) high.
600-750

r. A bisque shoulder headed ɔll, impressed with the Kling ꞏll 123 7, 20in (51cm) high.
2,250-3,000

A bisque domed shoulder eaded doll, probably by Bahr & roschild, 14in (36cm) high.
750-900

Two swivel headed pressed shoulder bisque fashionable dolls:
l. With white kid body, possibly by Francois Gaultier, incised 7 at back of head and shoulder, c1875, 24in (61cm) **$3,000-3,750**
r. With white gusseted kid leather body, probably Jumeau, unmarked, c1875, 35in (89cm) high, together with wooden trunk.
$5,250-7,500

bisque swivel headed arisienne doll, with kid body, 1½in (29cm) high.
1,200-1,800

Two dome headed shoulder bisque dolls:
l. With fabric body, composition lower arms and legs, in original outfit, German, c1885, incised 5 at base of shoulder plate, 14in (36cm) high **$1,050-1,350**
r. With white kid body, dressed in original clothes, Simon & Halbig, incised S&H 3/ 950, c1888, 15in (38cm) high.
$750-1,200

A bisque headed clockwork child automaton, sitting in a wooden tub, some damage, by Roullet & Decamps, 13in (33cm) high.
$1,050-1,350

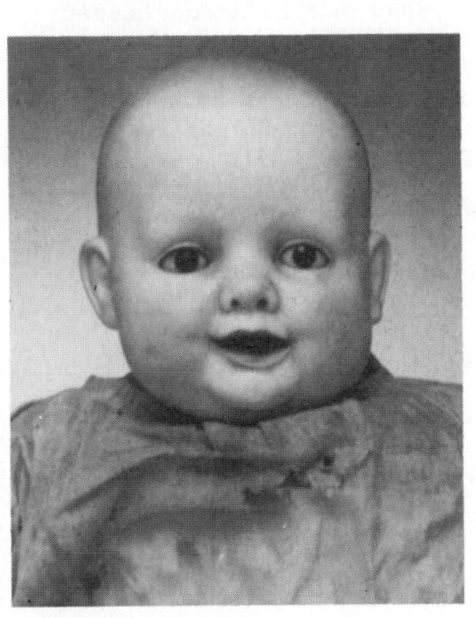

A bisque headed 'Bonnie Babe' doll, with fabric body and composition arms and legs, damaged, by Alt Beck & Gottschalk, incised Copr by Georgene Averill Germany 1005/3652/5, c1926, 22in (56cm) high.
$750-900

A googly-eyed bisque headed doll, with 5-piece bent limb composition body, Hertel Schwab, incised 165-9, c1914, 16in (41cm) high. **$4,500-6,000**

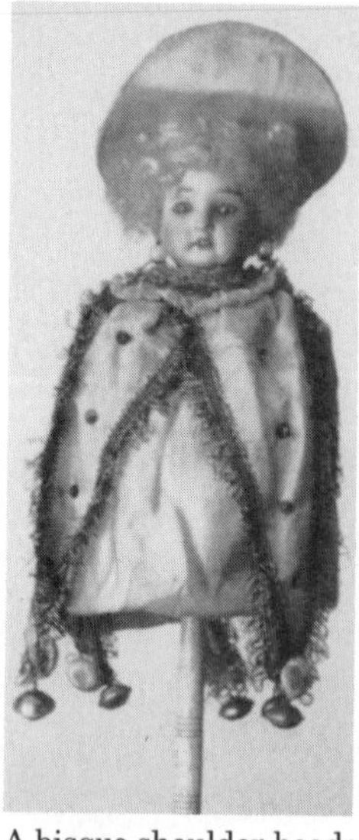

A bisque shoulder headed marotte, in original pink silk hat and streamers, with bone handle and whistle, 11in (28cm) high.
$600-750

Three bisque head dolls:
l. A girl doll, marked Armand Marseille 390, 19in (48cm) high
$300-375
c. A character doll, marked S.F.B.J. 236 PARIS, 20in (51cm) high **$750-1,200**
r. A googly-eyed girl character doll, Armand Marseille, marked Germany 323 A 2/0 M, 15in (38cm) high.
$1,200-1,800

A bisque headed marotte, with bone whistle handle, wearing original sequin and metal braid decorated hat and streamers, impressed Limoges, France, 13i (33cm) high.
$600-750

A bisque swivel headed Parisienne, with kid body, impressed 4 on shoulder, label on body A La Galerie Vivienne, Mon Guillard, Jeux & Jouets, Rémond Seur, 4 Rue Nve. des Petits Champs 4, Paris, c1875.
$1,800-2,700

Papier Mâché

A papier mâché shoulder headed doll, with kid body, wood limbs, wearing original muslin, lace and net frock, Sonneberg under dome, c1840, 16in (41cm) high.
$1,200-1,800

Two papier mâché shoulder dolls
l. With kid body, wood lower limbs, in original costume, German, mid-19thC, 14in (36cm)
$1,050-1,350
r. With cloth body, wearing elaborate headdress, German, mid-19thC, 16in (41cm).
$1,200-1,800

A papier mâché shoulder headed doll, with kid body and wearing original muslin dress with net overskirt, c1850, 12in (31cm) high.
$1,200-1,800

A papier mâché headed doll, with kid body, wood limbs, in original pink cotton lace trimmed frock, in shadow box with bocage of flowers, shells and mirrors, c1850, 13in (33cm) high.
$1,050-1,350

.F.B.J.

n S.F.B.J. doll, French, 16in 41cm) high.
375-525

. bisque headed character doll, ith jointed wood and omposition toddler body, npressed S.F.B.J. 236, 17½in 44cm) high.
1,200-1,800

François Gaultier

A swivel head pressed shoulder bisque fashionable doll, with fabric body, incised 7 to back of head and shoulder, possibly Gaultier, c1870, damaged, 26in (66cm) high.
$3,000-4,500

A swivel head bisque shoulder plate doll, with kid body and bisque lower arms, marked 11 FG in cartouche, 28in (71cm) high.
$5,250-7,500

Jumeau

A Jumeau doll, c1910, 22in (56cm).
$1,800-2,700

A bisque headed musical automaton figure of a standing girl, by Lambert, the head stamped Tête Jumeau, 18in (46cm) high.
$3,000-4,500

A bisque headed bébé, with jointed wood and papier mâché body, slight damage, stamped in red Tête Jumeau, shoes marked Bébé Jumeau Deposé, 17in (43cm) high.
$2,700-3,300

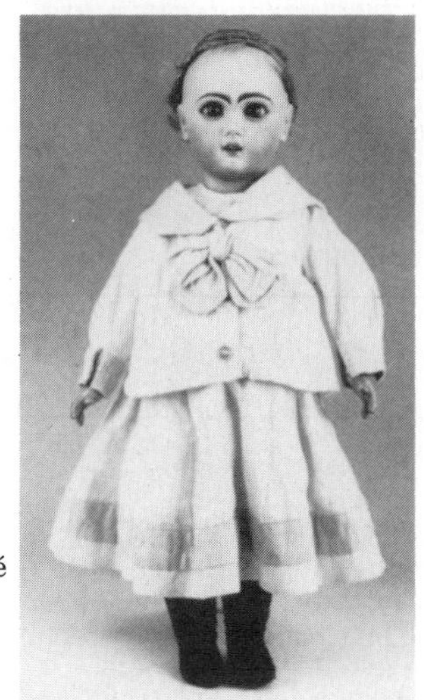

A bisque headed bébé, with jointed wood and papier mâché body, damaged, impressed 8, stamped in blue on body Bébé Jumeau, 19in (48cm) high.
$1,800-2,700

J. D. Kestner

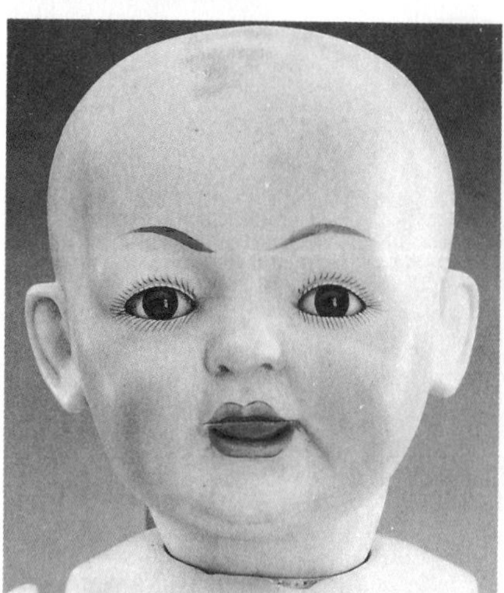

A bisque character doll, with curved limb composition body, probably by Kestner, German, c1897, 17½in (44cm).
$600-750

A bisque headed child doll, with jointed body and printed cotton outfit, impressed H 12 152, by Kestner. 22in (56cm) high.
$1,050-1,350

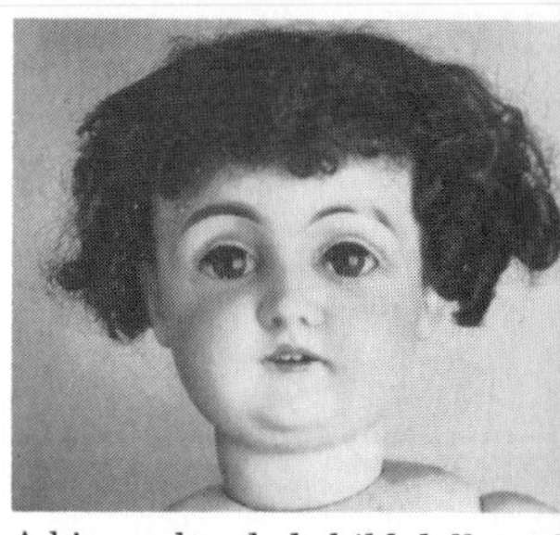

A bisque headed child doll, with jointed composition body, impressed L 15, by Kestner, 26in (66cm) high.
$750-900

Did you know?
MILLER'S Antiques Price Guide builds up year by year to form the most comprehensive photo reference library available.

Kammer & Reinhardt/ Simon & Halbig

A Kammer & Reinhardt bisque headed character doll, with jointed wood and composition body, replaced wig and clothes, incised 114/46, c1909, 16in (41cm) high.
$7,500-9,000

A Roullet et Decamps walking doll, with a Simon & Halbig bisque head, with key wind mechanism inoperative, incised RD, c1890, 16½in (42cm).
$600-750

A swivel head bisque shoulder fashionable doll, with gusseted kid body, incised 0 to back of head, c1885, 11in (28cm) high, together with some extra clothes and accessories, and a Simon & Halbig bisque head character doll, incised 122/36, damaged, 14in (36cm) high. **$2,250-3,000**

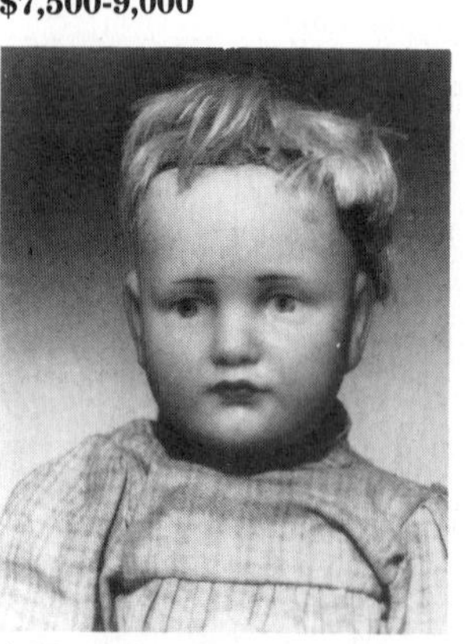

A bisque headed character doll, with jointed wood and composition body, Kammer & Reinhardt, 'Hans' incised 114/26, c1909, 10½in (26cm) high.
$2,250-3,000

A Kammer & Reinhardt/Simon & Halbig bisque headed doll, with composition jointed body.
$450-600

A Kammer & Reinhardt/Simon & Halbig, bisque doll, with ball jointed wood and composition body, impressed 117n 70, c1916, 27½in (70cm). **$1,500-2,250**

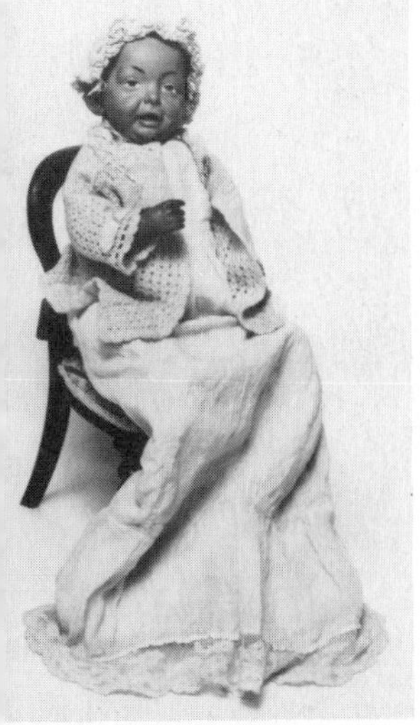

A black Kaiser baby doll, marked K * R 100, c1900, 14in (36cm).
$1,050-1,350

A bisque headed child doll, with composition jointed toddler body, impressed K*R Simon & Halbig 90, 34in (86cm) high.
$1,500-2,250

A pair of rubber headed character dolls, with cloth bodies and original clothes, embossed K*R Germany 873 30, 18in (46cm).
$900-1,500

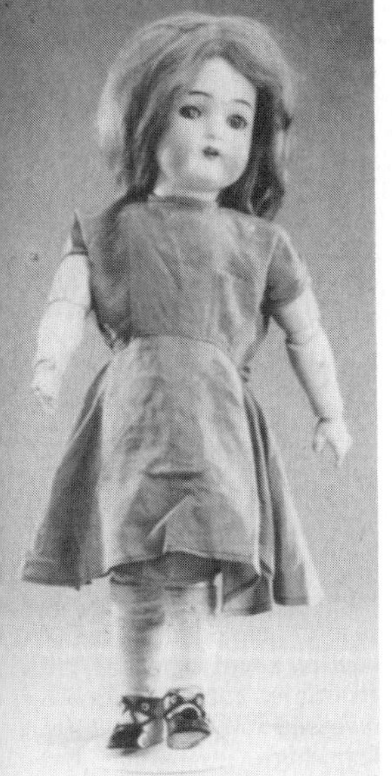

A Kammer & Reinhardt/Simon & Halbig, walking, talking bisque doll, with ball jointed wood and composition body, and voice box, impressed 403, c1910, 20in (51cm).
$750-900

A bisque headed child doll, with jointed wood and composition body, impressed Simon & Halbig K*R 70, 28in (71cm) and a red woollen dressing gown.

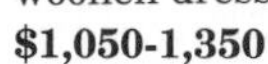

$1,050-1,350

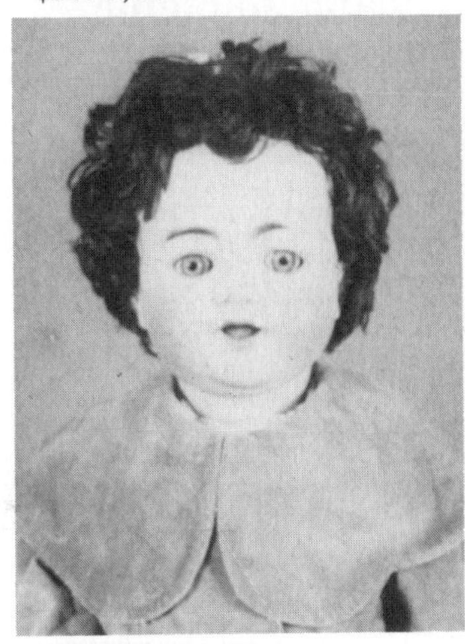

A Kammer & Reinhardt bisque headed character baby doll, with bent limb composition body, flirting eyes and quivering tongue, wig replaced, 126, with 3 spare dresses, c1920, 23in (59cm).
$450-600

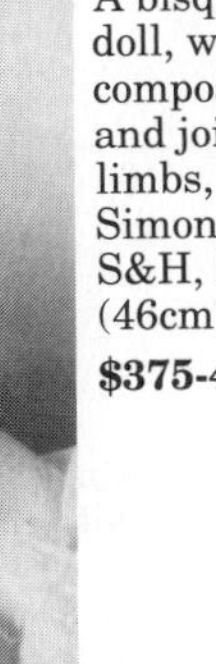

A bisque headed doll, with composition body and jointed limbs, marked Simon & Halbig, S&H, 8, 18in (46cm).
$375-450

Lenci

Two Lenci painted felt character dolls:
l. Wearing original frock and jacket, 165 Series, 25in (64cm) high, and 2 hats, **$600-750**
r. With mohair wig, wearing original frock, worn, probably 165 Series, c1930, 25in (64cm) high.
$375-525

Four Lenci felt dolls:
l. Dressed as a Russian, c1920, 18in (46cm). **$900-1,050**
c. back. Dressed as a German, c1920, 16in (41cm). **$900-1,500**
c. front. A black doll, c1920, 15½in (39cm). **$1,050-1,350**
r. Dressed as an Oriental, c1925, 24in (61cm). **$2,250-3,000**

A group of 4 Lenci dolls:
l. Dressed as a Dutch girl, c1930, 16½in (42cm). **$750-1,200**
c. back. Dressed as a Tyrolean, c1930, 16in (41cm). **$750-1,200**
c. front. Dressed as an Eastern European, c1930, 16in (41cm). **$750-1,200**
r. Dressed as a Dutch boy, c1930 18in (45cm). **$900-1,500**

Armand Marseille

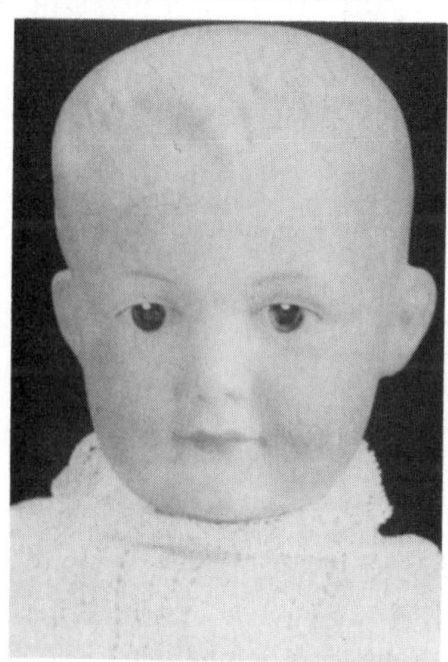

An Armand Marseille bisque character doll, with curved limb composition body, impressed 500 A3M, c1910, 12in (31cm).
$750-1,200

An Armand Marseille Oriental baby doll, 9in (23cm).
$750-1,200

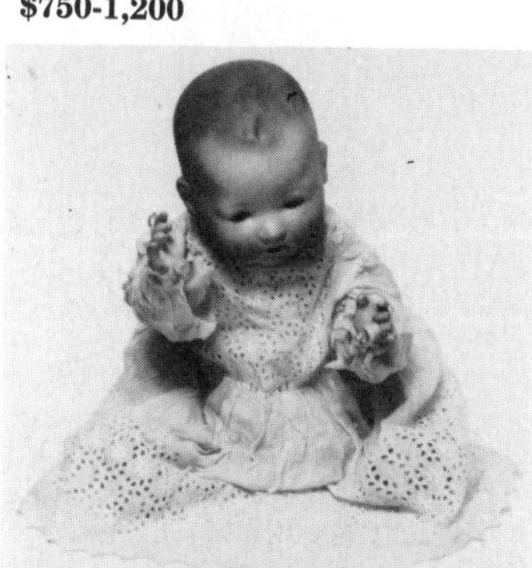

An Armand Marseille open mouth dream baby doll, c1915, 16in (41cm). **$150-225**

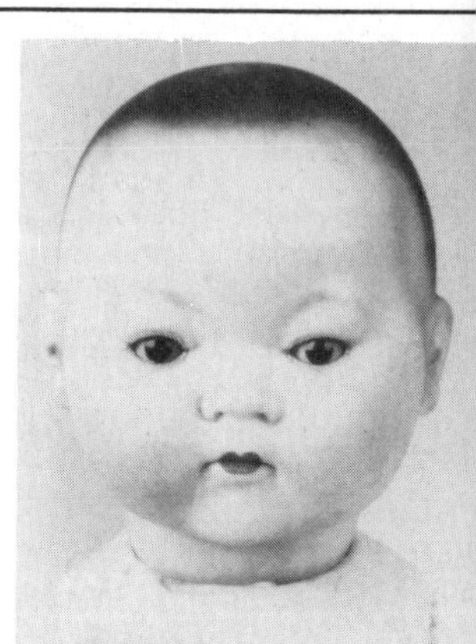

A bisque headed character doll, modelled as an Oriental, with bent limbed composition body, impressed AM 353/4K, 14in (36cm) high.
$1,200-1,500

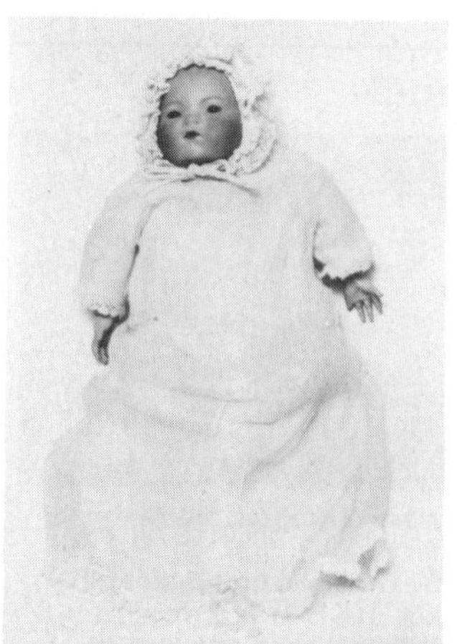

An Armand Marseille closed mouth Dream Baby doll, c1910, 14in (36cm).
$300-375

Two Armand Marseille bisque headed dolls, with composition jointed bodies:
l. Marked A9M-390, 26in (66cm) high. **$150-225**
r. Marked A3M-996, 15in (38cm) high. **$135-150**

An Armand Marseille doll, c1910, 9in (23cm).
$300-375

/liscellaneous

. cased doll, c1890, 18½in (47cm)
igh.
105-120

. case of small dolls, c1890, 6½in
16cm) high.
50-75

. set of Snow White and the Seven Dwarfs, all with
ainted felt heads, and Chad Valley labels,
now White 17in (43cm) high, the dwarfs 6½in
16cm) high. **$2,250-3,000**

An autoperipateticus walking doll, good working order, c1862, 9½in (24cm), in original box.
$450-600

Two German dolls, marked W&C, possibly Louis Wolf & Co, with fabric bodies, composition arms, both dressed in 1920s style clothes, 19in (48cm).
$300-375

A lace shop cased doll, c1890, 15in (38cm) high.
$150-180

An American clockwork animated store window display figure of a black boy, mechanism possibly replaced, early 20thC, 7in (18cm) high.
$1,200-1,800

A case of small dolls, c1890, 5in (13cm) high.
$50-75

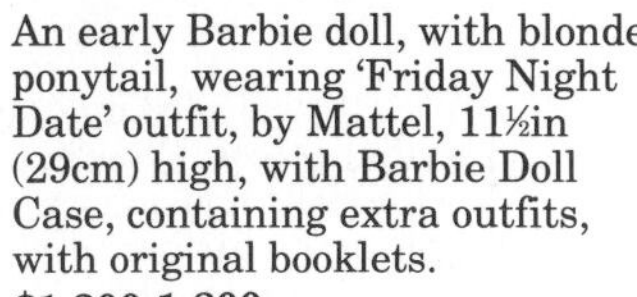

An early Barbie doll, with blonde ponytail, wearing 'Friday Night Date' outfit, by Mattel, 11½in (29cm) high, with Barbie Doll Case, containing extra outfits, with original booklets.
$1,200-1,800

An autoperipateticus clockwork walking doll, c1890, 9in (23cm).
$600-750

A German doll, modelled as an Oriental, c1910, 12in (31cm).
$750-900

An Ichimatsu doll, Japan, c1915 18in (46cm). **$225-255**

A turned and carved painted wood doll, wearing white frock, blue silk bonnet and red woollen slippers, early 19thC, 12in (31cm) high.
$1,800-2,700

A composition headed portrait doll, modelled as Shirley Temple, embossed 18 Shirley Temple Ideal N&T Cop, 18in (46cm) high, the box and dress with Reliable of Canada Shirley Temple label and name tag.
$900-1,500

A black painted doll's pram, needing restoration, late 19thC
$90-105

A pair of doll's riding boots, leather with wooden trees, 1½in (4cm) high.
$50-75

A set of felt headed Snow White and the Seven Dwarfs, all with painted felt faces, with Chad Valley labels, Snow White 16in (41cm) high, the dwarfs 6in (15cm) high.
$750-1,200

Dolls Houses

A set of tooled card miniature furniture and 3 similar pieces, French, late 19thC. **$750-9**
A set of dolls house furniture upholstered in purple and 4 further miniature pieces, French and Anglo-Indian, late 19thC. **$600-750**

A Napoleonic prisoner-of-war model of a Georgian house, designed as a casket with removable tray and roof, in stained pine with bone details, 12in (31cm). **$2,250-3,000**

A painted wooden dolls house, with set back alcove, original floor and wallpapers, curtains and blinds, 18½in (47cm) wide, pencilled number on base 983/1, with a bisque headed dolls house doll, 5in (13cm) high, and a group of blue upholstered furniture. **$750-1,200**

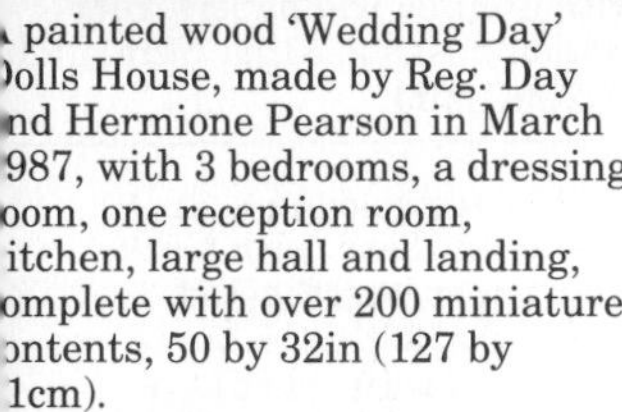

ι painted wood 'Wedding Day' ⟩olls House, made by Reg. Day ·nd Hermione Pearson in March 987, with 3 bedrooms, a dressing ·oom, one reception room, ·itchen, large hall and landing, ·omplete with over 200 miniature ·ontents, 50 by 32in (127 by 1cm). **2,700-3,300**

'his dolls house and its contents ·ere mentioned in articles in 'nternational Dolls House News', ιutumn and Winter 1986, Spring ·nd Summer 1987. Also Dolls Iouse World, issue No. 3 1989. 'his was sold on behalf of Save ·he Children Fund in September 992.

An architect designed and built mock Tudor dolls house, English, initialled AFB and 1932 on one side and AB 1929 on the other side, made by Sidney Brakspeare, younger son of W.H. Brakspeare, hinged panels in the roof and side opening to fitted interior, together with 12 bisque dolls house dolls and a large collection of contemporary furnishings, fixtures and accessories, late 1920s, 33 by 46 by 34in (84 by 117 by 86cm). **$1,500-2,250**

A painted wood dolls house, open on 3 sides, with 6 rooms and attic, with original wall and floor papers, Gottschalk, 25in (61cm) high. **$1,800-2,700**

A wooden dolls house, in the form of a town house, with front opening to reveal 4 rooms, slight damage, together with a quantity of furniture and effects, some damage, 30in (76cm) high. **$750-900**

Make the Most of Miller's

CONDITION is absolutely vital when assessing the value of an antique. Damaged pieces on the whole appreciate much less than perfect examples. However a rare, desirable piece may command a high price even when damaged.

A wooden dolls house, in the form of a traditional Hong Kong house, on 2 floors, carved façade, double front door and balcony, hinged side and rear openings, revealing staircases to each floor and roof, the flat roof with carved pierced gallery, c1920, with its wooden packing case.
$450-600

A wooden dolls house, in American family style, on 2 floors, the façade with porch, 2 bay windows and 3 with arched pediments, the hinged façade opening to reveal 4 rooms, mounted on wood base, together with a small quantity of furniture, 28½in (73cm) high.
$3,000-4,500

A painted wood toy poultry shop, with coloured flower transfer decoration and marble printed paper covered slab, by Christian Hacker, dated 1897, with original German pencilled number on base 152/1, 12in (31cm) wide.
$1,500-2,250

A group of Mexican dolls and artifacts, in 2 display cases, containing 6 dolls, with fabric covered soft bodies and painted features, mid-19thC, dolls 11½in (29cm) high, and an Indian hunter, a terracotta figure of a man and a similar figure of a woman, inscribed Ano 1857.
$750-1,200

A late Victorian wooden dolls house, in the form of a Villa, on 2 floors, opening to reveal 4 rooms, with original wallpapers, rear section missing, 31in (79cm) high.
$1,200-1,500

TEDDY BEARS

A Farnell golden plush covered teddy bear, with black glass eyes, cardboard-lined feet, swivel head, elongated jointed limbs, hump, growler and swing tag attached to chest, c1915, 14in (36cm) high.
$1,500-2,250

A Steiff honey golden plush covered teddy bear, with black boot button eyes, elongated jointed limbs, felt pads, hump and button in ear with remains of white label, c1908, 12in (31cm) high. **$1,800-2,700**

A plush hump back teddy bear, complete with original glass eyes, early 20thC, 13½in (34cm) high.
$180-225

An Edwardian early Steiff mechanical teddy bear, with button in the ear, boot button eyes, hand stitched nose and embroidered claws, 12in (31cm) high. **$750-900**

A Steiff golden honey plush
overed teddy bear, with black
oot button eyes, pronounced cut
nuzzle, black horizontally
titched nose, black stitched
nouth and claws, swivel head,
longated jointed limbs, felt paw
ads, hump and button in ear,
vorn and repaired, c1910, 12½in
32cm) high. **$900-1,500**
. A Steiff golden plush covered
entre seam teddy bear, with
lack boot button eyes,
ronounced snout, black stitched
ose, mouth and claws, swivel
ead, elongated jointed limbs, felt
ads, large paws and feet, and a
ump, damaged, c1910, 20in
51cm) high. **$1,200-1,500**
. A Steiff honey golden plush
overed teddy bear, with black
oot button eyes, pronounced
nout, black stitched nose, mouth
nd claws, swivel head, hump and
longated jointed limbs, repaired,
1910, 11½in (29cm) high.
$1,050-1,350

A cased 'Player's' bear, c1890, 15in (38cm) high.
$135-150

A set of Steiff plush covered bear ninepins, on turned wood bases, the king pin wearing a crimson felt covered robe and crown, 10in (25cm) high. **$3,000-3,750**

A Schuco bellhop Yes/No golden plush covered teddy bear, dressed in red felt jacket, black felt trousers and red felt cap, glass eye, swivel head, jointed limbs and cardboard-lined feet, damaged, c1923, 14in (36cm) high. **$900-1,500**

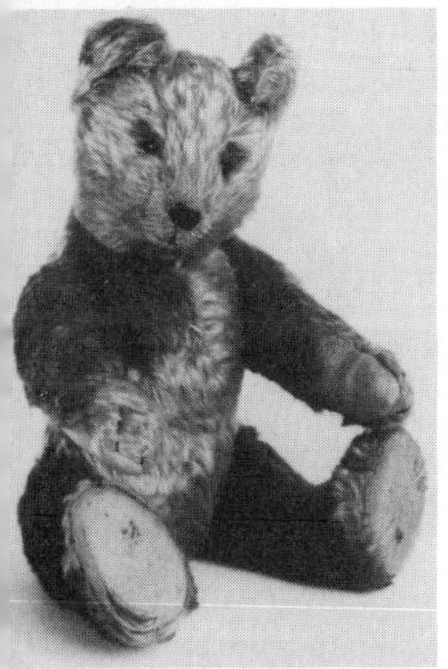

rich golden plush covered teddy
ear, with swivel head, jointed
mbs, curved paws, cardboard
ned feet, felt pads and hump,
3in (33cm) high.
600-750

A Gerbrüder Bing honey plush covered teddy bear, with black boot button eyes, pronounced snout, black horizontally stitched nose, black stitched mouth and claws, swivel head, elongated jointed limbs, felt pads and pewter button attached to side of body, c1914, 14in (36cm) high.
$1,800-2,700

An early Steiff golden plush covered teddy bear, with black shoe-button eyes, pronounced snout, remains of sealing wax nose, horizontal seam from ear to ear, black stitched claws, swivel head, elongated jointed limbs, felt pads, pronounced hump and metal rod jointing, slight wear, 1905, 19in (48cm) high.
$6,000-8,250

A German golden short plush covered pull-along bear, with black glass eyes, black stitched nose, mouth and claws, the bear modelled on all fours attached to metal frame, with four wooden wheels, repaired, c1915, 28in (71cm) long, and a hand coloured photograph of the bear with a former owner, framed and glazed, 46 x 26in (116.5 x 66cm).
$1,200-1,800

TOYS
Automata

A French bisque shoulder-headed automaton figure of an organ grinder, with closed mouth, fixed blue eyes, pierced ears, blonde wig, contemporary clothes and wooden base, c1880, 17in (43cm) high.
$2,700-3,300

A French gilt metal singing bird automaton, late 19thC, 22in (56cm) high.
$1,800-2,700

A French singing bird automaton with coin-operated mechanism, the bird with mottled brown plumage, contained in a gilt brass cage and on oak octagonal base with single drawer and foliate mounts, late 19thC, 23in (59cm) high.
$2,250-3,000

Slot Machines

A Buckley Bones 5c gambling machine, mechanical crap game with side play handle, two metal tables, jackpot, case painted red, c1935, 10in (25.5cm) high.
$3,000-4,500

A Jennings Rainbow 1c trade simulator, penny flip, with jackpot, glazed cast aluminium case, pinned blue flash, c1930, 20in (51cm) high.
$1,500-2,250

l. A Jennings 10c three reel Governor slot machine, the chromed front inset with orange plastic panels, marked for the Nevada Club Lake Tahoe, c1960, 27in (68.5cm) high.
$1,200-1,800
r. A Mills Castle 10c three reel slot machine, cast front with serial number 428135, painted red and blue, with oak sides and base, c1930, 26in (66cm) high.
$600-750

A Mills Automatic Dice 25c gambling machine, operating as a dice table game, with blue painted cast front with roulette form wheel, original stand, oak case, 6 coin slots correspond to numbers on wheel, c1935, 18in (45.5cm) high. **$4,500-6,000**

A Watling Rol-A-Top three reel 5c slot machine, gold award model with 2 column mint vendor, the decorative cast front brightly painted, with twin jackpots, top with 3 skill buttons, side play handle, restored by Squires and Corrie, mid-1930, 26½in (67.5cm) high.
$3,000-4,500

Make the most of Millers's

Unless otherwise stated, any description which refers to 'a set' or 'a pair' includes a valuation for the entire set or the pair, even though the illustration may show only a single item.

A Mills Chicago upright single heel slot machine, the oak case ith copper finish cast metal ements and legs, glass covering entral wheel reverse painted ith an image of the symbol of e city of Chicago, wheel with isible stop arm and ratchet heel, with 'Dewey' cast coin slots t top, restored, c1900, 66in 167.5cm) high. **$3,000-4,500**

A Wurlitzer Colonial jukebox Iodel 780, with maple case, heel motif to lower portion, lazed top, playing 24 selections, ith 5, 10, and 25 cent coin slides, 1940, 60½in (154cm) high. **3,000-3,750**

A Mills one wheel 'On the quare' upright slot machine, estored oak case with moulded elief details, cast metal details ncluding coin cup, coin slots, ront relief plaque, feet, mirrored anel in centre, upper portion vith coloured gambling wheel vith visible ratchet and stop arm, arly 20thC, 69in (175cm) high. **7,500-9,000**

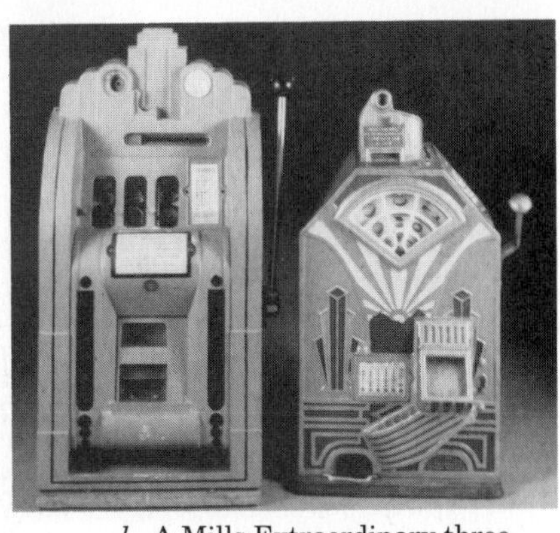

l. A Mills Extraordinary three reel bell slot machine, with 3 skill buttons, jackpot, side handle, front re-painted olive green and black, with oak sides, serial No. 417307, c1930, 29in (73.5cm) high.
$600-750

r. A Jennings Little Duke three reel 1c slot machine, reels visible in fan-shaped window at top, with jackpot win table, decorative cast front, side play handle, oak sides and base, front numbered 5946, c1930, 25in (63.5cm) high.
$1,050-1,350

A Jennings Peacock three reel 5c slot machine, with double jackpot, 2 column mint vendor, cast front painted black, gold and red, side play handle, oak sides and base, serial number 110366, restored by Squires & Corrie, San Mateo, California, c1932, 27in (68.5cm) high.
$5,250-7,500

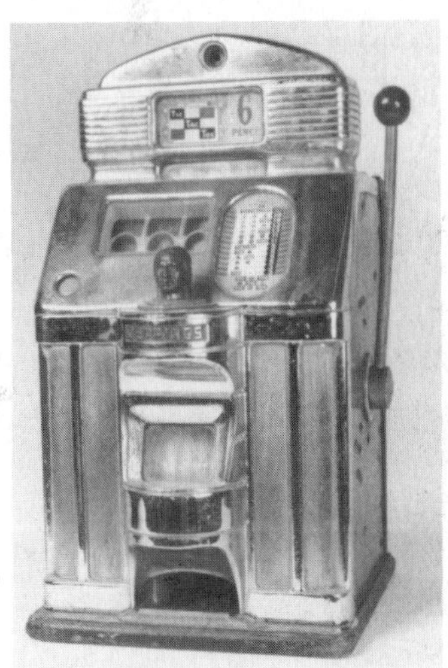

A Jennings chrome fruit machine, c1950.
$750-900

Mills Chicago one wheel pright slot machine, front everser painted with the emblem f the city of Chicago at the centre f the roulette type wheel, carved ak case with cast metal ecorative elements, coin slots, egs, jackpot, side carrying andles, play handle, restored, he case numbered 16725, c1900, 5½in (166cm) high.
$9,000-10,000

Rocking Horses

A child's Victorian cream and brown painted toy horse, 33in (84cm) long.
$135-150

A carved and painted pine horse pull-along toy, probably American, the stylised figure of a dappled grey horse with real horsehair mane and tail, leather ears and saddle, mounted on a platform with 4 cast-iron wheels, late 19thC, 28½in (72.5cm) long.
$1,800-2,700

A German hide covered skewbald trotting horse, with black mane and tail, remains of original leather saddle and bridle, mounted on wheeled red painted platform with detachable rocker base, damaged, c1910, 31in (79cm) high.
$375-525

A Victorian wooden rocking hors repainted white with black spots red corduroy and leather saddle, remains of bridle, mounted on black curved wood rockers, restored, 35in (90cm) high.
$600-750

A painted wood rocking horse, on trestle base, with saddle, leather reins and stirrups and remains of mane and tail, repainted, c1910, 44in (112cm) long.
$450-600

Transport

A hobbyhorse and wheel stand, early 19thC.
$750-1,200

An American carved and painted pine tricycle cart, with a horse's head, hand brakes, the seat painted with a yellow house on a red ground, mounted on 3 rolling red painted wheels, late 19thC, 37in (94cm) long.
$5,250-7,500

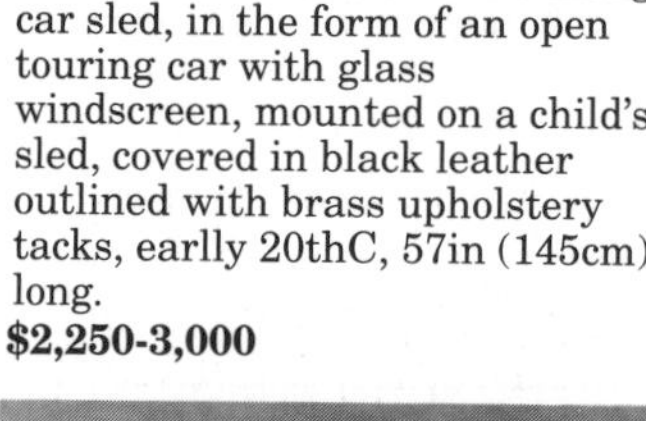

An American carved wood and leather child's two-seater touring car sled, in the form of an open touring car with glass windscreen, mounted on a child's sled, covered in black leather outlined with brass upholstery tacks, early 20thC, 57in (145cm) long.
$2,250-3,000

An American carved painted pine wrought iron child's sled, painted yellow with black pinstripes and signed in calligraphy 'LEWIS', on wrought iron runners, late 19thC, 22in (56cm). **$750-900**

An American carved painted pine and wrought iron child's sled, the sled painted red with yellow pinstripes, the runners painted green with stencilled initials 'I.J.T.', with stellate devices, late 19thC, 37in (94cm) long.
$1,800-2,700

An Allwin two-seater pedal car, with wooden chassis, wood and metal body, chain drive, radially spoked wire wheels with rubber tyres, fold-flat windscreen, opening doors, wood rimmed steering wheel, hand claxon horn petrol can, dummy instrument panel, radiator mascot, original leather cloth upholstery, dark blue finish with black wings, restored, c1920, 64in (162cm) long. **$7,500-9,000**

A veteran pedal car, wood with metal fittings, chain drive and rat trap pedals, wood artillery-type wheels with rubber tyres, wood rimmed steering wheel, adjustable seat, imitation ventilator, yellow and black with blue interior, black and red lining repaired, one tyre missing, c1905, 38in (96.5cm) long.
$2,700-3,300

An Auburn double cowl
ıaeton child's pedal car, with
›el body painted in brown, beige
d white, chrome details, brown
ıther seats, windscreen, steel
ıeels with pneumatic tyres,
adlights, adjustable spotlight,
ınnet ornament, double pedal
›adle propulsion, restored,
935, 55in (140cm) long.
,500-6,000

An SSJ Duesenberg pedal car,
ve grey and red exterior with
rome details, including
ndscreen, headlights, radiator
p, spoked wheels, rubber white
ıll tyres, spare tyre, brown
ıther interior, steering, front
d back bumpers, running
ards, treadle drive pedals,
nulated gauges on dashboard,
stored, c1935, 58in (147cm)
ng.
5,000-18,000

A Bentley 4½ litre pedal car, with steel chassis and body, treadle drive, wire spoked wheels with pneumatic tyres, headlamps with stone guards, external break lever, fabric covered body, bucket seat, louvred bonnet, imitation hood, British Racing green with tan upholstery, c1980, 56in (142cm) long.
$3,000-3,750

l. An Auburn double cowl Phaeton child's pedal car, with steel body painted dark maroon and wine red, chrome details, disc wheels with solid black rubber tyres, front bumper, boot at back, 2 seats with black leather upholstery, windscreen, cast steering wheel, single front pedal treadle power, c1932, 62in (158cm) long.

r. A Durant pedal car, with grey and black metal body with chrome details, black leather seat, treadle pedal motion, steel disc wheels with solid black rubber tyres, windscreen, luggage rack, side vents, steering wheel, spare wheel, radiator cap, 'Durant' written over radiator, restored, late 1920s, 42½in (108cm) long.
$6,000-8,250

A Toledo bi-wing pedal plane,
› steel body painted bright
llow, red wings and tail, lined
ange, chromed propeller, disc
ıeels with black rubber tyres,
dals, steering wheel adjusting
ıaller rear wheel, restored,
915, 41in (104cm) long.
,250-3,000

A Toledo Falcon pedal plane,
› steel body painted yellow with
l wing and tail fins, black
pporting struts, cast steering
ıeel, double disc wheels with
ıck rubber rims, treadle pedal
ɔpulsion, restored and
painted, c1930, 63in (160cm)
ng.
,200-1,500

Austin A40 pedal car, c1940.
00-750

A Ferrari Testarossa child's motorised two-seater car, by Agostini, Series No. 042, with steel chassis, fibreglass body, Briggs & Stratton 5hp single cylinder engine with V-belt drive to rear axle, cast aluminium wheels with pneumatic tyres, leather rimmed steering wheel, speedometer and rev. counter, upholstered bucket seats, opening rear panel to give access to engine, coil spring independent suspension, self starter and pull start, hydraulic disc brakes, forward and reverse gears, electric lights, pop-up headlamps, horn, rack and pinion steering, Ferrari red with cream upholstery, 1987, 114in (290cm) long.
$10,500-12,000

A Lines Bros Vauxhall pedal car, wood and sheet metal, treadle drive, wire wheels with solid rubber tyres, leaf springs, opening door, dummy instrument panel, damaged, c1935, 54in (138cm) long.
$1,050-1,350

A scratch built Bugatti Type 35 child's electric racing car, with steel chassis, fibreglass body, electric motor with chain drive to rear axle, radially spoked wire wheels with pneumatic tyres, wood rimmed steering wheel, aero screen, working front suspension, external brake lever operating brakes to rear wheels, French blue body with silver wheels and brown upholstery, English, 1960s, 62in (158cm) long.
$2,250-3,000

A Mercedes-Benz S.S. 38/250 one-third scale child's motorised car, with steel chassis, steel and aluminium body, 50cc Honda petrol engine with 3 gears driving rear axle, wire spoked wheels with pneumatic tyres, working lights, horn, fold flat windscreen, imitation engine, opening bonnet, external exhaust pipes, rack and pinion steering, dummy shock absorbers, rear mounted spare wheel, disc brake, cream body with red leatherette interior, chrome plated radiator grille, lights and wheels, c1990, 72in (183cm) long.
$7,500-9,000
This model was specially commissioned as a 'one off'.

A ½ scale model of a Morris Minc convertible child's car, with fibreglass body, 50cc transmissic drive to rear axle, disc type wheels with pneumatic tyres, folding hood, electric lights, almond green, 68in (173cm) long
$2,250-3,000

A Lines Bros Vauxhall pedal car, wood with metal bonnet and wings, wire spoked wheels with pneumatic tyres, headlamps, dummy instrument panel, brown finish, requiring restoration, c1935, 54½in (139cm) long.
$750-1,200

An Austin J40 Roadster pedal ca c1950.
$900-1,500

Tinplate

A Märklin clockwork painted tinplate four-wheel 'steeplecab' locomotive, V1022, finished in grey and black with straw lining, white rivets and red window frames, with opening doors and headlamp, damaged, c1904.
$2,250-3,000

A Carette clockwork lithographed tinplate limousine, finished in red with white lining and gold detailing, with reverse gear and lever, lever-operated brake, opening doors, chauffeur, glass windscreen and detailed interior, damaged, c1913, 12½in (32cm) long. **$1,800-2,700**

A Lehmann AHA delivery van, EPL 550, lithographed in red an yellow with cream lining, blue uniformed driver, opening rear doors, front steering and spring motor, damaged, c1910, 5in (13.5cm) long.
$600-750

A Günthermann clockwork painted and lithographed tinplate closed four-seat tourer, with bellows action, steering, jockey wheel brake, headlights and white rubber tyres, damaged, c1908, 8½in (21.5cm) long.
$1,500-2,250

Miller's is a price GUIDE not a price LIST

An American carved and painted pine and tin touring car, with 4 men seated inside, and a carved and painted pine toy soldier, early 20thC, car 17½in (44.5cm) long.
$1,500-2,250

A German tinplate saloon car, probably by Bub, lithographed in burgundy and black, with details including headlamps and sidelamps, handbrake, toolbox, hinged passenger doors, clockwork mechanism to rear axle, lever operated brake to rear wheel, early 1920s, 10½in (27cm) long.
$2,250-3,000

CIJ clockwork painted tinplate
lfa Romeo P2 Racing Car,
nished in blue, racing number 2,
ith operating steering and
andbrake, dummy drum brakes,
nock-on hubs, 'Excelsior' shock
osorbers and crank handle,
amaged, c1927, 21in (53cm)
ng, and a key.
1,500-2,250

A Bing tinplate saloon car, with clockwork mechanism, damaged, 15in (38cm) long.
$600-750

A Bing tinplate and clockwork limousine, finished in yellow with red lining, black roof, pressed tin balloon tyres, liveried chauffeur, 14½in (37cm) long.
$1,200-1,500

CIJ clockwork painted tinplate
lfa Romeo P2 Racing Car,
nished in turquoise, with
perating steering and
andbrake, damaged, c1928, 21in
3cm) long.
3,000-3,750

An Arnold clockwork armoured car, with matchstick firing guns, grey camouflage lithography, inserted driver, and another with large aerial, WH196, German, both late 1930s, both 9½in (24cm) long. **$900-1,500**

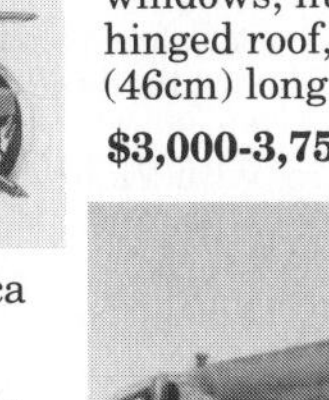

A Victory pull-along limousine sweet tin, lithographed in green and black, with passengers to windows, number plate VCL.A1, hinged roof, damaged, c1915, 18in (46cm) long.
$3,000-3,750

A Märklin 1108 G armoured constructor car, finished in camouflage colours, with rotating turret, front steering and clockwork motor, damaged, c1930, 15in (38cm) long.
$1,800-2,700

Günthermann tinplate Sedanca
e Ville, lithographed in dark
reen with black roof and light
reen lining, with blue uniformed
hauffeur, opening rear doors and
pring motor, damaged, c1920,
0in (25cm) long.
750-1,200

A JEP Delage tinplate saloon car, finished in maroon with lighter lining, black roof and running boards, headlamps and spotlamp, adjustable front axle, pressed tin wheels, steering wheel, gear lever and clockwork motor, damaged, c1920, 13in (34cm) long.
$750-900

Marx lithographed tinplate
harlie McCarthy and Mortimer
nerd Private Car, American,
1939, 16in (41cm) long.
1,050-1,350

A Märklin painted tinplate swimming bath, Cat. Ref. 1207, damaged, c1900, 17in (43cm) long.
$750-1,200

A Lehmann clockwork lithographed tinplate Adam the porter, EPL No. 689, with sack trolley and trunk.
$900-1,500

l. A Marusan battery powered tinplate Cadillac car, No. 2203, cream with a dark green roof, damaged, c1950, 12in (31cm) long, with original box.
$750-1,200
r. A Schuco Mercedes 2205 Convertible Elektro Hydrocar, No. 5720, battery powered, cream with red upholstery, in original box.
$600-750

A Bing tinplate gauge O Railzeppelin', damaged, c1934, 11in (28cm) long.
$375-525

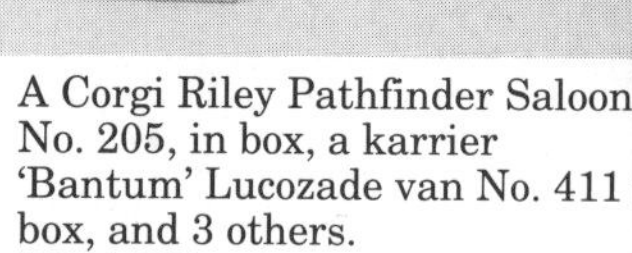

A Corgi Riley Pathfinder Saloon No. 205, in box, a karrier 'Bantum' Lucozade van No. 411 in box, and 3 others.
$225-255
A Dinky Pullmore Car Transporter, No. 982, in box, and a Triang Mini Series 2 Road Roller.
$135-150

A collection of Dinky Toys, including a No. 923 Heinz Bedford Van, No. 943 Leyland Octopus Esso Tanker, No. 967 BBC TV Control Room, in original boxes. **$750-1,200** and a collection of Dinky Toys, including No. 501 Foden Diesel Wagon, No. 504 Foden Tanker, No. 555 Fire Engine, No. 582 Transporter with ramp, No. 47 Road Signs, No. 771 Road Signs, and No. 27K Hay Rake, all in original boxes.
$750-1,200

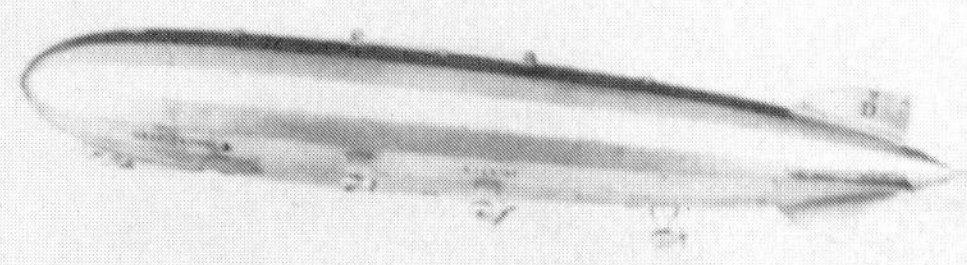

A Märklin clockwork painted tinplate Graf Zeppelin Airship D- LZ 127, Cat. Ref. 5406, with five underslung engines and forward cabin, damaged, c1937, 16in (41cm) long.
$1,050-1,350

A Bing clockwork painted tinplate Plunging Pike, Cat. Ref. 8412, damaged, c1906, 14½in (37cm) long.
$600-750

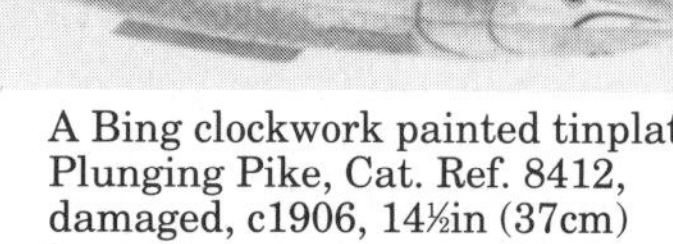

A Schuco clockwork lithographed tinplate and fabric Fox with Goose in Basket, No. 969, Clown with Violin, No. 986/2, a Monkey Drummer, No. 985/1, and a Mouse.
$600-750

An A.B.M. tinplate ferris wheel, German, damaged, c1910, 10in (25cm) high.
$375-525

A Harper Hoop-La mechanical bank, English, chipped, c1920, 8½in (21.5cm) long.
$600-750

A Lehmann painted tinplate and fabric Dancing Sailor, EPL No. 535, with Brandenburg cap tally, with swaying action, in original box.
$600-750

A Schuco clockwork tinplate and fabric figure, possibly religious representing St. Peter, damaged, c1930.
$375-525

liscellaneous

painted wood Noah's Ark, with
pproximately 70 painted wooden
nimals and 8 figures, Sonneberg,
6in (41cm) long.
1,200-1,800

A painted wood Noah's Ark, damaged, German, mid-19thC, 20in (50cm) long.
$600-750

painted wood Noah's Ark, with
iding side and animals including
eavers and leopards, Sonneberg,
te 19thC, ark 21in (53cm) long.
,200-1,800

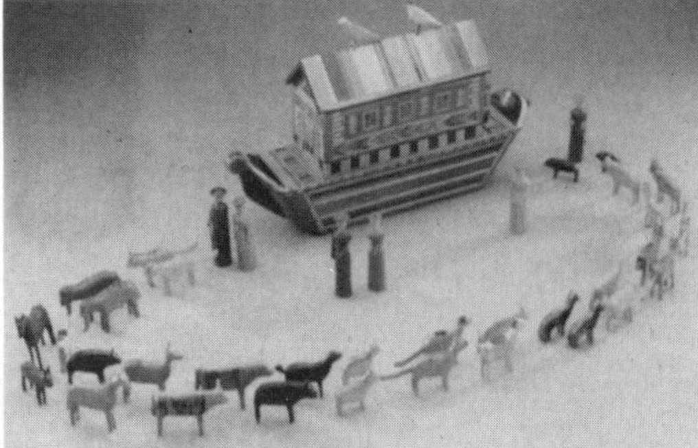

A small straw work Noah's Ark, with 6 figures and 62 painted wood animals, German, c1900, ark 9½in (24cm) long.
$1,200-1,800

painted wooden Noah's Ark,
id-19thC, 14½in (37cm) wide,
d a print of 3 children playing
ith the same ark.
1,800-2,700

A Dinky Toys Railway Accessories Set No. 3, Railway Passengers, and Set No. 4 Engineering Staff, in original plain grey boxes, dated '6-40', 1940, and 2 other figures.
$600-750

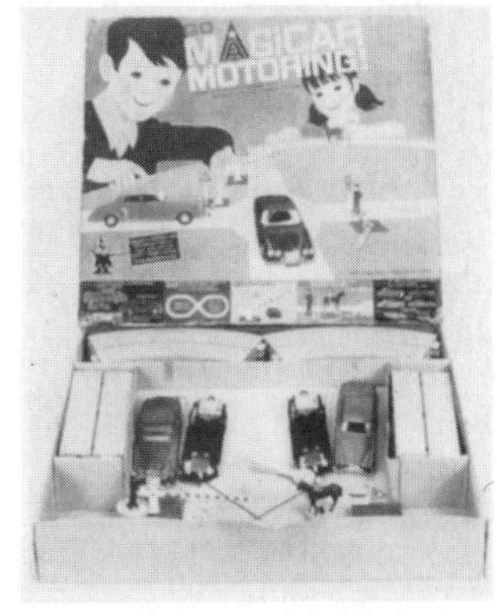

A Spot-On Magicar battery operated Set No. MG2, containing a plastic green Jaguar Mk10, and a red Rolls-Royce Silver Cloud, in original box, c1965.
$300-375

n Erzgebirge market place,
ight damage, German, in
riginal box, box 9½in (24cm) long.
750-1,200

A hollow-cast toy cavalry, including Scots Greys, Dragoons, Indian Lancers, Hussars, and Infantry, including Plughanded Highlanders, Japanese and others, by W. Britain.
$375-525

Three finger puppets.
$90-105

Five French glove puppets, heads 6in (15cm) high.
$375-450

A Mickey Mouse doll, Regd. No. 750611, repaired, early 20thC, 13in (33cm) high.
$375-450

A Steiff Peter Rabbit, button in ear, wearing original blue felt jacket, c1910, 8in (20cm) high.
$375-450

A Mickey Mouse doll, Regd. No 7500M, c1930, 7½in (19cm) high
$225-300

A Tamany William 'Boss' Tweed cast iron novelty money bank, 6in (15cm) high.
$375-525

A Corgi Toys shop display stand, with 7 cream and blue metal shelves revolving around a central column, with trade mark top and black wooden base, each model affixed and with numbered and priced label, c1960, 34in (86cm) high.
$3,000-3,750

A Dean's Rag Book Company velveteen Dismal Desmond, in seated position with red felt tongue, 1926, 6in (15cm) high.
$300-375

A Schuco mascot poodle, swivel head and jointed limbs, 1950, 2½in (6.5cm) high, and another.
$300-375

. collection of Rosenthal
'hunderbird's models, c1960, in
riginal boxes.
720-1,000

. Chad Valley Noddy toy tea set, c1956.
180-225

A large quantity of Meccano parts, Meccano clockwork motor and instruction booklets.
$750-900

A Corgi Gift Set 40, The Avengers, comprising John Steed's vintage Bentley, and Emma Peel's Lotus Elan S2, with figures and 3 umbrellas, in original display box.
$4,500-6,000

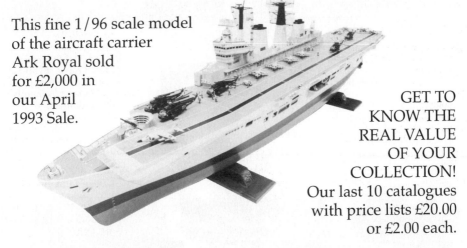

Chess Sets

An American carved and painted wood chess set, the pieces as various solders of World War I, 20thC, figures 5½in (14cm) high.
$2,700-3,300

A Chinese stained ivory chess set, in a black and gold lacquered fold-over case, in a leather travelling case.
$1,050-1,350

An English pre-Staunton style rosewood and lightwood chess se 19thC.
$135-150

MODELS
Rail

A gauge I three-rail electric model of the MR Class 2P 4-4-0 locomotive and tender No. 483, converted from clockwork, by Bing for Bassett-Lowke, damaged, 21in (54cm) long.
$750-1,200

A two-rail electric model of the DR Class 96 0-8-0 and 0-8-0 articulated side tank locomotive No. 96 021, with original external fittings and original paintwork, by Bockholt for Fulgurex, damaged.
$3,000-4,500

A Bing painted tinplate spirit-fired 'stork-leg' type locomotive and tender, with early trademar on smokebox, a Second Class coach, in original box, and a quantity of track, a funnel and pan, c1902, and a later lithographed LNWR Open Wago 4123. **$1,200-1,800**

A three-rail electric model of the GNR Atlantic 4-4-2 locomotive and tender No. 251, converted from clockwork, by Bing for Bassett-Lowke, damaged, 23in (59cm) long.
$1,050-1,350

Miller's is a price GUIDE not a price LIST

A hand built gauge O electric 4-6-0 locomotive, No. 6167, finished in LNER green livery with matching six-wheeled tender.
$375-525

The prototype live steam spirit fired model of the GNR Stirling Single No. 1, built by Bassett-Lowke Railways Ltd, c1968, 20in (50cm) long.
$2,700-3,300
Limited edition No. 3156/5000 Bassett-Lowke Railways Catalogue commemorating the Flying Scotsman's Tour of the USA, 1969.

A collection of American outline twin bogie box freight cars, by J. & M. Models Ltd.
$1,200-1,500

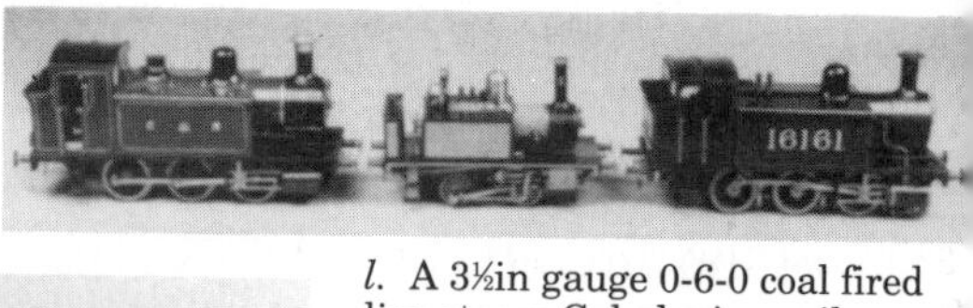

l. A 3½in gauge 0-6-0 coal fired live steam Caledonian railway tank locomotive. **$750-1,200**
c. A 3½in gauge 0-4-0 coal fired live steam tank locomotive 'Gladys'. **$750-1,200**
r. A 3½in gauge 0-6-0 coal figured live steam Caledonian Railway tank locomotive, No. 16161.
$750-1,200

The LNWR Jumbo 2-4-0 No. 860 Merrie Carlisle, no motor, and the Whales 4-6-0 No. 1990 North Western, and the Webb 2-4-2 coal tank No. 2524, painted and lined by A. Brackenborough.
$300-375

two-rail electric model of the Union Pacific ailroad 4-8-0 and 0-8-4 articulated locomotive ıd tender No. 4023 'Big Boy', with original xternal fittings in original paintwork, by Aster r Fulgurex, No. 38/45, some minor damage,)in (127cm) long. **$5,250-7,500**

A Hornby gauge O electric Princess Elizabeth locomotive and tender, in original LMS maroon livery and original box, c1936. **$2,700-3,300**

quantity of gauge O railway ems, including a Hornby six-volt ectric 4-4-0 Bramham Moor comotive, 2 LNER coaches, ullman brake composite and ırriage, parts of a Hornby Flying cotsman, and rolling stock. ;,250-3,000

A two-rail electric model of the DB Class 01 4-6-2 locomotive and tender No. 01 173-4, by Aster for Fulgurex No. 46/50, 1981, 30in (76cm) long. **$2,250-3,000**

A Märklin gauge II handpainted tinplate bogie L&NWR guard's passenger full brake, wheels replaced, c1902. **$1,200-1,800**

A Märklin for Gamages gauge I spirit fired 4-4-2 North British Atlantic locomotive and tender, No. 4021, and matching six-wheeled tender, on display track, c1913. **$2,250-3,000**

3½in gauge static model of a 4-6-0 L&NWR comotive 'Experiment', with six-wheeled tender, ıounted on a section of track on a wooden base. **1,200-1,800**

A live steam gas fired model of the K Bay Sts B Class 52/6 4-4-4 locomotive and tender No. 3201, by Aster for Fulgurex, No. 81.100, 1981, 26½in (67cm) long. **$2,700-3,300**

The GWR 0-6-0 pannier tank No. 1568, and the 45xx Class 2-6-2 side tank, both unpainted brass, by Samhongsa and Doujin. **$150-225**

The CR 4-6-0 No. 903 Cardean, the NBR 0-6-0 No. 706 and the NER Z Class 4-4-2 No. 127, all professionally painted and lined. **$120-135**

The LNER (ex-NER) Class Z 4-4-2 No. 2164, the ex-GCR Raven Atlantic 4-4-2 No. 6101 and the GNR Ivatt small boiler 4-4-2 No. 259, all professionally painted. **$300-375**

The LB & SCR Baltic 4-6-4 side tank No. 328 Charles C. Macrae, painted and lined by A. Brackenborough and the SR Class J1 4-6-2 side tank No. 325, professionally painted.
$150-180

A Bing gauge I 4-6-2 clockwork locomotive, with matching eight- wheeled tender, diner, passenger carriage and brake van, together with a gauge I LNER Third Class brake composite, a Midland guard's van and LNWR van. **$1,800-2,700**

Sea

A builder's mirror-back half model of the armed single screw cargo ship SS Newminster Abbey, built by Tyne Iron Shipbuilding Company Ltd., Willington Quay-on-Tyne for Messrs. Fisher Renwick & Co., Newcastle-on-Tyne, finished in pink, black, white and varnish with gold plated fittings and mounted on front silvered mirror, in original mahogany case, 52½in (133.5cm) long.
$10,500-12,000

An electric powered ½in:1ft scal wood and glass model of the Nigerian River launch Teal of Lagos, on a stand, 51in (129.5cm long.
$450-600

A French prisoner of war bone and horn model of a 100-gun ship of the line, mounted on a parquetry base with 4 carved bone feet, restored, early 19thC, 10 by 12in (25 by 31cm).
$10,500-13,500

A builder's half block model of the SS Elettrico of Palermo, built by Alexr. Steven & Sons, Ship Builders and Engineers, Glasgow, Yard No. 306, 1887, finished in varnish and black with gilded scroll bow and stern decoration, 76in (193cm) long.
$3,000-4,500

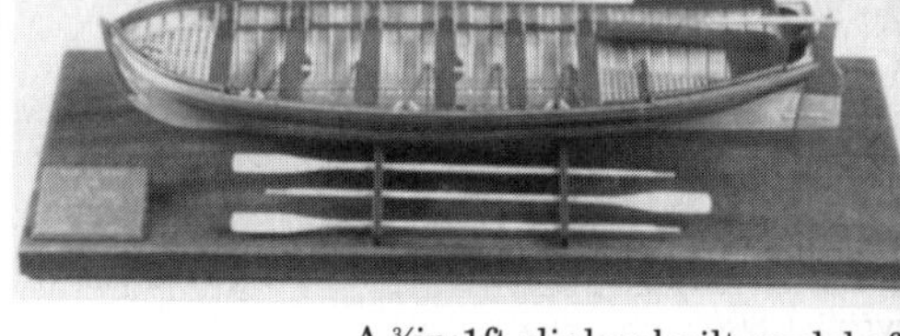

A ¾in:1ft clinker built model of a man-o'-war yawl, built by R. Phillips, finished in varnish, contrasting woods and white to the waterline and mounted in a cradle with oars displayed, with certificate, on a display base, c1800, 21in (54cm) long.
$2,250-3,000

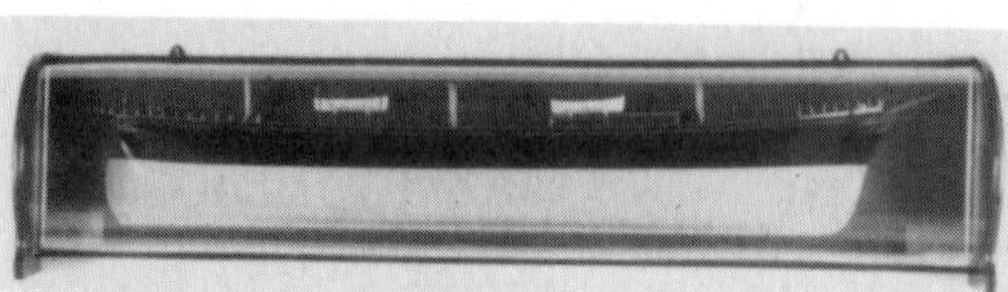

A builder's half model of the three-masted cargo sailing ship yacht No. 118, built by W. Doxford & Sons, Shipbuilders and Marine Engineers, Sunderland, finished in light brown to the waterline, black, white and varnish, in glazed case, 67in (170cm) long.
$4,500-6,000

A rigged wooden model of the four-masted barque Viking of Mariehamm, of c1907, on a stand, in a glazed oak showcase, 31½in (80cm) long.
$600-750

Viking of 2670 gross tons was built by Burmeister and Wain, Copenhagen, for Gustav Erikson.

wood and metal static display)del of R.M.S. Titanic, the hull ıished in red, black, white and llow, with 3 shafts and opellers and mounted on 2 rned wood columns, on a splay base, 72in (183cm) long.
,250-3,000

A display model of the harbour tug Hercules owned by the Boston Towboat Company, the hull fitted with single screw and rudder, finished in green, black, red and grey and mounted on 2 turned columns, on inlaid mahogany base and brass bound glazed case, 10½ by 15½in (26 by 39.5cm).
$1,050-1,350

A waterline display model of the Thames spritsail barge Nelson of London, built by W. H. Cook, mounted on a painted moulded seascape, in a glazed case, 15 by 14½in (38 by 37cm).
$450-600

fully planked and framed spirit ed live steam sailing model of e river launch Lady of the Lake, cluding oil can, hammer, anners, fire irons and tools, hull ıished in green, white and rnish, 39in (99cm) long.
,250-3,000

A fully planked and framed wood and brass model of the 37ft 6in Rother Class lifeboat J. Reginald Corah, No. 37-31, built by N.W.B. Portlock, the hull fitted with twin three-bladed propellers, lifting rudder, slipway skids, fenders, anchor and bow fender, finished in R.N.L.I. livery with gilded letter, on a stand, 40in (101cm).
$2,250-3,000

A fully rigged and planked model of H.M.S. Victory, built by I. R. Aitken, with open gun ports in the hull, a carved stern and quarter gallery detailing, finished in natural wood with gilded decoration, on a stand in a mahogany glazed case, 35 by 49in (89 by 124.5cm).
$1,500-2,250

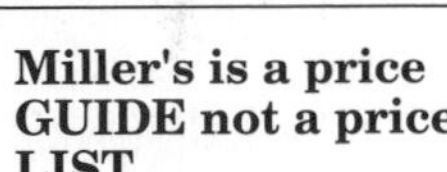

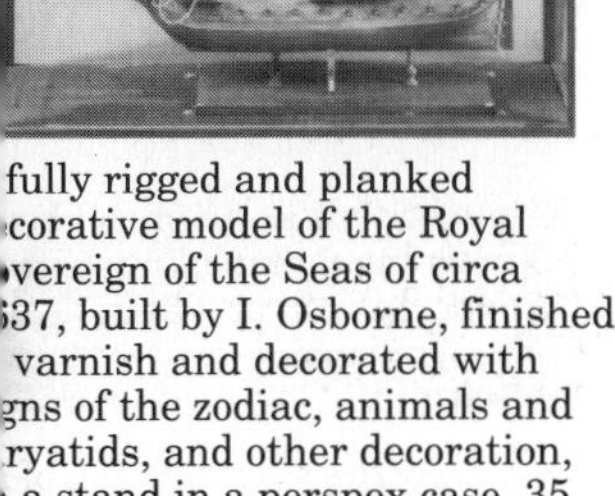

fully rigged and planked corative model of the Royal vereign of the Seas of circa 537, built by I. Osborne, finished varnish and decorated with gns of the zodiac, animals and ryatids, and other decoration, a stand in a perspex case, 35 40½in (89 by 103cm).
750-1,200

planked and framed model of a oman warship of circa 50BC., ilt by J. Robinson, in a glazed se on a stand, 38in (96.5cm) ng.
,050-1,350

A static scale display model of the Norwegian barquentine Jutta of Holmerstrand of c1890, built by K. Britten, the hull with decorated bow and transom, simulated plating and planked bulwarks, finished in green and white, mounted on a slipway, on inlaid wood base, in a glazed case, 18in (46cm) long.
$2,700-3,300

A 1:24 scale planked and framed fully rigged model of the Belgian yawl rigged pilot cutter No. 2 Astrid of Oostende, built by K. Britten, finished in pink, black, blue, and varnish, with white sails, on a stand, 40½ by 48in (102 by 122cm).
$1,500-2,250

A carved, partially planked, fully framed, unrigged model of a third rate of 70 guns of c1700, built by P. Rumsey, finished in black and natural wood with flower and foliate decoration, in a glazed case, 27in (68.5cm) long.
$1,800-2,700

A 25ft:1in scale wood and metal waterline model of the single screw brig-rigged iron steamship Clan Alpine of 1878, built by R. Wilson, with documentation, in a glazed ca with a fitted carrying case, 17½in (44.5cm) long. **$900-1,500**

A display model of the America paddle steamer MT Washingto mounted on 2 turned columns a wood base, in mahogany glazed case with satinwood inlay, with opening doors, locks and table with tapered legs on raised pan 30 by 72in (76 by 183cm).
$3,000-4,500

Air

A metal display model of the Lockheed C-5A Galaxy of Military Airlift Command, with stand, 18in (46cm) wingspan, and a pewter model of an F14 in original packing.
$150-180

An uncovered ⅛th scale wood, plastic and metal static display model of a Sopwith Camel FI., finished in varnish with polished cowlings, 42in (106.5cm) wingspan.
$1,500-2,250

A very detailed uncovered ⅛th scale mainly wood and metal static display model of a Fokke DRI., finished in varnish and polished brightwork, 36in (91cm wingspan.
$2,700-3,300

A very detailed uncovered ⅛th scale mainly wood and metal static display model of an SE5a., finished in green and varnish, 40in (101.5cm) wingspan.
$1,200-1,800

A detailed flying scale model of a Blackburn monoplane, finished i clear dope and silver, 55½in (141cm) wingspan.
$750-900

A flying scale model of the Bleriot monoplane No. 23, finished in white and varnish with Swiss markings, built by A. McKay, 104in (265cm) wingspan.
$450-600

A detailed flying scale model of a FE.8, Serial No. 6411, finished in RFC camouflage, 94in (239cm) wingspan.
$2,700-3,300

No. 6411 was originally built by Darracq Motor Engineering Ltd.

detailed flying scale model of an E.5A Serial No. B4615, built by McKay, with fabric covered ooden airframe with dummy cing, finished in RFC amouflage, 80in (203cm) ingspan.
900-1,500

A flying scale model of a Bleriot XI monoplane, finished in varnish and clear dope, 108in (274cm) wingspan. **$900-1,500**

A detailed flying scale model of Messerschmitt Bf 109 F-4 Werke No. 7629, of 10JG.2 with wooden airframe, flying and control surfaces, canopy with armoured windscreen and instrument panel, dummy radiator, oil cooler and exhaust stubs and retractable rubber tyred undercarriage, finished in Luftewaffe camouflage, 63in (160cm) wingspan.
$1,800-2,700

detailed flying scale model of a iemens Schuckert D.IV single eat, with fabric and wood overed wooden airframe, finished lozenge and olive green amouflage, 55in (140cm) ingspan.
2,250-3,000

A fine and detailed flying scale model of the Hansa Brandenburg KDW D.I. single seat bi-plane, Serial No. 28.60, finished in cream and varnish, 56½in (143.5cm) wingspan.
$750-900

A flying scale model of a Sopwith Taperwing Camel, with twin dummy machine guns and fitted with single cylinder glow-plug engine, 42in (107cm) wingspan.
$750-900

detailed flying scale model of de avilland DH 82 A Tiger Moth, erial No. DF-1AB RCO-U, nished in RAF yellow livery, 5in (165cm) wingspan.
750-900

A fine and detailed flying scale model of Siemens Schuckert D.IV single seat fighter, Code No. LO!, finished in lozenge camouflage, orange and silver, 83in (211cm) wingspan.
$1,800-2,700

partially complete flying scale odel of an SE5A, the uncovered ooden airframe with rubber yred undercarriage, working ontrol surfaces flying and control ires, windscreen, dummy rocker overs and propeller, finished in arnish, 79in (201cm) wingspan.
600-750

A detailed and well finished flying scale model of the Antonov An 2, Reg letters SP-ANC, finished in cream, red, white and pale blue lining, 84in (213.5cm) wingspan.
$1,200-1,800

WEATHERVANES

A moulded copper American eagle weathervane, probably New England, in a green painted wood pedestal base, weathered to an all-over verdigris, some repaired bullet holes, late 19thC, overall height 72in (183cm).
$2,700-3,300

An American moulded copper Goddess of Liberty weathervane, mounted on a rod secured in a white painted pine pyramid base, weathered with verdigris, some repairs, early 20thC, 82in (208cm) high overall. **$7,500-9,000**

An American carved and incised pine Fish weathervane, mounted on a rod on a painted pine base, c1900, 35in (89cm) long.
$2,250-3,000

An American carved and painted pine Angel Gabriel weathervane, probably New England, mounted on a wrought-iron rod above a carved pine ball, the whole on a black metal base, late 19thC, 22in (56cm) long.
$4,500-6,000

An American painted copper horned cow weathervane, mounted on a rod supported in a white wood standard, 25in (63.5cm) wide.
$1,800-2,700

An American moulded copper and zinc 'folky' prancing horse weathervane, weathered to an all-over verdigris with some repaired bullet holes, late 19thC, 35in (89cm) long.
$3,000-3,750

A moulded copper and zinc running horse weathervane, probably by Harris & Co., Boston, Massachusetts, mounted on a rod on a black metal base, with old yellow polychrome and traces of original gilding, late 19thC, 43in (109cm) long.
$7,500-9,000

An American moulded and gilde copper rooster weathervane, probably New England, weathered to an all-over verdigr with touches of gilding, late 19thC, 46in (118cm) high overal
$2,250-3,000

An American painted sheet-iron rooster weathervane, red with traces of original gilding, body and tail riveted together, 19thC 19½in (49.5cm) long.
$2,700-3,300

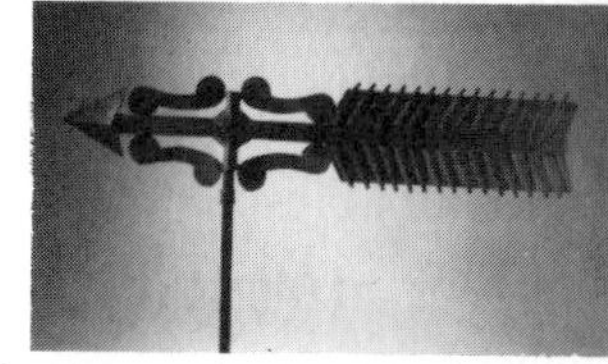

An American moulded and painted copper arrow banner weathervane, the shaft with shee copper curlicues and ridged tail terminating in a moulded arrow head with traces of gilding and old yellow paint, late 19thC, 49in (125cm) long.
$2,250-3,000

An American small-scale moulded and gilded copper standing horse weathervane, standing on an arrow directional, covered in gilding, late 19thC, 20½in (52cm) long. **$1,200-1,800**

ARMS & ARMOUR
Armour

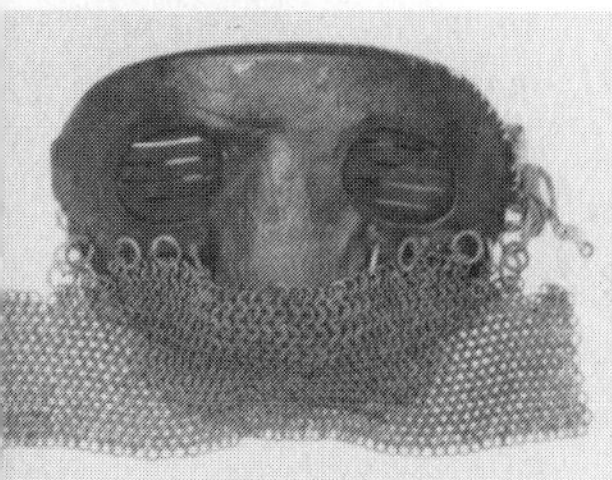

WWI tank driver's anti-shrapnel mask, leather covered with eye slits, chain mail skirt, securing ribbons and original label stating 'The curvature of this mask may be adjusted to your face by slightly bending'.
$225-300

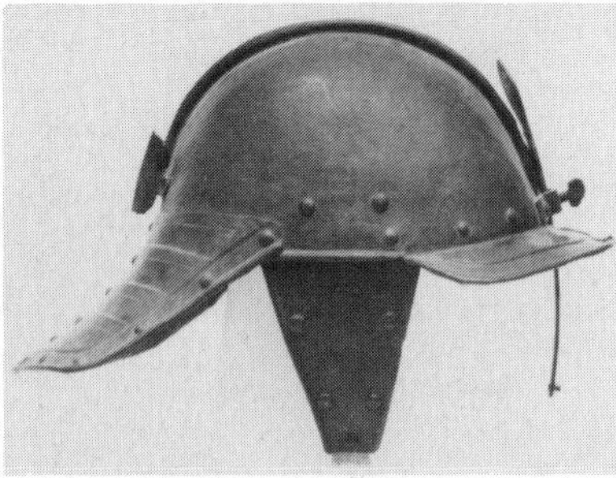

A Cromwellian trooper's lobster tail helmet, the skull and peak formed in 2 halves with low comb, armourer's mark to peak, sliding nasal bar secured by thumbscrew, plume socket at rear of skull, one piece neck guard, well restored ear flaps.
$1,500-2,250

A Cromwellian-style lobster pot helmet with face guard, 19thC.
$225-300

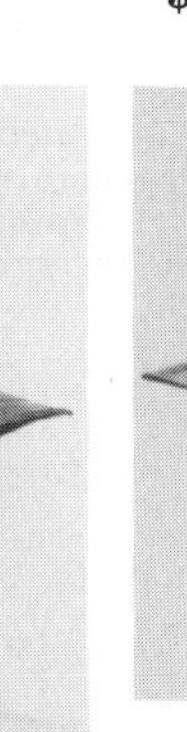

A burgonet, forged from one-piece iron, with peak and pierced ear flaps, late 16thC, 13in (33cm) high.
$500-750

A Cromwellian lobster tail helmet, one-piece skull embossed with 6 radial flutes, neck guard decorated with plain iron studs and retaining original leather lined inner borders, adjustable nasal bar with wing nut securing screw, pierced ear flaps, restored, with an iron wall mounting bracket.
$1,050-1,350

An Indian khulah khud, the one-piece bowl chiselled overall with flowering foliage having gold damascened borders, the edge chiselled with silver, twin plume sockets, sliding nasal bar with palmette finials, tall top spike all gold damascened en-suite, the camail of butted rings with some copper rings for decorative effect, c1800. **$1,200-1,500**

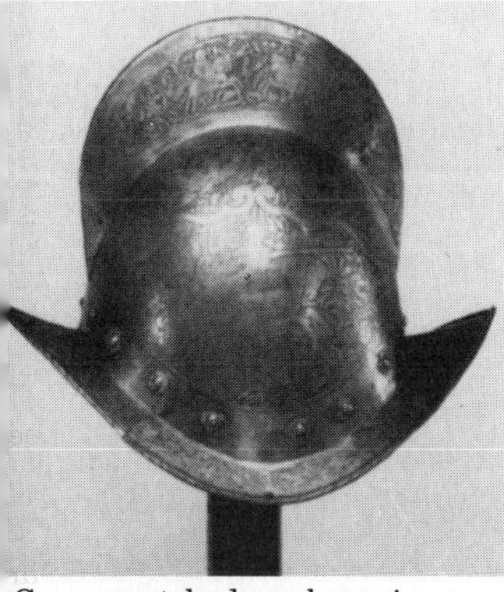

A German etched comb morion, with one-piece skull rising to a cabled comb, the base with a row of lining rivets each with pewter rosette shaped washer (some incomplete), the brim struck with Nuremberg mark and maker's mark MR conjoined and turned and roped at the edge, late 16thC, 11in (28cm) high.
$2,250-3,000

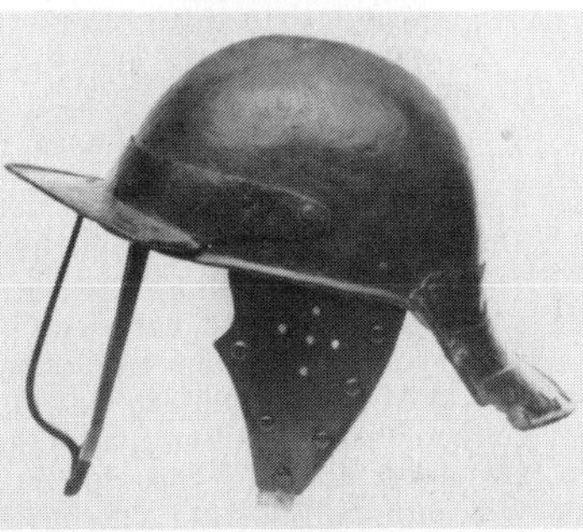

A Cromwellian trooper's lobster tail helmet, the skull formed in 2 halves with overlapping join, hinged peak stamped with initials 'IH', triple bar face guard, one piece neck guard, shaped 'Roman Style' ear flaps.
$2,250-3,000

A German lobster tail pot helmet, with bowl shaped skull formed in one piece and embossed with 5 radial ribs, pointed peak with turned edge and pierced for the moveable nasal bar, neck guard of 4 upward lapping cusped lames, and pierced cheek-pieces, the surface blackened throughout, late 17thC, 9in (23cm).
$1,200-1,800

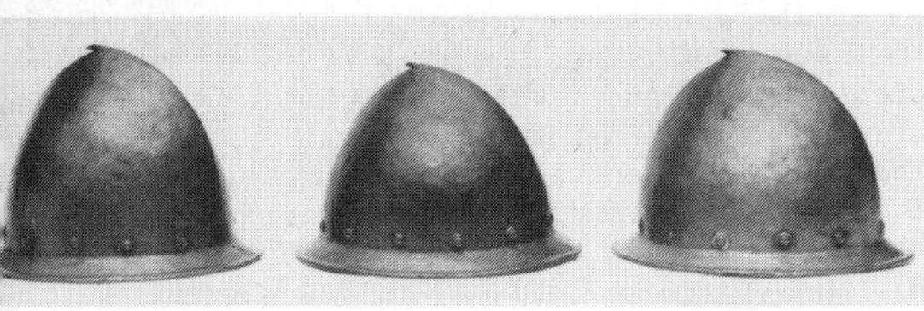

Three cabasset helmets, each formed in one piece, pear stalk finial to crown, brass rosettes, some damage, c1600.
$225-300

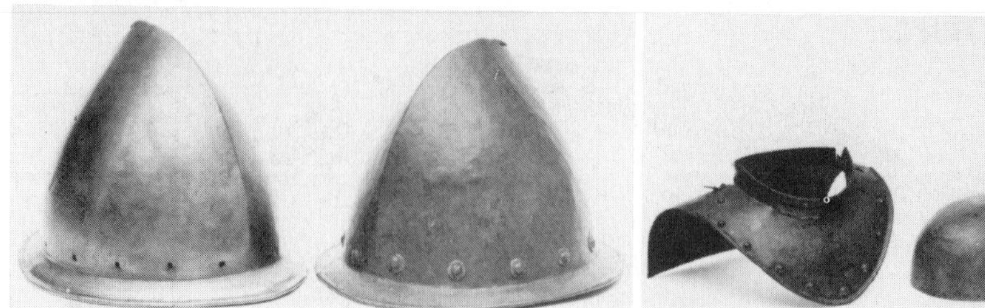

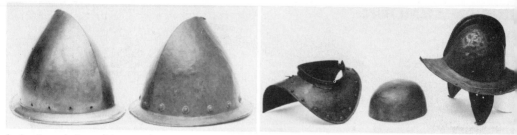

l. A cabasset, formed in one piece, 'pear stalk' finial to crown, brim struck with armourer's mark of a crowned shield containing 3 trees, c1600. **$225-300**
r. A cabasset, formed in one piece, 'pear stalk' finial to crown, brass rosettes around base, c1600. **$150-180**

l. A two-piece gorget, front plate with roped edge and later rivetted border, back with straight roped edge, roped edge to neck, keyhole and stud fastening, probably 17thC. **$225-300**
c. An English Civil War period steel hat liner 'secret' of simple skull cap form, brim pierced for sewing inside a Royalist hat, small slot for suspension thong. **$450-600**
r. A pikeman's pot, the skull formed in 2 halves with raised comb and recessed border to brim restored ear flaps, mid-17thC. **$1,800-2,700**

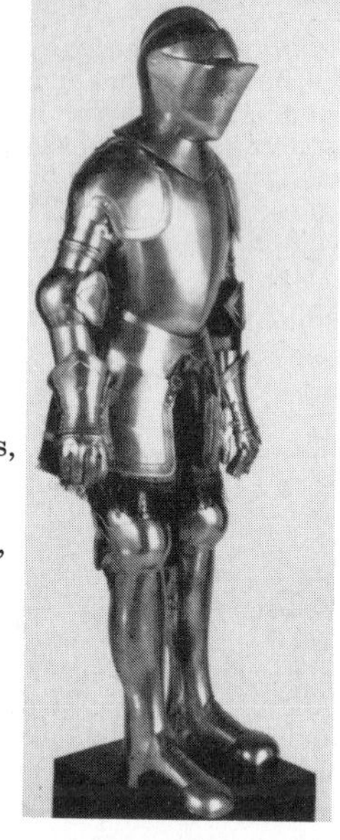

A child's full armour, well detailed and articulated throughout, including hinged visored close helmet, fingered gauntlets and bear paw sabatons, the edges turned and roped throughout, mounted on a dummy, together with a halberd, late 16thC style, 53½in (136cm) high. **$3,000-3,750**

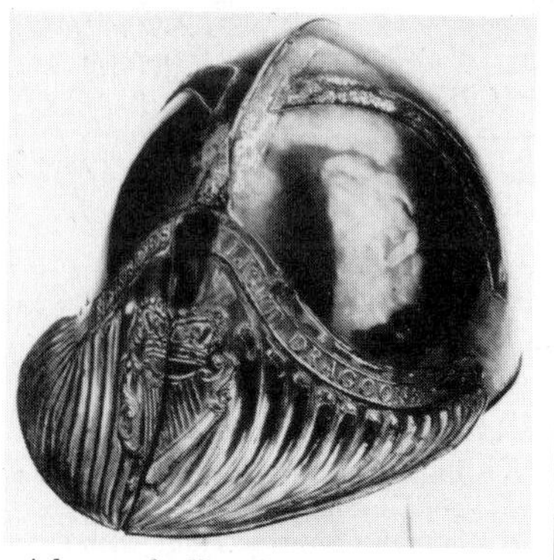

A brass skull and front plate with peak of a very rare Irish volunteer cavalry helmet, the front plate with repoussé title scroll Newtown Ardes Light Dragoons above the crowned female Harp which extends down on to the fluted peak, the skull formed in 2 halves with curved iron reinforcing bands of slightly rounded section extending up towards the top seam, the interior coated with black lacquer, minor repairs, c1780.
$5,250-7,500

This unit, called variously the Newtownard Light Dragoons and the Newtownard Troop of Horse, is known to have been in existence in 1783 and it may have been raised as early as 1778 along with the Newtown Ards Infantry (1778-92) but such very small local units (probably only Troop strength) are often not recorded in great detail. The graceful and distinctive shape of this helmet may possibly have been inspired by a French design of c1770 for Dragoons.

An Italian infantry breast plate, formed with medial ridge with 3 articulated lower plates each cusped at the centre and carrying a skirt of one plate, turned and roped at the neck and moveable gussets and with recessed borders, c1560, and a gorget for wear independent of armour, early 17thC.
$2,700-3,300

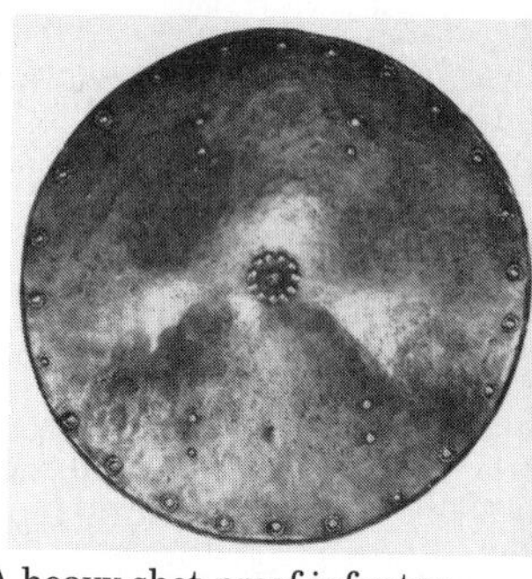

A heavy shot-proof infantry shield, of circular convex form, with raised flanged edge, struck with Nuremberg mark and maker's mark, 2 initials above a figure, studded with lining rivets with decorative brass washers, and fitted with small faceted onion-shaped boss on a decorative steel washer, damaged and restored, late 16thC, 22in (56cm) diam. **$3,000-4,500**

A German full armour, in late Gothic style, well made throughout, including visored sallet, bevor attached to the breast-plate by a staple, fully articulated arm and leg defences, the sabatons fitted with spurs and decorated throughout with sprays of fluting and pierced ornament at the edges, mounted on a dummy, together with a rapier, in 16thC style.
$15,000-22,500

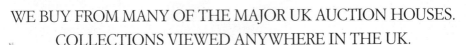

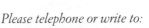

An Italian composed half armour, mainly early 17thC.
$10,500-13,500

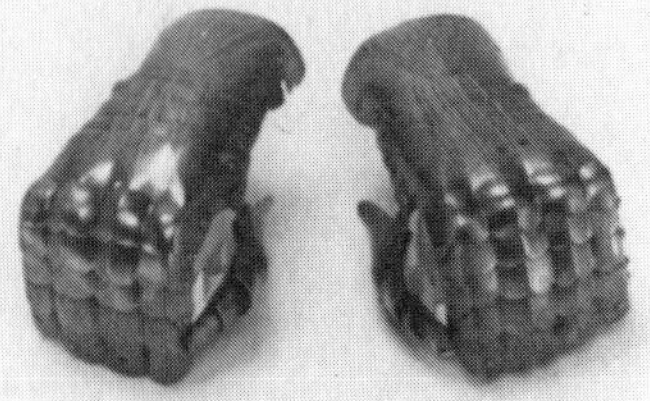

A pair of German composite mitten gauntlets, each comprising short cuffs with recessed border and embossed with chevron pattern of fluting, articulated metacarpus of 5 plates, embossed with differing pattern of fluting and embossed for the ulna, articulated embossed fluted knuckles and finger defences with cusped edges and hinged articulated thumb defences, repaired, c1510, 9in (23cm).
$4,500-6,000

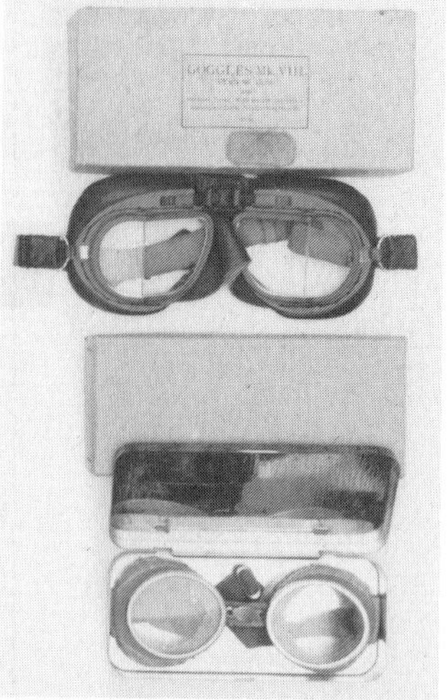

top A pair of RAF goggles, Mk VIII, with spare reflective pattern spare lenses, in their original cardboard carton, with printed caption. 1940. **$105-120**
bottom A pair of WWII dispatch rider's goggles, in original issue packet and tin dated 1944.
$50-75

An American silver-mounted parade saddle, by Edward H. Bohlin, Hollywood, California, made for Martinka Ballrooms Inc., Mamkateo Minnesota, with the cantle fully encased in silver and chased with flowers and scrolls, the horn embossed with a buffalo mask, and the seat and upper fenders finely tooled with rose foliage, the jockey and skirt entirely covered with chased shaped silver plaques, and including matching breast plate, reins and enclosed stirrups, c1930. **$15,000-18,000**

A pair of Mexican large iron stirrups of so-called 'Conquistador' type, of characteristic T-shaped form, decorated throughout with pierced and low relief patterns of flowers and scrolls, and the upper wings fitted with brass globular finials at the corners, 18thC, 18in (45cm).
$3,000-3,750

A French cuirassier's helmet, repaired, and a companion brea and back plate, heavy breast plate, the back plate with brass shoulder chain fastenings and leather retaining strap, plain brass stud decoration, mid-19th
$1,050-1,350

Headdress

An Edward VII officer's lance cap of The 12th (Prince of Wales's Royal) Lancers, in tin case, with name plate 'WR Styles Esq., 12th Royal Lancers', (Lt. 3.1.09), together with good scarlet feather plume in gilt flame socket, in tin case.
$4,500-6,000

A Victorian officer's black patent leather helmet of the Queen's Own Worcestershire Yeomanry, worn c1850-71, with silver plated mounts, including comb with ventilated sides, chin chain and lion's head ear bosses, gilt helme plate on a silver plated back plate, red and white hair plume screw fitted to the top of the comb, damaged.
$900-1,500

An other rank's rifle green ıako of The Cameronians, black ıtent leather peak, plaited cord ıd acorns trim, blackened bugle)rn badge and mullet on cord ›ss, leather chin strap, black ıir plume, leather lining, WD amp for 1912. **$225-300**

A Victorian officer's blue cloth ›iked helmet of the 3rd ınarkshire Rifle Volunteers, ith silver plated mounts, leather ıcked chin chain and ear ›settes, helmet plate, leather ıing, worn. **600-750**

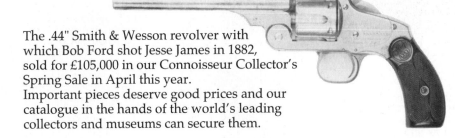

l. An officer's feather bonnet of The Argyll and Sutherland Highlanders, red and white diced wool headband, 6 tails, silver plated badge on rosette, white feather plume, leather chin strap, leather and silk lining, damaged. **$600-750**

r. A cuirassier's steel helmet of the Garde de Paris, with brass peak binding, minor damage. **$1,050-1,350**

The 4th Battalion Oxfordshire and Buckinghamshire Light Infantry seized this helmet in the 1914-18 war.

An Imperial German Garde du Corps Fahnrich's helmet, tombak skull stamped inside 'B.H. Osang Dresden, 1915', German silver helmet plate with part enamelled centre, front and rear peaks lined with red cloth, peak German silver trim mount stamped 'K', neck guard stamped '56'. **$4,500-6,000**

l. An Imperial German Prussian M 1897 pickelhaube, as worn by Guard Infantry or Railway Battalions, white metal helmet plate, removeable spike and mounts, both cockades, leather lining and chin strap.
$375-450
c. A scarce Imperial Prussian other rank's lance cap (tschapka), with silvered line eagle helmet plate, leather backed brass chin scales, leather lining, damaged.
$600-750
r. A Prussian Infantry Reserve Senior NCO's pickelhaube, with brass eagle helmet plate with white metal Landswehr cross, leather backed chin scales and mounts, both cockades, leather and silk lining.
$375-450

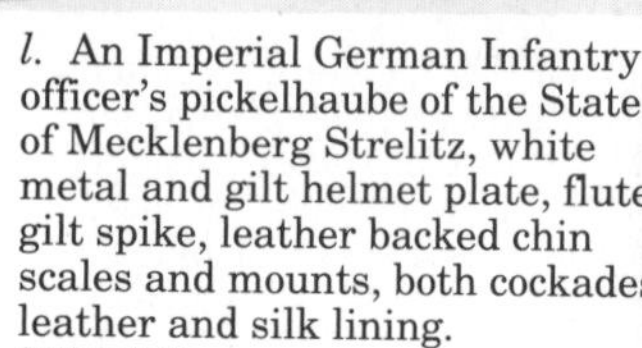

l. An Imperial German Infantry officer's pickelhaube of the State of Mecklenberg Strelitz, white metal and gilt helmet plate, flute gilt spike, leather backed chin scales and mounts, both cockades leather and silk lining.
$600-750
r. An Imperial Austrian army officer's shako, gilt Imperial eagle helmet plate, bullion cockade wit 'FJI' cypher, bullion cloth band, bullion embroidered peak, silk and leather lining, damaged.
$150-225

A British Consular white Wolseley helmet, retailed by Army & Navy Co-operative Stores, with narrow cream leather chin strap and both the undress white dome mount and alternative gilt spike with acanthus base and detachable gilt Royal Arms badge, in its metal case marked G.H. Selous 24.
$375-525

A bearskin cap properly constructed to boy's size, pierced to receive a plume on either side, with patent leather lining to the graduated brass chin chain, and a Welsh Guard's other rank's plume, an NCO's peaked forage cap of the Irish Guards dated 1962, and another of the Coldsteam Guards, dated 1965.
$2,700-3,300

A feather bonnet of the Black Watch, with four 'tails' of black ostrich feather and with wool dicing bearing other rank's pattern regimental badge and 9in red feather hackle and with crimson leather internal headband impressed with maker' name Marshall & Aitken, Edinburgh and an other rank's full dress Kilmarnock, of small size, of heavy dark blue nap cloth with red tourie and diced band with black bow at back and black rosette at side to which is fastened a refitted black cock's feather, and KC King's Own Scottish Borderers badge, bonnet lining bearing W.D. broad arrow and issue marks for January 1913. **$300-375**

l. An RAF officer's barathea service dress cap of Air Rank, with gilt bullion embroidery badge with gilt eagle, peak heavily gilt embroidered, worn by Air Vice Marshal H. N. Thornton, with a studio photograph of the officer wearing the cap.
$105-120
r. A Victorian officer's rifle green peaked drill cap of the 4th Berkshire Rifle Volunteers, embroidered badge, silver wire embroidered peak, braid piping to crown, black oak leaf mohair band, inside of peak marked 'E. Morland', with black oilskin foul weather cover.
$300-375

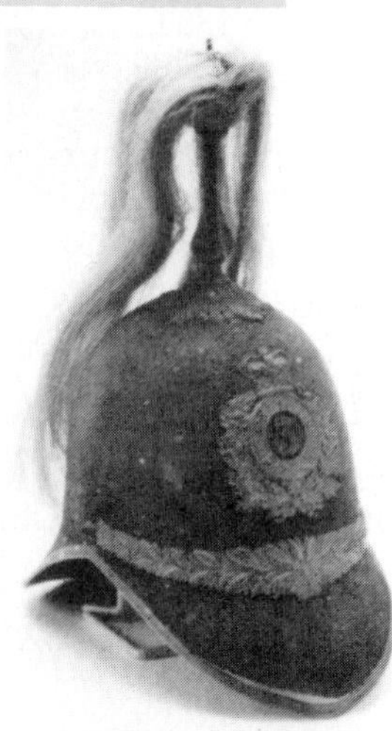

A Victorian black cloth plumed helmet of the 3rd Devon Light Horse, with red and white horsehair plume, Queen's Crown badge with garter and oak leaf border, similar strapwork and plain brass rim, hand written label with the name Pearse, chinstrap missing.
$2,250-3,000

An other rank's pattern busby ' the Queen's Own Oxfordshire ussars with Mantua purple bag, immed with Russia braid, the ısby encircled with triple white ord lines below the white corded ɔss at front and retaining ırnished white metal chin chain, hite over Mantua purple hair lume with white metal socket nd ring and red leather label nside crown) of The S & W lilitary Equipment Corporation td., London, all contained in a etal headdress case.
225-300

A cloth helmet of the 1st xfordshire Light Horse olunteers, trimmed with white etal including comb, rose bosses etaining a velvet-lined chin ıain, edging to patent leather ront peak (no trim), and QVC rown above the badge.
1,200-1,800

Jniform

ιn officer's full dress uniform tems of the Shropshire Yeomanry 'avalry, and a pair of blue veralls, all by Hawkes & Co., 14 'iccadilly, with gold oak leaf lace tripes in metal uniform trunk to I. R. Williams, Esq.
$2,250-3,000

n 1890 Henry Rupert Williams late Lieut. 3rd Bn. Shropshire ight Infantry) was a 2nd Lieut. n the Shropshire Yeomanry.

Miller's is a price GUIDE not a price LIST

A collection of Battle of Arnhem red beret medals, identity tags and field jacket of Staff Sergeant Dudley Pearson, with material relating to him and to the battle.
$1,050-1,350

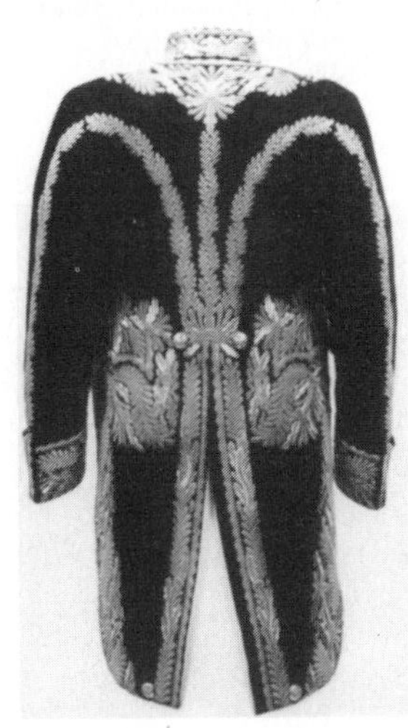

A Field Officer's old style mess jacket of the Westmoreland and Cumberland Yeomanry, scarlet with white facings and trimmed with silver lace, a peaked cap, and a small watercolour attributed to Percy Reynolds.
$450-600

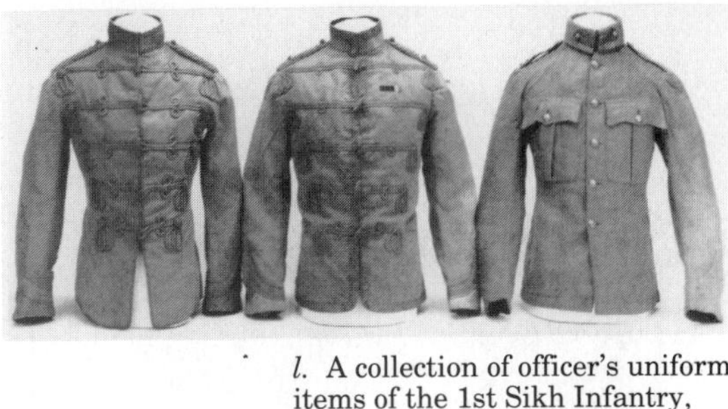

l. A collection of officer's uniform items of the 1st Sikh Infantry, Punjab Frontier Force, worn by W. H. Manning, including full dress tunic with matching Field Officer's braid, matching pantaloons, patrol jacket with Major's crowns, 2 pairs of overalls, mess waistcoat and jacket, two officer's Rifles pattern swords, and a plaited brown leather sword knot with acorn in steel scabbard.
$1,200-1,500

r. A further collection of khaki uniform items worn by W. H. Manning, including serge frock of Boer War shade of khaki, a similar frock but in khaki drill, another khaki drill frock, 2 slightly later khaki drill frocks, a Sam Browne belt with brace and frog, a scabbard for mameluke shape blade, and a plaited brown leather sword knot.
$450-600

l. A Victorian Lieutenant's full dress uniform of the Royal Naval Artillery Volunteers 1887-91, comprising: cocked hat, tail coat and gilt epaulettes. **$900-1,500**

r. A Victorian Royal Naval Midshipman's coatee, c1840.
$750-900

A British Ambassador's very richly embroidered full dress coatee, with gilt K.C. Royal Arms buttons and label of Gieves Ltd. to Sir C. F. W. Russell.
$3,000- 4,500

Sir Claude Russell, KCMG was Ambassador to Portugal 1931-35. He had been a Third Secretary at the time of Queen Victoria's death.

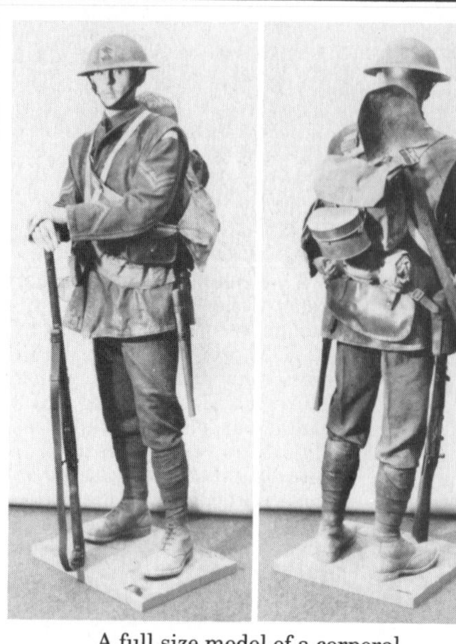

A full size model of a corporal, 20th (Service) Bn The King's Liverpool Regt (The 'Liverpool Pals') as serving with the 30th Division in France, 1916, in full khaki uniform, carrying full equipment, with SMLE rifle.
$1,800-2,700

l. An officer's busby of the 10th Royal Hussars, with scarlet bag trimmed with Russia, by Hawkes & Co., 14 Piccadilly, in a metal busby case with brass plate engraved 'The Honble. G. B. Portman, 10th Royal Hussars'.
$1,050-1,350

The Hon. George Berkeley Portman (born 1875) Captain 10th Hussars, served as ADC to the Viceroy of India 1901-02 after serving in the South African War. He had joined the regiment in 1895. He served again in WWI and despite being the sixth son of Viscount Portman, he succeeded to the title in 1946.

r. An officer's rare cloth helmet of the 2nd (Berwickshire) Volunteer Battalion, the King's Own Scottish Borderers, in a small metal helmet case with brass plaque engraved 'C. Hope Esqre, 60th Rifles', a leather pouch with Victorian K.O.S.B. badge, a leather sabretache to match, a pair of nickel-plated box spurs with straight neck, and a pair of swan neck spurs, and a swagger cane of the Harrow School O.T.C.
$1,050-1,350

Colonel Charles Hope (born 1850) commanded the 2nd Vol. Bn., King's Own Scottish Borderers and earned the Volunteer Decoration. He had earlier served in the 60th Rifles, attaining the rank of Captain and later in life became Lord Lieutenant of Berwickshire.

l. A Lewes Home Guard private's blouse. **$50-75**
r. A WWII Corporal's khaki battle dress blouse of the 23rd (Lewes) Sussex Home Guard, with Home Guard/SX/23 shoulder titles, marksman's badge on left cuff, factory label dated Feb. 1942, name inside 'E. H. S. Longhurst, Bx 48', and a pair of overalls. **$120-135**

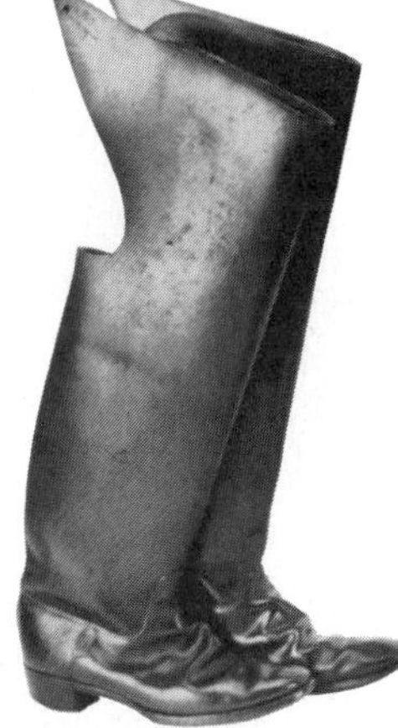

A pair of trooper's tall jack boots of the 2nd Life Guards, dated 1906, each stamped 2nd L.G. and 11.06 and with issue number 247?, 26in (66cm) high.
$120-135

A sporran.
$25-40

An officer's blue cloth saddle cloth of the 1st Life Guards, altered and sewn on to heavy dark blue cloth backing, 47 by 46in (119 by 116.5cm).
$750-900

Miller's is a price GUIDE not a price LIST

n officer's fine blue cloth helmet f the Prince of Wales's Leinster egiment, with gilt K. C. helmet late, gilt chin chain and label of oth Cater & Co., 56 Pall Mall nd T. McBride & Sons, full dress ınic, overalls, sword slings and lain crimson sash all on a male gure, mess vest, jacket, a pair of lack boots and a white waistcoat.
1,050-1,350
Villiam Evans became an Honorary Lieutenant in the einster Regt. (1st and 2nd Bns) ı May 1914 and was serving as 'uartermaster of the regiment's th Battalion in June 1916.

l. The coronet and robes of a baron, including a silver coronet by Henry Tessier, London 1901, Coronation robe of crimson velvet trimmed with white fur, matching sleeveless surcoat with label of Wilkinson & Son Ltd., Robe Makers to Her Majesty, with name Lord Currie, G.C.B., heavy red baize bag with tassels and similar label, and Parliamentary robe of scarlet cloth trimmed with white fur and gold lace.
$1,200-1,800
The Rt. Hon. Philip H. W. Currie, P.C. was created a baron in 1899 having earlier been Ambassador in Constantinople (1873-78), and then in Rome.

r. The mantle of a Knight Grand Commander of the Most Eminent Order of the Indian Empire, in deep blue satin lined with white silk, and a white cord cordon with large blue and gold tassels.
$1,500-2,250

A Victorian officer's full dress embroidered sabretache of the 21st Hussars, French grey cloth, gilt lace border, embroidered crown/VR/21H in circle/laurel wreath. **$375-525**

A corporal's full dress scarlet coatee of the Warwickshire Yeomanry, inscribed inside lining of right shoulder 'D. Sarjeant 1st Troop', c1840.
$1,800-2,700

. Royal Horse Artillery other ank's busby with scarlet bag (no lume), full dress jacket and ellow cord caplines, together ith a pair of Artillery Officer's veralls and non-regulation boots, ll on a male figure.
450-600

A British Civil/Diplomatic full dress coatee of the 2nd class, with rich gold embroidery, by Eade, Peckover & Co., 27a Sackville Street, label dated 16.8.1939, but owner's name unclear, a cocked hat, and a pair of trousers with wide gold oak leaf lace stripes, all in a metal trunk.
$900-1,500

Batons & Truncheons

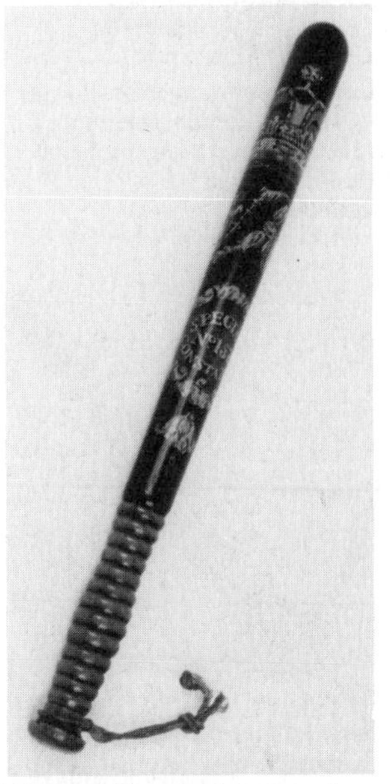

A Special Constable's truncheon, 19thC, 17½in (44.5cm) long.
$225-300

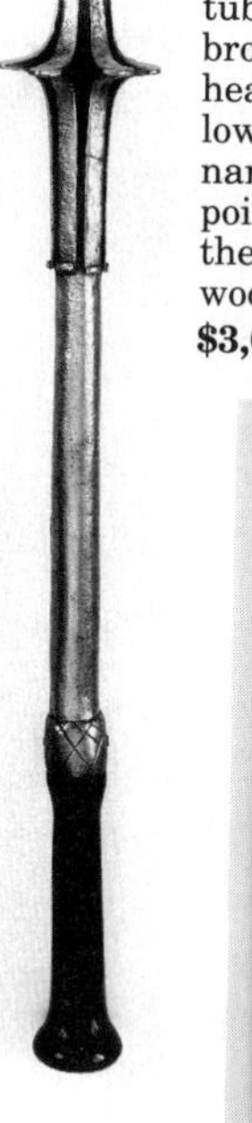

A Gothic steel mace, with short tubular haft applied with raised bronze collar at the the base, the head formed of 6 applied robust low flanges, each rising to a narrow triangular horizontal point swelling in section towards the end, and fitted with modern wooden grip, 15thC, 19in (48cm).
$3,000-4,500

A William IV Special Constable truncheon, 18in (46cm) long.
$225-300

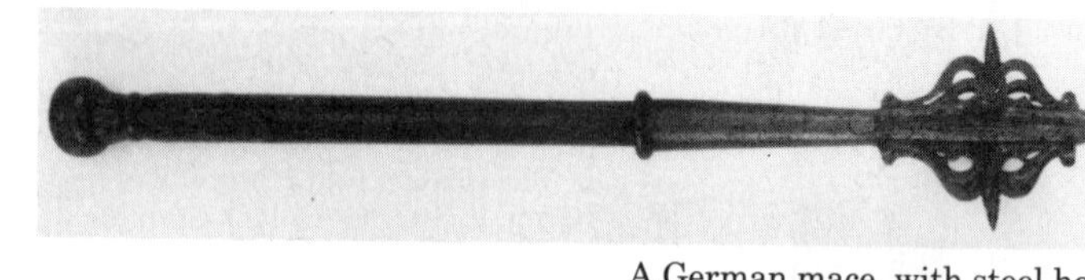

A German mace, with steel head formed with tapering tubular socket and moulded pointed finia applied with 6 pierced shaped flanges formed with a narrow point of diamond section, and modern carved wooden haft, damaged, mid-16thC, head 11in (28cm).
$2,700-3,300

A military fife, probably German, of turned black wood stamped with a small eagle mark and J. Link, ?Eissenfels? and dated 1915, with white metal mounts in its substantial black leather case with heavy brass caps, the case 16in (41.5cm) long.
$180-225

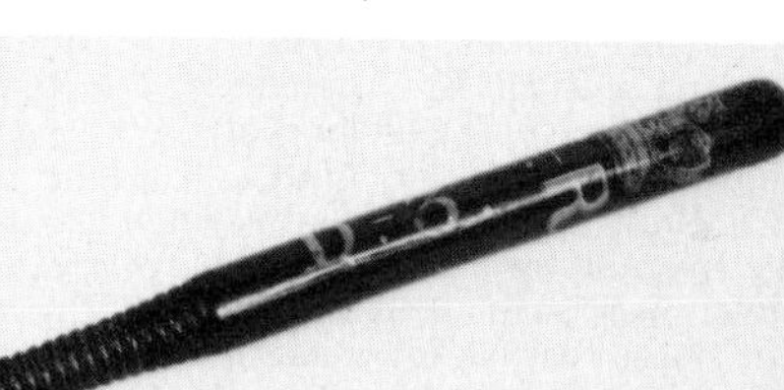

A Victorian truncheon, 16in (41cm) long.
$225-300

Crossbows

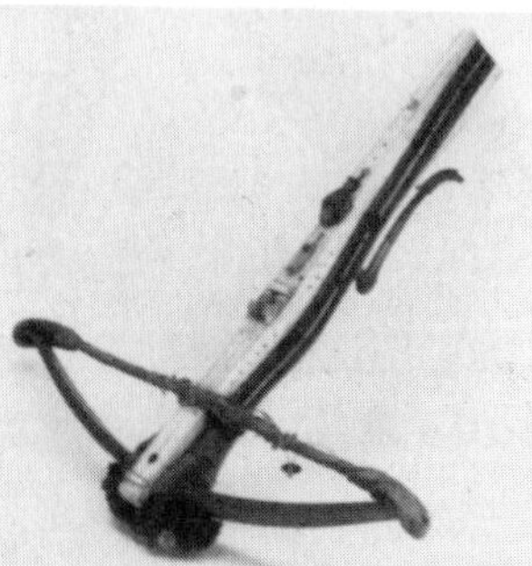

A German sporting crossbow, with original cords, string and 6 woollen tassels, 24in (60.5cm) long.
$7,500-9,000

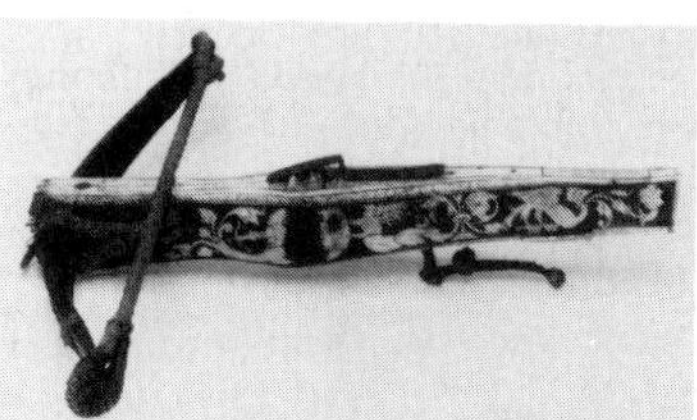

A German sporting crossbow, dated 1564, damaged, bow 25½in (65cm).
$9,000-10,000

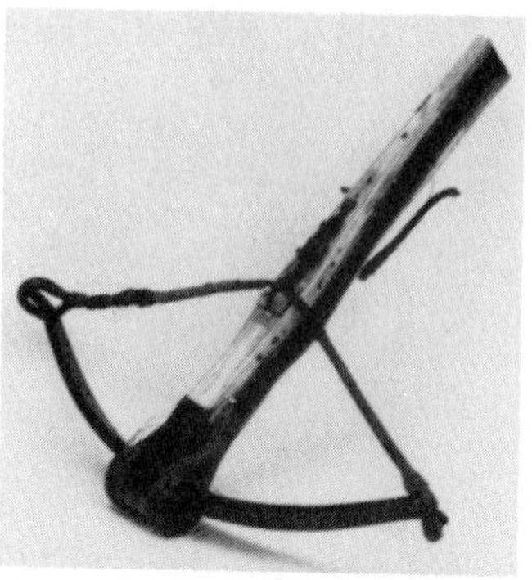

A German sporting crossbow, with robust steel bow struck with maker's initial H, damaged, early 17thC, 24in (61cm).
$4,500-6,000

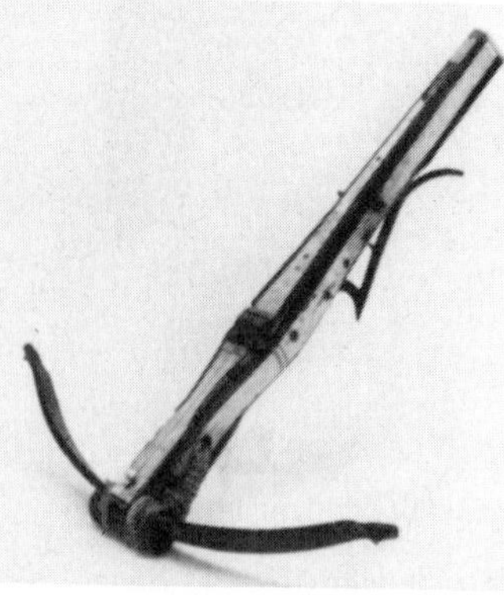

A German sporting crossbow, altered, late 16thC, 20in (51cm) long, and a target crossbow, signed Luanonne, French or Swiss, mid-19thC, sights and string missing, 32in (81cm) long.
$3,000-3,750

Daggers & Knives

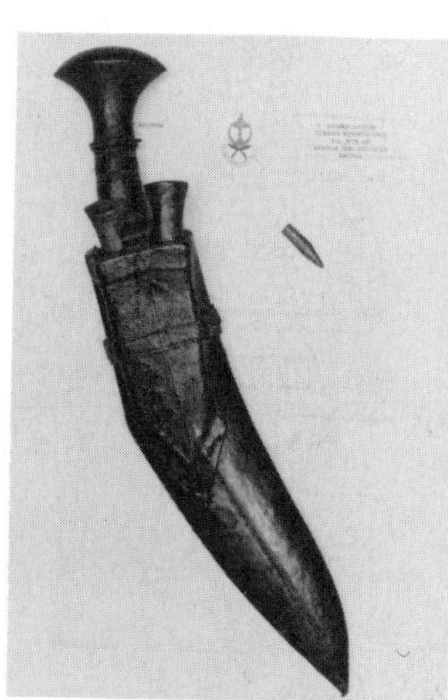

A Gurkha kukri belonging to Major Rambahadur Limbu VC, MVO, who won his Victoria Cross as Lance Corporal in Indonesia with the 10th Princess Mary's Own Gurkha Rifles during their 1963-66 posting, with a letter of authenticity from Major Limbu, 4 signed colour photos of the kukri and a framed history of the regiment.
$450-600

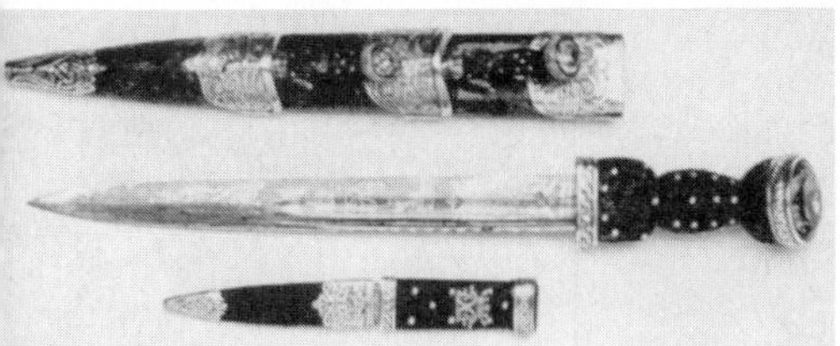

A George V Highland officer's dirk, by Brook & Son, straight single edged 11¼in blade with scalloped back, etched with crowned GR cypher and Argyll & Sutherland crests, carved black hardwood grip with basket weave and foliate design inset with silver studs, silver mounts, coloured stone pommel, in its matching silver mounted sheath with knife and fork, contained in its japanned metal case with matching skean dhu.
$1,800-2,700

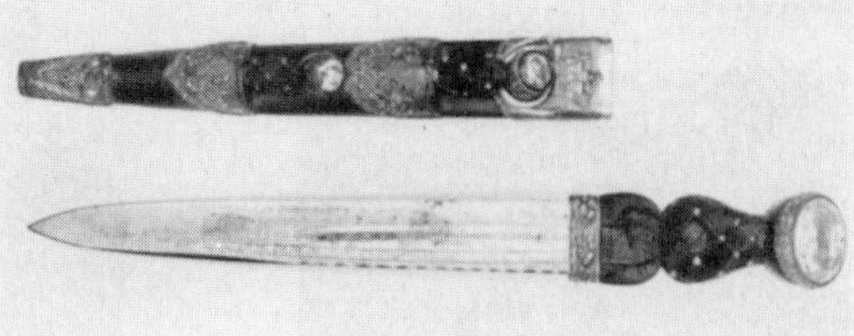

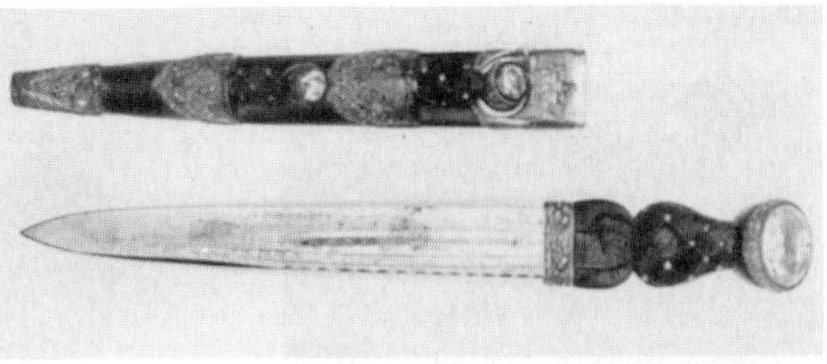

A Scottish officer's dirk of the 71st Highland Light Infantry, straight single edged 10½in (26cm) blade, with broad and narrow fullers, with companion knife and fork, defective.
$1,200-1,800

A bowie knife, signed Edmundo White y ca, Valparaiso, 16½in (42.5cm), and another, signed Harrison Bros & Howson, in original leather sheath, 11in (28cm), both late 19thC.
$4,500-6,000

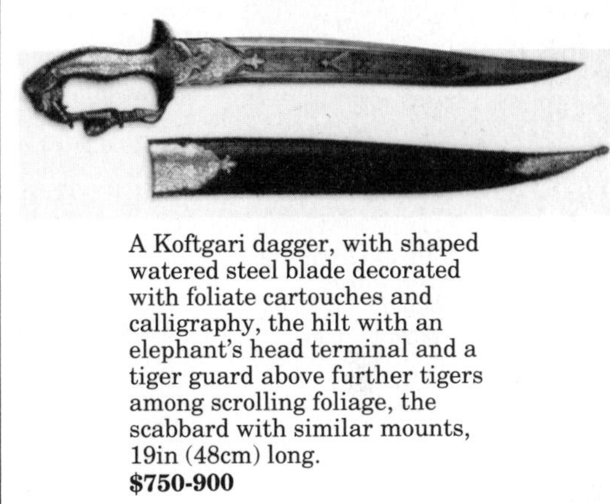

A Koftgari dagger, with shaped watered steel blade decorated with foliate cartouches and calligraphy, the hilt with an elephant's head terminal and a tiger guard above further tigers among scrolling foliage, the scabbard with similar mounts, 19in (48cm) long.
$750-900

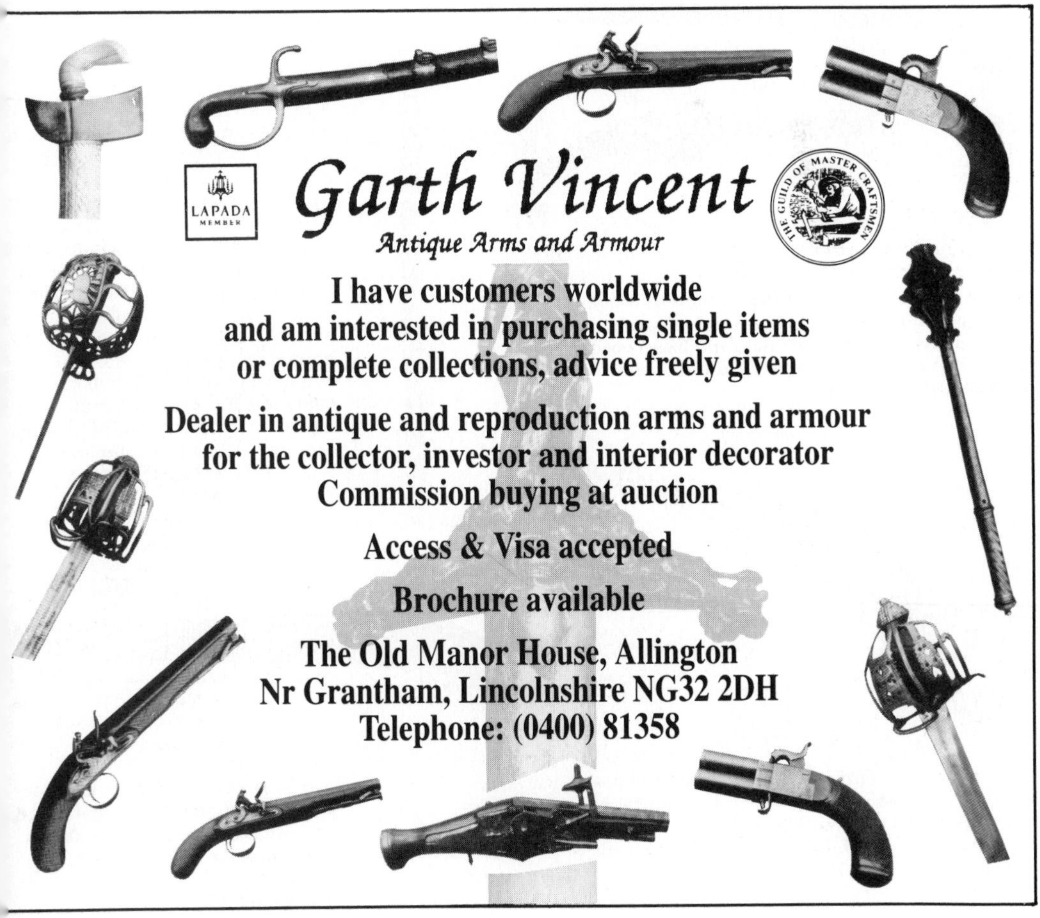

Powder Flasks

The relief designs on the front are common to a group of flasks of similar type attributed on stylistic grounds to either Augsburg or Nuremberg. Some of the hunting scenes are possibly based on woodcuts by Jost Amman of Nuremberg (1539-91).

A North African powder flask, the nozzle formed of turned horn, 9in (23cm), and a group of 8 Middle Eastern powder flasks and priming flasks, 18th/19thC.
$750-900

A German gilt bronze powder flask, Augsburg or Nuremberg, fitted with 4 gilt bronze rings for suspension, original gilding throughout, late 16thC, 8in (20.5cm). **$15,000-18,000**

Miller's is a price GUIDE not a price LIST

A factory engraved Colt .45 model 1911 self loading pistol, No. C135835, with 5in. barrel, slide with patent dates to 1913, profusely engraved overall with foliate scrolls, the breech and frame inlaid with fine scrolls of gold, ivory grips, retaining much original finish, certificate of proof, in its leather holster bearing Abercrombie & Fitch trademark.
$6,000-8,250

This pistol was supplied to Colt's New York office on February 2, 1924, for delivery to Abercrombie & Fitch, the famous New York sporting goods dealer. Factory records confirm that this pistol was factory engraved with ivory stocks and blue finish. The pistol is sold with a label stating that it was 'Presented to Sir Hubert-Gough, by American citizens helping to arm the Home Guard in June 1940' and that it was later presented to an officer with the Ulster Rifles 'used by him with good results in the invasion of Germany, 1945'.

Pistols

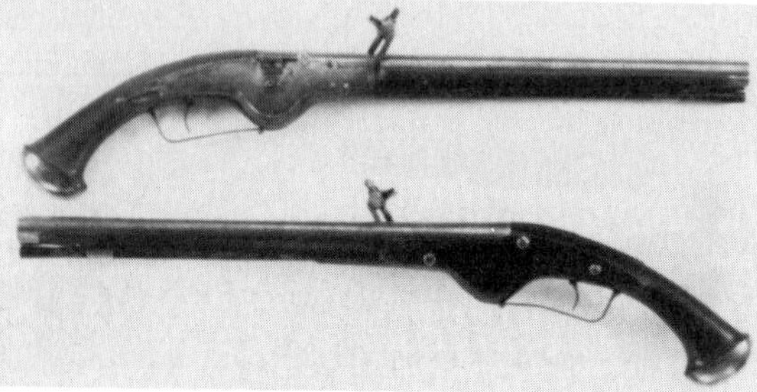

A pair of military wheel lock holster pistols, unsigned, Dutch or German, with long barrels struck on the breech with the letter P, with internal wheels and dog springs, domed oval steel pommel caps, steel trigger guards, ramrod pipes and fore-end caps, and later wooden ramrods, some damage, c1660, 25in (63.5cm).
$6,000-8,250

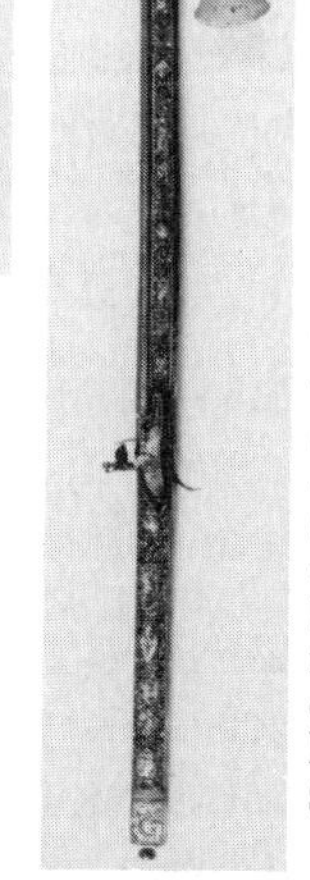

A Silesian flintlock axe-pistol with two-stage barrel formed with a full-length flat, struck with a mark, WB conjoined, and fitted with in-curved axe-blade and four-pronged pean over the muzzle, flat bevelled lock, straight walnut haft profusely inlaid with traditional patterns of staghorn scrolls and pellets inhabited by animals and both human and animal grotesque masks, staghorn pommel engraved with busts of a Turk and a female figure, fitted with iron finial, and original iron ramrod, damaged, late 17thC, 35½in (90.5cm).
$5,250-6,000

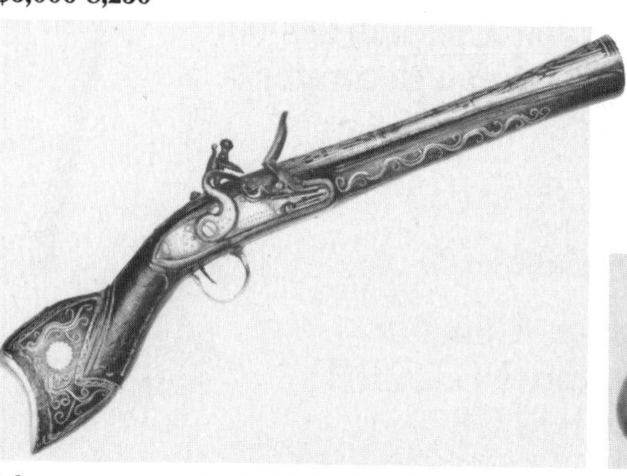

A brass mounted Turkish flintlock blunderbuss pistol, with flared 11in steel barrel, extensively silver inlaid overall, small brass maker's cartouche at breech, full stocked, engraved lock, brass furniture, c1800, 19in (48cm).
$600-750

A pair of Flemish flintlock holster pistols by Niquet Lejeune à Liège, and original wooden ramrods, some damage, c1740, 17½in (44.5cm).
$4,500-6,000

. Japanese small snap-matchlock
istol, with plain wooden stock,
nd button trigger, 18th/19thC,
½in (19cm).
3,000-4,500

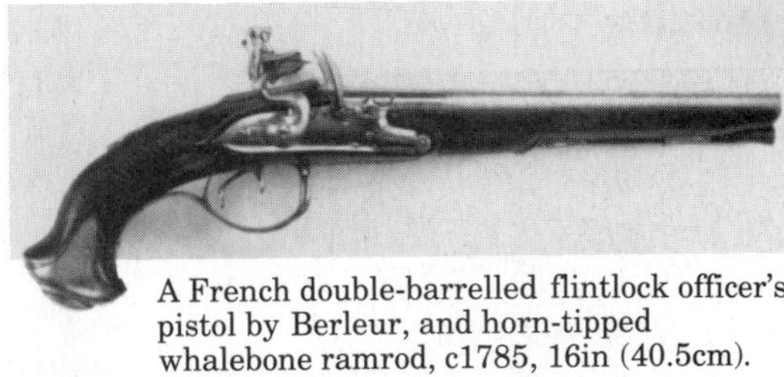

A French double-barrelled flintlock officer's pistol by Berleur, and horn-tipped whalebone ramrod, c1785, 16in (40.5cm).
$1,800-2,700

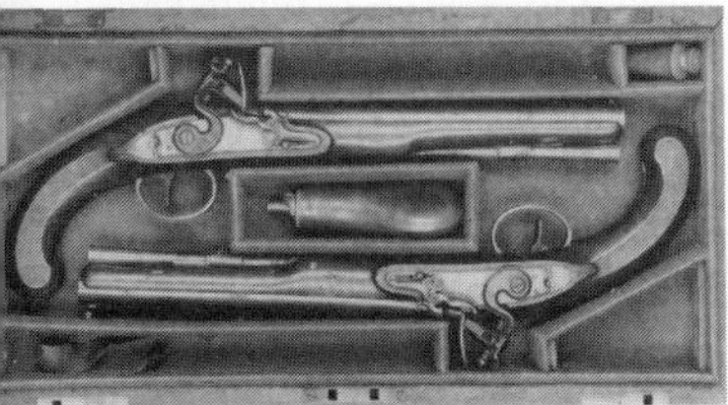

. pair of 28-bore flintlock duelling
istols by Probin, sighted
wamped barrels 9in, stepped
olted locks with rollers to frizen
prings set triggers full stocked
ith Wogden type butts with oval
lver escutcheons engraved C.P.,
arrels refinished, contained in
heir fitted mahogany case with
owder flask and oil bottle.
3,000-4,500

A Westley Richards & Co. .300 (H & H rimless magnum) detachable boxlock ejector rifle, No. T4016, with a canvas case.
$9,000-12,000
The rifle was rebarrelled in 1976 by the makers.

ifles

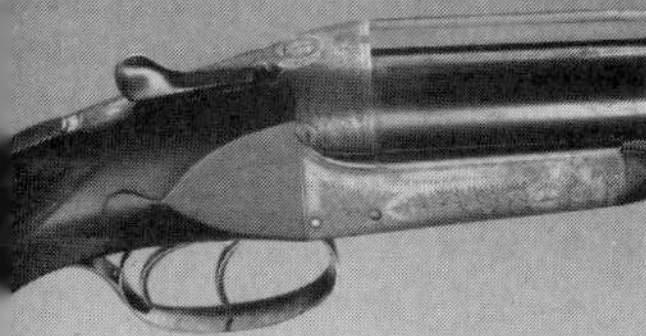

William Evans .360 boxlock
ector rifle, No. 9140, with 26in
hopper lump barrels, filed rib
ith leaf sights to 300, with a
anvas case.
6,000-8,250

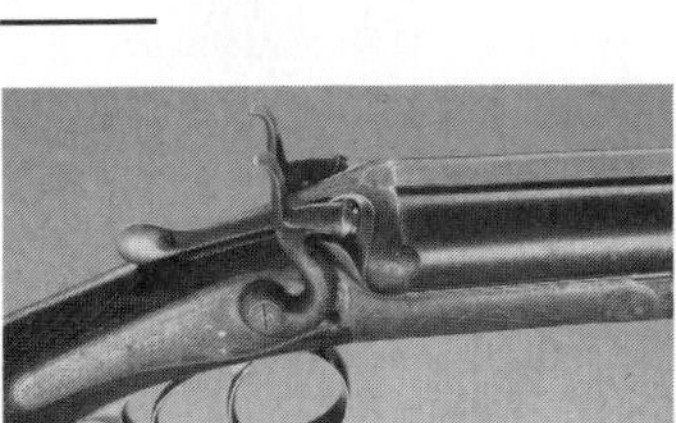

A Gye & Moncrieff .577/500 hammer rifle, No. 1211, in its oak and leather case.
$3,000-3,750
The gun case label is inscribed 'Won at Wimbledon 1878 at the Running Deer - seven shots, 4 bulls eyes and 3 centres. A. Stuart, Wortley'. Possibly a contributor to various sporting books such as 'Fur, Feather and Fin', and the 'Badminton Library'.

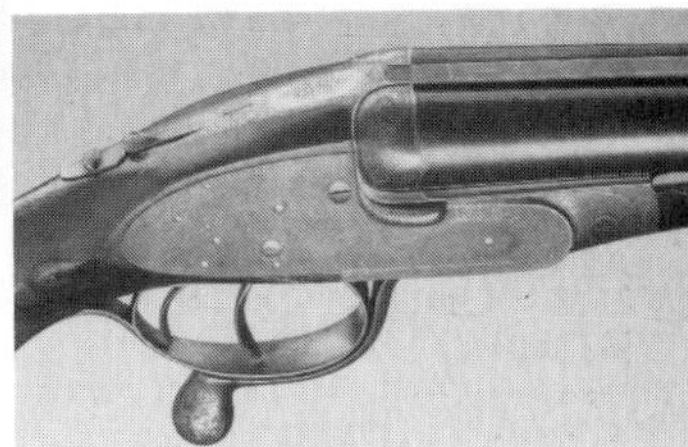

A J. Purdey & Sons .303 self-opening sidelock non-ejector rifle, No. 16202, with 25½in barrels.
$6,000-8,250

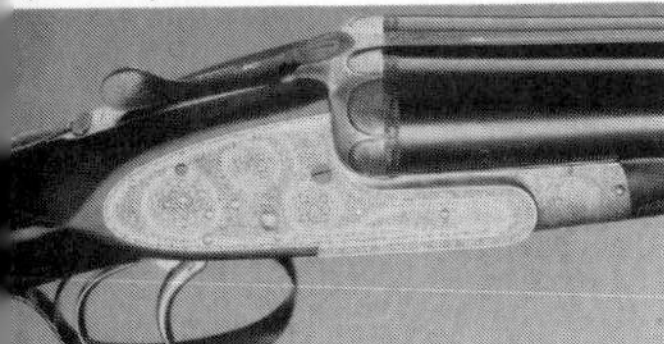

An incomplete pair of J. Woodward & Sons 12-bore (2½in) sidelock ejector guns, Nos. 6248/9, in oak and leather case with J. Purdey & Sons label.
$7,500-9,000

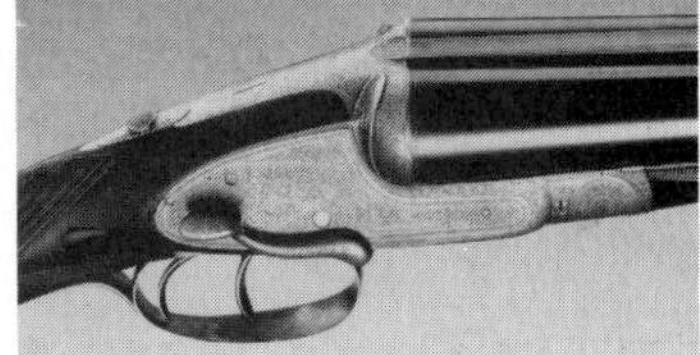

A Stephen Grant & Sons 12-bore (2½in) sidelock ejector gun, No. 6086.
$6,000-8,250

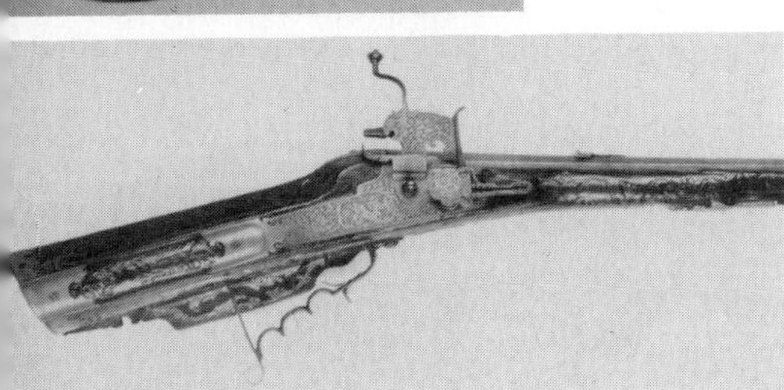

. European .55 wheel-lock rifle,
eavy octagonal barrel 27½in, lock
ith concealed wheel and sliding
over etched with battle scene,
ll stocked with carved foliate
ecoration and bone inlay, sliding
atch box cover, brass furniture,
laid bone panel depicting
untress with dog and rifle, some
amage and restoration.
2,250-3,000

A William Evans 12-bore side-by-side shotgun with sidelock ejector mechanism, No. 7525 and No. 1 of a pair (from Purdey's, 63 Pall Mall, St James's, London, 47in (119cm).
$2,700-3,300

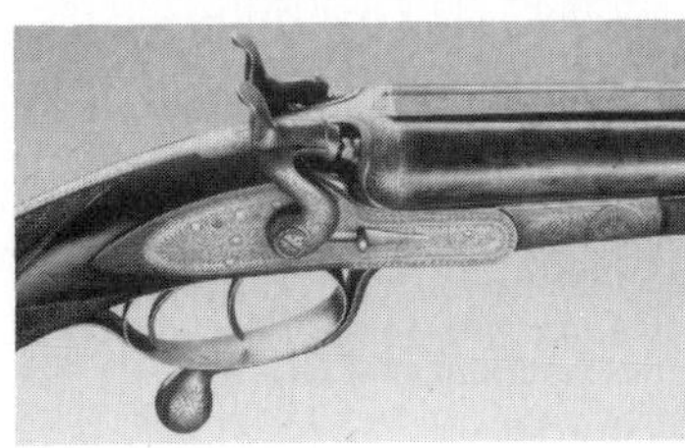

An Alex. Henry .450 (3¼in) hammer rifle, No. 6342, in its oak case.
$2,700-3,300

Swords

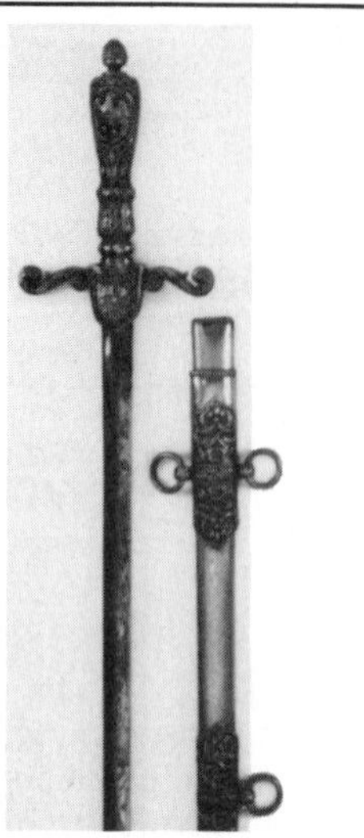

A Historic American Medical Officer's pattern dress sword, carried by Assistant Surgeon Holmes Offley Paulding, a participant in the 1874 expedition against the Sioux, with slender straight etched blade by the Ames Mfg. Co., regulation brass hilt applied with the silver letters MS on one langet and inscribed by the owner 'H.O.P., U.S.A., 1874', on the other, and in its original nickel-plated scabbard with regulation mounts, blade rubbed, blade 28in (71cm) long.
$4,500-6,000

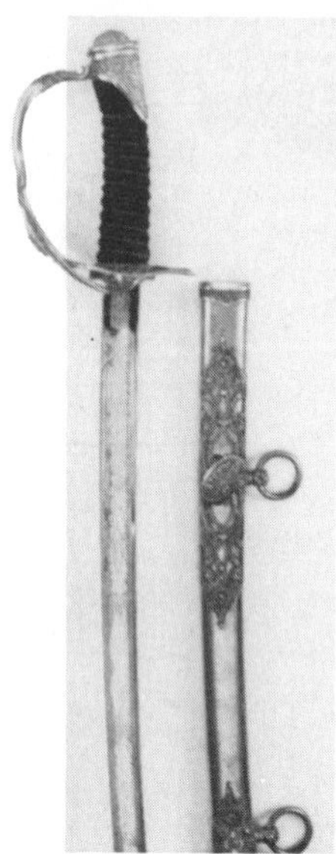

An American Cavalry Officer's dress sabre, with slender curved highly polished blade struck with maker's mark, a helmet, signed by the retailer 'The M.C. Lilley & Co., Columbus, O.', etched with the owner's name 'Capt. L. P. Hunt, 10th Cavalry U.S.A.', with its original sword knot and belt, c1870, blade 32in (81cm) long.
$1,800-2,700
Captain L. P. Hunt was a graduate of West Point and fought in the Civil War. The sword belonged to his great-great-grandson.

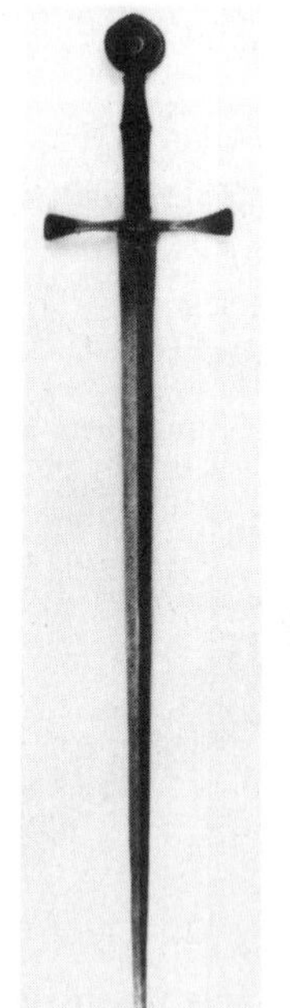

A composite broadsword, with iron guard with robust quillons with horizontally recurved spatulate terminals, large wheel pommel with associated bevelled edges, and later grip, late 15th/early 16thC, blade 36in (91cm) long.
$4,800-5,700

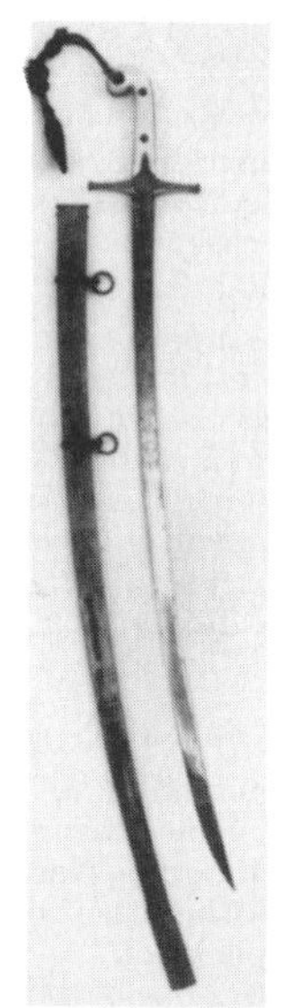

The late Victorian General Officer's pattern mameluke sword of Major-General Sir John Gatacre, K.C.B., with 30in (76cm) blade by Joel Edwards, Hanover Street, Hanover Square, London, well etched with crown, VR cypher, cross sword and baton etc. and laurel and oak sprays raised in relief, gilt hilt with ivory grips and full dress sword-knot in its nickel-plated scabbard.
$600-750
Sir John Gatacre, 1841-1932, KCB 1907, CB 1887, had served in the Indian Mutiny campaign in 1858 and was one of its last survivors at his death. He also served in China 1860, Afghanistan 1879-80 and Burma 1886-88 receiving all 3 medals and ending his long Indian Army career as Colonel of Outram's Rifles.

Miscellaneous

A Naga 'Dao' cutting weapon an belt, the weapon made of wood with dyed dogs' hair, the belt of woven fibre with shell detail, early 20thC.
$300-375

An Elizabeth II painted bass drum of the 1st Bn. Coldstream Guards, bearing Royal Arms, regimental badges and battle honour scrolls 'Tangier 1680' to 'Italy 1943-45', by George Potter Aldershot.
$750-900

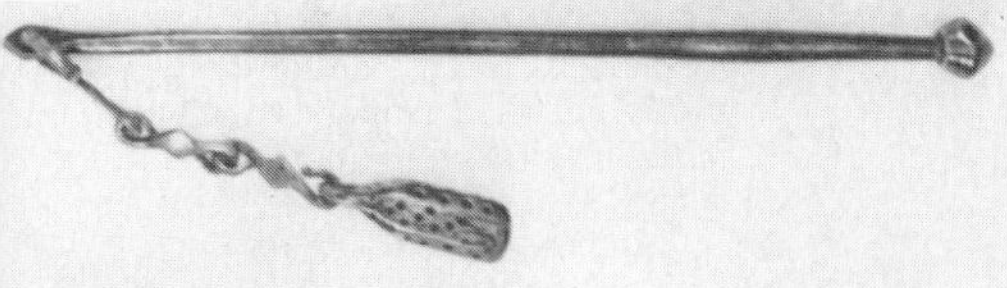

n all-steel military flail, with mark, possibly the aker's, 16th/early 17thC, haft 22in (56.5cm) long.
4,500-6,000

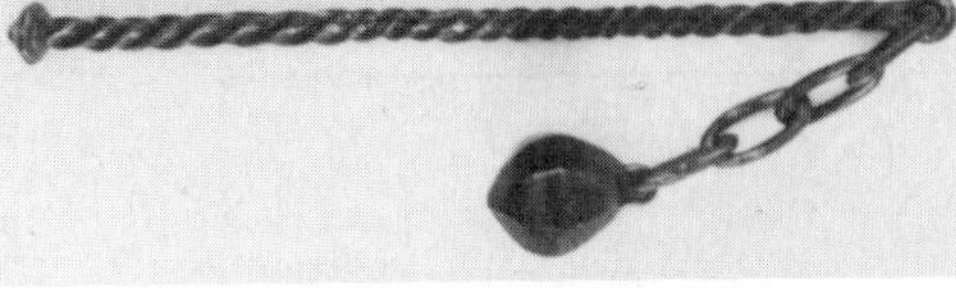

An all-steel military flail, with the haft formed of one rod doubled over and twisted in a boldly wrythen pattern, fitted with small compressed faceted finial, short chain of 4 oval links, and very heavy globular head of octagonal section, late 16th/early 17thC, haft 21in (53.5cm) long.
$2,700-3,300

MEDALS & ORDERS

Reading Police Bravery medal, warded to P.C. Arthur Searle, une 6th 1911, Bronze Medal, vith Borough of Reading Arms nd Reading Police above and For Bravery below, the reverse ngraved as above including For Stopping/Runaway Horse, and 8 ther medals.
450-600

An Afghanistan silver award medal, the reverse engraved in 4 lines, Shere Ali to his Soldiers, 1876.
$90-105

An East and West African Police Shooting Medal, 1927, No. 1204, 2nd Grade Sergeant Taibu, Tanganyika Police, by Asprey of London, the plain reverse with engraved recipient details, and 3 loops for wearing.
$135-150

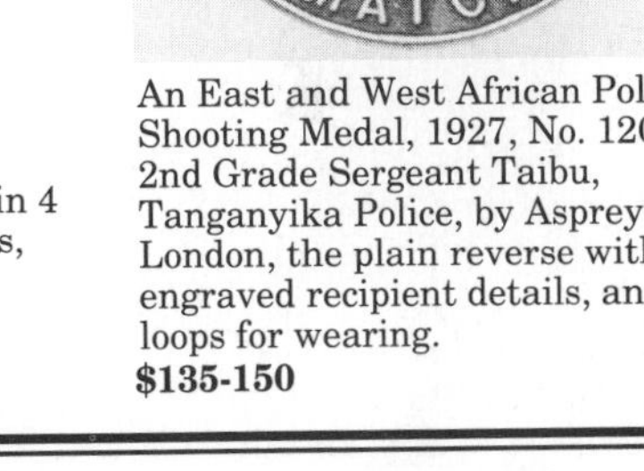

The Most Honourable Order of the Bath, Civil Division, a William IV Grand Cross (G.C.B.) Investiture sash badge by John James Edington, gold, hallmarks for London 1833, maker's mark on suspension, 1½in (3.5cm) wide.
$3,000-3,750

Prior to 1847 the Civil Division of this Order comprised one class.

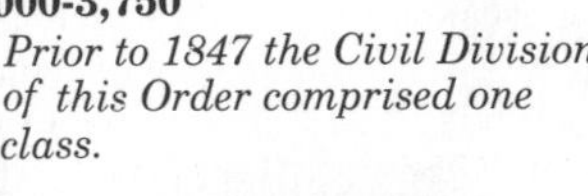

The Most Eminent Order of the Indian Empire, 1st large type, companion's breast badge with India on petals, gold and enamel, with its gold riband bar.
$900-1,500

Russia, Order of St Stanislaus, First Class 'Non-Christian' badge by Kordess, St Petersburg, gold and enamel, maker's mark on reverse, St Petersburg and gold '56' mark on ring, 6.5cm.
$1,500-2,250

A Hero of the Soviet Union gold breast badge, officially No. 2418.
$1,800-2,700

Russia, Order of St Anne, Second Class badge with 'black' enamel, gold and enamel, gold '56' mark on ring, 4.5cm wide.

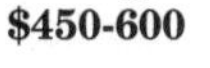

$450-600

Russia, Order of St Vladimir, Second Class neck badge with swords, by Edouard, St Petersburg, gold and enamel, maker's mark beneath enamel on reverse, atelier mark ET on suspension ring and loop, 4.5cm wide. **$600-750**

Russia, Order of St Andrew, gold and enamel badge, lacking crown, some restoration, early 19thC.
$3,000-4,500

Russia, Defence of Port Arthur 1904-5, silver and enamel cross by Edouard, St Petersburg, a Red Cross badge, silver and enamel, and a miniature badge of the Order of St Stanislaus in gold and enamel.
$600-750

Sweden, Order of the Vasa, Commander's badge, gold and enamel, 6cm wide, and Commander's star, silver, 8cm wide.
$600-750

Russia, Order of the White Eagle badge, by Keibel, St Petersburg, gold and enamel, maker's mark and 'kokoshnik' mark for 1896-1908 on suspension, slight damage, late 19thC, 2⅜in (6cm) wide.
$6,000-8,250

Spain, a rare Talavera Cross including crown suspension, gold and enamel, the white enamel cross with 'Talavera/28.de/Julio/de 1809' in gold letters on the arms on both sides, slight damage, 3.7cm wide.
$750-1,200

A cross in this size is very rare.

'RANSPORT

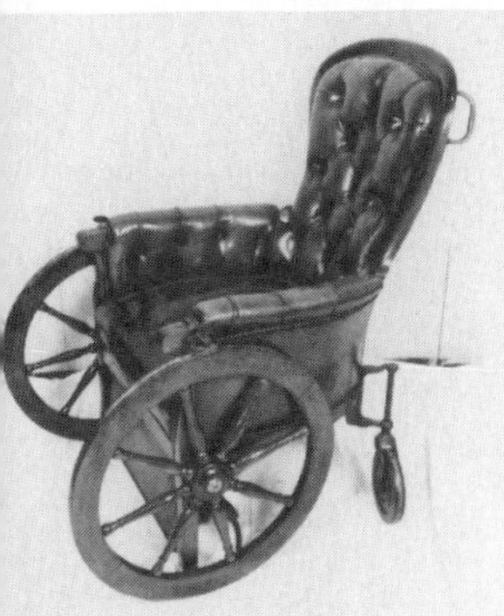

A leather buttoned invalid's wheelchair, with a chamberpot in the seat, c1890, 26½in (67.5cm) wide.
$3,000-3,750

A delivery cycle, c1930.
$300-375

An old pushchair, 17in (43cm) wide.
$225-300

'ransport Memorabilia

. Brooklands B.A.R.C. Trophy, ·ith silver-gilt interior and xterior decoration, scroll andles, detachable domed cover ·ith finial, engraved with .A.R.C. Brooklands crest and ıscriptions on cup and cover, by 'illiam Comyns, London 1912, 1in (28cm) high, 76oz.
1,500-2,250

'he inscription on the cup reads: st Prize, The 7th 100mph Short 'andicap, 13th July 1912', the ıscription on the cover: 'The 'alcolm Campbell Trophy' and 'resented by Donald Campbell to ıe committee of the West Ham oys & Amateur Boxing Club for nnual award'.

A collection of enamelled rally plaques for the Scottish Rally, 1937, 1938, 1939 and 1953, lapel badges for 1934, 1935, 1936, 1937, 1938 and 1939, and badges for the Irish Rally of 1937 and 1938.
$450-600

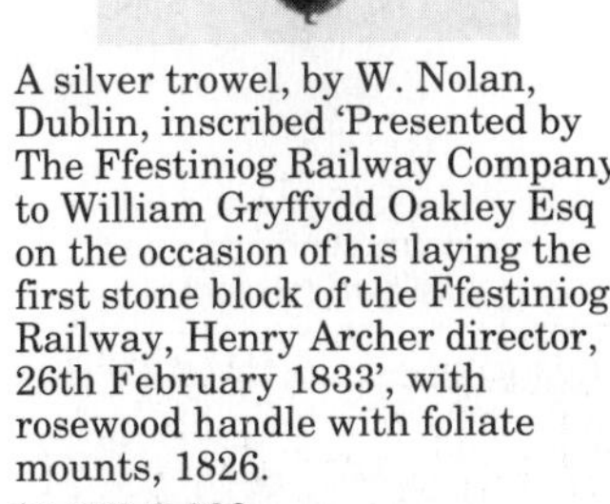

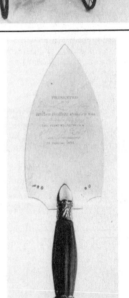

A silver trowel, by W. Nolan, Dublin, inscribed 'Presented by The Ffestiniog Railway Company to William Gryffydd Oakley Esq on the occasion of his laying the first stone block of the Ffestiniog Railway, Henry Archer director, 26th February 1833', with rosewood handle with foliate mounts, 1826.
$2,250-3,000

ı rude devil mascot, with tail wept back around the body, hoof eet and horns on the head, brass ainted in red and mounted on isplay base, c1925, 5in (12.5cm) igh.
600-750

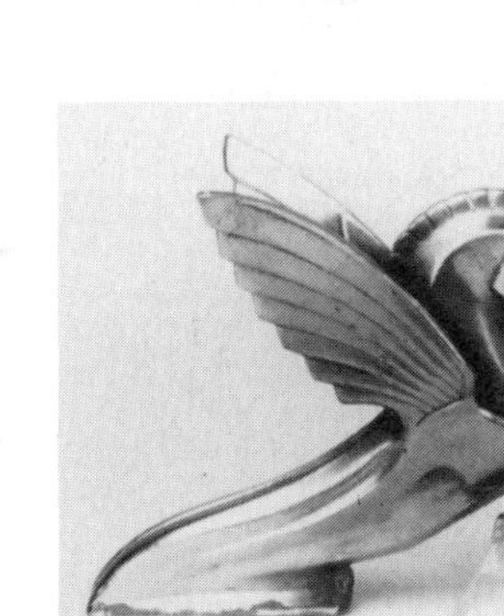

A chromium plated brass Pegasus mascot, the horse's body with stylised wings, c1930, 4½in (11.5cm) high.
$225-300

Miller's is a price GUIDE not a price LIST

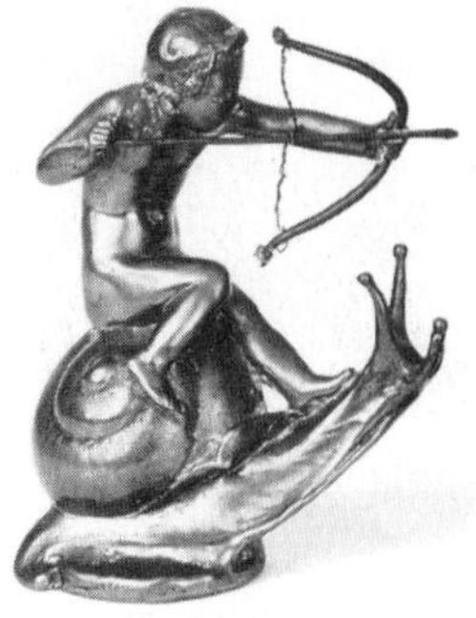

A Cupid and snail brass mascot, Cupid with bow and arrow seated on the snail's shell and resting a foot on its neck, mounted on a radiator cap, 5½in (14cm) high.
$375-450

A chromium plated leaping fox mascot, support and display base, Asprey retail mark on the support, 7½in (19cm) long.
$225-255

A London Brighton South Coast Railway Royal train locomotive dummy buffer lamp, polished brass handle, silvered lens bezel with opaque bull's-eye lens, mounting bracket to reverse, in original black with gold fine lined hand painted finish with Prince of Wales feathers and railway company heraldic device 1897, 16in (41cm) high, including handle.
$1,200-1,500

A bronze owl mascot, with wings spread, unpainted, mounted on a radiator cap, c1930, 6in (14.5cm) wingspan.
$300-375

A chromium plated bronze stylised squirrel mascot, eating a nut, signed 'Brau', mounted on a radiator cap, c1920, 4½in (11.5cm) high.
$450-600

A chromium plated flying goose mascot, stamped A. E. L. (A. E. Lejeune), and signed Ch. Paillet 4in (10.5cm) high.
$180-225

A GWR Hall Class cast brass lettered nameplate No. 4983, built 1931, withdrawn 1962.
$3,000-4,500

JEWELLERY

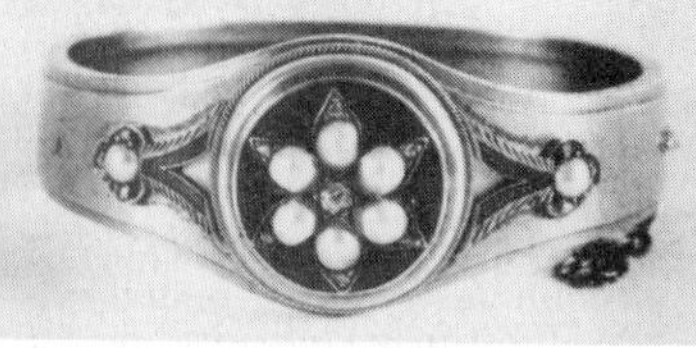

A mid-Victorian gold and blue enamelled diamond and pearl bangle, with portrait locket obverse.
$1,200-1,800

A Scottish agate bangle, surmounted with Royal Scottish badge, c1860.
$375-525

A gold and carbuncle brooch, with quatrefoliate design and a smaller drop at the front in similar design from serpentine pendant chains, a locket compartment at the back, late 19thC, with case.
$750-900

A gold and seed pearl hinged bangle, set with seed pearls in enamelled borders and with scrollwork engraved decoration on a snap clasp, the back glazed with a photographic locket compartment, mid-19thC.
$900-1,500

Diamond jewellery has an intrinsic as well as an antique value. Do not rely solely on the glass-scratch test for diamonds since there are other less valuable stones which will produce similar effects!

Good size diamonds fetch more than small ones or off-cuts, and 'brilliant cut' is preferred to the 'rose cut' which has fewer facets.

. white gold floral spray brooch, ›t with diamonds , rubies and meralds, 2in (6cm) wide.
2,250-3,000

 diamond bracelet, of three iple panels, connected by 6 oval nks, set with 143 brilliant cut iamonds and 24 baguettes.
9,000-12,000

. Mexican necklace and bracelet et, formed of circular plaques ach with ribbed decoration and et with an amethyst cabochon, Iexican marks and '925', 15 and ½in (38 and 17cm) long.
225-300

. gentleman's bog oak kilt pin, in he form of a dirk, with rose gold nounts, set with foiled citrines, 1850, 4in (10cm) long.
300-375

A brooch, set with central diamond within a circle of 8 smaller diamonds, converted from pendant.
$5,250-6,000

A clip-on brooch, set with large diamonds, 16 smaller diamonds and small sapphires.
$4,500-6,000

A Victorian Scottish silver and agate brooch, surmounted by crossed belts and crown, with small garnets, registration mark, c1867, 2½in (6cm).
$225-300

A 1.85ct diamond solitaire set 18ct white gold ring, the stone containing carbon inclusions just off centre.
$2,250-3,000

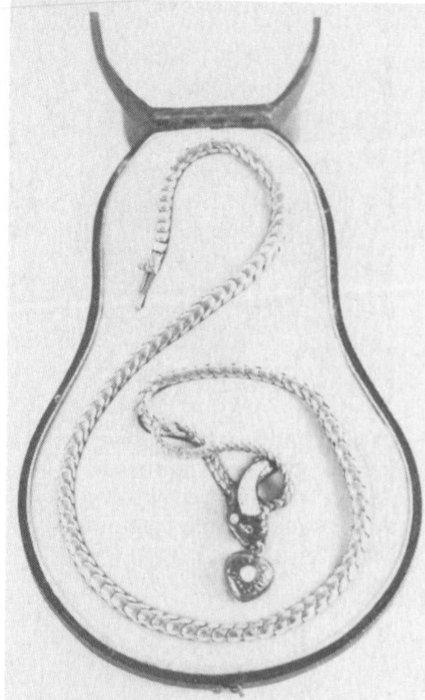

A Victorian gold and blue enamelled, flexible snake necklace, set with seed pearls.
$1,800-2,700

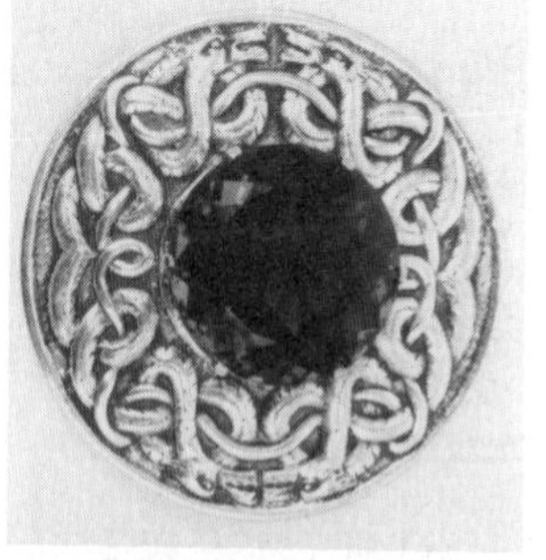

A Scottish silver plaid brooch, set with smokey quartz, in Celtic revival design, c1900, 3½in (9cm) diam.
$375-450

A pearl and diamond brooch, in an interwoven and scrolling design with foliate terminals, set with a large pearl at the centre, the end with a row of further pearls, set with large and small cushion shaped diamonds throughout, c1870.
$3,000-3,750

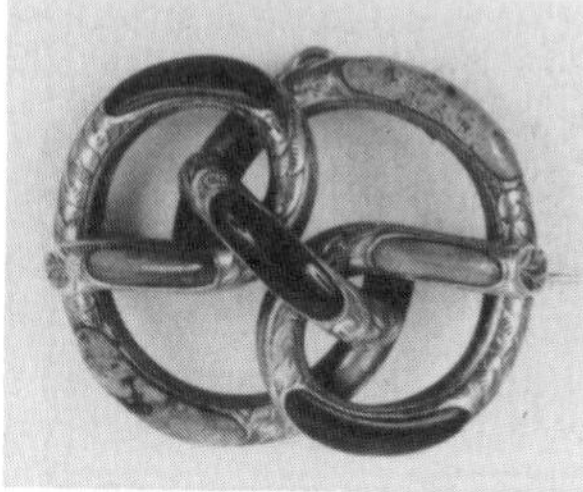

A silver knot brooch, set with Perthshire agate, c1860, 2in (5cm) wide.
$225-255

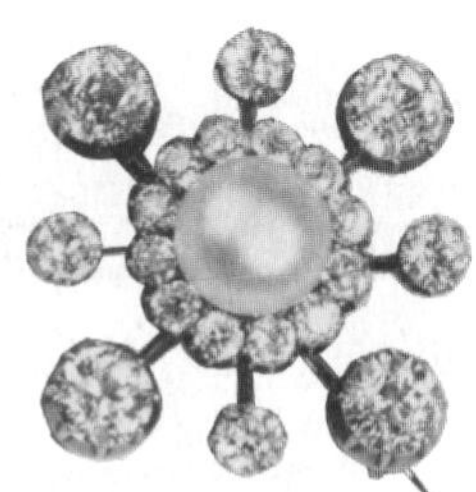

A star brooch, set with central pearl surrounded by 20 diamonds, converted from a pendant.
$3,000-3,750

A gold and turquoise brooch, designed as a bow, with turquoise forget-me-not flowerheads, the front with a circular pendant locket, glazed at the back, c1850, and case.
$600-750

A necklace and pendant, formed from a snake's skeleton of brown/amber tone partly set with silver gilt vertebrae and amber beads, the pendant in rock crystal carved with a snake and mounted in silver gilt set with an amber cabochon, maker's mark EC, for Eileen Coyne, London 1987.
$375-450

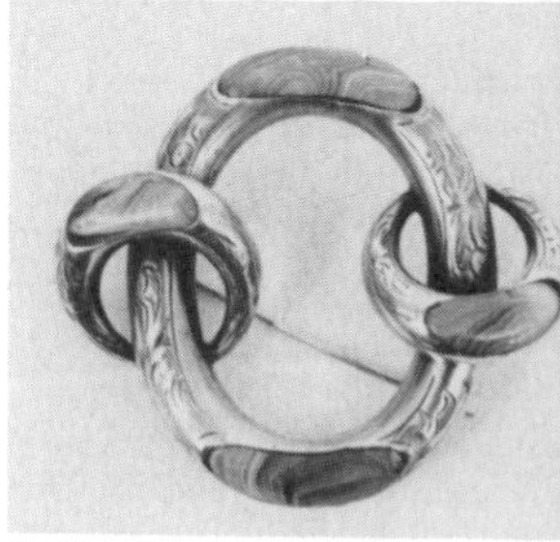

A silver and agate Celtic knot brooch, set with Montrose gre agate, c1850.
$225-300

A brass annular brooch, with zoomorphic design, c1800, copy of a much earlier brooch, 4½in (11cm) diam.
$225-300

Miller's is a price GUIDE not a price LIST

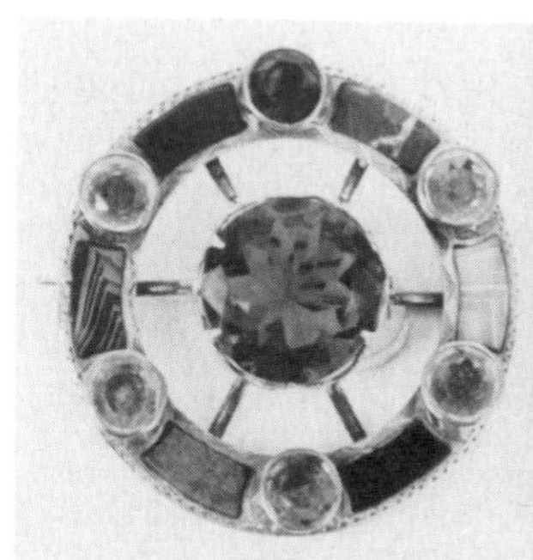

A Scottish agate brooch and earring set, with central garnet and amethyst and cairngorm surround, c1860.
$450-600

;ALCULATORS

\ Millionaire calculator, No. 2708, by Hans W. Egli, Zurich, in valnut case, with English nstructions on lid, 26½in (67cm) vide.
;1,500-2,250

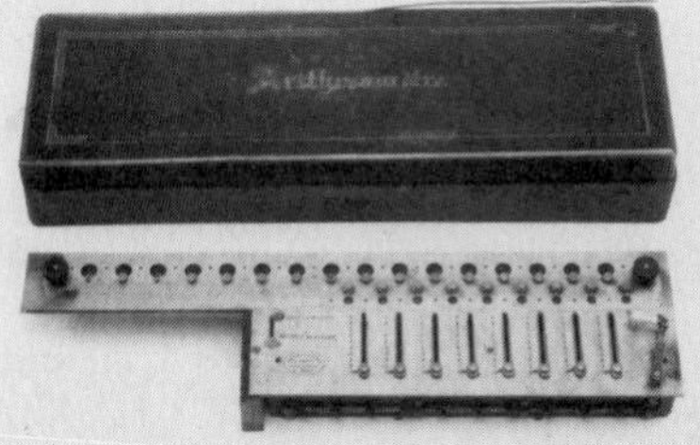

A Thomas De Colmar arithmometer, No. 700, with 16 digital displays, 8 sliding indices and winding handle, in ebonised case, with brass reinforcements and inlaid in brass to the lid, case distressed, c1860, 23½in (60cm) wide.
$3,000-4,500

An Arter, Dixon & Co. Guthrie's Patent Gem calculator, the pocket calculator with wooden board inset with sliding indices, the reverse with printed set of instructions, patented 1890, 9 by 4¼in (22 by 10.5cm).
$600-750

PENS & ARTISTS' MATERIALS

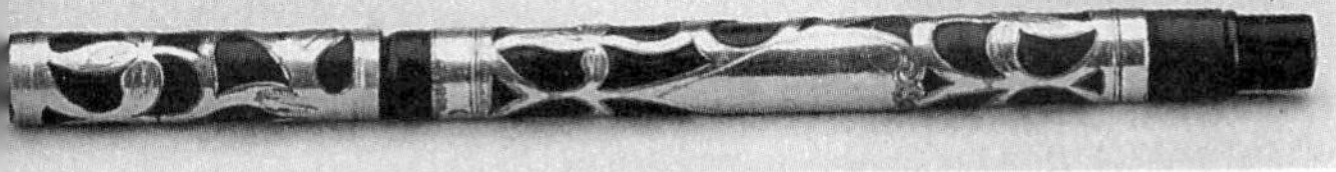

\ De La Rue Onoto fountain pen, vith plunger fill, over/under knib, ;ilt metal overlay, 6in (15cm).
'135-150

\n artist's pine paint cabinet, ainted black, fitted with 29 lrawers, each lettered in white, 7½ by 30in (121 by 76cm).
1,800-2,700

A satinwood easel, with pegs, early 20thC, 60in (152cm) high.
$450-600

Did you know?
MILLER'S Antiques Price Guide builds up year by year to form the most comprehensive photo reference library available.

'en tools, a knockout block, a ib/feed fitter, a '51' nib fitter, a norkel retractor, a sac stretcher nd a pair of rubber nosed pliers.
105-120

TYPEWRITERS

A Sennatus typewriter, German, 1928, 10¼in (26cm) wide.
$225-300

A Hammond typewriter, early 1900, 14in (36cm) wide.
$180-225

A Bennett typewriter, American, early 1900, 11in (28cm) wide.
$150-180

A Columbia Model 2 typewriter, with type wheel, indicator dial and nickelled base, American, in mahogany case.
$3,000-4,500

A Moya Visible No.2 typewriter, with oxydised top plate and mahogany case.
$2,250-3,000

An early Hammond typewriter, in 14in (36cm) oak case.
$150-225

An Active typewriter, with sliding typewheel, steel frame and leatherette case, German, early 20thC.
$450-600

A Lambert typewriter, No. 5618, with blue and gilt lining, by Gramophone & Typewriter Ltd, also oak case and accessories.
$600-750

Typewriters

- Patents were taken out on typewriters as early as 1828 in America, but Remington made the first commercially successful machine in 1873. As soon as the office potential was realised, demand soared and hundreds of manufacturers filed patents after 1890.
- Collectors look for pioneering machines which represent a stage in the development of typewriters, and rare pre-1900 models. Post-1914 machines hold little interest for collectors.
- Patent numbers are a useful guide to date; most machines were produced within three years of the patent being filed.
- Early manufacturers of note include Fitch, Yost, New Century, Williams, Empire, Fay-Sho, Oliver, Crandall and Blick.
- Condition is paramount in assessing value, and a perfect machine, with contemporary ribbon, undamaged transfer motifs, gilding, enamelling and paintwork sells for much more than a damaged or restored item. Accessories, such as instruction manual and carrying case, add further value. Avoid machines with defective nickelling to the metal parts which is expensive to repair or restore.

A Blick typewriter, American retailed in Britain, 13in (33cm) wide.
$105-120

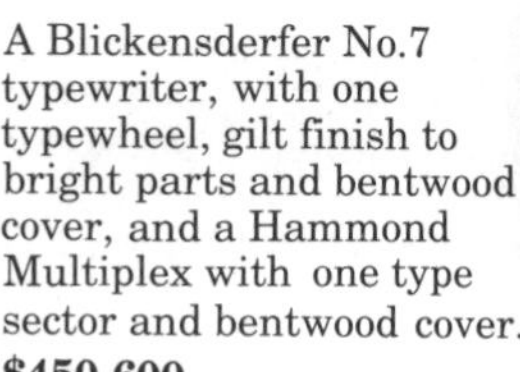

A Blickensderfer No.7 typewriter, with one typewheel, gilt finish to bright parts and bentwood cover, and a Hammond Multiplex with one type sector and bentwood cover.
$450-600

SPORT
Billiards

.n English oak full size
illiard/dining table, by
urroughes & Watts, c1880.
15,000-22,500

.n English oak, full size billiard
able, by Orme & Sons, 1902.
22,500-30,000

. Peruvian mahogany full size billiard table,
y George Wright, c1890.
7,500-9,000

. Brazilian mahogany billiard/dining table,
08in (274cm).
4,500-6,000

An English oak billiard/dining table, by E.J. Riley, c1920, 72in (183cm).
$3,000-4,500

A Peruvian mahogany billiard/ dining table, by Burroughes & Watts, c1890, 84in (213cm).
$4,500-6,000

A Brazilian mahogany full size billiard table, by Burroughes & Watts, c1860.
$7,500-9,000

Baseball

A grey flannel baseball uniform, with purple trim, no identification tags, no later than 1920 due to the style, excellent condition.
$600-750

Lou Gehrig bronze statue, signed by R.P. Daus and numbered 1 of 50, marble base and labelled 'The Pride of the Yankees', painted blue No. 4 on the Gehrig jersey reverse and home insignia on front, manufactured by Del Zornada, 16in (41cm) high.
$3,000-4,500

A 1922/23 St. Louis Cardinals jersey, worn by Pat Rooney, with staining around logo, otherwise in excellent condition, no name, with socks. **$750-1,200**

The last jersey worn by Mickey Mantle, 1968 Wilson brand New York Yankees #7 road style flannel.
$75,000-105,000

Presented by Mantle to a close friend along with a newspaper article dated Friday, September 20, 1968, picturing Mantle circling the bases after his 535th home run while wearing this uniform.

Rollie Fingers 1970 Oakland A's road flannel vest style jersey, worn by the premier relief pitcher, autographed in the collar, original and unrestored, one button missing, with letter of authenticity.
$3,000-4,500

A pen and ink cartoon by Roy Ullyett, signed, overmounted in green, framed and glazed, 16½ by 25in (42 by 64cm) overall.
$135-150

Harmon Killebrew 1970 Minnesota Twins road flannel uniform, worn by Hall of Famer and 500 Home Run Hitter, 'Killebrew' stitched in collar, tail and waistband, autographed on the front, original and unrestored with 2 letters of authenticity.
$7,500-9,000

Christy Mathewson Fad-A-Way Bubble Gum box, produced by American Chicle Co, extremely rare, cWWI, 7½in (19cm) wide.
$750-900

1959 Frank Malzone complete ome uniform, Boston Red Sox by im McAuliffe, size 42, shows ght game use.
600-750

A baseball, autographed by Pete Rose and three others.
$750-1,200

The three other signatures on this ball are those of the men who were instrumental in sending baseball's all-time hit leader to prison.

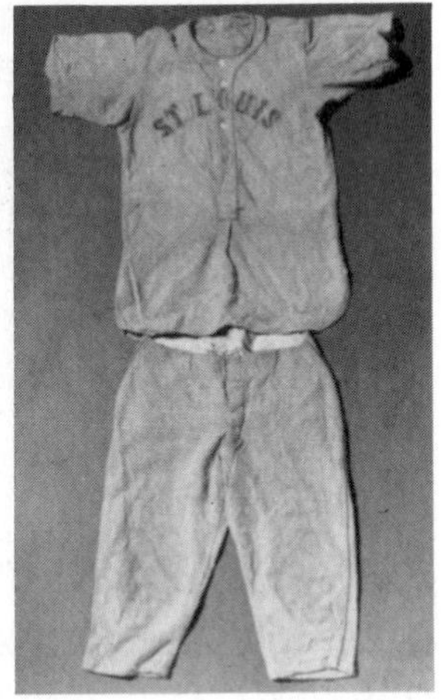

A 1931 St. Louis Browns road style uniform, by Rawlings, shirt worn by catcher Jack Crouch, name in tail, shows heavy wear, pants worn by outfielder Frank Waddey, name in waist.
$750-1,200

Hillerich and Bradsby M110 ickey Mantle signature bat, ith 'Mickey Mantle No. 7 under gnature imprint.
750-900

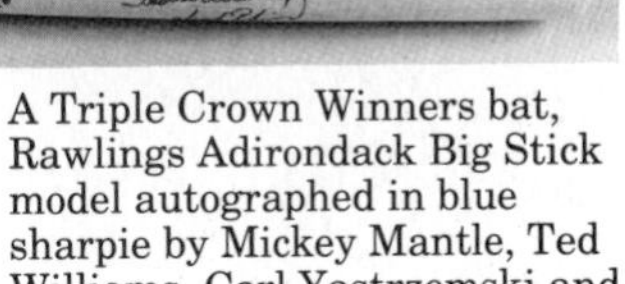

A Triple Crown Winners bat, Rawlings Adirondack Big Stick model autographed in blue sharpie by Mickey Mantle, Ted Williams, Carl Yastrzemski and Frank Robinson, the only living Triple Crown Winners.
$1,050-1,350

An official International League ball, signed in ballpoint pen Satchel Paige under the Wilson logo.
$600-750

batting helmet worn by Hank aron in early 1970s Atlanta raves, autographed, made by BC, size 7⅛, 44 and Aaron ritten in marker pen on inside, tyle worn when hitting homer 15, shows light wear, utographed on peak.
1,800-2,700

A 1969 New York Mets Team Ball, World Champion 'Miracle Mets,' 30 signatures including Seaver and Hodges, and a letter of authenticity from club Vice President and General Manager John Murphy on official Mets Stationery from 1969.
$1,800-2,700

Rod Carew's game worn batting helmet of the 1980's California Angels, made by ABC, size 7¼, 'Carew' identi-tape on peak, worn.
$450-600

Cricket

Twelve Continental porcelain coloured bisque cricketing figures, after D'Aquino, including F. Trueman, D. Lilly, W. G. Grace, I. Botham, and V. Richards, on circular bases with wooden stands, 8 to 13in (20 to 33cm) high.
$1,200-1,800

Geoff Boycott, a print by Stead, signed by both Stead and Boycott in pencil to image, LE 687/850, framed and glazed, 24 by 18in (61 by 46cm) overall.
$135-150

Vanity Fair, 'In his Father's Steps' (Lord Dalmeny), by Spy, 22nd September 1904, overmounted in green, 13 by 19in (33 by 48cm) overall.
$150-225

Vanity Fair, 'English Cricket' (The Honourable A. Lyttelton), b Spy, 20th September 1884, overmounted in green, 13 by 19i (33 by 48cm) overall.
$300-375

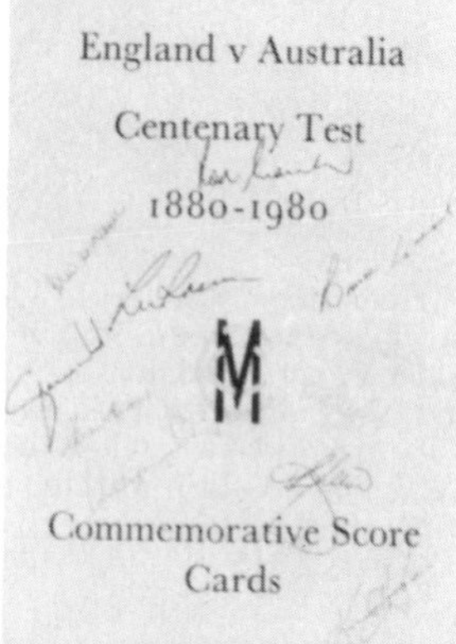

A presentation folder containing 2 silk commemorative scorecards issued for the England v. Austrialia Centenary Test, 1880-1980, signed to the cover of the folder by Allan Border, Graham Yallop, Greg Chappell, Graeme Wood, Ray Bright, Ashley Mallett, Kim Hughes etc., being the complete Australian team in this match, Lords 1980, 11 signatures in total.
$90-105

Vanity Fair, W. G. Grace by Spy, 'Cricket', 9th June 1877, overmounted in burgundy, framed and glazed, 15 by 18½in (38 by 47cm) overall.
$225-300

Vanity Fair, 'Tom' (Tom Hayward), by Spy, overmounted in green, 13 by 19in (33 by 48cm overall.
$300-375

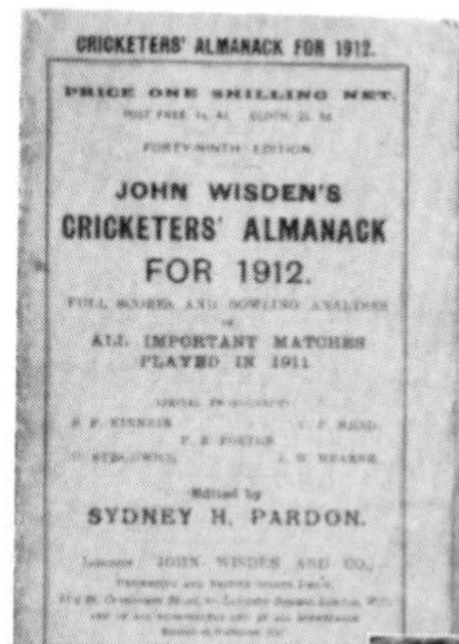

CRICKETERS' ALMANACK FOR 1912.

PRICE ONE SHILLING NET.

JOHN WISDEN'S
CRICKETERS' ALMANACK
FOR 1912.

ALL IMPORTANT MATCHES
PLAYED IN 1911.

SYDNEY H. PARDON.

John Wisden's Cricketers' Almanack for 1912 paper wrappers, some damage.
$105-120

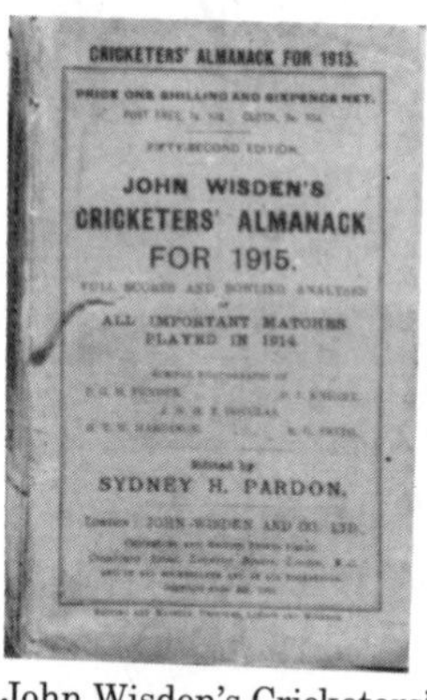

CRICKETERS' ALMANACK FOR 1915.

JOHN WISDEN'S
CRICKETERS' ALMANACK
FOR 1915.

ALL IMPORTANT MATCHES
PLAYED IN 1914

Edited by
SYDNEY H. PARDON.

John Wisden's Cricketers' Almanack for 1915, paper wrappers, spine worn.
$120-135

BADMINTON
CRICKET CLUB

OPENING OF THE
MEMORIAL
GROUND

SUNDAY, JULY 4th, 1948

Hours of play:
12 noon to 6.30 p.m.
Followed by
AN OPEN AIR SERVICE

A programme for the opening of the Memorial Ground, Badminton Cricket Club, 4th July 1948, signed to cover by Walter R. Hammond, Neil Harvey, Charles J. Barnett, John Arlott, W. J. O'Reilly, T. W. Goddard, etc., 14 signatures in total, some damage.
$150-180

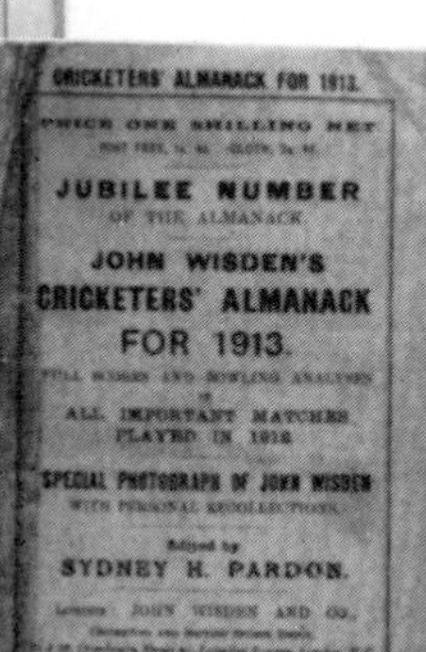

CRICKETERS' ALMANACK FOR 1913.

PRICE ONE SHILLING NET

JUBILEE NUMBER

JOHN WISDEN'S
CRICKETERS' ALMANACK
FOR 1913.

ALL IMPORTANT MATCHES
PLAYED IN 1912

SPECIAL PHOTOGRAPH OF JOHN WISDEN

SYDNEY H. PARDON.

John Wisden's Cricketers' Almanack for 1913, cover laminated.
$90-105

cricket ball, on an ebony display tand with mounted white metal laque engraved 'J. B. Hobbs from ıe Somerset XI. He scored his 26th Century from this Ball. omerset v. Surrey at Taunton. ug. 15, 17, 18, 1925'.
1,200-1,800
his ball came from J. B. Hobbs y direct descent. Wisden records: 'his was the match rendered rever memorable by the triumph f Hobbs who playing innings of 01 and 101 not out, equalled on ıe Monday morning W. G. race's aggregate of 126 centuries first-class cricket, and on the uesday afternoon beat the Grand Old Man's' record.'

A full size cricket bat, signed to reverse by England and Australia 1926, New Zealand 1927 and Lancashire, all 53 signatures bold and clear, in a custom-made wood and glazed display case.
$750-900

A miniature bat, issued to commemorate Sir Len Hutton's Test record of 364 against the Australians, 1938, with facsimile signatures of the Australian team on the front and the England team on the reverse, with a cartoon by Tom Webster, in the original Gradidge box.
$135-150

A full size cricket bat, signed by 5 of the Nations of the 1983 World Cup on the front and back, 54 signatures in all.
$150-180

A full size cricket bat signed by the 15 1991 bowlers taking 10 wickets in a match, including Lawrence, Medleycott, Younis, Stephenson, Akram, Tufnell, Foster, etc., with statistical data.
$120-135

A Thorne's Extra Super Crème Toffee tin, issued as a souvenir of the Australians' visit to England in 1926, with circular portraits of all the team, probably Melbourne Cricket Ground on the lid.
$225-255

full size cricket bat, signed by he 16 1991 players scoring 200 or ıore runs in an innings, ıcluding Malik, Gatting, Moxon, zharuddin, Barnett, Gooch, 'Olivera, etc., with statistical ata.
150-180

Fishing

l. A Hardy Altex No. 2 Mk 5 reel, with optional check.
$90-105
r. A Young's Ambidex reel, with full bale arm.
$40-60

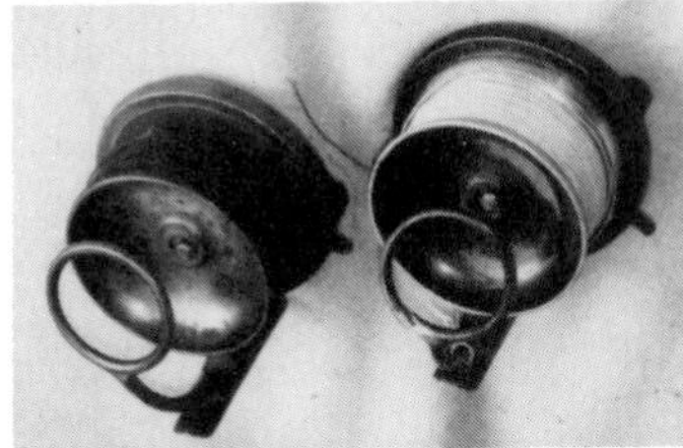

A pair of Malloch patent swivelling casting reels, designed for salmon spinning:
l. Aluminium.
$40-60
r. Brass.
CPT
$90-105

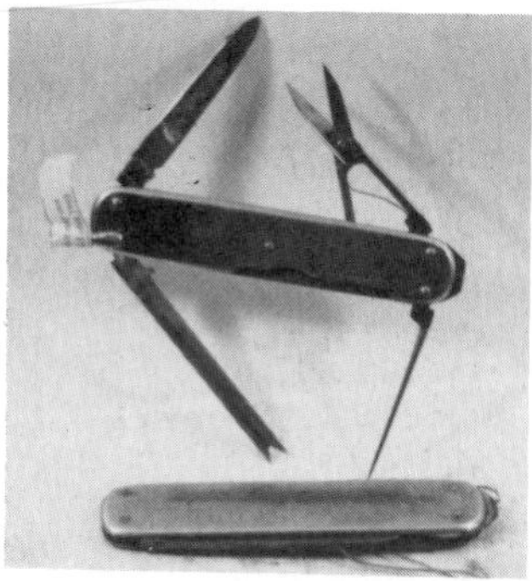

A knife, made by Fred Shaw, who was one of the greatest fishermen in about 1905.
$25-40

A 2⅝in Hardy Perfect fishing reel, brass faced, with ivorine handle, c1900.
$3,000-3,750

A 4¼in Hardy Perfect fishing ree all brass, made between 1896-1900.
$225-255

A 3in brass fishing reel, made in France.
$50-75

A 2¾in Hardy Silex Multiplier, c1920.
$150-225

A 3⅛in Hardy Perfect fishing ree with ivorine handle and narrow drum, c1900.
$135-150

A 3in Allcock fishing reel, The Marvel, post WWII.
$25-40

A 3⅞in Hardy fishing feel, The Taupo, made just after WWII for New Zealand.
$150-225

A pair of Decantelle spinnin centre-pin fishing reels:
l. French. **$90-105**
r. Hardy. **$180-225**

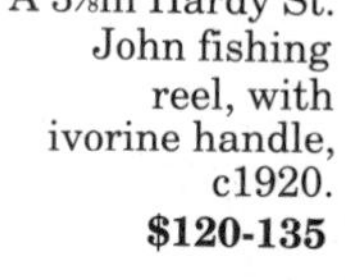

A 3⅞in Hardy St. John fishing reel, with ivorine handle, c1920.
$120-135

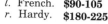

Three ABU of Sweden fishing reels:
top l. A Cardinal 66. **$50-75**
bottom l. A Cardinal 44X.
$90-105
r. An ABU 6000 Multiplier with a case. **$150-225**

There are many models similar to this 6000 worth over twice this amount.

A collection of creels:
l. Tin with sliding brass cover/fish hole. **$105-120**
r. Tin with ventilated fish hole.
$90-105
c. top. Fine split wicker. **$25-40**
c. bottom. Huntley & Palmer biscuit tin. **$225-255**

Hardy Silex No. 2 fishing reel, irst model of 1910, with knurled rum release nut.
120-135

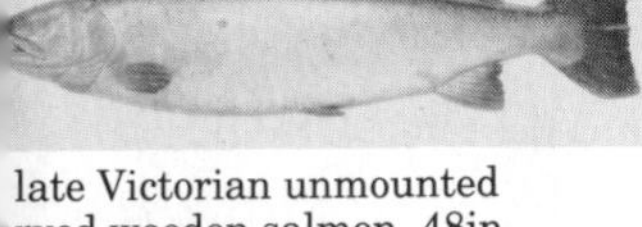

Victorian carved wooden lmon with scale, fin and gill etail, naturalistically decorated, 3in (122cm) long.
2,250-3,000

late Victorian unmounted rved wooden salmon, 48in 22cm) long.
2,250-3,000

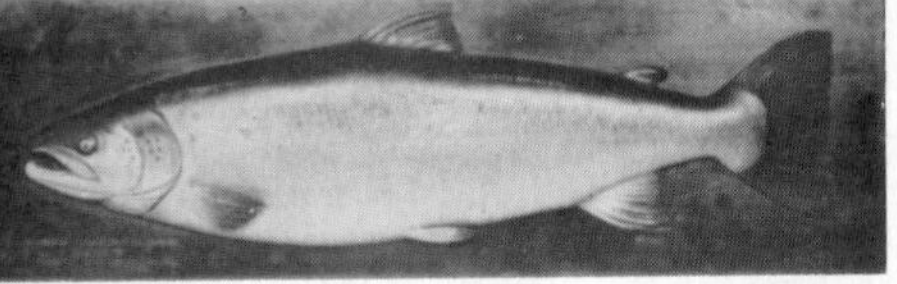

carved wooden salmon, 1929, 1in (104cm) long.
1,500-2,250

carved and painted wood model lmon, on black painted pine ackboard, inscribed 'Weight 4lbs, length 48in, girth 26in, ught by Captain J. P. Law, ept. 1903'.
3,000-3,750

fishing rod, with bamboo roach ole, c1930, 84in (213cm) long.
40-60

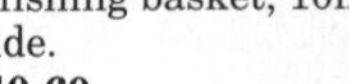

A fishing basket, 10in (25cm) wide.
$40-60

A fishing net, with cane handle and brass fitting, c1930, 50in (127cm) long.
$40-60

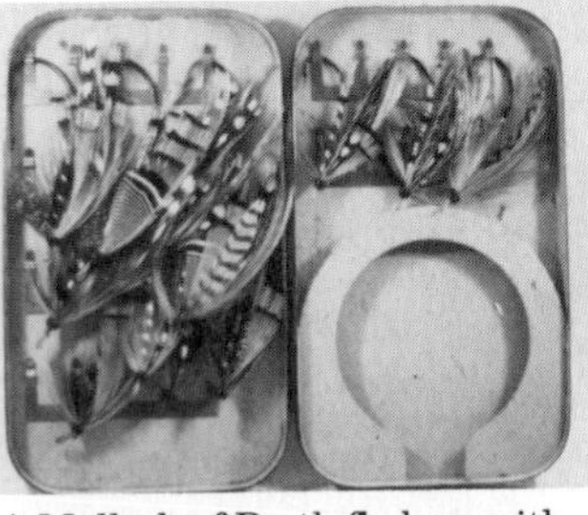

A Malloch of Perth fly box, with 30 clips, 13 gut-eyed salmon flies.
$90-105

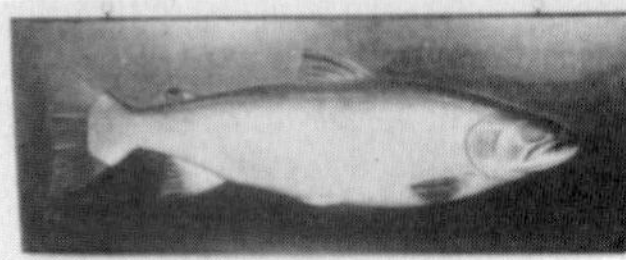

A carved wooden salmon, 1879, 40in (101.5cm) long.
$3,000-3,750

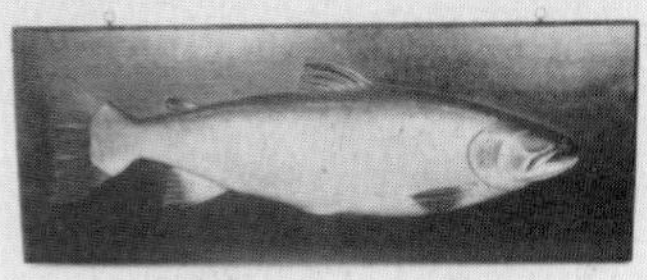

A carved wooden salmon inscribed on the backboard 'Caught by Herbert Peel Esq. of Taliaris on the River Cothy, 9th May 1879, weight 27lbs, length of fish 40in (101.5cm)'.
$3,000-3,750

Football

An official souvenir programme of the F.A. Cup Final, Aston Villa v. Newcastle United, Empire Stadium Wembley, 1924, front tissue cover missing.
$375-525

An official programme of the F.A. International match, England v. Scotland, Empire Stadium, Wembley, 14th April 1934, with relevant song sheet.
$90-105

An official souvenir programme of the F.A. Cup Final, Bolton Wanderers v. West Ham United, Empire Stadium, Wembley,, 28th April 1923, being the first Cup Final held at Wembley.
$750-1,200

An official souvenir programme of the F.A. Cup Final, Preston North End v. Huddersfield Town, Stamford Bridge, 29th April 1922.
$750-900

A random hammered gutta golf ball, by Allan Robertson.
$22,500-30,000

Vanity Fair, Mr Horace Hutchinson, by Spy, 19th July 1890, overmounted in green, 1 by 13in (48 by 33cm) overall.
$180-225

Golf

A composite set of 6 silver golf buttons, by Villiers & Jackson, cast with 2 golfers in open landscapes, within a matt border inscribed 'Brough Golf Club', 3 dated 1908 (Birmingham 1907), one dated 1910 (Birmingham 1909), one dated 1911 (Birmingham 1910), and one dated 1912 (Birmingham 1908), each 1in (2.5cm) diam., 42gr.
$300-375

A Robert L. Jones model Spalding putter, left handed, leather grip, wooden shaft, the handle engraved 'Babe Ruth'.
$15,000-18,000

A silver plated stemmed golf ball condiment set.
$90-105

Walt Disney poster, Pinocchio, half
ıeet, unfolded, framed, 1940, 22 by
3in (56 by 71cm).
,750-7,500

Paramount poster for Every
ay's A Holiday, one sheet, linen
acked, 1938, 41 by 27in (104 by
9cm).
2,250-3,000

A Paramount poster for
The Runaway, one sheet,
linen backed, 1926, 41 by
27in (104 by 69cm).
$1,500-2,250

A United Artists poster for The
Circus, one sheet, linen backed, 41
by 27in (104 by 69cm).
$18,000-20,000

A Warner Brothers poster for
Jezebel, 'other company', one
sheet, linen backed, 1938, 27 by
41in (69 by 104cm).
$3,750-4,500

A Warner Brothers poster
for Bordertown, one sheet,
paper backed, 1934, 41 by
27in (104 by 69cm).
$9,000-10,500

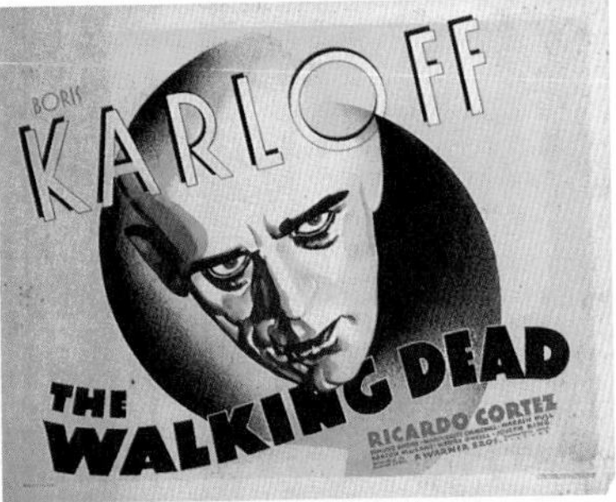

A Warner Brothers poster for The
Walking Dead, half sheet, unfolded,
1936, 22 by 28in (56 by 71cm).
$3,750-4,500

l. A Universal poster for Son Of
Frankenstein, three sheet, linen backed,
1939, 41 by 81in (104 by 206cm).
$11,500-12,500

A 20th Century Fox
poster for Lifeboat, one
sheet, linen backed,
1943, 41 by 27in (104
by 69cm).
$2,250-3,000

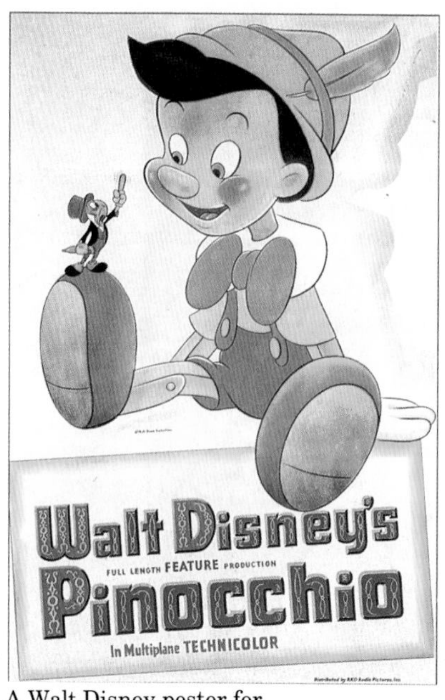

A Walt Disney poster for Pinocchio, one sheet, linen backed, 1940, 41 by 27in (104 by 69cm).
$6,000-7,500

An RKO poster for Notorious!, one sheet, linen backed, 1946, 41 by 27in (104 by 69cm).
$2,000-3,000

A United Artists window card, for Modern Times, unfolded, 1936.
$1,500-3,000

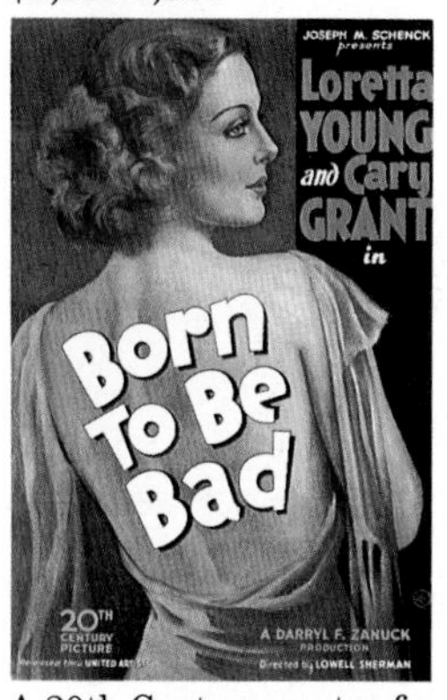

A 20th Century poster for Born To Be Bad, one sheet, linen backed, 1934, 41 by 27in (104 by 69cm).
$3,000-4,000

A Fox poster for Call Her Savage, one sheet, linen backed, 1932, 41 by 27in (104 by 69cm).
$1,300-1,600

A set of 8 Universal lobby cards for The Old Dark House, 1932, 14 by 11in (36 by 28cm) each.
$12,000-13,500

A First National poster for 3 On A Match, one sheet, paper backed, 1932, 41 by 27in (104 by 69cm).
$3,000-4,500

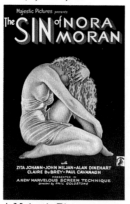

A Majestic Pictures poster for The Sin of Nora Moran, one sheet, linen backed, 1933. **$20,000-22,500**

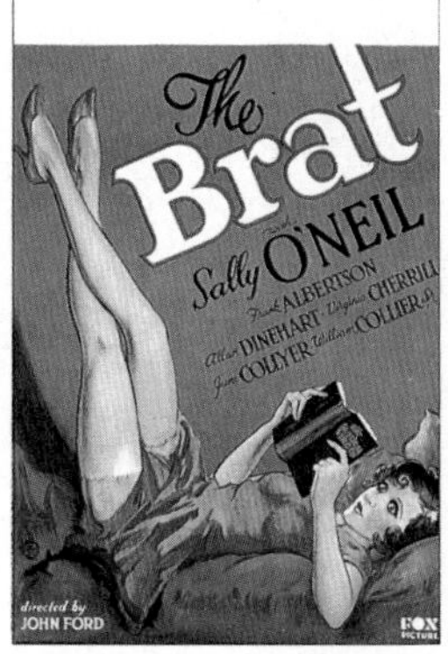

A Fox poster for The Brat, one sheet, linen backed, 1931. **$2,250-3,000**

l. A Gaumont British poster for Secret Agent, half sheet, folded, 1936, 28 by 22in (71 by 56cm).
$1,500-1,800

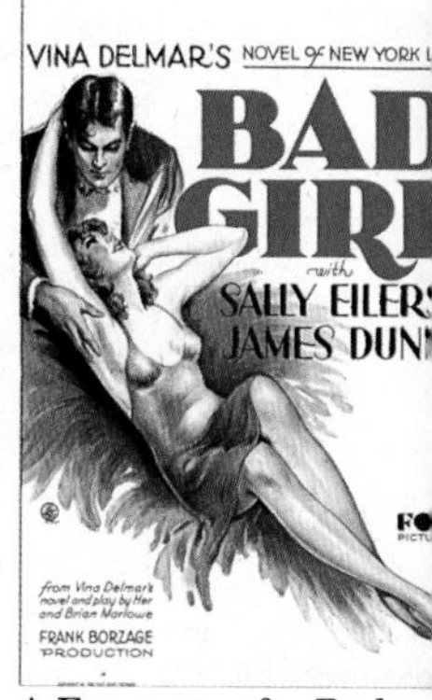

A Fox poster for Bad Girl, one sheet, linen backed, 1931, 41 by 27in (104 by 69cm).
$2,500-3,500

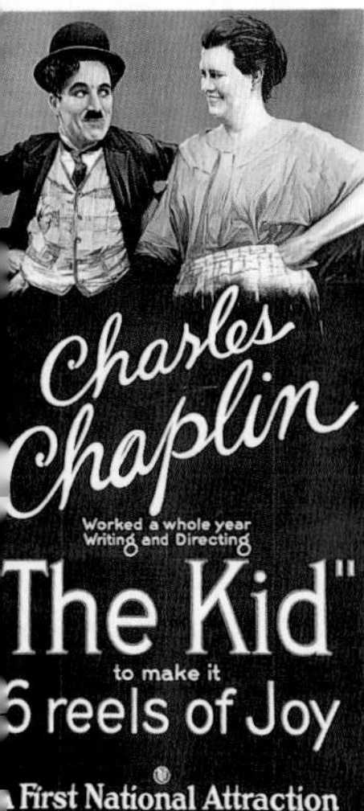

First National poster
r The Kid, three sheet,
nen backed, 1921, 81 by
.in (206 by 104cm).
,500-8,500

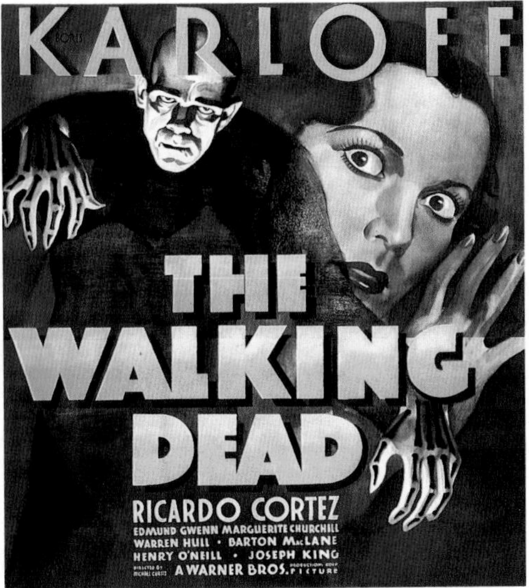

A Warner Brothers poster for The Walking Dead, six sheet, linen backed, 1936, 81 by 81in (206 by 206cm).
$30,000-35,000

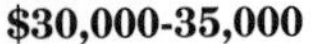

A Walt Disney poster for Dumbo, three sheet, linen backed, 1941, 81 by 41in (206 by 104cm).
$20,000-22,500

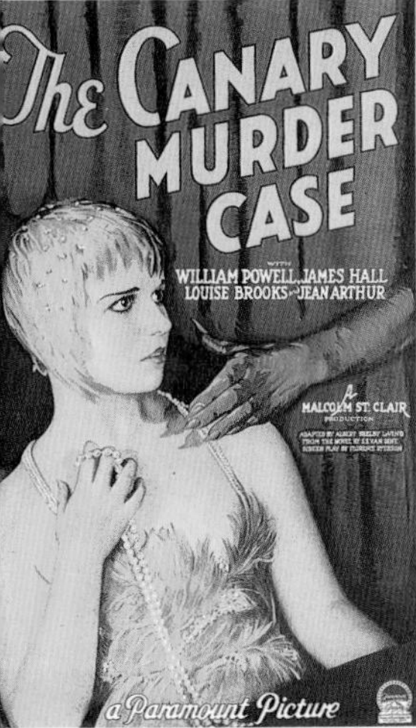

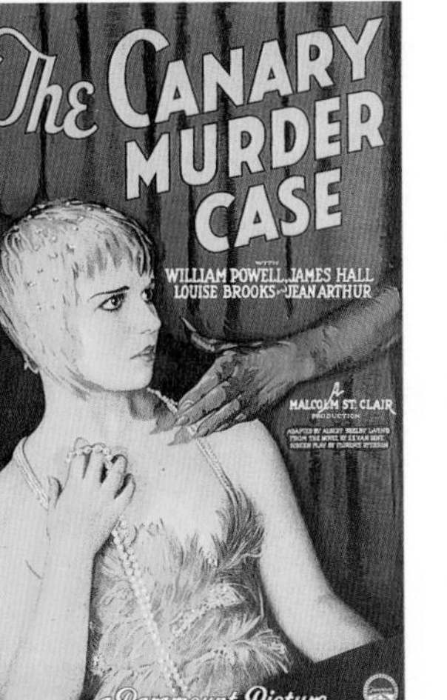

Paramount poster for
he Canary Murder
ase, one sheet, paper
acked, 1929.
30,000-34,000

An MGM poster for The Wizard Of Oz, half sheet, unfolded, paper backed, 1939, 28 by 22in (71 by 56cm).
$20,000-22,500

A Gaumont British poster for The 39 Steps, one sheet, paper backed, 1935, 41 by 27in (104 by 69cm).
$15,000-18,000

Gaumont British
oster for The Lady
anishes, one sheet,
nen backed, 1938, 41
y 27in (104 by 69cm).
10,000-11,500

A United Artists poster for Things To Come, six sheet, linen backed, 1936, 81 by 81in (206 by 206cm).
$22,000-27,000

A Paramount poster for She Done Him Wrong, three sheet, linen backed, 1933, 81 by 41in (206 by 104cm).
$5,250-6,750

A stoneware lidded jar, by Dame Lucie Rie, impressed LR seal, c1975, 9in (23cm) high. **$6,000-7,500**

A stoneware vase by Bernard Leach, the upper part glazed, impressed BL and St Ives seals, 14½in (37cm) high. **$4,500-5,500**

A stoneware chest of drawers with reindeer, by Ian Godfrey, surmounted 2 detachable houses, with carved reindeer lid and 2-part wagon lid, 8in (20cm) high. **$1,500-2,250**

A porcelain vase, by Dame Lucie Rie, impressed LR seal, c1978, 10in (25cm). **$4,000-5,000**

A stoneware dish, 'The Pilgrim', by Bernard Leach, with stencils of a pilgrim against mountain and sky, impressed BL and St Ives seals, c1967, 12in (31cm) diam. **$4,000-5,000**

A porcelain bowl, by Dame Lucie Rie, th well below rim glazed white with a band circular and a wide band of radiating inlay, impressed LR seal, c1968, 10in (25cm) diam. **$6,000-7,500**

A stoneware Noah's Ark bowl and lidded urn, by Elizabeth Fritsch, c1976, bowl 13½in (34cm) wide. **$11,500-12,500**

A porcelain bowl, by Shinobu Kawase, pale celadon glaze, 12in (31cm) wide, with signed wood box. **$3,000-4,000**

A shiny green porcelain bowl, by Dame Lucie Rie, with golden bronze runs, impressed LR seal, c1983, 9in (23cm) diam. **$5,500-6,500**

A tin glazed earthenware vessel, inscribed James Tower '80, with name label 'Spray', 21½in (54cm) high. **$2,500-3,500**

A stoneware composite form, by Hans Coper, impressed H seal, c1965, 6in (16cm) high. **$5,500-6,500**

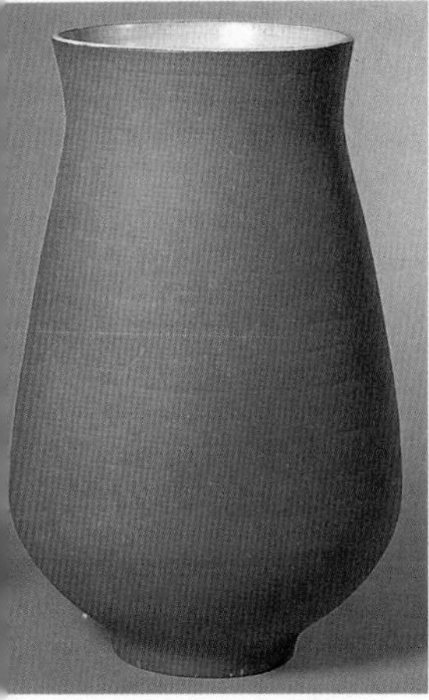

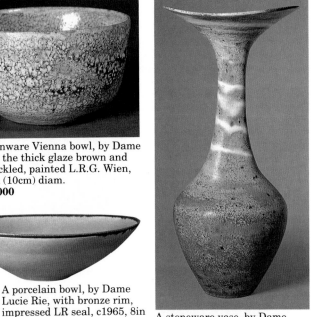

red earthenware vase, by ame Lucie Rie, glazed beige interior, impressed LR al, c1948, 9in (23cm) high.
,750-4,500

An earthenware Vienna bowl, by Dame Lucie Rie, the thick glaze brown and beige, speckled, painted L.R.G. Wien, c1930, 4in (10cm) diam.
$2,250-3,000

A stoneware vase, by Dame Lucie Rie, of different clays forming spiral, impressed LR seal, 14in (36cm) high.
$15,000-16,500

A porcelain bowl, by Dame Lucie Rie, with bronze rim, impressed LR seal, c1965, 8in (20cm) wide.
$2,250-3,000

golden bronze and white porcelain owl, by Dame Lucie Rie, sgraffito diating lines inside, impressed LR al, c1982, 8in (20cm) diam.
,750-4,500

A stoneware vase, by Ian Godfrey, deeply carved, the base with carved animals, 10in (25cm) high.
$2,250-3,000

A stoneware rounded bottle vase, by Katherine Pleydell Bouverie, covered with a glaze, impressed KPB seal, 13in (33cm) high.
$3,000-3,750

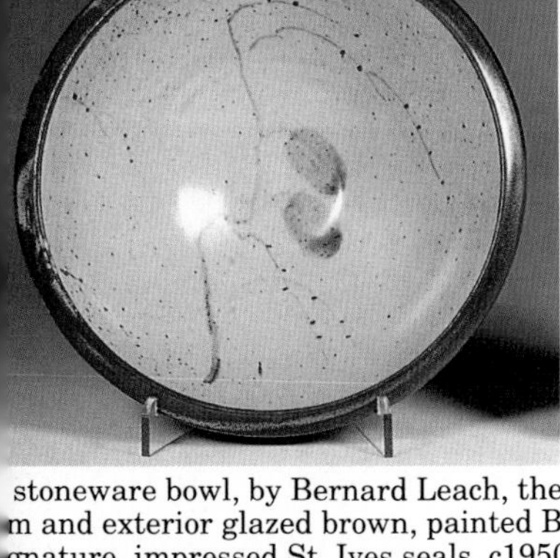

stoneware bowl, by Bernard Leach, the m and exterior glazed brown, painted BL gnature, impressed St. Ives seals, c1950, in (31cm) diam. **$2,250-3,000**

porcelain bowl, by Dame Lucie Rie, manganese ith radiating sgraffito, the foot and well glazed hite, impressed LR seal, c1965, 8in (20cm) diam.
,500-9,000

A stoneware pot, by Hans Coper, glazed white with matt brown abstract design to exterior, the foot with sgraffito, impressed HC seal, c1955. **$4,500-5,500**

A stoneware vase, by Katharine Pleydell Bouverie, with carved panels, impressed KPB seal, 9in (23cm) high.
$3,000-3,750

A stoneware 'egg-on-stand' form, by Hans Coper, with interior flower holder, impressed HC seal, c1975.
$6,000-7,500

A stoneware dish, by Shoji Hamada kaki, upper surface with resist stepped cross pattern, 10½in (26cm) square, with signed wood box.
$3,000-3,750

An stoneware pouring bowl, by Yu Fujiwara, the textured surface distinguished by 3 orange circles to interior, 11in (28cm) diam.
$3,750-4,500

A stoneware 'egg-on-stand' form by Hans Coper, with dark brown interior and flower holder, impressed HC seal, c1975, 5in (13cm) high. **$6,000-7,500**

A stoneware slab bottle, by Bernard Leach, impressed BL and St. Ives seals, stamped England, c1953.
$2,250-3,000

A stoneware vase by Hans Coper, with dark brown interior, damaged and restored, impressed HC seal, c1958, 12in (31cm) high.
$3,000-3,750

A goblet, by Ian Godfrey, with a band of 3 carved antelopes, 8in (20cm) high
$1,500-2,250

A black vessel form, by Hans Coper, on cylindrical base, impressed HC seal, c1975, 14½in (37cm) high.
$30,000-33,000

A porcelain manganese bowl, by Dame Lucie Rie, impressed LR seal, c1965, 6in (15cm) diam.
$2,500-3,500

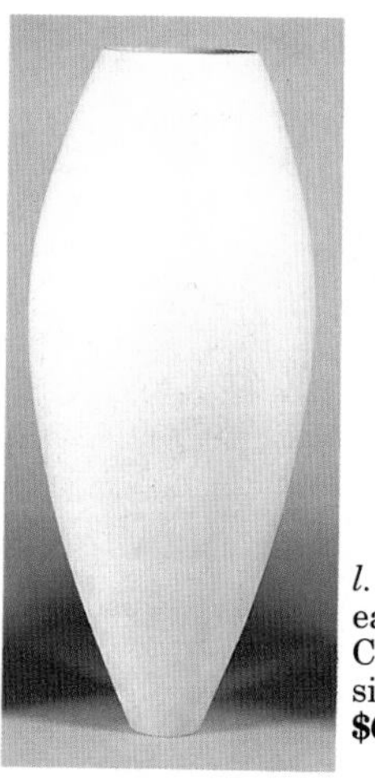

l. A coiled white earthenware vessel form, by Christine Jones, incised signature, 18in (46cm) high.
$600-750

stoneware vessel, by John
ard, impressed JW seal,
½in (32cm) high.
,250-3,000

A stoneware bowl, by Dame Lucie Rie, yellow and brown interior, impressed LR seal, c1965, 5in (13cm) diam. **$4,500-5,250**

A porcelain manganese bowl, by Dame Lucie Rie, impressed LR seal, c1965, 6in (15cm) diam.
$2,500-3,500

stoneware vase, by
ame Lucie Rie,
ith thick green
aze, impressed LR
al, c1980, 11in
8cm) high.
,250-3,000

A stoneware handled ram jug, by Ian Godfrey, with mottled running green and grey glaze, 9½in (24cm) high.
$750-950

An antelope vase, by Ian Godfrey, incised with foliate pattern above carved animal.
$2,250-3,000

A stoneware fox box, by Ian Godfrey, the lid with donkeys, ram and birds, 7in (17cm) high.
$1,200-1,500

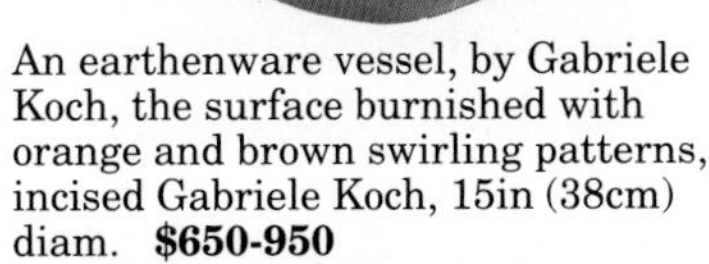

An earthenware vessel, by Gabriele Koch, the surface burnished with orange and brown swirling patterns, incised Gabriele Koch, 15in (38cm) diam. **$650-950**

Raku square lidded vessel, by
eiko Hasagawa, glazed lustrous
ue green, impressed potter's
al, 11in (28cm) high, with
gned wood box.
00-1,200

A stoneware cut sided bottle, by Shoji Hamada, tenmoku glaze over red body, c1951, 11in (28cm) high.
$6,000-6,750

A stoneware four-handled covered bowl, by Ian Godfrey, handles carved, lid and base with small applied discs and incised marks, 5in (13cm) high. **$1,200-1,500**

A builder's model of the turret deck steamers Sutherland and Argyll, by W. Doxford & Sons Ltd, Sunderland, for the Sutherland Steamship Co. Ltd, 13 by 44in (33 by 112cm), in original mahogany glazed case. **$12,000-13,500**

An exhibition standard 2in scale model of the Burrell double crank 'Gold Medal' tractor, engine No. 3846, built by K.C. Beszant, c1911. **$10,500-12,000**

A Märklin gauge O spirit fired 4-6-2 Pacific locomotive and tender, No. HR 4920, finished in black with gilt lining and factory fitted electric light, with matching 8-wheeled tender, some repairs and paint loss, c1928.
$6,750-7,500

A detailed exhibition standard 5in gauge model of th Great Western Railway Armstrong 4-4-0 locomotive and tender, No 16, 'Brunel', built by J F Bowman, 14 by 61½in (36 by 156cm). **$6,750-7,500**

A French prisoner-of-war copper and boxwood model of a 92-gun Ship of the Line, 8 by 12½in (20 by 32cm), in ebonised glazed case. **$5,250-7,500**

A planked and rigged early 19thC model of a American armed topsail schooner, 35 by 55in (89 by 140cm).
$18,000-19,500

A builder's exhibition half model of the S.S. Reginald Hanson, the semi-circular glazed case labelled Screw Steamer by John Young Short, M.I.N.A. of Short Brothers, 1877, 16½ by 64½in (42 by 163cm).
$5,250-6,750

A Märklin gauge I 'La France' 4-4-2 clockwork locomotive and tender, No. 102 restored and repainted, German, c1906.
$2,250-3,000

l. An exhibition standard 5/16in:1ft scale metal display model of the 'V' Class destroyer H.M.S. 'Vega', Pennant No.L41, built by Norman Peters, 17 by 58½in (43 by 148cm).
$18,000-19,500

Tipp limousine, with green uniformed chauffeur, ectric front and rear lights, front steering, opening ·ar doors, clockwork motor and number plate 10962, ›me damage, German, c1930. **$600-900**

. Hartnig & Vogel chocolate tin/pull-along delivery an, with hinged roof, damaged, German, 1910, 18in ‹6cm). **$16,000-17,500**

Distler Shell petrol tanker and trailer, with green ıniformed driver, number plate JD 1614, the tanks with ınged ends, clockwork motor, German, 1920s, tanker ‹in (28cm), trailer 6in (15cm) long. **$2,300-2,500**

CIJ clockwork painted tinplate Alfa Romeo P2 ıcing car, with operating steering and handbrake, xcelsior shock absorbers, in original box, c1927, 1in (53cm) long. **$4,500-6,000**

l. A Matarazzo YPF petrol tanker, with clockwork motor, Argentinian, 1930s, scratched, 11in (28cm) long. **$600-750**

A Carette limousine, with black uniformed chauffeur, front steering, twin handbrakes, opening rear doors, some rust, German, c1911, 16in (41cm) long. **$5,250-6,750**

A boxed No.174 petrol tanker, probably by Wells, with blue uniformed driver and clockwork motor, English, 1930s, good condition, 10in (25cm). **$1,350-1,500**

A Minerva open top double decker bus, lithographed in orange, red and yellow, some repainting, English, 1930s, 8in (20cm) long. **$2,250-3,000**

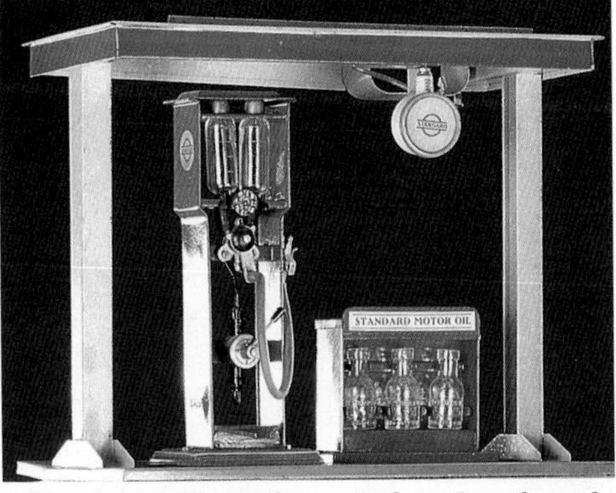

A Standard doll's tinplate petrol station, the red pump with twin glass reservoirs, an oil bin with 3 glass bottles, under metal canopy with electrically illuminated sign, German, 1930s. **$4,000-5,250**

A Bing four-seater open tourer, with adjustable steering and clockwork motor, c1912, good condition, 12½in (32cm). **$2,250-3,000**

A Jumeau bisque headed bébé, with jointed wood and papier mâché body, 29in (74cm) high.
$3,000-4,500

A brown bisque swivel headed bébé, with bisque arms and black kid body, impressed BRU Jne.
Est. $6,000-9,000

A bisque headed googlie-eyed character doll, with jointed wood and composition body, impressed F 10 J.D.K. 221, damaged.
$5,500-6,750

l. A bisque headed bébé Parlant Automatique, by Steiner, c1890. **$1,800-2,250** *r.* A Steiner bisque headed bébé, c1880.
$4,000-5,000

A spray painted character boy 'Gypsy' doll, impressed Heubach Koppelsdorf 452.0, 16in (41cm) high.
$1,000-1,500

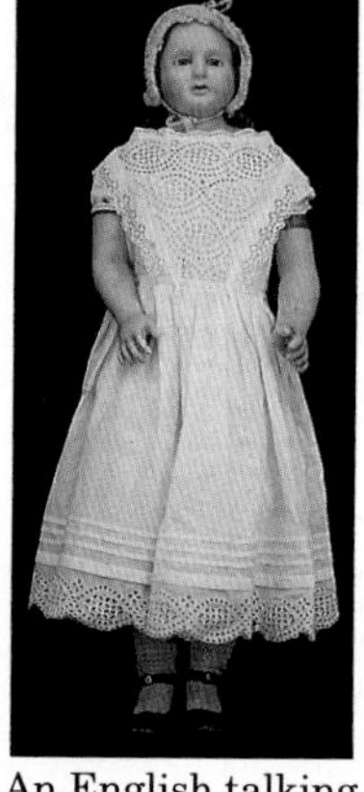

An English talking doll, with wax over papier mâché shoulder head, voice box inoperative, mid-19thC.
$4,000-5,000

A musical hand operated toy, when the handle is turned the clowns move their heads and appear to play instruments, impressed SPB in star H, in glass case.
$3,750-4,500

Two bisque headed bébé dolls:
l. J. Steiner Fre A15. **$5,500-6,750**
r. impressedC N 4 J Steiner, clockwork walking mechanism inoperative.
$3,750-5,250

A bisque headed bébé, with jointed wood and papier mâché, voice box, impressed Bru Jne R12, damaged and repaired, 25in (64cm) high.
Est. $9,000-12,000

A bisque swivel headed bébé, with kid body, bisque arms and wooden legs, impressed Bru Jne 8, finger and thumb broken, c1875, 22in (56cm) high.
$24,000-27,000

A bisque headed bébé Mothereau, with painted hollow cast lead body, wooden upper limbs, impressed B 4 M, c1880.
Est. $12,000-15,000

A J.M. pressed bisque doll, with fixed lass paperweight eyes, real hair wig over ork pate, ball jointed wood and papier nâché body, original satin dress, npressed 5 J stylised mushroom M, 'rench, c1880, 24in (62cm).
14,250-15,500

A Danel et Cie moulded bisque Paris ébé, real hair wig over cork pate, jointed ood and composition body, stamped Tête)eposée Paris Bébé, 1890, 27½in (70cm).
6,750-8,250

A Roullet et Decamps musical automaton of a mask seller, French, c1910, 41in (104cm) high.
$100,000-105,000

A William and Mary painted wooden doll, with peg joints to hips and knees, upper arms of cloth, wearing original clothes, replacement real hair wig, c1700, 16in (41cm). **$50,000-55,000**

bisque headed bébé, with fixed blue yes, pierced ears, blonde wig, jointed ody, transfer mark Deposé Tête umeau, 26½in (68cm) high.
st. $9,000-12,000

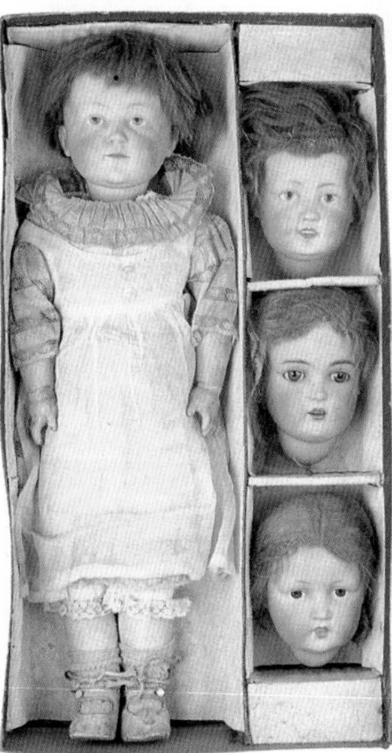

A boxed set by Kestner, comprising a bisque headed character doll and 3 interchangeable bisque heads.
$12,000-13,500

A Bru bisque swivel headed mannequin, c1890. **$16,000-18,000** holding a bisque headed Bébé du Louvre, c1892.
$3,000-3,750

Two French dolls:
l. A Jumeau Triste pressed bisque doll, c1875, 22in (56cm).
$10,500-13,500
r. A Jules Steiner C Series pressed bisque doll, stamped Le Petit Parisien Bébé Steiner, c1880, 23in (59cm).
$3,000-4,500

Two bisque headed bébés:
l. Danel & Cie. **$4,500-7,500**
r. May Frères Cie.
Est. $7,500-9,000

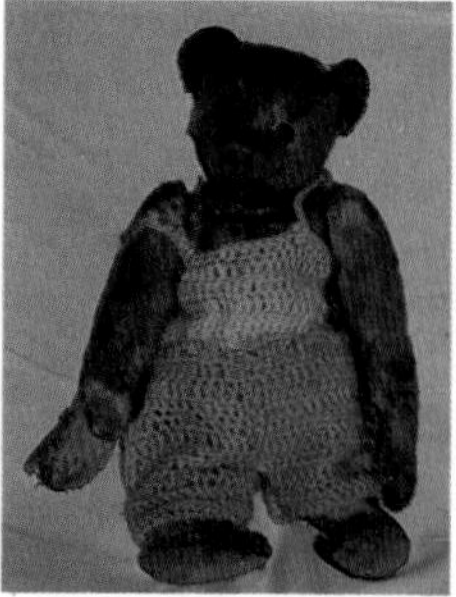

An early plush teddy bear, with hump back, 12in (31cm) high.
$300-375

l. 'Dicky', a Steiff white plush covered teddy bear, hump and button in ear, slight damage, 1930, 12in (31cm) high.
$5,250-6,750
r. 'Cedric', a Steiff cinnamon plush covered centre seam teddy bear, c1906, 16½in (42cm) high.
$2,500-4,000

A Steiff gold plush covered teddy bear, with swivel head, elongated shaped ar and legs, hump and button in ear, c1910, 12½in (32cm high. **$2,000-2,500**

A Steiff white curly plush covered teddy bear, with swivel head, elongated jointed shaped arms and legs, and hump, c1915, 24in (61cm). **$5,250-6,000**

A Rupert bear on a tricycle, by Chiltern Toys, 1950s, 11in (28cm).
$200-225

A Steiff honey golden plush covered centre seam teddy bear, with swivel head, elongated jointed arms and legs, and hump, growler inoperative, c1908, 16in (41cm). **$4,500-5,250**

A Steiff off white teddy bear, with button, one of the first with glass eyes, c1910, 18in (46cm).
$3,000-4,500

A group of teddy bears, the 3 on the left all Steiff, with ear buttons: *l.* 18in (46cm), c1925. **$1,200-1,500** *c. l.* 1905, 21in (53cm). **$2,250-3,000** and *c. r.* 24in (61cm) 1920. **$5,250-6,750** and *r.* probably German, c1910, 16in (41cm). **$750-1,000**

l. A Glockenspiel white long plush covered musical teddy bear, by Helvetic Co, c1925, 18in (46cm).
r. A Steiff white plush covered teddy bear, c1915, 24in (61cm) high.
$3,000-3,750 each

A cotton plush 'Sooty Type' squeaking bear, possibly Dutch, 24in (62cm).
$200-270

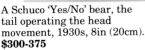

A Schuco 'Yes/No' bear, the tail operating the head movement, 1930s, 8in (20cm).
$300-375

An American purple mohair bear, soft stuffed with kapok, c1920,21in (54cm).
$600-700

r. Two Steiff honey gold plush covered bears, with black button eyes, swivel heads, ear buttons, c1910, 29 and 30in (74 and 76cm) high. *l.* **$2,250-3,000** *r.* **$6,000-7,500**

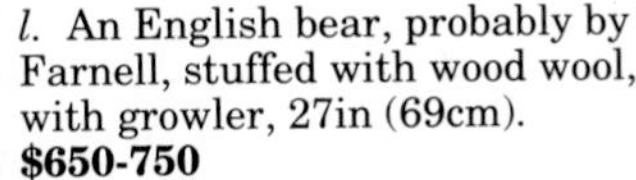

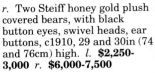

l. An English bear, probably by Farnell, stuffed with wood wool, with growler, 27in (69cm).
$650-750

A Dentzel carved second row jumper in the Philadelphia style, with original dappled body paint, restored, 52in (132cm) high. **$9,000-12,000**

A German boxed set of painted composition toy soldiers from the Franco-Prussian war, including cavalry and Zoaves, some set in scenes with rocks and trees, late 19thC, infantryman 3in (8cm) high, in original box. **$2,250-2,750**

A Märklin Russian carousel, hand painted and with hand-turned mechanism, cylinder musical accompaniment, in blue casing with gilt lining, German, c1904, 21in (53cm) high. **$93,000-102,000**

A German toy 'Englisches Theater', the 4 painted carved wood figures with articulated arms, the painted reversible backdrop with 7 wing inserts, canvas curtain, c1820, 19in (48cm) high. **$6,750-8,250**

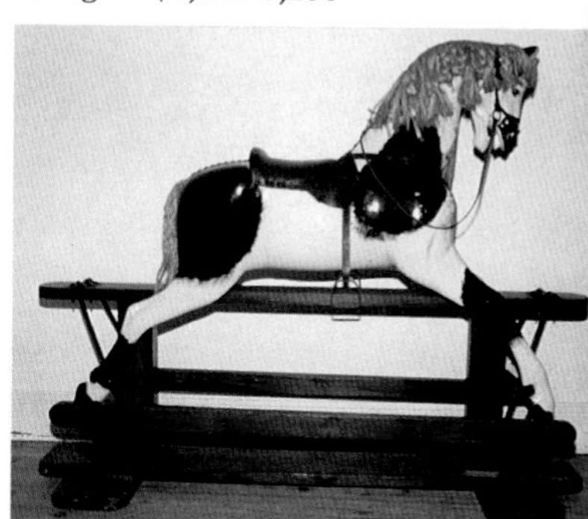

A rocking horse, on stretcher stand. **$450-600**

A carved and painted pine outside row standing carousel horse, by Gustav Dentzel & Co, Germantown, Philadelphia, c1895. **$23,000-27,000**

A French lithographed tinplate 'Holland' liner biscuit tin, with 3 funnels, twin masts and pennants, on 4 wheels, c1905. **$1,200-1,500**

A Giant in the Tower cast iron money bank, No. 196844, damaged, c1880, 9½in (24cm) high.
$5,250-6,000

A Mickey Mouse tinplate organ grinder toy, probably by Distler, the piano with clockwork motor, Mickey's tail missing, 6in (15.5cm) long, and other toys. **$3,750-4,500**

An American painted pine chequerboard, late 19thC, 15in (38.5cm) square.
$1,800-2,250

An Anglo-Indian ebony and ivory games board, in the form of 2 books entitled History of Persia 1 and 2, possibly Vizagapatam, restored, early 19thC, 18in (46cm) wide.
$4,500-5,250

A Yoshia Mighty Robot, with plastic head, on a rotating wheeled turntable, Japanese, c1960, 12in (31cm).
$1,350-1,800

An American carved and painted pine and metal toy village, including 8 individual buildings, c1900, church 25in (63.5cm) high.
$3,000-3,750

Two Japanese attacking Martian robots, c1960, 9 and 11in (23 and 28cm) high.
$600-750

A carved and painted pine and sheet metal American eagle birdhouse, made by E. G. James, Mingo County, West Virginia, c1920, 53in (135cm) high.
$8,250-9,000

Two carved and painted pine circus advertising figures of a tiger and a zebra, Cole Brothers Circus, Indiana, c1920, 59in (150cm) high.
$9,750-10,500 each

l. A carved and painted pine barber's pole and advertising sign, signed Amos K. Ross & Sons, New Jersey, c1930, 56in (141cm) high. **$18,000-19,000**

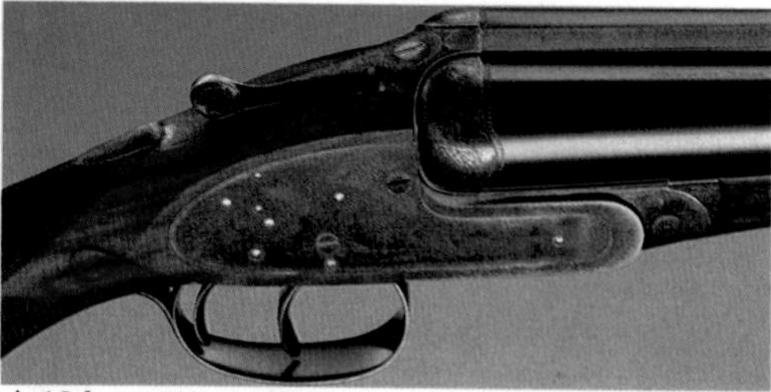

A 12-bore 2¾in self-opening sidelock ejector pigeon gun, No. 22873, J. Purdey & Sons, with 30in (76cm) Whitworth steel chopper lump barrels, 14⅝in replacement stock, semi-pistol grip, oak and leather case. **$10,000-12,000**

A pair of 12-bore 2¾in L70 grade sidelock ejector guns, No. 54830/1, W.W. Greener, with 30in (76cm) Whitworth steel barrels, in their oak and leather case. **$11,250-12,750**

A pair of 12-bore 2½in sidelock ejector guns, Nos. 7177/8, by John Dickson & Son, 28in (71cm) barrels, No. 1 with replacement barrels by the makers, in their leather case.
$7,500-10,500

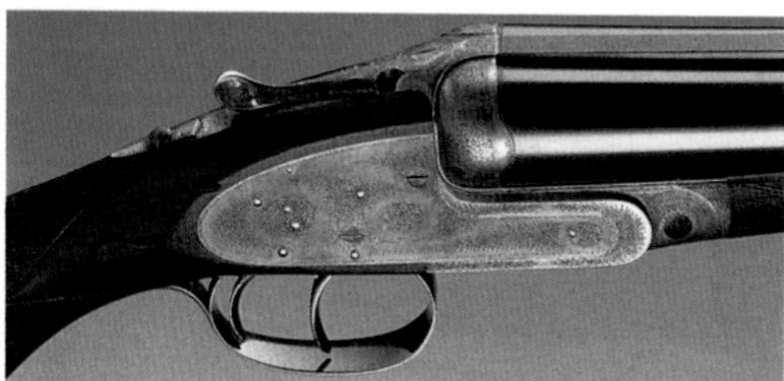

A 12-bore 2¾in self-opening sidelock ejector gun, No. 25589, by J. Purdey & Sons, with 30in (76cm) chopper lump barrels, full choke borings, with pistol grip, in its oak and leather case.
$11,250-12,750

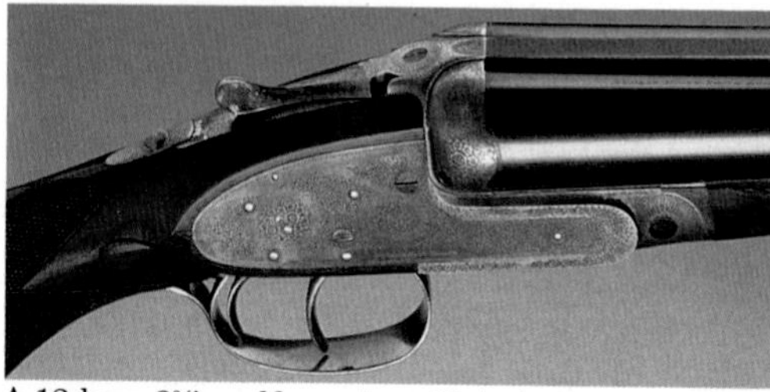

A 12-bore 2¾in self-opening sidelock ejector gun, No. 25590, by J. Purdey & Sons, with 30in (76cm) chopper lump barrels, about improved cylinder and ½ choke borings, in its oak and leather case.
$8,250-9,750

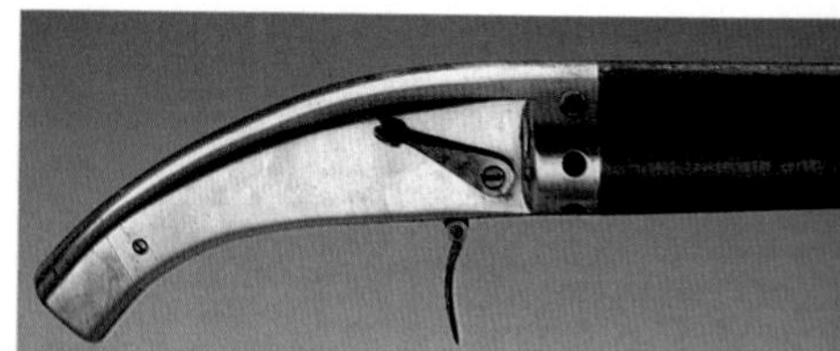

A single barrelled 2-bore Moore and Grey's type screw-breech punt gun, 76in (193cm) tapered barrel, in wooden case, with cleaning rod and 6 rechargeable brass cases, primed with .320 blank cartridges. **$2,250-3,000**

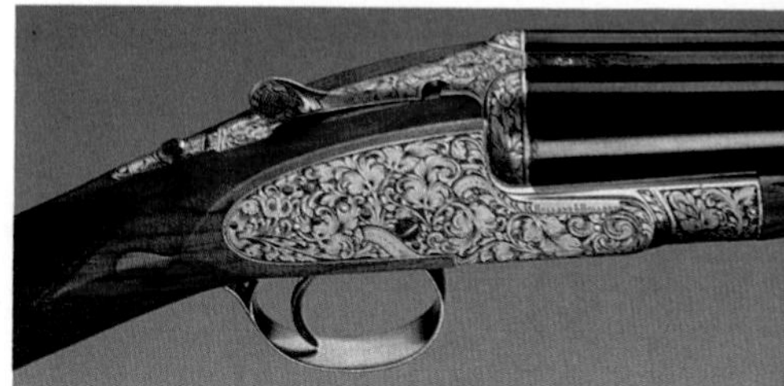

A set of 3 Caspard engraved 20-bore 2¾in (7cm) Roya de luxe model single trigger self-opening detachable sidelock ejector guns, Nos. 40444/5/6, by Holland & Holland, 28in (71cm) chopper lump barrels, in their oak and leather case, 1978. **$108,00-112,500**

A 12-bore 2¾in Royal model single trigger self-opening detachable sidelock ejector gun, No. 40006, by Holland & Holland, extra 30in (76cm) chopper lump barrels, in lightweight leather case.
$16,500-21,000

A pair of 12-bore 2½in self-opening single trigger sidelock ejector guns, Nos. 19196/7, by J. Purdey & Sons, with 29½in (75cm) Whitworth steel chopper lump barrels, about ¼ and ½ choke borings, in their oak and leather case. **$20,000-22,500**

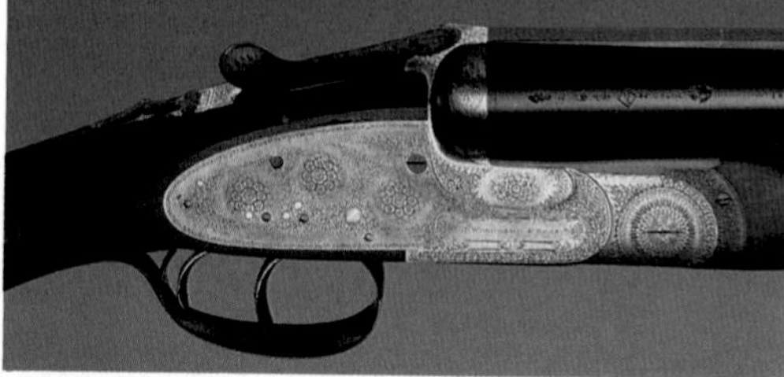

A 12-bore 2¾in sidelock ejector over/under gun, No. 6842, by J. Woodward & Sons, with 30in (76cm) barrels, ½ and ¾ choke borings, Prince of Wales grip, in its oak and leather case.
$15,000-22,500

\ wooden Tyrolean pavis, bearing he arms of the League of St George, c1470-90, face overpainted n 19thC, 47in (119cm).
30,000-33,000

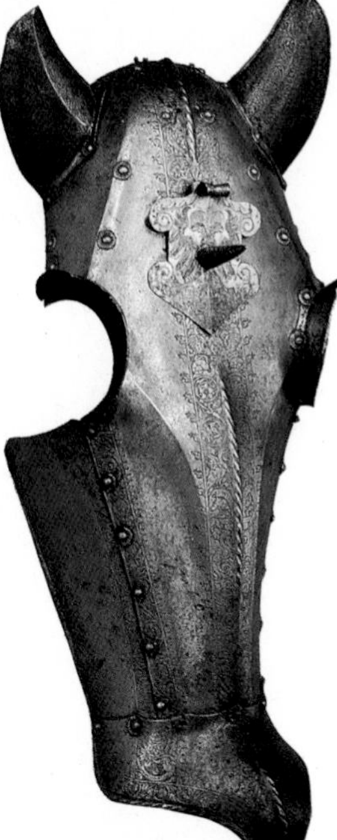
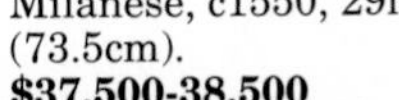

A North Italian etched shanfron, probably Milanese, c1550, 29in (73.5cm).
$37,500-38,500

A German fluted composed part-armour, comprising gorget of 4 plates front and rear, hinged at side, c1510-1520.
$15,000-16,500

A German comb morion of the Trabantenleibgarde of the Electors of Saxony, Nuremberg, maker's initials MR, c1580-91, 11in (30cm) high.
$13,500-14,250

Russia, Order of St Andrew, badge, gold and enamel, mid-19thC, 4in (9.5cm) high.
$8,250-9,000

Russia, Order of Alexander Nevsky, a non-Christian set of nsignia 'with diamonds', badge in gold and enamel with diamonds and suspension loop, and star, of flexible sew-on type with brooch pin, in silver, gold and enamel, set with diamonds. **$19,000-19,500**

An Italian Savoyard closed burgonet, early 17thC, 13in (33cm) high.
$9,000-9,750

An Italian embossed triple-combed burgonet from the Guard of Pier Luigi Farnese, Duke of Parma and Piacenza, c1545, 10in (25cm) high.
$42,000-45,000

Russia, Order of St George, Second Class gold and enamel neck badge, 2in (5cm).
$9,000-9,750

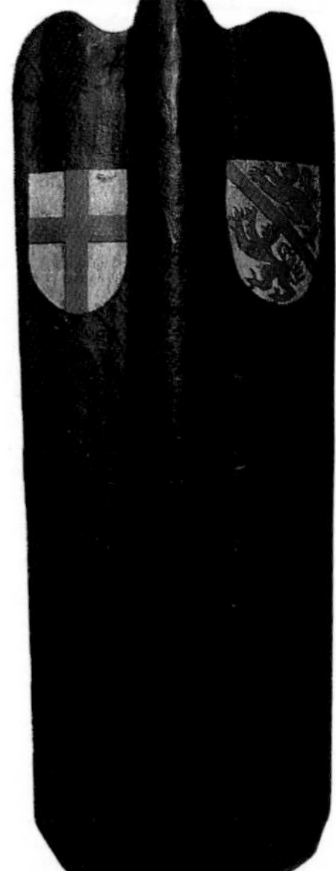

A Swiss pavis, with arms of the League of St George and town of Winterthur, c1460, 44in (112cm).
$30,000-37,500

A tapestry, woven in wools and silks, in the Soho style of John Vanderbank, 106½in by 84in (270 by 213cm).
$15,000-18,000

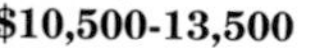

A Flemish Old Testament tapestry, perhaps Enghien, c1600, 122 by 103in (310 by 262cm).
$10,500-13,500

The Crowning of Solomon, a tapestry woven with the anointing of Solomon, late 16thC, Flemish, perhaps Oudenard 134 by 130in (340 by 330cm).
$18,000-22,500

A Flemish Old Testament tapestry, perhaps from the story of Joseph, in 4-sided floral border, Antwerp or Bruges, c1630, 120 by 124in (305 by 315cm).
$18,000-22,500

An Italian silk needlework armorial hanging, worked with an unidentified arms surrounded by flowering arabesques, with small birds, on an ivory field, early 18thC, 93 by 90in (236 by 229cm).
$9,750-12,000

The Sacrificial Offerings of Solomon, Flemish, perhaps Oudenarde, late 16thC, 134 b 102in (340 by 259cm).
$22,500-27,000

A South German tapestry antependium of The Crucifixion, with inscriptions and detail of the costume in metal thread, Upper Rhine or Alsace, late 15thC, 42½in by 80½in (108 by 204cm).
$15,000-22,500

l. A needlework picture of St. Joseph's Academy, attributed to Mary Devine, St. Joseph's Academy, Emmitsburg, Maryland, torn, c1826, 16 by 19in (41 by 48cm).
$9,500-12,000

A set of 6 painted canvas 'tapestries', with genre scenes and children playing, in the manner of Antoine Watteau, French, mid-18thC, each approx. 108 by 72in (274 by 183cm). **$46,000-52,000**

A Brussels tapestry, woven in silks and wools, with a battle scene in a pass, within conforming acanthus and vine leaf borders on a red ground, early 18thC, 140 by 151in (356 by 384). **$24,000-30,000**

A Brussels tapestry, woven in silks and wools, with Moses in a basket before Pharoah's daughter, with borders, early 18thC, 140 by 150in (356 by 383cm). **$22,500-30,000**

A London 'Teniers' Seasons tapestry, depicting autumn,with a sable border, attributed to the workshop of John Vanderbank, early 18thC, 116 by 168in (295 by 427cm). **$49,500-57,000**

An Aubusson Old Testament tapestry, depicting a processional triumph, left side border original, late 17thC, remaining associated and of later date, 110 by 161in (279 by 409cm). **$12,000-13,500**

l. A tapestry of The Procession of the Ark of The Covenant, Flemish, late 16thC, 134 by 152in (340 by 386cm). **$28,500-33,000**

An Aubusson mythological hunting tapestry, outer blue selvage renewed, extensive minor repairs, late 17thC, 111 by 180in (282 by 457cm). **$18,000-21,000**

A Flemish tapestry of Solomon and the Queen of Sheba, late 16thC. **$39,000-45,000**

A Brussels armorial tapestry portière, woven with the arms of Alesmanini of Padua, late 17thC, 134 by 93in (340 by 236cm). **$12,000-18,000**

A South German tapestry fragment, of Virgin and Child, early 16thC. **$12,000-18,000**

A needlework cushion, worked with scrollwork and 2 horses on an eau-de-nil ground, with bobble fringe, c1730, 24in (60cm) wide. **$4,500-4,750**

A needlework cushion, worked with strapwork and stylised foliage on a cream ground with red bobble fringe, c1730, 19in (49cm) wide. **$900-1,200**

A needlework cushion, worked with figures and animals in medieval style on a beige ground, 19thC, 30in (77cm) wide. **$2,500-2,750**

A needlework cushion, worked partly in petit point with a lady in a garden within a border of strapwork and scrollwork, with red bobble fringe, c1700, 24in (62cm) high. **$1,500-2,250**

Two pairs of tapestry cushions, woven with flowers and leaves, 17thC, largest 14in (35cm) square. **$1,000-1,500**

An Aubusson tapestry cushion, woven with an urn of flowers, with 18thC gold fringe, c1780, 23in (59cm) high. **$4,750-5,750**

A needlework cushion, woven with flowers, leaves and grenades, with yellow bobble fringe, c1720, 15in (39cm) wide. **$1,800-2,000**

A needlework cushion, with flowers and leaves on a blue reserve within yellow and brown borders with yellow bobble fringe, c1730, 18½in (47cm). **$2,750-3,000**

A Victorian cushion, 19thC, 18in (46cm) square. **$375-450**

A needlework cushion, worked with flowers and leaves on a yellow ground with deep red fringe, 15in (39cm) wide. **$750-900**

A needlework cushion, worked with bizarre scrolls on a buff coloured ground, with multi-coloured fringe, c1710, 19in (48cm). **$1,200-1,400**

A needlework cushion, worked with a river god in a landscape, borders re-worked, part early 18thC, 21in (54cm). **$750-900**

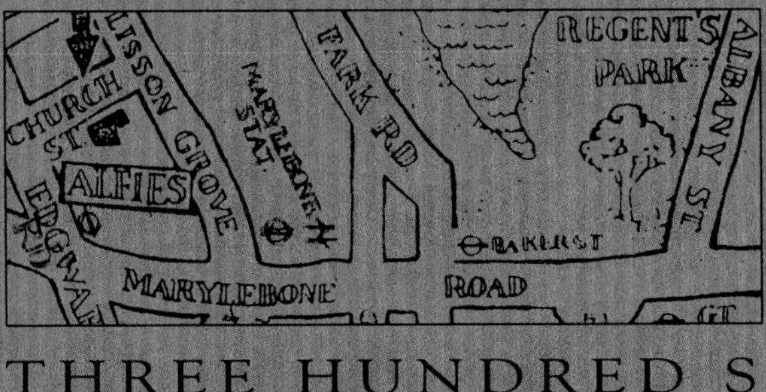

An American pictorial rug, signed Augustine W. Phillips, probably Pennsylvania, some damage, c1830, 54 by 62in (137 by 158cm).
$14,250-15,000

A cotton and broderie perse Star of Bethlehem quilt, Southern, probably Alabama, early 19thC, 112 by 107in (285 by 272cm).
$7,500-9,000

A needlework sampler, signed and dated Elizabeth H. Beale's Work, 1832, probably Pennsylvania, 21½ by 23½in (54.5 by 59.5cm).
$15,500-16,500

An American pictorial hooked rug, worked with prancing horses, initialled 'MM', New England, late 19thC, 40 by 61in (102 by 154cm). **$3,750-4,500**

A calico and chintz Star of Bethlehem quilt, probably from Pennsylvania, some staining and discolouration, mid-19thC, 116 by 114in (295 by 290cm).
$7,500-9,000

An American floral hooked rug, probably New England, early 19thC, 49 by 62in (125 by 158cm).
$7,500-8,250

A pieced and appliquéd cotton quilt top, Pennsylvania, each square with a different picture and with various flower and fruit motifs, early 19thC, 88 by 86in (224 by 218cm).
$6,500-8,000

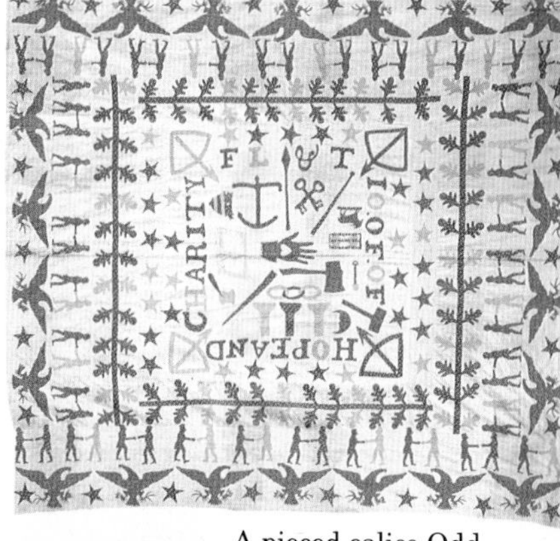

A pieced calico Odd-Fellows quilt top, made by Charlotte Gardner, New York or New Jersey, late 19thC, 104 by 92in (264 by 234cm).
$3,000-3,750

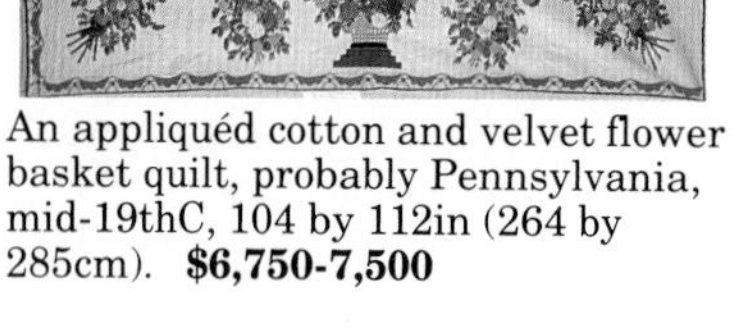
An appliquéd cotton and velvet flower basket quilt, probably Pennsylvania, mid-19thC, 104 by 112in (264 by 285cm). **$6,750-7,500**

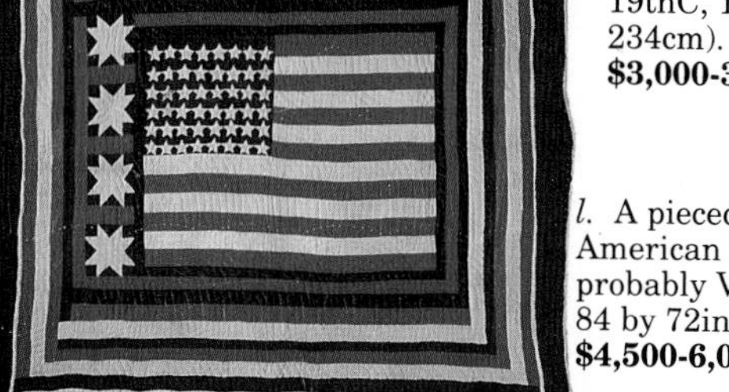
l. A pieced and appliquéd American flag quilt, probably Virginia, c1920, 84 by 72in (213 by 183cm).
$4,500-6,000

diamond bracelet, designed as rectangular panels pieced in a bow design, set hroughout with circular cut stones, connected by similarly set smaller rectangular nks, c1930, 7in (18cm) long. **$8,000-9,750**

A green tourmaline and diamond brooch/pendant, the step cut tourmaline set within brilliant cut diamonds. **$5,250-6,000**

diamond bracelet, designed as a line of oblong panels in a geometrical pattern, ach set with a baguette and 8 cut stones, c1930, 7in (18cm). **$8,000-9,500**

Sardonyx ameo, gold, half earl and enamel rooch/pendant, vith Athena vearing a helmet, 1870. **4,000-5,500**

A three-coloured gold cannetille and gem set bracelet, designed as 5 cartouche shaped panels, each set with an oval rock crystal within a scrolled border of gold cannetille, maker's mark JV in a lozenge, c1825, with later case. **$6,750-7,500**

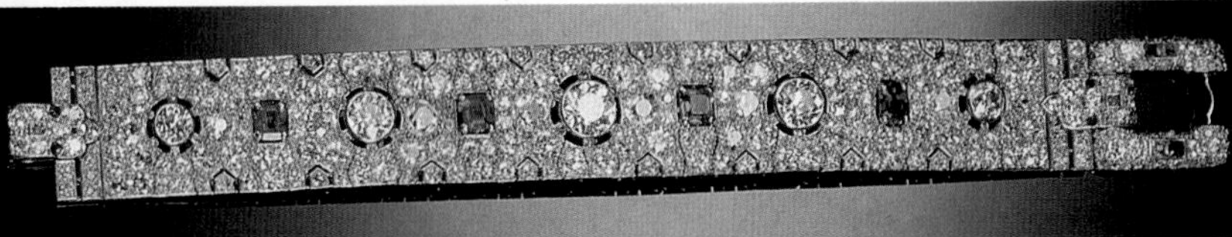

An emerald and diamond bracelet, by Cartier, the articulated band pierced and pavé set with cushion shaped, eight and brilliant cut diamonds, unsigned, 1927, 7in (17.5cm) long, in a fitted case. **$45,000-52,500**

l. A gold hinged locket brooch, with emerald and rose diamonds, 19thC. **$1,400-2,200**

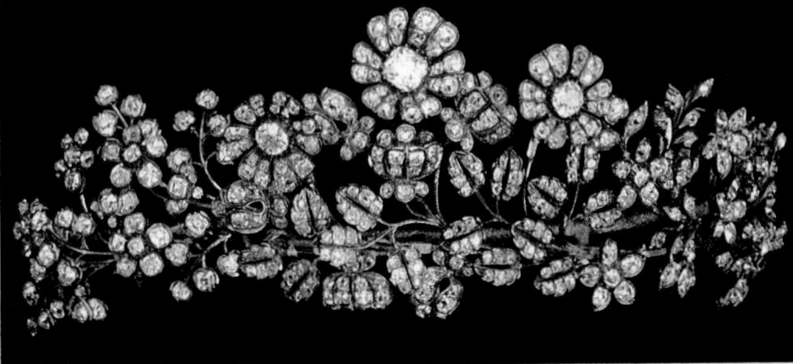

A diamond tiara, designed as a spray of leaves and wild roses, set with cushion shaped diamonds, repaired, mid-19thC. **$13,500-15,000**

l. An 18ct gold diamond flower clip brooch, pavé set and with circular cut diamonds, Mauboussin. **$48,000-52,500**

r. A pair of diamond pendant earrings, designed as stylised ribbon bows supporting dart motifs, set with baguette and brilliant cut stones. **$2,500-4,000**

A Cartier emerald and diamond bracelet, composed of 3 emerald and diamond clusters, set with cabochon emeralds with borders of diamonds, c1935, in maker's case. **$45,000-52,500**

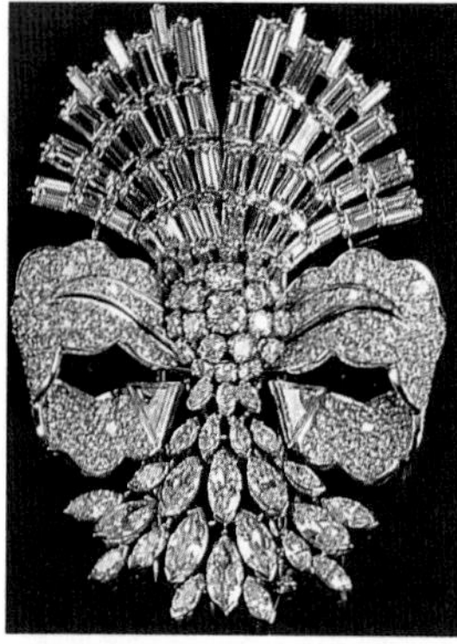

A diamond clip, designed as a stylised wheat sheaf, set with baguette and navette diamonds, tied by a ribbon bow. **$14,250-15,000**

A sapphire and diamond flowerhead clip brooch, with 7 calibré cut sapphire petals and a circular cut diamond pistil. **$39,000-42,000**

A 18ct gold, ruby and diamond brooch, signed Kutchinsky, hallmark for 1961, c1960. **$3,250-3,750**

A diamond brooch of looped ribbon and fringe design, with brilliant cut and baguette diamonds, c1950. **$7,500-9,000**

A ruby and diamond clip, designed as a pair of stylised calla lilies and foliage, and a matching pair of earclips, c1950. **$3,000-3,750**

A Russian gold crucifix pendant, each arm set with an oval amethyst and diamond 3 stone points, Christ in centre with rose diamond cluster halo, hallmarks for St Petersburg 1869. **$4,500-5,250**

A diamond and wood flower clip brooch, with amourette wood petals and circular cut diamond pistil to 18ct gold stem, signed VCA, 1969. **$2,500-3,000**

An emerald and diamond brooch/pendant, c1910. **$4,500-5,250**

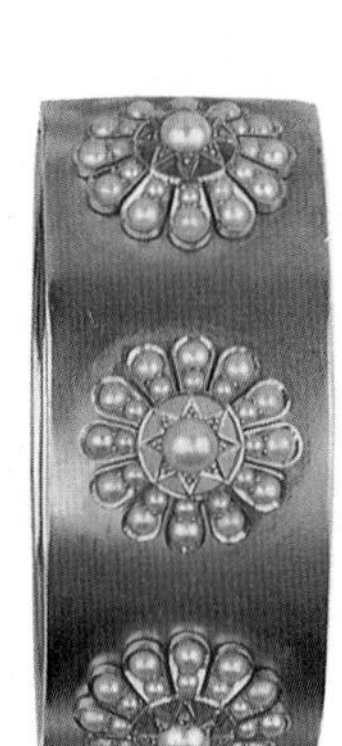

A Victorian gold broad hinged bangle, with triple half pearl applied flowerhead motifs. **$2,000-3,000**

A diamond plaque brooch, set throughout with baguette and brilliant cut stones, by Cartier, London, c1930. **$7,750-8,750**

A Victorian gold circular locket back brooch, with drop shape banded agate and half pearl quatrefoil motif. **$600-700**

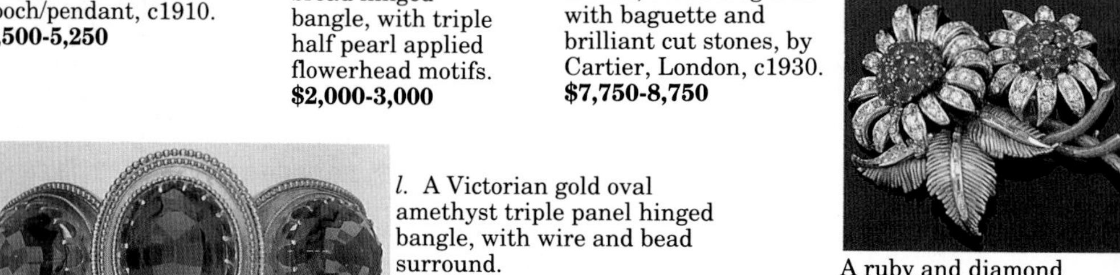

l. A Victorian gold oval amethyst triple panel hinged bangle, with wire and bead surround. **$2,500-3,000**

A ruby and diamond brooch, designed as a stylised spray of chrysanthemum, c1940. **$5,250-6,000**

Iiscellaneous

fencing mask.
l5-25

Staffordshire pearlware ʼlindrical mug, printed in black ıd coloured with a boxing scene ithin a leaf cartouche, inscribed Iumphreys and Mendoza, ıghting at Odiham in Hampshire ı Wednesday Jan. 9th 1788', ɛlow named cartouches, c1800, n (13cm) high.
l,200-1,500

Did you know?
MILLER'S Antiques Price Guide builds up year by year to form the most comprehensive photo reference library available.

pair of curling stones, c1920, ʼin (25cm) diam.

ʼ0-105

A 13oz 'Streamline' tennis racket, the slim main shaft supported by 2 diagonal shafts running from the handle to either side of the head with the intention of making it more aerodynamic, made by Hazells Ltd, London, designed by Bunny Austen, c1930.
$180-225

Ali Muhammed, signed photograph, colour, full length in boxing pose, 8 by 10in (20 by 25cm).
$50-75

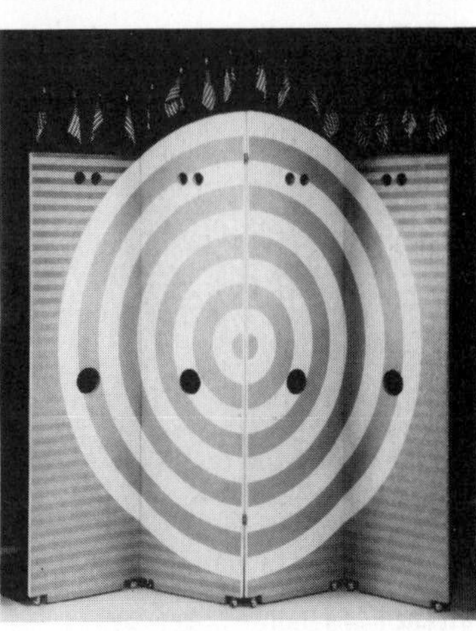

A Dan Friedman target screen with holes, c1984.
$1,500-2,250

Vanity Fair, Thrice Champion (Reginald Frank Doherty), by Spy, issued 1st September 1904, contemporary framing and glazing, 20 by 12in (51 by 31cm) overall. **$120-135**

A set of Young's jockey scales, with velvet upholstered chair with brass arm rests, mounted on an oak base, with a set of brass weights and scales adjacent, on 4 turned oak legs, late 19thC, 35in (91cm) wide. **$2,700-3,300**

ORIENTAL
Cloisonné

A pair of Japanese wireless cloisonné oviform vases, each decorated with numerous egrets on lime green grounds, restored, 5in (12.5cm) high.
$150-225

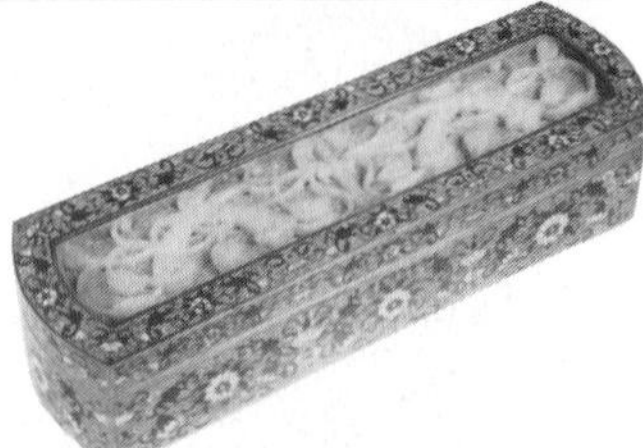

A Chinese cloisonné box and cover, with pierced celadon jade inset top, carved with trumpet-shaped flowers and leaves on a pierced trellis ground, the sides decorated with stylised peony flowerheads on a turquoise ground, incised with Qianlong four-character mark, 11½in (29.5cm) wide.
$750-900

A pair of Japanese cloisonné vases, decorated in silver wire with birds in flight among bamboo and flowering daisies on black grounds between bands of stiff leaves, 10in (25cm) high.
$600-750

A pair of Japanese cloisonné decorated chargers, with turquoise grounds within foliate borders, 17in (43cm) diam.
$900-1,500

A pair of Japanese cloisonné vases, with silver rims decorated on cream, mustard, goldstone and green grounds below bands of stylised insects and flowerheads, 7in (17.5cm) high.
$9,000-10,000

A large cloisonné vase, the black ground decorated with pale pink chrysanthemums and a pheasant, slight pitting, Meiji period, 47in (120cm) high, later wood stand.
$3,000-3,750

A pair of Chinese cloisonné wall vases, modelled as baskets with overturned rims, each decorated with a rural scene within a central cartouche surrounded by a turquoise ground of lotus flowers, 9in (22.5cm).
$750-900

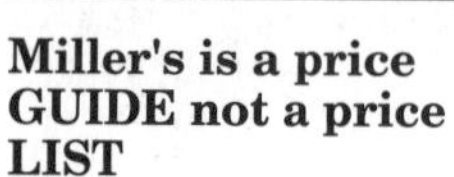

Miller's is a price GUIDE not a price LIST

A Chinese cloisonné baluster vase on tall foot, decorated with stylised scrolling lotus and leafy tendrils on a turquoise ground, some damage, 17in (43cm) high.
$600-750

A Japanese cloisonné vase and cover, with bud finial, on 4 feet with silver mounts and liner, decorated with alternating panels of coiled dragons and ho-o among clouds on coloured goldstone grounds, surrounded by bands of flowerheads and foliage on a black ground, finial damaged, 5in (12.5cm) high.
$450-600

'urniture

lacquered and inlaid wood
.binet, with silver mounts,
ımaged, Meiji period, 25in
3.5cm) wide.
;,000-8,250

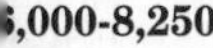

Japanese padouk wood and
cquer netsuke cabinet,
ecorated with bone, mother-of-
arl and abalone shell, 44in
12cm) wide.
,050-1,350

Japanese lacquered brass
ounted black, aubergine and gilt
cquer chest, with a later calico-
.ed interior, on a George III
twood stand with square legs
d later ebonised block feet,
stored, the chest late 17thC,
in (109cm) wide.
,800-2,700

A Chinese red lacquered steatite screen, carved to one side with two figures in a punt beside a figure and a buffalo on the bank and another figure crossing a bridge in a rocky mountainous landscape with pavilions, 22½in (57cm) high.
$1,800-2,700

A Chinese Export black and gilt lacquer cabinet-on-stand, on a George III ebonised stand with plain frieze and on canted square legs, the cabinet constructed in England using Chinese Export panels, damaged, early 18thC, 67in (170cm) high.
$3,000-4,500

A pair of Chinese cabinets, each with two red lacquer doors with circular brass lock plates and escutcheons, the interior with drawers and shelves, 19thC, 41in (104cm) wide. **$4,500-6,000**

A Chinese Export black and polychrome cabinet-on-stand, on an English black and polychrome japanned stand, with panelled frieze decorated with flowers, on chamfered square legs, the doors and stand 18thC, 61½in (156cm) high. **$2,250-3,000**

A Japanese carved wood and shibayama two-fold screen, the gold lacquered panels inlaid in mother-of-pearl and hardstone with peacocks and flowering shrubs, the reverse carved with swimming carp and terrapins, 11½in (29.5cm) high.
$2,250-3,000

A Chinese Export brown lacquer and gilt decorated work table, with all-over figures and scrolling foliage, rounded lid enclosing fitted interior and upholstered well on turned uprights and dual paw feet, 25in (63.5cm) wide.
$1,200-1,500

A Chinese Export black and gilt lacquer eight-leaf screen, depicting an extensive panoramic scene, the broad foliate scroll-filled panelled border with smaller scenes and foliate panels, the reverse with bamboo and other trees and perching birds amidst a broad foliate border, mid-19thC, each leaf 83½ x 22in (212.5 x 55cm).
$7,500-9,000

Inros

A kiriwood two-case inro, decorated in gold and black, after Shibata Zeshin, 19thC, 3in (8cm), with an ivory netsuke in the form of a tigress and cub, the ivory lightly stained and the eyes of mother-of-pearl, signed Hakuryu.
$7,500-9,000

A silver ground four-case inro, with ginji ground and decorated with 3 prancing horses in sumie togidashi, after the painting by Hogen Hakugyoku, the interior of nashiji, signed Jokasai, early 19thC, 3½in (9cm), with silvered metal ojime, carved with 2 rats in a double gourd, unsigned.
$22,500-30,000

A four-case inro, with a rich dark brown ground, decorated in gold takamakie and inlaid mother-of-pearl, signed Koma Kyuhaku saku, 19thC, 3in (8cm).
$22,500-30,000

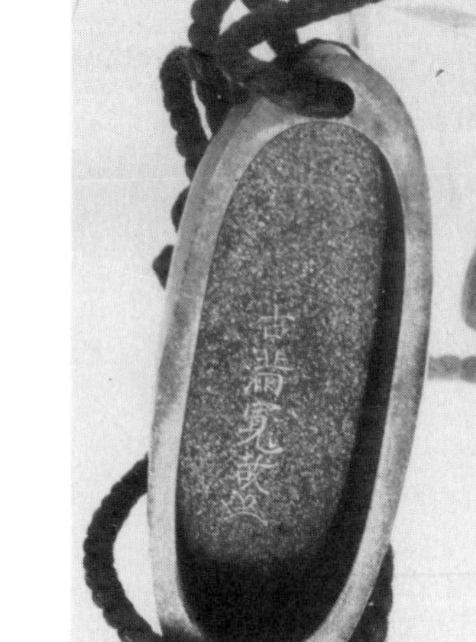

A gold and black lacquer four-case inro decorated in iroe hiramakie, takamakie and silver details with 6 grazing horses, one dappled, on a roironuri ground, the interior in nashiji, slight wear, signed Koma Kansai, 3in (9cm) long.
$7,500-9,000

A Guri lacquer four-case inro, deeply carved through numerou layers of red, black and ochre lacquer with a symmetrical design of formal scrolls, the interior of black lacquer, unsigned, 4in (11cm), with plai carnelian ojime, two-part manj carved with a scroll design in Guri lacquer, unsigned.
$6,000-8,250

An ivory and gold lacquer four-case inro, decorated in hiramaki takamakie and aogai with a peacock and peahen among flowering peony issuing from pierced rockwork, signed, 3½in (9cm) long, ivory ojime attached.
$1,500-2,250

A gold lacquer four-case inro decorated in hiramakie, togidashi, silver and coloured kirigane with huts and pagodas beside pine and willow trees beside a mountainous river landscape, the reverse with a similar scene with a shrine below birds in flights, all on a nashiji ground, the interior in nashiji, 3in (9cm) long, jadeite ojime attached.
$1,200-1,800

A black lacquered three-case inro, in black and silver takamakie with slight gold lacquer details, the interior of nashiji, signed in seal form Gi..., 19thC, 3½in (8.5cm), the metal ojime of bamboo form, inlaid with a snail, signed Temmin; Kagamibuta, the wood bowl bearing a shibuichi plate, carved and inlaid with Jurojin holding a tama, details in gold, unsigned.
$30,000-45,000

A six-case inro, with bright red ground, decorated with an asymmetrical design of kozuka and kogai, showing various designs in gold and coloured takamakie with details of kirigane and silver hirame, the interior of roiro with matt gold lacquer risers, signed Jokasai, 19thC, 4in (10cm), plain ojime, Hako-netsuke, lacquered in kinji and red nunome, decorated with snow covered berried plants in gold and silver takamakie, signed Yoyusai.
$22,500-30,000

A gold lacquer five-case inro with metal inlay, signed Kakosai Shozan, 19thC, 4in (10cm), the lacquered netsuke in the form of 2 peaches attached to a stalk with a leaf, a ladybird to one side, unsigned.
$15,000-18,000

ory

Japanese ivory box and cover, th flowerhead finial carved in ief with flowering rysanthemums and peony iong foliage, signed, 3in (8cm) gh.
00-750

A Chinese ivory figure of a standing bearded Shoulao, wearing long flowing robes, holding a peach in one hand and a staff in the other with a gourd suspended from it, small chips, 8½in (21.5cm) high, with a fitted wood stand.
$450-600

A Tokyo School carved ivory figure of a boy, on a plain oval base, slight damage, signed, Meiji period, 11½in (29cm) high, and a wood stand.
$2,250-3,000

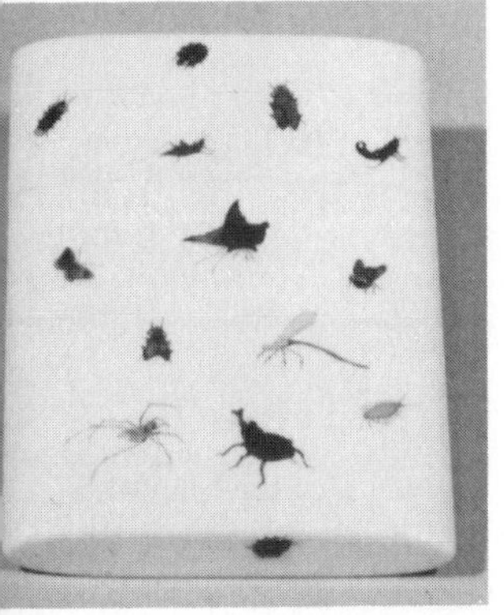

ı Oriental ivory card case, with tachable lid, decorated with sects in mother-of-pearl and mi-precious stones, in low relief, ½in (11cm) wide.
00-1,500

An ivory okimono of a farmer, kneeling on a mat and pulling husks of corn through 2 bamboo sections, next to a boy standing before baskets and boxes, slight damage, signed on a red lacquer tablet, 3in (8cm) wide.
$900-1,500

A Cantonese ivory hinged box and cover, carved with panels of numerous figures in gardens at various activities, below pine and wisteria and before further figures in pagodas, slight damage, 10in (25cm) wide.
$1,200-1,800

A large Chinese sectional ivory group carving of a battle scene, with 4 warriors mounted on galloping horses before castellated city walls defended by warriors, beside groups of towering rockwork and trees, restored, 46in (116.5cm) wide, on a wood base with pierced balustrade.
$7,500-9,000

An ivory okimono of a rat catcher, the details stained black, slight damage, signed, 3in (7.5cm) wide.
$1,200-1,800

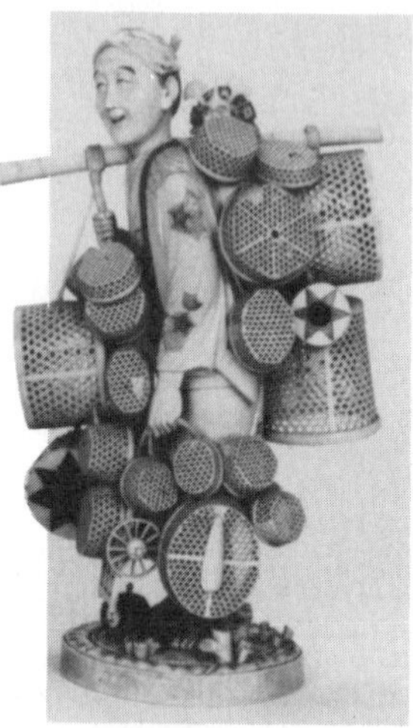

An ivory model of a basket seller, his wares slung across his shoulder on a bamboo pole, signed Hotoda, some old damage, late 19thC, 14in (36cm) high.
$4,500-6,000

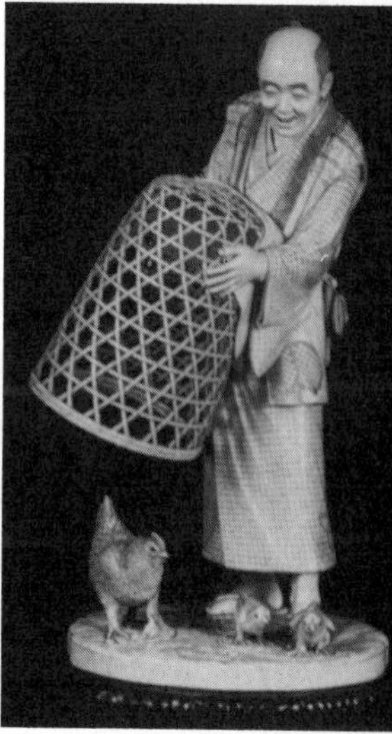

An ivory okimono of a farmer and poultry, the details incised and slightly stained, signed Shomin, Meiji period, damaged, 11½in (29cm) high, with a wood stand.
$5,250-7,500

An inlaid ivory okimono of a seated scholar, the details stained black, signed, 3in (7cm) high.
$1,050-1,350

Make the Most of Miller's

In Millers we do NOT just reprint saleroom estimates. We work from realised prices, either from an auction room or a dealer. Our consultants then work out a realistic price range for a similar piece. This is to try to avoid repeating freak results - either low or high.

A Chinese ivory wrist rest, carved in relief with boys playing Blind Man's Buff among pine trees and rockwork, 7in (18cm) wide, on a wood stand.
$375-525

A Japanese ivory carving of a man, holding a teapot in one hand and a teabowl in the other, beside a tied sack, signed, 2½in (6.5cm) high. **$375-525**

An ivory model of a peach seller and child, a basket of fruit around his neck, slight damage, signed Ikkosai Shizuhide, late 19thC, 10½in (27cm) high.
$3,000-3,750

Japanese sectional ivory rving of a farmer, carrying a sket and guiding 4 geese across bridge, the details aturalistically rendered, slight amage, signed, 15in (38cm) long.
1,200-1,800

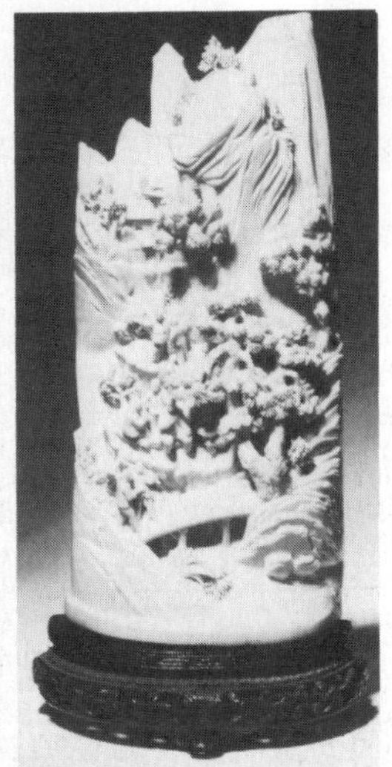

Chinese ivory mountain group, eeply carved with 2 figures ossing a bridge over a stream elow further figures in nversation, and a retreat among attered pine and crags, 8in 0cm) high, on a wood stand.
1,050-1,350

Chinese ivory pear-shaped jug nd cover, carved with insects mong peony and other foliage suing from rockwork, the handle nd body with lines of alligraphy, slight damage, ianlong four-character mark and the period, 4in (10cm) high.
1,050-1,350

A Japanese ivory carving of a woodcutter, carrying a pile of sticks on a rope-bound wooden frame on his back, an axe to his side, the details stained, signed on a red lacquer tablet, 6in (15cm) high.
$375-525

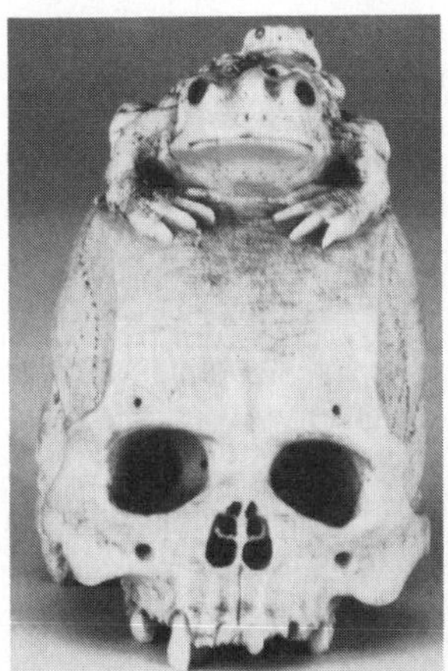

An ivory okimono modelled as a skull, with a toad and young crouched on top, the eyes inlaid in horn and details well defined, signed, 2in (5cm) high.
$750-1,200

A Japanese ivory tusk vase and cover, carved and stained with 4 tigers attacking an elephant, the cover with elephant knop, a white metal mount to the base below a seal signature, the whole supported on a hardwood lotus carved stand, 16in (40.5cm) high.
$1,050-1,350

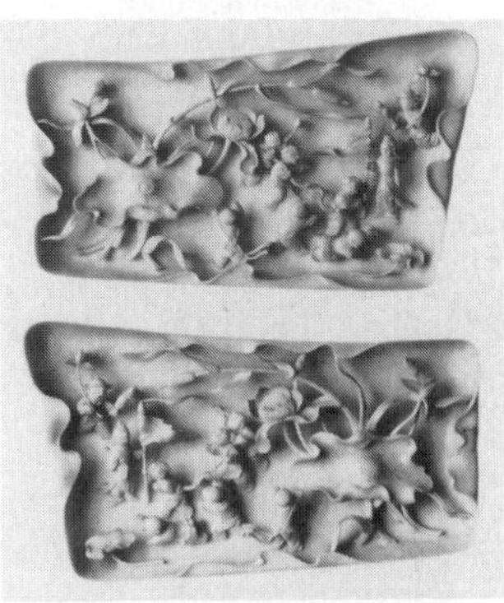

A pair of Chinese ivory panels carved in relief with boys and figures holding flags among flowering lotus branches, 7in (18cm) wide.
$1,800-2,700

Jade

A Chinese white jade group carving of 3 bearded Immortals and boy attendant on rockwork beside a crane, before a pine tree, 18thC, 5in (12cm) wide.
$1,200-1,800

A Chinese celadon jade pouring vessel with dark brown inclusions, carved in archaic style in the form of a three-legged mythological animal, carved to the rear in relief with coiled dragons, 6in (15cm) long.
$1,050-1,350

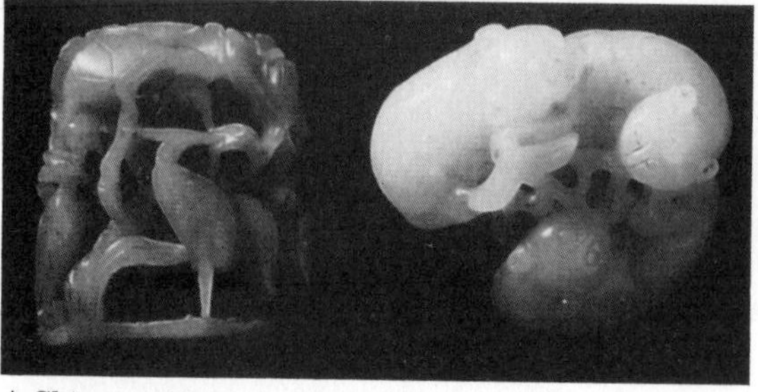

A Chinese white jade carving of 3 cats, clutching a spray of fungus, 18thC, 2in (5cm) wide, and a greyish celadon jade hat finial carved and pierced with cranes standing among lotus leaves, base chipped, Ming Dynasty, 1½in (4cm) high.
$450-600

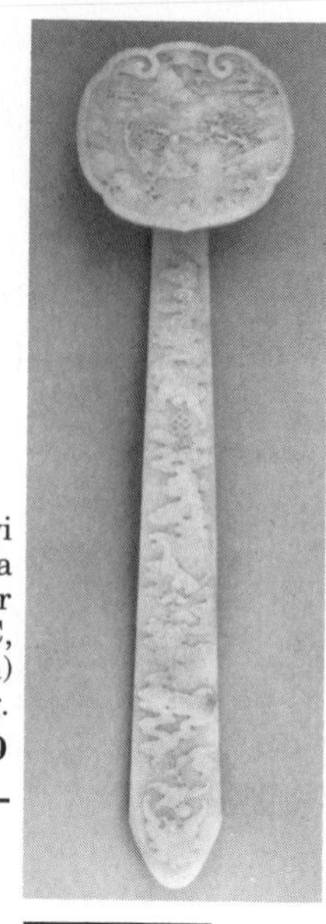

A Chinese jade myi sceptre, carved with a figure in a river landscape, 19thC, 19in (48cm) long.
$6,000-8,250

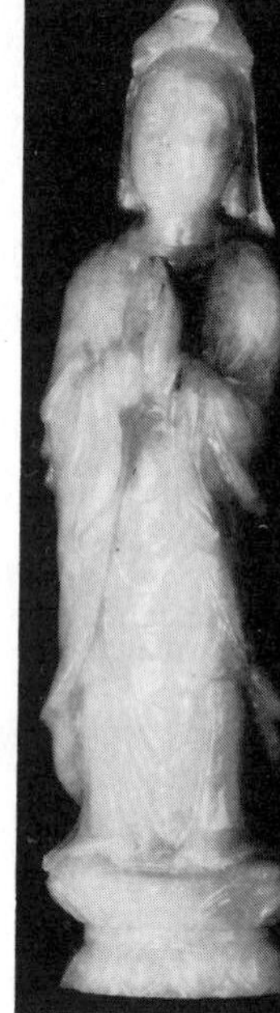

A Chinese jadeite carving of a standing Guanyin, with pale green and mauve inclusions, the figure wearing high headdress, flowing robes and holding her hands before her, on a double lotus base, 4½in (11.5cm) high.
$750-1,200

Lacquer

A pair of Chinese red lacquer boxes and domed covers, decorated with a panel of children at play in a landscape on a dense diaper ground, 3in (8cm) diam., and a shaped triangular red lacquer box and cover decorated with a jardinière of flowers, the sides with T-pattern, 18th/19thC, 3½in (9cm) wide.
$375-525

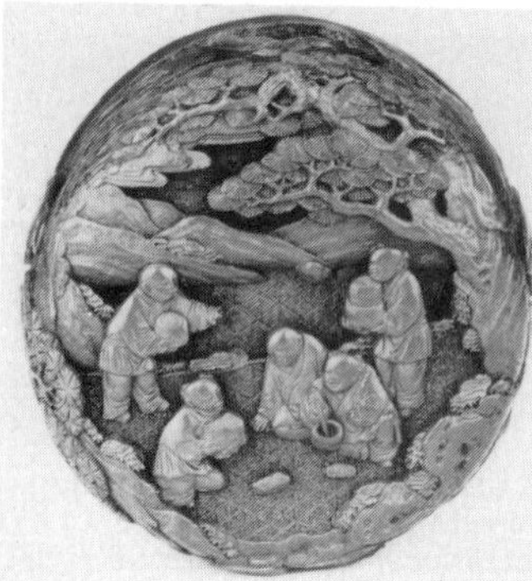

A Chinese red lacquer box and related cover, slight crack to rim, 18thC, 3in (8cm) diam.
$600-750

A Japanese gold, red and black lacquer group of a clump of lotus in bud, flower and pod issuing from a jardinière, decorated in coloured lacquer with butterflies in flight above flowerheads, 15in (38cm) high, and another similar issuing from a hexagonal jardinière decorated with foliate cartouches, slight damage, 14½in (37cm) high.
$450-600

A lacquer Shodana with stand, arranged asymmetrically with shelves, 2 sliding and 5 hinged doors, one curved, 3 drawers, decorated in gold hiramakie, takamakie, togidashi and kirigane with landscapes, flowers and figures, the body with flora motifs, 19thC, 24in (60.5cm), on a later black painted stand.
$7,500-9,000

l. A Chinese red lacquer box and domed cover, carved to both sides with flowering peony branches among leaves, rim chipped, 16th/17thC, 3½in (9cm) diam.
$1,200-1,500
r. A Mughal lapiz lazuli rounded triangular pendant carved in relief with flowering tulip branches flanked by 2 swans, 4in (10cm) high.
$450-600

A Tsuishu study of a shishi, carved red lacquer, the lion-dog lying on a rounded rectangular mat, its head lowered to the right, the mat carved beneath with a formal design in Chinese style, unsigned, late 18th/early 19thC, 1½in (4cm).
$1,500-2,250

n inlaid lacquer panel, lacquered
ı takamakie and hiramakie on a
oiro ground, with ferocious shishi
mong rocks and peony, harassed
y 2 warriors with carved ivory
ices and hands, their armoured
odies in relief with kirikane
etails, all under a prunus tree
ith mother-of-pearl blossom,
urrounded by a natural gnarled
ood frame, lacquer cracked,
leiji period, 38½in (98cm) wide.
1,500-2,250

A lacquered helmet, of Tobi-gashira form, decorated on the roiro ground in gold takamakie with a shishi prancing among peonies, the eyes inlaid in mother-of-pearl, damaged, 11½in (29cm).
$4,500-6,000

A Japanese gold lacquered kodansu, all-over decorated in raised gilt with mother-of-pearl inlay and with silver coloured metal hinges and clasp, damaged, enclosing 3 drawers with tea dust lacquer interiors, with a signed mother-of-pearl plaque, 3in (8cm) wide. **$4,500-6,000**

letal

. Japanese bronze tripod censer,
ith loop handles, decorated to
ıe neck in silver and gilt
irazogan with a continuous
cene of cockerels and hens
mong flowers and sparrows
erched in maple branches, above
band of key pattern, 9in (23cm)
ide.
900-1,500

A bronze figure of a warrior, signed Miyao with seal, sword possible restored, by Miyao Esuke of Tokyo, Meiji period, on a gilt wood base, 15in (38cm) overall.
$4,500-6,000

A Chinese bronze tripod censer of bombé form, with loop handles, traces of gilding, Xuande six-character mark within a coiled dragon to the base, 6½in (16.5cm) wide.
$600-750

. late Ming gilt bronze figure of
n immortal, wearing a leaf belt
bove a pleated skirt with
ecorated border, holding a censer
n one hand, on a rockwork base,
arly 17thC, 13in (33cm) high.
1,050-1,350

A bronze model of a seated smoker, signed Kaneda chu zo no ki, Meiji period, 17in (42.5cm) high.
$2,250-3,000

A bronze model of a woman feeding a pigeon, signed Kazumasa, Meiji period, 20in (51cm).
$1,500-2,250

A pair of bronze figures of workmen, with gilt details, signed on a rectangular tablet Miyao with seal, the ladle of the first added, each set on a giltwood base, Meiji period, 8in (21cm) overall.
$3,000-4,500

A pair of Japanese bronze mode of rats, one signed, 6½in (16.5cm long, on giltwood stands.
$1,200-1,500

l. A bronze figure of a growling tiger, Meiji period, 26in (66cm) long.
$1,800-2,700
r. A bronze group, cast as an elephant being attacked by a pai of tigers, the elephant with 'ivory tusks, Meiji period, 17in (43cm) long.
$1,200-1,500

A bronze figure of a fisherman, with gilt details, signed on a rectangular tablet Miyao with seal, a possibly a weighing stick missing from one hand, by Miyao Esuke of Tokyo, Meiji period, on a gilt wood base, 12in (30cm) overall.
$1,800-2,700

A Japanese bronze model of a rabbit leaning forward, the fur markings well delineated, 8in (20cm) long.
$900-1,500

A Japanese bronze model of a rat resting its paws on a nut, signed, 7in (18cm) long.
$900-1,500

A Japanese gilt bronze group of an eagle, with outstretched wings alighting on a branch, the feathers well delineated, 27½in (70.5cm) wide.
$2,700-3,300

A Japanese bronze model of a seated monkey, holding a peach and gazing upwards, wearing a short jacket decorated with geometric patterns, 7in (18cm) high, and an Indonesian bronze model of a monkey.
$900-1,500

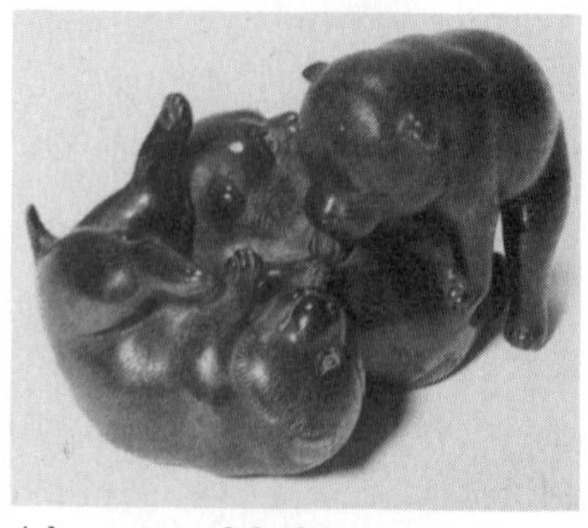

A bronze model of 3 puppies, playing in a group, 2 with eyes inlaid in gilt, signed Nihon koku Maruki sei, by Maruki, Meiji period, 3in (8cm) high.
$2,250-3,000

A Chinese bronze pagoda, with 7 tiers, late 18thC, 100in (254cm) high.
$12,000-15,000

Japanese bronze koro, on 4 feet,
op section missing, damaged,
6in (142cm) high.
2,250-3,000

Japanese bronze globular
ardinière, on 5 feet, decorated in
akazogan with a continuous
rocession of elephants, signed
eiya, 8in (20cm) wide.
1,200-1,800

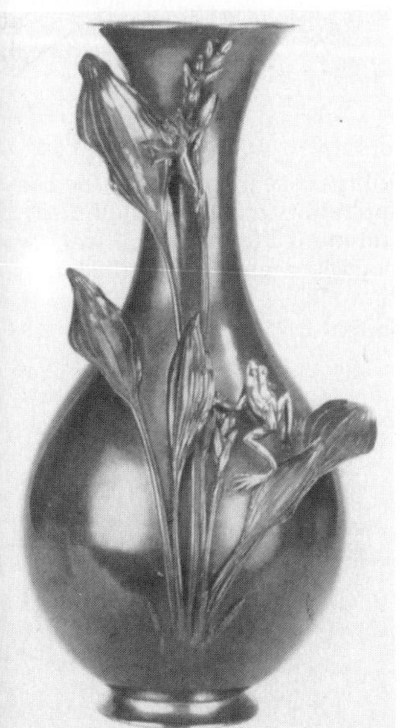

Japanese green and red
atinated bronze tapering pear-
haped vase, with tall neck and
laring rim, decorated in high
elief with a frog clambering on a
lowering lily, signed, polished in
arts, 16in (41cm) high.
600-750

A Chinese bronze double gourd vessel, on 2 feet cast as branches, decorated in relief with numerous squirrels among fruiting vine, some wear, probably Qianlong, 7in (17cm) high.
$450-600

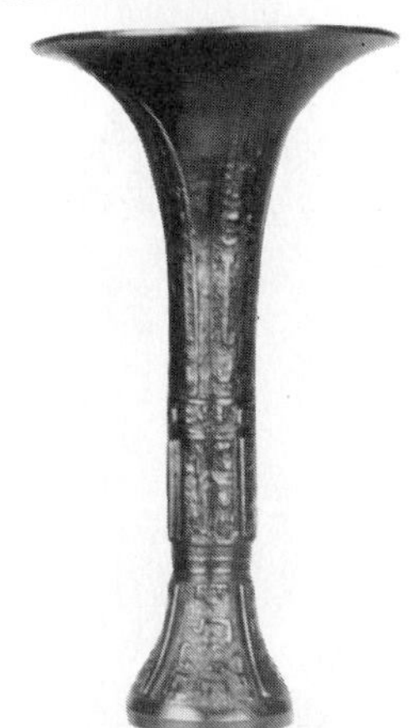

A Chinese bronze gu-shaped vase decorated with leaf-shaped panels of stylised taotie on key-pattern grounds interspersed with flanges, some wear, Ming Dynasty, 13in (33cm) high.
$225-300

A bronze teapot and cover decorated in iroe hirazogan with fruiting vine, the finial with a squirrel, signed Dai Nihon Kyoto Goro zo saku, late 19thC, 7in (18cm) high.
$1,800-2,700

A Japanese blue patinated bronze squat baluster vase, with shouldered neck decorated all-over with leafy branches, some wear, signed, 8in (20cm) high.
$600-750

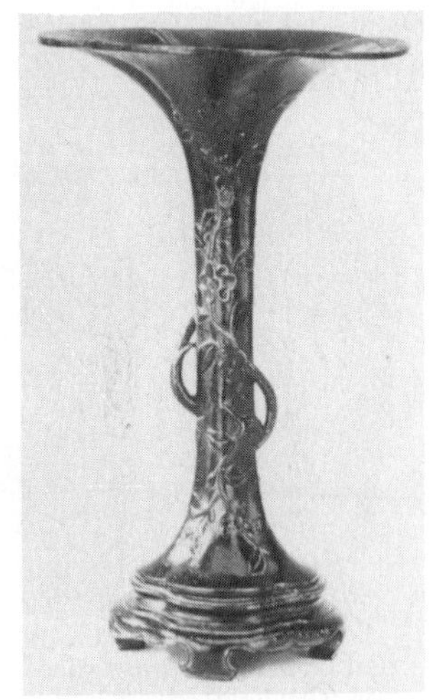

A Chinese bronze trumpet shaped vase, the body of quatrefoil form, decorated in relief with flowering prunus branches, some wear, Kangxi, 11in (28cm) high, on a wood stand.
$375-525

A pair of Japanese gilt bronze baluster vases, each with a coiled dragon to the neck above Kinko reading a scroll and riding on the back of a large carp and a figure beside a crane among pine and rockwork, 23½in (60cm) high, on large wood stands with inset marble tops.
$2,250-3,000

A pair of Japanese onlaid bronze vases, decorated in silver, gilt and copper hirazogan and takazogan with cranes, a kingfisher and a swallow in flight among lotus and reeds, damaged, one signed, 6½in (16.5cm) high.
$600-750

A pair of Oriental brass vases inlaid with gold, silver and copper, depicting a cockerel in a tree, c1920.
$375-450

A Chinese iron head of Buddha, the hair worn in a bun and decorated with flowerhead motifs, set on a wooden bust, worn, 14thC, head 8½in (21.5cm) high.
$600-750

A silver plated copper model of a hawk, slightly worn, signed Hide Nao, Meiji period, 19in (48cm) overall.
$2,700-3,300

A pair of Japanese bronze pear-shaped hexagonal vases, with foliate rims, decorated and patinated in part green relief with flowering irises issuing from streams, signed, both drilled, 14in (36cm) high.
$600-750

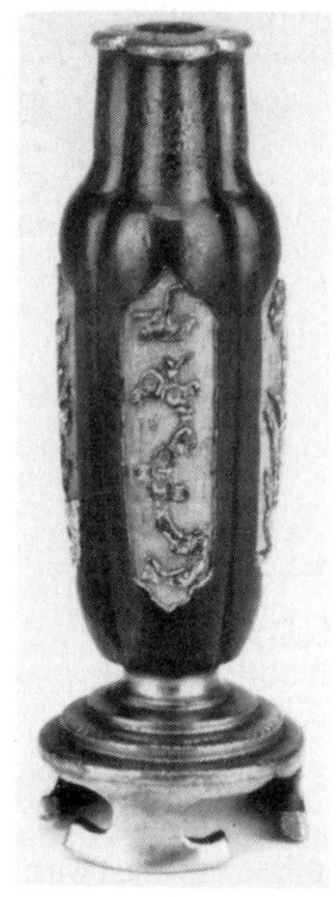

A Chinese gilt copper joss-stick holder, on a spreading pierced foot, the sides decorated with shaped panels of birds among prunus, the neck with simulated marble effect, Kangxi.
$300-375

A Japanese pierced silver dish, mounted with central shibayama panel, decorated with a vase of flowers on a table, surrounded by 6 smaller shaped panels similarly decorated, signed, 12in (31cm) diam. **$2,250-3,000**

A pair of Japanese silver and copper models of standing cranes, the details well delineated, minor dents, signed, 12in (31cm) high.
$4,800-5,700

A Japanese punch bowl, the body applied with chrysanthemums and mon, 3 foliate scroll feet, two character marks, 13in (32cm) diam, 97oz.
$3,000-3,750

A Japanese copper circular box and domed cover, with gilt rims, onlaid in gilt and silver hirazogan and takazogan, with 2 peahens perched on pierced rockwork beside flowering rose branches, signed, 5½in (14cm) diam.
$375-525

A silver pipe and case, the pipe engraved with bamboo, chrysanthemum and grasses, the hinged case with similar motifs among rocks, and with branch shaped cord attachment, signed Wakayama Hidemasa zo, worn, Meiji period, 9in (23cm) long.
$2,250-3,000

Two articulated models of insects, one signed (Miochin) Muneyoshi, 19thC, 2½in (6.5cm) long.
$3,000-3,750

A silver mounted pipe, applied in takazogan with small birds above peonies, signed Terumichi saku, rubbed, Meiji period, 10½in (27cm) long.
$1,200-1,800

Netsuke

A buffalo horn netsuke, modelled as a standing figure of Hotei lifting a sack containing a boy, old wear, 2in (5cm) high.
$450-600

An ivory netsuke, modelled as a reclining karashishi and cub on an oval base, the details well defined and eyes inlaid in horn, 1½in (4cm) wide.
$450-600

A Japanese boxwood netsuke, carved as a bird emerging from an egg, signed, 1½in (4cm) wide.
$750-900

A kagamibuta wood netsuke, the bronze disc decorated in hirazogan, takazogan and gilt, with 2 old women examining a scroll, signed Mitsuharu, 1in (3cm) diam., and an oval bronze flint netsuke, the hinged lid opening to reveal a striker, the cover decorated with flowerheads, 1½in (4cm) wide.
$900-1,500

Three similar painted wood netsuke, carved in Hobori technique, all modelled as standing figures of actors wearing long wigs, robes and masks, minor wear, 1 signed, 2¾in (7cm) high.
$150-180

Two lacquered wood mask netsuke, the first of a Ranryo variant with a dragon headdress, lacquered red with gold lacquer eyes, the reverse of polished wood, the second of Shishiguchi, lacquered in Negoro style, the eyes and teeth of gold lacquer and the reverse of roiro, the first signed Koshin, 1½in (4cm) high.
$1,050-1,350

Three mask netsuke, the first of red lacquer, depicting a smiling man, the second of Negoro style lacquer, depicting Shishiguchi, the eyes of gold lacquer, the third of stoneware, depicting Daikoku, his hat glazed dark green, the third with impressed mark Sekisen, 1¾in (4.5cm) high.
$900-1,500

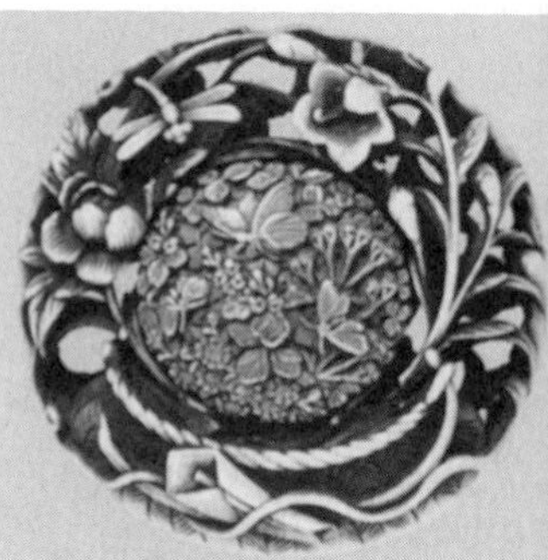

A kagamibuta, the bowl of walrus ivory, the small solid gold plate delicately carved in relief with butterflies among flowering cherry, the bowl signed in relief Tomin, 19thC, 1½in (4cm).
$2,700-3,300

Kagamibuta

A Kagamibuta is a netsuke that incorporates metalwork.

A kagamibuta, the tsuishu bowl carved in relief in Chinese style, inlaid in silver takazogan with a heron wading in a stream with fallen leaves in gold takazogan, signed Ichijo saku, 1½in (3.5cm).
$3,000-3,750

A kagamibuta, the wood bowl bearing a silver plate, carved in relief with a tiger standing on a rock beneath a waterfall, details in gold, signed on a gilt tablet Toju, 19thC, 2in (5cm).
$1,200-1,500

A kagamibuta, the tagasayan wood bowl bearing a gold plate hammered in relief, signed Yoshiteru saku, 19thC, 1½in (4cm) high. **$4,500-6,000**

A kagamibuta, the horn bowl bearing a gold plate, carved and inlaid with a squirrel leaping towards a hanging grapevine with large leaves, in silver, copper and shakudo takazogan, signed on reverse Jitokusai saku, 19thC, 1½in (4cm).
$1,800-2,700

A kagamibuta, the horn bowl bearing an ivory plate in the form of a tiger curled in a circle as it bites its hind leg, the ivory slightly worn and the eye pupils inlaid, signed in an oval reserve Hoshin, 1½in (4cm). **$3,000-4,500**

A two-part ivory manju, inlaid in gold takazogan with a ferry boat bearing a noblewoman and attendant and an overhanging cherry tree carved in relief, signed on an inlaid silver table Hakuo, 19thC, 2in (4.5cm).
$1,800-2,700

A kagamibuta, the horn bowl bearing a bronze plate, stamped in relief, with a gilt bronze ojime depicting a foreign fisherman, 19thC, 1in (3cm).
$1,200-1,800

Manju

A manju is a netsuke of round flat form carved in relief and is named after similarly shaped sweetmeats.

kagamibuta, the ivory bowl
rved and pierced, details in
ld, silver and shibuichi, the
wl signed Ikkeisai Hogyoku
ith kao, 19thC, 2in (5cm).
,200-1,500

kagamibuta, the ivory bowl
aring a shakudo plate, carved
relief with Jurojin standing on
cloud and holding a fan, details
2 shades of gold hirazogan,
gned Shumin with kao, 19thC,
n (4.5cm). **$2,250-3,000**

Vood

wood group of three masks, of
kame and Oni, backed by that of
uaku, rendered in stained wood,
gned Soko to, late 19th/early
thC, 2in (3.5cm).
,800-2,700

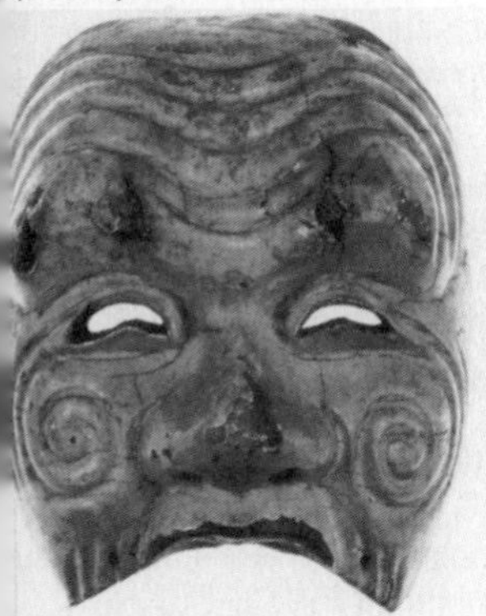

Japanese painted and gessoed
od mask of Uba, lower jaw
issing, 7in (18cm) high.
00-375

A Japanese wood and ivory group, of a cockerel and hen perched on a tree stump and rock, the cockerel with trailing tail feathers, with mother-of-pearl inlaid eyes, minor chips, 10½in (26.5cm) high overall.
$1,050-1,350

A Chinese burlwood brushpot, modelled as a gnarled tree stump, the details naturalistically rendered, 18thC, 6½in (17cm).
$600-750

A wood study of a snail, signed with ukibori characters Odawara ju Shigeharu, 19thC, 1½in (4cm).
$3,000-4,500

A wood study of a tiger, the wood slightly worn and the eyes inlaid, signed Kokei, early 19thC, 1½in (4cm). **$3,000-3,750**

A wood study of a snake and gourd, the wood stained for effect, signed Sukenaga, 19thC, 1½in (4cm). **$7,500-9,000**

A wood figure of Gama Sennin, the wood lightly stained and the eyes of pale translucent horn with dark pupils, signed Soshin, early 19thC, 2½in (6cm).
$3,000-4,500

Miscellaneous

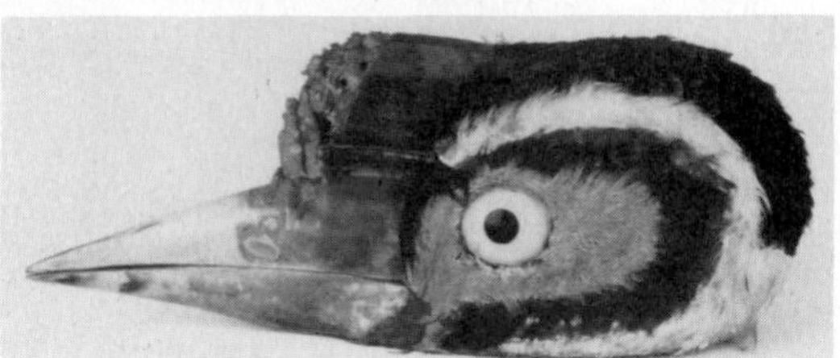

A Chinese toucan head, the beak carved and pierced with figures seated around a table before a pavilion and trees, with feathers attached and inset glass eyes, 10in (25cm) overall. **$750-1,200**

TRIBAL ART

A Middle Mochica figural vessel, lying on his right side with hands placed on his knees, wearing a cloak in the form of a peanut shell with punctate and ridged texture, painted in reddish brown, A.D. 200-500, 8in (20.5cm) high.
$750-900

A Mochica figural vessel, the dwarf figure dominated by the large head on top of the crouching legs, a stirrup spout on top, and painted overall in deep orange and tan, A.D. 200-500, 8½in (21.5cm) high. **$750-1,200**

A Vicus double-bodied vessel, the whistling vessel surmounted by a seated male figure, connected to a globular vessel, painted in reddish brown and black, A.D. 100-300, 12½in (32cm) long.
$1,200-1,500

A Middle Mochica figural vessel, painted in brownish orange and cream, A.D. 200-500, 10in (26cm) long. **$750-1,200**

A Middle Mochica erotic vessel, seated cross-legged, wearing a striped tunic and turban, painted overall in cream and brown, A.D. 200-500, 9in (23cm) high.
$1,800-2,700

A Middle Mochica figural vessel, painted overall in cream and brown, A.D. 200-500, 10in (25.5cm) high.
$2,250-3,000

A Nazca polychrome bridge-spout vessel, boldly painted in maroon, grey, reddish brown, white and black, A.D. 200-500, 8½in (21.5cm) high. **$1,500-2,250**

A Recuay vessel, painted in orange and cream, A.D. 100-300, 12in (30.5cm) high.
$900-1,500

A Nazca polychrome bridge-spout vessel, painted in white, black, deep red, grey and shades of brown on a cream ground, A.D. 200-500, 7in (18cm) high.
$750-1,200

A Vicus figural vessel, the supine male figure with arms outstretched, with a large central opening, painted in brownish orange with resist decoration in cream, A.D. 100-300, 11in (28.5cm) long. **$375-450**

Two Middle Mochica vessels, each painted in brown, A.D. 200-500, 8 and 10in (20.5 and 25cm) high.
$1,050-1,350

A Mochica double-bodied effigy vessel, in the form of a howling sea lion with head craning straight up, connected to a cylindrical vessel, painted overall in reddish brown, A.D. 200-500, 8½in (22cm) high.
$750-900

A Paracas painted and incised bowl, Ocucaje region, the straight sides with geometric patterns painted alternately in ochre, olive green, white, deep red and umber, 300-100 B.C., 7in (18cm) diam.
$1,500-2,250

A Mayan tripod vessel, Escuintla region, Early Classic, circa A.D. 250-450, 12½in (32cm) diam.
$9,000-10,000

A Mayan polychrome cylinder vase, painted in dark orange, white, black and grey against a pale orange ground, Late Classic, circa A.D. 550-950, 9in (23cm) high.
$4,500-6,000

A Middle Mochica portrait head vessel, the dignitary with upraised head and composed expression, painted overall in brown and cream, A.D. 200-500, 9½in (24.5cm) high.
$1,200-1,500

A pair of Mayan orangeware tripod vessels, Early Classic, circa A.D. 250-450, 6½in (17cm) high.
$1,500-2,250

A Middle Mochica vessel, painted overall in white and brown, A.D. 200-500, 9in (23cm) high.
$1,200-1,800

A Middle Mochica square vessel, painted with an orange brown growling feline on all four sides, the spout flanked by two striped lizards with curling tails, on a tan ground, A.D. 200-500, 8in (21cm) high.
$1,500-2,250

A Viru/Salinar effigy vessel, the standing bird with wings outspread, clenched taloned feet, incised feathers marking the end of the tail and wings, painted in shades of cream, pink and reddish brown, 500-300 B.C., 7in (18cm) high.
$1,050-1,350

A Chancay vessel, with pear-shaped body, painted in cream and black with a striped pattern, the handle in the form of a nursing pampas cat, A.D. 1100-1400, 16½in (42cm) high.
$1,200-1,500

A Mayan polychrome vessel, Highlands, painted overall in deep orange, black and white on a bright orange ground, with dark orange bands above and below, Late Classic, circa A.D. 550-950, 7in (17cm) high.
$4,500-6,000

A Chancay figural vessel, holding a cup in both hands, raised legs indicated in relief, adorned with facial tattoos and crested headband, painted in cream, brown and black, A.D. 1100-1400, 13in (33cm) high. **$750-900**

A Mayan orangeware cylinder vase, painted with two wading cormorants in white and black against a rich orange ground, with palmette leaves encircling the rim, Late Classic, circa A.D. 550-950, 6in (15cm) high.
$6,000-8,250

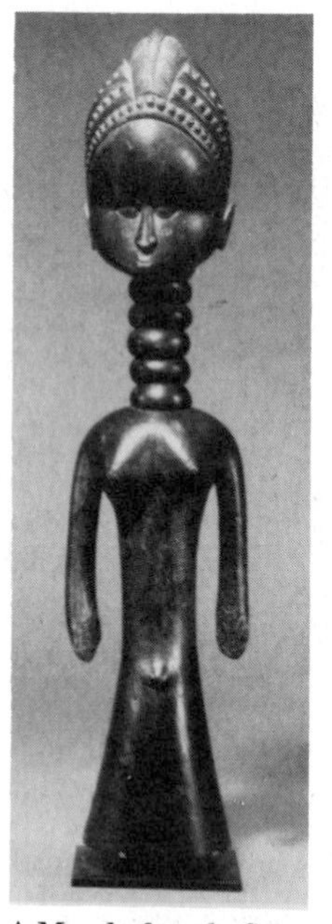

A Mende female figure, of typical form, with aged dark brown patina, 21in (54cm) high.
$6,000-8,250

A Colima dog, painted overall in reddish brown, Protoclassic, circa 100 B.C. - A.D. 250, 10½in (26.5cm) long.
$2,250-3,000

A Colima turtle, painted overall in reddish brown, Protoclassic, circa 100 B.C. - A.D. 250, 13in (33cm) long.
$2,250-3,000

A Mayan polychrome bowl, painted on both sides with a codex style panel, in white, black and deep orange, Late Classic, circa A.D. 550-950, 6½in (16cm) high.
$3,000-3,750

A Colima dog, painted overall in red, Protoclassic, circa 100 B.C. - A.D. 250, 16½in (42cm) long.
$3,000-4,500

A Jalisco seated couple, Ameca style, her breasts decorated with tattoos, each painted overall in tan with details in black, Protoclassic, circa 100 B.C. - A.D. 250, 16½ and 17in (42 and 43cm) high.
$7,500-9,000

. Middle Chavin incised vessel, ne large globular body carved ith a dense pattern of a stylised eline, with lunate eyes, claws ared and upturned tail, repaired, 000-700 B.C., 9in (23.5cm) high.
1,050-1,350

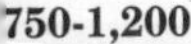

Chinesco female figurine, :ouching and leaning forward ightly, wearing jewellery, ainted in cream and orange, rotoclassic, 100 B.C. - A.D. 250, n (17.5cm) high.
750-1,200

Mayan polychrome cylinder ssel, painted in cream, black d reddish brown, with a band of yphs round the rim, Late assic, A.D. 550-950, 8in (21cm) gh. **$3,000-4,500**

A Veracruz priest, Remojadas, Classic, wearing a skirt and cape, beaded necklace, ear-spools, and incised turban, circa A.D. 450-650, 13in (33.5cm) high.
$1,800-2,700

A Veracruz priest, Remojadas, with areas highlighted by 'chapapote', Early Classic, circa A.D. 250-450, 19in (49cm) high.
$2,250-3,000

A Zacatecas musician, playing a drum held between his knees, wearing tasselled earrings with horns arching from his head, painted overall in reddish brown, black and cream, repaired, Early Classic, A.D. 250-450, 13in (33cm) high.
$1,500-2,250

A Veracruz smiling figure, Dicha Tuerta type, painted overall in orange-brown with decorative details in white and deep orange, Late Classic, circa A.D. 500-950, 9in (22cm) high.
$9,000-12,000

A Chinesco standing female figure, painted overall in reddish brown with geometric details in black on a white ground, Protoclassic, 100 B.C. - A.D. 250, 10in (26cm) high.
$1,500-2,250

A Jalisco female figure, Ameca style, painted overall in cream, Protoclassic, circa 100 B.C. - A.D. 250, 19in (48cm) high.
$3,000-4,500

A Veracruz standing warrior, Remojadas, wearing a tasseled headband, cord necklace and loincloth, areas covered with black chapapote, Classic, circa A.D. 450-650, 23in (58cm) high.
$1,800-2,700

A late Preclassic stone figure, Highlands, seated on a four-legged stepped throne with hands held firmly to the sides, muscular sloping shoulders, the shaven head with sunken eyes, parted lips, painted in greenish black serpentine, circa 300-100 B.C., 9in (23cm) high.
$4,500-6,000

A Chinesco seated figure, wearing armbands and painted overall in orange and buff, Protoclassic, 100 B.C. - A.D. 250, 9in (23cm) high.
$1,800-2,700

A Mende helmet mask, with aged black patina with traces of encrustation, 14in (35.5cm) high.
$2,250-3,000

A Chancay female figure, standing on large flattened feet with short arms upraised, broad face highlighted by upward flaring eyemask, painted overall in cream and black, A.D. 1100-1400, 22in (56cm) high.
$1,500-2,250

Three Trobriand seated figures, all with narrow arms and legs, their heads resting on their arms, the zig-zag carving with lime colouration, largest 9in (23cm) high.
$450-600

A Lega mask, with arched forehead pierced around the rim for attachment, aged white mottled patina, 7½in (19cm) hig
$1,800-2,700

An Ibibio mask, the dark brow patina with traces of white pigment, 8in (20cm) high.
$2,250-3,000

A Tlatilco female figurine, with striped decoration in red and ochre, Middle Preclassic, 1150-550 B.C., 6½in (16.5cm) high.
$450-600

Zacatecas female figure, ·aning forward with both arms ı her waist, beaded breasts, earing ear-spools, painted in ·ange and tan, Early Classic, .D. 250-450, 12½in (32cm) high.
,800-2,700

A Tlatilco female figure, Middle Preclassic, painted overall in brown with remains of ochre pigment, 1150-550 B.C., 12½in (32cm) high.
$750-900

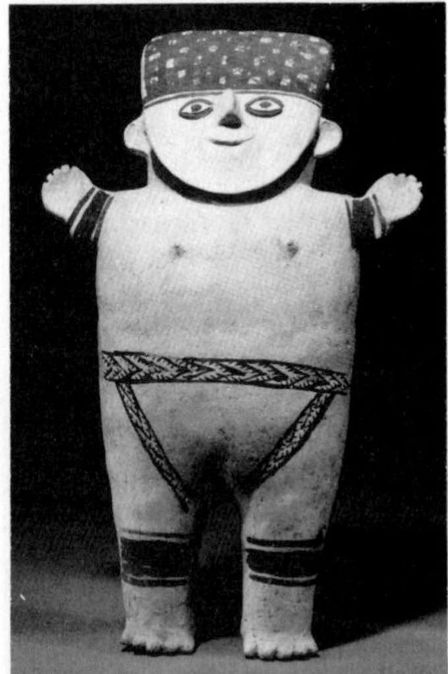

A Chancay standing female figure, with smiling face, small arms upraised, wearing chevron patterned loincloth and chequered headband, painted overall in white and brown, 19in (48cm) high.
$1,800-2,700

Nayarit standing mother and hild, the youthful mother holding er child on her shoulders, its rms upraised and legs extended n her neck, both with smiling xpressions, with remains of eddish brown, Protoclassic, 100 .C. - A.D. 250, 14in (35.5cm) igh.
1,800-2,700

An Easter Islands female figure, the eyes with shell and obsidian inlay, with rich dark brown glossy patina, 18½in (47cm) high.
$3,000-3,750

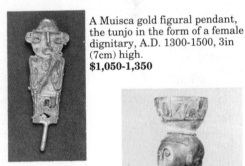

A Muisca gold figural pendant, the tunjo in the form of a female dignitary, A.D. 1300-1500, 3in (7cm) high.
$1,050-1,350

A Baga maternity group, the female figure seated on an oval chair, with a boy and girl seated on either side, the mother wearing an amulet necklace, balancing a deep bowl on her head, polychrome decoration overall, 26½in (67cm) high.
$1,800-2,700

n International style gold triple nimal pendant, A.D. 500-1000, in (5cm) wide.
1,050-1,350

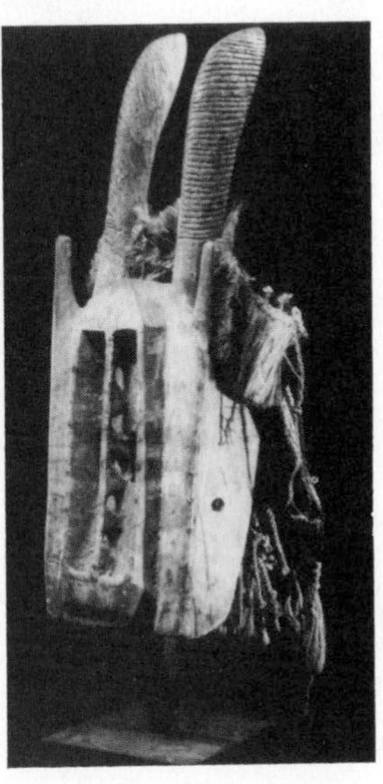

A Dogon wood face mask, representing an antelope, with weathered light brown patina, remains of red and black pigment, 25in (64cm) high.
$6,000-8,250

A Muisca gold figural ornament, the tunjo in the form of a female seated on a throne with filigree birds perched on top, wearing a pectoral and multi-stranded necklace, A.D. 1300-1500, 2in (5cm) high.
$1,050-1,350

A Guerrero stone mask, in Chontal style with naturally rendered features, in speckled grey andesite, pierced at the temples for suspension, Late Preclassic, 300-100 B.C., 4in (9.5cm) high.
$2,250-3,000

A Cameroons mask, the facial features well modelled, incised scarification representing a beard, the coiffure arranged in looped tresses, crusty dark patina, 15in (38cm) high.
$600-750

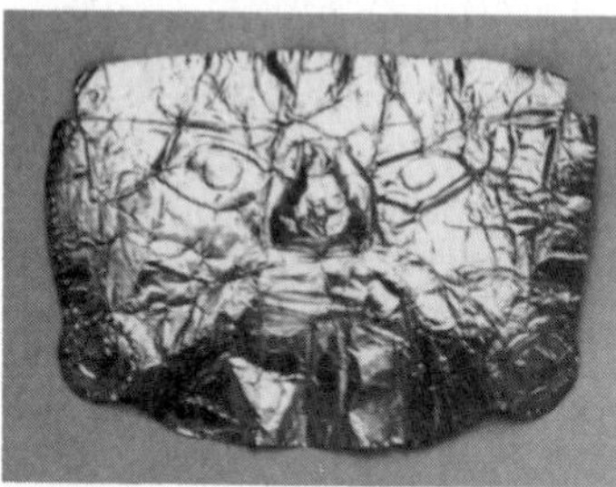
A Chimu gold mask, Sicán, the ears and spools embossed with beadwork, pierced in 4 pairs for attachment, A.D. 1100-1400, 10in (26cm) wide.
$3,000-4,500

Three Colombian gold ornaments, including a Sinú gold frog, a Sinú gold nose U-shaped ornament, and an International style double-headed bird pendant, A.D. 500-1000, 1in (2.5cm) long.
$1,200-1,500

A Teotihuacan stone mask, bright green translucent tecali, remains of 4 suspension holes at the back of the head, Classic, circa A.D. 450-650, 5in (13.5cm) high.
$6,000-8,250

A Chimu gold and lapis necklace, with hemispherical and lenticular beads interspersed with lapis lazuli beads and with 3 repoussé standing warriors, circa A.D. 1100-1400, 29in (74cm) long overall. **$2,700-3,300**

A pair of Kiwai Island figures, both standing on squared feet, both smiling, traces of ochre-re colour, weathered patina, legs with slight erosion, 28½in and 32in (72.5 and 82cm) high.
$3,000-4,500

A Muisca gold figural ornamen A.D. 1300-1500, 6in (15.5cm) lo
$1,500-2,250

A Lower Sepik mask, the beake nose pierced along the edges, flared nostrils, with a narrow arrow shaped mouth, woven rattan beard, old brown patina, 15in (38cm) high.
$1,500-2,250

\ Yoruba Gelede mask, the
lliptical eyes with pierced pupils,
nouth slightly open revealing
eeth, incised scarification on the
heeks and forehead, cross
atched coiffure with large
opknot, thick polychrome patina,
1in (28cm) high.
$750-1,200

Two pairs of Tairona gold ornaments, A.D. 1000-1500, each 2 and 1in (4.5 and 2.5cm) long.
$750-1,200

A Chancay painted mummy mask, the natural wood sack painted in shaded orange with a facial configuration, with copper features stitched on, and dark brown wool eyelashes emerging from under the eyes, wearing a woollen tapestry headband and a red cotton turban with long ochre wool tresses hanging downwards, A.D. 1100-1400, 22in (56cm) high.
$1,500-2,250

Twelve Colombian gold ornaments, including 10 Tolima pendants, 4 in the form of avians and 5 as highly stylised human figures, and 2 Muisca tunjos, 1 to 2½in (2.5 to 6.5cm) long.
$1,200-1,500

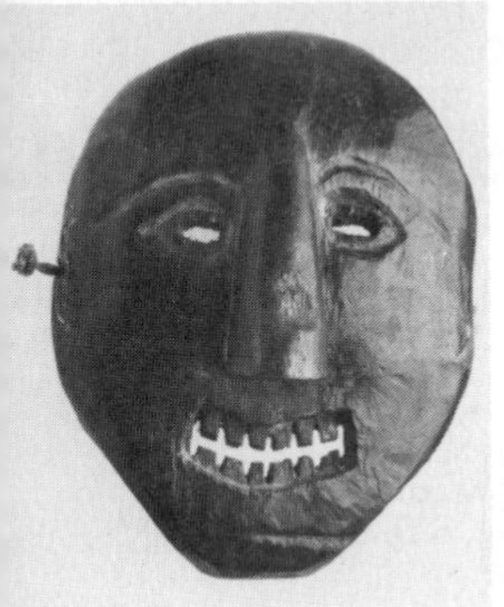

A Dancutta tribal mask from the Rae people, Nepal, early 19thC.
$375-525

A Bwa helmet mask, the stylised
oird's face with a projecting
diamond shaped beak, 3 pointed
knops on the reverse, weathered
polychrome colouration, native
hide repairs, 39½in (100cm) high.
$750-1,200

A Bwa mask, with broad swept back crescent horns, lower jaw missing, impressed triangular decoration overall, polychrome decoration, worn patina, repaired, 26½in (67cm) high.
$1,200-1,500

An Eastern Coastal Sepik mask, the broad nose with stylised nose ornament, narrow pierced eyes and mouth, a tapered projection at the base, weathered patina, ochre colouration, 12in (43cm) high.
$1,200-1,800

A Mayan jade pendant, carved with a cross-legged truncated figure with a serene expression, with a zoomorphic headdress, in veined pale apple green, drilled at the sides for suspension, Late Classic, circa A.D. 550-950, 2in (5.5cm) high.
$2,250-3,000

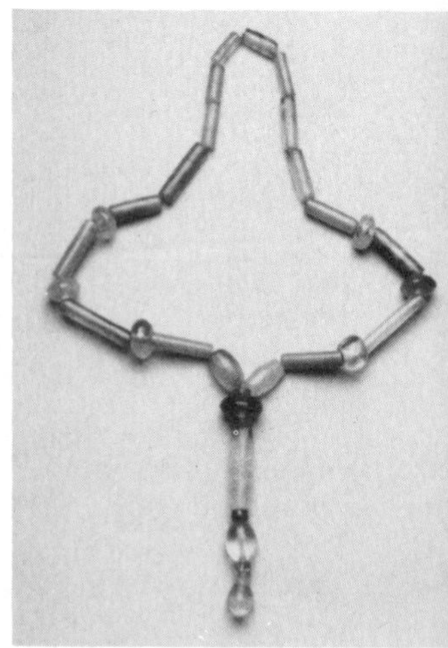

A Tairona rock crystal necklace, A.D. 1000-1500, 31in (79cm) long overall.
$1,200-1,500

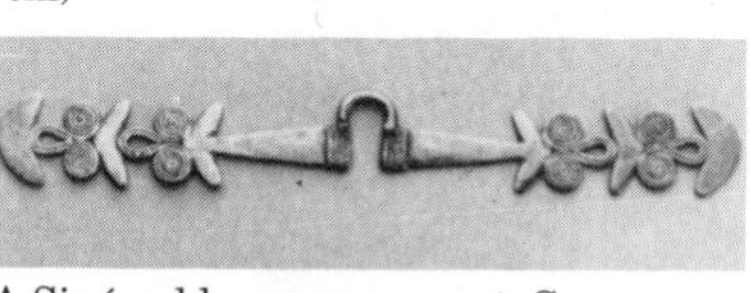

A Sinú gold nose ornament, Sucre region, A.D. 500-1000, 7½in (19cm) long.
$1,050-1,350

Two Sinú gold nose ornaments, A.D. 500-1000, 4 and 5in (9.5 and 12cm) long.
$1,500-2,250

A Yoruba Epa mask, the janiform helmet with broad elliptical eyes, wide open mouth, with a leopard standing over an antelope, tail arched, ochre, black and sienna, 52in (132cm) high.
$1,050-1,350

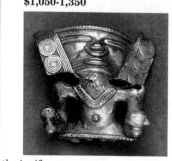

A Sinú gold figural pendant fragment, the shaman holding rattles in each hand, wearing a necklace and nose ring, A.D. 500-1000, 3in (7.5cm) wide.
$1,200-1,500

A Colombian gold face pendant, possibly Quimbaya, with 4 projecting armatures with ring dangles, 2 loops for suspension, A.D. 500-1000, 1½in (4cm) wide.
$2,700-3,300

A Carchi gold feline ear ornament, Esmeraldas Coast, embossed with head of snarling feline deity, encircled by repoussé roundels and tiny beadwork, A.D. 1000-1500, 3½in (9cm) diam.
$750-900

A Tairona carnelian bead necklace, composed of a strand of 44 graduated globular beads in variegated colours, A.D. 1000-1500, 25in (63.5cm) long overall.
$1,800-2,700

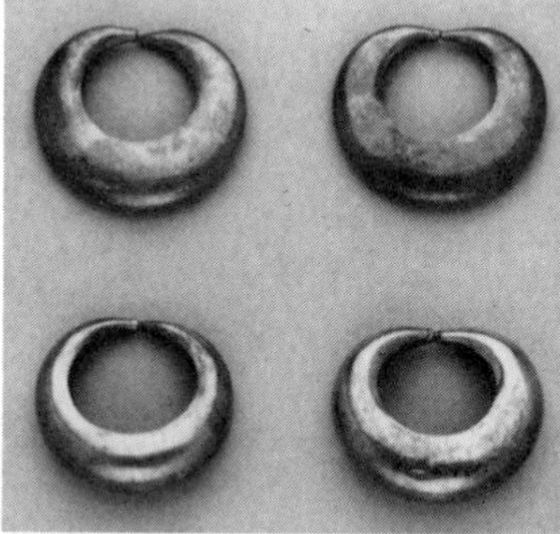

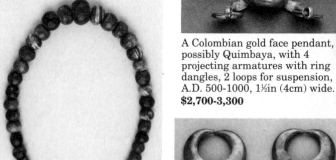

Two pairs of Tairona gold ear ornaments, A.D. 1000-1500, 2½in (6.5cm) wide.
$1,050-1,350

\ Tairona gold butterfly shaped
ıose ornament, A.D. 1000-1500,
in (8cm) wide.
1,200-1,500

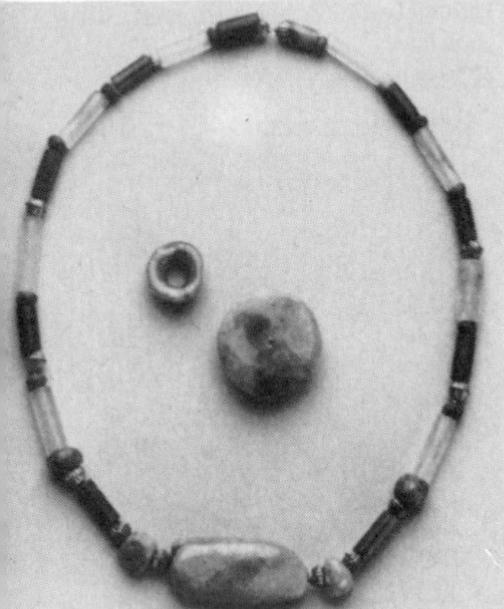

'hree Mayan jade ornaments,
ıcluding a single apple green
arflare, a small ear-spool with
eins of apple green, and an apple
reen bead strung to a necklace of
'airona rock crystal and
arnelian beads, Late Classic,
.D. 550-950, 1 to 2in (2 to 4.5cm)
ng.
,050-1,350

wo Mayan jade pendants, and a
osta Rican stone pendant in the
rm of a stylised bird in profile,
ate Classic, A.D. 550-950, 1½ to
in (3.5 to 8cm) long.
750-1,200

A Fon brass ceremonial staff, the finial with a saucer-shaped platform, over 4 tiers of conical brass bells, with 6 birds standing on the rim, another raised area at the centre, with 4 chameleons to the sides, and a leopard at the top, 52in (132cm) high.
$600-750

Three Dayak shields, one with an old label on the lower part reading 'Kenyah Tribe Borneo', 47 to 50in (119 to 126cm) high.
$600-750

A Chacay shirt panel, the cushma half woven in camelid wool in bright shades of pink, teal blue, yellow, lavender, cream, orange, green, pale blue, plum and brown, circa A.D. 1100-1400, 42in (107cm) long.
$4,500-6,000

A South Coast feather ornament, probably Nazca, the individual braids attached to green parrot feathers, possibly used as a tassel, A.D. 600-700, 11½in (29cm) wide.
$750-900

A Mayan jade bead necklace, composed of a strand of tubular and globular beads, with a single ear-spool as central pendant, in shades of pale green stone, Late Classic, A.D. 550-950, 16in (41cm) long.
$1,050-1,350

A Fiji rootstock club, the head with 10 broad flanges, the shaft with sennit binding, the grip with incised zig-zag decoration overall, fine glossy red-brown patina, 45in (115cm) long.
$750-1,200

An Inca bag, tapestry weave in camelid wool on a cotton ground, with a long fringe below and fringed tassels at each side, in bright shades of deep red, plum, ochre, yellow, mauve, brown and white, A.D. 1470-1532, 19in (48.5cm) long.
$3,000-3,750

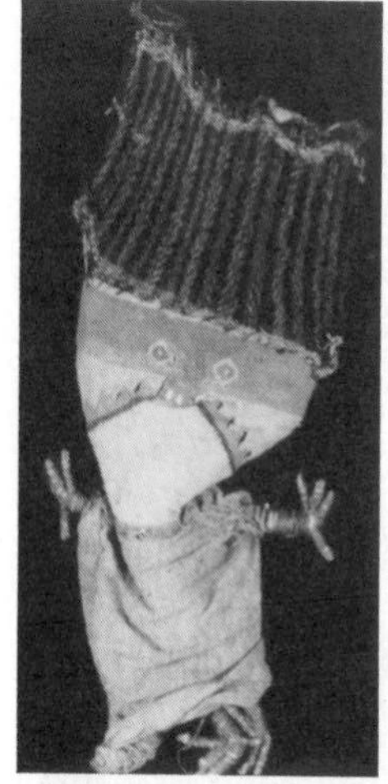

A Chancay textile doll, supported on a reed structure, the face woven in cream, ochre, red and brown, with a stepped pattern along the cheeks, the gauze weave headdress in shades of teal blue, yellow and brown, A.D. 1100-1300, 17½in (44.5cm) mounted.
$1,500-2,250

A Huari pile hat, in bright shades of teal blue, red, ochre, green brown and white, circa A.D. 700-1000, 5in (12cm) high including peak.
$5,250-7,500

A Huari pile hat, in blue, ochre, shades of green, white, dark brown and claret, A.D. 700-1000, 5in (13cm) high with tassels.
$750-1,200

A Yoruba bronze Ogboni staff, the finial as an elongated seated male figure smoking a pipe, holding a staff of office, 3 tiers of conical rattles, dark bronze patina, 59in (150cm) high.
$600-750

An Igbo headdress, surmounted by a Colonial style hat, kaolin colouration with black and red highlights, 26in (66cm) high.
$2,700-3,300

An Asmat shield, North West region, with 2 central stylised figures with elongated arms, with scrolled and curvilinear carving overall, lime, black and ochre colouration, 67in (170cm).
$3,000-4,500

A Central Coast textile panel, woven in cotton, slit tapestry in shades of tan, cream and blue-green, Pachacamac, A.D. 1000-1500, 37in (94cm) long.
$1,200-1,800

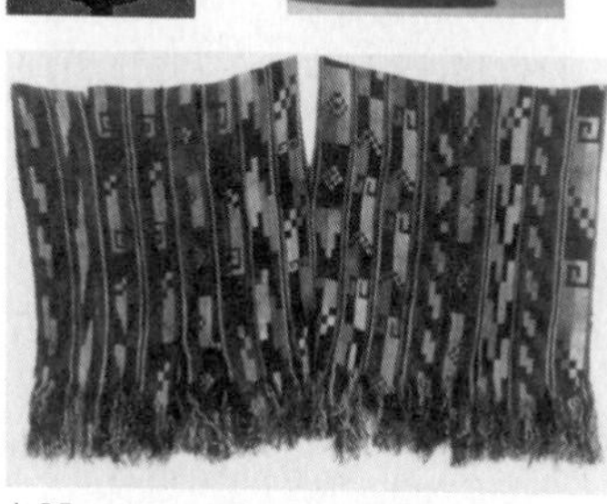

A Nazca poncho, in shades of ochre, red, orange and brown in camelid wool, in double cloth weave, A.D. 200-500, 37in (94.5cm) wide.
$1,200-1,800

A North Central Coast textile panel, possibly Chimu, woven in slit tapestry in camelid wood, in bright shades of wine red, rose, brown, tan, white and yellow, circa A.D. 1100-1400, 31in (79cm) long.
$1,050-1,350

A Chacay embroidered textile fragment, on plain cotton ground, sewn with 2 standing figures wearing tunics and downturned helmets, striped edges with fringes, with a row of birds in pink, yellow, black and white at the top, A.D. 1100-1300, 34½in (87.5cm) wide.
$1,500-2,250

A Chancay mantle fragment, in camelid wool in bright shades of olive brown, pink, red, yellow and dark brown, A.D. 1100-1400, 48in (121cm) wide.
$2,250-3,000

A Chancay painted textile fragment, woven in natural cotton and painted with a spotted pampas cat with bared talons and long curling tail, grasping a human in its jaws, A.D. 1100-1400, 15in (37.5cm) wide.
$1,500-2,250

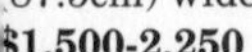

A Chancay gauze textile, in white cotton, A.D. 1100-1400, 89in (226cm) wide.
$1,500-2,250

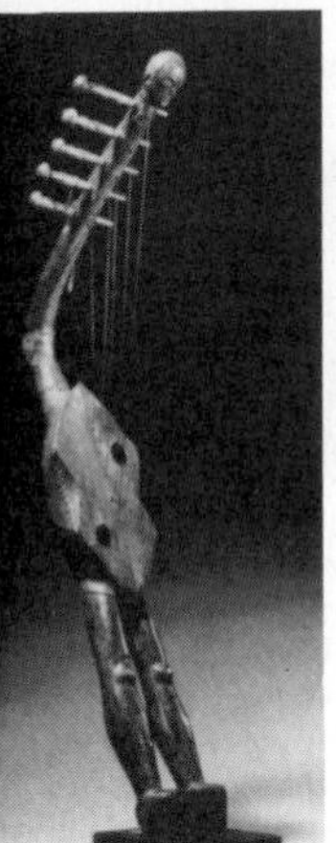

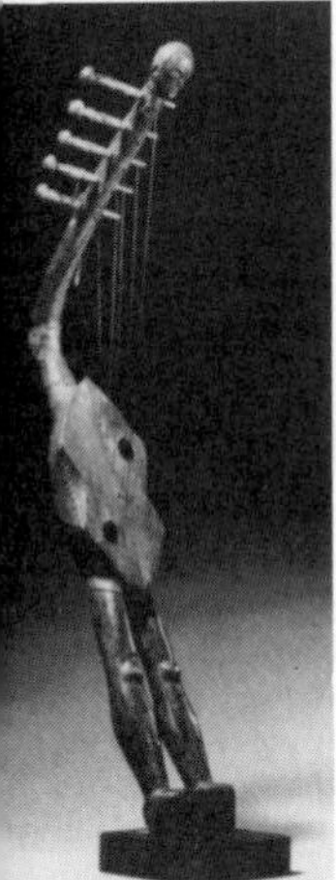

A Ngbaka harp in the form of a stylised human figure, with 5 wooden pegs inset down the sides of the neck, dark brown aged patina, 29in (74cm) high.
$4,500-6,000

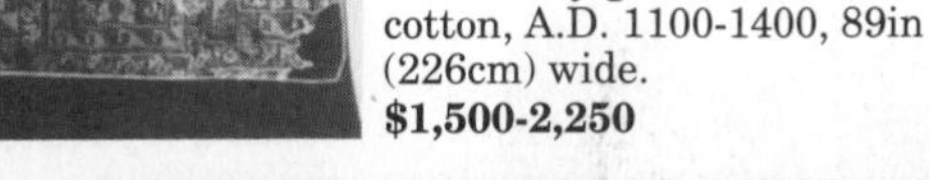

A Maori feather box, of canoe-like form, with flattened lid, decorated overall in shallow relief with linear and scrolling motifs, a tiki head on each end, a pair of miniature arms below one of the heads, the eyes inset with haliotis shell discs, light brown patina on the lid with dark oily patina on both ends, 17in (43cm) long.
$2,250-3,000

A feather box was made to hold ornaments that had been worn on the head of a chief and were thus 'taou'. The box was hung in the rafters of the house, out of the way so that people in the house were not endangered.

Miller's is a price GUIDE not a price LIST

A Yoruba Egungun headdress, 17½in (44.5cm) high.
$1,050-1,350

A Baule door, with a protruding tapered point on each side of the right edge for insertion, decorated in low relief with a large fish with thin, gaping mouth bearing teeth, one almong-shaped eye, rows of superimposed triangles representing the scales, 2 pairs of fins decorated with rows of parallel lines, the tail decorated in a similar fashion, fine aged patina, 60½in (154cm) high.
$4,500-6,000

A South Coast feathered tunic, woven in deep red, blue, olive green and shades of brown in a striped pattern, the front overlaid with 4 rows of green and pink parrot feathers, A.D. 700-1000, 27in (69cm) wide.
$900-1,050

MARINE MEMORABILIA

A brass cased Chetwynd & Clark's patent marine liquid filled compass, No. 445, by Kelvin & James White Ltd., 18 Cambridge Street, Glasgow, in a mahogany case, 12½in (32cm) wide.
$450-600

A ship's bulkhead clock, with brass case, the silvered dial signed The Toledo Shipbuilding Company, Toledo, Ohio, No.4212, the escutcheon inscribed The Ashcroft MFD Co., New York, subsidiary seconds dial, separately wound twin barrels, lever movement signed Seth Thomas, Thomaston, Conn.
$900-1,500

A ship's carved wood figurehead, in the form of a female torso, the crowned head with flowing tresses draped over the shoulders and below the bust, with a scroll below, finished in white, 44in (112cm) high.
$9,000-10,000

A ship's carved wood figurehead, in the form of a female torso, with arms by her side, holding sea shells and wearing a low cut dress with C-scroll and foliate decoration, finished in various colours, repainted, 19thC, 57in (145cm) high.
$7,500-9,000

A Seth Thomas ship's bell strike bulkhead clock, in a circular brass case, with silvered dial, Roman hour numerals, seconds dial, blued steel hands, repeat strike control, the brass bell suspended beneath, 10½in (26cm) high.
$750-900

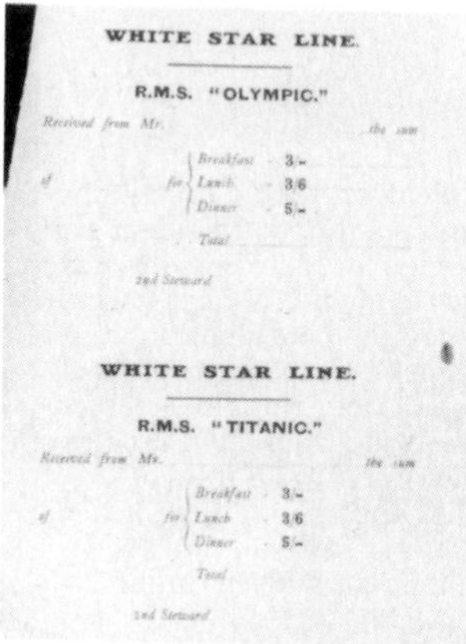

WHITE STAR LINE.

R.M.S. "OLYMPIC."

Received from Mr. the sum

of for Breakfast 3/- Lunch 3/6 Dinner 5/-

Total

2nd Steward

WHITE STAR LINE.

R.M.S. "TITANIC."

Received from Mr. the sum

of for Breakfast 3/- Lunch 3/6 Dinner 5/-

Total

2nd Steward

Two ship's copper and brass navigation lights, 'Not Under Command' with plaques embosse with a castle on the shore, waves and a ship, one stamped 887, the other 889, both with original oil lamps and chimneys, 23in (58.5cm) high.
$450-600

A German Imperial Navy bulkhead clock, the silvered dial signed and numbered A Schuchmann Wilhelmshaven 3738, and 'M' beneath the crown, Roman hour numerals, seconds dial, blued hands, mounted on oval shaped mahogany backboar
$750-900

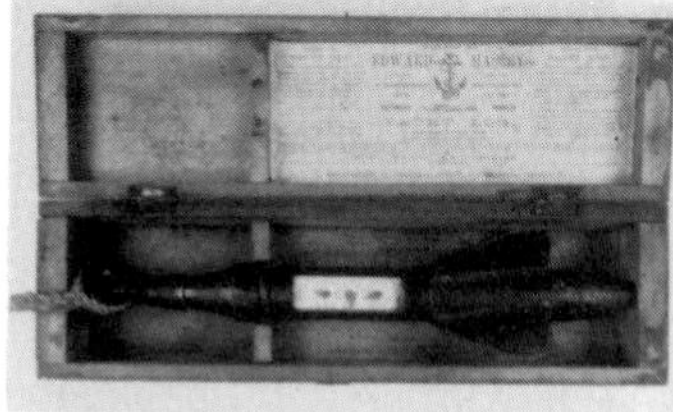

An Edward Massey ship's log, of torpedo shape with tail fins, signed lengthwise Edwd Massey's New Patent Yacht Log 16035, with a rotating slide shutter covering white enamel register comprising 3 'distance run' dials, inscribed New Yacht Log 'Edwd Massey' LLL (for 'Log, Lead and Look Out'), with a length of towing line, in a wooden storage box with a series of trade labels, 15½in (44.5cm) long.
$750-900

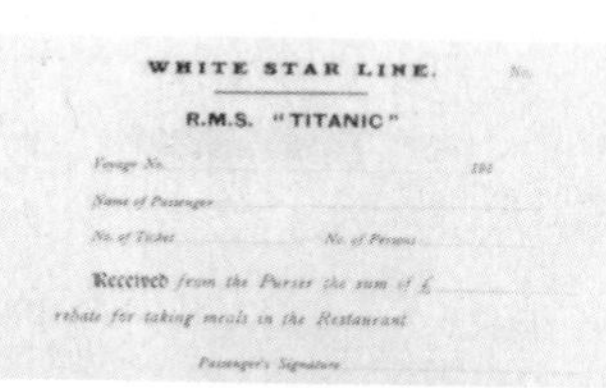

WHITE STAR LINE. No.

R.M.S. "TITANIC"

Voyage No. 191

Name of Passenger

No. of Ticket No. of Persons

Received from the Purser the sum of £

rebate for taking meals in the Restaurant

Passenger's Signature

Four unused receipts, each headed 'White Star Line RMS Titanic', and 2 '2nd Steward' receipts for meal payments, on one sheet.
$600-750

White Star Line.

R.M.S. "TITANIC" RESTAURANT.

Date........ Couvert........ Table........

Signature........

R.M.S. "Titanic" Restaurant

. small size folded board card, he front cover reading 'RMS 'itanic', 'Restaurant' above a epia tinted lithograph of a white ulled vessel in full sail, with ıscription below reading 'White tar Training Ship Mersey', the nside page area blank, 3 by 4½in 3 by 11.5cm), and an orange oloured table order form, unused, eaded 'White Start Line RMS 'itanic Restaurant'.
600-750

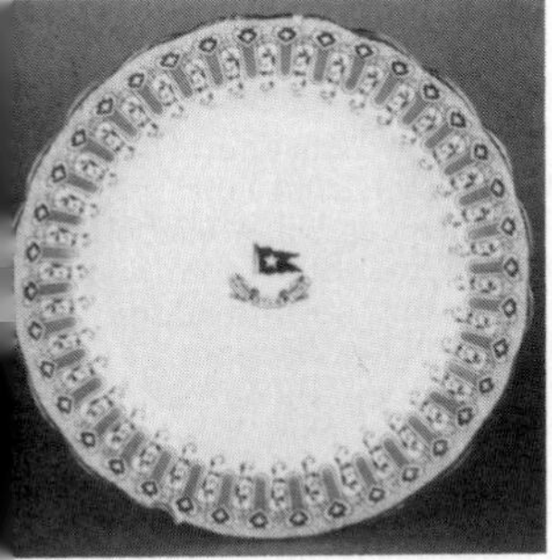

. pair of White Star Line orcelain plates, the centres mbossed with the company's ame and house flag, with urquoise tongue motif below a 'ave gilt line rim, mark of tonier & Co. Ltd., Liverpool, light wear, 7½in (19.5cm) diam.
375-525

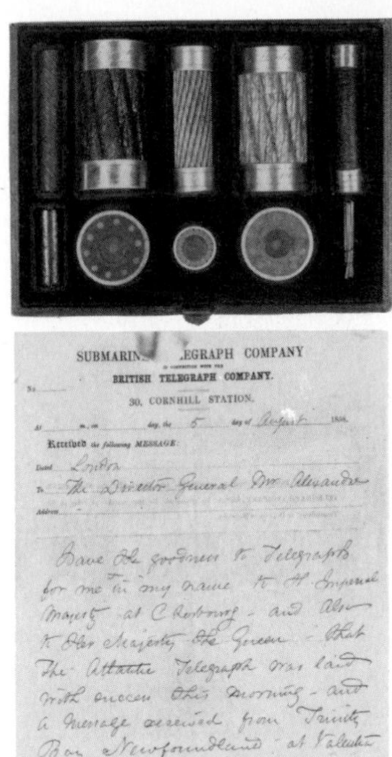
SUBMARIN[E TE]LEGRAPH COMPANY
BRITISH TELEGRAPH COMPANY.
30, CORNHILL STATION.

At .... day, the 5 day of August 1858.

Received the following MESSAGE:

Dated London

To The Director General Mr Alexander

Address........

Have the goodness to Telegraph for me in my name to H. Imperial Majesty at Cherbourg - and also to Her Majesty the Queen - that the Atlantic Telegraph was laid with success this morning - and a message received from Trinity Bay Newfoundland - at Valentia Bay Ireland

Brett

No Inquiry respecting this Message can be attended to without the production of this Paper.

A historically important collection of 'Atlantic Telegraph Cable' ephemera, including sample lengths of the cable laid in 1858, 1865 and 1866, a short length of the first submarine cable between Dover & Cap Grinez dated February 1850, in a velvet lined box, original correspondence and ephemera connected with John Watkins Brett, including photographs, silver commemorative plaques, a Submarine Telegraph Company Message Form dated 5th August 1858 to the Director General from Brett confirming that the first telegraph message had been received that morning at Valentia Bay, Ireland, from Trinity Bay, Newfoundland, a fob on a card made from a cross-section of the Atlantic cable associated with the message, 3 metal buttons, a publication of 1858, another dated 1950, and a catalogue of the sale of Brett's property dated April 5 1864, all in a velvet lined attaché case. **$2,250-3,000**

An unused off-white card, headed 'RMS Titanic' embossed with red White Star Line house flag above the cypher of the Oceanic Steam Navigation Company in gold, 4½ by 6in (10.5 by 15.5cm).
$375-525

John Watkins and Jacob Brett: The achievement of laying the first submarine cable of practical significance was due to the enterprise of 2 brothers, Jacob and John Watkins Brett. Jacob, the younger brother (1808-98) was an engineer. It was undoubtedly his initial interest which first attracted his elder brother, John Watkins, and induced him to take an active part in the enterprise. John Watkins Brett (1805-65) was originally in business as an antique dealer and, being a comparatively wealthy man, he was in a position to supply a proportion of the finance necessary to enable the project to go forward.

An embossed white metal plaque, signed F. Lanastre, depicting Admiral Lord Nelson being carried from the quarter deck of HMS Victory, with officers and seamen, with a mast, sails and rigging in the background and lettered under 'England Expects Every Man Will Do His Duty', 12½ by 13in (32 by 33cm), framed and glazed for wall hanging.
$450-600

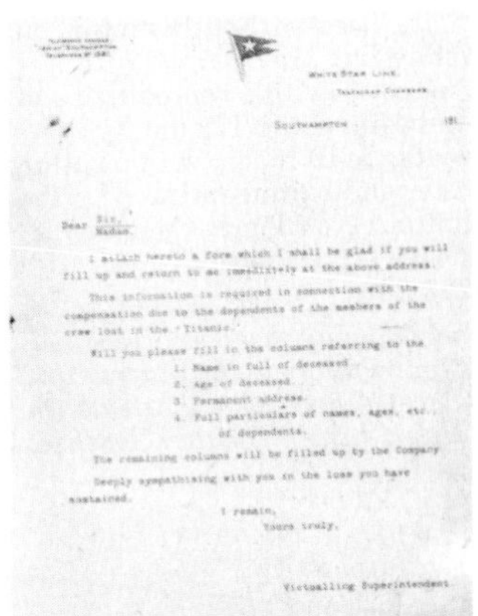
White Star Line.
Trafalgar Chambers

Southampton 191

Dear Sir, Madam.

I attach hereto a form which I shall be glad if you will fill up and return to me immediately at the above address.

This information is required in connection with the compensation due to the dependents of the members of the crew lost in the 'Titanic'.

Will you please fill in the columns referring to the

1. Name in full of deceased
2. Age of deceased.
3. Permanent address.
4. Full particulars of names, ages, etc., of dependents.

The remaining columns will be filled up by the Company.

Deeply sympathising with you in the loss you have sustained.

I remain,
Yours truly,

Victualling Superintendent

A headed White Star Line form letter, with coloured house flag and address Trafalgar Chambers, Southampton, blank dated 191-, addressed to dependents of crew members lost on the Titanic, asking for particulars of the deceased and dependents to be given on an enclosed form, unissued (no form attached), 8 by 10in (20 by 25.5cm).
$225-255

l. A diving suit, knife missing.
$2,250-3,000
r. A diving suit, comprising: copper and brass helmet, canvas on rubber suit, pair of weighted boots, front and back weights and a diver's knife in a brass sheath, probably made by Boehl of St Petersburg.
$3,000-3,750

A souvenir programme from the Titanic Relief Fund Special Benefit Matinée Concert, at the Palace Theatre, Southampton, on Wednesday May 8th 1912, the front cover with a reproduction of a painting of the Titanic. by Montague B. Black, with a sailing cutter and barque, printed by the Southampton Times Company, 6 by 10in (16 by 25cm).
$225-300

The following theatres are named as contributors to the programme: Palace, Hippodrome, Portsmouth Empire, King's Theatre, Southsea.

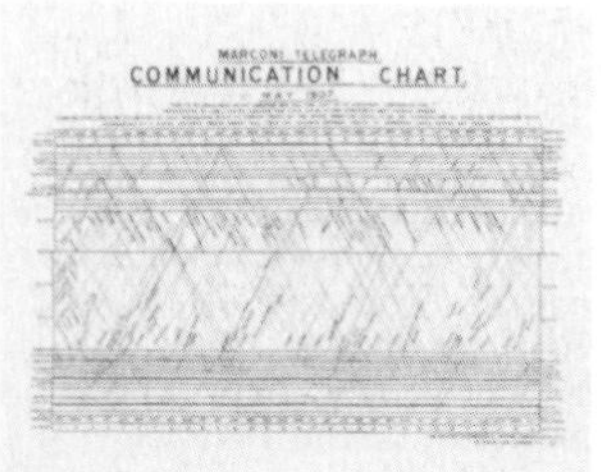

An early Marconi Telegraph Communication Chart, for May 1907, listing famous ships of the era.
$105-120

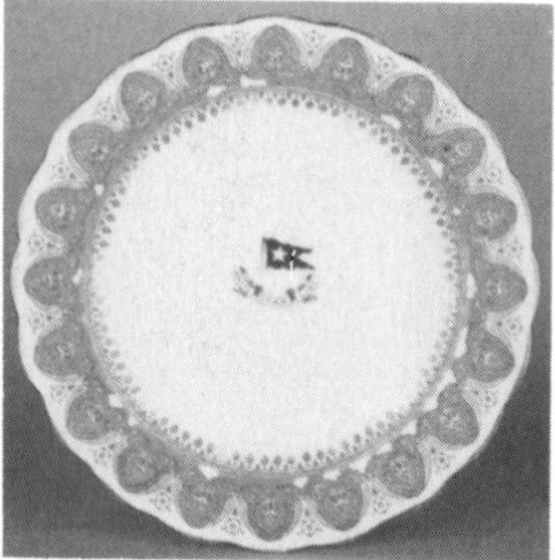

A pair of English porcelain plates made for the White Star Line, the centres embellished with the company's house flag above a scroll inscribed 'White Star Line', the arcaded border printed in brown and finished with turquoise below a wave gilt line rim, mark of Stonier & Co. Ltd. Liverpool, slight wear, 9in (23cm) diam.
$600-750

ROYAL ALBERT HALL

Under the Auspices of the Orchestral Association.

THE "TITANIC" BAND
MEMORIAL CONCERT
FRIDAY, 24th MAY, 1912 (Empire Day) at 3 p.m.

THE PHILHARMONIC ORCHESTRA.
THE QUEEN'S HALL ORCHESTRA.
THE LONDON SYMPHONY ORCHESTRA.
THE NEW SYMPHONY ORCHESTRA.
THE BEECHAM SYMPHONY ORCHESTRA.
THE ROYAL OPERA ORCHESTRA.
THE LONDON OPERA HOUSE ORCHESTRA.

SIR EDWARD ELGAR, O.M.
SIR HENRY J. WOOD
Mr. LANDON RONALD
Mr. THOMAS BEECHAM
Mr. PERCY PITT
M. FRITZ ERNALDY
and
Herr MENGELBERG
Madame ADA CROSSLEY.

A Titanic Band Memorial Concert programme, under the Auspices of The Orchestral Association, Royal Albert Hall, Friday 24th May 1912 (Empire Day), at 3pm, with all 478 musicians named.
$225-300

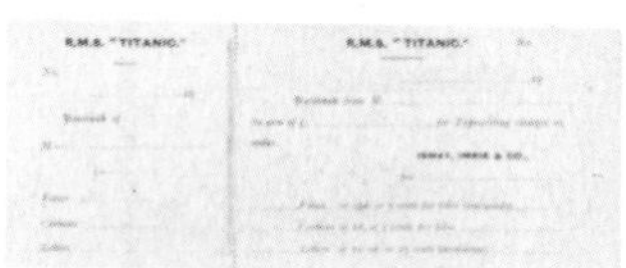

Two 'Typewriting Charges' receipts, attached to stubs, unused, headed 'RMS Titanic' and reading 'Received from M ... the sum of ... for Typewriting Charges as under, Ismay Imrie & Co'.
$450-600

A coloured Titanic postcard, published by the Success Post Card Co, New York, No. 1115, depicting the ship's port side, signed by 5 survivors.
$225-255

A silver plated metal figure of Neptune, seated on a rock with a shell back rest, crowned, holding a trident, 9in (23cm) high, on a wood plinth. **$450-600**

A White Star Line empty matchbox, the front label with their house flag below a scroll reading 'White Star Line', and above another scroll reading 'Safety Matches' beneath 'Prepared Specially for use on board White Star Steamers', 'Made in Sweden'.
$600-750

It is understood that this belonged to a survivor, Mr Tommy Knowles, the Firemen's messman, of Fanner's Lane, Lymington. It was in his pocket when he left the Titanic in Collapsible 'D'. This provenance was provided by direct family descent through his daughter, Miss Dorothy Knowles, who died in 1992.

ʀOCK & POP

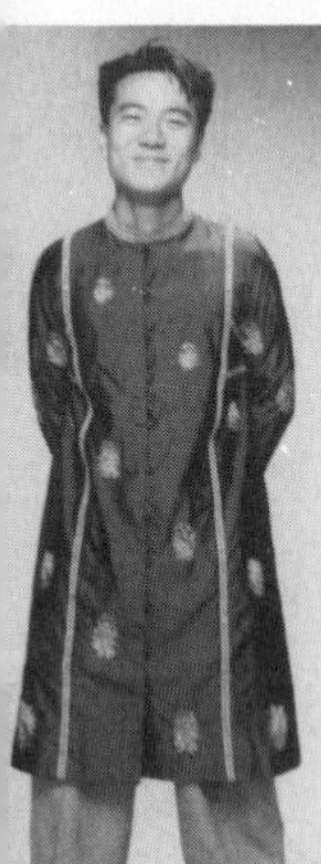

An embroidered blue satin robe, worn by John Lennon, with label Savita/Lowndes Lodge, Cadogan Place/London SW1, c1967, 40in (102cm) long.
$9,000-12,000
This robe was worn by John Lennon for the cover of the September 22, 1967 issue of Time Magazine. Apparently the robe was a gift by a photographer who worked on the shoot which provided the artist, Gerald Scarfe, with the photographs necessary to paint the picture which was to become the cover. A colour copy of the magazine cover which shows Lennon wearing the robe is included.

signed and inscribed ıotograph of Paul McCartney, so signed by Linda McCartney, by 4in (15 by 10cm).
225-300

collection of autographed ntage Motown albums, cluding Michael Jackson.
,700-3,300

A Stevie Wonder performance-worn red stage suit, cotton with rhinestones running along the length of the legs, and cuffs, silver beading on the chest and epaulets, worn late 1970s and 1980s, together with 3 photographs of the entertainer wearing the suit on stage, 64in (163cm) long.
$2,250-3,000

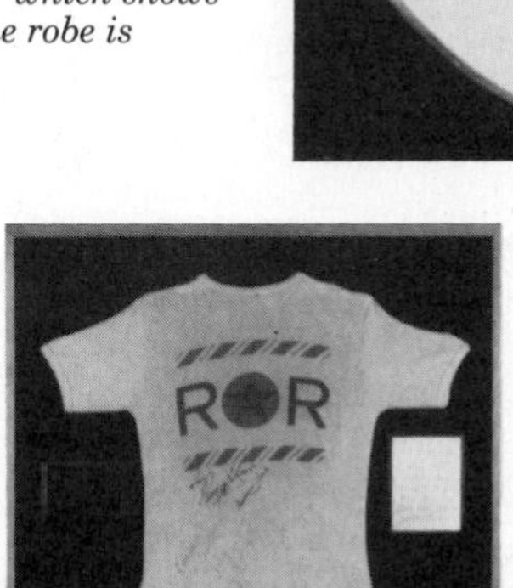

An ROR logo T-shirt, signed by Paul McCartney, Ringo Starr, and George Harrison, inscriptions are: Love Ringo Starr/Barbara Bach xxx/Love Linda McCartney 1983/Love From Paul McCartney with caricature drawing/Yoko Ono Lennon/George Harrison, framed with 2 plaques stating where and who signed the shirt, 1983, 29 by 33in (74 by 84cm).
$1,050-1,350
ROR stands for Richard Starkey and Robin Williams both of whom owned a furniture store in California in the 1980s. The shirt was signed December 1, 1983 by the celebrities in London at the Dorchester Hotel when they signed the final agreement to dissolve the Beatles.

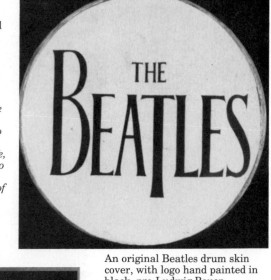

An original Beatles drum skin cover, with logo hand painted in black, pre-Ludwig Rouer, mounted on black velvet covered board, c1960, 26in (66cm) diam.
$15,000-22,500
With a letter of authenticity by Chris Farlowe, noted English rhythm and blues singer. Farlowe is best known for his work with Mick Jagger in the mid-1960s. This drum skin was given to Farlowe at an early 'Ready Steady Go' TV show, where he was performing on the same show as The Beatles.

A signed and inscribed Michael Jackson album record sleeve, 'Bad' record still present.
$105-120

A black felt hat, worn on stage by Michael Jackson during his 'Bad' tour, together with a signed photograph of him, 16½ by 16in (42 by 41cm).
$2,250-3,000

A set of Beatles 'Bobbing Head' dolls, hand painted, wearing grey-blue collarless suits, on gold bases with facsimile signatures, by Car Mascots Inc., 1964, each doll 8in (20cm) high.
$1,050-1,350

A collection of 15 signed pop celebrity photographs, includir Mick Jagger, Michael Jackson, The Doobie Brothers, Marv Johnson, Shirley Bassey, Fred Payne, Nancy Sinatra, Janet Jackson, Whitney Houston, Donna Summer, Paula Abdul, The Four Tops, Chuck Berry, Rufus Thomas, Chaka Kahn, A Green, in one binder.
$1,200-1,800

A signed photograph of Freddie Mercury, 8 by 10in (20 by 25cm).
$225-255

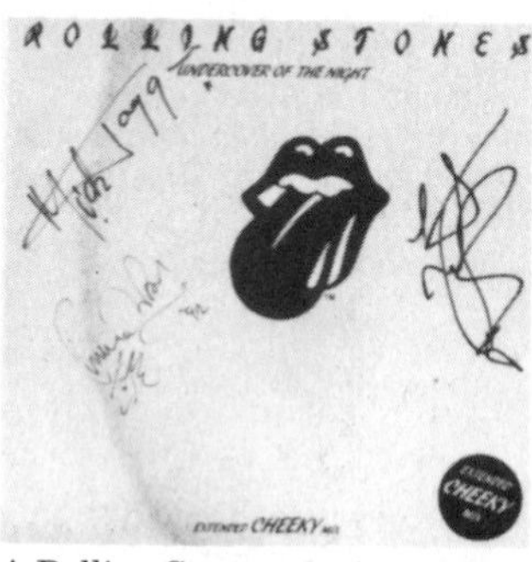

A set of The Dave Clark Five dolls, by Remco Industries, Inc., in their original box, 1964, with a promotional Pixerama Foldbook with 12 glossy pictures of the band, including a Herman of Herman's Hermits promotional doll, in original costume, with an 'I Love Herman's Hermits' button, together with a 3-dimensional promotional display of Bobby Sherman.
$1,500-2,250

A red 2920 Everlast boxing glo inscribed To Walter/Sly Stalon together with the Platinum CB Award presented to Walter Winneck for sale of more than million copies of Scotti Brother single 'Eye Of The Tiger' matte and framed, 16 by 12in (41 by 31cm).
$375-525

The RIAA Gold Single Award presented to Labelle for 'Lady Marmalade' and 20th Century Fox Records Platinum Single Award for 'It's Ecstasy When You Lay Down Next To Me', presented to Dick Bozzle, both matted and framed, 16½ by 13in (42 by 33cm) and 15 by 12in (38 by 31cm).
$750-900

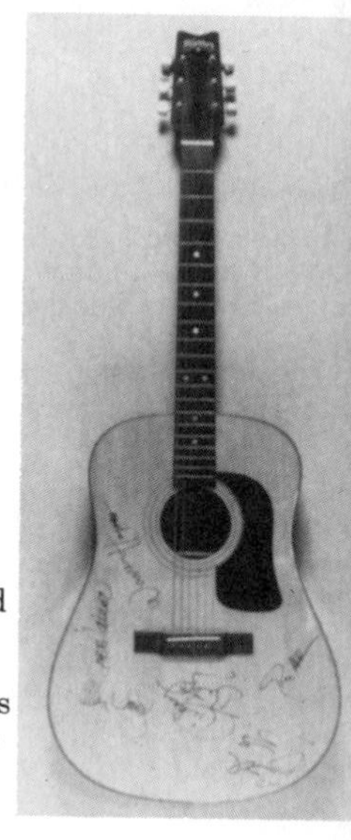

A Rolling Stones single record sleeve, signed to front cover by Mick Jagger, Charlie Watts and Ron Wood only, the record 'Undercover of the Night' no longer present.
$120-135

An Allman Brothers autographed guitar, the D 10N Washburn acoustic guitar serial No. 9106000836, 6 string instruments inscribed by all 6 members of the band.
$2,700-3,300

A signed photograph of Freddie Mercury, 8 by 10in (20 by 25cm).
$135-150

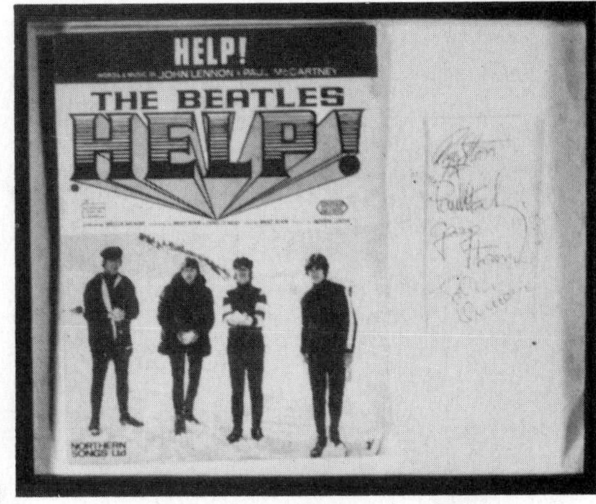

A card signed by all 4 Beatles, laid down alongside a song sheet for Help and featuring a photograph, framed, 13 by 16in (33 by 41cm) overall. **$750-900**

A signed Michael Jackson single record sleeve, featuring colour photo of Jackson, 'Leave me Alone' record still present.
$150-180

A miscellaneous group of Rock 'N' Roll promotional props, including a life-size cardboard cut-out of Elton John in cricket outfit.
$600-750

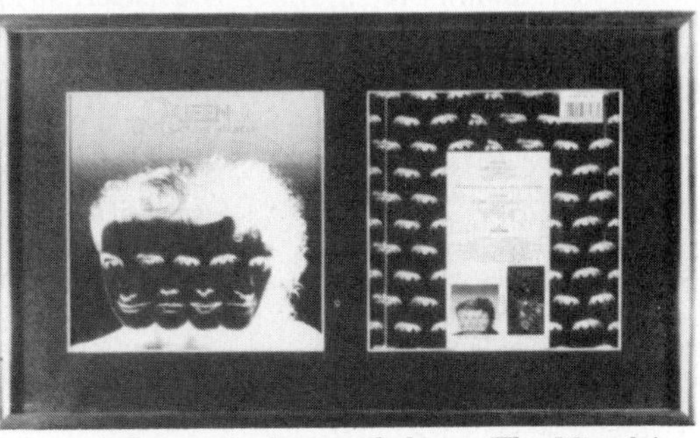

A Queen single record sleeve, 'The Miracle', signed to reverse, overmounted in black alongside the front cover of the same sleeve, framed and glazed, 11 by 19½in (28 by 49cm) overall.
$225-300

;inema & Film

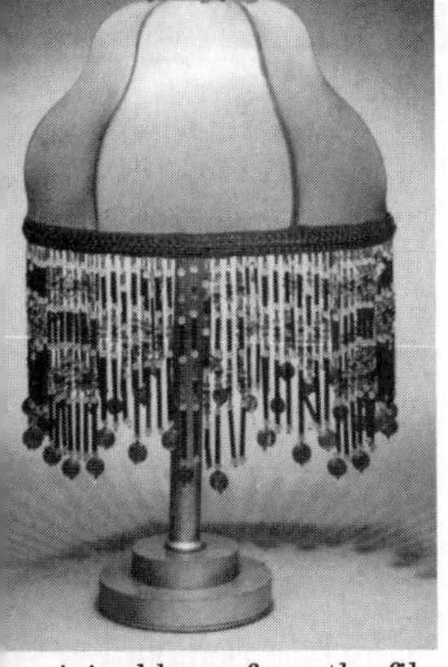

ı original lamp from the film ;asablanca' by Warner Bros, ›42, used as a prop in Rick's ıfé, marked on the bottom ;asablanca 007, 17in (43cm) high.
;2,000-15,000

:cluding 10 movie stills, with ıotographs of the lamp in Rick's ıfé, with a pop-up book entitled ıe Great Movies Live, which has ›op-up from Casablanca ıowing a café scene with the ımp. The lamp was acquired ›m a retired Warner Bros set ·corator.

Harrison Ford's hat from 'Indiana Jones and The Raiders of The Lost Ark', 1980, in beige felt with brown band, interior leather band with indistinct gold lettering, water stained, together with a Continuity Script, issued 18th May, 1980, an aluminium Arab style dagger from the film, with curving blade, 14in (36cm), and a cannon shell from 'The Last Crusade' realistically painted, 19in (48cm).
$1,200-1,500

With a letter confirming that the hat was given to the vendor by Harrison Ford as a memento, after filming on location in Tunisia.

The black leather jacket worn by Arnold Schwarzenegger in 'Terminator 2: Judgment Day', with bullet holes, traces of 'blood' and heavy scuffing, right hand pocket marked in white 1A.Prep.Mall, together with 8 black and white or colour publicity stills and a colour promotional poster, 40 by 27in (102 by 69cm).
$10,500-13,500

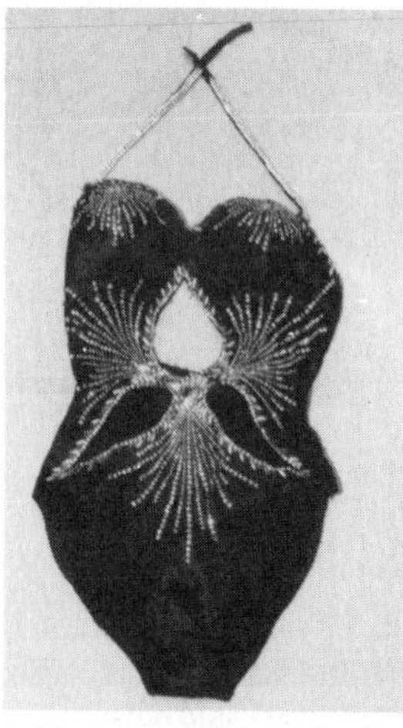

A black leotard worn by Jane Russell from 'The French Line', RKO 1953, designed by Jane Russell and Howard Greer, decorated with rhinestones and ovals cut out at the torso.
$3,000-3,750
This leotard caused worldwide censorship for years because it was so revealing. According to MFB from 'Halliwell's Film Guide' "...her clothes appear to stay put just as long as she agrees not to burst out of them..." This item includes a Japanese advertisement for the movie with Jane Russell wearing the leotard.

Harry Davenport's personal screen play for 'Gone With The Wind', inscribed by David O. Selznick, 1939, inscribed in blue ink on inside cover, for Harry Davenport, in appreciation of a splendid performance, David O. Selznick Xmas, 1939, the 256 page leather bound copy of the screen play embossed in gold, Gone With The Wind/Screen Play/Harry Davenport, includes original Carthay Circle Theatre programmes for 'Gone With The Wind', 11 by 9in (28 by 23cm).
$7,500-9,000
Harry Davenport played Doctor Meade in this film.

A cigarette case and lighter give to Sam K. Winston by Marlene Dietrich, in silver and gold coloured metal, black enamel outer with red, black and white rectangles/squares decoration down right edge, the interior inscribed 'To Sam Marlene Christmas 1931', with matching Dunhill lighter, French, 1931, 3 by 3in (9 by 8cm).
$3,000-3,750
Sam K. Winston adapted the so 'Falling In Love Again' into English from the German for Dietrich, he was also film editor on 'The Blue Angel'.

A 'Pulse' rifle used in the films, 'Alien' and 'Alien 3', in black metal with webbing strap extending butt, with certificate of de-activation, 32in (81cm) long with butt extended.
$3,000-3,750

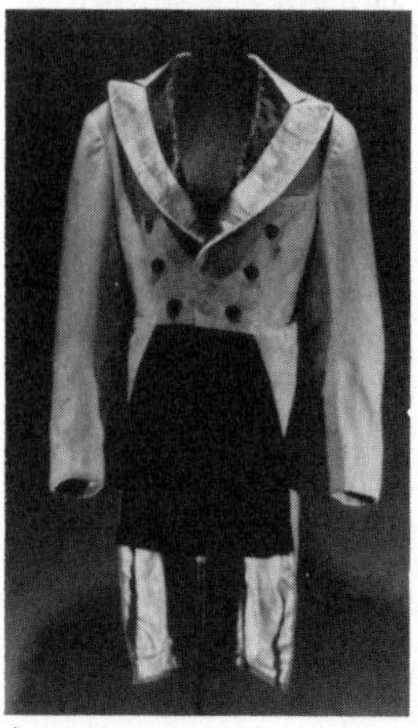

A costume worn by one of the munchkins in 'The Wizard of Oz', Metro Goldwyn Mayer, 1938, 40in (102cm) long.
$1,800-2,700

A black velvet gown worn by Vivien Leigh in 'Lady Hamilton', United Artists, 1941, designed by René Hubert, trimmed with black lace and crystal beading.
$3,000-3,750
Including a movie still of the actress wearing the dress.

A collection of letters, signed photographs and cablegrams relating to Laurel and Hardy, 1930s.
$900-1,500
In 1912 a young, unemployed Stan Jefferson teamed up with comedy musician Ted Leo to become 'The Barto Brothers - the Rum'uns from Rome' and was subsequently asked by Bob Reed, acrobat and silent film and character actor to join one of his comedy troupes, 'The Seven Komils'. They played unsuccessfully in Holland and Belgium and, some 20 years later, Ted Leo (now Ted Desmond, leader of a Glasgow dance band) met Jimmy Reed, a well known local cinema manager: in their discussion Ted mentioned the success in Hollywood of 'Arthur Jefferson's young son Stan...',and it was then that Jimmy realised that the familiar looking face on screen was that of Stan Laurel, who had worked with him and hi father in 'The Seven Komiks'. He wrote to Stan and the resulting letters etc. are these.

\ letter and 2 signed photographs
of Laurel and Hardy, 1940/50s,
he letter written in blue ink by
Stan Laurel on a sheet of The
Central Hotel Glasgow headed
paper, dated 11-3-52, the
photograph signed, the reverse of
he smaller with a note dated
12/4/47, by Laurel, the larger
photograph 5 by 7in (13 by 18cm).
$750-900

signed photograph of Laurence
livier in Richard III costume, 10
8in (25 by 20cm).
'0-145

black straw hat worn by Vivien
eigh in 'Gone With The Wind',
IGM, 1939, scalloped at the back
nd with a wide light pink silk
bbon across the front, label with
ar's name.
4,800-5,700
*'ith a movie still of Vivien Leigh
earing the hat.*

Leonard Nimoy's ears from 'Star Trek III:The Search for Spock', Paramount Pictures, 1984, with a note of authenticity from Leonard Nimoy and an autographed photograph.
$1,200-1,500

A signed colour photograph of Brigitte Bardot, 10 by 8in (25 by 20cm).
$50-75

A cigarette case, once owned by Errol Flynn, Elgin, inscribed EF on the front and engraved Good Luck Errol/ J.(John) Barrymore, on the inside, 4 by 3in (10 by 8cm).
$5,250-7,500
This comes with a letter of authenticity by Robert Slatzer, a personal friend of Errol Flynn.

A signed and inscribed sepia photograph of Marlene Dietrich, 1943, 9½ by 7½in (24 by 19cm).
$120-135

A large collection of letters and other material relating to Vivien Leigh, 1930s to 1960s.
$4,500-6,000

A black velvet gown worn by Marilyn Monroe in 'The Fireball', 20th Century Fox, 1950, with self covered belt, label with the star's name.
$5,250-7,500
Including a photograph of the star wearing the gown.

A pink dress worn by Marilyn Monroe in 'Niagra', 20th Century Fox, 1952, linen, tight fitting dress with a halter top, label with star's name.
$5,250-6,000
This dress is famous for being known as 'wiggle dress' in one of Marilyn Monroe's first big parts. With a movie still and postcard of Marilyn Monroe wearing the dress.

The blue and white cotton dress worn by Judy Garland in 'The Wizard of Oz', MGM, by costume designer Adrian, together with a white petticoat and 2 blue socks with red stains, label with star's name, 1939.
$45,000-60,000

A black lace dress worn by Jean Harlow in 'Libelled Lady', MGM, 1936, designed by Dolly Tree, lined with pale pink silk crêpe, torn, studio label.
$3,000-4,500

A black silk negligée wo
by Marilyn Monroe in
'Niagra' with an applied
pink rose at the bodice,
label with the star's nam
$7,500-9,000
Including a wardrobe photograph of Marilyn Monroe wearing the dress.

ADVERTISING

Cadbury's Bourn-Vita, 'The Goodnight Drink that Becomes Tomorrow's Energy', photographic showcard, 25 by 30in (64 by 76cm).
$50-75

A wall mounted advertisement plaque, with chef and bottle of Liebig, 'Mijne beste hulp!', with 6 screw holes, slight stains.
$150-180

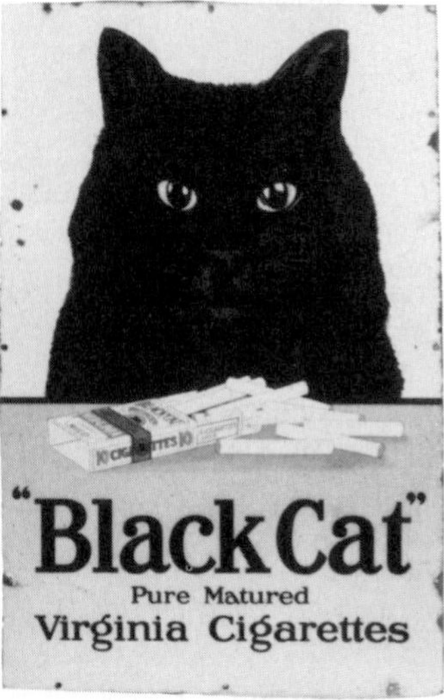

Black Cat Pure Matured Virginia Cigarettes, 36 by 24in (92 by 61cm).
$225-300

GREETINGS CARD

Two 3-dimensional chromolithographic pop-up valentine cards, c1885.
$225-255

An early hand made Rebus card, watercolour pen and ink, each fold opening to reveal a verse, the centre with 7 hearts, c1825, 4 by 4in (10 by 10cm).
$450-600

hand coloured, embossed and
ərced paperlace card, stamp
ırked Mossman, elaborately
plied with silver and gilded
tails, fabric flowers, leaves and
ke pearls, with printed
scription, c1870, 7 by 5in (18 by
cm), in original box addressed
James Parlance Esq., Wood
llas, Fallowfield, with 3 one
nny stamps.
25-300

An embossed and pierced paperlace valentine card, stamp marked Dobbs, hand coloured, titled in manuscript 'The Seal of Love', the standing seal singing 'Come to my Arms/Our love & bliss/Shall then be/Sealed with a/kiss', lifting to reveal a concealed message 'You are the Joy/Of my heart', c1850, 7 by 4½in (18 by 11cm), with contemporary envelope.
$300-375

Two hanging valentine cards, one heart-shaped card, with automobile suspended by a silk ribbon at the base, by Raphael Tuck & Sons, c1902, and a similar hanging valentine card with a keyhole, together with another novelty valentine card by Ernest Nister. **$450-600**

vo embossed and pierced
perlace cards, both stamp
arked Dobbs Kidd & Co., one
ntre applied with hand coloured
ums, lifting to reveal
scription, c1866, 8 by 5in (20 by
cm). **$225-300**

Two embossed and pierced paperlace cards, one stamp marked Mullord, both with original stamped addressed envelopes, c1860.
$150-180

A devotional card of delicate pin-prick work creating parchment paperlace, with an original watercolour head and shoulder portrait of 'S Rosina', written in gold and decorated with flowers, the borders edged in gold, c1810, 5 by 3in (13 by 8cm), and an embossed envelope with a one penny stamp, post marked Liverpool 13 Feb 69.
$375-450

ıree embossed and paperlace
ılentine cards, stamp marked
ansell, all with chromo-
hographic and hand coloured
tails, c1850, 5 by 3½in (13 by
m). **$135-150**

Two chromolithographic pop-up cards, one in form of a Venetian bridge, the other an ornate gilt table, with vases of flowers, a goldfish bowl and an opened letter, c1870. **$300-375**

ANIMATION ART & POSTERS

Hanna-Barbera

The Flintstones, Fred and Wilma storyboard, graphite and coloured pencil on paper, in common mount, 1960s, each 7 by 9in (18 by 23cm).
$600-750

Scooby Doo jumps on to a tabl gouache on full celluloid applie to a watercolour production background, 1970s, 10½ by 31½ (26 by 80cm).
$900-1,500

Scooby Doo and Shaggy, gouache on multi-celluloic set up applied to a watercolour production background, 7½ by 9½in (19 by 24cm).
$600-750

MGM

'Pup On A Picnic', 1955, Spike, Tyke, Tom and Jerry, gouache on multi-celluloid set up applied to a watercolour production background, 9 by 12in (23 by 31cm).
$1,200-1,500

'Fit To Be Tied' 1950, Spike walks Tom on a lead as Jerry rings a bell, gouache on multi-celluloid set up applied to a watercolour production background, 9 by 11½in (23 by 29cm).
$3,000-3,750

Miller's is a price GUIDE not a price LIST

'Feedin' The Kiddie', 1957, Tom, Jerry and kiddie mouse, gouach on full celluloid applied to a han prepared background, 8½ by 11i (21 by 28cm). **$900-1,500**

Walt Disney

'Winnie The Pooh and Tigger Too' 1974, U.S., one sheet, 41 by 27in (104 by 69cm).
$750-900

Vinnie The Pooh and The Honey ree', 1966, Rabbit fixes a sign, ouache on full celluloid applied a hand prepared background, 3½ by 16½in (34 by 42cm).
600-750

'Winnie The Pooh and The Honey Tree', 1966, Rabbit strides out, gouache on full celluloid applied to a hand prepared background, 10½ by 12½in (26 by 32cm).
$720-1,000

Vinnie The Pooh', 1970s, Winnie ne Pooh and Rabbit watch hristopher Robin playing his rum, gouache on full celluloid pplied to a hand prepared ackground, 9 by 11in (23 by 9cm).
600-750

'Winnie The Pooh, 1980s, Pooh, Tigger, Piglet and Owl build Eeyore's house, gouache on full celluloid applied to a watercolour production background, unframed, 10 by 14½in (25 by 37cm).
$1,200-1,500

'Winnie The Pooh and The Honey Tree', 1966, Christopher Robin, Kanga and Eeyore pull Pooh from the tree, gouache on full celluloid applied to a hand prepared background, 13½ by 16½in (34 by 42cm).
$1,500-2,250

'Pooh And Friends', February 14, 1976, Pooh and friends including Tigger and Rabbit, original artwork for 'Disneyland Magazine', watercolour on board, 16½ by 14½in (42 by 37cm).
$450-600

'Winnie The Pooh and The Blustery Day', 1968, Winnie the Pooh, an animation drawing, graphite on paper, unframed, 10½ by 12½in (26 by 32cm).
$300-375

'Jungle Book', 1967, King Louie, gouache on full celluloid applied to a hand prepared background, 10½ by 12½in (26 by 32cm).
$600-750

'Jungle Book', 1967, Mowgli, gouache on full celluloid applied to a hand prepared background, 7½ by 9½in (19 by 24cm).
$375-450

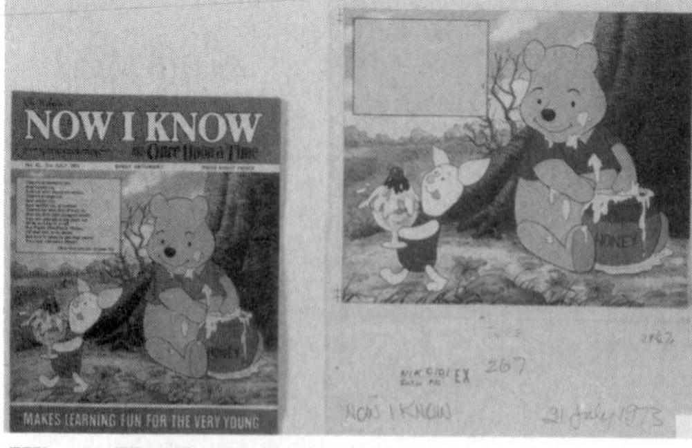

'Winnie The Pooh', Pooh with a pot of honey and Piglet with an ice cream sundae, artwork for a magazine cover, gouache on paper, and a corresponding copy of the magazine, largest 16 by 14in (41 by 36cm).
$600-750

Jungle Book
1967

'Jungle Book', 1967, Baby Elephant walks, gouache on partial celluloid applied to a hand prepared background, 4 by 5in (10 by 13cm).
$375-525

Peter Pan
1953

'Peter Pan', 1953, Michael as an Indian, gouache on full celluloid applied to a hand prepared background, 12½ by 16½in (26 by 42cm). **$600-750**

Jungle Book
1967

'Jungle Book', 1967, King Louie with his arms open, gouache on full celluloid, 12 by 16in (31 by 41cm).
$600-750

Jungle Book
1967

'Jungle Book', 1967, King Louie and Baloo danc gouache on full celluloid applied to a hand prepared background, 11 by 13½in (28 by 34cm
$1,050-1,350

Jungle Book
1967

'Jungle Book', 1967, Bagheera, gouache on full celluloid applied to a hand prepared background, 10½ by 12½in (26 by 32cm).
$600-750

Jungle Book
1967

'Jungle Book', 1967, Mowgli and Mowgli with Rama, 2 celluloids, both gouache on full celluloid applied to a hand prepared background, 10½ by 12½in (26 by 32cm).
$600-750

'Jungle Book', 1967, Mowgli and Baloo, gouache on full celluloid applied to a printed Disneyland background, 9 by 11in (23 by 28cm).
$750-900

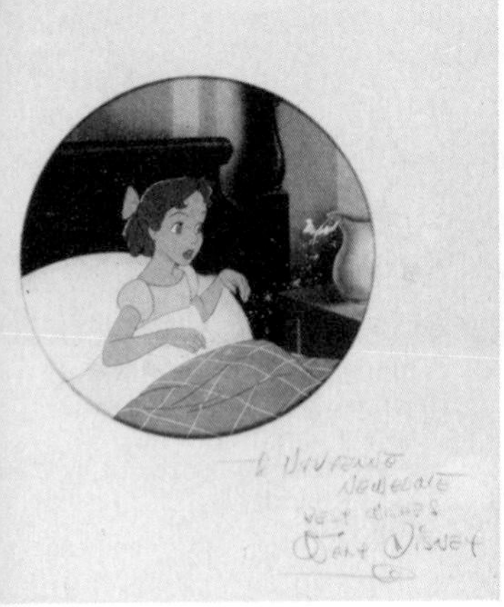

eter Pan', 1953, gouache on immed celluloid, Wendy and nkerbell, Courvoisier set up ith mount stamped WDP iginal, film title in pencil and gned and inscribed in brown ayon by Walt Disney, 8in (20cm) am.
,000-3,750

he recipient of this celluloid was journalist who met Disney and rote an article for 'Woman' agazine which appeared in ctober 1952. It sold, with a hotocopy of that article and a tter, on Walt Disney Mickey 'ouse Ltd, London, headed aper, dated 4th May, 1953, ating, ...'Walt Disney has tographed the enclosed artwork hich I hope you will accept with ır best wishes and thanks...'.

Jungle Book
1967

'Jungle Book', 1967, a monkey attendant, gouache on full celluloid applied to a hand prepared background, 11 by 13½in (28 by 34cm).
$375-525

Peter Pan
1953

'Peter Pan', 1953, Michael, John and The Lost Boys tied up with rope, gouache on full celluloid applied to a hand prepared background, 12 by 14in (31 by 36cm).
$600-750

'Peter Pan', 1953, Peter Pan wears an Indian headdress, Peter Pan sits cross-legged and Peter Pan stands with limbs out-stretched, 4 celluloids, 2 gouache on full celluloid, 2 gouache on trimmed celluloid, unframed, largest 12½ by 16in (32 by 41cm).
$1,200-1,800

eter Pan', 1953, The Crocodile, ı animation drawing, graphite ıd coloured pencil on paper, ıframed, 12½ by 15½in (32 by)cm).
75-450

'Peter Pan', 1953, Wendy flies, Peter Pan points, Wendy half-length close up, Tinkerbell looks surprised and Tinkerbell unconscious, 5 celluloids, each gouache on trimmed celluloid, unframed, largest 9 by 8in (23 by 20cm).
$1,500-2,250

ady and The Tramp', 1955, Lady ıd Jock, and 3 other animation ough drawings, coloured pencil ı paper, unframed, 12½ by 15½in 2 by 39cm).
600-750

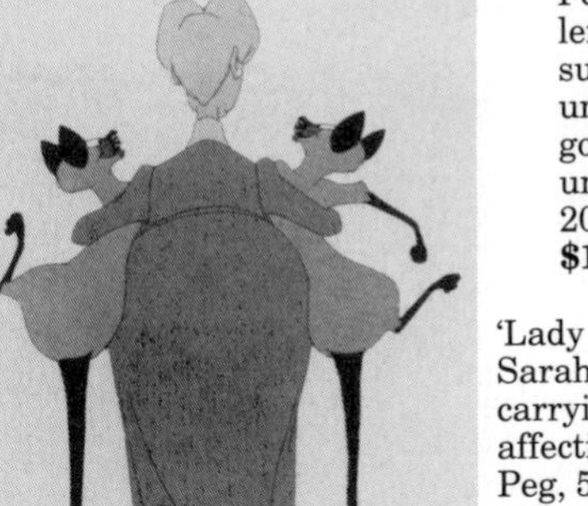

'Lady and The Tramp', 1955, Aunt Sarah carrying Lady, Aunt Sarah carrying Si and Am, Tony smiles affectionately, the Professor and Peg, 5 celluloids, each gouache on full celluloid, unframed, 12½ by 16in (32 by 41cm).
$2,250-3,000

'Lady and the Tramp', 1955, 2 publicity celluloids, Lady and The Tramp, both gouache on celluloid, 11 by 8½in (28 by 21cm).
$900-1,500
These 2 celluloids were sent for reference purposes to the porcelain manufacturers George Wade & Son, Stoke-on-Trent, who modelled ceramic figures on them.

'Dumbo', 1970s, Dumbo and friends, original artwork for 'Disneyland Magazine', watercolour on board, 13 by 27½in (33 by 70cm).
$600-750

'Lady and The Tramp', 1955, Toughy, Boris and Pedro sing, gouache on full celluloid applied to a hand prepared background, 10½ by 12½in (26 by 32cm).
$1,200-1,800

'Lady and The Tramp', 1955, The Tramp looks surprised, the Tramp looks inquisitive, the Tramp looks happy, Lady holds a ball in her mouth and a puppy runs, 5 celluloids, each gouache on full celluloid, unframed, 12½ by 16in (32 by 41cm).
$2,700-3,300

'Alice in Wonderland', 1951, Alice talks to the Mad Hatter, gouache on full celluloid, 6 by 9in (15 by 23cm).
$600-750

'Lady and The Tramp', 1955, Bull the Bulldog, gouache on full celluloid applied to a hand prepared background, 10½ by 12½in (26 by 32cm).
$600-750

'Alice in Wonderland', 1951, Alice, an animation drawing, brown pencil on paper, 5 by 3½in (13 by 9cm).
$300-375

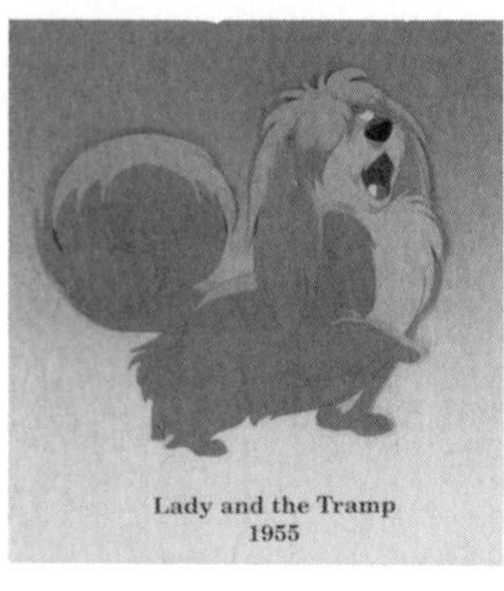

'Lady and The Tramp', 1955, Peg struts, gouache on full celluloid, 7½ by 9½in (19 by 24cm).
$1,500-2,250

'Sleeping Beauty', 1959, King Hubert, gouache on full celluloid applied to hand prepared backgrounds, 7½ by 9½in (19 by 24cm).
$375-450

lice in Wonderland', 1970s, ice with the Mad Hatter, Alice ith Dodo, original book ustrations, watercolour, 15½ by in (39 by 28cm) and similar.
105-120

leeping Beauty', 1959, Flora, auna and Merryweather, uache on full celluloid, nframed, 9½ by 10in (24 by 5cm).
450-600

umbo', 1941, A black crow quawking, a storyboard drawing, raphite on paper, 5 by 7in (13 by 8cm).
750-900

'Dumbo', 1941, Straw Hat Crow and Preacher Crow dance, gouache on full celluloid, unframed, 10 by 12in (25 by 31cm). **$900-1,500**

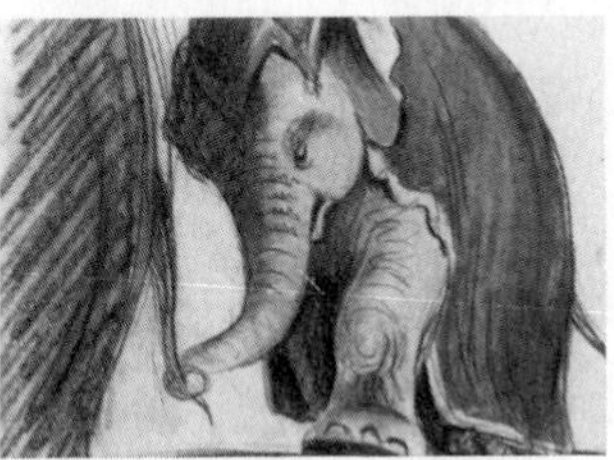

'Dumbo', 1941, Mrs Jumbo (Dumbo's mother), a concept drawing, charcoal on paper, 5 by 7in (13 by 18cm).
$900-1,050

'Snow White and The Seven Dwarfs', 1937, Doc, Bashful and Dopey, model sheet drawing, 9 by 12in (23 by 31cm).
$750-1,200

'Snow White and The Seven Dwarfs, 1937, The Witch, an animation drawing, unframed, 10 by 12in (25cm by 31cm).
$750-900

'Snow White and The Seven Dwarfs', 1937, The Witch clutches the poisoned apple, an animation drawing, graphite and coloured pencil on paper, unframed, 12½ by 15½in (32 by 39cm).
$1,800-2,700

'Snow White and The Seven Dwarfs', 1937, Three bluebirds on a branch, gouache on full celluloid applied to a Courvoisier airbrush background, unframed, 5 by 5in (13 by 13cm).
$900-1,500

'Snow White and The Seven Dwarfs', 1937, Doc, and Doc with Bashful, 2 storyboard drawings, graphite and coloured pencil on paper, 7 by 9in (18 by 23cm) and similar.
$750-1,200

'Snow White and The Seven Dwarfs, 1937, Grumpy, a model sheet drawing, graphite on paper, 10 by 12in (25 by 31cm).
$1,050-1,350

'Snow White and The Seven Dwarfs', 1937, Snow White surrounded by the Seven Dwarfs and forest animals, by Disney artist Fred Moore, a preliminary drawing for the poster released for the film, graphite and coloured pencil on paper, unframed, 11 by 15in (28 by 38cm).
$5,250-6,000

A similar image appears in the book: Walt Disney, The Illusion of Life.

'Snow White and The Seven Dwarfs', 1937, Grumpy whittling, a storyboard drawing, graphite and coloured pencil on paper, 7 by 7½in (18 by 19cm).
$1,800-2,700

'Snow White and The Seven Dwarfs', 1937, Dopey carries a dustpan full of diamonds, gouache on full celluloid applied to a Courvoisier airbrush background, 7 by 7in (18 by 18cm).
$2,700-3,300

'Snow White and The Seven Dwarfs', 1937, Sleepy, gouache o multi-celluloid set up applied to a Courvoisier wood veneer background, 5½ by 5½in (14 by 14cm).
$1,500-2,250

'Snow White and The Seven Dwarfs', 1937, Dopey, an animation drawing, graphite an coloured pencil on paper, unframed, 10 by 12in (25 by 31cm).
$600-750

'Snow White and The Seven Dwarfs', 1937, Dwarfs at work in the mine, original book illustration, watercolour, 16½ by 25in (42 by 66cm).
$600-750

'Snow White and The Seven Dwarfs', 1937, Snow White, 2 character drawings, graphite and coloured pencil on paper, unframed, 10 by 12in (25 by 31cm). **$600-750**

'Snow White and The Seven Dwarfs, 1937, Snow White dances with Dopey, Doc, Sneezy and Bashful, gouache on partial celluloids applied to a Courvoisier wood veneer background, 10½ by 13in (26 by 33cm).
$15,000-22,500

This celluloid is believed to have been the only piece to have been kept by the Courvoisier family.

'Snow White and The Seven Dwarfs', 1937, Five Dwarfs march, an animation drawing, coloured pencil and graphite on paper, 12 by 18in (31 by 46cm).
$900-1,500

'Snow White and The Seven Dwarfs', 1937, The Seven Dwarfs look down over the bannister, gouache on full celluloid applied to a Courvoisier wood veneer background, 5½ by 7½in (14 by 19cm).
$2,700-3,300

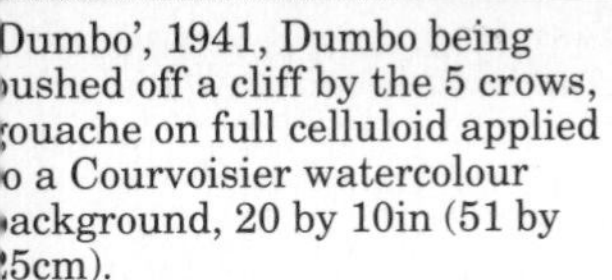

Dumbo', 1941, Dumbo being
ushed off a cliff by the 5 crows,
ouache on full celluloid applied
o a Courvoisier watercolour
ackground, 20 by 10in (51 by
5cm).
3,000-4,500

'Snow White and The Seven Dwarfs, 1937, Grumpy sits on a barrel, gouache on partial celluloid applied to a Courvoisier wood veneer background, 8 by 5½in (20 by 14cm).
$3,000-4,500

'antasia', 1940, Mlle. Upanova in
hree ballet positions, 3
toryboard drawings, coloured
encil and graphite on paper, in
ommon mount, 35½ by 8in (90 by
0cm).
750-1,200

'Fantasia', 1940, Centaurettes and Fauns frolick, an animation drawing, graphite and coloured pencil on paper, unframed, 9 by 12in (23 by 31cm).
$9,000-12,000

'Fantasia', 1940, Flying Cherub, gouache on partial celluloid, unframed, 7½ by 9½in (19 by 24cm).
$750-900

'Fantasia', 1940, A herd of baby Unicorns, gouache on trimmed celluloid applied to a hand prepared background, unframed, 10 by 13in (25 by 33cm).
$2,250-3,000

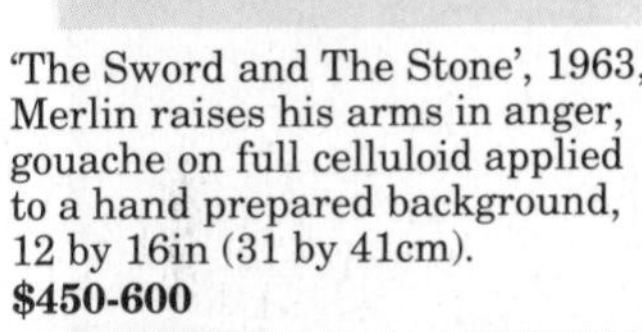

'The Sword and The Stone', 1963, Merlin raises his arms in anger, gouache on full celluloid applied to a hand prepared background, 12 by 16in (31 by 41cm).
$450-600

'The Sword and The Stone', 1963, The orphan boy Wart, gouache on full celluloid applied to a hand prepared background, 10½ by 9in (26 by 23cm).
$450-600

'Fantasia', 1940, Mlle. Upanova, gouache on full celluloid applied to a Courvoisier watercolour and airbrush background, 8½ by 10½in (21 by 26cm).
$1,800-2,700

'Pinocchio', 1940, Pinocchio as a boy, animation drawings, graphite on paper, unframed, 10 by 12in (25 by 31cm).
$1,050-1,350

'Mickey's Circus', Mickey and Donald falling, 2 animation drawings, both graphite and coloured pencil on paper, in common mount, largest 6½ by 5in (16 by 13cm).
$900-1,500

'Pinocchio', 1940, Jiminy Cricket with yo-yo, a pair of animation drawings, coloured pencil on paper, 12½ by 15½in (32 by 39cm).
$750-1,200

'Pinocchio', 1940, Figaro smiles, gouache on full celluloid applied to a hand prepared background, 10 by 12in (25 by 31cm).
$1,200-1,500

'Donald's Golf Game, 1938, Donald shoos a bird off the tee, gouache on partial celluloids applied to a watercolour production background, 7½ by 10in (19 by 25cm).
$4,500-6,000

'Pinocchio', 1940, Pinocchio in various positions, 2 model sheet drawings, graphite on paper, in common mount with a printed model sheet, largest 9½ by 11in (24 by 28cm).
$1,200-1,800

'Duck Pimples', 1945, U.S. one sheet, folded, 41 by 27in (104 by 69cm).
$900-1,500

Unknown production, 1950s, Donald Duck with telephone, publicity celluloid, gouache on partial celluloid applied to a hand prepared background, 9½ by 7½in (24 by 19cm).
$900-1,500

signed pen and ink sketch of
Iickey Mouse by Walt Disney, 4
y 3½in (10 by 9cm).
3,000-3,750

Mickey Mouse 20th anniversary
rawing, 1948, graphite, coloured
encil and wash on paper, 11 by
in (28 by 20cm).
450-600

Iickey Mouse Club', 1950s,
anger Rex and his bears,
ouache on multi-celluloid set up
r the opening of 'The Mickey
Iouse Club Show', 11 by 9in (28
y 23cm).
900-1,500

A drawing of Mickey Mouse by Walt Disney, in grey crayon, signed and dedicated by the artist, folding crease and small nick, 7½ by 5in (19 by 12cm).
$4,800-5,700

'Mickey and The Beanstalk', late 1940s, Mickey holds the box with the magic beans, original artwork for promotional purposes, graphite and coloured pencil on paper, 13 by 11½in (33 by 29cm).
$1,800-2,700

A television production, Mickey as the Sorcerer's Apprentice, gouache on full celluloid, 9 by 7½in (23 by 19cm).
$1,050-1,350

'Canine Caddy', 1941, Mickey Mouse, a model sheet drawing, coloured pencil, 10 by 12in (25 by 31cm).
$900-1,500

'Mickey's Fire Brigade', Mickey tangled in a firehose, an animation drawing, graphite and coloured pencil on paper, 10 by 12in (25 by 31cm).
$450-600

'Building a Building', 1933, Minnie Mouse and her boxed lunch cart, 2 animation drawings, both graphite and coloured pencil on paper, unframed, 9½ by 11½in (24 by 29cm).
$450-600

'The Flying Mouse', 1934, a bat, gouache on partial celluloid applied to a hand prepared background, 7½ by 9½in (19 by 24cm). **$1,050-1,350**

A television production, Mickey, the Sorcerer's Apprentice doffs his hat, gouache on full celluloid, 9 by 7in (23 by 18cm).
$750-1,200

Warner Bros

Unknown production, 1980s, Bugs Bunny with bow tie; and Bugs Bunny commercial celluloid for Dr. Pepper, both gouache on full celluloid, unframed, 10½ by 12½in (26 by 32cm).
$750-1,200

Unknown production, 1950s, Elmer Fudd, gouache on full celluloid, unframed, 10 by 12½in (25 by 32cm).
$450-600

Unknown production, 1950s, Daffy Duck raises one foot in the air, gouache on full celluloid, unframed, 10 by 12½in (25 by 32cm). **$450-600**

Unknown production, 1970s, Sylvester faces right; and Sylvester looks into a garbage can, both gouache on full celluloid applied to hand prepared backgrounds, 9½ by 12½in (24 by 32cm). **$600-750**

Unknown production, 1960s, The Roadrunner, gouache on full celluloid applied to a watercolour production background, 9½ by 11½in (24 by 29cm).
$2,700-3,300

'Super-Rabbit', 1943, Bugs Bunny as Super-Rabbit, a publicity title celluloid, gouache on full celluloid, 9 by 11in (23 by 28cm).
$900-1,500

Unknown production, 1950s, Daffy Duck holds a box, gouache on full celluloid, unframed, 10 by 12½in (25 by 32cm).
$450-600

A Bugs Bunny Cartoon Revue poster, U.S. one sheet, folded, 4 by 27in (104 by 69cm).
$600-750

Unknown production, 1950s, Bugs Bunny, gouache on full celluloid, the celluloid signed Chuck Jones, unframed, 10½ by 12½in (26 by 32cm).
$1,050-1,350

Unknown production, 1950s, Daffy Duck, gouache on full celluloid, 10 by 12½in (25 by 32cm).
$600-750

Jnknown production 1950s, Daffy)uck holds a footprint stamp, ;ouache on trimmed celluloid, unframed, 10 by 12½in (25 by ;2cm).
;750-900

Unknown production, 1950s, Sylvester hangs from a wire, gouache on full celluloid, 10 by 12in (25 by 31cm).
$600-750

Unknown production, 1950s, Yosemite Sam, gouache on full celluloid, unframed, 10 by 12½in (25 by 32cm).
$450-600

Jnknown production, 1950s, ;ylvester prepares to run, ;ouache on full celluloid, unframed, 10 by 12½in (25 by ;2cm).
;600-750

'Tennessee Tuxedo and Underdog', 1960s, 2 storyboard flip books with text, one for Tennessee Tuxedo and his tales 'Catch a falling Hammock', the other for 'Underdog RiffRaffVille part 3', both pen, ink and pencil on paper, unframed, 8 by 5in (20 by 12cm).
$600-750

A Charles Schultz signed wax crayon drawing, Psychiatric Help, The Doctor Is In, 36 by 30in (92 by 77cm).
$1,050-1,350

Miscellaneous

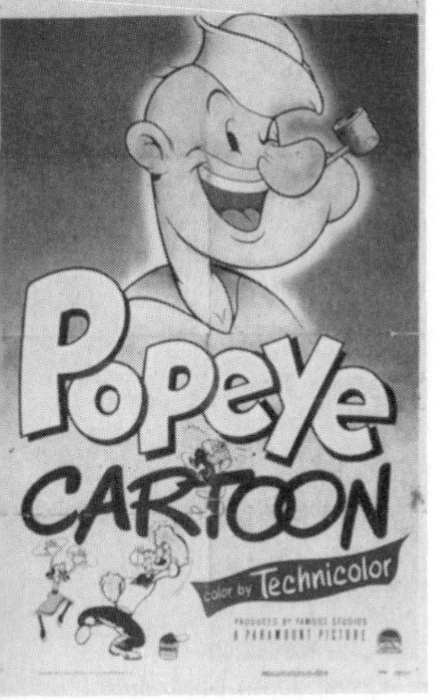

A 'Popeye Cartoon' poster, ?aramount, 1950, U.S. one sheet, 'olded, 41 by 27in (104 by 69cm).
;450-600

Thirty model sheets from various studios, characters include Popeye, Bluto, Sweet Pea and Olive Oyl, Snuffy Smith, Wimpey, Babey Google, Babey Huey, Casper the Friendly Ghost and others, all unframed, largest 14 by 15½in (36 by 39cm). **$1,050-1,350**

A poster for 'Mr Bug Goes To Town', Paramount, 1941, U.S. one sheet, folded, 41 by 27in (104 by 69cm).
$450-600

Two Louis Wain signed pen and ink drawings, 'Fighting like Cat and Dog', 10½ by 10in (27 by 25cm) and 10 by 15½in (25 by 39.5cm).
$450-600

A collection of 5 WWI recruitment posters, comprising: No. 111 'Take Up The Sword Of Justice', No. 35 'There Is Still A Place For You', No. 17 'Your King & Country Need You', No. 122 'There's Room For You' and 'Happy New Year To Our Gallant Soldiers', minor damage.
$450-600

A collection of 7 WWI recruiting posters, including: No. 96 'Enlist Today', No. 11 'Follow Me', No. 84 'At The Front', No. 108 'Britain Needs You At Once', and Nos. 58, 53 and 61, minor damage.
$300-375

A Strike poster, 1940, artwork, graphite, watercolour and wash on illustration board, 28 by 22in (72 by 56cm).
$450-600

Miller's is a price GUIDE not a price LIST

EPHEMERA
Autographs

A postcard of Charles Chaplin, signed in white ink, slight smudge. **$150-225**

A signed sepia photograph of Basil Rathbone, by Chidnoff of New York, slight damage, 4½ by 5½in (12 by 14cm).
$150-180

A signed sepia photograph of Sydney Greenstreet, 7 by 5in (17.5 by 12.5cm).
$225-300

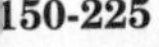

signed photograph of Bertrand ussell, 6 by 4in (15 by 10cm).

150-225

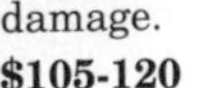

A signed postcard of Cary Grant, slight damage.

$105-120

A signed colour photograph of Jon-Erik Hexum, 8 by 10in (20 by 25cm).

$135-150

A signed postcard of Peter Sellers, dated 1963 in another hand, some creasing.

$50-75

A signed postcard of Tony Hancock.

$120-135

A signed colour photograph of Freddie Mercury, with advert base for 'I was born to love you', 6 by 10½in (15 by 26.5cm).

$120-135

n individually signed nd inscribed postcard f Stan Laurel nd Oliver Hardy.

375-525

A signed postcard of Margaret Rutherford.

$50-75

A signed photograph of Mother Teresa, 8 by 10in (20 by 25cm).

$120-135

A signed programme cover by Judy Garland, at the Dominion Theatre, October/November 1957, slight damage.
$375-525

A signed colour photograph of Elizabeth Taylor, 8 by 10in (20 by 25cm).
$50-75

A signed photograph of Ingrid Bergman, 8 by 10in (20 by 25cm
$105-120

A signed magazine photograph of Leslie Howard, taken from the Picturegoer Summer Annual, 8½ by 11½in (21 by 29cm).
$120-135

A photograph of Grace Kelly, modern reproduction signed in later years, 8 by 10in (20 by 25cm).
$180-225

A signed photograph of Vivien Leigh by Vickers, 6½ by 4½in (1 by 11cm).
$50-75

A signed colour photograph of Naomi Campbell, 8 by 10in (20 by 25cm).
$50-75

A signed photograph of Alfred Hitchcock, 8½ by 11in (21.5 by 28cm).
$300-375

A signed photograph of Kathleen Ferrier by Fayer, 4½ by 3½in (10 x 8cm).
$300-375

A signed and inscribed photograph of Cary Grant, 8 by 10in (20 by 25cm).
$120-135

.IGHTING

Louis XIV style polished steel nd silvered eight-light handelier, with central baluster em with scrolling caryatid ipports, scrolling foliate candle rms and beaded drip pans, above liate volutes with foliate finial, ectrified, late 19thC, 38in 7cm) high.
,000-12,000

An Empire style bronze and ormolu ten-light chandelier, the sconces with anthemion, the branches with chased, winged cherub head mounts, the central well with flaming urn finial and acanthine pineapple terminal, with chain suspension and corona, 16½in (42cm) diam.
$1,050-1,350

l. A set of French 5 gilt bronze two-light wall appliqués of fruiting vine, foliate and ribbon bow, beaded drip pans, 19thC, 21½in (54cm).
$2,250-3,000
r. A pair of French gilt bronze three-light wall appliqués, neo-classical motifs including ribbon bows, serpents, laurel foliage, paterae, mask of pan and musical trophies, lacking one capital, 19thC, 25in (64cm).
$2,250-3,000

Victorian brass and cranberry lass oil lamp, with brass orinthian column with foliate apital, fluted pillar and stepped quare base, together with clear lass chimney, 27in (68.5cm).
450-600

A Victorian Disraeli bronze figure lamp, 27½in (70cm) high.
$750-1,200

A brass and cranberry glass twin branch student's lamp, c1880, 32in (81cm) high.
$2,250-3,000

A pair of five-light corinthian column candelabra, each on beaded and stepped square base and square plinth applied with rams' masks, urns and husk swags, the foliate scroll branches terminating in shaped drip pans, vase shaped sockets and detachable nozzles, the central light with detachable flame extinguisher, 29in (74cm) high.
$3,000-3,750

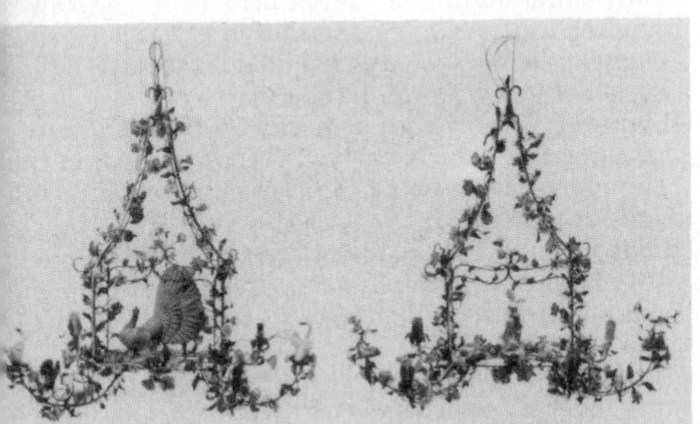

pair of Continental gilt metal and porcelain ounted chandeliers, the 6 branches and rectangular ame in the form of scrolling leaves and each ounted with Meissen style porcelain birds, figures, nimals and flowerheads, 30in (76cm) high.
3,000-4,500

A garniture of a pair of four-light candelabra and matching pair of candlesticks, the scrolling branches chased with berried foliage, the tapering columns with rams' masks and floral swags, the conforming shaped bases inset with porcelain plaques, the candelabra 16½in (42cm) high, the candlesticks 10½in (26cm) high.
$1,800-2,700

GLOSSARY

We have attempted here to define some of the terms that you will come across in this book. If there are any terms or technicalities you would like explained or you feel should be included in future, please let us know.

Aalto, Alvar (1898-1976): Finnish Art Deco architect and furniture designer, noted especially for his bentwood chairs, made from the 1930s onwards.

acid engraving: Technique of decorating glass by coating it in resin, incising a design and exposing the revealed areas to hydrochloric acid fumes.

acid-gilding: 19thC technique for decorating pottery whereby the surface is etched with hydrofluoric acid and the low-relief pattern gilded.

acorn knop: Wine glass stem moulding in the shape of an upturned acorn - the cup uppermost.

Adam, Robert (1728-1792): A Scottish born architect who created a neo-classical architectural and decorative style of furniture.

Admiral jug: Toby jug depicting an admiral; originally to commemorate Lord Howe's victory over the French in 1794.

agate ware: 18thC pottery, veined or marbled to resemble the mineral agate.

air-beaded: Glass containing bubbles of air, like strings of beads.

air-twist: Helical decoration in the stem of wine glasses, developed 1740-70, in which an air bubble in the glass is drawn out and twisted to form complex spirals, e.g. lace twist, multiple spiral, spiral gauze, corkscrew multi-ply, cable, etc.

ale glass: Drinking glass with tall stem and tall narrow bowl, capacity 3-4 fluid ounces, used for strong beer, sometimes decorated with barley ears and hops, 18thC.

all-bisque doll: One with body and limbs as well as head of biscuit-fired ceramic.

Ansbach: Factory specialising in large, colourful faience ornaments from the 1730s, and porcelain tableware late 18th and 19thC.

antiquities: Generally accepted to mean objects made before AD600 in Europe, and of ancient Egyptian, Greek or Roman origin. Also used to cover the pre-Columbian era in the Americas and the products of civilisations now extinct.

architect's table: Table or desk, the top of which rises at the back to provide an angled working area.

Arita (1): Blue and white Japanese pottery imported from the mid-17thC and much imitated by European makers.

Arita (2): Japanese 18thC porcelain, typically with flower-basket pattern in blue, red and gold, also called Imari ware after the port from which it was exported.

armoire: A large French cupboard or wardrobe, usually of monumental character.

associated (1): Term used of a set of silverware in which one part is of the same design but not originally made for it - e.g. of a teapot and associated stand.

associated (2): Of weapons, any part which is not original.

Aubusson: French town producing tapestries, and tapestry-weave carpets, since 17thC although formal workshops were not established until c1743.

automata: Any moving toy or decorative object, usually powered by a clockwork mechanism.

baleen: Whalebone, used 18th and 19thC for buttons, and also carved into ornaments by sailors.

ball jointed doll: One with ball-jointed limbs, able to swivel in all directions, as opposed to stiff jointed.

baluster stem: Glass with a swelling stem, like an architectural baluster: 'true' if the thicker swelling is beneath, 'inverted' if above. From late 17thC.

barley twist: Form of turning popular in late 17thC which resembles a spiral of rope.

basaltes: Black porcelain invented by Josiah Wedgwood with a polished, stone-like finish; modern reproductions are called basalt wares.

Bauhaus: Influential German artistic style which was inspired by new industrial materials, such as stainless steel, with the emphasis on cubic, unadorned shapes. The term was coined by the architect Gropius who became director of the Weimar School of Arts and Crafts in 1919, and renamed it the Bauhaus.

bébé: French dolls made by Bru and others in the latter half 19thC, modelled on actual children of 8-12 years of age.

Belleek: Very thin and iridescent parian ware, originally made at Belleek, in Ireland, late 19thC.

bisque: French term for biscuit ware, or unglazed porcelain.

Bizarre: Name of a highly-colourful range of Art Deco tableware designed by Clarice Cliff and manufactured by the Staffordshire potter, A.J. Wilkinson Ltd, in the 1930s.

bladed knop: Knop with a concave outward curve, culminating in a sharp edge.

bonheur du jour: Small French writing table of delicate proportions with a raised back comprising a cabinet or shelves.

Bow: Important London porcelain factory producing blue and white wares 1749-76, and polychrome wares 1754 onwards; early work shows Chinese influence (peony and chrysanthemum flower decorations), later work in Meissen style.

bowfront: An outwardly curving front.

bracket clock: Originally a 17thC clock which had to be set high up on a bracket because of the length of the weights; now generally applied to any small mantel or table clock.

bracket foot: A type of foot for case pieces which appears somewhat shaped as a right-angled bracket below the front edge.

Brameld: Family that acquired the Rockingham factory, Yorkshire, early 19thC; producers of the fine bone china noted for its rich enamelling and gilt decoration.

Bristol: Important porcelain factory established c1749, producing delftware, and (c1770) enamelled and gilded wares decorated with flowers and swags. Also, 17th and 18thC delftwares (bowls, figure groups, jugs) produced by several factories in the area.

Bru & Cie: Leading French doll maker 1866-99; noted for dolls in elaborate contemporary costumes.

bureau: Writing desk with either a fall, a cylinder or a tambour front.

bureau bookcase: Bureau with a glazed-fronted bookcase fitted above it.

ureau cabinet: Bureau with a solid-doored or mirrored cabinet fitted above it, often containing further fitted cupboards and drawers.
ureau de dame: Writing desk of delicate appearance and designed for use by ladies. Usually raised above slender cabriole legs and with one or two external drawers.
ureau-plat: French writing table with a flat top and drawers in the frieze.
abriole leg: Tail curving leg subject to many designs and produced with club, pad, paw, claw-and-ball, and scroll feet.
addy: Usually silver (but also of ceramic, wood or enamel) container for tea with a lead-lined compartment; often two compartments with a spoon and glass bowl for blending two types of leaf.
amaieu: Porcelain decoration using different tones of the one colour.
ameo glass: A sandwich of coloured glass which is then cut or etched away to create a multi-colour design in relief. An ancient technique rediscovered by Emile Gallé and popular with Art Nouveau and Art Deco glassmakers in the early 20thC.
andle slide: Small wooden slide designed to carry a candlestick.
ardew, Michael (1901-83): English art potter, taught by Bernard Leach, and inspired by Oriental porcelain. Worked at the Winchcombe Pottery 1926-39.
arlton House desk: A distinct type of writing desk which has a raised back with drawers which extend forward at the sides to create an 'enclosed' central writing area.
arlton Ware: Brand name of Art Nouveau pottery made by Wiltshaw and Robinson, a Stoke-on-Trent pottery founded in 1897.
arousel figures: Horses and other animals from fairground carousels or roundabouts, usually classified as either 'jumpers' or 'standers'.
arriage clock: Originally one fitted with a device to ensure that the jolts common in the days of coach travel would not interfere with the oscillations of the balance spring. Now any small portable oblong clock of rectangular form, popular from the 19thC to the present day.
artel clock: An 18thC French wall clock in the shape of a shield, often with a gilded bronze case and elaborately ornamented in rococo style.
artouche: An ornate tablet or shield surrounded by scrollwork and foliage, often bearing a maker's name, inscription or coat-of-arms.
astelli: Maiolica from the Abruzzi region of Italy, noted for delicate landscapes painted by members of the Grue family.
aughley: Shropshire factory, established c1750, producing porcelain very like that of Worcester, including early willow-pattern, often embellished by gilding.
eladon: Chinese stonewares with an opaque grey-green glaze, first made in the Sung dynasty and still made today, principally in Korea.
ellaret: Lidded container on legs designed to hold wine. The interior is often divided into sections for individual bottles.
entrepiece: Silver ornament, usually decorative rather than functional, designed to occupy the centre of a dining table.
Chaffers, Richard & Partners: Liverpool pottery manufacturer, operating around 1754-65, producing earthenwares resembling china and modelled on Worcester forms.
haise longue: An elongated chair, the seat long enough to support the sitter's legs.
hamplevé: Enamelling on copper or bronze, similar to cloisonné, in which a glass paste is applied to the hollowed-out design, fired and ground smooth.
character doll: One with a naturalistic face, especially laughing, crying, pouting, etc.
character jug: Earthenware jugs and sometimes mugs, widely made in 18th and 19thC, depicting a popular character, such as a politician, general, jockey or actor.
chesterfield: Type of large over-stuffed sofa introduced in late 19thC.
cheval mirror: Large toilet mirror in a frame with four legs, the mirror being pivoted and adjustable within the frame. Also known as a horse dressing glass and a psyche. Made c1750 onwards.
chiffonier: Generally a twin door cupboard with one or two drawers above and surmounted by shelves.
child's furniture: Mainly small-scale furniture for children to use, as distinct from toy furniture.
Chin dynasty: period in Chinese history AD1115-1260.
Chinese export porcelain: 16th to 18thC wares made in China specifically for export and often to European designs.
Chinese Imari: Chinese imitations of Japanese blue, red and gold painted Imari wares, made from the early 18thC.
Ch'ing dynasty: From 1644 to 1912, the period during which much decorated Chinese porcelain was exported to Europe.
chinoiserie: The fashion, prevailing in the late 18thC, for Chinese-style ornamentation on porcelain, wallpapers and fabrics, furniture and garden architecture.
chryselephantine: Originally made of gold and ivory, but now used for Art Deco statues made of ivory and another metal, typically bronze and very desirable.
Cliff, Clarice (1899-1972): Employed by A.J. Wilkinson Ltd, the pottery at Newport, Staffordshire, as artistic director in the 1930s. Designer of the colourful 'Bizarre' and 'Fantasque' ranges of mass-produced china.
clock garniture: A matching group of clock and vases or candelabra made for the mantel shelf. Often highly ornate.
cloisonné: Enamelling on metal with divisions in the design separated by lines of fine brass wire. A speciality of the Limoges region of France in the Middle Ages, and of Chinese craftsmen to the present day.
Coalport china: Porcelain manufactured at Coalbrookdale, Shropshire, from the 1790s, noted for the translucent felspathic wares produced from 1820 and the delicate colours of the figure groups.
coffer: In strict definition a coffer is a travelling trunk which is banded with metalwork and covered with leather or other material. However, the word tends to be used quite freely to describe chests of various kinds.
Commedia dell'Arte: Figures from traditional Italian theatre (Harlequin, Columbine, Scaramouche, Pantaloon) often depicted in porcelain groups in 18thC.
compound twist: In a wine glass stem, any air-twist made of multiple spirals; e.g. lace twist, gauze and multi-ply.
console table: Decorative side table with no back legs, being supported against the wall by brackets.
cordial glass: Smaller version of a wine glass, with a thick stem, heavy foot and small bowl; evolved 17thC for strong drink.
country furniture: General term for furniture made by provincial craftsmen; cottage furniture and especially that made of pine, oak, elm and the fruitwoods.

credenza: Used today to describe a type of side cabinet which is highly decorated and shaped. Originally it was an Italian sideboard used as a serving table.
crested china: Pottery decorated with colourful heraldic crests, first made by Goss but, by 1880, being produced in quantity by manufacturers throughout the UK and in Germany.
cup and cover: Carved decoration found on the bulbous turned legs of some Elizabethan furniture.
cut glass: Glass carved with revolving wheels and abrasive to create sharp-edged facets that reflect and refract light so as to sparkle and achieve a prismatic (rainbow) effect. Revived Bohemia 17thC, and common until superseded by pressed glass for utilitarian objects.
Cymric: The trade-name used by Liberty & Company for a mass produced range of silverware, inspired by Celtic art, introduced in 1899, and often incorporating enamelled pictorial plaques.
cypher: An impressed or painted mark on porcelain which gives the year of manufacture; each factory had its own set of codes; used principally mid to late 19thC.
davenport (1): Small writing desk with a sloping top and a series of real and false drawers below. Some have a writing surface which slides forward and rising compartments at the rear.
davenport (2): American term for a day bed or reclining sofa with headrest.
Davenport (3): Important factory at Longport, Staffordshire, founded 1793 by John Davenport; originally manufactured earthenware, but noted from 1820 for very fine botanical wares and Imari style decoration.
day bed: Couch with one sloped end to support the head and back whilst reclined. Either upholstered or caned and sometimes with six or eight legs. Made from 16thC until the mid-18thC. Also known in the U.S. as a davenport.
Delft: Dutch tin glazed earthenwares named after the town of Delft, the principal production centre. 16thC Delft shows Chinese influence but by 17thC the designs are based on Dutch landscapes. Similar pottery made in England from the late 16thC is usually termed 'delftware'.
Della Robbia: Florentine Renaissance sculptor who invented technique of applying vitreous glaze to terracotta; English art pottery made at Birkenhead, late 19thC, in imitation of his work.
Denby: Stoneware made by Bourne & Son, at Denby, 19thC; also known as Bourne pottery.
Derby: Important porcelain factory founded 1756, producing very fine figure groups - often called English Meissen - as well as painted wares decorated with landscapes and botanical scenes.
die-stamping: Method of mass producing a design on metal by machine which passes sheet metal between a steel die and a drop hammer. Used for forming toys as well as stamping cutlery etc.
Dresser, Christopher (1835-1904): Influential English pottery and glass designer who was inspired by Japanese art and worked for Tiffany as well as the pottery firms of Ault, Linthorpe and Pilkington.
drop-in seat: Upholstered chair seat which is supported on the seat rails but which can be lifted out independently.
Du Paquier: Porcelain from Vienna, especially chinoiserie wares produced early 18thC.
écuelle: 17thC vessel, usually of silver, but also of ceramic for serving soup. Has a shallow, circular bowl with two handles and a domed cover. It often comes complete with a stand.
eglomisé: Painting on glass, associated with clock faces: often the reverse side of the glass is covered in gold or silver leaf through which a pattern is engraved and then painted black.
electroplate: The process of using electrical current to coat a base metal or alloy with silver, invented 1830s and gradually superseding Sheffield plate.
enamel (1): In ceramics, a second coloured but translucent glaze laid over the first glaze.
enamel (2): Coloured glass, applied to metal, ceramic or glass in paste form and then fired for decorative effect.
EPNS: Electroplated nickel silver; i.e. nickel alloy covered with a layer of silver using the electroplate process.
etched glass: Technique of cutting layers of glass away, using acid, much favoured by Art Nouveau and Art Deco glassmakers. Such sculpture in high relief is known as deep etched, and layers of multi-coloured glass were often treated in this way to make cameo glass.
fairings: Mould-made figure groups in cheap porcelain, produced in great quantity in the 19th and 20thC, especially in Germany; often humorous or sentimental. So called because they were sold, or given as prizes, at fairs.
famille jaune: 'Yellow family'; Chinese porcelain vessels in which yellow is the predominant ground colour.
famille noire: 'Black family'; Chinese porcelain in which black is the predominant ground colour.
famille rose: 'Pink family'; Chinese porcelain vessels with an enamel (overglaze) of pink to purple tones.
famille verte: 'Green family'; Chinese porcelain with a green enamel (overglaze), laid over yellows, blues, purples and iron red.
Fantasque: Name of a colourful range of household china designed by Clarice Cliff and manufactured in the 1930s by the Staffordshire pottery, A.J. Wilkinson Ltd.
fauteuil: French open-armed drawing room armchair.
filigree: Lacy openwork of silver or gold thread, produced in large quantities since end 19thC.
flatware: Collective name for flat pottery, such as plates, trenchers and trays, as opposed to cups, vases and bowls.
frosted glass: Glass with a surface pattern made to resemble frost patterns or snow-crystals; common on pressed glass vessels for serving cold confections.
Fulda: Factory at Hessen that produced some of Germany's best faience in the mid-18thC; in the late 18thC turned to producing Meissen-style porcelain.
fusee: 18thC clockwork invention; a cone shaped drum, linked to the spring barrel by a length of gut or chain. The shape compensates for the declining strength of the mainspring thus ensuring constant timekeeping.
Gallé, Emile (1846-1904): Father of the French Art Nouveau movement and founder of a talented circle of designers based around Nancy. Simultaneously, in the 1880s, he designed delicate furniture embellished with marquetry and began experimenting with new glass techniques. In 1889, he developed cameo glass; in 1897 'marquetry in glass', or 'marqeutrie de verre'. After his death, factories continued to produce his wares, signed Gallé but marked with a star, until the 1930s.
gilding: Process of applying thin gold foil to a surface. There are two methods. Oil gilding involves the use of linseed oil and is applied directly onto the woodwork. Water gilding requires the wood to be painted with gesso.

Glasgow School: Originally the name of the Glasgow School of Art at which Charles Rennie Mackintosh studied in the 1880s, and whose new buildings he designed in the 1890s. Now used to describe the style developed by Mackintosh and his followers, a simplified linear form of Art Nouveau highly influential on Continental work of the period.

grisaille: Type of monochrome used to decorate furniture during the 18thC.

hall chair: Strongly constructed chair which lacks intricate ornament and upholstery, being designed to stand in a hall to accommodate messengers and other callers in outdoor clothing. At the same time it had to be attractive enough to impress more important callers and was often carved with a crest or coat-of-arms for this purpose.

hallmark: Collective term for all the marks found on silver or gold consisting of an assay office, quality, date and maker's marks; sometimes the term is used only of the assay office mark.

handkerchief table: Table with a triangular top and a single triangular leaf. This arrangement enables it to fit into a corner when closed and form a square when opened.

hard paste: True porcelain made of china stone (petuntse) and kaolin; the formula was long known to, and kept secret by, Chinese potters but only discovered in the 1750s in England, from where it spread to the rest of Europe and the Americas.

harewood: Sycamore which has been stained a greenish colour is known as harewood. It is used mainly as an inlay wood and was known as silverwood in the 18thC.

Hirado: Japanese porcelain with figure and landscape painting in blue on a white body, often depicting boys at play, made exclusively for the Lords of Hirado, near Arita, mid-18th to mid-19thC.

hiramakie: Flat decoration in Japanese lacquerware, as opposed to carving or relief.

Hornby: manufacturers of clockwork and electric locomotives from c1910, best known today for the 'Dublo' range, introduced mid-1940s.

Indianische Blumen: Indian flowers; painting on porcelain in the Oriental style, especially on mid-18thC Meissen and Höchst.

intaglio: Incised gem-stone, often set in a ring, used in antiquity and during the Renaissance as a seal. Any incised decoration; the opposite of carving in relief.

ironstone: Stoneware, patented 1813 by Charles James Mason, containing ground glassy slag, a by-product of iron smelting, for extra strength.

ivory porcelain: Development of 19thC, similar to parian but ivory coloured in biscuit form.

Jacobite: Wine glasses engraved with symbols of the Jacobites (supporters of Prince Charles Edward Stuart's claim to the English throne). Genuine examples date to between 1746 and 1788. Countless later copies and forgeries exist.

Jumeau, Pierre François: Important French doll maker noted for 'Parisiennes', active 1842-99.

Kakiemon: Family of 17thC Japanese potters who produced wares decorated with flowers and figures on a white ground in distinctive colours: azure, yellow, turquoise and soft red. Widely imitated in Europe.

kashgai: Rugs woven by Iranian nomadic tribes, notable for the springy lustrous texture, and finely detailed rectilinear designs.

kelim: Flat woven rugs lacking a pile; also the flat woven fringe used to finish off the ends of a pile carpet.

kneehole desk: Writing desk with a space between the drawer pedestals for the user's legs.

knop (1): Knob, protuberance or swelling in the stem of a wine glass, of various forms which can be used as an aid to dating and provenance.

knop (2): In furniture, a swelling on an upright member.

Knox, Archibald (1864-1931): English designer of the Cymric range of silverware and Tudric pewter for Liberty's store in London, responsible for some 400 different designs.

Lalique, René (1860-1945): French designer of Art Nouveau jewellery in gold, silver and enamel, who founded his own workshop in Paris in 1885. After 1900 he turned to making figures in crystal and opalescent glass. From 1920 he emerged as the leading Art Deco glass maker, and his factory produced a huge range of designs.

lambing chair: Sturdy chair with a low seat traditionally used by shepherds at lambing time. It has tall enclosed sides for protection against draughts.

Lazy Susan: Another name for a dumb waiter.

Leach, Bernard (1887-1979): Father of English craft pottery who studied in China and Japan in order to master Oriental glazing techniques.

Lenci: Italian company manufacturing dolls with pressed felt faces in Turin in the 1920s, noted for the sideways glance of the painted eyes.

Liberty & Co.: Principal outlet for Art Nouveau designs in England. Arthur Lasenby Liberty (1843-1917) founded his furniture and drapery shop in 1875. Later he commissioned designs exclusive to his store, including Cymric silver and Tudric pewter, which gave rise to a distinctive 'Liberty style'.

linenfold: Carved decoration which resembles folded linen.

Liverpool: Important pottery production centre from the mid-18thC, noted for blue painted delftware punch bowls, and early porcelain produced by several different factories, now eagerly collected.

longcase clock: First made c1660 in England, a tall clock consisting of a case which houses the weights or pendulum and a hood housing the movement and dial. In U.S.A. also known as a tallcase clock.

lyre clock: Early 19thC American pendulum clock, its shape resembling that of a lyre.

majolica: Often used, in error, as an alternative spelling for maiolica; correctly, a richly-enamelled stoneware with high relief decoration developed by Minton, mid-19thC.

mantel clock: Clock provided with feet to stand on the mantelpiece.

Martinware: Art pottery made by the Martin brothers between 1873 and 1914, characterised by grotesque human and animal figures in stoneware.

medicine chest: Used by itinerant medics from 17thC, usually with compartments, labelled bottles, spoons and balances.

Meiji: Period in Japanese history 1868 to 1912, when the nation's art was much influenced by contact with the West, and much was made specifically for export.

mihrab: Prayer niche with a pointed arch; the motif which distinguishes a prayer rug from other types.

Mei ping: Chinese for cherry blossom, used to describe a tall vase, with high shoulders, small neck and narrow mouth, used to display flowering branches.

millefiori: Multi-coloured, or mosaic, glass, made since antiquity by fusing a number of coloured glass rods into a cane, and cutting off thin sections; much used to ornament paperweights.

Ming dynasty: Period in Chinese history from 1368 to 1644.

Minton: Pottery established by Thomas Minton, at Stoke-on-Trent, in late 18thC. Originally produced earthenwares and creamware; then, most famously, bone china. After 1850 the company produced fine copies of Renaissance maiolica and, in 1870, set up the Minton Art Pottery Studio in London as a training academy for young designers, producing fine Art Nouveau work.
Moorcroft, William (1872-1946): Staffordshire art potter, who worked for MacIntyre & Co. from 1898, and set up independently in 1913. Known for colourful vases with floral designs and his 'Florian' and 'Aurelian' wares.
Moore, Bernard: Founder of art pottery based in Longton, Staffordshire, c1900 specialising in unusual glaze effects.
Morris, William (1834-96): Regarded as the progenitor of the Art Nouveau style. The company Morris, Marshall and Faulkner (later simply Morris & Co.) was founded in 1861 to produce wallpaper, stained glass, chintz carpets and tapestries. The origins of his style can be traced to medieval Gothic, but his organic flowers and bird motifs encouraged later artists to seek inspiration for their designs in nature.
netsuke: Japanese carved toggles made to secure sagemono ('hanging things') to the obi (waist belt) from a cord; usually of ivory, lacquer, silver or wood, from the 16thC.
New Hall: Late 18thC potters' co-operative in Staffordshire making porcelain and bone china wares.
ormolu: Strictly, gilded bronze or brass but sometimes used loosely of any yellow metal. Originally used for furniture handles and mounts but, from the 18thC, for ink stands, candlesticks, clock cases, etc.
overlay: In cased glass, the top layer, usually engraved to reveal a different coloured layer beneath.
overmantel: Area above the shelf on a mantelpiece, often consisting of a mirror in an ornate frame, or some architectural feature in wood or stone
over stuffed: Descriptive of upholstered furniture where the covering extends over the frame of the seat.
ovolo: Moulding of convex quarter-circle section. Sometimes found around the edges of drawers to form a small overlap onto the carcase.
Parisienne doll: French bisque head doll with a stuffed kid leather body, made by various manufacturers 1860s to 1880s.
pate: Crown of a doll's head into which the hair is stitched, usually of cork in the better quality dolls.
pâte-sur-pâte: 19thC Sèvres porcelain technique, much copied, of applying slip decoration to the body before firing.
Pembroke table: Small table with two short drop leaves along its length. Named after the Countess of Pembroke who is said to have been the first to order one. Also once known as a breakfast table.
percussion lock: Early 19thC firearm, one of the first to be fired by the impact of a sharp-nosed hammer on the cartridge cap.
pewter: Alloy of tin and lead; the higher the tin content the higher the quality; sometimes with small quantities of antimony added to make it hard with a highly polished surface.
pier glass: Mirror designed to be fixed to the pier, or wall, between two tall window openings, often partnered by a matching pier table. Made from mid-17thC.
Pilkington: Associated with the Lancashire glass factory, this pottery produced Art Nouveau ceramics in the early 20thC, remarkable for its iridescent and colourful glazes.
Pinxton: Soft-paste porcelain imitating Derby, made in Nottingham by William Billingsley, from c1800.
plate: Old fashioned term, still occasionally used, to describe gold and silver vessels; not to be confused with 'Sheffield plate', or plated vessels generally, in which silver is fused to a base metal alloy.
pole screen: Small adjustable screen mounted on a pole and designed to stand in front of an open fire to shield a lady's face from the heat.
portrait doll: One modelled on a well known figure.
poupard: Doll without legs, often mounted on a stick; popular in 19thC.
poured wax doll: One made by pouring molten wax on to a mould.
powder flask: Device for measuring out a precise quantity of priming powder made to be suspended from a musketeer's belt or bandolier and often ornately decorated. Sporting flasks are often made of antler and carved with hunting scenes.
powder horn: Cow horn hollowed out, blocked at the wide end with a wooden plug and fitted with a measuring device at the narrow end, used by musketeers for dispensing a precise quantity of priming powder.
pressed glass: Early 19thC invention, exploited rapidly in America, whereby mechanical pressure was used to form glassware in a mould, instead of using compressed air.
puzzle jug: Delftware form made from the 17thC on with several spouts and a syphon system, none of which will pour unless the others are blocked.
Qing: Alternative spelling of Ch'ing - the dynasty that ruled China from 1644 to 1916.
quarter clock: One which strikes the quarter and half hours as well as the full hours.
Quimper faience: From the factory in Brittany, France, established late 17thC and closely modelled on Rouen wares.
rack: Tall superstructure above a dresser.
refectory table: Modern term for the long dining tables of the 17thC and later.
regulator: Clock of great accuracy, thus sometimes used for controlling or checking other time pieces.
rummer/roemer: Originally 16th/17thC German wide bowled wine glass on a thick stem, decorated with prunts, on a base of concentric glass coils, often in green glass (waldglas). Widely copied throughout Europe in many forms.
sabre leg: Elegant curving leg associated with furniture of the Regency period but first appearing near the end of the 18thC. Also known as Trafalgar leg.
St. Cloud: Factory near Paris, famous for soft-paste porcelain in the first half of the 18thC, decorated in Kakiemon style and imitation blanc-de-chine.
salon chair: General term to describe a French or French style armchair.
scent bottle: Small, portable flask of flattened pear shape, made of silver, rock crystal, porcelain or glass.
Scots pine: Rather plain light yellowish wood with a straight grain. It is much used for carcases and drawer linings. Normally referred to simply as pine. Also known as deal.
seal bottle: Wine bottles with an applied glass medallion or seal personalised with the owner's name, initials, coat-of-arms or a date. Produced from the early 17th to the mid-19thC when bottles were relatively expensive.
secrétaire bookcase: Secrétaire with a bookcase fitted above it.

SFBJ: Société de Fabrication de Bébés et Jouets; doll maker founded 1899 by merging the businesses of Jumeau, Bru and others. Products regarded as inferior to those of the original makers.

Sheraton revival: Descriptive of furniture produced in the style of Sheraton when his designs gained revived interest during the Edwardian period.

silver table: Small rectangular table designed for use in the dining room. They usually have a fretwork gallery.

Six Dynasties: Period in Chinese history AD265-589.

six-hour dial: One with only six divisions instead of twelve, often with the hours 1 - 6 in Roman numerals and 7 - 12 superimposed in Arabic numerals.

snuff box: Box made to contain snuff in silver, or any other material: early examples have an integral rasp and spoon, from 17thC.

sofa table: Type of drop leaf table which developed from the Pembroke table. It was designed to stand behind a sofa, so is long and thin with two short drop leaves at the ends and two drawers in the frieze.

softwood: One of two basic categories in which all timbers are classified. The softwoods are conifers which generally have leaves in the form of evergreen needles.

spelter: Zinc treated to look like bronze and much used as an inexpensive substitute in Art Nouveau appliqué ornament and Art Deco figures.

Steiff, Margarete: Maker of dolls and highly prized teddy bears, she first exhibited at Leipzig, 1903, but died 1909. The company she founded continued to mass produce toys, dolls and bears for export. Products can be identified by the 'Steiff' button trademark, usually in the ear.

stirrup cup: Silver cup, without handles, so-called because it was served, containing a suitable beverage, to huntsmen in the saddle, prior to their moving off. Often made in the shape of an animal's head.

Sung dynasty: Ruling Chinese dynasty from AD960-1279.

table clock: Early type of domestic clock, some say the predecessor of the watch, in which the dial is set vertically: often of drum shape.

tallboy: Chest of drawers raised upon another chest of drawers. Also known as a chest-on-chest.

T'ang dynasty: Period in Chinese history AD618-906 during which porcelain was first developed.

tazza: Wide but shallow bowl on a stem with a foot; ceramic and metal tazzas were made in antiquity and the form was revived by Venetian glassmakers in 15thC. Also made in silver from 16thC.

tea kettle: Silver, or other metal, vessel intended for boiling water at the table. Designed to sit over a spirit lamp, it sometimes had a rounded base instead of flat.

teapoy: Piece of furniture in the form of a tea caddy on legs, with a hinged lid opening to reveal caddies, mixing bowl and other tea drinking accessories.

tear: Tear-drop shaped air bubble in the stem of an early 18thC wine glass, from which the air-twist evolved.

tester: Wooden canopy over a bedstead which is supported on either two or four posts. It may extend fully over the bed and be known as a full tester, or only over the bedhead half and be known as a half tester.

tin glaze: Glassy white glaze of tin oxide; re-introduced to Europe in 14thC by Moorish potters; the characteristic glaze of delftware, faience and maiolica.

Toby jug: Originally a jug in the form of a man in a tricorn hat, first made by Ralph Wood of Burslem, mid-18thC; since produced in great quantity in many different forms.

transfer printed: Ceramic decoration technique perfected mid-18thC and used widely thereafter for mass produced wares. An engraved design is printed on to paper (the bat) using the ink consisting of glaze mixed with oil; the paper is then laid over the body of the vessel and burns off in firing, leaving an outline, usually in blue. Sometimes the outline was coloured in by hand.

trefoil: Three-cusped figure which resembles a symmetrical three-lobed leaf or flower.

tripod table: Descriptive of any table with a three-legged base but generally used to describe only small tables of this kind.

tsuba: Guard of a Japanese sword, usually consisting of an ornamented plate.

tulipwood: Yellow brown wood with reddish stripe imported from Central and South America and used as a veneer and for inlay and crossbanding. It is related to rosewood and kingwood.

Venetian glass: Fine soda glass and coloured glass blown and pinched into highly ornamented vessels of intricate form, made in Venice, and widely copied from 15thC.

verge escapement: Oldest form of escapement, found on clocks as early as AD1300 and still in use 1900. Consisting of a bar (the verge) with two flag shaped pallets that rock in an out of the teeth of the crown or escape wheel to regulate the movement.

vesta case: Ornate flat case of silver or other metal for carrying vestas, an early form of match. From mid-19thC.

vitrine: French display cabinet which is often of bombé or serpentine outline and ornately decorated with marquetry and ormolu.

washstand: Stand designed to hold a basin for washing in the bedroom. Generally of two types. Either three or four uprights supporting a circular top to hold the basin and with a triangular shelf with a drawer. Or as a cupboard raised on four legs with a basin let into the top, sometimes with enclosing flaps. Also known as a basin stand.

Wedgwood: Pottery founded by Josiah Wedgwood (1730-95) at Stoke-on-Trent and noted for numerous innovations; especially creamware, basaltes, and pearlware; perhaps best known for jasperware, the blue stonewares decorated with white relief scenes from late 18thC.

Wellington chest: Distinct type of tall, narrow chest of drawers. They usually have either six or seven thin drawers one above the other and a hinged and lockable flap over one side to prevent them from opening. Made in the 19thC.

whatnot: Tall stand of four or five shelves and sometimes a drawer in addition. Some were made to stand in a corner. Used for the display of ornaments and known in Victorian times as an omnium.

WMF: Short for the Austrian Württembergishe Metallwarenfabrik, one of the principal producers of Art Nouveau silver and silverplated objects, early 20thC.

yew: Hard, deep reddish brown wood used both as a veneer and solid. It is very resistant to woodworm and turns well.

Yuan dynasty: Period in Chinese history AD1280-1368 during which the art of underglaze painting was developed.

DIRECTORY OF SPECIALISTS

This directory is in no way complete. If you wish to be included in next year's directory or if you have a change of address or telephone number, please telephone Miller's advertising department by June 1994. Finally we would advise readers to make contact by telephone before a visit, therefore avoiding a wasted journey, which nowadays is both time consuming and expensive.

ARCHITECTURAL

Cheshire

Nostalgia,
61 Shaw Heath,
Stockport.
Tel: 061 477 7706

Devon

Ashburton Marbles,
Grate Hall,
North Street,
Ashburton.
Tel: 0364 53189

Sussex

Brighton Architectural Salvage,
33 Gloucester Road,
Brighton.
Tel: 0273 681656

Worcestershire

Holloways,
Lower Court,
Suckley.
Tel: 0886 884665

ARMS & MILITARIA

Lincolnshire

Garth Vincent,
The Old Manor House,
Allington,
Nr Grantham.
Tel: 0400 81358

Oxfordshire

Peter Norden Antiques,
61 High Street,
Burford.
Tel: 099 382 2121

Surrey

West Street Antiques,
63 West Street,
Dorking.
Tel: 0306 883487

Sussex

Wallis & Wallis,
West Street Galleries,
Lewes.
Tel: 0273 480208

West Yorkshire

Andrew Spencer Bottomley,
The Coach House,
Thongs Bridge,
Holmfirth.
Tel: 0484 685234

BABY CARRIAGES

Essex

Basildon Baby Carriage,
83 Tyefields,
Pitsea,
Basildon.
Tel: 0268 729803
(By appointment only).
1950's coachbuilt baby carriages made and restored.

BAROMETERS

Devon

Barometer World,
Quicksilver Barn,
Merton,
Okehampton.
Tel: 08053 443

Wiltshire

P A Oxley,
The Old Rectory,
Cherhill,
Nr Calne.
Tel: 0249 816227

BOOKS

Middlesex

John Ives,
5 Normanhurst Drive,
Twickenham.
Tel: 081 892 6265
Reference books.

BOXES & TREEN

Oxfordshire

Peter Norden Antiques,
61 High Street,
Burford.
Tel: 099 382 2121

CARPETS

Yorkshire

Gordon Reece Gallery,
Finkle Street,
Knaresborough.
Tel: 0423 866219

CLOCKS

London

The Clock Clinic,
85 Lower Richmond Road,
London SW15.
Tel: 081 788 1407

Cheshire

Coppelia Antiques,
Holford Lodge,
Plumley Moor Road,
Plumley,
Cheshire.
Tel: 0565 722197

Essex

Its About Time, 863
London Road, Westcliff-on-Sea.
Tel: 0702 72574

Gloucestershire

Gerard Campbell,
Maple House,
Market Place,
Lechlade.
Tel: 0367 252267

Jonathan Beech,
Nurses Cottage,
Ampney Crucis,
Nr Cirencester.
Tel: 0285 851495

Kent

Derek Robert Antiques,
25 Shipbourne Road,
Tonbridge.
Tel: 0732 358986

Somerset

Exmoor Clock Workshop,
Wyndham House,
High Street,
Porlock.
Tel: 0643 863091

Surrey

Brian Clisby,
86b Tilford Road,
Farnham.
Tel: 0252 716436

The Clock Shop,
64 Church Street,
Weybridge.
Tel: 0932 840407/855503

Horological Workshops,
204 Worplesdon Road,
Guildford.
Tel: 0483 576496

Sussex

Samuel Orr Fine Clocks,
36 High Street,
Hurstpierpoint.
Tel: 0273 832081

Tyne & Wear

Hazel Cottage Clocks,
Eachwick,
Dalton,
Newcastle-on-Tyne.
Tel: 0661 852415

Wiltshire

P A Oxley,
The Old Rectory,
Cherhill,
Nr Calne.
Tel: 0249 816227

Allan Smith Clocks,
Amity Cottage,
162 Beechcroft Road,
Upper Stratton,
Swindon.
Tel: 0793 822977

Yorkshire

Haworth Antiques,
Harrogate Road,
Huby,
Nr Leeds.
Tel: 0423 734293

Brian Loomes,
Calf Haugh Farm,
Pateley Bridge.
Tel: 0423 711163

DECORATIVE ARTS

London

Arenski,
Stand 107,
Grays Antique Market,
58 Davies St,
W1.
Tel: 071 499 6824
Fax: 081 202 3075

The Collector,
9 Church Street
NW8
Tel: 071 706 4586

De Verzamelaar (The Collector),
1st floor,
Georgian Village,
Camden Passage,
N1.
Tel: 071 359 3322/
071 376 3852.
Gouda pottery.

Phillips,
101 New Bond St,
W1.
Tel: 071 629 6602

Sylvia Powell Decorative Arts,
28 The Mall,
Camden Passage,
Islington, N1.
Tel: 071 354 2977;
Fax 081 458 2769

Zeitgeist Antiques,
58 Kensington Church Street, W8
Tel: 071 938 4817

Bedfordshire

Rumours Decorative Arts,
10 The Mall,
Upper St,
Camden Passage,
Islington, N1.
Tel: 0582 873561
Moorcroft.

Gt Manchester

A S Antiques,
26 Broad Street,
Pendleton,
Salford,
Manchester.
Tel: 061 737 5938

Kent
St Clere Antiques,
Rhencullen,
Hollywood Lane,
West Kingsdown
Tel: 0474 853630
Carltonware.

Warwickshire
Rich Designs,
11 Union Street,
Stratford on Avon
Tel: 0789 772111/261612
Clarice Cliff.

Yorkshire
Muir Hewitt,
Halifax Antiques Centre,
Queens Road
Mills/Gibbet Street,
Halifax.
Tel: 0422 366657
Clarice Cliff.

DESKS

Surrey
Dorking Desk Shop, 41
West Street, Dorking.
Tel: 0306 883327

Sussex
Artisan,
4 The Parade,
Valley Drive,
Brighton.
Tel 0273 557418
Desk leathers.

Warwickshire
Don Spencer Antiques,
36a Market Place,
Warwick.
Tel: 0926 407989/499857

DINING TABLES

Kent
La Trobe & Bigwood
Antiques,
Tel: 0892 863840

Pantiles Spa Antiques,
4, 5, 6 Union House,
The Pantiles,
Tunbridge Wells.
Tel: 0892 541377

DOULTONWARE

London
The Collector,
9 Church St, NW8.
Tel: 071 706 4586

EPHEMERA

Nottinghamshire
T Vennett-Smith,
11 Nottingham Road,
Gotham.
Tel: 0602 830541

EXPORTERS

Devon
McBains of Exeter,
Exeter Airport,
Clyst Honiton,
Exeter.
Tel: 0392 366261

Essex
F G Bruschweller
(Antiques) Ltd,
41-67 Lower Lambricks,
Rayleigh.
Tel: 0268 773761

Lincolnshire
MC Trading Co,
Stanhope Road,
Horncastle.
Tel: 0507 524524

North Humberside
Geoffrey Mole,
400 Wincolmlee,
Hull.
Tel: 0482 27858

Shropshire
Swainbank Antique
Exporters,
Lord Hills Estate,
Coton Hill,
Coton,
Whitchurch.
Tel: 0948 880534;
Fax: 0948 880342

Suffolk
Wrentham Antiques,
40-44 High Street,
Wrentham.
Tel: 0502 75583
Full container, packing and courier service available.

Sussex
Bexhill Antique
Exporters,
56 Turkey Rd,
Bexhill.
Tel: 0424 225103

British Antique
Exporters Ltd,
School Close,
Queen Elizabeth Avenue,
Burgess Hill.
Tel: 0444 245577

The Old Mint House,
High Street,
Pevensey,
Nr Eastbourne.
Tel: 0323 762337

West Midlands
L P Furniture,
Lime Lane,
Pelsall, Walsall.
Tel/Fax: 0543 370256

Martin Taylor Antiques,
140B Tettenhall Road,
Wolverhampton.
Tel: 0902 751166

FISHING

Scotland
Jamie Maxtone Graham,
Lyne Haugh,
Lyne Station,
Peebles.
Tel: 07214 304

FURNITURE

London
Arenski,
Stand 107,
Grays Antique Market,
58 Davies St, W1.
Tel: 071 499 6824; Fax
081 202 3075

Oola Boola Antiques,
166 Tower Bridge Road,
SE1.
Tel: 071 403 0794

The Old Cinema,
160 Chiswick High Road,
W4.
Tel: 081 995 4166

Cambridgeshire
Simon & Penny Rumble,
The Old School,
Chittering.
Tel: 0223 861831

Cheshire
Richmond Galleries,
Watergate Building,
New Crane St,
off Sealand Road,
Chester.
Tel: 0244 317602

Cumbria
Anthemion,
Cartmel,
Grange Over Sands.
Tel: 05395 36295/36234

Derbyshire
Nimbus Antiques,
5 Lower Macclesfield
Road,
Whaley Bridge.
Tel: 0663 734248/732118

Hampshire
Cedar Antiques,
High Street,
Hartley Wintney.
Tel: 0252 843252

Millers of Chelsea Ltd,
Netherbrook House,
Christchurch Road,
Ringwood.
Tel: 0425 472062

Hertfordshire
Collins Antiques,
Corner House,
Wheathamstead.
Tel: 058 283 3111

Kent
Pantiles Spa Antiques,
4/5/6 Union House,
The Pantiles,
Royal Tunbridge Wells.
Tel: 0892 541377

The Old Bakery
Antiques,
St Davids Bridge,
Cranbrook.
Tel: 0580 713103

Lancashire
Preston Antique Centre,
The Mill New Hall Lane,
Preston.
Tel: 0772 794498

Lincolnshire
The MC Trading
Company,
Stanhope Road,
Horncastle.
Tel: 0507 524524

Middlesex
Robert Phelps Ltd,
133-135 St Margarets Rd,
East Twickenham.
Tel: 081 892 1778

Norfolk
Old Curiosity Shop,
South Walsham.
Tel: 0605 49204

Northants
Paul Hopwell,
30 High Street,
West Haddon.
Tel: 0788 510636

Oxfordshire
Rupert Hitchcock,
The Garth,
Warpsgrove,
Nr Chalgrove,
Oxford.
Tel: 0865 890241

Peter Norden Antiques,
61 High Street,
Burford.
Tel: 099 382 2121

Shropshire
BAFRA,
The Old School,
Longnor,
Shrewsbury.
Tel: 0743 718162.

Somerset
The Granary Galleries,
Court House,
Ash Priors,
Nr Bishops Lydeard,
Taunton.
Tel: 0823 432402

Suffolk
Hubbard Antiques,
16 St Margarets Green,
Ipswich.
Tel: 0473 226033

Oswald Simpson,
Hall Street,
Long Melford.
Tel: 0787 277512

Surrey
J Hartley Antiques Ltd,
186 High Street,
Ripley.
Tel: 0483 224318

Ripley Antiques,
67 High Street,
Ripley.
Tel: 0483 224981

Wych House Antiques,
Wych Hill,
Woking.
Tel: 0483 764636

Sussex

British Antique Exporters Ltd,
School Close,
Queen Elizabeth Avenue,
Burgess Hill.
Tel: 0444 245577

Dycheling Antiques,
34 High Street,
Ditchling,
Hassocks.
Tel: 0273 842929
Chairs.

Lakeside,
The Old Cement Works,
South Heighton,
New Haven.
Tel: 0273 513326

Latimer Road Antiques,
144 Latimer Road,
Eastbourne.
Tel 0323 417777

The Old Mint House,
High Street,
Pevensey,
Eastbourne.
Tel: 0323 762337

Warwickshire

Apollo Antiques,
The Saltisiford,
Birmingham Road,
Warwick.
Tel: 0926 494746

Don Spencer Antiques,
Unit 2,
20 Cherry Street,
Warwick.
Tel: 0926 499857

West Midlands

L P Furniture (Mids) Ltd,
152 Lime Lane,
Pelsall,
Nr Walsall.
Tel: 0543 370256

Wiltshire

Ray Coggins,
1 Fore Street,
Westbury.
Tel: 0373 826574

GAMES/SPORT

London

Donay Antiques,
35 Camden Passage, N1.
Tel: 071 359 1880
Games, paint boxes, pinball machines.

Somerset

Fenwick Billiards Company,
Tonedale Mills,
Wellington
Tel: 0823 660770

GLASS

London

Arenski,
Stand 107
Grays Antiques Market,
58 Davies St, W1.
Tel: 071 499 6824

Avon

Somervale Antiques,
6 Radstock Road,
Midsomer Norton,
Bath.
Tel: 0761 412686

Hampshire

Stockbridge Antiques,
High Street,
Stockbridge.
Tel: 0264 810829

GOSS & CRESTED CHINA

East Yorkshire

The Crested China Co,
The Station House,
Driffield.
Tel: 0377 47042

HUMIDIFIERS

London

Air Improvement Centre,
23 Denbigh Street, SW1.
Tel: 071 834 2834

LIGHTING

London

Allegras 'Lighthouse' Antiques,
75-77 Ridgway,
Wimbledon Village,
SW19.
Tel: 081 946 2050

LOSS ADJUSTERS & VALUERS

London

Cunningham Hart,
59 Compton Road,
Islington, N1.
Tel 071 354 3504

METALWARE

Oxfordshire

Peter Norden Antiques,
61 High Street,
Burford.
Tel: 099 382 2121

MOORCROFT

London

Rumours Decorative Arts,
10 The Mall,
Upper St,
Camden Passage,
Islington, N1.
Tel: 0582 873561/0836 277274

PACKERS & SHIPPERS

London

Featherston Shipping Ltd,
24 Hampton House,
15-17 Ingate Place, SW8.
Tel: 071 720 0422

Hedley's Humpers,
Units 3 & 4,
97 Victoria Road, NW10.
Tel: 081 965 8733

Wingate & Johnson Ltd,
134 Queens Road, SE15
Tel: 071 732 8123

Avon

A J Williams (Shipping),
607 Sixth Avenue,
Central Business Park,
Petherton Road,
Hengrove,
Bristol.
Tel: 0275 892166

Dorset

Alan Franklin Transport,
27 Blackmoor Road,
Ebblake Industrial Estate,
Verwood.
Tel: 0202 826539

Middlesex

Burlington/Vulcan Fine Art Packers & Shippers,
Unit 8,
Ascot Road,
Clockhouse Lane,
Feltham.
Tel: 0784 244152

PIANOS

Avon

Piano Export,
Bridge Road,
Kingswood,
Bristol.
Tel: 0272 568300

PINE

Bucks

For Pine,
340 Berkhampstead Rd,
Chesham.
Tel: 0494 776119

Cheshire

Richmond Galleries,
Watergate Building, New Crane St,
off Sealand Road,
Chester.
Tel: 0244 317602.
Pine, country and Spanish furniture.

Devon

Chancery Antiques,
8-10 Barrington Street,
Tiverton.
Tel: 0884 252416

Dorset

Overhill Antiques and Old Pine Warehouse,
Wareham Road,
Holton Heath,
Poole.
Tel: 0202 621818

Hampshire

Millers of Chelsea Antiques Ltd,
Netherbrook House,
86 Christchurch Road,
Ringwood.
Tel: 0425 472062

The Pine Cellars,
39 Jewry St,
Winchester.
Tel: 0926 777546

Humberside

Bell Antiques,
68 Harold Street,
Grimsby.
Tel: 0472 695110

Kent

Country Pine Antique C
The Barn,
Upper Bush Farm,
Upper Bush Road,
Upper Bush,
Nr Rochester.
Tel: 0634 717982

Up Country,
The Old Corn Stores,
68 St Johns Road,
Tunbridge Wells.
Tel: 0892 523341/0323 487167

Lancashire

Enloc Antiques,
Birchenlee Mill,
Lenches Road,
Colne.
Tel: 0282 867101

Northants

The Country Pine Shop,
Northampton Road,
West Haddon.
Tel: 0788 510430

Surrey

Wych House Antiques,
Wych Hill,
Woking.
Tel: 0483 764636

Sussex

Ann Lingard,
Ropewalk Antiques,
Ropewalk,
Rye.
Tel: 0797 223486

Graham Price Antiques Ltd,
Unit 4,
Chaucer Industrial Estate,
Dittons Road,
Polegate.
Tel: 0323 487167

Wiltshire

Ray Coggins Antiques,
1 Fore Street,
Westbury.
Tel: 0273 826574

Worcestershire

S W Antiques,
Abbey Showrooms,
Newlands,
Pershore.
Tel: 0286 555580

Ireland

Delvin Farm Galleries,
Gormonston,
Co Meath.
Tel: 010 3531 841 2285

onans Antiques,
rowe Street,
ort,
County Galway.
Tel: 010 353 9131 407

Daniel P Meaney,
Alpine House,
Carlow Road,
Abbeyleix,
Co Laois.
Tel: 0502 31348

Old Court Pine,
Old Court,
ollon,
County Louth.
Tel: 010 353 41 26270

omerville Antiques,
oysdale,
illanley,
allina,
Co Mayo.
Tel: 010 353 96 36275

Wales

The Pot Board,
0 King Street,
Carmarthen,
Dyfed.
Tel: 0267 236623

Ireland

Daniel P Meaney,
Alpine House,
Carlow Road,
Abbeyleix,
Co Laois.
Tel: 0502 31348

The Netherlands

acques van der Tol bv,
Antiek & Curiosa,
Antennestraat 34,
Almere Stad.
Tel: 010 31 3653 62050

PORCELAIN

Lancashire

Robert Antiques.
Tel: 0253 827798

Northants

Peter Jackson Antiques,
Market Place,
Brackley.
Tel: 0993 882415/0280
703259

Nottinghamshire

Breck Antiques,
726 Mansfield Road,
Nottingham.
Tel: 0602 605263/621197
Derby porcelain.

Shropshire

Teme Valley Antiques,
The Bull Ring,
Ludlow.
Tel: 0584 874686

POTTERY

London

Jonathan Horne,
66B & C Kensington
Church St, W8.
Tel: 071 221 5658

Valerie Howard,
131E Kensington Church
Street,
London W8.
Tel: 071 727 7995/792
9702
Mason's & Quimper pottery.

MS Antiques,
40 Gordon Place,
Holland St, W8.
Tel: 071 937 0793

Sue Norman,
L4 Antiquarius,
135 Kings Road, SW3.
Tel: 071 352 7212/081
820 4677
Blue & white transfer ware.

Jacqueline Oosthuizen,
23 Cale Street, SW3 *and*
1st floor,
Georgian Village,
Camden Passage, N1.
Tel: 071 352 6071/071
376 3852/071 226 5393

Rogers de Rin,
76 Royal Hospital Road,
SW3.
Tel: 071 352 9007
Wemyss Ware.

Humberside

Crested China Company,
The Station House,
Driffield.
Tel: 0377 47042

Tyne & Wear

Ian Sharp Antiques,
23 Front Street,
Tynemouth.
Tel: 091 296 0656
Maling ware & lustre ware.

Warwickshire

Janice Paull,
Beehive House,
125 Warwick Road,
Kenilworth.
Tel: 0926 55253
Mason's Ironstone.

PUBLICATIONS

London

Antiques Trade Gazette,
17 Whitcomb Street,
WC2.
Tel: 071 930 9958

Midlands

Antiques Bulletin,
HP Publishing,
2 Hampton Court Road,
Harborne,
Birmingham.
Tel: 021 428 2555

RESTORATION

London

BAFRA,
37 Upper Addison
Gardens,
Holland Park, W14.
Tel: 071 371 4586

Peter Binnington,
68 Battersea High Street,
Battersea,
SW11.
Tel 071 223 9192/0622
752273
Marquetry, gilding and verre églomisé.

Crawley Studios,
39 Wood Vale,
SE23.
Tel: 081 299 4121
Painted furniture, papier mâché, tôle ware, lacquer & gilding.

Glens Antiques,
Restoration,
Unit 12,
Windsor Centre,
Windsor Grove,
West Norwood, SE27.
Tel: 081 766 6789.
Gilding and woodcarving picture frames.

Avon

M & S Bradbury,
The Barn,
Hanham Lane,
Paulton.
Tel: 0761 418910.
Antique furniture restorers.

Jane Way Restorations,
6 Foxcombe Road,
Weston,
Bath.
Tel: 0225 446770
Porcelain

Cheshire

A Allen Antique
Restorers,
Buxton Road,
Newtown,
Newmills.
Tel: 0663 745274.
Boule, marquetry, walnut, oak, veneering, upholstery.

Devon

Barometer World,
Quicksilver Barn,
Merton,
Okehampton.
Tel: 08053 443

Dorset

Richard Owen,
Blackwoods,
805 Christchurch Road,
Bournemouth.
Tel: 0202 434800.
Fine furniture restoration & conservation.

Richard Bolton,
Ashtree Cottage,
Whitecross,
Netherbury,
Bridport.
Tel: 0308 88474.
Antique furniture.

Tolpuddle Antique
Restorers,
The Stables,
Southover House,
Tolpuddle,
Dorchester.
Tel: 0305 848739.
Furniture, clocks, barometers.

Essex

Clive Beardall,
104b High Street,
Maldon.
Tel: 0621 857890
Period furniture.

Lomas Pigeon & Co Ltd,
1 Beehive Lane,
Chelmsford.
Tel: 0245 353708
Furniture, picture framing, restoration of rocking horses.

Gloucestershire

Keith Bawden,
Mews Workshops,
Montpellier Retreat,
Cheltenham.
Tel: 0242 230320
Furniture, carving, upholstery, chair reproduction.

Andrew Lelliott,
6 Tetbury Hill,
Avening,
Tetbury.
Tel: 0453 835783/832652
Comprehensive service included on the Conservation Unit Register of the Museums & Galleries Commission.

Hampshire

David C E Lewry,
Wychelms,
66 Gorran Avenue,
Rowner,
Gosport.
Tel: 0329 286901
Furniture.

Hereford & Worcester

Phillip Slater,
93 Hewell Road,
Barnt Green,
Nr Birmingham.
Tel: 021 445 4942
Furniture & clocks.

Bryan Wigington,
Chapel Schoolroom,
1 Heol-y-Dwr,
Hay on Wye,
Hereford.
Tel: 0497 820545.
Furniture.

Hertfordshire

Charles Perry
Restorations Ltd,
Praewood Farm,
Hemel Hempstead Road,
St Albans.
Tel: 0727 853487/Fax
846668

Kent

Antique Restorations,
The Old Wheelwright's Shop,
Brasted Forge,
Brasted,
Westerham.
Tel: 0959 563863
Furniture, upholstery, longcase and bracket clocks, antique and fine art, disaster emergency unit.

T M Akers,
The Forge,
39 Chancery Lane,
Beckenham.
Tel 081 650 9179
Longcase and bracket clocks, cabinet making, french polishing.

Martin Body,
71 Bower Mount Road,
Maidstone.
Tel: 0622 752273
Giltwood restoration, frames, architectural ornaments, water or oil gilded.

Timothy Long Restoration,
26 High Street,
Seal,
Nr Sevenoaks.
Tel: 0732 762606
Cabinet restoration, polishing, upholstery, brass & steel cabinet fittings.

Middlesex

Antique Restorations,
45 Windmill Road,
Brentford.
Tel: 081 568 5249
Decorative artists, carvers & gilders.

Norfolk

David Bartram,
The Raveningham Centre,
Castell Farm,
Beccles Road,
Raveningham.
Tel: 050 846 721
18th & 19thC English furniture - rosewood & walnut, inlay and turning.

R N Larwood,
Fine Antique Restoration & Conservation of Furniture,
The Oaks,
Station Road,
Larling,
Norwich.
Tel: 0953 717937

Oxfordshire

Alistair Frayling-Cork,
Antiques & Period Furniture Restoration,
2 Mill Lane,
Wallingford.
Tel: 0491 826221

Colin Piper Restoration,
Highfield House,
The Greens,
Leafield,
Witney.
Tel: 0993 87593.
Restoration and conservation of fine antique furniture.

Shropshire

Richard Higgins,
The Old School,
Longnor,
Nr Shrewsbury.
Tel: 0743 718162
Furniture, clock, barometers, movements, dials and cases, carving, rush / cane seating.

Somerset

Nicholas Bridges,
68 Lower Street,
Merriott.
Tel: 0460 74672
Cabinet making, polishing, carving, marquetry, veneering, upholstery, gilding, brass casting.

J Burrell,
Westerfield House,
Seavington St Mary,
Ilminster.
Tel 0460 240610
Furniture, carving, marquetry, wax polishing.

P Hacker,
Castle House,
Bennetts Field,
Moor Lane,
Wincanton.
Tel: 0963 33884
Antique furniture restoration.

Suffolk

Denzil Grant,
Suffolk Fine Arts Ltd,
Hubbards Corner,
Bradfield St George,
Nr Bury St Edmunds.
Tel: 0449 736576;
Fax 0449 737679

Sussex

Albert Plumb,
Practical Craftsman,
31 Whyke Lane,
Chichester.
Tel: 0243 788468
Furniture, boulle, marquetry.

Wiltshire

William Cook,
High Trees,
Savernake Forest,
Nr Marlborough.
Tel: 0672 413017/071 736 4329
Furniture.

Worcestershire

Malvern Studios,
56 Cowleigh Road,
Malvern.
Tel: 0684 574913
Furniture.

Yorkshire

Rodney F Kemble,
16 Crag Vale Terrace,
Glusburn,
Nr Keighley.
Tel: 0535 636954
Furniture, clock cases.

SCIENTIFIC INSTRUMENTS

Scotland

Michael Bennett-Levy,
Monkton House,
Old Craighall,
Musselburgh,
Mid Lothian.
Tel: 031 665 5753

SERVICES

London

Studio & TV Hire,
3 Ariel Way, W12.
Tel: 081 749 3445

Thesaurus Group Ltd,
76 Gloucester Place, W1.
Tel: 071 487 3401

Hampshire

Securikey Ltd,
PO Box 18,
Aldershot.
Tel: 0252 311888,
fax 0252 343950

Herefordshire

ID-Link Ltd,
PO Box 99,
Ross-on-Wye.
Tel: 0989 769399
Security.

Middlesex

John Ives,
5 Normanhurst Drive,
Twickenham.
Tel: 081 892 6265
Reference books.

Sussex

Artisan,
4 The Parade,
Valley Drive,
Brighton.
Tel: 0273 557418
Desk leathers.

West Midlands

Retro Products,
The Yard,
Star Street,
Lye,
Nr Stourbridge.
Tel: 0384 373332/894042
Brass handles and accessories.

SILVER

Shropshire

Teme Valley Antiques,
1 The Bull Ring,
Ludlow.
Tel: 0584 874686

STAFFORDSHIRE POTTERY

London

Jonathan Horne,
66B & C Kensington,
Church St,
W8.
Tel: 071 221 5658

M S Antiques,
40 Gordon Place,
Holland Street, W8.
Tel: 071 937 0793

Jacqueline Oosthuizen,
1st floor,
Georgian Village,
Camden Passage, N1.
and
23 Cale St,
SW3
Tel: 071 352 6071/071 376 3852/071 226 5393

Lancashire

Roy W Bunn Antiques,
34-36 Church Street,
Barnoldswick,
Colne.
Tel: 0282 813703

Suffolk

John Read,
29 Lark Rise,
Martlesham Heath,
Ipswich.
Tel: 0473 624897

TEDDY BEARS

Oxfordshire

Teddy Bears of Witney,
99 High Street,
Witney.
Tel: 0993 702616

TELEPHONES

Essex

The Old Telephone Co,
The Old Granary,
Battlebridge Antiques Centre,
Nr Wickford.
Tel: 0268 734005

TOYS

Sussex

Wallis & Wallis,
West Street Galleries,
Lewes.
Tel: 0273 480208

TRIBAL ART

Yorkshire

Gordon Reece Gallery,
Finkle Street,
Knaresborough.
Tel: 0423 866219

WATCHES

London

Pieces of Time,
Grays in the Mews,
1-7 Davies Mews, W1.
Tel: 071 629 2422

WINE RELATED ITEMS

Bedfordshire

Christopher Sykes,
The Old Parsonage,
Woburn,
Milton Keynes.
Tel: 0525 290259

FAIR ORGANISERS

Surrey

Cultural Exhibitions,
8 Meadrow,
Godalming.
Tel: 0483 422562

MARKETS & CENTRES

London

Alfies Antique Market,
13-25 Church Street,
NW8.
Tel: 071 723 6066

Grays Antique Markets,
1-7 Davies Mews & 58
Davies Street, W1.
Tel: 071 629 7034/7036

Lancashire

Preston Antique Centre,
The Mill,
New Hall Lane,
Preston.
Tel: 0772 794498

Lincolnshire

The Hemswell Antiques
Centre,
Caenby Corner Estate,
Hemswell Cliff,
Gainsborough.
Tel: 0427 668389

Sussex

Bexhill Antiques Centre,
Old Town,
Bexhill.
Tel: 0424 210182/225103

Yorkshire

The Emporium,
77 Walmgate,
York
Tel: 0904 634124

A pair of carved Bath stone lions, each seated on associated composition stone base, 19thC, 44in (112cm).
$3,000-3,750

Auctioneers
the South of England

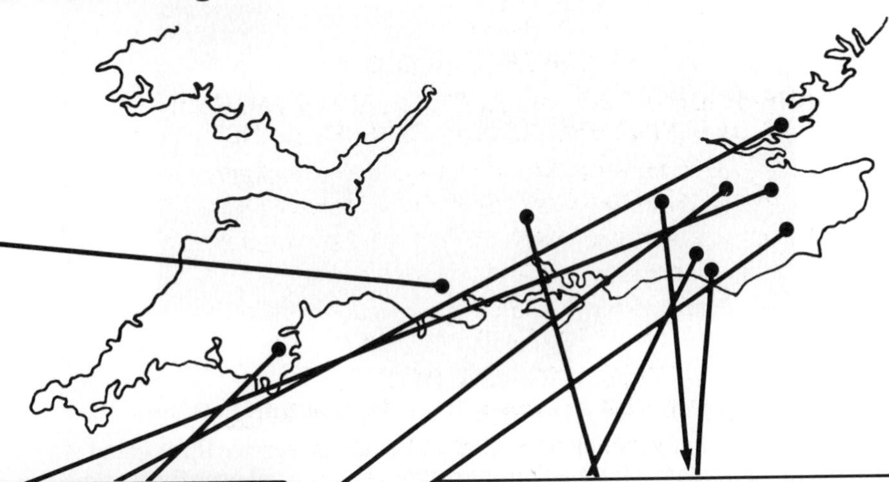

IBBETT MOSELY

25 High Street, SEVENOAKS 456731

A Regular Programme of Sales

of Antique, Victorian and Edwardian Furniture, Works of Art, Silver, Glass, Watches, China, Musical Instruments, Jewellery, etc. etc.

Held in our Saleroom at Sevenoaks.

Also valuations carried out for Probate, Insurance and Family Division.

Complete house clearances undertaken with personal supervision.

Storage facilities available for short periods pending sale.

Chattel Auctions and Valuations

P. F. Windibank

FINE ART AUCTIONEERS & VALUERS

18-20 Reigate Road
Dorking
Surrey RH4 1SG

Tel: (0306) 884556/876280
Fax: (0306) 884669

Established 1945

(Established 1925)

Auctioneers & Estate Agents

The long established Family Firm. Well experienced in Auctioneering and property matters.

Regular Monthly Auctions

18 Bridge Street, Andover (0264) 323417

THE Sussex Auction Galleries

ANTIQUE AND REPRODUCTION FURNITURE AND EFFECTS

EVERY LAST WEDNESDAY OF THE MONTH

59 Perrymount Road
Haywards Heath, Sussex

Telephone: (0444) 414935
Fax: (0444) 450402

JULIAN DAWSON

Regular sales of
ANTIQUE FURNITURE AND EFFECTS

Weekly sales of
ANTIQUE & MODERN FURNITURE, BRIC-A-BRAC etc.
every Monday at 11 am

Auction Offices, 56 High Street. Lewes. Tel. Lewes 478221
Salerooms, Garden Street, Lewes, Sussex.

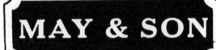

tioneers

outh of England

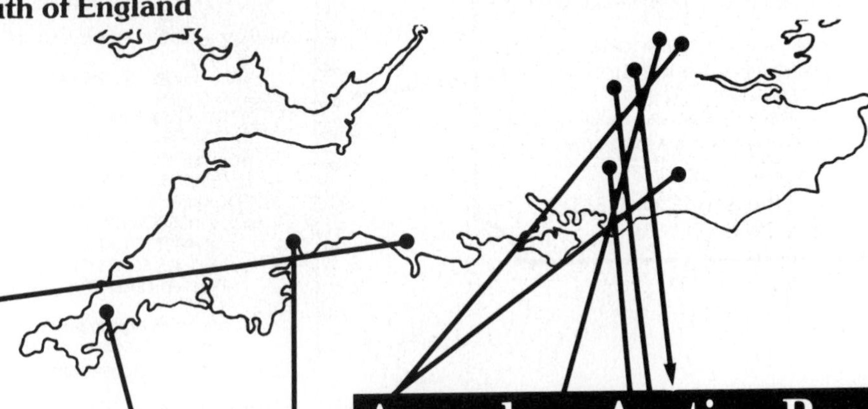

Auctioneers

the South of England

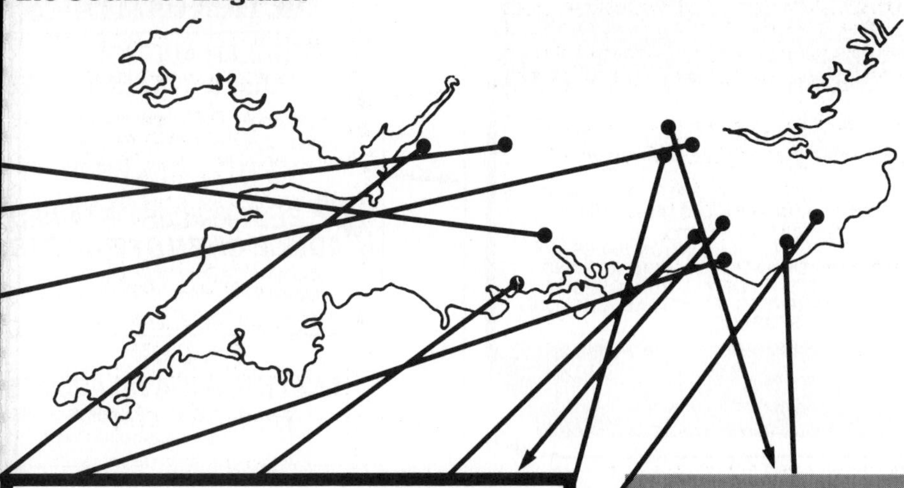

COOPER HIRST AUCTIONS

Chartered Surveyors
Auctioneers and Valuers

- ★ REGULAR ANTIQUE SALES
- ★ HOUSEHOLD FURNITURE AND EFFECTS Every TUESDAY at 10.00am (Viewing from 8.30am)
- ★ TIMBER, BUILDING MATERIALS, DIY, PLANT, MACHINERY AND VEHICLES. Every FRIDAY at 10.00am (Viewing from 8.30am)
- ★ BANKRUPTCY AND LIQUIDATION SALES ★
- ★ VALUATIONS OF ANTIQUES, FINE ART AND OTHER CHATTELS FOR ALL PURPOSES
- ★ HOUSE CLEARANCES, REMOVALS AND LONG/SHORT TERM STORAGE

THE GRANARY SALEROOM
VICTORIA ROAD, CHELMSFORD
Tel: 0245 260535

ASCENT AUCTION GALLERIES

REGULAR AUCTIONS OF ANTIQUES & COLLECTABLES

Period English & Continental Furniture, Silver, Jewellery, Gold, Oil Paintings, Watercolours, Ceramics, Carpets, ETC.

ADVICE GIVEN BY EXPERTS

Insurance, Tax and Probate valuations.
Auction terms or best Cash Prices paid.
Carriage arranged all areas at local rates.

Telephone
HASTINGS (0424) 420275
11-12 EAST ASCENT, ST. LEONARDS-ON-SEA
(Find us to the rear of Marine Court)

Gorringes Auction Galleries

Member of the Society

of Fine Art Auctioneers

MONTHLY AUCTION SALES

Period Furniture, Porcelain, Glass, Objects of Vertu, Silver Plate Jewellery, Books, Works of Art, Oriental Carpets
Valuations for Insurance, Probate, Family Division and Sale by Auction
Auction Sales conducted in Private Residences

15 NORTH STREET, LEWES, SUSSEX
Tel: (0273) 472503

MICHAEL STAINER LTD

Fine Art Auctioneers and Valuers
Regular Auctions
Removal and Sale of Entire House Contents
Valuations for Probate
Insurance and Family Division

For Expert Advice Contact:
Michael Stainer F.S.V.A.
Nicholas Stainer F.N.A.E.A.
(0202) 309999
St. Andrews Hall
Wolverton Road, Boscombe
Bournemouth BH7 6HT

CRITERION AUCTION ROOMS

53 ESSEX ROAD, ISLINGTON
LONDON N1
Tel: 071-359 5707 Fax: 071-354 9843

Auctions of General Antiques and Decorative Items every Monday at 6.00pm

on view:
FRIDAY – 4pm-8pm
SATURDAY – 11am-3pm
SUNDAY – 11am-3pm
MONDAY – 10am onwards

DALKEITH AUCTION
BOURNEMOUTH

MONTHLY COLLECTORS SALES
POSTCARDS, CIGARETTE CARDS, EPHEMERA AND OTHER COLLECTORS ITEMS

NO FURNITURE

POSTAL BIDDING FACILITIES

For First Free Catalogue
TEL: (0202) 292905
or write to:
Dalkeith Auctions, Dalkeith Hall
Dalkeith Steps, Rear 81 Old Christchurch Road
Bournemouth BH1 1YL

Watson Bull & Porter Auction Rooms

ANTIQUES & FINE ARTS AUCTION
79 Regent Street, Shanklin
Isle of Wight PO37 7AP
Telephone: (0983) 863441
Fax: (0983) 863890

uctioneers
e South of England

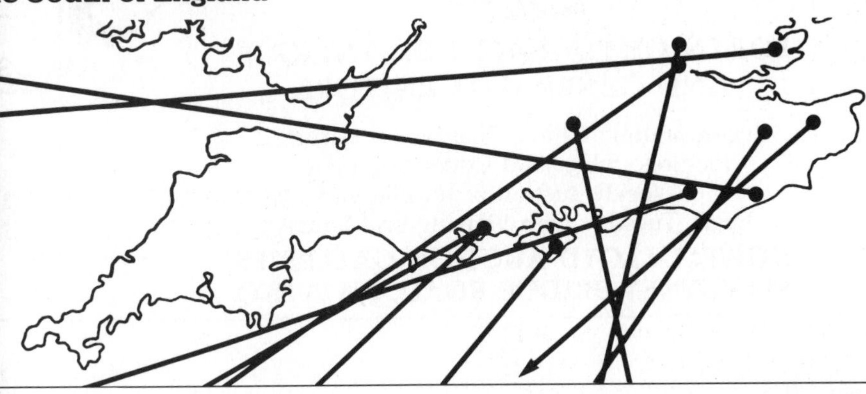

Auctioneers
n the South of England

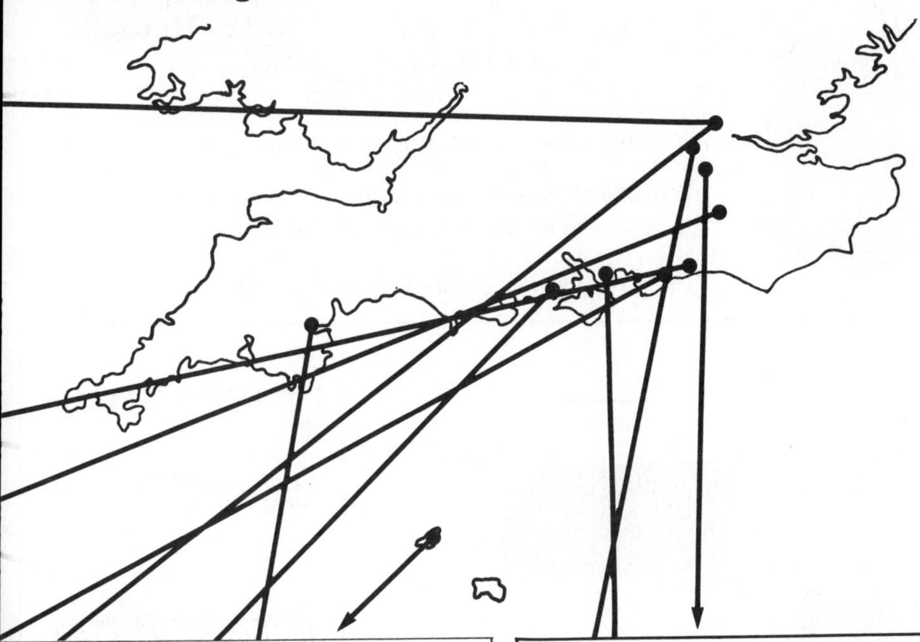

Auctioneers
in the Midlands

ROGERS JONES CO.

FURNITURE & FINE ART AUCTIONEERS
Probate & Insurance Valuers

Antique Furniture Collectables and Paintings every last Tuesday in the month

Regular Specialist Sales of 'Welsh' Fine Art

SHIPPING AND GENERAL SALES ON FOLLOWING TWO TUESDAYS

The Saleroom, 33 Abergele Road, Colwyn Bay, Clwyd LL29 7RU
Telephone (0492) 532176 24 hrs.
Fax (0492) 533308.

Arthur Johnson & sons

The Largest Furniture Auction Complex in the Midlands

(0602) 869128 Meadow Lane Nottingham

The NOTTINGHAM AUCTION CENTRE

6 SPECIALIST SALEROOMS
Around 2,000 lots every Saturday
(Over 1,000 lots Antique & Export Furniture
Gold, Silver, Ceramics, Collectables, etc)

Nigel Ward & Morris

CHARTERED SURVEYORS
AUCTIONEERS AND VALUERS

Regular monthly auctions of Antiques, Objects d'Art & Collectables
Household Furniture & Effects

On the premises marquee sales

STUART HOUSE
18 GLOUCESTER ROAD
ROSS-ON-WYE
HEREFORDSHIRE HR9 5BU
(0989) 768320

THE BORDER PROPERTY CENTRE
PONTRILAS
HEREFORD HR2 0EH
(0981) 240140

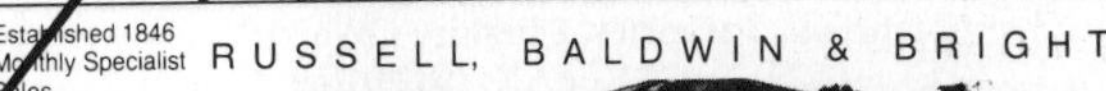

Established 1846
Monthly Specialist Sales
FURNITURE
WORKS of ART
PORCELAIN & POTTERY
SILVER
PEWTER
CLOCKS
MUSICAL BOXES
BRONZES
BOOKS and PICTURES
BYGONES
ORIENTAL CARPETS

VALUATIONS for all purposes carried out by our qualified staff.
SALES by AUCTION of the contents of Town and Country Houses conducted throughout the West Midlands and Wales.

Enquiries to: The Fine Art Saleroom, Ryelands Rd., Leominster, Herefordshire HR6 8NZ. (0568) 611166 Fax (0568) 611802. Also at Portland Room, Malvern. Tel (0684) 893933

HOLLOWAY'S
Furniture & Fine Art Auctioneers & Valuers

SALES THROUGHOUT THE YEAR
at least twice monthly
Also Special Sales for Silver and Jewellery
Pictures and Automobilia

Free Pre-Sale Advice

Auction room opposite multi-storey car park
(5 minutes M40 Junction 11)

49 PARSONS STREET, BANBURY
OXFORDSHIRE OX16 8PF
Tel: (0295) 253197. Fax: (0295) 252642
and at Streatley, Berkshire

SALEROOM
20 The Square, RETFORD, Nottinghamshire DN22 6BX
(0777) 708633 Fax (0777) 709299

OFFICES
65 Regent Street, CAMBRIDGE CB2 1AB
(0223) 327592
1 Princes Square, HARROGATE, North Yorkshire HG1 1ND
(0423) 500566
42 Silver Street, LINCOLN LN2 1TA
(0522) 536666
21 St Annes Road West, LYTHAM ST ANNES, Lancashire FY8 1SB
(0253) 780202
5 Regent Street, NOTTINGHAM NG1 5BW
(0602) 508833
1 St James' Row, SHEFFIELD S1 1WZ
(0742) 728728

6-8 Specialist Sales held each month
Catalogues available individually or by subscription

Fine Art Auctioneers

Auctioneers covering the North West
Valuations for Probate and Insurance
Monthly Antique Auctions
Weekly General Sales

Head Office and Auction Galleries
29 HOLT STREET, WREXHAM, CLWYD
LL13 8DH TEL: (0978) 353553

CATO CRANE & Co.

AUCTIONEERS & VALUERS
FINE ART – ANTIQUES
GENERAL DOMESTIC
FURNISHINGS
REGULAR ANTIQUE AUCTIONS
FREE PRE-SALE ADVICE
HIGHLY COMPETITIVE FEES
HOUSE CLEARANCE SERVICE AVAILABLE
Telephone John Crane
Liverpool Auction Rooms 051-709 5559
Wirral 051-342 2321
& North Wales 0244 317400
6 STANHOPE ST., LIVERPOOL L8 5RF

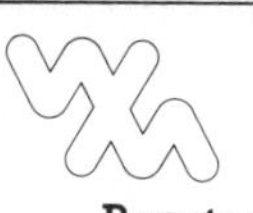

Wright-Manley

Beeston Sales Centre, Near Tarporley,
Cheshire CW6 9NJ

Regular Furniture and Fine Art Sales

Fortnightly Collective Sales of
Antique and Modern Furniture

Information: Gerald Tilston
Tel: (0829) 260318

FINE ART AUCTIONEERS & VALUERS

Weekly Auctions of Victorian, Later Furnishings and Effects
Bi-monthly Auctions of Fine Art and Antiques
BIRCHALL'S – WE VALUE THE THINGS YOU TREASURE

Cotebrook, Tarporley, Cheshire CW6 9DY
TEL: (0829) 760754 FAX: (0829) 760547

GOLDINGS

THE GRANTHAM AUCTION ROOMS

INDEPENDENT
Auctioneers & Valuers

Geo. III painted satinwood secretaire bookcase
SOLD FOR £13,000

BI-MONTHLY CATALOGUED
ANTIQUE & FINE ART SALES
with flexible commission rates and swift payment

FORTNIGHTLY SALES OF
GENERAL FURNITURE & EFFECTS

VALUATIONS
for
Sale, Probate and Insurance

OLD WHARF ROAD, GRANTHAM
LINCOLNSHIRE NG31 7AA
Tel: (0476) 65118. Fax: (0476) 590998

THOS. WM. GAZE & SON

ESTABLISHED 1857

AUCTIONS

2000 LOTS EVERY FRIDAY
at the
DISS AUCTION ROOMS
including

500 LOTS. ANTIQUES and COLLECTABLES
400 LOTS. SHIPPING, BARN CLEARANCES and ARCHITECTURAL
500 LOTS. MODERN FURNITURE and EFFECTS
Specialist Sales throughout the year
Catalogues Available

AUCTION ROOMS, ROYDON ROAD, DISS, NORFOLK. TEL: (0379) 650306

AUDSLEY'S AUCTIONS

Auctioneers of Antiques, Fine Arts
and Household Furniture and Effects

Specialist Catalogue Sales of Antiques and Fine Arts
Fortnightly Sales of Antiques and Household Furniture & Effects
Periodic Sales of Insurance Salvage and Liquidation Stocks

Office and Auction Salerooms
11 Morris Lane, Kirkstall, Leeds LS5 3JT

Telephone:
(0532) 758787

Auctioneers

the Midlands

Auctioneers
n Scotland and he North of England

DIRECTORY OF AUCTIONEERS

This directory is by no means complete. Any auctioneer who holds frequent sales should contact us for inclusion in the next Edition. Entries must be received by April 1994. There is, of course, no charge for this listing. Entries will be repeated in subsequent editions unless we are requested otherwise.

London

Academy Auctioneers & Valuers,
Northcote House,
Northcote Avenue, Ealing, W5
Tel: 081 579 7466

Bonhams, Montpelier Galleries,
Montpelier Street,
Knightsbridge, SW7
Tel: 071 584 9161

Bonhams, Lots Road,
Chelsea, SW10
Tel: 071 351 7111

Christie Manson & Woods Ltd,
8 King Street,
St James's, SW1
Tel: 071 839 9060

Christie's Robson Lowe,
47 Duke Street,
St James's, SW1
Tel: 071 839 4034/5

Christie's South Kensington Ltd,
85 Old Brompton Road, SW7
Tel: 071 581 7611

City Forum Auctioneers,
108 Belsize Avenue, NW3
Tel: 071 433 1305

Criterion Salerooms,
53 Essex Road,
Islington, N1
Tel: 071 359 5707

Dowell Lloyd & Co,
118 Putney Bridge Road, SW15
Tel: 081 788 7777

Forrest & Co,
79-85 Cobbold Road,
Leytonstone, E11
Tel: 081 534 2931

Stanley Gibbons Auctions Ltd,
399 Strand, WC2
Tel: 071 836 8444

Glendining's,
101 New Bond Street, W1
Tel: 071 493 2445

Hamptons Fine Art Auctioneers and Valuers,
6 Arlington Street, SW1
Tel: 071 493 8222

Harmers of London Stamp Auctioneers Ltd, 91 New Bond Street, W1
Tel: 071 629 0218

Hornsey Auctions Ltd,
91 New Bond Street, W1
Tel: 071 629 0218

Hornsey Auctions Ltd,
54/56 High Street, Hornsey, N8
Tel: 081 340 5334

Jackson-Stops & Staff,
14 Curzon Street, W1
Tel: 071 499 6291

Lots Road Chelsea Auction Galleries,
71 Lots Road, Worlds End,
Chelsea, SW10
Tel: 071 351 7771

MacGregor Nash & Co,
Lodge House, 9-17 Lodge Lane, North Finchley, N12
Tel: 081 445 9000

Thomas Moore,
217-219 Greenwich High Road, SE10
Tel: 081 858 7848

John Nicholson,
20 The Ridgway,
Wimbledon Village, SW19
Tel: 081 944 5575

Onslow's,
Metrostore,
Townmead Road, SW6
Tel: 071 793 0240

Palmers,
New Octagon House,
17-31 Gibbons Road,E15
Tel: 081 555 0517

Phillips,
Blenstock House,
7 Blenheim Street,
New Bond Street, W1
Tel: 071 629 6602 and
10 Salem Road, W2
Tel: 071 229 9090

Rippon Boswell & Co,
The Arcade, South Kensington Station, SW7
Tel: 071 589 4242

Rosebery's Fine Art Ltd,
Old Railway Booking Hall,
Crystal Palace Station Road, SE19
Tel: 081 778 4024

Sotheby's,
34-35 New Bond Street, W1
Tel: 071 493 8080

Southgate Auction Rooms,55 High Street,
Southgate N14
Tel: 081 886 7888

Town & Country House Auctions,
42A Nightingale Grove, SE13
Tel: 081 852 3145

Avon

Alder King, Black Horse Agencies,
The Old Malthouse,
Comfortable Place,
Upper Bristol Road, Bath
Tel: 0225 447933

Aldridges, Bath,
The Auction Galleries,
130-132 Walcot Street, Bath
Tel: 0225 462830 & 462839

Bristol Auction Rooms,
St Johns Place, Apsley Road, Clifton, Bristol
Tel: 0272 737201

Clevedon Salerooms,
Herbert Road, Clevedon
Tel: 0275 876699

Phillips Auction Rooms of Bath, 1 Old King Street, Bath
Tel: 0225 310609

Phillips Fine Art Auctioneers,
71 Oakfield Road, Clifton, Bristol
Tel: 0272 734052

Taviner's Ltd,
Prewett Street, Redcliffe, Bristol
Tel: 0272 265996

Woodspring Auction Rooms,
Churchill Road,
Weston-super-Mare
Tel: 0934 628419

Bedfordshire

Wilson Peacock,
The Auction Centre, 26 Newnham Street, Bedford
Tel: 0234 266366

Berkshire

Dreweatt Neate,
Donnington Priory,
Donnington, Newbury
Tel: 0635 31234

R. Elliott,
Chancellors, 32 High Street, Ascot
Tel: 0344 872588

Holloway's,
12 High Street, Streatley, Reading
Tel: 0491 872318

Martin & Pole,
12 Milton Street,
Wokingham
Tel: 0734 790460

Thimbleby & Shorland,
31 Great Knollys Street, Reading
Tel: 0734 508611

Duncan Vincent Fine Art & Chattel Auctioneers,
105 London Street, Reading
Tel: 0734 594748

Buckinghamshire

Amersham Auction Rooms,
Station Road, Amersham
Tel: 0494 729292

Bourne End Auctions Rooms, Station Approach, Bourne End
Tel: 0628 531500

Hamptons,
10 Burkes Parade,
Beaconsfield
Tel: 0494 672969

Geo Wigley & Sons,
Winslow Sale Room,
Market Square, Winslow
Tel: 029 671 2717

Cambridgeshire

Cheffins Grain & Comins,
2 Clifton Road, Cambridge
Tel: 0223 358721/213343

Goldsmiths,
15 Market Place, Oundle.
Tel: 0832 272349

Grounds & Co,
2 Nene Quay, Wisbech
Tel: 0945 585041

Hammond & Co,
Cambridge Place, off Hills Road, Cambridge
Tel: 0223 356067

Maxey & Son,
1-3 South Brink, Wisbech
Tel: 0945 584609

Phillips Auctioneers,
Station Road, St. Ives
Tel: 0480 68144

Cheshire

F.W. Allen & Sons,
Central Buildings
15/15A Station Road,
Cheadle Hulme,
Tel: 061 485 4121

Andrew Hilditch & Son,
Hanover House, 1A The Square, Sandbach
Tel: 0270 762048/767246

Birchalls,
Cotebrook,
Tarporley
Tel: 0829 760754

Robert I Heyes,
Hatton Buildings, Lightfoot Street, Hoole, Chester
Tel: 0244 328941

Highams Auctions, Waterloo House, Waterloo Road,
Stalybridge
Tel: 061 338 8698 also at:

Southgate House, Southgate Street, Rhodes Bank,
Oldham Tel: 061 626 1021

Frank R Marshall & Co,
Marshall House, Church Hill, Knutsford
Tel: 0565 653284

Phillips North West,
New House, 150 Christleton Road, Chester
Tel: 0244 313936

Phillips Fine Art Auctioneers,
Trinity House, 114 Northenden Road, Sale,
Manchester
Tel: 061 962 9237

Rothwell & Co (Auctioneers),
Waterloo House
Waterloo Road
Stalybridge
Tel: 061 303 2924

Henry Spencer Inc. Peter Wilson,
Victoria Gallery, Market Street, Nantwich
Tel: 0270 623878

Wright Manley,
Beeston Sales Centre,
3 High Street, Tarporley
Tel: 0829 260318

Cleveland

Lithgow Sons & Partners,
The Auction Houses,
Station Road, Stokesley,
Middlesbrough
Tel: 0642 710158 & 710326

Cornwall

Eric Distin Chartered
Surveyors,
4 Fore Street
Saltash

Jeffery's,
5 Fore Street, Lostwithiel
Tel: 0208 872245

Lambrays,
incorporating
R J Hamm ASVA
Polmorla Walk, The Platt,
Wadebridge
Tel: 020 881 3593

W H Lane & Son,
St Mary's Auction Rooms,
5 Morrab Road, Penzance
Tel: 0736 61447

David Lay,
Penzance Auction House,
Alverton, Penzance
Tel: 0736 61414

Phillips Cornwall,
Cornubia Hall, Par
Tel: 072 681 4047

Pooley and Rogers,
Regent Auction Rooms,
Abbey Street, Penzance
Tel: 0736 68814

Truro Auction Centre,
Calenick Street,
Truro
Tel: 0872 260020

Cumbria

Cumbria Auction Rooms,
12 Lowther Street, Carlisle
Tel: 0228 25259

Mitchells,
The Furniture Hall,
47 Station Road,
Cockermouth
Tel: 0900 827800

Alfred Mossops & Co,
Loughrigg Villa, Kelsick
Road, Ambleside
Tel: 05394 33015

James Thompson,
64 Main Street, Kirkby
Lonsdale
Tel: 05242 71555

Thomson, Roddick &
Laurie,
24 Lowther Street, Carlisle
Tel: 0228 28939/39636

Derbyshire

Richardson & Linnell Ltd,
The Auction Office,
Cattle Market,
Chequers Road,
Derby
Tel: 0332 296369

Noel Wheatcroft & Son,
The Matlock Auction
Gallery,
39 Dale Road, Matlock
Tel: 0629 584591

Devon

Bearnes,
Avenue Road, Torquay
Tel: 0803 296277

Bonhams West Country,
Devon Fine Art Auction
House,
Dowell Street, Honiton
Tel: 0404 41872

Michael J Bowman,
6 Haccombe House, Nr
Netherton, Newton Abbot
Tel: 0626 872890

Eric Distin,
Chartered Surveyors,
54 Fore Street, Saltash
Tel: 0752 843768/842355

Peter J Eley,
Western House, 98-100
High Street, Sidmouth
Tel: 0395 513006

Robin A Fenner & Co,
Fine Art & Antique
Auctioneers,
The Stannary Gallery,
Drake Road, Tavistock
Tel: 0822 617799/617800

Kings Auctioneers,
Pinnbrook Units,
Venny Bridge,
Pinhoe, Exeter
Tel: 0392 460644

Kingsbridge Auction Sales,
85 Fore Street, Kingsbridge
Tel: 0548 856829

McBain's of Exeter,
Exeter Airport,
Clyst Honiton
Tel: 0392 66261

Michael Newman,
Kinterbury House,
St Andrew's Cross,
Plymouth
Tel: 0752 669298

Phillips,
Alphin Brook Road,
Alphington, Exeter
Tel: 0392 439025 and
Armada Street, North Hill,
Plymouth
Tel: 0752 673504

Potbury's,
High Street, Sidmouth
Tel: 0395 515555

Rendells,
Stone Park, Ashburton
Tel: 0364 653017

G S Shobrook & Co,
20 Western Approach,
Plymouth
Tel: 0752 663341

John Smale & Co,
11 High Street, Barnstaple
Tel: 0271 42000/42916

South Street Auctions,
Newport,
Barnstaple
Tel: 0271 788581/850337

Martin Spencer-Thomas,
Church Street Auction
Rooms, Exmouth
Tel: 0395 267403

Taylors,
Honiton Galleries, 205
High Street, Honiton
Tel: 0404 42404

Ward & Chowen,
1 Church Lane, Tavistock
Tel: 0822 612458

Whitton & Laing,
32 Okehampton Street,
Exeter
Tel: 0392 52621

Dorset

Cottees, Bullock & Lees,
The Market, East Street,
Wareham
Tel: 0929 554915/552826

Dalkeith Auctions,
Dalkeith Hall,
Dalkeith Steps,
Rear of 81 Old
Christchurch Road,
Bournemouth
Tel: 0202 292905

HY Duke & Son,
The Dorchester Fine Art
Salerooms, Dorchester
Tel: 0305 265080
also at:
The Weymouth Saleroom,
St Nicholas Street,
Weymouth
Tel: 0305 761499

Garnet Langton Auctions,
Burlington Arcade,
Bournemouth
Tel: 0202 552352

House & Son,
Lansdowne House,
Christchurch Road,
Bournemouth
Tel: 0202 556232

William Morey & Sons,
The Saleroom, St Michaels
Lane, Bridport
Tel: 0308 22078

Riddetts of Bournemouth,
26 Richmond Hill, The
Square,
Bournemouth
Tel: 0202 555686

Southern Counties
Auctioneers,
Shaftesbury Livestock
Market,
Christy's Lane, Shaftesbury
Tel: 0747 51735

Michael Stainer Ltd,
St Andrew Hall,
Wolverton Road,
Boscombe,
Bournemouth
Tel: 0202 309999

County Durham

Denis Edkins,
Auckland Auction Room,
58 Kingsway,
Bishop Auckland
Tel: 0388 603095

Thomas Watson & Son,
Northumberland Street,
Darlington
Tel: 0325 462559/463485

Wingate Auction Co,
Station Lane, Station
Town, Wingate
Tel: 0429 837245

Essex

Abridge Auction Rooms,
Market Place, Abridge
Tel: 099281 2107/3113

Black Horse Agencies,
Ambrose, 149 High Road,
Loughton Tel: 081 502 3951

William H Brown,
The Auction Rooms,
11-14 East Hill
Colchester
Tel: 0206 868070

Cooper Hirst,
The Granary Saleroom,
Victoria Road,
Chelmsford
Tel: 0245 260535

Grays Auction Rooms,
Ye Old Bake House, Alfred
Street, Grays
Tel: 0375 381181

Hamptons Fine Art/J.M.
Welch & Son,
The Old Town Hall,
Great Dunmow
Tel: 0371 873014

Leigh Auction Rooms.
88-90 Pall Mall,
Leigh-on-Sea,
Tel: 0702 77051

Saffron Walden Saleroom,
1 Market Street,
Saffron Walden
Tel: 0799 513281

Gloucestershire

Bruton, Knowles & Co,
111 Eastgate Street,
Gloucester
Tel: 0452 521267

Fraser Glennie & Partners,
The Old Rectory,
Siddington,
Nr Cirencester
Tel: 0285 659677

Hobbs & Chambers,
Market Place,
Cirencester
Tel: 0285 654736 also at:
15 Royal Crescent,
Cheltenham
Tel: 0242 513722

Ken Lawson t/as
Specialised Postcard
Auctions,
25 Gloucester Street,
Cirencester
Tel: 0285 659057

Mallams,
26 Grosvenor Street,
Cheltenham
Tel: 0242 235712

Moore, Allen & Innocent,
33 Castle Street,
Cirencester
Tel: 0285 65183

Wotton Auction Rooms,
Tabernacle Road,
Wotton-under-Edge
Tel: 0453 844733

Hampshire

Andover Saleroom,
41A London Street,
Andover
Tel: 0264 364820

Fox & Sons,
5 & 7 Salisbury Street,
Fordingbridge
Tel: 0425 652121

Hants & Berks Auctions,
82, 84 Sarum Hill,
Basingstoke
Tel: 0256 840707
also at:
Heckfield Village Hall,
Heckfield

Jacobs & Hunt,
Lavant Street, Petersfield
Tel: 0730 62744/5

George Kidner,
The Old School,
The Square,
Pennington,
Lymington
Tel: 0590 670070

May & Son,
18 Bridge Street, Andover
Tel: 0264 323417

D M Nesbit & Co,
7 Clarendon Road,
Southsea
Tel: 0705 864321

New Forest Auction Rooms,
Emsworth Road,
Lymington
Tel: 0590 677225

Odiham Auction Sales,
The Eagle Works,
Rear of Hartley Wintney Garages,
High Street,
Hartley Wintney
Tel: 0252 844410

Phillips Fine Art Auctioneers,
54 Southampton Road,
Ringwood
Tel: 04254 473333 also at:
The Red House, Hyde Street,
Winchester
Tel: 0962 862515

The Romsey Auction Rooms, 86 The Hundred,
Romsey
Tel. 0794 513331

Hereford & Worcs

Broadway Auctions,
41-43 High Street,
Broadway
Tel: 0386 852456

Carless & Co,
58 Lowesmoor, Worcester
Tel: 0905 612449

Andrew Grant,
St Mark's House,
St Mark's Close, Worcester
Tel: 0905 357547

Griffiths & Co,
57 Foregate Street,
Worcester
Tel: 0905 26464

Hamptons,
69 Church Street, Malvern
Tel: 0684 892314

Philip Laney & Jolly,
12a Worcester Road,
Gt Malvern
Tel: 0684 892322

Phipps & Pritchard,
Bank Buildings,
Kidderminster
Tel: 0562 822244/6 & 822187

Russell, Baldwin & Bright,
Fine Art Saleroom,
Ryelands Road, Leominster
Tel: 0568 611166

Village Auctions,
Sychampton Community Centre, Ombersley
Tel: 0905 421007

Nigel Ward & Morris,
Stuart House, 18 Gloucester Road, Ross-on-Wye
Tel: 0989 768320

Richard Williams,
2 High Street, Pershore
Tel: 0386 554031

Hertfordshire

Bayles,
Childs Farm, Cottered,
Buntingford
Tel: 076 381 256

Brown & Merry,
41 High Street, Tring
Tel: 044 282 6446

Hitchin Auctions Ltd,
The Corn Exchange,
Market Place,
Hitchin
Tel: 0462 442151

Andrew Pickford,
42 St Andrew Street,
Hertford
Tel: 0992 583508

Pamela & Barry Auctions,
The Village Hall, High Street, Sandridge,
St Albans
Tel: 0727 861180

Sworders,
Northgate End Salerooms,
Bishops Stortford
Tel: 0279 651388

Humberside North

Gilbert Baitson, FSVA, The Edwardian Auction Galleries, Wiltshire Road,
Hull Tel: 0482 500500

H Evans & Sons,
1 Parliament Street, Hull
Tel: 0482 23033

Humberside South

Dickinson, Davy & Markham,
10 Wrawby Street, Brigg
Tel: 0652 653666

Isle of Man

Chrystals Auctions,
Majestic Hotel, Onchan
Tel: 0624 673986

Isle of Wight

Phillips Fine Art Auctioneers,
Cross Street Salerooms,
Newport
Tel: 0983 822031

Watson Bull & Porter,
Isle of Wight Auction Rooms, 79 Regent Street,
Shanklin
Tel: 0983 863 441

Ways Auction House,
Garfield Road, Ryde
Tel: 0983 62255

Kent

Albert Andrews Auctions & Sales,
Maiden Lane, Crayford
Tel: 0322 528868

Bracketts,
27-29 High Street,
Tunbridge Wells
Tel: 0892 533733

Canterbury Auction Galleries,
40 Station Road West,
Canterbury
Tel: 0227 763337

Mervyn Carey,
Twysden Cottage,
Benenden, Cranbrook
Tel: 0580 240283

Stewart Gore,
100-102 Northdown Road,
Margate
Tel: 0843 221528/9

Halifax Property Services,
Fine Art Department,
53 High Street, Tenterden
Tel: 0580 763200
also at:
15 Cattle Market,
Sandwich
Tel: 0304 614369

Edwin Hall,
Valley Antiques,
Lyminge, Folkestone
Tel: 0303 862134

Hobbs Parker,
Romney House, Ashford Market, Elwick Road,
Ashford
Tel: 0233 622222

Ibbett Mosely,
125 High Street, Sevenoaks
Tel: 0732 452246

Kent Sales,
'Giffords', Holmesdale Road, South Darenth
Tel: 0322 864919

Lambert & Foster,
102 High Street, Tenterden
Tel: 0580 762083/763233

Lawrence Butler & Co, (inc. F W Butler & Co.),
Fine Art Salerooms, Butler House, 86 High Street,
Hythe
Tel: 0303 266022/3

B J Norris,
"The Quest", West Street,
Harrietsham,
Nr Maidstone
Tel: 0622 859515

Phillips,
11 Bayle Parade,
Folkestone
Tel: 0303 45555

Phillips Fine Art Auctioneers,
49 London Road, Sevenoaks
Tel: 0732 740310

Michael Shortall,
Auction Centres,
Highgate, Hawkhurst
Tel: 0580 753463

Town & Country House Auctions, North House,
Oakley Road,
Bromley Common
Tel: 081 462 1735

Walter & Randall,
7-13 New Road, Chatham
Tel: 0634 841233

Peter S Williams, FSVA,
Orchard End, Sutton Valence, Maidstone
Tel: 0622 842350

Lancashire

Artingstall & Hind,
29 Cobden Street,
Pendleton, Salford
Tel: 061 736 5682

Capes Dunn & Co,
The Auction Galleries,
38 Charles Street,
Manchester
Tel: 061 273 6060/1911

Charles Edwards & Co,
4/8 Lynwood Road,
Blackburn
Tel: 0254 691748

Entwistle Green,
The Galleries, Kingsway,
Ansdell, Lytham St Annes
Tel: 0253 735442

Robt. Fairhurst & Son,
39 Mawdsley Street, Bolton
Tel: 0204 28452/28453

Highams Auctions,
Southgate House,
Southgate Street, Rhodes Bank, Oldham
Tel: 061 626 1021

McKennas, formerly Hothersall, Forrest, McKenna & Sons,
Bank Salerooms, Harris Court, Clitheroe
Tel: 0200 25446/22695

Mills & Radcliffe,
101 Union Street, Oldham
Tel: 061 624 1072

David Palamountain,
1-3 Osborne Grove,
Morecambe
Tel: 0524 423941

J R Parkinson Son & Hamer Auctions,
The Auction Rooms,
Rochdale Road, Bury
Tel: 061 761 1612/7372

Phillips,
Trinity House, 114 Northenden Road, Sale,
Manchester
Tel: 061 962 9237

Smythe, Son & Walker,
174 Victoria road West,
Cleveleys
Tel: 0253 852184 & 854084

Warren & Wignall Ltd,
The Mill, Earnshaw Bridge
Leyland Lane, Leyland
Tel: 0772 453252/451430

Leicestershire

Churchgate Auctions,
The Churchgate Saleroom,
66 Churchgate, Leicester
Tel: 0533 621416

Gildings,
64 Roman Way,
Market Harborough
Tel: 0858 410 414

Noton Salerooms,
76 South Street, Oakham
Tel: 0572 722681

David Stanley Auctions,
Stordon Grange,
Osgathorpe, Loughborough
Tel: 0530 222320

William H Brown,
The Warner Auction Rooms,
16/18 Halford Street,
Leicester Tel: 0533 519777

Lincolnshire

Bourne Auction Rooms,
Spalding Road, Bourne
Tel: 0778 422686

Dowse,
89 Mary Street, Scunthorpe
Tel: 0724 842569/842039

Goldings,
The Saleroom,
Old Wharf Road,
Grantham
Tel: 0476 65118

Thomas Mawer & Son,
63 Monks Road, Lincoln
Tel: 0522 524984

Henry Spencer & Sons,
42 Silver Street, Lincoln
Tel: 0522 536666

Marilyn Swain Auctions,
The Old Barracks,
Sandon Road,
Grantham
Tel: 0476 68861

John H Walter,
1 Mint Lane, Lincoln
Tel: 0522 525454

lerseyside

ato Crane & Co,
verpool Auction Rooms,
Stanhope Street,
verpool
el: 051 709 5559

artley & Co,
& 14 Moss Street,
verpool
el: 051 263 6472/1865

ingsley & Co,
5 The Quadrant, Hoylake,
irral Tel: 051 632 5821

uthwaite & Litherland,
ingsway Galleries,
ontenoy Street, Liverpool
el: 051 236 6561/

orralls,
-15 Seel Street, Liverpool
el: 051 709 2950

lorfolk

wings,
arket Place, Reepham,
orwich Tel: 0603 870473

hos Wm Gaze & Son ,
Market Hill, Diss
el: 0379 651931

igel F Hedge,
B Market Place, North
alsham Tel: 0692 402881

A Key,
Market Place, Aylsham
el: 0263 733195

ilhams,
aker Street, Gorleston,
reat Yarmouth
el: 0493 662152 & 600700

mes Norwich Auctions
d,
Timberhill, Norwich
el: 0603 624817/625369

lorthants

orby & Co,
-32 Brook Street, Raunds
el: 0933 623722

eathcote Ball & Co,
bion Auction Rooms, Old
bion Brewery,
ommercial Street,
orthampton
el: 0604 37263

owery's,
Bridge Street,
orthampton
el: 0604 21561

erry's Auctioneers,
he Old Corn Exchange,
attle Market, 14 Bridge
reet, Northampton
el: 0604 32266

oreton Pinkney,
High Street, Daventry
el: 0327 703917

outham & Sons,
orn Exchange, Thrapston,
ettering
el: 08012 4486

Wilford Ltd,
idland Road,
ellingborough

lorthumberland

ouis Johnson Auctioneers,
orpeth Tel: 0670 513025

Nottinghamshire

Arthur Johnson & Sons Ltd,
The Nottingham Auction Rooms, The Cattle Market,
Meadow Lane, Nottingham
Tel: 0602 869128

Neales of Nottingham,
192 Mansfield Road,
Nottingham
Tel: 0602 624141

John Pye & Sons,
Corn Exchange, Cattle
Market, London Road,
Nottingham
Tel: 0602 866261

C B Sheppard & Son,
The Auction Galleries,
Chatsworth Street, Sutton-in-Ashfield
Tel: 0773 872419

Henry Spencer & Sons Ltd,
20 The Square, Retford
Tel: 0777 708633

T Vennett-Smith,
11 Nottingham Road,
Gotham Tel: 0602 830541

Oxfordshire

Green & Co,
33 Market Place, Wantage
Tel: 02357 3561/2

Holloways,
49 Parsons Street, Banbury
Tel: 0295 253197/8

Mallams,
24 St Michael's Street,
Oxford Tel: 0865 241358

Messengers,
27 Sheep Street, Bicester
Tel: 08692 52901

Phillips Inc Brooks,
39 Park End Street, Oxford
Tel: 0865 723524

Simmons & Sons,
32 Bell Street,
Henley-on-Thames
Tel: 0491 571111

Shropshire

Cooper & Green,
3 Barker Street,
Shrewsbury
Tel: 0743 232244

Ludlow Antique Auctions
Ltd, 29 Corve Street,
Ludlow
Tel: 0584 875157

McCartneys,
25 Corve Street, Ludlow
Tel: 0584 872636

Perry & Phillips,
Newmarket Salerooms,
Newmarket Buildings,
Listley Street, Bridgnorth
Tel: 07462 762248

Somerset

Dores, The Auction Mart,
Vicarage Street, Frome
Tel: 0373 62257

John Fleming,
4 & 8 Fore Street,
Dulverton
Tel: 0398 23597

Greenslades,
13 Hamet Street, Taunton
Tel: 0823 277121also at:
Priory Saleroom,
Winchester Street, Taunton

Gribble Booth & Taylor,
13 The Parade, Minehead
Tel: 0643 702281

Black Horse Agencies,
Alder King, 25 Market
Place, Wells
Tel: 0749 73002

Lawrences of Crewkerne,
South Street,
Crewkerne
Tel: 0460 73041

The London Cigarette Card
Co Ltd,
Sutton Road, Somerton
Tel: 0458 73452

Frome Auction Rooms,
Frome Market,
Standerwick, Nr Frome
Tel: 0373 831010

Nuttall Richards & Co,
The Square, Axbridge
Tel: 0934 732969

Wellington Salerooms,
Mantle Street, Wellington
Tel: 0823 664815

Wells Auction Rooms,
66/68 Southover, Wells
Tel: 0749 678094

Staffordshire

Bagshaws,
17 High Street, Uttoxeter
Tel: 0889 562811

Hall & Lloyd,
South Street Auction
Rooms, Stafford
Tel: 0785 58176

Louis Taylor,
Britannia House, 10 Town
Road, Hanley, Stoke-on-Trent
Tel: 0782 260222

Wintertons,
Lichfield Auction Centre,
Woodend Lane, Fradley,
Lichfield
Tel: 0543 263256

Suffolk

Abbotts (East Anglia) Ltd,
The Hill, Wickham Market,
Woodbridge
Tel: 0728 746321

Boardman Fine Art,
Station Road Corner,
Haverhill Tel: 0440 730414

Diamond, Mills & Co,
117 Hamilton Road,
Felixstowe Tel: 0394
282281

William H Brown,
Ashford House,
Saxmundham
Tel: 0728 603232

Lacy Scott,
Fine Art Department, The
Auction Centre, 10
Risbygate Street, Bury St
Edmunds
Tel: 0284 763531

Neal Sons & Fletcher,
26 Church Street,
Woodbridge
Tel: 0394 382263

Olivers, Olivers Rooms,
Burkitts Lane, Sudbury
Tel: 0787 880305

Phillips,
Dover House, Wilsey
Street, Ipswich
Tel: 0473 255137

Surrey

ABC Auctions,
Central Avenue,
West Molesey,
Tel: 081 941 5545

Chancellors,
74 London Road,
Kingston upon Thames,
Tel: 081 541 4139

Clark Gammon,
The Guildford Auction
Rooms, Bedford Road,
Guildford Tel: 0483 66458

Crows Auction Gallery,
Rear of Dorking Halls,
Reigate Road, Dorking
Tel: 0306 740382

Croydon Auction Rooms
(Rosan & Co)
144-150 London Road,
Croydon
Tel: 081 688 1123/4/5

Ewbank Fine Art,
Welbeck House, High
Street, Guildford
Tel: 0483 232134

Hamptons, Fine Art
Auctioneers & Valuers, 93
High Street, Godalming
Tel: 04834 23567

Lawrences,
Norfolk House, 80 High
Street, Bletchingley
Tel: 0883 743323

John Nicholson,
1 Crossways Court,
Haslemere Road,
Fernhurst, Haslemere Tel:
0428 653727

Parkins,
18 Malden Road, Cheam,
Surrey
Tel: 081 644 6633 & 612

Phillips Fine Art
Auctioneers, Millmead,
Guildford
Tel: 0483 504030

Richmond & Surrey
Auctions, Kew Road,
Rear of Richmond Station,
Richmond
Tel: 081 948 6677

Wentworth Auction
Galleries, 21 Station
Approach, Virginia Water
Tel: 0344 843711

P F Windibank,
Dorking Halls, 18-20
Reigate Road, Dorking
Tel: 0306 884556

Sussex - East

Ascent Auction Galleries,
11-12 East Ascent, St
Leonards-on-Sea
Tel: 0424 420275

Burstow & Hewett,
Abbey Auction Galleries
and Granary Salerooms,
Battle
Tel: 0424 772374/772302

Clifford Dann Auction
Galleries,
20-21 High Street, Lewes
Tel: 0273 480111

Fryers Auction Galleries,
Terminus Road, Bexhill-on-Sea
Tel: 04[illegible] 212994

Gor[illegible]nges Auction
Galleries,
15 North Street, Lewes
Tel: 0273 472503

Graves, Son & Pilcher, Fine
Arts, 71 Church Road, Hove
Tel: 0273 735266

Edgar Horn's Fine Art Auctioneers,
46-50 South Street, Eastbourne
Tel: 0323 410419

Hove Auction Galleries,
1 Weston Road, Hove
Tel: 0273 736207

Raymond P Inman,
Auction Galleries, 35 & 40 Temple Street, Brighton
Tel: 0273 774777

Lewes Auction Rooms, (Julian Dawson),
56 High Street, Lewes
Tel: 0273 478221

Rye Auction Galleries,
Rock Channel, Rye
Tel: 0797 222124

Wallis & Wallis,
West Street Auction Galleries, Lewes
Tel: 0273 480208

Watsons,
Heathfield Furniture Salerooms, The Market, Burwash Road, Heathfield
Tel: 0435 862132

Sussex - West

John Bellman,
New Pound, Wisborough Green, Billingshurst
Tel: 0403 700858

Peter Cheney,
Western Road Auction Rooms, Western Road, Littlehampton
Tel: 0903 722264/713418

Denham's,
Horsham Auction Galleries, Warnham, Horsham
Tel: 0403 255699/253837

R H Ellis & Sons,
44-46 High Street, Worthing
Tel: 0903 38999

Francis,
Star Industrial Estate, Partridge Green, Horsham
Tel: 0403 710567

Midhurst Auction Rooms,
Bepton Road, Midhurst
Tel: 073081 2456

Phillips Fine Art Auctioneers,
Baffins Hall, Baffins Lane, Chichester
Tel: 0243 787548

Sotheby's in Sussex,
Summers Place, Billingshurst
Tel: 0403 783933

Stride & Son,
Southdown House, St John's Street, Chichester
Tel: 0243 780207

Sussex Auction Galleries,
59 Perrymount Road, Haywards Heath
Tel: 0444 414935

Worthing Auction Galleries,
31 Chatsworth Road, Worthing
Tel: 0903 205565

Tyne & Wear

Anderson & Garland,
The Fine Art Sale Rooms, Marlborough House, Marlborough Crescent, Newcastle-upon-Tyne
Tel: 091 232 6278

Boldon Auction Galleries,
24a Front Street, East Boldon
Tel: 091 537 2630

Thomas N Miller,
18-22 Gallowgate, Newcastle-upon-Tyne
Tel: 091 232 5617

Sneddons,
Sunderland Auction Rooms, 30 Villiers Street, Sunderland
Tel: 091 514 5931

Warwickshire

Bigwood Auctioneers Ltd,
The Old School, Tiddington, Stratford-upon-Avon
Tel: 0789 269415

John Briggs & Calder,
133 Long Street, Atherstone
Tel: 0827 718911

Locke & England,
18 Guy Street, Leamington Spa Tel: 0926 427988

West Midlands

Biddle & Webb,
Icknield Square, Ladywood Middleway, Birmingham
Tel: 021 455 8042

Cariss Residential,
20-22 High Street, Kings Heath, Birmingham
Tel: 021 444 0088

Ronald E Clare,
Clare's Auction Rooms, 70 Park Street, Birmingham
Tel: 021 643 0226

Frank H Fellows & Sons,
Augusta House, 19 Augusta Street, Hockley, Birmingham
Tel: 021 212 2131

Giles Haywood,
The Auction House, St Johns Road, Stourbridge
Tel: 0384 370891

James & Lister Lea,
42 Bull Street, Birmingham
Tel: 021 200 1100

Phillips,
The Old House, Station Road, Knowle, Solihull
Tel: 0564 776151

K Stuart Swash, FSVA,
Stamford House, 2 Waterloo Road, Wolverhampton
Tel: 0902 710626

Walker Barnett & Hill,
3 Waterloo Road, Wolverhampton
Tel: 0902 773531

Weller & Dufty Ltd,
141 Bromsgrove Street, Birmingham
Tel: 021 692 1414

Wiltshire

Hamptons,
20 High Street, Marlborough
Tel: 0672 513471

Swindon Auction Rooms,
The Planks (off The Square), Old Town, Swindon
Tel: 0793 615915

Dominic Winter,
The Old School, Maxwell Street, Swindon
Tel: 0793 611340

Woolley & Wallis,
The Castle Auction Mart, Castle Street, Salisbury
Tel: 0722 411422

Yorkshire - East

Dee & Atkinson,
The Exchange, Driffield
Tel: 0377 43151

Yorkshire-North

Boulton & Cooper (Fine Arts),
St Michael's House, Market Place, Malton
Tel: 0653 696151

H C Chapman & Son,
The Auction Mart, North Street, Scarborough
Tel: 0723 372424

Cundalls,
The Cattle Market, 17 Market Place, Malton
Tel: 0653 697820

M W Darwin & Sons,
The Dales Furniture Hall, Bedale
Tel: 0677 422846

GA Fine Art & Chattels,
Royal Auction Rooms, Queen Street, Scarborough
Tel: 0723 353581

Hutchinson Scott,
The Grange, Marton-Le-Moor, Ripon
Tel: 0423 324264

Christopher Matthews,
23 Mount Street, Harrogate
Tel: 0423 871756

Morphets of Harrogate,
4-6 Albert Street, Harrogate
Tel: 0423 530030

Nationwide Fine Arts,
27 Flowergate, Whitby
Tel: 0947 603433

Stephenson & Son,
Livestock Centre, Murton, York
Tel: 0904 489731

Geoffrey Summersgill, ASVA,
8 Front Street, Acomb, York
Tel: 0904 791131

Tennants,
Harmby Road, Leyburn
Tel: 0969 23780

Thompson's Auctioneers,
Dales Saleroom, The Dale Hall, Hampsthwaite, Harrogate
Tel: 0423 770741

D Wombell & Son, Bell Hall, Escrick, York
Tel: 090 487 531

Yorkshire-South

Eadon Lockwood & Riddle
Western Saleroom, Crookes, Sheffield
Tel: 0742 686294
William H Brown,
10 Regent Street, Barnsley
Tel: 0226 733456

William H Brown,
Stanilands Auction Room, 28 Nether Hall Road, Doncaster
Tel: 0302 367766

Roland Orchard,
Fine Art & Chattels Valuers & Auctioneers, 55 Copley Road, Doncaster (call Monday)
Tel: 0302 340499

Henry Spencer & Sons Ltd
1 St James Row, Sheffield
Tel: 0742 728728

Wilkinson & Beighton,
Woodhouse Green, Thurcroft, Nr Rotherham
Tel: 0709 700005

Yorkshire - West

Audsley's Auctions (C R Kemp BSc),
11 Morris Lane, Kirkstall, Leeds 5
Tel: 0532 758787

de Rome,
12 New John Street, Westgate, Bradford
Tel: 0274 734116

Eddisons,
Auction Rooms, 4-6 High Street, Huddersfield
Tel: 0484 533151

Andrew Hartley,
Victoria Hall Salerooms, Little Lane, Ilkley
Tel: 0943 816363

Malcolms No. 1 Auctioneer & Valuers,
7 Finkle Hill, Sherburn-in-Elmet, Nr Leeds
Tel: 0977 684971/685334 (24 hours)

Whitby Auction Rooms,
West End Saleroom, The Paddock, Whitby
Tel: 0947 603433

New Bond Street Auctions,
76 Harry Street, Batley Car, Dewsbury
Tel: 0924 469381

Phillips,
17a East Parade, Leeds
Tel: 0532 448011

John H Raby & Son,
The Sale Rooms, 21 St Mary's Road, Manningham, Bradford
Tel: 0274 491121

Windle & Co,
The Four Ashes, 535 Great Horton Road, Bradford
Tel: 0274 572998

Channel Islands

Langlois Auctioneers & Valuers,
Westway Chambers, 39 Don Street, St Helier, Jersey
Tel: 0534 22441

La Gallais Auctions Ltd,
36 Hillgrove Street, St Helier, Jersey
Tel: 0534 66689

Martel, Maides & Le Pelley, 50 High Street, St Peter Port, Guernsey Tel: 0481 713463

Ireland

James Adam & Sons, 26 St Stephens Green, Dublin 2 Tel: 010 3531 760261

Mealys, Chatsworth Street, Castle Comer Co. Kilkenny Tel: 010 353 564 1229

Northern Ireland

Dunmurry Auctions Ltd, Barbour Gardens, Dunmurry, Belfast Tel: 0232 602815/6

Morgans Auctions Ltd, Duncrue Crescent, Duncrue Road, Belfast Tel: 0232 771552

Temple Auctions Limited, 133 Carryduff Road, Temple, Lisburn, Co. Antrim Tel: 0846 638777

Scotland

John Anderson, 33 Cross Street, Fraserburgh, Aberdeenshire Tel: 0346 28878

Christie's Scotland, 164-166 Bath Street, Glasgow Tel: 041 332 8134

B L Fenton & Sons, Forebank Auction Halls, 84 Victoria Road, Dundee Tel: 0382 26227

Frasers (Auctioneers), 28-30 Church Street, Inverness Tel: 0463 232395

William Hardie Ltd, 141 West Regent Street, Glasgow Tel: 041 221 6780/248 6237

J & J Howe, 24 Commercial Street, Alyth, Perthshire Tel: 08283 2594

Loves Auction Rooms, The Auction Galleries, 52-54 Canal Street, Perth Tel: 0738 33337

Robert McTear & Co (Auctioneers & Valuers) Ltd, Royal Exchange Salerooms, 6 North Court, St. Vincent Place, Glasgow Tel: 041 221 4456

Mainstreet Trading, Mainstreet, St Boswells, Melrose, Roxburghshire Tel: 0835 23978

John Milne, 9 North Silver Street, Aberdeen Tel: 0224 639336

Robert Paterson & Son , 8 Orchard Street, Paisley, Renfrewshire Tel: 041 889 2435

Phillips in Scotland, 207 Bath Street, Glasgow Tel: 041 221 8377 also at: 65 George Street, Edinburgh Tel: 031 225 2266

L S Smellie & Sons Ltd, Within the Furniture Market, Lower Auchingramont Road, Hamilton Tel: 0698 282007

Thomson, Roddick & Laurie, 20 Murray Street, Annan Tel: 0461 202575

West Perthshire Auctions, Dundas Street, Cowie, Perthshire

Wales

Dodds Property World, Victoria Auction Galleries, 9 Chester Street, Mold, Clwyd Tel: 0352 752552

Graham H Evans, FRICS, FRVA, Auction Sales Centre, The Market Place, Kilgetty, Dyfed Tel: 0834 812793 & 811151

Spencer's John Francis, Curiosity Salerooms, 19 King Street, Carmarthen Tel: 0267 233456

Roger Jones & Co, 33 Abergele Road, Colwyn Bay, Clwyd Tel: 0492 532176

King Thomas, Lloyd Jones & Company, 36 High Street, Lampeter, Dyfed Tel: 0570 422550

Morgan Evans & Co. Ltd, 30 Church Street, Llangefni, Anglesey, Gwynedd Tel: 0248 723303/77582

Morris Marshall & Poole, 10 Broad Street, Newtown, Powys Tel: 0686 625900

Phillips in Wales Fine Art Auctioneers, 9-10 Westgate Street, Cardiff Tel: 0222 396453

Rennies, 1 Agincourt Street, Monmouth Tel: 0600 712916

Wingett's, 29 Holt Street, Wrexham, Clwyd Tel: 0978 353553

A Steiff tousled gold plush teddy bear, pewter stud in left ear, with brown and black glass eyes, hump, elongated limbs with felt pads, damaged, c1920, 20in (51cm).
$3,000-3,750

A Steiff blonde plush teddy bear, with brown stitched snout, black button eyes, hump back and swivel jointed body with excelsior filling, slight wear, button missing, c1908, 26½in (68cm) high.
$7,500-9,000

A Schuco panda, with black and white mohair-over-metal face, body and limbs, black bead eyes, black stitched nose and mouth, swivel head and jointed limbs, c1950, 3½in (8.5cm) high.
$225-255

A Steiff beige plush teddy bear, with stitched snout, black button eyes, hump back and swivel jointed body with excelsior stuffing, button missing, worn, c1910, 16in (41cm) high.
$1,200-1,800

INDEX TO ADVERTISERS

INDEX

Italic page numbers denote information and pointer boxes

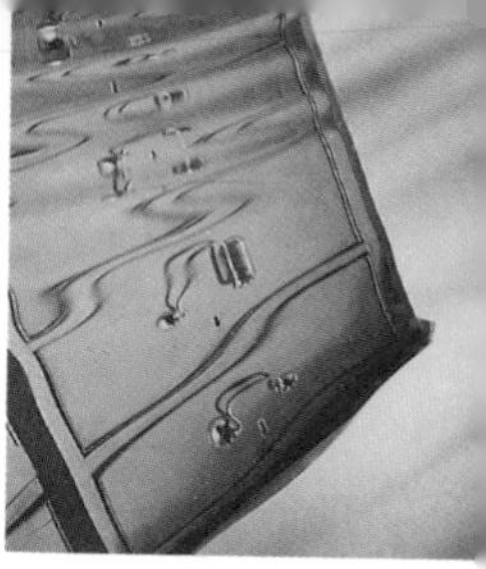

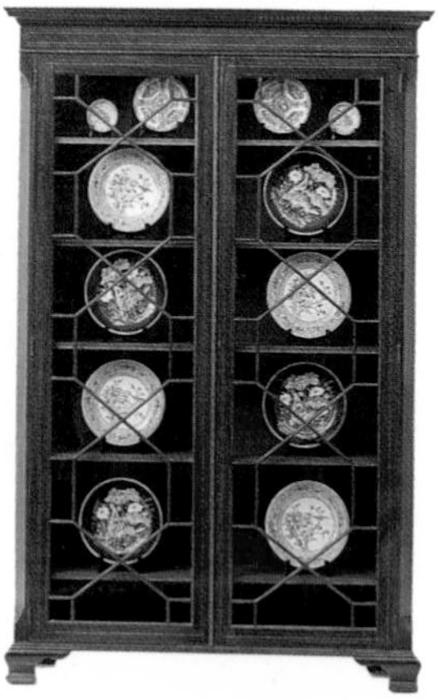